Handbook of Anticipation

Roberto Poli
Editor

Handbook of Anticipation

Theoretical and Applied Aspects of the
Use of Future in Decision Making

Volume 1

With 289 Figures and 38 Tables

 Springer

Editor
Roberto Poli
Department of Sociology and Social Research
University of Trento
Trento, Italy

ISBN 978-3-319-91553-1   ISBN 978-3-319-91554-8 (eBook)
ISBN 978-3-319-91555-5 (print and electronic bundle)
https://doi.org/10.1007/978-3-319-91554-8

This Springer imprint is published by the registered company Springer Nature Switzerland AG
The registered company address is: Gewerbestrasse 11, 6330 Cham, Switzerland

Preface

The aim of the *Handbook of Anticipation* is to establish anticipation of the future as a legitimate topic of research – as an object of empirical study, as a subject for theorization, and as a practice with real-world implications.

An anticipatory behavior is a behavior that "uses" the future in its actual decisional process. It is the process of using the future in the present, which includes a forward-looking stance and the use of that forward-looking stance to effect a change in the present.

It is our thesis that behavior is primarily anticipatory, and reactive behavior is only a secondary – albeit important – component of behavior. A system behaving in an anticipatory way – an anticipatory system – takes its decisions in the present according to anticipations about something that may eventually happen in the future.

Our understanding of anticipation is still cursory, and the novelty of the perspective may conceal the difficulty implied by this otherwise refreshingly new vision. Nonetheless, anticipation is increasingly at the heart of urgent contemporary debates, from climate change to economic crisis. Anticipatory capabilities of individuals and communities can enhance the overall sense-making process and improve decision-making, strategy formation, and societal resilience.

While anticipation has been widely studied within a number of different disciplines – including biology and cognitive and social sciences – and under different names, in fields such as anthropology, futures studies, management, political science, cultural studies, and philosophy, to date there have been few systematic attempts to build a thorough understanding of different types of anticipations and their uses. This handbook is the first systematic exploration of the theory and practice of anticipation.

The handbook encompasses natural, formal, and social systems that intentionally or unintentionally use ideas of a future to act in the present, with a broad focus on humans, institutions, and human-designed systems. Our aim is to enhance the repertoire of resources for developing ideas of the future, and for expanding and deepening the ability to use the future.

Some questions that the handbook intends to address are the following: When does anticipation occur in behavior and life? What types of anticipation can be distinguished? What properties of our environment change the pertinence of different types of anticipation? What structures and processes are necessary for anticipatory action? What is the behavioral impact of anticipation?

The handbook is divided into four main parts: Introducing Anticipation, Understanding Anticipation, Contexts of Anticipatory Practices, and Enhancing Anticipation. Introducing Anticipation will set the focus of the handbook. Understanding Anticipation and Contexts of Anticipatory Practices present both what we already know about anticipation and cutting edge chapters on what is emergent and what people are working on, and how they are working on it. The former part will keep a disciplinary focus, while the latter will give more attention to field activities and constraints. Throughout these chapters, the handbook explores the different scales and cultures of anticipation. Finally, Enhancing Anticipation is the toolkit part, the educational section – how to do, assess, improve and judge the use of anticipatory practice in different contexts, make mature and informed decisions about when different anticipatory tools are appropriately used.

Trento, Italy   Roberto Poli
June 2019

Contents

Volume 2

About the Editor

Roberto Poli (Ph.D. Utrecht) was awarded the first UNESCO Chair in Anticipatory Systems, is fellow of WAAS – World Academy of Art and Science, and STIAS – Stellenbosch Institute for Advanced Study. Poli is editor-in-chief of Axiomathes (Springer) and editor of the series Categories (De Gruyter) and Anticipation Science (Springer). Poli heads the master's programme in social foresight. Poli's research interests include:

- Anticipatory systems, i.e., systems able to take decisions according to their possible future development (R. Poli, Introduction to Anticipation Studies, Springer 2017).
- Ontology, in both its traditional philosophical understanding and the new, computer-oriented, understanding (Alwis. Ontology for Knowledge Engineers, PhD Thesis, Utrecht, 2001; Theory and Applications of Ontology, 2 vol. Springer 2010).

Poli has published 6 books, edited or co-edited more than 20 books or journal special issues, and published more than 250 scientific papers.

List of External Reviewers

Peter Ache Institute for Management Research, Radboud University, Nijmegen, The Netherlands

Jan M. Ahrend Department of Computer Science, University of Oxford, Oxford, UK

Liliana Albertazzi Laboratory of Experimental Phenomenology, Department of Humanities, University of Trento, Trento, Italy

Angela Ales Bello Rome and Italian Center of Phenomenology, Pontifical Lateran University, Rome, Italy

Adrian Baker Nairn Healthcare Group, Nairn, Nairnshire, UK

Roberto Belloni Department of Sociology and Social Research, University of Trento, Trento, Italy

Stefano Benati Department of Sociology and Social Research, University of Trento, Trento, Italy

Mark H. Bickhard Lehigh University, Bethlehem, PA, USA

Peter Bishop University of Houston, Houston, TX, USA
Teach the Future, Sacramento, CA, USA

Marcus Bussey Faculty of Arts, Business and Law, University of the Sunshine Coast, Maroochydore, QLD, Australia

Flaviano Celaschi Department of Architecture, University of Bologna, Bologna, Italy

Manuela Celi Dipartimento di Design, Politecnico di Milano, Milan, Italy

Roy Clouser The College of New Jersey, Ewing, NJ, USA

Nathaniel Coleman School of Architecture, Planning and Landscape, Newcastle University, Newcastle upon, Tyne, UK

Ariel Colonomos CNRS – Centre de Recherches Internationales, Sciences Po, Paris, France

Giovanni Emanuele Corazza Marconi Institute for Creativity, University of Bologna, Bologna, Italy

Andrew Curry SOIF (School of International Futures), London, UK

Osvaldo Da Pos Department of Psychology, University of Padua, Padua, Italy

Mario Diani Department of Sociology and Social Research, University of Trento, Trento, Italy

Andrée Ehresmann Faculté des Sciences, Mathématiques LAMFA, Université de Picardie Jules Verne, Amiens, France

Jane I. Guyer John Hopkins University, Baltimore, MD, USA

Keri Facer School of Education, University of Bristol, Bristol, UK

Daniele Fanzini Department of Architecture, Built Environment and Construction Engineering, Politecnico di Milano, Milan, Italy

Elena Formia Department of Architecture, University of Bologna, Bologna, Italy

Ted Fuller University of Lincoln, Brayford Pool, Lincoln, UK

Iacopo Hachen International School for Advanced Studies (SISSA), Trieste, Italy

Lars Geer Hammershøj Department of Education (DPU), Aarhus University, Campus Emdrup, Copenhagen, NV, Denmark

Tanja Hichert Centre for Complex Systems in Transition, University of Stellenbosch, Stellenbosch, South Africa

Anthony Hodgson Centre for Environmental Change and Human Resilience, School of Social Sciences, University of Dundee, Dundee, UK

International Futures Forum, Aberdour, Fife, UK

Decision Integrity Limited, Pitlochry, Perthshire, UK

Jan-Hendrik S. Hofmeyr Centre for Complex Systems in Transition and Department of Biochemistry, University of Stellenbosch, Stellenbosch, South Africa

Timothy L. Hubbard Department of Psychology, Arizona State University, AZ, USA

David Huron Arts and Humanities Distinguished Professor, School of Music & Center for Cognitive and Brain Sciences, Ohio State University, Columbus, OH, USA

Gonzalo Iparraguirre University of Buenos Aires, Buenos Aires, Argentina

Paolo Jedlowski University of Calabria, Arcavacata, Italy

Marina Jirotka Department of Computer Science, University of Oxford, Oxford, UK

J. Scott Jordan Department of Psychology, Institute for Prospective Cognition, Illinois State University, Normal, IL, USA

Achilles Kameas School of Science & Technology, Hellenic Open University, Patras, Greece

Sandra Kemp Ruskin-Library, Museum and Research Centre, University of Lancaster, Lancaster, UK

Georgios Kolliarakis German Council on Foreign Relations, Berlin, Germany

Fabián Labra-Spröhnle Clinical Research Programme, School of Biological Sciences, Victoria University of Wellington, Wellington, New Zealand

Genevieve Liveley University of Bristol, Bristol, UK

Carlos Lopez-Galviz Institute for Social Futures, Lancaster University, Lancaster, UK

A. H. Louie Ottawa, ON, Canada

Stellenbosch Institute for Advanced Study (stias), Wallenberg Research Centre at Stellenbosch University, Stellenbosch, South Africa

Andrew Cyprian Love Glenstal Abbey, Co. Limerick, Munster, Ireland

Giuliana Mandich Università di Cagliari, Cagliari, Italy

Riccardo Manzotti IULM, Milano, Italy

Gerald Midgley Centre for Systems Studies, Business School, University of Hull, Hull, UK

School of Innovation, Design and Engineering, Mälardalen University, Eskilstuna, Sweden

Victoria Business School, Victoria University of Wellington, Wellington, New Zealand

School of Political and Social Sciences, University of Canterbury, Christchurch, New Zealand

School of Agriculture and Food Sciences, University of Queensland, Brisbane, QLD, Australia

Riel Miller Social and Human Sciences Sector, UNESCO, Paris, France

Victor Vahidi Motti World Futures Studies Federation, Tehran, Iran

Winston P. Nagan University of Florida Levin College of Law, Florida, FL, USA

Slawomir J. Nasuto Division of Biomedical Sciences and Biomedical Engineering, School of Biological Sciences, University of Reading, Reading, UK

Deborah Osberg Graduate School of Education, University of Exeter, Exeter, Devon, UK

Heikki Patomäki Faculty of Social Sciences, University of Helsinki, Helsinki, Finland

Angela Piccini School of Arts, University of Bristol, Bristol, UK

Adrian Pop National University of Political Science and Public Administration, Bucharest, Romania

Fabiola Riccardini Department of Statistical Production, ISTAT, Italian Statistical Institute, Rome, Italy

Michael Rovatsos School of Informatics, The University of Edinburgh, Edinburgh, UK

Neantro Saavedra-Rivano University of Tsukuba, Tsukuba, Japan
University of Brasilia, Brasilia, Brazil

Richard Sandford University College London, London, UK

Andrzej M. J. Skulimowski Department of Automatic Control and Biomedical Engineering, AGH University of Science and Technology, Krakow, Poland
International Centre for Decision Sciences and Forecasting, Progress and Business Foundation, Krakow, Poland

Thomas O. Staiger Department of Medicine, University of Washington, Seattle, WA, USA

John Supko Department of Music, Duke University, Durham, NC, USA

John A. Sweeney Narxoz University Almaty, Almaty, Kazakhstan

Mark Swilling Stellenbosch University, Stellenbosch, South Africa

Efstathios Tapinos Aston University, Birmingham, UK

Hardin B. C. Tibbs Synthesys Strategic Consulting Ltd., Cambridge, UK

Ilkka Tuomi Meaning Processing, Helsinki, Finland
Stellenbosch Institute for Advanced Study (stias), Wallenberg Research Centre at Stellenbosch University, Stellenbosch, South Africa

Liisa Välikangas Aalto University, Helsinki, Finland
Hanken School of Economics, Helsinki, Finland

Ruud van den Bos Department of Animal Ecology and Physiology, Institute for Water and Wetland Research, Radboud University, Nijmegen, The Netherlands

Dewald van Niekerk Faculty of Natural and Agricultural Sciences, Unit for Environmental Sciences and Management, North-West University, Potchefstroom, South Africa

Dhanraj Vishwanath School of Psychology and Neuroscience, University of St. Andrews, Fife, UK

Daniel Visser University of Cape Town, Cape Town, South Africa

Joseph Voros Faculty of Business and Law, Swinburne Business School, Swinburne University of Technology, Hawthorn, VIC, Australia

Jennifer A. Wagner-Lawlor Department of Women's, Gender and Sexuality Studies and English, The Pennsylvania State University, University Park, PA, USA

Eric Weislogel Saint Joseph's University, Philadelphia, PA, USA

Markku Wilenius School of Economics, Finland Futures Research Centre, University of Turku, Turku, Finland

Angela Wilkinson Said Business School, University of Oxford, Oxford, UK
World Energy Council, London, UK

Alan F. T. Winfield Bristol Robotics Laboratory, University of the West of England, Bristol, UK

Mike Yearworth Centre for Simulation, Analytics & Modelling (CSAM), Business School, University of Exeter, Exeter, UK

Alf Zimmer Department of Psychology, University of Regensburg, Regensburg, Germany

Contributors

Peter Ache Institute for Management Research, Radboud University, Nijmegen, The Netherlands

Cash Ahenakew University of British Columbia, Vancouver, BC, Canada

Jan M. Ahrend Department of Computer Science, University of Oxford, Oxford, UK

Liliana Albertazzi Laboratory of Experimental Phenomenology, Department of Humanities, University of Trento, Trento, Italy

Tom Erik Arnkil Finnish National Institute for Health and Welfare, Helsinki, Finland
Pro & Re Ltd, Helsinki, Finland
Dialogical Practice Institute, Kanagawa, Japan

Adrian Baker Nairn Healthcare Group, Nairn, Nairnshire, UK

Mary Tuti Baker Cogut Institute for the Humanities, Brown University, Providence, RI, USA

Stefano Benati Department of Sociology and Social Research, University of Trento, Trento, Italy

Isabella Bergamini Facultad de Ingeniería, Universidad Panamericana, Zapopan, Jalisco, Mexico

Mark H. Bickhard Lehigh University, Bethlehem, PA, USA

Peter Bishop University of Houston, Houston, TX, USA
Teach the Future, Sacramento, CA, USA

Ruud van den Bos Department of Animal Ecology and Physiology, Institute for Water and Wetland Research, Radboud University, Nijmegen, The Netherlands

Marcus Bussey Faculty of Arts, Business and Law, University of the Sunshine Coast, Maroochydore, QLD, Australia

Marie-Hélène Caillol European Laboratory of Political Anticipation (LEAP), Paris, France

Flaviano Celaschi Department of Architecture, University of Bologna, Bologna, Italy

Manuela Celi Dipartimento di Design, Politecnico di Milano, Milan, Italy

Sylvaine Mercuri Chapuis Esdes, The Business School of Ucly, Lyon, France

Nathaniel Coleman School of Architecture, Planning and Landscape, Newcastle University, Newcastle upon Tyne, UK

Chiara Colombi Department of Design, Politecnico di Milano, Milan, Italy

Ariel Colonomos CNRS – Centre de Recherches Internationales, Sciences Po, Paris, France

Giovanni Emanuele Corazza Marconi Institute for Creativity, University of Bologna, Bologna, Italy

Cornelia Daheim Future Impacts Consulting, Cologne, Germany

Vanessa de Oliveira Andreotti University of British Columbia, Vancouver, BC, Canada

Yannick Dujardin Applied Futures Researcher, Erasmushogeschool Brussel, Anderlecht, Belgium

Jake Dunagan Governance Futures Lab, Institute for the Future, Palo Alto, CA, USA

Nick Dunn Lancaster University, Lancaster, UK

Andrée Ehresmann Faculté des Sciences, Mathématiques LAMFA, Université de Picardie Jules Verne, Amiens, France

Ken Eklund Writerguy, CA, USA

Kristel Van der Elst The Global Foresight Group, Geneva, Switzerland
The College of Europe, Brügge, Germany

Keri Facer School of Education, University of Bristol, Bristol, UK

Daniele Fanzini Department of Architecture, Built Environment and Construction Engineering, Politecnico di Milano, Milan, Italy

Jan Faye Department of Media, Cognition and Communication, University of Copenhagen, Copenhagen, Denmark

Ulrike Felt Department of Science and Technology Studies and Research Platform on Responsible Research and Innovation in Academic Practice, University of Vienna, Vienna, Austria

Elena Formia Department of Architecture, University of Bologna, Bologna, Italy

Ted Fuller University of Lincoln, Brayford Pool, Lincoln, UK

Antonio Furlanetto SKOPÌA, University of Trento, Trento, Italy

Thomas Gauthier Haute école de gestion de Genève, HES-SO, University of Applied Sciences Western Switzerland, Carouge, Switzerland

Emlyon business school, Écully, France

Mario Giampietro Institut de Ciència i Tecnologia Ambientals, Universitat Autònoma de Barcelona, Bellaterra, Spain

Institució Catalana de Recerca i Estudis Avançats (ICREA), Barcelona, Spain

Jane I. Guyer John Hopkins University, Baltimore, MD, USA

Iacopo Hachen International School for Advanced Studies (SISSA), Trieste, Italy

Verena V. Hafner Department of Computer Science, Humboldt-Universität zu Berlin, Berlin, Germany

Maarten Hajer Urban Futures Studio, Utrecht University, Utrecht, The Netherlands

Trevor Haldenby The Mission Business Inc., Toronto, ON, Canada

Craig Hammer The World Bank, Washington, DC, USA

Lars Geer Hammershøj Department of Education (DPU), Aarhus University, Campus Emdrup, Copenhagen, NV, Denmark

Yoshikatsu Hayashi Division of Biomedical Sciences and Biomedical Engineering, School of Biological Sciences, University of Reading, Reading, UK

Hemi Hireme Te Whare Wananga O Awanuiarangi, Whakatane, New Zealand

Anthony Hodgson Centre for Environmental Change and Human Resilience, School of Social Sciences, University of Dundee, Dundee, Scotland, UK

International Futures Forum, Aberdour, Fife, Scotland, UK

Decision Integrity Limited, Pitlochry, Perthshire, Scotland, UK

Jan-Hendrik S. Hofmeyr Centre for Complex Systems in Transition and Department of Biochemistry, University of Stellenbosch, Stellenbosch, South Africa

Roberto Iñiguez Flores Industrial Design Department, Tecnológico de Monterrey, Guadalajara, México

Gonzalo Iparraguirre University of Buenos Aires, Buenos Aires, Argentina

Paolo Jedlowski University of Calabria, Arcavacata, Italy

Marina Jirotka Department of Computer Science, University of Oxford, Oxford, UK

John J. Kineman University of Colorado, Boulder, CO, USA

Georgios Kolliarakis German Council on Foreign Relations, Berlin, Germany

Patricia A. Kritek Department of Medicine, Division of Pulmonary and Critical Care, University of Washington, Seattle, WA, USA

Sofi Kurki University of Turku, School of Economics, Finland Futures Research Centre, Turku, Finland

Fabián Labra-Spröhnle Clinical Research Programme, School of Biological Sciences, Victoria University of Wellington, Wellington, New Zealand

Ruth León Morán Industrial Design Department, Tecnológico de Monterrey, Guadalajara, México

Genevieve Liveley University of Bristol, Bristol, UK

Carlos Lopez-Galviz Institute for Social Futures, Lancaster University, Lancaster, UK

A. H. Louie Ottawa, ON, Canada
Stellenbosch Institute for Advanced Study (stiα̃s), Wallenberg Research Centre at Stellenbosch University, Stellenbosch, South Africa

Andrew Cyprian Love Glenstal Abbey, Co. Limerick, Munster, Ireland

Gang Luo Department of Biomedical Informatics and Medical Education, University of Washington, Seattle, WA, USA

Giuliana Mandich Università di Cagliari, Cagliari, Italy

Carl Mika University of Waikato, Hamilton, New Zealand

Riel Miller Social and Human Sciences Sector, UNESCO, Paris, France

Neville Morley Department of Classics and Ancient History, University of Exeter, Exeter, UK

Andrew Morrison Centre for Design Research, Oslo School of Architecture and Design, Oslo, Norway

Victor Vahidi Motti World Futures Studies Federation, Tehran, Iran

Winston P. Nagan University of Florida Levin College of Law, Florida, FL, USA

Slawomir J. Nasuto Division of Biomedical Sciences and Biomedical Engineering, School of Biological Sciences, University of Reading, Reading, UK

Astrid Nordin Lancaster University, Lancaster, UK

Deborah Osberg Graduate School of Education, University of Exeter, Exeter, Devon, UK

Heikki Patomäki Faculty of Social Sciences, University of Helsinki, Helsinki, Finland

Markus Paukku Amsterdam Business School, Amsterdam, The Netherlands

C. Anthony Pfaff Strategic Studies Institute, U.S. Army War College, Carlisle, PA, USA

Edgar Pieterse African Centre for Cities, University of Cape Town, Cape Town, South Africa

Roberto Poli Department of Sociology and Social Research, University of Trento, Trento, Italy

Adrian Pop National University of Political Science and Public Administration, Bucharest, Romania

Fabiola Riccardini Department of Statistical Production, ISTAT, Italian Statistical Institute, Rome, Italy

Aaron B. Rosa Competence Center Foresight, Fraunhofer Institute for Systems and Innovation Research (ISI), Karlsruhe, Germany

Irina Rotaru Department of Architecture, Built Environment and Construction Engineering, Politecnico di Milano, Milan, Italy

Michael Rovatsos School of Informatics, The University of Edinburgh, Edinburgh, UK

Richard Sandford University College London, London, UK

J. Scott Jordan Department of Psychology, Institute for Prospective Cognition, Illinois State University, Normal, IL, USA

Cynthia Selin School for the Future of Innovation in Society and the School of Sustainability, Arizona State University, Tempe, AZ, USA

Kaethe Selkirk School for the Future of Innovation in Society, Arizona State University, Tempe, AZ, USA

B. Sharpe International Futures Forum, Aberdour, Fife, UK

Andrzej M. J. Skulimowski Department of Automatic Control and Biomedical Engineering, AGH University of Science and Technology, Krakow, Poland
International Centre for Decision Sciences and Forecasting, Progress and Business Foundation, Krakow, Poland

Thomas O. Staiger Department of Medicine, University of Washington, Seattle, WA, USA

Gina Stovall Second Nature, CA, USA

John Supko Department of Music, Duke University, Durham, NC, USA

John A. Sweeney Narxoz University Almaty, Almaty, Kazakhstan

Mark Swilling Stellenbosch University, Stellenbosch, South Africa

Efstathios Tapinos Aston University, Birmingham, UK

Peter Tarczy-Hornoch Department of Biomedical Informatics and Medical Education, Department of Pediatrics, Division of Neonatology, Department of Computer Science and Engineering, University of Washington, Seattle, WA, USA

Aïda Terblanché-Greeff Unit for Environmental Sciences and Management, Faculty of Natural and Agricultural Sciences, North-West University, Potchefstroom, South Africa

Hardin B. C. Tibbs Synthesys Strategic Consulting Ltd., Cambridge, UK

Ilkka Tuomi Meaning Processing, Helsinki, Finland

Stellenbosch Institute for Advanced Study (STIAS), Wallenberg Research Centre at Stellenbosch University, Stellenbosch, South Africa

Dewald van Niekerk Faculty of Natural and Agricultural Sciences, Unit for Environmental Sciences and Management, North-West University, Potchefstroom, South Africa

Liisa Välikangas Aalto University, Helsinki, Finland

Hanken School of Economics, Helsinki, Finland

Dhanraj Vishwanath School of Psychology and Neuroscience, University of St. Andrews, Fife, UK

Daniel Visser University of Cape Town, Cape Town, South Africa

Joseph Voros Faculty of Business and Law, Swinburne Business School, Swinburne University of Technology, Hawthorn, VIC, Australia

Jennifer A. Wagner-Lawlor Department of Women's, Gender and Sexuality Studies and English, The Pennsylvania State University, University Park, PA, USA

Markku Wilenius School of Economics, Finland Futures Research Centre, University of Turku, Turku, Finland

Angela Wilkinson Said Business School, University of Oxford, Oxford, UK

World Energy Council, London, UK

Alan F. T. Winfield Bristol Robotics Laboratory, University of the West of England, Bristol, UK

Guy Yeomans Arctic Futures, London, UK

Danila Zindato Department of Design, Politecnico di Milano, Milan, Italy

Part I

Introducing Anticipation

Introducing Anticipation

1

Roberto Poli

Contents

Abstract

Anticipation occurs when the future is used in action. The anticipatory processes that allow the future to become part of actions in the present may be either internal or external. Watching a weather forecast and behaving accordingly is to use an external model; actions taken on the basis of subjectively constructed psychological expectations are internal. It is our thesis that behavior is primarily anticipatory, while reactive behavior is only a secondary – albeit important – component of behavior. Therefore, behavior is almost always goal-oriented rather than being stimulus-driven. Anticipation comes in many different guises. The simplest distinction is between explicit and implicit anticipation. Explicit anticipations are those of which the system is aware. Implicit anticipations, by contrast, work below the threshold of awareness. Anticipatory systems show forms of impredicativity, that is the presence of self-referential cycles in their

I thank Anthony Hodgson, Jan-Hendrik Hofmeyr, Gonzalo Iparraguirre, Scott Jordan, Achilles Kameas, Aloisius Louie, Riel Miller, and Thomas Staiger for their comments to a previous version of this chapter.

R. Poli (✉)
Department of Sociology and Social Research, University of Trento, Trento, Italy
e-mail: roberto.poli@unitn.it

© Springer Nature Switzerland AG 2019
R. Poli (ed.), *Handbook of Anticipation*,
https://doi.org/10.1007/978-3-319-91554-8_1

constitution. The main distinction within self-referential systems is between incomplete and complete forms of self-reference. Logical forms of self-reference are typically incomplete because they need an external interpreter. Complete forms of self-reference do not require an external interpreter because all their components are 'defined' – that is 'produced' – within the system itself.

Keywords

Anticipation · Anticipatory system · Forecast · Foresight · Latent · Impredicative system · Self-reference · Robert Rosen

Introduction

The aim of this handbook is to establish anticipation of the future as a legitimate topic of research.

Anticipation comes in different guises. As a lay term it refers to all forward-looking attitudes and activities. As a technical term, it takes on two different meanings: as a distinct aspect of futures studies that goes beyond forecast and foresight modeling, and as the qualifier "anticipatory" in the expression "anticipatory systems." These two meanings of "anticipation" belong to two different frameworks. As different as they are, we take care to identically define these two acceptations of anticipation in order to facilitate their mutual translation (Poli 2017).

Anticipation occurs when the future is used in action. From this perspective, anticipation consists of two necessary but distinct components: a forward-looking attitude and the use of the former's result for action. A weather forecast in itself is not anticipatory in our sense. Watching a weather forecast and, as a consequence taking an umbrella before going to work is instead an anticipatory behavior.

Anticipation's two components are consistent with Rosen's definition: "An anticipatory system is a system containing a predictive model of itself and/or its environment, which allows the system to change state at an instant in accord with the model's predictions pertaining to a later instant" (Rosen 2012, pp. 8, 313, originally published in 1985).

With reference to the three-level framework presented in the next section, the expression "predictive model" covers the level of forecasts only. It is my contention, however, that anticipation uses both forecasts and foresights.

The anticipatory processes and models that allow the future to become part of actions in the present may be either internal or external. Watching a weather forecast and behaving accordingly is to use an external model; actions taken on the basis of subjectively constructed psychological expectations are internal.

Internal anticipation is particularly important for understanding the anticipatory behavior of people, groups, organizations, and institutions. A major issue concerning internal anticipation is its origin: where does internal anticipation come from? We will see that this apparently minor issue serves as a dividing line that distinguishes radically different theoretical perspectives.

As relevant as anticipation may be for action, no anticipation is a guarantee of success. Continuing with the previous example, taking an umbrella before going to work does not guarantee that it will rain. While anticipation helps to develop more sophisticated courses of action, and is required for understanding much individual and social behavior, anticipation is not always correct. First and foremost, anticipation is a feature characterizing the behavior of suitably defined complex systems.

It is our thesis that behavior is primarily anticipatory, while reactive behavior is only a secondary – albeit important – component of behavior. A system behaving in an anticipatory way – an anticipatory system – makes decisions in the present according to "anticipations" about something that may eventually happen in the future. This *handbook* presents the theory and practices of anticipation and shows that anticipation is a serious topic of research. One of the key starting points for this research is the contention that the currently dominant theories of time and causation are unable to incorporate anticipation and, therefore, are in need of serious revision.

When first confronted with the proposition that anticipation is a subject worthy of research, most people seem to think that anticipation is a feature that human beings possess because we are such highly complex and wonderfully sophisticated cognitive agents. That is not what the theory of anticipation claims. Indeed, the major surprise embedded in the theory of anticipation is that anticipation is a widespread phenomenon present in and characterizing *most* types of real systems. Life in all its varieties is anticipatory; the brain works in an anticipatory way; the mind is obviously anticipatory; society and some of its structures are anticipatory; even nonliving or nonbiological systems can be anticipatory. All this often comes as a surprise.

If all that is true, and providing that the necessary supporting evidence is offered, it follows that a proper understanding of anticipation necessitates the adoption of new scientific (as well as philosophical) frameworks.

To date there have been few systematic attempts to pursue a thorough understanding of different types and uses of anticipation.

After years of neglect, interest in the study of anticipation is gaining momentum (Poli 2014a, b, 2017). To quote a few *recent* developments, Martin Seligman's prospection theory deserves special mention (Seligman et al. 2013). Seligman, former President of the American Psychological Association, has recently proposed developing a "science of prospection" with the aim of changing psychology from a primarily past-oriented field to a primarily future-oriented one. Another example is Jens Beckert, Director of the Max Planck Institute for the Study of Societies, whose recent work argues for including fictions in the architecture of economics and calls attention to the need to reconsider the way in which economics looks at the future. According to textbook economics, activities are pursued or avoided according to expectations of optimal outcomes. However, "under conditions of fundamental uncertainty, expectations cannot be understood as being determined through calculation of optimal choices taking into account all available information, but rather are based on contingent interpretations of the situation in the context of prevailing institutional structures, cultural templates, and social networks" (Beckert 2013, p. 325). Here Beckert introduces the concept of fictional expectation – referring to "present imaginaries of future situations that provide orientation in decision making *despite* the incalculability of outcomes" (Beckert 2013, p. 325).

In the field of anthropology, Arjun Appadurai, a most distinguished contemporary anthropologist, proposes reshaping anthropology and begins by asking how societies – past and recent – construe the future as a cultural fact (Appadurai 2013). While it is true that "the intellectual infrastructure of anthropology ... remains substantially shaped by the lens of pastness," Appadurai notes that "the subjects of anthropology have increasingly been those of the present and of the world we live in: ethnographies of science, technology, state, law, markets, and finance" (Appadurai 2013, p. 285). In order to develop "a general point of view about humans as future-makers and of futures as cultural facts" – continues Appadurai – "we need to construct an understanding of the future by examining the interactions between three notable human preoccupations that shape the future as a cultural fact, (namely) ... imagination, anticipation and aspiration" (Appadurai 2013, p. 286), even if "we have not yet found ways to articulate how anticipation, imagination, and aspiration come together in the work of future-making" (Appadurai 2013, p. 298).

As a final example, the social psychologist Kenneth Gergen asks whether the practice itself of scientific research may generate futures (Gergen 2015). While "traditional" research may inquire into "the causes of prejudice, aggression, human happiness, aging, and so on because these are commonly shared terms for understanding the world," the questions supporting future-generating research are much more difficult to raise because the latter research is "about what does not yet exist, or about ways of life that could be created" (Gergen 2015, p. 293). Ultimately, future-generating research is about possible futures and how to realize them. "The aim of research would not be to illuminate *what is*, but to create *what is to become*. Herein lies the essence of a future forming orientation to research" (Gergen 2015, p. 294). The very idea of future-forming research runs counter to the methodological divide between "social" and "sociological" problems and suggests that the future is far from being something "there" – as something that is in some way given – and agents will simply have to "go there." The alternative possibility is that futures themselves can be generated and consumed, and this possibility opens new avenues for research and action (Poli 2015).

Under different denominations, and often without knowing of Rosen's work, all the abovementioned scholars recognize the importance of and need for anticipatory systems and processes. Other recent developments are more aware of Rosen's ideas, such as the collections of essays by Baianu (2006), Mikulecky (2007), and Nadin (2015, 2016), and the books by Louie (2009) and (2013). We may also mention the UNESCO chair in Anticipatory Systems (http://projectanticipation.org) and the endeavor to establish a full-fledged "Discipline of Anticipation" (Miller et al. 2017).

The Three Levels of Futures Study

I shall distinguish among forecasting, foresight, and anticipation. The same division into three main levels has been proposed by Tuomi (2013). Tuomi distinguishes among "forecasting," "foresight 1.0," and "foresight 2.0." This last is also called "next-generation or design-based foresight" and fully includes the main ideas underlying anticipation, such as futures literacy and complexity/impredicativity (Miller et al. 2017).

The first level (forecasting) is the properly predictive component of futures study. Its models tend to adopt either a very short – as with econometric models – or a very long – as with climate change models – temporal window. It is often quantitative, even point-based, and starts from an underlying assumption of continuity: the system under study will continue to work more or less as it has been working so far because its structure remains essentially the same, or the laws governing it remain the same. The relevant futures are all past-based, as happen for time-series extrapolations or projection from cross-sectional samples.

The second layer (foresight) includes most traditional futures studies. It is not predictive, and for this reason the main output of most foresight exercises is the production of a variety of possible futures. Foresight is often qualitative; moreover, it includes and even focuses on discontinuities. As practiced, foresight usually shows a limited acceptance of complexity. Foresight exercises are primarily used to challenge the mindset of decision makers by exploring possible futures. Alternatively, normative futures can be used. The difference between explorative scenarios and normative scenarios is that the former work in a forward attitude from the present to the future while the latter work backward from the future to the present. Moreover, while the method of exploratory scenarios produces a variety of different, mutually incompatible scenarios, the method of normative scenarios selects a given scenario and works backward towards its necessary conditions.

The third level (anticipation, aka foresight 2.0 or design-based foresight) is grounded on the outcomes resulting from forecast and foresight models and aims at implementing them into decisions and actions. By exploiting a variety of models, anticipation shares some of the features of foresight, namely that it is nonpredictive, qualitative, and focused on discontinuity. The distinguishing features of anticipation in futures study are those that are becoming known as "futures literacy" (Miller 2006, 2007; Miller et al. 2017), together with a full acceptation of impredicativity (see below for further details).

Explicit Versus Implicit Anticipations

Anticipation comes in many different guises. The simplest distinction is between explicit and implicit anticipation. Explicit anticipations are those of which the system is aware. Implicit anticipations, by contrast, work below the threshold of awareness. They may be active within the system without the system itself being aware of them. Implicit anticipations are properties of the system, intrinsic to its functioning. Consider an organism's *schemata*. By determining the ways in which the organism looks at its environment, *schemata* are anticipatory. Schemata construct anticipations of what to expect and thus enable the organism to *actually perceive* the expected information.

Most anticipations work as acquired habits either through evolution (as in biological anticipation) or learning (as in most cases of psychological and social anticipation). Evolution-based anticipations are difficult to change, for obvious reasons. However, as difficult as they are to change, they may evolve, and this raises the question as to whether we can eventually contribute to bend evolution.

According to the theory of anticipation, behavior is almost always *goal-oriented* rather than being *stimulus-driven*. Anticipation runs contrary to the claim that psychic processes in general are determined by stimuli (i.e., it is at odds with both behaviorism and most of current cognitive psychology).

If behavior is indeed goal-oriented, this implies that changes in behavior are filtered by the system's identity. Anticipation within systems is based on controllers detecting the working conditions of the system itself (i.e., feed-forward controllers). Changes in the system's working patterns are therefore projected by feed-forward controllers into new anticipations.

Anticipation shows that reality includes not only what is actually given but also dispositions, habits, tendencies, and the forces generating them. That is to say, reality includes latents (Poli 2011, 2017). Even if latents may not be actually detectable in any given situation, they can nevertheless be there. Latents may become actual, if proper triggering conditions are in place, or they may get lost in the process. The simplest case of latents is given by dispositions, which can be described under the label "what would happen if" (what would happen if sugar were added to a liquid). Occasionally, latents can be perceived even when they are not exercised. They form a kind of halo around persons and situations. Individual and group decisions are often based on the perception of latents. The lack of a general theory of latents, however, makes it difficult both to organize systematically the psychological data already available and to guide research towards a better understanding of the less known aspects of the perception of latents. Be that as it may, a major difference between the behavior of people and the behavior of institutions is that the latter seems remarkably less able to perceive and make sense of latents.

As far as explicit anticipation is concerned, the reflexive side of explicit anticipation becomes visible as the difference between looking into the future and taking account of the consequences of that looking, i.e., as the impact of anticipation on current behavior. The types or aspects of behavior that can be modified through anticipation are exemplifications of normative behavior. If the system evaluates its own evolution as positive (according to its own criteria), it will maintain its behavioral patterns; conversely, if the system evaluates its own evolution as negative, it may seek to change its behavioral patterns in order to prevent the occurrence of the anticipated negative results. This is only a first step, however, because we all know how poorly "understanding" scores in changing behavior. Anyway, from an evolutionary point of view, explicit anticipation is an advantage because it enables more rapid goal-directed processing.

The other side of the coin, however, is that focused goal-oriented behavior usually gives rise to inattentional blindness, i.e., the incapacity to perceive things that are in plain sight (Simons and Chabris 1999). Patterns constrain attention, govern the boundary of relevance, and they direct attention to preestablished foci. The more efficient the pattern, the more likely is the outcome of an overrestricted focus of attention. The more efficient the behavioral patterns are, the more rigid they become.

Anticipation exhibits a variety of temporal patterns, from microanticipations embedded in perception to usually longer forms of social anticipation, ranging from seconds to years and decades.

A major question is whether explicit anticipations depend – or to what extent they may depend – on implicit ones (Riegler 2003). The apparently obvious answer that explicit anticipation depends – at least to some extent – on implicit anticipation may beg the question. For it may well turn out that the two forms of anticipation are based either on entirely different enabling conditions, or on different subsystems.

Where Do Models Come From?

Consider the capacity of an organism to navigate its environment, e.g., through its perceptions. The organism's percepts work as models of the environment. In this regard, two major options compete, which may be called the "representational" and the "presentational" perspective points. The former is the mainstream position accepted by most practitioners of cognitive science and branches into many other fields, including computer science and the social sciences. The main problem for the representational position is the question about where the modeling capacity of the representational system comes from. Apparently, most think that these capacities are wired in the hosting system. All the efforts to understand perceptions as entirely governed by and reduced to brain processes pertain to this position. The alternative position – called after Albertazzi (2006) "presentational" – introduces two divides: from one side, the distinction is made between the processes pertaining to the mind and the processes of the brain that underlie, make possible, or bear mental processes. There is a categorical divide between these two layers, as shown by the fact that their observables are different. To provide but an exemplification concerning color perception, the difference between warm and cold colors has no neurological correspondence (Albertazzi and Poli 2014).

The second divide is between first-level and higher-order cognitive processes. From the point of view of the perceptor, the former are naturally endowed with meaning since their first appearances, while the latter are higher order recodification of the former's outcomes. The difference between first-level and higher-order cognitive processes depends upon processes unfolding in the "time of presentness," known also as "specious present" or "moment now" and processes unfolding in wider temporal windows.

To the best of my knowledge, the presentational position has two main defenders: Albertazzi's experimental phenomenology (Albertazzi, 2006, 2013) and Bickhard's interactivism (Bickhard 2009, 2015a, b; Bickhard and Terveen 1995). For both of them, the main problem that the representational position is unable to address can be seen through two different yet deeply related questions, namely: where do meanings come from? And, where do models come from?

From a representational point of view, meanings (or the first person perspective) and models come from an interpreter; that is from an external system. As soon one asks – where do the interpreter's meanings and models come from? – it is apparent that an infinite regress begins. In this regard, it is immaterial whether the regress is spatial or temporal (as with evolutionary explanations). In both cases an explanation based on some form of infinite regress is far from being satisfactory. To get rid of infinite regresses, sooner or later a first meaning or model must be found. In this regard, representational perspectives runs into troubles; they do not have a clue about the first, initial origin of meaning and therefore the representational perspectives are unable to explain how a natural system could have ever begun developing its capacities to perceive and make sense of its environment. On the other hand, for the presentational point of view, processes in the first person perspective are meaningful, because meanings are generated from the processes themselves.

If, at least occasionally, semantics is internal, the problem of the self-generation of models becomes a central issue and cannot be put aside. Not by chance, perhaps, this issue is more visible in cognitive science than in any other research field.

Another way to describe the difference between the representational and the presentational strategies is to resort to the difference between syntax and semantics. The representational perspective focuses on the manipulation of symbols and therefore on syntax. Its problem is where the semantics comes from. On the other hand, the presentational perspective focuses on semantics, and it can allow itself ample leeway about which syntactical constraints to adopt. The latter can opportunistically exploit whatever "machinery" is available, without getting committed to any of them. From a biological point of view, this phenomenon is often called "plasticity."

As soon as the distinction between presentation and representation is mapped into the difference between semantics and syntax, other close oppositions pop up, such as the difference between function and structure and the difference between subsystem and element. While these oppositions are different, it is also patent that they closely resemble one another. To wit, elements go hand in hand with structure and composition rules and therefore are focused on syntax, while subsystems are functional in nature and therefore more context-dependent and are focused on semantics (Poli 2017).

Apropos the Impredicativity of Anticipatory Systems

Since the dawn of modern science, science has grown, dramatically improving its methods and developing new theoretical frames. I see no reason to believe that the science of twenty-first century will be less creative and surprising than the science of the twentieth century.

As far as the last decades are considered, the most pervasive development of science goes under complexity theory – however defined. As a first approximation, a complex system is a system with many interacting parts and complexity derives from feedback cycles among the system's parts as well as the subsequent collective emergence of new properties and behaviors. Chaos theory adds a different strand to this picture: the introduction of an unavoidable degree of uncertainty due to the required and impossible condition of measuring the system's initial conditions with infinite precision.

A bird's eye glance at contemporary science may describe twentieth-century science as characterized by the move from a science primarily based on linear models to a science progressively based on nonlinear models. Both complexity and chaos converge on showing the unavoidability of uncertainty – whether it is embedded into feedback cycles and emergence or in the infinite precision of initial conditions. This focus on modeling techniques subsumes a variety of subtler differences. To wit, linear models assume that even grossly simplified representations of real phenomena are nevertheless helpful proxies supporting the dominant "command and control" attitude. Complexity, on the other hand, shows that uncertainty is unavoidable and the command and control attitude is a no go.

A subtler transformation is ongoing, however: a transformation working on a deeper level than the move from linear to nonlinear models and patently much less visible than it. This presently less visible transformation, if successful, may impact the very idea of science in a vastly more relevant way than the move from linear to nonlinear modeling techniques.

As a matter of fact, both linear and nonlinear techniques are forms of predicative modeling. The difference between predicative and impredicative systems (and models and definitions) is pervasive and often considered of marginal interest. To wit, the underlying unproven assumption is that the vast majority of systems is predicative and only marginal, borderline systems are impredicative. As a matter of fact, the transformation I am alluding to calls attention to the opposite possibility: the unquestioned belief in the predicativity of most systems may prove to be illusory – a kind of self-inflicted form of groupthink. As a matter of fact, many disciplines, including sociology, anthropology, and biology, exhibit varieties of self-reference, the primary source of impredicativity (Bartlett 1987, p. 6).

The very idea that most systems are indeed impredicative opens new avenues to science. Moreover, it may help addressing some of the most egregious failures of contemporary science. The possibility to deepen and extend science as well as the possibility to address daunting obstructions of present science is serious enough reasons for a deep and thorough investigation of the difference between predicative and impredicative science.

In logic, the definition of an object is impredicative if it directly or indirectly refers to the object itself. This self-referentiality of impredicativity is the feature that has raised most doubts against impredicativity. Sometimes, impredicativity gives rise to paradoxes (the most notable of them is Russell's paradox of the set of all sets that do not contain themselves as elements), although impredicativities are usually harmless and are regularly used in mathematics. The reduction of mathematics to its predicative fraction (i.e., to recursive functions or algorithms) corresponds to a major curtailment of the capacity of mathematics. While Feferman (1998, 2005) has shown that a large part of classical mathematics can be reconstructed without using impredicative definitions, there is a great deal of mathematics that goes beyond the limits of the rote, mechanical repetition of a set of rules.

Furthermore, many natural systems do indeed show forms of impredicativity, that is the presence of self-referential cycles in their constitution. Organisms generate the very parts they are made of; minds produce the psychological processes they are based on; societies produce the roles or patterns of actions they are made of. If it is true that biological, psychological, and social systems are indeed impredicative, we have room for doing science and perhaps finding common grounds among otherwise widely isolated disciplines.

One may note that the presence of the closure manifested by impredicativity is always flanked by twin forms of openness. An organism self-produces its own parts but needs food and usually other enabling (and constraining) environmental supports; a mind self-generates its psychological processes but needs a supporting organism and usually a brain; a society self-produces its roles but needs people to populate them. Every system requires admissible environments (possibly in the form of other more encompassing systems). But once the supporting or enabling (as well as constraining) capacity of the environment is provided, the impredicative cycle characterizing the system proceeds in its own way.

We shall say that impredicative systems are open to material causation (such as food for organisms). The nature of the closure defining impredicative systems raises deep questions. For the time being, let us suppose that the impredicative cycle includes efficient causes. For reasons that will become apparent in due time, we shall call hierarchical a cycle that includes efficient causes.

The main distinction within impredicative or self-referential systems is between incomplete and complete forms of self-reference. Logical forms of self-reference (such as the well-known Epimenides paradox) are typically incomplete because they need an external interpreter able to make sense of expressions like "this," "sentence," and "falsity." These cases of self-reference do not refer to themselves only but also and necessarily to something else, namely an external interpreter. On the other hand, complete self-reference pertains to systems whose terms are all defined within the system. Complete forms of self-reference do not require an external interpreter because all their components are "defined" – that is "produced" – within the system itself (Lofgren 1968). Moreover, according to Lofgren (1968), complete self-reference is independent from set theory and can therefore be added as a new primitive. Apart from the pioneering efforts of Rosen, and usually without his idea that impredicativity is the next paradigmatic frontier of science, the issue of impredicativity has received some attention. See a. o. Aczel (1988), Barwise and Etchemendy (1987), Kampis (1995), Varela (1974). If impredicativity is indeed of such general relevance as we claim, at least some systems should be self-referentially complete, i.e., they should be such that their semantics self-emerge without the need of an external interpreter. As a matter of fact, we claim that the vast majority of systems work this way. Either one of the sources of meaning, i.e., semantics, is internal or life, mind, and society are not only meaningless but also impossible.

Unsurprisingly, many properties of impredicative systems are still unknown and suitable research programs must be developed. Specifically, we know very little of nested or tangled impredicative systems, such as the organism – mind – society encapsulation (Poli 2001). On the other hand, some results are nevertheless available.

Since the internal cycle defining an impredicative system can be taken as an implicit model of the system itself, the next step is between those systems that are able to use that model as opposed to those systems that are unable to make use of the model. We shall call anticipatory the systems of the first type. The class of impredicative systems can then be divided into the subclasses of anticipatory and nonanticipatory systems.

In its turn, anticipatory systems can be distinguished between the systems in which all their efficient causes are closed within hierarchical cycles and the systems in which only some of the efficient causes are closed within hierarchical cycles. The former systems will be called CLEF (closed to efficient causation). A major issue is: which systems are CLEF? (i.e., impredicative, anticipatory and CLEF). According to Robert Rosen, living systems are CLEF. I for one claim that also psychological and social systems are CLEF, which implies that (1) psychological and social systems are living systems as well, or (2) further *formal* distinctions should be found distinguishing these three classes of systems, or (3) their difference stems from the *realization*, i.e., implementation into different material systems (which amounts saying that matter matters, at least derivatively), or (4) further conditions of both types (formal and material) are needed.

What these cases have in common is an idea of system different from that characterizing artifacts or mechanisms. To build, say, a house, one starts from a whole series of materials (bricks, concrete, tiles, doors, windows, etc.) and assembles them appropriately. Organisms and society are not "built" this way. Since their beginnings, they have always been systems (or wholes) and they generate within themselves all the relational and functional structures they need.

The techniques developed by predicative science, what we have called the linear and nonlinear modeling techniques, can be used for impredicative science as well, providing that one clearly acknowledges that these techniques provide partial, fragmented models of aspects of the encompassing impredicative system. Even so, they can be dramatically helpful. At the same time, it is fair to state that predicative modeling techniques can also be deeply dangerous if understood as capturing the nature or intrinsic complexity of an impredicative system.

The important lesson to be learned is that impredicative science does not throw away the capacities and the results of predicative science. On the other hand, impredicative science is more general than predicative sciences: it shows that predicative science deals with specific cases. In other words, an impredicative system can always be modeled predicatively, by severing some of its temporal, spatial, or functional connections.

Predicative systems can simulate any system behavior. Given any system behavior, providing that it can be described sufficiently accurately, there is a predicative system which exhibits precisely this behavior (Rosen 2012, p. 10). The manner in which the behavior is naturally generated is utterly immaterial. What matters is only the simulation. The underlying reason deals with the fact that any function can be approximated arbitrarily closely by functions canonically constructed out of a suitably chosen "basis set" whose members have a special form (such as polynomials, trigonometric functions).

In the same way as the denumerably infinite cannot be reached by adding +1 as many times as one likes, but requires a transition to the limit, impredicative systems do not arise from adding a new part or a new feedback loop to any given system, even if this operation is repeated times and again. The passage from predicative to impredicative systems implies the crossing of a threshold, the transition to a limit. This amounts to saying that the difference between predicative and impredicative systems is sharp: a system is either predicative or impredicative and the latter do not emerge from the former by making them more and more, even bewilderingly, complicated. Impredicativity originates in self-referential cycles not in the number of parts. This means that an impredicative system may be based on a smaller number of parts than a predicative one.

Further, impredicative systems may and usually do contain predicative systems, without being themselves predicative. The most obvious instance is provided by organisms, which contain endless chemical machines without being themselves (only) chemical machines. Consider by way of an exemplification the Na-K pump within cell membranes governing the exchange of ions. While each "machine" is predicative, the whole system is impredicative. This explains both why the usual modeling techniques can be used within impredicative science and their limitations.

The transition to the limit characterizing impredicative science helps in making visible other aspects of this new acceptation of science. Notably, the modeling efforts suitable to predicative and impredicative science follow two different strategies. Predicative science facilitates a bottom-up development of models, from field cases to their mathematical coding. Models can then be patched together, after which new abstractions may pave the way towards new models, etc. While this strategy is pestered by inconsistencies and failures, and after a while the efforts to scaling it up become more and more ineffective, major alternatives are not apparent. Impredicative science works the other way round: the starting point is a formal, impredicative model and the main question becomes the specification of the conditions for its realization. This also means that numbers are not used as starting point for developing models; eventually they are used as test beds for verifying how good a model is. Within impredicative science, quality and relation work on a deeper level than quantity and individuality.

Summary

A better and more complete understanding of anticipation and its effects will improve theories and models of individual and collective human behavior and its consequences. The ability to anticipate in complex environments may improve the resilience of societies under threat from a global proliferation of agents and forces by articulating insecurities through anticipatory processes.

The explicit recognition of anticipation opens new scientific perspectives. To mention but two apparently opposed and disconnected outcomes, anticipation both rehabilitates the Aristotelian theory of causes (including a version of the final cause) and generates an innovative understanding of complexity. And from these arises a new, vastly more general acceptance of science.

It is evident that our understanding of anticipation is still cursory and that the novelty of the perspective may conceal the difficulties implied by this otherwise refreshingly new vision. Nonetheless, anticipation is increasingly at the heart of urgent contemporary debates, from climate change to economic instability. Anticipatory capabilities of individuals and communities may enhance the overall sense-making process and improve decision-making, strategy formation, and societal resilience. I will be satisfied if this handbook provides some of its readers with the motives and tools for developing more inclusive forward-looking perspectives.

References

Aczel, P. (1988). *Non-well-founded sets*. Stanford: CSLI.

Albertazzi, L. (2006). *Immanent realism*. Dordrecht: Kluwer.

Albertazzi, L. (Ed.). (2013). *Handbook of experimental phenomenology. Visual perception of shape, space and appearance*. Chichester: Wiley-Blackwell.

Albertazzi, L., & Poli, R. (2014). Multi-leveled objects: Color as a case study. *Frontiers in Psychology, 5*, 592. https://doi.org/10.3389/fpsyg.2014.00592.

Appadurai, A. (2013). *The future as cultural fact*. London: Verso.

Baianu, I. (Ed.). (2006). Complex systems biology and life's logic in memory of Robert Rosen. *Axiomathes, 16*(1–2).

Bartlett, S. J. (1987). Varieties of self-reference. In S. J. Bartlett & P. Suber (Eds.), *Self-reference. Reflections on reflexivity* (pp. 5–28). Dordrecht: Martinus Nijhoff.

Barwise, J., & Etchemendy, J. (1987). *The liar: An essay on truth and circularity*. New York: Oxford University Press.

Beckert, J. (2013). Capitalism as a system of expectations: Toward a sociological microfoundation of political economy. *Politics and Society, 41*(3), 323–350.

Bickhard, M. H. (2009). The interactivist model. *Synthese, 166*(3), 547–591.

Bickhard, M. H. (2015a). Toward a model of functional brain processes I: Central nervous system functional micro-architecture. *Axiomathes, 22*(3), 217–238.

Bickhard, M. H. (2015b). Toward a model of functional brain processes II: Central nervous system functional macro-architecture. *Axiomathes, 22*(4), 377–407.

Bickhard, M. H., & Terveen, L. (1995). *Foundational issues in artificial intelligence and cognitive science. Impasse and solution*. Amsterdam: Elsevier.

Feferman, S. (1998). Weyl vindicated: Das Kontinuum seventy years later. In S. Feferman (Ed.), *In the light of logic* (pp. 249–283). Oxford: Oxford University Press.

Feferman, S. (2005). Predicativity. In S. Shapiro (Ed.), *The Oxford handbook of the philosophy of mathematics and logic* (pp. 590–624). Oxford: Oxford University Press.

Gergen, K. J. (2015). From mirroring to world-making: Research as future forming. *Journal for the Theory of Social Behavior, 45*(3), 287–310.

Kampis, G. (1995). Computability, self-reference and self-amendment. *Communication and Cognition – Artificial Intelligence, 12*(1–2), 91–109.

Lofgren, L. (1968). An axiomatic explanation of complete self-reproduction. *Bulletin of Mathematical Biophysics, 30*, 415–425.

Louie, A. H. (2009). *More than life itself*. Frankfurt: Ontos Verlag.

Louie, A. H. (2013). *The reflection of life. Functional entailment and imminence in relational biology*. New York: Springer.

Mikulecky, D. C. (Ed.). (2007). System theory and biocomplexity (Commemorative issue, Robert Rosen). *Chemistry and Biodiversity, 4*.

Miller, R. (2006). *From trends to futures literacy. Reclaiming the future.* Paper presented at the Centre for Strategic Education, Seminar Series Paper No. 160.

Miller, R. (2007). Futures literacy: A hybrid strategic scenario method. *Futures, 39*(4), 341–362. https://doi.org/10.1016/j.futures.2006.12.001.

Miller, R., Poli, R., & Rossel, P. (2017). The discipline of anticipation. Exploring key issues. In R. Miller (Ed.), *Transforming the future: Anticipation in the 21st century.* UNESCO/Routledge: Paris/Oxford.

Nadin, M. (Ed.). (2015). *Anticipation: Learning from the past.* Dordrecht: Springer.

Nadin, M. (Ed.). (2016). *Anticipation across disciplines.* Dordrecht: Springer.

Poli, R. (2001). The basic problem of the theory of levels of reality. *Axiomathes, 12*(3–4), 261–283.

Poli, R. (2011). Steps toward an explicit ontology of the future. *Journal of Futures Studies, 16*(1), 67–78.

Poli, R. (2014a). Anticipation: A New Thread for the Human and Social Sciences? *Cadmus, 2*(3), 23–36.

Poli, R. (2014b). Anticipation: What about turning the human and social sciences upside down? *Futures, 64*, 15–18.

Poli, R. (2015). The implicit future orientation of the capability approach. *Futures, 71*, 105–113.

Poli, R. (2017). *Introduction to anticipation studies.* Dordrecht: Springer.

Riegler, A. (2003). Whose anticipations? In M. V. Butz, O. Sigaud, & P. Gerard (Eds.), *Anticipatory behavior in adaptive learning systems* (pp. 11–22). Berlin: Springer.

Rosen, R. (2012). *Anticipatory systems. Philosophical, mathematical, and methodological foundations* (2nd ed.). New York: Springer.

Seligman, M. E. P., Railton, P., Baumeister, R. F., & Sripada, C. (2013). Navigating into the future or driven by the past. *Perspectives on Psychological Science, 8*(2), 119–141. https://doi.org/10.1177/1745691612474317.

Simons, D. J., & Chabris, C. F. (1999). Gorillas in our midst: Sustained inattentional blindness for dynamic events. *Perception, 28*, 1059–1074.

Tuomi, I. (2013). *Next-generation foresight in anticipatory organizations.* Paper presented at the European Forum on Forward-Looking Activities (EFFLA). European Commission.

Varela, F. (1974). A calculus for self-reference. *International Journal of General Systems, 1*(2), 5–24.

Complex Systems

2

A. H. Louie and Roberto Poli

Contents

Abstract

Traditional modes of system representation as dynamical systems, involving fixed sets of states together with imposed dynamical laws, pertain only to a meagre subclass of natural systems. This reductionistic paradigm leaves no room for final causes; constrained thus are the simple systems. Members of their complementary collection, natural systems having mathematical models that are not dynamical systems, are the complex systems. Complex systems, containing hierarchical cycles in their entailment networks, can only be approx-

A. H. Louie (✉)
Ottawa, ON, Canada

Stellenbosch Institute for Advanced Study (STIAS), Wallenberg Research Centre at Stellenbosch University, Stellenbosch, South Africa
e-mail: connect@ahlouie.com

R. Poli
Department of Sociology and Social Research, University of Trento, Trento, Italy
e-mail: roberto.poli@unitn.it

© Springer Nature Switzerland AG 2019
R. Poli (ed.), *Handbook of Anticipation*,
https://doi.org/10.1007/978-3-319-91554-8_3

imated and simulated, locally and temporarily, by simple ones. Anticipatory systems are, in this specific sense, complex, hence this introductory chapter on Complex Systems in the *Handbook of Anticipation*.

Keywords
Complex system · Simple system · Anticipatory system · Dynamical system · Impredicativity · Closed path of efficient causation · Hierarchical cycle · Emergence · Difference in kind · Simulability · Algorithm

Complexitas

There is no unique definition of 'complexity'.

The only agreement is that scholars disagree: there are almost as many definitions of 'complexity' as schools involved in the study of the topic. The babel of the usage of the *avant-garde* word 'complexity' and all its derivatives is evident. A common intersection, however, of all characterizations of 'complexity' contains as the very minimum the requisite

$$\text{emergence of phenomena from a plurality of interactions.} \qquad (1)$$

A complex system entails emergent novelties, things that are surprising, unexpected, and apparently unpredictable. A simple (i.e., noncomplex) system does not engender these counterintuitive things. But complexity is not employable as an explanatory principle of (1), 'complexity' and 'emergence' being fashionable labels of the same concept. It is the *source(s)* and the *cause(s)* of this 'emergence' in (1) that are the contentions of what constitute 'complexity'.

This chapter on Complex Systems is not meant to be a comprehensive survey of this vast subject. It is, after all, a chapter appearing in *The Handbook of Anticipation*, so the presentation will be on the connection between anticipation and complexity, with emphasis on one species of the latter. This particular species of complexity explicated herein is *impredicativity*, and is proposed in the Rashevsky–Rosen school of *relational biology* as a necessary condition for life:

$$\textit{Complexitas viventia producit.} \qquad (2)$$

Complexity brings forth living beings. More explicitly, a living system anticipates, and an anticipatory system is impredicative (complex):

$$\text{Impredicativity} \supset \text{Anticipation} \supset \text{Life} \qquad (3)$$

(See the ▶ Chaps. 1, "Introducing Anticipation," ▶ 10, "Relational Biology," and ▶ 45, "Mathematical Foundations of Anticipatory Systems" in this *Handbook* for further explorations of these inclusions.) We shall begin informally with an exposition on the strategies of studying complexity before homing in on the mathematical intricacies of the beyond-algorithmicity that is impredicativity.

The antonymy of 'simple' and 'complex' (used as attributes of natural systems) has been studied in many modes and contexts, by natural scientists, social scientists, mathematicians, and myriad others. But their various distinctions, just as many other dealings with differences, may be broadly classified as either 'difference in degree' or 'difference in kind'.

If one takes a material view of nature, and believes that physics equips one with universal laws that encompass all (natural) systems, then there is only one kind of 'system' (namely, a subset of the universe), whence 'simple' and 'complex' only differ in degree. A representative proponent of this stereotypical view is von Neumann (1951, 1956), who contended that 'complexity' is a measurable (or even computable) quantity of systems that might be used to totally order them, i.e., that complexity was a kind of taxonomic index, or ranking, of systems. Further, he suggested that there was a critical value, or *threshold*, of complexity. Below this threshold were simple systems that behaved in their conventional mechanical modes, and above the threshold populated complex systems that were capable of manifesting new, counterintuitive, unanticipated modes of behavior. In this scenario, (a necessarily finite number of) repetitions (and removals) of rote operations sufficed to cross the (unavoidably fuzzy) threshold, to carry systems from one realm to the other (and back). This in-degree difference between simple and complex devolved into the equivocation of complexity with 'complication': the more constituent elementary units a system had, and the more elaborate the modes of interconnection between them were, the 'more complex' the system was. Note that the in-degree difference allows the possibility of the comparative 'more complex'.

On the other hand, an in-kind difference between the class of simple systems and the class of complex systems would require an absolute partition of the universe into two complementary sets. In the universe U of natural systems, one defines the collection P of simple systems as all those natural systems that satisfy a specific property p:

$$P = \{x \in U : p(x)\}. \tag{4}$$

(See ▶ Chap. 10, "Relational Biology" in this *Handbook* for an explication of the Axiom of Specification and other nuances of set theory). For an in-kind distinction, one defines the collection of complex systems as its complement, the set P^c of all the natural systems that do *not* satisfy the property p; equivalently, all those that satisfy the property $\neg p$ (*not p*), i.e.:

$$\begin{aligned} P^c &= \{x \in U : \neg\, p(x)\} \\ &= \{x \in U : x \notin P\} = U \sim P. \end{aligned} \tag{5}$$

The partition $\langle\, P \,|\, P^c \,\rangle$ of U then entails an 'impermeable' boundary: a system is either simple or complex (but not both), and the two categories of simple systems and complex systems are mutually exclusive. From the outset, a dichotomy is established; a complex system is defined as a system that is not simple, and vice versa. In-kind difference is absolute: a natural system is complex or it is not; there is no 'more complex' in-degree comparisons among systems.

As an illustration, consider the cardinality of sets. An in-degree difference between simple and complex is akin to the classification of the size of sets into 'small' versus 'big'. Instinctively, a set containing a few elements is small, while a set containing, say, a googolplex of elements is big; but the transition from small to big is fuzzy, it being context dependent. (Is 2703068 a small number, or a big number? How about 2703069?) Contrariwise, an in-kind difference between simple and complex systems is analogous to the distinction between 'finite' and 'infinite' sets. The partition between finite sets and infinite sets is impermeable. Infinite is not 'big finite': from within the finite realm, (a finite, however big, number of) repetitions of mechanistic operations such as 'add one element' will not make a finite set infinite.

Analysis and Synthesis

How should one study a given natural system? The conventional strategy is to break down the system into its constituent elements. If the resulting elements are still too complicated, the same procedure is repeated until one arrives at simple-enough elements to be able to understand them. Ideally, once the 'elementary' elements or particles have been found, the original system can be reconstituted from them.

This strategy goes back to Descartes's methodological rules. It is based on two implicit and usually tacit assumptions. The first assumption is that fragmentation implies simplification: that is, the idea is that particles are indeed *simpler* than the system they compose. In this regard, it is worth noting that elementary-particle physics is apparently as good a counterexample as any other. The second assumption is that fragmentation does not eliminate *essential* information. Otherwise stated, the implicit assumption is that all the relevant properties of a system can be recovered by taking into account its elements and their relations.

This strategy of system analysis has even been elevated to the *principle* of composition, one of the fundamental assumptions of classical science. According to the principle of composition, a given entity under analytical investigation is decomposed into parts. The guiding idea is that the entity is literally made of these parts and can be reconstructed from them, and decomposition into parts misses no relevant information. This assumption is universally valid, providing that the following conditions are respected: (*a*) the interactions among the parts do not exist or are negligible, (*b*) the relations describing the behavior of the parts are linear, and (*c*) the whole resulting from the parts does not perform any functional behavior. These are, however, very severe restrictions; very few natural systems meet them. The parts of a system are in interaction, their relations in general are nonlinear, and systems are encapsulated within other systems. Systems so restricted, described as "not organized complexity," are well represented in classic physics, and systems not so restricted (almost all natural systems), "organized complexity," are well represented in biology (Weaver 1948).

Fundamental for organized complexities is the concept of hierarchical order, according to which systems are decomposable into subsystems and these into further sub-subsystems. One cannot fail to note that the starting point of this new vision is the system (the whole) and that systems are decomposed into subsystems, not into elements or atomic components.

While the suggestion is proposed that this divide-and-rule strategy has proved immensely successful, the systems that are entirely governed by their elements (from below, so to speak) are rare. The vast majority of systems follows a different pattern: these systems depend not only on their elements but also on the system that results from them and eventually also on higher-order systems of which they are parts (e.g., organisms, communities) (Poli 2011; Rosen 1985a). The fact is that analysis through fragmentation may inadvertently destroy the relational linkages that are crucial in the study of many kinds of systems (such as 'living' ones). Other forms of analysis (e.g., through 'subsystems') may offer better results. Synthesis, on the other hand, is a natural procedure with which to study emergence: the (unanticipated) relational connections that appear when a multitude of component systems interact. The main problem is that at least some systems cannot be fragmented without losing relevant information.

Admittedly, our understanding of non-fragmentable systems is still deficient: there is no denying that robust methods of subsystem analysis and synthesis need to be developed. Anyway, the availability of both strategies (analytic and synthetic) will enable the development of a more articulated, integral, respectful, and responsible vision of the world.

Analysis and synthesis are the two general strategies to which we may resort to understand any given system. The former strategy claims that a system is what results from its parts (look downward), while the latter strategy claims that a system is what results from the higher systems to which it pertains (look upward) (Poli 2011, 2017).

System Theory

In the same sense in which the Copernican revolution was far more than the ability to better calculate, albeit slightly, the movement of the planets, and relativity has been much more than an explanation of a small number of recalcitrant physical phenomena, the introduction of system theory is more than the study of nonlinear dynamics. What systems bring in and make visible is the idea of complexity. However, something more is at stake, namely, the difference between predicative and impredicative science.

System theory faces its difficulties too. In fact, system theory has raised both enthusiastic appreciations and even more severe denigrations. For a scathing attack on the whole "systems movement," see, e.g., Lilienfeld (1978). As Midgley (2003, *p.* xxxv) notes,

Although Lilienfeld's book might have been a little hysterical, it struck a chord with a social science research community that was aware of some of the expensive failures and disastrous social experiments being perpetrated in city planning departments in the name of systems [*sic*] thinking.

The systemic perspective encounters resistance from other directions as well. Many scientific questions have the annoying habit of crossing departmental and faculty boundaries. Not by chance, having learnt to properly frame one's questions is customarily taken as indicative of successful training. The subsequent fragmentation into more and more restricted areas of specialization has provided such an astonishing amount of results that it almost annuls the possibility of any alternative strategy. The very idea that one science could have something to learn from another science – say sociology from biology, or the other way round – is dismissed out of hand. Dissenting voices have been feeble and substantially ineffective. The common wisdom is that there is only one universal science, namely, physics. To this end, biology deals with inordinately rare contingencies, and, say, sociology deals with second-order inordinately rare contingencies and therefore lacks any general value.

Out of darkness emerges a robust alternative strategy. Nicolas Rashevsky (1899–1972) initiated relational biology in the 1950s, and the subject was subsequently expanded and fine-tuned by his student Robert Rosen (1934–1998). Rosen explicitly posed two disturbing questions: Is physics indeed the most general science? Do we not have something to learn not only from the differences among sciences but also from their similarities?

The first question raises the possibility that physics could be very special – even inordinately so – and that a proper understanding of the duality between 'speciality' and 'generality' opens new avenues for science. The second question entails the distinction between two different modes of analysis, the structural and the functional. Learning to distinguish the two modes and to use them properly will become the gateway to a new vision of science.

A promising strategy is to distinguish between what a system is *made of* (structure) and what a system is *made for* (function) (Rosen 1971). The former attitude is isolative; the latter is relational. To fix ideas, the distinction is introduced between two different modes of *analysis*: the analysis of a system into its elements and the analysis of a system into its subsystems. One should be careful to avoid the assumption that each functional activity implies a given structure that supports it. In fact, the relation is far from being one-to-one; eventually a many-to-many relation is implied, in the sense that each function can be implemented by different structures and each structure can express different functions.

For an illustrative example, consider a production company. To survive and develop, the company should perform a variety of different functional activities, including designing new products, producing, storing, and distributing them, managing employees and workers, etc. Any of these activities may be performed by a specialized unit, or it may be split among a variety of units in many different ways. Companies make different choices in this regard. All the possibly different structural choices notwithstanding, the functions to be performed are analogous. Structures divide, functions unify.

One of the major differences between analysis via elements and analysis via subsystems is the following: given a system S, there is only one maximal set of component elements, while there are many ways to decompose the system S into functional subsystems, both at different hierarchical levels and from different perspectives. This difference underlies Rosen's claim that "there are many ways for a system of entailment to be complex; only one way for it to be simple" (Rosen 1991b).

To compound the problem, the functional perspective is not limited to the subsystem–system relation. The system itself enters into functional relations with its environment or, better, with other systems in its environment. And, as the case may be, it can establish different functional relations with different systems. Moreover, different functional subsystems can develop different functional relations among themselves. The social realm offers as many relevant exemplifications as one may wish: one may consider functional subsystems such as the economic, political, legal, scientific ones, etc., and the network of their functional interdependencies.

Each subsystem has its own models – one could say its own codes. However, to communicate with other subsystems or the overall systems, a given subsystem cannot but exploit the structures to which it has access.

An awkward and often misunderstood issue emerges here. The problem is the difference between 'doing' something and 'making sense' of what is done. Beside the difference between *ex ante* and *ex post* sense-making, i.e., between the sense of an action before it is performed and the different sense that it may acquire after it has been performed (Schutz 1967), all the systems' interactions depend on, and can be performed only through, their material structures. What a system *does* depends on its structure; what a system *means* depends on its functional interconnections.

Note that the very distinction between structural and functional organization is an outcome of the interaction with our scientific and technological capacities. Apparently, nature does not distinguish them in the same way as we do. Consider, for instance, an airplane and a bird. The airplane distinguishes the engine (power) and the lift mechanisms (the airfoil) and segregates them into separate 'organs'. The bird, instead, unifies the propeller and the airfoil into a single organ, the wing. As Rosen notes, "there is no physical mechanism which can dissect the bird wing apart in such a way that the functions are separated" (Rosen 1974). Interestingly, holograms are the only artifacts similar to natural organs.

We have seen the difference between analysis through fragmentation into elements and analysis through distinction into subsystems. Before entering into further details, the reader should take notice that the distinction between analysis through *elements* and analysis through *subsystems* is not exhaustive. A third kind of analysis should be considered, namely, analysis though separation into natural *levels*. Levels here correspond to what has elsewhere been called 'levels of reality' as distinguished from either levels of organization or levels of representation (Gnoli and Poli 2004; Poli 1998, 2001, 2006, 2007, 2011).

The availability of different kinds of analysis (and, likewise, different kinds of synthesis) shows that different strategies can be used. It is therefore important to understand the capacities and the limitations of each strategy.

The following two examples reveal something more of the tangled network resulting from the interactions among system, subsystem, structure, and function. In the case of the 'vertical' relation exemplified by the subsystem-system situation, the relevant structure automatically pertains to both of them. Even if what the structure does can be (and usually is) interpreted differently, because the system and the subsystem may adopt different models, the presence of a shared structural unit forces a level of mutual adjustment. On the other hand, the 'horizontal' relation between systems (or subsystems) is much more subject to misunderstanding, in the sense that more translations are required: the communication from system S_1 to system S_2 includes the translation from S_1 to the structure $\delta(S_1)$ of S_1 that should interact with a corresponding structure $\delta(S_2)$ of S_2, the translation between $\delta(S_1)$ and $\delta(S_2)$, and finally the translation between $\delta(S_2)$ and S_2:

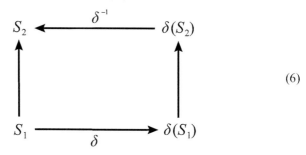

$$(6)$$

Not only may each of these translations go awry, the selection itself of the structures that materially open a channel between the two systems is also a source of possible mistakes. Therefore, the unfolding of $S_1 \to S_2$ into the composition $S_1 \to \delta(S_1) \to \delta(S_2) \to S_2$ is far from being a trivial affair. It is even more complex when one realizes that, as far as social systems in particular are concerned, the value of the usual 'structural map' $S \to \delta(S)$ is rarely uniquely determined, it often being instead of the type $S \to \{\delta_1(S), \delta_2(S), \ldots, \delta_n(S)\}$. On the connection between set-valued mappings and anticipation, see Louie (2013) and Poli (2017).

Systems and Subsystems

Each subsystem uses only some of the degrees of freedom of the overall system. As a consequence, the dynamics of the subsystem and the dynamics of the overall system may and usually do diverge. The dynamic equations of the overall system include all the system's degrees of freedom. Similarly, the dynamic equations of the subsystem include all the subsystem's degrees of freedom. However, since the degrees of freedom of the subsystem is smaller than that of the overall system, the question arises as to the roles performed by the system's degree of freedom that do not contribute to the subsystem's dynamics. They may characterize other subsystems, and in general they are free to interact with other subsystems and even with other systems in the environment of the overall system. What they do, however, is outside the window of relevance of the subsystem (given by its degrees of freedom), so that they may follow codes incomprehensible from the point of view of the subsystem.

Systems (or subsystems) endowed with different models read the same underlying situation differently. "Our choice of models … is important because it affects how we think about the world" (Maynard Smith 1987, *p.* 120). Essentially, this is the source of both innovation and conflict. The following question arises: "how can the behaviors of different systems, perceiving the same set of circumstances but equipped with different models, be integrated?" (Rosen 1979). To begin with, conflict is a natural outcome of any differentiated society. Not only do different underlying models see the situation differently (e.g., because different observables are encoded and/or the observables are differently structured), but they generate different anticipations about the future evolution of the situation.

Not surprisingly, "most of what we call 'conflict' arises not so much in an objective situation, but in the fact that widely different predictive models of that situation are harbored by the parties to the conflict" (Rosen 1984). Indeed, many *objective* differences, such as those connected to the social division of labor, the differences in social capital (economic, cultural, relational; Bourdieu 1984); gender, age, health – that is, all the variants of social differentiation – contribute to the development of different models and are therefore sources of possible conflicts. One way to mitigate conflicts is to develop strategies for the embedding of partial individual and group models in more comprehensive ones.

Models

It is now time to address the question: "to study social systems, why should one study biological ones?" (Rosen 1979, 1984). The converse question may be raised as well: "to study biological systems, why should one study social ones?" And, more generally, the basic question is: "to study a system of type X, why should one study a system of type Y?" As Rosen notes, science is replete with relevant exemplifications. To mention but one of the examples presented by Rosen, in order to understand biological membranes, biologists study collodion films, ultrathin glass, and ion exchangers. This and many other similar cases show that it is simply untrue that "the only thing about a system which is important is the arrangement of matter within it." In fact, if it were so, "how does it happen that the study of such 'model systems' is possible at all?" (Rosen 1974).

A condition is needed for this to make sense, namely, that the two systems, as different as they are from a structural (material) point of view, are nevertheless similar enough from a functional point of view, so that one can learn something about the behavior of one system by looking at the behavior of the other.

The simplest way to exploit this intuition is to understand the dynamics of a given system as a representative of a class of systems with the same dynamics. When different systems (and related subsystems) have the same dynamics, one can use the knowledge arising from any of them to better understand any other system of the class. Since different sciences are usually differently successful in understanding different aspects of the relevant systems, each of them can have something analogous to offer to its fellow sciences.

Besides the possibility of using materially different systems (such as a biological and a social one) pertaining to the same dynamic class in such a way that one could be used to gain better understanding of the other, the same idea can be exploited for hierarchically organized systems. When different levels of organization of a biological or social system pertain to the same dynamic class, the level that is better understood can be used as a specimen for those that are less understood.

Models anticipate. In fact, the anticipatory exploitation of models is possibly the single most important reason for developing models. According to Rosen, "An anticipatory system is a system containing a predictive model of itself and/or its environment, which allows it to change state at an instant in accord with the model's predictions pertaining to a later instant" (Rosen 1985a, *p.* 339). This definition states that anticipation concerns the capacity exhibited by some systems to tune their behavior according to a model of the future evolution of themselves or the environment in which they are embedded.

The following quote, after Rosen (1979), helps developing a somewhat more concrete grasp of the situation:

> The vehicle by which we anticipate is in fact a *model*, which enables us to pull the future into the present. The stimulus for our action is in fact not simply the sight of the bear; it is the prediction or output of our model under these conditions ... This simple example contains the essence of anticipatory behavior. It involves the concept of *feedforward*, rather than feedback. The distinction between feedforward and feedback is important, and is as follows. In a feedback system, as we have seen, control is error-actuated, and serves to correct a system performance which is already deteriorating. In a feedforward system, on the other hand, system behavior is *preset*, according to some model relating present inputs to their predicted outcomes. ... The essence of a feedforward system, then, is that present change of state is determined by an anticipated future state, computed in accordance with some internal model of the world.

As natural as model-based anticipation may appear, its potentialities are restrained by the main assumption hidden in the modelling of physical systems championed by Newton: namely, that the dynamics of a natural system depends exclusively on present and past states of the system. No future information is ever allowed to play any role whatever. This is captured by what Rosen (1991a, *p.* 49) succinctly calls

The Zeroth Commandment *Thou shalt not allow the future to affect the present.*

For the most part, physics may consider only present states and present forces; biological, psychological, and social systems need to include also past states and forces (memory). This is already a first major difference between physical (or nonliving) and living systems. The inclusion of memory, however relevant it may be, is still not sufficient for precise distinction between nonliving and living systems. Memory-based systems can still be purely mechanical systems. Living systems require more, namely, future states and forces. It is simply impossible to perform even the simplest action without involving in one way or another the future as an active force. Therefore, underlying the idea of anticipation is

Anticipatory System's Main Assumption *Future states may determine present changes of state.*

Causes, Complexity, and Dynamics

The explicit introduction of anticipation into the scientific framework developed by Rosen rehabilitates the supposedly antiquated Aristotelian theory of the four causes: material, formal, efficient, and final. Even more importantly, Rosen advances the Aristotelian theory by showing not only that the causes can overlap with but even merge into one another. Two steps are needed to arrive at this result. The first step is to find a way to show how the first three Aristotelian causes are customarily translated into the machinery of physics. Rosen's translation in this regard is to embed the material cause in the state space, the formal cause in the space of parameters, and the efficient cause in the family of operators (Rosen 1984). The second step adds anticipation as the scientific counterpart of the final cause. The Newtonian framework does not have room for anticipation. The claim is therefore advanced that Newtonian science is too limited a framework to give proper account of the structures of reality. A more general new framework is needed, one able to include all the causes at work in reality. One may note that the theory of Memory Evolutive Systems arrives at the same result. Specifically, the merging of the causes is a consequence of the "Iterated Complexification Theorem" (see Ehresmann and Vanbremeersch 2007, Chap. 4, Sect. 6.1).

During the past few decades, the idea has been repeatedly put forward of using the network of causes to distinguish between complex and complicated systems. It is often claimed that complicated systems originate from causes that can be individually distinguished, can be addressed piece by piece, and that for each input to the system there is a proportionate output. On the other hand, complex systems result from networks of multiple interacting causes that cannot be individually distinguished, must be addressed as entire systems (i.e., they cannot be addressed piecemeal), and are such that small inputs may result in disproportionate effects. Unfortunately, the theoretical support for these claims is fragmented and often lacks the generality required to be fully convincing.

An intimately connected issue is the mutual transmutation of the causes, generating the collapse of the framework supporting the theory of dynamic systems. Dynamic theories have two components: instantaneous states (the values of observables at a given time point) collected into the system's state space and the modification in time of the state space (i.e., the changes of the values of states of the system) as captured by dynamic equations. When the different categories of cause are mutually interrelated, new states emerge and others may disappear. As a result, the system no longer has a preestablished, fixed once-and-for-all, state space. As soon as the state space changes, the idea of a set of dynamical equations able to capture the dynamics of the system vanishes as well.

A different way to present the same problem is to say that we do not have a dynamic theory of functional systems. The dynamic frameworks that we can exploit are limited to structural systems. The failure of the theory of dynamic systems opens interesting new avenues, among them the ontological priority of open systems over closed ones. In this regard, it is worth noting that the very idea of open system is relational, in the sense that it makes no reference to particles. Even more interestingly, the failure of the theory of dynamic system paves the way for a full-fledged theory on the emergence of new, higher-order systems from underlying preceding systems. One may note that the emergence of new systems follows a characteristic pattern: often the new emergent system is initially simpler ('more primitive' in a suitable sense of 'primitive') than the systems from which it results; then, once generated, it starts its own developmental trajectory and in time acquires new capacities.

Rosen's relational-biologic framework is the only one proposed so far that is wide enough to fully resolve the above issues. The move from predicative to impredicative science suffices. *Impredicativity*, indeed, is the definitive 'complexity'; it encompasses anticipation and life (see inclusions (3) above). And on this πέτρα the Rashevsky–Rosen school of relational biology is built. It is thus toward a formal exposition of this topic that we now turn.

Beyond Algorithms

The Rashevsky–Rosen school of relational biology resides definitively on the in-kind difference moiety of the simple-versus-complex distinction. The introduction of the Rosen essay (Rosen 1985b) serves as its manifesto:

> The thrust of this essay is that the theory of organisms, and of what we shall call *complex systems* in general, requires a circle of ideas and methods that, from the very outset, depart radically from those taken as axiomatic for the past 300 years.
>
> What we shall conclude can be stated succinctly here at the outset, as follows.
>
> 1. Our current systems [*sic*] theory, including all that presently constitutes physics or physical science, deals exclusively with a very special class of systems that I shall call *simple systems* or *mechanisms*.
> 2. Organisms, and many other kinds of material systems, are not mechanisms in this sense. Rather, they belong to a different (and much larger) class of systems, which we shall call *complex*.
> 3. Thus the relation between contemporary physics and biology is not, as everyone routinely supposes, that of general to particular.
> 4. To describe complex systems in general, and organisms *a fortiori*, an entirely novel kind of mathematical language is necessary.
> 5. A simple system can only *approximate* to a complex one, locally and temporarily, just as, e.g., a tangent plane can only approximate to a nonplanar surface locally and temporarily. Thus in a certain sense, a complex system can be regarded as a kind of global limit of its approximating simple subsystems.
> 6. Complex systems, unlike simple ones, admit a category of final causation, or anticipation, in a perfectly rigorous and nonmystical way.

One may offer the explicit.

Definition A natural system is a *simple system* if all of its models are simulable.

Definition A natural system is a *complex system* if it is not a simple system.

Here is a terse explanation of the terms, in their formal incarnations, appearing in the definitions. (Most of them are discussed in detail in the ▶ Chaps. 10, "Relational Biology" and ▶ 45, "Mathematical Foundations of Anticipatory Systems" in this

Handbook. We shall also have more to say about them presently in this introductory chapter.) A *model* is a commutative encoding and decoding between two systems in a *modelling relation*. A model is *simulable* if it is "definable by an algorithm." (There is no need to get into the intricacies of algorithms here. It suffices to note that the crucial characterization of algorithmic and simulable as applied to formal systems is that these are concepts restricted by *finitude*, whence their simplicity. A *formal system* is "an object in the universe of mathematics." It includes, but is not limited and therefore not equivocated to, Hilbert's formalism. In this context, then, a simple system is a natural system with the property that every formal system that encodes it through the modelling relation is simulable.

Let U be the universe of natural systems and let $N \in U$. Let M be a model of N (i.e., $M \in \mathbf{C}(N)$; see ▶ Chap. 45, "Mathematical Foundations of Anticipatory Systems" in this *Handbook* for the notations). Further, let $s(M)$ be the property 'M is simulable'. Then, by definition, the collection of all simple systems is

$$S = \{N \in U : \forall M \in \mathbf{C}(N)\, s(M)\}. \tag{7}$$

The negation of the statement 'all models are simulable' is 'there exists a nonsimulable model'; the complementary set, the collection of all complex systems, is accordingly

$$S^c = \{N \in U : \exists M \in \mathbf{C}(N)\, \neg s(M)\}. \tag{8}$$

As a consequence of our in-kind distinction between simple systems and complex systems, we do not equate 'complexity' with mere 'complication'. A simple mathematical example serves to illustrate the difference between the two terms. There are many methods of matrix inversion, and they are all algorithmic. The mechanism to calculate the inverse of an (invertible) $n \times n$ matrix is, therefore, simple. For small n, say up to 20, one may feasibly do the inversion 'by hand' (i.e., with pencil and paper). For larger n, modern electronic computers pick up the baton with alacrity. Whatever the size of n, the same simple-in-principle algorithms apply. For very large n, however, the matrix inversion problem becomes 'complicated'. 'Technical difficulties' include the polynomial computation time (viz., the usual 'it won't finish before the end of the universe' hyperboles), computer memory and page-faulting issues, and numerical errors due to truncation and magnitude-disparity cancellations. These 'complications', however, do not negate the fact that the processes are algorithmic and therefore *simple* (i.e., by definition *not complex*) and, indeed, some of the difficulties will disappear (or at least diminish) with technological advances. The corresponding 'complex' problem would be, say, the calculation of the inverse operator on an infinite-dimensional Hilbert space; then, of course, the problem requires a completely different solution and is not the algorithmic extension to 'invert the $n \times n$ matrix but with $n = \infty$'.

The simple system/complex system partition is an ontological divide. But how does one epistemologically distinguish the simple from the complex? Since one cannot practically check *all* models of a system for simulability, how does one recognize a simplex system when one sees one? Chapter 8 of Rosen (1991a) and

Chap. 8 of Louie (2009) contain expositions and mathematical proofs of the consequences of simplicity of systems. The reader is cordially invited to consult these two works, especially for explanation of those terms that appear below but are not explicitly defined. We will not repeat the philosophical and formal discussions here but will only give a summary of the conclusions.

These are properties of a simple system:

Theorem *If a natural system N is a simple system, then*

i. *N has a unique largest model M^{max}.*
ii. *N has a finite set $\{M_i^{min}\}$ of minimal models.*
iii. *The maximal model is equivalent to the direct sum of the minimal ones, $M^{max} = \bigoplus_i M_i^{min}$, and is therefore a synthetic model.*
iv. *Analytic and synthetic models coincide in the category $\mathbf{C}(N)$.*
v. *Every property of N is fractionable.*

A simple system contains no closed path of efficient causation (hierarchical cycle). The five statements in the following theorem are equivalent to one another. (See ▶ Chap. 10, "Relational Biology" in this *Handbook* for the definitions and notations.)

Theorem
i. *If all models of a natural system N are simulable, then there can be no closed path of efficient causation in N.*
ii. *There can be no hierarchical cycle in a simple system.*
iii. *If a closed path of efficient causation exists in a natural system N, then N cannot be a simple system.*
iv. *If a closed path of efficient causation exists in a natural system, then it has a model that is not simulable.*
v. *In (the relational diagram of) a simple system, there cannot be a cycle that contains two or more solid-headed arrows.*

Simplicity of systems therefore has an equivalent, and graphically verifiable, characterization (Fig. 1).

Theorem *A natural system has no closed path of efficient causation if and only if all of its models are simulable.*

Toward Impredicativity

A complex system is one in which there must exist closed paths of efficient causation. Such hierarchical cycles cannot exist in a simple system; therein lies its feebleness, in the sense that there is insufficient entailment structure in a simple system to close a cycle of hierarchical compositions. In mathematics, cycles of this kind are manifested by impredicativities, or self-references – indeed, by the inability

Fig. 1 Entailment network of a sample simple system: no closed path of efficient causation (The *green cycle* is a closed path of material causation, a sequential cycle)

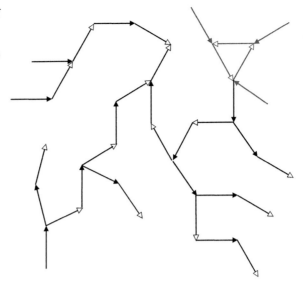

to internalize every referent. Simplicity is thus equivalent to predicativity. (*Predicativity* is complete, algorithmic, inferential syntacticization. *Impredicativity*, its antonym, is the property of a self-referential definition and may entail ambiguities. Cf. ► Chaps. 1, "Introducing Anticipation" and ► 10, "Relational Biology" in this *Handbook*.) One has, therefore, the following collection of five equivalent statements:

S i. N is a simple system.
S ii. N has no closed path of efficient causation.
S iii. All models of N are simulable.
S iv. N has no hierarchical cycle.
S v. N is a predicative system.

Complementarily, one also has the following set of five equivalent statements (Fig. 2):

S^c i. N is a complex system.
S^c ii. N contains a closed path of efficient causation.
S^c iii. N has a nonsimulable model.
S^c iv. N contains a hierarchical cycle.
S^c v. N is an impredicative system.

Theorem *A natural system is impredicative (i.e., 'complex') if and only if it contains a closed path of efficient causation. A natural system is predicative (i.e., 'simple') if and only if it contains no closed path of efficient causation.*

In view of this last Theorem, every appearance of the characterization 'all models are simulable' heretofore may be replaced by 'has no closed path of efficient causation', or equivalently 'has no hierarchical cycle', or equivalently 'predicative' (taking care, obviously, in rephrasing to avoid redundancies). So all discussions of

Fig. 2 Entailment network of
a sample complex system,
with a closed path of efficient
causation (shown in *red*)

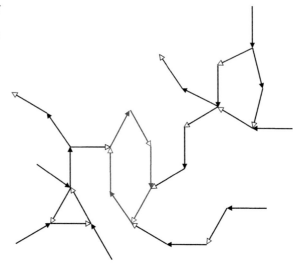

simple systems may be taken without ever mentioning simulability (computability, effectiveness, 'evaluability by a mathematical (Turing) machine', or any other similar computing-theoretic concepts). In fact, the only property of simulability that is used in the proofs of the above theorems is the obvious fact and almost-tautological statement that the program of a simulable model must be of *finite* length. It is opportune to reemphasize that complex systems are 'noncomputable' in the 'non-algorithmic' sense. A suitably altered definition of computability (e.g., drop the finitude requirement, or if ever a true 'heuristic computer' is developed) can make complexity (indeed, anything at all) computable.

Although it has been proven (in Rosen 1991a and Louie 2009) that certain processes are not simulable, it is really beside the point! The sidetrack into the domain of the Church–Turing thesis is incidental. The most important conclusion is that causal entailment patterns *without* and *with* closed paths of efficient causation are *different in kind* and that the barrier between the two classes is 'nonporous': "there are no purely syntactic operations that will take us across the barrier at all." The in-kind difference of predicativity and impredicativity is the very dichotomy between simple systems and complex systems.

The Newtonian paradigm invariably images natural systems as dynamical systems, dual structures consisting of sets of states and imposed dynamical laws. However much the languages that one uses to construct system models of whatever kind may differ, in detail and emphasis, all represent paraphrases of the language of Newtonian mechanics. Two separate ingredients are necessary for the process of system description; they are: (i) a specification of what the system is like at any particular instant of time, with the associated concept of the *instantaneous state* of the system, and (ii) a specification of how the system changes state, as a function of present or past states and of the forces imposed on the system, i.e., the *dynamics*. The characterization of the instantaneous state involves the specification of an appropriate set of *state variables*, while the characterization of how the system changes state involves a specification of the *equations of motion* of the system. Further, each natural system has a maximal image, which behaves like a free object (in the mathematical sense), and of which all formal models of the natural system are homomorphic images. All dynamical systems are simulable. In this regime, therefore, all natural systems are simple. Stated otherwise, a natural system is simple if a single description (namely, its maximal dynamical system model) suffices to account for its processes (and all one's interactions with it).

Relational biology contends that there are natural systems that possess mathematical images that are not dynamical systems; these are the impredicative complex systems. There is, in particular, no maximal description of a complex system. Complexity is a consequence of the plurality of inequivalent models. Complexity is not an intrinsic property of systems but, rather, arises from qualitatively different possible interactions. A complex system offers a multitude of partial descriptions, each an appropriate model of a different aspect of its behavior under consideration. A complex system cannot be completely and consistently described as a whole but admits a plethora of (mutually independent) partial descriptions. Each partial description represents a *subsystem* and by itself appears to model a simple system. A living system is complex. An anticipatory system is complex. A social system is complex. They are complex because one can interact with them in many ways, with no singular model sufficient for their complete characterization.

On the other hand, because complexity is subjective, depending entirely on modes of available interactions, *any* system can be made complex. A rock is usually considered a simple system, since one can only interact with it in a few mechanistic ways. Indeed, as a Newtonian particle it can be completely characterized as a simple dynamical system. However, for a geologist, say, who is equipped to interact with the rock in a multiplicity of distinct ways, a rock becomes a complex system.

It is important to note that while a complex system admits many models that are simple subsystems, the former is not a superposition of the latter. This inherent non-invertibility that a complex system is not the synthesis of its analytic parts may in fact be taken as a definition of our species of complexity that is impredicativity. (The reader is cordially invited to read Sects. 7.43–7.49 of Louie 2009 for an exposition on the amphibology of analysis and synthesis.) This departure from superposition (or 'direct sum') is the root cause that defeats attempts to characterize complexity in reductionistic terms (which have been successful for simple systems).

Summary

Life $\subset$ Anticipation $\subset$ **Impredicativity**

Complexity is reflected in the absence of a single overreaching system description. An immanent cause of complex systems is the multiplicity of partial descriptions, each one by itself a simple system. That is, each partial description accords with the

Newtonian paradigm of a dynamical system, a state set with imposed dynamical laws.

Complexity manifests itself operationally through the failure of these partial descriptions, either individually or collectively, to account for the whole system's behavior. That is to say, a simple subsystem of a complex system is always more open to interaction than it would have been if it were merely a simple system. Such a failure to conform to predictions based on simple models is equivalent to the emergence of new modes of system behavior. Emergence manifests itself as a qualitative difference (rather than a mere quantitative difference) between what is expected and what is observed.

Closed paths of efficient causation provide a rigorous platform on which to discuss categories of final causation. This kind of finality, in turn, is scaffolding for the exploration of function (which dictates structure) and anticipation (in which the end entails the means). In short, causality in a complex system can also include what an effect entails rather than exclusively what entails the effect.

Acknowledgments   We dedicate this exposition on impredicativity to Robert Rosen (1934–1998), iconoclastic mathematical biologist, whose permeating presence in this Handbook of Anticipation is keenly felt. His next monograph would have been Complexity.

References

Bourdieu, P. (1984). *Distinction: A social critique of the judgment of taste.* Harvard: Harvard University Press.

Ehresmann, A. C., & Vanbremeersch, J. (2007). *Memory evolutive systems: Hierarchy, emergence, cognition.* Amsterdam: Elsevier.

Gnoli, C., & Poli, R. (2004). Levels of reality and levels of representation. *Knowledge Organization, 31*(3), 151–160.

Lilienfeld, R. (1978). *The rise of systems theory: An ideological analysis.* New York: John Wiley and Sons.

Louie, A. H. (2009). *More than life itself: A synthetic continuation in relation biology.* Frankfurt: Ontos.

Louie, A. H. (2013). *The reflection of life: Functional entailment and imminence in relational biology.* New York: Springer.

Maynard Smith, J. (1987). How to model evolution. In J. Dupré (Ed.), *The latest on the best* (pp. 119–131). Cambridge, MA: MIT Press.

Midgley, G. (2003). *Systems thinking. Volume 1. General systems theory, cybernetics and complexity.* London: Sage.

Poli, R. (1998). Levels. *Axiomathes, 9*(1–2), 197–211.

Poli, R. (2001). The basic problem of the theory of levels of reality. *Axiomathes, 12*(3–4), 261–283.

Poli, R. (2006). First steps in experimental phenomenology. In A. Loula, R. Gudwin, & J. Queiroz (Eds.), *Artificial cognition systems* (pp. 358–386). Hersey: Idea Group Publishing.

Poli, R. (2007). Three obstructions: Forms of causation, chronotopoids, and levels of reality. *Axiomathes, 17*(1), 1–18.

Poli, R. (2011). Analysis–synthesis. In V. Petrov (Ed.), *Ontological landscapes* (pp. 19–42). Frankfurt: Ontos.

Poli, R. (2017). *Introduction to anticipation studies.* Dordrecht: Springer.

Rosen, R. (1971, November 22). *The polarity between structure and function* (Center for the study of democratic institutions discussion paper). Santa Barbara: CSDI.

Rosen, R. (1974). Biological systems as organizational paradigms. *International Journal of General Systems, 1*(3), 165–174.

Rosen, R. (1979). Old trends and new trends in general systems research. *International Journal of General Systems, 5*(3), 173–184.

Rosen, R. (1984). *On social-biological homologies* (Collaborative paper for International Institute for Applied Systems Analysis). Laxenburg.

Rosen, R. (1985a). *Anticipatory systems: Philosophical, mathematical, and methodological foundations.* Oxford: Pergamon; (2012) 2nd ed., New York: Springer.

Rosen, R. (1985b). Organisms as causal systems which are not mechanisms: An essay into the nature of complexity. In R. Rosen (Ed.), *Theoretical biology and complexity: Three essays on the natural philosophy of complex systems* (pp. 165–203). Orlando: Academic.

Rosen, R. (1991a). *Life itself: A comprehensive inquiry into the nature, origin, and fabrication of life.* New York: Columbia University Press.

Rosen, R. (1991b). What can we know? In J. L. Casti & A. Karlqvist (Eds.), *Beyond belief: Randomness, prediction and explanation in science* (pp. 1–13). Boca Raton: CRC Press.

Schutz, A. (1967). *The phenomenology of the social world.* Evanston: Northwestern University Press.

von Neumann, J. (1951). The general and logical theory of automata. In L. A. Jeffress (Ed.), *Cerebral mechanisms in behavior* (pp. 1–49). New York: Wiley.

von Neumann, J. (1956). Probabilistic logics and the synthesis of reliable organisms from unreliable components. In C. E. Shannon & J. McCarthy (Eds.), *Automata studies* (pp. 43–98). Princeton: Princeton University Press.

Weaver, W. (1948). Science and complexity. *American Scientist, 36*, 536–544.

Ontological Expansion

3

Ilkka Tuomi

Contents

Abstract

Much of science and philosophy is based on the assumption that a reality exists that is independent of who observes it (realism) or that this reality is primarily a construction of the mind (idealism). In both cases, the reality is often assumed to be static, and large bodies of philosophical literature exist that study what can we know about this reality. This chapter proposes a different approach, arguing that reality is continuously expanding. Innovation and evolution create things that did not exist before. We have data or facts only about things that already exist, and the

I. Tuomi (✉)
Meaning Processing, Helsinki, Finland

Stellenbosch Institute for Advanced Study (STIAS), Wallenberg Research Centre at Stellenbosch University, Stellenbosch, South Africa
e-mail: ilkka.tuomi@meaningprocessing.com

© Springer Nature Switzerland AG 2019
R. Poli (ed.), *Handbook of Anticipation*,
https://doi.org/10.1007/978-3-319-91554-8_4

traditional epistemic theories of realism and idealism therefore have little to say about the nature of innovation, qualitative novelty, and creative evolution.

In many practical areas of concern, such as strategy and policy development, design, and innovation management and impact assessment, emerging futures play a central role. This chapter studies how realities expand and become real. It characterizes three main principles—functional shift, constant creation, and relational ontology—that underpin ontological expansion. It then discusses the dynamics of this expansion in the context of learning, narrative chronotopes, innovation theory, and the cognitive theory of "dominants" proposed by A.A. Ukhtomsky in the first decades of the 20th century. The chapter then suggests ways in which the key processes of ontological expansion can be formally modeled, using concepts from category theory.

Keywords

Innovation · Evolution · Anticipatory systems · Chronotope · Unpredictability · Relational ontology · Functional shift · Constant creation · Bergsonism · Cultural-historical activity theory · Memory Evolutive systems · futures literacy · Futures studies · Business strategy · Policy development · Category theory · Emergence

Introduction

Fifteen years ago presidents did not tweet. There was no Twitter. In the last 15 years, Twitter, YouTube, Facebook, WhatsApp, Google, and big data analytics have changed our world. What is real and important today did not exist 15 years ago.

In this chapter we discuss how both theory and practice of foresight and anticipatory processes change when we understand the dynamics of changing reality. *Ontology* is in philosophy the study of being, becoming, and existence. In the next pages, I shall merge insights from some relatively unknown but highly relevant thinkers coming from disciplines ranging from philosophy to neurophysiology, literary theory, cultural-historical theory of cognitive development, and the mathematics of category theory. The fundamental claim that motivates the concept of ontological expansion is that not only new ideas and inventions pop up in our world but also reality itself is in the process of becoming. The philosophical foundation for ontological expansion, therefore, provides a radically different starting point from conventional discussions on epistemology, knowledge, and our knowledge about future. Most importantly, as we can observe only things that already exist, there can be no empirical facts or data about things that generate ontological expansion. No statistical data or scientific observation could have predicted the truly novel, creative, and emergent aspects of tweeting before Twitter existed. We have facts only about things that repeat the past. New methods and new foresight practices are therefore needed to understand futures that do not exist yet.

The idea of ontological expansion is both obvious and difficult. The next section illustrates ontological expansion using the history of telephone as an example and shows how our conceptual models of creativity and emergence are based on deeply rooted cultural models. The still dominant model of creativity that is represented, for example, in the first chapter of the Bible underpins many stories about modern innovators. This model, however, is in stark contrast with current research on innovation processes. Unlike the model provided in the Bible, a model of constant creation provides a useful starting point for understanding ontological expansion. The dynamics of emergence can be clarified using the concept of functional shift, originating in the final edition of Darwin's *On the Origin of Species*. The model of constant creation leads to one of the fundamental ideas motivating the concept of ontological expansion, the idea that ontology is relational and that models of reality, in other words science, in general require formalisms that can capture reality as a relational phenomenon. Relational ontology is based on the observation that what is "real" for a living being depends on its capacity to act. A living being is an integral part of the reality it observes and perceives. Instead of a clean separation between "subjects" and "objects" they mutually construct each other in the ongoing process of action.

The philosopher Henri Bergson proposed such a relational view on ontology around the turn of the twentieth century. It was incompatible with both idealism and realism, and though extremely influential in the first decades of the twentieth century, it was almost completely wiped out of philosophical textbooks after the Second World War. Bergson's work provides a useful starting point to understand relational ontologies, also because it underpins important later contributions.

Bergson and his work on memory, time, and creative evolution helps us understand what ontological expansion is from biological and cognitive points of view. The following sections will then focus on the dynamics of ontological expansion. The cultural-historical psychology of Lev Vygotsky suggests that ontological expansion occurs in three different time horizons, as biological evolution, as cultural development, and as ontogenic development when the cognitive processes of a child mature and develop. Mikhail Bakhtin's work on chronotopes, embedded in speech genres and literary forms, provides nice examples of how written texts and the time-space organization of stories have generated alternative forms of ontological reality. Bakhtin's work is interesting in the context of studies in anticipation also because it has clear links with recent work on "next-generation" foresight and futures literacy.

Beyond some isolated observations, the Vygotskian cultural-historical model of cognitive development and learning did not explicitly address innovation. More recent contributions in this tradition, in particular Engeström's (1987) model of expansive learning, have influenced research on knowledge creation and innovation. The multifocal model of innovation (Tuomi 2002) is one of these and, indeed, was based on viewing innovation as ontological expansion in a relational ontology. As the multifocal model was developed in the context of Internet-related innovations, it highlights ontological expansion in the context of rapidly changing socially shared but heterogeneous ontologies. The multifocal model emphasized the mutual dependency of the emergence of new social practices and technical artifacts that enable them, to the point of claiming that innovation becomes real only when social practice changes. It did, however, to a large extent skip over the question of "invention," as a process that finds tentative solutions to practical problems and imaginary possibilities. There is a huge literature on creativity in existence today; this chapter, however, takes a different starting point congruent with the idea of relational ontology. This is the relatively little-known theory of "dominants" by the Russian neurophysiologist Alexei A. Ukhtomsky (c.f. Sokolova 2015; Zueva and Zuev 2015). Ukhtomsky's ideas have very close similarity with the Bergsonian analysis of perception, memory, and cognition, and it is no accident that they also had impact on Bakhtin and Vygotsky. In fact, Bakhtin learned about the idea of chronotope from Ukhtomsky.

Relational ontology is in many ways incompatible with conventional idealistic and realistic ontologies. The belief in data and facts as the sources of knowledge is fundamental for science, and it has extraordinary impact in the modern world, including policy-making, economic forecasting, and strategic planning. This impact has in recent years been greatly amplified by computational tools and big data. The specific episte-mology that underpins modern thinking is, however, a very special kind of epistemol-ogy, based on physical models of the world that originate with Newton and Leibniz. As Robert Rosen's (1958a, b) early work on living and anticipatory systems showed, this Newtonian approach does not capture the essential characteristics of living organisms. This observation was the starting point of relational biology developed by Rosen's mentor Nicolas Rashevsky (1954), but Rosen was able to put this idea into a rigorous theoretical framework using the then new mathematical formalism, category theory. Category theory is a highly abstract mathematical formalism that erects the edifice of mathematics on foundations that are very different from the conventional ones. It has therefore a very steep learning curve. This chapter will therefore describe category theory only in very broad terms, focusing on the motivation to use it. This is, however, useful as category theory provides a very strong starting point for studying relational and emergent phenomena (Ehresmann and Vanbremeersch 2007; Louie 2009). Ehresmann and Vanbremeersch's work on *Memory Evolutive Systems* is of particular interest in the present context, as it can be understood as a category-theoretic imple-mentation of some key elements of Ukhtomsky's theory of dominants. The theory of dominants, in turn, can be linked back to relational ontology, innovation, and ontolog-ical expansion. Its category-theoretic interpretation therefore leads to new insights on the possibilities and practices of anticipatory activities.

The next sections introduce three key principles that underpin the idea of ontological expansion. These are illustrated in the contexts of technical innovation, biology, and philosophy, respectively. After that, we explore different ways of understanding the dynamics of change in expanding ontologies, moving from Vygotskian cultural-histor-ical theory of cognitive development to Bakhtinian chronotopes and Ukhtomsky's theory of dominants. The final section then focuses on the question how ontological expansion can be modeled and studied using category-theoretic concepts.

The Three Principles of Ontological Expansion

Three key concepts characterize ontological expansion. These are *constant creation*, *functional shift*, and *relational ontology*. The following sections illus-trate these basic concepts. The next three sections focus on innovation, evolution, and philosophy, respectively, and also show that these become linked in a new conceptual framework that is needed to understand what ontological expansion is and what makes it happen.

The Principle of Constant Creation

Innovation creates things that did not exist before. Fifteen years ago, we had no YouTube, Facebook, Instagram, Uber, or Airbnb. There were no bloggers or vloggers. Clouds were still in the sky. Crowdfunding, block chains, synthetic genomes, and designer babies were unregulated and unheard of. iPod was just to be released, iPad did not exist, and mobile apps were still to be invented.

There is nothing new here. We all know that the world is changing. This world, however, is in stark contrast with the commonsense idea that the world exists independent of humans. The various refinements of this commonsense idea are known as philosophical realism. Many varieties of realism exist today, but the task of knowing is in this tradition understood to be about uncovering and discovering truths about the world. Empirical sciences, in this view, gradually develop increasingly accurate models of natural phenomena, ultimately ending in the discovery of fundamental laws that cover the regularities of the world.

Although realism is a natural attitude for the human intellect, the empirical model of knowledge acquisition does not easily apply in a world where innovation creates novelty. How could knowledge converge toward eternal laws that describe the phenomenon and dynamics of tweeting or the next big thing that emerges after it? If facts are accurate representations of reality or attributes of objects floating in it, how can there be facts of a reality that is in the process of making?

Yet, our observable reality is full of objects that did not exist before. Steam engines, airplanes, submarines, satellites, gravitons, genetic scissors, computer viruses, and tweeting were not there for Kepler, Galileo, or Newton to observe. The set of objects that form the reality is constantly increasing, the attributes of existing objects are constantly refined and reinterpreted, and their characteristics evolve in a continuous process.

We often think that when a new innovative gadget emerges, it is introduced and embedded in an extant reality, in an absolute and inert coordinate system where every object finds its place. The reality remains the same, and novelty is just a new object or phenomenon that now enriches it. This view is so deeply ingrained in our culture, language, and scientific and philosophical systems that it is often taken as the only possibility. To be able to talk about novelty and creation, we need a background context that stays the same and allows us to see something that does not.

In this static background, a realist puts things and objects. Common sense reflects culture and its stories, and it is not surprising that Western commonsense realism can be found from the first pages of the Bible, in the Book of Genesis. The 1769 version of King James Bible tells us how cattle and beasts are created:

> And God said, Let the earth bring forth the living creature after his kind, cattle, and creeping thing, and beast of the earth after his kind: and it was so.

And God made the beast of the earth after his kind, and cattle after their kind, and every thing that creepeth upon the earth after his kind: and God saw that [it was] good.

This model of creativity assumes that as new entities are brought to life, their nature is well-defined. Someone – in this case God – knows where to put the thing in the existing system of being. Cattle, in this model, can clearly be separated from beasts. All the creation can be categorized at the moment of creation. Snakes will be snakes, and cattle will always be cattle.

This is a very special model of creativity and it comes with a very special ontology. It requires a god that at the point of creation has a perfect blueprint of the world to be. Although the proper place for objects and animals in this world may not always be known to humans, God knows. In the Western history, science thus becomes an enterprise that aims at getting closer and closer to revealing the perfect plan of an omniscient creator.

In the history of science and philosophy, this model underpins positivism and empiricist views on reality as something external to us and independent of our action. Because innovation, creativity, or human action does not really matter, this world can gradually be "discovered." The god of creation, in this model, does not rethink or revise her plans. There is nothing to be learned or observed because everything is known at the point of original creation. The change in reality can only be gradual unfolding and maturation of already encoded futures, and true novelty is impossible because for an all-knowing god nothing can be unknown or surprising.

In the history of theological thinking, there have been many attempts to address the apparent contradiction between ongoing change and an omniscient creator. The Book of Genesis, however, provides a very clear characterization of the dynamics of realistic ontology. In human practice, this model of creation is not very convincing, however. From the historical record, we know that what used to be a beast can now be cattle. The "beastiness" of cattle cannot be found by just studying the animal in question. Whether something is cattle depends on its relation to historical human practices. If we scream and run away, we may call it a beast; if we milk it, it becomes cattle. We domesticate wild animals and technologies, and after they are domesticated, they are not anymore what they used to be. If the Book of Genesis would have been written by modern students of innovation, it would have focused on relations between things. The things, themselves, would have been defined by exactly these relations, instead of the internal characteristics and attributes of the thing.

The process of domestication is clearly visible when we study the history of innovation and technology (Lie and Sørensen 1996; Silverstone and Haddon 1996). For innovations that change the world, the socially and economically critical innovative step is often located in the "downstream" where potential users of new technical opportunities figure out new ways of integrating technology with their ongoing social practices (Tuomi 2012). "Inventors" may be granted patents, but often they have no idea of what their inventions will look like when they start to make a difference. History shows that innovative ideas abound, parallel innovation and re-invention is frequent, and unintended uses often become key drivers of development. Socially and economically important innovations are often invented several times before they eventually start to matter. In history of science, this is known as Stigler's Law of Eponymy (Stigler 1999). In its strongest form it says: "No scientific discovery is named after its original discoverer."

The true innovative step, in general, occurs when a potential user group finds a meaningful way to integrate latent innovative opportunities in the current social practice. Innovation thus does not occur when some heroic innovator or creator comes up with a new brilliant idea or a new animal species; instead, it happens when social practice changes (Tuomi 2002). Stories of innovation and technical change, therefore, often mislocate the locus of innovation to some original creator that resembles the creator of the Genesis. History also shows that human innovators are not omniscient; they rarely understand or control the future uses of invention. On the contrary, innovations acquire new attributes and new characteristics in a historical process that is essentially unpredictable and thus able to generate true novelty and new realities. This process is nicely illustrated in the history of telephone.

If asked about the history of the telephone, many technology students can easily name Alexander Graham Bell as its inventor. Yet, in his patent application from 1876, Bell tells us what the telephone is about:

> By these instruments two or more telegraphic signals or messages may be sent simultaneously over the same circuit without interfering with one another.

Toward the end of his patent application, Bell, however, reserves the right to use his invention also for yet to be imagined uses:

> I desire here to remark that there are many other uses to which these instruments may be put, such as the simultaneous transmission of musical notes, differing in loudness as well as in pitch, and the telegraphic transmission of noises or sounds of any kind. (Bell 1876)

As Fischer (1992) has documented in detail, for many decades after the telephone was invented, it was marketed mainly for business use. It was often understood either as a new form of telegraphy or a broadcast medium. Telephone entrepreneurs tried to use the telephone to broadcast news, concerts, church services, weather reports, and stores' sales announcements. The telephone was also expected to be used for voting campaigns, long-distance Christian-Science healing, and to broadcast lullabies to put babies to sleep.

Social conversations and "visiting" over the telephone were not the uses that telephone was supposed to serve, and for almost the first five decades, the industry actively discouraged such use. The social use of the telephone was basically invented by housewives, in particular in the US Midwest, around the first decade of the twentieth century. As we now know, the invention of the telephone did not stop there. An essentially similar story about continuous innovation can be told about almost all important innovations. If an innovation is socially important, it almost by definition generates qualitatively new social practices that did not exist before. At the same time, the material embodiment of innovation becomes a carrier and a symbol of such revolutionary new practices.

Constant creation, therefore, means that no one has a full blueprint of reality. The uses of beasts, telephones, and the Internet evolve and enable new social practices and new systems of meaning. After they exist, we use them to make sense of the world that has just emerged.

The Principle of Functional Shift

This gradual process of emergence and its relation to ontological expansion can easily be understood in a biological context. After Darwin published *On the Origin of Species* in 1859, one of the most substantial critiques of the idea of natural selection was elaborated by George Mivart, in his 1871 book *On the Genesis of Species* (Mivart 1871). In particular, Mivart presented a strong argument against natural selection in the first chapter of the book, entitled "The Incompetency of 'Natural Selection' to Account for the Incipient Stages of Useful Structures."

Mivart argued that natural selection may well select useful biological structures such as wings, eyes, and the resemblance of an insect to a stick or a dead leaf. Selection of such useful structures obviously makes sense. But how can such complex evolutionary structures be selected in their incipient stages? A proto-bird cannot fly with incipient wings. If evolution produces wings in a gradual process that generates the required complex structures, how can such nonfunctioning intermediate structures be preferred in the process of natural selection? In other words, how could natural selection produce animals with wings and eyes?

In the final sixth edition of *The Origin of Species* in 1872, Darwin thanked Mivart for his excellent characterization of the problem and added a full chapter to address Mivart's arguments. Darwin's answer was *functional shift,* and he illustrated this concept with numerous examples. He argued, for example, that insects evolved wings from their breathing organs, stating that "It is therefore highly probable that in this great class organs which once served for respiration have been actually converted into organs of flight."

A more current theory is that wings developed out of structures that earlier functioned to maintain body temperature. In fact, Kingslover and Koehl (1985) showed experimentally that the aerodynamic benefit for wings increases as the size of the wings grows and that small wings are not useful for flying. In contrast, the thermal control benefits of wings start already with small wings, grow with the size of wings, but as the size approaches a critical size, there is no more benefit from bigger wings. In other words, in the process of evolution, small wings can well emerge as structures beneficial for temperature control, become larger as larger wings are increasingly useful, but can start to function as structures for flying as they become large enough.

At such a transition point, functional shift occurs. Functional shift, however, is not just about the emergence of new interesting functionality in a living organism. The capability for flying opens up an entirely new domain of action and being. Similarly, when a functional shift occurs that makes a pre-existing structure available for vision, a new reality of seeing, a world of vision, emerges with new forms of possible interaction with this reality. It has qualitatively new "objects" and new dimensions of "space" and "movement" that did not exist before.

The epistemological consequences of this observation are profound, indeed. Even if we would have all the possible knowledge and facts about the reality as it was *before* the functional shift, this would not make it possible to know the reality as it exists *after* the functional shift. With all the data and facts available in year 2000, we would not be able to say anything about the truly novel aspects of tweeting because Twitter did not exist yet. Functional shift can therefore lead to deep unpredictability and ontological expansion (Tuomi 2012).

The dynamic of Darwinian functional shifts occurs in a slow evolutionary process over tens of thousands of years. As soon as we give up popular retrospective histories of heroic innovators who invent the future of telephony, steam engines, and light bulbs, the same dynamic of functional shifts is easily observed in the history of technical change. When the World Wide Web emerged in 1990 as a rudimentary document management system, it lacked almost all functionality that is typically expected from document management systems, such as access control, system management functionality, and support for collaboration and content management. As a document management system, it was clearly a failure. However, because it lacked capabilities for central control and because it made already existing functionality of the Internet easily accessible, its users rapidly invented a growing set of uses and functions for the Web. In this process, these "downstream" innovators transformed the idea of the Web and generated new realities. Ontological expansion, therefore, is nothing new, and it has always been there; the rapid disruption and reconfiguration of social practices enabled by global communication networks, however, now makes it difficult to avoid.

The Principle of Relational Ontology

But how do such emerging realities look from a point of view of a bird who has just acquired wings, or from a point of a view of a president who has just acquired a Twitter account? What is the "ontology" of the animal that we call a bird after it starts to fly? In the Darwinian world, this question does not arise because evolution operates in glacial pace. Around the time of Darwin's death, Henri Bergson, however, proposed a radically different approach to understanding evolution and ontology (Bergson 1983, 1988). The Bergsonian ontology is relational, in the sense that it tightly couples the capabilities of perception to capabilities of action. As capabilities to act change in the course of evolution of each species, new ontological realms emerge. As a result, a cat lives in a different ontology than a bat.

For simple animals such as insects, capabilities to act are instinctive and expressed in the physiological structure of the body. For humans and some other animals, capabilities to act can also be generated by modifying the material environment. Humans, in particular, shape their environment into tools for action and gain new functionality without changing their physiological structure. To do this, they have developed a way of knowing the environment that is different from instinctive knowledge. Bergson calls this intelligence. Because of its original task, shaping the environment for useful purposes, intelligence, however, has become unable to generate knowledge about continuous processes. Intelligence can describe in excellent detail the inorganic world, but it struggles with the creative nature of evolution and living processes because it has developed to address a different need. In particular, Bergson shows that intelligence struggles with the concepts of time and space.

The relational nature of Bergsonian ontology is most clearly visible in his discussions about simple organisms and instinct. Ontology is an abstract philosophical concept that is often tangled with historical debates about human mind and matter. The Bergsonian approach, however, allows us to see ontologies as they emerge in their most primitive forms. This biological entry point to deep philosophical problems has been strongly resisted by many leading twentieth-century philosophers.

Bergson was probably the most internationally famous philosopher in the world in the first two decades of the twentieth century. When he gave a lecture in New York in 1913, parts of the city were choked by "the first traffic jam of the brand-new automotive age" (Gunter 1983, p. xvii). At the height of his fame, according to the historian R.C. Grogin, people made pilgrimages to Bergson's summer home in Switzerland where "locks of his hair at the local barber's were treated as holy relics" (quoted in Antliff 1993, p. 4). Yet, after the Second World War, Bergson rapidly disappeared from philosophy textbooks. Partly this was because "Bergsonism" was widely used in political and cultural fights, and partly because Bergson developed a philosophy that contradicted key beliefs of idealism, scientific empiricism, and the emerging logical positivism. The resulting antagonism is well represented in Russell's History of Western Thought. At the end of his chapter on Bergson, Russell states:

> There is no room in this philosophy for the moment of contemplative insight when, rising above the animal life, we become conscious of the great ends that redeem man from the life of the brutes. Those to whom activity without purpose seem a sufficient good will find in Bergson's books a pleasing picture of the universe. But those to whom action, if it is to be of any value, must be inspired by some vision, by some imaginative foreshadowing of a world less painful, less unjust, less full of strife than the world of our everyday life, those, in a word, whose action is built on contemplation, will find in this philosophy nothing of what they seek, and will not regret that there is no reason to think it true. (Russell 1946, pp. 764–765)

Russell was one of the key proponents of the idea that logic is the foundation of philosophy. Logic, in turn, was clearly a uniquely human activity, closely related to abstract mathematics. Bergson, in contrast, spent considerable effort in describing how perception and cognition emerge in the simplest living forms, eventually evolving into higher forms of conceptual thinking that, for example, underpin science and logic. One could, therefore, read Bergson as explaining logic in terms of amoebas and insects. This clearly did not appeal to Russell. More devastating, however, was Bergson's claim that empiricism and idealism were fundamentally flawed because they assumed that reality is somehow "represented" in the human mind or cognition. As the logical approach to philosophy essentially claimed that philosophy only dealt with representations, the Bergsonian critique meant that

Russell and his colleagues had misunderstood what philosophy can be. This, apparently, was too much for Russell, and therefore he naturally misinterpreted what Bergson was trying to say. (Alfred North Whitehead, together with Russell, published the groundbreaking *Principia Mathematica* between 1910 and 1913, which tried to derive all mathematical truths from basic logical axioms. In contrast to Russell, Whitehead (1978) went on to develop his highly original process philosophy largely influenced by Bergson.) Following his advice, most philosophers in the second half of the last century simply believed that Bergson was an irrelevant philosopher of mystical "vitalism," which Bergson himself, in fact, explicitly rejected.

Bergson proposed an alternative to the two predominant philosophies in the Western history, idealism and realism. He adopted a view where living beings generate their realities in an interaction with the world. Bergson argued that perception and cognition are not oriented toward theoretical contemplation; instead, they are products of evolution where perception and cognition are oriented toward action. We perceive the world as a potential for action, and what we perceive depends on our capabilities to act. In simpler animals, the capabilities for action are based on physiological characteristics and the body; in human beings, the "tools and organs for action" are manufactured from materials that exist outside the body.

Bergson rejected realism that assumed that the reality consists of objects with well-defined attributes that are independent of observation. He, however, also rejected idealism, which assumed that reality is produced in the mind. Both realists and idealists had assumed that the problems of epistemology can be approached by studying how the reality is represented in the mind, and whether the representations somehow are accurate or true. According to Bergson, we live in a reality and not in its representation, and philosophies that focus on studying representations will never understand cognition, knowing, or life.

Starting from biological considerations, Bergson argued that the historical evolutionary emergence of cognition is tightly coupled with emerging forms of action. From an evolutionary point of view, it makes no sense to have perceptional capabilities that cannot make a difference. An amoeba therefore lives in a world that consists of directions toward food and away from it. How "far" things in this universe are depends on how quickly the amoeba can reach them. It perceives this world as directions toward and away from food because it is able to move where the food is. The world, in this sense, "represents" itself to the amoeba, as a set of edible and nonedible things in a time-space of distances from these things, but it is not separately represented in the cognition of the amoeba. The perceiver and its world are results of a shared process of coevolution, where the needs of an organism, its functional capabilities, and its reality have shaped each other's development.

To understand advanced forms of human thinking, such as language and science, we have to note that evolution has taken two essentially different ways to know the reality. One Bergson calls "instinctive" the other "intelligent." Both have their limitations. Using a wealth of biological examples, Bergson argues that intelligence produces knowledge that will be unable to describe the essential characteristics of life, evolution, innovation, and creativity. Intellect, as understood by Bergson, always necessarily turns back to history to explain the future and therefore misses those aspects of the future that cannot be described as repetition of the past.

Instead of the "objects" of realists, Bergson argues that reality consists of real "images" that are "filtered" based on the perceiver's capabilities to act. The "reality" is thus a "reflection" of its perceiver, who is also part of this reality. Whereas a realist's "object" or "thing" has attributes that are intrinsic parts of the object, Bergson argues that the attributes of an image consist of all the possible interactions that can exist with the image. (This interdependence has devastating impact on the idea that propositional logic can be used to formalize knowledge. Because of this, Kitaro Nishida, the founder of the Kyoto School of Japanese philosophy, argued that we need a new type of "paradoxical" logic that avoids the assumption of subject-object distinction (Nishida 1987; Nishitani 1991).) From this set of possibilities, each perceiver can perceive those that can make a difference. This theoretical set of all possible observables corresponds to "pure perception." The "objects" of "pure perception," thus, consist of "images" that exist in a reality spawned between the "external" and the "internal," and both are elements of the same process of living.

Bergson, thus, makes a radical turn, finding both idealism and realism dead ends. Idealists and realists both assumed that reality is either in the mind or in the external world. Bergson showed that external and internal are both generated in a historical process of evolution that makes them complementary pieces of a bigger picture. Only if we forget this historical process does the dualism between "internal" and "external" or "mind" and "body" start to look like a problem. Instead of studying a philosophical mind that contemplates the objects of the world or its own representations of it, Bergson claims that both the mind and the world can only be understood by studying the evolutionary path of perception, driven by biological needs and the capabilities of a living body to fulfill these.

This is why mollusks, insects, and monocellular organisms enter philosophy. An amoeba has "instinctive" knowledge about its world, and in the case of an amoeba, this knowledge is linked to its relatively simple physiological characteristics. Instinct is thus tightly bound with special biological structures that make specific forms of action possible. Instinctive knowledge can be highly complex, as, for example, in insects that have specialized structures and behaviors that allow them to interact with their environment. Bergson uses the paralyzing instinct of wasps as an example:

> We know that the different species of hymenoptera that have this paralyzing instinct lay their eggs in spiders, beetles or caterpillars, which, having first been subjected by the wasp to a skilful surgical operation, will go on living motionless a certain number of days, and thus provide the larvae with fresh meat. In the sting which they give to the nerve-centres of their victim, in order to destroy its power of moving without killing it, these different species of hymenoptera take into account, so to speak, the different species of prey they respectively attack. The Scolia, which attacks a larva of the rosebeetle, sting it in one point only, but in this point the motor ganglia are concentrated, and those ganglia alone: the stinging of other ganglia might cause death and putrefaction, which it must avoid. The yellow-winged Sphex, which has chosen the cricket for its victim, knows that the cricket has three nerve-centres which serve its three pairs of legs – or at least it acts as if it knew this. It stings the insect first under the neck, then behind the prothorax, and then where the thorax joins the abdomen. The Ammophila Hirsuta gives nine successive strokes of its sting upon nine nerve-centres of its caterpillar. . .

> The general theme is 'the necessity of paralysis without killing'; the variations are subordinated to the structure of the victim on which they are played. (Bergson 1983, p. 172)

Instinctive knowledge is generated in evolution, and it is embedded in the structure of the living organism in question. It is oriented toward the practical needs of the organism. The structures involved in instincts, such as the sting of a wasp, are "tools" and instruments that enable specific kinds of action and which have a specialized function in the life of the organism. Bergson, however, points out that an alternative form of knowing characterizes humans and some other animals. Evolution, according to Bergson, has taken two divergent paths, one leading to instincts and one leading to intelligence. Whereas instinct uses the functionality of the biological body as its instrument, intelligence uses external resources to construct instruments for action. Thus, Bergson states, the human species should not be called *Homo sapiens* but *Homo faber*:

> In short, intelligence, considered in what seems to be its original feature, is the faculty of manufacturing artificial objects, especially tools to make tools, and of indefinitely varying their manufacture. (Bergson 1983, p. 139)

Intellect, therefore, develops to address the same practical needs as instinct, but it has a fundamentally different approach. It requires that the world is perceived as a potential tool and instrument. Instinct has direct knowledge of the world, whereas intelligence provides a mediated view of it, as something that can be used as a potential instrument to achieve the objectives of action. Bergson argues that the original starting point of intelligence is to perceive the world as extended solid objects and possible ways to grasp the world and break it into components that can be assembled into useful instruments. Intellect, therefore, has a tendency to see the world as a set of independent things, discontinuities, and possible breaking points. It tries to atomize and decompose the world, break it into elementary units, and to recompose it according to the needs of action.

To do this, it has to stop the world and understand time and space in a very special way. From a continuous reality and flux of life, intelligence has to construct separate entities. Intellect therefore splits processes into chains of static states that can be labeled using the ticks of a mechanical clock, and it makes space a set of non-overlapping points where extended material bodies can be accurately located.

The benefits of this approach are extraordinary. Intellect allows evolution to free itself from physiological change and the instinctive actions afforded by the body. It generates a new dynamic of evolutionary development and produces new realities that expand faster than any instinctive development would make possible. Whereas instinct is the current end point of a long history or coevolution expressed in the functional structure of the body, intellect generates instruments that are only loosely coupled with the body of their user. Because of this loose coupling, they can move and acquire new uses. Whereas instinct has intimate knowledge about matter that it interacts with, intelligence operates with abstract forms of matter that can be combined into useful things (Bergson 1983, p. 149). Intelligence, therefore, gains freedom from the actual concrete material reality. Instead of pure "images" of reality, it becomes able to operate on the relations of these images.

Yet, the benefits of intellect come with limitations. As the faculty of intelligence requires that the world is perceived as a set of discontinuities, it can only perceive the world as a sequence of static states. It can only view continuous processes as if they would consist of beads of a necklace strung on a thread. Because of this, intellect is unable to understand the essential characteristics that separate inanimate mechanical things from living processes. The knowledge that is generated by intelligence is unable to grasp emergence and creativity in evolution and life. As Bergson puts it:

> Here again, thinking consists in reconstituting, and, naturally, it is with given elements, and consequently with stable elements, that we reconstitute. So that, though we may do our best to imitate the mobility of becoming by an addition that is ever going on, becoming itself slips through our fingers just when we think we are holding it tight.

> Precisely because it is always trying to reconstitute, and to reconstitute with what is given, the intellect lets what is new in each moment of history escape. It does not admit the unforeseeable. It rejects all creation. That definite antecedents bring forth a definite consequent, calculable as a function of them, is what satisfies our intellect. In both cases we have to do with the known which is combined with the known, in short with the old which is repeated. (Bergson 1983, p. 163)

Bergson illustrated the problem with the mathematical problem of representing continuous curves as sequences of straight lines. At each point in the curve, we can draw its tangent, and with an increasing number of points, we can approximate the curve with increasing accuracy.

> A very small element of a curve is very near being a straight line. And the smaller it is, the nearer. In the limit, it may be termed a part of the curve or a part of the straight line, as you please, for in each of its points a curve coincides with its tangent. (Bergson 1983, p. 31)

Similarly, the continuous living process can in each point of time be described using physical and chemical forces, as depicted by analytical sciences and differential equations of motion. From this local description of a process, however, we cannot get to the a more global description of the phenomenon that we are interested in. Such points are, Bergson notes, only views taken by a mind which imagines stops at various moments of the movement that generates the curve. In reality, life is no more made of physicochemical elements than a curve is composed of straight lines.

In mathematical terms, Bergson therefore argues that an infinite sequence of straight lines is not a curve. Indeed, category theory shows that Bergson was right; a "limit" of such a sequence is qualitatively different from its components. Joseph Schumpeter (2005, p. 138) put the same point in the context of innovation economics: "Add as many mail-coaches as you please, you will never get a railroad by so doing."

Bergson pointed out that intelligence generates systems of signs and that, in contrast to social animals such as ants that have instinctive signs, an intelligent sign is highly mobile. As the intelligent sign is not fixed by instinct and biological structure, it can point to other signs and become reflexive. Furthermore, as humans live in a society and their roles are not fixed by their phenotype, as it is for ants, humans need a language that allows them to coordinate action and learn the functionality that is needed for different social roles. Human ontology, therefore, becomes to a large extent dependent on the evolution of language. This, however, is only the intelligent part of the reality. It has a different dynamic than instinctive reality that lacks the mobility of intelligence but, in contrast to intelligence, still retains its direct connection with life as a process. Whereas the ontology generated by intelligence may to a philosopher seem to be the full reality, in it are only those things that can exist as potential tools for our action. The existence of "objects" in this intelligent reality is made possible only because this layer of ontology is built on top of a more primitive biological ontology. Whereas intelligence makes a cut out of this reality, creating an ontology where subjects and objects are separated, intelligence, itself, is made possible by the process of life. This process is characterized by action and interaction, where subjects and objects emerge as integrated elements of a mutual process of coevolution. A fundamental driver in the evolution of this deeper ontology is the process of life that continuously generates new relations between the living being and its reality. The subjects and objects of reality are expressions of life, and in a constant dialog.

Dynamics of Ontological Expansion

Humans live in a reality that is both biological and social, and social reality is both mediated and made possible by language and the social division of labor. Although Hegel was right in stating that the world is a process, he made a crucial mistake in assuming that the human mind can only understand the ongoing change through ideas. Thus, states Engels (1907), despite its great service, the Hegelian system was "a colossal miscarriage" that turned things upside down. Even the most abstract ideas of human mind, including logic and mathematics, are born in a historical process of development where humans and their societies address practical and very material concerns. Engel's unfinished essay "The Part Played by Labour in the Transition from Ape to Man" (1966, Chap. 9) told an influential story of human development, arguing that the development of human brain and society were products of productive labor and that this process of development continuously opens up new realities. Labor, states Engels in the beginning of his essay, "is the prime basic condition for all human existence, and this to such an extent that, in a sense, we have to say that labour created man himself."

Thus, independent of the Bergsonian focus on action-oriented perception and cognition, also Engels emphasized the importance of action for the development of human mind, arguing that the mind and the things it thinks about are inseparable and related elements of nature. We should regard things not as stable and rigid objects; instead, we should focus on the connections between things and their pictures in mind, "their concatenation, their coming into being and passing away" (Engels 1907). Whereas labor in the early phases of human history was mainly about individual effort, in the more recent development of human thought and brain, according to Engels, the social division of labor has played a crucial role. When the essay was published as a chapter in Dialectics of Nature, first in Russian in 1925, it had a decisive impact on the way in which Soviet thinkers understood the dynamic connection between society, culture, and the development of cognition. This emphasis on action as socially constituted activity also becomes a key element in the cultural-historical activity theory developed by Vygotsky and his followers.

Vygotsky's Three Planes of Development

This link between social and thus essentially human forms of being, language, and socially meaningful action was an important theme in Vygotsky's work on developmental psychology in the 1920s (Vygotsky 1978, 1986; van der Veer and Valsiner 1994; Kozulin 1990). Vygotsky argued that advanced forms of human cognition are enabled by historically and culturally evolved conceptual systems and material tools that the cognition uses. Based on a large number of experiments with development of thought processes in children, Vygotsky formulated a "general genetic law of development." This stated that "higher forms" of thinking appear first on the level of social interaction and only afterward become internalized, at the same time radically changing the processes of thinking. As Vygotsky puts it:

> The general law of development says that awareness and deliberate control appear only during a very advanced stage in the development of a mental function, after it has been used and practiced unconsciously and spontaneously. In order to subject a function to intellectual and volitional control, we must first possess it. (Vygotsky 1986, p. 168)

In Bergsonian terms, instinctive and intuitive knowledge precedes intelligent knowing. We need to know the world before we can think and talk about it. Vygotsky's "higher forms of thinking," however, are not simply upgraded versions of already existing cognitive functionality. On the contrary, the advanced forms of cognition represent qualitatively new systems of psychological functions (Vygotsky and Luria 1994, p. 162). In the process of development, earlier functionality becomes combined in a qualitatively new complex that makes new types of thinking possible. We saw a similar functional shift on the level of phenotype in the emergence of wings. Wings open up a new world and new categories of objects associated with this world. The emergence of higher forms of cognition is enabled by the social use of symbols and concepts, and the resulting new forms of cognition also generate new realities.

For Vygotsky, the general genetic law of development implies that cognition is not something that can be locked inside the human head. This is in stark contrast with most conventional views of psychology and cognition. (As Wertsch and Tulviste (1996, p. 55) point out, the contemporary use of terms such as cognition, memory and attention implicitly assume that these are individual phenomena. When we want to talk about phenomena that occur on the social plane, some modifiers must therefore be added. Because of this, terms such as "socially shared cognition," "socially distributed cognition," and "collective memory" have become popular. For Vygotsky, advanced forms of cognition emerge on the social plane and such modifiers would not make sense.) According to Vygotsky, in the development of a child, social interaction is primary, and children learn to communicate with speech before they learn to use words in thinking. Similarly, a child has practical forms of thinking that do not require verbalization or concepts. A radical transition occurs, however, when practical thought and speech start to interact, and at this juncture, words become internalized tools for thinking and behavioral control. At the same time, conceptual thinking and intergenerational transfer and accumulation of its outcomes become possible. In the development of a child, this process is seen as ontogenetic development and learning.

In "primitive" cultures, some traces of this historical evolution are still visible. Vygotsky was particularly interested in "auxiliary memory tools," such as the golden figurines of West African storytellers that reminded the storyteller about a specific tale, or the ancient Peruvian *kvinus* that record stories and messages in knots of a string. Such cognitive tools and artifacts enable human cognition to move to a level of symbolic thinking, where thought is only indirectly connected with the current reality. The Bergsonian "intelligent sign," therefore, becomes in the Vygotskian framework possible when thought is externalized as a material artifact and then internalized again as abstract and generalized representation of that thought. Most importantly, action is not anymore directed toward present needs and immediately perceived environment. In contrast with chimpanzees and birds that can use tools to respond to their immediate needs, human action becomes mediated by symbol systems and thus free from current needs. In contrast to apes, humans, therefore, can also make tools that address the expected future (Vygotsky and Luria 1994, p. 165).

In the Vygotskian model, human development therefore occurs on three different planes: as the slow evolutionary development of the biological phenotype, as individual ontogenic maturation and learning that makes a newborn child a culturally competent adult, and as historical processes of sociocultural change. Because the higher cognitive functions are historically or "genetically" based on social interaction, understanding cultural-historical processes is critically important for a coherent theory of the human psyche. This link between historical sociocultural development – and thus the current organization of society – and mental processes means that human knowing is inherently a social phenomenon. Bergson pointed out that knowing depends on the knower's possibilities for action and cannot be reduced to a relation between an abstract "mind" and the reality it perceives. In the Vygotskian cultural-historical view, possible forms of meaningful action depend on the current social structure. Knowing, cognition, and ontology can fully be described only in relation to a social structure and the products of cultural processes. When intelligence becomes able to use words, not only in social communication but also internally to control behavior and thought, it transforms cognition to levels that are not available to other animals.

Bakhtinian Chronotopes and Cultural Forms of Ontology

Vygotsky's illustrations of social, cultural, and historical factors in the development of human thought imply that different cultures and cultures in different historical time periods have different realities. In a very practical sense, this was the focus of

Vygotsky's contemporary Mikhail Bakhtin in his studies of literary chronotopes (Bakhtin 1981).

For Bakhtin, different forms of literary genres have different concepts of time and space. Stories in different genres make sense in the context of specific and often unarticulated structures of time-space that makes events meaningful. Inspired by Alexei Ukhtomsky's work on neural physiology and his concept of chronotope (Chebanov 2015), Bakhtin showed how different historical forms of literature had produced increasingly complex forms of time-space, culminating in the Dostoevsky's multi-voiced novels where different chronotopes generate new realities through dialogical relations.

Bakhtin suggested that the ancient novel developed three major chronotopes. For example, in the five completely surviving "ancient novels of ordeal," written under the Roman Empire between the second and sixth centuries, the chronotope consists of "an alien world in adventure-time" (Bakhtin 1981, p. 89). In these Greek romances, the adventures leave no trace and affect nothing. The heroes and heroines do not change, mature, or even age as a result of their adventures. There is no inherent reason why the string of adventures and surprising events could not have occurred in a different order. According to Bakhtin, time in Greek romances, therefore, is "reversible." Time is a crucial factor in this literary genre, but not because it would underpin change, becoming, or emergence, as in the nineteenth-century novel; it is important because rescues and critical turning points occur at the last possible moment. Thus, Bakhtin notes, this genre is characterized by the use of expressions such as "suddenly" and "at the last moment." As Morson and Emerson put it:

> This is a world in which simultaneity, random contingency, miraculous coincidence, and sheer change play a key role. Wars happen unexpectedly and without apparent cause at crucial moments; storms come from nowhere to cause fatal shipwrecks. The time of the Greek romance is therefore … a time in which irrational forces erupt into human life to change its course… If a war should break out, it does not matter which war or why; and nothing that happens to the hero and heroine in any way shapes or reflects the historical process, which remains entirely abstract, just another source of random disruptive forces. That is one reason why adventuristic plots are so easy to adapt by authors of different countries and eras and so difficult to date accurately. (Morson and Emerson 1990, p. 378)

In the Greek romance time is reversible or repeatable, and also place becomes abstract and undifferentiated. A sea is needed for a shipwreck, but which sea makes no difference. Surprising events and incredible miracles require an alien country, but any alien country will do.

In the Greek romance, the hero travels in alien time-spaces where almost anything can happen because everyday constraints are not there. One thing stays the same, however. This is the hero himself. Events happen to the hero but his actions have no influence on them. As Bakhtin notes, in this chronotope individuals are completely passive and the actions of heroes and heroines "are reduced to enforced movement through space (escape, persecution, quests); that is, to a change in spatial location" (Bakhtin 1981, p. 105). Although the hero goes through adventures, these do not change him; instead, they represent tests that illustrate that the hero, indeed, is a hero.

> The novel as a whole, and each adventure in it, affirms who the hero and heroine are. The plot is a sort of judicial proceeding verifying innocence; and indeed judicially shaped rhetoric of the time is used in Greek romances and was clearly important in developing their ethos. The more severe the test, the greater the proof of the protagonists' integrity. (Morson and Emerson 1990, p. 381)

Another form of chronotope can be found in what Bakhtin calls "the adventure novel of everyday life." An example of this is in *The Golden Ass* of Apuleius, the only Ancient Roman novel written in Latin that has survived in its entirety. While trying to perform a spell that would metamorphose the protagonist Lucius into a bird, he accidentally turns into an ass. This leads to a long chain of adventures before finally a goddess gives Lucius advice how to become a man again.

In the chronotope of *The Golden Ass*, the chronotope of Greek romance is still strongly present. The logic of change, however, is subordinated to another higher logic, where the hero's adventures become elements in an overarching story of the protagonist's crisis and redemption. The hero at the beginning of the story is different from the one at the end, and change is represented as a process of metamorphosis that first makes Lucius an ass and, after all the adventures, human again. Time, therefore, becomes irreversible.

A third type of chronotope can be found in ancient biographies and autobiographies. Bakhtin argued that in the early antiquity there was no difference between autobiographies and biographies. This was because the characteristics of an individual were assumed to equal his publicly visible characteristics. There was no concept of "private" person as we may now understand it, and no "internal perspective" that could have differentiated autobiographies from biographies. In this chronotope of the public square, an individual was understood to be totally open to public gaze, and nothing in him could avoid being subject to public control and evaluation. In this chronotope, private emotions and thoughts did not exist simply because such concepts were as meaningless as a round square.

Beyond these three early chronotopes, Bakhtin elaborated in great detail the gradual and complex development of literary genres and their chronotopes, contrasting these with the nineteenth-century novel. In particular, Bakhtin saw the culmination of these developments in Dostoevsky's novels, where many voices and many chronotopes generate a complex system of emergent meanings. In the resulting chronotope, the actors are in a constant state of becoming and, perhaps more importantly, emerge in a dialogical relation with other actors.

Bakhtin's claim was that the historical development of literary genres has enabled new forms of thinking and knowing. Dostoevsky was a culmination of this process because Bakhtin understood life as a dialogical process where subjects and their environments are in constant interaction and generate each other. In fact, Bakhtin believed that important new forms of thinking emerge first as new literary forms. (This resembles Vygotsky's claim that a child first learns to speak and then only later in ontogenic development does she or he internalize the advanced forms of thought that language enables. Although there are close similarities in the works of Bakhtin and Vygotsky, it seems that they did not know each other (Kozulin p. 180).)

Literature reflects emerging realities, and provides resources for making sense of them. As the social life is fundamentally linguistic, literature provides the chronotopes that define what in that world is real. New forms of literary genres, therefore, imply new ontologies, where action, individuality, causality, and time-space are interpreted in a new way. Today, we can use a rich archive of these chronotopes. Fictive heroes, such as Indiana Jones, can now freely move in a time-space where ancient and recent past is fused in alien landscapes that we all already know.

Although Bakhtin's work centered on history of literature, it was motivated by essentially ethical concerns. In Bakhtin's view, humans exist in constant dialog with their environment, from the level of biology all the way up to social life. Although "dialog" is often understood as a conversation between two speakers, Bakhtin's concept of dialog is deeply rooted in his views on the nature of reality. A living cell is in a dialog with its environment, constantly observing everything that the cell can observe; from this pure perception, it makes sense by selecting one response among all the possible ones, at the same time reducing and organizing its ambience into a meaningful reality. Similarly, a human being is constantly engaged in its material and social world, trying to interpret it and make sense out of it.

This dialogical view generates a relational view of existence. A perceiving subject and a perceived "object" exist only as mutually constituted elements in interaction. Thus, when idealists or realists take either the subject or the object as the primary starting points for understanding knowledge or existence, they end up in positions that cannot explain either. A deep current in Bakhtin's work is the question what is action, agency, and responsibility in a world where the future is not determined by the subject or by its environment but constitute elements of the same dialogical relation.

Ontological Expansion in the Multifocal Model of Innovation

Bakhtin focused on cultural evolution, represented and enabled by literary and narrative forms, arguing that new chronotopes and new realities developed through the creative acts of authors. Written texts were rich stocks of knowledge and meaning that enabled people in a culture to make sense of their world. More importantly, he also argued that, based on culturally accumulated stocks of stories and meaning, we all are authors writing what exists, in a dialog with the world in which we live. There are no "universal" languages; instead language consists of a multitude of speech genres, each with their own chronotopes and systems of meaning.

This multi-voiced and dialogical view also underpins the multifocal innovation model (Tuomi 2002, Chap. 2). Innovation, in this view, is a process that creates new concepts, first as externalized artifacts and tools and then internalized as concepts and words that can be used to make sense of the expanded reality. In the context of different communities of users, each with their own practice-related systems of meaning, innovation and its functionality is interpreted differently.

In contrast to the conventional heroic model of innovation where a creator comes up with revolutionary new things such as steam engines, paper clips, or the World

Wide Web, the multifocal innovation model is based on the view that innovation requires social learning, sensemaking, and change in social practice. (The multifocal model is therefore also aligned with enactivist views on social cognition. The foundations of the multifocal model are discussed in detail in Tuomi (1999), which applies an action-oriented view of knowing to theory of organizational knowledge management and knowledge creation.) Innovation becomes real when potential users figure out what the still latent possibilities of a new material artifact could mean for them. For example, they may figure out that it is possible to talk with friends using a thing called a "telephone," or they can start to use computer networks for email. Innovation is in this view a sensemaking process, and the focus of sensemaking is in the existing communities of practice. The critical resources that make innovation possible, therefore, are not in the "upstream" where inventors come up with great new ideas; instead, it is in the "downstream" where potential users invent new interpretations about what the emerging functionality could mean in the context of the current system of meaning.

Beyond history of technology and innovation, the multifocal model is informed by research on social construction of technology and Vygotskian models of learning. In particular, the multifocal model is based on the claim that when potential users try and make sense of latent possibilities, they do it in the context of local meaning systems. These local meaning systems, in turn, are related to social practices. The multifocal model assumes that knowledge, meaning, and intelligence are developmentally grounded in practical action, as Bergson argued, and meaningful action in human societies is intrinsically social and based on established and evolving forms of division of labor. As a first approximation, the multifocal model therefore assumes that systems of meaning are organized around activity- and practice-related communities. New inventions, as it were, are thrown into a field of interdependent communities of practice that form systems of social division of labor, and some of these communities realize some emerging but still latent possibilities in their ongoing activity. At different points in the evolution of innovation, different communities can drive its development, and the same material artifact, for example, a telephone, can evolve along different trajectories in different communities. A "phone" can thus have very different functionalities for a taxi driver, a parent, a teenager, or a farmer in rural Africa.

The concept of "community of practice" emerged toward the end of the 1980s in ethnographic studies on how Xerox technicians learned to maintain copying machines. In these studies, Julian Orr (1996) showed that knowledge and skills required to keep a copying machine running were learned by participating in the informal community of maintenance technicians rather than through formal training or reading the manuals. The skills of the trade were learned around discussions around coffee and lunch breaks and with the help of more competent colleagues. Lave and Wenger (1991) put this in the Vygotskian context, arguing that novice community members develop their skills and knowledge by moving in a "zone of proximal development" toward higher levels of competence guided by more competent community members. Similar emphasis on the importance of social learning processes and local meaning systems has been suggested by other researchers, for example, as communities of practitioners in technology development, as thought communities in the history of science, and as epistemic cultures in ethnographic studies on knowledge generation practices in science (Brown and Duguid 1991; Constant 1984; Fleck 1979; Knorr Cetina 1999; Schön 1983).

Lave and Wenger introduced communities of practice to describe learning and identity development in specialized professional groups, focusing on the social and cognitive structure of the groups themselves. The existence of such specialized groups, of course, implicitly assumes a broader social system that makes specialization possible. An alternative approach is to focus on interactions among "networked communities of practice." Such a broader perspective is useful when we try to understand how and why communities of practice and their ontologies change. Whereas the original focus of communities of practice research was on increasing mastery of existing community-specific competences and knowledge, thus implicitly interpreting learning as "socialization" into an existing local culture, a broader "networks of communities" – view focuses on interactions between communities that generate new forms of activity and social practice. In contrast with learning as "acquisition of knowledge," the multifocal innovation model naturally adopts this view of learning as creation of new knowledge.

Partly because of the legacy of Engels and compatibility with contemporary political doctrines, Vygotsky and his followers strongly emphasized the importance of social division of labor in the development of human cognition and knowledge. After Vygotsky's death in 1934, the link between learning, cognition, and the Marxist focus on social division of labor become elaborated in the cultural-historical activity theory, in particular in the shape formulated by Vygotsky's colleague Alexei Leont'ev (1978). Inspired by this earlier work on cultural-historical activity theory, Engeström (1987) developed a more detailed structural model of activity and an associated model of "expansive learning," with a particular emphasis on conflicts and contradictions that drive and constrain change.

In the context of ontological expansion, Engeström's model is interesting for two reasons. First, Engeström argued that internal contradictions in human activity generate a dynamic that constantly produces new forms of activity. Human activity has an internal structure that leads to a continuously expanding ontology. Although Bergson was right claiming that the human species should be called Homo faber, more accurately it should be called Homo creativus. Whereas we normally understand creativity as a characteristic of individuals, Engeström's model of expansive learning suggests that creativity and change are already embedded in the dynamics of all socially organized activity, essentially independent of any individual drive for creation. Ontological expansion, therefore, is an unalienable characteristic of all social systems, and creativity and innovation are unavoidable. From this point of view, the expansion of ontology is a natural phenomenon in all social systems, and the primary question is not why it happens but why ontological expansion does not lead to ontological "explosion." To understand the dynamics of ontological expansion, we, therefore, have to explain what constrains this dynamic. In terms in innovation research, the question is not what makes innovation happen but what makes it exceptional and difficult. Second, Engeström applied his cultural-historical model of activity in the domain of learning, arguing that a historically new form of learning is emerging in response to the development of advanced capitalism. If Engeström is right, ontology is now expanding in a qualitatively different way from earlier historical periods. One way of putting this is to say that the dynamics and conditions of change, indeed, have changed. (One way to link macroeconomic development with ontological expansion is to view dominant cultural ontologies as products of an underlying techno-economic structure. Ontological expansion, therefore, becomes constrained by the speed of change of these institutionalized social structures. This is essentially the Freeman-Perez interpretation of long cycles in economic development (Freeman and Louçã 2001; Perez 1985, 2002).)

The multifocal model of innovation adapts somewhat eclectically complementary ideas from cultural-historical activity theory and from research on communities of practice. A major difference between activity theory and the communities or practice model of activity is that activity theory assumes a heterogeneous system of knowledge and meaning (Tuomi 1999, Chap. 9). Activity-theoretic models therefore require an implicit system of division of labor. In contrast, prototypical communities of practice are homogeneous systems of meaning and specialization, where differences exist as levels of expertise and community-specific knowledge. The multifocal model retains the idea that development occurs by integrating new practical and symbolic means into practice and that this integration is driven by internal contradictions and external conflict. On the other hand, it emphasizes the point that communities of practice have their idiosyncratic systems of meaning that enable their members to communicate in the same language. The "struggles" and "contradictions" that result in the development of new technology-mediated practices, therefore, to an important extent reflect the different interpretations of different communities of practice. Because each community has different stocks of knowledge and meaning available, embedded in its stories and their chronotopes, the realization of innovation often becomes a question of which of the possible stories is culturally the most powerful. This, of course, to a great extent depends on the practical impact. In the multifocal model, however, innovation is not only realized to solve problems and release tensions. On the contrary, innovation is also driven by creativity, curiosity, and experimentation that leads to unpredictable surprises and emotional delight.

Ukhtomsky's Theory of Dominants

The discussion above indicates that reality is a deeply relational phenomenon. For humans, much of this reality is inherently social and based on historical and culturally accumulated stocks of meaning. Historically evolving forms of social collaboration, coordination, and specialization lead to social practices and systems of meaning that provide the foundation for social change and innovation. As Vygotsky showed, advanced forms of adult human thought are enabled by these systems of meaning, which in the Bakhtinian context can be called genres. The biological roots of relational ontologies and their evolution from the simplest living organisms to human cognition were, in turn, outlined in the Bergsonian account of perception, time, instinct, and intellect. In this section, these threads are woven together in the context of Alexei Ukhtomsky's "theory of dominants," developed in the first decades of the twentieth century (Sokolova 2015; Zueva and Zuev 2015).

Ukhtomsky's highly original work has major implications for a variety of research fields, ranging from pure philosophy and sociology to brain studies and artificial intelligence. Ukhtomsky's work, however, to a large extent remains to be rediscovered. (For an important collection of articles that explore Ukhtomsky's work, see Nadin (2015). Ukhtomsky's concept of chronotope became the starting point for Bakhtin, and his work was also well known to Vygotsky and his followers. In discussing development as an evolutionary change in phenotypes, Vygotsky quotes at length Ukhtomsky, pointing out that "One might say that the whole task of man and his behavior is the construction and cultivation of new instincts" (Luria and Vygotsky 1992, p. 3).) In this section, I use Ukhtomsky's concept of dominants to show that ontological expansion can be understood as the emergence of a new dominant. There is a close similarity between Bergson's description of pure perception and "images" of the ambient world and Ukhtomsky's concept of dominants. Based on his research, Ukhtomsky, however, proposed an essentially neurophysiological model of the formation of these images. In contrast to Bergson, Ukhtomsky also extended this model beyond epistemology and ethics to social phenomena.

Already early in his research career, Ukhtomsky noted an anomaly in experiments that were supposed to illustrate the theory of reflexes. When the nerves of a dog were electrically stimulated, the reaction was not always predictable. Ukhtomsky realized that the state of the animal played an important part in generating the response. In contrast to contemporary ideas on reflex conditioning and studies on localization of brain functions, Ukhtomsky came to the conclusion that the brain is a dynamically organized system, where different nerve centers form transient functional constellations. Different constellations or neural ensembles inhibit and excite each other based on the internal state of the animal and influences from its environment. In this process, one constellation becomes "dominant" and determines the action of the animal, at the same time suppressing other potential actions.

To understand the concept of dominant, one may think of a simple reflex arc where external stimulus produces an action. In the simplest interpretation, the action is a function of the stimulus. Excitation from sensory nerves arrives in a neural ganglion, which in turn activates appropriate behavior. If, however, instead of this simple chain, the effect of the sensory activation is influenced by other neural ganglia, the outcome will depend also on the activity of these other ganglia. We can then ask, which of these has the most decisive influence on the realized activity. This ganglion that "selects" one action from a set of all possible actions we can call the dominant one.

In Ukhtomsky's view, such "ganglia," however, are not just spatial bundles of interconnected neurons. They are dynamic functional centers of activity, distributed in the structures of the brain and even beyond the neural system in the whole organism. The functional constellation or temporary ensemble that at each point in time determines action is what Ukhtomsky calls the "dominant."

This is a highly unorthodox view. For Ukhtomsky, perception is not just a function of sensory inputs. Instead, a living organism perceives its ambience through a collection of historically accumulated activity patterns. In perception, the ambience arouses or "triggers" dominants, and, depending on the state of the perceiver and its ambience, one of these becomes the dominant that selects present action. If the action confirms that the dominant was appropriate, the neural connections that excite the dominant and inhibit its alternatives can be strengthened. Moreover, dominants are not spatially localized; instead, they are distributed across neural networks as dynamical patterns. This model, therefore, resembles self-organizing neural network models, for example, Kohonen's self-organized maps (1998). In contrast to most currently popular neural AI models, Ukhtomsky's theory of dominants, however, is based on a functional description where cognitive activity is connected with action. (Functional description means that a system is described in terms of its impact on a larger system, i.e., a context or environment that exists beyond the system boundaries. As Rosen (e.g., 1991, Chap. 5) has explained, a functional description requires an essentially "semantic" description that cannot be derived from purely "syntactic" characteristics of the system itself. For example, the functioning of a biological organ such as the heart can only be understood in the context of a body where the heart is a functional component. This also means that functional descriptions lead to system models that cannot be expressed using algorithmic programs that syntactically manipulate system states (Rosen 1987). For a definitive mathematical discussion on this subject, see Louie (2009, pt. III) and the chapters written by Louie in this Handbook ▶ Chaps. 2, "Complex Systems," ▶ 45, "Mathematical Foundations of Anticipatory Systems," and ▶ 10, "Relational Biology.") Although the activation of a dominant implies that some neurons and some areas of the brain are active, there is therefore no simple mapping between the areas of the brain and its functions. Functional cognitive components are distributed, generated as collective and coordinated activity of the underpinning components that realize them, and the same set of neurons can play a role in many different dominants. Furthermore, a dominant consists of the state of the organism beyond just the cells in its brain. A dominant is jointly produced by the internal and external elements of reality, which together activate the dominant.

This concept of dominants was extensively elaborated by Ukhtomsky during the 1920s in an attempt to create a unified view of physics, biology, society, and ethics. It implies a relational ontology, where the biological subject and its ambience are in constant interaction and resonate with each other. Most interestingly, Ukhtomsky's concept of dominance leads to a view where anticipation is the foundation of ontology. A real object is always a potential object of action and therefore always a prediction of what this object will be. When the various sensory inputs generate a "primary image" of the environment, it activates neural centers based on memory traces created in earlier experience. As the various centers activate and inhibit each other, a dominant formation of activity emerges together with a "secondary synthesis" that produces an "integral image" of perception. Integral images are models of reality that are partly based on experienced reality and memory, partly on the current environment and situation, but always oriented toward the future outcomes of action (Sokolova 2015, p. 125). Dominants, in this sense, are expectations of reality. However, because objects are integral images that arise when the ambience activates a dominant, and dominants are products of past experience, we can only perceive what already exists. When we talk about goals, we always talk about anticipated future. When we think about causal relations, we always think about the past as it used to be. As Ukhtomsky states:

> Full-fledged human thought is always directed towards the future, it is always pragmatic and purposeful – man can devote himself to an exclusively causal description of reality only in abstraction and reduction, when you can turn your attention exclusively to past events and when present reality is just a repetition of the past. (quoted in Zueva and Zuev 2015, p. 32)

As Zueva and Zuev note, Ukhtomsky therefore saw the role or logics, verbal argumentation, and formal methods in science not as a method to expand knowledge but to explain, verify, and systematize what is already known. Intuition, or the "play of dominants," is, according to Ukhtomsky, the true source of new knowing.

One of the key ideas of Ukhtomsky was that dominants are not only found in neural processes. Human thought is influenced by cultural and historically developed dominants that amplify some patterns of activity and inhibit others. From an ethical point of view, the idea that dominants underpin also our perception of others implies that what we see in others is more a reflection of ourselves than the true nature of other persons. Ethics, therefore, is not about finding moral rules that others should follow; instead, it is about listening the world and developing the dominants that enable ethical development. (Bakhtin's dialogical ethics, of course, bears close similarity to Ukhtomsky here, as well as to the ethics of Buber (2000) and Levinas (1969).)

After Stalin's "the year of great breakthrough" started to wipe out Russian intelligentsia in 1929, Ukhtomsky focused on physiological studies. In these studies he also tried to develop models of dominants as systems of nonlinear oscillators. In retrospect, this approach can be seen as doomed. A relational ontology requires a formalism that is able to describe relational phenomena. Such a formalism was developed only in the 1940s. It is known as category theory, and it is the formalism that also underpins Robert Rosen's work on anticipatory systems (Louie 2009, 2010; Rosen 1985). In the next section, I briefly highlight the potential of this formalism for modeling the emergence of Ukhtomskian dominants and ontological expansion, more generally.

A Category-Theoretic Approach to Modeling Ontological Expansion

To clearly describe what happens when ontology expands, we need to turn to a science that specializes in clear and well-defined descriptions. In this section we therefore briefly put the above discussion in a mathematical context. Whereas mathematics is often assumed to deal with numbers and quantities by non-mathematicians, in this section we refer to a different kind of mathematics, known as category theory. Category theory has sometimes been called "metamathematics" as it can be used to study different formal systems and their relations. Beyond just providing a language that can clarify the concepts that we are talking about, mathematical constructs that category theorists have developed since the 1940s are surprisingly relevant for understanding ontological expansion.

Category theory is a very powerful but also abstract branch of mathematics. It was originally developed to solve difficult topological problems by mapping them into easier to solve algebraic problems. To do this, category theory had to abstract away the specificities of one mathematical structure and show how the structure can be represented in another mathematical structure that on the surface appeared quite different. Since then, category theory has been used in studies of pure mathematics, as well as in many different domains ranging from physics and philosophy to biology and computer science (Awodey 2010).

The strength of category theory follows from the fact that it represents mathematical and other structures in a relational way. A commonsense approach to represent objects of a system is to describe the internal characteristics of the objects. For example, the solar system can be described as planets that have a mass and, at each point in time, a location in a trajectory around the Sun. In more accurate models, the planets may be composed of solid materials, gases, and water, each with their physical properties. Category theory, in contrast, represents all characteristics of objects as relations that an object has in the system. "Objects" in category theory do not have any hidden inner structure; instead, all the characteristics of the system are represented as the structure of the system.

A category-theoretic system, therefore, consists of objects that are related to the other objects in the system. As the objects do not have any hidden internal structure, they can be drawn on a paper as simple dots. The relations, in turn, can be drawn as links or arrows between the objects. A category-theoretic representation thus consists of dots connected with arrows. On a piece of paper, a category looks like a network graph. Although category theory studies mathematical structures called "categories," the objects that constitute these categories can be of many different kinds as long as some basic axioms remain valid. A category-theoretic model of a living organism, for example, could have atoms, molecules, cells, and food as its objects. "Food," in turn, would be represented, not by its internal composition or recipe but by its effect on the organism. When the effects are fully represented as relations to other objects in the system, no additional information can be gained by putting the object under a microscope and peeking inside it.

Category theory was originally concerned with structure-preserving mappings between systems. When a category is represented as a graph with vertices and directed arrows between them, a basic question in category theory is how to compare two different graphs. In particular, category theory is interested in studying those mappings between graphs that maintain the essential category-theoretic structure of the graph. When that is the case, mathematical statements about one "graph" can be "transported" to the other "graph." As the graph can actually be a representation of a complete mathematical domain, for example, the category of all topological spaces, the category of all possible sets, the category of relations, or the category of finite sets with specified mappings between their elements, knowledge about one mathematical domain can be mapped to other mathematical domains when the category-theoretic structure is preserved.

To make this possible, category theory abstracts two of the most basic structural characteristics of mathematical functions that map points in its source domain to its target domain (known as "co-domain" in category-theoretic terms). First, functions can be combined or "chained." Second, there always exists an "identity function" that maps each value to itself. Category theory translates these into a requirement that for each chain of arrows in a graph, there has to be a unique "composite" arrow and to the requirement that there has to be an "identity" arrow. Using these simple but highly abstract elements, category theory builds up a mathematical formalism that is able to talk about the similarities among vastly diverse domains of mathematics. The strength of category theory follows from the fact that many difficult mathematical problems can be shown to be equal to problems in other mathematical domains, where they can be easily solved.

Much of work in category theory is, indeed, pure and abstract mathematics. Beyond mathematics itself, category-theoretic models can, however, be built for many other types of systems. One of the first applications of category theory was Robert Rosen's (1958b) model of a minimal functional structure of a living cell. Rosen was able to show that there can exist systems that can maintain their own functional structure, thus making the system an autonomous functional unit. Such systems, however, lead to category-theoretic models that cannot be simulated by computers without losing their essential category-theoretic structure (Louie 2009; Rosen 1991). Since then, category-theoretic models have been widely used, first for studying logical formalisms and then for computer science, quantum theory, and, for example, modeling cognitive and neural processes.

Of particular interest in the context of ontological expansion is the work on *Memory Evolutive Systems* by Ehresmann and Vanbremeersch (2007). It provides a category-theoretic model of human cognition that can be interpreted as a proper formalization of Ukhtomsky's theory of dominants. Below, ontological expansion is interpreted as the formation of Ukhtomskian dominants, using category-theoretic concepts. This provides a solid and well-developed mathematical formalism for studying ontological expansion, creative learning, and innovation. Moreover, category-theoretic concepts can naturally be applied to devising robust methodologies for empirical studies of anticipatory systems and processes (Ehresmann et al. forthcoming).

A common characteristic of models of complex systems is that they are hierarchical. (Here we use the term "complexity" in a somewhat loose manner, focusing on the intuitive idea of emergence as something that is "more than a sum of its parts." Rosen definssed complex systems as systems that have models that cannot be algorithmically computed. Rosennean complexity, therefore, is associated with self-referentiality and impredicativity. Ehresmann and Vanbremeersch use a different definition based on category-theoretic system characteristics. Most current work on complex systems focuses on systems models that are "difficult to compute" but which Rosen would call complicated simple systems or mechanisms.) For example, a living cell is typically understood to consist of components such as atoms, molecules, and organelles. Molecules are understood to be organized bundles of atoms, and organelles are understood to be organized bundles of molecules. If a cell is interpreted as a category-theoretic system, we may then ask what is the relation between a molecule and its constituent atoms.

Atoms in a molecule are not only random bundles but they are structurally organized. Each atom in a molecule constrains the "freedom of interactions" of other atoms in the molecule and makes their interactions with the rest of the system different from what they would be without the organization of the molecule. Atoms in a molecule thus implement an interconnected pattern. If the category includes an object – we may call it a "molecule" – that has the same effect on the rest of the system as the underlying pattern of interlinked atoms, this object can be understood as a "higher-level" object. It is "composed" of the lower-level objects but qualitatively different from them as the effects of the higher-level object represent coordinated and synergistic effects of its constituent elements. Thus, a molecule is qualitatively different from atoms, and a stone bridge is different from the stones that were used to construct it. A bridge does not fall down because the stones that compose it constrain each other's movement and restrict their free fall. The bridge, therefore, is a collective product of linkages that exist between the stones. We may call these linkages "the organization" of the bridge, and if they are taken away, the bridge comes crumbling down.

In category theory, a "simplest possible" object that has the same effects that an underlying pattern of objects is called a *colimit*. In the special case that there are no linkages among the constituent elements of a colimit, a colimit equals the "sum" of its unconnected elements. In general, however, a colimit is the "smallest" object that is "more than a sum" of its components. Another way of putting this is to say that a colimit, in general, is the smallest thing that cannot be reduced to its constituent elements. It is "more" than a sum of its parts because its elements are not independent but form an organized system. As Ehresmann and Vanbremeersch have emphasized, the concept of colimit is therefore highly relevant for modeling emergence.

This also explains why category theory is a central piece in studying functional shift and constant creation in the relational ontologies of living systems. Classical physics and sciences it inspired are essentially atomistic, trying to derive system characteristics from the characteristics of the underlying objects. The mathematics that they use is inherently unable to take into account organizational linkages that make qualitatively new and more complex objects possible. In a category-theoretic framework, atomistic systems emerge as very special kinds of systems, defined by their lack of organization. As biology, sociology, economy, and cognition consist almost without exception of highly organized phenomena, category theory both explains why physical models frequently fail to capture such phenomena and also provides a more coherent starting point for their study.

A category-theoretic model of a natural system may thus have patterns of objects that generate "collective" effects. In some models, the category that is used to model the system may not have a colimit that represents these collective effects. The collective may remain informal, for example, a temporary association of people working together. It is, however, also possible that over time this informal collective transforms into a more stable structure and may gain its own identity. The resulting system can then be modeled as an enlarged category that explicitly models the emergent organization. As Ehresmann and Vanbremeersch show, in general, the modeling of organized and evolving systems therefore requires that we describe how categories change, while retaining some of their essential characteristics. In category theory, such "structure-preserving" mappings from one category to another are called "functors," and large bodies of mathematical literature exist that describe how they behave and how they can be used.

In category-theoretic terms, the emergence of a Ukhtomskian "dominant" may therefore be interpreted as the emergence of a colimit. In a neural system, a dominant represents the collective effects of the underlying pattern of neural activity, which in turn is structured by previous experience. In contrast to many computer-inspired models of cognition, there is no separate "processor," "memory," or miniature "homunculus" sitting inside the brain making decisions. Instead, previous experiences are sedimented in the inhibitory and excitatory propensities of the neural structure, as well as in the rest of the body and its culturally and historically accumulated material extensions.

As both Ukhtomsky and Bergson stated, we can perceive the present only as repetition of what we already have experienced. A category-theoretic interpretation of dominants, however, shows that this is not the whole story. When an underlying pattern of neural activity becomes "institutionalized" and gains its own identity as a colimit of the pattern, it starts to represent qualitatively new characteristics that cannot be reduced to the characteristics of the underlying elements. In particular, when a single colimit is a colimit of several independent patterns, it is not possible to tell what was the underpinning pattern that activated the dominant. When such "complex" colimits emerge, experience and perception can become "decoupled." Imagination, in particular, may be understood as the active reconfiguration of neural patterns and a search for new dominants associated with increasingly effective possibilities for action.

As Ukhtomsky pointed out, the concept of dominants can be extended to social and cultural domains. A category-theoretic model of neural dominants can be mapped to different domains if the category-theoretic structure is retained. To the extent that a "functorial" mapping can be found, it does not matter whether the objects of the category are neurons, humans, or social institutions. Although there may be no "collective mind" perceiving its reality as a potential object for action, social action is constituted by patterns of acts that jointly produce socially meaningful outcomes. Without coordination, interaction, and constraints between individual acts, collective production would not be possible. In category-theoretic terms, extensions of Ukhtomsky's concept of dominant toward social and cultural domains are therefore natural. In particular, there is no need to "reduce" social phenomena to the characteristics of specific individuals or to the atoms that constitute them. In fact, except in some extraordinary cases, such a reduction is mathematically impossible. Category theory shows that in a hierarchical system lower-level objects do not have attributes that emerge when these lower-level objects form organized wholes. Perfect knowledge about the characteristics of lower-level objects, therefore, is not enough to characterize the system. In other words, even the most careful study of an animal will not tell us whether it is cattle or a beast; beasts live in a category where a pattern of animals and humans jointly generate a new phenomenological domain. In this world, beasts are created millions of years after the most terrible of Earth's sons, Kronos, is born. More accurately, beasts are created when in human history the underlying relations between cows and humans become institutionalized in productive social practice that differentiates cattle as something distinct from beasts.

In the context of the multifocal innovation model, ontological expansion can then be interpreted as the emergence of a new pattern of social practice that is institutionalized enough that our commonsense models of the reality include its colimit as one of its objects. In practice, this means that we have invented a word and a concept that labels the object. When such a new practice is enabled by new functional artifacts, for example, a telephone or the Internet, the artifact may also act as a "boundary object" (Star 2010) that links several relatively independent practices. In such a situation, many alternative interpretations of "proper" use and appropriate conceptualization may emerge. Each interested community of practice interprets the novel functional possibilities using its local system of meanings, in its own ontological reality, and in this process some interpretations may become culturally dominant. When that happens, it becomes easy to tell retrospective stories that are full of meaning, understandable, and easy to believe, but which often lack the historical detail that would spoil the expected storyline.

Summary

In this chapter we have provided a broad and multidisciplinary introduction to ontological expansion, exploring the historical basis of the concept. We started by characterizing three key principles, continuous creation, functional shift, and relational ontology that clarify what ontological expansion is. We then focused on a more detailed discussion on what drives change in ontology. Vygotsky's cultural-historical model of development illustrated that ontological expansion occurs at social, individual and evolutionary levels. Bakhtin's work on literary chronotopes was used to show that important elements of social ontology and its time-space organization are embedded in evolving speech genres, literary forms, and stories. Returning back to the starting point of this chapter, innovation, we then used the multifocal innovation model as an example of how new realities emerge in the context of multiple communities of practice, each with their own systems of meaning and conceptions of reality.

Ukhtomsky's theory of neural dominants is in many ways incompatible with much of current brain research and many recent neural network models. It is, however, highly compatible with the principles of continuous creation, functional shift, and relational ontology. Using some key ideas from the mathematical theory of categories, we illustrated that Ukhtomsky's theory of dominants can be put on a very strong formal foundation and that it easily extends to social and cultural domains. The theory of dominants, interpreted in a category-theoretic framework, therefore provides a very practical starting point for studying ontological expansion. As ontological expansion and the deep unpredictability it generates are important challenges for anticipatory practices, these starting points can also lead to new models in the theory and practice of anticipation and foresight.

This account of ontological expansion, therefore, has three immediate implications for research and practice on anticipatory systems and processes. First, we don't have facts or data about things that do not exist yet. Extrapolations based on historical data cannot provide knowledge about qualitatively new aspects of the future. What counts as qualitatively new depends on practical impact. When innovation increases the efficiency of an existing practice, predictive models of the future may for the time being be accurate; when it transforms and reorganizes practices and systems of meaning, predictive models become misleading and obscure the present. They talk about the reality as it used to be and lack words to talk about things that are new. When the emergent novelty has dramatic consequences, innovation researchers talk about radical and disruptive innovation. Because revolutions and disruptions can only be observed after they already have visible impact, many exercises in foresight have missed important qualitative changes. In particular, predictive mathematical models are fundamentally unable to predict disruption, revolution, and true novelty. At best, such models are able to show how the future would look like if nothing important happens.

Second, category theory provides a rich and well-developed formalism for describing and studying relational systems. As the founder of Kyoto School of philosophy Kitaro Nishida argued in the first decades of the last century, Western philosophical thinking took a wrong turn with Aristotle, when the separation of subjects and objects became the starting point for epistemology and ontology (Nishida 1987). It is a curious historical fact that this division between subjects and objects has been critically studied mainly by thinkers who have been interested in the philosophy or religion and ethics. In the case of Nishida, this critique was based on an attempt to synthesize Zen Buddhist conceptions of reality with European phenomenology, Bergson, and American pragmatism. For Ukhtomsky and Bakhtin, the starting point was Russian Orthodox thinkers. As the modern empirical science is deeply grounded in the Aristotelian distinction, only highly original thinkers have been able to question this foundation of Newtonian science. Category theory, however, provides a well-established formalism that can move scientists beyond the Newtonian world, toward domains where organization and relational systems can be explored and understood. Society, economy, biology, brains, and the Internet are replete with such systems.

Third, category-theoretic models provide interesting opportunities for studying how we can learn to know futures that do not exist yet. The basic category-theoretic operations that generate colimits can be implemented in actual foresight practice. Different approaches to foresight processes assume different chronotopes, and better understanding of the characteristics of these chronotopes can be understood as improved futures literacy (Miller 2007). Foresight methods that assume relational ontologies and build on category-theoretic concepts are able to invent futures that remain beyond the grasp of more traditional approaches. This opens up interesting new avenues for conceptual and practical research on "next-generation" foresight. In the relational approach, future becomes an ontological thing instead of an epistemic thing. Conventional challenges of anticipatory processes therefore appear in new light. For example, if the future is about making futures instead of knowing them, the challenge of translating future-oriented knowledge and intelligence into action and "actionable knowledge" disappears. We may invent the future, even when we do not know it.

References

Antliff, M. (1993). *Inventing Bergson: Cultural politics and the Parisian avant-garde*. Princeton: Princeton University Press.

Awodey, S. (2010). *Category theory*. Oxford: Oxford University Press.

Bakhtin, M. (1981). Forms of time and of the chronotope in the novel: Notes toward a historical poetics. In M. Holquist (Ed.), *The dialogic imagination: Four essays by M.M. Bakhtin* (pp. 84–258). Austin: University of Texas Press.

Bell, A.G. (1876). Improvement in telegraphy. In Coe, L. (1995). *The telephone and its many inventors*. Jefferson, N.C.: McFarland, Appendix 10.

Bergson, H. (1983). *Creative evolution (first edition 1907)*. Lanham: University Press of America.

Bergson, H. (1988). *Matter and memory (first edition 1896)*. New York: Zone Books.

Brown, J. S., & Duguid, P. (1991). Organizational learning and communities of practice: Toward a unified view of working, learning, and innovation. *Organization Science, 2*(1), 40–57.

Buber, M. (2000). *I and Thou*. New York: Free Press.

Chebanov, S. V. (2015). Ukhtomsky's idea of chronotope as frame of anticipation. In M. Nadin (Ed.), *Anticipation: Learning from the past – the Russian/Soviet contributions to the science of anticipation* (pp. 137–150). Cham: Springer.

Constant, E. W. (1984). Communities and hierarchies: Structure in the practice of science and technology. In R. Laudan (Ed.), *The nature of technological knowledge: Are models of scientific change relevant?* (pp. 27–46). Dordrecht: Reidel.

Ehresmann, A. C., & Vanbremeersch, J.-P. (2007). *Memory evolutive systems*. Amsterdam: Elsevier.

Ehresmann, A., Tuomi, I., Miller, R., Béjean, M., & Vanbremeersch, P. (forthcoming). Towards a formal framework for describing collective intelligence knowledge creation processes that "Use-the-future." In *Transforming the future: Anticipation in the 21st century* (p. Ch. 3). Paris: Routledge/UNESCO.

Engels, F. (1907). *"Anti-Duehring" (Original title: Herrn Eugen Dührings Umwältzung der Wissenschaft, 1878)*. Chicago: Charles H. Kerr & Company. Retrieved from http://www.guten berg.org/ebooks/31933.

Engels, F. (1966). *Dialectics of nature*. Moscow: Progress Publishers.

Engeström, Y. (1987). *Learning by expanding: An activity theoretical approach to developmental work research*. Helsinki: Orienta Konsultit.

Fischer, C. S. (1992). *America calling: A social history of telephone to 1940*. Berkeley: University of California Press.

Fleck, L. (1979). *Genesis and development of a scientific fact*. Chicago: The University of Chicago Press.

Freeman, C., & Louçã, F. (2001). *As time goes by: From the industrial revolutions to the information revolution*. Oxford: Oxford University Press.

Gunter, P. A. Y. (1983). Introduction to the UPA edition: Philosophical method and biological time. In H. Bergson (Ed.), *Creative evolution* (pp. xvii–xvli). Lanham: University Press of America.

Kingslover, J. G., & Koehl, M. A. R. (1985). Aerodynamics, thermoregulation, and the evolution of insect wings: Differential scaling and evolutionary change. *Evolution, 39*(3), 488–504. https://doi.org/10.2307/2408648.

Knorr Cetina, K. (1999). *Epistemic cultures: How the sciences make knowledge.* Cambridge, MA: Harvard University Press.

Kohonen, T. (1998). The self-organizing map. *Neurocomputing, 21*(1), 1–6. https://doi.org/10.1016/S0925-2312(98)00030-7.

Kozulin, A. (1990). *Vygotsky's psychology: A biography of ideas.* Cambridge, MA: Harvard University Press.

Lave, J., & Wenger, E. (1991). *Situated learning: Legitimate peripheral participation.* Cambridge: Cambridge University Press.

Leont'ev, A. N. (1978). *Activity, consciousness, and personality.* Englewood Cliffs: Prentice-Hall.

Levinas, E. (1969). *Totality and infinity.* Pittsburgh: Duquesne University Press.

Lie, M., & Sørensen, K. H. (1996). *Making technology our own? Domesticating technology into everyday life.* Oslo: Scandinavian University Press.

Louie, A. H. (2009). *More than life itself: A synthetic continuation in relational biology.* Frankfurt: Ontos Verlag.

Louie, A. H. (2010). Robert Rosen's anticipatory systems. *Foresight, 12*(3), 18–29.

Luria, A. R., & Vygotsky, L. (1992). *Ape, primitive man, and child: Essays in the history of behavior.* Hemel Hempstead: Harvester Wheatsheaf.

Miller, R. (2007). Futures literacy: A hybrid strategic scenario method. *Futures, 39*(4), 341–362. https://doi.org/10.1016/j.futures.2006.12.001.

Mivart, G. (1871). *On the genesis of species.* London: Macmillan and Co. Retrieved from http://www.gutenberg.org/ebooks/20818.

Morson, G. S., & Emerson, C. (1990). *Mikhail Bakhtin: Creation of Prosaics.* Stanford: Stanford University Press.

Nadin, M. (Ed.). (2015). *Anticipation: Learning from the past – the Russian/Soviet contributions to the science of anticipation.* Cham: Springer.

Nishida, K. (1987). *Last writings: Nothingness and the religious worldview.* Honolulu: University of Hawaii Press.

Nishitani, K. (1991). *Nishida Kitaro.* Berkeley: University of California Press.

Orr, J. E. (1996). *Talking about machines: An ethnography of a modern job.* Ithaca: Cornell University Press.

Perez, C. (1985). Microelectronics, long waves and world structural change: New perspectives for developing countries. *World Development, 13*(3), 441–463.

Perez, C. (2002). *Technological revolutions and financial capital: The dynamics of bubbles and golden ages.* Cheltenham: Edward Elgar.

Rashevsky, N. (1954). Topology and life: In search of general mathematical principles in biology and sociology. *Bulletin of Mathematical Biophysics, 16*, 317–348.

Rosen, R. (1958a). A relational theory of biological systems. *Bulletin of Mathematical Biophysics, 20*, 245–260.

Rosen, R. (1958b). The representation of biological system from the standpoint of the theory of categories. *Bulletin of Mathematical Biophysics, 20*, 317–341.

Rosen, R. (1985). *Anticipatory systems: Philosophical, mathematical and methodological foundations.* Oxford: Pergamon Press.

Rosen, R. (1987). On the scope of syntactics in mathematics and science: The machine metaphor. In J. L. Casti & A. Karlqvist (Eds.), *Real brains, artificial minds* (pp. 1–23). New York: Elsevier.

Rosen, R. (1991). *Life itself: A comprehensible inquiry into the nature, origin and fabrication of life.* New York: Columbia University Press.

Russell, B. (1946). *History of western philosophy.* London: Unwin Paperbacks.

Schön, D. A. (1983). *The reflective practitioner.* New York: Basic Books.

Schumpeter, J. A. (2005). The analysis of economic change. Reprinted from review of economic statistics, May 1935, 2–10. In R. V. Clemence (Ed.), *Essays on entrepreneurs, innovations, business cycles and the evolution of capitalism* (pp. 134–149). New Brunswick: Transaction Publishers.

Silverstone, R., & Haddon, L. (1996). Design and the domestication of information and communication technologies: Technical change and everyday life. In L. Silverstone & R. Mansell (Eds.), *Communication by design: The politics of information and communication technologies* (pp. 44–74). Oxford: Oxford University Press.

Sokolova, L. V. (2015). On the legacy and life of academician Alexei A. Ukhtomsky. In M. Nadin (Ed.), *Anticipation: Learning from the past – the Russian/Soviet contributions to the science of anticipation* (pp. 113–136). Cham: Springer.

Star, S. L. (2010). This is not a boundary object: Reflections on the origin of a concept. *Science, Technology & Human Values, 35*(5), 601–617. https://doi.org/10.1177/0162243910377624.

Stigler, S. M. (1999). *Statistics on the table: The history of statistical concepts and methods.* Cambridge, MA: Harvard University Press.

Tuomi, I. (1999). *Corporate knowledge: Theory and practice of intelligent organizations.* Helsinki: Metaxis.

Tuomi, I. (2002). *Networks of innovation: Change and meaning in the age of the internet.* Oxford: Oxford University Press.

Tuomi, I. (2012). Foresight in an unpredictable world. *Technology Analysis & Strategic Management, 24*(8), 735–751. https://doi.org/10.1080/09537325.2012.715476.

van der Veer, R., & Valsiner, J. (1994). *Understanding Vygotsky: A quest for synthesis.* Cambridge, MA: Blackwell Publishers.

Vygotsky, L. (1978). *Mind in society: The development of higher psychological processes.* Cambridge, MA: Harvard University Press.

Vygotsky, L. (1986). *Thought and language.* Cambridge, MA: The MIT Press.

Vygotsky, L., & Luria, A. (1994). Tool and symbol in child development. In R. van der Veer & J. Valsiner (Eds.), *The Vygotsky reader* (pp. 99–174). Oxford: Blackwell Publishers.

Wertsch, J. V., & Tulviste, P. (1996). L.S. Vygotsky and contemporary development of psychology. In H. Daniels (Ed.), *An introduction to Vygotsky* (pp. 53–74). London: Routledge.

Whitehead, A. N. (1978). *Process and reality: An essay in cosmology.* (Corrected Edition). New York: Free Press.

Zueva, E. Y., & Zuev, K. B. (2015). The concept of dominance by A.A. Ukhtomsky and anticipation. In M. Nadin (Ed.), *Anticipation: Learning from the past – the Russian/Soviet contributions to the science of anticipation* (pp. 13–35). Cham: Springer.

Futures Literacy: The Capacity to Diversify Conscious Human Anticipation

4

Riel Miller and Richard Sandford

Contents

Abstract

This chapter offers an introduction to a capability called Futures Literacy (FL), a framework for making sense of the anticipatory assumptions that distinguish different kinds of FL, and one specific research tool called Futures Literacy Laboratories (FLL) that has been designed to explore anticipatory assumptions. The chapter points to the following conclusions. First, FL is a practical skill that develops as people gain a better understanding of anticipatory assumptions. Second, our understanding of anticipatory assumptions requires a robust theory of anticipatory systems and processes. Third, FL has potentially important implications for the conceptualization and deployment of human agency, particularly with respect to our relationship to complexity.

R. Miller (✉)
Social and Human Sciences Sector, UNESCO, Paris, France
e-mail: r.miller@unesco.org

R. Sandford
University College London, London, UK

© Springer Nature Switzerland AG 2019
R. Poli (ed.), *Handbook of Anticipation*,
https://doi.org/10.1007/978-3-319-91554-8_77

Keywords
Futures literacy · Futures studies · Complexity · Foresight · Human agency ·
Collective intelligence · Futures literacy laboratories · Leadership ·
Management · Decision-making · Policy · Sustainability · Resilience ·
Transformation

Futures Literacy as Anticipation

Futures Literacy (FL) (Note: The capitalization of the term Futures Literacy and
Futures Literate is for the purposes of signalling the distinctive nature of this skill
in the context of its initial emergence. Such demarcation may eventually disappear
once the unfamiliar becomes familiar.) is a human capability, similar to the
currently much more familiar form of "literacy," the ability to read and write. FL
is a skill, and like all skills, it must be learned. Someone who is Futures Literate has
learned how to consciously and deliberately "use-the-future" for different reasons
and in different ways depending on the context. Conceptualizing the ability to
"use-the-future" (i.e., FL) in this instrumental fashion makes clear the roots of FL
in the "anticipatory systems and processes" perspective as per the Robert Rosen
formulation cited by Roberto Poli at the outset of this handbook: "An anticipatory
system is a system containing a predictive model of itself and/or its environment,
which allows it to change state at an instant in accord with the model's predictions
pertaining to a later instant" (Rosen 1985, p. 339). Along with many of the authors
in this volume, we believe that this hypothesis is a critical step towards integrating
both time into our understanding of life and creativity (as nondeterministic novelty) into our understanding of complexity (Bergson Kaufmann, DeLanda, Poli,
and Akomolafe).

Taking the Rosen perspective on anticipatory systems and processes as a
starting point also draws attention to the difference between conscious and
nonconscious "use-of-the-future." Although for some it may seem self-evident,
it is important to underscore that there is a fundamental difference between, on
the one hand, the nonconscious anticipatory systems and processes that characterize an amoeba or a tree and, on the other hand, learned human anticipation as
conscious and deliberate Futures Literacy (FL). This reinforces the point that FL
is a skill that must be acquired in order to be manifested. Skills are learned, in part
by doing, even if the processes and outcomes that characterize a skill can be
described or observed in a passive way (DeLanda 2006, p. 80). As a result,
deploying a skill involves, of necessity, explicit situational and performative
decisions. In the case of FL, these decisions are about why to "use-the-future"
and how to imagine it. Consequently, a Futures Literate person satisfies Rosen's
definition of an anticipatory system because they activate their knowledge of why
and how to "use-the-future" – a form of model – to "change state in accord with
the model." Call it anticipation of anticipation.

Such conscious human anticipation, as distinct from reflex and unconscious
expressions, covers a broad range of reasons and methods, from the predictive and

locked-in kind that Rosen mentions to the nonpredictive – Anticipation for Emergence (AfE) – that make up a critical part of the Futures Literacy Framework presented in this chapter (Fig. 1). When it comes to FL, the "change of state" that constitutes the action arising from the functioning of an anticipatory system is the action of thought or perception that occurs prior to taking any external action understood in the conventional way as a physical or virtual commitment. Thus, exercising one's FL is a form of anticipatory action, the choice of why and how to "use-the-future," that occurs before actually imagining any specific futures or making bets, on imagined futures, that are external to the mind. As a result, conscious human anticipatory systems and processes can include "uses-of-the-future" that go beyond the constraints imposed when the futures we imagine are confined to the probable and desirable. In the Futures Literacy Framework (Miller 2018), as depicted in Fig. 1, conscious human anticipation encompasses both the conventional and familiar Anticipation for the Future (AfF) and rarely considered Anticipation for Emergence (AfE). Futures imagined in the latter category are not constructed with the goal of inventing ex-ante probable or normative outcomes. Stated more exactly, futures imagined when the aim is AfE adopt narrative and analytical assumptions that are as open as appropriate and feasible to invention and novelty, improvisation and ephemerality. As Roberto Poli explains:

> …if we expand our consideration of change to fully incorporate novelty – discontinuity that is unknowable in advance – there is the challenge of being in two (or more) frames at once. How to develop the capacity to see and act in ways that take incompatible systems into account? These are situations where taking the point-of-view of one system not only renders

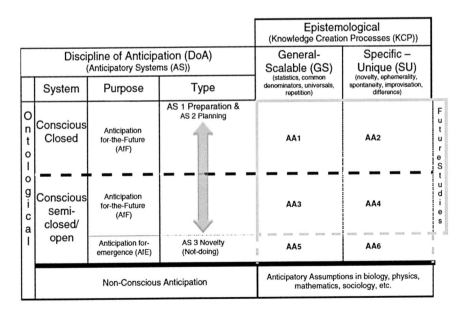

Fig. 1 The Futures Literacy Framework (Miller, 2018)

the other invisible but often expresses an existential conflict with the new system. The problem that surfaces here is dramatically urgent: while we well know how to build a bureaucratic structure meant to act within the existing framework of agency – i.e. we know how to use the future for optimization and contingency – we are still in the deepest fog about how to build anticipatory structures able to deal organically with complex problems and systems. (Poli 2017, p. 185).

Figure 2 offers one way of depicting an expansion of human agency beyond preparation and planning; to instrumentalize the future differently, to identify conscious "uses-of-the-future" that do not exclusively originate from the goal of realizing a particular future. Figure 2 attempts to provide a categorical map for locating "where" human agency can potentially play a role, without at all claiming that the outcomes from the exercise of such agency can be known in advance. As odd and yet as obvious as it may seem, it is crucial to repeat that the exercise of Futures Literacy through the choice and intervention of any particular set of anticipatory systems and processes, like the selection of a filter for looking at the world, cannot be done on the basis of prior knowledge of what will happen. We cannot see what we will see before

Locating Human Agency in the Context of Repetition and Difference in Complexity						
		Repetition in system conditions		Difference in system conditions		
Agency		Specificity	Generality	Incremental internal	Novel internal	Non-contiguous external
Non-conscious	Inertia	Improvisation, spontaneity, invention, serendipity				
	Reflex adaptation					
	Chance					
	Ignorance					
Conscious	Preservation through continuity	Success in achieving stasis without change		Endogenous change – within system reform to maintain system conditions		Co-existence
	Preservation through discontinuity	Success in achieving stasis with change				Disruptive coexistence
	Exploiting novelty					Transformation

Fig. 2 Locating human agency in the context of repetition and difference in complexity

we see it and so the selection of the filter is in this sense arbitrary. Perhaps, it is the case that in order to be good at detecting change and recognizing patterns, humans rather automatically rotate filters – like when the optometrist checks a patient's vision. Maybe the evolutionary steps that stack-up behind our relatively young and immature species have provided us with anticipation patterns of anticipation that are effective at an evolutionary level. Just like trees that lose leaves as winter arrives. Yet, as powerful as the evolutionary processes may be, the point of Futures Literacy is to see if we can consciously, through the development of scientific hypotheses and testing, both understand the world a bit more – particularly novelty – and enhance our capacity to be free (Sen 2011). Figure 2 is one foray towards mapping this ambition.

Figure 2 helps to map different ways human agency might "use-the-future" with respect to repetition and difference, but it does not and cannot claim that "success" or causal impact can be established *ex ante* (even in cases where the likelihood of predictive success – such as the sun rising tomorrow – appears extremely high). Accepting such unescapable uncertainty often generates considerable discomfort or rejection from within the currently dominant conventional mind-set, and seems to attack the motivational underpinnings and basic functioning of human agency (Ogilvy 2011) that depends on establishing, at least with some degree of probability, that "best laid plans" will in fact "make-a-difference." But what research into Futures Literacy shows is that this association between probability and outcomes can be intermediated differently. By running experiments, Futures Literacy Laboratories (see section "Futures Literacy as Anticipation"), that expose the anticipatory assumptions upon which Futures Literacy functions, it may be possible to find ways of accepting the radical equality of uncertainty as a way to more fully embrace complexity.

The evidence generated by these labs does not deny or ignore the critical relationship between assumptions that allow for the calculation of probability and the choices that humans make on that basis. Quite the contrary, since the action-learning processes deployed in labs to develop participants' Futures Literacy are designed to render conventional Anticipation for Future (AfF) reasons and methods for "using-the-future" more explicit. Then, building on a better awareness of AfF anticipatory assumptions, it becomes easier to develop and explore other reasons and methods for "using–the-future," including those related to Anticipation for Emergence (AfE). In this way, the acquisition of Futures Literacy makes "walking-on-two-legs" or alternating between AfF and AfE a question of choice. And, by rendering this choice explicit, Futures Literacy opens up the potential to imagine and construct human agency, at least in part, outside a causal deterministic framing. In other words, outside the logical constraints imposed by anticipation that uses the past to determine probable and preferable targets for human agency. These are indeed two different "legs." When "using-the-future" to sense and make-sense of aspects of the present that are invisible or nonsensical on the basis of probable or preferable futures, it is necessary to seek inspiration from outside the logic of probability and preference. A task that appears, in most cases, to be of no interest from the point-of-view of Anticipation for the Future (AfF).

Discovering the value and logic of Anticipation for Emergence is rendered even stranger, from the perspective of AfF by the fact that when we act to choose different anticipatory systems and processes there is no way to know if we are making the right choice. In other words, we can only experiment. The observation that much of the time the experiments work out as expected does not deny our fundamental ignorance at the moment we select a particular set of anticipatory assumptions and processes. From the stance of AfF, it is disturbing that the only aspect of this process that is amenable to being less blind is the choice of anticipatory systems and processes. In other words, we can be a bit more Futures Literate. Still, this begs the question, so what? If the future is complex and fundamentally uncertain, what good does it do to be aware that we can acquire the capacity to choose different filters or not? The answer offered here may not be particularly satisfying from the point of view of the old determinist, colonize-the-future perspective, but it provides a reasonable rationale for becoming Futures Literate. In a nutshell, people who are Futures Illiterate run a double risk. One possibility is that they get stuck using one or a limited set of filters without even being aware. Two is that they are unable to consciously and deliberatively "use-the-future" to search analytically, systematically, and more intentionally serendipitously for meaning in the emergent present. This makes them less able to: ask new questions, sense and make-sense of novelty, appreciate ephemerality because its connection to already imagined futures is not evident, and in general, improvise on the basis of constantly emerging unknowables – the wellspring of uncertainty that makes up the difference and repetition of the emergent present.

Of course, being Futures Literate or Illiterate does not change the indeterminate nature of complex emergence. Consequently, there is no way to be certain if in the end being skilled or unskilled in anticipatory systems and processes will play a role in better or worse outcomes. Humanity's resilience, for instance, will always be an open question – since uncertainty is the only certainty. But, we do have proof-of-concept level evidence (Miller 2018) that being Futures Literate does "make-a-difference" for why and how people "use-the-future" and that the acquisition of this skill has an impact when it comes to detecting and inventing novelty as ontological expansion (Tuomi 2017). Obviously, this novelty can only exist once it has emerged, or at least the conditions for the "creative" moment (Boden 2003) are in place. There is still no way to really know if we will "make-a-difference," but as we shift onto the leg that uses the assumptions that seek probable futures, one of those probabilities can be greater openness to novelty. By getting better at "using-the-future" by switching between AfF and AfE, it seems we can also enhance our capacity to sense and make-sense of novelty. Once again, it is worth stressing that getting better at a means for perceiving the world does not guarantee better outcomes.

Whatever the rationale, the only way to gain a better understanding of the nature and role of conscious human anticipation is to conduct further research (Poli 2017). The contribution to such an endeavor made by this chapter and the on-going work around Futures Literacy (Miller 2018) is to focus on discerning the attributes of the capacity to "use-the-future" for different reasons and in different ways in different contexts. The rest of this chapter provides an initial look at research along these lines.

It offers a brief overview of the Futures Literacy Framework (FLF), used to define and work with anticipatory assumptions, and describes some preliminary evidence that suggests Futures Literacy Laboratories are one productive methodological format for conducting research into anticipatory assumptions. The chapter concludes by examining the relevance for policy formation of getting better at determining the assumptions that define "strategic boxes."

The Futures Literacy Framework (FLF)

The Futures Literacy Framework (FLF) presented in Fig. 1 below has the ambition of providing "handles" or descriptors for characterizing the attributes and utility for a broad range of anticipatory systems and processes (This section leans heavily on Miller (2018, Chap. 1).). The goal of the FLF is not only descriptive but also to assist with the explicit choices of conscious human anticipation. To continue the analogy to filters, the FLF assists with the effort to match filters to contexts, tools to tasks. The FLF is one way of discerning different reasons for deploying our imaginations – "using-the-future" – and applying relevant methods for describing these imaginary worlds. The FLF as can be seen in Fig. 1 classifies anticipatory systems and process along two axes – the ontological and epistemological, with a bias to diving deeper into conscious human "uses-of-the-future." The ontological categories are on the left-hand side and the epistemological ones are on the upper right. Drawing the intersection between these two sets of characteristics situates FL in six distinct clusters of anticipatory assumptions (AA1 to AA6).

This framework for describing why and how people "use-the-future" is useful because it contributes to:

- Developing FL by helping to construct the learning processes that enable people to "use-the-future" in different ways depending on aims, means, and context
- Exploring FL by helping to identify existing and new topics for research
- Determining the best methods to conduct research into FL by helping to select the appropriate design criteria
- FL as a practice by helping to determine which tools for thinking about the future are most appropriate for the kind of future being thought about in a given context

Anticipatory Assumptions

The FLF describes anticipatory systems and processes on the basis of a common unit of analysis: anticipatory assumptions (AA). The relevance of the term "assumption" is relatively obvious in the context of the future since by definition the future does not yet exist. The future is imaginary, generated out of a set of assumptions, whether such premises define the (For a more in-depth discussion of so-called "block time," in which the past, present, and future all coexist, see the chapter by Tibbs in this handbook. For the purposes of this chapter, however, it is assumed that at a practical level, even if the future may exist simultaneously with the present, it is not accessible for the purposes of consciously deliberative human anticipatory activities.) "possibility space" of a predicted future that is locked into nonconscious anticipatory systems and processes, at least for the present iteration, or conscious flights of fancy, the gamut of fictional inventions that humans exercise constantly. Putting AA at the analytical center of efforts to understand anticipatory systems and processes also makes it easier to take into account the point raised above about the distinction between conscious and nonconscious anticipation. When anticipation occurs without explicit conscious imagining, such as with trees or single-cell creatures or through the functioning of capitalist competition, the AA at a systemic level are of an inherently nonvolitional-, nonagency-based character. This is why the bottom of Fig. 1 designates nonconscious anticipation as the kind of imaginary futures that are relevant to fields like biology, physics, mathematics, sociology, economics, etc. In these fields, the later-than-now, at an ontological "what-is-it?" level is defined and incorporated into anticipatory systems, at least up until very recently, by exclusively nonconscious evolutionary processes.

AA are also the descriptive and analytical building blocks of research into FL because conscious human anticipation can only occur on the basis of AA of one kind or another. AA are what enable people to describe and invent imaginary futures. The frames and models that are used to invent the content of the fictions that are conscious human anticipation can be described using AA. This means that FL can be described as the capacity to identify, design, target, and deploy AA. One of the virtues of designating AA as the theoretical and practical core of human anticipatory capabilities (FL) is that AA can be described and situated on the basis of the intersection of different Anticipatory Systems and Knowledge Creation Processes, as per the FLF depicted in Fig. 1. Conscious anticipation is fundamentally about producing fiction. As a result, the KCP that are relevant are restricted to those frames (Kahneman 2012; Lakoff 2006; Bakhtin 1981; Goffman 1974) that enable meaningful descriptions of imaginary futures.

Initial Evidence from Futures Literacy Laboratories

This section briefly summarizes some of the evidence generated by some of the FLL (This initial research was conducted at the beginning of UNESCO's efforts to explore Futures Literacy, starting in 2012 and running through 2014, as discussed in Miller (2014)) run at the outset of UNESCO's efforts to explore anticipatory systems and processes. The results examined in this section focus primarily on two issues: one the extent to which people's anticipatory assumptions were revealed by being participants in FLL and what were the signs, if any that participants were becoming FL.

Overview of the FLL Format and Data Collected

The core features of the FLL process, as presented to participants, reflected a set of common design principles that underpin each distinct FLL. These design principles were informed by previous work undertaken in a number of different settings. In particular, initial evidence of the nature and role of "futures literacy" emerged from work at the OECD's International Futures Programme that provided an opportunity to experiment and observe both collective intelligence knowledge creation and using the future together (Miller 2007). Efforts to elaborate and test the role and nature of anticipatory systems continued through experiments conducted by the Irish and Romanian governments as well as the European Commission (Miller et al. 2010; Miller and Storper 2008; Miller 2010). This work also connected researchers from a range of disciplines and designer/facilitators who started building communities of practice around different aspects of anticipatory systems and processes. Many of the researchers were part of an informal network called FuMee that emerged from a larger undertaking funded by the European Commission's COST program (http://www.cost.eu/COST_Actions/isch/A22). Many of the practitioners were part of the Association of Professional Futurists or the Futures Oriented Technology Assessment network sponsored by the European Commission's Joint Research Centres. All of these different strands of action-research were drawn together with the launch of the Scoping Global/Local Anticipatory Capacities project undertaken by UNESCO and sponsored by The Rockefeller Foundation, CGEE Brazil, and Innovation Norway (Miller 2014). The core purpose of this project was to engage with participants' anticipatory systems and processes in order to generate new information and specific questions regarding the nature of the way people use the future, through exploring specific topical issues in context.

These aims were given practical expression by undertaking FLL. The intention was that the FLL would materially contribute to efforts to address specific local concerns, tackling a complex, dilemma-filled situation not considered effectively tractable through traditional planning approaches. Each Lab was designed in collaboration with a local sponsor with a remit to address such a topic, convening local stakeholders (NGOs, policy makers, academics, activists, citizens) in a process running, in most cases, over 1 or 2 days. The Lab took as a starting point the existing assumptions and practices regarding the future that participants brought with them to the event, situating them within a domain of inquiry set by local priorities and concerns. Through making these existing future-facing ideas visible to participants, setting them in a novel and unfamiliar frame to examine and assess them anew, and using this reframing process to generate new questions regarding the topic under consideration, the process aimed to produce new perspectives on this domain, and to demonstrate the value of engaging with uncertainty and using the future differently. All FLLs were custom designed to take into account the specificity of each context. Reflecting the aspiration that the process embody the principles of enquiry through action learning, there was an overarching general architecture to the cognitive process – a learning-curve structure that guided the sequencing of the heuristics or a generic agenda. The following is a typical example of the design of an FLL event as a collective intelligence knowledge creation process that "uses-the-future."

Phase One: Revealing Existing Anticipatory Assumptions

In groups, participants discuss their understanding of the subject and their current beliefs and ideas about its future development. The conversation is conducted in two parts that distinguish hopes or preferred futures from likely or predicted futures. Afterwards, these breakout groups report back to a plenary session, sharing their imaginings of likely and hoped for futures: the facilitators help lead a discussion that identifies and elaborates the anticipatory assumptions as articulated by the participants – the largely tacit models used to imagine the future become more explicit.

The entire process relies on the same source, the "collective intelligence" of the group, or shared meaning-making through a conversational process that obliges participants to examine and articulate what they imagine about the future of the chosen topic. Such conversations can be more or less structured, longer or shorter, mined for meaning or just skimmed, but in most cases comprise the easy (or at least less-steep) part of the learning curve. This is when people make their assumptions explicit and try to find common meanings without necessarily seeking agreement or consensus.

Phase Two: Reframing, Inventing New Anticipatory Assumptions

In this phase, participants take a further step in developing their understanding of the nature and role of the anticipatory assumptions they use to frame their imaginations and how the imaginary future can influence their perceptions, priorities, and actions. In this way, the collective intelligence process continues to develop their FL. Again, in practice, there are as many ways to undertake a reframing exercise as there are contexts. The central aim, however, is to enable participants to gain a better understanding of the nature and role of anticipatory assumptions by projecting themselves into a scenario or narrative that is radically discontinuous from the most familiar or dominant imaginaries or narratives. Then, on the basis of these "odd" or difficult to assimilate anticipatory assumptions, the participants try to describe the systems, structure and modes of agency, forms and mechanisms of knowledge creation, and use, processes of communication, elements of social structures for trust and so on. The challenge of the reframing exercise is to enable participants to immerse themselves fully in this "alternative" scenario through a process of "rigorous imagining": the aim is not to explore the ways in which such a scenario might come to pass, nor to assess the extent to which such a scenario might be likely or desirable, but to accept it and "think oneself into it" as completely as one is able.

One heuristic, deployed in a number of events, uses a detailed framework constructed to be radically different from current models of societal functioning, called the "learning intensive society" (LIS) (Miller 2006). Participants are provided with a series of analytical tools that enable them to describe a society in which the processes and structures of production and consumption have been fundamentally transformed. On this basis, enabled by technological and capability changes, learning becomes the predominant value creating activity: society operates as a dynamic and continually shifting set of interacting networks in which identities are more fluid, people participate in a culture of creative experimentation and rapid failure, and learning is something that happens continuously through this process. The LIS scenario is intended to challenge fundamental ideas about responsibility, agency, causality and the nature of the self, giving participants the opportunity to reexamine their anticipatory assumptions, and thereby gain a better understanding of how the models they use and the ensuing ideas about the future alter their perception of the present, in addition to providing indications of the methods and communities they work with when using the future.

Phase Three: New Questions, a Capacity to Think About Changes in the Conditions of Change

In the third phase of the process, participants are invited to revisit the anticipatory assumptions they articulated during the first phase and reconsider their models for describing the imaginary future in the light of a heightened awareness produced during the second phase of the process. The reframing phase offered participants a new vocabulary or palette with which to imagine and describe the future, making it possible to ask new questions that might, in the context of the old frame, have seemed unimportant or inconsistent or unimaginable. This session gives participants a direct experience of the way our sense of the current moment is shaped in part by the models and expectations we use to think about what happens next. Once again, the purpose is to provide participants with an opportunity to articulate their anticipatory assumptions and become more aware of how the future enters into the perceptions and activities of their specific community of practice.

Data Collected

The intention throughout the Networking to Improve Global/Local Anticipatory Capacities project (Miller 2014) was to use FLL to generate data that would inform the sponsors' understandings of the way different groups make use of the future, and of the effectiveness of the process in developing FL. A set of general research tools intended to support this process were drafted by members of the project design committee (Miller 2014). For a variety of reasons, including significant differences across places and cultures in the ways time and the future are represented and approached, a crucial design parameter for the design of FLL is co-created contextualization. Collective intelligence knowledge creation processes that "use-the-future" cannot work if the design does not take into account differences and variations in the organization and expectations of each context. Such customization, while indicative of the degree to which each event was a local product rather than implemented top-down, limits the ability to assess the relationship between formally identical processes and specific outcomes. With this in mind, a number of surveys were carried out in order to generate qualitative data that could be analyzed for indications that the sought-for impact was achieved. In addition, several summary reports were created by the organizers and facilitators of various events.

There are consequently a number of caveats regarding the data presented here, given the contingencies surrounding its production. The survey responses from each event (what might be considered "primary" sources, consisting of participants' reports) are in general from a subset of those participating, in response to surveys written in English that offer a number of leading questions and assume particular understandings of key concepts. The reports from organizers (which might be considered "secondary" sources) are necessarily partial and mediated accounts from a particular perspective. There is little empirical data available (some of the sessions were recorded, but resources for in-depth analysis were not available). The data shared should be understood as arising from different cultural and societal contexts, and not representative of the entire population of those attending these events (indeed, given the low response rates it should be understood as representing a minority). Consequently, the claims made from the analysis will be limited.

The data examined here is drawn from the following material:

Item	Event	Responses
Post-event survey	Youth to Adult Transition, Paris	13
Pre-event survey	Future of Cities, Paris	13
Post-event survey	Future of Cities, Paris	14
Post-event survey	Future of Universities, Sao Paolo	24
Event report	Future of Universities, Sao Paolo	–
Event report	Future of Local Labour Markets, Bogota (see case studies)	–

Analysis

The analysis of the evidence generated by the participants in FLL is structured around two research questions, derived from the aims of the Networking to Improve Global/Local Anticipatory Capacities project:

1. Do participants reveal anticipatory assumptions they use to imagine the future?
2. Are there indicators that participants have developed an understanding of FL?

Textual analysis of the responses to the Paris post-event survey (the item with the richest material from respondents) was carried out using a thematic coding approach. The research focus was embedded in the structure of the forms employed by participants to generate their responses, making it possible to begin by applying descriptive codes to participants' responses, then clustering these emergent themes into key categories that spoke to the overarching research questions. Having produced a set of codes capable of organizing responses in relation to this analytic focus, they were used to analyze the remaining surveys from the Future Cities event and Sao Paolo, producing a revised iteration of the set of codes used to understand participants' representations of the process they went through during the event. This set of codes were used to structure an investigation of the reports from Sao Paolo and Bogota, looking for the presence of similar themes in the observations of the report authors.

Findings

In this section, we describe what can be seen of the nature of the anticipatory assumptions from participants' responses and assess the indications that they have developed FL. We briefly discuss the reflexive anticipatory assumptions made visible, the different framings of the future employed by participants, the different ways in which they suggest they use-the-future, the motivations that are offered for using-the-future, and their responses to the notion of FL.

Reflecting on Personal Anticipatory Assumptions

Any investigation into the assumptions towards the future held by participants using the data collected will be limited, since the surveys presented a predefined and limited set of stances towards the future for respondents to choose among. A change between the options selected by participants before and after the events would be a relevant indicator, assuming that they originally held a different perspective towards the future. This was visible in a few cases: for example, in the Future Cities event, one respondent offered these two responses to a question about how they think about uncertainty.

Pre: The future is uncertain. I look at the future sometimes with fear.
Post: Uncertainty – is not a threat, can be taken as a challenge.

A colleague at the same event noted that they were now able to:

take the time to question some of my own (and shared) assumptions that I use in my work in education/training policy about what young people will "need" to live, learn, be citizens, and work in the 21st century.

Others reported a new awareness of their thoughts towards the future.

When I think about the future, I think of many challenges of different sort: environmentally, politically, economically. At the same time I have a quite optimistic image of the future and for example when thinking about environment many new technologies come to my mind.

After the Paris event, some participants noted a change in the way they considered the future:

New awareness of complexity of defining what an adult is; of the tension between social and administrative definitions and personal and tacit understanding and needs. Became aware of my own habits of mind about the subject through my interactions with the group and seeing their presuppositions.
It made me question the definitions and social norms we adhere to when thinking about what characterizes that transition.
The workshop facilitated my out-of-the-box thinking about what those terms mean, whether they should mean anything at all, who defines those categories, and how they are shaped by and influence other systems.
Became aware of my own habits of mind about the subject through my interactions with the group and seeing their presuppositions the future as a construct is a very effective tool to make me aware of my own 'idées reçues' *(received ideas)* and also to loosen and stir up my creativity.

And this respondent from the Future Cities event got to the heart of the issue:

After the workshop I had a feeling of uncertainty: I understood that the dominant structures in life (the paradigm) are not fixed and taken for granted. I now understand that this can be a source for real new ideas and insights. I guess that these methods really enable you to think out of the box.

Frames from Personal and Professional Futures

Participants noted a variety of ways in which they were asked to make use of the future in their personal and professional lives:

> I use and think about the future all the time. For planning things, making decision, imagining projects
>
> I usually use the results of data mining, participate in building scenarios and morphological analysis in urban and territorial design and planning, given that data mining, scenario methods and morphological analysis have the same meaning for an architect/planner, as I am, and for a 'future expert'
>
> Managing risk
>
> I have to think about my future first and how to plan what I want to do and be

There are, even in these short quotes, a range of approaches to the future: "imagining" projects and thinking about "my future," creating visions of a desired future; planning and decision-making, projecting ideas of a desired future forwards from the present; "managing risk," envisaging different futures with varying degrees of probability and preparing accordingly. One respondent names a set of techniques associated with formal planning practices used across disciplines. It can be seen, here, how different communities of practice might develop a practical familiarity with particular techniques and approaches towards the future that resonate with the concerns of the group. Indeed, two such communities are named – architects and urban planners, and "future experts" – and their overlapping interest in specific tools noted. These tools might be considered "boundary objects" (Star and Griesemer 1989), facilitating the exchange of knowledge and ideas across different contexts.

Different Ways of Using the Future

Some participants' responses suggested different approaches towards their "use-of-the-future":

> I try to pay particular attention to the present and try not to lock myself into projections and imaginings about the future
>
> The workshop has confirmed what I thought deep inside, that the future is not linear and that anticipating the evolution of things can help in designing my future

The issue here is not especially disciplinary – the concern is not immediately with asking whether engineers share a sense of the future with chemists or historians, for example, but rather with how different modes of knowing the future interact within subjects. These participants identify a number of different modes of knowing the future that coexist: internal intuition ("what I thought deep inside"), constraining "projections and imaginings," the contemporary technosocial problematique that frames our thinking about future conditions ("many challenges of different sort"), and personal visions that might be as much affective and dispositional as grounded in content ("a quite optimistic image of the future"). Again, these different ways of imagining the future are not presented here as inconsistent or in conflict with one another: as set out earlier, the FLF recognizes that individuals have multiple ways of considering the future, whether formally as described above or on a more personal level.

Motivations for Using-the-Future

For many participants, engaging in anticipatory thinking was naturally linked to their wider concerns about social justice and the survival of future generations:

> The main questions I have are concerned with global equity and if we will manage to share what we have so that people in the developing world can also have an adequate level of well-being.
>   I wish humans will survive forever on the planet. That's why I give a great importance to future literacy (decision making capacity) and the endeavour to change the conditions of change.
>   Do we need existing institutions (governments, rules, traditions, etc.) or can we create new systems which could lead to more creative, happier, healthier, equal societies?

Here two characterizations of agency can be seen: action intended to create change and action intended to create the conditions for the desired change. Both are part of AfF, in different clusters – the former in AA1 and the latter in AA3.

Developing Futures Literacy

The notion of "futures literacy" appealed to many participants. One, at the Future Cities event described it as how:

> to learn how to use the future in a better way. (For myself, for the society I am living in.)

While another at the Youth to Adult Transitions FLL in Paris was pleased to have learned about the existence of formal future studies.

> It is great to know that there is a field that welcomes and encourages uncertainty, spontaneity, and a break from existing patterns in regards to futures-thinking

Some participants used language that recalled notions of complexity and emergence, concepts at the heart of futures literacy. One participant described their new understanding of

> how [systems] are shaped by and influence other systems.

While others showed an awareness of the nature of connected factors:

> I am more aware of the importance of networks (people, videos, internet, FaceBook, etc.) in the exchange of knowledge and skills impacted by many different evolving factors

New questions regarding the subjects of the workshops were generated:

What can we do with education in order to adapt to the transition to an evolving world?
    How will universities and firms adapt to this new system of learning skills and studying?
Who decides? What is responsibility? What are the parameters of childhood?
    How and by whom to judge the completion of transition process? What happens if the "young" is unable to complete the transition for "adult"? Is he/she regarded as failure of adulthood due to the transition?

There was reference made by participants to the value of embedding futures literacy within institutions (particularly universities – perhaps unsurprising given the number of attendees affiliated with academic institutions):

> The main contribution can be teaching them "Future Literacy" which is an original idea and not used a lot in the curricula of universities.
>
>   All these can be done by arranging some courses (short term, longer term, summer schools etc) covering these issues. I am working in a university that my organization is partly doing this directly or indirectly through different activities.
>
>   My job is to help my institution 'develop' and so a big part of my function is encouraging (goading!) people into looking ahead and attempting to set objectives in the future

The immediate conclusion suggested, then, is that, notwithstanding the many limitations with respect to the collection of data, there is preliminary evidence that the FLL events did make the attributes and role of anticipatory assumptions clearer, and that they have the potential to develop the kind of FL described in the first section of this chapter.

Conclusion

In this chapter, we have offered an introduction to the idea of FL as a capability and FLL as a tool for revealing two aspects of FL: the shift from tacit to explicit anticipatory assumptions by participants and indications from participants that they have developed an understanding of FL. In exploring these key aspects of FL, we analyzed some limited preliminary data generated through surveys completed by FLL participants, identifying responses that indicated a new awareness of their anticipatory assumptions, and changes in the way they represented the future. While the available data is still rudimentary, it does provide affirmative answers to the research questions. Participants in FLL did reveal assumptions regarding the future that were previously tacit and provided a venue for them to engage with notions of complexity, uncertainty, and possibility that enlarged their perceptions of the present. This offers a proof-of-concept level illustration of the potential of FLL processes to build FL and develop peoples' capacity to make "use-of-the-future" in their decision-making processes. This is a preliminary conclusion, and it is clear that much additional research into the ideas introduced here is needed in order to generate evidence of the different attributes of FL as a capability and FLL as an effective and efficient tool for researching, learning, and applying FL.

Even at this early stage in the research, it is worth drawing attention to the implications of FL for understanding the relationship of human agency to both perception (search) and decision-making (choice). Figure 3 offers one way of explaining how being better able to "use-the-future" can be useful. Succinctly, FL is one way to sense and understand change because the identification of anticipatory assumptions and the related imaginary futures generates clearer differentiation of endogenous changes that pertain to systemic continuity from exogenous changes that may be "weak signals" of systemic discontinuity. In more prosaic terms, we can think of this as a way of both generating items on a menu as well as categorizing them according to different courses. As everyone knows, putting an item on a menu and assigning it to the category of appetizer, main course or dessert, does not determine what someone will choose from the menu, nor in what order. And of course, many people skip dessert altogether. Furthermore, as every restaurant goer knows, what we imagine when we order may or may not correspond to what is delivered.

FL does not overcome the unknowability of outcomes, the fundamental inability to know if there will even be consequences of a particular choice (will what we ordered actually arrive), and if there are consequences will there be any congruence with what was intended or expected (did it taste as hoped). What FL does offer is greater clarity and capability to "use-the-future" in ways that take into account the differences of perception and choice that arise when planning, preparing or exploring novelty. FL as a capability enables people to understand

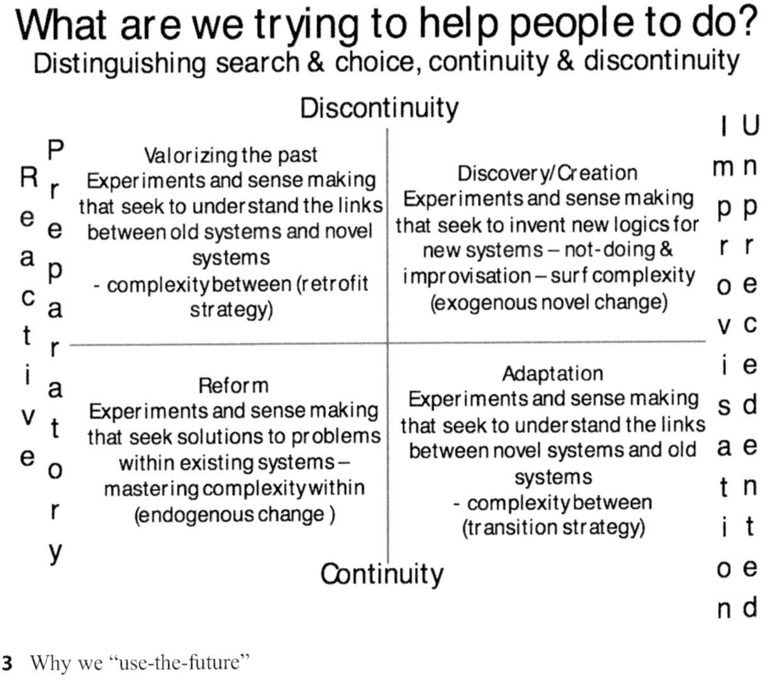

What are we trying to help people to do?
Distinguishing search & choice, continuity & discontinuity

Fig. 3 Why we "use-the-future"

that the choice of reasons and methods for thinking about the future alter what we see and do. Being futures literate changes the meaning of trying to "make a difference," be it through policies or laws or norms as collective actions, or through the personal experiential and performative dimensions of meaning making and interconnectedness.

FL makes the role of the imaginary future explicit and thereby allows us to choose among different anticipatory systems and processes depending on what we are trying to do. As Fig. 3 attempts to illustrate, it could be a desire to reform or adapt or valorize the past or sense and make-sense of novelty. Each of which has value, none is inherently better than the other. Only the complex evolving world of which we are a part invites us to understand all four spheres of human agency and FL assists with that rich challenge.

In closing, it is important to underscore that the work presented here on the nature and potential of FL is not proposed as a way to exclude particular approaches to "using-the-future." As Poli (2013) points out, there are many varieties of futures work, and some have more in common with practices such as medicine or architecture which do not necessarily require a theoretical base in order to make important contributions to society. What can be claimed here is that engaging with a theoretical perspective on anticipation and the future in order to design and interpret the outcomes of FLL shows some additional benefit. Using anticipatory systems theory offers a deeper understanding of the thought processes set in motion by FLL and provides frameworks for distinguishing different ways of knowing the future and ontological tools for resolving what seem to be inconsistent or contradictory representations of the future (in particular, the notions of categories of the future, levels of reality, and the "thick present"). Engaging with theory also helps articulate more compelling arguments for developing the capacity to make use of the future: it offers an account of why some forms of knowing the future fail to support decision-making, by illustrating the contexts in which linear or probabilistic thinking is not appropriate, making a case for developing other ways of knowing the future, and it reveals something of the nature of our moral obligation towards the future, making the limits of our agency better known to us and illustrating the need to give proper consideration to why and how we use the future, rather than leaving it unexamined.

References

Bakhtin, M. (1981). Forms of time and of the Chronotope in the novel: Notes toward a historical poetics. In M. Holquist (Ed.), *The dialogic imagination: Four essays by M.M. Bakhtin* (pp. 84–258). University of Texas Press: Austin.

Boden, M. (2003). The creative mind: Myths and mechanisms (2 ed.). Routledge: UK. ISBN 978-0415314527.

DeLanda, M. (2006). *A new philosophy of society: Assemblage theory and social complexity* (1st ed.). London/New York: Continuum.

DeLanda, M. (2016). Assemblage Theory, Edinburgh University Press, ISBN-13: 978-1474413633

Goffman, E. (1974). *Frame analysis: An essay on the organization of experience* (1st ed.). Boston: Northeastern University Press.

Kahneman, D. (2012). *Thinking, fast and slow*. London: Penguin Press. Retrieved from www. greenpenguin.co.uk.

Lakoff, G. (2006). Simple framing: An introduction to framing and its uses in politics. Retrieved 1 Aug 2017 from http://archives.evergreen.edu/webpages/curricular/2006-2007/languageof politics/files/languageofpolitics/Simple_Framing_Rockridge_Institute.pdf

Miller, R. (2006). Equity in the 21st century learning intensive society: Is schooling part of the solution. *Foresight, 8*(4), 13–22, Emerald. https://doi.org/10.1108/1463668061068200.

Miller, R. (2007). Futures literacy: A hybrid strategic scenario method. *Futures, 39*(4), 341–362. https://doi.org/10.1016/j.futures.2006.12.001.

Miller, R. (2010). Which anticipatory system for university foresight? A postscript. In A. Curaj (Ed.) *The For-Uni blueprint*. Editura Academiei Române: France. ISBN 978-973-27-1965-7.

Miller, R., Poli, R., Rossel, P. (2013). "The discipline of anticipation: Exploring key issues". Working paper 1, Networking to improve global/local anticipatory capacities, a scoping exercise: narrative report; 2014 - 230316e.pdf, UNESCO

Miller, R. (2014). Networking to improve global/local anticipatory capacities – a scoping exercise. UNESCO. Retrieved 09/10/2018 from http://unesdoc.unesco.org/images/0023/002303/230316e.pdf

Miller, R. (Ed.). (2018). *Transforming the future (open access)*. London: Routledge.

Miller, R. & Storper, M. (2008). Near and Far: Imagining the Future of Telepresence, Commissioned Research, Cisco Systems, available: https://www.researchgate.net/publication/48911257_Near_and_far_imagining_the_future_of_TelePresence

Miller, R., O'Connell, L., O'Donnell, R. (2010). Futures Ireland: A case study in building futures literacy. In M. Aaltonen (Ed.), *Robustness: Anticipatory and Adaptive Human Systems*. American Emergent Publications. Retrieved from https://www.researchgate.net/publication/285131731_Futures_Ireland_A_Case_Study_in_Building_Futures_Literacy

Miller, R., Poli, R., Rossel, P. (2013). *The discipline of anticipation: Exploring key issues.* Working paper 1, Local/global capabilities scoping project. Paris: UNESCO/Rockefeller.

Miller, R., Shapiro, H., Hilding-Hamann, K-E. School's over: learning spaces in Europe in 2020: *An Imagining Exercise on the Future of Learning*, Report number: EUR Number: 23532 EN, ISBN: 978-92-79-10053-6.

Ogilvy, J. (2011). Facing the fold: From the eclipse of Utopia to the restoration of hope. *Foresight, 13*, 7. https://doi.org/10.1108/14636811111153931.

Poli, R. (2009). The complexity of anticipation. *Balkan Journal of Philosophy, 1*(1), 19–29.

Poli, R. (2010). The many aspects of anticipation. *Foresight, 12*(3), 7–17.

Poli, R. (2011). Steps toward an explicit ontology of the future. *Journal of Futures Studies, 16* (1), 67–78.

Poli, R. (2013). The theoretical basis of futures studies. *On the Horizon, 12*, 1.

Poli, R. (2014). Anticipation. *Using the Future for Understanding the Present*. Opening lecture to the conference "Anticipation: Complexity and The Future", Stellenbosch, 18 Mar 2014.

Poli, R. (2015). Relational science, complexity and anticipation. Introduction to Robert Rosen, *Selected Papers on Social Systems*. De Gruyter: Germany.

Poli, R. (2017). Introduction to anticipation studies. Springer: Germany. https://doi.org/10.1007/978-3-319-63023-6.

Rosen, R. (1985). *Anticipatory systems: Philosophical, mathematical, and methodological foundations*. Oxford: Permagon Press.

Sen, A. (2011). *Development as freedom*. Random: House.

Star, S., & Griesemer, J. (1989). Institutional ecology, 'translations' and boundary objects: Amateurs and professionals in Berkeley's Museum of Vertebrate Zoology, 1907-39. *Social Studies of Science, 19*(3), 387–420. https://doi.org/10.1177/030631289019003001.

Tuomi, I. (2017). "Ontological Expansion." In Handbook of Anticipation, edited by Roberto Poli, 1–35. Cham: Springer International Publishing. https://doi.org/10.1007/978-3-319-31737-3_4-1.

Anticipation and the Normative Stance

5

Ted Fuller

Contents

Abstract

The connection between anticipation and norms is that anticipation has causal power to change social norms and social norms have causal power in framing anticipation. In the stabilization or transformation of social norms, anticipation can be seen as a causal mechanism. I take further Rosen's characterizations of anticipatory systems as having "almost an ethical character" to suggest that in the domain of the social, ethics, as values inherent in inferential judgments, act on the disposition to anticipate. The agent's disposition to anticipate creates dynamic activity guided by the modeling relations between agent and environment. Modeling relations are intersubjectively formed. Judgments about desirable or undesirable effects of environmental change, relative to the agent (i.e., relative to values), lead to anticipatory action. Following a critical realist methodology (Bhaskar, Archer, Elder-Vass, Sawyer), the causal effects of such individual actions within a group tend to stabilize and amplify emergent change or extinguish short-lived (ephemeral) emergent properties. Modeling relations are emergent. Anticipation is a key framing activity in social emergence and therefore in human self-emancipation.

T. Fuller (✉)
University of Lincoln, Brayford Pool, Lincoln, UK
e-mail: tfuller@lincoln.ac.uk

© Springer Nature Switzerland AG 2019
R. Poli (ed.), *Handbook of Anticipation*,
https://doi.org/10.1007/978-3-319-91554-8_6

93

Keywords

Normative · Anticipation · Emergence · Critial realism · Ethics · Values ·
Transformation · Dispositions · Modeling relations · Rosen · Causation

Introduction

This contribution to the *Handbook of Anticipation* considers the ways that
anticipation invokes or maintains relatively stable behavior. Most discussion of
anticipation relates to changes and responses to sensed changes external to the
actor or system, for example, changes in the "external environment." My
approach to this question of stability and associated normativity arises from my
long-standing interest in emergence as being significant in understanding how
futures are produced from the present.

The term "normative" is used here to mean *relating to or deriving from a
recognized standard and applied to behavior and to judgments*. The term "normative" has a variety of meanings and can relate to ethical questions of which values are
"good" or "bad," or more generally to what values are taken as "social values." The
role of cultural values is central to structural functionalist theories of social structure
(Parsons 1961). The thesis in this chapter is that human anticipation, which includes
the effectuation of actions, involves judgments. Judgments are influenced by normative values as constructed by the actor. The construction of what is normative
involves social practice, i.e., interaction between people and between institutions.
Social norms are inherent and hidden in languages, are contested, are negotiated.
Norms are dynamic; there are evident deviations between practices and the rhetoric
of espoused values. What is operationalized as "the norm" is not fixed. Norms also
vary between groups of people: subcultures, nations, ethnic groups, religious communities, professional practitioners, etc. Norms are dynamic, and the relationship
between anticipation and the normative is dynamic. The processes of anticipation, I
suggest, create or add to the dynamism of social norms.

The sections of this chapter provide the following. Firstly anticipation is framed
through Robert Rosen's work on anticipatory systems, but in particular noting the
concern Rosen had for normativity as ethical good and the ways in which his
systemic models relate to norms and values.

The second theme is that of emergence as a theory of social change. This section
is grounded in a critical realist philosophy after Roy Bhaskar that sees emergence as
an explanation of the possibility of human self-emancipation. More specifically, I
follow Margaret Archer's theory on morphogenesis and the developments of this by
R. Keith Sawyer and Dave Elder-Vass. My contribution to this work is to suggest
that anticipation is inherent in the causal power of social structure.

I then turn to a more empirical question of what is being anticipated that might
change society. I discuss the role of value and values in anticipatory inferences,
suggesting that what is taken as value is central to the inferential logic of anticipatory
systems. This then leads to a discussion of ways in which anticipation is causal and
what effect it has on the stabilizing or destabilizing of social norms.

Anticipating Good, Anticipating Harm

Taking Rosen's work as one point of departure, anticipation involves inference. In an anticipatory system, the modeling relations synthesize entailments in a natural system by inferential entailments in a formal system. The relational model is a set of inferential entailments. Inference is a judgmental process, whether conscious or unconscious, cognitive or psychomotor, reasoned or "felt." Inference, at the point of action (of the effector in the case of an anticipatory system), is an internal and individualistic process – internal to the "system." However, the causal influences on human inferential reasoning are social. The way that anticipating entities (agents or systems or actors) form their inferences is through the experience of the interactions with their environment, i.e., other entities. The judgments in inference are socially produced. Rosen called the process of forming inferential entailments "encoding" and the making of judgments "decoding," i.e., decoding from the inferential entailments back into actions in the natural system with which the anticipatory system is engaged. Figure 1, taken from Rosen 1985, p. 72, illustrates this.

As a mapping process, encoding and decoding may not appear to have ethical characteristics. However, Rosen raised the question of normative values in his work, firstly pointing out that anticipatory systems assumed an "almost ethical character."

"The character of a predictive model assumes almost an ethical character even in a purely abstract context. We might even say that the models embodied in an anticipatory system are what comprise its individuality; what distinguish it uniquely from other systems. As we have seen, a change in these models is a change of identity. . .". (Rosen et al. 2012, p. 370)

Secondly Rosen had an enduring ethical concern about policy and planning as a form of anticipation. He was influenced in this by Robert Hutchins, one-time president of the University of Chicago and founder of the Center for the Study of Democratic Institutions, Santa Barbara, USA. The center's work was oriented to the discovery of the "means and ends of human society" and its common good. Robert Hutchins posed the central question "What should we do?" The question related to both the technology of planning and the norms that accompanied policy and

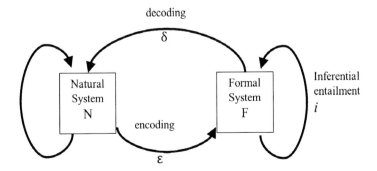

Fig. 1 Inferential entailment in anticipatory systems. Source: Rosen (1985, p. 72)

decision-making. Rosen later asserted that "ought is of the essence" in anticipatory systems: "Without a conception of 'ought,' there could be no guide to politics" (Rosen et al. 2012, p. 1).

As suggested elsewhere (Fuller 2017), the way in which "ought" is manifest in Rosen's model is in the "programming" of the effectors in an anticipatory system, that is, the "specification of a dynamics on [effectors] which will convert the input information from the model (i.e. information about the future state of the system) into a specific modification of the dynamics of the system." (Rosen 1974, p. 46). Such programming is related to an "arbitrary choice" with respect to the identification of "desirable" and "undesirable" regions. These regions are within the state space of the system. The effectors act when the trajectory of the system moves away from desirable region toward an undesirable region. The choice of what is desirable or undesirable, Rosen said, represents "a kind of constraint added from the outside, and enters into the planning process in an equally weighty fashion as does the model and the effector system" (Rosen 1974, p. 6), reproduced in (Rosen et al. 2012, p. 13).

The use of the terms desirable and undesirable makes explicit the value judgments inherent in anticipatory systems. What constitutes "desirable" will depend on context and the character of the anticipatory system. The sustaining of life needs fairly basic resources, and a lack of these would be "undesirable" for "life itself" (a synonym for anticipatory systems in Rosen's terms). At the more human and social level what is "desirable" is more complex, in the sense that human agency produces a range of desires and motivations in regard to these desires. Here is a clear sense of Rosen's acceptance of normative values as inherent in anticipatory systems – that what is desirable has causal effect on the programming of the effectors, i.e., on the actions taken as a result of inferences made about the changing environment. Whether the desires of a particular actor are normative to the ecology of actors rather than only themselves is an empirical question. However, we can detect normative behavior in social contexts, subgroups, professions, religions, etc. as being relatively stable.

Emergence and Anticipation

I argue here that the causal effects of what is desirable and undesirable shape the emergence of changes in the environment. I link two dynamics, anticipation and emergence, by the interacting effects of each on the other. If actors (or anticipatory systems) are interrelating in an ecology of actors, then each will have a sense of what is desirable and undesirable for themselves. Whether or not their inferential logic is correct is not relevant, but inferences have power because they act on the effector. Thus, anticipation of a change in value of something significant – something of greater or lesser desirability or undesirability than currently exists – motivates action.

For the purposes of this paper, I take emergence to be in its weak form. That is to say, ontological emergence: the appearance of an emergent property produced through interactions of something other than the emergent property, and that the emergent property has features which are novel from the features that produced them. In certain kinds of emergence, the emergents are also autonomous from the features that produced them and have a form of holism in themselves. See Humphreys (2016, p. 26) for further explanation. Common to the variety of accounts of emergence is the idea of layers or levels, such that "higher" forms of organizing are built upon – emerge from and are different to – "lower" forms of organizing. Our world is populated by things or entities, which in turn are composed of entities, and hence the higher levels have emerged from relationships between lower levels. An example of this is Sawyer's (2005, p. 211) representation of social emergence, reproduced in Fig. 2 and asserting that social structure (high level) is formed from individuals and interactions (lower levels). Sawyer's ideas draw from Archer's work on morphogenesis described later. What can be seen from the figure is that while social structure is emergent from individuals and their interactions, "top-down" causal relationships between the higher levels of structure (social structure) and individual agency are also possible. That is, the emergent properties produced from the "bottom-up" by individual interactions have autonomous and independent causal power on the features from which they emerged. This duality is a feature of stronger forms of emergence.

This chapter does not attempt to explain or theorize emergence, a topic that others are much more capable of explaining. However, the paper takes emergence as a process or complex of processes through which structural change occurs and through which new forms of order or stability are produced.

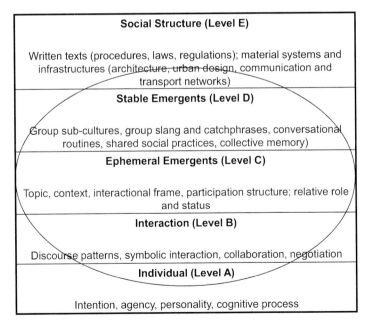

Fig. 2 The Emergence Paradigm (Sawyer 2005, p. 211), showing the "circle of emergence" (p. 220), i.e., that area which is subject to social emergence

The layers in Sawyer's framework between interactions and social structure is the space where emergence occurs. Interactions (level B) produce new forms of interactional frame, for example, which are in Sawyer's words "ephemeral," i.e., short-lived. Some of these "ephemeral emergents" become stabilized in such continuing forms, for example, as conversational routines. Following this, some of the stable emergent forms (which Sawyer refers to with the noun "an emergent") become institutionalized as social structures. This is a simple model which, as presented here, does not say much about what causes emergence or stability. Sawyer's exposition is much more thorough and well developed relating to what he calls the Emergence Paradigm, which, as the figure illustrates, sits between interaction and social structure and:

> [...] "takes from the Interaction Paradigm (sic) the close empirical focus on processes of symbolic interactionism and it takes from the Structure Paradigm (sic) the belief that emergent social phenomena are ontologically distinct and have autonomous causal influence on individuals. [...] The Emergence Paradigm attempts to explain the causal forces that originate in an emergent that was created by the participants. Emergence Paradigm research focusses on the micro-interactional mechanism by which shared social phenomena emerge and on how those emergents constrain those mechanisms". (Sawyer 2005, pp. 212–213)

Sawyer's reference to causal forces and interactional mechanisms reflects Archer's morphogenesis, a critical realist perspective applied to understanding the dynamical developments in the nature of human society (Archer 1995). In short, Archer offered an explanation for the transformation of social structure based on Roy Bhaskar's ontological realism which is "premised explicitly upon emergence" (Archer 1995, p. 136). Archer develops Buckley's concepts of morphogenetic/morphostatic processes (Buckley 1967). She presents these as in a cyclic form, stating that temporality is a necessity because social structures "are in a space/time *flow*" (Bhaskar 1983, p. 93). Morphogenesis theorizes structural elaboration or transformation, and morphostasis theorizes structural reproduction, both of which occur in the flow of sociocultural interactions within pre-existing structural conditioning. The inclusion of this area of theory in this chapter is simply to illustrate the significance of emergence in the transformation of society, including the transformation of social norms through social interaction. Archer's thesis is that emergent properties are relational. I will link this idea to the relational nature of anticipation and anticipatory systems which have causal power over the "effector" in the system, i.e., over what agential actions are taken.

Elder-Vass builds on Archer's approach by offering an alternative formulation of the argument for emergence. His critique of Archer's morphogenesis is that it does not explain how an entity can possess emergent properties. Morphogenesis explains the development of a set of relations over time but not the causal power at a particular point in time (Elder-Vass 2007, p. 30). Elder-Vass makes a case for what he calls the "redescription principle," which is that the causal powers of an entity arise from (i) the parts of the entity, (ii) the relations between those parts, and (iii) the relations between those parts only when they are organized into the emergent form. Without the third aspect, causal explanation would only be a redescription of the parts and their relations. With Elder-Vass' formulation, the emergent form of the whole has causal power because the parts and their relations are contained within it. I suggest that anticipation is active in the relation between parts and that it is inherent in the particular relations of the emergent form. I will return to this argument when considering the effects of anticipation in relational and organizational settings.

Furthermore, Elder-Vass makes a significant contribution to understanding the relationships between anticipation, emergence, and social norms. He notes from the Collins Dictionary of Sociology (Jary and Jary 2005) that norms and roles are characteristic of the arrangements of large numbers of people into social institutions and also that this implies social institutions can be identified by empirical regularities of behavior. These empirical regularities, he says, are "effects" and not causes. Elder-Vass argues that the only representations or beliefs held in social institutions are the individual normative beliefs of the individuals concerned. There are no collective representations existing separate to those held by individuals. Social institutions, suggests Elder-Vass, are not entities, but properties of social groups and that "each member of the group that enacts normative practices holds a normative belief endorsing the practice" (Elder-Vass 2008, p. 290). He refers to such an entity as a "norm group." The normative practices of the individuals within a norm group create emergent social institutions:

> "In this emergentist view of social institutions, then, this type of social structure is causally effective because real social entities (norm groups) have emergent properties (institutions) that arise from the way their parts (human individuals) are related to each other (through their mutual commitment to endorse and enforce the practice concerned)." (Elder-Vass 2008, p. 292)

Elder-Vass extends this theorization of norm groups as norm circles in his later book (Elder-Vass 2010), stating that "Normative social institutions [...] are an emergent causal power of norm circles." The norm circle is an entity:

> "that has an emergent property or causal power; the tendency to increase conformity by its members to the norm. The property is the institution and the causal power is the capability that the group has to affect the behavior of individuals. That causal power is implemented through the members of the group, although it is a power of the group, and when its members act in support of the norm, it is the group (as well as the member concerned) that acts." (Elder-Vass 2010, p. 124)

All of the above discussion on group norms is orientated toward stability of behavior and values within the group. However, it also sets up the basis for considering how norms change, i.e., how social structures change. Both Archer and Bhaskar offer theories for change in social structures: Archer through a morphogenetic cycle and Bhaskar through a transformational model of social activity (TMSA) (Archer 1995, pp. 154–161). Both are temporal as well as relational. The approaches share what Elder-Vass refers to as "two critical moments," one where individual actions are affected by pre-existing social institutions and one where they act to reproduce or transform the social structure concerned. Such actions, argues

Elder-Vass, have multiple influences, not simply determined by the values and practices of the particular group circle or social structure involved. Other more powerful influences may change the dominant beliefs of an individual; other more powerful influences may loosen any group sanctions for norm transgressions by individuals. Significant changes external to the group may cause a weakening of social institutional power that guides the shared practices and for the model that each individual has of this environment to become obsolete.

Theorizing social structure from an emergentist perspective provides an explanation of structural change – of changes in norms over time – as occurring through human agency. Human agency is influenced by the social structure in which that agency takes place and is influenced by the agent's relations with other social institutions, other norm circles, in other social structures. The causal powers include the individual's capacity and capability to act, their recognition of alternative practices to the norm, and the stabilizing effects of the social institution in which this relational action takes place. The relevance of this to the arguments set out here in relation to anticipation is twofold. Firstly is the question of how modeling relation are constructed and evolve and secondly with regard to the link between value or norms and actions that reproduce or transform practices. I suggest that the individual's anticipation of value is material in this process.

Anticipation of Value

The central theme of relational emergence in this chapter, and the relevance of anticipation thereon, is continued by consideration of the psychology of anticipation, in particular, the characterization of *Homo Prospectus* (Seligman et al. 2016). The (well-informed) belief these authors hold is that "the unrivaled human ability to be guided by imagining alternatives stretching into the future – prospection – uniquely describes *Homo sapiens*." (p. ix). This initially appears as a more cognate deliberative account of anticipation compared to Rosen, for whom anticipation was a feature of "life itself," not just the life of humankind. The authors offer a list of propositions with regard to prospection, which take the position that the human mind and body are pulled more by the future than driven by the past, that human agency "metabolizes the past and present into projected futures." Their list of propositions includes prospective notions of perception, memory, emotion, happiness, morality, clinical disorder, and knowledge.

Seligman et al. contribute to understanding relations between prospection, emergence, and social norms. One of their propositions is this: "what if morality is not evaluation of the present action, but the prediction of character and its thrust into the future?" (p. x). Morality and social norms, as with laws and technologies, add structure to the future, making otherwise unavailable actions and outcomes possible (Railton 2016, p. 22). A causal force in this, they imply, is the idea of a future benefit or costs which regulates or motivates action. "To want to take an action because we like the idea of what that action might yield, even if that is remote in time or novel in character." (p. 21). The drive toward action is thus anticipatory. Railton argues that the "system biology" with the features necessary for making and acting on moral judgment is the affective system – human emotion. This is the system capable of representing and comparing the values at stake and allocating efforts, such that our values serve to "orient and move us." The affective system involves "attention, perception, memory, inference and action-readiness in a coordinated way" (p. 24).

Furthermore, although their concern is human psychology from a prospective point of view, they explicitly recognize the significance that collective psychology has in shaping social structures and norms. Returning to a theme of Elder-Vass, albeit implicitly, Roy Baumeister suggests that:

"In a sense, the future [is a] product of collective imagination and agreement. The Group imagines it together [. . .] people in the group cooperate to impose their collective imagination on top of some physical or anticipated facts". (Baumeister 2016)

The "sense" that is referred to above is not that people walk around with precisely the same images in mind nor share interpretations of possible futures arising from collective agreement. The "sense" refers to the social construction of the future, that individuals' realities are shared as is their sense of futures because the future is *culturally constructed*, for example, via human conventions. "The future is neither an objective, inhuman prospect nor a product of solitary imagination." (p. 136). This sentiment has considerable resonance with Appadurai's notion of the future as cultural fact (Appadurai 2013). Baumeister offers an example of the complex of human imagining and interactions that produce one-passenger air flight moving through different time zones. The relative stability of human conventions (education, religion, money) leads to expectations and trust. Collaboration is feasible in these circumstances, and collaboration, planning, and the sharing of knowledge open up possibilities for different, better, futures. In other words human culture is prospective – filled with possibilities and constructed to achieve these.

To summarize the above short tour of literature thus far, societies exist and develop through structures and institutions, which involve norms, shared values, collective actions, and prospection. Interpretative and action-oriented anticipation in the human species is influenced by engagement in social structures. Inherent in both interpretation and action are norms and values. Such norms are not necessarily what is best for society as a whole – social justice remains a contested and at time unfulfilled space – but group norms will be seen by the subgroups as desirable for them. To belong to a subgroup is to accept and behave in a manner consistent with the dominant values, whatever other beliefs are held. Social structures are stable but not fixed; they evolve. The transformation of social structures involves acts of human agency (e.g., morphogenesis). Social emergence arises through interaction of entities (e.g., agents), and the emerging new patterns of interaction may initially be ephemeral, short-lived, and limited to subgroups (e.g., norm circles). Some emergent patterns stabilize and develop as social form (e.g., institution) which itself has causal power through the normative practices enacted by each member. If normativity is prospective (following Seligman), morality may be the "prediction of character thrust into the future," i.e., a future cost or benefit. The transformation of society (e.g., social institutions or structures) is thus culturally constructed as striving for better futures. The next section elaborates this idea though anticipation as a causal mechanism.

Anticipation as Causal Mechanism

The idea of causal mechanisms is realist, specifically critical realism and the work of Roy Bhaskar. Bhaskar's causal powers theory (among other things) separates the concept of real causal power and actual causation. Actual causation can be caused by combinations of real causal powers. Bhaskar identifies real causal powers with "relatively enduring structures and mechanisms" that are "nothing other than the ways of acting of things" [and these things] "are complex objects in virtue of which they possess an ensemble of tendencies, liabilities and powers" (Bhaskar 1975, pp. 50–51) in (Elder-Vass 2010, p. 45). What we observe empirically may be the outcome of interacting causal powers. Elder-Vass (p. 45) argues, after Mumford (2008, p. 140), that real causal powers are emergent properties.

Working within this realist, emergentist framework, I briefly introduce the idea of dispositional realism. Objects or entities possess dispositions, i.e., some inherent quality that may be causal in particular circumstances. Borghini and Williams explain it thus:

> "Sometimes referred to as a 'power', or 'propensity', a disposition is the ability of an object to bring about some state of affairs (its 'manifestation'), when met with the appropriate stimulus. This stimulus (typically) consists in an arrangement of other objects; the other objects being such that they too have dispositions, and it is owing to the complementary dispositions of the objects involved that they mutually produce their manifestation. Dispositions are characterised by the manifestations they produce, and hence are for that manifestation. For example, the disposition fragility has as its manifestation a shattering or breaking of the fragile object, so fragility is a disposition for shattering or breaking. [...] 'Dispositional realism' refers to any theory of dispositions that claims that an object has a disposition in virtue of some state or property of the object." (Borghini and Williams 2008, p. 23)

Disposition is an inherent quality and not relational. It has causal potency which may be made actual by virtue of relations with other entities and causal powers. Borghini and Williams develop from this an account of *possibility* on the understanding that dispositionality is the source of causal potency. Bhaskar describes dispositional realism as the specific form of modal realism. Modal realism takes the realist position that entities have disposition, i.e., causal powers that are transcendental from the particular actual world context in which they are observed as being situated. Such inherent dispositions transcend the specific context, albeit that in a difference context they might not be realized or manifest because of the arrangements to other objects and their dispositions. Thus, modal realism is epistemically consistent with alternative futures, a world of possibilities, where there are other possibilities than what exists now. "There is another world, but it is in this one [...] as a possibility it is enfolded within the things and

structures that we have in this world, and so this world could be different."
(Bhaskar and Hartwig 2010, p. 66). For Bhaskar, modal realism is indispensable
for concrete utopianism and for human freedom.

If, as Rosen, Gilbert and Wilson (2007), Seligman, and others assert, anticipation
(or prospection) is existential, that it is a characteristic of "life itself," then anticipation can be described as a disposition. Perhaps more specifically, prospection and
acting upon anticipations are dispositional. The nature of the particularities of what
is anticipated is ontological; it depends on the situation. The nature of an actual
anticipation and its effects are empirical. The point is that all living things have such
dispositions, even when they are not manifest because of the specifics of a situation.

Taking Bhaskar's position that "states and dispositions may properly be said to be
causes" (Bhaskar 1978/1998, p. 92), one can argue that anticipation is causal, or
rather the disposition to act on anticipation is causal. Anticipation is entailed in the
causal process. Anticipation is a causal mechanism. Actual cause depends on how
the mechanism acts in particular circumstances. Anticipatory causation is not deterministic nor necessarily consistent, nor therefore reliably predictable. Although,
when circumstances are stable, a tendency for agents to reproduce structures, rather
than seek to transform them, means that behaviors may be predictable in the sense of
empirically observable regularities.

Stabilizing Ephemeral Emergents: The Becoming of Norms

We have reached the final stage in this reasoning of the relationship between
anticipation and the normative stance. The question we return to is that posed by
Elder-Vass: what causal mechanisms reproduce or transform society? In addressing
this question, I return to Sawyer's "circle of emergence" (Fig. 2) which characterizes
emergence, or an emergent property, as having varying possible states of ephemerality. Social structure is stable, not ephemeral. What is it that transforms short-lived,
temporary presence into something more sustained? What are the causal mechanisms for stabilizing ephemeral emergents?

This question of cause brings us back to anticipation. Anticipation it is argued,
following Rosen, Gilbert, and others, is dispositional, existential, and part of the
temporality of being. Anticipation is a process of sensing and interpreting "external"
information in relation to the actor's (or anticipatory system's) internal model. When
presented with new information or experiences, the inferential process makes judgments about the salience of that information and its consequences; judgments with
regard to whether this information, or this experience, or this deviation from the
norm, has desirable or undesirable consequences. Thus, the anticipation of an end
effect will cause a response, either to accept and adapt to absorb the new condition or
to try to reject or try to amend the condition. I suggest that this process is at least a
partial explanation for transformations in social structure. The empirical nature of
how knowledge of a change in modeling relations is actually sensed and responded
to would benefit from further research.

Philosophically, causation as a result of the perception or judgments of future consequences is consistent with Aristotle's "final cause," which as Rosen commented is defined in terms of something entailed by the effect. "All the troubles occasioned by the concept of finality spring from this curious fact" (Rosen 1991, p. 133). It is also consistent with the teleological characteristic of Aquinas' (1225–1274) fifth cause, namely, the "exemplary cause"; see (Louie 2008) in Aquinas' Summa Theologica translated thus:

> "Whereas in other agents (the form of the thing to be made pre-exists) according to intelligible being, as in those that act by the intellect; and thus the likeness of a house pre-exists in the mind of the builder. And this may be called the idea of the house, since the builder intends to build his house like to the form conceived in his mind." (Aquinas 1485: Part 1 15. Q1)

While using the term "teleological," it should not be presumed that this gives any particular closure of the future. Arguably, the existence "in the mind" and also in social discourses of a set of norm beliefs and values does inhibit some possible futures. However, I argue here that the dynamical manifestation of what is taken as "norm," associated with the emergence of new legitimized meanings and novel practices, maintains the intrinsic openness of the future. The same processes also foreclose some possible futures. The emergence of what is normative involves social and political processes which are open to corruption and power in myriad ways. One might say that what becomes successfully established as social norms colonizes the anticipatory capacity of society but ethically should not foreclose future possibilities. The implications of this are profound. Governance on humanity's futures necessitates governance and education with respect to the ontologies of anticipation, what is anticipated and by what means.

Those familiar with Bloch's philosophy in *The Principle of Hope*, etc. will see the connections between this the critical realist position that separates the real from the potential. As Poli writes in this handbook (Poli 2018), Bloch's claim was that the "real continuously unfolds, and it may well be that the true nature of the real has still to surface. Furthermore, the conditions making the true nature of the real possible may still be pending in the sense that they may be still under formation." Bhaskar's aim was an emancipatory philosophy which, in his view, requires an explanation that depends on emergence:

> "It is only if social phenomena are genuinely emergent that realist explanations in the human sciences are justified; and it is only if these conditions are satisfied that there is any possibility of human self-emancipation worthy of the name. But, conversely, emergent phenomena require realist explanations and realist explanations possess emancipatory implications. Emancipation depends upon explanation depends upon emergence." (Bhaskar 1986, pp. 103–104)

The relations between explanation and anticipation are important, though not the subject of this chapter, except in terms of an explanation of the role of anticipation in the normative stance. Explanations, i.e., knowledge of why things occur, inform anticipation. Anticipations based on poor, weak, or downright inaccurate explanations will lead to a widening between the assumed world and the actual world. Anticipation based on "the wrong model" may give the illusion of progress and emancipation but will not achieve it. The questions of what constitutes the "right model" as well as what the "right model" ought to be remain crucial to the framing of human futures.

To consider the role of anticipation in the social process of establishing, maintaining, or changing norms, I take as a basic model the morphogenesis/morphostatic duality proposed by Archer. This model asserts that social action can be stabilizing or transformational, depending on the actions of the actors involved. Inherent in the notion of transformation is that actions leading to transformation are destabilizing, in the sense that transformation is a post hoc state. The preceding text shows that interpretation of circumstances or conditions is an anticipatory modality of action. The modality of anticipation is a process that mediates between sense (knowledge sensed in multiple ways) and action, or "effecting" in the terms of anticipatory systems. One significant function of this anticipatory mode is evaluative, seeking to understand if a particular situation or changing context is desirable or undesirable and how to act. Logically, the evaluative criterion in relation to anticipated future states is how valuable that possible future state is to the actor. The evaluation framework used by the actor is influenced by the norms and values of the "group circle" (Elder-Vass), though not in a closed way, as discussed earlier. Within that group circle, the criterion is, logically, the anticipated consequences for the group's existential being and related identity, longevity, quality, purpose, etc. In short, the anticipation of value stabilizes practices in relation to ephemeral emergent properties. The anticipation of greater value arising from emergent practices or properties tends toward a destabilizing of the norm and transforming to another stabilized state. The anticipation of reduced value, as threats or loss, leads to action that conserves stable practices, i.e., morphostasis. Loss aversion has been shown to be a somewhat stronger motive than possible gains (Tversky and Kahneman 1992; Kahneman and Tversky 1979).

What is taken as value in this evaluative process, in this anticipatory modality, is an empirical question, based on extant norms and associated practices, but influenced by norms external to the group circle experienced by group members. Let us return to Hutchin's question, "what should be done?" i.e., are there particular norms and values and associated practices that are of greater worthiness or virtue than others? Can group circle norms be somehow suboptimal to the wider good? This of course is a core question of moral philosophy, and it is abundantly clear that default normative practices, preferences, and underlying values between different groups can be in conflict. Power arises from the assertion and maintenance of particular norms. Normativity and ethical choice are culturally political phenomena. Anticipation has causal power in the politics of ethical choice because it is a mode of action that makes judgments.

Anticipation as described above offers a contribution to theories of emergence. This chapter has taken a critical realist perspective to social change, and in that context, anticipation acts to support the redescription principle (Elder-Vass 2007). The arguments could have been set in a range of theories, relying on the evidence that anticipation is an observable phenomenon and the entities produced through that process have material, ontological status. Anticipation produces sensory or imaginative responses by the actor. It is a process that is sensory, engaging cognitive and affective inferences and which modifies actions or practices. The imaginings, sensory-affective responses, and disruptions of everyday practices associated with anticipation are emergent and exist, if only temporarily, along with extant and emergent entities. In addition, anticipated futures and the evaluation of these exist as emergent discourse or interplay between group members, as demonstrated by Sawyer (see Fig. 2). While this state of being exists, these ephemeral emergent entities and the anticipatory sense associated with an inferred (future) state have ontological existence, and, being material, they have causal power over extant entities.

The causal power of anticipation by virtue of its relation to values and norms in the evaluation of possible future states can be observed in transformational practices, in particular in the way that narratives are intentionally shaped and promoted by those in transformational roles, such as leaders, entrepreneurs, politicians, and activists. This may manifest as narratives of hope, of promised utopias, of security, and of better lives. Or narratives may convey fear, threat, uncertainty, and loss. Influence on the inferential modality of anticipation is a political imperative. Economic and monetary systems on which humankind depends for development are dependent on imaginaries; on the expectation of future value, whether as the result of new technologies; or the payment of interest on loans. Social systems depend on trust for their stability and flourishing. The relationship between anticipation and norms is not a passive relationship nor necessarily a natural one.

Impredicativity, i.e., where internal causality is self-defined and thus not predicated on causes in the environment, is to be avoided. Powerful narration of particular prospects can form and modify modeling relations; our inferential judgments about the world made in the process of our actions. The avoidance of impredicativity requires a continuous critical reframing of the "modeling relations" (between inference mechanisms and natural systems) to prevent a divergence between assumed reality and experienced reality.

Summary

Normativity, *relating to or deriving from a recognized standard and applied to behavior and to judgments*, is assumed to be significant in the maintenance of social structures. Transformations in social norms are possible and associated with changes in practices. Norms, with associated values and practices, are socially reproduced and socially transformed. The question of what "causes" these to be reproduced or transformed is a central one to understanding social change. This chapter takes an emergence perspective on social change, i.e., that changes in patterns of practice of social interaction are emergent from extant practice and can exert power over extant practices.

The link between social emergence and anticipation is drawn from Rosen's theory of inferential modeling relations contained within his theorizing of anticipatory systems. In the context of human society, it applies when a particular human actor or agent makes inferential judgments about the desirability of changes in their relations to others and to their environment. The disposition to anticipate other possibilities may be causal with respect to a change produced, where the agent has, and uses, power to respond to an anticipated change. The extent to which such a disposition leads to action will depend on context.

From a critical realist perspective, anticipation is a causal mechanism in the process of emergence. At the same time, the state of an anticipatory system, involving inferential logic, modeling relations, and actions of effectors, is dynamic, emergent, and inherently formative of emergent practices.

Anticipation can act to stabilize practices to avoid undesirable outcomes or to destabilize practices in a transformational process. Transformation is a process of destabilizing and restabilizing. The appearance of ephemeral (short-lived) emergent norms can be stabilized by the actions of individuals within the group in anticipation of future value. Similarly, existing norms can be maintained, while ephemeral emergents are extinguished by reactions to an anticipated loss in value.

The anticipatory mode of normative judgment is material in the stabilizing and transformation of human society. In the methodological context of this paper, dispositions to anticipate and the anticipatory actions initiated by this anticipation provide some explanation of morphogenesis and morphostasis.

With regard to anticipation and the normative stance, a case is offered that anticipation is inherent in the formation and stabilizing of normative practices.

References

Appadurai, A. (2013). *The future as cultural fact: Essays on the global condition.* New York/London: Verso Books.

Aquinas, T. (1485). *Summa Theologica* (trans: Province FotED). Benzinger Brothers Printers to the Holy Apostolic See.

Archer, M. S. (1995). *Realist social theory : The morphogenetic approach.* Cambridge: Cambridge University Press.

Baumeister, R. F. (2016). Collective prospection: The social construction of the future. In M. E. P. Seligman, P. Railton, R. F. Baumeister, & C. Sripada (Eds.), *Homo prospectus* (p. xiv). New York: Oxford University Press, 384 pages.

Bhaskar, R. (1975). *A realist theory of science.* Leeds: Books.

Bhaskar, R. (1978/1998). *The possibility of naturalism: A philosophical critique of the contemporary human sciences. Critical realism – interventions* (3rd edn). London/New York: Routledge.

Bhaskar, R. (1983). Beef, structure and place: Notes from a critical naturalist perspective. *Journal for the Theory of Social Behaviour, 13*(1), 81–96. https://doi.org/10.1111/j.1468-5914.1983.tb00464.x.

Bhaskar, R. (1986). *Scientific realism and human emancipation.* London: Verso.

Bhaskar, R., & Hartwig, M. (2010). *The formation of critical realism: A personal perspective.* London: Routledge.

Borghini, A., & Williams, N. E. (2008). A dispositional theory of possibility. *Dialectica, 62*(1), 21–41.

Buckley, W. F. (1967). Sociology and modern systems theory. Prentice Hall, Englewood Cliffs, N.J.

Elder-Vass, D. (2007). For emergence: Refining Archer's account of social structure. *Journal for the Theory of Social Behaviour, 37*(1), 25–44.

Elder-Vass, D. (2008). Integrating institutional, relational and embodied structure: An emergentist perspective. *British Journal of Sociology, 59*(2), 281–299.

Elder-Vass, D. (2010). *The causal power of social structures : Emergence, structure and agency*. Cambridge: Cambridge University Press.

Fuller, T. (2017). Anxious relationships: The unmarked futures for post-normal scenarios in anticipatory systems. *Technological Forecasting and Social Change, 124*(2017), 41–50. https://doi.org/10.1016/j.techfore.2016.07.045.

Gilbert, D. T., & Wilson, T. D. (2007). Prospection: Experiencing the future. *Science, 317*(5843), 1351–1354. https://doi.org/10.1126/science.1144161.

Humphreys, P. (2016). *Emergence*. New York: Oxford University Press.

Jary, D., & Jary, J. (2005). *Collins dictionary of sociology* (4th ed.). Glasgow: Collins.

Kahneman, D., & Tversky, A. (1979). Prospect theory: An analysis of decision under risk. *Econometrica, 47*, 263–291.

Louie, A. H. (2008). Functional entailment and immanent causation in relational biology. *Axiomathes, 18*(3), 289–302. https://doi.org/10.1007/s10516-008-9047-y.

Mumford, S. (2008). Powers, dispositions, properties or a causal realist manifesto. In R. Groff (Ed.), *Revitalizing causality: Realism about causality in philosophy and social science* (pp. 139–151). London: Routledge.

Parsons, T. (1961). *Theories of society; foundations of modern sociological theory*. New York: Free Press of Glencoe.

Poli, R. (2018). Anticipation and the philosophy of the future. In R. Poli (Ed.), *Handbook of anticipation*. New York: Springer.

Railton, P. (2016). Introduction. In M. E. P. Seligman, P. Railton, R. F. Baumeister, & C. Sripada (Eds.), *Homo prospectus* (p. xiv). New York: Oxford University Press, 384 pages.

Rosen, R. (1974). Planning, management, policies and strategies: Four fuzzy concepts. *International Journal of General Systems, 1*(4), 245–252. https://doi.org/10.1080/03081077408960784.

Rosen, R. (1985). *Anticipatory systems: philosophical, mathematical and methodological foundations*. Oxford: Pergamon.

Rosen, R. (1991). Life itself: a comprehensive inquiry into the nature, origin, and fabrication of life. New York; Chichester: Columbia University Press.

Rosen, R., Rosen, J., Kineman, J. J., & Nadin, M. (2012). *Anticipatory systems : Philosophical, mathematical, and methodological foundations* (2nd ed.). New York/London: Springer.

Sawyer, R. K. (2005). *Social emergence: Societies as complex systems*. Cambridge: Cambridge University Press.

Seligman, M. E. P., Railton, P., Baumeister, R. F., & Sripada, C. (2016). *Homo prospectus*. New York: Oxford University Press.

Tversky, A., & Kahneman, D. (1992). Advances in prospect theory: Cumulative representation of uncertainty. *Journal of Risk and Uncertainty, 5*(4), 297–323. https://doi.org/10.1007/BF00122574.

Anticipation and the Philosophy of the Future

6

Roberto Poli

Contents

Abstract

A philosophy of the future sees the world as an unfinished process, as a continuous tendency toward new horizons. Within this process, what matters most is the tendency itself, more than its starting and ending points. To understand this situation, one needs an ontology of the not-yet, of being as processual, and therefore of being understood as an incomplete, still unfolding reality, indeterminate with respect to its endpoint, leaving room for entirely new determinations as well as for growing or maturing ones. A philosophy of the future provides

R. Poli (✉)
Department of Sociology and Social Research, University of Trento, Trento, Italy
e-mail: roberto.poli@unitn.it

© Springer Nature Switzerland AG 2019
R. Poli (ed.), *Handbook of Anticipation*,
https://doi.org/10.1007/978-3-319-91554-8_10

guidance for distinguishing genuine from not genuine futures. Similarly, it distinguishes between utopia as focused on the endpoint and utopia as focused on everyday life, especially its humblest, tiniest aspects – which is a way of saying that the roots of the future are in the present, if only we learn to see them.

Keywords
Ernst Bloch · Latency · Tendency · Horizon · Real possibility · Not-yet · Daydream · Utopia

Introduction

Philosophers have widely contributed to anticipation, albeit under different denominations and within different frameworks. Chapter 5 of Poli (2017b) presents a sample of the contributions to the understanding of the future developed by twentieth-century philosophers, including Bergson, Husserl, Mead, Whitehead, Peirce, Jonas, Heidegger, Deleuze, Bloch, and Hartmann. All but the last two are summarily presented. I pay closer attention to Bloch and Hartmann because, to my knowledge, they have gone deeper and farther than any other.

My other contributions to this *Handbook* have examined different aspects of the openness of the future. Notably, *Introducing anticipation* (Poli 2017a) is focused on the complexity and impredicativity of natural systems. The subsequent theorem, according to which the lattice of models of an impredicative system does not admit Top (the most general model, subsuming all the others), clarifies the meaning of complexity from an anticipatory point of view. The chapter on *Complex systems* (Louie and Poli 2017) explores in detail the anticipatory understanding of complexity.

Time and temporality (Poli 2017d) shows the complexity of the category of time by calling attention to the difference between the pure and the qualified understanding of time. The former hinges on metaphysics; the latter depends on the type of the real processes that are unfolding in time. As far as social time is concerned, that chapter shows that the relations among the temporal modes of past, present, and future are much more tangled – that is, complex – than usually understood.

The chapter on *Anticipatory risk management* (Furlanetto and Poli 2017) addresses the openness of the future the other way round. Precisely because the future is open, efforts to tame the future by conquering it from the past are deemed to fail. The confusion between risk and uncertainty comes to the fore here. By blurring the distinction between risk and uncertainty and addressing uncertainty as if it were risk, the illusion is created that the future has been tamed. Put in another way, statistical modeling is dangerous (when improperly used; that is, when used beyond its boundaries).

The present chapter digs deeper than any of the already-mentioned chapters and addresses the ontological reasons that explain why the future is intrinsically open. Even less than with the previous explorations, these reasons have almost nothing to do with lack of information – that is, with epistemological issues. A different and possibly complementary perspective has been developed by Tuomi in his excellent *Ontological expansion* (Tuomi 2017).

I shall rely here on Bloch's understanding of concrete utopias. While Popper's propensities may also be considered (Popper 1990), I shall leave his contribution for another occasion (see however Poli 2010a, 2013).

The World as an Incomplete Process

The thinker who has conducted the most extensive categorical analyses of the future has undoubtedly been Ernst Bloch. His entire work is dedicated to the future, from the early *Geist der Utopie*, to his magnum opus *Principle of hope* (Bloch 1995), to the *Tübinger Einleitung in die Philosophie* (partially translated as (Bloch 1970)) and *Experimentum mundi*.

From an ontological perspective, Bloch (as well as Hartmann, see (Poli 2012)) frames ontological categories as neither the most universal predicates nor a priori functions of the intellect. Instead, ontological categories are modes of being, the innermost determinations of being (on categories as modes or principles of being see Poli 2007, 2009, 2010b, 2011a, 2012). Bloch adds that ontological categories are categories of the not-yet-being, because the main feature of real being is its openness to the future. Precisely for this reason, Bloch's ontology can be termed the "ontology of the not-yet." See in particular Chaps. 17–20 of Bloch (1995) and Chap. 23 of Bloch (1963). For a clarification of the categories used to develop such an ontology, see Bloch (1980). Bloch's *Principle of Hope* (Bloch 1995) is the best approximation that I know to an encyclopedia of the categories of the future.

Bloch is more focused on the realm of the real than on being in general (which includes both the real and the ideal). Bloch's main claim is that the realm of reality is far from being a given – that is, completed – totality. On the contrary, the real continuously unfolds, and it may well be that the true nature of the real has still to surface. Furthermore, the conditions making the true nature of the real possible may still be pending in the sense that they may be still in formation. Bloch's claim goes deeper than the idea that the true nature of the real is hidden, waiting for triggers able to activate and make it visible. Bloch's position is more radical than this: it amounts to the claim that, at least in some cases, the conditions making the true real possible are still entirely lacking. From this point of view, the idea arises that the laws of sociology, psychology, biology, or even those of physics may change together with the maturing of their ontological conditions.

The "real" that interests Bloch most is the real of social and, secondarily, psychological being. While his categorical framework does not exclude the possibility that the conditions making the lower layers of reality possible may still be unfolding or under formation, Bloch's interest is focused on the realization of human beings.

The World as an Experiment

As just said, Bloch sees the world as an unfinished process, the main reason being that the processes that are the world continue to unfold. Precisely because the world is an unfinished process, it can be taken as an experiment – an *Experimentum mundi*, as the title of Bloch's last major work reads.

Being in a proper experimental mode, it is still undecided whether the world will arrive at some positive outcome or end in disaster – at least *for us*. That is, the experiment that is the world may fail (again, for us).

Since the world's horizon is still undecided, one may claim that: "the world itself is not yet at home." On the contrary, the world is in a state of continuous tendency toward new horizons, even if these horizons are far from being crystal-clear, visible, or well-defined endpoints. The tendency toward a horizon shows that the processual unfolding of the world is neither random nor blind but includes a direction.

Latency, Tendency, and Horizon

In order to understand the ontological nature of the world, what matters most is the tendency itself, more than its starting and ending points. However, in order to figure out the details of this ontology, a clarification of the starting and ending points of the tendency is needed. In Bloch's terminology, these are respectively called "latency" and "horizon."

To understand this tangled situation, one needs an ontology of the not-yet, of being as processual, and therefore of being understood as an incomplete, still unfolding reality, indeterminate with respect to its endpoint, leaving room within its core (starting point) for entirely new determinations as well as for growing or maturing ones.

Real Possibility

The modal category of possibility thus moves to central stage. Possibility here is understood as "real" possibility and not merely as "conceptual" possibility. That is, real possibility is possibility grounded in the real processes of the world and it is different from possibility as conceptual variation.

Following Aristotle, Bloch distinguishes between *dynamei on*, "possible being," and *katà to dynatòn*, "according to possibility." Possible being is wider than being according to possibility. One can understand possible being (*dynamei on*) as "possible in general," while being according to possibility (*katà to dynatòn*) is what governs the passage from general possibility to actuality.

Bloch further distinguishes what is objectively possible from what is really possible. Objectively possible is everything whose occurrence cannot be excluded on the basis of the present, partial knowledge of its actual conditions. Instead, something is really possible when its conditions are not yet fully assembled within the object itself. This may imply that the said conditions are still maturing or even that they are still entirely lacking. Real possibility comes in different guises: as the initial not-yet, as partial conditioning, as subjective capacity, and as the sea of possibility surrounding existents.

Entities Are Categorically Open

The future as an ontological category makes sense only if entities are categorically open – that is to say, only if new determinations can be superimposed on an entity's previous determinations. This means that the ontological nature of entities is not thoroughly established. New determinations can always appear. Entities are never totally given in advance, and they have some kind of tendency toward the future. Just as understanding the past often helps the understanding of actually given situations, prefiguring the future may also aid understanding of actually given situations. As a preliminary note, it is important to distinguish the problem of missing information (the entity is imperfectly or only partially known) from the problem of the entity's categorical openness, that is, to conditions of the entity that have still to mature. The former is an epistemological problem and does not bother Bloch (or Hartmann for that matter). The latter is a truly ontological problem.

"Categorical openness" means that the entity is not maximally determined; some of its aspects are still hidden. Better: some of its determinations may still be lacking. The difference is that hidden components are there, waiting for proper triggers to activate them. On the other hand, lacking components relate to incompletely present conditions and aspects. Their incompleteness may be ascribed either to still maturing conditions or to new conditions that may subsequently arise (Poli 2006b, 2011b).

Not-Yet

The future-oriented category of the not-yet is anchored in the processual nature of the world. According to Bloch, everything becomes. The not-yet is the direction, the goal toward which everything aims. A description of the present (or, for that matter, the past) state of the world which does not include its not-yet is defective. It lacks the most authentic dimension of being, its *aspiration* toward completion.

The processualistic basis of the not-yet means that the identity of entities is not present internally to them, and for this reason entities must go outside themselves. For the time being, let me note that the process of going outside to find one's identity requires a direction – but it does not have to be a predetermined or a once-and-forever pre-established endpoint. On the contrary, the endpoint may be present generically and, properly speaking, it may even not exist. Therefore, the endpoint is not an attractor, at least not an attractor in the sense in which the term is used in the theory of dynamic systems. The not-yet works as a pulling force taking everything out of itself, without, however, acting from an explicitly pre-given ending point and with a pre-established intensity. On the side of the entity, the endpoint is its *horizon*; the force is called *latent* or *latency*, as in the expression "the latency of things"; and the direction is *tendency*.

While the latency of things refers to the force driving them to acquire their true identity – to be what they will become, that is the identity of becoming – the not-yet of things is precisely this identity as seen by the entity still lacking it. Modally, the not-yet is the real possibility of the thing, what the thing can really become. "Really" here refers to the conditions that make achieving given targets possible – respectively, impossible – where possibilities are concrete, partial conditions of realization.

Realizations depend on two series of conditions: possibilities, or active powers able to change things; and potentialities or the passive capacities that things have to be transformed. Real possibility – the category of categories, as Bloch says – is partial conditioning. These partial conditions are open to the future as anticipations of open possibilities.

Categorical Groups

Bloch distinguishes different groups of categories: dimensional categories (time and space); objectivizing categories (cause, latent finality, substance); the categories of the stages of processes, their partial and provisional outcomes, including occasional pauses and "trials"; the categories of the different "sectors" or "spheres" of reality, what, after Hartmann, I call "levels of reality." To the usual understanding of levels as centered on types of beings (physical, biological, psychological, social) Bloch adds differences based on periods and epochs. Finally, the categories of the "going out of itself" in order to become itself should be considered. This group includes the categories of the not-yet, latency, and tendency.

As regards the dimensional category of time, the innermost structure of time is given by the series of its "nows," where each now is unique and unrepeatable. For Bloch, the pure now is the most obscure moment, the moment that is so close to the entity to be literally invisible. In the same sense in which the blind area of the eye is what makes vision possible, the nows are what make the real world possible, the constitutive condition of its existence. Processual entities that are internally incomplete must go outside the now. The not-yet of the now works as its open context, enlightening the now to itself. Tendency and latency are the two modes of the openness toward the not-yet. Determinants arise from the process of going outside things-in-the-now, starting from the positional determinations of succession and contiguity.

Bloch's now is not the present. The now does not last, while the present lasts for a while. The present is more than an instantaneous now, because it includes the pasts from which it derives and the futures in which it enters. Moreover, presents can have different durations. As Bloch explicitly says, there is no univocal delimitation of the present. Entire years and even decades have been counted as presents.

The outward unfolding of things is centered on the process of becoming, not on its already realized outcomes. The new emerges in the now into the present; the present then is creative, it is the open frame where the new may unfold.

On the contrary, the past is closed, it has become. As customary as it is, this description of the past is far from being complete. Presents have their futures, both as components of the presents themselves and as subsequent generated presents. When presents fall into pasts, the futures intertwined with them fall into the past as well. Memories of the futures locked into past presents can still ring out in subsequent presents. Past presents include sold off futures, mute futures, and futures that still have a voice. Antiquity for the Renaissance was less "closed" than antiquity for the Middle Ages. The productive nexus between the present era and a previous era is always a nexus that includes the future that was embedded in the past era. In this sense, even archaic archetypes may continue to be productive, perhaps as fragments needing later integrations.

It results from these remarks that the logic of "before" and "after" does not capture time. Time is more than a linear series of chronometric moments. Apart from the nexuses linking past futures to present futures, temporalities also depend on the events in them, and these events are organized in levels of reality and their multifarious relations.

On distinguishing chronometric time and real time, the possibility arises of delays or accelerations of the latter with respect to the former. The real time of living or social beings may show their backwardness, their being left behind by the clock of biological or social history; or it can show their forwardness, their capacity to open new avenues and act as precursors (Poli 2017c).

Causality for Bloch is more than connection between completely determined events. The most interesting cases are those of causal nexuses in which one can intervene and thereby produce new effects. According to Hartmann's ontological terminology, this is a case of "overforming." While we cannot modify the laws of physics, we can exploit them for our purposes (e.g., building a bridge): physical causal determinations are overformed by our intentional determinations.

To be noted is that, together with Hartmann, Bloch understands causality as a creative process (Poli 2012).

Causes should not be confused with conditions. The latter have different degrees of maturation, while the former do not. Something can be more or less conditioned. The claim of something that is more or less caused makes no sense. Partial conditioning makes sense; partial causation does not.

Bloch distinguishes among law, tendency, and latency. Law is the realm of repetition; where law dominates, novelties are lacking. By contrast, tendency is openness to the new; it is the source of ontological creativity. Tendencies need subjective interventions. An interesting generalization of Bloch's framework includes the idea of tendency as intervention by other levels of reality: that is, overformation of the lower levels by the higher ones. In this case, the interplay between law and tendency becomes the difference between determining processes working within a given level of reality and determining processes among levels of reality (on levels of reality see (Poli 2001, 2006a, 2007).

Finally, latency is the ground of tendency. The unfolding whole, the whole in movement, the whole together with its tendency, includes latency as the ground from which tendency arises. According to Bloch, latents are not entities; even less are they closed and hidden factors or components, things that need to be unpacked; nor is a latent a hidden force sleeping on a tensed spring that could be awakened by releasing the spring.

Latency is the way in which the still nonexistent aim manifests itself in the tendency. It is anticipation of the endpoint.

Horizon and Front

On subjecting the openness of entities to closer scrutiny, further categories emerge, the most important being those of horizon and front.

As we have seen, everything real, being temporal, tends toward something else. The concept of *horizon* – as opposed to the concept of boundary used to distinguish a system from its environment – suits our purpose precisely. As Luhmann notes, "the essential characteristics of an horizon is that we can never touch it, never get at it, never surpass it, but that in spite of that, it contributes to the definition of the situation" (Luhmann 1976).

The entity's horizon delimits that fragment of the space of possibilities whose conditions are maturing. As its conditions mature, the entity's horizon moves ahead. Without horizons, entities are dead. They may still continue along their trajectories, but no real novelty can ever appear: everything is forever fixed. Horizons have fronts – "areas" where novelties appear. The front is the growing, maturing, changing section of the horizon.

Affects

Turning to psychological determinants, Bloch distinguishes different kinds of affects, notably "completed" and "virtual" ones. Completed affects have a limited cognitive component and include envy, greed, and reverence. Virtual affects, on the other hand, have wide cognitive aspects and include fear, hope, and faith. The anticipatory component of virtual affects is incomparably wider than the anticipatory component of completed affects. The latter refer to a closed or inauthentic future – that is, a future without real novelties. Virtual affects refer instead to open or authentic futures, the futures of the not-yet.

The not-yet-conscious heads toward something new that is springing up. It has nothing to do with memory or something already met and subsequently forgotten. Anticipation molds both hope and fear. Furthermore, as already pointed out, a proper understanding of anticipation requires an ontology of the not-yet (Poli 2006b). In its turn, this requires an understanding of being as something that is categorically open and dynamic. Only at this point does hope become a principle truly categorizing the human condition.

Nightdreams and Daydreams

To be noted is Bloch's emphasis on the sharp contrast between nightdreams and daydreams. While the former presuppose a weakening of the ego and repeat, albeit in an often unrecognizable manner, what has already happened, the latter are dreams of a better life. Differently from nightdreams, daydreams produce images and projects that may require further elaboration more than interpretation. The range of daydreams is very wide and may include dreams based on crude, deviant, or paralyzing images, as well as dreams that may be as enabling as a scientific discovery or an art product. However, the typical feature of daydreams – as opposed to nightdreams – is that they usually are not oppressive. Moreover, as already mentioned, the ego in daydreams is weakened much less than it is in nightdreams.

Under the name of "mind-wanderings" and without any awareness of the analysis developed by Bloch, daydreams have been subjected to careful experimental research. For a recent contribution, see, e.g., Stawarczyk et al. (2013). Interestingly, daydreaming is a quite frequent phenomenon and may represent from 20 to 50 percent of our daily thinking time (Kane et al. 2007). Unfortunately, however, "there is surprisingly little data on the content and phenomenological features of mind-wandering episodes" (Stawarczyk et al. 2013). What is known is that "most mind-wandering episodes are oriented toward the future" (Smallwood et al. 2009; Stawarczyk et al. 2011). Apparently, "an important function of mind-wandering is to enable the anticipation and planning of personally relevant future goals" (Stawarczyk et al. 2011, 2013; Baird et al. 2011). While the language is obviously different from Bloch's expressionist style, and the theoretical aims are patently very different as well, what I see is the beginning of a preliminary experimental confirmation of some of the intuitions underlying Bloch's position (Poli 2017b).

Authentic and Nonauthentic Futures

Futures can either be authentic or nonauthentic. Nonauthentic futures are repetitive futures, futures without novelties. Moreover, nonauthentic futures come to us as schemata, while authentic futures are embedded in dawning, unfolding events.

One of the major tasks of an ontology of the future is to provide guidance for distinguishing genuine from not genuine futures, open from closed, unadulterated from deceptive, adulterated futures. The latter include features such as repetitive, forecast, macrotrend, risk. The former include novelty, foresight, visioning, and uncertainty. Within the two lists, terms are counterpoints to one another: repetition against novelty, forecast against foresight, macrotrend against visioning, and risk against uncertainty. This table of oppositions underlines in particular two of my other contributions to this handbook (Furlanetto and Poli 2017; Poli 2017a).

Concrete Utopias

The main aim of Bloch's *Principle of Hope* is to develop the idea of "concrete utopia." A utopia is said to be concrete when it is able to anticipate the not-yet-conscious and to use it within the not-yet-become that is latent in the ongoing historical processes. Interestingly, however, Bloch turns the idea of utopia from a millennial type change to a component of daily life. In this regard, Appadurai notes that "Ernst Bloch's grand work on hope marked a transition in European social thought from a preoccupation with utopias, radical revolution, and millennial change to more nuanced engagements with hope as a feature of quotidian social life and with the conditions for its cultivation" (Appadurai 2013). In other words, Bloch distinguishes between utopia as focused on the endpoint and utopia as focused on everyday life, especially its humblest, tiniest aspects – which is a way of saying that the roots of the future are in the present, if only we learn to see them.

References

Appadurai, A. (2013). *The future as cultural fact*. London: Verso.

Baird, B., Smallwood, J., & Schooler, J. W. (2011). Back to the future: Autobiographical planning and the functionality of mind-wandering. *Consciousness and Cognition, 20*, 1604–1611.

Bloch, E. (1963). *Tuebinger Einleitung in die Philosophie*. Berlin: Suhrkamp Verlag.

Bloch, E. (1970). *A philosophy of the future*. New York: Herder and Herder.

Bloch, E. (1980). *Experimentum mundi*. Brescia: Queriniana.

Bloch, E. (1995). *The principle of hope*. Cambridge, MA: The MIT Press.

Furlanetto, A., & Poli, R. (2017). ARM-anticipatory risk management. In R. Poli (Ed.), *Handbook of anticipation*. New York: Springer.

Kane, M. J., Brown, L. H., McVay, J. C., Silvia, P. J., Myin-Germeys, I., & Kwapil, T. R. (2007). For whom the mind wanders, and when: An experience-sampling study of working memory and executive control in daily life. *Psychological Science, 18*, 614–621.

Louie, A. H., & Poli, R. (2017). Complex systems. In R. Poli (Ed.), *Handbook of anticipation*. New York: Springer.

Luhmann, N. (1976). The future cannot begin: Temporal structures in modern society. *Social Research, 43*, 130–152.

Poli, R. (2001). The basic problem of the theory of levels of reality. *Axiomathes, 12*(3–4), 261–283.

Poli, R. (2006a). Levels of reality and the psychological stratum. *Revue Internationale de Philosophie, 61*(2), 163–180.

Poli, R. (2006b). The ontology of what is not there. In J. Malinowski & A. Pietruszczak (Eds.), *Essays in logic and ontology* (pp. 73–80). Amsterdam: Rodopi.

Poli, R. (2007). Three obstructions: Forms of causation, chronotopoids, and levels of reality. *Axiomathes, 17*(1), 1–18.

Poli, R. (2009). A glimpse into the sphere of ideal being: The ontological status of values. In B. Centi & W. Huemer (Eds.), *Values and ontology: Problems and perspectives* (pp. 155–170). Heusenstamm: Ontos Verlag.

Poli, R. (2010a). An introduction to the ontology of anticipation. *Futures, 42*(7), 769–776.

Poli, R. (2010b). Ontology: The categorial stance. In R. Poli & J. Seibt (Eds.), *Theory and application of ontology. Vol 1: Philosophical perspectives* (Vol. 1, pp. 1–22). Berlin: Springer.

Poli, R. (2011a). Ontological categories, latents and the irrational. In J. Cumpa & E. Tegtmeier (Eds.), *Ontological categories* (pp. 153–163). Heusenhamm: Ontos Verlag.

Poli, R. (2011b). Step toward an explicit ontology of the future. *Journal of Future Studies, 16*(1), 67–78.

Poli, R. (2012). Nicolai Hartmann. In E. N. Zalta (Ed.), *The stanford encyclopedia of philosophy*, Stanford, Stanford University, (Fall 2012 Edition).

Poli, R. (2013). Overcoming divides. *On the Horizon, 21*(1), 3–14.

Poli, R. (2017a). Introducing anticipation. In R. Poli (Ed.), *Handbook of anticipation*. New York: Springer.

Poli, R. (2017b). *Introduction to anticipation studies*. Dordrecht: Springer.

Poli, R. (2017c). Social time as a multidimensional category. *World Futures Review, 9*(1), 19–25.

Poli, R. (2017d). Time and temporality. In R. Poli (Ed.), *Handbook of anticipation*. New York: Springer.

Popper, K. R. (1990). *A world of propensities*. Bristol: Thoemmes.

Smallwood, J., Nind, L., & O'Connor, R. C. (2009). When is your head at? An exploration of the factors associated with the temporal focus of the wandering mind. *Consciousness and Cognition, 18*, 118–125.

Stawarczyk, D., Majerus, S., Maj, M., Van Der Linden, M., & D'Argembeau, A. (2011). Mind-wandering: Phenomenology and function as assessed with a novel experience sampling method. *Acta Psychologica, 136*, 370–381.

Stawarczyk, D., Cassol, H., & D'Augembeau, A. (2013). Phenomenology of future-oriented mind-wandering. *Frontiers in Psychology, 4*, 425.

Tuomi, I. (2017). Ontological expansion. In R. Poli (Ed.), *Handbook of anticipation*. New York: Springer.

Part II

Understanding Anticipation

Backward Causation

7

Jan Faye

Contents

Abstract

The ability to anticipate the future is of great benefit to any organism. Whenever such a foreseeing takes place, it typically happens because an organism has been able to learn about some regularity in the past and then uses this information to expect some happenings in the future. Modern human beings have perfected this capacity far beyond any other animal by getting to know the laws by which nature operates. But it is still based on past experience that even human beings are able to say something about the future. So every form of anticipation of the future relies on inductive reasoning based on knowledge of causal processes in the past. Both these processes and the processes by which we learn to anticipate the future are common in the sense that it is always an earlier cause that brings about a later

J. Faye (✉)

Department of Media, Cognition and Communication, University of Copenhagen, Copenhagen, Denmark

e-mail: faye@hum.ku.dk

© Springer Nature Switzerland AG 2019   121

R. Poli (ed.), *Handbook of Anticipation*,

https://doi.org/10.1007/978-3-319-91554-8_50

effect. The ability to anticipate depends on the fact that our cognitive faculties only work on information that stems from the past. Had it been possible for us to receive reliable information about the future, the ability of anticipation might not have existed or might have been less faulty than it sometimes is.

Keywords
Anticipation · Backward causation · Causation · Time

Anticipation concerns with our cognitive capacities to penetrade into the future, but it would be a mistake to believe that some actual forms of anticipation operate based on backward causation. The present entry argues that backward causation is a coherent concept and explores the consequences this notion has for our understanding of time and causation. But it also concludes that no empirical evidence seems to support the existence of processes going backward in time.

It is therefore understandable that people have speculated about the possibility of having direct knowledge of the future. If one could have access to the future, we might be able to know what is going to happen instead of predicting what is going to happen. Throughout history soothsayers, shamans, and other psychic people have claimed that they were able to see directly into the future. In modern time the so-called psychic research has maintained that such examples of foreknowledge or precognition are genuine enough and claim that experiments show that such phenomena really exist. Regardless of the truth of these claims, which has not been proven to most scientists' satisfaction, their truth would require both that the future is real so that we could get information about it and that this information could be handed down to us in an accessible way. If space and time are four dimensional that would be by backward causation.

Aristotle separated four types of causes (explanations): (1) the material cause being that out of which things are made, (2) the formal cause being the account of what kind of structure a thing has, (3) the efficient cause being that which is the main source of making changes in the world, and (4) the final cause being the end by which a thing is done (Aristotle 1955). Today when thinking of normal causation, we usually identify it with Aristotle's efficient cause. The cause is what changes things, and this change is then the effect of the cause. Moreover, we take the cause to be earlier than its effect. So the Aristotelian efficient cause corresponds to forward causation. It might therefore be tempting to identify the Aristotelian final cause with backward causation. But a final cause should not be considered the same as a backward cause.

A final cause, if we accept its existence, may mean different things. Originally it refers to the purpose of an action that guides or draws the action toward fulfilling that very purpose. In a modern context, one may either think of a final cause as a form of attractor or a form of energetic equilibrium or take it to be an intentional cause of action. In the first case, the thinking refers to a principle of nature according to which a physical system always, whenever possible, moves toward an internal state in which it occupies minimal energy. The second case involves people's ability to imagine their own and others' wants and then intentionally put their action behind those wishes to realize the aims of the wishes. However, none of these suggested cases of final causes fit the notion of backward causation since their causal development takes place forward in time.

The above remarks indicate that the concept of backward causation as used here refers to the inverse order of some possible chains of cause and effect in time. This is how the concept is understood in physics, metaphysics, and philosophy of science. In other contexts one may find expressions such as "backward loop" and "retroaction," and perhaps even "backward causation," but in each of these cases, the meaning is that in complex systems, some parts of the system influence each other via feedback mechanisms. In all of those kinds of circuit processes of causes and effects, the temporal order of cause and effect is the same.

If anything, backward causation corresponds to the Aristotelian efficient cause reversed in time. The main idea is simply that the only conceptual difference between forward and backward causation is the direction of the causal efficacy in time. In a forward situation, the efficiency passes from the past to the future, whereas in a backward situation, it goes from the future to the past. As long as one regard backward causation as something that may characterize information-generating processes in a hypothetical world different from the actual world, then the conceptual conflict with what else we believe about time and causation would not be very challenging. The real task comes from the idea that backward causation could exist alongside forward causation. So what would it take for backward causation to be possible in a world like ours?

We may divide the conceptual task to be solved into two sets of questions: one concerning the nature of time and the other specifically related to causation itself. David Hume famously defined the cause as that event in a general regularity between two events that is earlier than the other. It is clear, however, that such a definition excludes that it makes sense to talk about the causal direction being opposite of what it normally is. Backward causation is possible only if this analytic connection between time and causation is relinquished. Making sense of backward causation requires that the direction of causation is definable independently of the direction of time.

The Nature of Time

Time has occupied the human mind ever since the dawn of mankind. We are born, grow up, and become older and die, and we experience everything around us constantly changing, like ourselves. We also believe that the world does not stop existing when we have passed away just like we know that it existed before we were born. But is time more than these restless changes, and why is our experience limited to what is present? These are hard questions. Already Saint Augustine acknowledged that time is one of the enigmas of our life that is difficult to grasp. He famously wrote: "What then is time? If no one asks me, I know what it is. If I wish to explain it to him who asks, I do not know" (Augustine 2006). To this day, philosophers and scientists attempt to understand what time is; however, due to the non-experiential nature of such questions, little agreement can be found among them.

Presentism

In the philosophical discussion figures three basic theories about how we should understand time. Only one of them is consistent with a notion of backward causation. The first view, called *presentism*, is sometimes associated with common sense. It holds that only present events exist. Past events have been, but exist no longer. Future events do not yet exist; they are only real once they become present. Thus present events are real until they pass away and become unreal. Some also associate this view with the passage of time. Events are real so far as they occur now, but which moment of time that is now constantly changes. Therefore which events that are real and which are not constantly change, too. This is the passage of time. The common argument for such a shifting now is an appeal to our immediate experience, which changes all the time. We have no perceptual experience of what we did yesterday and no perceptual experience of what we are going to do tomorrow. We only have experiences of what happens now.

It is clear that as part of her presumptions, the presentist believes that no future events can cause a present event. If future events are not real, and have never been real, they cannot initiate anything that occurs now. The problem for the present, however, is that she may fall victim to a similar objection with respect to forward causation. How can a past event initiate anything that occurs now if past events, just like future events, do not exist? The reply that it once existed seems not acceptable because the fact of the matter seems to be that causation in both cases would be a relation between a real and an unreal event.

For the presentist the distinction between the past, the present, and the future is absolute and universal. For instance, if an event occurs now, it is neither past nor future. Innocent as the statement may seem, it nevertheless hides a potentially devastating thread. More than 100 years ago, the British philosopher John McTaggart proposed an argument that apparently undermines presentism. He even argued that more than presentism was at stake. It was time itself that could be shown to be unreal (McTaggart 1908). McTaggart realized that we can represent the temporal order of moments with the help of two sets of predicates. One way of ordering the moments, which he called the A-series, is carried out by using predicates like "is present," "is past," or "is future," where each of these predicates can be expressed by verbs and their various tempi in the natural languages. The other way of representing them, which he named the B-series, is done with the help of the predicates "is earlier than," "simultaneous with," and "later than" with respect to the temporal dating of the moments. The presentist position can only be stated in the A-series terms, but McTaggart also believed that the description of time without them would be no description at all.

His argument for the unreality of time goes like this: (1) The A-series is essential for time; (2) the reality of time requires the reality of the A-series; and (3) the A-series is inconsistent. Therefore (4) time cannot be real (because something inconsistent cannot exist). No philosopher would now accept McTaggert's argument, but for different reasons. Presentists may accept (1) and (2) but would deny (3). Non-presentists would accept (3) as true but claim that (1) is false. They do not believe, as McTaggert did, that the A-series is necessary for having real change. They would argue that real change can take place within the B-series.

As mentioned, most non-presentists think that McTaggert had an important insight when he argued that time in the form of the A-series is inconsistent. So what was his argument for premise (3)? Here is how I understand his argument: He tells us that "the characteristics of the A series are mutually incompatible and yet all true of every term" (page 470). In other words, the same moment is in the future, in the present, and in the past. Nonetheless being future, being present, and being past are incompatible features. Every moment must be characterized by one or the other, but no moment can be characterized by more than one of them. In spite of this, we must say that every moment has all features. Therefore we have a contradiction. The inconsistency arises because of our understanding of time in terms of the A-series takes being future, being present, or being past to be inherent properties of the moments (and therefore of the events occurring at these moments). We can escape the conclusion only if we relate the attribution of being future, present, and past in relation to another moment. This particular moment is now present; it was shortly before in the future and will be shortly afterward in the past. So this moment is in the future, in the present, or in the past with respect to another moment which happens now. This means that we have to introduce another A-series to which the first one can relate.

The proposal solves the problem with the internal inconsistency by seeing the transitory properties like being future, being present, and being past in relation to other times and not as in relation to themselves. This move demands a further temporal ordering. The new one also has to be an A-series involving the same tensed facts. With respect to this A-series, any moment must have all the new A-series properties. This generates a new inconsistency. In order to escape that situation, we must introduce an even further A-series. The conclusion is that the contradiction cannot be solved because the position of a moment in an A-series cannot be relativized within the A-series itself. Tensed facts are due to immanent features of time itself and cannot be relativized. If we attempt to relativize them in terms of a new A-series, we run into an infinite regress. We either have to accept the inconsistency or the infinite regress. In recent time many non-presentists have cited this argument in support of their own position that, although time is real, tensed facts are not real. The A-series does not represent time.

Possibilism

The second view about the nature of time, *possibilism* or *the growing block universe*, doesn't face the same problems. The proponent of this view holds that the past is just as real as the present. It is only the future that is in its own making and therefore not yet real. We can, for instance, change the future but cannot change the past. The future consists of possibilities, some of which will be actualized the moment they become present. In this way the universe adds new events to its existence all the time. There are several arguments in favor of such a theory.

One argument points to the fact that we are able to perceive past events. In old days nobody knew anything about the velocity of light, so people believed that a perceived event took place exactly at the time it was perceived to happen. But today we know that celestial events far away from the Earth do not occur at the time of their observation. Apparently we are able to perceive long-gone events if these events do not exist in our vicinity. Another argument that most people agree upon is that present sentences about the past are always true or false just like present sentences about the present. If I say that my daughter was at scout camp yesterday or she is there right now, most people will insist that I say something which is either true or false. But this is possible only if there exists something that makes these statements true or false. The past and the present have to be real.

By contrast we have present sentences about future events. Here many people would hesitate since they believe that free will demands that at least not every present sentence about the future is true or false. If somebody has not yet made up his mind whether or not he will visit a friend tomorrow, nothing exists today that can make it either true or false that this person is going to see a friend tomorrow. Moreover, nobody has observed future events. Since radiation of light, like other causal processes, moves forward in time, and nothing else gives us immediate access to the future, the possibilitist or adherent of the growing universe view concludes that nothing exists in the future that could provide us with such an epistemic access.

Possibilism can easily account for forward causation. It consists of a relation between two real events. But backward causation is an incoherent notion according to this theory. No future event is yet real or determinate, and no present and determinate event can stand in a causal relation to something that is not real or determinate. Possibilism seems also to be able to explain real change because assuming that it not yet determinate what the future will be and that it is determinate what the present and the past are, then real change happens the very moment some possibilities become actualized in the present.

Eternalism

The only conceptual framework that can incorporate the idea that the future may affect the present is the third view called *eternalism*. It holds that all events regardless of when they occur are real. There is no substantial difference between the past, the present, and the future. Everything is on par with everything else. Usually the eternalist argues that being past, present, or future is not a quality of the events themselves. These predicates do not even signify modes of existence. Instead they express our temporal relations to the items we are talking about. If these items occur earlier than the statements by which we mention them, we consider them to be past, and if they occur simultaneously with such statements, we regard them to be present, and finally, if they occur later than such statements, we take them to be future.

It is not part of the eternalist view that future events already exist, even though they occur tenselessly at a later time. An event that occurs tenselessly at a later time does not occur now, and therefore it makes no sense to say that it already occurs.

Precisely the same holds with respect to past events. Unless one is inconsistent, nobody would say that past events, which occur tenselessly at an earlier time, still exist now. Believing that present statements about the past are true or false, because something in the past makes them true or false, does not imply a belief that this truth-making state of affairs has to exist now. In support both the possibilist and the eternalist may point to the fact that a statement about some spatial distant events is true or false irrespective of the truth-making fact does not exist right there where the statement is made.

The eternalist understanding of time is that of the three views, that is furthest away from common sense. "Fair enough," one might say since it is also the only view that permits backward causation (which nobody has experienced). The view implies that not only statements about the past and the present but also about the futures can be true or false. The implication seems to indicate that people are unable to change decisions if it is already true that what they are going to decide tomorrow. If the future is determinate, we cannot just change it. In fact the objection seems to be much more threatening for the eternalist than merely challenging our free will. If backward causation were possible, it would require that the present events could cause changes in the past. Many will think of such a consequence as unacceptable.

This raises an obvious riddle: How is it possible for the eternalist to consistently claim that both the past and the future are determinate and at the same time maintain that backward causation as well as free will is possible within such a conceptual framework? The eternalist's answer comes in two steps. First, she accepts that we cannot change the past, or the future, but will argue that we may have the ability to influence the past to be what it was as we have the ability to influence the future to be what it is going to be. Second, she does not need to deny human free will. Because if it is possible to influence the future to be what it is going to be, it is human decisions that causally determine human actions and the result of these actions. Thus, the position of the eternalist is not internally inconsistent in any lethal way.

But what are the arguments in support of eternalism? Here the eternalist most often draws on the special theory of relativity put forward by Albert Einstein in 1905. The theory is based to two fundamental principles: (1) the velocity of light is the same for all observers regardless of the velocity of the light source, and (2) the laws of nature should be similar to all observers regardless of whether they are at rest or moving with a constant velocity. In addition, Einstein chose to define simultaneity in terms of the exchange of information by light signals. Such a choice was based on a reasonable physical requirement that synchronization of clocks between distant observers had to rely on some physical medium and could not take place merely in our thoughts. And since the velocity light in vacuum is constant, and it is also the maximal velocity any signal can have, it is not only a reasonable but also the only compelling choice. The consequence is that there is no absolute simultaneity. Whether or not two events occur at the same time depends on the observer's velocity in case these two events are not causally connectable. Hence, with no absolute simultaneity, there can be no absolute now.

One could indeed attempt to separate the relativistic concept of simultaneity and a notion of a now. But which possible criteria could provide us with such a separation?

If we say that our present awareness is actually present because what it is aware of occurs now, how then can we distinguish between our present awareness from the one we have at other times, and which is present at these other times? Each and every time a new awareness occurs, it is always present due to the fact that it occurs at a particular now. But every time the now is the same; in fact we cannot use it to distinguish one experience from another. Furthermore how can we decide whether your present awareness and my present awareness are occurring at the same now? Apparently, the only criterion we have is to say that a particular awareness A is present at the particular time it occurs, and another particular awareness that occurs at any given time is not present if it is not simultaneous with A. An experience is by definition present whenever one is aware of it. Think of a present experience A and a present experience B. Both experiences have the same content. What distinguishes them is that nobody can have them at the same time, that is, they are not simultaneous with one another. So we can only define the now in terms of simultaneity of awareness. Given this definition we can easily determine what it means for two different observers to be present at the same time and what it means for two experiences of the same observer not to be present at the same time.

The special theory of relativity allows different observers to see causally inconnectable events in a different temporal order. Assume Alice and Bob observe two different events P and Q that cannot be connected by any light signal. Then it follows that Alice may experience P before Q, whereas Bob, who is an observer in motion in relation to Alice, will see them in the reverse order so that Q occurs before P. So when Alice judges P to be past and Q to be present measured with respect to her clock, Bob might consider Q to be in the past, while P is still in the future measured according to his clock. The distinction between the past, the present, and the future is no longer universal but varies according to the velocity of the observer. This consequence is not a theoretical fluke of relativity but an observable prediction that has been confirmed by experiments.

With scientific support in his baggage, the eternalist seems to be vindicated in his claim that the future is just as real as the present and the past. The conceptual framework of the eternalist has the necessary temporal means to deal with backward causation. But backward causation is in no way a quotidian phenomenon. This fact cries out for an explanation. In response some philosophers argue that backward causation in itself is not a coherent concept, and we cannot experience what is incoherent; other will argue that it is, but that it does not correspond to anything real. They see it like our concept of a unicorn which does not correspond to a real animal. Finally there are those who believe that the concept is coherent, and it might be empirically possible to discover cases of backward causation.

Causation

Before one can address any question about backward causation, it is important to know what causation is. According to Hume causation is the regularity between events. If the same kind of event is always followed by another kind of events, there exists a causal connection between these two types of events. Hume was occupied with what we can immediately experience, so he never asked himself about the possibility of backward causation. He therefore defined the cause as the event that precedes the other, which is the effect (Hume 1748[2000]). Later many philosophers have maintained that there is more to causation than a mere regularity. All regularities could be accidental if a cause is not responsible for its effect by bringing about this event. So causality is a modal notion, they would say, which means the causal relation has to be understood in terms of necessity and counterfactuals. The effect does not only follow the cause, the cause is necessary for the effect to occur. This necessity can then be cashed out by saying that had the cause not occurred, the effect would not have occurred. The suggestion is that an analysis along these lines better enables us to understand causation than Hume's idea of regularity.

Hume was not entirely resistant to this kind of argument. But he believed that these modal features were a result of our habits of thinking that humans force onto their experience. Immanuel Kant picked up Hume's idea by making causation into one of the category of understanding. Kant regarded these categories as being a priori concepts in virtue of which we understand nature (Kant 1787[2007]). Whenever we get to experience something, say a particular instance of causation, our mind applies the category of causation on the sense impressions. However, it is of no great significance for our understanding of backward causation that several modern philosophers oppose Hume and Kant by holding that the characteristics of causation are not due to the manner in which we grasp our sense impressions but come from a full comprehension of how the modal structures of the world really is. The nature of causation is not a vital issue. What is important is that we can pin down some criteria which can be used to differentiate the cause from its effect. Only if we can point to some robust criteria that are recognizable to everyone can we decide that backward causation is a coherent notion.

The Bilking Argument

The wanted criteria are to be found in our ability to manipulate and intervene in a causal process. In virtue of our action, we can bring about a certain effect by producing its cause. Actions themselves may be regarded as causes. Whatever one thinks of actions as causing the action itself can give rise to a cause that generates an effect. I put some fertilizer on my lawn to improve the growth of the grass. If we know the causal relation between two types of events, we can use this knowledge to produce new events. But apart from using the cause to produce the effect, we can also intervene in the causal relation. If I had abstained from putting fertilizer on my lawn, it would have had no effect on the grass. So if I prevent a cause from happening, I also prevent the effect from happening. However, it is also possible to intervene in the causal relationship, after the alleged cause has occurred, and thereby hinder the expected effect from occurring. These various actions of manipulation give us knowledge of what counts as the cause and the effect in a causal relationship.

Most people will undoubtedly accept that these are the operational criteria by which we can determine whether or not an observed regularity conceals a causal connection. The knowledge of causation does not arise from perception alone but in combination with our ability to interact with our surroundings. Some philosophers have considered this to be fatal for any coherent understanding of backward causation.

The modern philosophical discussion of backward causation began in the middle of 1950s with an exchange of papers between the two British philosophers Michael Dummett and Antony Flew. The former was open for such a possibility whereas the latter was utterly against (Dummett 1954; Flew 1954). A couple of years later, the British-American philosopher Max Back raised his skepticism in the form of a challenge that goes under the name *the bilking argument* (Black 1956). Imagine, Black said, that E occurs earlier than C and that C purportedly causes E. In such a situation, it is possible to intervene in the series of events after E has occurred, but before C is expected to take place such that C is prevented from happening. Thus we would have a situation in which E is not caused by C and therefore cannot be an example of backward causation after all. Bilking the future cause could in principle take place each time we were facing a putative example of backward causation. Therefore Black believed that our ability to bilk a future cause jeopardized the whole conception of backward causation.

With respect to forward causation, nothing corresponds to the bilking argument. In situations of normal, forward causation, one can, knowing the appropriate laws of nature, prevent a particular cause from happening with the result that its alleged effect would not happen either. Also one can intervene into the processes after the purported cause has occurred with the result that the purported effect will not occur, but we cannot intervene after the effect occurs. The reason is that after one knows that the effect has happened, one does know that the cause must have happened, and nobody can change the past. A parallel case to backward causation is possible only if we think of someone who has the same knowledge of the future as we have of the past. However, such a precognition must involve backward causation. But since the bilking argument is a challenge to the very conception of backward causality, introducing foreknowledge in one's response cannot be permissible as a counterargument.

Even so, several responses to the bilking argument are available (Faye 1989). First we have the *intervention-is-not-actually-possible* argument: if it is a fact that a particular future cause C is what brings about an earlier effect E, then it is impossible for anything to intervene. Even if we assume that backward causation is open for direct human manipulation, we must in this particular case fail in all of our attempts to interfere with C. For whatever reason we have to miss, if it is a fact that C causes E, we cannot intervene because that would be equivalent to changing the future. The person who wants to intervene might be distracted, become ill, suffer from an accident, fall death, etc. If C actually causes E, nothing can stop that event from doing so. Indeed in those circumstances, in which somebody is successful in preventing C, it is obvious that E cannot be caused by C. Still, if E occurs it must be because E is either determined by another future cause C^* (and therefore would have been overdetermined if *C* had not been prevented from occurring) or alternatively determined by an earlier cause *C***. Such an answer is not in any way inaccurate but it is not very satisfactory.

Behind the bilking argument lies the assumption that humans are able to intervene after the alleged effect has happened. Such a capability may sometimes fail, but it cannot always fail, because this would implicate that we have no such capacity. In most situations we have to be able to interact with the processes after we have identified the alleged effect. This is what having a capacity means. So what does that tell us? It tells us, one might argue, that if backward causation is real, we do not have the ability to intervene in that kind of causal processes. Each time somebody precludes a purported future cause from happening, that person is actually not interacting with backward causation. There cannot be this kind of processes to act on if no future cause exists, so it must be an illusion that we have the ability to have influence on them. This arises a completely new problem, namely, how we can establish backward causation if not by intervention, since our operational criteria for having causal knowledge are based on intervention and manipulation.

A second response might therefore be the *intervention-is-not-physically-possible* argument. This argument is different from the one above in the sense that the first argument presupposed that human beings could physically interact with backward causal processes but sometimes were excluded from actually doing so for accidental reasons. In those situations an earlier event could not be caused by a future event. The invention-is-not-physically-possible argument assumes that it technically lies outside human control to interfere with backward causation.

Intervention and manipulation require that humans directly or indirectly can experience the events and processes that may be object for such interaction. Typically humans experience the world via their sense organs which all operate on the basis of processes that move forward in time. The same holds for our own actions. They are also causally directed toward the future and away from the past. Hence, if humans were to be able to deliberately interfere with backward causation, we must be able to identify both the present effect and the future cause in the normal perceptual way, just as our actions must be physically efficacious on the series of events that constitutes backward causation. Is this possible? It seems so but only indirectly.

In the literature on backward causation, one can sometimes meet a thought experiment called the Newcomb paradox. In fact the paradox was invented for a different purpose within decision theory, but it offers a good illustration of a possible situation in which we may discover backward causation without being directly able to interact with the backward causal link itself. But let us make the argument simple and construct a less complicated thought experiment.

Assume Bob claims that he is able to anticipate with absolute certainty what is going to happen even though he does not know how he is able to do so. Alice, on the other hand, is doubtful. Bob and Alice therefore agree to put Bob's acclaimed abilities to the test. Bob is asked to take part in the following way. Sitting in front of a computer screen, he looks, say, at ten different symbols at the computer screen. The only task for him is to make his choice about which of the ten symbols will be displayed at the screen after he had made up his mind. When his decision is taken, Bob marks the symbol on the screen and presses a bottom indicating that he has made his guess. This activates the internal parts of the computer to run a random-number-generator program, and depending on which number is generated, a particular symbol is displayed at the screen two seconds after Bob's choice. In order to gain robust statistical data, Alice and Bob must repeat the experiment over and over again. Now, assume that much to her surprise, Alice discovers that each time Bob has selected a symbol, his choice exactly corresponds with the symbol that is randomly picked afterward by the computer. As Bob claimed he is able to anticipate the future 100%.

If this thought experiment had been a real scientific test, Alice is allowed, based on the statistics of the experiment, to draw the conclusion that there is something in the world that gives Bob access to the future. Everything she and Bob can control is within the range of the normal senses. They can see the symbols, he can mark his choice on the screen, and they can visually register the succeeding symbol at the screen. Also the internal mechanisms of the computer run forward in time. It is only the assumed process going backward in time from the one picked-up symbol at the screen and Bob's previous choice that they don't have direct epistemic access to. That there is such a process is what the random number generator should guarantee, but at the same, it is also the only process that is out of Alice and Bob's physical control.

The upshot seems to be that it is possible for us to establish the existence of backward causation regardless of whether we have any physical means to get our hands on the series of events between the two for us perceptual events X and Y such as Bob's choice and the appearance of a symbol at the screen. If there is a perfect correlation between X and Y, and X and Y are not correlated because of forward causation (the random number generator excludes that), it is rational to assume that the correlation appears because some backward causation is involved. Indeed, in most sciences, less than a perfect correlation will suffice as significant to establish a correlation that is not regarded accidental.

Note also that it is possible to manipulate X and Y indirectly in virtue of normal actions. Alice may attempt to fool Bob by sometimes letting the random number generator abstain from selecting a symbol. Without Y, and if Y is truly the cause of X, Bob must at these occasions pass on his choice of any symbol. This brings us back to the first response to the bilking argument because it is not completely outside of Alice's range to bilk Bob's predictions.

Imagine Alice deciding to install into her computer a program that sometimes jams the computer a second after Bob is expected to have made his choice of a symbol. What will she observe? A little handful of possible scenarios crops up: (1) If Alice earlier has tested Bob rigorously and found that until now he has predicted with accuracy which symbol will be displayed subsequently at the computer screen, she will observe under the new circumstances no response from Bob those times the computer is about to jam. (2) If she has already before discovered that Bob's hits were highly significant but not absolutely certain, she might see under the new circumstances some responses from Bob, even though the computer is jammed shortly afterward. (3) She has tested Bob with a result as indicated (1) or (2), but surprisingly for her, Bob now begins to produce a lot of responses. Finally (4) she had never tested Bob before, but he produces a lot of responses even when the computer is jammed afterward.

The appropriate interpretation of scenario (1) and (2) proves to be that Alice cannot physically bilk a future cause in spite of her attempts to do so. If there will be no cause, there would not have been an effect. The only rational thing for Alice to conclude is therefore that Bob is able to anticipate future events, and it must involve backward causation. It is also rational for her to interpret scenario (3) such that the new circumstances, which she deliberately have created, somehow obstruct Bob's ability to foresee a future event, since he is able to do so under other circumstances. This would be a form of bilking a future cause, but because she already knows that without the bilking Bob's ability has satisfactorily been proven, she is not incoherent or irrational in insisting that this form of bilking proves nothing against backward causation. Based on the evidence of the machine bilking in the scenario (4), Alice is prima facie justified in concluding that Bob is not able to foretell the future. Scenario (4) looks very much like the situation we began to discuss in connection with Black's original bilking argument. But we can also see now that given this scenario, it can be too hasty of Alice to reject backward causation altogether. As long as she has not carried out a complete series of experiments as she did in scenario (1), (2), or (3), and the outcome of these experiments showed no correlation between Bob's answer and the succeeding symbol, she cannot rationally rule out that backward causation is possible under some circumstances.

After Black proposed his bilking argument in the attempt to show that backward causation was in conflict with our basic criteria of causal knowledge, and therefore was an incoherent concept, more sophisticated versions of the argument have been produced to exclude it from being meaningful. A more recent example has been provided by the British philosopher Hugh Mellor who is an eternalist but nevertheless believes that he can exclude backward causation a priori (Mellor 1991). To the best of my conviction, these examples fail altogether to demonstrate anything of relevance. The fundamental strategy behind the bilking argument rests on an intuitive belief we all have that we can in principle deliberately interfere with every future event. The proponent of this strategy then supplies us with a scenario in which every event has been arranged beforehand such that the arrangement rules out backward causation. What a surprise until one realizes that the proponent is fiddling with the cause of events.

A World of Paradoxes

In a world in which backward causation exists, alongside forward causation could indeed be a strange world full of paradoxes. But it would be bizarre only if we can manipulate those processes that might go backward in time. Some of the same paradoxes would appear in case we could travel in time. Suppose Alice can manipulate processes going backward in time, what then could happen if she were to attempt to effect the past? It depends on how much she knows about the past. Note that knowledge is always true beliefs. The more she knows, the less free she seems to be influencing the past, because she knows that it is impossible for her to change what has already happened. If she already knows that something happened, or something didn't happen, then why should she later deliberately make any effort in order to bring about what happened, or what didn't happen? It happened or didn't happen.

Similar considerations hold with respect to the future. The more Bob knows what is going to happen in the future, the less free he seems to be to act intentionally. In case he had full knowledge of the future, he would apparently not be motivated to act at all. However, full knowledge may include that he was actually responsible for a future event, but then the outcome of his deliberation could not be actions that did not bring about this event. To be free to act means that one is able to entertain alternatives and choose that option one believes is best in the given situation. So knowing which of the purported alternatives that actually occurred or actually will occur would restrict both Alice's and Bob's possibilities of actions. They couldn't have that kind of freedom we have if they had full knowledge about the past or the future.

That knowledge about what has happened and what is going to happen excludes freedom of action explains the so-called grandfather paradox. Alice knows that her grandfather must have lived, because she is alive, but that he does not live today. Furthermore, she knows that her grandfather sometimes in the past had killed her grandmother when her father was young. Some rumors say that her grandfather died shortly afterward and that he probably committed suicide; other rumors say that he disappeared and might still be alive. Now, assume Alice harbors a hostile attitude against her grandfather for the reason that he killed her grandmother and she therefore wishes to stop him. This implies that even if we grant Alice the physical resources to warn her grandmother or to stop her grandfather, she would not change the past. The weird thing is, however, that Alice would not be free to stop her grandfather before his dreadful deed by killing him, but she might be free to kill him afterward. So what might have been suicide was in fact she who successfully had her revenge.

Lucky for us we do not live in such a world where we have just as much knowledge of the future as we have of the past. Epistemically, the future is rather open for deliberation due to the fact that we have only little knowledge of what will happen and that we have never experienced an effect before its cause. Thus we are free to act toward the future but not toward the past. It would be extremely complicated to live in a world in which we have just as much knowledge of the future as of the past, and even more so if we had the physical resources to influence the past like we have the resources to influence the future. A world in which human cognitive abilities and capacity of action were not asymmetrically orientated in time is beyond our imagination. From this lack of conception, the conclusion does not follow that backward causation could not exist in a world in which humans exist. The inference that can be made is that if backward causation is real, (1) it cannot work on the macroscopic level of human actions and cognitive experience, or (2) it has a nature very different from those processes that constitute human actions and experiences so that humans have great difficulties of discovering their existence.

The Nature of Backward Causation

Nobody really knows for sure what backward causation would look like. Nobody really knows what kinds of processes would constitute going backward in time if such processes exist at all. Knowledge of the existence of backward causation may come from two possible sources. It could be obtained either by experience or by a theoretical account of some physical phenomena which could not be explained otherwise.

The experience of backward causation is very rare indeed, so rare that no genuine phenomenon requiring a description in opposition to familiar phenomena seems to exist. The whole complex of cognitive operations of our brain – including the physical processes by which an organism receives signals from the environment and by which the organism emits signals to the environment (action and speech) – is structured such that earlier events cause later event. This observation explains why all of our experiences are of past events and not of future events. Today the scientific consensus among psychologists and statisticians is that reliable experiments of human extrasensory perception such as precognition have not been demonstrated. More generally biology has been able to explain biological evolution in terms of natural selection and adaptation with no use of backward causation. All biological evidence points to the fact that the evolution is accidental, and the selection of some generic variations over others is not shaped by any future cause.

Turning to the basic science of the physical world, exotic speculations sometimes suggest solutions that involve backward causation. But as long as there is no experimental evidence that reveals backward causation as a real phenomenon, it is difficult to give a qualified guess about what would physically constitute backward causation. Theoretically two options seem available: (1) the causal direction of common physical processes is determined by their boundary conditions; for backward causation to be real, some very unusual sets of boundary conditions among these processes must be satisfied. (2) The causal direction of any physical process is determined by the kind of stuff or energy that takes part in the process, for instance, no common physical particles can participate in backward causation.

Examples of the first option could be the decrease of entropy in closed systems or the contraction of spherical waves. The cream and the coffee would start to separate after they have been mixed, or the outgoing waves from a stone dropped in a pond would turn around and start to shrink after having first expanded outward. For something like this to happen to a physical system, it requires that the movements of all spatially separated particles that make up such a macroscopic system instantaneously undergo a coherent coordination. Such coordination cannot be established by any known physical force. Therefore if it happens, it must happen by chance, and since the probability of that is almost zero, we never observe anything like that on the macroscopic scale. On the microscopic scale, however, among the processes of elementary particles, the probabilities of boundary conditions that lead to backward causation might be different. This remains, however, unproven.

The other option rejects the idea that backward causation has something to do with the boundary conditions. It insists that the dynamics of backward causation cannot be accomplished by ordinary matter and has looked for very strange forms of stuff. One proposal has been the so-called tachyons, hypothetical particles that always move with a velocity greater than light. If such particles existed, and no observation indicates this, they would by some observers according to the theory of relativity be seen as if they were going backward in time. Another proposal introduces particles that permanently have negative mass and energy in contrast to ordinary matter that always carries positive mass and energy. But again this is pure speculation since no one really knows whether or not a question concerning backward causation has a definite physical answer.

Conclusion

In summary, backward causation seems to be a consistent concept. Obviously, such a notion meshes with our commonsense intuition of time and causation, but during our recent history, science has often discovered that the world is not exactly how common sense lays it out. Neither the concept of time nor the concept of causation necessarily excludes the possibility that some processes could go backward in time. But one thing is that backward causation may be conceptually consistent; another thing is whether there is anything in the world that corresponds to such a notion. This is something we still have to see. Explaining human anticipation as a result of backward causation is not a real prospect.

References

Aristotle. (1955). *Physics*. The Ross-edition. Oxford: Oxford University Press.
Augustine. (2006). *Confessions*. Indianapolis: Hackett Publishing.
Black, M. (1956). Why cannot an effect precede its cause. *Analysis, 16*, 49–58.
Dummett, M. (1954). Can an effect precede its cause? *Proceedings of the Aristotelian Society, 28*, 27–44.
Faye, J. (1989). *The reality of the future*. Odense: Odense University Press.
Flew, A. (1954). Can an effect precede its cause? *Proceedings of the Aristotelian Society, 28*, 45–62.
Hume, D. (1748[2000]). *An enquiry concerning human understanding*. Oxford: Oxford University Press.
Kant, I. (1787[2007]). *The Critue of the Pure Reasons*. Translated by Norman Kemp Smith. London: Palgrave-Macmillan.
McTaggart, J. M. E. (1908). The unreality of time. *Mind, 17*(68), 457–474.
Mellor, H. (1991). Causation and the direction of time. *Erkenntnis, 35*, 191–203.

Anticipation: Some Notes

8

John Supko

Abstract

In musical discourse, the word "anticipation" can suggest two separate, yet not unrelated, analytical approaches. The first is ancient, and concerns a device of melody and its harmonic implications. The second is nascent, though already well-documented, and concerns the way the human brain, trained by a lifetime of listening, hears and interprets musical information. This chapter enlists both approaches to investigate the various ways composers, intuitively or intentionally, prepare the ear for fulfillment and deception alike. It begins with a rudimentary example of an anticipation tone, and then expands the classical notion of this phenomenon by tracing its variants in works spanning two centuries of Western music history. It concludes with a postscript that offers a vision of music's future, in which anticipation acquires new meaning and creates new challenges.

Keywords

Analysis · Anticipation tone · Artificial intelligence · Cadence · Counterpoint · David Huron · Erik Satie · Ernest Chausson · Gap-fill principle · Harmonic implication · Harmony · IRCAM · Leonard Meyer · Melody · Meter · Michael Nyman · Milton Babbitt · Mozart · Music-as-software · Music cognition · Music history · Music technology · Music theory · Non-harmonic note · Ornament · Philip Glass · Score following · Schoenberg · Schumann

Among the admirable features of Ernest Chausson's music recommended by Jean Gallois in his New Grove entry for the composer are:

J. Supko (✉)
Department of Music, Duke University, Durham, NC, USA
e-mail: john.supko@duke.edu

© Springer Nature Switzerland AG 2019
R. Poli (ed.), *Handbook of Anticipation*,
https://doi.org/10.1007/978-3-319-91554-8_47

well-constructed three- and four-note chords, remote but effective modulations that turn
easily about the 5th degree either chromatically or enharmonically, grace notes, appoggiaturas, anticipations, even certain rhythms (crotchet + triplet) and 7th chords that became the
composer's hallmark, as well as the 11th chords that blossom in the final string quartet. (Jean
Gallois, "Chausson, Ernest." *Grove Music Online*, ed. Deane Root, accessed 2 Sept. 2016,
http://www.oxfordmusiconline.com)

This little catalog is an accurate résumé, in technical terms, of Chausson's musical
language. It manages to capture something of the elusiveness and originality of
Chausson's often sensuous, "iridescent" music. But however alive to the details of
musical description Gallois was, he (or his editors) apparently overlooked an ambiguous repetition, the proximate recurrence of the word "anticipation": "There are
anticipations also of Ravel in *Serre d'ennui*, a song of 1893, and of Koechlin's *La
prière du mort* in *Oraison*, of 1895"(Ibid.) The two usages of "anticipation," which
share the same paragraph, mean different things, of course. The initial usage is
analytical, referring to the harmonic and rhythmic behavior of a single note in a
musical context; the second is a rhetorical reference to Chausson as historical
precursor to Ravel and Koechlin. I point out this authorial oversight because it is a
deceptively arbitrary, and thus, to me, irresistible, way into the topic at hand, and
because its potential to create confusion mirrors the misunderstandings I have already
had (indeed, any musician might have) when discussing this subject with colleagues:

A: I'm writing an article about anticipation in music.
B: That'll be a short one. I'll bet it's eagerly awaited, haha.

The prospective short article my playful colleague had in mind would contain,
presumably, the entirety of a music dictionary entry, or a counterpoint manual
description:

Anticipation. An unaccented NON-HARMONIC NOTE, sometimes regarded as an ornament, that belongs to and is repeated in the harmony immediately following; an extra
statement of an entire chord on a preceding weak beat is called 'rhythmic anticipation.'
("Anticipation." *Grove Music Online*, ed. Deane Root, accessed 2 Sept. 2016, http://www.
oxfordmusiconline.com.)

If the old adage concerning truth and jest is to be believed, there is not much to
say beyond describing the function of the anticipation note, and any novice counterpoint student should know how to do that. But I couldn't help thinking that this
tiny ornamental detail might repay extended reflection from the perspective of a
composer. I wanted to investigate how much information it could contain, to know if
it might tell me something about music I would have otherwise overlooked. This
chapter therefore begins with a rudimentary example of an anticipation tone, and
then traces its variants (as well as broader issues of musical anticipation) in works
spanning two centuries of Western music history. (I have endeavored, insofar as it
was possible, to write for a nonspecialist audience, a readership that I imagine will be
comprised of interested scholarly amateur musicians and nonmusicians alike. This
chapter is not a work of music theory or musicology, but its observations draw from

both fields. The rehearsal of some basic analytic concepts has therefore been necessary. It will be useful for the reader to be able to read music.) I conclude with a postscript that offers a vision of music's future, in which anticipation acquires new meaning and creates new challenges.

Let's begin by returning to the music dictionary entry for anticipation. I supplement it with a straightforward musical illustration (Ex. 1) below. As in poetic meter, musical meter is divided into strong and weak beats. For example, in 4/4 time, beats 1 and 3 are strong, and 2 and 4 are weak. Events occurring on strong beats are by definition emphasized or metrically "accented." These events predictably reinforce a work's given meter. By contrast, activity falling on weak beats is often associated with surprise or pleasure — a kind of musical legerde-main — since this activity occurs between the strong beats that give music its metrical identity. (In his seminal book, *Sweet Expectation: Music and the Psychology of Expectation*, cognitive musicologist David Huron examines the neuroscience of musical surprise. He states: "I have noted that there are different expressions of surprise and that these expressions echo the primordial behaviors of *fight*, *flight*, and *freeze*. Musical surprises are capable of initiating these responses, but the responses themselves are short-lived because an ensuing appraisal ultimately judges the stimuli as nonthreatening. The appraisal response inhibits the full expression of fight, flight, or freeze and also prevents the individual from becoming consciously aware of their brief brush with fear. Instead, the listener is left with a corresponding response of frisson, laughter, or awe." David Huron, *Sweet Anticipation: Music and the Psychology of Expectation* (Cambridge, US: Bradford, 2008), 39.)

Example 1

In Example 1 the four beats of the measure are indicated above the staff. We see clearly that the four notes on (strong) beat 1 correspond to a D major triad: D in bass and tenor, F-sharp in alto, A in soprano. The lower three voices hold this D major chord for two full beats, while the top voice holds its A for half a beat less, changing to a G just after the arrival of (weak) beat 2. The soprano's beat 2 has been subdivided into two eighth notes. The first eighth note is elided with the A, which is represented by the dot. The new soprano note G occurs on the second eighth note of beat 2, the weakest of weak positions, that is, the unaccented second half of unaccented beat 2. On beat 3, the soprano comes back into alignment with the other voices on a new sonority. The bass leaps up from D to G, the tenor leaps down from D to B, the alto moves up from F-sharp up to G, and the soprano, which had already reached G by the end of beat 2, repeats its note. This repetition, combined with the foregoing metrical information, reveals the soprano's first G to be the anticipation note. What it anticipates is the G major triad on beat 3, the full-fledged harmonization of the initial, premature G.

Recall the music dictionary's fervent assertion that an anticipation is a "NON-HARMONIC NOTE." This means that the anticipation will not fit into the prevailing harmony in which it first appears. That is exactly what we find in Example 1. For half a beat, the soprano's anticipatory G creates a grating dissonance – an interval of a minor second – against the alto's F-sharp, and a less strident dissonance – a perfect fourth – with the lower two voices. To complicate further this tiny slice of musical time, its harmonic tension is coupled with the suggestion of rhythmic tension.

Observe the feeling of dislocation produced by Example 2 in the context of its given meter of 4/4. Instead of anticipating the G-major chord with one note on beat 2.5 in the soprano, the entire chord arrives on that very weak offbeat and sustains into beats 3 and 4 to fill out the measure.

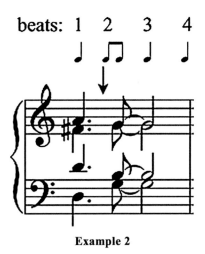

Example 2

In Example 1, the single anticipation note is but a hint of this metrical awkwardness. (If we remove the ties from beats 2.5 into 3 as in Example 3, the awkwardness disappears; this is the "rhythmic anticipation" to which the dictionary entry above refers.) But we cannot decouple the rhythmic aspect of the anticipation from the harmonic context; the two exist symbiotically. This symbiosis can be generally described in three stages referring to Example 1:

1. Strong beat, harmonic preparation (beat 1): the D major chord is also the dominant (V) of G major, which exhibits a general tendency towards G major (I) via the leading tone F-sharp;
2. Weak beat, nonharmonic anticipation (beat 2.5): the imminent G-major chord is partially and prematurely sounded by the soprano, creating dissonances with the other 3 voices, namely the alto's F-sharp leading tone;
3. Strong beat, harmonic resolution (beat 3): the soprano resounds its G, the alto moves up by step to the same G from F-sharp, and rest of the voices fill out the triad.

It is important to point out that the initial D major chord could have moved elsewhere: its general tendency to proceed to the tonic G major is not strictly inevitable, only statistically probable. (See Huron, *Sweet Anticipation*, 251. Huron provides a table of harmonic probabilities based on a sample of Baroque music.) The intervention of the soprano's anticipatory G, however, makes this trajectory nearly unavoidable. (Shortly we will observe how Chausson modifies the anticipations highlighted by Gallois so that the consonant resolution reharmonizes the anticipation note to surprising effect.) The anticipation simply intensifies a latent potential.

Example 3

Without a broader musical context, however, we are not likely to learn much more about anticipations from Example 1. Moreover, composers' use of such subtle note-level details is never as straightforward as a theoretical example. The anticipations at the beginning of the *Minuetto* movement of Mozart's *String Quartet No. 17 in B-flat Major, K. 458*, commonly called the "The Hunt," arise within a useful expanse of rich harmonic and rhythmic features, which we will now briefly consider.

The *minuetto, menuetto, minuette*, or minuet is a dance of French provenance that found its way into the instrumental repertoire as a codified, undanced musical form. By the late seventeenth century it was most often paired with a secondary section called a "trio." (For a discussion of the minuet and trio form in the eighteenth century, see William E. Caplin, *Classical Form: A Theory of Formal Functions for the Instrumental Music of Haydn, Mozart, and Beethoven* (New York: Oxford University Press, 1988), 219–230.) There is astonishing motivic variety in minuets, even those written by composers of the same era, such as Haydn and Mozart, but the rhythmic feature that they usually share is an emphasis on the first beat of every measure in strict 3/4 time. This extra emphasis, a reminder of the form's terpsichorean origins, gives each measure a consistently front-heavy rhythmic orientation in a meter where beat 1 was already strong and the remaining two beats weak. As I have already noted, weak beats are the composer's playground. In his *Minuetto*, Mozart's imagination luxuriates in two adjacent weak beats in every measure.

Example 4 (Mozart, *String Quartet No. 17 in B-flat Major, K.458: Minuetto, mm. 1-6*)

After the *Minuetto*'s relatively staid first bar we find an almost immediate transfer of musical interest away from the downbeat. In measure 2, the first violin interjects a trill on beat 2; then, in measure 3, after an apparent return to sober emphasis on beat 1, in which the two violins hold C and F for two full beats, the violins and the cello suddenly make a gigantic leap up into a half-diminished 7th chord (completed by the viola) on beat 3. To heighten the dramatic effect of this leap, Mozart has added a dynamic marking – "sf," *sforzando*, "with sudden emphasis" – that essentially forces the ear to hear the normally weak beat 3 as a strong beat. Compare this dissonant 7th chord, made more strident by the dynamic indication, to the straightforward D major triad from which our first anticipation emerged in Example 1. We are but three measures into the *Minuetto* and yet Mozart seems already to be playing with our sense of musical perception. Not only is the violins' double anticipation prepared on an "artificial" strong beat, this *sforzando* chord effectively makes beat 3 of measure 3 sound like beat 1 of a new measure. (This phenomenon is known as a "dynamic accent." For a discussion of dynamic accents in the context of musical surprise, see Huron, *Sweet Anticipation*, 295.) This metric displacement continues, as similar *sforzando* + anticipation figures appear in measures 4 and 5 (see Example 5).

Example 5 (metric displacements)

The effect of these metric displacements is akin to a musical pun, a *double entendre* in which the anticipation notes play a subtle yet crucial role. We hear the *sforzando* chords seem to reposition the downbeat starting in measure 3, yet the sixteenth note anticipations that immediately follow lend a sense of inevitability to the notated downbeats in measures 4, 5, and 6. Mozart's dynamics and phrasing thus overlay a new grouping of beats onto the traditional metric pattern of the minuet, a pattern that the anticipation notes nevertheless reinforce.

Let's turn now to a dramatic, and more ambiguous, use of anticipation notes from the canon of German *lieder*. Robert Schumann's song *Ich grolle nicht* (*I bear no grudge*) is the seventh in his 1840 cycle of Heinrich Heine settings entitled *Dichterliebe* (*A Poet's Love*). The song is notable for the aching dissonances that seem to betray the singer's true state of mind in spite of what he sings. Although Schumann has the lover repeatedly exclaim, "I bear no grudge" (more times, it should be noted, than Heine himself allowed in the original version of his poem), the reluctance of the vocal line to leave certain notes, even as the piano accompaniment plods on, suggests a psychological inability to let go. The dissonances between voice and piano resulting from this reluctance imbue the song with added tension. At other times the voice lurches forward, beating the accompaniment to a new note (and thus implying a new harmony) by a fractional beat. It is the skillful use of anticipation notes that lend these moments of the song a contrasting yet subtle sense of impatience.

The first anticipation is found in measure 5; it is the last note, the A on the syllable "-nes" of "verlor'nes" ("lost"). Upon inspecting this measure, perhaps the first detail that strikes us about the eighth note A is that it occurs in a weak (unaccented) metrical position almost as late as possible in the measure. (In the first measure, the piano accompaniment establishes an unchanging eighth-note grid, which persists unabated until the last measure. This grid clearly demarcates 8 metric positions for each measure, and the A in measure 5 occupies the eighth position. The only later position possible would be the last sixteenth note of the measure, but Schumann interestingly reserves the few sixteenth notes in this song for moments that do not coincide with anticipations.) As we saw in the Mozart *Minuetto*, the confluence of rhythmic and harmonic details reveals the anticipation note to be a contradiction of sorts: it is a late metrical event with respect to the measure in which it is found, but it is a premature harmonic event with respect to the subsequent measure. And because the anticipation belongs harmonically to the following measure, it results in a dissonance against the rest of the notes sounding when it appears.

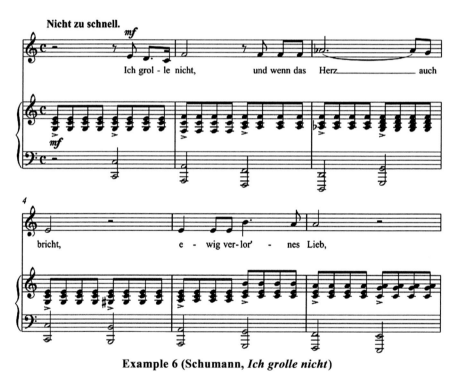

Example 6 (Schumann, *Ich grolle nicht*)

In measure 5 of *Ich grolle nicht*, the anticipation tone is freighted with several layers of harmonic ambiguity in relation to the piano's chordal accompaniment. To appreciate the anticipation's place in the unsettled terrain of Schumann's song, we will need to disentangle a few strands of harmonic information. Measure 5 begins with two unequivocal beats in A minor: the voice sings *e-wig ver-* ("eternally lo[st]") on a repeating E, doubling the fifth of the piano's pulsating root-position A minor triad in the right hand; the piano's left hand holds the octave-doubled root A. On beat 3 of the measure, the left hand's octaves descend by step to G. At this moment, the voice leaps up to a B, and the right hand of the piano keeps two notes (A and E) from the previous A minor triad and doubles the singer's B. This sonority, and especially the doubled B, creates considerable harmonic tension. According to Leonard Meyer's pioneering approach to musical analysis from the perspective of Gestalt psychology – particularly the "gap-fill principle" (See Leonard B. Meyer, *Emotion and Meaning in Music* (Chicago: University of Chicago Press, 1973), 130–135.) – the voice's upward leap of a perfect fifth creates the expectation of subsequent downward motion. But this melodic counterpoise is only one reason the ear can expect an A to follow the dotted quarter note B in the voice. We can consider this B an appoggiatura, that is, an accented nonharmonic tone approached by leap and usually resolving down by step. Because of their "sudden and bold" effect appoggiaturas tend to be brief in duration (Leonard G. Ratner, *Harmony: Structure and Style* (New York: McGraw-Hill, 1962), 162.). The longer the duration, the "bolder" the effect. Strikingly, Schumann prolongs this appoggiatura for 1.5 beats before resolving it on the A. But the A is not simply the appoggiatura's resolution, it is also the anticipation of the next sonority. In this way, Schumann transforms the expected resolution of an appoggiatura into a cue for further expectation in the form of an anticipation note.

The elision of a resolution note with an anticipation note is not, however, the last notable detail of this passage. The relative independence of all three of the song's moving parts (the voice and the accompaniment's right and left hands) produces further ambiguities. We can note the stepwise descending bassline – we might even consider this a diatonic lament bass – and the aching extended harmonies it produces with the right hand's pulsating chords (For a discussion of this particular version of the lament bass, see Mark Ellis, *A Chord in Time: The Evolution of the Augmented Sixth from Monteverdi to Mahler* (Surrey, UK: Ashgate, 2010), 200.). We can analyze these harmonies privileging either the linear or vertical perspective. The different conclusions we reach from either analysis underscores the considerable ambiguity with which Schumann endows this music. Adding up all sounding notes vertically on beat 3 of measure 5 would suggest that this sonority is a C major 7th chord in second inversion. But perhaps this vertical analysis does not give us the full story. Might it explain away too quickly the B as simply the seventh of a chord build on C? Given the voice's dramatic approach to the B by a leap of a perfect fifth, and its immediate instability – its tendency to move to A – perhaps it makes more sense to analyze the entirety of measure 5 as an elaborated A minor (7th) sonority (Taking into account the octave G in the bass on beats 3 and 4.). To be sure, the first two beats of the measure are clearly in A minor, and the right hand on beats 3 and 4 sustains the C and E of A minor. We hear the B over those two notes so poignantly precisely because it is not A but seems to yearn for it, the classic effect of an appoggiatura. Of course, most appoggiaturas resolve more quickly than this one does, and without the repetitions we see in the right-hand part.

It is perhaps enough simply to point out these competing harmonic interpretations of the passage, since their mutual viability demonstrates the ambiguity of the music. But we have been investigating the role of anticipation notes in musical discourse, and it would seem that the anticipation note A favors the vertical (C major 7th) interpretation of beats 3 and 4 over the linear one (A minor 7th). Recall once more that the anticipation is a nonharmonic tone. The A is only nonharmonic if the second half of measure 5 is a C major 7th chord. But rather than simply anticipating the next harmony in measure 6, as we have seen, the anticipation note A is also the delayed resolution of the B appoggiatura. In this single eighth note A, Schumann has encapsulated an extraordinary amount of perceptual information.

I began this chapter by drawing attention to a tiny linguistic ambiguity in a description of Ernest Chausson's music. Before concluding this examination of note-level anticipation and shifting to a discussion of the broader aspects of musical expectation, it seems fitting to spend a moment with the music of this undeservedly neglected French composer.

Chausson wrote his *Quelques danses, Op. 26* for piano in 1896, just 3 years before his accidental death at the age of 44. There are many exquisite details in this graciously wistful and luminous music, but I will limit my discussion to two, two-bar passages in the second dance, the *Sarabande*. Like the minuet, the sarabande originated as a dance, but its entry into the Western canon of instrumental forms followed a more circuitous, mysterious route, possibly beginning in North Africa and reaching France via Spain and Italy. Along the way, what was once a fast, sensuous display became a slower and chaster entertainment. The sarabande also shares the minuet's triple meter, but whereas the latter dance emphasizes the downbeat of each *measure*, the sarabande often emphasizes the second beat of each *phrase*.

This initial emphasis of beat 2 is exactly what we find in the first phrase of Chausson's sarabande. Not only do the dynamic markings indicate that beat 2 is the loudest moment of the measure, the syncopation on beat 1 adds gentle rhythmic momentum to the second beat as the notes get louder. Although this sixteenth note D at the end of beat 1 fits the rhythmic profile of an anticipation note, it does not, as a clear member of the initial B-flat major chord, meet the harmonic criterion for an anticipation. This is a crucial point, because there is nothing about this repeated D that suggests its subsequent reharmonization, something we have seen in the anticipations from Mozart and Schumann. Indeed, when the D is repeated for a third time on beat 2, it is the most strikingly unexpected feature of that harmony, the detail that lends the chord an exotic flare.

Example 7 (Chausson, *Quelques danses, Op. 26: Sarabande*, mm. 1-4)

As with the Schumann example, we can consider the material in measures 1–2 of Chausson's *Sarabande* both vertically and linearly. Computing the notes occurring directly on beat 2, we find an unusual sonority, possibly the result of Chausson's study of Gabriel Fauré's harmonic procedures, and/or his admiration for the music of his friend, Claude Debussy. We can call this sonority an altered 11th chord: a dominant 7th chord built on A-flat, with the melodic note D as a raised (augmented) 11th and the subsequent B-flat on the second half of beat 2 contributing the 9th of the chord. The linear view of this passage would treat the melodic D and B-flat as "changing tones," that is, consecutive non-chord tones (upper and lower neighbors) in relation to the chord tone C on beat 3. By excluding the D and B-flat from the prevailing harmony, the reemergence of the D at the end of the triplet on beat 3, and its subsequent reharmonization on the downbeat of measure 2, identifies this note's function as an anticipation. What it anticipates is the G minor triad, the relative minor, in the next bar. The exclusion of D and B-flat from the harmony in measure 1 helps us to see how Chausson arrives at this G minor chord: the A-flat major-minor 7th chord resolves as a German augmented 6th chord. (We would typically expect this sonority, which is borrowed from C minor, to resolve to that key's dominant chord, G major. Instead, Chausson uses the modal resolution to G minor as the initiation of a modal tonicization of G minor (the submediant) itself.

Example 8 (reduction of *Sarabande,* mm.1-2)

As brief as it is, the D anticipation note in measure 1 plays a key role in maintaining a sense of harmonic trajectory. Jean Gallois notes that some critics accused Chausson's music of being "vague, disjointed, incomprehensible, harmful." Leaving aside the exaggerated subjectivity of these accusations, an analysis of a passage even as brief as the present one demonstrates Chausson's subtle, innovative, and eminently coherent musical mind. It is the last D in measure 1, the anticipation, that prompts the listener to hear the preceding sonority as a German augmented 6th chord and not a secondary dominant that will potentially move the harmony precipitously into D-flat major. The tritone the anticipation creates with the A-flat in the bass demands a downward resolution to a perfect 5th between D and G. Likewise, the major 2nd (a notated 9th) between the anticipation D and the left hand's C, not to mention the major 7th created with the right hand's E-flat, make resolutions to B-flat and D respectively, nearly unavoidable.

The ear's ability to hear and instantly process information such as a dominant 7th chord resolution arises effortlessly from the listener's lived experience, a lifetime spent immersed in music – both listened to attentively and heard passively – in which the occurrence of these note-level behaviors is statistically significant. The anticipation note is simply an indicator or predictor of these statistically probable harmonic events. The composer's derailment of the anticipated outcome by what amounts to a harmonic pun makes the listening experience more pleasurable. But it is important to point out that in Chausson's day, the proliferation of ever more extended harmonies – that is, triads and 7th chords elaborated by accumulations of added tones – and increasingly modulatory harmony, contributed to the weakening and eventual breakdown of the tonal system. Composers were gradually abandoning the strategy of creating dramatic interest through the tension and resolution of tonal harmonic progressions. Instead, composers began to treat notes and harmonies as loci of aesthetic interest in and of themselves – *l'harmonie pour l'harmonie*, to paraphrase the slogan made famous by Théophile Gautier. This approach, which produced increasingly unpredictable harmonic results, reached its zenith in the methodical dismantlement of tonality inherent in Arnold Schoenberg's 12-tone system in the first quarter of the twentieth century. An investigation of anticipatory details in Schoenberg's music is still to come, but there are few observations we can make in Chausson's *Sarabande*, and in French music of the period. We will pause briefly to consider some of these details now.

Another characteristic of the sarabande form is the tendency of its phrases to be constructed in eight-bar groups. Chausson's *Sarabande* is no exception. When the syncopated motif returns in measure 9, however, it is transposed to the dominant key area of F major. But this is no rote transposition: the theme is reharmonized and revoiced. These elaborations also bear upon our hearing of the anticipation note, now transposed up a perfect 5th to A.

Example 9 (*Sarabande*, mm. 9-10)

Besides the transposition, the first discrepancy we notice between measures 1 and 9 is the revoicing of the major triad on beat 1. We note not only the prominent descending 6ths in the right hand of measure 9 but also a difference in chord quality: a half-diminished 7th chord built on G now occupies beat 2. For the second time, Chausson has placed an ambiguous chord on the second beat of the theme. This particular sonority is rich with harmonic possibility: will it resolve (a) to the dominant of A-flat major; or (b) to the dominant of F minor or F major? (See Example 10.)

Example 10

Choice (a) is attractive because it leads back to the German augmented 6th chord (marked here with an asterisk) that we first encountered in measure 1. But rather than retrace his steps, Chausson moves from the G half-diminished 7th chord to a C dominant 7th chord beneath the two eighth notes + triplet figure. (Refer again to Example 9.) In this new harmonization, the F, a non-chord tone B-flat in measure 1 (Example 7), is now clearly a chord tone. The syncopated cadential motion from the G half-diminished 7th chord to the C dominant 7th chord clarifies the nature of the final A eighth note in the measure: it is a non-chord-tone, a clear anticipation of the next measure.

Before the A resounds in measure 10, we feel sure that the imminent chord will be an F major triad. Any confusion the G half-diminished 7th chord borrowed from the parallel minor might have caused has been resolved by the A-natural anticipation note – or at least we think! Our anticipation of F major is beautifully set up by the rhythmic interplay between the hands: the offbeat C dominant 7th chord and the triplet-eighth note A. The dominant 7th chord generates a strong pull toward F; in turn, the anticipation's dissonance is created by the partial and premature encroachment of the tonic upon the dominant. In the end, however, we ought not to have been so sure of ourselves. The ground shifts – or rather drops away – to reveal a harmonization of the anticipation note A not as the third of F major but as the root of an A minor triad. (Refer once more to Example 9.)

The effect of this unusual harmonic progression – C dominant 7th to A minor – is jarring. But what saves the music from "incoherence" is the anticipation. At the very least, we expect a repeated A, and this expectation is fulfilled. The fact that A is a common tone between F major and A minor makes the substitution plausible. (In terms of voice leading, Chausson could have easily written a descent from B-flat to A in the left hand to mitigate further this startling progression, but the B-flat steps up to C instead.) But the harmonic information below the anticipation gives no hint that a substitution of A minor for F major will occur. Rather, the statistical likelihood of dominant-tonic progressions informs the way we hear the anticipated note in bar 10. Chausson's daring and innovative harmonic bait-and-switch depends therefore on the listener's "correct" hearing of the anticipation.

It is easy to imagine the disorienting harmonic effect of music in which similar chord substitutions proliferate. The tonal moorings progressively loosen until they lose their hold on the ship of music altogether. In the harmonic experiments of composers as disparate as Fauré and Satie, we can observe this tonal "loosening" – merely yet elegantly evoked here by Chausson – at a moment just before the ropes slipped the bollards definitively. It will be worthwhile to examine how the ear navigates the music from this period of transitional harmony before venturing into the storm-tossed waters of atonality.

In our study of the anticipation note, we have observed its ability to initiate a predictive collaboration between ear and brain, enlisting the statistical aspect of musical memory. Instantaneously and reflexively comparing sound patterns heard in the present with those stored in long-term memory (See Ray Kurzweil, *How to Create a Mind*, (New York: Penguin Books, 2012), 34–74, and Huron, *Sweet Anticipation*, 21), the listener is continuously updating (predicting, confirming, correcting) an expected future version of music in real time. Sometimes the ear is wrong, of course, and it is these "failure[s] of expectation" (Huron, *Sweet Anticipation*, 21) that often elicit pleasurable listening experiences. But the aesthetic value and efficacy of surprise in Western music has historically stood in inverse proportion to its frequency. Put another way, the more surprises, the less pleasurable (and more disorienting) the music becomes. Although almost never expressed in these terms, the absence of reasonable predictability accounts for the greater part of the popular and critical indignities suffered by composers such as Schoenberg and Webern. When critics speak of musical "coherence," the delicate and elusive balance of expectation fulfillment and failure figures prominently in their estimation. So, too, does the correlated balance of repetition and variation, since repetition can be perceived as a marker of structural importance or a detail that betrays a lack of ideas or skill.

In the musical examples encountered thus far we can observe the general trend of increasing challenges to the ear-brain predictive apparatus. Mozart's genius was the well-chosen moment of deviation from expected conventions. Schumann's exploration of music's potential to convey emotional or psychological information at odds with a text led him into more daring harmonic territory. Chausson's experiments, like those of his contemporary Emmanuel Chabrier, were largely confined to unusual but easily parsable harmonizations of melodic notes, and reveal an increasingly sensual approach to harmony. The ascendance of the composer's subjectivity over conventions of harmony and counterpoint resulted in a decrease in the listener's ability to anticipate correctly these aspects of a composition. At a certain point, harmonic progression becomes chord collection, and anticipation becomes more difficult.

Example 11 (Satie, *Harmonies*)

Our ability to make split-second predictions about what we see or hear is due to the pattern-seeking cognitive function of the human brain. When we listen to music, the mind is perpetually alert to potential patterns in the notes. (These patterns acquire meaning and are learned through enculturation. See Huron, *Sweet Anticipation, 3*.) Even in as idiosyncratic a context as Satie's *Harmonies* of 1906 (see Example 11 above), the ears of a trained musician or keen amateur are likely to catch the downward groups (2, 3, and 4 notes) in the lowest voice of the left hand. But even this general downward trend has its anomalies: leaps, repetitions, major versus minor seconds. Satie is not particularly concerned with maintaining tonal order in his little piano piece; neither does he think in terms of modulatory harmony. What does preoccupy him, however, is the concatenation of adjacent harmonies according to his various subjective ideas about harmonic intervals, the way one chord moves to the next. (See Chap. 9, *Compositional systems and other sources of inspiration*, in Robert Orledge, *Satie the Composer* (Cambridge: Cambridge University Press, 1990.)) In this concatenation model, musical meaning arises in a fashion similar to linguistic meaning arising from a Markov chain. Nevertheless, Satie's singular approach to harmony did not preclude the use of tonal procedures such as leading-tone motion or dominant-tonic resolutions, and we can hear these phenomena either hinted at or in full effect in works from every period of his career. The result is music that never completely defies the listener's faculty of anticipation, principally because Satie's categorical avoidance of developmental harmony means that repetition often "does duty for development." (This is an observation Steven Whiting makes regarding some of the earliest works of Satie, but I have argued elsewhere that this approach to repetition is characteristic of Satie's entire œuvre. See Steven Whiting, *Satie the Bohemian: From Cabaret to Concert Hall* (Oxford: Oxford University Press, 1999), 65.) And repetition breeds anticipation.

By design, the harmonic innovations of the Second Viennese School made anticipatory listening decidedly more difficult, if not impossible. The human ear-brain predictive apparatus relies on enculturated patterns of musical information as it tries to determine the statistical likelihood of future musical events. There are, of course, fewer of these patterns in the music of Schoenberg et al. save those they allow. But the expressionism of Schoenberg's counterpoint is nothing if not fractured, collapsed, overgrown ruins from the tonal past. (See Ethan Haimo,

Schoenberg's Transformation of Musical Language (Cambridge, UK: Cambridge University Press, 2006), for a detailed investigation of Schoenberg's links with past musical practice and his subsequent efforts to break from it.) His early atonal works make this fact plain, but the ear can easily miss anticipatory cues if the music is not sensitively performed. Momentary flashes of tonal harmony run through the first of Schoenberg's *Drei Klavierstücke, Op. 11* of 1909. We hear the first in measure 3, where somehow we know that the rhythmically anticipated F in the right hand will descend a half-step to E. The F in measure 2 is not technically classifiable as a true anticipation, however. There's no way of knowing that the F will resound in measure 3. But when the D-flat and A-natural appear under this suspended F, we hear the three upper notes as an augmented triad tending towards resolution as a major triad (Example 12). (The B-flat is primarily coloristic here; it does not contribute to the sense of anticipation that the F will move to E.)

Example 12 (Schoenberg, *Drei Klavierstücke*,
***Op. 11: No. 1 Mäßig*, mm. 1-3)**

Fleeting moments of tonal function like this one are recognizable in large part because of Schoenberg's handling of register. Note that the melody in the top voice of measures 1–3 is constrained to a perfect 5th (starting on B and ending on E). The close proximity of the melodic notes allows the ear to hear the unstable melodic tritone between the initial note B and the repeating F. (A comparable outline of a tritone subsequently occurs in the right hand of measure 5 going into measure 6 (E-C-B-flat-B-natural).) Similarly, the melodic line's registral proximity to the trichord in the lower voices in measure 3 allows the F to acquire a further tonal reference, namely as a member of the unstable augmented sonority (A-C-sharp/D-flat-F) over the B-flat in the bass. When Schoenberg begins to experiment with registral displacements, however, the ear's ability to listen predictively is strained. Leonard Meyer's "gap-fill" theory suggests a compelling explanation for this difficulty by way of a quotation from the early experimental psychologist Henry J. Watt: "To pass over a note immediately creates a desire for it. . ." If this is true, then it follows that the larger the leap is, the more notes are "desired." And the manifold "desire" created by large leaps risks destroying entirely the sense of tonal expectation.

Although tonal harmonizations of chromatic scale segments, known collectively as the "omnibus progression," have existed at least since the Baroque era, these harmonizations are subjective adaptations: there is no single harmonization implied by the chromatic scale. Played on its own, however, the unbroken sequence of minor 2nds does nevertheless produce an immediate, sustained, and almost primordial sense of expectation. This is perhaps explained by the minor 2nd's role as a leading tone. Simply put, the chromatic scale sounds like an endless chain of leading tones. (Repetition breeds anticipation.) Ethan Haimo has explored the effects of registral displacement on chromatic scale segments in another passage (measures 34–8, Example 13) of *No. 1 Mäßig* from *Drei Klavierstücke*:

This chromatic scale does not unfold in a single register. Rather, as he has done in prior works (although never as systematically as here), Schoenberg states the chromatic scale by alternating between a lower and upper register. This has the obvious consequence of creating two other indeterminate scale segments: whole tone scale segments in the different registers. (Haimo, *Schoenberg's Transformation of Musical Language*, 313)

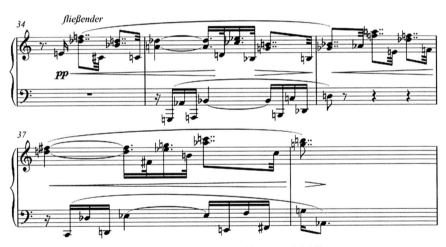

Example 13 (*No. 1 Mäßig*, mm. 34-38)

There is a strong sense of inevitability in this passage. The hands play sequential gestures converging in contrary motion at the end of the first phrase, and then the sequences move in similar motion – ascending, the left hand's direction since measure 35 – at the end of the second phrase. It seems clear that the passage's inevitability derives more from the consistent intervallic and rhythmic patterning than from any sense of anticipation arising from the composite harmony. The left hand has three features that give it a predictable shape: (1) the chromatic scale, which is also partitioned, as Haimo notes, into whole tone scale segments (another symmetrical scale); (2) the leaps in alternating directions, corresponding to Leonard Meyer's "gap-fill" rule; and the rhythmic pattern of three sixteenth notes followed by a long duration or rests (Of course, the left hand figure, were it to continue indefinitely, would never fill itself in completely given the size and direction of the alternating leaps.).

Admittedly, Meyer's "gap-fill" rule has quite limited applicability in case of the large left-hand leaps of measures 35–38. A large leap implies subsequent movement in the opposite direction as a means of maintaining "completeness" or equilibrium in a melodic line. This "completeness" constrains a melody's pitch space and guarantees a melody's legibility. But the presumption of the "gap-fill" rule is that leaps will be relatively rare, otherwise any notion of equilibrium would be irrelevant. In measures 34–38 alone, we can easily observe the disjunct quality of Schoenberg's motivic writing. When, later in the century, Milton Babbitt and other composers expanded the organizational reach of serialism to include register, among other elements, the ensuing music effectively obliterated one of the last cues for anticipatory listening: registrally constrained melody. (The work of Christopher Hasty, specifically his concept of "rhythmic projection," might possibly be used to determine if anticipatory rhythmic cues are nevertheless present in Babbitt's music.) The first measures of Babbitt's *Composition for Four Instruments* (1948) demonstrate this new, systematic approach to motivic construction (Example 14).

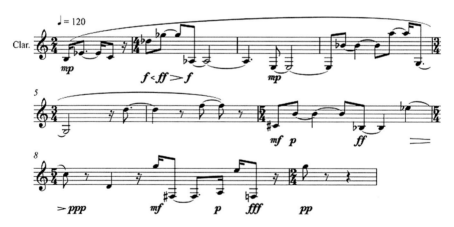

Example 14 (Babbitt, *Composition for Four Instruments*, mm.1-9)

As we now know, the prominence and influence of serialism rose and fell in the second half of the twentieth century, mostly within the walls of universities and other institutions. In the meantime, some composers outside those walls were taking another look at tonality and developing new approaches for composing music with tonal centers. Embedded in these approaches were new ways of treating anticipatory listening: the existence of a tonal center implies the listener's experience of hearing the tendency of certain notes to move toward or away from the central pitch. This renewed interest in anticipatory listening did not, for the most part, result in wholesale adoption of functional harmony, although historical appropriation and parody were by no means uncommon. Instead, many composers such as Philip Glass, Steve Reich, and Terry Riley carried out the return to tonality with an often extreme economy of means: limited pitches, prolonged repetition with little varia- tion, rhythmic uniformity, etc. Much of this music treated tonal function as an object to be investigated. These tonal investigations often had the effect of prolonging the sense of anticipation indefinitely, long enough for the anticipation to become an end (a feeling) in and of itself.

One example of minimalist prolongation of tonal anticipation, and its ambig- uous effects on the listening experience, is found in the second movement of Glass's *Symphony No. 2 in C Minor* (1994). This movement begins in A minor with oscillating thirds (A-C) in the violins over a pedal E in the violas and bassoons, pitches that create a classic 6-4 sonority. The effect of beginning on this unstable sonority – and sustaining it for two measures – lends the music a slight tension, an atmosphere of expectation. This atmosphere is also supported by the muted orchestration with which Glass limns his harmonies. The instability of the 6-4 sonority arises from the perfect 4th above the bass (E and A). By convention, the top note of this interval resolves down by half-step to the major 3rd, the essential component of the dominant sonority (E major here) in a cadential progression. After two measures of the 6-4, however, the subsequent chord – a root position A minor triad created by the change of bass notes – recontextualizes the 6-4 as the beginning of a simple A minor arpeggiation, that is, two A minor triads with changing bass notes. Is the 6-4 meant to be heard as a weak dominant function or as part of an arpeggiation? A subsequent repetition of these initial 4 bars only thickens the plot. The 6-4 sonority returns in measure 9, but the heretofore consistent allotment of two measures per chord is interrupted in measure 10 by a surprising move in the bass up to F. Since the E pedal is retained from the previous chord, the resulting sonority is a major 7th chord built on F. This surprise is followed by another: the appearance of A-flat in measure 11. In one possible hearing of the passage, this note (written G-sharp) has been expected since the beginning of the movement as a consequence of the initial 6-4 sonority. The subsequent repetitions of the 6-4 served simultaneously to establish A minor as the key area and prolong the instability of the 6-4. The respelling of the G-sharp leading tone as A-flat temporarily diverts the harmony away from A minor: the violas and bassoons descend accordingly to E-flat, creating an A-flat major 6-4 chord. The bass note F from measure 10 returns in measure 12 while all other notes remain in place, resulting in a minor-minor 7th chord built on F. (Refer to Example 15.)

Example 15 (Glass, *Symphony No. 2 in C Minor: Mvt. II.*, mm. 1-18; transposed score)

In measure 12, the harmony seems poised to move towards C minor, but none of the normal harmonic expectations has so far been fulfilled. Instead of moving from the F minor 7th to a dominant sonority on G (the statistically likely choice), Glass returns to the opening A minor 6-4 sonority. Far from an unimaginative return to previous material, the progression from F minor 7 to A minor 6-4 amounts to a sophisticated harmonic ruse, which has the effect of further intensifying the instability of the recurring A minor 6-4 sonority and establishing it as cadential. We can analyze this progression as the resolution of an altered German augmented 6th chord to a cadential 6-4 (Example 16). The disappearance of the double basses on the lower octave E adds to the subtlety of this progression.

**Example 16 (*Mvt. II*, mm. 12-12 respelled as aug.
6th resolving to A minor 6-4)**

In measure 15, the previous A-flat is respelled as G-sharp, oscillating with C in the violins and harmonized as an augmented C chord. To this chord is added the recurring bass note F, resulting in a pungent minor-major 7th sonority in measure 16. When the violas and bassoons descend to D in measure 17, implying a half-diminished 7th chord on D, the harmony appears once more to turn towards C minor. Although spelled with a G-sharp instead of an A-flat, this chord outlines a half-diminished 7th chord on D (the supertonic of C minor), suggesting a subsequent move to a cadential G dominant sonority. This time, Glass accedes to our expectation, but in the most ambiguous of ways. In measure 18, while the D in the violas and first bassoon continues to sound under the violins' G-sharp-C oscillations, the basses step up to a grinding G-natural in measure 18. The resulting dissonant tetrachord is therefore a collision of the half-diminished supertonic chord with the root of the chord it implies, the dominant G (Example 17). When this "collision chord" is followed by the now-familiar A minor 6-4 sonority, the expected arrival on C minor is foiled. In the process, Glass appears to have invented new species of deceptive cadence: A minor (instead of A-flat major) substituted for C minor.

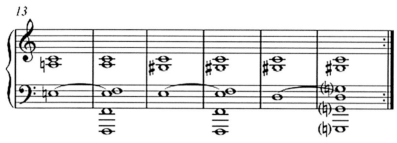

Example 17 (Mvt. II., mm. 13-18)

With an ambiguous tonic sonority almost always voiced in second inversion and repeatedly thwarted tonal function, Glass has effectively fused the instability and expectation of cadential movement with the illusion of harmonic stasis. The passage in measures 1–18 does not seem to lead anywhere except back into itself. It is a closed circle, but one in which there is nevertheless an alluring atmosphere of anticipation.

The use of extended durations and delayed resolutions, essentially a manipulation of the dramatic elements of tonal syntax, finds aleatoric expression in Michael Nyman's 1975 work for multiple pianos, *1–100*. In performance, four or more pianists play from the same part, which Pwyll ap Siôn describes as having

> an unswerving internal logic and independence. Its 100-chord. . . sequence forms a structural grid from which a Baroque-style harmonic process gradually unfolds. The pattern's cyclical movement is characterized by an oblique motion in the bass, rising up a perfect fourth then falling by a perfect or diminished fifth interval, and usually harmonized by major or minor chords, or permutations thereof. The use of alternative fifths intervals allows the chord sequence to either remain within a previously established harmonic area or shift across into related ones. (Pwyll ap Siôn, *The Music of Michael Nyman: Texts, Contexts and Intertexts* (Surrey, UK: Ashgate, 2007), 46)

As the harmonic sequences progress through various key areas, the chords accumulate added tones, resulting in an intriguing stylistic metamorphosis from Baroque to jazz chords. These chords also gradually traverse the keyboard from high to low register. This latter detail has major implications not only for the timbral profile of the work but also for the performance. Brian Eno, whose record label Obscure Records released the first recording of *1–100* on *Decay Music* (*Obscure No. 5*) in 1976, describes a faithful performance:

> A player is instructed to move on to his next chord only when he can no longer hear his last. As this judgment is dependent on a number of variables (how loud the chord was played, how good the hearing of the player is, what the piano is like, the point at which you decide that the chord is no longer audible), the four players rapidly fall out of sync with one another. What happens after this is that unique and delicate clusters of up to four different chords are formed, or rapid sequences of chords are followed by long silences. (Brian Eno quoted in Christoph Cox and Daniel Warner, eds., *Audio Culture: Readings in Modern Music* (New York: Continuum, 2006), 230.)

Naturally, the higher the chord, the shorter the decay time; the pianists' attacks will thus occur in relatively close proximity. As the chord progression descends, however, the attacks spread out more and more in time as each player waits longer for the chords to decay before moving on. In making the work's harmonic rhythm dependent on the unpredictable acoustic, physical, and perceptual factors Eno describes, Nyman forces the listener to observe the workings of the tonal machinery objectively, out of reach of any momentum the modulatory progressions might normally generate. A dominant 7th chord might persist for 8 seconds or more before resolving, enough time for harmonic tension to fade, anticipation to evaporate. When the resolution does eventually arrive, it might be accompanied by a flurry of other chords from the other pianos, or it might be altered by the simultaneous sounding of these chords. By including an aspect of disruptive uncertainty in the performance instructions of *1–100*, Nyman transforms the experience of listening to historically derivative – even clichéd – material into an occasion of sonic discovery.

Perhaps the greatest insight *1–100* offers is the aesthetic potential of delayed and deflected anticipation. It is not the familiar chord changes that hold our attention. Apart from the Baroque-to-jazz shapeshifting, which occurs so gradually as to be imperceptible, there is scant nuance or novelty in the voicings or ambit of these chords. Rather, it is the proliferation of unpredictable collisions, skirmishes, antiphonies, and near-silences, in spite of the straightforward chord progressions, that captivate and disorient the ear. Musical anticipation is here a thing to be toyed with in an arbitrary, yet convincing, way. The result is a music that seems to be indifferent to the listener's anticipation, but which in fact could not exist without it.

Behind this chapter lies another, unwritten essay. Because it does not yet exist, let's call it *Anticipatory Problems in the Future of Music*. This hidden essay takes up where the present one leaves off. That is to say, after the death of anticipation. Isn't that where we are now? I have attempted to write a pocket biography of anticipation, starting with a depiction of its early life as a tiny note (Mozart), then its turbulent adolescence (Schumann), the treacheries and dissolutions of its adulthood (Chausson, Schoenberg), and finally its death and transfiguration (Babbitt, Glass, Nyman). You'll forgive me if I seem to be conflating anticipation (note) with anticipation (concept). We began, after all, with a similar linguistic confusion. But there really is not a difference; it is simply a matter of proportion. The copious amount of perceptual information squeezed into a sliver of time in Mozart's "Hunt" quartet is stretched and warped over several measures in Glass's symphony. Viewed from the perspective of music history, a tiny black dot becomes an impression, a feeling, an atmosphere. Anticipation (note) becomes anticipation (concept).

The hidden essay would take a different approach (if only for my own, purely self-interested, reasons), investigating the history and problems of human-computer musical interaction. I spend a good deal of time every day thinking about how dumb computers are and how smart musicians are; or how dumb humans are and how smart computers are. It is really the same problem: what computers know is vast and indiscriminate; what humans know is limited and magical. Imagine you were a composer interested in musical collaboration between humans and computers, in making something vast and magical. The first step would be to find a way for humans and computers to make music together. Composers have been working on this problem for more than half a century, but the computer has yet to become the undisputed expressive equal of its human counterparts.

The first compositions exploring this terrain were pieces for human performers and recorded electronic sounds, such as those by Babbitt and Mario Davidovsky (1960s). Then came the early interactive systems, like the one designed by composer David Behrman on a KIM-1 Microcomputer for his work *On the Other Ocean* (1977). The composer and trombonist George Lewis started developing his Voyager software system in 1986 and continues to make his own innovative contributions today. ("'Voyager' is a nonhierarchical, interactive musical environment that privileges improvisation. In Voyager, improvisors engage in dialogue with a computer-driven, interactive 'virtual improvising orchestra.'" George Lewis, *Too Many Notes: Computers, Complexity and Culture in Voyager*, Leonardo Vol. 10, No. 1, 33–39 (2000).) At IRCAM in Paris, the composer Pierre Boulez started working with engineer Andrew Gerzso to design electronic systems for his music in the early 1980s, notably for *Répons* (1981). In 1997, this collaboration culminated in an interactive system for Boulez's violin work *An-thèmes 2*. (Boulez describes the function of this system in the program note: "*Anthèmes II* adopte également une approche live; c'est pourquoi tout le matériau électronique est généré en temps réel pendant la représentation.")

The work on the system for *Anthèmes 2* led to further developments at IRCAM, particularly in the area of "score following" capabilities. Today, a team headed by computer scientist Arshia Cont, an IRCAM affiliate, is leading research into computational score following with the development of the software Antescofo (2007–present), designed in collaboration with composer Marco Stroppa. Like some of the earlier systems, Antescofo can listen to a human performance and identify the notes played, using that information to trigger subsequent musical events. But it can do much more: with a musical score input in advance, Antescofo can use the performance data to follow the musician's playing in real time and adjust to fluctuations in tempo. This is perhaps the first example of a computer system successfully anticipating aspects of human performance. (The name "Antescofo" is a portmanteau of "Anticipatory Score Following.") Another IRCAM-developed system, Jérôme Nika's improteK software (2013–present), adds generative improvisatory capability to its anticipatory function (improteK captures and analyzes live performance and generates real-time improvisations, which are reintegrated into the live performance.)

With remarkable perseverance and ingenuity, musicians and scientists like Cont and Nika have largely overcome many of the technical challenges of human-computer musical performance, particularly those related to data capture and synchronicity. Their systems are truly capable of anticipating human musical activity in terms of note attack and even harmonic probability. But these technical achievements suggest ever more elusive goals, and they are quite similar to goals preoccupying current AI and deep learning research: the computer's development of aesthetic preferences ("taste," "personality") that would inform its live performance; a capacity for higher-order musical thinking regarding form, affect, style, etc.; multisensory data and biofeedback analysis; the ability to compose and revise – not simply improvise – in real time, maintaining long-range formal coherence; in short, a technology that evolves from reaction to discourse.

A discursive, artificial musical intelligence would not only be able to anticipate the actions of a human collaborator, it would also anticipate the human thought process behind those actions: why is the human's playing becoming faster? softer? more dissonant? What are the aesthetic implications of such observations? Do I (the computer) follow, divert, or interrupt the trajectory of the human's performance? What shared musical or cultural references might influence my decision? These are the kinds of unspoken questions human improvisors ask and answer – subconsciously and instantaneously – during a performance.

Beyond these highly specialized performative issues lie more broadly applicable questions as well. In the future, I expect that when we listen to music, we will be listening to software, not fixed recordings. (As early as 1996 Brian Eno suggested: "I think it's possible that our grandchildren will look at us in wonder and say: 'You mean you used to listen to exactly the same thing over and over again?'" Andy Oldfield, *Brian Eno's generation game*, The Independent (28 July 1996).) Using data such as biofeedback, software will be able to anticipate a listener's reactions to the music and make appropriate modifications to it. We can imagine what some of these modifications might entail: shortening or lengthening the duration of a song; changing the tempo globally or momentarily; changing the timbre, key, instrumentation, and performers (including vocalists).

When music begins to be widely consumed as software, as I believe it one day will be, composers will have to grapple with profound conceptual challenges if they wish to participate in this evolution of their art. The process of composing "music-as-software" that is capable of anticipatory adaptation to individual listeners' neurobiology will be unlike any working methods most composers today employ. "Music-as-software" will likely be conceived as a collection of musical behaviors and events governed by probabilities that are in turn modified by the analysis of biofeedback. The calibration of these probabilities will become part of the composition process, reflecting the composer's personal aesthetic values. No longer will the unique identity of a musical work be dependent upon the exact sequence notes and rhythms permanently recorded in the hardcopy score, but rather upon the unique patterns of behavior with which the composer endows the software. This new way of working will apply considerable tension to the conventional definition of composition, indeed, to the very origin of the word, i.e., *componere*, "to put together." In music-as-software, the "putting-together" will be the computer's job. And it will happen differently at each listening and for each listener.

Whether or not this will be a good development for music is an unavoidable, if essentially pointless, debate to come. Societal trends regarding media consumption are on an irreversible course towards the infinitely customizable, individual experience. This trend, when considered together with advances in technology, especially artificial intelligence, suggests software will change the nature of music in the way the printing press changed literature and photography changed painting. Composers and listeners alike will have at their disposal virtually limitless computational power to reimagine the experience of making and listening to music. As with prior advances in music technology – the piano, the metronome, the notation system – this future potential promises to produce new and startling works of music. But just what these new works might sound like is something the entire history of music has not prepared us to anticipate.

Where to Begin? Surveying Anticipation in Neuroscience: An Essential Roadmapping Toolkit

9

Fabián Labra-Spröhnle

"To begin at the beginning:"
Dylan Thomas. 'Under milk wood'.

Contents

Abstract

This paper introduces a basic tool kit derived from "systematic reviews" in clinical research and from "genetic epistemology." The purpose of this tool kit is to establish a bird's-eye view of some fundamental landmarks and grounding notions, directly related to the subject of "anticipation" in neuroscience. This tool kit is particularly aimed at helping scholars orient within the plethora of published literature in neuroscience and to facilitate the identification and analysis of notions underpinning the subject of "anticipation." The methodological and

F. Labra-Spröhnle (✉)
Clinical Research Programme, School of Biological Sciences, Victoria University of Wellington, Wellington, New Zealand
e-mail: flabra@xtra.co.nz

© Springer Nature Switzerland AG 2019
R. Poli (ed.), *Handbook of Anticipation*,
https://doi.org/10.1007/978-3-319-91554-8_19

epistemological foundations for the tool kit are scrutinized and condensed in two sequential procedures: a "scouting systematic review" and a "fast-track episte-mological analysis." To examine the performance of this tool kit, an example of its application is provided. As a result, important landmarks and grounding notions, within the subject of "cognitive anticipation," have been identified. Despite this method's value, it is concluded that it should be used with caution, for it is not meant to replace a full systematic review, and it does not give an exhaustive epistemological analysis.

Keywords

Anticipation · Cognitive anticipation · Inferences · Epistemology · Neuroscience · Mind · Conjectures

Introduction

The field of neuroscience has become a vast territory, spanning from the natural world to the artificial and synthetic (Davis et al. 2016; Jaeger and Jung 2015). As a result, navigating this theoretical, methodological, and experimental landscape has become a critical issue for the advancement of the discipline.

The breadth of this territory is determined by two orthogonal and interdependent dimensions:

(i) The first is quantitative. It concerns the plethora of published literature in neuroscience that thwarts its full revision. To manage this problem, some initiatives are already in place aimed at engineering navigational and organizing tools to deal with the overwhelming amount of information (cf. Silva et al. 2013).

One concerning shortcoming of these proposals is how to manage the "paradigm-dependent" character of experiments, observations, and data gathering. These ele-ments, once collected and mapped, are assumed to be more or less "commensurable" (Kuhn 1996), in order to "fit" into a unified map to show meaningful connections between them. This situation leads us to the next dimension.

(ii) The second is qualitative. It concerns the diversity and complexity of the notional content and practices in neuroscience. This dimension is difficult to deal with, since we have to go beyond a simple information retrieval process. This process requires hermeneutic procedures to make sense of ideas and notions at play, i.e., to interpret theories, methods, experiments, and data, in a wider paradigmatic context (Kuhn 1996).

In this dimension most of the notional content is derived from or associated with the "mind-body problem" and its related solutions. Traditionally, one of the prime goals of neuroscience has been to provide an account of this problem (in terms of explanation, prediction, and modeling), i.e., of how the body, its neural structures, and their functioning are related to mental functions (cognition, affection, and conation) (Hilgard 1980).

To get a profitable orientation when dealing with the notional entanglement of the mind-body problem, some scholars have advised to carry out a conceptual analysis and a critique of the theoretical landmarks and grounding notions at play, including their historical inception and development, i.e., an epistemological analysis (Labra-Spröhnle 2016b; Marková and Berrios 2016; Overton 2015; Piaget 1963).

However, to perform a fair epistemological analysis is a very demanding task mainly because of two reasons: firstly, it depends on how well the quantitative dimension is managed and, secondly, it depends on the insightful treatment of the qualitative dimension, i.e., on the pertinent allocation of boundaries by researchers.

In summary, the way we handle these two dimensions has direct impact on how we gather information and analyze knowledge available at present. *A fortiori*, dealing with these dimensions, influences the practice of designing "research road maps," tracing new routes of inquiry and planning new experiments.

Main Objective

Given the breadth and complexity of the neuroscience landscape, the development of orienting tools and strategies that could assist during the retrieval and analysis of the current literature has become a desideratum.

Therefore, the main purpose of this paper is to suggest and trial orienting strategies and navigational tools (a basic "road-mapping tool kit"), in order to establish a cursory overview of some fundamental landmarks and grounding notions directly related to the subject of anticipation in neuroscience. This basic "road-mapping tool kit" should provide assistance in retrospective and prospective research.

Anticipation in Neuroscience

"Anticipation in neuroscience" could be understood as any "future-oriented action, decision, or behaviour based on a (implicit or explicit) prediction" (Pezzulo et al. 2008) in reference to any subject of inquiry within the field of neuroscience.

As a subject matter, anticipation is a ubiquitous topic; anticipatory phenomena are embedded within and scattered through almost all the main research areas in neuroscience. Much of the acquired knowledge in this particular subject has been obtained indirectly. Notions regarding anticipation are a *sine qua non* element in the description and explanation of any goal-directed process that develops in time. Anticipatory and comparing mechanisms play a fundamental role in creating, guiding, and controlling the interactions of living agents with the environment.

Despite of the key role played by anticipatory mechanisms, its notion has been occasionally neglected and relegated as troublesome (Nadin 2015c; Seligman et al. 2013). The acknowledgement of the subversive power of anticipation and some of its closely associated concepts (e.g., teleology) have led in some extreme cases to its overt censorship. Only recent initiatives have been promoting and rescuing anticipation studies, bringing them to the foreground as an important and autonomous field of research (Nadin 2015a, b).

An understanding of the anticipatory phenomena in neuroscience is directly linked and subordinated to the different views and solutions given to the aforementioned "mind-body problem." Thus, an epistemological analysis seems to be a suitable initial strategy to get a primary overview of some theoretical landmarks and notions that underpin the subject of anticipation in neuroscience.

In practical terms the feasibility of this task rests in the implementation of an expeditious procedure, to gather and scrutinize the raw information. Thus, the first step is to perform a "systematic review" (Gough et al. 2012) and thereafter to proceed with an epistemological survey of the collected data.

However, the task of performing a systematic review and a proper epistemological analysis is very demanding, due to the vastness of the field of neuroscience and its inherent complex notions. To make this undertaking tractable, two sequential procedures are proposed: the first one is to perform a "scouting systematic review" (see method section Rationale) and the second one is a "fast-track epistemological analyses." Regarding this last procedure, it is proposed that tools and strategies that can be derived from "genetic epistemology" (GE) should be used. This procedure is the heart of the proposal and deserves a special treatment to justify it.

Justification of Theoretical Approach (Fast-Track Epistemological Analyses)

The justification to use this approach rests in the following GE tenets:

GE have a line of work congruous with a non-reductionist, "integrative approach," that suits the nature of the phenomena investigated by neuroscience, particularly anticipatory events. This integrative approach is supported by:

(i) A naturalistic "principle of continuity" (geared by a mechanism of differentiation and integrations), which states that (a) the center of life is a self-regulating process and that (b) there is a continuity and isomorphism of this process throughout all goal-directed activities of living creatures.
This type of organization is "found at all levels from the regulations of the genome to those of behaviour" (Piaget 1974). These self-regulating mechanisms consist of a "combinatory system" of anticipations and retroactions.
(ii) GE is a developmental and evolutionary framework.
(iii) The assumption of the explanatory irreducibility of mental experience leads to a methodological commitment, i.e., "psychophysiological parallelism," in which mental phenomena are treated in twofold manner, i.e., as simultaneously psychological (in which the elements given to conscious experience are connected by "implications") and neurological (in which the connection between the elements is "causal").
If the elements of these two realms are abstracted, only their "relational" aspect remains, and what can be observed is the formation of a gradual and

developmental "isomorphism between implications and causality." This position favors *relational* thinking and parlance in which: "no appeal must be made
to entities, faculties or factors beyond the relations themselves and their interconnections" (Piaget 2007).
(iv) The "principle of continuity" guarantees that anticipatory mechanisms play a
central role at all levels in the analysis of phenomena (diachronically and
synchronically).
(v) The last insights advanced by Piaget in his posthumous published works extend
the continuity principle to certain mechanisms found at a physical-chemical
level, like those in Prigogines' dissipative structures. Piaget countersigned by
Prigogine acknowledged at least five close analogies between cognitive equilibria and "dissipative structures"(Piaget 1980a).

In fact, there are at least five close analogies between these "dissipative structures" and what
we consider equilibrations and cognitive equilibria. In the first place, these structures
concern dynamic equilibria which include interchanges with the outside; these are quite
different from equilibria without interchange. Secondly, it is these interchanges which
stabilize the structures through regulations. Thirdly, equilibration as such is characterized,
in both cases, by a form of "a self-organization. " Fourthly, the states, at given points in time,
having passed through a series of unstable states, can be understood only on the basis of their
past history. Finally, and most importantly, the stability of a system is a function of its
complexity. (Piaget and Garcia 1988)

Conclusion

(i) Using heuristic tools derived from GE (further discussed in the following
sections) may assist scholars to perform a "scouting systematic review" and a
"fast-track epistemological analysis" of anticipation's grounding notions and
thus facilitate the making of a cursory roadmap of "anticipation in neuroscience."
(ii) Both an epistemological awareness of fundamental assumptions and the making
explicit of starting points (a kind of "zero milestone" in all scientific inquiry)
and their generating mechanisms may serve to orientate and to suggest further
solutions, explanations, and experimental work.

Outline of the Following Sections
2 Epistemological tools.
2.1 This subsection summarizes the theoretical framework and some empirical
evidence (psychogenetic and historical-critical) that support and assist the selection of "epistemological tools."
2.2 This subsection establishes the methods and "epistemological tools" that will be
used to identify landmarks and outline some grounding notions of anticipation in
neuroscience.
3 Scouting systematic review and fast-track epistemological analysis.
3.1 This subsection is presented as a proof of concept and illustrates the use of the
tools already described; a "scouting systematic review" and an abbreviated "fast-

track epistemological analysis" are performed. Important landmark and diverse grounding notions that underpin some anticipations research in neuroscience are identified.

4 Conclusions and Warnings.

Epistemological Tools

In an essay entitled "What does it mean to orient oneself in thinking?" Kant noticed that no matter how abstract we conceive our notions to be, they are always attached to our experience, since they are born from it and also because their function is to be "serviceable for experiential uses" (Kant 1998). Moreover, Kant stated that if we remove all the sensible content from these notions, what is left over are just some overarching maxims or rules for thinking in general, like those that gave origin to general logic. Kant surmises that numerous heuristic methods could be extracted from the practical and experiential use of our operations of understanding and reason, or as he put it:

> ... many heuristic methods of thinking perhaps lie hidden in the experiential use of our understanding and reason; if we carefully extract these methods from that experience, they could well enrich philosophy with many useful maxims even in abstract thinking (Kant 1998).

In particular, Kant recalls Mendelssohn's principle, "namely, the maxim that it is necessary to orient oneself in the speculative use of reason [...] by means of a certain guideline which he sometimes called common sense or healthy reason, and some-times plain understanding." Likewise, the next subsection exposes theory and evidence that will inform the guidelines for teasing out "grounding notions" under-pinning anticipation research in neuroscience.

Genetic Epistemology: Abstraction and Generalization Processes

Genetic epistemology (GE) is an experimental and theoretical discipline that aims to study the growth of knowledge, both at the individual level (the conceptual devel-opment at different stages of their psychological growth) and historical level (col-lective scientific notions held during different historical periods).

The choice of studying this matter at these two levels is supported by the view that the constructive processes of knowledge are similar in both cases.

GE combine methods from the history of science and psychogenesis. By these means GE relates the experimental study of the intellectual development in children to the historical-critical analysis of scientific concepts. Briefly in the words of Piaget, the founder of GE:

> GENETIC EPISTEMOLOGY attempts to explain knowledge, and in particular scientific knowledge, on the basis of its history, its sociogenesis, and especially the psychological origins of the notions and operations upon which it is based. (Piaget 1971)

Recently, GE has been scrutinized as a valid approach to tackle the history of science (Winstanley 2016). Despite this reevaluation, it was concluded that GE cannot totally be dismiss a legitimate style of inquiry into the history of science. As it often happens with Piaget's ideas, this criticism has overlooked one of the main tenets of Piaget's theoretical framework, i.e., the continuity of life's general organizing function.

Life's self-regulating activity is expressed in cognitive processes that "seem, then, to be at one and the same time the outcome of organic autoregulation, reflecting its essential mechanisms, and the most highly differentiated organs of this regulation at the core of interactions with the environment" (Piaget 1974).

One of the main principles of GE is that children, like scientists, have to actively manipulate their environment in order to construct knowledge. According to Piaget:

> Knowing does not really imply making a copy of reality but, rather, reacting to it and transforming it (either apparently or effectively) in such a way as to include it functionally in the transformation systems with which these acts are linked. (Piaget 1974)

This statement conveys the idea that knowledge is built up from the practical interaction between the agent and the world. This interaction is organized in sensory-motor patterns (action schemata), which drives and regulates behavior.

Within this framework, abstraction and generalization processes have a central role during the construction of knowledge. Since Aristotle, abstraction processes have been identified as one of the fundamental mechanisms responsible for concept formation. Notwithstanding, the term "abstraction" as it is commonly used nowadays was introduced by Boethius in the early sixth century. Boethius defined "abstraction" as the mental operation by which only certain aspects, which are relevant for a particular purpose, are extracted from an observable phenomenon.

When Piaget was experimentally dealing with the problem of concept formation in children, and also analyzing the creation of scientific concepts (in mathematics and in physics), he noticed the striking similarity between the abstraction mechanisms involved in the creation of concepts at both levels (Piaget and Campell 2014; Piaget and Garcia 1988). Piaget described two main kinds of abstractions processes, namely, empirical abstraction and reflecting abstraction.

Empirical Abstraction

Empirical abstraction corresponds to what Aristotle and Boethius framed as a generic variety of processes that participates in the formation of concepts (Wiener 1980). In Piaget's words:

> The kind of abstraction that ranges over physical objects or the material aspects of one's own action (such as movements, pushes, and the like) we will call 'empirical.' Let us note right away that this type of abstraction, even in its most elementary forms, cannot be a pure 'read-off' of data from the environment. To abstract any property whatsoever from an object, such as its weight or its colour, the knowing subject must already be using instruments of assimilation (meanings and acts of putting into relation) that depend on sensorimotor or conceptual schemes. And such schemes are constructed in advance by the subject, not furnished by the object.

> However, these schemes are only instrumentally necessary for empirical abstraction. Empirical abstraction does not range over the schemes themselves; it aims only at the data that remain external to them. The facts are the content; the knowing subject's schemes merely embody the forms that make it possible to grasp that content. (Piaget and Campell 2014)

To illustrate his concept of "instruments of assimilation," Piaget bracketed two examples worth commenting on: "meanings" and "acts of putting into relation." Before dwelling into these examples however, some of Piaget's basic notions need to be established.

The most basic instruments of cognitive assimilation are "action schemata." When a living being interacts in a goal-directed manner with the world (by acting upon it), there are two interdependent processes that could arise from this interaction: "assimilation" and "accommodation." Both of these processes make up the primary mechanism of knowledge acquisition.

To elaborate on these, let's examine the act of grasping an object (e.g., a pebble). This act consists of an ordered sequence of discrete actions that form a pattern (a script or choreography). Piaget referred to this pattern as "action schemata" and expressed it as follows:

> We shall apply the term 'action schemata' to whatever, in an action, can thus be transposed, generalized, or differentiated from one situation to another: in other words, whatever there is in common between various repetitions or superpositions of the same action. (Piaget 1974)

This notion can be further illustrated via the following examples:

If a grasping scheme is applied to a pebble, and the pebble allows this (in the sense that the scheme is accepted by this object), then it may be said that the object has been "assimilated" by and into this schema. Now suppose that the same grasping schemata is applied to a ripe apricot. Because this object requires a different amount of pressure to grasp it, the scheme has to be modified accordingly. In this case, the original action schemata (that was applied to the pebble) was "accommodated" to the new object (apricot).

It should be noted here that there are also cases where a grasping schema can be applied, but the object does not accept it. These objects consist of those that cannot be grasped, for example, a soap bubble or a shadow.

Following these notions, and returning to the concept of "instruments of assimilation," it now becomes possible to explain how "action schemata" are the origin of meanings.

The meaning of "graspable," for instance, is actualized through the application of grasping schemata upon objects (cf. Piaget 1950), whereby the meaning's "extension" and "intension" are determined by assimilation and accommodation, respectively. In general, complex arrangements of schema give origin to complex meanings at the sensory-motor level, and complex sets of "operations" give rise to meanings at higher cognitive levels (Piaget et al. 2013).

Now to recall the last example of "instruments of assimilation" given by Piaget, i.e., the "acts of putting into relation," a brief explanation will be given to clarify this concept. Aside from generating "meaning," the application of action schemata to new objects or content furthermore implies "the act of putting into relation," namely, the act of relating old content with new content. In general, any correspondence or comparison (metric and non-metric) rests on acts of "putting into relation."

For example, consider the act of manually weighting two pebbles, by comparing the subjective feeling of each, with the hand. In this case the "act of putting into relation" refers to the act of relating the weight (directly derived from the application of sensory-motor schemata) of one pebble with the other.

Notwithstanding, "action schemata" can be extended by the use of material tools (like auxiliary objects, scripts, diagrams, devices, and machines). These tools act as mediators, facilitators, or enhancers of the practical action performed upon the world, by the cognitive agent. At the same time, material tools embody actions and operations derived from the direct interaction between the agent and the world.

To elaborate with an example, evaluate the act of grasping little things with the hand. Once an object, such as a grain of sand, becomes too small to be grasped with the hand, a tool like tweezers (which embody the act of grasping) can serve to extend this act and aid in this regard. Likewise, the act of comparing the weights of pebbles could be enhanced with a tool embodying that action, such as a weighing scale. It is apparent from both examples that physical tools can support and extend the range of our operation in the world.

However, there are also nonmaterial tools that fulfil the same purpose. Consider a more complex task (instead of one isolated action), where the agent has to order a sequence of acts. In this case, a nonmaterial tool (e.g., symbolic), such as a verbal formula or written script, like a complex self-directive utterance (Luria 1982) or a cooking recipe, respectively, can aid the sequencing process.

In summary, "meanings" and "acts of putting into relation" are examples of instruments of assimilation derived from action schemata. These action schemata can either be directly exerted by the subject upon the world or else mediated by the use of material and/or nonmaterial tools.

Reflecting Abstraction

In the "Introduction à l'épistémologie génétique. Vol. 1: la pensée mathématique" (Piaget 1950), Piaget critiques Helmholtz's idea about the origin of the concept of number. According to Helmholtz, the notion of number is abstracted from the sequence of conscious acts. Instead, Piaget states that this notion is derived from a variety of abstractions that arise from the subject's coordination of actions; he called this type of abstraction "reflecting abstraction."[1]

Piaget went on to experimentally study "reflecting abstraction" by examining the formation and development of concepts in children and in science (Piaget and Campell 2014; Piaget and Garcia 1988). From these studies, he concluded that:

---

[1]A similar and earlier notion, was held by Locke in Book II, chapter VI (Of simple ideas of reflection) of his essay "An Essay Concerning Human Understanding" (Locke 1998)

> Reflecting abstraction proceeds from the actions or operations of the knowing subject and transfers to a higher plane what has been taken from a lower level of activity; it leads to differentiations that necessarily imply new, generalizing compositions at the higher level. (Piaget and Campell 2014)

Piaget also held that "reflecting abstraction" is a *sui generis*, process for knowledge construction, which functionally corresponds, in part, to biological and neural mechanisms.[2]

According to the same author, "reflecting abstraction" differs from "empirical abstraction," in the following way:

> By contrast, 'reflecting' abstraction ranges over those very forms and over all of the subject's cognitive activities (schemes or coordinations of actions, operations, cognitive structures, etc.). Reflecting abstraction separates out certain characteristics of those cognitive activities and uses them for other ends (new adaptations, new problems, etc.). It is 'reflecting' in two complementary senses. First, it transposes onto a higher plane what it borrows from the lower level (for instance, in conceptualizing an action). We will call this transfer or projection a *reflechissement*. Second, it must therefore reconstruct on the new level B what was taken from the previous level A. or establish a relationship between the elements extracted from A and those already situated in B. This reorganization that is forced by the projection will be called a reflection in the strict sense. (Piaget and Campell 2014)

Remarking the twofold functioning of "reflecting" abstraction, at every level of cognitive development, Piaget continues:

> Reflecting abstraction, with its two components projection and reflection, can be observed at every major stage of development. During the sensorimotor substages. . . toddlers can solve problems by borrowing certain coordinations from previously constructed cognitive structures and reorganizing them in light of new data. In these cases, we have no idea what the knowing subject becomes conscious of. By contrast, at the higher levels, when reflection is a product of thinking as this is normally understood, it becomes necessary to make a further distinction. There is reflecting abstraction as a constructive process, and there is its retroactive thematization which then becomes a reflection on the reflection. In these cases, we will speak of 'reflected abstraction' or reflecting thought. (Piaget and Campell 2014)

When knowledge shifts from a lowest level to a higher level, the advancement is firstly enacted only at an instrumental level (pure "know-how") without cognizance. Only in later phases, this instrumental advancement is thematized giving birth to new concepts and theories. These thematizations prompt reflecting abstraction to "reflected abstraction."

To finalize, he introduces the idea that "reflecting abstraction" could spring from the actions or operation embodied in material tools, used by the subject:

---

[2]It was Hughlings Jackson and Sherrington, inspired by Herbert Spencer's evolutionary ideas, that first describe these mechanisms, which are driven by "differentiation" and "integration" processes, and produce "the integration of lower structures into the structure of the subsequence stage to form a hierarchy whose levels correspond to the successive phases of growth" (Piaget 1974)

It is useful to add a final distinction. At those developmental levels that are representational but preoperational, as well as at the level of concrete operations, it sometimes happens that the knowing subject cannot carry out some constructions (which later on will become purely deductive) without relying constantly on their observable results (cf., using the abacus for the first numerical operations). In that case we will speak of 'pseudo-empirical abstractions.'

While the results are read off from material objects, as is the case with empirical abstraction, the observed properties are actually introduced into these objects by the activities of the subject. Consequently, we are in the presence of a variety of reflecting abstraction that operates with the aid of observables that are external, on the one hand, but that are constructed by reflecting abstraction, on the other. By contrast, the properties covered by empirical abstraction were already in the objects before the subject engaged in any act of observation. (Piaget and Campell 2014)

Generalization Processes

"Generalization processes," as defined by Piaget, are closely related to the abstractions already discussed in the above subsection; in addition, they are also instruments for the construction of knowledge. There are two main forms of generalization, each springing from one type of abstraction:

(i) Firstly, "inductive generalization" is derived from the content obtained by "empirical abstractions." This kind of generalization is purely "extensional" with regard to its content and is responsible for the formal transition from some to all, or from particular to general laws in the empirical realm.

(ii) Secondly, "constructive generalizations" is derived from "reflecting abstractions." This generalization entails a widening of the extension and intension of its content. It is furthermore responsible for new synthesis and invention of new meanings in the formal and the empirical realm.

Psychogenesis and the History of Science

For more than a decade, Piaget conducted comparative studies following the program of GE (Bringuier and Piaget 1989), on the formation and development of concepts in children and in science (Piaget and Garcia 1988).

The main findings from this research identified several common elements among these two levels of analysis; Piaget classified these elements into three groups, namely, (i) instruments, (ii) processes and (iii) mechanisms:

(i) Key "instruments" of knowledge acquisition, generated by "assimilation" and "accommodation," are "abstractions" and "generalizations."

(ii) The most important "process" is the "search of reasons" that support "abstractions" and "generalizations." This is expressed by the search for "causes" in empirical science (physical realities) and the search for "proofs" or demonstrations in formal science (logic-mathematical realities).

This "search of reasons" is bound to another process, i.e., an "inferential activity," which gives rise to the "possible" and the "necessary." From this duality, a third fundamental process arises, namely, the twofold movement that drives "assimilation" and "accommodation" and which produces a dynamic "equilibrium" between "differentiations" and "integrations."

(iii) There are three common mechanisms: "intrafigural," "interfigural," and "trans-figural" relationships.

Piaget develops this in the following quote:

> For larger periods of history, obviously one does not find any stage-by-stage parallelism, but one can search for common mechanisms. For instance, the history of Western geometry bears witness to a process of structuration whose steps are those of a centration on an emphasis by Euclid on simply intrafigural relationships, then a construction of interfigural relationships with Cartesian coordinate systems, and then finally a progressive algebrization by Klein. Now one finds, on a small scale, a similar process in children, who naturally begin with the 'intrafigural' but who discover around their seventh year that in order to determinate a point on a plane, one measurement is not sufficient, but two are necessary, and they must be orthogonally arranged. After this 'interfigural' stage (which is necessary also for the construction of horizontal lines) follows that which we can call the 'transfigural' stage, in which the properties to be discovered cannot be read on a single diagram. but necessitate a deduction or a calculation (for example, mechanical curves, relative motions, and so on). (Piaget 1980b)

As a corollary to the former theoretical exposition, it should be remarked that "reflecting abstraction" and its variants can be derived not only from the direct use of actions performed by the subject but also from the actions and operations embodied in the material and/or nonmaterial tools that the subject uses to interact with the world. An example regarding the use of tools in this sense was discussed by Piaget in the last part of section "Reflecting Abstraction," where he explains how the use of the abacus can support "abstraction" processes. He goes on to say, with the aid of a different example, that:

> the subject can have no knowledge of objects except by acting on them. To "establish" what a weight is, one has to perform the muscular action of feeling it, and, in so doing, one sets up a balance which supplies the weight by means of a collection of metric relations. (cf. Pag 336. Piaget 1974)

In concordance with this, recent publications in neuroscience and the history of science that are completely oblivious to Piaget's advancements show awareness of the role of tools, diagrams, and techniques, in the formation of theory in neuroscience (Borck 2016; Uttal 2016). In an emblematic insight, Uttal affirms that: "An emerging generalization is that our theories are, too a much greater degree than we appreciate, creatures of whatever technology is available at any stage of history." Furthermore, the same author affirms that "the course of scientific history quickly makes clear that an array of influential instruments has guided the historical progress of the biological sciences and lately the cognitive neurosciences" (Uttal 2016).

However, the most instructive example of "reflecting abstraction" derived from tools, during the formation of concepts and theories in neuroscience, was provided by the "tools-to-theories" research program, carried out by Gerd Gigerenzer. This will be the subject of the next subsection (Gigerenzer 1991).

The Tools-to-Theories Heuristic

In the foreword of Piaget and García's (1988) "Psychogenesis and the History of Science," Barbel Inhelder commented on some findings related to "abstraction and generalization processes":

> These mechanisms and instruments of progress have been illustrated by the great number of behaviors children adopt in solving problems. They turned out to be of a more general nature so that they can serve as a heuristic for analyses in depth of the historical sequences in the evolution of certain aspects of mathematical and physical thinking. (Piaget and Garcia 1988)

Following a similar insight, Gigerenzer stated in "From tools to theories: A heuristic of discovery in cognitive psychology" that:

> The power of tools to shape, or even to become, theoretical concepts is an issue largely ignored in both the history and philosophy of science. (Gigerenzer 1991)

Gigerenzer was unaware of the work of Piaget and García regarding the role of "reflecting abstraction" in the formation of concepts and theories in science. Nonetheless, he provided one of the best examples of the enactment of "reflecting abstraction." Gigerenzer depicted how diverse concepts of mind and behavior have been abstracted from statistical tools and other experimental procedures used in neuroscience (Gigerenzer 1987). In this way, he provided further evidence for the role of "reflecting abstraction" as a constructive process and its retroactive thematization. Concordant with the aims of this paper, and to our benefit, Gigerenzer dwells on some particular tools that give rise to concepts directly linked to anticipation. The aim of the next subsection is to elaborate on this matter.

Mind as an Intuitive Statistician

According to Gigerenzer, the tools-to-theories heuristic, "explains the emergence of a broad range of cognitive theories, from the cognitive revolution of the 1960s up to the present, and it can be used to detect both limitations and new lines of development in current cognitive theories that investigate the mind as an 'intuitive statistician'" (Gigerenzer 1991).

In an earlier work, the same author postulated that the mechanism behind the formation of concepts and theories from tools rests on linguistic metaphors that lead to testable models (Gigerenzer 1987). However, Gigerenzer's conception of tools as simple sources of "metaphors" for theories of mind is even more fundamental than he recognized, for tools embody actions and operations, from which the process of "reflecting abstraction" can take place and thus allow for the buildup theories in science.

It is contended in this paper that Piaget's theory of "reflecting abstraction" provides a stronger explanatory framework than Gigerenzer's theory because (i) of its empirical evidence and (ii) it gives a more cogent base to Gigerenzer's findings (Piaget and Campell 2014; Piaget and Garcia 1988). As such, it is possible to explain that the most fundamental source of "metaphoric processes" is not "linguistic," but instead "pre-linguistic," i.e., due to "reflecting abstraction" processes, as shown by

Piaget in his studies on the formation of "analogies" (Piaget and Campell 2014). A quote by Piaget serves to illustrate this point:

> The construction of analogies makes an even prettier example of reflecting abstraction when we realize that their content, which ranges over the intrinsic properties of objects, is owed to a series of empirical abstraction. So the construction of analogies is essentially the construction of a form, and the facts we have reviewed clearly exhibit the steps by which this form is constructed. (Piaget and Campell 2014)

The fundamental and overarching role of "reflecting abstraction" processes as depicted by Piaget strongly supports similar and contemporary views in neuroscience (Uttal 2015, 2016), the history of science (Borck 2016), and epistemology. It is worthwhile to recognize that a particular branch within this orientation in epistemology, termed "epistemology of the concrete" (Daston 2000; Rheinberger 2010), deals with the study of how concepts in science are derived from the discipline's tools and practices. This method follows an analytical shift from the study of theory to the study of actions, procedures, and tools. Interestingly, a similar shift was made by Piaget in his studies of children, whereby the study of children's actions was privileged over the study of their theories about their actions. This allowed him to penetrate deeper onto the psychological phenomena under study. The present paper will take a similar methodological approach to tackle its aim; this will be elaborated in the following subsection.

Method and Tools

The methodological core of this paper's proposal is composed of two sequential procedures: a "scouting systematic review" and a "fast-track epistemological analysis."

(i) A scouting systematic review": gathering relevant information

"Systematic reviews" have been thoroughly dealt with in the literature and for this reason do not need to be detailed here; reference to texts such as "An Introduction to Systematic Reviews" (Gough et al. 2012) and "Systematic Reviews and Meta-Analysis" (Littell et al. 2008), illustrating the methods and tools used in systematic research, should suffice to clarify this matter. A brief explanation will nevertheless be offered at this point, in order to orient the reader.

A "scouting systematic review" is a variant of "scoping reviews":

> Scoping studies aim to map *rapidly* the key concepts underpinning a research area and the main sources and types of evidence available, and can be undertaken as standalone projects in their own right, especially where an area is complex or has not been reviewed comprehensively before. (Mays et al. 2001)

"Scoping reviews" therefore aim at establishing a cursory road map to assist scientific research, by suggesting further steps of inquiry; this is done by (a) visualizing the extent and distribution of the literature on a particular topic,

(b) determining the limits of the domain of enquiry, and (c) planning a further and more detailed review. Detailed guidelines of how to conduct a "scoping review" can be found in the area of research methodology, within the medical literature (Arksey and O'Malley 2005; O'Brien et al. 2016; Levac et al. 2010; Peters et al. 2015).

The basic procedure of a "scouting systematic review" consists in collecting "reviews" in the area of interest, in this case in "anticipation in neuroscience." In order to do this, it is very important to choose carefully (i) the "search keywords" and (ii) the right combination of these keywords that will be entered onto search engines like "Google Scholar." A tool which efficiently assists this method is the "Publish or Perish" software (available for free from the Internet), which retrieves and analyzes academic citations from different databases (Harzing 2011).

After this procedure, and taking a sort of "Lévy flight strategy" (Reynolds and Rhodes 2009) to navigate the searching field, a selection and examination of the references contained within the collected reviews should be carried out. This operation should be repeated, in order to form a nesting sequence of searches within the collected references.

(ii) A "fast-track epistemological analysis": guidelines

A "fast-track epistemological" analysis refers to the process of short-cutting or abbreviating an epistemological analysis, for example, by focusing on a particular element within the discipline of study. Thus, following the theoretical stance of this paper, and as preluded to in the previous section, the paramount focus in the epistemological analysis of the present paper will be on the particular "tools" and methods used by researchers.

The present fast-track analysis will consist of the following steps:

(a) Identify the tools, methods, and procedures embedded in the theoretical content of the subject under scrutiny, and illustrate instances of their presence.
(b) Obtain a primary understanding of the features, functioning, and mechanisms of these tools.
(c) Identify and analyze the actions and "operations" that are "abstracted," "reflected," and "thematized" from these tools.
(d) Identify the advantages and limitations of these tools within their particular scope and within theory construction.
(e) Summarize the most important findings, and recommend a course of navigation accordingly, in order to thoroughly investigate the references and plan new research.

Proof of Concept: A Brief Example

Anticipation in Neuroscience: Kilometer Zero Landmarks (Milestone)

In this section, an example of the application of the method (from section "Method and Tools") in the subject of anticipation in neuroscience is provided. Firstly, results will be discussed in terms of a "scouting review" and, secondly, in terms of a "fast-track epistemological analysis."

(i) "Scouting review"

The aim of this review is to find important landmarks and associated grounding notions that historically precede anticipatory research in neuroscience. Accordingly, the scouting review question is formulated as follows:

Since when, why, and how was the concept of mind equated to inferential activity (in its broadest sense)?

It is contended that answering this questions could help to "document the breadth and depth of the anticipation-related inquiry" (Nadin 2010). This question was prompted from previous reviews, but in particular from Gigerenzer's findings (Gigerenzer 1987). Gigerenzer noticed that the use of certain statistical tools led researchers to conceptualize mind as an "intuitive statistician." He showed how operations of mind could be equated to two main versions of statistical techniques of hypothesis testing, namely, Frequentist and Bayesian statistics (Gigerenzer 1992).

The same author convincingly showed that: "The spectrum of theories that model cognition after statistical inference ranges from auditory and visual perception to recognition in memory, and from speech perception to thinking and reasoning" (Gigerenzer and Sturm 2007). Nevertheless, Gigerenzer's findings are mainly limited to an "inductivist" view of inferences, since this view is embodied in the tools and techniques that he analyzed. Gigerenzer did not dwell into a broader notion of inferences and tools that can be associated with these processes. Nevertheless, his findings are crucial as an orienting clue for this review, because at the cognitive level, anticipatory activities are rendered by inferential processes. The notion of inferences therefore is central to anticipatory processes.

Noteworthy, the guiding questions and the searching keywords for this review are based on a wider notion of inferences than the one used by Gigerenzer. The concept used here is taken from Pierce and considers inferences as they happen during "processes of inquiry." Pierce defines it as follows:

> Confining ourselves to science, inference, in the broadest sense, is coextensive with the deliberate adoption, in any measure, of an assertion as true. For deliberation implies that the adoption is voluntary; and so consequently, the observation of perceptual facts that are forced upon us in experience is excluded. General principles, on the other hand, if deliberately adopted, must have been subjected to criticism; and any criticism of them that can be called scientific and that results in their acceptance must involve an argument in favor of their truth. My statement was that an inference, in the broadest sense, is a deliberate adoption, in any measure, of an assertion as true. The phrase 'in any measure' is not as clear as might be wished. 'Measure,' here translates modus. The modes of acceptance of an assertion that are traditionally recognized are the necessary, the possible, and the contingent. (Peirce 1998)

Based on this concept and on the scouting review question, the keywords used included mind, *mente*, inference, conjecture, anticipation, quantitative medicine, medicine history, and review. After performing multiple searches combining these terms, and inspecting the results, two key papers were selected:

"Nicolaus of Cusa, van Helmont, and Boyle: the first experiment of the Renaissance in quantitative biology and medicine," published in *the Journal of the History of Medicine and Allied Sciences* (Hoff 1964).

"On the beginnings of quantitative thinking in medicine (Nicolas of Cusa and the Idiot)," published in *History of Physiology: Proceedings of the 28th International Congress of Physiological Sciences, Budapest, 1980* (Schultheisz 2013).

These two papers were key for narrowing the scope of the search, in terms of its content and historical time. Searching keywords were extracted from these two papers, including Cusa, Cusanus, inference, conjecture, *mente*, and mind. A new search was carried out with these terms, and several papers and books were selected and inspected. The main finding was that Nicolaus Cusanus (1401–1464), also known as Nicholas of Cusa, was the first to put inferential activity at the center of mind, declaring that "mind is the form of inferential reasoning" (Cusa and Hopkins 1996a). The details and importance of this finding will be documented in the following subsection.

(ii) "Fast-track epistemological analysis"

This subsection will follow the guidelines from the section "Method and Tools":

(a) Identify the tools, methods, and procedures embedded in the theoretical content of the subject under scrutiny, and illustrate instances of their presence.

There is increased agreement among scholars from different disciplines that optical tools, instruments, and techniques, derived from linear perspective and the parametrization of visual space, played a fundamental role in the "rationalization of sight" (Ivins and Pèlerin 1973). Furthermore, this rationalization was recognized as one of the driving forces of the cultural and conceptual transition from medieval times to the modern world (Carman 2014; Denery II 2009; Edgerton 2009; Harries 2002; Hoff 2013).

It was in this transitional scenario that Nicholas of Cusa postulated a non-substantial, proactive, inference driven, functional, and developmental view of mind. What is more important for our purposes is his view of mind, which considers anticipatory activity as an essential feature (Cusa and Hopkins 1996a). Noteworthy, his notion of mind was informed by linear perspective methods and the mathematical operations that support them.

The following quotation taken from Nicholas of Cusa's *De Coniecturis* (On surmises) makes explicit reference to linear perspective and acknowledges its restrictions and ways to overcome them.

You now see that the positive assertions of the wise are surmises. For example, when with your very clear eyesight you, O Father, see before you the face of the Supreme Pontiff, our most holy lord, Pope Eugene IV, you form of it a positive assertion, which, in conformity with your sight, you maintain to be precise. But when you turn toward the root from whence the senses' discrimination flows—when you turn toward reason, I mean—you understand that the sense of sight partakes of [reason's] discriminating power with a degree-of-otherness that is contracted to the sense-organ. Consequently, you see the defect that characterizes the falling away from preciseness; for you contemplate the face not as it is [in itself] but in its otherness, according to your eye's angle, which differs from [that of] all the eyes of other living beings. Therefore, a surmise is a positive assertion that partakes—with a degree of otherness—of truth as it is [in itself]. However, just as by means of the oneness-of-reason the senses experience their own otherness and make surmises by freeing from precise oneness assertions about perceptible objects, so reason, by means of its root-oneness, viz., by means of the light of intelligence, discovers its own otherness and its falling away from preciseness into surmise. (Cusa and Hopkins 2000)

From this quotation it follows that precise absolute truth is unattainable; therefore, "every human affirmation about what is true is a surmise. For the increase in our apprehension of what is true is endless." In the same vein, Cassirer (2011) expands on Nicholas of Cusa's *De docta ignorantia*, by stating that "all of our empirical knowledge remains a 'probability', an attempt, a hypothesis which, from the very beginning, is reconciled to being superseded by better, more exact attempts."

According to Cusanus, mind's activity (spanning from simple perceptions to intellectual processes of enquiry) is determined by a process of creating surmises (hypothesis) and testing them by "comparing" (measuring) the accuracy of the presupposition about a thing (by anticipating a result), with the experienced thing (the actual result). Cusanus explains this idea in the following quote.

(The intellect insatiably desires to attain unto the true through scrutinizing all things by means of its innate faculty of inference.) Now, that from which no sound mind can withhold assent is, we have no doubt, most true. However, all those who make an investigation judge the uncertain proportionally, by means of a comparison with what is taken to be certain.

Therefore, every inquiry is comparative and uses the means of comparative relation. Now, when, the things investigated are able to be compared by means of a close proportional tracing back to what is taken to be [certain], our judgement apprehends easily; but when we need many intermediate steps, difficulty arises and hard work is required. (Cusa and Hopkins 1985)

Expanding on the idea of comparing, Cusanus declared in his *Idiota de mente* that: "Mind [*mens*] takes his name from measuring [*mensurare*]" (Cusa and Hopkins 1996a). From a functional and dynamic point of view, surmises are always interlocked with anticipatory and comparative (measuring) mechanisms.

Stressing the role of anticipation, De Cusa remarked in a text within his *Staticis Experimentis* that knowledge cannot be obtained solely by an inductive procedure, as it is usually conceptualized by empiricist views, i.e., inferred from data. Instead, he recognized that certain anticipatory capabilities in the knower motivate and guide the process of inquiry and the making sense of data.[3] In the words of Cusa:

---

[3]This outlook predated Kantian and Peircean views (cf. Giovanelli 2010; Peirce 1998). Moreover, the conceptual compatibility between Peirce and Cusa has been explicitly acknowledged by Debrock (1998)

There is no suitable way [for a surmise] to be made from weights, even though it is perhaps the case that the one giving the answer can gauge the weightiness of a [suitable] response only from the weightiness of the question. For the motivation for the questioning, on the part of the one posing the question, seems to be produced from a certain foreseeing of a future event, although [the questioner] does not see the source from which he is being motivated. (Cusa and Hopkins 1996b)

In an insightful review, concerning the possibility of a rational explanation to the *l' art of divination*, Parmentier (2011) pointed out the relation between the anticipatory capabilities described by Cusa and the theory of *petite perceptions* from Leibniz. In doing so, this author opened up a fruitful connection that could inspire the exploration of the origin of anticipatory phenomena, from a wider psychological point of view.

To conclude this step, it should be noted that Cusa's notion of mind was parsimoniously summarized by D'amico (2005), who furthermore observed that mind is the origin of conjectures (*origo coniecturae*) and the conjectural form of the world (*forma coniecturalis mundi*), that its own entity is due to conjectures (*entitas coniecturam suarum*), and that its functioning could be defined by mathematical operations.

(b) Obtain a primary understanding of the features, functioning, and mechanisms of these tools.

The Latin word *perspectiva* (perspective) means "seeing through" (Panofsky 1996). In general, perspective may be understood as a practical means for depicting the mutual, metric relationship, between the contours of objects (as they are actually located in space), and pictorially representing these relationships (Ivins and Pèlerin 1973). In particular, single-point linear perspective is a geometrical technique for creating the illusion of a three-dimensional visual space, on a planar two-dimensional surface. The technique and tools used in single-point linear perspective originated in Italy during the early Renaissance. Florentine architect Filippo Brunelleschi was the first to devise these and to experimentally demonstrate their empirical principles, while Florentine polymath Leon Battista Alberti was the first to document (in 1435) the mathematical underpinnings of single-point linear perspective, based on the mathematization of visual space, developed by Biagio Pelacani di Parma (Hoff 2013).

In order to represent things in a linear perspective, the canvas or drawing surface should be conceived like an open window, through which a scene is observed. A straight horizontal line is drawn on the canvas, in order to represent the horizon (thus separating the sky from the ground). Then straight orthogonal lines (visual lines) are drawn, to connect the observer's eye to a selected point in the distance, close to the center of the horizon line (this converging point is referred to as the vanishing point). These lines act like visual rays that link the observer's eye, to points on the edges of objects, to the vanishing point, thus creating the illusion of depth (Ivins and Pèlerin 1973).

(c) Identify and analyze the actions and "operations" that are "abstracted," "reflected," and "thematized" from these tools.

The most conspicuous actions and operations that may be abstracted from linear perspective are related to the displacement (in width, height, depth, and angle of view) of an observer's point of view, across a scene. These displacements are driven by the active visual search that occurs when inspecting a scene. This active exploration is similar to a questioning or inquiry processes (Spruit 2008). When these displacements are abstracted, they lead to as perspectivist view of knowledge, what Cusanus referred to as "learned ignorance" (Cusa and Hopkins 1985).

From a perspectivist stance, the adoption of a point of view is similar to the adoption of a surmise. In perspective, a point of view is related to others, by precise geometrical laws; likewise, a surmise is logically or analogically linked to other surmises. In addition, a point of view is not randomly established; instead, it is dependent on previous ones and guided by gaze anticipation, during the interactive process of viewing. In the same manner, a surmise is not randomly set and depends on previous surmises and guided by cognitive anticipations, during the process of inquiring.

Other important actions and operations that can be abstracted and thematized are related to the parametrization of space, which is directly related to geometrical operations that can be extended to the infinite (or to the "maximum" or "minimum" – in Cusano's words). A good example of these operations is given by Cusa, in order to illustrate his principle of "coincidence of the opposites":

> First of all, it is evident that an infinite line would be a straight line: The diameter of a circle is a straight line, and the circumference is a curved line which is greater than the diameter. So if the curved line becomes less curved in proportion to the increased circumference of the circle, then the circumference of the maximum circle, which cannot be greater, is minimally curved and therefore maximally straight. Hence, the minimum coincides with the maximum—to such an extent that we can visually recognize that it is necessary for the maximum line to be maximally straight and minimally curved. (Cusa and Hopkins 1985)

(d) Identify the advantages and limitations of these tools within their particular scope and within theory construction.

One of the fundamental advantages that linear perspective brought to the representation of visual space during the Renaissance was its "systemic" (in the sense of Bertalanffy's "systems theory") organization (Panofsky 1996). Within the scope of visual representation, this type of organization afforded the possibility to manage the visual space in a rigorous formal way; and within the scope of theory construction, it allowed scientific explanations, to shift from being "intrafigural" to "interfigural" (cf. Piaget and Garcia 1988).

Before the Renaissance, the representation of space was treated as an independent element, much like figures in a picture. In addition, the relationship among the elements in the picture (including the space) was mainly symbolic (Panofsky 1996). None of the earlier theories of space succeeded in depicting space as a "system" of relationships between width, depth, and height. In this respect, linear perspective was at the dawn of "systemic" and "relational" thinking. Since then, this new style of thought has had a pervasive influence in science.

This new style of thinking particularly influenced the theoretical notion of mind; befittingly, Cusa's concept of mind had a systemic, dynamic, dialectic, and functional character and thus was integrative – a view that accordingly was opposed to the "faculties'" theory of mind. In this regard, Bertalanffy rightly referred Cusanus as one of the first forerunners of 'system theory' (Bertalanffy 1968).

Another advantage derived from linear perspective, and specifically related to the "systematization of space," is the notion of "infinity." Within the scope of visual representation, this notion facilitated the construction of certain pictorial elements (e.g., vanishing point) (Panofsky 1996); and within the scope of theory construction, it permitted the formation of an intuitive notion of infinity beyond sensible representations.

During antiquity and medieval times, the notion of "infinity" was strongly informed by Christian theology; however, during the Renaissance and as a result of the mathematization of space, this notion adopted an empirical model. The importance of this achievement was paramount to the further developments in science and philosophy (Panofsky 1996). This shift in the notion of infinity led to a direct shift in the notion of truth, e.g., rejecting the Aristotelian "principle of excluded middle" (Cusa and Martinez 1994).

Taking part in this shift, Cusanus put forward a view of infinity (absolute maximum) abstracted (by reflecting abstraction) from geometrical operations that are akin to those that give origin to fractals (Cusa and Hopkins 1985). Intuitively, he acknowledged the contradictory properties inherent in such geometrical figures, when certain operations were applied, and infinitely extended, onto these. Furthermore, he realized that those ideal figures resisted any "rational" thinking of the time.[4]

The aforementioned advantages resulting from linear perspective gave rise to the radical change in the way that scholars have studied the natural world, for it led to the revolutionary shift from a contemplative science (*theoria*) to the active and experimental science (*praxis*) of today (Koyre 1968).

Importantly, within this transition, Cusa's ideas and their empirical directives established the beginnings of a "quantitative thinking in medicine" (Hoff 1964; Schultheisz 2013). His treatise *Idiota de staticis experimentis* (The layman on experiments done with weight scales) serves as a conclusive example of this orientation (Cusa and Hopkins 1996b).

Cusanus' ingenuity is especially portrayed in his "staticis experimentis," by two important affirmations. The first is that many normal and pathological human and animal behaviors are the result of, and expressed by, "harmonic proportions" and the

---

[4]Similarly, it is now recognized how difficult the concept of fractals was to grasp in the last century (Mandelbrot 1982)

second is that these proportions could be investigated by means of weights[5] (Cusa and Hopkins 1996b). The contemporary use of fractal methods in medicine and in many other fields is compelling evidence of this vision's fecundity (Ieva 2016; Labra-Spröhnle 2015, 2016a). In the following quote, Cusanus expresses his ideas regarding "harmonic proportions."

> Yes, all concordant harmonies are, in general, very accurately investigated by means of weights. Indeed, the weight of a thing is, properly speaking, a harmonic proportion that has arisen from various combinations of different things. Even the friendships and the animosities of animals (and of men) of the same respective species—as well as their customs and whatever [other] such thing—are weighed from harmonic concordances and from opposing dissonances. Likewise, too, both a man's health and his lack of health are weighed in terms of harmony—and so too are his flightiness and seriousness, his prudence and naiveté, and many other such things, if you pay careful attention. (Cusa and Hopkins 1996b)

One limitation of "single-point linear perspective" is that it provides the pictorial representation of a scene with only one fixed viewpoint at a time. This feature limits the power of this tool, to fully describe objects – whether dynamically, or from multiple, simultaneous viewpoints (like in Picasso's cubism).

Another limitation embodied in this tool is its exclusive dependency on the sense of vision (space) for abstracting concepts and the consequent devaluing of other senses as sources of abstractions. Wittgenstein's work (Krämer 2011), in particular his "Tractatus Logico- Philosophicus," exemplifies the continuation of this visual-projective reductionism, with the suggestion that visual space serves as a model for abstracting logic features (Wittgenstein and Russell 2007).

A further problem arising from this limitation is that the consequent representational view of space will promote by analogy representational views of mind and of anticipatory phenomena.

(e) Summarize the most important findings, and recommend a course of navigation accordingly, in order to thoroughly investigate the references and plan new research.

The "fast-track epistemological analysis" can be summarized in six main points:

(i) "Reflecting abstractions," derived from the techniques, tools, and mathematization of space, inherent in "single-point linear perspective," led to a revolutionary conceptual advancement during the Renaissance.

(ii) Nicholas of Cusa was aware of the power of analogies (reflecting abstractions) derived from geometrical tools. He made extensive use of the analogical method in order to overcome the limitations of Aristotelian logic (Cusa and

---

[5]A current enactment of this insight is the box-counting algorithm. Briefly, the "box-counting algorithm" is used for estimating several types of fractal dimensions; it consists in laying out grids of different sizes on a digital image and counting the number of boxes that contain pixels of interest, as well as the number of pixels per box. In other words, the main routine of this algorithm is to "weigh" the "pixel mass" of each box

Martinez 1994). In this regard, Cusanus pioneered the use of "diagrammatic thinking" (Cusa and Hopkins 1985).

(iii) Cusa abstracted his principle of "learned ignorance," from the operations associated with the displacement of an observer's viewpoint during the scanning of a scene. In addition, the same author noticed that a single viewpoint can never account for the entirety of a scene. The consequent projection of this idea to the realm of knowledge led to a perspectivist view of knowledge acquisition.

(iv) Equipped with his new concept of infinity (abstracted from geometrical operations that could be applied endlessly over finite figures), Cusanus abstracted one of his most important principles, namely, the "coincidence of the opposites."

(v) Using his two aforementioned principles (iii and iv), Cusanus postulated a non-faculty, creative, inferential, functional, and developmental view of mind – with anticipatory activity as one of its essential features.

(vi) Cusanus' notion of inferences (*coniectura*) seems to be compatible with several contemporary views on anticipation. Furthermore, his notion is an important landmark in its own right, with a historical and conceptual priority over other already-known accounts.

From these six points, it is suggested that the next course of navigation should consist in (a) revisiting Cusanus' notions and his work on "surmises" (Cusa and Hopkins 2000) and "actualized possibilities" (Hopkins 1986) and (b) examining the influence of some Neoplatonic scholars (given their importance as sources that influenced Cusanus' conceptions). It is believed that by studying these sources, scholars would be able to gain an insightful orientation on anticipatory phenomena, which concurrently would open up new possibilities of inquire.

Conclusions and Warnings

The history of science shows that mature and more advanced fields of science, like physics and mathematics, have been able to delineate their problems and tackle their internal crises, by retrospectively examining their grounding concepts. Most of the time, this task has been accomplished by an internal epistemological critique derived from the same discipline, rather than from philosophy (Piaget 1963).

In the same spirit, this paper introduces a basic tool kit derived from "systematic reviews," methodology, and "genetic epistemology," in order to orient scholars within the vast literature in neuroscience and aid the search and analysis of notions underpinning the subject of "anticipation." An example of the application of this tool kit to a real-life scenario (cognitive anticipation) was provided, in order to illustrate its performance. As a result, landmarks and grounding notions within the subject of cognitive anticipation were exposed.

Despite this method's advantage, it nonetheless ought to be used with caution, for it is not meant to replace a full systematic review, and it does not give an exhaustive epistemological analysis. This method represents only a primary step, in a more thoroughgoing process of appraisal and "work-up."

Finally, notwithstanding the importance of an epistemological analysis, a caveat must be placed. To advance in science does not inevitably require conceptual clarity and precise definitions; for sometimes, imprecisions and logical entanglements at the conceptual level drive to serendipitous discoveries. In other words, what could be critical in the "context of justification" is not the case in the "context of discovery" (Reichenbach 1938).

References

Arksey, H., & O'Malley, L. (2005). Scoping studies: Towards a methodological framework. *International Journal of Social Research Methodology, 8*(1), 19–32.

Bertalanffy, L. V. (1968). *General system theory: Foundations, development, applications* (1st ed.). New York: George Braziller.

Borck, C. (2016). Animating brains. *Medical History, 60*(3), 308–324. https://doi.org/10.1017/mdh.2016.25.

Bringuier, J. -C., & Piaget, J. (1989). *Conversations with Jean Piaget* (B. M. Gulati, Trans.). Chicago: University of Chicago Press.

Carman, C. H. (2014). *Leon Battista Alberti and Nicholas Cusanus: Towards an epistemology of vision for Italian Renaissance art and culture* (New ed.). Burlington: Routledge.

Cassirer, E. (2011). *The individual and the cosmos in Renaissance philosophy* (Unabridged ed.). Mineola: Dover Publications.

Cusa, C. N., & Hopkins, J. (1985). *Nicholas of Cusa on learned ignorance: A translation and an appraisal of De Docta Ignorantia* (2nd ed.). Minneapolis: The Arthur J. Banning Press.

Cusa, C. N., & Hopkins, J. (1996a). Idiota de mente (The layman on mind). In *Nicholas of Cusa on wisdom & knowledge* (pp. 530–601). Minneapolis: Arthur J. Banning Press.

Cusa, C. N., & Hopkins, J. (1996b). Idiota de staticis experimentis (The layman on experiments done with weight-scales). In *Nicholas of Cusa on wisdom & knowledge* (pp. 605–630). Minneapolis: Arthur J. Banning Press.

Cusa, C. N., & Hopkins, J. (2000). De Coniecturis (On surmises). In *Nicholas of Cusa on wisdom & knowledge* (Vol. 2, pp. 162–297). Minneapolis: Arthur J. Banning Press.

Cusa, N. de, & Martinez, R. (1994). Introduccion. In Servicios Editoriales de la Facultad de Ciencias, UNAM. (Eds). *El Juego de las Esferas* (pp. 7–45). México: UNAM.

D'Amico, C. (2005). Introduccion el dialogo idiota de mente: su lugar en la obra cusana. In J. Machetta & C. D'Amico (Eds). *Un Ignorante Discurre Acerca de La Mente* (pp. 21–27). Buenos Aires: Editorial Biblos.

Daston, L. (Ed.). (2000). *Biographies of scientific objects* (1st ed.). Chicago: University of Chicago Press.

Davis, F., Riedl, R., Brocke, J. vom, Léger, P. -M., & Randolph, A. (Eds.). (2016). *Information systems and neuroscience: Gmunden retreat on NeuroIS 2016* (1st ed. 2017 edition). Cham: Springer.

Debrock, G. (1998). El ingenioso enigma de la abducción. *Analogía Filosófica, 12*(1), 21–40.

Denery II, D. G. D. (2009). *Seeing and being seen in the later medieval world: Optics, theology and religious life* (1st ed). Cambridge/New York: Cambridge University Press.

Edgerton, S. Y. (2009). *The mirror, the window, and the telescope: How Renaissance linear perspective changed our vision of the universe* (1st ed.). Ithaca: Cornell University Press.

Gigerenzer, G. (1987). *Cognition as intuitive statistics* (D. J. Murray, Ed.). Hillsdale: Psychology Press.

Gigerenzer, G. (1991). From tools to theories: A heuristic of discovery in cognitive psychology. *Psychological Review, 98*(2), 254.

Gigerenzer, G. (1992). Discovery in cognitive psychology: New tools inspire new theories. *Science in Context, 5*(2), 329–350.

Gigerenzer, G., & Sturm, T. (2007). Tools= theories= data? On some circular dynamics in cognitive science. *Psychology's Territories,* 305–342.

Giovanelli, M. (2010). *Reality and negation – Kant's principle of anticipation of perception: An investigation of its impact on the post-Kantian debate.* Dordrecht: Springer.

Gough, D., Oliver, S., & Thomas, J. (Eds.). (2012). *An introduction to systematic reviews* (1st ed.). London/Thousand Oaks: SAGE Publications Ltd..

Harries, K. (2002). *Infinity and perspective* (Reprint ed.). Cambridge, MA: The MIT Press.

Harzing, A.-W. (2011). *The publish or perish book, part 1: A guide to the software.* Melbourne: Tarma Software Research.

Hilgard, E. R. (1980). The trilogy of mind: Cognition, affection, and conation. *Journal of the History of the Behavioral Sciences, 16*(2), 107–117.

Hoff, H. E. (1964). Nicolaus of Cusa, van Helmont, and Boyle: The first experiment of the Renaissance in quantitative biology and medicine. *Journal of the History of Medicine and Allied Sciences, 19*(2), 99–117.

Hoff, J. (2013). *The analogical turn: Rethinking modernity with Nicholas of Cusa.* Grand Rapids: Eerdmans.

Hopkins, J. (1986). *A concise introduction to the philosophy of Nicholas of Cusa* (3rd ed.). Minneapolis: Arthur J Banning Press.

Ieva, A. D. (2016). *The fractal geometry of the brain.* New York: Springer.

Ivins, W. M., & Pèlerin, J. (1973). *On the rationalization of sight: With an examination of three Renaissance texts on perspective* (Vol. 13). New York: Da Capo Pr.

Jaeger, D., & Jung, R. (Eds.). (2015). *Encyclopedia of computational neuroscience.* New York: Springer.

Kant, I. (1998). What does it mean to orient oneself in thinking? In A. Wood & G. Di Giovanni (Eds.), *Religion Within the Boundaries of Mere Reason: And Other Writings.* (pp. 3-14). Cambridge CB2 2RU: Cambridge University Press.

Koyre, A. (1968). *From the closed world to the infinite universe* (1st ed.). Baltimore: Johns Hopkins University Press.

Krämer, S. (2011). 'The Mind's Eye': Visualizing the Non-visual and the 'Epistemology of the Line'. In R. Heinrich, E. Nemeth, W. Pichler and D. Wagner (Eds.), Image and Imaging in Philosophy, Science and the Arts: Proceedings of the 33rd International Ludwig Wittgenstein-Symposium in Kirchberg, 2010. volume 2, (pp. 275–293). Frankfurt · Lancaster · Paris · New Brunswick. Ontos Verlag,

Kuhn, T. S. (1996). *The structure of scientific revolutions* (3rd ed.). Chicago: University of Chicago Press.

Labra-Spröhnle, F. (2015). The mind of a visionary: The morphology of cognitive anticipation as a cardinal symptom. In M. Nadin (Ed.), *Anticipation: Learning from the past.* (pp. 369–381). Cham: Springer.

Labra-Spröhnle, F. (2016a). Human, all too human: Euclidean and multifractal analysis in an experimental diagrammatic model of thinking. In M. Nadin (Ed.), *Anticipation across disciplines* (pp. 105–133). Cham: Springer.

Labra-Spröhnle, F. (2016b). Restoring the integrative value to the notion of executive function. Commentary on: "advancing understanding of executive function impairments and psychopathology: Bridging the gap between clinical and cognitive approaches". *Frontiers in Psychology, 6,* 2040.

Levac, D., Colquhoun, H., & O'Brien, K. K. (2010). Scoping studies: advancing the methodology. Implementation Science, 5, 69. https://doi.org/10.1186/1748-5908-5-69

Littell, J. H., Corcoran, J., & Pillai, V. (2008). *Systematic reviews and meta-analysis* (Poc ed.). Oxford/New York: Oxford University Press.

Locke, J. (1998). *An essay concerning human understanding* (R. Woolhouse, Ed., Reprint ed.). London: Penguin Classics.

Luria, A. R. (1982). *Language and cognition* (J. V. Wertsch, Ed., 1st ed.). Washington, DC/New York: Wiley.

Mandelbrot, B. (1982). *The fractal geometry of nature* (1st ed.). San Francisco: W. H. Freeman and Company.

Marková, I. S., & Berrios, G. E. (2016). Research in psychiatry: Concepts and conceptual analysis. *Psychopathology, 49*, 188–194.

Mays, N., Roberts, E., & Popay, J. (2001). Synthesising research evidence. In N. Fulop, P. Allen, A. Clarke, & N. Black (Eds.), *Studying the organisation and delivery of health services: Research methods* (pp. 188–220). London: Routledge.

Nadin, M. (2010). Anticipation. *International Journal of General Systems, 39*(1), 35–133.

Nadin, M. (Ed.). (2015a). *Anticipation across disciplines* (1st ed. 2016 edition). Cham: Springer.

Nadin, M. (Ed.). (2015b). *Anticipation: Learning from the past: The Russian/Soviet contributions to the science of anticipation* (1st ed. 2015 edition). Cham: Springer.

Nadin, M. (2015c). Introduction: Commitment to knowledge. In M. Nadin, (Ed). *Anticipation: Learning from the Past: The Russian/Soviet Contributions to the Science of Anticipation*. Vol. 25. (pp. 1–9). Cham. Springer.

O'Brien, K., Tricco, A. C., Lillie, E., Zarin, W., Colquhoun, H., Kastner, M., . . . Wilson, K. (2016). A scoping review on the conduct and reporting of scoping reviews. BMC Medical Research Methodology.16:15.

Overton, W. F. (2015). Taking conceptual analyses seriously. *Research in Human Development, 12* (3–4), 163–171.

Panofsky, E. (1996). *Perspective as symbolic form* (C. S. Wood, Trans., Rev. ed.). New York/ Cambridge, MA: Zone Books.

Parmentier, M. (2011). Leibniz et la perception du futur. *Revue de Métaphysique et de Morale, 2*, 221–233.

Peirce, C. S. (1998). On the logic of drawing history from ancient documents, especially from testimonies. In Peirce edition project (Ed.), *The essential peirce: Selected philosophical writings, (1893–1913)*. (Vol. 2, pp. 75–114).Bloomington: Indiana University Press.

Peters, M. D., Godfrey, C. M., Khalil, H., McInerney, P., Parker, D., & Soares, C. B. (2015). Guidance for conducting systematic scoping reviews. *International Journal of Evidence-Based Healthcare, 13*(3), 141–146.

Pezzulo, G., Butz, M. V., Castelfranchi, C., & Falcone, R. (Eds.). (2008). *The challenge of anticipation* (Vol. 5225). Berlin/Heidelberg: Springer. Retrieved from http://link.springer.com/ 10.1007/978-3-540-87702-8

Piaget, J. (1950). *Introduction à l'épistémologie génétique*. Paris: Presses Universitaires de France.

Piaget, J. (1963). Explanation in psychology and psychophysiological parallelism. In P. Fraisse & J. Piaget (Eds.), *Experimental psychology: Its scope and method* (Vol. I). New York: Basic Books.

Piaget, J. (1971). *Genetic epistemology* (E. Duckworth, Trans.). New York: W W Norton & Co Inc.

Piaget, J. (1974). *Biology and knowledge* (B. Walsh, Trans.). Chicago: University of Chicago Press.

Piaget, J. (1980a). *Epistemologia genetica y equilibracion*. Madrid: Editoriales De Derecho Reunidas.

Piaget, J. (1980b). The psychogenesis of knowledge and its epistemological significance. In M. Piattelli-Palmarini (Ed.), *Language and learning: The debate between Jean Piaget and Noam Chomsky* (pp. 1–23). Cambridge, MA: Harvard University Press.

Piaget, J. (2007). *The mechanisms of perception* (1st ed.). London: Routledge.

Piaget, J., & Campell, R. L. (2014). *Studies in reflecting abstraction*. Hove: Psychology Press.

Piaget, J., & Garcia, R. (1988). *Psychogenesis and the history of science* (H. Feider, Trans., First English language edition). New York: Columbia University Press.

Piaget, J., Garcia, R., & Davidson, P. (2013). *Toward a logic of meanings*. New York: Psychology Press.

Reichenbach, H. (1938). *Experience and prediction: An analysis of the foundations and the structure of knowledge*. Chicago: The University of Chicago Press.

Reynolds, A. M., & Rhodes, C. J. (2009). The Lévy flight paradigm: Random search patterns and mechanisms. *Ecology, 90*(4), 877–887.

Rheinberger, H.-J. (2010). *An epistemology of the concrete: Twentieth-century histories of life.* Durham: Duke University Press Books.

Schultheisz, E. (2013). On the beginnings of quantitative thinking in medicine (Nicolas of Cusa and the idiot). In E. Schultheisz (Ed.), *History of physiology: Proceedings of the 28th international congress of physiological sciences, Budapest, 1980* (pp. 1–7). Oxford: Pergamon.

Seligman, M. E., Railton, P., Baumeister, R. F., & Sripada, C. (2013). Navigating into the future or driven by the past. *Perspectives on Psychological Science, 8*(2), 119–141.

Silva, A. J., Landreth, A., & Bickle, J. (2013). *Engineering the next revolution in neuroscience: The new science of experiment planning* (1st ed.). Oxford: Oxford University Press.

Spruit, L. (2008). Renaissance views of active perception. In S. Knuuttila, P. Kärkkäinen (Eds.) *Theories of perception in medieval and early modern philosophy* (pp. 203–224). Dordrecht: Springer.

Uttal, W. R. (2015). *Macroneural theories in cognitive neuroscience* (1st ed.). New York: Psychology Press.

Uttal, W. R. (2016). *The neuron and the mind: Microneuronal theory and practice in cognitive neuroscience.* New York: Routledge.

Wiener, P. P. (Ed.). (1980). *Dictionary of the history of ideas* (Box ed.). New York: Macmillan Pub Co..

Winstanley, M. A. (2016). Genetic epistemology, a universalist approach to the history of science. *Journal of the Philosophy of History, 10,* 249–278. https://doi.org/10.1163/18722636-12341327

Wittgenstein, L., & Russell, B. (2007). *Tractatus Logico-Philosophicus* (C. K. Ogden, Trans.). New York: Cosimo Classics.

Relational Biology

10

A. H. Louie

Contents

Abstract

Relational biology is a study of life in terms of the organization of entailment relations in living systems, independent of any particular physical mechanism or material realization. Anticipation is the pivot on which the relational study of life

This chapter was written when I was a resident Fellow at the Stellenbosch Institute for Advanced Study (stias), South Africa, in February–April 2016. I thank the stias staff and my contemporary Fellows, especially those involved in the Complexity and Anticipation project, for their inspiration and, indeed, fellowship.

A. H. Louie (✉)
Ottawa, ON, Canada

Stellenbosch Institute for Advanced Study (stias), Wallenberg Research Centre at Stellenbosch University, Stellenbosch, South Africa
e-mail: connect@ahlouie.com

© Springer Nature Switzerland AG 2019
R. Poli (ed.), *Handbook of Anticipation*,
https://doi.org/10.1007/978-3-319-91554-8_17

191

revolves. An organism is the very example of an anticipatory system. Robert Rosen's systematic study of anticipation was founded under the auspices of his determined journey in relational biology, a quixotic adventure that is now continuing in the next generation and beyond.

Keywords

Relational biology · Living system · (M,R)-system · Clef system · Anticipatory system · Impredicative system · *Function dictates structure* · Closure to efficient causation · Metabolism–repair · Material entailment · Functional entailment · Hierarchical cycle

Life Anticipates

Anticipation is a necessary condition of life: *a living system anticipates*. This connection ultimately explains how the mathematical biologist Robert Rosen (1934–1998), in his lifelong quest of general principles that would answer the question "What is Life?", happened to write, en passant, many papers on anticipatory systems, culminating in his book *Anticipatory Systems: Philosophical, Mathematical, and Methodological Foundations* (Rosen 1985a).

Rosen was a stalwart of a specific school of mathematical biology called *relational biology*, the study of biology from the standpoint of 'organization of relations'. It was founded by Nicolas Rashevsky (1899–1972) in the 1950s, thence continued and flourished under his student Rosen (who was, incidentally, my PhD supervisor). The essence of reductionism in biology is to keep the matter of which an organism is made and throw away the organization, with the belief that, since physicochemical *structure implies function*, the reconstitution of the organization from the analytic material parts may be attempted. Relational biology, on the other hand, keeps the organization and throws away the matter; *function dictates structure*, whence material aspects are synthetically entailed.

For a thorough exploration of the Rashevsky–Rosen school of relational biology (and for a comprehensive illustration of the powers of our approach to the study of life), the reader is cordially invited to read the two books that I have (so far) written on the subject. The exploratory journey begins with the monograph *More Than Life Itself: A Synthetic Continuation in Relation Biology* (Louie 2009) and continues with the monograph *The Reflection of Life: Functional Entailment and Imminence in Relational Biology* (Louie 2013). The themes of the two books are, respectively, "What is life?" and "How do two lifeforms interact?". This present chapter of the *Handbook* is a terse introduction to relational biology, with emphasis on its connection to anticipation, the topic at hand.

Respectus

Rashevsky, in 1939, founded the *Bulletin of Mathematical Biophysics* (now the *Bulletin of Mathematical Biology*) after having been taken to task by the editor of a physiology journal because his submitted (and accepted) paper on nervous excitation did not contain "original experimental observations." Rashevsky, as a physicist, began, as was the norm at the time, with an essentially reductionistic view of the relation of biology to chemistry and physics. His successes at modeling specific biological processes, however, instead of reinforcing his reductionism began to gnaw at him in an increasingly something-is-missing sense. As he wrote in Rashevsky (1954):

> There is no record of a successful mathematical theory which would treat the integrated activities of the organism as a whole... this integrated activity of the organism is probably the most essential manifestation of life... These fundamental manifestations of life drop out from all our present theories of mathematical biology... We must look for a principle which connects the different physical phenomena involved and expresses the biological unity of the organism and of the organic world as a whole.

This now-classic 1954 paper ("Topology and Life") is generally acknowledged as the origin of relational biology. Indeed, Rashevsky first discussed therein the 'relational aspects' of biology. By 'relational' he meant an approach that was based on the algebraic, topological organizations of functions, as opposed to one based on the analytic, metric, mechanistic, physicochemical organizations of structures, the latter approach having theretofore dominated his subject of 'mathematical biophysics'.

Here is Rashevsky's basic idea: instead of starting with a mishmash of reductionistic fragments and attempting to find some a posteriori way of fitting them together to generate integrated biological behavior, he might try to represent this integrated behavior from the outset. Organisms are recognized as such because one can recognize homologies in their behaviors, regardless of the physical structures through which these behaviors are implemented. All organisms seek and ingest food, metabolize it to generate energy, adapt, reproduce, etc. Rashevsky sought to represent the integrated manifestation of these biological functions, common to all organisms, in mathematical terms. Through the basic and ubiquitous manifestation of such functions, organisms could be mapped ('biotopologically') into one another in such a way as to preserve these basic relations, and we could in fact hope to construct a unified theory of organisms in this fashion. In this way, he was led to an abstract topological structure that served as a kind of functional bauplan manifested by any system that might be called an 'organism'. Stated otherwise, one *begins* with an abstract structure, of which any specific organism constitutes a *realization*. The manner in which particular organisms relate to (or map onto) the bauplan then establishes their relations to one another.

Rashevsky coined the term *relational biology* to characterize this qualitative approach, as distinct from the quantitative approach that is *metric biology*. One of its crucial premises is this: experimenters (e.g., biochemists or molecular biologists) proceed by initially destroying all higher-level biological organization, leaving behind a purely physicochemical system to be studied entirely by physicochemical means. In other words, they proceed by abstracting away all organizational properties, hoping to recapture them in due course by synthetic arguments based on encoded data from their analytic models. The relational approach, on the other hand, proceeds in an exactly converse way; in effect, it initially abstracts away all purely physicochemical aspects, leaving behind a pure organization to be represented and studied entirely by mathematical means. The detailed physics and chemistry of such a system are to be recaptured later by a decoding process of *realization*. (For a detailed explication of encoding, decoding, model, and realization, consult the exposition on the modeling relation in ▶ Chap. 45, "Mathematical Foundations of Anticipatory Systems" in this *Handbook*.)

Premise

The principles of relational biology may thus be considered the operational inverse of reductionistic ideas. Relational biology is mathematical organization seeking realizations, and reductionistic biology is physicochemical process seeking models (Fig. 1).

One must understand that the 'relational' in 'relational biology' is not just an adjective with its common-usage sense of 'having an effect of a connection' (sometimes even misinterpreted as 'relative'). 'Relational' is more importantly used in its mathematical sense that 'a mathematical relation (subset of a product set) exists'.

Operational inverses relational biology and reductionistic biology may be, but it is important to note that we in the former are not antagonistic in any sense toward practitioners of the latter. One does not argue with success. Molecular biology, the poster child of reductionistic biology, is useful and has enjoyed popular success and increased our understanding of life by parts. It is, however, also evident that there are incomparably more aspects of natural systems that the physics of mechanisms is not equipped to explain. It is the overreaching reductionistic claim of genericity (that only material-based biology is biology) that is a misrepresentation and a falsehood.

Fig. 1 Relational biology decodes; reductionistic biology encodes

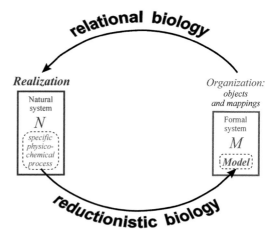

In relational biology we often propose not one model for a specific biological process, but many entirely different models that share a common formalism. It is the commonality that makes them all models for a particular biological process which is the true item of interest and not the detailed properties of any one of them. Thus our interest is not on the details of individual mechanisms (as important as these might be in many contexts), but on qualitative concepts of *behavior*, which may be variously realized: what needs to be isolated is what these mechanisms share that allows them to be realizations of a behavior.

In the rest of this chapter, I shall illustrate how relational biology attempts to answer the ultimate biological question, "What is life?". I will show how the concept of anticipation arises in this process. "What is life?" is a very terse ontological question. A slightly more explicit ontological formulation is "How is a living system different from a non-living one?" or, epistemologically, "What are the defining characteristics of a natural system for us to perceive it as being alive?". A relational-biologic answer will be of the form: "an organism is a material system that realizes a certain kind of relational pattern (whatever the particular material basis of that realization may be)." The exercise, then, is to find this specific relational pattern that defines life.

It is opportune here to point out the subtle difference between a *material system* (or a *physical system*) and a *natural system*. A material system is ontological, it being simply any physical object in the world. A natural system, on the other hand, is a part, whence a subset, of the external world and a collection of qualities, to which definite relations (of causal entailment) can be imputed. A natural system is, therefore, epistemological, since the partitioning of the external world and the formation of percepts and their relations are all mental constructs (and are therefore entailed by the bounds of mental constructs). In short, a natural system is a subjectively defined representation of a material system. Note also that the existence of causal entailment in a natural system is ontological, but the representation of causality, by arrows (i.e., as mappings), is epistemological.

Pegmata

I need some set-theoretic scaffolding to proceed.

Axiom of Specification   For any set U and any statement $p(x)$ about x, there exists a set P, the elements of which are exactly those $x \in U$ for which $p(x)$ is true.

To indicate the way P is obtained from the 'universe' U and the defining property p, the customary notation is

$$P = \{x \in U : p(x)\}. \tag{1}$$

The '$p(x)$' in (1) is understood (with the conventional omission of the predicate) to mean "'$p(x)$' is true"; it may also be read as "x has the property p." The axiom of specification says that a set is defined by the property that its elements must satisfy.

The set specified by the property p, $P = \{x : p(x)\}$, has as its *complement* the set specified by the property $\neg p$ (*not p*); i.e.,

$$P^c = \{x : \neg p(x)\} \; [\; = \{x \in U : x \notin P\} = U \sim P \;] \tag{2}$$

[the set consisting of elements of U that do *not* have the property p].

A property p is more interesting if both P and P^c are nonempty. If either every $x \in U$ or no $x \in U$ satisfies $p(x)$ (which means, respectively, that $\langle P = U, P^c = \varnothing \rangle$ or $\langle P = \varnothing, P^c = U \rangle$), then property p defines no new subset of U. More importantly, the pair $\langle P, P^c \rangle$ of sets that is a subset and its complement defines a *partition* of the universe U, in the sense that for each $x \in U$, either $x \in P$ or $x \in P^c$, but not both; for each $x \in U$, either x has the property p or it does not, but not both:

$$\forall x : [p(x) \vee \neg p(x)] \wedge [\neg(p(x) \wedge \neg p(x))]. \tag{3}$$

Stated otherwise, the 'barrier' between P and P^c is 'nonporous' (Fig. 2).

In our discourse (that of relational biology), the universe is the collection N of natural systems. An organism (in the sense of a general lifeform, a living system) is a natural system. So, if L is the collection of all organisms, then (Fig. 3)

$$L \subset N. \tag{4}$$

And trivially both L and $L^c = N \sim L$ are nonempty.

Now, the answer to the "What is life?" question should consist of a property ℓ such that a natural system x is alive if and only if $\ell(x)$ is true, i.e., iff 'x has the property ℓ':

$$L = \{x \in N : \ell(x)\}. \tag{5}$$

Let $P = \{x : p(x)\}$ and $Q = \{x : q(x)\}$, then

Fig. 2 A subset P and its complement P^c partition U

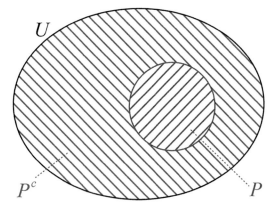

Fig. 3 The partition of life from nonlife

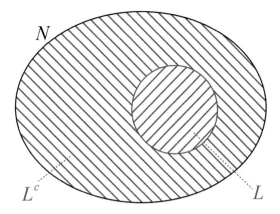

$$P \subset Q \quad \text{if and only if} \quad \forall x \; p(x) \Rightarrow q(x). \tag{6}$$

The equivalence (6) may be read as $P \subset Q$ if and only if p is *sufficient* for q, and also $P \subset Q$ if and only if q is *necessary* for p.

Thus, the quest to answer the "What is life?" question is the search for a precise definition of the 'living condition' ℓ that is necessary and sufficient. Explicitly, if q is *necessary* for ℓ, i.e., if

$$\forall x \; \ell(x) \Rightarrow q(x), \tag{7}$$

i.e., if a living system must have the property q, then (Fig. 4)

$$L \subset Q. \tag{8}$$

The exercise is then to further restrict the 'necessity'.

Conversely, if p is sufficient for ℓ, i.e., if

$$\forall x \; p(x) \Rightarrow \ell(x), \tag{9}$$

i.e., if a natural system has the property p, then it is living, and then (Fig. 5)

$$P \subset L. \tag{10}$$

In this case, the exercise is then to relax the 'sufficiency' to make it less stringent. Also, if one knows a sufficient condition for life, then it is in principle possible to realize the sufficiency thence fabricate life.

It is usually easier to discover necessary conditions q for life. The experimental verification simply consists of: remove condition q and the organism dies. Sufficient conditions are more difficult to come by.

Fig. 4 Necessity for life

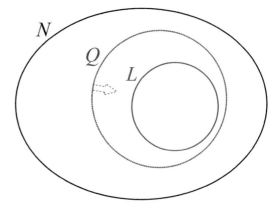

Fig. 5 Sufficiency for life

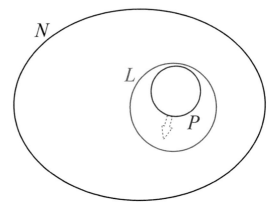

In any event, our strategy is to derive a set of individually necessary and jointly sufficient conditions for life. The set-theoretic motivation is that a set is the intersection of all its supersets:

$$A = \bigcap_{B \supset A} B. \tag{11}$$

We strive for a set of individually necessary conditions, viz.:

$$\ell \Rightarrow q_1, \quad \ell \Rightarrow q_2, \quad \ell \Rightarrow q_3, \quad \ldots ; \tag{12}$$

i.e.,

$$L \subset Q_1, \quad L \subset Q_2, \quad L \subset Q_3, \quad \ldots . \tag{13}$$

Then from these supersets Q_i of L, one may construct a descending chain of intersections,

$$Q_1 \supset Q_1 \cap Q_2 \supset Q_1 \cap Q_2 \cap Q_3 \supset \cdots \supset L, \tag{14}$$

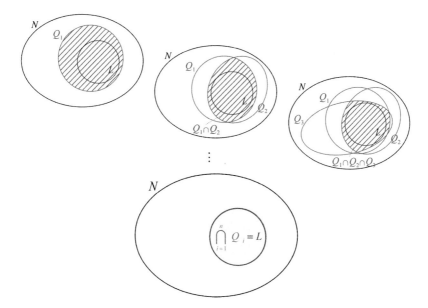

Fig. 6 Individually necessary and jointly sufficient conditions for life

that will ideally converge to L in the limit. In practice, however, one may not get the (necessarily finite) sequence to converge to L. All one can do is to find supersets $Q_1 \supset L, Q_2 \supset L, Q_3 \supset L, ..., Q_n \supset L$ (corresponding to necessary conditions $q_1, q_2, q_3, \ldots, q_n$), so that their intersection $\cap_{i=1}^n Q_i$ is *as close to L as one can achieve*. Then one *defines*

$$\ell = \bigwedge_{i=1}^n q_i \tag{15}$$

(whence

$$L = \bigcap_{i=1}^n Q_i), \tag{16}$$

and declares the joint sufficiency that all natural systems satisfying simultaneously the conditions $q_1, q_2, q_3, \ldots, q_n$ are alive. This may include some natural systems that are not obviously alive, but one defines them to be (Fig. 6).

Opera

Consider the following three properties of a natural system $x \in N$:

$$q_1(x) \quad = x \text{ is } \textit{impredicative};$$
$$q_2(x) \quad = x \text{ is } \textit{anticipatory};$$
$$q_3(x) \quad = x \text{ is } \textit{closed to efficient causation}.$$

Each defining term, of course, requires explanation, which I shall do presently. But let me first give an overview of the argument. It turns out that each of the three properties is a necessary condition for life, i.e.,

$$\ell \Rightarrow q_1, \quad \ell \Rightarrow q_2, \quad \ell \Rightarrow q_3. \tag{17}$$

But more than that, they are related by sequential implications:

$$\ell \Rightarrow q_3 \Rightarrow q_2 \Rightarrow q_1. \tag{18}$$

This means $Q_2 = Q_1 \cap Q_2$ and $Q_3 = Q_1 \cap Q_2 \cap Q_3$, and the three supersets Q_1, Q_2, and Q_3 of L form a descending chain:

$$Q_1 \supset Q_2 \supset Q_3 \supset L. \tag{19}$$

One then declares the sufficiency of q_3 for life that Q_3 is the closest that one gets to L in the relational-biologic approach and defines

$$L = Q_3, \tag{20}$$

which is the bold statement of

The Fundamental Theorem of Relational Biology *A natural system is an organism if and only if it is closed to efficient causation.*
Robert Rosen's lifetime's opera are embodied in his trilogy:

- *Fundamentals of Measurement and Representation of Natural Systems* (Rosen 1978)
- *Anticipatory Systems: Philosophical, Mathematical, and Methodological Foundations* (Rosen 1985a)
- *Life Itself: A Comprehensive Inquiry into the Nature, Origin, and Fabrication of Life* (Rosen 1991)

The following additional references are also notable milestones:

- "Some relational cell models: the metabolism–repair systems" (Rosen 1972)
- "Organisms as causal systems which are not mechanisms: an essay into the nature of complexity" (Rosen 1985b)
- *Essays on Life Itself* (Rosen 2000)

Historically, the condition q_2 (anticipation) was introduced in Rosen (1985a, although the first draft of the book was completed in 1979); condition q_1

(impredicativity) first appeared in Rosen (1985b) and then was explicated in detail along with condition q_3 (closure to efficient causation) in Rosen (1991). The various essays in Rosen (2000) further illustrate these conditions and their connections. Metabolism–repair systems, the very picture of closure to efficient causation, were the topic of Rosen's PhD thesis and his first published paper (Rosen 1958), and Rosen (1972) remains the most comprehensive treatise on this subject.

Anticipation

As mentioned at the outset, anticipation is a necessary condition for life: *a living system anticipates*. In Rosen (1985a), the Foreword contains the passage:

> ... biology is replete with situations in which organisms can generate and maintain internal predictive models of themselves and their environments, and utilize the predictions of these models about the future for purpose of control in the present. Many of the unique properties of organisms can really be understood only if these internal models are taken into account.

and in Section 1.1:

> ... obvious examples of anticipatory behavior abound in the biosphere at all levels of organization, and that much (if not most) conscious human behavior is also of this character.

One proclaims the

Axiom of Anticipation *Life is anticipatory.*

Anticipation is, of course, the *raison d'être* of the present *Handbook*. I shall provide a comprehensive exposition on Robert Rosen's theory of anticipatory systems in ▶ Chap. 45, "Mathematical Foundations of Anticipatory Systems." For now, as a stepping stone toward a characterization of life, it suffices to give a terse

Definition A natural system is an *anticipatory system* if

(i) it contains an *internal predictive model* of itself and its environment, $a\Box nd$
(ii) in accordance with the model's predictions, *antecedent actions* are taken.   Let

$$a(x) \;=\; x \text{ is an anticipatory system } (= q_2(x)),\tag{21}$$

whence

$$A = \{x \in N : a(x)\} = \text{the collection of all anticipatory systems.}\tag{22}$$

The axiom of anticipation thus says

Fig. 7 Life is anticipatory

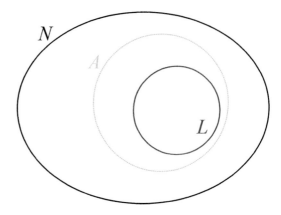

$$\forall x \ \ell(x) \Rightarrow a(x) \tag{23}$$

and (Fig. 7)

$$L \subset A. \tag{24}$$

One notes that all complementary sets are nonempty: for example, a simple mechanism is not anticipatory: umbrella $\in A^c = N \sim A$, and a socioeconomic system is a nonliving anticipatory system: SES $\in A \sim L$ (Fig. 8).

Impredicativity

In logic, the *predicate* is what is said or asserted about an object. It can take the role as either a property or a relation between entities. Thus *predicate calculus* is the type of symbolic logic that takes into account the contents (i.e., predicate) of a statement. The defining property $p(x)$ in $P = \{x \in U : p(x)\}$ (cf. (1) above) is an example of a predicate, since it *asserts* unambiguously the property that x must have in order to belong to the set P.

Contrariwise, a definition of an object is said to be *impredicative* if it invokes (mentions or quantifies over) the object itself being defined or perhaps another set which contains the object being defined. In other words, *impredicativity* is the property of a *self-referencing definition*. Impredicative definitions usually cannot be bypassed and are mostly harmless. But there are some that lead to paradoxes and may *entail ambiguities*.

Let the property i be defined thus

$$i(x) = x \text{ is an } impredicative \text{ system;} \tag{25}$$

then

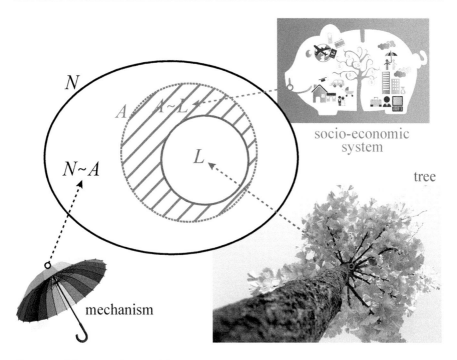

Fig. 8 Anticipatory and non-anticipatory systems

$$I = \{x \in N : i(x)\} = \text{the collection of all } \textit{impredicative } \text{natural systems.} \quad (26)$$

A natural system that is *not* impredicative is called *predicative*, whence

$$\begin{aligned} I^c \quad &= \{x \in N : \neg\, i(x)\} \\ &= \text{the collection of all } \textit{predicative } \text{natural systems.} \end{aligned} \quad (27)$$

Recall that there is a 'nonporous' boundary between I and I^c, which cannot be crossed at all in either direction. The partition is built into the set-theoretic logic. There are no purely syntactic operations, i.e., no finite number of rote repetitions that will produce predicativity from impredicativity, or vice versa (Fig. 9).

In Rosen's lexicon, members of I^c are *simple* systems (also called mechanisms), and members of I are *complex* systems. There are, alas, unfortunate derogatory connotations of the burdened terms: physics deals with simple systems; biology deals with complex systems. The dubious ordering 'complex > simple' entails an implied hierarchy of importance. Indeed, to have one's subject labeled 'simple' may be seen as a slight. Also, there are almost as many definitions of complexity as schools involved in the study of the topic, and the overused term 'complex(ity)' is consequently rendered quite meaningless. It is perhaps better off sticking with the 'neutral' adjectives of I^c = *predicative* systems and I = *impredicative* systems. An added advantage is that since 'predicativity' and 'impredicativity' are not words of

Fig. 9 *I* and *I*^{c} partition *N*

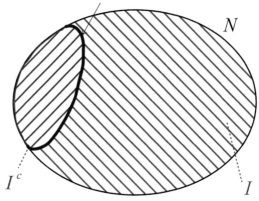

Fig. 10 $L \subset A \subset I$

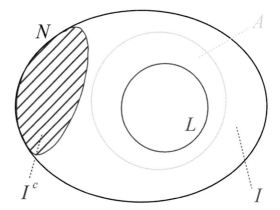

common usage, there is less chance of equivocation. For an alternate exposition on 'complex systems', see ► Chap. 2, "Complex Systems" in this *Handbook*.

For our purpose here of reaching a characterization of life, it is sufficient to consider the

Theorem *An anticipatory system must be impredicative; an impredicative system may (or may not) be anticipatory.*

(See ► Chap. 45, "Mathematical Foundations of Anticipatory Systems" in this *Handbook* for further discussion of this implication, $\forall x \; a(x) \Rightarrow i(x)$.) Thus one has the proper containment:

$$A \subset I. \tag{28}$$

Together with the containment $L \subset A$ from (24) above, one has the containments shown in Fig. 10.

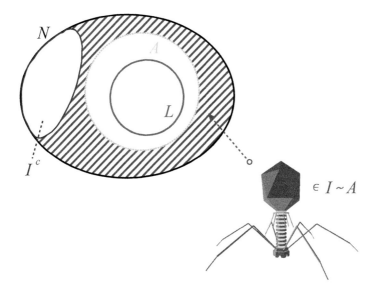

Fig. 11 Relational virology

A virus is impredicative but not anticipatory: virus $\in I \sim A$. This is because it is an isolated repair component (more on this later), but only uses the host's anticipatory processes to reproduce itself when joined (Fig. 11).

The proper containments (24) and (28) together say

$$L \subset (A \subset)I, \tag{29}$$

whence

Rosen's Theorem *An organism must be impredicative; an impredicative system may (or may not) be an organism.*

Impredicativity is a necessary condition of life, but not life itself.

Mappings and Their Relational Diagrams

Let $f : A \to B$ be a mapping from set A to set B; this situation may also be denoted $f \in H(A, B)$, where $H(A, B) \subset B^A$ is a *hom-set* (of mappings from A to B). When f is represented in the element-chasing version $f : a \mapsto b$ (where $a \in A$ and $b \in B$), its *relational diagram* may be drawn as a network with three *nodes* and two *directed edges*, i.e., a directed graph (or *digraph* for short):

$$f \underrightarrow{\hspace{2cm}} a \underrightarrow{\hspace{2cm}} b \tag{30}$$

The *hollow-headed arrow* denotes the *flow* from input (material cause) $a \in A$ to output (final cause) $b \in B$, whence the final cause of the mapping may be identified also as the hollow-headed arrow that terminates on the output:

$$\longrightarrow \!\!\!\!\triangleright b \tag{31}$$

The *solid-headed arrow* denotes the induction of or constraint upon the flow by the *processor* (efficient cause) f, whence the efficient cause of the mapping may be identified also as the *solid-headed arrow* that originates from the processor:

$$f \longrightarrow \tag{32}$$

The formal cause of the mapping may be identified as the *ordered pair* $\langle$ processor, flow $\rangle$ of the two kinds of arrows:

$$\longrightarrow \!\!\!\!\!\longrightarrow \!\!\!\!\triangleright \tag{33}$$

The processor and output relationship may be characterized 'f entails b', denoted by

$$f \vdash b \tag{34}$$

where $\vdash$ is called the *entailment symbol*. The efficient cause f, the processor of entailment $\vdash$ and at the tail of the solid-headed arrow, is *that which entails*. The final cause b, the target of entailment $\vdash$ and at the head of the hollow-headed arrow, is *that which is entailed*. A relational diagram is also called an *entailment network*.

The relational diagrams of mappings may *interact*: two mappings, with the appropriate domains and codomains, may be connected at different common nodes. (For an in-depth study on the various modes of connections, see Chap. 5 of Louie 2009 and Chap. 10 of Louie 2013.)

Composition of two mappings involves the combination of their digraphs in such a way that a final cause of one is relayed to become an ingredient of the other; i.e., when one mapping entails some component of the other. Two of the interactions of two mappings may be considered as compositions:

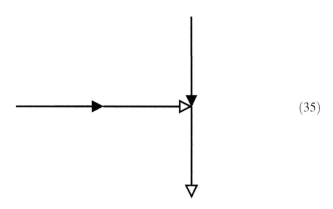

$$\tag{35}$$

and

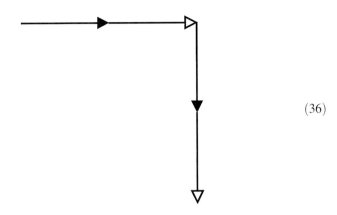

(36)

The relational interaction (35) arises when one has two mappings $f \in H(A, B)$ and $g \in H(X, A)$, whence *the codomain of g is the domain of f*. Let the element chases be $f : a \mapsto b$ (thus $f \vdash b$) and $g : x \mapsto a$ (thus $g \vdash a$), whence *the final cause of g is the material cause of f*. When that which is entailed is used as material cause (by another process), as is the case for '$\vdash a$' in $g : x \mapsto a$ followed by $f : a \mapsto b$, the entailment is called *material entailment*. The relational diagrams of these two mappings connect at the common node a as in

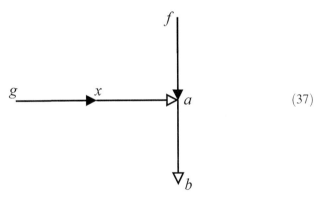

(37)

This *sequential composition* of relational diagrams represents the composite mapping $f \circ g \in H(X, B)$ with $f \circ g : x \mapsto b$ and has the abbreviated relational diagram:

(38)

whence the corresponding entailment diagram is

$$f \circ g \vdash b$$

(39)

($f \circ g$ entails b).

Next, the relational interaction (36) happens when one has two mappings $f \in H$ (A, B) and $g \in H(X, H(A, B))$, whence *the codomain of g contains f*. Because of this 'containment', the mapping g may be considered to occupy a higher 'hierarchical level' than the mapping f. Let the element chases be $f : a \mapsto b$ and $g : x \mapsto f$, whence *the final cause of g is the efficient cause of f*. When that which is entailed is an efficient cause (of another process), as is the case for '$\vdash f$' in $g : x \mapsto f$ (with $f : a \mapsto b$ in turn), the entailment is called *functional entailment*. In functional entailment, one has the *hierarchical composition* of relational diagrams

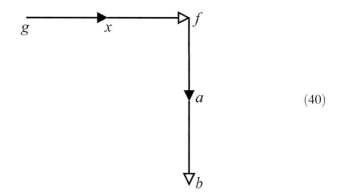

$$(40)$$

with the corresponding composition of entailment diagrams

$$g \vdash f \vdash b. \qquad (41)$$

Note that diagram (41) shows an iterative *entailment of an entailment*. A comparison of (39) and (41) reinforces the graphical differences of diagrams (35) and (36) and shows that sequential composition and hierarchical composition are different in kind: they are different both *formally* and *in content*.

Hierarchical Cycle

A formal system is an object in mathematics. ▶ Chapter 45, "Mathematical Foundations of Anticipatory Systems" in this *Handbook* contains a more detailed explanation. Here one may simply consider a formal system as a set S with a collection $\kappa(S)$ of mappings, so a formal system is the ordered pair $\langle S, \kappa(S) \rangle$. The mappings may compose to form a very complicated pattern of inferential entailment in a network. The various network topologies are explored in Chap. 6 of Louie 2009.

There is one mode of connection that is of special interest: when *two or more* hierarchical compositions are involved in a *cycle*, i.e., a closed path. (Note that a closed path in the directed graph sense means the arrows involved have a consistent direction.) This is called a *closed path of efficient causation*. In other words, a closed path of efficient causation is an entailment cycle that contains two or more efficient causes. Both the hierarchy of containment and the cycle are essential attributes of this closure.

For example, consider three mappings from a hierarchy of hom-sets,

$$f \in H(A,B), \quad g \in H\big(C,H(A,B)\big), \quad h \in H\Big(D,H\big(C,H(A,B)\big)\Big). \qquad (42)$$

Their hierarchical compositions form the relational diagram:

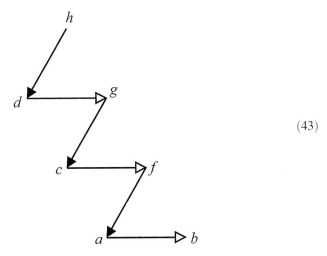

$$(43)$$

(where, naturally, $a \in A$, $b \in B$, $c \in C$, and $d \in D$). Now suppose there is a correspondence between the sets B and $H(D, H(C, H(A, B)))$. Then an isomorphic identification between b and h may be made, and a cycle of hierarchical compositions results

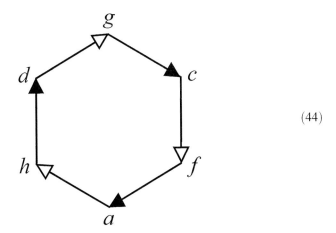

$$(44)$$

In diagram (44), one may say that the hierarchical compositions of the three maps $\{f, g, h\}$ are in *cyclic permutation*. The corresponding cyclic entailment pattern is

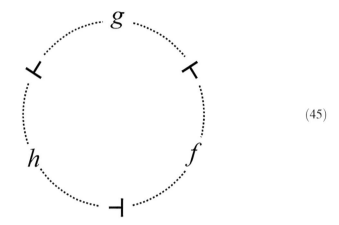

$$(45)$$

One may say that the diagram (45) represents the *cyclic entailments*:

$$\{\, g \vdash f, \ h \vdash g, \ f \vdash h \,\}. \tag{46}$$

Formally, one has the

Definition A *hierarchical cycle* is the relational diagram in graph-theoretic form of a closed path of efficient causation.

Impredicativity and Clef

Note that in a hierarchical cycle (e.g., arrow diagram (44)), there are *two or more solid-headed arrows* (since a closed path of efficient causation is defined as a cycle containing *two or more* hierarchical compositions). A hierarchical cycle is by definition the formal system representation (i.e., encoding) of a closed path of efficient causation in a natural system, so trivially one has the following

Lemma *A natural system has a model containing a hierarchical cycle if and only if it has a closed path of efficient causation.*

Because of this equivalence of a closed path of efficient causation in a natural system and a hierarchical cycle in its model, the term *hierarchical cycle*, although defined for formal systems, sometimes gets decoded back as an alternate description of the closed path of efficient causation itself. In other words, one may speak of a hierarchical cycle of inferential entailments as well as a hierarchical cycle of causal entailments.

Having a hierarchical cycle turns out to be equivalent to impredicativity:

Theorem *A natural system is impredicative* (i.e., *'complex'*) *if and only if it contains a closed path of efficient causation. A natural system is predicative* (i.e., *'simple'*) *if and only if it contains no closed path of efficient causation.*

Stated otherwise, a natural system is impredicative if and only if it has a model that contains a hierarchical cycle.

In formal systems, closed paths of efficient causation, i.e., cycles of entailment, are manifested by impredicatives (or 'self-references'). In science, where entailment means causality, causal cycles empower a rigorous study on categories of final causation, whence on *function* and *anticipation*. To say that something is a final cause of a process is *to require the process to entail something*. Final cause thus requires something of its effect. Indeed, a final cause of a process must *entail the entailment of the process itself*. (See, in particular, the discussion on 'immanent causation' in the last few sections of Chap. 5 of Louie 2009.) It is this peculiar reflexive character of final causation that links it intimately to impredicative, hierarchical cycles, in which the hierarchical compositions are precisely 'entailments of entailment'.

Note that an impredicative system only requires the *existence* of a hierarchical cycle that contains two or more processes. There may be many of its constituent processes that are not part of hierarchical cycles.

Definition A natural system is *closed to efficient causation* if its every efficient cause is entailed within the system.

Theorem *Closure to efficient causation for a natural system means it has a formal system model in which all of the efficient causes in its causal entailment structure are contained in closed paths; i.e., all efficient causes are components of hierarchical cycles.*

This theorem allows the description *closed to efficient causation* to be used on formal systems, those with all efficient causes involved in hierarchical cycles.

Let me emphasize that the predicates 'contains a closed path of efficient causation' and 'closed to efficient causation' are *not* equivalent. The class of systems that are closed to efficient causation forms a *proper subset* of the class of systems that contains a closed path of efficient causation. Members of the latter class, i.e., impredicative systems, are required to have only *some*, and not necessarily *all*, processes involved in hierarchical cycles.

Instead of the verbose 'closed-to-efficient-cause system' or 'systems that are closed to efficient causation', in Louie and Poli (2011), we have introduced a new term '*clef* system' (for *cl*osed to *ef*ficient causation) with the

Definition A natural system is *clef* if and only if it has a model that has all its processes contained in hierarchical cycles.

Analogously, a *clef* formal system is one that has all its mappings contained in hierarchical cycles. The word 'clef' means 'key', so this terminology has the added bonus of describing the importance of the class of *clef systems*.

Let

$$c(x) = x \text{ is a clef system.} \qquad (47)$$

Then

$$C = \{x \in N : c(x)\} \subset I \qquad (48)$$

with proper containment. In other words, the class of clef systems forms a proper subset of the class of impredicative systems.

Metabolism and Repair

As mentioned above, Robert Rosen, a stalwart in relational biology, devised in the 1950s a class of relational models called *metabolism–repair systems* ((M,R)-systems).

Relational biology has a functional view of life, expressed in terms of processes that organisms manifest, independent of the physical substrata on which they are carried out. An organism, being a system open to material causation, must have processes that are modes of interaction with the world. It must have inputs from the world, typical material inputs which supply energy and which provide the capacity for renewing the structure of the organism, whatever it might be. So it is a sine qua non that one has to have a *metabolic* apparatus. The word *metabolism* comes from the Greek *μεταβολή*, 'change', or *μεταβολισμός*, 'out-throw', i.e., an alteration or a relay of materials. Metabolism, in its most general form, is thus a mapping $f : x \mapsto y$ in which $\vdash y$ is material entailment.

An organism must also have a *genetic* apparatus, information carriers that tell how the products of metabolism are to be assembled. The genetic apparatus serves two functions: to produce the metabolic apparatus of the organism and to *re*produce it. Rosen called the genetic processes *repair*, which, in its most general form, is a mapping $f : x \mapsto y$ in which $\vdash y$ is functional entailment.

The English word 'repair' comes from the Latin *re + parare*, 'make ready again'. It is, of course, a word in common usage and means 'restore to good condition or proper functioning after damage or loss'; 'renovate or mend by replacing or fixing parts or by compensating for loss or exhaustion'; 'set right or make amends for loss, wrong, or error'. Rosen defined the technical usage of the term 'repair' in relational biology, precedently back in the beginnings of (M,R)-systems in the 1950s, to mean a hierarchical process for which 'the output of a mapping is itself a mapping'. This is the general telos of 'repair', that of an action taken to generate another action. The entailed process may possibly be previously existing, but repair does not have to be a 'return to normalcy' or 'restore to original condition'; the goal of 'the fix works' is more important. It is unfortunate (but ultimately irrelevant) that the technical term now, alas, suffers semantic equivocation because of its usage in molecular biology to insularly mean biochemical repair of a specific molecule, that of 'DNA (and sometimes RNA) repair'. This restricted usage is a very example of the meager appropriating the generic. Since the word 'repair' is not a specially coined word, its biological definition is not entitled to a universal decree. And in the absence of a default, Humpty Dumpty's rule applies: "When I use a word, it means just what I choose it to mean – neither more nor less."

To recap, our Unabashed Dictionary of Relational Biology defines

$$\begin{aligned} \textit{metabolism} &= \text{ material entailment,} \\ \textit{repair} &= \text{ functional entailment.} \end{aligned} \tag{49}$$

Anything that one would want to call 'alive' would have to have at least these two basic functions of M and R. (M,R)-systems began as a class of metaphorical, relational paradigms that define cells. It is, however, not much of a hyperbole to declare that all of Rosen's scientific work – his lifelong quest being the answer to the question "What is life?" – has arisen from a consideration of topics related to the study of (M,R)-systems.

Definition
(a) An *(M,R)-network* is an entailment network of a finite collection of metabolism and repair components.
(b) An *(M,R)-system* is an (M,R)-network that is closed to efficient causation.   *Not* every system is an (M,R)-network. This is because the terse definition (a) above has hidden some connection details; it has the verbose (and mathematically technical) expansion thus:

Definition *Metabolism* and *repair* are input-output systems that are connected as *components* into a network. They are formal systems with the following further category-theoretic structures.
 (i) A *metabolism component* is a formal system $M_i = \langle\, A_i, H(A_i, B_i)\,\rangle$.
 (ii) A *repair component* is a formal system $R_i = \langle\, Y_i, H(Y_i, H(A_i, B_i))\,\rangle$.
(iii) A *metabolism–repair network*, i.e., an *(M,R)-network*, is a finite collection of pairs of metabolism and repair components $\{(M_i, R_i) : i \in I\}$, connected in a model network. In particular, the outputs of a repair component R_i are observables in $H(A_i, B_i)$ of its corresponding metabolism component M_i. The metabolism components may be connected among themselves by their inputs and outputs (i.e., by $B_k \subset A_j$ for some j, $k \in I$). Repair components must receive at least one input from the outputs of the metabolism components of the network (i.e., $Y_i = \prod_{k=1}^{n} B_{i_k}$ with $n \geq 1$ and where each $i_k \in I$).

Note that the connections specified in (iii) are the *requisite* ones; an (M,R)-network may have additional interconnections among its components and with its environment.

This is not the place for an exposition on (M,R)-systems. In addition to the comprehensive reference Rosen (1972), the enthused reader may like to consult Chaps. 11–13 of Louie (2009) and Chap. 7 of Louie (2013). For illustrative purposes, here is an (M,R)-network with six pairs of metabolism–repair components (Fig. 12).

Fig. 12 A sample (M,R)-network

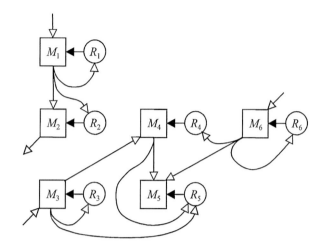

Let

$$m(x) \ = \ x \text{ is an } (\mathbf{M}, \mathbf{R})-\text{network}, \tag{50}$$

$$r(x) \ = \ x \text{ is an } (\mathbf{M}, \mathbf{R})-\text{system}, \tag{51}$$

$$M \ = \ \{\, x \in N : m(x) \,\} \ = \ (\mathbf{M}, \mathbf{R})-\text{networks}, \tag{52}$$

and

$$R \ = \ \{\, x \in N : r(x) \,\} \ = \ (\mathbf{M}, \mathbf{R})-\text{systems}. \tag{53}$$

Note that

$$N \sim M \neq \varnothing \tag{54}$$

because not all systems have the requisite structure in the definition of an (M,R)-network. In Sect. 13.14 of Louie (2009), I have shown that, however, an anticipatory system contains the necessary entailment, that for each $i \ \in \ I$ one must have $R_i \vdash M_i$ of an (M,R)-network, so

$$A \subset M. \tag{55}$$

Theorem *A anticipatory system is an (M,R)-network.*
    By definition, an (M,R)-system is an (M,R)-network that is clef:

$$R \ = \ M \cap C. \tag{56}$$

But in fact a clef system is a priori an (M,R)-network, because closure to efficient causation implies the repair $\vdash$ metabolism entailment, whence

$$C \subset M \qquad (57)$$

(cf. Sect. 8.28 in Louie 2013).

Theorem *A clef system is an (M,R)-network.*
Relations (56) and (57) then combine to imply

$$R = C; \qquad (58)$$

that is,

Theorem *A clef system is an* (M,R)-*system* (*and* vice versa).

Sufficiency

(M,R)-systems began as a class of metaphorical, relational paradigms that define cells.

Definition A *cell* is (at least) a material structure that realizes an (M,R)-system.
The class has since been generalized to model 'organisms', a term which is used in the sense of general living systems, including, in particular, cells. So, by definition,

$$L \subset R \qquad (59)$$

(a living system is an (M,R)-system).
In Louie (2012) (also Sect. 13.13 of Louie 2009), I have shown that

Theorem *An* (M,R)-*system is anticipatory.*
Thus with equality (58), one has

$$R = C \subset A. \qquad (60)$$

The Venn diagram is now (Fig. 13)
At this point, the question is, "Is the set $R \sim L$ empty?" Stated otherwise, "Is an (M,R)-system a sufficient characterization of life?" Rosen argued (in what were in effect concluding statements of his lifetime's work), for example, that "Any material system possessing such a graph [of an (M,R)-system] as a relational model (i.e., which *realizes* that graph) is accordingly an organism." (Section 10C of Rosen 1991) and "*Making a cell means constructing such a realization.* Conversely, I see no grounds for refusing to call such a realization an autonomous life form, whatever its material basis may be." (Chap. 17 of Rosen 2000). So he answered the question by *defining* (i.e., expanding) L so that

$$R \sim L = \varnothing, \qquad (61)$$

whence

$$L = R. \tag{62}$$

This is the

Postulate of Life *A natural system is an organism if and only if it realizes an (M,R)-system.*

Thus an (M,R)-system is the very model of life, and, conversely, life is the very realization of an (M,R)-system.

A union of interacting (M,R)-systems (or better, their *join* in the *lattice* of (M,R)-systems; cf. Sects. 2.1 and 7.28 in Louie 2009) is itself an (M,R)-system. A multicellular organism has a life of its own, apart from the fact that the cells that comprise it are alive. Similarly, in some sense an ecosystem of interacting organisms is itself an organism. In particular, a symbiotic union of organisms may itself be considered an organism (cf. Sect. 11.12 in Louie 2013).

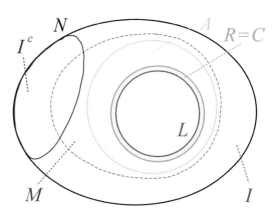

Fig. 13 Necessary and (almost) sufficient conditions for life

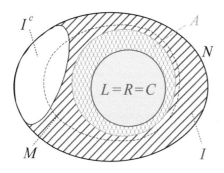

Fig. 14 The taxonomy

Systems	
N =	natural
I =	impredicative (complex)
I^c =	predicative (simple)
A =	anticipatory
M =	(M,R)-networks
R =	(M,R)-systems
C =	clef (closed to efficient causation)
L =	living

Fig. 15 The triumvirate

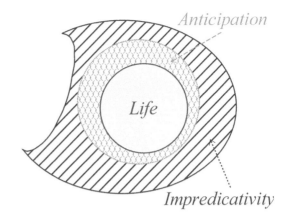

The equalities (58) ($R = C$) and (62) ($L = R$) together imply

$$L = C, \tag{63}$$

which is

The Fundamental Theorem of Relational Biology *A natural system is an organism if and only if it is closed to efficient causation.*

Here is, then, the final taxonomy with the necessary and sufficient condition for life (Fig. 14):

$$\text{Impredicativity} \supset \text{Anticipation} \supset \text{Life}. \tag{64}$$

Anticipation holds a pivotal role in the relational biology exercise of the characterization of life. So hereby it is duly noted (Fig. 15).

Summary

$$\textbf{Life} \subset \text{Anticipation} \subset \text{Impredicativity}$$

Life anticipates. Robert Rosen's theory of anticipatory systems arose out of his quest to characterize life using the tools of relational biology. The connection explains the presence of a ▶ Chap. 10, "Relational Biology" in this *Handbook*. In this chapter, I show how three necessary conditions for life – impredicativity, anticipation, and closure to efficient causation – become jointly sufficient to distinguish a living system from a nonliving one.

References

Louie, A. H. (2009). *More than life itself: A synthetic continuation in relation biology.* Frankfurt: ontos.

Louie, A. H. (2012). Anticipation in (M,R)-systems. *International Journal of General Systems, 41,* 5–22.

Louie, A. H. (2013). *The reflection of life: Functional entailment and imminence in relational biology.* New York: Springer.

Louie, A. H., & Poli, R. (2011). The spread of hierarchical cycles. *International Journal of General Systems, 40,* 237–261.

Rashevsky, N. (1954). Topology and life: In search of general mathematical principles in biology and sociology. *Bulletin of Mathematical Biophysics, 16,* 317–348.

Rosen, R. (1958). A relational theory of biological systems. *Bulletin of Mathematical Biophysics, 20,* 245–260.

Rosen, R. (1972). Some relational cell models: The metabolism-repair systems. In R. Rosen (Ed.), *Foundations of mathematical biology* (Vol. 2, pp. 217–253). New York: Academic.

Rosen, R. (1978). *Fundamentals of measurement and representation of natural systems.* New York: North-Holland.

Rosen, R. (1985a). *Anticipatory systems: Philosophical, mathematical, and methodological foundations.* Oxford: Pergamon; (2012) 2nd ed., New York: Springer.

Rosen, R. (1985b). Organisms as causal systems which are not mechanisms: An essay into the nature of complexity. In R. Rosen (Ed.), *Theoretical biology and complexity: Three essays on the natural philosophy of complex systems* (pp. 165–203). Orlando FL: Academic.

Rosen, R. (1991). *Life itself: A comprehensive inquiry into the nature, origin, and fabrication of life.* New York: Columbia University Press.

Rosen, R. (2000). *Essays on life itself.* New York: Columbia University Press.

Basic Biological Anticipation

11

Jan-Hendrik S. Hofmeyr

Contents

Abstract

Living organisms persist as functional wholes far beyond the individual lifetimes of their functional components. They achieve this by taking antecedent action, continuously fabricating themselves in anticipation of a future nonfunctional and deleterious internal state. This property of self-fabrication is the most basic expression of biological anticipation and of life itself. Self-fabricating systems must be closed to efficient causation, and in this chapter, I identify the classes of efficient biochemical causes in the cell and show how they are organized in a hierarchical cycle, the hallmark of a system closed to efficient causation. Broadly speaking, the three classes of efficient causes are the *enzyme catalysts* of covalent metabolic chemistry, the *intracellular milieu* that drives the supramolecular processes of chaperone-assisted folding and self-assembly of polypeptides and nucleic acids into functional catalysts and transporters, and the *membrane transporters* that maintain the intracellular milieu, in particular its electrolyte composition.

J.-H. S. Hofmeyr (✉)
Centre for Complex Systems in Transition and Department of Biochemistry, University of Stellenbosch, Stellenbosch, South Africa
e-mail: jhsh@sun.ac.za

© Springer Nature Switzerland AG 2019
R. Poli (ed.), *Handbook of Anticipation*,
https://doi.org/10.1007/978-3-319-91554-8_51

Keywords
Biological anticipation · Closure to efficient causation · Hierarchical cycle ·
Covalent chemistry · Supramolecular chemistry · Intracellular milieu

Introduction

All living organisms are constructed from fragile materials, yet they persist as functional wholes far beyond the individual lifetimes of their functional components. They must therefore have the ability to autonomously rebuild themselves in anticipation of the fact that they will deteriorate it they don't. Organisms therefore conform to Rosen's (1985) definition of an anticipatory system, in the sense that they take antecedent action by continuously fabricating themselves in anticipation of a future deleterious internal state. This property of self-fabrication underlies all higher properties of life, such as growth, adaptation, and reproduction, and is the most basic expression of biological anticipation, and of life itself.

The purpose of this chapter is to figure out how, at a molecular level, the living cell, the unit of life, accomplishes this remarkable and defining feat. To the best of my knowledge, this has not been done yet, except for my own preliminary attempt in Hofmeyr (2007). The concept of self-fabrication as *the* feature that distinguishes life from nonlife is of course not new and originated with Rosen's (1958a, b, 1959, 1991) metabolism-repair or (M,R)-systems and Maturana and Varela's (1980) related concept of autopoiesis, both of which focus on the self-fabricating nature of living systems. The relationship between (M,R) systems and autopoietic systems has since been explicated by Letelier et al. (2003). Maturana and Varela also emphasized that an autopoietic system forms a concrete unity in space in which the self-fabricating network is encapsulated. However, neither Rosen nor Maturana and Varela, nor, for that matter, anybody who has since published on this topic, has delved deeply enough into the biochemical underbelly of the cell to pinpoint exactly how the cellular processes form a self-fabricating organization.

With his (M,R)-systems and his formalization of the four Aristotelean causes (material, efficient, formal, final), Rosen gave us the theoretical tools with which to model causal entailment and self-fabrication at an abstract level (Rosen 1991; Louie 2009, 2013). The crucial result is that closure to efficient causation is a necessary condition for self-fabrication, and thus for life. Following Rosen, Aloisius Louie, in his handbook ► Chap. 10, "Relational Biology" (which is ideal background reading for the present discussion), defines a *cell* as "(at least) a material structure that realizes an (M,R)-system," and shows that an (M,R)-system is closed to efficient causation and hence anticipatory. However, the mappings in Rosen's (M,R)-diagram, especially the so-called replication map, have been notoriously problematic to realize in terms of real biochemical processes. At journey's end of this chapter, I hope to have shone new light on this matter.

From a biochemical point of view, what I therefore set out to do is identify the sets of efficient causes in the cell and show that the functional organization of cellular processes is closed to these efficient causes. In the jargon of relational biology, I set out to show how all the efficient causes participate in a so-called *hierarchical cycle*, the hallmark of a system closed to efficient causation (Louie 2009, Louie's handbook ► Chap. 10, "Relational Biology").

The Hierarchical Cycle in the Cell

Before attempting to identify the sets of efficient causes that form a hierarchical cycle, I lay out the cell's underlying network of material transformations, its metabolism. The term *metabolism* usually conjures up the image of a huge network of coupled, enzyme-catalyzed reactions depicted on the wall-charts that typically adorn biochemistry lecture halls. Despite the apparent complexity of this network, it can be simplified considerably to show the functional organization of the metabolic processes (Fig. 1). The degradative processes of catabolism break down nutrients (carbohydrates, proteins, lipids) to yield carbon skeletons, chemical energy (high ATP/ADP ratio or high energy charge), and reducing equivalents (high NADPH/NADP$^+$ ratio), which in turn are used by anabolism to synthesize the building blocks for macromolecular synthesis: *amino acids* for proteins, *nucleotides* for DNA and RNA, *fatty acids* for lipids. Catabolism and anabolism form the core of *intermediary metabolism* in all heterotrophic organisms. Both photoheterotrophes and photoautotrophes require the addition of a photochemical block, while photoautotrophes require a further block (the Calvin cycle) which produces sugars that are inputs to the catabolic block. Nevertheless, for the purpose of the present analysis, the whole of intermediary metabolism can be collapsed into the conversion of nutrients to the building blocks for macromolecular synthesis (a single arrow in Fig. 2).

What happens to the building blocks produced by intermediary metabolism? Figure 2 shows the processes relevant to this analysis, namely the maintenance of DNA integrity and the copying of DNA (combined in a single arrow), the production of the three major forms of RNA, namely ribosomal RNA (rRNA), messenger RNA (mRNA), and transfer RNA (tRNA), and the production of membrane lipids. Amino acids, in the form of aminoacyl-tRNAs, serve as substrates for the production of polypeptides. There are of course many other processes that also use products of catabolism and anabolism, but they are peripheral to this analysis and their exclusion does not affect its conclusions.

Efficient Cause 1: Enzymes and Ribosomes Catalyse Covalent Chemistry

The processes in Fig. 2 form the underlying network of *material causation* in the cell. From a chemical viewpoint, this is a *covalent reaction network* in which the bonds that are formed, broken, or rearranged are all covalent bonds. The individual biochemical reactions that comprise this network, while thermodynamically

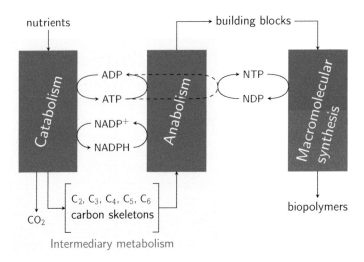

Fig. 1 The functional organization of metabolism. NTP and NDP represent nucleotide triphosphates and diphosphates. The triphosphates ATP, GTP, UTP, and CTP are used in macromolecular synthesis. *Blue* represents catalysis by enzymes, while *green* represents polypeptide synthesis by ribosomes (compare Fig. 2) (Adapted from Atkinson 1977)

Fig. 2 *Macromolecular synthesis* from monomeric building blocks. The *arrow* from nutrients to building blocks (amino acids, nucleotides, lipids) denotes intermediary metabolism in Fig. 1, while the other *arrows* comprise the macromolecular synthetic block. The *circular arrow* around mRNA represents the formation of mature mRNA through splicing, processing and editing. The substrates for polypeptide synthesis are the aminoacyl-tRNAs

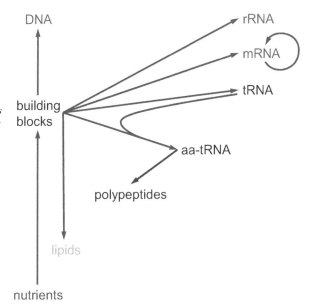

unstable, are kinetically stable and, in the absence of catalysts, proceed at negligible rates. For the network to be kinetically separable and independent from the greater network of spontaneous mass-action chemical transformations in which it is embedded, its reactions must operate on a timescale orders of magnitude faster than the side-reactions; the greater the time-scale separation, the smaller the effects of these side-reactions and the greater the degree of kinetic autonomy. This can only be achieved by efficient *catalysts* that are highly specific with respect to the substrates they recognize and the reactions they catalyze (Hofmeyr 2007). In the cell these specific catalysts are enzymes, membrane transporters, and supramolecular assemblies such as oligomeric enzymes, ribosomes, proteasomes, spliceosomes, nucleosomes, chaperones, and many others; they are all proteins or, in the case of ribosomes, spliceosomes and nucleosomes, nucleoproteins.

The dashed arrows in Fig. 3 make explicit the catalysis of the covalent chemical processes in Fig. 2 by enzymes and by ribosomes and the transport of nutrients across the cell membrane by transport proteins. Together they comprise the enzyme-catalyzed metabolism and the ribosome-catalyzed repair components of Rosen's (M,R)-system (the detailed biochemistry of the processes depicted in Figs. 1, 2, and 3 can be found in any modern biochemistry textbook and will not referenced here). Whereas the specificity of each enzyme is determined by the architecture of its active site, the specificity of ribosomal synthesis of polypeptides is determined by the ribonucleotide sequences of mature messenger RNAs, each mRNA specifying the amino acid sequence (primary structure) of a unique polypeptide. mRNA in noneukaryotic organisms is mature upon transcription, whereas in eukaryotic organisms its directly transcribed sequence (pre-mRNA) is processed into mature mRNA through a number of processes, including the splicing out of noncoding sequences and rearrangement of the coding sequences (the circular arrow around mRNA in Fig. 3).

Messenger RNA is but one class of RNA that is transcribed from DNA; the other two classes pertinent to this analysis are (i) rRNA, which forms the major structural component of ribosomes and is directly involved in its catalytic function (Steitz and Moore 2003), and (ii) the set of tRNAs. (Besides rRNA and tRNA there are also a host of other noncoding RNAs that fulfill important regulatory, processing, and protective functions, but their fabrication needs nothing more than an extra enzyme-catalyzed arrow from building blocks in Fig. 3.) Each tRNA is covalently coupled with high fidelity to a specific amino acid by an aminoacyl-tRNA synthetase to form an aminoacyl-tRNA (aa-tRNA); the set of aa-tRNAs are the substrates for ribosomal translation of mRNA sequences into polypeptides. The fixed relation between the unique anticodon sequence of three ribonucleotides on a tRNA and its cognate amino acid forms a rule of the genetic code. The set of 20 aminoacyl-tRNA synthetases that most cells possess, one for each amino acid, can therefore be regarded as the efficient cause of the genetic code; the genetic code is inscribed in the active sites of these crucial enzymes (Barbieri 2015).

In Fig. 3 the red dotted arrows emanating from DNA show that DNA acts as a template both for its own copying and error-correcting maintenance and for the synthesis of the different classes of RNA; the red dotted arrow emanating from mRNA shows that it acts as a template for the synthesis of polypeptides. These pathways for the transfer of sequence information from DNA can be regarded as the *formal cause* of polypeptide synthesis.

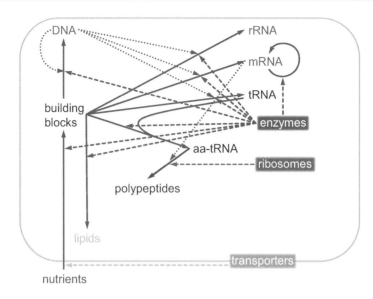

Fig. 3 *Catalysis* as efficient cause of metabolism, macromolecular fabrication, and nutrient transport. The *blue*, *green*, and *grey dashed arrows* indicate the processes that are catalyzed by enzymes, ribosomes, and nutrient transporters, respectively. The *red dotted arrows* show the role of *templates* in the copying and repair of DNA and in the synthesis of the different forms of RNA by transcription and of polypeptides by translation

Figure 3 also makes explicit the fact that nutrients need to be transported across the cell membrane by specific transport proteins.

The polypeptides formed by catalyzed covalent chemistry are as yet *non-functional*. We now turn to the processes that entail their functional state, i.e., the efficient causes that transform nonfunctional polypeptides into the functional catalysts and transporters that comprise efficient cause 1.

Efficient Cause 2: The Intracellular Milieu Enables Supramolecular Chemistry

In order to become functional, say as an enzyme, a newly synthesized polypeptide needs to fold into the correct three-dimensional conformation that forms the active binding and catalytic site. Higher-order structures such as proteasomes and chaperones need to self-assemble from pre-folded proteins, while ribosomes and spliceosomes need to self-assemble from pre-folded proteins and RNA. These processes of *folding* and *self-assembly* are driven by noncovalent interactions and are now called *supramolecular chemical processes* (Lehn 1995) (see Fig. 4).

The pioneering studies on ribonuclease in the 1950s and 1960s by Anfinsen, Sela, and White (Anfinsen 1973) and on the assembly of viruses by Caspar and Klug (1962) established that, given a watery environment with a specific pH, temperature,

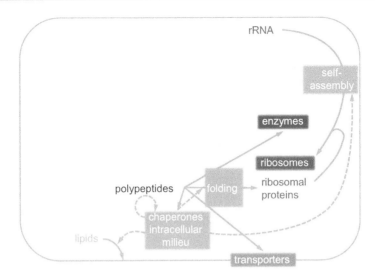

Fig. 4 The *supramolecular processes* of *polypeptide folding* and *macromolecular assembly* that generate *functional catalysts* such as enzymes, transporters, and ribosomes, as well as chaperones that assist in folding and self-assembly (the *yellow solid arrows*). The intracellular space is enclosed by the cell membrane, which is formed from lipids through processes involving self-assembly. Together, the *chaperones* and the membrane-delimited *intracellular milieu* act as efficient causes of folding and self-assembly (the *yellow dashed arrows*)

ionic strength, and electrolyte composition, the folding of polypeptides into their functional state is a spontaneous process that is determined by their amino acid sequences (primary structures). Similarly, the self-assembly of proteins and/or nucleic acids into higher-order structures is spontaneous, the specificity of the process being determined by the properties of the prefolded subunits. The generality of these facts has since been confirmed by the many studies that show that a very large number of pure denatured proteins refold or re-assemble spontaneously to their functional conformations when the denaturant is removed (Ellis et al. 1998). Nevertheless, while the specificity of folding and self-assembly is determined by the hydrogen bonding and electrostatic properties of the polypeptides and subunits themselves, the main driver for folding and assembly is the *hydrophobic force* exerted by the watery environment, which imparts an important agency to the intracellular milieu (intracellular meaning "inside the cell" and milieu the "environmental condition"). Furthermore, for the intracellular milieu to be effective as an efficient cause of supramolecular chemistry, its pH, temperature, ionic strength, and electrolyte composition have to be strictly maintained, since these factors determine the state of dissociation and solvation of functional groups on proteins and nucleic acids.

Since the discovery by Laskey et al. (1978) that the assembly of histones and DNA into nucleosomes is allowed only in the presence of a protein called nucleoplasmin that prevents aggregate formation, our understanding of protein folding and assembly has been enhanced dramatically. With the introduction of the concept of *molecular chaperone* "to describe a class of cellular proteins whose function is to ensure that the folding of certain other polypeptides and their assembly into oligomeric structures occur correctly" (Ellis 1987, p. 14), we have a new class of efficient causes of supramolecular chemistry. In a recent review, Ellis (2013) suggests "that it is more useful to think of a molecular chaperone as a function, rather than a molecule," a notion that fits perfectly with the idea that, in essence, chaperones can be regarded as catalysts of noncovalent folding and assembly since they assist these processes without becoming permanent components of the structures they help creating. Ellis (2013) suggests that the principle of spontaneous self-assembly should be replaced by the principle of *chaperone-assisted self-assembly*, thus retaining the principle of self-assembly while modifying it to include the need for chaperones that reduce unproductive side reactions, particularly aggregation.

Just like other proteins, chaperones can in principle fold and self-assemble spontaneously, but it is quite probable that it happens with the assistance of other chaperones ("cross-chaperoning"), perhaps even of themselves ("self-chaperoning"); this is suggested by the circular dashed arrow in Fig. 4. Some evidence for this was provided by Lissin et al. (1990) who showed that the chaperone GroEL re-assembles itself in an ATP-dependent process. To my knowledge there are at present no other published studies that explicitly address this issue. The assembly of ribosomes from proteins and rRNA is also assisted by chaperones (Woolford 2002; Karbstein 2010).

It is therefore clear that the efficient causes of the supramolecular processes of folding and self-assembly is an amalgam of, on the one hand, chaperones that prevent mis-folding, mis-assembly, and aggregation and, on the other, a conducive intracellular milieu made up of a pH-buffered solvent with a high dielectric constant (water) and a homeostatically maintained electrolyte composition that differs from that of the external environment. Factors such as macromolecular crowding (Ellis 2001) and the presence of enzyme cofactors (Wittung-Stafshede 2002) also contribute to the effectiveness of the intracellular milieu as efficient cause of supramolecular chemistry.

As depicted in Fig. 4, a controlled intracellular milieu would not exist were it not encapsulated by a barrier that distinguishes and isolates it from the extracellular environment. This barrier is of course the semi-permeable bilayer of lipids called the cell membrane, which contains, among others, proteins that selectively transport nutrients and electrolytes. The cell membrane can be thought of as forming part of the intracellular milieu in that it provides a two-dimensional lipophylic environment that is needed for membrane-bound proteins such as transporters to fold and self-assemble. As with folding, the formation of membranes from amphipathic lipids is a self-assembly process driven by the hydrophobic force of the watery surroundings.

We now have catalysis of covalent biochemistry (efficient cause 1) functionally entailed by the intracellular milieu and chaperones (efficient cause 2) through the supramolecular processes of folding and self-assembly of proteins and nucleic acids, which also account for the self-assembly of membrane lipids. To form a hierarchical cycle, we need to show that the intracellular milieu itself (efficient cause 2) is functionally entailed by efficient causes that have already been accounted for in Figs. 3 and 4.

Efficient Cause 3: Membrane Transport Maintains the Intracellular Milieu

The main differences between the intracellular and extracellular environments are the marked difference in electrolyte composition and the high intracellular protein concentration, the latter the main contributor to macromolecular crowding. In virtually all microbial, plant, and animal cells the intracellular pH is buffered near 7.2, the most important buffers being inorganic and organic phosphates and proteins, both of which have already been shown to be efficiently caused by metabolism. *Membrane transporters*, which are also already accounted for by protein synthesis and folding, maintain the intracellular electrolyte composition (Fig. 5).

The cytosolic concentration of K^+ is much higher than that of Na^+, while extracellularly the opposite holds. In most organisms, a Na^+/K^+-ATPase maintains the high potassium level inside cells while keeping sodium low. Intracellular Ca^{2+} is also strictly maintained as very low levels. The major intracellular anions are phosphates, sulfate, proteins, and amino acids, while Cl^- is the major extracellular

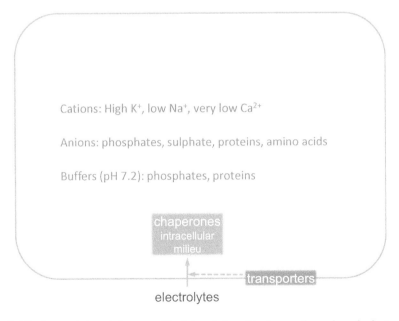

Fig. 5 The homeostatic maintenance of the intracellular milieu by *membrane-bound selective ion transporters* (*grey dashed arrow*), which act as the efficient cause of the electrolyte composition of the intracellular milieu (*grey solid arrow*)

Table 1 Typical ion concentrations in mammalian cytosol and blood (Lodish et al. 2013, p. 485) and in sea water (DOE 1994)

Ion	Cytosol (mM)	Blood (mM)	Sea water (mM)
Potassium	139	4	10
Sodium	12	145	469
Chloride	4	116	546
Bicarbonate	12	29	2
Amino acids in proteins	138	9	
Magnesium	0.8	1.5	53
Calcium	<0.0002	1.8	10

anion; in blood, bicarbonate is also a major anion. Table 1 shows the differences in electrolyte composition of the mammalian cytosol as compared to blood and sea water.

We have already seen that chaperones can be considered part of efficient causation of supramolecular chemistry by the intracellular milieu (efficient cause 2). Like all the other enzymes and transporters they have already been accounted for by polypeptide synthesis, folding and self-assembly.

Closure to Efficient Causation

When stitched together, as in Fig. 6, the three sets of efficient causes depicted in Figs. 3, 4, and 5 form a system in which all efficient causes are produced internally, i.e., a cycle that is closed to efficient causation – a hierarchical cycle.

At first glance this visual representation of the complete network of causation is complicated and difficult to decipher, but it can be simplified, as in Fig. 7, to a form in which the closure to efficient causation is immediately clear. What this representation also shows is the apparent presence in the cell of a constructor in the sense of Von Neumann. In Von Neumann and Burks (1966, Fifth Lecture), he described a theoretical kinematic automaton that could reproduce itself. The automaton consists of a *universal constructor* combined with the description of a machine. The constructor builds the machine from component parts according to its description. If supplied with its own description, the automaton can construct itself. The ribosome that makes polypeptides according to the information in mRNA seems obviously analogous to Von Neumann's constructor, but the analogy is at best partial. The polypeptides constructed by ribosomes are not yet molecular machines; they are still nonfunctional and need to fold, and, in the case of higher order structures, self-assemble in an environment that is conducive to these supramolecular processes. Von Neumann's constructor, given its own description, can make itself, but the ribosome cannot do this: it only makes the protein part of itself, which is not even the functional component: as noted above, ribosomes are ribozymes with rRNA performing the catalytic function. This new understanding of ribosomal function should, I hope, supersede the erroneous view that ribosomes can directly make

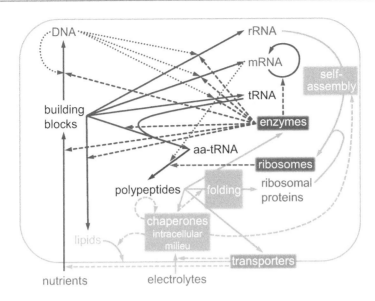

Fig. 6 The superposition of the three sets of efficient causes in Figs. 3, 4, and 5 provides a complete picture of the self-fabricating organization of the cell

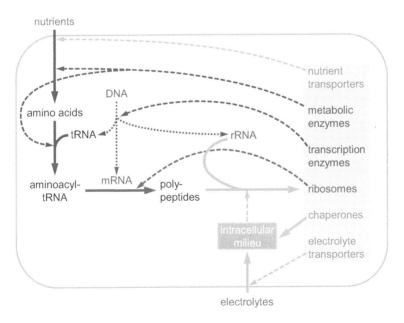

Fig. 7 An alternative view of the self-fabricating organization of the cell depicted in Fig. 6. It shows how all the efficient causes (*dashed arrows*) are produced in the cell, thereby forming an anticipatory hierarchical cycle. The *solid arrows* originate from material causes and the *red dotted arrows* depict formal causation by transfer of sequence information. Lipid and cell membrane synthesis in not included here. The scheme is an expanded version of Fig. 9 in Hofmeyr (2007)

themselves (since some examples of this view were published before the ribozyme nature of ribosomes was known and since the point of this discussion is not polemic I do not provide literature references).

For those readers of a more theoretical bent, the closed-to-efficient causal entailment structure that underlies self-fabrication of the cell is summarized in the diagram of mappings shown in Fig. 8. The catalytic mapping, e, includes metabolic and transcription enzymes, ribosomes, and nutrient transporters. As noted above, these macromolecules also contribute as proteins to aspects of the intracellular milieu, m, but the main efficient cause of m is t, the membrane transporters that maintain the intracellular electrolyte composition and ionic strength. As already noted, chaperones, c, which assist folding and self-assembly, are considered part of the intracellular milieu, but they are already accounted for by the efficient causes e and m that fabricate their structure and make them functional, also by cross-chaperoning or self-chaperoning. The intracellular milieu mapping should therefore more correctly be the product of m and c. It is possible to expand the diagram in Fig. 8a to a version that decomposes the mappings

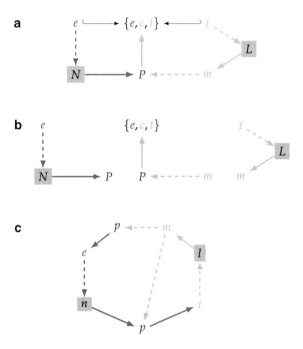

Fig. 8 (**a**) Diagram of the mappings that correspond to Figs. 6 and 7. The *dashed arrows* originate from efficient causes (the mappings e, t and m), the *solid arrows* originate from material causes N, P and L, while the *hooked arrows* to $\{e, c, t\}$ are inclusion mappings (the inclusion mapping from c to $\{e, c, t\}$ is not shown). N, nutrients (extracellular); L, electrolytes (extracellular); P, polypeptides; e, catalysts (enzymes – including nutrient transporters – and ribosomes); c, chaperones, t, electrolyte transporters; m, intracellular milieu, including chaperones. (**b**) Decomposition of the scheme in (**a**) into three mappings that respectively correspond from *left* to *right* to Figs. 3, 4, and 5. (**c**) Chasing elements through the diagram in (**a**) to form a cycle of hierarchical compositions (see Louie (2009) for the theory underlying such diagrams)

into all the details of Figs. 6 and 7, but this will be the subject of a separate publication. Here I just want to provide an abstract representation of how the three major efficient causes described above form the hierarchical cycle that is the most basic expression of biological anticipation and which forms the functional core of all cells, whether prokaryotic or eukaryotic, bacterial, plant, or animal.

While the purpose of this chapter was to analyze closure to efficient causation in terms of cellular biochemistry, we may nevertheless ask where Rosen's (1991) (M,R)-system fits into the present picture. Without going into detail here, the e mapping is a composition of the metabolism and repair components of Rosen's diagram and therefore accounts for both metabolism and genetics as in Fig. 3. However, the crucial difference is that the repair is not yet complete because the polypeptides in P are still nonfunctional, whereas in the (M,R)-system their functional state is just assumed and not explicitly accounted for as it is in my analysis. The central insight of my analysis is that closure to efficient causation is achieved through an intracellular milieu that serves as efficient cause of the supramolecular chemistry that makes the molecular machinery of the cell functional. In turn these molecular machines create and maintain the intracellular milieu and therefore serve as its efficient cause. What this analysis also makes explicit is that the existence of the intracellular milieu presupposes encapsulation by a self-assembling, semi-permeable isolating barrier that allows selective transport.

The idea that the matrix in which the functional components of a system are embedded can itself be a functional component of the system may be foreign to most readers, but the intracellular milieu actually fulfills Rosen's (1991) criteria for a functional component perfectly. First, it has an input (non-functional polypeptides and polynucleotides) from which it produces an output (functional catalysts and transporters), and second, changing its properties (such as its dielectric constant, pH, ionic strength, or electrolyte composition) affects the effectiveness with which it does this, and so changes the behavior of the system.

The critical reader may protest that the functional organization I describe in Figs. 6 and 7 only pertains to prokaryotic cells (Archaea and Bacteria). While it is true that these diagrams capture the essential details of the functional organization of prokaryotic cells, eukaryotic cells are just elaborations of that functional organization, the essence of which remains unchanged. Of course, the eukaryotic cell is structurally and functionally much more complex than the prokaryotic cell – consider, for example, compartmentation, the cytoskeleton, endomembranes, chromosomes and their remodeling, mRNA splicing and processing, more complex post-translational protein modification, specialized organelles, membrane trafficking, not to mention all the organic codes beyond the genetic code (Barbieri 2015) – but ultimately it remains just a more complicated exemplar of the same three sets of interlinked efficient causes: covalent catalysis by enzymes, supramolecular chemistry driven by the intracellular milieu, and maintenance of the intracellular milieu by membrane transport. Whereas Figs. 6 and 7 do not include these extra eukaryotic features, Fig. 8 applies to all living cell forms. If the Last Universal Common Ancestor (LUCA) was enclosed by a membrane (so creating an intracellular milieu) and had catalysts (whether protein or RNA or both) that needed the correct supramolecular chemistry to become functional (which depends on the intracellular milieu), then, in principle, Fig. 8 applies to LUCA as well, although some aspects of Figs. 6 and 7 most probably do not. Figure 8 therefore describes the core of the functional organization, if not of life itself, then at least of life as we know it.

Conclusion

In order to fabricate themselves, cells use a single, conceptually straightforward chemical process – polymerization – to create linear macromolecules that fold into functional three-dimensional structures that can self-assemble into higher-order molecular machines. The analysis presented above shows that to make this possible nature had to learn to harness both covalent carbon chemistry and non-covalent supramolecular chemistry. Covalent chemistry is effected by specific catalysts, while supramolecular chemistry is effected by a strictly-maintained intracellular milieu. The functional cellular architecture that ultimately evolved is what I would call a distributed Von Neuman constructor, distributed in the sense that it encompasses three efficient causes: template-directed polymerization to make non-functional polypeptides and polynucleotides (covalent chemistry informed by DNA/RNA sequence information), folding/self-assembly to make these macromolecules functional (supramolecular chemistry), and the maintenance of the intracellular milieu by encapsulation and membrane transport to make supramolecular chemistry possible. To create a link between the world of DNA/RNA sequences and the world of amino-acid sequences in polypeptides a chemical convention (the genetic code) had to be established. Together all of these processes are folded into a hierarchical cycle that forms the basis of basic biological anticipation.

The above analysis of basic biological anticipation also teaches us an important lesson about the functional organization and anticipatory nature of self-sustaining systems in general: in order to qualify for such a system, the relations between *structure, function*, and *context* must form a hierarchical cycle, allowing all three components to be generated from within the system itself. In Hofmeyr (2007) I suggested a mantra for systems biology: "Nothing in an organism makes sense except in the light of functional context." I now want to suggest that one can generalize this by replacing "organism" with "organization." As noted by many before me, we have much to learn from life itself.

References

Anfinsen, C. B. (1973). Principles that govern the folding of protein chains. *Science, 181*, 223–230.
Atkinson, D. E. (1977). *Cellular energy metabolism and its regulation*. New York: Academic.
Barbieri, M. (2015). *Code biology: A new science of life*. Heidelberg: Springer.
Caspar, D. L. D., & Klug, A. (1962). Physical principles in the construction of regular viruses. In L. Frisch (Ed.), *Cold Spring Harbor symposia on quantitative biology* (Vol. 27, pp. 1–24). Cold Spring Harbor: Cold Spring Harbor Laboratory Press.

DOE. (1994). *Handbook of methods for the analysis of the various parameters of the carbon dioxide system in sea water* [Version 2, ORNL/CDIAC-74]. U.S. Department of Energy. http://cdiac.ornl.gov/oceans/DOE_94.pdf.

Ellis, R. J. (1987). Proteins as molecular chaperones. *Nature, 328*, 378–379.

Ellis, R. J. (2001). Macromolecular crowding: An important but neglected aspect of the intracellular environment. *Current Opinion in Structural Biology, 11*, 114–119.

Ellis, R. J. (2013). Assembly chaperones: A perspective. *Philosophical Transactions of the Royal Society of London. Series B, Biological Sciences, 368*, 20110398.

Ellis, R. J., Dobson, C., & Hartl, F. U. (1998). Sequence does specify protein conformation. *Trends in Biochemical Sciences, 23*, 468.

Hofmeyr, J. H. S. (2007). The biochemical factory that autonomously fabricates itself: A systemsbiological view of the living cell, Chapter 10. In F. C. Boogerd, F. Bruggeman, J. H. S. Hofmeyr, & H. V. Westerhoff (Eds.), *Systems biology: Philosophical foundations* (pp. 217–242). Amsterdam: Elsevier.

Karbstein, K. (2010). Chaperoning ribosome assembly. *The Journal of Cell Biology, 189*, 11–12.

Laskey, R. A., Honda, B. M., Mills, A. D., & Finch, J. T. (1978). Nucleosomes are assembled by an acidic protein which binds histones and transfers them to DNA. *Nature, 275*, 416–420.

Lehn, J. M. (1995). *Supramolecular chemistry: Concepts and perspectives*. Weinheim: Wiley-VCH.

Letelier, J. C., Marn, G., & Mpodozis, J. (2003). Autopoietic and (M,R) systems. *Journal of Theoretical Biology, 222*(2), 261–272.

Lissin, N. M., Venyaminov, S. Y., & Girshovich, A. S. (1990). (Mg-ATP)-dependent self-assembly of molecular chaperone GroEL. *Nature, 348*, 339–341.

Lodish, H., Berk, A., Kaiser, C. A., Krieger, M., Bretscher, A., Ploegh, H., Amon, A., & Scott, M. P. (2013). *Molecular cell biology*. New York: W. H. Freeman.

Louie, A. H. (2009). *More than life itself. A synthetic continuation in relational biology*. Heusenstamm: Ontos Verlag.

Louie, A. H. (2013). *Reflection of life: Functional entailment and imminence in relational biology* (Systems science and engineering, Vol. 29). New York: Springer.

Maturana, H. R., & Varela, F. J. (1980). *Autopoiesis and cognition: The realisation of the living*. Dordrecht: D. Reidel Publishing Company.

Rosen, R. (1958a). A relational theory of biological systems. *The Bulletin of Mathematical Biophysics, 20*, 245–260.

Rosen, R. (1958b). The representation of biological systems from the standpoint of the theory of categories. *The Bulletin of Mathematical Biophysics, 20*, 317–341.

Rosen, R. (1959). A relational theory of biological systems II. *The Bulletin of Mathematical Biophysics, 21*, 109–128.

Rosen, R. (1985). *Anticipatory systems: Philosophical, mathematical & methodological foundations*. New York: Pergamon Press.

Rosen, R. (1991). *Life itself: A comprehensive inquiry into the nature, origin, and fabrication of life*. New York: Columbia University Press.

Steitz, T. A., & Moore, P. B. (2003). RNA, the first macromolecular catalyst: The ribosome is a ribozyme. *Trends in Biochemical Sciences, 28*(8), 411–418.

Von Neumann, J., & Burks, A. W. (1966). *Theory of self-reproducing automata*. Urbana: University of Illinois Press.

Wittung-Stafshede, P. (2002). Role of cofactors in protein folding. *Accounts of Chemical Research, 35*, 201–208.

Woolford, J. (2002). Chaperoning ribosome assembly. *Molecular Cell, 10*, 8–10.

Animal Anticipation: A Perspective

12

Ruud van den Bos

Contents

Abstract

Anticipatory behavior may be defined as behavior expressed in the "here and now" based upon expected events in the near future and information processed in the past. Hence, it suggests an element of awareness of past, present, and future on behalf of the subject. In this chapter I discuss two examples of animal behavior, which at first sight may equally qualify as anticipatory behavior: migrating south in the fall to survive harsh winter conditions and deciding to continue or stop foraging behavior in face of a potential threat, such as indicated by smells (or other signals) of a predator. I show that in many animal species, awareness is present, a global working space, allowing the animal to adjust behavior when stimuli have changed their value; the latter implies some idea of the notion of the future. In addition, I discuss that only the foraging-predator threat case may be labeled as anticipatory

R. van den Bos (✉)
Department of Animal Ecology and Physiology, Institute for Water and Wetland Research, Radboud University, Nijmegen, The Netherlands
e-mail: ruudvdbos@science.ru.nl

© Springer Nature Switzerland AG 2019
R. Poli (ed.), *Handbook of Anticipation*,
https://doi.org/10.1007/978-3-319-91554-8_18

235

behavior in the sense of containing an element of awareness of past, present, and future. This is framed in the wider context of decision-making.

Keywords
Animal behavior · Decision-making · Evolution · Intentional systems · Goal-directed behaviour

Introduction

As winter is approaching, some species of birds in the village I live in (close to Utrecht, the Netherlands) are preparing to move south. They will return springtime next year. Is this a case of anticipatory behavior? Winter may be a period of low temperatures, frozen lakes, and snow-covered land, with little food available. Migrating south to warmer and food-rich areas is a good way to deal with the upcoming harsh living conditions. In the introductory chapter of this handbook (see ► Chap. 1, "Introducing Anticipation"), Poli defines anticipatory behavior using the example of taking an umbrella while going for a walk after watching the weather forecast. The essential elements of the description are: "An anticipatory behavior is a behavior that 'uses' the future in its actual decision process. Anticipation as here understood includes two mandatory components: a forward-looking attitude and the use of the former's result for action" (see ► Chap. 1, "Introducing Anticipation"). Thus it seems that anticipatory behavior may be defined as behavior expressed in the "here and now" based upon expected events in the near future and information processed in the past. I use this as a general, descriptive, starting point of this chapter. At first sight bird migrating behavior seems to fit the description and may qualify as anticipatory behavior.

Now consider the following case. When an animal is foraging and senses that a predator may be nearby, say by its smell or other signals, what will it do? Let us take one step back and think of alternative scenarios. At the extreme ends, the animal either may blindly flee – a stimulus-response-like behavior – or may continue to forage, oblivious to the information the signal carries, an extreme form of risk-taking behavior. In between these extremes, we may think of the animal halting to assess the situation and then taking a decision to advance, to hide, to slowly retreat, or to flee, based on the strength of the signal and its reliability, its own internal state, etc. I will return in more detail to the different features of this example later on. For now, when we think of the umbrella example, one could argue that the outcome in the intermediate scenarios – a cost-benefit analysis – is close to what may be considered anticipatory behavior: it takes into account the future, the goals to be achieved, and uses this to take appropriate action now.

The description of anticipatory behavior suggests an element of awareness of past, present, and future on behalf of the subject. After all, to do what is needed in the "here and now" suggests an element of envisioning events in the future (see also ► Chap. 1, "Introducing Anticipation"). My guess would be that many people do not consider bird migration as an example of anticipatory behavior in the sense of a consciously taken course of action, but rather as an instinct to migrate, elicited by changes in temperature and day length affecting hormonal systems setting "behavioral and physiological wheels in motion." The foraging-predator threat course of action would more likely qualify as an example of a consciously taken course of action, i.e., anticipatory behavior, whatever the precise behavior chosen. But is there a difference, and if so, how can we differentiate one from the other and what do they mean? And does anticipatory behavior require awareness? Could migratory behavior be called anticipatory behavior, but then at a different level? Here, I will expand on this using the umbrella example a number of times in this chapter to illustrate the point in animal research.

In general one problem with animal behavior is that we cannot ask the animal's punctuations directly, but that only the behavioral end product is visible. Yet, what we observe may not be how things really are, even how complicated and sophisticated it may look to us. So, we need models of the organization of behavior and critical experiments to analyze whether what we observe is anticipatory behavior in a conscious sense or not.

Here, I will first discuss how to study the issue of anticipatory behavior in animals and then using the umbrella/foraging/migration examples to define in more detail the relevant questions.

Private and Subjective Versus Public and Objective: Inferring from What You See

When applied to the level of subjects, it seems that anticipatory behavior as described above in one way or the other implies an element of awareness, a kind of global working space where information can be retained, even if shortly, "digested" and/or processed, before appropriate action is taken. Some image of the future or scenario enrolling in the future, in whatever way, must be there to choose an appropriate behavior in the present. Elsewhere (van den Bos 2000, 1997) I have argued, based on the fascinating work by among others the British psychologist Anthony Dickinson, that for understanding animal and human behavior, the concept of intentional systems may be a starting point to assess whether behavior is goal-directed or habit-like and whether reflection is present or not.

Three layers of intentional systems or behavioral modes may be envisioned: zero-order, first-order, and second-order, which amount respectively to systems or modes working on stimulus-response, action/stimulus-outcome (goal-directed behavior), and reflections (on the previous two levels). Thus some behaviors may be zero-order, while others are first-order or second-order. While some species may only have zero-order modes, others may possess all three. As subjects develop, these levels may develop in succession.

Anticipatory behavior assumes goal-directedness, but not necessarily reflection, although reflection may expand the time window over which actions may be considered and may widen the number of actions to be taken (see also ▶ Chap. 1, "Introducing Anticipation"). So when viewed from this perspective, anticipatory behavior may more likely be present in animals possessing at least first-order modes than only zero-order modes.

A point that has been central to discussions on whether nonhuman animals do have emotions or cognitive capacities, such as anticipatory behavior, is that it is impossible to know *what* or *how* nonhuman animals feel or think from their own, subjective, perspective. However, as I have argued elsewhere, the relevant research question is not *what/how* human or nonhuman animals feel or know (i.e., a *subjective* perspective, the private contents of mental states) but *that* they feel or know (i.e., an *objective* perspective, the fact that they have mental states) and how this is represented in their behavior and its associated circuits in the nervous system (van den Bos 1997, 2000, 2001; Braithwaite et al. 2013). In other words, emotion and cognition are not private properties just occurring by accident, for instance, in one individual, but fundamental properties of the organization of brain and behavior occurring in all individuals of a species (van den Bos 1997, 2000, 2001; Braithwaite et al. 2013). This also amounts to an important difference between zero-order and first−/second-order systems or modes: when, for instance, anticipatory behavior (goal-directedness) plays a role in the organization of behavior in human and nonhuman animals, then we should define conditions under which this is likely to be advantageous, the underlying neural circuits that are necessary for it to be present and the *critical* experiments that would show whether this is the case or not. So, anticipatory behavior becomes a construct open to investigation rather than something mysterious and closed to study. This does not take away the fact that differences may occur in *how* it is perceived (what might be called "the flavor") between individuals of one species or between species. Such variation may be related to differences in the way sensory information is processed, prior history, etc., which is discussed in detail elsewhere (Van den Bos 1997, 2000; Braithwaite et al. 2013).

Anticipatory Behavior: Affording Flexibility

Zero-Order

In classic ethology behavioral patterns related to motivational systems have been divided or labeled according to their successive or temporal occurrence in the sequence of behavioral patterns: preparatory behavior (sometimes called anticipatory behavior, which is more a temporally based descriptive label then) and consummatory behavior (see Spruijt et al. 2001 for discussion). Consummatory behavioral patterns encompass the final patterns, which lead to satisfying the needs which have set the wheels in motion, e.g., patterns related to handling and consumption of food or arriving in the area in the south to forage and survive the winter. Preparatory behavioral patterns encompass all patterns leading up to this final result, e.g., searching and hunting behavioral patterns or migratory behaviors. Many examples have been studied in great detail related to all relevant motivational systems: food, water, reproduction, temperature regulation, etc. (Spruijt et al. 2001). The preparatory behavioral patterns may at first sight look like anticipatory behavioral patterns as indicated above; after all the decision to act is because of some expected outcome or event in the future. However, the assumption is that these behavioral patterns have developed over evolutionary times, i.e., across many generations (including ancestral species), without the subject performing them having knowledge of its specific purpose. In the case of preparatory behavioral patterns, this can be seen as subjects still performing those behaviors even in conditions where those behaviors are not productive: birds start to prepare for migration in captivity when there is no need of doing so ("migratory restlessness").

Now the question is when external conditions change, how will this change behavior? For instance, when due to global warming, harsh winter conditions will slowly change to more temperate winter conditions or when food is gradually available earlier in spring. Will animals return earlier being aware of these changes, i.e., anticipate on these changes and change their behavior, or will changes occur by natural selection across generations? In the first case, the subject is aware that conditions have changed and changes its behavior accordingly. As some animals may do this better than others, differences in the population may occur. In the second case, the animal has no clue of these changes, and changes in behavior are brought about by selection on trait differences between subjects, leading to a shift in the population: as there is always a distribution in arrival time, say you have early, middle, and late "arrivers." Suppose that middle "arrivers" are currently more successful than either early or late "arrivers," as the peak of food availability co-occurs with middle "arrivers." When the peak shifts to earlier times, early "arrivers" may be more successful than middle and late "arrivers." This will lead to a shift in the distribution of "arrivers." So, adaptation then occurs across generations as long as variation in traits is present on which selection may act, as long as these changes do not overtax the systems of the animals (say the peak is not before any bird has arrived) and as long as behavior may be passed onto the next generation (in whatever way).

Given that migratory behavior (as discussed: moving south in fall and returning in spring) has characteristics of a zero-order mode, it is more likely that also changes herein occur based on unconscious rather than conscious notions. So in this sense, long-term changes in behavior (e.g., being late or early) are based on changes in their adaptive value in the current context (which one pays off) and not based on any conscious notion of the future ("food is available earlier, so I should leave now"). Hence they may not qualify as anticipatory behaviors as used in sense of conscious behaviors. It has been suggested that zero-mode behaviors are critically related to survival and ultimately reproduction of the subject with which all subjects are endowed, albeit with individual variation in performance (Spruijt et al. 2001). Hence, they are called species-specific behaviors. I return to this following the next section.

First-Order

Defining the Context
As mentioned above, in the Introduction to this handbook (see ▶ Chap. 1, "Introducing Anticipation"), Poli uses the example of a person taking an umbrella with

him or her after watching the weather forecast as an instance of anticipatory behavior: in view of things that might happen, a precautionary measure is taken. I elaborate on this a little more here.

First, the person decides upon watching the weather forecast to bring an umbrella. We assume that getting wet matters to the subject; otherwise the behavior would serve no purpose, and that the umbrella is suited for staying dry. Now we also assume that the weather forecast is sufficiently predictive for the person's decision to bring an umbrella. On the part of the person, this entails an element of learning to judge and use information: that is, how many times has the forecast been correct in the past, to be used for a decision to be taken now, and related to something that may happen in the future. This is relevant, especially in the context of its consequences in situations where the expected outcome does not match the action: (1) the person is not bringing an umbrella (the weather forecast says that no rain will come), but it rains on the way, and (2) the person is bringing an umbrella (the weather forecast says that rain will come), but it does not rain. Now this may not seem like a big deal; the story becomes different when you place this in the context of a cost-benefit analysis. We assumed that getting wet mattered to the subject. Take the first mismatch: suppose the person is off to a job interview for a prestigious job in an expensive suit and on his walk to the interview, he gets soaking wet, making a poor impression on his interviewers and in addition ruining the suit. Take the second mismatch: suppose that the umbrella is an antique one that costs a fortune and bringing it idly may enhance the risk of damaging it or of getting it stolen. It is obvious that the decision is affected by the amount of money the subject has.

So, what to do then depends upon the costs and benefits – we can frame that in the amount of money won or lost – associated with different options, and hence information feeding decisions are critical. This is exactly the problem all living creatures are facing: a limited budget (available energy in this case), decisions to be taken on different courses of action (cost-benefit analyses of matching and non-matching situations), and information needed for the decision to be taken (how predictive is information obtained).

Critically here, the umbrella example is framed in the wider context of decision-making (see also ► Chap. 1, "Introducing Anticipation") and uncertainty reduction of which the outcome may differ according to the different costs and benefits. Underlying animal behavior is the question of allocation of resources (the economy of behavior; Spruijt et al. 2001). Thus, referring to the example mentioned in the Introduction, when an animal is facing a threat yet is hungry, the outcome may depend on the strength of the threat and how hungry the subject is. The outcome may differ due to the different weights of these elements. Hence, anticipatory behavior may be seen in the wider context of flexibility of behavior: to do what is optimal given (a) information based on past experiences, (b) what is to be expected in future, and (c) which costs and benefits are at stake. To show that such punctuations may occur, it needs to be shown that animals are capable of a form of future prospect. Some studies suggest this to the case as will be discussed in the following sections.

The Case of Conditioning

Delay Versus Trace
Under both delay conditioning and trace conditioning Pavlovian conditioning procedures, subjects prepare for an upcoming event, i.e., shocks, air puffs, or food, by acquiring conditioned responses, such as freezing, closure of the eyelid, or approaching the area where food will arrive when the cue comes on. A clear difference is present between delay and trace conditioning: in delay conditioning the offset of the conditioned stimulus occurs later than the onset of the unconditioned stimulus (i.e., they overlap in time), while in trace conditioning a temporal gap exists between the offset of the conditioned stimulus and the onset of the unconditioned stimulus (i.e., they are separated in time). Studies in humans have shown that trace conditioning critically depends on awareness, while delay conditioning does not; that trace conditioning is susceptible to distraction, while delay conditioning is not; and that trace conditioning requires more higher-order networks (prefrontal and temporal lobe structures) than delay conditioning (Carter et al. 2003; Clark and Squire 1998, 2004; Knight et al. 2004; Weike et al. 2007). Animal studies, including studies in fish species, have basically confirmed these differences in conditioning paradigms and have thereby implicated that awareness in these species may be likely (e.g., Han et al. 2003; Nilsson et al. 2008a, b, 2010; Nordgreen et al. 2010; reviews: Broglio et al. 2005; Salas et al. 2006; Vargas et al. 2009).

Expectations
Thus while animals seem to be able to associate stimuli across a temporal window, suggesting awareness or a global working space, the next question is whether subjects have an expectation of what is going to happen when a cue comes on. Observations in the context of appetitive trace conditioning have indicated that subjects have acquired knowledge of the emotional value of the upcoming event. Thus, Spruijt, van der Harst, and coworkers (van der Harst et al. 2003) have shown that the hyperactive behavior of rats, measured as transitions between behavioral patterns, in the interval between the onset of the cue and arrival of the reward is proportional to the (expected) rewarding properties of the stimulus. Interestingly, the expression of this anticipatory, hyperactive, behavior was species-specific as well as context-specific. Thus, while in rats an upcoming reward elicited hyperactive behavior, it elicited hypoactive behavior in cats in the laboratory yet hyperactive behavior in the home setting (van den Bos et al. 2003). In several conditioning paradigms, it has been shown that fish anticipate on a food reward to arrive (cod: Nilsson et al. 2008a, b; halibut: Nilsson et al. 2010). Interestingly, this behavior was also species-specific, i.e., hyperactive behavior in cod, "hypoactive" behavior in halibut (Nilsson et al. 2008a, b; 2010), and time interval dependent (halibut: Nilsson et al. 2010).

Accordingly, while the underlying expected reward may be similar across species and between contexts, the behavioral expression may be different. This may reflect the zero-order nature of these behaviors, i.e., behaviors associated with hunting (Van den Bos et al. 2003; Nilsson et al. 2010). Thus, the level of expression of these behaviors (*how much*) may reflect the first-order nature (knowing what will come), while *what* is being expressed may reflect the zero-order nature.

Changing Behavior

While this conditioning-induced behavior may suggest a level of knowledge of the rewarding value of the upcoming event, it would be more powerful to demonstrate that rats change their reward-related behavior, when the reward has, for instance, been devalued in the meantime. Thus, when rats would see or hear the Pavlovian cue, announcing the upcoming reward, they should modify their behavior when the reward was devalued prior to the experiment. For this lower value would generate a conflict with the reward-related learned behavior, and animals should adjust their behavior accordingly. When this can be shown to occur, it is strong evidence that they are aware of the changed value, that they anticipate the outcome of the action, and that they are able to incorporate this knowledge into their ongoing behavior. When rats would not change their behavior, this shows that their behavior is stimulus-response driven rather than goal-directed. This so-called goal-directed behavior paradigm is up to now one of the most powerful paradigms to show that experiences may play a role in the organization of behavior (Dickinson and Balleine 1994).

Pietersen, Maes, and van den Bos (unpublished data) have shown that rats adjust their food magazine approach behavior when sugar pellets were devalued in a Pavlovian conditioning paradigm. Thus, rats were first trained to associate a tone with the arrival of sugar pellets in a classic Skinner box setup. When rats clearly showed that they increased their time spent in the food magazine contingent upon the presentation of the tone, sugar pellets were devalued. The latter was done by allowing rats to consume sugar pellets in their home cage and injecting them with lithium chloride (LiCl; controls received saline) immediately thereafter. LiCl induces gastric malaise in rats, and upon representation of the sugar pellets in a subsequent session in their home cage, they express a strong dislike for the sugar pellets and do not consume them (conditioned taste aversion; see Dickinson and Balleine 1994). Critically, the LiCl-induced change in value occurred outside the context of the Skinner box, rendering any stimuli or behavioral patterns inherent to the devaluation procedure as irrelevant for measuring potential changes in behavior in the Skinner box. When conditioned taste aversion was established, rats were reintroduced into the Skinner box, and the tone was presented to assess the behavior of the rats. No sugar pellets were present upon presentation of the tone to prevent any relearning of the value of the sugar pellets, i.e., the experiment was run as an extinction phase. The data show that the LiCl-treated rats spent less time in the food magazine contingent upon the presentation of the tone than saline-treated rats. Thus, this experiment showed that rats adjusted their behavior by combining new information (pellets have lost their rewarding value) with earlier acquired behavior (tone predicts the arrival of sugar pellets which are rewarding) to change ongoing behavior.

In an elegant series of experiments, Dickinson, Balleine, and coworkers have shown that rats similarly modify their operant behavior to obtain rewards after devaluation of the rewards, either using conditioned taste aversion or satiety-specific procedures (Balleine and Dickinson 1998, 2000; Balleine and O'Doherty 2010;

Dickinson and Balleine 1994, 2008). They have included many control experiments to show that the behavioral adjustments were selective, i.e., only the operant behavior contingent on the devalued reward was changed, and that the behavior was changed as a result of disliking the pellets.

In both goal-directed behavior paradigms, a critical feature is that insensitivity to changes may be caused by prolonged training or overtraining in the first phase, i.e., the behavioral response has already become a stimulus-response or habit before devaluation (Quinn et al. 2007). This renders the behavior insensitive to changes in reward value.

These goal-directed behavior paradigms may be framed in the wider context of decision-making paradigms where optimal long-term strategies need to be deduced from changes in moment-to-moment information, which could be either positive or negative: elsewhere I have discussed this as well as its underlying neuro-architecture in detail (van den Bos et al. 2014). In addition, these paradigms concur with the elegant work by Cabanac and coworkers (Cabanac 1971, 1979, 1992, 2008; Cabanac et al. 2009) who have shown that (changes in) emotions are critical in optimization of long-term behavior, also shown by Damasio, Bechara, and colleagues (Bechara et al. 1994, 1997; Bechara 2005; Damasio 1994; see also van den Bos et al. 2014).

Across different species it seems that awareness and first-order behavior may be found in vertebrates (see Braithwaite et al. 2013; Nordgreen et al. 2010), although not all authors agree on this (Cabanac et al. 2009); data for invertebrates are not conclusive as yet.

Afterthoughts and Perspectives

In this chapter I have discussed two examples, which at first sight may equally qualify as anticipatory behavior: migrating south to survive harsh winters and deciding to continue or stop foraging behavior while facing a potential threat. I have shown that in animal species awareness is present, a global working space, allowing the animal to adjust behavior when stimuli have changed their value; the latter implies an idea of a notion of the future. These examples are clearly framed in different time windows. As indicated, migratory behavior is indiscriminately shown by all subjects of a species (species-specific behavior), the product of selection across many generations. Changing behavior based on prior experiences is a unique event of the subject as it depends on its own history. You may say that all subjects possess the ability to adjust, but what and how to adjust is more of a private matter.

Nature's "Solutions"

Migration is critical to survival when conditions are harsh. As indicated above selection on variation in this trait allows for changes in the distribution of the trait to occur without requiring any knowledge on the subject's part. However, this would not qualify as anticipatory behavior dependent on awareness. At best one could argue that nature's first "solution" to the problem of how to deal with changes in the future is selection on traits: as long as there is variation, as long as changes are within the adaptive range (not overtaxing the capacities of the subjects), and as long as changes in behaviors may be passed on to next generations (in whatever way: genetic, rearing, cultural), then future changes can be dealt with, even without the subject having a clue about one or the other. Maybe the fact that animals have little possibilities in their life to learn these contingencies, selection on specific behavioral traits secures survival.

Nature's second "solution" to cope with changes in the future was to endow all subjects with awareness, a global working space, of course also brought about by natural selection, allowing to process information privately in the subject's own lifetime, and without defining the optimal solution on each and single event. This would qualify as anticipatory behavior as being dependent on awareness. Animals have ample opportunities for learning for this to be effective.

A second-order mode, emerging relatively late in the animal kingdom (see de Veer and van den Bos 1999), but not discussed here, is the third "solution" as it expands going back and forth between here and now, future, and past. This is especially true when structured communicative options support this, such as language.

I am not intending here to suggest that this has been a logical process. We only observe the end product of a long history of "experiments" in nature, which we may describe to the best of our abilities, yet not claiming to be able to reconstruct this in linear fashion. For instance, the possibility may be entertained that migratory behavior started as a first-order behavior but then across generations became a zero-order behavior. As an example, it is known that goal-directed behavior may become stimulus-like behavior or a habit across many trials. Thus when tested later in the series of trials, the behavior is resistant to change when values have changed, while early in the series it is susceptible to change (Quinn et al. 2007). It is often very difficult to assess the origin of behavioral patterns. So behaviors that we view now as zero-order may have initially been first-order behaviors.

Implicit and Explicit Anticipation

As to other conceptual frameworks and/or terminology, the distinction between *implicit* and *explicit* anticipation is relevant here. Implicit anticipation has been defined as "In implicit anticipation the agent do not produces expectations, but still exhibits anticipatory behavior which are for example selected by evolution to deal with the future; anticipation is functional but not represented" (Pezzulo 2008, page 189). Thus implicit anticipation is qualified by its functionality as a behavior. The bird migratory example, or in general zero-order intentional behavior, would qualify for this. In contrast explicit anticipation has been defined using representations: "In order to do so, the agent has to anticipate (at least to a certain degree of abstraction) the state of affairs to achieve in order to prepare its resources; once this is done, the goal state acts as a regulatory mechanism for the system" (Pezzulo 2008, page 214). The foraging-predator conflict as well as goal-directed paradigms, or in general first-order intentional (and second-order intentional) behavior, would qualify for this. So this distinction would amount, as indicated above, to a specific behavior expressed by all subjects of a species, but blind as to its goal (implicit), and as a capacity to be used at the level of the subject of which the outcome varies with time and context (explicit). Poli uses a similar distinction in the Introduction regarding the subject's awareness (see ► Chap. 1, "Introducing Anticipation"): "Explicit anticipations are those of which the system is aware. Implicit anticipations, by contrast, work below the threshold of awareness." Regardless of different terminologies or conceptual frameworks, the critical element in animal (and human) studies is to design experiments that differentiate one from the other, such as paradigms described here (see also, e.g., Pezzulo et al. 2013). This is not at all an easy job. For instance, different subjects may use different strategies to solve the task, especially when tasks have multiple degrees of freedom, and hence, several alternative ways of solving the problem may exist. This makes interpreting differences between experimental paradigms difficult. Or subjects use different strategies in succession to solve tasks switching between one and the other as they continue, again making comparisons difficult. Dickinson, Balleine, and coworkers have nicely shown how to optimize such experimental paradigms (Balleine and Dickinson 1998, 2000; Balleine and O'Doherty 2010; Dickinson and Balleine 1994, 2008).

Final Remark

As a final general remark, all organisms are physically bound to the "here and now." Anticipatory behavior allows for escaping this limitation by uniting the "here and now," the lived past, and the to be lived future. As the imagined future is in a way carved from elements of the past, anticipatory behavior allows for flexibility and innovation by recombining these elements into adaptive and new behavior, which is suited to the particular situation. This is not to say that the subject is aware of all the details of these elements or their origin: flexibility, innovation, and visions of future may also arise out of free-floating and wild associations, as we may sometimes witness in humans.

Summary

In sum, (explicit) anticipation, as an awareness-dependent activity, may be studied in animals using a mind-brain-behaviour framework from which critical experiments and critical field observations follow. Using such rigour, future studies should help in unravelling when (explicit) anticipation has evolved and how this is distributed in the animal kingdom.

References

Balleine, B. W., & Dickinson, A. (1998). Goal-directed instrumental action: Contingency and incentive learning and their cortical substrates. *Neuropharmacology, 37*, 407–419.

Balleine, B. W., & Dickinson, A. (2000). The effect of lesions of the insular cortex on instrumental conditioning: Evidence for a role in incentive memory. *The Journal of Neuroscience, 20*, 8954–8964.

Balleine, B. W., & O'Doherty, J. P. (2010). Human and rodent homologies in action control: Corticostriatal determinants of goal-directed and habitual action. *Neuropsychopharmacology, 35*, 48–69.

Bechara, A. (2005). Decision making, impulse control and loss of will power to resist drugs: A neurocognitive perspective. *Nature Neuroscience, 8*, 1458–1463.

Bechara, A., Damasio, A. R., Damasio, H., & Anderson, S. W. (1994). Insensitivity to future consequences following damage to human prefrontal cortex. *Cognition, 50*, 7–15.

Bechara, A., Damasio, H., Tranel, D., & Damasio, A. R. (1997). Deciding advantageously before knowing the advantageous strategy. *Science, 275*, 1293–1295.

Braithwaite, V. A., Huntingford, F., & van den Bos, R. (2013). Variation in emotion and cognition among fishes. *Journal of Agricultural and Environmental Ethics, 26*, 7–23.

Broglio, C., Gomez, A., Duran, E., Ocana, F. M., Jimenez-Moya, F., & Rodrıguez, S. C. (2005). Hallmarks of a common forebrain vertebrate plan: Specialized pallial areas for spatial, temporal and emotional memory in actinopterygian fish. *Brain Research Bulletin, 66*, 277–281.

Cabanac, M. (1971). Physiological role of pleasure. *Science, 173*, 1103–1107.

Cabanac, M. (1979). Sensory pleasure. *Quarterly Review of Biology, 54*, 1–29.

Cabanac, M. (1992). Pleasure: The common currency. *Journal of Theoretical Biology, 155*, 173–200.

Cabanac, M. (2008). The dialectics of pleasure. In M. L. Kringelbach & K. C. Berridge (Eds.), *Pleasures of the brain. The neural basis of taste, smell and other rewards* (pp. 113–124). Oxford: Oxford University Press.

Cabanac, M., Cabanac, A. J., & Parent, A. (2009). The emergence of consciousness in phylogeny. *Behavioural Brain Research, 198*, 267–272.

Carter, R. M., Hofstotter, C., Tsuchiya, N., & Koch, C. (2003). Working memory and fear conditioning. *Proceedings National Academy of Sciences (USA), 100*, 1399–1404.

Clark, R. E., & Squire, L. R. (1998). Classical conditioning and brain systems: The role of awareness. *Science, 280*, 77–81.

Clark, R. E., & Squire, L. R. (2004). The importance of awareness for eyeblink conditioning is conditional: Theoretical comment on Bellebaum and Daum. *Behavioral Neuroscience, 118*, 1466–1468.

Damasio, A. R. (1994). *Descartes' error. Emotion, reason and the human brain*. New York: Avon Books.

de Veer, M. W., & van den Bos, R. (1999). A critical review of methodology and interpretation of mirror self recognition research in nonhuman primates. *Animal Behaviour, 58*, 459–468.

Dickinson, A., & Balleine, B. (1994). Motivational control of goal-directed action. *Animal Learning and Behavior, 22*, 1–18.

Dickinson, A., & Balleine, B. (2008). The cognitive/motivational interface. In M. L. Kringelbach & K. C. Berridge (Eds.), *Pleasures of the brain. The neural basis of taste, smell and other rewards* (pp. 74–84). Oxford: Oxford University Press.

Han, C. J., O'Tuathaigh, C. M., van Trigt, L., Quinn, J. J., Fanselow, M. S., Mongeau, R., et al. (2003). Trace but not delay fear conditioning requires attention and the anterior cingulate cortex. *Proceedings National Academy of Sciences (USA), 100*(22), 13087–13092.

Knight, D. C., Cheng, D. T., Smith, C. N., Stein, E. A., & Helmstetter, F. J. (2004). Neural substrates mediating human delay and trace fear conditioning. *The Journal of Neuroscience, 24*(1), 218–228.

Nilsson, J., Kristiansen, T. S., Fosseidengen, J. E., Ferno, A., & van den Bos, R. (2008a). Learning in cod (*Gadus morhua*): Long trace interval retention. *Animal Cognition, 11*, 215–222.

Nilsson, J., Kristiansen, T. S., Fosseidengen, J. E., Fernö, A., & van den Bos, R. (2008b). Sign and goal-tracking in Atlantic cod (*Gadus morhua*). *Animal Cognition, 11*, 651–659.

Nilsson, J., Kristiansen, T. S., Fosseidengen, J. E., Stien, L. H., Fernö, A., & van den Bos, R. (2010). Learning and anticipatory behaviour in a "sit-and-wait" predator: The Atlantic halibut. *Behavioural Processes, 83*, 257–266.

Nordgreen, J., Janczak, A. M., Hovland, A. L., Ranheim, B., & Horsberg, T. E. (2010). Trace classical conditioning in rainbow trout (*Oncorhynchus mykiss*): What do they learn? *Animal Cognition, 13*, 303–309.

Pezzulo, G. (2008). Coordinating with the future: The anticipatory nature of representation. *Minds and Machines, 8*, 179–225. https://doi.org/10.1007/s11023-008-9095-5.

Pezzulo, G., Rigoli, F., & Chersi, F. (2013). The mixed instrumental controller: Using value of information to combine habitual choice and mental simulation. *Frontiers in Psychology, 4*, 92. https://doi.org/10.3389/fpsyg.2013.00092.

Quinn, J. J., Hitchcott, P. K., Umeda, E. A., Arnold, A. P., & Taylor, J. R. (2007). Sex chromosome complement regulates habit formation. *Nature Neuroscience, 10*, 1398–1400.

Salas, C., Broglio, C., Duran, E., Gomez, A., Ocana, F. M., Jimenez-Moya, F., et al. (2006). Neuropsychology of learning and memory in teleost fish. *Zebrafish, 3*, 157–171.

Spruijt, B. M., van den Bos, R., & Pijlman, F. (2001). A concept of welfare based on how the brain evaluates its own activity: Anticipatory behavior as an indicator for this activity. *Applied Animal Behaviour Science, 72*, 145–171.

van den Bos, R. (1997). Reflections on the organisation of mind, brain and behavior. In M. Dol, S. Kasanmoentalib, S. Lijmbach, E. Rivas, & R. van den Bos (Eds.), *Animal consciousness and animal ethics; perspectives from the Netherlands, Animals in Philosophy and Science* (Vol. 1, pp. 144–166). Assen: Van Gorcum.

van den Bos, R. (2000). General organizational principles of the brain as key to the study of animal consciousness. *Psyche, 6*, published on-line at http://psyche.cs.monash.edu.au/v6/psyche-6-05-vandenbos.html

van den Bos, R. (2001). The hierarchical organization of the brain as a key to the study of consciousness in human and non-human animals: Phylogenetic implications. *Animal Welfare, 10*, S246–S247.

van den Bos, R., Koot, S., & de Visser, L. (2014). A rodent version of the Iowa gambling task: 7 years of progress. *Frontiers in Psychology, 5*, 203.

van den Bos, R., Meijer, M. K., Van Renselaar, J. P., Van der Harst, J. E., & Spruijt, B. M. (2003). Anticipation is differently expressed in rats (*Rattus Norvegicus*) and domestic cats (*Felis silvestrus cattus*) in the same Pavlovian conditioning paradigm. *Behavioural Brain Research, 141*, 83–89.

van der Harst, J. E., Fermont, P. C. J., Bilstra, A. E., & Spruijt, B. M. (2003). Access to enriched housing is rewarding to rats as reflected by their anticipatory behaviour. *Animal Behaviour, 66*, 493–504.

Vargas, J. P., Lopez, J. C., & Portavella, M. (2009). What are the functions of fish brain pallium? *Brain Research Bulletin, 79*, 436–440.

Weike, A. I., Schupp, H. T., & Hamm, A. O. (2007). Fear acquisition requires awareness in trace but not delay conditioning. *Psychophysiology, 44*, 170–180.

Anticipation in Neurocybernetics

13

Slawomir J. Nasuto and Yoshikatsu Hayashi

Contents

Abstract

There is an increasing recognition in cognitive sciences of the need to account for the fundamental role of anticipation; an ability exhibited by living systems to orient toward future. Anticipation has been even proposed in psychology as the foundational building block of cognition. More recently, cognitive sciences and philosophy of mind have seen proliferation of theories varying in flavor and emphasis but common in postulating the fundamental role of predictive inference in the brain's function. These accounts are steeped in computational cognitive paradigm and a contributing factor to their rapid gains in popularity is their consistency with the mechanistic view dominant in sciences. However, due to this very computational commitment, these accounts face serious philosophical problems, in common with other computational approaches, in their inability to provide a satisfactory explanation of the most fundamental properties of our

S. J. Nasuto (✉) · Y. Hayashi
Division of Biomedical Sciences and Biomedical Engineering, School of Biological Sciences, University of Reading, Reading, UK
e-mail: s.j.nasuto@reading.ac.uk; y.hayashi@reading.ac.uk

© Springer Nature Switzerland AG 2019
R. Poli (ed.), *Handbook of Anticipation*,
https://doi.org/10.1007/978-3-319-91554-8_61

249

mental life. Robert Rosen offered an alternative account of living systems, which inextricably links life and cognition. His postulate is to extend narrowly constructed mechanistic (and henceforth computational) account beyond classical Newtonian mechanics to a framework recognizing that living systems constitute a distinct class of complex systems and positioning anticipation as the fundamental characteristics distinguishing them from inanimate ones. Anticipating synchronization, a recently discovered intriguing behavior of some dynamical systems, offers a possibility of explaining anticipation from ground up, based on simple features abundant in living systems in general, and in the nervous system, in particular. A review of the studies investigating the anticipating synchronization and its extensions is provided, and a special emphasis is placed on the investigations concerned with its neurobiological plausibility. The core definition of anticipation according to Rosen postulates the ability of an organism to change its behavior in view of potential future outcomes. Thus, an overview is included of research on motion coordination that is grounded in dynamics and also concerned with the role of anticipation in movement.

Keywords
Anticipation · Anticipatory systems · Anticipating synchronization · Neurocybernetics

Introduction

Anticipation seems to be one of the fundamental cognitive capacities used by organisms in their strive for survival. Essentially, one could even propose that the entire concept of natural evolution is about promoting biological solutions that support persistence into the future rather than merely existence in the present moment. In psychology, prospection, an ability to plan or to remember to do things in future, has been recognized as one of the cognitive capacities, on par with other faculties such as attention, memory, or perception. However, recently some psychologists have been calling for a fundamental refocusing of psychology and cognitive science placing prospection at their very core (Seligman et al. 2013). Beyond the purely empirical approaches amassing evidence for observed phenomena and providing their descriptive explanations, prospective behaviors have also been offered explanatory accounts in terms of computational models. Many such models have been put forward, especially to explain motor control and planning, where insights from control theory and machine learning approaches to analogous problems abound. Modern science is dominated by reductionist methodology where mechanistic explanation is an ultimate goal and computational models are perfectly consistent with it. Yet, computational and mechanistic explanations leave many thinkers uncomfortable, as such accounts do not seem to be able to offer satisfactory explanations of fundamental properties of living organisms, such as their complexity, their capacity for autonomous, goal-oriented behavior, and ability to adapt in an almost open ended fashion to varying environmental conditions.

It is the recognition of such apparent shortcomings that was motivating researchers developing alternative frameworks in cognitive science (Nasuto and Hayashi 2016a). For example, autopoietic enactivism, building on work of Maturana and Varela, linked the circular organization of living systems with cognition (Maturana and Varela 1991), while Bickhard's interactivism sought explanation for the circular organization of far from equilibrium thermodynamical systems and pointed to the resulting anticipatory coupling between the organism and the environment as the starting point for normative behavior (Bickhard 2009). Theoretical biologist Robert Rosen proposed that living systems are fundamentally anticipating in lieu of the complexity of their circular organization (closure to efficient causation) (Rosen 2012). His model of living systems as anticipating systems delineated boundary between living, complex systems and inanimate, hence simple, objects. It also created a link between cognition and organization of living organisms and effectively proposed that anticipation is a joint characteristics of both.

This chapter approaches the problem of anticipation from the perspective of neurocybernetics (Wiener and Schadé 1963). Neurocybernetics was defined by Norbert Wiener as a branch of cybernetics, a field of study he championed, integrating within a single framework investigations of communication and control mechanisms in artificial and living systems. Wiener considered neurocybernetics to be a part of cybernetics specifically concerned with explaining behavior of organisms via analyzing and characterizing sensory-motor feedback loops. In its essence, neurocybernetics tries to characterize the interactions along the neural pathways in terms of information flow they underpin, and the operation of the pathways' neural constituents in terms of dynamical systems. Control, an ability to drive the entire system toward some desired goal, is achieved via identification of appropriate inputs to the actuators, given the current state of the system. In contrast to control of man-made systems, where control is an external input to the dynamical system, the plant, in neurocybernetics, the controlling signal itself is a result of activity of the nervous system and stems from the whole-system's, an organism's, goals or drives. This naturally places dynamical systems as a natural framework, within which one can formulate laws governing operation of the nervous system from the neurocybernetics perspective.

Dynamical systems originate from the field of Newtonian mechanics and in fact significant part of natural laws postulated by physics to govern the evolution of matter have the form of dynamical equations. Although the dynamical systems theory has been abstracted and generalized beyond physics, it inherits the intriguing potential of its predecessor of capturing the actual natural laws governing the system in question rather than merely providing their computational description. A dynamical system is specified as a relationship between the current state of the system and its future state short time ahead. The fundamental notion is that of the state space with coordinates corresponding to the variables specifying any potential system's configuration at any point in time. Deterministic dynamical systems have unique way of evolving into the future from a given current state. A deterministic dynamical system over continuous time is generally defined as a flow

$$\phi : T \times M \to M, \tag{1}$$

where M is a manifold on which dynamical system evolves and T is a segment of time. If, for any given initial point, a flow describing the dynamics of a system can be solved, a collection of all the points on the evolution path of the system is known as its trajectory or orbit,

$$X(t) = \phi_t(X(0)), \tag{2}$$

and under some additional assumptions including differentiability, the orbit is a solution of a differential equation,

$$\dot{X}(t) = f(X). \tag{3}$$

If the derivative defining the differential equation is first order, the corresponding equation is an ordinary differential equation and if the right hand side of Eq. (3) does not change with time then the equation is called autonomous. It is possible to define the dynamical system using other types of differential equations. Higher order differential equations are defined using higher order derivatives, although these can be transformed into systems of ordinary differential equations, thus defining the dynamical system in a suitably higher-dimensional state space. Nonautonomous differential equations are obtained if the right hand side of the differential equation changes with time. This may be the case if the system's evolution rule is not fixed in time, or if the system is driven by an external input. Such dynamical systems may again be analyzed by constructing a corresponding higher dimensional system which is autonomous, although theory of nonautonomous dynamical systems requires nontrivial extensions of concepts developed for autonomous systems, for example, long-term behavior. The state space of a dynamical system described by ordinary differential equations is a finite dimensional manifold. Typically, these arise if the evolution of the system in question is memoryless and depends only on the current state. On the other hand, if the evolution, captured by the derivative, is dependent on the past values, the state space of such dynamical systems is infinite dimensional and the systems are known as time-delay systems. Delays arise naturally in physical systems where interactions propagate with finite speed along the communication paths and are also introduced by finite response times of actuators and sensors. Dynamical systems with delays exhibit rich and complicated behavior, and are of interest from both mathematical and control-engineering perspectives. For example, they often exhibit memory phenomena, where their current behavior is affected by the history of their evolution up to the present time, a property that in computational terms would normally be accounted for with some form of explicit memory. More-over, delayed dynamical systems also pose additional challenges from the perspective of control and often require specific control methods going beyond classical controller designed for systems with an instantaneous time evolution. Nevertheless, delays are not always detrimental and their presence may also be beneficial for controlling the system. It is this context that is explored in the current chapter – the presence of delays in a specific type of dynamical systems affording them a form of anticipatory characteristics is one of the main points of discussion. Dynamical systems theory as a subset of mathematics concerned itself mostly with the study of autonomous dynamical systems and investigated rich types of behavior that they can exhibit. Both, systems evolving in continuous time and discrete time steps have been studied. One of the most important concepts is that of a long-term behavior of system trajectories and the nature of the subsets, or attractors, of the state space that govern it. Until the discovery of chaotic dynamical systems, attractors were believed to be relatively simple geometrical objects, for example, points, corresponding to equilibria or closed trajectories corresponding to limit cycles. Discovery of chaotic dynamics, due to nonlinearities present in the equations describing the dynamical system, led to realization that such sets may have very complicated, fractal structure, so-called strange attractors.

A fundamental notion studied in dynamical systems is that of asymptotic stability, which implies that the system subjected to a sufficiently small perturbation returns to its original trajectory after sufficiently long time. Global stability requires stability for any initial state. The dynamical systems theory invokes a qualitative or geometric view of the system behavior, and of particular importance is a long-term behavior of system trajectories near attractors. Depending on whether trajectories asymptotically converge to, or are diverging from attractors, one can talk about asymptotically stable, respectively unstable, attractors. Nonlinear dynamical systems may exhibit particularly rich dynamical behavior. For example, several attractors may be present in the state space, and the system behavior may be affected by their respective geometric, topological, and stability properties as its trajectory traverses the state space. Many complex systems can be described as collectives of dynamical systems interacting with each other and such interactions, or couplings, give rise to very interesting, emergent dynamical behaviors. A fundamental notion in this context is that of synchronization, whereby the constituent dynamical systems start tracing similar trajectories in the state space. This implies that the relative positions between states of the evolving components become fixed. Such coordinated evolution may involve all the components, or only a subset of them, and it may stabilize after an initial period of uncoordinated evolutions through the state space, or may wax and wane intermittently. Collective behavior of fireflies or synchronization of cells giving rise to circadian rhythms are examples of synchronous dynamics. Synchronization can result in rich dynamical patterns showing both spatial and temporal complexity and is particularly relevant for study of the nervous system, in which coordinated activity of various oscillations is paramount for its overall behavior and function.

Control theory is more concerned with the input-output dynamical systems, as these are more explicitly reflecting the basic premise of this theory – determining what is the nature of the inputs that need to drive a dynamical system in order to obtain a desired behavior, given some measured information about the system's state, its output. Although much of control theory has been developed under the assumption that the system to be controlled, the plant, is linear, nonlinear control theory has been building tools for systems exhibiting rich nonlinear dynamics. Many concepts from nonlinear dynamical systems theory have been used in nonlinear control, and chaotic systems, systems with delays, as well as complex systems comprised of many coupled dynamical components continue to offer fertile ground for developing new analysis tools for understanding, and control, of such systems. Further entry points to this vast area of research are Jordan et al. (2007), Wiggins (2006), and Khalil (2002).

Dynamical systems have been proposed as an alternative to the dominant computational view and the number of cognitive phenomena that it purports to explain have been growing (Ward and Press 2002; Port and Van Gelder 1998), although prospection is still most frequently discussed within predictive framework (Clark 2013), invoking notion of simulation (Hesslow 2012), basically all consistent with computational view of cognition (Vernon et al. 2015). This chapter elaborates the notion that, within the concept of neurocybernetics, it is also possible to provide an account of anticipatory behavior of living systems, parsimonious with dynamical cognitive science, and that a specific type of dynamics may constitute building blocks of Rosenian theory of anticipation.

Most of the studies of intelligent behavior are conducted on organisms equipped with the nervous system. In context of Rosen's theory of anticipating systems, several questions require elucidation – is there an evidence of anticipatory behavior, what processes could constitute building blocks of Rosen's account, and what is the evidence for their presence in the nervous system.

The next section "Anticipatory Systems," will provide a brief exposition of the central tenets of Rosen's anticipatory systems definition and will then introduce recently proposed dynamical process, anticipating synchronization, as an intriguing candidate component which may be a dynamical building block of the anticipatory capacity postulated by Rosen. Subsequently, basic properties of anticipating synchronization will be reviewed in the section "Anticipating Synchronization," alongside extensions and generalizations of the basic definition. The section "Anticipating Synchronization in Neural Systems," will outline theoretical investigations of putative neural mechanisms implementing anticipating synchronization. One of the fundamental functions, where anticipation may be pivotal is motor control and coordination, and the next section "Empirical Evidence," will review literature pertaining to the motor control and the anticipation before the final section "Summary," will offer summary and concluding remarks.

Anticipatory Systems

The conceptual framework put forward by Robert Rosen has been far reaching (Rosen 2012). The modern science is based on the assumption that physics is at the heart of the natural sciences, with the latter seeking mechanistic, hence essentially reducible to physics, explanations as the ultimate account of natural phenomena.

Rosen suggested that although physics has been very successful in explaining natural phenomena involving inanimate objects and processes, such a framework

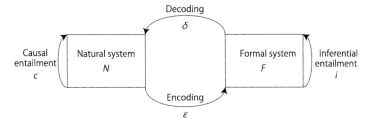

Fig. 1 The representation of the modeling and the simulation relation. (Modified from Nasuto and Hayashi 2016b)

should be extended in order to provide a satisfactory account of living. He proposed an alternative view, in which physics, biology, and other natural sciences are all specialized instantiations of a science of complex systems. Only parts of complex systems, according to Rosen, can be approximated or simulated by simple systems. The latter are the object of study of physics, whereas the objects of study of biology and other sciences involving living systems are complex. It has to be noted that Rosen considered complex systems as different in kind from physical systems which, however complicated, would not fulfill his definition of complexity. The distinction rests on the nondecomposability of the complex systems. The simple systems can be decomposed into constituents and the information about the whole system can be recovered from the information gleaned about them. In the complex system, the relationships between its components are essential for understanding the whole system. The essential characteristics of complex systems according to Rosen is that they are closed to efficient causation (Louie 2009), a concept related to self-referential nature of autopoietic definition of living by Maturana and Varela, which has continued to form a central backbone of the autopoietic enactivism (Stewart et al. 2010; Thompson 2010). Other chapters in this volume provide a more in-depth discussion of the central concepts related to Rosen's theory (Louie 2019; Louie and Poli 2019).

A central role in Rosen's framework, constructed in order to understand the natural systems, is played by the concept of modeling and its distinction from simulation; see Fig. 1.

According to Rosen, both model and simulation impose a systematic mapping between their states and those of the natural system they are meant to represent. However, in addition for a model, that relationship must also determine correspondence between causal relationships between states in the natural system and those in its model. No such strict relationship is required of the simulation. This distinction provides an opportunity to differentiate complex and simple/physical systems by a criterion determining whether their properties are well reflected using modeling or simulation relation. Complex systems, according to Rosen, do not have a priori well-defined state space, which is one of the most basic postulates of physics and a necessary starting point for any simulation. This is related to the fact that in complex systems the distinction between different notions of causality, e.g., material and efficient case, are blurred and indeed different components may not have a fixed causal role but may play different roles in different circumstances. This characteristic may afford complex systems flexibility and degrees of freedom in response to the environmental factors which simulations can only approximate by making specific a priori fixed commitments to the state space representation and the causal roles of the involved variables. Thus, according to Rosen, a physical system, for which it makes sense to speak of well-defined state space and for which the causal roles of state variables are fixed and distinct, can in principle be well simulated. However, for complex systems there may exist simulations which are locally and/or transiently good approximators, but nevertheless there exist no simulation of the complex system as a whole.

Rosen's endeavor to characterize the living systems resulted in postulating that their fundamental characteristic is their ability to anticipate, which is a consequence of their specific complex organization (closure to efficient causation). Thus, anticipatory systems can not only react to the past and present circumstances, but they can also modify their behavior in response to the anticipated future. The concept central to his definition of anticipatory systems is the modeling relation introduced above.

Thus, anticipatory systems are postulated to contain, and be able to use, models of themselves and of their environment and use their predictions about future in shaping their current behavior; they are capable of orienting themselves toward the future as much as they can react to the current and past conditions. The definition of anticipatory systems has subtle but profound implications. For a system to be anticipatory, it must be able to incorporate the model predictions about specific future conditions in shaping its current behavior; mere prediction capability is not enough. Moreover, the anticipation is a universal property; it implies capacity to pull the future into present behavior under a wide range of possible future scenarios – after all future is not determined. This characteristic is subtle and may be difficult to appreciate, if one tries to conceptualize it from the perspective of what is available at the present moment in time. Such a mind frame forces thinking about potential evolution of specific present state and present environmental variables, which often can be constrained enough to account for with a suitable (computational) predictive simulation. If the environmental interaction is stereotypical and constrained to be of such a simple (in Rosen's terms) kind, it may well be that it can be described by simulation, in which case computational predictive model may very well provide an appropriate description of the anticipatory system ability to orient itself to the future in such a situation. Interestingly, it is the notion of simulation that underpins the computational accounts of predictive processing in the brain (Butz et al. 2007; Pezzulo et al. 2009) that goes hand in hand with the modern empirical methodology of predefining the initial conditions and constraining experimental variables.

Anticipatory systems are complex, and living systems are anticipatory (Louie 2009). Thus, a question of special interest here is, in the context of organisms equipped with the nervous system, if one can identify the building blocks that may account for their capacity to contain internal anticipatory models. In Nasuto and Hayashi (2016b), a discussion of some possible building blocks has been presented. The next section will focus on one of these by introducing the definition of a specific dynamical phenomenon, an anticipating synchronization, and its extensions and will overview some of its known formal properties.

Anticipating Synchronization

In this chapter, a particular emphasis will be placed on the recently introduced model of synchronous dynamical behavior called anticipating synchronization (Voss 2000). Anticipating synchronization relies on a particular coupling between sufficiently similar dynamical systems, in which recurrent connections and delays play fundamental role in their apparently paradoxical behavior. Anticipating synchronization is a form of synchronous behavior between two dynamical systems coupled in a master–slave configuration. The direction of the interaction between these systems seems to imply that, should such coupling result in the slave's entrainment by the master, slave would retrace master's trajectory after some delay; master precedes the slave in their state space evolution. What is observed in the case of anticipating synchronization is, counterintuitively, quite the opposite – the nature of the coupling between these systems makes the slave precede the master. Arguably, the nervous system abounds in biological components which can be considered as dynamical systems subject to massive recurrent interactions limited by finite speed and hence conduction delays; all the ingredients necessary for the anticipating synchronization. This, together with some properties and extensions of the basic anticipating synchronization concept discussed in recent literature, makes it a particularly intriguing candidate model for building blocks of anticipatory capacity in Rosen's sense. In informal terms, anticipating synchronization relies on the delayed dynamical systems capacity to behave in a way that traditionally, in computational terms, is modeled by postulation of a memory storage. Systems with memory can store information about the past behavior of their inputs and may have the capacity to adapt their behavior accordingly, in advance of impending inputs. Such adaptation will largely depend on the complexity of the memory and the ability of the system to extract information about the past. Memory and internal models allow computational systems to predict future values of inputs, and if performed in a continuous fashion in time, trace the input trajectory before it is actually realized. Anticipating synchronization, a dynamical model introduced by Voss can provide an analogous account of such behavior because of the aforementioned memory-like behavior afforded by some dynamical systems subject to delays (Voss 2000). In other words, and somewhat simplistically, a slave system subject to self-delay, acts as a system with memory, which remembers the regularities in the master behavior and is thus able to entrain to master's future state space trajectory, rather than trailing behind it that would be typical of a memoryless slave system. Voss proposed two formulations, both consisting of two systems, a master and a slave, interacting via unidirectional coupling. In the first scheme, the master, X, is a system modeled with a delayed differential equation and the slave, Y, is a memoryless system driven by the master.

Fig. 2 Diagram of an
anticipating synchronization,
in which master system is
unidirectionally driving the
slave system. (Modified from
Nasuto and Hayashi 2016b)

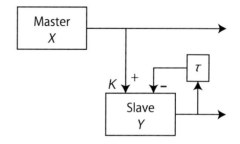

$$\dot{X} = -aX + f(X(t-\tau)) \tag{4}$$

$$\dot{Y} = -aY + f(X). \tag{5}$$

In the long term, the system asymptotically settles onto a globally stable synchronization manifold, a set $\{(X, Y) : X = Y_\tau\}$, where $Y_\tau := Y(t - \tau)$. The name stresses the fact, that this subset of the state space of the enlarged system consisting of the master and the slave is defined by the points corresponding to cojoint evolution of the master and slave in a fixed relationship with respect to each other. Under shifting of the time by τ, it follows that points of this set fulfill the condition, $Y(t) = X(t + \tau)$, implying that the synchronization manifold delineates a subset of the state space of the system on which the slave traces, or anticipates, the future trajectory of the master. The anticipating synchronization in this form does not dependent on the details of master dynamics, which suggests that it could, in principle, be observed for complex systems exhibiting chaotic behavior or long-term memory characteristics (Voss 2000).

The second form of the anticipating synchronization introduced by Voss consists of a memoryless master, X, which drives a slave system, Y, equipped with a delayed self-coupling, see Fig. 2,

$$\dot{X} = f(X) \tag{6}$$

$$\dot{Y} = f(Y) + K(X - Y_\tau). \tag{7}$$

Here, the anticipatory behavior relies on the coupling term $K(X - Y_\tau)$ between the current state of the master and a past value of the slave. Again, this term drives the dynamics toward the synchronization manifold and it disappears on it, leading to the joint evolution of the master–slave system, where the current state of the slave coincides with the future state of the master. Voss characterized numerically the stability region of the anticipating synchronization in the parameter space spanned by the coupling strength, K, and the delay, τ.

Further characterization of the anticipating synchronization properties have been discussed by Calvo et al., who analyzed anticipating synchronization assuming linearity of the master and slave vector fields, essentially assuming linear form of the differential equations (Calvo et al. 2004). This allowed them to concentrate on the essential characteristics of the anticipating synchronization coupling. They conclude that nonlinearity is not essential to understand the principles behind anticipating synchronization, and, in fact, it may be detrimental to achieve anticipation. They assume the control perspective and derive the transfer functions, as well as the feedforward and feedback gains formulations for the involved systems which eventually allows them to derive the stability condition in the (K, τ) parameters analogous to the one found numerically by Voss.

In a number of papers, Oguchi and Nijmeijer combined the anticipating synchronization-based predictive control with tools from differential geometry in order to define control schemes for nonlinear retarded systems (Oguchi 2007, 2017; Oguchi and Nijmeijer 2005a, b, 2006). Retarded systems constitute a class of systems with delays, where delays are present in state variables rather than in the input.

Their starting point is a formulation of a state predictor for nonlinear time-delay systems. Systems with delays have attracted a lot of interest in physics, biology, and social sciences, where various interactions present may be complex, nonlinear, and subject to delays. Modern control theory has explored tools from differential geometry in order to analyze nonlinear systems and propose their control schemes. Different forms of linearizations have proven particularly useful in this context. However, such approaches are not directly applicable to time-delay systems. Extensions of the control schemes using input–output linearization generalized for nonlinear systems with input delays have been constructed by introducing state predictors, such as Smith's predictor. Oguchi and Nijmeier recognized potential of using instead the anticipating synchronization scheme for the state prediction without a need for a separate numerical integration. The results presented by these authors are among the first demonstrations that state anticipating synchronization is not just of theoretical interest but can be employed effectively to perform specific functions – in this case, forming part of a predictive control scheme.

To this end, they extended the formulation of the systems subject to anticipating synchronization to systems with an output, in the form of differential-difference equations,

$$
\begin{aligned}
\dot{X}(t) &= aX(t) + f(Y(t - \tau)) \\
Y(t) &= h(X(t)),
\end{aligned}
\tag{8}
$$

and hence proposed, for such systems, a state predictor scheme based on anticipating synchronization.

Finite spectrum assignment control method developed for linear retarded systems has been applied by Oguchi to a class of retarded nonlinear systems by extending notions of Lie derivative and Lie bracket to, respectively, delayed state derivative and delayed state bracket, in order to extend the exact linearization control to retarded nonlinear systems described by difference-differential equations (Oguchi 2007). In Oguchi and Nijmeijer (2005a), he further extended this method to nonlinear systems, for which his state linearization technique transforms the retarded system into one with delay in the input.

Thus, Oguchi considered the following formulation of a nonlinear system with input delays to be controlled (Oguchi 2017),

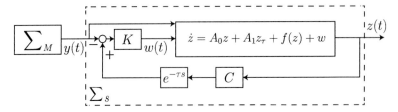

Fig. 3 Diagram of the state prediction scheme. (Modified from Oguchi 2017)

$$\dot{X}(t) = f(X(t), u(t - \tau)),$$
$$Y(t) = cX(t). \tag{9}$$

Here, the system defined by the state variable, X, generates an output, Y, and is subject to a control input, u. These authors assumed that the system (9) is such that in case of no delay, $\tau = 0$, there exists a closed loop control with a control input, $u = \gamma(X(t))$, that achieves a stable control of this system.

For nonzero delays in the system inputs, they introduced predictor, Z, based on anticipating synchronization,

$$\dot{Z}(t) = f(Z(t), u(t)) + K(cZ(t - \tau) - Y(t)), \tag{10}$$

illustrated in Fig. 3.

Such transformed system can be then stabilized using anticipating synchronization-based predictor (Oguchi 2017). Thus, in this control scheme, the anticipating synchronization-based predictor is used to estimate the future value, $X(t + \tau)$ of the state variable, X, and output of the predictor is used in the control feedback loop instead of the system state. The controller is given by $u(t) = \gamma(Z(t))$. The anticipating synchronization-based predictive control schematic is illustrated in Fig. 4.

This is interesting, as it implies that anticipating synchronization is a useful tool to design control schemes, or to describe in control theoretic terms the behavior of, a wide variety of linear and nonlinear systems exhibiting delays.

Although AS can be used within predictive control as shown by Oguchi and Nijmeijer, existing predictive controllers cannot be used to implement or replace a strongly anticipating AS controller. Firstly, there is no one element within the AS paradigm that can be replaced with a predictive model, as anticipation is a result of the continuous interaction between the master and slave. Secondly, and more importantly, there is no single predictive controller with fixed parameters that would exhibit equivalent behavior to the strongly anticipating control proposed by Stepp and Turvey, where the controller anticipates in proportion to the real feedback delay within the system (Stepp and Turvey 2010).

Eberle et al. hypothesized that a control scheme based directly on the strong anticipation principle and utilizing AS can be designed by coupling a correctly designed dynamical system to the real output of the plant through the sensors – a sensory coupling (Eberle et al. 2018). Because the sensed output of the plant is subject to both, the delays introduced by the plant itself (feedback delay, τ_f) and

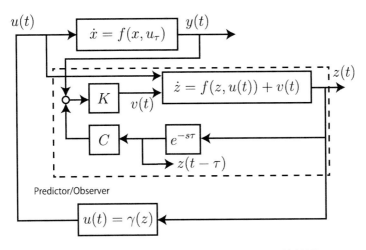

Fig. 4 Diagram of the predictor/control scheme. (Modified from Oguchi 2017)

those that result from sensory processing (sensory delay, τ), the anticipation period will always be equal to the true delay within the system.

Thanks to a "sensory coupling" between an internal dynamical system and the true dynamics of the plant, delays within the control loop are seamlessly counteracted by a matching degree of anticipation, ensuring that the robot's response neither lags nor becomes unstable (Fig. 5). This holds true even if the delay changes mid-execution, with no need to change a corresponding parameter within the internal model. In the "parallel" system introduced in that paper, the sensory coupling is fed to the plant concurrently (or "in parallel") with the primary control signal to enable anticipation (Eberle et al. 2018).

In particular, the "parallel" system exhibits robustness to both unpredictable delay and unmodelled disturbances, while its internal system's dynamics are not specific to the chaotic target in this tracking task, meaning it is not limited to tracking only one possible target. This fact indicates that strong anticipation through coupling with the body dynamics alone could be a useful paradigm for tasks in highly unstructured environments (Eberle et al. 2018).

This parallel model is considered to be one possible implementation of the well-known "Comparator Model," the neurocognitive comparator mechanism proposed to underpin the sense of agency (Fig. 6) (Haggard 2017). Sense of agency is a well-known notion in cognitive neuroscience, reflecting our everyday experience of knowing what we are doing and feeling responsible for our own actions, and via them, having subjective experience of being in control of our environment. Sense of agency is both a mental and neural state, and the question how these two dimensions are related is of utmost importance. That relationship must at one end encompass subjective experience of being in control and ipso facto at the other end, the operation of the sensory-motor loops exerting successful control of the intended actions. It is the latter that has been the focus of control theoretic accounts such as the "Comparator Model." In the context of the parallel model introduced in Eberle et

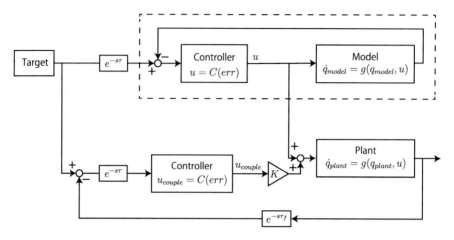

Fig. 5 Parallel configuration of the control scheme incorporating the anticipating synchronization

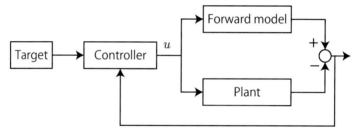

Fig. 6 The schematic block diagram of the comparator model

al. (2018), its feedback control loop, a comparison between the actual state resulting from the motion and the estimated state calculated by the internal model, allows to calculate a motor error (comparator), which is fed back to the system to improve its functioning (see, for example, Synofzik et al. 2007). On the basis of a given motor command, the internal model predicts the outcome of one's own behavior (predicted state).

The preceding discussion points to an interesting conclusion, that classical predictive models may be reconstituted in a manner much more steeped in dynamics and coupling, often with anticipating synchronization providing predictive capacity.

The original formulation of anticipating synchronization assumes that the slave dynamics is identical to that of the master or, in other words, from the control theoretic perspective, that the master dynamics is completely known. This is however often not the case, and lack of a complete knowledge of the precise master dynamics may pose problems for the stability of theoretical control schemes when deployed to real systems. Another source of uncertainty is due to possible random perturbations affecting the master. Such uncertainties, either due to lack of knowledge or randomness, may be represented as additional perturbative terms. It is an important problem in control theory to consider the control of systems subject to perturbations. Thus, Oguchi and Nijmeijer also considered the control problem of system with uncertainties (Oguchi and Nijmeijer 2006),

$$\dot{X}(t) = f(t, X_t) + g(t, X_t), \tag{11}$$

where $g(t, X_t)$ is a term representing the master uncertainty or perturbations, and derived various conditions for the stability of the state predictor, Z, based on anticipating synchronization under these conditions. Interestingly, this also constitutes one of the first theoretical results showing that anticipating synchronization can take place with nonidentical master and slave systems.

As such, the study by Oguchi and Nijmeijer complements the empirical studies of Ciszak et al., who demonstrated anticipating synchronization in system where both the master and the slave were subjected to common and uncommon external forcing noise input (Ciszak et al. 2004a), and investigated numerically the stability region of anticipating synchronization manifold for such systems.

Further extension along similar lines was investigated by Stepp and Frank, who studied the problem of estimating anticipating synchronization variability due to relative balance between deterministic coupling of the slave with the master, and its coupling with a stochastic force. This case also results in master and slave being subject to somewhat different dynamics and the authors propose an estimation method for identifying the coupling parameters and the variance of forcing noise (Stepp and Frank 2009).

In a series of recent papers, Voss also considered an extension of the anticipating synchronization toward the case of nonidentical master and slave systems (Voss 2016b, c, 2018). In Voss (2016b), the slave is defined as a linear relaxation system driven by the master via the usual anticipatory coupling with a delay

$$Y(t) = aY(t) + K(X(t) - Y(t - \tau)).$$

Voss showed that such anticipatory relaxation dynamics can successfully cope with a smooth but random stationary signal, X, in terms of predicting the signal on average as well as anticipating accurately most of its peaks. This performance is frequency specific and according to Voss could be explained in terms of the negative group delay. Another limitation implied by the particularly simple form of the slave dynamics is that, in general, it confers shorter anticipation horizon than possible in the original formulation of anticipating synchronization. Voss explored extending the relaxation dynamics to discrete delay induced negative group delay systems with a single delay coupling (Voss 2016c) and universal negative group delay filters with multiple delayed coupled feedback terms (Voss 2018).

The extension of anticipating synchronization toward mismatched master and slave dynamics is interesting, as it is hard to expect that brain systems that could be coupled with some delays would be exactly identical, thus this line of investigation of anticipatory dynamics increases viability of anticipating synchronization as a framework to understand cognitive and neural dynamics (Stepp and Turvey 2010).

The above generalizations of anticipating synchronization focused on the relationships between master and slave dynamics, preserving the original form of the coupling between these systems. Another form of extension of the basic anticipating synchronization definition has been considered by Stepp and Frank (2009). Interestingly, they observe that the linear coupling term between master and slave in the original formulation of anticipating synchronization, $K(X - Y_t)$, could be considered as a linear term of a Taylor expansion approximation of a more general nonlinear coupling. This allows them to consider further extension of anticipating synchronization, where couplings could be of different form. Specifically, they consider the system subject to periodic boundary conditions, for which they conclude that an analogue first order approximation of the general coupling would be the lowest sine function of a Fourier expansion. Thus, they effectively introduce a Kuramoto model with harmonic and anharmonic oscillators subject to a non-instantaneous coupling.

Pyragas and Pyragienė introduced a different coupling that exploited the particular form of the master dynamical system's attractor (Pyragas and Pyragienė 2008). This allows them to achieve significantly longer anticipating horizon than possible with the original coupling scheme introduced in the original formulation of anticipating synchronization.

Recognizing limitations of the anticipating horizon achievable with the standard anticipating synchronization, Voss introduced an extension of the system, whereby he showed that a cascade of unidirectionally coupled slave systems can achieve anticipation on time scales exceeding the characteristic time scales of the chaotic dynamics (Voss 2001) (Fig. 7).

The equations for a chain of m unidirectionally coupled slave systems are

$$\dot{\mathbf{X}}_1 = \mathbf{f}(\mathbf{X}_1) \tag{12}$$
$$\dot{\mathbf{X}}_i = \mathbf{f}(\mathbf{X}_i) + \mathbf{K}(\mathbf{X}_{i-1} - \mathbf{X}_{i,\tau}), \quad i = 2, \dots, m+1.$$

The anticipation in coupled oscillator's chains amplifies the noncausal effect, as all but one slave are not being causally connected with the master. Ciszak et al. also observed that the cascading of slaves proposed by Voss (2001) improves anticipating synchronization in excitable systems subject to uncommon forcing.

Although the original anticipating synchronization scheme relies on the presence of a delay, a number of studies investigated the phenomenon relaxing this requirement. For example, Corron et al. (2005) performed a first order approximation to the delay line and obtained anticipatory effect in the resulting non-delayed system. Pyragas and Pyragienė used conceptually similar approach to remove the delay by approximating a pure delay line by Pade approximation; effectively a low-dimensional filter (Pyragienė and Pyragas 2017).

Hayashi et al. suggest that an interesting insight into the anticipating synchronization can be obtained by the renormalization of the time scale in a driven system (Hayashi et al. 2016). Their approach directly links the feedback delay of the driven

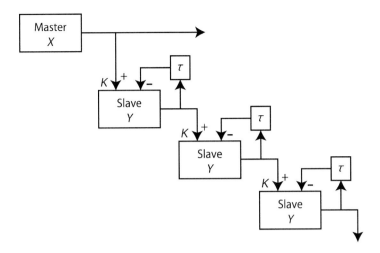

Fig. 7 Cascade of anticipating synchronization systems. (Modified from Nasuto and Hayashi 2016b)

system with the renormalized time scale of the driven system by performing the first order expansion of the time-delay term in the slave system.

The following points summarize the method of renormalized time step, extending the paradigm of anticipating synchronization:

1. Larger time scale amounts to the faster evolution of the state variable of the driven system based on the internal dynamics.
2. Coupling term drives the state variable of the driven systems to be synchronized with one of the driver.
3. Interplay between internal dynamics and coupling term gives rise to the anticipating or lagging synchronization of the driven system.

The stability of the state variable and the presence of anticipating manifold are guaranteed by $K > \alpha$ and $K\tau < 1$ for the linear case of master and slave dynamics ($f(X) = \alpha X$). Multidimensional nonlinear cases were also studied in Hayashi et al. (2016).

From the numerically obtained stability diagrams, the renormalized time scale of the driven system led to an alternative method to induce the anticipating synchronization when the time-delay term is not available to the driven system. These results imply that the different time scales of the dynamical systems can be considered as different clocks governing their temporal evolution. Depending on the sign of τ, the time evolution of the driven system can be anticipating or lagging with respect to the driver system. When the dynamical systems evolve according to the different clocks that interact unidirectionally, the anticipating synchronization can appear without any time-delays. Therefore, this approach will further expand this interesting paradigm toward a wider range of dynamical scenarios.

Anticipating Synchronization in Neural Systems

Another line of investigation of anticipating synchronization focused on its potential relevance for modeling neural systems. One of the first efforts to study if anticipating synchronization could be instantiated in neural-like system was performed by Ciszak and colleagues (Ciszak et al. 2003). They recapitulated the anticipation synchronization system with Hodgkin-Huxley and FitzhHugh-Nagumo model, neurons subject to identical random input, and observed that excitable systems are also capable of anticipatory behavior; that is, the "slave" neuron with delayed self-feedback would fire the same spike trains as the master neuron but ahead of it. This is not a simple trivial application of the same anticipating synchronization principle, as the active system driven by a noisy input is much harder to anticipate than a low dimensional but continuously changing chaotic system. Ciszak et al. account for the anticipatory behavior in the slave by lowering its firing threshold due to delayed self-coupling (Ciszak et al. 2004a). The anticipating synchronization can also be realized for larger coupling values even when master and slave are driven by different realizations of white noise, and the anticipating synchronization quality can be improved by cascading several slave model neurons (Ciszak et al. 2004b). This is also one of the first papers that invoked anticipating synchronization as a hypothetical mechanisms accounting for the experimentally observed phenomenon of zero-lag synchronization in the nervous system; the presence of simultaneous oscillations in cortical areas separated by orders of millimeters distances. Voss, in line with his extensions of anticipating synchronization toward nonidentical master and slave systems via anticipatory relaxation dynamics, has shown that a leaky integrator, one of the simplest and most popular models of neurons, can also exhibit the negative group delay when equipped with recurrent delayed self-inhibition (Voss 2016a). Consequently, even such simple modeled systems are capable of predicting lower frequency components of their inputs. Interestingly, Voss demonstrated this capacity by integrating the model, using as its input the experimentally recorded local field potential (LFP) data. The leaky integrator was capable of predicting the lower frequency of the LFPs, whereas it lagged with respect to the higher frequency components.

In order to claim biological plausibility of anticipating synchronization, other defining characteristics should also be accounted for in computational models in a biologically plausible manner. There is a great variability of neuron types in the nervous system, each with different set of biophysical properties affecting neurons' dynamical properties. Even within the same class, there is a considerable variability between neurons; hence any explanation invoking neural dynamics must be able to cope with such variability. In Pyragiené and Pyragas (2013), they showed that anticipating synchronization is robust to differences between master and slave neurons; the result that, for excitable dynamical systems such as model neurons,

Fig. 8 Master–slave–interneuron motif. (Modified from Matias et al. 2011)

parallels control theoretic extension of anticipating synchronization by Oguchi toward systems with uncertainty (Oguchi and Nijmeijer 2006). Moreover, as long as the slave's natural mean frequency is greater than the natural frequency of a master neuron, approximate anticipating spike synchronization will follow (Pyragienė and Pyragas 2013). Interestingly, they also have shown that, under these conditions, anticipation can be achieved without a need for delayed self-feedback in the coupling. The delayed self-feedback is an important characteristic of the anticipating synchronization, so it is important to consider what biologically plausible constituents could play its role.

An alternative approach to replacing the delayed slave self-feedback was investigated in a series of papers by Matias and colleagues (Matias et al. 2011, 2014, 2016; Mirasso et al. 2017).

As these authors note, although seemingly anticipating synchronization constituent characteristics – dynamics, coupling, and delayed self-feedback – are ubiquitous in the brain, in addition to neural-like dynamics, the latter two also need to be instantiated in a biologically plausible way. Motivated by such considerations, they propose to replace a diffusive coupling by models of chemical synapses and the delayed self-feedback of the slave's membrane potential by a neural motif of excitatory-inhibitory loop (Matias et al. 2011). Thus, the excitatory master and slave neurons are forming unidirectional chain connected by AMPA synapses and terminating on the inhibitory interneuron, which provides an inhibitory feedback onto the slave neuron via $GABA_A$ synapse; see Fig. 8.

The authors investigated an occurrence and a dependence of the anticipating synchronization on parameters characterizing chemical synapses and their interplay with the noise input (Matias et al. 2011, 2016). They concluded that the system transitions from delayed to anticipatory synchronization, as the inhibitory synapse from the inhibitory interneuron to the slave increases in strength. Such control of the fluctuations of the precedence of spiking by master and slave may play an important role in regulating the effects of spike timing dependent plasticity.

Moreover, anticipating synchronization may thus be achieved without use of explicit delay mechanisms, paralleling example mechanism introduced in Hayashi et al. (2016).

The authors also investigated effects of the mutual excitatory coupling between the master and the slave and concluded that, the anticipating synchronization behavior can, in fact, be stabilized by the presence of a slave-to-master synapse, whereas if the system is in the delayed synchronization regime (i.e., the master leads the slave), increasing the excitatory coupling from the slave to the master can switch the system's behavior to anticipating synchronization mode. The implication of these results is that under some circumstances mutually interacting excitatory and inhibitory neurons may be regarded as a single dynamical unit leading the activity of excitatory neurons to which it is connected. Taken together with the results reported in Pyragienė and Pyragas (2013), it implies that care needs to be taken in inferring the direction of flow and causal interactions on the basis of multi electrode spike time or time series statistics.

This theme is investigated further in Matias et al. (2014), where the master-slave-interneuron model from Matias et al. (2011) is extended to the populations of excitatory and inhibitory neurons, such that connectivity between the populations recapitulates the motif analyzed in the previous paper. This model is then used in order to analyze the local field potential data obtained by Brovelli et al. from monkeys during a cognitive GO/NO–GO task (Brovelli et al. 2004). The model was able to capture qualitative properties of the empirical coherence and Granger causality spectra, as well as the interaction time-delay (obtained from the phase, at which the peak of the coherence spectrum occurs). In particular, the model was able to reproduce the lack of consistent relationship between the direction of interaction, as indicated by the Granger causality, and the relative phase of activities observed experimentally. One important implication is that any inference of the direction of information flow in the brain needs to take into account not only the anatomical connectivity but also excitation to inhibition balance. Given the potential fluctuations of the latter, it offers a flexible mechanism of dynamic organization of synchronization patterns, irrespective of structural connectivity.

The preceding discussion suggests an important role the strength of synaptic couplings plays in coordinating synchronization dynamics within the anticipating synchronization framework. In addition to the use of excitable dynamics in order to define a master and a slave, a consideration should be given to the methods of tuning the connection gains. In case of anticipating synchronization, this amounts to an investigation whether the coupling strength gain could be tuned in a manner consistent with models of synaptic plasticity. Matias and colleagues investigated the interplay between a form of synaptic plasticity, the spike timing dependent plasticity (STDP), and the anticipating synchronization in Matias et al. (2015). They augmented the neural motif and population level models of anticipating synchronization based on the inhibitory loop (Matias et al. 2011, 2014, 2016), by STDP of the excitatory synapses and showed that STDP is not detrimental to anticipating synchronization. Moreover, the transition from anticipating to delayed synchronization could be controlled by tuning the local inhibition within the receiving population, and STDP interacted synergistically with such transitions. They also demonstrated that the synaptic plasticity results in such model systems in a near zero-lag synchronization; hence, the model may account for occurrence of such dynamical behavior regime between distant brain areas found empirically.

The computational investigations discussed in this section concentrated on modeling the anticipating synchronization in systems designed to address the feasibility of existence of such dynamic behavior in neural circuitry. The models also afforded investigation of the formal dependence of the anticipatory dynamics on various neurobiologically motivated model properties or even to provide a qualitative account for experimentally observed data. However, they stopped short

Fig. 9 Predict, prevent, control scheme. (Modified from Ciszak et al. 2009)

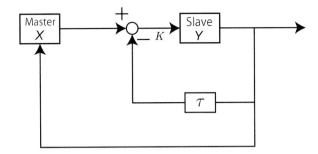

at addressing the possibility of construction of neurobiologically plausible antici-pating synchronization system in which anticipatory behavior would play a functional role.

In Ciszak et al. (2009), they addressed such a problem by proposing a neurobio-logically motivated simple motif capable of performing a control task. The problem considered is to prevent the unwanted spiking activity of an excitable system. The authors used in their study two models – Adler and FitzHugh-Nagumo systems, often used to represent simple model neurons with class I or II excitability, respec-tively, effectively accounting for different dynamical mechanisms of spike genera-tion: a saddle-node bifurcation for class I and a Hopf bifurcation for class II. They achieved the task by putting the excitable system in an anticipating synchronization master–slave configuration, with the output from the slave system providing the control signal back to the master, see Fig. 9.

Thus, they have demonstrated the successful operation of this predict-prevent control method, whereby the slave system would make the prediction of the impending spike of the master, and that prediction would trigger a corrective signal inhibiting the master's imminent firing. This work thus constitutes an interesting bridge between, on the one hand the attempts to use anticipating synchronization in a control theory setting as discussed in the previous section, and on the other hand the exploration of neurobiologically motivated implementation of anticipatory behavior outlined in the current section. This also motivates an overview of the work on the importance of anticipation to explain cognitive phenomena, particularly in movement coordination, which will be the focus of the subsequent section.

Empirical Evidence

There is a broad recognition in psychological literature of the importance of future-oriented cognition, and many studies in psychology are concerned with various forms of prospection. Planning, decision making, goal-oriented behaviors are all future oriented activities. This led some researchers to claim that the foundations of psychological sciences should be revisited and prospection should be considered as the founding block of psychology and not just one of its cornerstones (Seligman et al. 2013).

There has been somewhat similar resurgence of interest in cognitive neuroscience and philosophy of mind, following in footsteps of Helmholtz, to consider the brain as a hypothesis generator. For example, Daniel Dennett has discussed in his book *Darwin's Dangerous Idea: Evolution and the Meaning of Life* (Dennett 1996) a system for categorizing the various organisms' capacities for acting in the world. At the very bottom of this system are creatures only capable of reacting to the external world. Individuals may be hardwired in their responses but collectively entire species, subject to natural variability, are able to survive, under natural selection. Organisms at higher levels of hierarchy are more able to select in which way they may respond to the environmental factors, perhaps even going beyond the limitations imposed by biological constraints.

Recently, the predictive brain hypothesis is stirring a lot of excitement in cognitive science and philosophy of mind (Clark 2015). The reason for this renewed interest is growing hope, within some sections of the scientific community, that the recent formulation of this hypothesis may provide a unified view of the brain and the mind, and thus may be able to bring back into a single fold philosophy of mind, neuroscience, and cognitive sciences.

Typically though, and including the attempts mentioned above, given strong links between the mode of explanation dominating in cognitive science and the information processing metaphor, empirical findings and their explanations are discussed in computational terms, for example, when cognitive processes or brain systems are considered to represent expectations of future outcomes or to perform predictions.

Various recent flavors of the predictive brain account, e.g., predictive coding or predictive processing, propose mechanistic accounts of cognitive processing in terms of some form of a statistical, or even Bayesian as some would have it, inference. The latter is not a passive response of inert computational brain machinery to the sensory flux (feedforward processing), but requires an active inference, where the perception is affected by the prior knowledge and mental states instantiated by internal models and feedback loops, and the brain is actively seeking to minimize the prediction errors, either by modifying the models or by acting in the world.

The predictive processing provides explanations of cognitive phenomena in dynamic terms, such as feedback and action, but uses them in a very computational manner, and the discourse remains couched in computational semantics.

In spite of huge interest, these theories seem to be generating in cognitive science and philosophy of mind; they are not without problems. Even among researchers accepting computational account of brain function, there are some that voice concerns regarding equating predictive coding and Bayesian inference (Aitchison and Lengyel 2017). As Aichison and Lengyel argue, predictive coding may be orthogonal to Bayesian inference, in the sense that they may serve different computations. Interestingly, Aichison and Lengyel propose that predictive coding should be better understood in terms of neural motifs that emerge at different levels of the brain and subserve different functions.

From the perspective put forward by Rosen, the problem with the predictive brain theories may have more to do with the very use of computational framework as their starting point and taking it, together with the predictive brain theory, as the ultimate account of the mind, rather than a *description* of its operation under some specific fixed circumstances. An implication of Rosen's theory is that an ability of living systems to anticipate the future should not, in general, be reduced to a computational expectation or a prediction (even if the latter may be an appropriate *description* of cognitive processing, sufficiently accurate in very contrived laboratory settings, where all the variables are constrained and predefined).

Somewhat similarly to Rosen, a dynamic view of cognition sheds the computational metaphor and proposes instead that the most appropriate way of describing the operation of the nervous system is in dynamical systems terms. In this spirit, Stepp and Turvey provide overview of anticipating synchronization in their argument against computation and representation as the foundational explanations in cognitive science (Stepp and Turvey 2010). It is perhaps not surprising that the dynamical view is most naturally reconciled with cognitive function involving dynamics par excellence, i.e., movement coordination and control. This section will review some work that discusses movement coordination and will link it with dynamical and anticipatory accounts.

Anticipation in Movement Coordination

Living systems have to flexibly adjust themselves to the changes in the environment. However, it is impossible to fully model the environmental dynamics to simulate the imminent changes. To anticipate the future changes of dynamical environment, it is necessary to perceive velocity and acceleration of the environmental variables in real time. This amounts to some measure of time flow, implying that the time step has to be generated within the central nervous systems. In fact, there is evidence that populations of medial motor area neurons participate in estimating timing intervals on the order of seconds and, interestingly, some neurons show anticipatory preparatory buildup of activity before the actual motor action initiation (Mita et al. 2009). However, due to the speed limitation of the action potential transmission, sensory-motor systems are inevitably subject to the time-delays of a few hundred milliseconds. The consideration above gives rise to the fundamental questions about the human perception of time, such as the judgment of a chronological order of the external events and of motor coordination in response to the external events. The following sections overview various experimental paradigms aimed at revealing the mechanisms of the sensory-motor coordination in humans responding to the dynamical environment. Considering a vast amount of the literature on the subject, the focus in this section is set on those studies, which showed the anticipatory behavior in the sensory-motor coordination.

Anticipating Tapping

Timing mechanisms in the sensory-motor systems can be revealed by the repetitive motion in response to external stimulation. The simplest psychophysics experiment, called tapping experiment, involves the participant tapping or flexing their index finger in response to the auditory or visual stimulation at a certain frequency (Repp 2005).

Engström et al. found in the tapping experiments, the behavioral mode transition from the reactive to anticipatory mode, when the frequency of the auditory stimuli increased (Engstrom 1996). The reactive mode is a consequence of the time-delay in sensory-motor system, i.e., the participant simply perceives the auditory stimulation, and reacts to it by finger flexion, whereas the anticipatory mode represents the fact that the human motion can actually precede the external stimulation, i.e., the participant flexes their index finger before the auditory stimulation. The antici-patory mode itself has been studied for many years and termed a Negative Mean Synchrony (NMS), but Engström et al. were the first to provide an explanation of mode transition using the double-well potential (Engstrom 1996). This approach fits in synergetic and nonlinear dynamic frameworks and follows the success of the Haken-Kelso-Bunz (HKB) model, which explains the phase transition in the index finger motion.

Adopting a more engineering approach, Mates suggested the feedback control loops based on the correction of phase and cycle time with respect to the external stimulation (Mates 1994). The most basic part of a set of equations is a simple linear model to determine the cycle time (an inter-tap time interval), $C(n + 1)$, based on the cycle time at the n_{th} tapping, $C(n)$, and the synchronization error, $S_E(n)$, of the n_{th} tap with respect to the external signal. The equation defining the model is given below:

$$C(n + 1) = C(n) + KS_E(n),   \tag{13}$$

where K is a gain parameter.

The originality of his approach stems from the assumption of an internal time keeper based on the human perception of the errors between the timing of the stimulation and the action. The feedback model introduced by Mates could success-fully demonstrate the NMS, even though it included the time-delay in the sensory-motor loops (Mates 1994).

Recent studies in neuroscience reported that basal ganglia and cerebellum may play a role in the timing mechanisms of the sensory-motor systems (Middleton 2000). These two regions have mutual connections with cortex. Kawato suggested that cerebellum plays an important role in forming an internal predictive model, as well as in learning process (Kawato 1999). The comparison between tapping motion and repetition of self-motion showed that the participant's brain under the former paradigm showed higher activity in the supplementary motor area and the sensori-motor cortex, indicating that timing mechanisms coupled to the external stimulation should involve wider area of the brain for sensory-motor coordination (Ikegami et al. 2010). It is tempting to think that the different neuronal circuits separately perform the process of phase and cycle time correction (Mates 1994), i.e., the loop between basal ganglia and cerebellum should be responsible for unconscious motor coordi-nation, whereas the loop between the motor cortex and the prefrontal cortex for the processing more cognitive aspects of movement.

Experimental and theoretical evidence imply that timing mechanisms rely on feedback control for error corrections, and amount to making a decision for one-step ahead, based on the information available at present. These feedback models and the mode transition represented by HKB model do not require any computation of internal models, i.e., dynamical coupling with the environmental dynamics can induce appropriate behavioral patterns.

Anticipation in Tracking

The frequency of transition to anticipatory mode in tapping experiments indicates that the internal rhythm is generated with the motor command prior to the external stimulation. As a next step to reveal the switching mechanisms from the reactive to anticipatory mode, tracking experiments, in which sensory-motor loops are coupled to continuous environmental dynamics, would be appropriate to be explored.

Ishida and Sawada performed the target tracking experiments to quantify the dynamical error correction during target motion subject to the unpredictable changes (Ishida and Sawada 2013). The participants controlling the visual tracer were asked to track the visual target moving periodically in a 1D space, by minimizing the relative phase difference between the target and the tracer. The perturbation of the target motion was introduced by a sudden change in target frequency, and the resultant transient phase difference was measured.

The main finding of this study was that when the tracer preceded the target on average, the transient errors were minimized. This implies that human's self-motion precedes the target motion so that the participant can adapt to an unexpected changes in the environment. The mechanism behind such behavior, named "Proactive Control," characterized the functionality of the anticipatory mode by revealing, in a dynamical sense, the benefit of being ahead of the environment. To account for such anticipatory behavior, these authors proposed the visual-motor control law as follows:

$$\frac{dX(t)}{dt} = K(Y(t) - X(t)) + \gamma \dot{Y}, \tag{14}$$

where $X(t)$ and $Y(t)$ represent the position of the tracer and of the target, respectively. The first term is the feedback control term for the positional error control with the gain parameter K, and the second term is the feed forward term for the target velocity with the gain parameter γ. The basic idea is that by perceiving the target velocity, humans can speed up their tracer so that the position of the tracer precedes the target on average. This simple mechanism could also explain the experimentally observed minimization of the dynamical error co-occurring with the average precedence of the tracer with respect to the target.

Following this pioneering work, in order to suppress the positional correction or the reactive mode, and to quantify the kinematics of the anticipatory mode, Hayashi et al. performed intermittent tracking experiments, in which participants were asked to continue tracing the target in spite of the target intermittently disappearing (Hayashi et al. 2011, 2015). Their findings can be summarized as follows:

1. When the position control is suppressed as the information flow from the environment becomes intermittent, anticipatory mode starts to function, and internal rhythm is generated to serve as an internal clock.
2. When the information flow is completely shut down, the internal clock ticks faster, and tracking velocity increases, resulting in the tracker preceding the target motion.
3. The precedence of tracking motion in the intermittent condition is subject to the feedback control of the positional error. However, on average, the tracer motion precedes the target motion.

Anticipation in Mutual Tapping/Tracking

Extending the tapping paradigm of single subjects, Hayashi and Kondo performed mutual tapping experiments with two humans to investigate the conditions required for synchronized motion (Hayashi and Kondo 2013). In the mutual tapping experiments, the participants were asked to maintain the tapping at the provided initial guiding frequency for five taps and thereafter following the light cue to synchronize their taps' onsets without presence of an external periodic reference signal.

A transition from an alternate mode to a synchronization mode was discovered under the same conditions, as when a single subject changed from a reactive mode to an anticipatory mode in the single tapping experiments. The experimental results suggest that the cycle time for each tapping motion is tuned by a proportional control that is based on synchronization errors and cycle time errors. As the tapping frequency increases, a mathematical model based on feedback control in the sensory-motor closed loop predicts a discrete mode transition as the gain factors of the proportional control decrease, Eq. (15). This indicates that as the frequency of tapping increases in mutual tapping, sensitivity or precision over the synchronization errors decreases, leading to mutual synchronization, i.e., they tap at the same time.

To summarize, Hayashi and Kondo found that the combination of the first and second order error correction in synchronization errors is the key for the convergence to synchronization in mutual tapping, as shown in Eq. (15) below:

$$
\begin{aligned}
C_A(n+1) &= C_A(n) + K_{A,1}S_{E,A}(n) + K_{A,2}S_{E,A}(n-1), \\
C_B(n+1) &= C_B(n) + K_{B,1}S_{E,B}(n) + K_{B,2}S_{E,B}(n-1),
\end{aligned}
\tag{15}
$$

where $C_A(n)$ and $C_B(n)$ represent the cycle time of subject A and B, respectively.

As the frequency in mutual tapping increases, we observed a mode transition from the alternate mode to the synchronization mode. The tapping mechanism is found to be a proportional control of the cycle time correction based on the synchronization error and the cycle time error. A mathematical model based on feedback control in the sensory-motor closed loop predicts a mode transition from

Fig. 10 Mutual tracking experiments. Two participants were asked to synchronize the motion of tracers. (Modified from Hayashi and Sawada 2013)

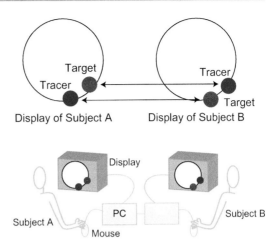

the divergence to synchronization as the gain factors of the proportional control decrease when the tapping frequency increases, demonstrating that the second order correction of the synchronization error, $S_E(n - 1)$, plays a major role in mutual synchronization, tuning the cycle time of tapping.

Considering the knowledge obtained in the mutual tapping experiments, a possibility arises that an active mode transition might also occur in the continuous motion while two subjects are interacting, for example, in the mutual target tracking experiments. Hayashi and Sawada undertook a study to reveal what kind of mode appears in the sensory-motor system, when a participant was asked to track the hand position of the partner at various mean tracking frequencies (Fig. 10) (Hayashi and Sawada 2013).

The experimental results showed that a transition from a mutual error-correction mode to a synchronization mode occurred at the frequencies corresponding to those observed at the transition from a reactive error-correction mode to a proactive anticipatory mode, reported previously with the single subjects in the target tracking experiments (Hayashi et al. 2011; Ishida and Sawada 2013). The mathematical formulation of the proposed control mechanism suggested that in the mutual error-correction mode, the time-delay in sensory-motor coupling dominates the mutual motion in correcting the relative phase distance, and in the synchronization mode, the rhythm generation was formulated as a feedforward mechanism to synchronize the mutual coordination of hands (Hayashi and Sawada 2013).

Anticipatory mode in tapping/tracking experiments, in which the body motion occurs prior to the reference signal, has been previously reported when a periodic target signal was shown to the subjects at relatively high frequencies. As discussed in the preceding section, the mechanisms underlying the anticipatory mode have been accounted for within three frameworks: (1) dynamics governed by a double-well potential; (2) feedback control; and (3) proactive control (feedforward control).

Independent from the approaches originating from the tapping experiments to investigate the nature of sensory-motor coupling in humans, anticipating synchronization was used in an attempt to shed a new light onto the paradigm of tracking experiments (Stepp 2009).

In order to investigate if humans might use the anticipating synchronization, Stepp performed the target tracking experiments with chaotic target (Stepp 2009). The underlying idea is that chaotic tracking motion extends the motion paradigm beyond a simple target tracking with a dominant rhythmic movement. By introducing the time-delay between the hand motion and the tracer motion (delayed visual feedback of their own movements), these authors aimed at inducing the anticipating synchronization resulting in the precedence of tracer with respect to the chaotic target. Using 6 values of delay from 20 ms to 1 s, evidence shows that (a) participants are able to synchronize with a chaotic target, even with some amount of applied delay, (b) task performance varies systematically with applied delay, and (c) the same systematic dependence is predicted for systems exhibiting anticipating synchronization (Stepp 2009). However, even though their results clearly indicated the ability of humans to compensate the visual time-delay of their own movements with respect to the tracer, the tracer itself did not precede the chaotic target.

Using a robotic arm consisting of two planar links, Eberle et al. showed, by calculating the phase diagram of the time-delay and the precedence of the hand motion, that the internal model of the body dynamics could indeed lead to the anticipating synchronization, if it was implemented in "Parallel" to the dynamics of body plant (Eberle et al. 2018). This study is essentially the demonstration of how the anticipating synchronization may arise in tracking experiments, where the time-delay is introduced between hand motion and visual feedback (Stepp 2009).

These new lines of research in anticipating synchronization give rise to two fundamental questions: (1) Can humans learn the target and plant dynamics and use them as internal models? and (2) What is the fundamental role of the inevitable time-delay in sensor-motor systems, when the dynamics is governed by the internal model coupled to the master dynamics? As one possible approach, an interesting insight into the anticipating synchronization can be obtained by renormalizing the time scale in the driven system (Hayashi et al. 2016). This approach directly links the feedback delay of the driven system with the effects of time scale renormalization, identifying the main component in the anticipating synchronization paradigm and suggesting an alternative method to generate the anticipating and the lagging synchronization. Thus, expanding the delay term, $Y(t - \tau)$ in Eq. (7), one can obtain

$$\frac{dY(t)}{dt^*} = f(Y(t)) + K(X(t) - Y(t)), \tag{16}$$

where $t^* = t/(1 - K\tau)$ is a renormalized time in the driven system. From $K > 0$ and $\tau > 0$, we obtain $0 < 1 - K\tau < 1$, which leads to the property of the renormalized time, $t < t^*$. This outcome suggests that the time scale of the driven system should be larger than that of the driver system, i.e., the effect of the time-delayed variable in the coupling term can be equivalently replaced by the renormalized time in the driven system dynamics, after performing the first order expansion (Hayashi et al. 2016). From the numerically obtained stability diagrams, the renormalized time scale of the driven system was demonstrated to be the alternative method to induce the anticipating synchronization when the time-delay term is not available to the driven system.

A more general understanding of the anticipatory mode may result from considering how the internal time within the biological system, as discussed earlier, is related to the renormalized time. The results reported above have an important implication that the different time scales of the dynamical systems can be considered as different clocks governing the speed of their temporal evolution, i.e., depending on the sign of τ, the time evolution of the driven system can be anticipating or lagging with respect to the driver system, when the dynamical systems running based on the different clocks interact unidirectionally.

In behavioral sciences, the feedforward model or the internal predictive model is motivated by the assumption that the feedback delays destabilize the controlled objects. Internal models have been widely adopted to explain the human motion overcoming the time-delay in the sensory-motor systems (Kawato 1999). Kawato concluded that forward internal models can predict sensory consequences from efference copies of issued motor commands and that inverse internal models can calculate necessary feedforward motor commands from desired trajectory information. However, this approach underestimates the dynamical aspects of motion, and might be considered as a static mapping between the positions in work space and the sequence of motor commands.

Even though Stepp's attempt at using anticipating synchronization to account for human sensory-motor coupling is confined to capturing the data regularities (Stepp 2009), his emphasis on the importance of the dynamical coupling with the changing environment should be considered, to make a link between human behavior and dynamical systems. For example, in the mutual interactions experiments, Hayashi and Kondo found that humans follow the feedback control to tune the cycle time based on the synchronization errors, and that the gain parameters change as a function of tapping frequency (Hayashi and Kondo 2013). From the perspective of renormalization of internal time, they found that the tuning of the gain parameters can be attributed to the internal time scale to detect the cycle time of tapping motion. Also, the mathematical modeling of Mates explicitly modeled the internal time clock (Mates 1994). In the case of tracking experiments, the gain factor γ in Eq. (14) can be renormalized into the time scale for velocity of self-motion.

Therefore, the flexible adjustment of the internal time scales to anticipate the changing environment could be a fundamental property of the living systems, for which "orienting toward the future" is a crucial characteristics.

Summary

In this chapter, a brief review was given of the main concepts behind Robert Rosen's proposal that the living systems have the inherent capacity to sense and react to the future possible modes of interactions with the environment. Complex, information-rich, but dynamic, environment may require organisms to achieve a balance between complexity, necessary to be able to capture and act on the environmental regularities, and ability to adjust to the ever changing flux of environmental interactions. A dynamical concept of anticipating synchronization proposed by Voss was introduced in this chapter alongside an outline of the computational studies exploring its properties and putative neurobiologically plausible implementations. Any interactions with the environment must involve an action, hence ultimately a motoric response. Thus, a discussion followed, of the movement coordination from the perspective of dynamics and anticipation.

Evidence of the living systems' capacity for orienting toward the future comes typically from studies conceived in the traditional scientific framework, designing the experiments and interpreting the results by defining a priori the variables responsible for the observed phenomenon and ignoring all other factors or relegating them to the role of unwanted confounds. This results in a reduction of an inherently open living system, capable of interacting with the world according to any available affordances that may be required to achieve the desired result, to a closed subsystem's description with few predefined inputs and outputs. Thus, this empirical framework has already preselected the mode of explanation before the data have even been collected.

This is not an approach that Rosen would advocate, although appreciation to why his theories necessitate this divergence is not easy, in spite of Rosen being quite vocal about such implications for the philosophy and epistemology of science. Two important but perhaps overlooked aspects of his work need to be considered, in order to evaluate properly the putative implications of his work.

One has to do with his anticipatory system definition of living, which contains a subtle but crucial distinction between what he defines as a model versus a mere simulation. The latter is tantamount to instantiating some form of computation, or mechanistic implementation of the behavior of a priori defined and fixed variables.

Living organisms evolved for millions of years in an open-ended fashion – the modes of interactions with the environment were not predefined, the rules of engagement not set a priori. No holds barred battle for survival requires using whatever it takes, and those with capacity to use any means necessary will acquire an evolutionary edge against those that are set in the ways of solving a given survival problem. Very specific and stable ecological niche may result in very fixed ways of solving a problem; hence under this scenario, evolution may amount to a refinement, or optimization, of the solution mechanism. However, relying on just such a way of dealing with the problem may prove catastrophic, if niche is significantly altered. In general, in complex, dynamic, and information-rich but less stable environment, the best prospect for survival may not be offered by optimization of a fixed strategy, but an open-ended capacity to respond to the environmental interactions.

Second, taking Rosenian definition of anticipatory systems in isolation from the rest of his body of work may well result in an incomplete appreciation of the scope of its implications. His minimal definition of life, based on its most fundamental building blocks, is that of (M,R)-systems, that is meant to capture the essence of the biochemical network of reactions and pathways closed to efficient causation that, according to Rosen, is a quintessential organizational property of a living system – a system that is otherwise open to material and energy flux from the environment. The (M,R)-systems definition states what are the requirements on the organizational complexity of the system to be living, whereas anticipatory systems definition spells out the essential functional consequence of such a complexity – the open-ended ability to sense, and act on, future possibilities. Nevertheless, both are attempting to provide, effectively complementary, characterizations of living systems. It is the (M,R)-systems definition, which provides a potential bridge between dynamics and Rosen's thinking. Although the latter was steeped in relational biology and category theory (Louie 2009), nevertheless differential equations models are common in capturing the properties of biochemical reactions.

In this context, an overview was provided of dynamical systems' variants implementing the novel concept of anticipating synchronization introduced by Voss as a very intriguing building block that may subserve organization of anticipatory capacity. Special attention was given to the numerical explorations investigating the possibility of such dynamics to be implemented in neural motifs.

Although anticipating synchronization may have the potential to be a constituent of Rosen's definition of anticipatory systems, to be fair, it could also be used in computational, predictive models of brain function. After all, using dynamical systems does not automatically obviate the objections against computational account of intentionality (Preston and Bishop 2002) and in fact more general frameworks encompassing various forms of computations, including digital and analogue varieties, have been proposed (Spencer et al. 2013). Thus, the crux of the matter is not in the unique nature of anticipating synchronization and its ability to explain observed phenomena, but in how it might be a part of the larger organization of the living system and furnishing it with the complexity required to exhibit anticipatory behavior. Here, the real-time dynamic coupling between the body and the environment, of the type proposed in ecological psychology, when supported by anticipating synchronization, may result in a strong anticipation, a concept bridging ecological psychology and Rosenian school of thought (Stepp and Turvey 2010). The language of dynamical systems seems more promising than computational framework, as it is dynamics that is closer to capture the essence of natural processes, be it physical, chemical, or biological. Computations that may be afforded by such processes should be their emergent consequences and indeed may help us a posteriori to understand and systematize the richness of the ways living systems may have interacted with their environments.

The efforts to understand the interplay between the living systems' capacity to react to future possibilities afforded by dynamic environments and the evolution are already taking place, resulting in the characterization of the complexity levels of the organisms that survive such pressures (see, e.g., Marzen and Crutchfield 2018; Seoane and Solé 2018), although, because of the computational tractability constraints, such models concentrate on simpler organisms. Nevertheless, simplicity is a relative term; even a unicellular living organism belongs to a class of complex systems defined by Rosen, and distinct from a complexity class, to which belong all inanimate objects and processes.

Anticipation is observed across different levels of the phylogenetic tree and organizational complexity (Nasuto and Hayashi 2016a). Anticipating synchronization may be a dynamical systems model candidate to account for at least some of such capacity, but it certainly is not the only alternative (see other examples provided in Nasuto and Hayashi 2016b) or model of anticipatory motor coordination discussed in this chapter. What makes anticipating synchronization appealing is the ubiquity of its defining characteristics in the nervous system and a relative robustness of its behavior, as discussed earlier.

Anticipation may involve responses of the entire organism, linking complex physiological and behavioral adaptations (Buck 2018), and there is an increasing recognition of the importance of extending our understanding of organism regulation beyond homeostasis to allostatic control, in which hormonal interactions with brain mechanisms contribute to anticipatory regulation of body states (Sterling 2012).

There are many empirical studies exploring the importance of future outcomes to immediate behavior of organisms, although most of them are interpreted in terms of expectations and predictions (Butz et al. 2007; Pezzulo et al. 2009). Brain mechanisms must be playing an important role in moderating anticipation and various preparatory brain activities that subserve preparation for future action have been reported for a long time (Nasuto and Hayashi 2016a; van Boxtel and Böcker 2004).

Synchronous oscillations within prefrontal cortex have been implicated in anticipatory stimulus attention (Liang and Wang 2003), especially interesting phenomenon, given the ability of anticipating synchronization to subserve zero-lag synchronization. Recently observed in the primary visual cortex, time-compressed anticipatory preplay of the stimulus sequence (Ekman et al. 2017) provides an intriguing possibility for neural mechanism responsible for time renormalization consequence of anticipating synchronization as reported in analytic studies (Hayashi et al. 2016) and observed in computational modeling of neural motifs (Matias et al. 2016). Studies of posterior parietal cortex neurons in rats, consistent with findings in monkeys and humans, indicate that their activity is related more to the prior stimulus history, than to the ongoing sensory input (Akrami et al. 2018). However, this evidence is not implying a simple working memory function of the posterior parietal cortex, but rather may support anticipatory effects of the past sensory input history on the present performance.

The evidence from such studies, together with evaluation of prior experiments originally interpreted from the predictive computational perspective, as well as the new experiments that will explicitly probe the living systems' abilities to orient to potential future outcomes, will all be needed in order to critically evaluate the Rosenian theory of anticipation. Such a research program will entail characterization of organism's complexity required at different levels of phylogenetic organization to exhibit anticipation, and answering the fundamental question – whether it is indeed the case that anticipation in Rosen's sense is a necessary characteristics of life or, otherwise, at what levels and under what circumstances the computational predictive accounts may do just fine, and under what conditions Rosenian view will prevail.

References

Aitchison, L., & Lengyel, M. (2017). With or without you: Predictive coding and Bayesian inference in the brain. *Current Opinion in Neurobiology, 46*, 219–227. https://doi.org/10.1016/j.conb.2017.08.010. (Computational Neuroscience).

Akrami, A., Kopec, C. D., Diamond, M. E., & Brody, C. D. (2018). Posterior parietal cortex represents sensory history and mediates its effects on behaviour. *Nature, 554*, 368–372. https://doi.org/10.1038/nature25510.

Bickhard, M. H. (2009). The biological foundations of cognitive science. *New Ideas in Psychology, 27*(1), 75–84. https://doi.org/10.1016/j.newideapsych.2008.04.001.

Brovelli, A., Ding, M., Ledberg, A., Chen, Y., Nakamura, R., & Bressler, S. L. (2004). Beta oscillations in a large-scale sensorimotor cortical network: Directional influences revealed by granger causality. *Proceedings of the National Academy of Sciences, 101*(26), 9849–9854. https://doi.org/10.1073/pnas.0308538101.

Buck, C. L. (2018). Hibernation: Life in the fast lane. *eLife, 7*, e35029.

Butz, M., Sigaud, O., Pezzulo, G., & Baldassarre, G. (2007). *Anticipatory behavior in adaptive learning systems: From brains to individual and social behavior.* Berlin/Heidelberg: Springer.

Calvo, O., Chialvo, D., Eguíluz, V., Mirasso, C., & Toral, R. (2004). Anticipated synchronization: A metaphorical linear view. *Chaos, 14*, 7–13. https://doi.org/10.1063/1.1620991.

Ciszak, M., Calvo, O., Masoller, C., Mirasso, C. R., & Toral, R. (2003). Anticipating the response of excitable systems driven by random forcing. *Physical Review Letters, 90*, 204102. https://doi.org/10.1103/PhysRevLett.90.204102.

Ciszak, M., Marino, F., Toral, R., & Balle, S. (2004a). Dynamical mechanism of anticipating synchronization in excitable systems. *Physical Review Letters, 93*, 114102. https://doi.org/10.1103/PhysRevLett.93.114102.

Ciszak, M., Toral, R., & Mirasso, C. (2004b). Coupling and feedback effects in excitable systems: Anticipated synchronization. *Modern Physics Letters B, 18*(23), 1135–1155. https://doi.org/10.1142/S0217984904007694.

Ciszak, M., Mirasso, C. R., Toral, R., & Calvo, O. (2009). Predict-prevent control method for perturbed excitable systems. *Physical Review E, 79*, 046203. https://doi.org/10.1103/PhysRevE.79.046203.

Clark, A. (2013). Whatever next? Predictive brains, situated agents, and the future of cognitive science. *Behavioral and Brain Sciences, 36*(3), 181–204. https://doi.org/10.1017/S0140525X12000477.

Clark, A. (2015). *Surfing uncertainty: Prediction, action, and the embodied mind.* Oxford University Press. Retrieved from https://books.google.co.uk/books?id=TnqECgAAQBAJ.

Corron, N. J., Blakely, J. N., & Pethel, S. D. (2005). Lag and anticipating synchronization without time-delay coupling. *Chaos: An Interdisciplinary Journal of Nonlinear Science, 15*(2), 023110. https://doi.org/10.1063/1.1898597.

Dennett, D. (1996). *Darwin's dangerous idea: Evolution and the meanings of life.* Simon & Schuster. Retrieved from https://books.google.co.uk/books?id=FvRqtnpVotwC.

Eberle, H., Nasuto, S., & Hayashi, Y. (2018). Anticipation from sensation: Using anticipating synchronisation to stabilise a system with inherent sensory delay. *Royal Society Open Science, 5*, 171314.

Ekman, M., Kok, P., & de Lange, F. P. (2017). Time-compressed preplay of anticipated events in human primary visual cortex. *Nature Communications, 8*, 15276. https://doi.org/10.1038/ncomms15276.

Engstrom, D. (1996). Reaction-anticipation transitions in human perception-action patterns. *Human Movement Science, 15*, 809–832.

Haggard, P. (2017). Sense of agency in the human brain [Journal Article]. *Nature Reviews Neuroscience, 18*, 196. https://doi.org/10.1038/nrn.2017.14.

Hayashi, Y., & Kondo, T. (2013). Mechanism for synchronized motion between two humans in mutual tapping experiments: Transition from alternative mode to synchronization mode. *Physical Review E, 88*(2), 022715.

Hayashi, Y., & Sawada, Y. (2013). Transition from an anti-phase error-correction-mode to a synchronization mode in the mutual hand tracking. *Physical Review E, 88*(2), 022704.

Hayashi, Y., Tamura, Y., Sase, K., Sugawara, K., & Sawada, Y. (2011). Intermittently-visual tracking experiments reveal the roles of error-correction and predictive mechanisms in the human visual-motor control system. *Transactions of the Society of Instrument and Control Engineers, 46*(7), 391–400.

Hayashi, Y., Blake, J., & Nasuto, S. (2015). Anticipatory engineering: Anticipation in sensory-motor systems of human. In *Anticipation across disciplines* (Cognitive systems monographs). Switzerland: Springer International Publishing.

Hayashi, Y., Nasuto, S. J., & Eberle, H. (2016). Renormalized time scale for anticipating and lagging synchronization. *Physical Review E, 93*(5), 052229.

Hesslow, G. (2012). The current status of the simulation theory of cognition. *Brain Research, 1428*, 71–79. https://doi.org/10.1016/j.brainres.2011.06.026. Retrieved from http://www.sciencedir ect.com/science/article/pii/S0006899311011309. (The Cognitive Neuroscience of Thought).

Ikegami, T., Hirashima, M., Taga, G., & Nozaki, D. (2010). Asymmetric transfer of visuomotor learning between discrete and rhythmic movements. *The Journal of Neuroscience, 30*(12), 4515–4521.

Ishida, F., & Sawada, Y. (2013). Human hand moves proactively to the external stimulus; An evolutional strategy for minimizing transient error. *Physical Review E, 93*, 168105.

Jordan, D., Smith, P., & Smith, P. (2007). *Nonlinear ordinary differential equations: An introduction for scientists and engineers*. Oxford: Oxford University Press. Retrieved from https://books.google.co.uk/books?id=KpASDAAAQBAJ.

Kawato, M. (1999). Internal models for motor control and trajectory planning. *Current Opinion in Neurobiology, 9*, 718.

Khalil, H. (2002). *Nonlinear systems* (3rd ed.). New Jersey: Prentice Hall.

Liang, H., & Wang, H. (2003). Top-down anticipatory control in prefrontal cortex. *Theory in Biosciences, 122*(1), 70–86. https://doi.org/10.1007/s12064-003-0038-7.

Louie, A. H. (2009). *More than life itself: A synthetic continuation in relational biology*. ontos verlag, Frankfurt [now De Gruyter, Berlin].

Louie, A. H. (2010). Robert Rosen's anticipatory systems. *Foresight, 12*(3), 18–29.

Louie, A. H. (2019). Relational biology. In R. Poli (Ed.), *Handbook of anticipation: Theoretical and applied aspects of the use of future in decision making* (pp. 1–28). Cham: Springer International Publishing.

Louie, A. H., & Poli, R. (2019). Complex systems. In R. Poli (Ed.), *Handbook of anticipation: Theoretical and applied aspects of the use of future in decision making* (pp. 1–19). Cham: Springer International Publishing.

Marzen, S. E., & Crutchfield, J. P. (2018). Optimized bacteria are environmental prediction engines. Phys. Rev. E 98, 012408.

Mates, J. (1994). A model of synchronization of motor acts to a stimulus sequence. I. Timing and error corrections. *Biological Cybernetics, 70*(5), 463–473.

Matias, F. S., Carelli, P. V., Mirasso, C. R., & Copelli, M. (2011). Anticipated synchronization in a biologically plausible model of neuronal motifs. *Physical Review E, 84*, 021922. https://doi.org/10.1103/PhysRevE.84.021922.

Matias, F. S., Gollo, L. L., Carelli, P. V., Bressler, S. L., Copelli, M., & Mirasso, C. R. (2014). Modeling positive granger causality and negative phase lag between cortical areas. *NeuroImage, 99*, 411–418. https://doi.org/10.1016/j.neuroimage.2014.05.063.

Matias, F. S., Carelli, P. V., Mirasso, C. R., & Copelli, M. (2015). Self-organized near-zero-lag synchronization induced by spike-timing dependent plasticity in cortical populations. *PLoS One, 10*(10), 1–18. https://doi.org/10.1371/journal.pone.0140504.

Matias, F. S., Gollo, L. L., Carelli, P. V., Mirasso, C. R., & Copelli, M. (2016). Inhibitory loop robustly induces anticipated synchronization in neuronal microcircuits. *Physical Review E, 94*, 042411. https://doi.org/10.1103/PhysRevE.94.042411.

Maturana, H., & Varela, F. (1991). *Autopoiesis and cognition: The realization of the living*. Springer Netherlands.

Middleton, A. (2000). Basal ganglia and cereberllar loops: Motor and cognitive circuits. *Brain Research Reviews, 31*, 236–250.

Mirasso, C. R., Carelli, P. V., Pereira, T., Matias, F. S., & Copelli, M. (2017). Anticipated and zero-lag synchronization in motifs of delay-coupled systems. *Chaos: An Interdisciplinary Journal of Nonlinear Science, 27*(11), 114305. https://doi.org/10.1063/1.5006932.

Mita, A., Mushiake, H., Shima, K., Matsuzaka, Y., & Tanji, J. (2009). Interval time coding by neurons in the presupplementary and supplementary motor areas. *Nature Neuroscience, 12*, 502–507.

Nasuto, S. J., & Hayashi, Y. (2016a). Anticipation: Beyond synthetic biology and cognitive robotics. *BioSystems, 148*, 22–31.

Nasuto, S. J., & Hayashi, Y. (2016b). Synapses in digital medium: Computational investigations of neural basis of anticipation. In M. Nadin (Ed.), *Anticipation across disciplines* (pp. 187–201). Cham: Springer International Publishing.

Oguchi, T. (2007). A finite spectrum assignment for retarded non-linear systems and its solvability condition. *International Journal of Control, 80*(6), 898–907. https://doi.org/10.1080/1749951 0701204166.

Oguchi, T. (2017). Anticipating synchronization and state predictor for nonlinear systems. In N. van de Wouw, E. Lefeber, & I. Lopez Arteaga (Eds.), *Nonlinear systems: Techniques for dynamical analysis and control* (pp. 103–122). Cham: Springer International Publishing.

Oguchi, T., & Nijmeijer, H. (2005a). Control of nonlinear systems with time-delay using state predictor based on synchronization. In *Proceedings of the ENOC 2005* (pp. 1150–1156).

Oguchi, T., & Nijmeijer, H. (2005b). Prediction of chaotic behavior. *IEEE Transactions on Circuits and Systems, 52-I*(11), 2464–2472. https://doi.org/10.1109/TCSI.2005.853396.

Oguchi, T., & Nijmeijer, H. (2006). Anticipating synchronization of nonlinear systems with uncertainties. *IFAC Proceedings Volumes, 39*(10), 290–295. https://doi.org/10.3182/20060710-3-IT-4901.00048. (6th IFAC Workshop on Time Delay Systems).

Pezzulo, G., Butz, M., Sigaud, O., & Baldassarre, G. (2009). *Anticipatory behavior in adaptive learning systems: From psychological theories to artificial cognitive systems*. Berlin/Heidelberg: Springer.

Port, R., & Van Gelder, T. (1998). *Mind as motion: Explorations in the dynamics of cognition*. MIT Press. Retrieved from https://books.google.co.uk/books?id=rY2IPwAACAAJ.

Preston, J., & Bishop, M. (2002). *Views into the Chinese room: New essays on Searle and artificial intelligence*. Clarendon Press. Retrieved from https://books.google.co.uk/books?id=0V6Pw UrH2aYC.

Pyragas, K., & Pyragienė, T. (2008). Coupling design for a long-term anticipating synchronization of chaos. *Physical Review E, 78*, 046217. https://doi.org/10.1103/PhysRevE.78.046217.

Pyragienė, T., & Pyragas, K. (2013). Anticipating spike synchronization in nonidentical chaotic neurons. *Nonlinear Dynamics, 74*(1), 297–306.

Pyragienė, T., & Pyragas, K. (2017). Anticipatory synchronization via low-dimensional filters. *Physics Letters A, 381*(22), 1893–1898. https://doi.org/10.1016/j.physleta.2017.04.005.

Repp, B. (2005). Sensorimotor synchronization. A review of the tapping literature. *Psychonomic Bulletin Review, 12*(6), 969–992.

Rosen, R. (2012). Anticipatory systems. In *Anticipatory systems* (pp. 313–370). New York: Springer.

Seligman, M. E., Railton, P., Baumeister, R. F., & Sripada, C. (2013). Navigating into the future or driven by the past. *Perspectives on Psychological Science, 8*(2), 119–141.

Seoane, L. F., & Solé, R. V. (2018). Information theory, predictability and the emergence of complex life. *Open Science, 5*(2). https://doi.org/10.1098/rsos.172221.

Spencer, M. C., Roesch, E. B., Nasuto, S. J., Tanay, T., & Bishop, J. M. (2013, March). Abstract platforms of computation. In *Aisb 2013* (pp. 25–32). Exeter. Retrieved from http://centaur. reading.ac.uk/35696/. (Published in: The 6th AISB symposium on computing and philosophy: The scandal of computation – What is computation? Mark Bishop and Yasemin J. Erden (editors) AISB Convention 2013, University of Exeter, 3–5 April 2013. Published by The Society for the Study of Artificial Intelligence and the Simulation of Behaviour. http://www. aisb.org.uk. ISBN: 9781908187314).

Stepp, N. (2009). Anticipation in feedback-delayed manual tracking of a chaotic oscillator. *Experimental Brain Research, 198*, 521.

Stepp, N., & Frank, T. (2009). A data-analysis method for decomposing synchronization variability of anticipatory systems into stochastic and deterministic components. *The European Physical Journal B-Condensed Matter and Complex Systems, 67*(2), 251–257.

Stepp, N., & Turvey, M. (2010). On strong anticipation. *Cognitive Systems Research, 11*(2), 148–164. https://doi.org/10.1016/j.cogsys.2009.03.003.

Sterling, P. (2012). Allostasis: A model of predictive regulation. *Physiology & Behavior, 106*(1), 5–15. https://doi.org/10.1016/j.physbeh.2011.06.004. (Allostasis and Allostatic Load).

Stewart, J., Gapenne, O., & Di Paolo, E. (2010). *Enaction: Toward a new paradigm for cognitive science*. Cambridge, MA: MIT Press.

Synofzik, M., Vosgerau, G., & Newen, G. (2007). Beyond the comparator model: A multifactorial two-step account of agency. *Consciousness and Cognition, 17*(1), 219–239.

Thompson, E. (2010). *Mind in life: Biology, phenomenology, and the sciences of mind*. Cambridge, MA: Harvard University Press.

van Boxtel, G. J., & Böcker, K. B. (2004). Cortical measures of anticipation. *Journal of Psychophysiology, 18*(2–3), 61–76. https://doi.org/10.1027/0269-8803.18.23.61.

Vernon, D., Beetz, M., & Sandini, G. (2015). Prospection in cognition: The case for joint episodic-procedural memory in cognitive robotics. *Frontiers in Robotics and AI, 2*, 19. https://doi.org/ 10.3389/frobt.2015.00019. Retrieved from https://www.frontiersin.org/article/10.3389/frobt. 2015.00019.

Voss, H. U. (2000). Anticipating chaotic synchronization. *Physical Review E, 61*, 5115–5119. https://doi.org/10.1103/PhysRevE.61.5115.

Voss, H. U. (2001). Dynamic long-term anticipation of chaotic states. *Physical Review Letters, 87*, 014102. https://doi.org/10.1103/PhysRevLett.87.014102.

Voss, H. U. (2016a). The leaky integrator with recurrent inhibition as a predictor. *Neural Computation, 28*, 1498.

Voss, H. U. (2016b). Signal prediction by anticipatory relaxation dynamics. *Physical Review E, 93*(3), 030201. https://doi.org/10.1103/PhysRevE.93.030201.

Voss, H. U. (2016c). A simple predictor based on delay-induced negative group delay. *ArXiv e-prints*.

Voss, H. U. (2018). A delayed-feedback filter with negative group delay, Chaos: An Interdisciplinary Journal of Nonlinear Science 28, 113113.

Ward, L., & Press, M. (2002). *Dynamical cognitive science*. MIT Press. Retrieved from https:// books.google.co.uk/books?id=g1ZMAoWGYesC.

Wiener, N., & Schadé, J. (1963). Introduction to neurocybernetics. In N. Wiener & J. Schadé (Eds.), *Progress in Brain Research, 2*, p. 1–7. Elsevier. https://doi.org/10.1016/S0079-6123(08) 62055-5. Retrieved from http://www.sciencedirect.com/science/article/pii/S007961230862 0555.

Wiggins, S. (2006). *Introduction to applied nonlinear dynamical systems and chaos*. New York: Springer. Retrieved from https://books.google.co.uk/books?id=YhXnBwAAQBAJ.

Microgenesis of Anticipation: Windowing the Present

14

Liliana Albertazzi

Contents

Abstract

This chapter analyses the micro-genesis of anticipation in awareness and shows how the internal determinants of anticipation construe our perception of empirical reality. Rooted in the psychic present, anticipation occurs in very short durations. Anticipation develops in phases allowing temporal and spatial displacements, and it includes an internal model of itself. Examples are given from visual, acoustic and motion perception, showing the anticipatory structure of awareness in subjective space-time. Finally, anticipation in perception throws light on the deep roots of semantics.

Keywords

Anticipation · Awareness · Contextual perceptions · Embedded future · Microgenesis · Subjective space-time

L. Albertazzi (✉)
Laboratory of Experimental Phenomenology, Department of Humanities, University of Trento, Trento, Italy
e-mail: liliana.albertazzi@unitn.it

© Springer Nature Switzerland AG 2019
R. Poli (ed.), *Handbook of Anticipation*,
https://doi.org/10.1007/978-3-319-91554-8_13

Plurivocity in the Concept Anticipation

Anticipation is necessary for survival. Specifically, life itself is anticipatory, as a necessary condition for being alive (Rosen 1985/2012, 1991; Louie 2009, 2013). There are, however, different anticipatory strategies that a living organism can put into action. A rather simple case of anticipatory behavior is based on past experience. Hence it is a kind of inferential reasoning and is explainable in terms of forecasting. For example, knowing that, notwithstanding their appealing colorful appearances, certain mushrooms or berries are poisonous enables an animal to avoid gathering them and eating them. This type of anticipation is fairly explained on the basis of the theory of adaptation and evolution. Another kind of anticipation is future oriented (foresight), i.e., the analytical exploration of possible futures. This type of anticipation, however, usually includes neither complexity nor the understanding of the nature of the structural psychological components responsible for the phenomenon. A third type of anticipation is based on future expectation, which means adopting a forward-looking stance and using it to change the present conditions. In other words, implementing future scenarios in our actual behavior requires a good deal of imagination, but it must be grounded in the present conditions (Appadurai 2013; Louie 2016; Louie and Poli 2011; Poli 2011, 2012, 2014a, b, 2017). This handbook is explicitly conceived in these terms (Poli 2017). A fourth kind of anticipation, related to this view, and taking the psychological determinants of anticipation into consideration, is responsible for how we actually experience the environment. Because it is rooted in our perceptual and mental structures, it follows specific laws of subjective completion in awareness (Kanizsa 1979; Libet 2004; Wertheimer 1912/2012). This kind of anticipation, which occurs in very short durations, is unavoidable in the construction of our empirical reality and also embeds fringes of the future (Husserl 1966/1991, 1939/1973). Furthermore, it is not reducible to psychophysical and/or neurophysiological behavior, because it contains an internal and predictive model of itself, which is not explained by external causes (Albertazzi 2013, 2015; Albertazzi and Louie 2016; Poli 2017). In this chapter I shall deal with this kind of anticipation, highlighting the peculiarity of its microgenetic format as distinct from anticipation as inference and/or prediction.

Anticipation as Inferential Reasoning

In science, most understanding and explanation of human behavior in relation to the information present in the environment are currently given in terms of inferential behavior. In other words, anticipation is framed as a general inferential attitude based on already stored data, such as memory traces, and/or following the logical inference of the type "if smoke, then fire" (Lukasiewicz 1934/1970; Mates 1953). However, the anticipation occurring in perceptual phenomena is not merely a recovery of past experience on which to forecast: if smoke, then fire; if clouds, then rain; and if war, then death. This kind of anticipation, as correctly noted by Hume (1975), can produce probabilistic predictions based on an inferential reasoning, but not that kind of certainty based on the uncontroversial evidence of what is given in actual awareness, which is complex, qualitative, and meaningful wholes, not a sum of sense data.

Also in perception studies, as in other research fields, inferentialism is currently the dominant viewpoint based on probabilistic computations (Gregory 1998; Rock 1977, 1983). The ecological perspective (Gibson 1954), a widely held mainstream view some decades ago, which suggests a direct access to the physical information to be found in the environment, has been almost completely superseded by the probabilistic viewpoint, augmented by the development of the so-called computational predictive models. Inferentialism maintains that, in perceiving, our brain regularly and continuously applies probabilistic hypotheses based on past experience to the surrounding physical environment in order to make sense of it. Perception theory has therefore become largely a Bayesian simulation analysis of the metrical aspects (cues) of physical reality, considered as the proper objects of both natural science and human perception, according to the tenets of the computational theory of vision (Marr 1982). However, this framework draws no semantic distinction between the meaning externally assigned to the metric stimulus by scientists and those internally perceived by subjects in awareness, for the simple reason that they are assumed to coincide: the stimulus essentially becomes a description of the perceptual presentation and vice versa (Albertazzi et al. 2010; Vishwanath 2005).

Because of the exponential increase of computational techniques and algorithmic models in scientific inquiry, the boundary between reality and simulation of reality has become evanescent. Moreover, it has further excluded the analysis of the qualitative aspects of perceiving as immediately and directly given in our experience. This comes as no surprise because of the Galilean-Newtonian idea of science, which excludes, by default, the consideration of (subjective) secondary properties relative to color, taste, flavor, etc. (Galileo 1623/1957). Interestingly, however, the inferentialist conception produces an odd consequence. It would seem that our brain – constantly engaged in a sort of wager on the meaning of the stimuli that it receives and that it can only sensorially detect and elaborate through neural electrochemical paths – is also continuously making mistakes. One thinks of the *pervasive* presence of the so-called perceptual illusions in the environment, primarily the phenomenon of partial occlusion of objects by other objects, of surfaces by other surfaces, or the phenomenon of masking, where objects lose their identity in the context of other objects (Figs. 1 and 2).

The usual explanation of the constitutive ambiguity and "illusory" character of our perception is that, for example, phenomena such as the so-called apparent size (Ebbinghaus 1902; Müller-Lyer 1889; Ponzo 1912), apparent movement (Wertheimer 1912; Kenkel 1913), or apparent causality (Michotte 1954; Michotte et al. 1963) remind us of the discrepancy between the physical objective reality of the stimuli and the probabilistic interpretation that we are able to give of them. Each of these labels (apparent movement, size, causality), then, consists of different phenomena characterized by their own specific structure. In other words, they are not equivalent. For example, the term "apparent movement" blurs a diversified series of perceptive events

Fig. 1 One sees a square partially covering a triangle partially covering a circle

Fig. 2 The star is no more retrievable in the configuration to the right (Metzger 1975/2006)

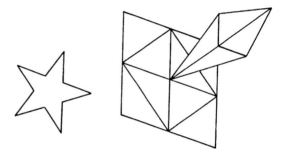

comprising several phenomena such as objectless movement (or φ movement), configurational movement (β movement, see below), movement with replacement, induced movement, gamma movement, anorthoscopic movement, stereokinetic movement (see below), autokinesis, aftereffect movement, etc. (Palmer 1999, Chap. 10. See also: http://epunix.biols.sussex.ac.uk/Home/George_Mather/Movement/index.htm). Conceptually, the inferentialist approach conceives *anticipation as an activity of scorekeeping*; factually, it reveals a constitutive fragility of our capacity to orient ourselves in the environment surrounding us, and its scant reliability. Within the probabilistic framework, however, it is entirely inexplicable why, for example, once I know on the basis of past experience (say, because I myself drew them) that the vertical lines of the Hering illusion are parallel, I compellingly see them as curved (Hering 1920/1964). And the same holds for other "illusions" (Fig. 3).

There are several unquestioned assumptions at the foundations of inferentialism and its concept of anticipation. For example, the assumptions that the ontologically unique objective reality is described by physics, that our perception of reality is ruled by psychophysical laws of behavioral response to physical stimuli according to a linear and unidirectional order of cause and effect, that the same predictive models are a product of causally efficient laws based on previous information, and that the perception of qualities is not a matter for scientific analysis, because it is subjective and not explainable in terms of third person account. However, when we realize that

Fig. 3 The two parallel lines appear to diverge (Hering/ Wundt). https://commons. wikimedia.org/wiki/File: Hering_illusion.svg

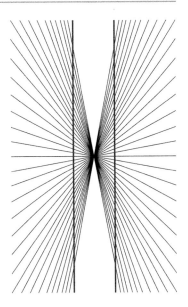

species very different from ours are "victims" of the same "illusions" (Sovrano et al. 2014, 2015), the mainstream explanation becomes even more puzzling: should we believe that this widespread erroneous behavior in living organisms is induced by nature?

Put briefly, the inferentialist explanation of structural perceptual ambiguity is cumbersome and ecologically implausible. Yet its computational applicability (for restricted purposes), consisting in the mere transformation of syntactic structures into other syntactic structures, makes it difficult to dismiss in current science. Most of all, an inferentialist viewpoint on reality only partially explains what it means *to perceive, which is essentially a conscious, subjective, meaningful, qualitative process imbued with value and emotional tone, and dynamically anticipating the lines of its forward potential deployment.* We live neither in a static present nor in a series of unrelated snapshots. Unity of consciousness is an assumption necessary to explain our conscious life, and it implies anticipatory processes already in its microstructures.

Beyond Inferences and Representations

The best way out of the theoretical quagmire of inferentialism is the adoption of a radical standpoint starting again from what one perceives *as it is given* in actual seeing, hearing, touching, etc., and in its cross-modal interactions. To be radical, however, one has to accept that what we experience in awareness are essentially not metric stimuli as such, but qualitative phenomena given *in presence* and *with evidence* (Brentano 1874/1995; Albertazzi 2013). What humans and/or living beings perceive is not totally reducible to physical information. It also comprises those aspects of perception that make sense to them, primarily the qualitative dimensions necessary for the interaction between the species and the environment. Not only is the process that occurs in perceiving nonlinear, in that it works on several dimensions at different levels of granularity, but it is also impredicative, in the sense that the laws of its internal deployment are embedded in it. The dimensions of subjective experience, in fact, appear to behave as components of a self-referential system (Albertazzi and Louie 2016) ruled by internal laws and specific kinds of causation – final causes included. These processes are apparent in the dynamic of whole/part organization of the percept (Albertazzi 2017, in press), where *the whole anticipates and influences the role of the parts*, or in the phenomenon of *Prägnanz* of shapes, i.e., the tendency to reach the best configuration out of potentially (physically) indefinite numbers of possible configurations if considered from an inferential viewpoint (Wertheimer 1923). The inferentialist approach, as said, attributes an important role for knowing our environment to conscious and unconscious inferences. As regards unconscious phenomena, Brentano lucidly observed in the formative period of psychophysics that a psychic phenomenon as such is necessarily conscious; otherwise, it is another kind of phenomenon, i.e., a physiological one (Brentano 1874/1995). (Needless to say, Brentano never denied the *correlation* between (neuro)physiology and psychology.) As to conscious phenomena, Brentano analyzed the nature of an act of *presentation* as a conscious phenomenon, internally given, of qualitative contents and internal relations, and totally distinct from the concept of *representation* of a stimulus (i.e., of an external objective reality) mainstream in science today. In Brentano's theory of consciousness, the phenomena appearing in awareness, such as visual appearances, forms of grouping and multistability, relationships of similarity, etc., are subjective, purely mental phenomena. To make the point clear, Brentano's conception is the opposite of eliminative materialism, which maintains that subjective mental phenomena are reducible to the physical events of neural cells (Singer 2000). However, the activity of nerve cells, even at the cortical level, does not necessarily trigger a subjective experience, which is an idea that goes in favor of Brentano's view. For example, the neuroscientist Libet has shown that there are short trains of electrical impulses, of about 100 ms that arrive at the cerebral cortex where they induce a response by nerve cells, although without triggering any subjective experience (Libet 1973, 1985; Libet et al. 1991, and below). In other words, what occurs at the level of brain circuits does not explain the nature of qualitative, conscious awareness.

Currently, scientists are still trying to shed light on the nature of consciousness from a systematic and experimental viewpoint. They do so by relying on different methodologies and techniques. In this field, however, it seems difficult to reach agreement. Neuroscience has not made significant progress within this framework because it has essentially changed the reference from one kind of simulating computer (the mind) to another (the brain), which is assumed to behave according to inferential-probabilistic principles, rather than logical-deductive ones. However, doubts have been raised concerning the digital computational nature of the brain, because of statistical variations in movement and brain cell death (Edelman 2004) and because mental functions do not necessarily have to be algorithmic (Penrose 1989).

A distinctive feature of our conscious experiences is that, strictly speaking, they are not "states" at all, as conceived, for example, in a Marrian approach of standard cognitive science. This approach, in fact, considers the body to be a physiological substrate in a wetware computer running the algorithm proposed by artificial intelligence that causes certain brain locations to be in certain *states.* All our perceptual and mental contents are subjectively, temporally, and dynamically deploying in the present: they are subjective *events,* taking place in brief durations (standardly of about 700 ms, whose maximum limits are 2–3 s: see, e.g., Pöppel and Bao 2014). These events extend in subjective space. They are ruled by specific laws of organization which are responsible also for phenomena of temporal and spatial displacement of the perceived stimuli and of which *the future, although in a handful of msec, shapes the appearance* (Albertazzi 1999, 2001, 2011; Benussi 1913; Fraisse 1957/ 1964; Vicario 2003; and below). Consciousness does not occur in discrete, atomic, linearly successive, unrelated snapshots like the states of an algorithmic machine. Perception, instead, is a *process of anticipation* that continuously produces the next thread (i.e., the next "now") of perceptual experience while the current one fades away. As Wertheimer pointed out long ago, our mental life is made of processes (*Gestalten*) and part/processes experienced in continuity (Wertheimer 1923; Albertazzi 2006). Present consciousness (also termed "psychic present," "specious present," "psychic time," "subjective time," "time of presentness," "time of contemporaneity," "experienced time," "duration," "interval of indifference," etc.) (see Stern 1897; James 1890/1950; Benussi 1913; Libet 2004) and its mental events, however, are equivocal terms in current science. Of the dozen or so *definitions* of psychic present to be found in the literature, none explains what *being consciously present* means. On the other hand, mental events have a grammar of their own. Metzger gave a provisional taxonomy with which to start classifying them according to specific characteristics (Metzger 1941). He distinguished among stationary, nonstationary, quasi-stationary, and quasi-continuous events, all of which share the basic trait of *not being static states.* Some of these events, such as *nonstationary* and *quasi-continuous events*, are very interesting from the viewpoint of the microstructure of anticipation and of the type of causality ruling their appearance.

The Future in the Present

Nonstationary events occur when the stimulation is not constant, as in movement perception or in the change of a quality: for example, a visual line that elongates or is misshapen, a surface that changes color, and the variety of multistable figures. The well-known phenomena of bistability like the old/young woman and the duck/rabbit illusions, or Michotte's parallelepiped (Michotte 1948/1991) pertain to these events (Fig. 4).

Among these illusions, the Necker cube (the natural appearance of crystals, in fact) furnishes a great deal of information on the microgenesis of appearances in the present, as to its anticipatory phases, the behavior of the visible parts, and the inner causality of the whole (Kopferman 1930). Each perceptual *phase* in see*ing* a

Necker's cube according to its embedded different vistas refers to a segment of the temporal object deploying in the presentation (Fig. 5).

During the temporal unfolding of the subjective presentation of a Necker cube, its different appearances are each time *anticipated* by the virtual viewpoint in subjective space assumed by the observer, due to the plurivocal nature of the object. The Necker cube, in fact, can appear to be entirely flat, like a hexagon divided by diagonals or radiuses; or when it is rotated in 3D, it appears to be a cube or a six-sided pyramid. Specifically, in the 2D hexagon configuration, all the internal lines behave as radiuses, or as diagonals from the enclosing boundary lines; the six border points have the same function, unlike the midpoint, and the six inner triangles have the same role, while the inner surface is only the base. In this mode of appearance of the Necker cube, the variation also follows the symmetry of the parts. In the case of the 3D cube configuration, instead, all the lines have the same function as the sides of the cube; all the points have the same function as points of the cube, and the midpoint becomes an angle point. Finally, when the 3D figure is seen as a pyramid, the role of the parts is similar to that in 2D; the inner "base" surface has a stronger role than in 2D (it is not divided into triangles, but forms a whole: an intermediate unity between the triangles and the pyramid), and the mid-point is seen as a dot. There is no unilinear, unidirectional causality to produce a univocal appearance of "the" Necker cube! From time to time, it *is* a flat hexagonal surface,

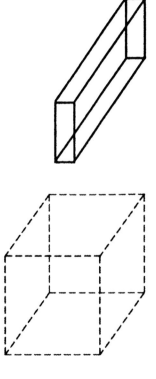

Fig. 4 The parallelepiped appears to "stand up," with one base attached to the paper and the rest of the body elevated in the space above the sheet. One sees a truncated pyramid (Michotte 1948)

Fig. 5 The figure may appear as a transparent cube leaned on a table, or as a cube hanged on the ceiling, or as a box on the floor of which one can see the inner parts through the top

like a coat of arms, a regular solid bounded by six flat faces or, better, a box-shaped object. A Necker cube, like any other object of a conscious presentation, is not an objective representation of a stimulus! Patently, this phenomenon is a paradigmatic example of the inner structure of a presentation, which in its temporal unfolding anticipates potential appearances of the same physical stimulus.

Consider the Penrose (so-called impossible) triangle (Fig. 6).

Here again in a visual presentation, there are multiple perceptions shifting in 2D, 3D, and 4D as inner parts of the whole "triangle" appearance, which as such does not remain stable in the visual field. In this case, the triangle's different partial appearances are *anticipated by subjective different visual bounding* because of the continuous attentional shifts of the observer directed to potential different bounds: the visual shifting produces the appearance of different wholes, although they always remain incomplete. In fact, on all three sides, one extremity is seen to be a modally completed behind another, and consequently, each intersecting pair appears to have a precise 3D orientation. If one hides any of the vertices, one can see a 3D structure with three segments, each pointing in the direction of the axes (x, y, z) and therefore at 90° to each other. The triangle's "impossibility" is due to the two nonadjacent segments of this structure *being seen* to meet in the third vertex when the lines that they define in 3D space clearly should not have any points in common. Note that if one hides any one side of the triangle (i.e., two vertices), it is possible to complete the triangular structure appropriately. This is because the two remaining sides define a 2D structure only (namely, a plane), any two points of which can be simply connected by a third segment. This phenomenon is another good example of the spatial grammar of an *implicit anticipation* (of "a triangular shape") which resides in the foundational subjective structure of perception. It also shows the presence of *phases (part of)* correlated in a deploying unitary presentation. Once again, explaining this phenomenon in terms of a direct reflection/representation of the well-structured behavior of the physical world would be an error: what one sees is internally construed in the present awareness.

Other phenomena interesting from the point of view of anticipation are *quasi-continuous events* exhibiting an evolving pattern with and island of stability: consider, for example, a vortex or fireworks. A paradigmatic example of these phenomena is provided by stereokinetic shapes (Musatti 1924, 1955, 1975; for a detailed discussion of the phenomenon, see Albertazzi 2004; Vezzani et al. 2015). Stereokinetic shapes show the tendency, in awareness, for slowly rotating complex planes

Fig. 6 The triangle does not show any anomaly if seen sequentially. Focusing on its 3D structure, however, it appears as an impossible object https://en.wikipedia.org/wiki/Penrose_triangle

to anticipate and develop into solid bodies moving in three-dimensional space (Fig. 7).

For example, given a black disc on which a white ellipse is drawn, and put in slow rotation, what one sees is first the rotation of the ellipse upon itself; then a *deforming elastic ring*; then a *rigid disc (a coin with finite thickness) seen at an angle, of which the closest point to the observer is constantly changing* (3D); and finally *an inverting* disc (3D).

In particular, stereokinetic movements evidence the nature of the continuous movement ruled by the law of common fate (again a final cause) that characterizes a large part of perceived movement. In fact, because common fate induces the components involved to assume the role of a figure, it is responsible for anticipation the percept of a single constantly moving figure (i.e., a whole), rather than a complex of distinct elements in relative movement (i.e., parts as pieces).

Another paradigmatic example of the unitary anticipation of a visual phenomenon through internal phases and relations is provided by stroboscopic movement (or β motion) (Wertheimer 1912/2012; Kenkel 1913; Beck et al. 1977), a phenomenon that deploys in five phases.

This phenomenon, which is classified among the so-called apparent motions, consists of *one perceived moving* light which takes up the two *physically stationary* lights that light in succession at a very short interstimulus interval (ISI) of about 50 ms. The perceived movement in this phenomenon is a whole that belongs to both light spots, which are no longer perceivable as two distinct and independent stimuli. Also in this case, a Gestalt law of whole/part organization (again ruled by a final cause) operates. The whole that is seen is classically something different from (and more than) the sum of the parts: the one moving light is something new and unpredictable, forming the viewpoint of the characteristics of the physical cues (Fig. 8).

Stroboscopic movement is particularly interesting from the point of view of its cause, because the classic notion of causality does not apply in this case. In fact, the light *moves* from A to B only if spot B lights up. Consequently, the cause of movement for spot A is something happening in spot B, but spot B lights up after spot A has been

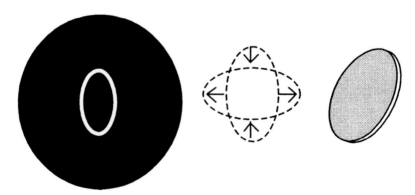

Fig. 7 Placed in slow rotation, after a while the 2D ellipsis appears as an elastic ring, then a disc stably oriented and shifted in space (Musatti 1955, pp. 16–19)

Fig. 8 Five phases of activation of two lights (l_1, l_2). Interstimulus interval (ISI) is the duration of phase c. White discs = light off; black discs = light on. If ISI < 10 ms, one sees two fixed lights. If ISI > 500 ms, one sees two fixed lights alternatively present to the right or to the left. If ISI ca 50 ms, one sees one light in motion from left to right (β movement) (Image in Vicario 2005, p. 186)

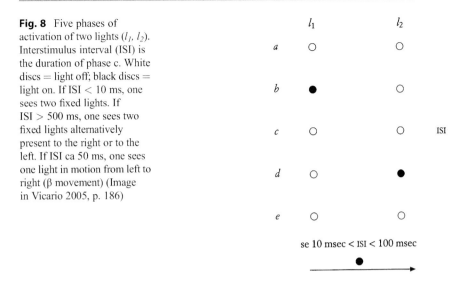

turned off: hence the cause of the departure of A is *somehow in the future* of A (by ca 50 ms)! In other words, we perceive the beginning of the movement of a spot of light before we perceive its arrival at its final standpoint. The phenomenon again shows that causality in awareness is not strictly ruled by the before-after relation, but depends on a relational structure. In fact, the non-independent parts of the event simultaneously cause the event, and what happens afterwards influences what happens before (though within well-established temporal boundaries). The β movement shows how a visual presentation actually develops on a brief present-time scale in anticipating phases of the final percept. These varieties of phenomena of so-called apparent movement also show that the perception of movement does not derive from the memory of experiencing an object that has changed place (the Zenonian-logical thesis). They are not atomic objects in a space container but effects of perceptual organization in the visual field (Koffka 1935/1999, ch. 3).

A related phenomenon is the so-called window effect, whereby *what comes afterwards has an effect on what comes before* (Vicario and Zambianchi 1998). The effect consists in a rectangular luminous surface in the darkness that deploys as in Fig. 9, according to three different phases.

In a first phase *a*, the surface expands from ds to sn: only the "head" of the surface is in motion, while its "tail" is at rest, and the phase *a* lasts until the surface reaches it maximum length. In the second phase *b*, three events may occur: b_1, the tail starts moving before the head has stopped, rendering the time interval st < 0; b_2, the tail starts moving in the same instant in which the head stops, rendering the time interval st = 0; in b_3, the tail starts moving some time after the stop of the head, rendering the time interval st > 0. In the third phase *c*, the head is immobile, and the tail is in motion until it reaches the head, making the surface disappear. Consider now the phase b_3: the strip in motion arrives from ds, and in a short time, its head reaches the margin of the surface to the left. At this point the head can do two things: (a) stop at

Fig. 9 Evolution of the
stimuli in the window effect
(Vicario 1964. Image in
Vicario 2005, p. 60)

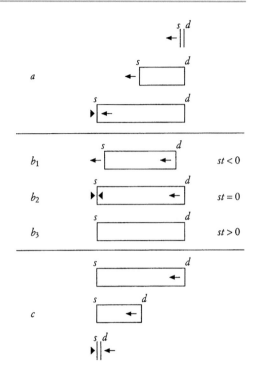

the margin and (b) continue behind the margin. The event which decides whether (a) or (b) will occur is the moment in which the tails appear, which can follow within 100 ms, within 300 ms, or within whatever interval of physical time. If the tail appears within 100 ms, the head will have passed behind the margin; if the tail appears within 300 ms or more, the head will have remained at the margin. Put briefly, the behavior of the head of the strip, at a certain instant of physical time, depends on the physical instant in which the tail appears, which, however, is still to come! In other words, also for this event, pertaining to the microstructure of intervals, *the cause is in the future*!

Other interesting examples of what may happen in the microgenesis of events in consciousness – in comparison with the "objectivity" and the linear succession of the stimuli according to the instants of metric time – are provided by temporal displacements in acoustic (and visual) perception, which show the capacity of consciousness to anticipate (and also to delay) at qualitative perceptual level in the order of the physical stimuli. These phenomena relate to the fact that, for example, a sequence of very brief stimuli can be perceived as a whole and that the different qualitative saliences of the stimuli of the sequence may cause their rearrangement in the perceived succession. Briefly, what happens is that elements perceptually more relevant from a qualitative viewpoint may be *heard* (or *seen*) before (negative displacement) or after (positive displacement) the perceptually less relevant ones (Benussi 1913). Experiments conducted with triplets of very brief noises, consisting of two even and one odd elements (A1-B-A2) (Rubin 1949), or with triplets of pure tones well separated in tonal space and in the absence of interstimulus intervals (H1 = 1760 Hz; L = 82.4 Hz; H2 = 1568 Hz) (Vicario 1982) have shown that temporal displacements are facilitated in the former case by the *similarity* between the two As, in concurrence with small durations for B and for the interval between B and A2, and that for triplets lasting 300 ms (100 ms for each member of them); as in the latter case, observers report hearing first the two high tones and then the low one (the odd element undergoes a positive displacement).

It is thus apparent that the perceived succession itself is a whole (a Gestalt), its appearance depending more on *the internal qualitative relations* among its components (such as similarity, tonal proximity, etc.) than on the physical sequence of stimuli. This also means that the perceived sounds in the actual presentation have undergone a *reorganization* of the order of the sequence of the stimuli, according to the qualitative level of grouping: some components *are perceived in advance* relatively to their physical sequence because, for example, "sounds" group together, pushing away "noises" (Fig. 10).

Interestingly, the phenomenon does not occur at macro-level, i.e., when the stimuli are presented with different temporal lengths (say, of seconds). Specifically, if A1 and A2 are prolonged to 1 s each, no temporal displacement occurs. One hears a succession A1-A2 without continuity, and the element B is heard as somehow "floating in an elsewhere" difficult to localize temporally as a "lateral" presence. The simultaneity can extend to succession as well, if it is perceived in a unitary duration (Benussi 1913; Fraisse 1957/1964). Notwithstanding the fact that phenomena of temporal displacement occur in the microgenesis of conscious presence, the role of tonal salience and of the internal relations among the components is at work also in the case of extended acoustic durations such as melodies (see Hachen and Albertazzi, this handbook).

All these phenomena show that the anticipatory structure of consciousness relative to a subjective spatiotemporal field (the psychic present) does not deploy

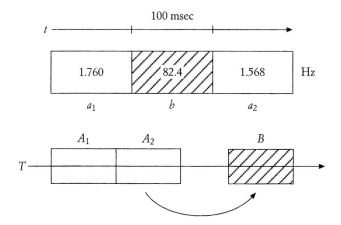

Fig. 10 Above, the disposition of the stimuli to observe a temporal dislocation. Below, what one hears. *t* axis of physical time; *T* axis of the phenomenal time (Image in Vicario 2005, p. 112)

in instants of metric time such as t_1, t_2, and t_n, but in thick moments of time characterized by different durations and positions according to the specific phenomenon, and with embedded fringes of anticipation. The microgenetic analysis of phenomena in consciousness shows that we deal with a deformable subjective space/time extension, *tuned to the specific context* with limited contents, and dynamically unfolding, to produce an actually *becoming* object, i.e., a specific type of event not necessarily mapped on the physical stimuli.

The leveled series of brief durations occurring in the micro- and macrogenesis of a presentation were already identified by Benussi (1913) and Calabresi (1930) at the beginning of the last century. They are very short durations (from 90 to 234–252 ms), short durations (from 234–252 to 585–630 ms), intermediate durations (from 585–630 to 1080–1170 ms), long durations (from 1080–1170 to 2070 ms), and extremely long durations (2070 ms) (Benussi 1913, pp. 9–24). From these analyses it emerges that the *units* of phenomenic time are those temporal extensions with a maximum extension of *about* 100 ms. Their distinguishing feature, as we have seen in the above phenomena, is that below 100 ms, there is no longer any correlation between the real order of the sequence of physical stimuli and the order of perceived events, which remains above the maximum threshold of minimal perceptibility. Furthermore, the units of phenomenic time into which the temporal parts of the presentation are divided cannot be the instants of physical time, because the phenomenic perception of the successions does not have the same duration as the objective sequence of the stimuli. Several of these durations characterizing the abovementioned phenomena have been recently confirmed at computational (Rensink 2002) and neurophysiological level (Libet et al. 1992).

The rationale for these and other phenomena – such as the so-called *representational momentum*, in which the starting location of a moving dot is judged to be *displaced forward* in the direction of motion (Freyd and Finke 1984; Hubbard and Barucha 1988); or the Frölich effect (Frölich 1923), which consists in a fast-moving stimulus whose location is *displaced forward* – is that the perception of an *order* in a succession of stimuli is given by its inner qualitative location in awareness. Also in these cases, the position of an element in a perceived succession is determined not so much by the linear sequence of stimuli as by its phenomenic salience: the greater the salience, the greater is the likeliness that the element is perceived *in anticipation* (and/or delay) *over the others*, i.e., having *temporal advantage*. Here anticipation clearly does not mean forecasting or formulating probability hypotheses based on past experience of the phenomenon. Anticipation is shown to be a *structural dimension of the present*. The causes governing these specific phenomena are qualitative, ranging from similarity to tonal proximity and internal organization.

Conclusions

The golden rule in conducting systematic and experimental research on perceptual phenomena is, as suggested by Kanizsa (1991), careful avoidance of the stimulus error, i.e., the error of substituting the list of the characteristics of the stimulus (what one epistemologically "knows") for the description of direct unbiased experience (what one "sees"). From the previous exemplifications, we may conclude that conscious perception in its microstructure shows the presence of *anticipatory structures*. Psychophysical and neurophysiological research has made it possible to identify temporal durations of an act of perceiving (Pöppel and Bao 2014; Pöppel and Logothetis 1986), and even the temporal delay necessary for a sensory stimulus to become conscious (of about 500 ms) (Libet et al. 1992). However, detecting at brain level the presence of temporal windows of about 20–30 ms (so-called relaxation oscillations) representing the logistical basis on which to integrate spatial and visual information, and identifying temporal windows of about 3.2 s (with a subjective variability) which constitute the specious present, signifies detecting the presence of *syntactic* mechanisms at neurophysiological level. These are logistical functions that reduce sensory noise or uncertainty through elementary integration units and open the sensory channel for new information. What these functions do is deliver a frame for subjective time, or at least for some temporal phenomena: they do not say anything about either the qualitative experience of subjective time, its temporal qualitative displacements, its experienced length and continuity, or the individuation of a self. Current research in this field affirms that the *continuity* of the flow of time is *due to the semantics* (Pöppel 2009), but again what semantics is remains unsaid (unless one considers again symbolic syntactic structures). In fact, even today, there is no evidence that consciousness phenomena are explainable in terms of the physics that we currently know, as honest researchers confirm (Libet 2004). The brain may be a necessary but not a sufficient condition for conscious experience and its anticipatory behavior.

Acknowledgments The author thanks the director and the scientific board of STIAS (Stellenbosch Institute for Advanced Study, Wallenberg Research Centre at Stellenbosch University, Stellenbosch, South Africa) for providing the perfect environment in which to write this chapter during the author's visit in February to April 2016.

References

Albertazzi, L. (1999). The time of presentness. A chapter in positivistic and descriptive psychology. *Axiomathes, 10*(1–3), 49–74.

Albertazzi, L. (2001). The primitives of presentation. Parts, wholes and psychophysics. In L. Albertazzi (Ed.), *The dawn of cognitive science. Early European contributors* (pp. 29–60). Dordrecht: Kluwer.

Albertazzi, L. (2004). Stereokinetic shapes and their shadow. *Perception, 33*, 1437–1452.

Albertazzi, L. (2006). Das rein Figurale – the shadowy scheme of the form. *Gestalt Theory, 28*(1–2), 123–151.

Albertazzi, L. (2011). Renata Calabresi. The experimental analysis of the present. *History of Psychology*. 1093–4510/11/$12.00. https://doi.org/10.1037/a0021104

Albertazzi, L. (2013). Appearances from an experimental viewpoint. In L. Albertazzi (Ed.), *The Wiley Blackwell handbook of experimental phenomenology. Visual perception of shape, space and appearance* (pp. 267–290). Chichester: Wiley.

Albertazzi, L. (2015). A science of qualities. *Biological Theory, 10*, 188–199. https://doi.org/10.1007/s13752-015-0213-3.

Albertazzi, L. (2017, in press). Brentano's Aristotelian concept of consciousness. In D. Jacquette (Ed.), *The Bloomsbury companion to consciousness*. London: Bloomsbury Publish House.

Albertazzi, L., & Louie, A. (2016). A mathematical science of qualities: A sequel. *Biological Theory*. London: Bloomsbury Publishing House. https://doi.org/10.1007/s13752-016-0248-0.

Albertazzi, L., van Tonder, G., & Vishwanath, D. (2010). Information in perception. In L. Albertazzi, G. van Tonder, & D. Vishwanath (Eds.), *Perception beyond inference. The information content of perceptual processes* (pp. 1–26). Cambridge, MA: MIT Press.

Appadurai, A. (2013). *The future as cultural fact*. London: Verso.

Beck, J., Elsner, A., & Silverstein, C. (1977). Position uncertainty and the perception of apparent movement. *Perception & Psychophysics, 21*(1), 33–38. https://doi.org/10.3758/BF03199464.

Benussi, V. (1913). *Die Psychologie der Zeitauffassung*. Leipzig: Hölder.

Brentano, F. (1874/1995). *Psychology from an empirical standpoint*, ed. by L. McAlister. London: Routledge (Tr. of the 2nd ed. with an Introduction and notes by O. Kraus, Leipzig 1924. 1rst German ed. 1874, Leipzig: Duncker & Humblot).

Calabresi, R. (1930). *La determinazione del presente psichico* [The determination of the psychic present] Firenze: Bemporad.

Ebbinghaus, H. (1902). *Grundzüge der Psychologie*. Leipzig: Veit.

Edelman, G. M. (2004). *Wider than the sky. The phenomenal gift of consciousness*. New Haven: Yale University Press.

Fraisse, P. (1957/1964). *Psychologie du temps*. Paris: PUF. Eng. Tr. 1964. *The psychology of time*. London: Eyre and Spottiswoode.

Freyd, J. J., & Finke, R. A. (1984). Representational momentum. *Journal of Experimental Psychology: Learning, Memory and Cognition, 10*, 126–132.

Frölich, F. W. (1923). Über die Messung der Empfindungszeit. *Zeitschrift für Sinnespsychologie, 54*, 58–78.

Galilei, G. (1623/1957). *The Assayer*, translated by Stillman Drake. In *Discoveries and opinions of Galileo* (pp. 237–238). New York: Doubleday & Co.

Gibson, J. J. (1954). A theory of pictorial perception. *Audio-Visual Communication Review, 1*, 3–23.

Gregory, R. L. (1998). *Eye and the brain. The psychology of seeing* (5th ed.). Oxford: Oxford University Press.

Hering, E. E. (1920/1964). *Outlines of a theory of the light sense*. Trans. L. M. Hurvich, D. Jameson. Cambridge, MA: Harvard University Press. [Tr. of *Zur Lehre vom Lichtsinn*]

Hubbard, T., & Bharucha, J. J. (1988). Judged displacement in apparent vertical and horizontal motion. *Perception & Psychophysics, 44*(3), 211–221.

Hume, D. (1975). *Enquiries concerning human understanding and concerning the principles of morals*, ed. by L. A. Selby-Bigge (3rd ed.), revised by P. H. Nidditch. Oxford: Clarendon Press.

Husserl, E. (1939/1973). *Erfahrung und Urteil. Untersuchungen zur Genealogie der Logik*, ed. by L. Landgrebe. Prag: Academia Verlag (En. tr. 1973 by Spencer Churchill, Evanston: Northwestern University Press).

Husserl, E. (1966/1991). *Zur Phänomenologie des inneren Zeitbewusstseins*, ed. by R. Boehm Den. Haag: Martinus Nijhoff (En. tr. 1991 by John B. Brough, Dordrecht: Kluwer).

James, W. (1890/1950). *Principles of psychology*, 2 vols. Boston: Holt and Co. Repr. New York: Dover Publications 1950 (1st ed. 1890).

Kanizsa, G. (1979). *Organization in vision*. New York: Praeger.

Kanizsa, G. (1991). *Vedere e pensare* [seeing and thinking]. Bologna: Il Mulino.

Kenkel, F. (1913). Untersuchungen über den Zusammenhang zwischen Erscheinungsgrösse und Ercheinungsbewegung bei einigen sogennanten optischen Täuschungen. *Zeitschrift für Psychologie, 67*, 358–449.

Koffka, K. (1935/1999). *Principles of gestalt psychology*. London: Lund Humphries (Reprint 1999, London: Routledge).

Kopferman, G. (1930). Psychologische Untersuchungen über die Wirkung zweidimensionaler Darstellungen körperlicher Gebilde. *Psychologische Foschung, 13*, 293–364.

Libet, B. (1973). Electrical stimulation of cortex in human subjects and conscious sensory aspects. In A. Iggo (Ed.), *Handbook of sensory physiology* (pp. 743–790). Berlin: Springer Verlag.

Libet, B. (1985). Unconscious cerebral initiative and the role of conscious will in voluntary action. *Behavioural and Brain Sciences, 8*, 529–566.

Libet, B. (2004). *Mind time. The temporal factors in consciousness.* Cambridge, MA: Harvard University Press.

Libet, B., Pearl, D. K., Morledge, D. E., Gleason, C. A., Hosobuchi, Y., & Barbara, N. M. (1991). Control of the transition form sensory detection to sensory awareness in man by the duration of a thalamic stimulus: The cerebral 'time-on' factor. *Brain, 114*, 1731–1757.

Libet, B., Wright Jr., E. W., Feinstein, B., & Peral, D. K. (1992). Retroactive enhancement of a skin sensation by a delayed cortical stimulus in man: Evidence for delay of a conscious sensory experience. *Consciousness and Cognition, 1*, 367–375.

Louie, A. H. (2009). *More than life itself: A synthetic continuation in relational biology.* Frankfurt: Ontos Verlag.

Louie, A. H. (2013). *The reflection of life: Functional entailment and imminence in relational biology.* Frankfurt/New York: Springer.

Louie, A. H. (2016) Mathematical foundations of anticipatory systems, in this *Handbook*.

Louie, A. H., & Poli, R. (2011). The spread of hierarchical cycles. *International Journal of General Systems, 40*(3), 237–261. https://doi.org/10.1080/03081079.2010.550579.

Lukasiewicz, J. (1934/1970). On the history of the logic of propositions. In L. Borkowski (Ed.), *Jan Lukasiewicz Selected works.* Amsterdam: North-Holland.

Marr, D. (1982). *Vision: A computational investigation into the human representation and processing of visual information.* New York: W. H. Freeman.

Mates, B. (1953). *Stoic logic.* Berkeley and Los Angeles: University of California Press.

Metzger, W. (1941). *Psychologie.* Darmstadt: Steinkopff.

Metzger, W. (1975/2006). *Gesetze des Sehens.* Frankfurt a.Main: Kramer (En. tr. 2006 by Lothar Spillmann, Steve Lehar, Mimsey Stromeyer, and Michael Wertheimer, Cambridge Mass.: MIT Press).

Michotte, A. (1948/1991). The psychological enigma of perspective in outline pictures. Tr. in G. Thines, A. Costall, and G. Butterworth (Eds.) (1991), *Michotte's experimental phenomenology of perception.* Hillsdale: Erlbaum.

Michotte, A. (1954). *La perception de la causalité.* Louvain: Publications Universitaires de Louvain.

Michotte, A., Thinès, G., & Crabbé, G. (1963). *Les compléments amodaux des structures perceptives.* Paris: Béatrice Nauwelaerts.

Müller-Lyer, F. C. (1889). Optische Urteilstäuschungen. *Archiv für Anatomie und Physiologie. Physiologische Abteilung, 2*, 263–270.

Musatti, C. L. (1924). Sui fenomeni stereocinetici [On stereokinetic phenomena]. *Archivio Italiano di Psicologia, 3*, 105–120.

Musatti, C. L. (1955). La stereocinesi e la struttura dello spazio visibile [Stereokinesis and the structure of visible space]. *Rivista di Psicologia, 49*, 3–57.

Musatti, C. L. (1975). Stereokinetic phenomena and their interpretation. In G. B. D'Arcais (Ed.), *Studies in perception, Festschrift for Fabio Metelli* (pp. 166–189). Milan: Martello-Giunti.

Palmer, S. (1999). *Vision science. From photons to phenomenology.* Cambridge, MA: MIT Press.

Penrose, R. (1989). *The Emperor's new mind: Concerning computers, minds and the laws of physics.* Oxford: Oxford University Press.

Poli, R. (2011). Steps toward an explicit ontology of the future. *Journal of Futures Studies, 16*(1), 67–78.

Poli, R. (2012). Complexity, acceleration and anticipation. *Emergence: Complexity and Organization, 14*(4), 124–138.

Poli, R. (2014a). Anticipation: A new thread for the human and social sciences? *Cadmus, 2*(3), 23–36.

Poli, R. (2014b). Anticipation: What about turning the human and social sciences upside down? *Futures, 64*, 15–18.

Poli, R. (2017). *Introduction to anticipation studies*. Dordrecht: Springer.

Ponzo, M. (1912). Rapports de contraste angulaire et l'appréciation de grandeur des astres à l'horizon. *Archivio Italiano di Biologia, 58*, 327–329.

Pöppel, E. (2009). Pre-semantically defined temporal windows for cognitive processing. *Philosophical Transactions of the Royal Society of London: Series B, Biological Sciences, 363*, 1887–1896.

Pöppel, E., & Bao, Y. (2014). Temporal windows as a bridge from objective to subjective time. In V. Arstila & D. LLyod (Eds.), *Subjective time* (pp. 241–262). Cambridge, MA: MIT Press.

Pöppel, E., & Logothetis, N. (1986). Neuronal oscillations in the human brain. Discontinuous initiations of pursuit eye movements indicate at 30hz temporal framework for visual information processing. *Naturwissenschaften, 73*, 267–268.

Rensink, R. A. (2002). Change detection. *Annual Review of Psychology, 53*, 245–277.

Rock, I. (1977). In defence of unconscious inferences. In W. Epstein (Ed.), *Stability and constancy in visual perception: Mechanism and processes* (pp. 321–373). New York: Wiley.

Rock, I. (1983). *The logic of perception*. Cambridge, MA: MIT Press.

Rosen, R. (1985). *Anticipatory systems: Philosophical, mathematical, and methodological foundations* (2nd ed.). Oxford: Pergamon Press; (2012), New York: Springer.

Rosen, R. (1991). *Life itself: A comprehensive inquiry into the nature, origin, and fabrication of life*. New York: Columbia University Press.

Rubin, E. (1949). Geräuschverschiebungsversuche. In E. Rubin (Ed.), *Experimenta psychologica* (pp. 305–347). Copenhagen: Munskgaard.

Singer, W. (2000). Phenomenal awareness and consciousness from a neurobiological perspective. In T. Metzinger (Ed.), *Neuronal correlates of consciousness* (pp. 121–137). Cambridge, MA: MIT Press.

Sovrano, V. A., Albertazzi, L., & Rosa Salva, O. (2014). The Ebbinghaus illusion in a fish (*Xenotoca eiseni*). *Animal Cognition*. https://doi.org/10.1007/s10071-014-0821-5.

Sovrano, V. A., Da Pos, O., & Albertazzi, L. (2015). The Müller-Lyer illusion in the teleost fish (*Xenotoca eiseni*). *Animal Cognition*. https://doi.org/10.1007/s10071-015-0917-6.

Stern, L. W. (1897). Psychische Präsenzzeit. *Zeitschrift für Psychologie und Physiologie der Sinnesorgane, 22*, 13–22.

Vezzani, S., Kramer, P., & Bressan, P. (2015). Stereokinetic effect, kinetic depth effect, and structure from motion. In J. Wagemans (Ed.), *Handbook of perceptual organization* (pp. 521–540). Oxford: Oxford University Press.

Vicario, G. B. (1964). Analisi sperimentale di un caso di movimento apparente (experimental analysis of an apparent movement). *Rivista di Psicologia, 58*, 133–189.

Vicario, G. B. (1982). Some observations in the auditory field. In J. Beck (Ed.), *Organization and representation in perception* (pp. 269–283). Hillsdale: Lawrence Erlbaum Associates.

Vicario, G. B. (2003). Temporal displacement. In R. Buccheri, M. Saniga, & W. M. Stuckey (Eds.), *The nature of time: Geometry, physics, and perception* (pp. 53–66). Dordrecht: Springer.

Vicario, G. B. (2005). *Il tempo (time)*. Bologna: Il Mulino.

Vicario, G. B., & Zambianchi, E. (1998). Some experimental observations on instantaneousness and durableness of events in the visual field. *Teorie e Modelli, 3*, 39–57.

Vishwanath, D. (2005). The epistemological status of vision science and its implications for design. *Axiomathes, 3*(15), 399–486. https://doi.org/10.1007/s10516-0044-5445-y.

Wertheimer, M. (1912/2012). Experimentelle Studien über das Sehen von Bewegung. *Zeitschrift für Psychologie 61*, 161–265. En. tr. by M. Wertheimer, K. W. Watkins. In L. Spillmann (Ed.), *Max Wertheimer, On perceived motion and figural organization* (pp. 1–92). Cambridge, MA: MIT Press.

Wertheimer, M. (1923). Laws of organization in perceptual forms. *Psychologische Forschung 4*, 301–350. En. tr. in W. E. Ellis (1938), *A source book of gestalt psychology* (pp. 71–94). London: Routledge.

The Anticipatory Structure of Perceptual Systems

15

Dhanraj Vishwanath

Contents

Abstract

Recent developments in AI suggest that highly complex forms of prediction implicit in human cognitive and perceptual processes can be efficiently replicated in artificial systems. Within cognitive science, it has long been accepted that natural perceptual systems incorporate some form of predictive behaviour. Conventional models of perception construe such prediction to occur either at the level of inference and detection (predictive coding) or in the learning of sensory and motor interdependencies (sensorimotor contingency). In this chapter I argue that prediction as construed in these artificial systems and models of perception does not capture the true anticipatory nature of natural perceptual systems. I suggest that an understanding of the anticipatory structure of perceptual systems requires a more nuanced understanding of the steps required for the evolution of natural perceptual systems.

D. Vishwanath (✉)
School of Psychology and Neuroscience, University of St. Andrews, Fife, UK
e-mail: dv10@st-andrews.ac.uk

© Springer Nature Switzerland AG 2019
R. Poli (ed.), *Handbook of Anticipation*,
https://doi.org/10.1007/978-3-319-91554-8_71

Keywords

Perception · Anticipation · Visual space perception · Sensorimotor contigency · AI · Predictive Coding

Introduction

As you walk toward the airport departure area, the door automatically opens anticipating your intention to walk through it. On a wet snowy day, as you apply the brakes on your car, the antilock braking system (ABS) senses the relative rotational speed of the wheels, anticipates a possible wheel lock and skid, and activates a specific pattern of braking. An AI (Artifical Intelligence) system utilizing deep learning, Alpha Go (Silver et al. 2016), recently demonstrated the ability to defeat the world's best player of the board game Go by, in effect, learning the space of possible moves given the current board position and determining and executing the best possible next move. The existence of these exponentially complex examples of predictive behaviour in artificial systems suggests that we have a sophisticated technical understanding of *anticipation* and how to achieve it in artificial systems. Does this imply that we have sufficient understanding of the nature of anticipation to decipher the basic principles underlying the workings of the most sophisticated anticipatory entity in existence, the human mind?

I want to argue that these achievements in artificial predictive systems are not of the kind that can help us understand the nature of anticipation constituted in human or animal perceptual systems and that an unquestioning fascination with these, albeit technically stellar achievements, can potentially serve to obscure a true understanding of natural anticipatory systems.

The examples in the introductory paragraph above do indeed mimic many types of predictive behaviors in humans. These range from the reflexive visual looming response (Schiff et al. 1962) to the complex predictive behaviors of limbs that allow an athlete to engage in trail running over complex macro and micro terrain based primarily on peripheral visual input. They range from the anticipatory nature with which eye movements are deployed (McMurray and Aslin 2004; Kowler 2011) to the cognitive processes that engage when playing chess (Charness 1992). But importantly, these examples of anticipatory behavior in humans, once translated to the domain of artificial systems, are specifically of the type where the features/categories of the input space and possible values of output space are well-defined and can be prescribed, even if often extremely complex (e.g., the dynamic visual input of the ground terrain in trail running and resulting limb movements). In many such well-specified domains, artificial systems have indeed yielded predictive behavior mimicking the capacities of humans.

Yet much of human anticipation is unscripted, with ill-defined or unspecified features or variables of either the input or output space. For example, how does an artist determine that his or her choice of material, subject matter, and execution will constitute a true breakthrough in artistic expression in the specific sociocultural context they operate (often entailing choices never made before)? How does a scientist determine what scientific question is worth pursuing – which question to ask rather than answer? How does a mathematician choose a particular problem domain from the arcana of mathematics where there is no obvious adaptive output? These examples entail anticipation in complex cognitive processing domains, but even the most basic processes of the mind, such as visual perception (of space, time, and objects), appear to have intrinsically anticipatory structure.

In comparing the two different classes of anticipatory behaviors (artificial and natural), one could say that while artificial anticipatory systems have successfully demonstrated ways in which the *past can be efficiently summarized* to generate predictive behaviour given a well-defined input/output space, natural systems, like the human mind, demonstrate a capacity to, in effect, *divine the future* from ill-defined input structure and output goals; what Poli (▶ Chap. 1, "Introducing Anticipation," this volume) highlights as the difference between forecasting and foresight.

The distinction between these two forms of anticipation mirror the longstanding and hard to reconcile distinctions in science and philosophy between *predicative and impredicative* systems (see ▶ Chap. 1, "Introducing Anticipation" by R. Poli, this volume; Albertazzi and Louie 2016; ▶ Chap. 14, "Microgenesis of Anticipation: Windowing the Present" by L. Albertazzi, this volume), *quantitative and qualitative* perceptual information (see ▶ Chap. 14, "Microgenesis of Anticipation: Windowing the Present" by L. Albertazzi, this volume; Albertazzi et al. 2011; Vishwanath 2005), and *declarative and non-declarative* information (see Vishwanath in preparation). In all these dichotomies (impredicative vs. predicative; qualitative vs. quantitative; declarative vs. non-declarative), as in the domain of anticipation, there is the tendency to assume that increasingly sophisticated variants of the former will eventually capture the full functional nature of the latter: That impredicative systems can eventually be described in terms of highly sophisticated variants of predicative ones (see ▶ Chap. 1, "Introducing Anticipation" by R. Poli, this volume) or that qualitative perceptual information is simply a complex collection of well-defined quantitative structures (see ▶ Chap. 14, "Microgenesis of Anticipation: Windowing the Present" by L. Albertazzi, this volume; Albertazzi et al. 2011; Vishwanath 2005). In a similar vein, we are tempted to assume that true anticipation (the human mind) is simply a complex variant of the sort of predictive behaviour already achieved in artificial systems.

Evolution of a Sensing and Perceiving Organism

In order to interrogate more closely the distinction between what I call quasi-anticipatory (predictive) and true anticipatory systems, I restrict myself to the domain of perception. Consider the hypothetical evolution of a sentient perceiving organism in Fig. 1 (from Vishwanath 2013). More specifically, consider the basic and necessary stages required for the evolution of the capacity for visual perception and awareness (a key component of anticipation in most sentient organisms), starting from the most primitive motile light-sensing organism to the sophisticated perceptual apparatus of the human. It is generally acknowledged that brain-like structures

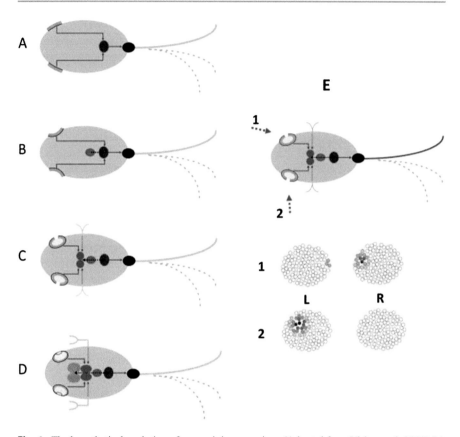

Fig. 1 The hypothetical evolution of a perceiving organism. (Adapted from Vishwanath 2013) (**a**) A simple organism with light-sensitive photoreceptor sheets linked to its locomotor apparatus. The red oval represents a neural "relay" and the black oval "musculature." (**b**) A slightly more advanced organism with a cup eye that improves directional discrimination of light. It has also evolved neural apparatus (green oval) that modulates light-mediated locomotion based on current adaptive needs. (**c**) A still more advanced organism with a pinhole eye that provides high-resolution discrimination of light direction, as well as a sophisticated neural "map" relating light patterns, locomotion, past behavior, and adaptive consequences (blue circles). The organism also has rudimentary tactile receptors linked to the map. (**d**) A sophisticated "perceiving" organism with an advanced lens eye and tactile apparatus. The organism has evolved the apparatus (yellow ovals) to consciously monitor, in real time, the state of the activity/information in the advanced neural "maps." It is this information that the organism "sees," not the external world. (**e**) Top panel: A simple organism receives light from one of two directions (1 or 2). Bottom panels: Activation patterns on the left and right photoreceptor array as a result of light entering the eyes from one of two directions (1 or 2) assuming parallel rays. Darker spots indicate higher activation

evolved only in organisms that required whole-body movement for sustenance and reproduction. Figure 1 (adapted from Vishwanath 2013) shows the hypothetical stages of the evolution of the sensory and neural apparatus of a generic light-sensing, water-borne organism indicating the hypothesized evolution of neural processing for increasingly sophisticated sense-mediated behavior and perception. Panel A shows an organism with a simple reflexive linkage between light sensing and axial loco-motion. Activity in the photo-sensitive array is relayed to a motor coordinator, which in turn relays an efferent neural signal to the "musculature" (motor plant) causing a pattern of adaptive "tail flips" that alters or initiates the movement of the organism, toward or away from the source of light; predicting, for instance, presence of nutrients or predators. The reaction of our primitive light-activated organism is driven simply by the presence of light and its relative direction, nothing about the internal state of the organism or external context modulates the fixed stereotypic pattern of tail flips (creating patterns of light with a flashlight while the creature in a lab tank produces the same behavior). This type of "anticipation" can therefore be seen as mirroring the airport-door example in the introductory paragraph above. The door opens regardless of whether one intends to cross the threshold or not; e.g., it would do so even if one were simply standing in front of it waiting for someone or lighting a cigarette.

This process (Fig. 1a) is simple enough to capture what appear to be important constituents of a reflexive process. Hence, we feel comfortable that this sort of anticipatory process is easily understood and replicated artificially. A step beyond this would be an organism that does not move willy-nilly based on the presence of light but whose light-activated locomotion is modulated by internal states such as arousal, satiety, vigilance, etc. This could occur through the evolution of a "modu-lator" controlling the activity of the motor coordinator. It can be thought to be akin to the ABS device alluded to in the introduction, which involves a reflex-like action based on a complex state-monitoring process. Again, given the apparent similarity in the nature of anticipatory behavior in the artificial device and organism, we might conclude that this variety of anticipation is also well understood.

Greater sophistication in state-based modulation of reflexive sensory-motor activity will no doubt be accompanied by a corresponding evolution in sophisticated sensory apparatus (improved directional light resolution of the receptor sheet) as well as more sophisticated neural apparatus that can subserve this (see Land and Nilsson 2012). Such sophisticated neural apparatus might, for example, incorporate information regarding adaptive success based on the reflex actions and may be linked the pattern of information both from the light-sensing apparatus as well as past patterns of movement (see, e.g., Wehner 2003) which will likely lead to sensory-motor maps in which complex photo-sensor activation patterns begin to be encoded in real time in locomotion-relevant terms (path integration). These "maps," in communication with the "state-modulator," could determine ever more sophisticated patterns of light-modulated anticipatory motor behavior. Note that some of these might not be maps in the conventional sense but much more rudimentary mecha-nisms (see Wehner et al. 2006). The evolution of photo-sensing will likely be matched with a parallel development of other sensory apparatus and their associated "maps" such as pressure sensors (the "fins"), swim bladders, epithelial hair cells, and so forth. This will now engage, on an evolutionary time scale, complex co-calibra-tions of the sensory-motor maps based on inter- and intra-modal sensory feedback during motor activity, allowing for ever more complex modes of transmodal antic-ipatory behavior. The information in these structures in effect "represent" some mapping between receptor activation patterns, locomotion, and the pattern of real-time physiological or sensory consequences of the sense-mediated actions. At a coarse grain, such consequences could, for example, be a shift in the state of satiety. At a fine grain, it might be the level of correspondence between the patterns of activity of the pressure receptors (or pressure maps) with those "predicted" by the visual maps; or perhaps the change in the pattern of activity of the photoreceptors predicted within the visual maps themselves.

This far more complex anticipatory mechanism and behavior might at first glance be seen as akin to, and perhaps similar in technical complexity to, the Alpha Go program (Silver et al. 2016). Alpha Go, like our 3rd stage sensing organism, has evolved some sort of encoding of the complex space of moves and patterns of the go board based on iterative learning; but there are crucial differences. The encoding and functional behavior of the organism constitutes–in a critical sense–an *impredicative system*, where the informational contents of the encodings are self-referential (see ▶ Chap. 1, "Introducing Anticipation" by R. Poli, this volume; Albertazzi and Louie 2016). On the other hand, the Alpha Go program, however complex (and however undecipherable or opaque the information or states constituted by the "hidden layers" of the network), is still, taken together, *a predicative system*: the "meaning" or "content" of the critical input/output components are externally specified and validated. In the artificial device, the undecipherable internal states, whose content ultimately derive from a pre-specification of the desired input/output structure and functional goals, are not only parasitic on external definition but relevant only for the highly circumscribed problem domain. The system did not evolve its own goals as our 3rd stage organism has done, and thus the anticipatory nature of the two is critically different. Despite the complexity and sophistication of the encodings within the Alpha Go program, it cannot adapt to other problem spaces, although the general computational approach used to instantiate such a program (deep learning) will no doubt translate to other similar restricted problem domains (e.g., image recognition).

The problem is actually worse. It turns out that even the anticipatory behaviors of the organisms in steps 1 and 2, which appear uncontroversial and mundane when viewed from the lens of a predicative (artificial) system, are, in fact, not commensurate with such seemingly equivalent artificial systems. Even the simplest anticipatory behaviors in natural systems have to also be considered as impredicative in nature because they originate in a system that is self-referential: the organism does not have an external agent specifying the input/output variables, format, features, etc. This suggests that the capacity to simply mimic reflexive or state-dependent anticipatory sensory-motor mechanisms does not automatically constitute a true understanding of the anticipatory nature of natural systems or their mode of instantiation.

What is important to note is that the incommensurability of the theories underlying artificial anticipatory systems and natural systems is evident even before we have begun to discuss the much more complex nature of anticipation constituted by the human perceptual system.

In order for the evolutionary steps in Fig. 1a–c to have eventually resulted in the visual system and perceptual capacity that we humans have, somewhere on this evolutionary trajectory, the organism must have developed a capacity to have *conscious access* to the information and structures constituted in the neural maps and related activity that have evolved on an evolutionary time scale. More specifically, somewhere between the complex anticipatory sensory-motor capacities *without* conscious awareness (stage 3) and the perceptual capacities of humans (conscious awareness of space), there has to have been the inception of mechanisms that allow the organism to consciously monitor, in real time, the information content constituted in its own neural states in order to *volitionally plan* behavior. This stage is shown in Fig. 1d.

Based on considering the conjectured evolution of a sentient animal in Fig. 1a–d, conscious visual perception (of space and objects) can now be loosely defined as *the real-time awareness of the anticipatory information constituted in the sensory-motor maps*. The information is intrinsically anticipatory and impredicative since it has evolved from self-referential processes that, from the very start, are anticipatory (a simple sensory-motor reflex). This implies that what the organism "sees" is not an image of the external environment nor is it a "direct perception" of objects and properties in some objectively definable "external world." Rather, what the organism "sees" is the information constituted in the complex structures or "maps" encoding an adaptive anticipatory sensory-motor linkage. What the organism perceives is the complex subjective space of possible intentional actions along with an anticipation of their consequences. We refer to this as *subjective* because the content does not derive from any externally defined objective feature space. The content of this map will be contingent on the specific sensory and motoric capacities of the animal, its adaptive needs, the nature of the organisms it evolved from, and intrinsic constraints in neural signaling and connectivity – thus, "subjective" rather than "objective." While the "environment" that the animal "sees" based on this capacity for awareness is no doubt contingent on the current state of physical stimulation at the receptor surfaces (and therefore correlated to the state of the external physical world), it is not in any useful sense a "re-presentation" of it.

In contrast, standard approaches to perception science construe what is perceived by an organism (e.g., a human) to be, more or less, a faithful re-presentation of a subset of objective properties of external environment (usually specified in the terms of the constructs of physics) internally encoded in terms of certain "features" instantiated in single (or collections of) neurons (see Vishwanath 2005). These properties of the external physical environment range from, say, the dimensions and curvature of a surface, the wavelength distribution of its electromagnetic emittance, the distance among objects, and what have you. The features internally instantiated are, in the ontological sense, assumed to be essentially the same constructs (dimensions, curvature, distance) encoded or "detected" by certain (collections of) neurons. In some cases, according to the standard model, such features are construed to have no objective epistemic content but are merely epiphenomenal qualia (e.g., the appearance of a specific color, say 'red'). They are deemed to have no functional significance apart from co-occurring with the instantiation of useful epistemic information (the detection of a surface geometry and particular reflectance distribution). The standard model implies that an artificial perceptual system could "do without" these epiphenomenal, qualitative states and still be considered a more-or-less successful emulation of a natural perceptual system.

At higher levels of representation, in the standard approach, the input/output relationship is cast, not in terms of a "re-presentation" but a "re-cognition": The determination of an entities identity (e.g., a particular shape, an object's category, a material category, etc.). For example, the internal re-presentation of the physical feature dimensions of roughness, albedo, curvature, hardness, etc. might end up activating a higher level "feature" that constitutes the "re-cognition" of a specific material, say, marble.

According to the standard non-anticipatory model of perception, what is perceived is akin to a set of estimates of numerical values (size, distance, depth, curvature, albedo, roughness, aspect ratio, and what have you) and a set of labels that signify the presence of a particular entity or feature (square, circle, red, tree, sky, marble, etc.); see Vishwanath 2005.

An important aspect of theoretical and empirical approaches in this standard model is that the content to be explained (the re-presentation or re-cognition) is stripped of all so-called subjective or qualitative content (e.g., the redness of red, the visual continuity of a surface, the subjective impression of space).

Artificial versus Natural Anticipatory Systems

Building an artificial system that can achieve the transposition from a pattern of light intensity values (at the eye or a camera) to an output of numerical values and labels signifying the contents of the scene that gave rise to the image (to be interpreted by a subsequent agent) is no doubt an enormously complex computational problem. This difficult problem was, in fact, the basis for many of the original developments in AI upon which recent instantiations (deep learning) strongly depend. Advances in information processing software and hardware have led to great success in models of re-cognition (e.g., image processing and object recognition). Such advances have reinforced that view that the model used in standard artificial intelligence work (re-presentation, re-cognition) is a valid model of the human mind for the empirical perceptual sciences (c.f., Vishwanath 2005).

However, modeling a perceptual system and its anticipatory nature on this basis (or on the perception-as-action account; see below) suffers from the same flaw as equating the automatic door, the ABS system, and the Alpha Go program to the first three stages of our hypothetical organisms in terms of their respective anticipatory capacities and behavior. In each of the artificial cases, the information constituted in the variables within the artificial system *do not in and of themselves have any anticipatory content* but only acquire them due to their *interpretation and specification by an external agent*; in other words, *the anticipation is not constituted within the internal encodings and states.* For example, the data (or data structures) generated by the braking sensors are not in and of themselves anticipatory but instead feed into a rule set devised externally by the engineer that initiates an action. The internal states of the Alpha Go program are not in themselves anticipatory, but only determine an output that is translated into a plan of action (based on some maximization or minimization rule) devised externally by the engineer. The information in the internal states or output are only anticipatory from the viewpoint of an external agent that devised the system, namely, the engineer.

Similarly, because re-presentation and re-cognition (at any specified level) in standard models of perception, in effect, reduce to the output of a set of numerical values and labels necessarily implies that there is nothing anticipatory in the *content of the perceptual output in the absence of an extra-perceptual interpretive mechanism*. Perceptual information in these models is simply an output constituted by a feature value or learned causal model, as defined external to the system. It is only once this output is assessed and matched against memory by the higher-order mental processes that anticipatory information or meaning is inferred ("red [value of feature variable COLOUR] fruit [re-cognised value of feature variable OBJECT] are ripe and nutritious [higher order inference based on past experience of feature values and outcomes of related behaviours], so reach out and grab one [motor command based on inferential outcome]").

To understand more specifically the difference between non-anticipatory "features," "re-presentation," and "inference"-based information in standard perception models and genuine anticipatory content within natural perceptual presentation, we return to our primitive organism in Figure 1.

Consider stage 3 (Fig. 1c). Despite the fact that we have a fairly sophisticated sensory device, and associated neural apparatus, it makes little sense to say that the content of the sensory-motor maps are an "inference" or "representation" about the outside world. While there is clearly some relationship between the objective external energy/matter flux and the patterns of activity on the receptors, at this stage it is far from a "representation" or "picture" of the external world as ordinarily construed. The activity of the receptors, even at the level of the retinae, is but one component of the evolving sensorimotor system which is shaped by many factors but primarily in relation to the motor coordinator, adaptive needs, and the intrinsic constraints of neural signaling and connectivity. Despite the fact that the pinhole eye at stage 3 optically projects an image on the photoreceptor array, it makes little sense to say that the neural apparatus has access to an "image" or a "picture" of its environment which it is trying to interpret or represent.

One might argue that at this stage it is not the contents of a complex "image" that is being registered or represented but something more simple like, say, the "direction" of the light source. But the claim of a re-presentation or encoding of a feature/variable as simple as "direction" is equally problematic. Figure 1e shows the organism in stage 2 (Fig. 1b) receiving light from a single source in two different scenarios. Light coming from each "direction" will cause a specific pattern of activation on the photoreceptor surface (shown by the shading of the dots representing individual receptors). This will be linked, via the rudimentary sensory-motor map, to a set of motor commands that alter the axial locomotion of the organism. Notice how, critically, the content of the sensory-motor apparatus that we (as an external observer) might label as "representing" directions "left" or "right" is meaningless within the system itself without reference to locomotion (i.e., a rudimentary anticipatory response). "Left" (as we construe an internal representational state as an external observer or engineer) is simply the causation of a certain pattern of tail activity and "Right" is another. The two values (left and right) of the feature (direction), considered from the internal workings of the organism, are meaningless outside of the locomotive consequences of the differential light stimulation. It is not as though motor mechanisms peer at objectively meaningful content from the sensory system (direction, say, 30 deg. "left" or 45 deg. "right" with respect to body axis) and then activate the appropriate tail flip, or, that the sensory mechanism has "recovered" or "detected" the direction of light which is then fed onward for sensory guided motor activity. Rather, the patterns in the rudimentary sensory-motor apparatus have gained "meaning" or content only throughout the anticipatory linkage between directional light sensitivity and locomotion (a–c in Fig. 1).

Similarly, the neural encodings in the more advanced organism's sensory-motor map are not objective "representations" of the external light environment; they are a complex encoding of the linkage between sensor activity and locomotion that anticipates adaptive needs. In contrast, for an artificial system mimicking the behavior of this organism, the encoded variable or feature "direction" takes on specific $(+/-)$ values where the value of the variable constitutes the objective output information (which then feeds into a "yaw" vector specifying an accompanying leftward or rightward turn). Such declarative constructs cannot, in principle, exist within the information structure constituted in the natural organism, even though we might offhandedly label a specific neuron to be a "left detector" or "right detector" or a "yaw" neuron. This is because the input, output, and intermediary information form an impredicative system without reference to externally specified input parameters or output features/variables (direction, yaw).

Any simple consideration of the evolution of natural perceptual/cognitive systems shows how it is problematic to view even the most simplistic perceptual capacity (the sense of visual direction) in terms of post hoc constructs like (direction), values (left, right, degrees), and causal models (direction vector provides input to yaw vector). In a similar vein, the more elaborate aspects, such as the visual perception of shape, surfaces, and space, cannot usefully be construed in terms of geometry (Euclidean space) and features (direction, distance) re-presenting the self-same objective external constructs. For example, the internal encoding of the percept of a surface or shape cannot be usefully thought of as a collection of values specifying its geometry (e.g., length, curvature, z-scale or depth relief, affine class, etc.) but must, necessarily, entail the phenomenal awareness of a complex anticipatory structure providing a basis for *planning* motor actions (grasping, touching, reaching, caressing). This anticipatory structure cannot be described simply in terms of conventional geometry, because what is given in the perceptual phenomenology of surface and shape perception is not simply a "re-presentation" nor "re-cognition" of an external geometry as classified in physics or mathematics (see, Leyton 1984). Instead, we might define a visual SURFACE as the *phenomenological presentation of a complex "plan" that anticipates consequences to the perception of touch*. Note how this definition is self-referential to perception and thus opens the possibility to be understood in terms of an impredicative system where the information content of the object itself is anticipatory.

Similarly, the perception of depth or distance can be seen as an anticipation of movement duration/effort, not a re-presentation of effort, for if it was a representation, then it reduces in a trivial way to a representation of "locations of points." Points and temporal instants are reductive post hoc categorizations of time and space – both of which are absent in the actual act of perception which exemplifies a continuity (see Albertazzi 2002).

As also pointed out in the chapter in this volume by Albertazzi, perceptual qualities are in fact anticipatory patterns. For example, roughness, shininess, softness, and color might be thought to constitute what Poli (this volume) refers to as "latents" and where he emphasizes that the organism's view on the world consists of an anticipatory schemata. The latents may be implicit (e.g., subsidiary motor anticipations, subconscious feelings) or explicit (e.g., what is given in perceptual awareness (see ▶ Chap. 14, "Microgenesis of Anticipation: Windowing the Present" by L. Albertazzi, this volume)).

This aspect of anticipatory "future-oriented" schemata is not restricted to perceptual and higher-order cognitive processes, but there is increasing acknowledgment that other basic building blocks of cognition such as memory have to be viewed from an anticipatory lens. This is seen in the evolving definitions of one of the central constructs in memory research, namely, *episodic memory*. While original definitions specified this memory construct in terms of a re-presentation of features and feature values of past events "what," "when," and "where," it is now conceived increasingly as a much more complex mechanism that is essentially future oriented and anticipatory – the capacity for "mental time travel" (see Suddendorf et al. 2009).

Importantly, what anticipatory impredicative systems of perceptual and cognitive *presentation* also entail is that content is *generative and inexhaustive*. Given a specific visual scene, anticipatory planning based on perceptual and cognitive mechanisms proceeds not as a circumscribed and predetermined class of actions and outcomes (however large as in Alpha Go) but as a potentially infinite set of possible actions, many of unspecified outcome. This capacity opens the door for insight as is, for example, seen in the development of tool use.

In contrast, conventional approaches to perceptual and cognitive science which construe content in terms re-cognition and categorization – where "scene recognition" is the inference of a fixed categorical and geometric structure – cannot yield the sort of open-endedness of behaviors apparent in advanced animals and humans. This is because these fixed canonical categories and geometries are specified post hoc by the scientist or engineer based on *a deliberate reduction or compacting of the inexhaustive anticipatory structure that is actually given in perception*. The construal of perception in terms of representation of features and feature values is essentially positing a *derivative subset of the content given in perception* in the way language does. Indeed, any set of categories, however cleverly conceived, cannot exhaust the space of possibilities for categorization given in perceptual presentation. This intrinsic open-endedness and anticipatory nature of perceptual presentation is what allows the inference of, for example, the use of a key as a bottle opener (The term presentation is used here in the sense that perception entails a direct mental presentation of a phenomenal space imbued with objects and qualities. This phenomenal space is not a "re-presentation" that "stands in for," is "an inference to," or a "direct view of," an objective external reality. The usage derives from that in the literature on phenomenology originating in the Brentano School (see Albertazzi 2002, 2006).)

Planning action based on divining the future implies that no action is mandatory and that there is no absolute ground truth (i.e., most efficient summary of the past) to base a future action. The criteria that determine the right plan are not exhaustive or delimited, even though there is always a consequence. Moreover, at least in terms of anticipation in the human mind, there is the capacity to change the definition of the problem domain, if necessary, for example, nesting the current planning/problem space into a broader higher dimensional plan space. This is one of the central issues to be addressed in assessing the problematic use of artificial agents (forecast-based anticipation) in areas like medical diagnoses and policy-making, where the capacity to step out of the predefined hypothetical constructs originally based simply on summarizing past experience can turn out to be critical.

AI and Anticipatory Sensory/Cognitive Systems

It is precisely a lack of appreciation of the impredicative and necessarily anticipatory nature of information constituted in natural systems that afflicts both the AI and cognitive science approaches to understanding human perceptual/cognitive systems. For example, the approach in AI can be construed as one that aims to build a system that constitutes an efficient summary of behaviors of a natural system observed by an external agent, coded in terms of constructs (features, causal models) specified by the external agent.

Remarkably, even recent critiques of the standard AI approaches that point out the chasm between the behaviors that can be emulated currently by artificial systems and the capacities of the human mind (Lake et al. 2017) appear to miss this critical source of the problem. Lake et al. (2017) suggest that what is needed to fix or improve standard AI models is to build in "priors," "inductive biases," and "causal structures" similar in vein to what is implied to exist in the human perceptual/cognitive systems based on empirical work on perceptual/cognitive development. But the priors, biases, causal models, etc., that they mention are all consructs that arise from a model of perception/cognition that is in itself derived from the standard AI approach! One which relies on external specification of "features," "feature values," "causal structure," etc. Indeed Lake et al. appear to neglect the critical problem related to specification of priors and biases in terms of an externally specified feature or cue space that is already foreshadowed in Hume's problem of induction more than two centuries ago (see Vishwanath 2005). Their critique, while an enormously valuable and welcome analysis of the state of the art in AI, misses the fundamental distinction between a predicative model specified in terms of post hoc externally defined features/cues/values and the impredicative one that underlies natural anticipatory perceptual and cognitive systems.

What is interesting from the sociology of the interplay between the field of AI and cognitive psychology is the long history of the arguments, ranging from the early debates on the relative efficacy of neural networks in symbolic processing explaining human cognition (Fodor and Pylyshyn 1988) to the most recent one regarding the lack of causal modeling and structured priors in current AI (Lake et al. 2017). But what is almost always overlooked is that both standard AI *and* standard cognitive science both subscribe to the same delimited ontological/epistemological model, one that cannot, in principle, lead to a full understanding of the anticipatory human mind.

In recent times, technology has allowed standard AI to make gigantic leaps in engineering applied solutions (image parsing, object recognition, speech recognition, emulating delimited cognitive capacities, e.g., Alpha GO, robot locomotion), and there is again a developing subservience on the part of the cognitive sciences toward AI (as there was in the 1970s and 1980s). Specifically, there is the notion that standard AI, through brute force, will eventually lead to an emulation of the human mind. This is clearly seen in the hegemony of computational neuroscience in perceptual and cognitive sciences that have arguably led to the diminishment and relegation of efforts for *a pre-modeling theoretical understanding of the basic principles of psychological processes.*

Sensorimotor Contingency, Predictive Coding and Anticipation

An ancillary to the standard (inferential, representationalist) approach is the oft cited perception-as-action view championed by O'Regan and Noe (2001), as well as others. The idea central to this account, in which perception depends on "sensorimotor contingencies," suggests at first glance that it captures the sort of anticipatory structure of perception espoused here. In point of fact, the O' Regan and Noe (O'R&N) account and other associated theories suffer the same conceptual pitfalls as the standard (inferential, representationalist) model critiqued above. Neither approach captures the intrinsic impredicativity of natural perceptual systems, the subjective nature of perceptual information content, and the essential anticipatory nature of that content.

O'Regan and Noe's approach is, as they themselves admit, a variant of the Gibsonian idea of "direct perception." Namely, that perceptual experience arises out of a "direct sampling" of objective external information structure (3D Euclidean space, objects, surfaces, shape, etc.) constituted in the external world, prespecified independent of the observer. Like Gibsonianism, it contrasts with the standard approach in that it postulates that there is no "internal activation" or a "re-presentation" of that world. *The world simply sits there as "external memory,"* fully and objectively specified. According to O'Regan and Noe (2001), perception consists in the *manner and consequences of sensory sampling of this prespecified external world through the movements and motor actions of the observer.*

Real objects have properties such as size, shape, texture, and color, and they can be positioned in the three-dimensional world at different distances and angles with respect to an observer. Visual exploration provides ways of sampling these properties which differs from sampling via other sense...

Indeed, there is no "re"-presentation of the world inside the brain: the only pictorial or 3D version required is the real outside version. What is required, however, are methods for probing the outside world – and visual perception constitutes one mode via which it can be probed...

But it does bring forcibly to mind the fact that the perceived detail to be out there in the world, not in our head. Indeed, we take ourselves to be embedded in the environment and to have access to detail through active exploration...

The animal must be exploring the environment in a manner that is governed by the two main kinds of sensorimotor contingencies (those fixed by the visual apparatus, and those fixed by the character of objects).

According to O'R&N, it is these so-called sensorimotor contingencies, the pattern of changes of sensory array activation that occur due to movement and motor action (relative to the prespecified objects and properties in the worlds), that the observer phenomenally "experiences" as perception (without the need for any intermediary encoding or representation of properties). This is essentially a variant of Gibson's idea of perception as the *direct experience of changes in the optic array.*

It is easy to mistakenly interpret the sensorimotor contingencies account as capturing the sort of natural anticipatory structure espoused here. But even cursory inspection reveals that O'R&N's account *necessarily* reduces to the structure of predicative artificial systems. This is because in this account the so-called external world of the perception is already prespecified. O'R&N's "Real objects positioned in the three-dimensional world at different distances and angles with respect to an observer having properties such as size, shape, texture, and color," "real outside pictorial or 3D version," "perceived detail out there in the world," and "character of objects" form an objective, prespecified information structure residing for free in the external world and cannot therefore, by definition, be anticipatory, since anticipatory information *is always relative to an agent.*

Therefore, while the O'R&N account suggests a system where there is prediction of how the sensory apparatus can potentially sample the external world, and a prediction of how that sampling might change the sensory input, it is based on implicit assumption of a prespecified (predicative) informational structure of the external world.

This is in stark contrast to what is proposed here, where those very objects, properties, and characters, which the perceiver (and O'R&N) ascribes to an objective external world (3D space, objects, properties, details), are in fact wholly subjective, impredicative, and anticipatory. There is no fixed objective information or knowledge of sensor functionality available to the organism to build the sort of sensorimotor contingencies desired by O'R&N. This becomes clear in the examples they use as intuition pumps for explaining their hypothesis.

O'R&N employ the example of the visual contemplation and handling of a wine bottle. In this example, the shape of the bottle is already objectively prespecified externally (O'R&N's "character of the objects"), and the sensorimotor contingency simply predicts how the actuators will move in response to exploring the bottle by touch (wider grasp followed narrower grasp as one moves up the bottle) or eye movements will be deployed (follow a certain path of the given profile geometry contours) and the resulting change in visual input. But this is nothing more than the sort of sensorimotor contingency that an engineer might incorporate into the function of a robotic system, with bottle's "shape" and "properties" (hardness, smoothness) already prespecified within the system. O'R&N's sensorimotor account is therefore very far from the anticipatory perceptual system of the sort being championed here, where the nature of "shape," "hardness," "smoothness," and "3D," in themselves, forms a subjective and impredicative anticipatory structure that needs explanation.

O'R&N attempt to bolster their arguments by suggesting that their model provides a better understanding of *visual experience*. But their claim, namely, that perception (vision, touch) is something "we do," that "vision is a mode of exploration of the world that is mediated by knowledge of what we call sensorimotor contingencies" are rather obscure:

> But experiences, we have argued, are not states. They are ways of acting. . .
> They are things we do. There is no introspectively available property determining the character of one's experiential states, for there are no such states. Experience is something we do and its qualitative features are aspects of this activity.

According to O'R&N, this standpoint banishes the need to talk about subjective experiential states, because the experiential states (usually referred to as Qualia) are standardly implied to be associated with "representations" of properties of states or events in the world, and no such properties are represented in the sensorimotor contingency account. Their system is simply a mechanism of sampling the already *prespecified structure and detail* of the external world.

Things get even more obscure with O'R&N's idea that qualitative perceptual states involve "actively exercising mastery of these laws [of sensorimotor contingency]" or that seeing "'Red' is knowing the structure of the changes that 'red' causes," or that experiences are "'exercisings' of complicated capacities, not ongoing occurrences in the mind or brain."

Finally, O'R&N appear to have significantly misinterpreted some of the earlier philosophical proposals (e.g., Poincare 1905; Michotte 1948) which are, in fact, more closely and correctly aligned to the proposal of perceptual experience constituting a natural anticipatory system proposed here. For example, consider Poincare's statement quoted in their paper:

> To localize an object simply means to represent to oneself the movements that would be necessary to reach it. It is not a question of representing the movements themselves in space, but solely of representing to oneself the muscular sensations which accompany these movements and which do not presuppose the existence of space. (Poincare 1905, *La valeur de la science.* p. 47)

This is in fact more consistent with the proposal championed here, that perceptual experiences are subjective and anticipatory, and in opposition to O'R&N's proposal. Poincare, correctly, does not presume even the preexistence of space, which for O'R&N is given for free in the so-called external world. Instead, it is apparent that he takes localization as a subjective *presentation* ("the muscular sensation") rather than an encoding of the contingent array of movements within a preordained space as O'R&N propose.

Work preceding O'R&Ns account, cited in their paper, and similarly suggestive of anticipatory models (e.g., Hochberg (1968)) are subject to some of the same conceptual drawbacks as O'R&N's work. The ultimate appeal to a prespecified external information content in these proposals aligns them with the constructs of artificial predicative systems discussed earlier. Similarly, the O'R&N approach is in contrast to the "enactive" approach to perception champoined by Maturana and Varela (1989), and which inspired O'R&Ns theory. In the original enactive account, the organism plus environment is considers a closed impredicative system based on their notion of autopoesis, which is far from the notion of a prespecified, objective, god-given structure that is assumed in O'R&N.

A more recent and increasingly popular account of perception is that of 'Predictive Coding' (see Clark (2013) for a review). This approach construes 'prediction' as intrinsic to perceptual inference but once again, unfortunately, incorrectly relies on a predicative and naive-realist conception of perception. It, in effect, reduces to an artificial model of predictive (control) systems, rather than providing a useful basis for an anticipatory account of perceptual content. A more detailed critique of the problematic nature of this approach (predictive coding) as a model of perception is left to the reader as an exercise.

There are however other strains of an anticipatory account of perception coming out of philosophy that appear to remain agnostic to notions of objective or subjective information content and should be seen as sympathetic to idea of perception as anticipatory structure proposed here. In this account, for example, spatial content is construed as being subjective, and dispositions for engaging in motor behaviour are seen as being *constituively embedded* in the content of our visuo-spatial experiences (see Briscoe 2009).

In summary, the sensorimotor contingency (perception-as-action) and predictive coding accounts, while *suggestive* of the anticipatory model of perception championed here, in the end suffer from the same epistemological and ontological problems present in the standard (inferential, representational) models. Equally, they do not provide a coherent model to understand subjective visual experience, especially as a way to support an empirical research program. These approaches arise from an apparent misunderstanding of the necessary paths in the genesis of natural systems (Fig. 1) which we have seen must, in principle, be anticipatory and impredicative from the very start. Rather, these accounts are more consistent with the approach of an artificial intelligence researcher or engineer, an approach to building artificial models where input/output features/variables/values can be objectively prespecified.

Perception of Space as Anticipation

The standard view of the perception of space assumes a prespecified Euclidean 3D spatial structure external to the observer with an inherent objective metric. The *perception of space* is then simply a *representation* of this space. In the case of Gibson or the sensorimotor contingency account of O'R&N, it is even more problematic: space and its associated constructs (distance, direction, depth, objects, surfaces, size) is given directly for free *to* perception! In all these models, the content, or information, constituted in the perceptual presentation of space is thus non-anticipatory. The contents can however be engineered into a predictive system by linking to action in the manner of an artificial devices as we have discussed (as representation-guided action or sensorimotor contingencies).

An alternative is to view the contents of the perception of space (distance, depth, size, location) to be intrinsically anticipatory constructs that are not derived from the external world. For example, the impression of space characteristic of stereopsis has been proposed to be an anticipatory presentation of the potential for manipulation (Michotte 1948; Vishwanath 2011, 2014). Such an anticipatory subjective impression of space (spacing between, and extents of, objects) has been operationalized in psychophysical terms as visually derived depth relations scaled with egocentric metrics (Vishwanath 2014). This is what is conjectured to generate an impression of objects, and the spaces in between them, as tangible, immersive and real under binocular or stereoscopic viewing (stereopsis). It is in contrast to the standard view that stereopsis is simply the veridical *representation* of objective Euclidean external space inferred on the basis of binocular disparity cues, or as in the Gibsonian view, *directly seen*.

An important example from spatial memory research sheds further light on these important distinctions in perception of space as an anticipatory system. One of the major neurophysiological discoveries of the last decade has been that of the so-called grid cells in the medial entorhinal cortex (Hafting et al. 2005). These are individual neurons, discovered in the rat, which have a stereotypic firing pattern when the rat explores or forages over a bounded space. Specifically, a given grid cell or neuron fires when the animal is only at specific locations within the space, where these locations form a regular hexagonal grid. In other words, the receptive field of a specific cell is the nodes of a regular hexagonal grid distributed over delimited space. Remarkably, such grid cell firing occurs even in the dark, without visual input. Research thus far has concluded that these cells form the substrates for navigation and specifically a way for the animal to self-locate or navigate in space via path integration (Barry et al. 2007; Hafting et al. 2005; McNaughton et al. 2006). Specifically, the most popular interpretation of the firing pattern of grid cells is that their firing pattern matrix gains its *metrics* through path-integration-based computations utilizing inputs from cells coding direction, speed, and time of travel as well as input regarding the boundary conditions and that they are "part of a generalized, path-integration-based map of the spatial environment" (Hafting et al. 2005). However, the view of grid cells as supporting metrically accurate memory representation for path integration is challenged by the finding that the metrics of grid cells changes in different environments (e.g., different shape, Barry et al. 2007; Krupic et al. 2015) suggesting that they might not be able to provide a universal environment-invariant spatial metric for path-integration related navigation or as a reproducible representation of spatial location.

What is interesting is that work on grid cells has almost exclusively been conducted by researchers interested in memory representations. Path integration and navigation are spatial concepts associated with memory rather than perception. The potential implication of grid cells as a substrate for real-time perception of space, rather than one subserving memory guided navigation, has therefore generally been neglected.

It is interesting to consider grid cells from the context of our hypothetical organism in Fig. 1 and the proposed mapping to the mammalian brain. Since the medial entorhinal cortex (MEC) is part of the neocortex, it seem reasonable to propose that grid cells are not intrinsically part of mechanisms underlying memory of location (as in the hippocampus) but instead *underwrite the subjective and anticipatory real-time perception (awareness) of space* (which then feed into mechanisms underlying spatial memory).

Specifically, it is possible that the grid cells are later evolutionary mechanisms (part of the perceptual "awareness" module, stage 4 of our evolving organism in Fig. 1) involved in explicit perceptual presentation, rather than evolutionarily early rudimentary representations that yield *implicit egocentric metric computations* for path-integrative navigation or spatially relevant memory traces (the sensorimotor maps in the stage 3 of our organism). It is well established that highly accurate path-integration-based navigation is already present in organisms that lack structures like the neocortex but only have protocerebrums. Importantly, evidence suggests that such path-integration mechanism may be more rudimentary than a map-like representation evident in grid cells (Wehner et al. 2006).

Specifically, a novel conjecture would be that the medial entorhinal cortex is the locus where visually (or auditorily) generated presentation of relative spatial order or layout arising in the sensory cortices becomes imbued with an egocentric metric to generate a perceptual presentation (awareness) of spatial location that is intrinsically anticipatory in terms of locomotion. Instead of thinking of grid cells as underlying a representation of the animals spatial location that is mainly utilized by navigational and spatial memory mechanisms (as typically construed in the literature), the alternative conjecture I am making here is that grid cells contribute to the *real-time perception of space as a predictive anticipatory presentation of ambulatory distances to locations in that space.* (This is in line with Poincare's definition of space in the quote given in the previous section of this chapter as a kind of anticipation of movement.)

Based on this conjecture, the ontogenetic calibration of grid cell metrics with movement should then not to be thought of as a process to yield accurate "representation" of location for path-integrative navigation mechanisms or self-location in space but instead as the process of calibrating *the anticipation of movement implicit in the perception of space* with the consequences of actual movement.

Such a space may be distinct and dissociable from egocentric presentation of objects and space that anticipates visually guided manual action (reaching, grasping) alluded to earlier in association with stereopsis. Recent preliminary neurophysiological data has localized putative neural mechanisms underlying the qualitative experience of stereopsis in the posterior parietal (dorsal) regions (Vishwanath et al. in preparation). In contrast, the MEC, where grid cells are located, is situated in a quite different area, the medial region of the temporal lobe of the neocortex.

Conclusion

The sort of information and capacity that has evolved in the perceptual apparatus of sentient organisms is that of *an anticipatory system that allows planning on the basis of divining futures*, rather than providing the basis for what is essentially a *reflexive action based on a complex analysis and efficient summary of the past*. This *divining of futures* should not be seen solely in terms of effortful cognitive activity that we as humans have first-person experience of. Rather, we must recognize that the default perceptual presentation (consisting of, among other things, space, objects, surface, and color) is in itself a divination of the future. While modern AI has a workable understanding of the informational transaction involved in reflexes based on efficient past summary and has become proficient at building predictive systems that operate on this basis, understanding the nature of the informational transaction in natural anticipatory perceptual systems and the proficiency to replicate them still remain the major challenge.

References

Albertazzi, L. (2002). *Unfolding perceptual continua*. Amsterdam: Benjamins Publishing Company.

Albertazzi, L. (2006). Introduction to visual spaces. In L. Albertazzi (Ed.), *Visual thought. The depictive space of perception* (pp. 3–34). Amsterdam: Benjamins.

Albertazzi, L., & Louie, A. H. (2016). A mathematical science of qualities: A sequel. *Biological Theory, 11*, 192.

Albertazzi, L., van Tonder, G., & Vishwanath, D. (2011). Information in perception. In L. Albertazzi, G. van Tonder, & D. Vishwanath (Eds.), *Perception beyond inference. The information content of perceptual processes* (pp. 1–26). Cambridge, MA: MIT Press.

Barry, C., Hayman, R., Burgess, N., & Jeffery, K. J. (2007). Experience-dependent rescaling of entorhinal grids. *Nature Neuroscience, 10*, 682–684.

Briscoe, R. (2009). Egocentric spatial representation in action and perception. *Philosophy and Phenomenological Research, 79*(2), 423–460.

Charness, N. (1992). The impact of chess research on cognitive science. *Psychological Research, 54*(1), 4–9.

Clark, A. (2013). Whatever next? Predictive brains, situated agents, and the future of cognitive science. *Behavioral Brain Sciences, 36*(3), 181–204. https://doi.org/10.1017/S0140525X12000477.

Fodor, J., & Pylyshyn, Z. (1988). Connectionism and cognitive architecture: A critical analysis. *Cognition, 28*, 3–71.

Hafting, T., Fyhn, M., Molden, S., Moser, M.-B., & Moser, E. I. (2005). Microstructure of a spatial map in the entorhinal cortex. *Nature, 436*, 801–806.

Hochberg, J. (1968). In the mind's eye. In R. N. Haber (Ed.), *Contemporary theory and research in visual perception*. Holt: Rinehart & Winston.

Kowler, E. (2011). Eye movements: The past 25 years. *Vision Research, 51*, 1457–1483.

Krupic, J., Bauza, M., Burton, S., Barry, C., & O'Keefe, J. (2015). Grid cell symmetry is shaped by environmental geometry. *Nature, 518*, 232–235.

Lake, B., Ullman, T., Tenenbaum, J., & Gershman, S. (2017). Building machines that learn and think like people. *Behavioral and Brain Sciences*, 40, E253. https://doi.org/10.1017/S0140525X16001837.

Land, M. F., & Nilsson, D. E. (2012). *Animal Eyes*. Oxford: Oxford University Press.

Leyton, M. (1984). Perceptual organization as nested control. *Biological Cybernetics, 51*(3), 141–153.

Maturana, H. R., & Varela, F. J. (1989/1992). *The tree of knowledge: The biological roots of human understanding*. Boston: Shambala.

McMurray, B., & Aslin, R. N. (2004). Anticipatory eye movements reveal Infants' auditory and visual categories. *Infancy, 6*, 203–229.

McNaughton, B. L., Battaglia, F. P., Jensen, O., Moser, E. I., & Moser, M.-B. (2006). Path integration and the neural basis of the "cognitive map". *Nature Reviews Neuroscience, 7*, 663–678.

Michotte, A. (1991/1948). The psychological enigma of perspective in outline pictures. In G. Thinès, A. Costall, & G. Butterworth (Eds.), *Michotte's experimental phenomenology of perception*. Hillsdale: Erlbaum.

O'Regan, J. K., & Noe, A. (2001). A sensorimotor account of vision and visual consciousness. *The Behavioral and Brain Sciences, 24*, 939–1031.

Poincaré, H. (1905). La valeur de la science. Paris: Flammarion.

Schiff, W., Caviness, J. A., & Gibson, J. J. (1962). Persistent fear responses in rhesus monkeys to the optical stimulus of 'looming'. *Science, 136*, 982–983.

Silver, D., et al. (2016). Mastering the game of go with deep neural networks and tree search. *Nature, 529*, 484–489.

Suddendorf, T., Addis, D. R., & Corballis, M. C. (2009). Mental time travel and the shaping of the human mind. *Philosophical Transactions of the Royal Society, B: Biological Sciences, 364*(1521), 1317–1324.

Vishwanath, D. (2005). The epistemological status of vision and its implications for design. *Axiomathes, 15*, 399–486.

Vishwanath, D. (2011). Information in surface and depth perception: Reconciling pictures and reality. In L. Albertazzi, G. van Tonder, & D. Vishwanath (Eds.), *Perception beyond inference, the information content of visual processes*. Cambridge: MIT Press.

Vishwanath, D. (2013). Experimental phenomenology of visual 3D space: Considerations from evolution, perception and philosophy. In L. Albertazzi (Ed.), *Wiley handbook of experimental phenomenology*. Chichester: Wiley-Blackwell.

Vishwanath, D. (2014). Toward a new theory of stereopsis. *Psychological Review, 121*, 151–178.

Vishwanath, D. (in preparation). Declarative and non-declarative information.

Vishwanath, D., Uji, M., Cavin, D., & Lingnau, A. (in preparation). Identifying the cortical locus of the subjective impression of stereopsis: An fMRI study.

Wehner, R. (2003). Desert ant navigation: How miniature brains solve complex tasks. *The Journal of Comparative Physiology A: Neuroethology, Sensory, Neural, and Behavioral Physiology, 189*, 579–588.

Wehner, R., Boyer, M., Loertscher, F., Sommer, S., & Menzi, U. (2006). Ant navigation: One-way routes rather than maps. *Current Biology, 16*, 75–79.

Anticipation and Representation

16

Mark H. Bickhard

Contents

Abstract

Anticipation or prediction is generally assumed to be based on some sort of representation. Such representations will be involved, for example, in a model – causal, statistical, dynamic (process), and other kinds of model – of the system or phenomena to be anticipated. This form of anticipation certainly exists, and is quite important.

M. H. Bickhard (✉)
Lehigh University, Bethlehem, PA, USA
e-mail: mhb0@Lehigh.EDU

© Springer Nature Switzerland AG 2019
R. Poli (ed.), *Handbook of Anticipation*,
https://doi.org/10.1007/978-3-319-91554-8_11

I will argue, however, that there is a more basic form of anticipation that does not require representation, but is, in fact, *constitutive* of representation. The intuition underlying this point is that anticipation can be true or false, thus, have truth value, and thus constitute representation in its own right. (The basic criterion here for being representational is "bearing truth value" – that is, being true or false.) But how such anticipation can occur without being based on representation itself will be my focus.

Keywords

Anticipation · Representation · Interactivism · Correspondence encoding

I will first address how anticipation can constitute representation, a bit about how this might be realized in the brain, mention a few consequences of the overall model for, for example, learning and development, and then turn in the second half of the discussion to some metaphysical issues that must be addressed in order to ground the model of representation.

Anticipation/Representation in Agents

Any complex agent must have some functional indications of what interactions are possible in the current situation; it can then select among these indications what to (try to) do next – it does not help to initiate an "open the refrigerator door" interaction if there is no refrigerator available (perhaps you are in the middle of a forest). So some form of sensitivity to the environment must be maintained, on the basis of which indications of possibility of interaction with that environment can be evoked or constructed.

Indications of interactive possibility are *anticipatory* in the sense that such an indication anticipates that, if the indicated interaction (kind) were to be engaged, that interaction would proceed as anticipated (within the range of anticipation). Such anticipations might be correct or incorrect. If engaged, they may or may not proceed as anticipated – the anticipations can be true or false. Anticipations of potential interactions, thus, have truth value: they are representational.

A frog, for example, might have indications that it could flick its tongue in one direction and eat (perhaps a fly) or in another direction and eat (a different fly) and perhaps yet a third direction (perhaps a worm). (One aspect of this notion might be approximated by production rules: If A, then do B. Production rules, however, do not have any intrinsic normativity, and in general are triggered, not selected. For a discussion of SOAR, see Bickhard and Terveen (1995).) It might select one of these, or perhaps none if, for example, a shadow of a hawk passes over the frog. Here there are at least three indications: indications can *branch* into multiple possibilities.

A frog might also have an indication that, if it were to move a little to the left, several more tongue flicking and eating possibilities would become accessible. In that sense, indications can conditionally *iterate* – in the example, conditional on moving to the left, several other potentialities open up.

A simple interactive anticipation constitutes a *primitive form* of representation, but it constitutes the basic form of emergence of *representational normativity*: having truth value. The frog examples, however, illustrate some basic resources for modeling more complex representation. In particular, branching and iterating anticipations can, in principle, yield complex webs of such anticipatory indications of possibility. Such complex webs are what we find in agents more complex than frogs, including, in particular, humans.

Representing (Small) Objects

The power of these resources can be illustrated with an example of small, manipulable objects – perhaps a child's toy wooden block. A small block offers multiple possibilities for visual scans, manipulations, throwing, chewing, and so on. The scans and manipulations, in particular, can constitute a subweb of anticipated possibilities with some special properties: (1) every scan or manipulation can be accessed conditional on appropriate intermediate interactions – for example, to get to some particular scan, an appropriate manipulation will bring that scan potentiality into view – so the subweb is internally completely reachable, every part reachable from every other part (with appropriate intermediate interactions), and (2) the potentialities of that subweb remain invariant under a range of other interactions and transformations. The block can be left on the floor or put away in the toy box, and the interactions can be reaccessed by returning to the room or retrieving the block from the toy box. The potentialities of the subweb are not invariant under all changes, however: crushing or burning the block eliminates the subweb potentialities, and the subweb would need to be changed. The internally reachable subweb with its crucial invariances constitutes a child's representation of the block. The general model of representation as anticipation, thus, has resources for addressing more complex representation. (This is Piaget's model of action-based representation, adapted to the interactivist model. Such adaptation is possible because both models are action-based. Another partial borrowing from Piaget addresses issues of abstract representation, such as for the number three (Bickhard 2009).)

Apperceiving

The overall web of anticipatory indications is called the organism's *situation knowledge* – knowledge of the (extended) interactive potentialities of its current situation. Situation knowledge is constantly changing due to the organism's interactions and other changes taking place in the environment. Situation knowledge, thus, must be constantly maintained and updated. These processes of maintenance and updating of situation knowledge are called *apperceiving*.

Apperception is based on the flow and internal outcomes of previous interactions, including interactions of kinds that are *specialized* for *differentiating* various properties of the environment – otherwise known as *perceiving*. (These are paradigmaticallly specialized in physiology by evolutionary processes: the classical sensory systems. But they also include nonphysiologically specialized forms of interaction, such as interpreting X-rays.) Apperceiving must be based on such interaction with the environment, including but not limited to pure differentiating interactions (perceiving), so that the apperceptive process can set up and modify the situation knowledge in appropriate ways. Sensitivity to the environment is necessary in order to anticipate correctly what possible interactions there are in that environment.

Such sensitivity to the environment is, in general, based on the flow and outcomes of interactions, but could be based on purely passive processing of inputs from that environment (such as pure visual input processing). Such passive input processing is the classic model of perception. *Pure* passive processing, however, rarely occurs, and is intrinsically less powerful than full interactions, including, for example, visual *interactions* with the ambient field of light – Gibson's ecological optics (Bickhard and Richie 1983) – not just visual *inputs*. (There is a resonance here with Gibson, including with the notion of affordances (indications of interactive potentiality), but also some basic differences – e.g., Gibsonian affordances cannot be linked into webs (Bickhard 2017): Gibson was opposed to models of mental processes, especially representational mental processes (Bickhard and Richie 1983).)

Contact

Apperceiving is also based on interactions that induce relevant *changes* in the environment, not only detections: these too must be kept track of in situation knowledge. Such actual interactions with environments, whether perceptual or not, constitute relevant sensitivity to those environments – relevant *contact* with those environments. Such contact does not itself have truth value: it differentiates, but what is differentiated is not thereby represented. (For a simple example: a vending machine might differentiate between dimes and quarters without thereby representing either dimes or quarters. Nevertheless, the differentiation can influence further processes in the machine.) It is the anticipations based on such contact that are representational, that have truth value, that have *aboutness* concerning the environment.

Differentiation

A word about differentiation: a (sub-)system engaged in an interaction with an environment will proceed in its internal dynamics in one way in some types of environments, and in other ways in other types of environments – perhaps ending up in particular internal "final" states depending on the courses of those interactions. If the process ends up in internal state A, for example, then it differentiates that it has been in contact with an A-type environment, rather than, say, a B-type environment.

Note that, on one hand, such differentiations of environments are necessary in order for the organism to successfully set up and engage in further interaction, and, on the other hand, there is nothing in such differences in dynamic flows (or in "final" internal states) that represents what has been differentiated. Functional differentiation (contact) is necessary, but does not itself constitute representation.

Content

Indications or anticipations of what might be done next, however, *do* constitute representation: they can be true or false. Furthermore, the anticipations will be borne out – they will be true – in some environments and not in others. An indication of the possibility of an interaction, thus, functionally presupposes that sufficient supporting conditions obtain in the environment. The sufficient supporting conditions are intrinsic and implicit in such anticipations: the presupposed support is internally related to the anticipation. Such presupposed support constitutes *content* that is attributed to the environment – is *about* the environment – attributed intrinsically by the nature of anticipation. The truth or falsity of the anticipation is grounded on the presence or absence of those supporting conditions.

So, contact and content are differentiated: they are differing aspects of the dynamics of an interactive agent.

It should be noted that in standard models, contact is via perception construed as passive input processing, and content is, supposedly, of what has been thereby differentiated: contact and content are identified (e.g., Carlson 2013). There is no future-oriented anticipation that is intrinsic to the nature of representation or perception in these models (they are not inter-action based), and, therefore they cannot account for the normativity of truth value that emerges with anticipation. (In spite of multiple attempts to do so (see, e.g., Cummins 1996; Dretske 1988; Fodor 1990; Millikan 1984, 1993; Bickhard 2009). This is especially the case for the issue of *system detectable* representational error (not just, supposedly, detectable from the perspective of an external observer). This issue has not been addressed at all in the general philosophical literature, but, without organism detectable error, there is no error guided interaction and no learning. There are some discussions in the broader literature that use words like "error" – e.g., in machine learning – but this is normative error only from the perspective of the designer or user of the system. There is no intrinsic error for the system (Bickhard 2009, 2015b, 2016).)

Motivation

Within situation knowledge, the organism selects and guides trajectories of interaction in accordance with other constraints, such as goals, or conditions such as hunger. This selection function is the function of *motivation*: what shall "I" do next. So, representation and motivation are different aspects of one underlying dynamic of selecting interactions within a space of (anticipated) possible interactive trajectories (Bickhard (2003)).

Any sort of complex agent must serve these functions of anticipation and selection, and evolution has constructed (and has to have constructed) ways in which complex agents can accomplish these functions. I turn now to a brief outline of how this might be accomplished in the brain.

Anticipation in the Brain

The key to modeling how the brain functions is to recognize that there are many kinds of relevant processes at multiple physical and temporal scales, and they are all dynamically coupled. (Models of brain functioning in terms, for example, of threshold switches linked via classical synapses – or other "information processing" equivalents – are simply false (Bickhard 2009, 2015a).) For example, there are small-scale and fast processes such as gap junctions and classical synapses, as well as larger-scale and slower processes such as volume transmitters and astrocyte processes (Bickhard 2015a, b).

The larger-scale, slower, processes are relatively constant at the fast scales of the smaller processes, and, thus, set parameters for those faster processes – they influence how the faster processes will proceed. The coupling is via multiple dynamics, including, for example, varying extra-neural concentrations of ions and transmitter substances. This set up, or microgenesis, of how other (generally faster) processes proceed is anticipatory. It is a preparation for what happens next, and, thus, anticipates that what happens will be within the bounds of what has been prepared for. Clearly, these functional microgenetic anticipations can turn out to be false – the actual course of processes may violate the microgenetic anticipatory preparedness. So, rather directly, brain processes are anticipatory in virtue of the facts that: (1) they can vary in their dynamics and (2) that there is a microgenetic set up for which dynamic (sub-) spaces they are prepared for – preparing for "this" range of dynamic possibilities as distinct from "that" range is anticipatory. And, thus, can be true or false.

Some Properties of Representing

This model of representing as constituted in particular kinds of functional anticipation captures the basic representational normativity of having truth value, and has resources for modeling more complex forms of representation. There are some properties and consequences of this interactive anticipatory model, however, that differ from others on offer in the contemporary literature.

One such difference is that anticipatory representing is *future oriented*, rather than past oriented: it is not a "spectator" model, attempting to look backward down the input stream (Dewey 1960; Tiles 1990). Action-based models – pragmatic models in general – share in this future orientation, but others do not.

In being future oriented, the model is intrinsically *modal*: anticipations are of potential, or possible, interactions. This is in contrast to standard models of representations of current actual objects, events, and properties that have no intrinsic modality.

Interactive representing is *emergent*: a dynamic organization serving the normative function of (inter-)action anticipation will emergently realize representational normativity. This is in contrast to standard models that must posit representation as having an innate base in particular organisms, but as having "emerged" in evolution – even though the models make it impossible for there to be any such emergence in evolution, any more than it is possible in learning and development, for example, Fodor's model (Bickhard 2009).

As mentioned, content in this model is *implicit*, rather than explicit. This is in contrast to encoding models, in which, for example, in order for an encoding to represent a chair, the content of "chair" has to be explicit and explicitly tied to the encoding (vehicle). (For several senses of "implicit" that are relevant to the model, see Bickhard (1998).)

Another difference is that both the possibility of error in representing and the possibility of *organism detectable error* are easily accounted for in the future-oriented model: engage in an indicated potentiality and "see" if it works out within the range of anticipation. Note that this detection of whether or not the actual flow of processes violates microgenetic anticipations can be accomplished strictly functionally, and, thus, does not require further representation.

This is in strong contrast to models in which simply accounting for the possibility of error is either impossible, or is possible only from the perspective of an external observer or user of the system. And in which the possibility of organism detectable error is not addressed at all. But, if organism detectable error could not occur, then error guided behavior and learning would not be possible. We know that error guided behavior and learning occur, so organism detectable error occurs, and, so, is possible. Thus any model that renders such error detection impossible is refuted (Bickhard 2009).

One further difference that I will mention has to do with consequences of the model for *learning and development*. Models that construe epistemic contact with the world in terms of the world somehow impressing itself into a passive mind, such as via transduction or induction, generally take some set of such "impressions" as foundational (and, usually, innate). (The classic version, of course, is Aristotle's analogy with a signet ring pressing its form into wax (Campbell 1992).) They can then differ in terms of how much, if any, further constructions on that foundational basis are required in order to account for development in the child (Allen and Bickhard 2011, 2013). Any such posited construction, however, is added "on top" of the basic foundation in order to attempt to account for what the foundation does not account for.

In contrast, with a future-oriented, action-based, anticipatory model, there is no temptation to assume that a competent interaction system can be impressed into a mind by the world – there is no plausibility to such a notion. System organization *must* be constructed: a constructivism is forced. Furthermore, absent prescience, that constructivism must be some sort of trial and error, variation and selection, constructivism: An (inter-)action based model forces an evolutionary epistemology (Campbell 1974).

Note that, if the microgenetic constructive processes in the brain are stabilized by successful anticipation, and destabilized by failure of anticipation, then this already constitutes a core evolutionary epistemology. Much more needs to be addressed, such as the dynamics of heuristic learning, creativity, and so on, but the evolutionary epistemological constructivism is accounted for (Bickhard and Campbell 1996).

Such a constructivism will manifest shorter time scale constructive dynamics as well as longer time scale constraints and enablings. Properties of the short time scale dynamics are the general subject matter of "learning" (e.g., some constructions making others more probable, such as in the case of what are called "associations"), while the longer time scale properties are the subject matter of "development" (such as some constructions being practically necessary – precursors or prerequisites – before others become possible). So, "learning" and "development" are differing temporal perspectives on one underlying constructivist dynamic (Bickhard 2006).

Encodingism

There is a general form for models of representation that contrasts with interactive anticipatory representation: these contrasting forms assume that representation is constituted as some special kind of correspondence that "encodes" whatever is being represented. These special correspondences are variously posited to be causal, lawful, informational, or structural, but they all posit some special kind of factual correspondence that is supposed to constitute a normative representation. (Such models, therefore, include computational symbol models, connectionist and neural correspondence models, semantic information processing models, and others (e.g., Bickhard 2009, 2014).)

Encodings certainly exist (and our contemporary economy would collapse without them), but, so I argue, they are necessarily *derivative* forms of representation. Thus, they cannot be the exhaustive form of representation, and they cannot be a foundational form of representation.

Encodings are stand-ins: they stand-in for other representations, generally changing the form of the "vehicle." Thus, ". . ." stands-in for "s" in Morse code, and that is useful because ". . ." can be sent over telegraph wires while "s" cannot. Similarly, neutrino counts in a North Dakota gold mine encode properties of fusion processes in the sun, and this is useful because those properties cannot be directly measured. In both cases, the encoding relationship holds only if an interpreter knows about both ends of the relationship and about the relationship itself. There is no way to have "original" epistemic access to "s" by studying ". . .", nor about sun-fusion properties by studying the raw data from the gold mine. Encodings must be interpreted, and interpretation requires that the encoding content – which is being borrowed via the (known) stand-in relation – is already available. Encodings cannot provide original or emergent content; they are derivative.

Nevertheless, models of representation have, for millennia, posited some form of encoding relationship as constituting *all* of representation. I call this assumption *encodingism*: the assumption that *all* representations are encodings. But encodingism models cannot account for the origins (the emergence) of representation (Representation did not exist 13 billion years ago, but it does now. It has to have emerged, so any model that renders that impossible is thereby refuted.); they require foundations, but cannot account for their own foundations; they cannot account for the possibility of error, and certainly not of organism detectable error; and so on (Bickhard 2009, 2014; Allen and Bickhard 2013). (For a few additonal relevant references, see Allen and Bickhard (2013; Bickhard 2000, in preparation; Freyd 1987, 1992; Freyd and Pantzer 1995; Shanon 1993).)

The Larger Model

The interactivist anticipatory model of representation arguably accounts for the nature of representation and avoids multiple problems that alternative models encounter. But representation and therefore assumptions about representation abound in studies of mental phenomena. Insofar as these assumptions are encodingist assumptions, then they are in error, and need to be corrected. But it is not always obvious where and in what way encodingism is presupposed, nor how to remove those presuppositions.

The general interactivist model has attempted to explore these presuppositions and to propose models that avoid them across many domains. These include, for example, language, perception, memory, learning, emotions, reflective consciousness, and others (Bickhard (2009)). This is not the occasion for reviewing those further developments in detail, but it should be noted that discovering and undoing encodingism presuppositions does not leave everything else in extant models unchanged.

Metaphysical Foundations

The model of anticipatory, interactive representation outlined above depends on the truth-value normativity of representation. And representational normativity, in turn, is grounded in the biological, functional normativity of action and action selection. It is "natural" to assume such biological normativity, but there are reasons and arguments to consider normativity, of any kind, to not be a part or property of the natural world – and perhaps to not exist at all (Bickhard 2009). So, if the above model is to be acceptable, its metaphysical foundations must be addressed. I turn now to these foundations.

In particular, I will argue that:

1. *Normativity* per se must be accounted for.
2. Which account requires *emergent* normativity.

3. Which requires *metaphysical* emergence more generally.
4. Which requires *process* metaphysics.
5. Which requires undoing millennia of background metaphysical substance and particle assumptions.

I will address these in reverse order.

Process

Heraclitus argued that everything is flux; Parmenides that change is not possible. Historically, Parmenides won. The impossibility of change, so Parmenides's argument went, is at the basic foundational metaphysical level, while the *appearance* of change occurs at nonbasic levels – such as in terms of varying *mixtures* of "stuffs" or substances, for example, earth, air, fire, and water (Empedocles), or in terms of varying *configurations* of basic "atoms" (Democritus). The most basic level, whether substances or atoms, does not and cannot change.

Aristotle introduced a sophisticated variant of this framework with notions of "substance" as "entity" (Campbell 1992; Gill 1989), comprised of matter and form. Descendants of this framework have been dominant since.

There are three basic, sequential consequences of this framework that I will focus on.

1. The default at "the" basic metaphysical level is no-change, stasis. Any (apparent) change requires explanation – for example, external cause.
2. Metaphysical emergence is not possible: no new substances or particles can be created, and mixtures of substances or configurations of particles are not basic – such mixtures or configurations are epiphenomenal. Any such metaphysical change at the level of basic substances or particles is precisely what is supposedly precluded by the Parmenidean argument. This assumption of the necessity for an unchanged substrate for change has been with us for millennia (Gill 1989).
3. The metaphysics of the natural world consists of substances or particles, and factual and causal relations among them. There is no place in the "natural" world viewed in this way for normativity, intentionality, or other "mental" phenomena. There is a split between the natural world and the world of mental processes and properties.

Given this metaphysical split, there are three possibilities: (1) assume two basic metaphysical realms, such as form and matter (Aristotle), or mental and physical kinds of "substance" (Descartes), and so on; (2) attempt to understand the world in terms of just the "mental" side of the split (e.g., Hegel, Green, Bradley), or (3) attempt to understand the world in terms of just the "material" side of the split (e.g., Hobbes, Hume). These three possibilities have framed much of metaphysics since Parmenides, with the "material" framework, in the form of assumed basic physical particles, being dominant in the contemporary world. (Note that most arguments *against* naturalism assume the same split – they have the general form of: some "mental" kind of phenomena exists and cannot be accounted for within a naturalist world, therefore naturalism must be false or at least incomplete (e.g., Wagner and Warner 1993; Caro and MacArthur 2004). But, if the split were artifactual from substance/particle metaphysics in the first place, and the split can be bridged with the two "sides" integrated by, perhaps, emergence, then these arguments too would be unsound.)

Such views, however, have basic flaws. For example, in a world consisting of just point particles, nothing would ever happen: point particles have zero probability of ever hitting each other, and there is no reason why they would ever approach or diverge or "hang on" to each other. Our world is a world in which things happen, so it cannot be a world of (just) point particles.

Perhaps ours is a world of point particles that interact via the forces induced by fields. This is, in fact, the dominant contemporary view. It already abandons the particle/substance metaphysical framework, though that is not often recognized: fields are neither particles nor substances, but, instead, are processes – back to Heraclitus. (Fields are intrinsically changing, while basic substances do not and cannot change.) (Another possibility would be extended particles, perhaps with hooks and eyes to hold them together if and when they become "hooked." But (1) this encounters fatal problems attempting to account for transmission of force through such particles, given the Special Theory of Relativity, and (2) there is still nothing to either attract or repel particles to or from each other without the introduction of something like fields.) (For process ontology, see Seibt (2003, 2009, 2012).)

Even more telling, there are no particles (Cao 1999; Halvorson and Clifton 2002; Hobson 2013; Huggett 2000; Weinberg 1977, 1995; Zee 2003). What are called particles are quantized interactions among field processes, and these quantizations are equivalent to the quantizations of the wavelengths in a guitar string: in spite of this quantization, there are no guitar sound particles.

So, both logic and our best physics refute particle models in favor of process models. (A pure point particle universe would be a universe in which nothing happened.)

Emergence

Once we have a metaphysics of process, however, we have overturned the first of the three consequences of a particle (or substance) metaphysics mentioned above, and, therefore, the following two consequences also become ungrounded. In a process metaphysics, *change* is the default, and it is any kind of stasis or stability that requires explanation. (A misunderstanding of this point yields the charge that process frameworks, thus Heraclitus' framework, yields irrational chaos – in a metaphysically bad sense of chaos.)

But stability is not precluded by a process metaphysics. In particular, organizations of process can, in important cases, remain stable *as organizations*. (Consider a candle flame: an organization of process that remains stable for some time period.)

So, there is no stasis at the level of process per se, but there can be stability of the organization of such "changingness."

Crucially, such organization is intrinsic to process. Process, for example, quantum field processes, have whatever influence on the world that they have in necessary part due to the organization of those field processes. In other words, process organization has "causal" influence on the world: it is not epiphenomenal.

So, differing organizations can have such differing influences. (Consider any two fields, classical or quantum, that have differing metric (or topological) organizations.) Such influences will be *emergent* in those organizations: emergence is not precluded by, but is grounded in, a process metaphysics. So, the second metaphysical consequence of the Parmenidean "no-change" metaphysics falls as a result of the failure of the first consequence. Change is the default, not stasis, and emergence is possible, not precluded.

But, if metaphysical emergence is possible, then perhaps normative and intentional emergence are possible, thus integrating via emergence the split metaphysics that we have inherited from Parmenides.

Normative Emergence

Emergence per se is the first step toward such an integration. Such a framework can account for emergence in the "natural" world, such as, perhaps, chemical attractions and repulsions. But, although emergence in a general sense is enabled by a process metaphysics, we still need a more particular model of the emergence of *normativity* in order to (begin) bridging the metaphysical gap between the "natural" and the "mental" realms. (I put such terms in quotes because they are commonly understood in a manner that already presupposes the split. But, if the natural world is integrated via emergence across physical and mental (and normative, etc.) realms, then the background assumption that "naturalism" is some form of physicalism that precludes normative phenomena fails.)

One of the fundamental problems in attempting to naturalize normativity is that normativity involves asymmetric differentiations, between good and bad, true and false, functional and dysfunctional, and so on. The laws of physics provide unbounded kinds of differentiation, of location, momentum, charge, etc., but there are no sources of normative asymmetry among these: there is no sense in which, or relative to which, any of these is intrinsically better or worse than others. ("Symmetry breaking" is of fundamental importance in physics, such as the breaking of magnetic symmetry in the formation of a bar magnet (and other more fundamental cases), but such "breaking" is in fact "breaking" precisely because it breaks the underlying symmetry of the relevant laws. And such "symmetry breaking" does not provide a normative assymetry. The laws of physics tend strongly to be symmetric; of special relevance here is time symmetry. The laws of thermodynamics provide (under some interpretations) a basic time asymmetry.)

There is one domain of physics, however, that can provide a ground for such asymmetry: thermodynamics. Thermodynamics provides a nonlinear asymmetric distinction that, so I argue, provides the ground for the asymmetries of normativity. The relevant basic thermodynamic distinction is between energy-well and non-energy-well stabilities of process organization – that is, between two differing kinds of organizational stability.

Energy-well stable process organizations are those that would require some above-threshold injection or impingement of energy to disrupt them. They are in an energy-well, and will remain stable unless and until something knocks them out of that well. An atom, for example (a contemporary atom, not a Democritean atom), will remain stable potentially for billions of years, if not disrupted. In particular, if an energy-well stable process organization is isolated from the environment, it will go to equilibrium and stay there, indefinitely.

In contrast, some kinds of organizations of process are far from thermodynamic equilibrium and are stable nevertheless. In contrast to the atom, these stable organizations cannot be isolated: if they are isolated, they go to equilibrium and cease to exist. They must be *maintained* in their far from equilibrium conditions, and this necessity for maintenance, in contrast to energy-well stabilities, is the asymmetric distinction that, so I argue, constitutes the ground for normativity.

A canonical example of a far from equilibrium stability is a candle flame, and this example illustrates two basic properties: (1) the flame self-organizes given appropriate far from equilibrium initial conditions – for example, a match held to a wick – and (2) the candle flame makes contributions to its own stability, to its own persistence: it maintains above combustion threshold temperature, induces convection, vaporizes wax in the wick, melts wax in the candle, and so on. This second property is a crucial property of some far from equilibrium organizations – they can be *self-maintenant*. (Not all far from equilibrium processes are self-maintenant. Consider, for example, a chemical vat held in far from equilibrium conditions by the external contributions of pumps injecting various chemicals into the vat, perhaps for the purpose of studying the self-organizations occuring in the vat.)

A still further form of complexity arises in systems that can shift what they are doing in order to maintain a condition of being self-maintenant in the face of changing conditions in or relations with the environment. A candle flame, for a contrasting example, has no options if it is running out of wax. A bacterium, on the other hand, can swim and maintain swimming if it is headed up a sugar gradient, but shift to tumbling if it is headed down a sugar gradient. Swimming is self-maintenant if heading in one orientation, but not if it is headed in the opposite orientation. Under "opposite orientation" conditions, tumbling is self-maintenant. (It should be clear that all living things are self-maintenant, and, in general, recursively self-maintenant.)

Normative Function

We already have here the outlines of a model of emergent normativity. It is a relative notion, relative to the (contributions) to stability of particular instances of a system or organism, not a God's eye view good or bad. In particular, contributions to the stability of a far from equilibrium system are *(normatively) functional*, relative to that stability. Note, first, that this does not presuppose that the system or its stability are normative per se, but functionality is a *relational property* of contributing to, or weakening, that stability – functionality is *in relation to* the (relative) stability of a particular process organization. Note also that this relativity can be different relative to different systems: for example, the heartbeat of a parasite is functionally positive for the parasite, but functionally negative for the host. (For comparison with and discussion of etiological models of function, see Bickhard (2009).)

From Function to Representing

With a model of normative functional emergence at hand, we can address the function of anticipatory *interaction indication* in complex agents, and, thus, the emergence of truth valued functioning: the emergence of representing. At this point, we have connected with and grounded the discussion of anticipatory representing in the first part of this discussion. So:

1. A process metaphysics is supported, even forced, by both logic and our best physics.
2. A process metaphysics makes emergence "natural."
3. A consideration of thermodynamics yields a model of normative emergence, in the form of (biological) function.
4. The function of indicating potentialities of interaction yields emergent truth value, thus representation.

Conclusions

Anticipation in the sense of functional preparedness, such as is involved in micro-genetic preparedness in the brain, has truth value that is not based on already available representation. Such anticipation, thus, constitutes an emergent form of representing, and it has resources for modeling more complex and sophisticated forms of representation, such as of objects. Anticipation, thus, can *constitute* representation.

This anticipatory truth value is based on a necessary ground of normative function – in particular, the agentive function of indicating what interactions might be possible under what interactive conditions. Such a model of normative biological function encounters potential metaphysical challenges of long-standing – since the Greeks, in fact.

The model of representation as anticipation, thus, cannot stand unless these potential metaphysical problems can be resolved. The resolution is outlined in terms of a series of steps establishing: (1) process metaphysics, thus, (2) the possibility of metaphysical emergence, thus, (3) the possibility of normative emergence via thermodynamic considerations, thus, (4) the agentive normative emergence of potential interaction anticipation.

Anticipation, thus, is the emergent ground of representation, without any necessity of being based on representation.

References

Allen, J. W. P., & Bickhard, M. H. (2011). Emergent constructivism. *Child Development Perspectives, 5*(3), 164–165. https://doi.org/10.1111/j.1750-8606.2011.00178.x. Invited.

Allen, J. W. P., & Bickhard, M. H. (2013). Stepping off the pendulum: Why only an action-based approach can transcend the nativist-empiricist debate. *Cognitive Development, 28*, 96–133.

Bickhard, M. H. (1998). Levels of representationality. *Journal of Experimental and Theoretical Artificial Intelligence, 10*(2), 179–215.

Bickhard, M. H. (2000). Review of B. Shanon, the representational and the presentational. *Minds and Machines, 10*(2), 313–317.

Bickhard, M. H. (2003). An integration of motivation and cognition. In L. Smith, C. Rogers, & P. Tomlinson (Eds.), *Development and motivation: Joint perspectives* (Monograph series II, pp. 41–56). Leicester: British Psychological Society.

Bickhard, M. H. (2006). Developmental normativity and normative development. In L. Smith & J. Voneche (Eds.), *Norms in human development* (pp. 57–76). Cambridge: Cambridge University Press.

Bickhard, M. H. (2009). The interactivist model. *Synthese, 166*(3), 547–591. https://doi.org/10.1007/s11229-008-9375-x.

Bickhard, M. H. (2014). What could cognition be, if not computation … or connectionism, or dynamic systems? *Journal of Theoretical and Philosophical Psychology, 35*(1), 53–66. https://doi.org/10.1037/a0038059.

Bickhard, M. H. (2015a). Toward a model of functional brain processes I: Central nervous system functional micro-architecture. *Axiomathes, 25*(3), 217–238.

Bickhard, M. H. (2015b). Toward a model of functional brain processes II: Central nervous system functional macro-architecture. *Axiomathes, 25*(4), 377–407.

Bickhard, M. H. (2016). The anticipatory brain: Two approaches. In V. C. Müller (Ed.), *Fundamental issues of artificial intelligence* (pp. 259–281). Cham: Springer.

Bickhard, M. H. (2017). Information, representation, biology. *Biosemiotics, 10*, 179. https://doi.org/10.1007/s12304-017-9296-5.

Bickhard, M. H. (in preparation). The whole person: Toward a naturalism of persons – Contributions to an ontological psychology.

Bickhard, M. H., & Campbell, R. L. (1996). Topologies of learning and development. *New Ideas in Psychology, 14*(2), 111–156.

Bickhard, M. H., & Richie, D. M. (1983). *On the nature of representation: A case study of James J. Gibson's theory of perception*. New York: Praeger.

Bickhard, M. H., & Terveen, L. (1995). *Foundational issues in artificial intelligence and cognitive science: Impasse and solution*. Amsterdam: Elsevier Scientific.

Campbell, D. T. (1974). Evolutionary epistemology. In P. A. Schilpp (Ed.), *The philosophy of Karl Popper* (pp. 413–463). LaSalle: Open Court.

Campbell, R. J. (1992). *Truth and historicity*. Oxford: Oxford University Press.

Cao, T. Y. (1999). *Conceptual foundations of quantum field theory*. Cambridge: Cambridge University Press.

Carlson, N. R. (2013). *Physiology of behavior* (11th ed.). Upper Saddle River: Pearson.

Cummins, R. (1996). *Representations, targets, and attitudes*. Cambridge, MA: MIT Press.

de Caro, M., & MacArthur, D. (2004). *Naturalism in question*. Cambridge, MA: Harvard.

Dewey, J. (1960/1929). *The quest for certainty*. New York: Capricorn Books.

Dretske, F. I. (1988). *Explaining behavior*. Cambridge, MA: MIT Press.

Fodor, J. A. (1990). *A theory of content and other essays*. Cambridge, MA: MIT Press.

Freyd, J. J. (1987). Dynamic mental representations. *Psychological Review, 94*(4), 427–438.

Freyd, J. J. (1992). Dynamic representations guiding adaptive behavior. In F. Macar, V. Pouthas, & W. J. Friedman (Eds.), *Time, action and cognition: Towards bridging the gap* (pp. 309–323). Dordrecht: Kluwer.

Freyd, J. J., & Pantzer, T. M. (1995). Static patterns moving in the mind. In S. M. Smith, T. B. Ward, & R. A. Finke (Eds.), *The creative cognition approach* (pp. 181–204). Cambridge, MA: MIT Press.

Gill, M.-L. (1989). *Aristotle on substance.* Princeton: Princeton University Press.

Halvorson, H., & Clifton, R. (2002). No place for particles in relativistic quantum theories? *Philosophy of Science, 69*(1), 1–28.

Hobson, A. (2013). There are no particles, there are only fields. *American Journal of Physics, 81*, 211. https://doi.org/10.1119/1.4789885.

Huggett, N. (2000). Philosophical foundations of quantum field theory. *The British Journal for the Philosophy of Science, 51*(Suppl), 617–637.

Millikan, R. G. (1984). *Language, thought, and other biological categories.* Cambridge, MA: MIT Press.

Millikan, R. G. (1993). *White queen psychology and other essays for Alice.* Cambridge, MA: MIT Press.

Seibt, J. (2003). Free process theory: Towards a typology of occurings. In J. Seibt (Ed.), *Process theories: Crossdisciplinary studies in dynamic categories* (pp. 23–55). Dordrecht: Kluwer.

Seibt, J. (2009). Forms of emergent interaction in general process theory. *Synthese, 166*(3), 479–512.

Seibt, J. (2012). *Process philosophy.* Stanford Encyclopedia of Philosophy: http://plato.stanford.edu/entries/process-philosophy/.

Shanon, B. (1993). *The representational and the presentational.* Hertfordshire: Harvester Wheatsheaf.

Tiles, J. E. (1990). *Dewey.* London: Routledge.

Wagner, S. J., & Warner, R. (Eds.). (1993). *Naturalism: A critical appraisal* (pp. 23–51). Notre Dame: University of Notre Dame Press.

Weinberg, S. (1977). The search for unity, notes for a history of quantum field theory. *Daedalus, 106*(4), 17–35.

Weinberg, S. (1995). *The quantum theory of fields* (Foundations, Vol. 1). Cambridge: Cambridge University Press.

Zee, A. (2003). *Quantum field theory in a nutshell.* Princeton: Princeton University Press.

Wild Anticipation: On the Evolution of Meaning

17

J. Scott Jordan

Contents

Abstract

The present paper offers an approach to anticipation and meaning, based on Wild Systems Theory (WST), which begins by describing organisms as self-sustaining energy transformation systems that constitute embodiments of context. This idea leads to the assertion that anticipation refers to a self-sustaining system's ability to prespecify and constrain the dynamic possibilities of its nested transformation systems. The paper describes how anticipation, defined as the prospective constraint of context, evolved from the small-scale contexts constrained by a single cell to the full-blown, self-aware prespecification and constraint of contexts (i.e., forward-looking thinking) exhibited in human anticipation. Specifically, anticipation scaled up because (1) the systems that phylogenetically entailed it (i.e., organisms) were simultaneous energy transformation systems whose status as such rendered them a possible energy source for potentially emergent energy transformation systems (i.e., plants and herbivores) and (2) as self-sustaining embodiments of context, such systems are naturally and necessarily "about" the contexts they embody. As a result, they

J. Scott Jordan (✉)
Department of Psychology, Institute for Prospective Cognition, Illinois State University, Normal, IL, USA
e-mail: jsjorda@ilstu.edu

© Springer Nature Switzerland AG 2019
R. Poli (ed.), *Handbook of Anticipation*,
https://doi.org/10.1007/978-3-319-91554-8_59

339

are inherently meaningful, and the phenomenon we refer to as consciousness, or self-awareness, is a phylogenetically scaled-up recursion of the self-sustaining prespecification and constraint of nested, dynamic possibilities we see in single-cell organisms.

Keywords

Self-sustaining systems · Wild systems theory · Embodiment · Prospective constraint · Meaning · Autocatalysis

Usually, when we discuss *anticipation*, we describe it in terms of a system's ability to generate forward-looking assumptions, ideas, and models that can be used to guide behavior in the present. Such a description seems noncontroversial: It is consistent with how we use the word *anticipation* in daily life, and researchers in different disciplines seem to know what it means in their field. Such a take on anticipation is evident in the arguments of Seligman et al. (2013), who claim that the century-old dogmas of behaviorism and psychoanalysis, which described behavior as being driven primarily by the past, will soon be overturned by the new science of *prospection*.

While I agree that systems capable of generating and using forward-looking models are clearly anticipatory, I am concerned that our seemingly straightforward take on the meaning of *anticipation* implies it is something a system *does*, as opposed to being constitutive of what a system *is*. This distinction is important, for if anticipation emerges only in the *doing*, and is not present in the *being*, we are not allowed to assert the system is inherently anticipatory, and this is precisely what Rosen (1985) and Hofmeyr (2007, ▶ "Basic Biological Anticipation," present volume) explicitly assert, while others seem to imply it (Kauffman 1995; Maturana and Varela 1980).

One reason people might find it hard to consider the notion that living systems *are* anticipation is because such a statement leaves one with comical images of highly intelligent amoebas, planning and scheming their way along a concentration gradient. Upon further reflection, however, we discover the joke emerges from the fact we have projected our own, human experience of anticipation, in all its cognitive glory, onto the dynamics of single-cell organisms and found the idea wanting. In short, one feels the notion of prospecting amoebas is silly because there is no way such simple systems could ever hope to entail the cognitive richness found in human anticipations. In what follows, I present an approach to describing living systems (i.e., Wild Systems Theory – WST) that is consistent with and is inspired by the ideas of Rosen (1985) and others who consider anticipatory dynamics as being constitutive of living systems. I first present WST's take on what livings systems are. I then describe WST's account of how human-level anticipation emerged phylogenetically out of the type of anticipation that constitutes single-cell organisms. In the end, I argue that the phylogenetic emergence of anticipation also works as an account for the evolution of meaning and what cognitive scientists refer to as consciousness and self-awareness.

Wild Systems Theory

WST is a theoretical approach to the nature of living systems that was developed specifically for cognitive science (Jordan and Day 2015; Jordan and Heidenreich 2010; Jordan and Ghin 2006) and has been applied to more general topics such as complex systems theory (Jordan and Day 2015; Jordan 2013a), education (Critchfield and Jordan 2014; Jordan and Ranade 2014), dance ethnology (Hahn and Jordan 2014, 2017), philosophy (Jordan 2009, 2010a, b, 2012, 2013b; Jordan and Day 2015; Jordan and Ghin 2006), communication studies (Jordan 2008a; Kinsbourne and Jordan 2009; Streeck and Jordan 2009), rhetoric (Jordan and Mays 2017), neuroscience (Jordan and Heidenreich 2010), archeology (Jordan 2008b), morality (Jordan and Wesselmann 2015), issues in popular culture (Jordan 2006; Wesselmann and Jordan 2016), and the issue of conceptual integration within the arts and the sciences (Jordan and Vandervert 1999; Jordan and Vinson 2012).

The reasons for developing WST stem mainly from a deep dissatisfaction with the hard naturalist (Gardner 2007) metaphysics that tends to underlie much of contemporary scholarship. In order to move away from the problematic, naturalist assertion that humans are constituted of physical bodies that entail mental properties, WST conceptualizes organisms as *multi-scale*, *self-sustaining*, and *embodiments of context*. Referring to a system as *self-sustaining*, it means the *work* (i.e., energy transformations) that constitutes the system recursively gives rise to and maintains the system as a whole. Kauffman (1995), who refers to this type of work as *autocatalysis*, proposes it as a possible explanation of the evolutionary emergence of life. Specifically, he postulates that living systems emerged in the prebiotic soup because certain networks of chemical reactions developed the ability to create catalysts for the reactions that produced the catalyst or for some other reaction in the network. Given such systems were constituted of autocatalytic work, Kauffman (1995) also referred to them as *self-metabolizing*. Hofmeyr (2007, ▶ "Basic Biological Anticipation," present volume) prefers the term *self-fabricating* and, based on extensive empirical detail, describes how, at the level of the cell, relations between structure, function, and internal context recursively generate a hierarchical cycle that allows all aspects of the hierarchy to be fabricated from the work of the hierarchy. Maturana and Varela (1980) coined the term *autopoiesis* to refer to living systems as a network of processes that continually regenerate and realize themselves in a way that constitutes the network as a concrete entity.

WST takes this notion of self-sustaining, self-metabolizing, self-fabricating, autopoeitic systems and makes the case that organisms beyond the scale of single-cell systems are constituted of *multiple scales* of self-sustaining work. Jordan and Vinson (2012) describe the multi-scale aspect of organisms in the following manner:

> At the chemical level, self-sustaining work has been referred to as autocatalysis (Kauffman 1995), the idea being that a self-sustaining chemical system is one in which reactions produce either their own catalysts or catalysts for some other reaction in the system. At the biological level, self-sustaining work has been referred to as autopoiesis (Maturana and Varela 1980), again, the idea being that a single cell constitutes a multi-scale system of work in which lower-scale chemical processes give rise to the larger biological whole of the cell which, in turn, provides a context in which the lower-scale work sustains itself and the whole

it gives rise to (Jordan and Ghin 2006). Hebb (1949) referred to the self-sustaining nature of neural networks as the "cell assembly," the idea being that neurons that fire together wire together. Jordan and Heidenreich (2010) recently cast this idea in terms of self-sustaining work by examining data that indicate the generation of action potentials increases nuclear transcription processes in neurons which, in turn, fosters synapse formation. At the behavioral level, Skinner (1976) referred to the self-sustaining nature of behavior as operant conditioning, the idea being that behaviors sustain themselves in one's behavioral repertoire as a function of the consequences they generate. Streeck and Jordan (2009) recently described communication as a dynamical self-sustaining system in which multi-scale events such as postural alignment, gesture, gaze, and speech produce outcomes that sustain an ongoing interaction. And finally, Odum (1988) and Vandervert (1995) used the notion of self-sustaining work to refer to ecologies in general (p. 235).

WST and Anticipation

An immediate advantage of taking the concept of self-sustaining work, and applying it to the various levels of an organism's organization, including behavior and cognition, is that it allows for a take on the meaning of *anticipation* that integrates the meanings asserted by Rosen (1985) and Hofmeyr (2007, ▶ "Basic Biological Anticipation," present volume) with those proposed by contemporary cognitive scientists such as Seligman et al. (2013). Specifically, WST describes anticipation in terms of the micro-macro synergies that constitute self-sustaining systems. Jordan and Ghin (2006) argue that the micro- and macrostates of the cell (i.e., the molecular structures comprising the whole, and the cell as a whole, respectively) are synergistically enmeshed such that interactions between the two keep the former in particular states. For example, the micro-level cell membrane proteins that allow food particles into the cell are kept in a "food intake" state via the macro-level transformations of the whole cell (e.g., swimming or tumbling, depending upon the species), and these macro-level phase transitions emerge out of the micro-level dynamics that comprise the cell as a whole. Because of such micro-macro synergy, the cell is capable of regulating the inputs to its cell membrane proteins.

Jordan and Ghin (2006) developed the notion of self-sustaining micro-macro synergies in order to distinguish such dynamics from those of *self-organizing systems*. As an example, in a self-organizing system such as a convection roll, the states of all the molecules in the system are simultaneously *about* both the other molecules in the system and the macro-level convection roll that emerges from the interactions between its constituent molecules. However, while the system does transform (i.e., dissipate) energy, its micro-macro synergies do not give rise to products that serve to sustain, fabricate, or replicate the convection roll state. Its dynamics do not keep it in a state that is far from thermodynamic equilibrium. Turn off the heat, and the convection roll disappears. Thus, while the micro-macro synergies that constitute convection rolls are clearly self-organizing, they are neither self-sustaining, self-fabricating, nor self-reproducing. Rather, the convection roll as a macro-level whole emerges and dissipates as energy flows through the system. In self-sustaining systems, the micro-macro synergies of the system intake, transform, and dissipate energy, and as they do so, some aspect of the system is sustained; the system does not dissipate. It keeps itself far from thermodynamic equilibrium, and it does so because its micro-macro synergies are self-fabricating, self-metabolizing, and self-reproducing.

Because self-sustaining systems are able to regulate their inputs and, as a result, sustain themselves, Jordan (2003a) claims they represented the phylogenetic emergence of end-directedness (i.e., intentionality):

> This activity can be non-vitalistically described as end-directedness because the system's micro-macro synergy is such that it will offset perturbation to the food intake state. The inherent ability of biological systems to offset perturbation to nested system states and, as a result, keep such states in specific states, constitutes the evolutionary emergence of end-directedness. (217)

The notion of self-sustaining end-directedness intimates such systems are, in some way, forward-looking. However, when we attempt to apply concepts such as *intentionality or anticipation* to the micro-macro synergies of a single cell, we feel hesitant because we are used to conceptualizing such concepts as information about the future utilized in present behavior, and it is hard to imagine where such information might be found in a single cell. In addition, we are used to thinking of single-cell organisms as *biochemical* systems that are simply slave to tropisms and, as a result, reactive systems, as opposed to being prospective. The notion of organisms as multi-scale, self-sustaining micro-macro synergies reframes our thinking about organisms, at every level, including behavior, cognition, and social interaction, into notions of regulatory, energy transformation dynamics, versus efficient-cause-driven thinking about individual reactions among individual chemical components, or individual neural networks, or individual, interacting humans.

Having made this conceptual maneuver, WST asserts that a micro-macro synergy's ability to sustain itself as a persistent whole across a time scale larger than the transformations that constitute it provides a means of addressing the nature of anticipation. Specifically, instead of conceptualizing anticipation as a bit of forward-looking information located somewhere in the system, WST proposes that a self-sustaining, micro-macro synergy's *work-contingent persistence* perpetually "keeps ahead" of (i.e., anticipates) the micro-level work of which it is constituted. Such "getting-ahead-of" does not mean the system has information about the future. It means, rather, that the system exists (i.e., sustains itself) within multiple time scales of energy transformation, simultaneously, and it is within the nesting of these different time scales of work that the phenomenon of anticipation emerges.

In the case of a single cell, the work at the chemical level (see Hofmeyr 2007, ▶ "Basic Biological Anticipation," this volume) takes place within a time scale that is shorter yet nested within the time scale of events encountered at the biological level (e.g., the cell as a whole, making its way through a concentration gradient). Within the relative disparity in the time scales at which these different, yet nested, scales of work are synergistically coupled, the slower, larger time scale of the biological work (i.e., the single cell as a whole and the dynamics of its interaction with its environment) *constrains* the dynamic possibilities of the chemical level work of which it is constituted. It is this notion of *self-sustaining constraint* that WST equates with *anticipation*.

Such constraint is ahead of the work that constitutes it because it perpetually prespecifies (i.e., constrains) the dynamic possibilities of the work. That is, at any given moment, the states of the cell limit the types of work (i.e., chemical reactions) that can occur in the system (e.g., only certain chemicals are allowed to enter the cell, certain chemicals are generated by the constrained work of the system, and certain chemicals are transported to specific locations in the cell). This ability to *dynamically constrain nested possibilities* emerges of out the system's ability to sustain itself as a whole across distinct yet nested time scales. Given this emphasis on time scales, it may be the case that our notion of anticipation being "information about the future" derives from our ability to constrain nested possibilities at multiple time scales. That is, anticipation might be more coherently and usefully described as our propensity for prespecifying and, as a result, constraining the contexts that constitute the brain, the body, and the world. In order for this idea to work, it has to be made clear how anticipation, defined as prospective constraint, evolved from the small-scale possibilities constrained by a single cell to the full-blown, self-aware prespecification of constraints (i.e., forward-looking thinking) exhibited in human anticipation. This task requires two steps. The first is to explain the phylogenetic scale-up of anticipation, and the second is an explanation of why human anticipation entails the phenomenal sense of looking forward (i.e., the sense of anticipating).

The Phylogenetic Scale-Up of Anticipation

WST's assertion that organisms constitute nested scales of self-sustaining work affords an approach to anticipation that focuses on the commonalities between the internal and external contexts of organisms – specifically, energy transformation dynamics. Such an approach stands in contrast to traditional models that conceptualize the external context as a *physical* world in which organisms constitute physical systems whose psychological properties are (1) identical with the physical (i.e., identity theory), (2) emergent from the physical (i.e., emergentism), (3) an informational property of certain causal relations (i.e., functionalism), or (4) an aspect of reality other than the physical (i.e., double-aspect theory and property dualism), all of which run into problems when attempting to establish the reality of the phenomenal sense of prespecification present in human anticipation (Jordan and Day 2015).

Anticipation and the evolution of internal contexts. Given WST's focus on energy transformation dynamics, the external context is conceptualized as a self-organizing energy transformation hierarchy (Odum 1988; Vandervert 1995). Such an approach to internal and external contexts reveals the dynamic homologies that transcend the phyla as well as the multi-scale energy transformation systems that constitute an individual organism. Based on these ideas, Jordan and Ghin (2006) assert *the fuel source dictates the consumer.* What this means is that as a result of being an energy transformation system, living systems are always available for "capture" by another system capable of using their encapsulated (i.e., embodied) energy for sustainment. To do so, however, the consuming system must be constituted in such a way that it is able to overcome all the constraints that need to be addressed to capture the fuel source. For example, the wide-scale availability of plant life afforded the emergence of systems able to sustain themselves on the chemical energy encapsulated in plants. Herbivores, therefore, constitute self-sustaining embodiments of the constraints that need to be addressed for a system to sustain itself on plant energy, while carnivores, in turn, constitute embodiments of the constraints involved in capturing herbivore energy.

The fuel source dictates the consumer provides a means of explaining how the anticipation (i.e., the prespecification of nested, dynamical possibilities) embodied in a single-cell organism, evolved into the forward-looking type of prespecification reflected in human cognition. Specifically, an important shift in the evolution of self-sustaining systems occurred when constraints dictated the consumer be able to propel itself, as whole, toward a fuel source, as is the case when an herbivore forages for plants, or a carnivore chases prey. Lotka (1945) recognized that in order for a predator to capture moving prey, the former has to propel itself on an *anticipatory* pursuit curve, in that it has to run toward a location the prey does not yet occupy. In short, it propels itself toward the prey's *future*.

Such forward-looking, anticipatory self-propulsion is possible because the predator has embodied the constraints of capturing a moving fuel source. An extremely important aspect of this embodiment is the ability of the predator's neurodynamics to embody patterns between movement commands leaving motor cortex and the immediate sensory consequences of the resultant movements (Desmurget and Grafton 2003; Grush 2004; Kawato et al. 1987; Wolpert et al. 1998). The embodiment of these command-feedback patterns is possible because the cortical areas involved in the motor command and the sensory feedback both innervate the same neurons in the cerebellum. As a result, what it means for the predator to learn to control its body in relation to moving prey, is that neural command-feedback patterns that lead to capture become embodied in the structure of its cerebral-cerebellar circuits, what are often referred to as forward and inverse models (Blakemore and Decety 2001; Blakemore et al. 2000; Golfinopoulos et al. 2009; Ito 2008; Iacoboni 2005; Koziol and Lutz 2013; Miall 2003; Shadmehr and Krakauer 2008; Wolpert et al. 2003), and/or cerebellar control models (Koziol et al. 2011). These cerebellar neurons recursively innervate the cortical neurons that innervate them. As a result, when a motor command is initiated, cortico-cerebellar loops recursively influence motor cortex at a time scale of roughly 10–20 ms. Since the time scale between motor commands and actual movement feedback is roughly 120 ms, the recursive innervation from the cerebellum (i.e., 10–20 ms) influences motor cortex on a faster time scale than actual feedback. This allows the organism to generate motor commands and control its propulsion via *virtual* feedback (Clark 1997; Grush 2004), what Paulin (1993) refers to dynamic state *estimation* and Kawato et al. refer to *anticipatory* motor error (1987). Common to the notions *virtual*, *estimation*, and *anticipatory* is the fact that they are about the future.

According to WST, it is possible to embody these forward-looking, command-feedback regularities within cortico-cerebellar loops because neural networks themselves function according to the principle of self-sustaining work – i.e., *neurons that fire together wire together* (Edelman 1987; Hebb 1949). Thus, events that give rise to repetitive neural patterns (i.e., command-feedback patterns in cerebral-cerebellar loops and their relationship to predator-prey patterns) become embodied within these self-sustaining neural patterns. In addition, all of this embodied work is naturally and necessarily about the entire multi-scale context that must be addressed in order for the work to sustain itself, including single neurons nested within neural circuits, which are nested within a neuromuscular architecture, which is nested within the organism as a whole. Because of this multi-scale, recursive embodiment, as well as its multi-scale coupling with the contexts in which the organism sustains itself, there is no epistemic divide between internal and external contexts. In short, organisms are reciprocally nested ecosystems of self-sustaining work.

Given this notion of multi-scale embodiment, one can see the *prespecification and constraint of nested possibilities* at every level. While a neural network prespecifies and constrains the possible states of its nested neurons, the collective constellation of other neural networks (i.e., the brain as a whole) likewise prespecifies and constrains the possible states of its nested neural networks. To complete the recursion, the body as a whole, and the manner in which it is organized in context, prespecifies and constrains the possible states of its nested neuromuscular architecture. In short, every scale of self-sustaining work prespecifies and constrains the possible states of the nested systems that constitute it. Anticipation resides at every level. Thus, organisms entail multiple forward-looking systems, with the magnitude of the *future* emerging out of the relative difference in the temporal scales entailed in the specific micro-macro synergies.

Anticipation and the evolution of external contexts. At first glance, one might assume WST's reliance on the notion of multi-scale embodiment leads to a solely internalist account of the evolutionary emergence of full-blown, phenomenal, human anticipation. It's actually the case, however, that while WST considers embodiment to have been *necessary* to such emergence, it does not claim it to have been *sufficient*. Rather, WST is based on a form of emergence known as *contextual emergence* (Bishop and Atmanspacher 2006) in which the emergence of a phenomenon necessitates certain lower-level properties (i.e., the self-sustaining dynamics of organisms) as well as the larger scale, contingent context in which the lower-level properties are nested (i.e., the larger-scale energy transformation hierarchy). This notion of contextual emergence implies that a scientific account of the phylogenetic emergence of self-sustaining systems cannot be reduced to only one level of transformation (e.g., the autocatalytic properties of certain chemical interactions) because the emergence of such networks necessitated the larger-scale context of the prebiotic soup.

While the contextual emergence of autocatalytic chemical networks seems to have initially been a fairly passive response to the conditions of the prebiotic soup, later emerging self-sustaining systems played a much more active role in generating the larger-scale contingent contexts that afforded their sustainment. Colonies of ants, for example, are able to sustain large-scale coordinations because individual ants excrete and detect pheromone (Dussutour et al. 2004). By changing their shared external context (i.e., releasing pheromone) the ants collectively generate and sustain the external conditions necessary to both individual and group sustainment.

As another example, many organisms generate auditory alterations of their external context (i.e., produce sounds) that influence social organization (i.e., the sustainment of social context). Certain insects, for example, generate synchronous or asynchronous sounds as a way to compete for mating partners (Gerhardt and Huber 2002). A male banded wren will generate calls that overlap those of another male wren in order to establish social hierarchies and sustain territorial boundaries (Hall et al. 2006). And female songbirds that hear their partner lose a vocal interaction are more likely to seek extra-pair copulations (Mennill et al. 2003). While on the one hand we tend to conceptualize such auditory events as "signals," on the other, we can see them as giving rise to and comprising an *auditory gradient*. Thus, just as colonies of ants generate and sustain chemical gradients, birds do so with auditory gradients. As a result, both species can be said to generate and sustain aspects of the larger-scale contingent contexts that afford their contextual emergence. In short, self-sustaining systems generate and sustain *coupled internal-external contexts*.

The ability to generate and sustain internal-external context couplings played an important role in the phylogenetic scale-up of anticipation, from the prespecification and constraint of nested possibilities entailed in single-cell organisms to the full-blown, forward-looking phenomenology entailed in human anticipation. Specifically, it turns out that areas of the human brain are actually open to direct external coupling with conspecifics. In macaque monkeys, brain areas involved in goal-oriented movement planning (i.e., area F5 of the frontal cortex) are also involved in the observation of goal-directed actions produced by another (Rizzolatti et al. 2002). Using fMRI, Calvo-Merino et al. (2005) found pre-motor neural systems in the human homologue of the macaque F5 that have similar response properties. Specifically, while participants watched videos of dancers, there was more pre-motor activation in expert observers than novices and even more if the expert observed a dance in the style they had mastered.

Collectively, these data indicate that humans share direct, goal-related internal-external coupling between plans and the outcomes they produce. Thus, as a group of individuals interact, they "see" each other in terms of the plans inherent in their collective actions. Elsewhere (Jordan and Ghin 2007) I have referred to this phenomenon as the coupling of *intentional contexts*, what one might also think of as intentional gradients.

In addition to being coupled in goal-related intentional contexts, data also indicate direct connections between individuals in terms of the neural systems involved in controlling movements. Grezes et al. (1998), for example, discovered that if participants observe body movements that are either meaningful or meaningless (e.g., slicing bread motions with or without the presence of bread, respectively), both types of movements give rise to increased activity in neural networks involved in the planning of movement dynamics (i.e., bilaterally, the occipito-temporal junction and superior occipital gyrus and, in left hemisphere, the middle temporal gyrus and the inferior parietal lobe). These findings indicate that the observation of another's movements results in the activation of brain processes one would use to generate those same movements oneself.

In terms of the notion of internal-external couplings, it seems that humans constrain and contextualize one another's *planning* states, both at the level of goal specification and movement kinematic specification. Said another way, interacting humans are directly coupled in multi-scale planning contexts, again, what one might refer to as *intentional gradients*. Kinsbourne (2002) refers to these coupling in terms of "resonance" and argues it constitutes the default value in human interaction. Kinsbourne was led to this statement by the observation that as caregivers interact with an infant, the multi-scale coupling of intentional contexts between the two affords the infant a space in which to learn the same action-effect contingencies. Later in life, as the brain develops inhibitory systems, we also develop the ability to "not" resonate to the action-effect contingencies of others.

The multi-scale coupling inherent in intentional contexts was, and is, recursively self-sustaining. That is, the "work" of engaging in multi-scale intentional coupling produces products that sustain such coupling. *Internally*, as already mentioned, neural networks emerge and function according to the principle of self-sustaining work (Hebb 1949; Edelman 1987). Thus, regularities embodied in self-sustaining neural dynamics are available for "capture" by newly emerging neural networks (Grush 2004). The aboutness of these new systems will necessarily constitute an abstraction from the aboutness embedded and sustained in the networks being tapped into. *Externally*, the human ability to become coupled in multi-scale intentional contexts affords the further ability, when coupled with the plasticity of neural networks, to embody regularities generated in these intentional contexts. Example of such regularities would be gestures and/or vocalizations that repeatedly occur during the sustainment of multi-scale intentional contexts (e.g., moving a couch together). As gesture and/or vocal patterns are associated (via neural embodiment) with the intentional contexts in which they occurred, they can then be generated intentionally as a means of more efficiently altering or varying the type of intentional contexts being sustained. That is, the generation and sustainment of intentional contexts (e.g., sitting around a campfire or sitting in a circle while making tools) affords groups the opportunity to constrain and contextualize one another's multi-scale planning states (i.e., goal and movement plans) and, potentially, discover new ways of being together (e.g., spoken or written language or dancing). And as these new, contextually emergent intentional contexts are repeatedly generated and sustained, their persistence makes it possible for more people to join the context and for new types of contexts to emerge.

At every level of such multi-scale intentional contexts, nested possibilities are constrained and prespecified. During a group dance, the movements of each dancer constrain and contextualize the dance possibilities of the other members. As the group develops a repeated pattern of dance, labelling the pattern with a gesture or written symbol will serve to prespecify and constrain the dance possibilities of the participants as they work to collectively perform the dance. As these new contexts emerge (e.g., spoken and written symbols), they would be more abstract than the intentional contexts from which they had been abstracted, because they would be about *possibilities* for such intentional contexts. In addition, they were (and still are) self-sustaining because by having a means of anticipatorily organizing intentional contexts, groups are able to get more energy per unit work (e.g., capture more prey during the hunt) as well as generate and sustain more sophisticated forms of group organization (i.e., governments).

The ability to engage in such *joint abstract intentional contexts* (i.e., culture) was, and is, meted out over time as members of an intentional context converge onto a shared pattern of events that come to anticipate (i.e., prespecify and constrain) the nested possibilities of group coordination. Thus, just as ant and bird coordinations necessitate the generation and sustainment of external pheromone and auditory contexts, respectively, joint, abstract intentional contexts in humans necessitate the generation of external intentional contexts.

As an example of WST's notion of *joint, abstract intentional contexts*, Streeck and Jordan (2009) reported a conversation analysis of the real-time, videotaped interactions between the owner of an auto body shop and his employees and customers. During the videoed interactions, the body alignments, postures, gestures, and utterances generated by participants were constrained and contextualized by the relationship between the two (e.g., customer and owner or employee and supervisor). In addition, different external contexts provided spaces in which these different role-constrained interactions occurred. For example, in one owner-customer interaction, the two stood in a face-to-face configuration near the back end of the car in question. As the owner took two steps backward, away from the car, the customer took two steps forward, toward the owner. The two then walked in synchrony, away from the car, in a side-by-side configuration for a few steps before the owner then slowed down and came to a stop while the customer, once she detected the change in gait, also came to a stop. The two then stood in a face-to-face configuration and continued their conversation regarding the auto. Streeck and Jordan asserted that the multi-scale behaviors generated by the two (i.e., body position, body dynamics, and utterances) emerged spontaneously and contextually as each member's behaviors constrained and contextualized the behaviors of the other. In addition, each level of the interaction was anticipatory in that the dynamics constrained its nested possibilities. Specifically, the coactors constrained and contextualized each other at the level of body postures (i.e., facing each other versus walking side by side), gestures (i.e., their gestures are coupled differently when walking side by side versus facing one another), and utterances (i.e., the words they generate vary as a function of whether or not they are walking side by side versus facing each other). According to Streeck and Jordan (2009):

Each participant in this "dynamic dance" constitutes a self-sustaining embodiment of the multiscale contexts in which she has had to, and continues to have to, sustain him- or herself. Given these enculturated bodies are naturally and necessarily "about" these multiscale contexts, the "dynamic dance" is one of fluid, multiscale, joint-sustainment, in multiple contexts simultaneously. (p. 454)

As another example:

While greeting an approaching customer, for example, the multiscale work of maintaining certain gaze and overall body configurations serves to sustain the immediate interactional context, as well as the larger-scale, culturally embedded context of one participant as customer and the other as sales person. Given that both of these scales of context are being sustained simultaneously, they can be said to be nested. The dynamics of the overall interaction, therefore, is never "about" just one level of context (e.g., the possible sale). Rather, it is simultaneously "about" all of the scales of embodied context the participants bring to bear during the interaction. (p. 454)

Wild Systems Theory and Phenomenal Anticipation

Over the course of cultural evolution, as intentional contexts became more and more inhabited by the artefacts necessary to the generation and sustainment of increasingly sophisticated intentional contexts (e.g., libraries, government buildings, art galleries, court houses), the sustainment challenges faced by humans also became more complex. Specifically, developing the ability to sustain oneself within such increasingly abstract contexts (e.g., the ability to be a "father' in the morning, a "teacher" during the day, a "customer" at the grocery story on the way home from work, and a father once more upon arriving home) necessitated the ability to distinguish one's own, internally generated abstract contexts (i.e., thoughts) from those in which one is embedded, and to sustain such thoughts according to pre-scribed roles in different contexts. These are the constraints that I believe forced the emergence of the "self" (Metzinger 2003; Ghin 2005), as well as the self-other distinction (Jordan 2003b; Jordan and Knoblich 2004; Knoblich and Jordan 2003). In short, the self, emerged as foreground amidst a background of abstract, embodied "others," and it did so in order to sustain itself with those others in these abstract intentional contexts (i.e., within a world of ideas).

The *self* garners its phenomenal properties the same way all self-sustaining systems do; from the fact they are naturally and necessarily "about" the contexts, they must embody in order to sustain themselves. Because WST conceptualizes organisms as multi-scale, self-sustaining embodiments of the multi-scale contexts within which they emerged and sustain themselves, it refers to them more tersely as self-sustaining *embodiments of context*. That is, the energy transformations of which they are comprised can be seen as internalizations, or embodiments, of the energy transformation dynamics in which they are embedded. Thus, the body and fins of a fish can be seen as an embodiment of the hydrodynamic properties of water, while the neuromuscular architecture of a human can be seen as an embodiment of the constraints that need to be addressed in order to propel a mass, as a whole, through a gravity field. Likewise, the identity (i.e., self) of an individual human can be seen as an embodiment of all the social constraints one must address to sustain oneself in a world of ideas. The point being made is that self-sustaining systems necessarily constitute embodiments of the phylogenetic, ontogenetic, cultural, social, and personal contexts in which they emerged and sustain themselves.

While the notion of organisms as embodiments of context may seem odd, Jordan et al. (2015) propose that one reason for its peculiarity might stem from our tendency to think of context as the host of yet-to-be measured background factors that allow for the foregrounding of an object or event. That is, we think of context as *background*, which allows us to assume the foregrounded object or event exists, as it does, independently of its background (i.e., context). Jordan et al. assert that such an approach to *context* frequently underlies our use of the concept *intrinsic*. For example, mass is often referred to as an intrinsic property because it does not vary with gravity, while weight does. We therefore treat weight as a relative, or *relational* property, and mass is treated as being non-relational, or inherent (i.e., intrinsic). Such an approach can lead one to believe that intrinsic properties are *context independent*, which is tantamount to asserting that intrinsic properties exist, as they do, completely independently of all other properties (i.e., independent of all context). Such a concern with the notion of intrinsic, context-independent properties is shared by many contemporary philosophers of science (Bauer 2011; Dehmelt 1989; Harré 1986; Jammer 2000; Prior et al. 1982; Schaffer 2003) who use phrases such as *externally grounded*, *ultra-grounding*, *global groundedness*, and *infinite levels of microstructure*. They create such concepts to provide informed alternatives to the notion there exist properties that are intrinsic in the sense they exist, as they are, independent of all context.

According to Jordan and Day (2015), it is our acceptance of context-independent intrinsicness that moves us away from the idea that context is *constitutive of* events and objects. Thus, when we focus on the foregrounded phenomenon (i.e., the event or the object), it becomes hard to see that the event or object is completely *context-dependent*, in the sense that its existence as an object or an event *emerges from* and *is continuously constrained by* the context in which it exists. In short, objects and events constitute embodiments of context. To some extent, one might argue that Rosen's (1985) introduction of the concept *relational biology* was an attempt to reframe our thinking about biological systems in ways that are more consistent with the idea of *embodied context*.

As embodiments of context, events, bodies, and organisms are naturally and necessarily constituted of, and *about*, the contexts they embody and in which they emerged. As a result, they do need to detect or process *information* from the environment in order be "about" their environment. Rather, they need to modulate and to be modulated by the contexts in which they sustain themselves. In short, embodiments of context are naturally and necessarily constituted of context and, as a result, aboutness. From this perspective, phenomena, we refer to via concepts such as consciousness, anticipation, and self-awareness, are actually phylogenetically scaled-up recursions on the embodied context (i.e., embodied aboutness) inherent in all self-sustaining embodied contexts (i.e., organisms). A possible reason for why human anticipation feels so forward-looking could be due to the distality of the contexts we are able to generate and sustain. In a similar vein, Pezzulo (2011) asserts that "...an organism's knowledge and representation ability originates from – and is grounded in – anticipation of sensorimotor interaction" (p. 80). While my dog and I can generate and sustain the intentional context of "playing fetch," my dog cannot anticipate (i.e., prespecify and constrain) the possibility of doing today within the anticipation of doing so at the same time tomorrow. As a result, my embodied context is able to be about contexts that are vastly more distal and remote than those of my dog. This, in turn, leads to my embodied aboutness being more abstract and distally referenced than that of my dog.

Conclusions

Clearly, WST's approach to anticipation is quite different from that of contemporary cognitive scientists who conceptualize it as information about the future that informs current behavior. By beginning with the idea of self-sustaining work, based the ideas of Rosen (1985), Maturana and Varela (1980), Kauffman (1995), and Hofmeyr (2007), WST is able to provide an account of how the anticipatory dynamics that constitute a single-cell organism phylogenetically scaled-up to the anticipation inherent in full-blown human phenomenology.

While WST might seem to imply that differences in embodied contexts (i.e., phenomenology) across the phyla are explained solely in terms of the evolution of internal, embodied contexts, Jordan (2008b) asserts that the sustainment of abstract contexts necessitates the emergence and sustainment of external contexts such as language and technology specifically and culture, in general. It is within this entire multi-scale, contextually emergent, self-sustaining system of work that nested sub-systems (i.e., individual humans) are able to generate and sustain abstract contexts. And at every level, anticipation is there, prespecifying and constraining the nested possibilities of the systems nested within it. In short, living systems are anticipation.

References

Bauer, W. (2011). An argument for the extrinsic grounding of mass. *Erkenntnis, 74*(1), 81–99.

Bishop, R., & Atmanspacher, H. (2006). Contextual emergence in the description of properties. *Foundations of Physics, 36*, 1753–1777.

Blakemore, S. J., & Decety, J. (2001). From the perception of action to the understanding of intention. *Nature Reviews Neuroscience, 2*, 561–567.

Blakemore, S.-J., Wolpert, D. M., & Frith, C. D. (2000). Why can't you tickle yourself? *Neuroreport, 11*, 11–16.

Calvo-Merino, B., Glaser, D. E., Grèzes, J., Passingham, R. E., & Haggard, P. (2005). Action observation and acquired motor skills: An fMRI study with expert dancers. *Cerebral Cortex, 158*, 1243–1249.

Clark, A. (1997). *Being there: Putting brain, body, and world together again*. London: MIT Press.

Critchfield, T. S., & Jordan, J. S. (2014). Prospective cognition in education and enculturation: An overview. *Journal of Cognitive Education and Psychology, 13*(2), 139–147.

Dehmelt, H. (1989). Triton,...Electron,..., Cosmon...: An infinite regression? *Proceedings of the National Academy of Sciences, 86*, 8618–8619.

Desmurget, M., & Grafton, S. (2003). Feedback or feedforward control: End of a dichotomy. In S. H. Johnson-Frey (Ed.), *Taking action: Cognitive neuroscience perspectives on intentional acts* (pp. 291–338). Cambridge, MA: MIT Press.

Dussutour, A., Fourcassie, V., Helbing, D., & Deneubourg, J. L. (2004). Optimal traffic organization in ants under crowded conditions. *Nature, 428*, 70–73.

Edelman, G. M. (1987). *Neural Darwinism: The theory of neuronal group selection*. Basic Books.

Gardner, S. (2007). The limits of naturalism and the metaphysics of German idealism. In E. Hammer (Ed.), *German idealism: Contemporary perspectives* (pp. 19–49). Abingdon: Routledge.

Gerhardt, H. C., & Huber, F. (2002). *Acoustic communication in insects and anurans*. Chicago: The University of Chicago Press.

Ghin, M. (2005). What a self could be. *Psyche, 11*(5), 1–10.

Golfinopoulos, E., Tourville, J. A., & Guenther, F. H. (2009). The integration of large-scale neural network modeling and functional brain imaging in speech motor control. *NeuroImage, 52*, 862–874.

Grezes, J., Costes, N., & Decety, J. (1998). Top-down effect of strategy on the perception of human biological motion: A PET investigation. *Cognitive Neuropsychology, 15*(6/7/8), 553–582.

Grush, R. (2004). The emulation theory of representation: Motor control, imagery, and perception. *Behavioral and Brain Sciences, 27*, 377–442.

Hahn, T., & Jordan, J. S. (2014). Anticipation and embodied knowledge: Observations of enculturating bodies. *Journal of Cognitive Education and Psychology, 13*(2), 272–284.

Hahn, T., & Jordan, J. S. (2017). Sensible objects: Intercorporeality and enactive knowing through things. In C. Meyer, J. Streeck, & J. S. Jordan (Eds). *Intercorporeality: Emerging socialities in interaction* (pp. 267–288). Oxford: Oxford University Press.

Hall, L., Illes, A., & Vehrencamp, S. L. (2006). Overlapping signals in banded wrens: Long-term effects of prior experience on males and females. *Behavioral Ecology, 17*, 260–269.

Harré, R. (1986). *Varieties of realism: A rationale for the natural sciences*. Oxford: Blackwell.

Hebb, D. O. (1949). *The organization of behavior: A neuropsychological theory*. New York: Wiley.

Hofmeyr, J. H. S. (2007). The biochemical factory that autonomously fabricates itself: A systems biological view of the living cell. *Systems biology: Philosophical foundations*, 217–242.

Iacoboni, M. (2005). Understanding others: Imitation, language and empathy. In S. Hurley & N. Chater (Eds.), *Perspectives on imitation: From mirror neurons to memes* (pp. 77–99). Cambridge, MA: MIT Press.

Ito, M. (2008). Control of mental activities by internal models in the cerebellum. *Nature Reviews Neuroscience, 9*, 304–313.

Jammer, M. (2000). *Concepts of mass in contemporary physics and philosophy*. Princeton: Princeton University Press.

Jordan, J. S. (2003a). The embodiment of intentionality. In W. Tschacher & J. Dauwalder (Eds.), *Dynamical systems approaches to embodied cognition* (pp. 201–228). Berlin: Springer Verlag.

Jordan, J. S. (2003b). Emergence of self and other in perception and action. *Consciousness and Cognition, 12*, 633–646.

Jordan, J. S. (2006). Born to be wild: Faust, Pinocchio and the Marlboro man meet the embodied other. *Mitteilungen, 3*, 5–19.

Jordan, J. S. (2008a). Toward a theory of embodied communication: Self-sustaining wild systems as embodied meaning. In I. Wachsmuth, M. Lenzen, & G. Knoblich (Eds.), *Embodied communication in human and machines* (pp. 53–75). Oxford: Oxford University Press.

Jordan, J. S. (2008b). Wild-agency: Nested intentionalities in neuroscience and archeology. *Philosophical Transactions of the Royal Society B (Biological Sciences), 363*, 1981–1991.

Jordan, J. S. (2009). Forward-looking aspects of perception-action coupling as a basis for embodied communication. *Discourse Processes, 46*, 127–144.

Jordan, J. S. (2010a). Wild systems theory: Overcoming the computational-ecological divide via self-sustaining systems. In *Proceedings of the 32nd annual meeting of the Cognitive Science Society*. Portland: Cognitive Science Society.

Jordan, J. S. (2010b). Shusterman, Merleau-Ponty, and Dewey: The role of pragmatism in the conversation of embodiment. *Action, Criticism & Theory for Music Education, 9*(1), 67–73.

Jordan, J. S. (2012). What's new in new realism: A review of Edwin Pierce's a new look at new realism [Review of the Book A New Look at New Realism]. *PsycCRITIQUES: Contemporary Psychology – APA Review of Books*, 57, Article 6.

Jordan, J. S. (2013a). Seeing through the noise: Where was this Guy headed? *Ecological Psychology, 25*, 219–225.

Jordan, J. S. (2013b). The wild ways of conscious will: What we do, how we do it, and why it has meaning. *Frontiers in Psychology, 4*.

Jordan, J. S., & Day, B. (2015). Wild systems theory as a 21st century coherence framework for cognitive science. In T. Metzinger & J. M. Windt (Eds.), *Open MIND: 21(T)*. Frankfurt: MIND Group. https://doi.org/10.15502/9783958570191.

Jordan, J. S., & Ghin, M. (2006). (Proto-) consciousness as a contextually-emergent property of self-sustaining systems. *Mind & Matter, 4*(1), 45–68.

Jordan, J. S., & Heidenreich, B. (2010). The intentional nature of self-sustaining systems. *Mind & Matter, 8*, 45–62.

Jordan, J. S., & Ghin, M. (2007). The role of control in a science of consciousness: Causality, regulation and selfsustainment. *Journal of Consciousness Studies, 14*(1–2), 177–197.

Jordan, J. S., & Knoblich, G. (2004). Spatial perception and control. *Psychonomic Bulletin and Review, 11*(1), 54–59.

Jordan, J. S., & Mays, C. (2017). Wild meaning: The intercorporeal nature of objects, bodies, and words. In C. Meyer, J. Streeck, & J. S. Jordan (Eds). *Intercorporeality: Emerging socialities in interaction* (pp. 361–378). Oxford: Oxford University Press.

Jordan, S., & Ranade, E. (2014). Multiscale entrainment: A primer in prospective cognition for educational researchers. *Journal of Cognitive Education and Psychology, 13*(2), 147–163.

Jordan, J.S., & Vandervert, L. (1999). Liberal education as a reflection of our assumptions regarding truth and consciousness: Time for an integrative philosophy. *Modeling Consciousness Across the Disciplines*, 307–331.

Jordan, J. S., & Vinson, D. (2012). After nature: On bodies, consciousness, and causality. *Journal of Consciousness Studies, 19*, 229–250.

Jordan, J. S., & Wesselmann, E. D. (2015). The contextually grounded nature of prosocial behavior: A multiscale, embodied approach to morality. In D. A. Schroeder & W. G. Graziano (Eds.), *The Oxford handbook of prosocial behavior*. New York: Oxford University Press. Published online November 2014. https://doi.org/10.1093/oxfordhb/9780195399813.013.031.

Jordan, J. S., Bai, J., Cialdella, V., & Schloesser, D. (2015). Foregrounding the context: Cognitive science as the study of embodied context. In E. Dzhafarov & J. S. Jordan (Eds.), *Contextuality from physics to psychology* (pp. 209–228). Berlin: Springer.

Kauffman, S. (1995). *At home in the universe*. New York: Oxford University Press.

Kawato, M., Furukawa, K., & Suzuki, R. (1987). A hierarchical neural-network model for control and learning of voluntary movement. *Biological Cybernetics, 57*(3), 169–185.

Kinsbourne, M. (2002). The role of imitation in body ownership and mental growth. In A. Meltzoff & W. Prinz (Eds.), *The imitative mind: Development, evolution, and brain bases* (pp. 311–330). New York: Oxford University Press.

Kinsbourne, M., & Jordan, J. S. (2009). Embodied anticipation: A neurodevelopmental interpretation. *Discourse Processes, 46*, 103–126.

Knoblich, G., & Jordan, J. S. (2003). Action coordination in groups and individuals: Learning anticipatory control. *Journal of Experimental Psychology: Learning, Memory, and Cognition, 29*(5), 1006–1016.

Koziol, L., & Lutz, J. (2013). From movement to thought: The development of executive function. *Applied Neuropsychology: Child, 2*(2), 104–115.

Koziol, L., Budding, D., & Chidekel, D. (2011). From movement to thought: Executive function, embodied cognition, and the cerebellum. *The Cerebellum, 11*, 505–525.

Lotka, A. J. (1945). The law of evolution as a maximal principle. *Human Biology, 17*, 167–194.

Maturana, H.R., & Varela, F.J. (1980). Problems in the neurophysiology of cognition. In *Autopoiesis and cognition* (pp. 41–47). Springer Netherlands.

Mennill, D. J., Ratcliffe, L. M., & Boag, P. T. (2003). Female eavesdropping on male song contests in songbirds. *Science, 296*, 873.

Metzinger, T. (2003). *Being no one. The self-model theory of subjectivity*. Cambridge, MA: MIT Press.

Miall, R. C. (2003). Connecting mirror neurons and forward models. *Neuroreport, 14*, 2135–2137.

Odum, H. T. (1988). Self-organization, transformity, and information. *Science, 242*, 132–1139.

Paulin, M. G. (1993). The role of the cerebellum in motor control and perception. *Brain, Behavior and Evolution, 41*(1), 39–50.

Prior, E., Pargetter, R., & Jackson, F. (1982). Three theses about dispositions. *American Philosophical Quarterly, 19*, 251–257.

Rizzolatti, G., Fadiga, L., Fogassi, L., & Gallese, V. (2002). From mirror neurons to imitation: Facts and speculations. In A. Meltzoff & W. Prinz (Eds.), *The imitative mind: Development, evolution, and brain bases* (pp. 247–266). New York: Oxford University Press.

Rosen, R. (1985). *Anticipatory systems: Philosophical, mathematical*. New York: Pergamon Press.

Schaffer, J. (2003). Is there a fundamental level? *Noûs, 37*(3), 498–517.

Seligman, M. E., Railton, P., Baumeister, R. F., & Sripada, C. (2013). Navigating into the future or driven by the past. *Perspectives on Psychological Science, 8*(2), 119–141.

Shadmehr, R., & Krakauer, J. W. (2008). A computational neuroanatomy for motor control. *Experimental Brain Research, 185*, 359–381.

Skinner, B. F. (1976). *About behaviorism*. New York: Vintage Books.

Streeck, J., & Jordan, J. S. (2009). Communication as a dynamical self-sustaining system: The importance of time-scales and nested contexts. *Communication Theory, 19*, 445–464.

Vandervert, L. (1995). Chaos theory and the evolution of consciousness and mind: A thermodynamic-holographic resolution to the mind-body problem. *New Ideas in Psychology, 13*(2), 107–127.

Wesselmann, E., & Jordan, J. S. (2016). Wild heroes: The complexity of being "moral". In T. Langley (Ed.), *The psychology of civil war* (pp. 111–124). New York: Sterling.

Wolpert, D. M., Miall, R. C., & Kawato, M. (1998). Internal models in the cerebellum. *Trends in Cognitive Sciences, 2*(9), 338–347.

Wolpert, D. M., Doya, K., & Kawato, M. (2003). A unifying computational framework for motor control and social interaction. *Philosophical Transactions of the Royal Society of London B Biological Sciences, 358*, 593–602.

Second-Order Anticipatory Systems

18

Anthony Hodgson

Contents

Abstract

This chapter introduces a new concept, the anticipatory present moment (APM) which offers a way of integrating Rosen's seminal model of the anticipatory system with post-Rosen developments in second-order cybernetics and the ontology of the present moment. The APM is a meta-model that enables systems thinking and futures thinking to be accommodated in a paradigm that transcends the contradiction between the science of systems based on evidence from the past with futures scenarios which derive from the psychology and mental models of practitioners trying to anticipate the future. As well as anticipatory systems

A. Hodgson (✉)
Centre for Environmental Change and Human Resilience, School of Social Sciences, University of Dundee, Dundee, Scotland, UK

International Futures Forum, Aberdour, Fife, Scotland, UK

Decision Integrity Limited, Pitlochry, Perthshire, Scotland, UK
e-mail: tony@decisionintegrity.co.uk

© Springer Nature Switzerland AG 2019
R. Poli (ed.), *Handbook of Anticipation*,
https://doi.org/10.1007/978-3-319-91554-8_97

theory, the APM arises from a transdisciplinary study including the phenomenology of time consciousness, boundary critique, scenario method, reperception as induction, and multidimensionality of time. The APM provides a conceptual framework which is stimulating fresh ideas about practices which support strategic decision-making.

Keywords

Anticipatory system · Second-order cybernetics · Present moment · Reperception · Time consciousness · Systems thinking · Futures thinking · Decision-making

Introduction

The aim of this chapter is to make a case for including a second-order perspective in research into anticipatory systems. Although Rosen's foundational definition and description establishes anticipation as a system that "uses the future," his definition was based on the inclusion of a predictive model of itself and its environment (Poli – Introduction to this handbook). In an ambiguous world of action in society where dominant conditions are increasingly complex, uncertain, and with multiple contradictions, prediction has limited validity. Hence, if anticipation as a discipline is to have value and impact, the nature of that anticipation needs to be well situated in the ambiguous world and able to contribute advantages. This requirement has been demonstrated, for example, by attempts to formulate anticipatory governance in both political and societal resilience (Fuerth and Faber 2012; Boyd et al. 2015).

Dealing with ambiguous situations necessarily involves the actor or observer. However, first-order reductionism leaves out the observer. The potential for introducing second-order cybernetics as an approach to anticipatory systems is that it includes the observer. Since anticipation incorporates the capacity to act in accord with, as well as perceive, the future (or some representation of it), then, from a second-order perspective, the state of the observer is a key factor in the functioning of an anticipatory system. This accords with the nature of second-order cybernetics (Foerster 1979; Scott 2004) the core of which is an inseparable triadic network of observer, society, and language (Muller 2016). This chapter explores the nature of that triadic network as related to the anticipatory system.

First, the first-order perspective on the anticipatory system is outlined and amplified by a second-order perspective; second, a brief description of second-order science is outlined; third, the transdisciplinary ingredients for constructing a second-order anticipatory system are proposed; and finally, a conjecture regarding the structure of a second-order system is introduced as the anticipatory present moment, APM (Hodgson 2016).

From First-Order to Second-Order Anticipatory Systems

Poli, in his review of the many forms of anticipation (Poli 2010), points out a fundamental issue in considering the nature of systems which are, in some way, able to anticipate the future. In what sense is the future there to be "made use of"? Considering this question from a second-order observer perspective requires a link between the nature of systems that function within a temporal order and the phenomenology of time consciousness: how are we aware of the future? To accommodate this question, Rosen's definition needs expanding in a way that offers the possibility of integration with the phenomenology of the present moment.

A necessary aspect of an anticipatory system is feedback in which effects are causes. A feedback loop will feed into the present of system information regarding past behavior of the system, which clearly can be of value in adjusting its present behavior. However, if the only information feeding back into the system is from the past, then it does not sufficiently meet the criteria for an explanation of anticipation. It is necessary that the system is able to adapt its behavior also incorporating information from the future. The simple term Rosen (1985) used for this additional loop is *feedforward*. The conventional interpretation of this feature is that the system operates with models of possible futures that go beyond those constructed simply from past information.

An analogy to feedforward in phenomenology is Husserl's (1991) notion of *protention*. This is a property of consciousness which anticipates as a lived experience a range of "what next?" which he distinguishes from imagination. The link with Husserl's model will be described on page 6.

Rosen's idea that an anticipatory system is one which contains an internal predictive model of itself and its environment goes beyond a reactive system based solely on feedback. Reactive systems can only respond to changes that have already happened and for effectiveness depend on a repeated environment or context. In contrast an anticipatory system not only responds this way but is in addition continually sense-making in the present and taking into account futures that have not yet happened.

A second-order development of the anticipatory system includes as part of the system an observer who is able to reflect and act on the consequence of anticipatory model assumptions. This opens up the possibility of creativity and acausal factors entering into the decisions of the system.

Figure 1 presents an extended version of Rosen's anticipatory system. In the diagram, S stands for system, which may be an individual organism, an ecosystem, or a social or economic system. At first view, S is an ordinary non-anticipatory dynamical system. M represents a model of S. In Rosen's account (1985), the behavior of S is considered to be taking place in conventional real time. The behavior of M, however, is taking place in a time variable which goes faster than real time. This means that after a fixed interval T, then M will have proceeded further along its behavioral trajectory than S. In this way, the behavior of M predicts the behavior of S; by looking at this stage of M at time T_1, we get information about the stages that S will be in at time T_2. M and S are set up to interact in specific ways.

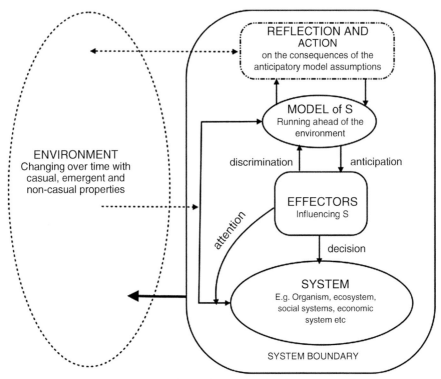

From First-oreder to Second-order Anticipatory System

Fig. 1 Second-order extension of Rosen's model

Suppose system M is equipped with a set E of effectors which allow it to operate either on S itself or on the environmental inputs to S, in such a way as to change the dynamical properties of S. The whole system will now be adaptive such that prospective future behaviors determine present changes of state. Anticipation would require the further property that M can discriminate between desirable and undesirable states and can change the dynamics of S in a way to avoid the undesirable region as well as cope with mutual possible trajectories in the future.

If S is a planning system, then we can make further propositions from this model. To be anticipatory beyond adaptability, the system needs to be open to interactions that enable M to be revised and extended beyond inherited experience (feedback), and the system needs M to be able to reframe and re-perceive its advance running in the light of an anomalous situation that is not yet experienced (feedforward). There is also the question as to whether, without openness to information from the future and in some sense "guessing futures," the system is fully anticipatory in an impredicative world in which time may be richer than simply a linear "block time" future.

From a second-order perspective, the case can be made that such anticipation is facilitated by the reflexive nature of an observing system which is able to ask itself what its view of the future is. In first-order science, the notion of anticipation is problematic due to what has been summarized as "the zeroth commandment" that future states cannot affect present changes of state. In second-order science, the nature of time and causality is open to reframing, and so the possibility of a theory of anticipation is more plausible. ("The idea of anticipation in science is controversial, because of "objective causality" pronounced in the "Zeroth Commandment": Thou shalt not allow future state to affect present change of state. Anticipation is almost always excluded from study at every level of system theory. The reasons for this rest on certain basic methodological presuppositions which have underlain "science" in the past few centuries: the essential basis on which "genuine scientific inquiry" rests is the principle of causality (which an anticipatory systems apparently violates); and "true objective science" cannot be argued from final cause (but an anticipatory system seems to embody a form of teleology)" (Louie 2010, p. 20).) Especially important in this view is the concept of inferential entailment in mathematics which is considered to correspond to forms of enactive relationship in biology as described in the emerging field of relational biology (Kineman and Poli, 2014) in which relational modeling emphasizes integration rather than mechanistic reduction.

   Louie (2010) considers that this "information from the future" is not actually from the future but is information about self, species, and the evolutionary environment encoded in the organization of living systems. This is the idea of model-based behavior where the model can contain aspects that are speculated future states not directly derivable from past causality. Having said that, Louie (2010) also makes a strong case for the admission of the "forbidden" concept of teleology to legitimately reenter science. Discussing this in the context of the Aristotelian four causes, he points out that three of them (material, efficient, and formal) are congruent with Newtonian physics, but the fourth, final cause, is conventionally rejected. However, the Newtonian paradigm itself violates the existential nature of time and therefore cannot be regarded as an adequate comprehensive frame for considering what is scientifically acceptable (Smolin 2013). The extension of dimensions beyond space-time leaves open more radical ways to consider what the future is that is being used in anticipatory systems (Hodgson 2013).

Transdisciplinary Expansion of Second-Order Anticipation

What is time? The ontology of time in philosophy has been largely concerned only with an ill-defined instant or with a timeless "eternal now." The question needs broadening out. An ontology of all present moments, including past and future states, is needed (Poli 2011). We can begin from our experience of the present, the actual "now." What exists in the human mind is our present moment, and this can be different according to the state of our consciousness. Our attention to the present can be constricted with very little content, or it can be very expansive with a multiplicity of impressions informing it. In the ordinary way, experience is of the content which is being actualized coupled with its traces of the past and expectations of the future. Within that personal present moment, freedom is limited by the commitments of the past and recognition of latent patterns of potential. If the commitments are high and the recognition is low, then the present moment is a conditioned state in which the self has little power of choice. This is one version of the "thin" present moment. It is, however, possible to transcend this conditioning by abandoning attachment to the current content of the present moment, expanding the consciousness, and thereby experiencing a larger present moment with more degrees of choice and freedom. This is the "thick" present moment. A sentient human walker resting at the bottom of a valley can, unlike a rock, bring to mind the destination over the hill and climb out – still conditioned by the physical situation but exercising freedom to transcend it. This is because the processes "inside" the walker are not wholly determined by the contextual processes of its environment as is the case with the rock.

The present moment in some way contains aspects of the future – future in the present. Containing the future in some existent way implies the idea that the future can influence the present in a distinct way beyond any modeling function such as is proposed in first-order anticipatory system theory. The status of both the present and the future are not the same in this context as in the conventional time line of the past, present, and future. In this alternate view, the key framing is a topological one of nested present moments of different scales of present moment. This means that what is contained in a larger present moment can be in the future of a smaller present moment. This is another way of interpreting that some "saw it coming," whereas many did not.

In Fig. 2, the present moment of a system is represented by a circle of which a time span is a diameter. In present moment theory, the future exists: but it does not exist within a small conditioned "thin" time slice. It exists in a greater "thick" time slice. Our future is not-yet-now for us, but it is already present as a latency. We cannot say that the future is "in" the future in a linear sense. What we can say is that an event that will occur in our future is already present in a larger present moment. The notion of present moment also implies sentience. This may be of differing degrees depending on the level of reality in focus.

The conjecture made here is that a systemic structure of a second-order anticipatory moment can be constructed from the integration of the following six aspects depicted in Fig. 2.

The anticipatory present moment, APM, brings together the following perspectives:

1. The phenomenology of time experience (Gell 1992)
2. The scenaric stance toward the future (Ogilvy 2011)
3. The ontology of the present moment (Hodgson 2013)
4. Boundary critique as a second-order notion (Midgley 2000)
5. The nature of anticipatory systems (Rosen 1985)
6. Meta learning through varieties of reperception (Wack 1985)

These aspects are described briefly in the following sections.

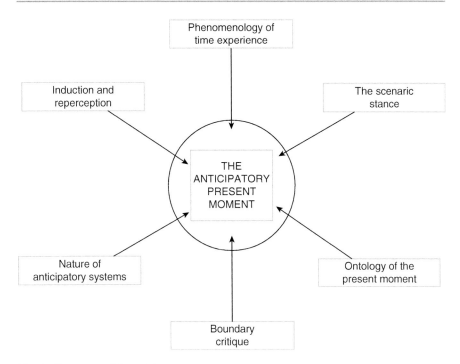

Fig. 2 Six aspects of the anticipatory present moment

Husserl's Model of Time Consciousness

Husserl developed his theory regarding the problem of the continuity of the perceptual present in contrast to the conventional idea that now is a "thin" present between the future and the past. Instead he saw it as a "thick" present (Gell 1992). For example, if we are listening to a note played on an instrument, we hear it as a continuous duration. When we are part way through, the sound of the first second is no longer audible. In terms of our experience, however, it is still a present tone that we are hearing. The meaning of the tone in, say, a musical work, is also evoked in relation to its future ending.

The immediate experience of the earlier part of the sound is not the same as a memory of that sound. There is a distinction between *retentions of experience* and memories of that experience. The present future of the sound is *protention* as an extended present. The idea of a knife-edge present, or a thin instant, is abandoned. Retentions are qualitatively different from memory reproductions in that they are all part of the current consciousness of the present. Protentions also contain elements of the emergent proximate future, which can be distinguished from fantasized futures. The present moment thus contains elements of conventional past and future, experienced as an extended now as in Fig. 3 (Gell 1992).

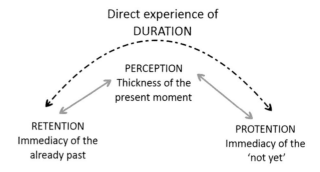

Fig. 3 Representation of Husserl's present

The Basic Nature of Anticipatory Systems

The phenomenology of the present as the properties of retention, perception, and protention serves to integrate anticipation in a reflexive way. It is necessary to extend the basic concept of feedback as applied in adaptive systems. A feedback loop will feed information into the present of a system regarding past relationships of the system, which has limitations of value in adjusting its present behavior to an unknown future. It is necessary that the system also has the property of feedforward in order to be able to adapt its behavior to be ready for the "not yet."

As previously stated an anticipatory system needs a way that information regarding the future can be acquired. One way is that an anticipatory system contains a predictive model of itself and its environment which enables it to make choices which are not entirely based on past information. Another way is that in some sense, aspects of the future already exist and therefore an anticipatory system can have the additional capacity to pick up information regarding the future which is neither inferential nor based on a predictive model; "using the future" could include perceiving an existent future. This requires two distinct channels of information input as shown in Fig. 4, one from the past retention side and the other from the future protention side.

The Ontology of the Present Moment

This topic is considered in some depth in my paper on the subject (Hodgson 2013). The essential features that need to be borne in mind for synthesis are recapitulated here. Poli's (2013) distinction between a thin and a thick present moment supports the idea that the present should be considered an extended duration that interfaces between the past and future, which is in contrast to it being a knife edge between the past and the future. The thickness of the present moment is related to a sense of dimensionality that is both measurable, in the sense of dimensionality in physics (Bohm 1980; Ferret 2010), and phenomenological, as in the Husserlian (1991) and Bergsonian (1910) notion of duration. Bennett (1966) extended this interpretation to six dimensions of experience: namely, traces and memories; interacting commitments; passive forms; active patterns; expectations and hopes; and capacity for creative decisions. This idea is summarized in Fig. 5.

Fig. 4 A phenomenological
view of anticipation

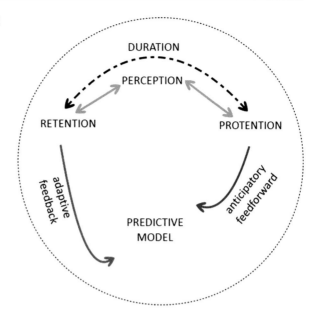

The Structure of Boundary Critique

The notion of boundary critique in systemic intervention (Midgley 2000; Ulrich 1994) addresses problematic situations with second-order reflections on boundaries. Consideration of a present moment implicitly assumes or defines the scope of a boundary in time. Psychologically this is determined by both the duration of attention and concern over time and the richness or variety of the content under consideration. A present moment is complex, nonlinear, and generative of emergent properties, including those influenced by the future. The boundaries of a system are defined by the limits of the knowledge that is taken as pertinent to the system in question.

In considering human systems as anticipatory systems, then, boundary critique can supply a rationale and method for supporting not only clarification of the system in question but also the present moment in which that system is being considered.

The basic representation in Fig. 6 of boundary critique by Midgley is a spatial diagram (see Fig. 6) circumscribing the domain of relevance and indicating that such a domain has a central value and identity. This is represented as the boundary of the anticipatory system. For the purposes of developing the anticipatory present moment concept, I am assuming a single boundary condition and introducing the time dimension. In this modified version, the "space" (content) of the system is represented in the plane orthogonal to the plane of the paper. The time dimension is the circle in the plane of the paper. This represents a duration with past, present, and future spread over time's arrow. Thus the boundary critique takes a space and time perspective. The significance of this is that not only do we make assumptions of boundaries of inclusion and exclusion, we also make assumptions of what is relevant

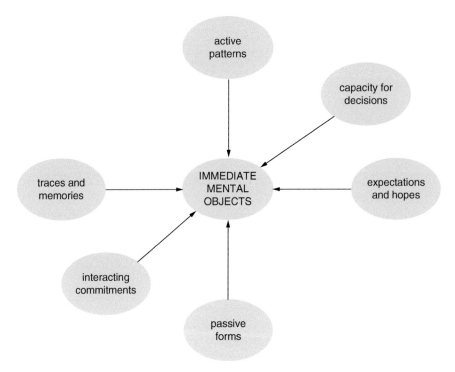

Fig. 5 The experience of the present moment, after Bennett (1966) and Hodgson (2013)

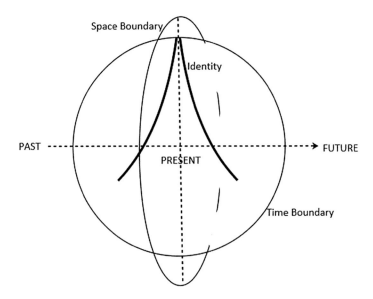

Fig. 6 Boundary critique with time in addition to space

in usually narrow time ranges. Put simply, without a time boundary critique, we may sacrifice the longer-term viable future to short term fixes.

Cognition and Perception

The decision-maker is actually more than just an observer. To take a decision is to commit to some interaction with the field of the decision and "bring forth a world." An investment decision depends on financial resources in the decision system potentially at the disposal of the decision-maker. Although observing and analyzing the situation, from a systemic point of view, the decision-maker is an integral component of that decision system. Markets are reflexive to the decision-makers who participate in them (Umpleby 2007).

We need to understand both feedback and feedforward in terms of cognition and induction. As described by Holland et al. (1986), the key trigger for induction is anomaly. This is the case where inductive learning is taking place stimulated by information from the past or previous experience. This is hard enough, but the challenge of induction in the anticipatory system is dealing with anomalies that have little or no basis in information from the past. Usually we are "future blind" in this respect. Holland et al. (1986) give the example of the falling "leaf" behaving in a self-propelled way from flower to flower provoking a reinterpretation as "butterfly." But, in a world where we have never seen self-propelled plant seeds (as in the movie Avatar), how do we anticipate such and adjust beliefs and behavior accordingly?

Stated as a paradox, the important distinction here is that anticipation needs the capacity to imagine the unimaginable and see the invisible (Toffler 1970). Entertaining multiple representations of a possible reality that has not yet happened is one way a system can become anticipatory. This is a challenge to cognitive and perceptual capabilities.

The Scenaric Stance

Ogilvy (2011) introduces the notion of the scenaric stance by which he means the simultaneous entertaining of multiple scenarios of the future that may be contradictory (e.g., both pessimistic and optimistic) and leaving room for the unknown and the creative. This frame of mind is also clearly consistent with opening to anomaly and contradiction, which can support anticipation. To practice this we need a capacity to embrace permanent ambiguity and to put our confidence in acting in the present but with a greatly enriched multidimensional experience of the present moment.

Reperceiving (Wack 1985; Burt 2010) is necessary to allow for the creative openness of our experience. This orientation accords with the "open future" that is part of the present moment concept, with this future being imagined within an enlarged (or "thick") present.

The Structure of the Anticipatory Present Moment

To summarize, the six key notions which underpin this synthesis between systems thinking and futures thinking implied in second-order anticipatory systems are:

- Multiple futures, not necessarily compatible, held in the consciousness of the present.
- Openness in that consciousness to the presence of choice and creative action.
- Capacity of the mind steady in its embrace of this openness and complexity.
- The implications of responsibility for choice in relation to the unfolding future.

These support the integrating concept of the notion of the present moment put forward here.

Figure 7 depicts the anticipatory present moment (APM). The circle represents the scale and extent of the present moment in question. It also represents the selection or identification of the relevant boundary conditions. The stimulus entering the circle on the left represents the influences of conventional causation from the past of this particular present moment. The response exiting the circle on the right represents the influence of the present moment in question on future conditions. The present moment in question is recognized as the experiential or phenomenological aspect of the self-agency of the system in question. This second-order observing self is taken to include a cognitive system represented by the components within the circle. The alphabetical

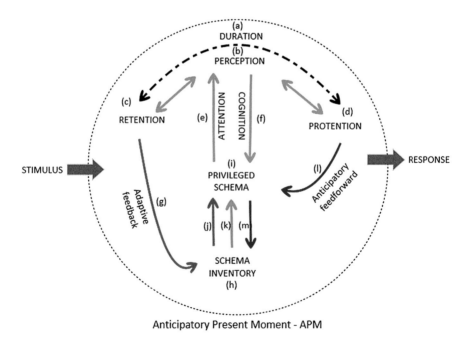

Anticipatory Present Moment - APM

Fig. 7 The anticipatory present moment (APM)

tags on the diagram reference to components of the diagram to the descriptions which follow.

The different components of this diagram are labeled (a), (b), (c), and so on. These aid the referencing to the diagram in the description that follows. Subsidiary perspectives of the diagram are given in Figs. 8, 9, and 10. The main components are:

(a) Duration – the fundamental experience of time consciousness
(b) Perception – what is seen to be present
(c) Retention – the active retrospective present
(d) Protention – the immediate sense of the future
(e) Attention – the directing of interest
(f) Cognition – the mental sense-making of the moment
(g) Adaptive feedback – adjusting to information from previous experience
(h) Schema inventory – the set of mental interpretations available in the mind
(i) Privileged schema – the selected interpretation of the moment
(j) Promotion of schema from past – recovery from previous history
(k) Promotion of schema from present – immediate interpretations of current "reality"
(l) Anticipatory feedforward – alertness to information from the dimensions of the future

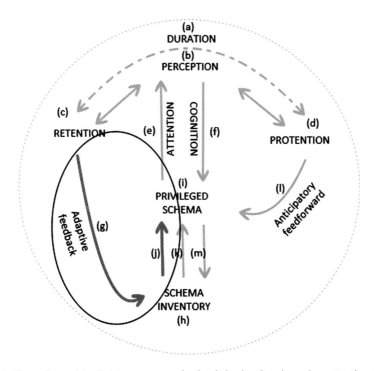

Fig. 8 The pathway (g) ➜ (j) represents adaptive behavior that determines attention (e) and perception (b)

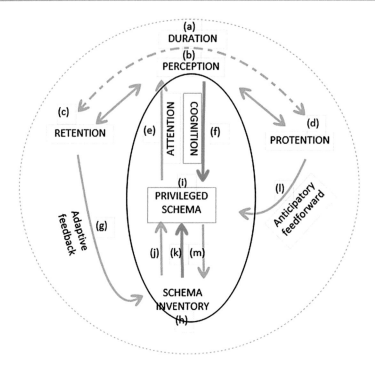

Fig. 9 The pathway cognition (f)→(k) represents the mainstream of choosing how to look at the situation

(m) Promotion of schema from future – innovative interpretations not extrapolated from accumulated experience – the anticipatory difference

This model can serve as a basis for interpreting reflexive decision-making. The APM thus incorporates the six threads, namely, the phenomenology of time experience, the scenaric stance, the ontology of the present moment, boundary critique, the nature of anticipatory systems, and the nature of induction and perception. The APM concept has more to it than simply the addition of these six factors; they have a dynamic interrelationship as depicted in the diagram.

Beginning with extended boundary critique, the dotted circle represents the boundary of both the system in question and the duration of the present moment. The notion of boundary critique is extended from the boundary of system space to include time span but, more than that, the span of all six dimensions of the present moment. The line is dotted to symbolize that the present moment system boundary is permeable to influences from a greater present moment within which it is contained and also subject to the judgment of the reflexive agent or subject at the heart of the system. So the concept of present moment contributes to framing the definition of the APM.

The phenomenological aspect of the APM is the experience of duration (a) which depends on the attention (e) and cognition (f) of the reflexive subject. Duration is the experience of the present as having more to it than simply the knife-edge instant between the past and the future. Attention (e) is the capacity to direct and sustain

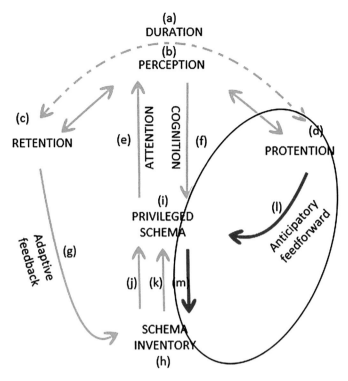

Fig. 10 The pathway anticipatory feedforward (l)→(m) represents the way additional degrees of freedom become available to the APM. (m) is the enrichment of the schema inventory by the learning brought about by anticipatory feedforward, which would not occur reliant on only adaptive feedback

interest in the present event (Ingold 1999). Cognition (f) is the capacity to configure and interpret the experience.

An important consideration here is the attention span of the subject. Husserl (Gel, 1992) considered this in terms of listening to a musical note lasting a matter of seconds differentiating the direct experience of hearing the sound into retention as distinct from memory and protention as distinct from imagination. The APM extends this to the range of factors in both past and future that the subject can sustain. In conventional terms, this can be related to time span capacity (Jacques 1988). In the context of systemic intervention, this span relates to the intended scope of improvement which in conventional terms is characterized as short, medium, or long term. Perception (b) is the engagement in the experience by a conscious self. Retention (c) is the presence in experience of temporally recent aspects of the currently ongoing event; note this is not the same as the reproduction of the experience in memory. Protention (d) is the counterpart to retention in the experience of anticipation of the currently ongoing event; note this is not the same as the imagination of a future.

Research into time and brain structure sheds some light on this at the neurobiological level, but the field is still unresolved. The APM implies that the time experience can range beyond the short intervals of neural impulses. The situation is summarized by Damasio (2014):

> ...mind time has to do with how we experience the passage of time and how we organise chronology. Despite the steady tick of the clock, duration can seem fast or slow, short or long. And this variability can happen on different scales, from decades, seasons, weeks and hours, down to the tiniest intervals of music – the span of a note or the moment of silence between two notes. We also place events in time, deciding when they occurred, in which order and on what scale, whether that of a lifetime or of a few seconds. (Damasio 2014, p. 42)

In the structure of APM, the first cybernetic dynamic is the adaption to feedback (g), which is the learning cycle of adaptation. This, in itself, is not anticipation but is essential for a viable system. Adaptive feedback is the capacity of the experiencing conscious self to take heed of and adjust behavior to what has recently occurred within their present moment.

The APM structure includes the capacity to learn from past experience. This can be seen as information, as coming from the retention side of duration, which in conventional terms is characterized as adaptation, learning from history. The APM also includes the capacity to receive information from the protention side of the present moment, learning from the future. This information contains elements which cannot be derived from the past. In some current thinking about the prospective capacities of mind and brain (see, e.g., Seligman et al. 2013), this is beginning to be acknowledged.

As an anticipatory system, able to incorporate both past and future into current choice, the APM exercises the intelligent flexibility of induction and reperception. Any reflexive mind has a repertoire or inventory of schema or mental models that inform behavior at different levels. Schema inventory is the repertoire of cognitive interpretations that are available to the conscious self. The term schema refers to some organized pattern of thought or mental model that organizes categories of information and the relationships among them. The term was given prominence by Piaget and taken up by von Glasersfeld (2001) in his radical constructivism. The role of schema in sense-making also features in Weik's theory (Weber and Glynn 2006). Schema should not be understood as equivalent to blueprints within the mind that are in some way implemented. The situation is far more dynamic and plastic than that; cognition is neither wholly schematic nor wholly interactive but some hybrid of the two. The plasticity of the brain seems to be constantly active with its inventory of schema as well as enacting, through the equivalent of simulation, much wider possibilities than those currently manifest. In the APM diagram, this is represented by the relationship between the schema inventory (h) and the privileged schema (i) in action at any particular moment, selected as appropriate.

In behavior which is principally adaptive, the privileged schema will be part of an existing historical repertoire which may well be applied in a novel way but is essentially based on past experience. In behavior which is anticipatory, the privileged schema may emerge from a shock factor which has invalidated the current repertoire as ill-fitting and inappropriate. Privileged schema is the automatically or consciously selected schema that is dominant in the current interpretation. We can suppose from this model that any authentic anticipatory behavior is always arising from some anomaly that challenges the habitual way of responding to situations or taking decisions that have strong implications for the future. These anomalies may come in several forms. An example is when, in a scenario planning exercise, the reflexive decision-maker sees propositions in a scenario that contradict his or her current strategic assumptions and therefore indicate possible future failure if not taken into account. If these scenario propositions are taken seriously enough, then a crisis of reperception is triggered. This is a nontrivial event since it almost certainly will also trigger psychological factors like denial and defensive routines (Argyris and Schon 1978) as well as entry into new opportunity space.

However, there can be internalized forms of anticipatory reperception that emerge from a more intuitive source. This can be observed externally in fields from competitive sport to entrepreneurial enterprise. A player in a ball game may have an uncanny capacity to be ahead of the game in just the right spot to make winning moves. An entrepreneur may have a hunch that something unbelievable will work against all conventional wisdom, risking with confidence seizing an opportunity overlooked or dismissed by others.

So in terms of the APM diagram, pathway cognition (f)➔(k) represents the mainstream of choosing how to look at the situation.

Conclusion

In summary, the APM reframes the anticipatory system as a second-order cybernetic system and sets the scene for new research in the discipline of anticipation related to decision-making, policy, and governance which all include the observer/actor/decider. The APM framework provides a heuristic for exploring different forms of conscious participation especially relevant to the human domain of practical affairs. These explorations include recognizing the importance of creativity in anticipatory governance, the role of the state of mind of the decision-maker in anticipation (e.g., in forms of mindfulness), and the need to stimulate reperception if the confirmation biases of entrenched belief systems are to be loosened up to better embrace the presented complexity and uncertainty of the world.

References

Argyris, C., & Schon, D. (1978). *Organisational learning*. Reading: Addison Wesley.
Bennett, J. G. (1966). *The dramatic universe* (Vol. 4). London: Hodder and Stoughton.
Bergson, H. (1910). *Time and free will: An essay on the immediate data of consciousness* (trans: Pogson, F. L.). London: George Allen and Unwin.
Bohm, D. (1980). *Wholeness and the implicate order*. London: Routledge & Kegan Paul.
Boyd, E., Borgstrom, S., Nykvist, B., & Stacewicz, I. A. (2015). Anticipatory governance for social-ecological resilience. *Ambio, 44*(Suppl 1), 149–161.
Burt, G. (2010). Revisiting and extending our understanding of Pierre Wack's the gentle art of re-perceiving. *Technological Forecasting and Social Change, 77*, 1476–1484.
Damasio, A. (2014). Remembering when. *Scientific American, 23*, 42–47.
Ferret, J. (2010). Anticipatory systems in physics. *Foresight, 12*(3), 30–37.

Fuerth, L., & Faber, E. M. H. (2012). *Anticipatory governance – Practical upgrades: Equipping the executive branch to cope with increasing speed and complexity of major challenges.* Washington, DC: Elliott School of International Affairs. Retrieved from http://forwardengagement.org/?option=com_content&view=article&id=6&Itemid=6.

Gell, A. (1992). *The anthropology of time: Cultural constructions of temporal maps and images.* Oxford: Berg.

Hodgson, A. (2013). Towards an ontology of the present moment. *On the Horizon, 21*(1), 24–38.

Hodgson, A. (2016). *Time, pattern, perception: Integrating systems and futures thinking.* PhD thesis, University of Hull.

Holland, J. H., Holyoak, K. J., Nisbett, R. E., & Thagard, P. R. (1986). *Induction: Processes of inference, learning and discovery.* Cambridge, MA: MIT Press.

Husserl, E. (1991). *On the phenomenology of the consciousness of internal time (1903–1917).* Dordrecht: Kluwer.

Ingold, T. (1999). *From the transmission of representation to the education of attention.* Department of Social Anthropology, University of Manchester.

Jacques, E. (1988). *Requisite organization: A Total system for effective managerial organization and managerial leadership for the 21st century.* Gloucester: Cason Hall.

Kineman, J. J., & Poli, R. (2014). Ecological literacy leadership. *Bulletin of the Ecological Society of America, 95*(1), 30–58.

Louie, A. H. (2010). Robert Rosen's anticipatory system. *Foresight, 12*(3), 18–29.

Midgley, G. (2000). *Systemic intervention; philosophy, methodology, and practice.* New York: Kluwer.

Muller, K. H. (2016). *Second-order science: The revolution of scientific structures* (p. p37). Wien: Edition Echoraum.

Ogilvy, J. (2011). Facing the fold: From the eclipse of utopia to the restoration of hope. *Foresight, 13*(4), 7–23.

Poli, R. (2010). The many aspects of anticipation. *Foresight, 12*(3), 7–17.

Poli, R. (2011). Steps toward an explicit ontology of the future. *Journal of Future Studies, 16*, 67–78.

Poli, R. (2013). Overcoming divides. *On the Horizon, 21*(1), 3–14.

Rosen, R. (1985). *Anticipatory systems: Philosophical, mathematical and methodological foundations.* New York: Pergammon Press.

Scott, B. (2004). Scott 2nd order cybernetics: An historical introduction. *Kybernetes, 33*(9/10), 1365–1378.

Seligman, M. E. P., Railton, P., Baumeister, R. F., & Sripada, C. (2013). Navigating into the future or driven by the past. *Perspectives on Psychological Science, 8*, 119–141.

Smolin, L. (2013). *Time reborn: From the crisis in physics to the future of the universe.* London: Penguin.

Toffler, A. (1970). *Future shock.* New York: Random House.

Ulrich, W. (1994). Can we secure future-responsive management through systems thinking and design? *Interfaces, 24*(4), 26–37.

Umpleby, S. (2007). Reflexivity in social systems: The theories of George Soros. *Systems Research and Behavioural Science, 24*, 515–522.

von Foerster, H. (1979). Cybernetics of cybernetics. In K. Kippendorf (Ed.), *Communication and control in society.* New York: Gordon and Breach.

von Glasersfeld, E. (2001). The radical constructivist view of science. *Foundations of Science, 6*(1–3), 31–43.

Wack, P. (1985). Scenarios: The gentle art of re-perceiving. *Harvard Business Review.*

Weber, K., & Glynn, M. A. (2006). Making sense with intuitions: Context thought and action in Karl Weik's theory. *Organization Studies, 27*(11), 163901660.

Anthropology and the Near-Future Concept 19

Jane I. Guyer

Contents

Abstract

My concept of the "near future" originates in a paper published in 2007, in the context of what US Federal Reserve Chairman Alan Greenspan called *The Age of Turbulence* (2007) in the economy. The coincidence of this economic concern, alongside a rising religious focus on "the end times," and secular concerns with the new millennium, global warming and political turbulence, became complex and contested themes for conceptualization. A calculable "near future" may be disappearing, as referring to a manageable range of rational planning of the postwar, 5-year-plan kind, with its confident expectation of making life better within a definite time frame, and by following a defined path. Instead, a "punctuated time" of multiple dates and commitments is being crafted and managed together by both individual people and collectivities, drawing more often on invocations of "apocalypse" as looming disaster, and "emergence" as an indeterminate process. Anthropological analysis has also inserted new questions about ontology: how do we conceptualize *ourselves* in these differently defined

J. I. Guyer (✉)
John Hopkins University, Baltimore, MD, USA
e-mail: jiguyer@jhu.edu

© Springer Nature Switzerland AG 2019
R. Poli (ed.), *Handbook of Anticipation*,
https://doi.org/10.1007/978-3-319-91554-8_69

transitional modes? My paper endorses and explores how "anticipation" can help to focus empirical exploration of the complexity of temporal concepts and processes, in the public sphere.

Keywords
Economy · Turbulence · Temporality · Religion · Ontology

Introduction

I introduced the concept of the "near future" in a plenary session paper delivered at the American Ethnological Society in 2005 and then published in (Guyer 2007). In the context of what US Federal Reserve Chairman Alan Greenspan called *The Age of Turbulence* (2007), the rising focus within certain religious circles of the concept of "the end times" and many concerns with the temporality of the new millennium and the writing and thinking about time in the public sphere and collective life had become complex and contested. Macroeconomics and religious thinking about the horizons of the long-term future seemed to share certain qualities. Even the words themselves moved across the different domains of social life in ways that purely analytical thinking generally avoids. Apocalypse,on a visible horizon of the future, was becoming a concept applied to many macro-dynamics, not only with its early etymological referent of "revelation" but then later "cataclysm," and then into vernacular language in an everyday mode, as these terms became increasingly performative. In that paper, I suggested that in this cultural-historical context, the "near future" was disappearing, as referring to a manageable range of rational planning and of the postwar, 5-year-plan kind, with its confident expectation of making life better within a definite time frame, and by following a defined path. This was being replaced, but still in a reasoning mode, by the "punctuatcd time" of multiple dates and commitments that had to be crafted and managed together by both individual people and collectivities. According to the records, that article has been widely cited in the 10 years since it was published. Ideally, my revisit to the concept would review the questions, observations, critiques, and new directions arising from all these direct engagements. However, the current paper simply highlights the conceptual innovations now being made in anthropological research, both on the formal sectors of finance, economy, and religion and in the conceptual repertoires of the people.

I introduced the "near future," then, to refer to a temporal frame for social and economic life that I noticed, from my own history, to have retreated from the public arena in favor of two others: the immediate and the long term. The immediate frame referred to decision-making, specific actions, and their predictable aims and conse-quences in the present. The long term referred to recognized forces playing out their logics toward a moment of "arrival" at a wholly new condition. In between the two, instead of a sense of living within 5-year plans, there had developed a sensibility to unpredictability. I called this, "punctuated time." It did have predictable dates to some of its dynamics, for specific people and actions, but there had grown up a profound sense that the interactions among date regimes would be complex and not entirely falling within the dynamics of the long term. Indeed, action in punctuated time could cause surprising turbulence when the different participants in one arena were also managing several others.

In one sense, then, I was advocating bringing a classic ethnographic mind-set to a topic of rising importance in our own Euro-American public and bureaucratically managed life, as well as being attentive to the people's own conceptualization of "the future." We would be particularly attentive to variable and shifting conceptual frameworks with respect to time as mobilized by different parties, manipulations of the words by those creating public rhetoric, and differences in the language itself, as used within and between communicative communities. Alan Greenspan's subtitle was *Adventures in a New World*, and the title of the book by Secretary of the Treasury, Henry Paulson, was *On the Brink* (2010), both metaphors expressing a departure from an expectation of confidence in the possible absolute precision of planning and prediction. "Adventures" and "the brink" are both implicitly open to happenstance. I attended to these "terms of debate versus words in circulation" in an article with that title (Guyer 2012), focusing on the terms that have temporal implications, such as "stability," "liquidity," and "flaw" in a "system."

Over the years since these "turns" and "turbulences" in our own economic world, there has developed a new vocabulary for what used to be "the near future" as a planned horizon. "Near" implies that one can see it and thereby actively create a path toward it, based on an understanding of oneself and of the terrain ahead, drawing on reasoned thought. The focus and terminology, in both academic and public life, have now shifted to a lived-in present where multiple dynamics interact in indeterminate ways, to produce a condition experienced as turbulence, crisis, confusion, and others that contain no clear temporal quality to them. Of course, *crisis* implies that it passes, since it is a pivotal point, used in ancient languages for turning points in the course of a disease. But the kinds of duration, direction, and chance of repetition are not clearly embedded in the meanings of these terms, unlike with terms based on an underlying concept of *evolution*, in which the future possibilities are already embedded in the present. Bill Maurer (2002) captured this complex sense of a present imbued with several conceptual regimes in a paper on financial artifacts: "Financial derivatives are credited with bringing to the fore a number of sociological and metaphysical problems for modernity, from the instantiation of particular modalities of risk to the destabilization of referentiality in knowledge-claims about the world" (2002, p. 15). So these new conditions are increasingly conceptualized as producing "emergent" novel combinations, from multiple intersections and mutual infusions, within short time frames that are not predictable and manageable through classic calculative rationality, and there may not even be definable and clear terms that can apply to these processes.

Classic anthropology worked with the concept of "the ethnographic present" as the source from which cultural patterns and political-ideational structures could be learned, since the cultures that our discipline was studying were approached as if they were in reproductive, rather than evolutionary historical, mode. In more recent years, anthropological work has moved into a new temporal mode by being deeply attentive to the present seen as indeterminate, even for its central actors, with qualities of emergence, both analytically and empirically. In their own ways, collectivities experience and create their conditions of being in such an uncertain world as we all inhabit in the twenty-first century. Both the scholars and the people may make *parts* of it predictable, by managing what appears to be under our own control. However, we know that many conditions, components, and concerns of others cannot be relied upon with certainty, either to contribute to or to disrupt predictability. While some of the new works do explicitly address questions of how to engage with "futures" which are now often expressed in the plural (see, later, my analysis of Goldstone and Obarrio's new collection entitled *African Futures.* 2016), they can also draw on some broader philosophical moves within our discipline with respect to a complexly interwoven *present* from which futures are emerging. I discuss this new "present" first.

Ontology and Etymology in Temporal Mode and a Recent Overview

Since questioning the "near future," I have found new inspirations coming from the cultures, and the new writing about them, which have always infused anthropological thought and theory. While that paper focused on concepts of time, it did not yet raise very clearly the ontological issues of *"who are we, now, in the present?"* experienced and contemplated in these different and changing temporal modes, *within* converging temporalities, in a new phase of history. Ontology has become a topic of great debate, mainly in other disciplines than anthropology, over this same time period, through what is referred to as "the ontological turn." For us, however, the move from social determinism with respect to shared conditions to an affective attention to a complex present is not an entirely new finding in the world. In a recent lecture, I explored this question empirically, under the title of *Shape-shifting and Thinking Within Transitions*, drawing on classic ethnography from the past: in this case, the main reference was to Victor Turner's (1967) description of his African friend, known as Muchona the Hornet. Muchona was a brilliant companion, whose mind buzzed intensely around every philosophical issue as well as around the drinks at a gathering. We have many classic and current ethnographic sources on shifting ontology, hence the possibility of beings moving from one self to another, so perhaps thinking differently *within* a transition or an indeterminate state of affairs than thinking only *about* it, from a stability of self.

The possibility of moving through different "selves" is quite widespread, as I illustrated from Amazonian and African sources, from Kafka's *Metamorphosis*, and from the folklore of the *dybbuk*. Even the thinking being who is predicting, reasoning, anticipating, and managing temporality might be, itself, changing in the process. The stable rational self of economics and the enduring soul of religious life are concepts that place the imagination in a more secure place of confident durational being than would a culture with an acceptance of shape-shifting and a world increasingly seen as indeterminate. We now have a set of resources on which to draw in order to mediate interpretations of "being now" and "being next," in temporal mode.

The most challenging new anthropological work on ontology and temporality can be found in the newly detailed studies in Amazonia. For example, Eduardo Kohn's ethnography on *How Forests Think* (2013) contains many referents to "the future," in a context where not only the people but also the forests do the thinking. He places "absence" within the experiential dynamics of the present: how to study "the relation of continuity and growth to absence...The future matters to living thoughts. It is a constituent feature of any kind of self" (p. 23). He concludes that there are many kinds of selves and, in this case, spiritual selves, in a "vast but fragile realm of relating . . . (in) a living future in relation to the deaths that make that future possible" (p. 218, 219). Kohn's example places relational presence and absence at the center of our understanding of the dynamics between present and future, which we already perceive to be complex in our so-called "modern" societies. Although his case is a specific ethnographic example, such examples can always provoke new thinking into other cases, for comparative purposes, as well as offering another analytical angle to bring to theory and method. The present is not only what is currently present but includes spaces experienced as absences. How absence plays its role in our own formalized temporal regimes, as they are managed in improvisational mode in many different contexts, is a question such ethnographic study can inspire.

By drawing on such deeply ethnographic works, in classic cultural milieus, new questions can arise about the near future in our more immediate contexts. The specific temporal referent of the "near future" has been responded to, and developed in new directions, for at least 10 years. Before reviewing this growth and enrichment, it is worth noting that the verbs associated with visions of the future have shifted: particularly moving from "predict" to "anticipate." Etymology helps us greatly with our nuanced shifts in the use of concepts with overlapping referents. To "predict" is to "say before" something happens, so to be specific about what it is expected to be and possibly also the time frame within which it will arrive. To "anticipate" is to "be aware of (something) coming," with the intimation that this could be prepared for, or forestalled, but with no intimation of a specific time frame or exact content. Prophecy, which was in the original title of the paper in order to allude to the recent infusion of a religious sensibility, has yet another etymological implication: to be able to understand the will of God (or the gods, in the plural).

In his important review of *The Future as Cultural Fact*, Arjun Appadurai navigates us through the application of three verbs: "aspiration, anticipation, imagination" (2013, p. 286), each of which will also involve emotion and sensation, hence an ontological sensibility to the specific nature of the present from which we reach forward in time. The evocations of each verb with respect to our approaches to the future – the time "yet to be" – can differ, since each may allow people, in their own ways, to "absorb newness into frames that they always carry with them before the fact" (Appadurai 2013, p. 285). But what, then, are those frames, how to do coexist, and who is crafting and re-crafting them for a shifting present? These are classic questions for an attentively ethnographic approach. With respect to the action that one or other of these verbs about the future would inspire, in another work,

Appadurai writes "Perhaps we are now ready for an anthropology of and for resistance, which takes the diversity of images of the good life into fuller account when discussing resistance, so that it becomes a matter not just of refusal but of culturally inflected aspiration"(2016, p. 3).

In his basic trilogy of concepts, anticipation does not refer to the outcome of rational planning, although it might be used to express a concern that something "predicted" might be accompanied by something else altogether, in complex intertwining. Appadurai (2013, pp. 293–299) connects it to the expectation of "risk" and to the work of Mary Douglas. For understanding any signs and portents of this, we may need prophets, diviners, or, in the present formalized world, people who can interpret the signs. This would put any clarity about the future into a domain of expertise, where special skills enable the reading of the signs of change. He points out, though, that the sensibilities can be different, according to whether this future is seen in terms of an "ethics of possibility," meaning "those ways if thinking, feeling and acting that increase the horizons of hope, that expand the field of the imagination, that produce what I have called the capacity to aspire, and that widen the field of informed, creative, and critical citizenship." He contrasts this with thinking in terms of an "ethics of probability ... those ways of thinking, feeling, and acting that flow out of ... the dangers of modern regimes of diagnosis, counting and accounting" (Appadurai 2013, p. 295). Hope is central to aspiration, but not to formal prediction, hence the centrality of indeterminacy and affect.

As we make this shift in emphasis from prediction to anticipation, the concept of time itself, and the course it follows, has also shifted. The concept of anticipation opens up both of the vistas: the directions of change, and the concepts of the process and pattern of change, to the broader and deeper indeterminacy that has moved into the space I had indicated as "the near future" with its punctuated time. Punctuated time has not disappeared, but it now contributes to the senses of confusion, emergence, and disorientation in the present, of which we begin to see more empirical evidence. Appadurai advocates an ethnographic approach to this empirical world. "(B)uilding a robust anthropology of the future ... will require a new conversation between approaches to liminal moments and persons, to the production of the everyday, and to the discursive processes by which violence, disaster and emergency are made tolerable" (2013, p. 288).

Temporal Terms: "Near," as "Next" and "Emergent," in Current Economies

In the Formal Terminology

We can turn, in ethnographic mode, to our current sense of indeterminacy within what might be termed "the foreseeable future" or "developmental stages": how people and formal organizations are looking ahead in varied ways, creating varied horizons, managed by various constituencies who are, nevertheless, in regular conversation and collaboration of one sort or another, in a varied set of what used to be called "central places." In our words of the current present, then, the time frame that used to be "near," as a visible horizon toward which we plan our moves, is now more commonly referred to as "next" and "emergent," in open and indeterminate mode. Both of these terms imply a trajectory toward a temporal point of reference for the future that has (a) no visible logical sequence – one step after the other – that can be theorized in advance and (b) no eventual form on the horizon that can be definitively shaped or defined in advance. "Next" and "emergent" have become terms used much more widely than in the past, even in the technical literature, which would once have been in rational, predictive mode. In African studies, we have a book entitled *The Next Africa. An Emerging Continent Becomes a Global Powerhouse* (Bright and Hruby (2015). And there is an economic index entitled EAGLES, Emerging and Growth Leading Economies, created in 2010, to indicate economies expected to "lead global growth in the next 10 years, and to provide important opportunities for investors." Is this "future" envisaged in the mode of "punctuated time," as I suggested earlier (dated debts, benchmarks, etc.)? Or have anthropologists and others discovered a yet more open form of imagination about time and being, in the formal sector, that bypasses all these older benchmarks? We would need ethnographic depth of attention to examine exactly how dated transactional obligations and general indeterminacy configure together over this new view of the "near future" in the formalized world of financialization.

In Anthropology and Social History

Next: In 1996, Katherine Verdery brought the question of "what comes next?" into our analytics when she asked this of Eastern Europe after the demise of the socialist model. So "next" came to refer to the immediacy of action in the context of a qualitative shift, with a still-indeterminate horizon rather than indicating a step on a predictable pathway. This did not exclude the possibility of the preservation or recuperation of elements from the past, in active terms of preservation and continuation, but she highlighted high-profiled novelties being created, within indeterminate systemic frameworks indicated by the question mark at the end of her title. She refers to "transitological thinking" (1996, p. 16) and notes that "'Capitalist' time must be rendered progressive and linear so that it can be forever speeded up" (1996, p. 57). What, then, replaces it or nuances it when the form of capitalism is shifting toward the globalized financial capitalism indicated by historians Massimo Amato and Luca Fantacci in their book on the current system, looked at in historical context: *Saving the Market from Capitalism* (2014)? They deeply question the directions that this "speeding up" of a globalized financial capitalism would take and suggest that a return to more localized monetized markets would be a great improvement: "the effective birth and bottom-up spreading of systems of complementary local currency would be grounded solely on the associative capacity and needs of local communities" (2014, p. 274).

In the same decade as Verdery's work, the 1990s, a team of anthropologists had addressed *Culture Through Time. Anthropological Approaches* (Ohnuki-Tierney

1990), arguing against seeing radical disjunctures too sharply, and especially in a globalizing world: "no island of history is unconnected to the rest of the world; every historical study must be situated in the context of the world" (1990, p. 24). In two famous sources on the Caribbean world, the continuing, although varied, relevance of the past, even the distant past, to a future that may not be clearly predictable is drawn sharply to our attention. Michel-Rolph Trouillot wrote of the dangers of *Silencing the Past* (1995), and Sidney Mintz is quoted as complaining that "new theories of transnationalism and globalization are not respectful enough of history" (1998, quoted in Baca et al. 2009, p. 15). In his article of 2002, Maurer had already launched some of the ideas I used, in his paper entitled "Repressed Futures. Financial derivatives' theological unconscious," thus laying the groundwork for the indeterminacy of past-present-future that has entered into both the analytical and the popular orientations to the future, in our own time.

The interwoven dynamics that account for the indeterminacy of the present, and therefore the "near" and the "next," have also been addressed in anthropology through the concept of "the contemporary." The complexity of being, seen within the ontological realm, and the complex world of the present in which that being lives are beginning to be brought together in the analytical development of an anthropology of "the contemporary." In James Faubion's (2016) very recent edited collection on "the contemporary," published in HAU Journal, we can trace out how current anthropology is reconceptualizing the literal etymological referent of "con" (together) "tempus" (time) to which I have referred here, so far, using the formal sector's self-depiction and the sense in which in-depth empirical works have engaged with the interweaving of disturbances which seems characteristic of the existential present. The ways in which current anthropological thought on *the contemporary* is providing a new set of concepts and orientations to temporality, anticipation, and the near future can be drawn out of the several contributions to Faubion's edited collection. Focused on the work of Paul Rabinow, Faubion quotes Rabinow as picking up exactly this quality, by arguing for "'a moving ratio of modernity, moving through the recent past and near future in a (non-linear) space,' through the lens of which both the 'traditional' and the 'modern' become 'historical'" (Faubion 2016, p. 372). The "nearness" of this particularly indeterminate future is the temporal reflection of the "recency" of the past, when both of these temporal concepts stand in relationship to an intermediating present that has neither exact form nor existential clarity nor a clear future. We hardly find any use of "near" to depict the past in this collection of observations on "the contemporary" as a key concept. Boellstorff writes of the contemporary as "an emergent relationship between modernity and the historically novel," "near the now." And he suggests that moving "through the recent past and the near future is emic" (2016, p. 379, 380), that is, thought in people's own meaningful terms, which may be quite varied, even within a particular socioeconomic space. Another contribution to this same collection of commentaries, by Deliss and Keck, turns us back to the concept of assemblages, to convey the relational meeting of things, some purposely fashioned and some coincidental to temporal dynamics. Clearly, these anthropologists have all suspended any indication of a straight linear course from past to future, such that the same concept, "near," could be used when tracking movement from one to the other in both directions, implicitly along a linear pathway. In vernacular usage, "recent" would seem to invoke a much less tight existential frame than "near" (to me or us). It can be used comparatively, inclusively, and as part of an implicitly critical conversation: "Didn't that happen more recently than you're telling me?"

In my own contribution to Faubion's collection, I take the concept of being "on the verge" (not unlike Paulson's "on the brink") from Rabinow's own work and developed an exploration of the intellectual trajectory from "the possible to the emergent." These two concepts would echo our own themes in the present collection: from prediction to anticipation, the latter being much less precisely definable, from the vantage point of particular actors, in particular places, at their particular moment of history, weaving together the strands of a nonlinear version of "the near future," which is then necessarily "emergent," even if there are aspects that may seem predictable or are promoted as such, especially in public and rhetorical life. In their own contribution to Faubion's collection, Deliss and Keck (2016) explicitly use the concept of anticipation to refer to the combining of expectation and indeterminacy with respect to a complex phenomenon, namely, "the anticipation of animal-engendered pandemics" (2016, p. 386). Which animals, which illnesses, in which regions, and becoming "pan" rather than simply "epi" are all issues left in the realm of the unknown.

One commentary on a yet broader process, the intensifying connection of China to Africa, by Achille Mbembe (2016), explicitly refers to the "interweaving" of different dynamics whereby "Africa (the South) and China (the East) are trying to weave the paths that tie both regions together in the present and the future"(Mbembe 2016, p. 229). This expresses an approach to the wider dynamics, which would complement my own orientation toward understanding the smaller arenas in which futures are being crafted out of the meetings of macro-dynamics originating outside their borders: anthropologists being "a presence and dedicated witness or . . . an instigator within the process of emergence" (Guyer 2016, p. 376).

Using these same terms to apply to the people's own social life, rather than primarily to the world at large, draws our attention to emergent socialities rather than self-consciously created, or publicly marketed, ideational forms. To ask what becomes "near" when "near" fades from collective consciousness is to ask about social distance and access as well as conceptual horizons. It is to invoke material and political urgencies as well as time-space schema. And out of an enormous potential range of ethnographic and theoretical work relevant to time, I hope this question can identify, and highlight, a field of practice that may arise in specific ways in the present world across a whole variety of domains, from law to livelihood. So the idea of the future as an emergent, indeterminate configuration of elements from the past, the present, and a range of current possibilities, plus unpredictables, on which we can only have an empirical traction through concepts such as "next" and the one I now turn to, "emergence," was already gaining some traction before my own article was published. It has been growing into the space of the "near future" ever since.

"*Emergence*," as the concept to depict processes within the condition of anticipation with no precisely predictable end, at least at the outset, was first of all a philosophical and scientific concept, before it moved into anthropology. I found its use as long as almost four centuries ago, in the title of cleric-poet John Donne's work, entitled *Devotions upon Emergent Occasions* (1624), which seemed to refer to surprises which stimulate such new and profound thoughts as one which has been quoted down the centuries: "No man is an island...Ask not for whom the bell tolls. It tolls for thee." Later the concept of *emergent* came to depict natural and other processes whereby disparate elements and conditions came together in the creation of "complex systems": not by central organizational forces but through ongoing interactions. One of the first importations of "emergence" into anthropology in the mid-twentieth century was in the reconsideration of human evolutionary pathways, as biological anthropology became increasingly sophisticated. John Pfeiffer wrote several versions of what used to be referred to as "human origins" under the title of *The Emergence of Man* (1969) and in its much later edition entitled *The Emergence of Humankind* (1985). Here he incorporates a human preference for shifting lives rather than stable structures. "Stability is not for us. . . . We have created in ourselves a new chronic restlessness, a process which continually works against equilibrium and an antihomeostasis" (Pfeiffer 1985, p. 9).

When evolutionary thinking was brought into the social and cultural sub-discipline of anthropology in the nineteenth century, it was turned into a series of "stages," from mobile hunter-gatherer society to various modes of agriculturalist and pastoralist societies, to permanent settlement and social hierarchy, through several states of that form into the industrial and national organizations of "modernity." There were phases of "revolution": agricultural, industrial, and other more specifically local ones. One aspect of the old version of evolutionism was an implication of directionality. "Primitive" societies would evolve or be managed – or forced – into "modern" societies. For a long period, those eras were assimilated to various versions of structuralism. In recent years, however, there has been a growing sense in socio-cultural anthropology that the structuralism that was so inspiring under the auspices of Claude Levi-Strauss had become only one strand in our disciplinary archive and those of its subdisciplines. As mentioned with respect to "the ontological turn," the indeterminacies of "being" are now imported into the analysis of political economy and collective life.

A strong statement on this configuration, in theory and in life, with respect to understanding Africa, is offered by Achille Mbembe, under the title of "The "New" Southern Question" (2016, p. 220), where "radical changes go hand in hand with various other gradual and subtle shifts ...within a condition of temporariness" (p. 222), which he sees producing "Collisions and Collusions" (p. 224). Except for work which profiles the people's own sense of direction, perhaps even toward the "end times" under religious leadership, the formal sector's participation in anticipation may be more confident in its projections in predictive mode toward the mid- to long-term while being less self-conscious and explicit about the living of a turbulent present. This would demand ethnographic attention to the conditions of our own formalized world.

Temporal Frames. Emergence implicitly does away with a clear pathway of steps and stages toward an evolutionary or developmental horizon. We can refer briefly, now, to certain popular works, by academics, which appear to be reclaiming an evolutionary philosophy that assumes some kind of an "endpoint" and anthropological works which are examining what this would mean to the people. Is the religious notion of "the end times" focusing us on examining people's own conceptions of this process, thereby infusing some aspects of the study of emergence?

The following section focuses first on the question of method, in times of transition, that has been raised in several different works. Then it examines two modes of new ethnographic enquiry and interpretation about the future: first, the present seen by the people as considerably more indeterminate than our past method assumed, under the guide of structural approaches to a comparative grid and a specific sequence of change, and, secondly, an appreciation of the relevance of affect, particularly hope and fearful concern, to people's orientation to "the near future" as a place along the way of an inevitable journey through time. I address the ethnography of an indeterminate present and an affective approach to the near future, in the following section. However, first of all, it is worth devoting a brief exposition to how evolutionary pathways are still in the great range of thinking on this challenging topic and especially in cross-disciplinary works aimed toward a varied reading public.

The most notable recent publication is historian Yuval Noah Harari's *Homo Deus. A Brief History of Tomorrow* (2015). Following his book entitled *Sapiens*, Harari points to a current transition in human anticipation, especially of the classic troubles such as famine, plague, and war, moving away from "consciousness" in a broad sense to "intelligence" in the narrow sense of data management. He tracks us moving from a religious framing of "what is to come" to a humanist framing in the pre-Enlightenment era, to what he calls "dataism" now. He ends with a question: "What will happen to society, politics and daily life when non-conscious but highly intelligent algorithms know us better than we know ourselves?" (2015, p. 397). Maybe people combine all these sources of inference about human time, in their own ways, for their own contexts. This would be an ethnographic question to ask of our scientific community and the public culture it informs. What are the components, in both knowledge and affect, of this "dataist" present?

Our own theoretical works do realize that we, as a discipline, are "in transition" (Boyer and Marcus 2015). They point out that we have a "proliferation of interests" (p. 9) that hardly lends themselves to a single encompassing theoretical framework. Following their lead, we could attend to this sense of ourselves not knowing a "near future," even for the disciplinary approaches to our subject matter let alone in the world, but seeing, rather, a proliferation of varied sites and subjects of anthropological interest. They argue in favor of a certain approach that we might see as emergent out of our direct experience in the indeterminate world of the present. They end their introduction, not with a question but with an advocacy of a method "of analytical experimentation that encourages a more organic interrelationship among field knowledge, ethnographic writing, and concept work" (2015, p. 11). Rational configuration and calculation become subject matter, not method, so we move now toward ethnographic understandings of configurations made by the people themselves.

Ethnography as Source: An Indeterminate Present and Affect Toward the Future

We have several works that combine these two domains of empirical study. The first to which I draw attention is Hiro Miyazaki's *The Method of Hope* (2004). Focusing on religious orientations and social life in Fiji, he captures exactly the qualities that move our understanding beyond both a "near future" of planning and a "punctuated time" of rigid commitments. He understands people to be creating a life that largely depends simply on being in "attendance," where "The moment of hope that emerged at the moment of abeyance of agency was, then, simultaneously open and closed" (2004, p. 106). Again, a complex of dynamics meet together, in possibly unexpected ways which need then to be crafted, to create futures. However, the presence of hope itself, in specific instances, opens up the possibility of its later recuperation in what he calls "repetition" and "replication" (p. 128), which create the possibility of performance and confidence in whatever the next step would be. He then applies this wisdom to disciplinary efforts to "bring into view the possibility of radical reorientation of knowledge," reignited by the "spark of hope" (2004, p. 149). Since then, Miyazaki has coedited another collection on hope, with Richard Swedberg, entitled *The Economy of Hope* (2016). We can expect a rising interest in this topic, for disciplinary practice as well as for empirical focus.

My own most recent contribution on the indeterminacies of the present is based on the condition of "confusion," from which orientations and actions have to emerge. In this work, and the collection of papers around this theme (Guyer 2015), we examine the cultural resources in different communities which could give criteria and terminologies to designate conditions that certain expertise could then try to solve, with respect to immediate mediation. For example, the Yoruba pantheon includes a god of confusion, Eshu, who inhabits the crossroads and has his own acolytes who know how to supplicate him to find a direction. His face is also carved on the diviner's tray for overseeing his predictions, or perhaps also anticipations, about the future, on which he offers advice as to how to act (Salami and Guyer 2015). The affect here is, first of all, deep concern but later a certain confidence that once the right actions and directions have been taken by the right people, with respect to the right spiritual powers, the trouble will settle back into a manageable order. All this is contextualized within a religious vision that hardly includes any ultimate horizon of "the end of days" or a developmental, evolutionary, model of gradual, incremental change. The whole of life is always constituted by person, event, power, expert wisdom, and their situational intersections at varying moments along sequences in life that are no longer rationally planned or religiously foreordained.

In yet another mode of designating the meeting of forces in the present, through which futures can be imagined and affectively approached, Janet Roitman (2014) responds to our own western sense of being taken up by "crisis" rather than by abeyance or confusion. She notes how "crisis is productive; it is the means to transgress and is necessary for change or transformation" (2014, p. 35). What it produces, she argues, is "narrative," rather than affect. "As an a priori, crisis is the place from which to posit a future" (2014, p. 70), presumably by the depth of its provocation and the limited archive of intellectual-cultural resources from which to start afresh. This makes it entirely different from a planned, or anticipated, "revolution." Here "a future" is in the singular, presumably chosen from several options, and able to encompass all the people and components that had been caught up in the "crisis." Later, with respect to visions of capitalism at this moment, she asks "Can we narrate a future without crisis?", crisis being a kind of "revelation" (2014, p. 89). Without crises, she implies that we would not create narratives, which then distinguishes narrative from plan. The phases, temporalities, and participations would be imaginative and persuasive, by re-enlivening the collective archive of knowledge. Roitman's work reviews a wide range of philosophical sources on how time emerges, and is periodized, mainly in Western thought but approached with an ethnographic sensibility as to context and a culturally sensitive approach to specific situational responses. In her case, she prioritizes narrative over affect, concluding that there can be "flashes, reversals, setbacks, duplications, parallels, recurrences, and reprises," thus letting loose the idea of a temporal progression in a certain direction and being more like what she calls a "dream" (2014, p. 96).

Here, by drawing ethnographic parallels with other domains, Roitman encourages us to bring a whole archive of possible analytics to bear on specific cases in the current world, where the "near future" appears indeterminate in different ways, in different places, due to the disturbed sense of the present from which futurity is projected. For example, on the theme of "dreams," we could return again, after Miyazaki's example, to the anthropological study of religious life among those who have taken up evangelical Christianity. The key scholar here is Joel Robbins (2004), who writes on how suffering "torment" in the present figures in the approaches of the Urapmin, in Papua New Guinea, to "what next."

In a more comprehensive review of a rapidly growing anthropology of the "near future," in attentive mode to local populations studied ethnographically, I could also pull out, from many sources, the evidence for specific themes, particularly the monetary and religious lives that Maurer and I both linked together, in the postmillennial moment. For example, there must be a new temporality to monetary transactions, in different contexts, as Charles Piot depicts in his book entitled *Remotely Global, Village Modernity in West Africa* (1999). Taking in a topically more wide-ranging vista, although still geographically focused, I review a new collection on Africa, whose title uses several of the concepts brought forward already: *African Futures. Essays on Crisis, Emergence, and Possibility* (Goldstone and Obarrio 2016). How do these concepts now coexist in the analytical and existential vocabulary?

Goldstone and Obarrio's approach exemplifies the novel directions I have introduced here. They introduce their collection as being about how scholarship might deal with "seemingly contradictory forecasts," drawing on an "untimely sensibility" (2016, p. 1, 17), how the people "think *within* paradoxes and complexities" (2016, p. 3), how life is "incessantly on the move" (p. 18), and how they see "excess proliferating" (p. 19). The index of paper titles could cover all the themes introduced above. Here are the key words: "otherwise" (Roitman); "crisis" and "affect"

(Larkin); "the productivity of crisis" (McKay); "money in the future" (Guyer); "forensics of capital" (Ralph); "imagining future war" (Hoffman); "hedging the future" (Piot); "entangled post-colonial futures" (Cole); "mobilizing uncertainty" (Simone); "the future of the local" (De Boeck); "changing mobilities" (Geschiere and Socpa); "time and again, future anterior" (Obarrio); "time, potential and value" (Weiss); and Africa in Theory (Mbembe). Summarizing the arguments of the papers, on their varying subject matters in various places, the editors conclude that the purpose is "taking the pulse of what is emerging before it becomes fully crystallized, discerning unexpected resonances between apparently unlike entities and oddly, counterintuitively entangled circumstances and events" (2016, pp. 17–18). Their final words to the Introduction can serve as a segue into my conclusion and link to this volume's theme, through Poli's own work: "the Africa glimpsed in these pages is one of creative practices of remembrance and anticipation – and also, to be sure, of active forgetting" (Goldstone and Obarrio 2016, p. 19).

Anticipation in the Mode of the Contemporary: Concluding Thoughts

There are clearly emerging frontiers in the anthropology of the near future. The present is seen as a convergence of multiple dynamics, not clearly predictable in their direction of change, and not even very clear in their conditions of convergence. The complexity of the experience of the present, with its presences, absences, and emergent qualities, many (although not all) of which are in indeterminate mode, arouses deep affective responses in "selves" that are also in indeterminate mode rather than the predictable life cycles described in classic ethnographies. My strongest inference here is that we are drawing increasingly on the full range of our ethnographic sources, on other disciplines such as history, philosophy, political economy, literature, and the arts, and combining their concepts and inspirations with those from the ethnography of other "futures." In the world out there, both formal and community based, we are finding that the present and near future are no longer experienced in firmly predictable ways, through stability and rationality. And even where there may be a modicum of confidence in anticipation, there has been a remarkable influx of uncertainty, a move from imaginable possibility to open vistas, and we can see an increased intensity of affect, confusions, and sudden crises. In all these cases, the ethnography suggests that people often call on some kind of narrative form, or poetic resonance, into which to place such experiences.

Indeed, narrative may be one aspect of the varied religious archives, rather than the doctrine and the rules, that makes popular religion increasingly attractive in a twenty-first century once seen as the pinnacle of a secular rational "modernity." Indeed, Nigerian writer Ben Okri has observed that the parables of the Bible are more powerful than the miraculous events, which he summarizes as follows: "All the great religions, all the great prophets, found it necessary to spread their message through stories, fables, parables. The Bible is one of the world's greatest fountains of fiction and dream" (1996, p. 19), followed by "Nations and peoples are largely the stories they tell themselves" (1996, p. 21). Exactly how narrative interpretations and configurations are done, and by whom, under present conditions of indeterminacy and intensified affect, remains a question to be explored further, when this exploration could take in a much broader comparative vista. With more sources, from more areas with their own narrative traditions and proverbial archives, we could ask how the specific temporalities of narrative are adapted and nuanced when people, institutions, and interpretive leaders bring them into the arenas of a "present" no longer thought of as stable, to infuse a future no longer seen as controllable through enlightenment-style rationality. Recent anthropology is pointing us in these directions of attentive focus.

Roberto Poli's work can orient us conceptually in some of the necessary directions of thought in our discipline. Drawing on the precision of Gurvitch's conceptualization of several temporal regimes, which may coexist, he writes that "groups, classes, and entire societies have their own 'preferred' times, those that better manifest the pace of their internal dynamics" (Poli 2017, p. 4). From our ethnographic experience, I would both heartily endorse this view and also add one category to the list: age and generation of experience. He writes that "The thick presents of social time are moments of becoming, and they refer to ongoing processes" (2016, p. 6). Working in Nigeria, I was recurrently made aware of the archive of experience that oral traditions conserve, which then makes "the elders," the wise and the experientially knowledgeable people, and, following Okri, the skilled storytellers, one particular repository of expertise on temporal processes. We can wonder whether something similar endures at all in fully literate contexts, where the experience of the "near past" (whatever time frame this indicates) can be recuperated, even by the youth, simply by reading. The generational process of ingrained affect through past experience being passed on (or not at all) through a variety of media would seem to be one further dimension of "near past-present-near future" temporal experience to be probed, for an era such as ours, for which the present is experientially mixed, processually uncertain, and affectively intense, possibly differently nuanced according to generation, location, and the media of memory and projection.

I conclude with Appadurai's (2016) implicit reminder that we, too, as anthropologists, are subject to the "mood swings" of the experiential present and the "emerging future." It poses many ethnographic and philosophical questions, whose guidance can be infused with the thought of others, colleagues in other disciplines, and all the subjects and subjectivities to which our archive of experience and imagination can be exposed in attentive mode.

Summary

The anthropology of the future has opened up to the complexity, and even the confusion, of the current economic, political and religious worlds in which people live, and through which their own sense of *being* is created and mobilized, both socially and situationally. The concept of *anticipation*, etymologically *thinking before*, is novel enough as an analytical term to help empirical studies to enrich the temporal processes they study, beyond the more reason-based or faith-based confidence in *prediction*, by attending to the combinations through which several conceptual repertoires are brought together in the public sphere.

References

Amato, M., & Fantacci, L. (2014). *Saving the market from capitalism*. Cambridge: Polity Press.

Appadurai, A. (2013). *The future as cultural fact. Essays on the global condition*. London: Verso.

Appadurai, A. (2016). Moodswings in the anthropology of the emerging future. *HAU Journal of Ethnographic Theory, 6*(2), 1–4.

Baca, G., Khan, A., & Palmié, S. (2009). *Empirical futures. anthropologists and historians engage the work of Sidney W. Mintz*. Chapel Hill: University of North Carolina Press.

Boyer, D., & Marcus, G. E. (2015). Introduction. New methodologies for a transformed discipline. In D. Boyer, J. Faubion, & G. E. Marcus (Eds.), *Theory can be more than it used to be. Learning anthropology's method in a time of transition* (pp. 1–11). Ithaca: Cornell University Press.

Bright, J., & Hruby, A. (2015). *The next Africa. An emerging continent becomes a global powerhouse*. New York: Thomas Dunne Books.

Faubion, J. (Ed.). (2016). On the anthropology of the contemporary. Addressing concepts, designs, and practices. *Hau: Journal of Ethnographic Theory, 6*(1), 371–402.

Goldstone, B., & Obarrio, J. (2016). *African futures. Essays on crisis, emergence, and possibility*. Chicago: University of Chicago Press.

Greenspan, A. (2007). *The age of turbulence. Adventures in a new world*. New York: Penguin Books.

Guyer, J. I. (2007). Prophecy and the near future: Thoughts on macroeconomic, evangelical and punctuated time. *American Ethnologist, 34*(3), 409–421.

Guyer, J. I. (2012). Terms of debate versus words in circulation: Some rhetorics of the crisis. In J. Carrier (Ed.), *Handbook of economic anthropology* (pp. 612–625). Cheltenham: Edward Elgar publishing.

Guyer, J. I. (2015). Introduction to the question: Is confusion a form? *Social Dynamics, 41*(1), 17–33.

Guyer, J. I. (2016). "On the verge": From the possible to the emergent. *HAU Journal*, see above, ed Faubion, 6(1), 373–377.

Harari, Y. N. (2015). *Homo Deus. A brief history of tomorrow*. London: Harvill Secker.

Kohn, E. (2013). *How forests think. Toward an anthropology beyond the human*. Berkeley: University of California Press.

Maurer, B. (2002). Repressed futures: Financial derivatives' theological unconscious. *Economy and Society, 31*(1), 15–36.

Mbembe, A. (2016). Africa in Theory. *In African Futures. Essays on Crisis, Emergence, and Possibility*. Brian Goldstone and Juan Obarrio (eds.) University of Chicago Press, 211–230

Miyazaki, H. (2004). *The method of hope. Anthropology, philosophy and Fijian knowledge*. Stanford: Stanford University Press.

Miyazaki, H., & Swedberg, R. (Eds.). (2016). *The economy of hope*. Philadelphia: University of Pennsylvania Press.

Ohnuki-Tierney, E. (1990). *Culture through time. Anthropological approaches*. Stanford: Stanford University Press.

Okri, B. (1996). *Birds of heaven*. London: Phoenix, division of Orion Books.

Paulson, H. (2010). *On the brink. Inside the race to stop the collapse of the global financial system*. New York: Business Plus.

Pfeiffer, J. (1969). *The emergence of man*. New York: Harper and Row.

Pfeiffer, J. (1985). *The emergence of humankind*. New York: Harper and Row.

Piot, C. (1999). *Remotely global. Village modernity in West Africa*. Chicago: University of Chicago Press.

Poli, R. (2017). Social Time as a Multidimensional Category. *World Future Review, 9*, 1–7.

Robbins, J. (2004). *Becoming sinners. Christianity and moral torment in a Papua New Guinea society*. Berkeley: University of California Press.

Roitman, J. (2014). *Anti-crisis*. Durham: Duke University Press.

Salami, K. K., & Guyer, J. I. (2015). Confusion and personification in Yoruba thought and practice. *Social Dynamics, 41*(1), 1–16.

Trouillot, M.-R. (1995). *Silencing the past. Power and the production of history*. Boston: Beacon Press.

Turner, V. (1967). Muchona the hornet, Chapter 6. In *The forest of symbols. Aspects of Ndembu ritual*. Ithaca: Cornell University Press.

Verdery, K. (1996). *What was socialism and what comes next?* Princeton: Princeton University Press.

Indigenous Knowledge Systems and Anticipation

20

Vanessa de Oliveira Andreotti, Carl Mika, Cash Ahenakew, and Hemi Hireme

Contents

Abstract

Indigenous people across the globe face a difficult paradox in their relationship with modernity. On the one hand, there is the necessity of surviving in an unsustainable system premised on colonial and imperialist violences carried out in the name of global capital, nation-states, and Enlightenment humanism. On the other hand, and at the same time, there is the necessity to keep alive possibilities of existence based on different metaphysics that can generate other ways of knowing/being. Indigenous knowledges have their own conceptualizations of temporality and futurity that are irreducible to those that orient modern Western knowledge. Yet, because of ongoing processes of colonization, Indigenous peoples have been compelled to negotiate Western ideas of time. We have also often

V. de Oliveira Andreotti (✉) · C. Ahenakew
University of British Columbia, Vancouver, BC, Canada
e-mail: vanessa.andreotti@ubc.ca; cash.ahenakew@ubc.ca

C. Mika
University of Waikato, Hamilton, New Zealand
e-mail: mika@waikato.ac.nz

H. Hireme
Te Whare Wananga O Awanuiarangi, Whakatane, New Zealand

© Springer Nature Switzerland AG 2019
R. Poli (ed.), *Handbook of Anticipation*,
https://doi.org/10.1007/978-3-319-91554-8_40

393

been designated as anachronistic within the particular anticipatory contours of Western thought, in which we are deemed "out of time" and consigned to disappear in order to make way for more "advanced" civilizations.

Keywords

Indigenous metaphysics · Counter-colonialism · Futurity · Anticipation · Knowledge · Being

Introduction

In the introduction to this book, Poli suggests, "Anticipatory capabilities of individuals and communities may enhance the overall sense-making process and improve decision-making, strategy formation, and societal resilience." However, the futures anticipated by those with the most systemic power tend to be those futures toward which the rest of us are compelled to move, and the sense- and decision-making processes they employ are neither timeless nor universal and are likely to be harmful. For instance, what if existing modes of anticipation ensure the resilience of our capitalist economic system in ways that contribute to climate instability, or conversely, that ensure the resilience of our ecosystem contributes to economic instability? Indigenous people have for centuries been navigating the worlds produced through colonial modes of anticipation, and our resilience has often been viewed as threatening to the resilience of Western societies, particularly settler societies like the USA, Canada, and New Zealand/Aotearoa (Baldwin 2012; Byrd 2011; Tuck and Gaztambide-Fernández 2013). Thus, it remains necessary to historicize and address the ethical and political dimensions of anticipation, in particular those related to what Poli describes as "latents" (dispositions, habits, tendencies) that tend to naturalize colonialism and are made to be invisible.

According to Poli, rather than presume that the future is preordained and predictable, "future-generating research is about possible futures and how to realize them." He suggests there are two approaches to this future-generating work: explorative, which starts from the present and imagines various possible futures, or normative, which imagines one possible future and tries to work backward in order to produce it. Our concern with both of these approaches is that any future imagined from within our contemporary colonial mode of sense-making will likely reproduce colonial relations – even if the intention is to do precisely the opposite. Certain futures are generally understood to be possible within this framework, while others are deemed to be unreasonable and unrealistic or are made invisible. However, now that climate change seriously threatens the ability for all of us to survive, we have noted a recent increase in interest in Indigenous knowledges in different disciplines. This interest seems to stem from a sense of crisis and urgency for alternatives. While there are positive aspects of the increase of visibility (and possibilities) for Indigenous struggles and peoples, this interest is also problematic. Even when Indigenous knowledges are treated as the source of inspiration, they may be instrumentalized within anticipatory practices as a means to rescue and resuscitate a system premised on harm, while the gifts of Indigenous ways of being remain illegible (Ahenakew 2016).

If Indigenous and decolonial futures appear impossible within Eurocentric anticipatory practices, they are nonetheless kept alive within Indigenous knowledge systems. These approaches to anticipation are neither exploratory nor normative in the sense that Poli describes, because they are grounded on different metaphysical referents that make it impossible to (over)determine the future in advance. In this chapter, we suggest that any conceptualization of "futures literacy" must undertake a more expansive and self-reflexive approach to anticipation not averse to paradoxes and incommensurabilities. Before we proceed, it is important to acknowledge that Indigenous groups adopt a broad spectrum of perspectives in relation to this topic; that Indigenous communities are also inherently heterogeneous; and that Indigenous knowledge systems are dynamic, complex, and interfaced with place.

We start our argument with a translation of a Māori story that equates the present of time with the process of "weaving." In line with this metaphor, this chapter has been written by multiple hands, waves of thinking, and styles of writing. This nonnormative and, at points, opaque approach that refuses standardization is intentionally meant to offer an experience for the readers that might create a productive form of discomfort that, in turn, can interrupt projective desires for understanding that remain caught within the cycle of colonial knowledge production that seeks to domesticate difference. Our Māori story is followed by a philosophical engagement with the concept of time. Next, we use the events at Standing Rock as a concrete illustration of notions of futurity and anticipation based on the Indigenous perspective we describe. We conclude with a few reflections on the implications of our argument for the field of anticipatory studies.

"The Future" in Speculative Indigenous Thought

There is a popular story told in Māori circles to illustrate the differences between anthropocentric orientations to the future grounded on ideas that can be traced to the European Enlightenment period and non-anthropocentric relational orientations that are often associated with Indigenous cultures. We recognize it is problematic to retell this story in this context of this chapter and in written form, using categories that are intelligible to non-Indigenous readers. We believe that this risk is educationally justified but would like to acknowledge that our use of the story is not intended to appease the non-Indigenous readers' desire for the approximation of "understanding" or authoritative knowledge about "the Other": we are not offering a window where readers can have a peak at another reality. On the contrary, our intention in telling our version of this story is to highlight incommensurabilities in the very terms of what is perceived as intelligible and possible to be "understood," as the "Other" reality we evoke is not based on the same fixation on the intellectualization, categorization, rationalization, objectification, and understanding of the world with a view to control it.

This Māori story says that people coming from the Enlightenment/anthropocentric orientation walk toward the future with their bodies moving "forward": they imagine something ahead of them and all steps they take are planned to achieve the imagined *teleological* end point. This would probably correlate with the normative approach to the future mentioned by Poli. Conversely, the story goes, Māori people walk backward toward the future with their bodies facing the past and with their ancestors facing them. The ancestors are those who have come before and those who are yet to come and those with longer temporalities of form. Needless to say, ancestors are not only human. Those who are walking in the present are weaving and being woven into a fabric of relationships. They can only see the weaving with peripheral vision as they are looking to the past and the ancestors to inform their braiding.

The threads of the braiding and the fabric are alive – there are no objects in the picture, and everything is animated and connected to ancestral genealogical fibers. The future does not exist, as it is the present that weaves the future into being (which becomes the present), at the same time, the future has already been, as those who are yet-to-come are also those who have-already-been (time is not linear). The patterns being formed in the fabric by this collective weaving can only be seen by the ancestors, who can see the patterns being woven through their vantage point and predict when the threads of the weaving are forming a problematic future to come. In that case, they can choose to intervene by communicating their concerns and advising on different weavings or not. They can also choose to let us figure things out and learn from the process. The responsibility of the weavers in relation to the future-to-come is threefold: to learn from the teachings of the past, to be attentive to the communications of the ancestors, and to weave accordingly in ways that secure the good quality of their braiding as part of a much larger piece of patterned fabric.

The fact that the weaver can only see what is being woven in the present with peripheral vision is extremely significant in our discussion, as it points to the fact that the Indigenous perspective represented here does not correlate with the exploratory approach presented by Poli. It points to a metaphysics where the world and the present are not self-evident, and where relationships are not mediated by knowledge, identity, or understanding, but by visceral interwovenness and ancestral responsibilities. This relationship to the world requires a multiplicity of senses rather than relying solely on "sense-making." The perception and relationship with language are also counterintuitive to European Enlightenment-based socializations; as language neither describes nor constructs the world, it rather serves as an animated buffer between individual and collective experiences and a wider reality that by definition cannot be apprehended by the human mind. In this sense, language/stories can be seen as the needles that knit the threads within the larger fabric of the world. If we were to translate what future anticipation would mean in this context, a first layer of interpretation would be that anticipation is connected to the responsibility to learn from seven prior generations in the weaving of the present so that seven generations ahead can continue to exist. Therefore, anticipation could be seen as us being prepared to fulfill our "grown-up" responsibilities toward ancestral elders and unborn babies and their families representing the past, present, and future simultaneously. We expand on this topic in the next section, focusing on the concept of time and offering different speculative layers of translation/interpretation of anticipation.

Indigenous Philosophical Considerations of "Time"

Discussions about time in Indigenous contexts are challenging for various reasons, and there are several points to be addressed that academic language can only hint at. Firstly, despite our resistance to the categorizing of time (which we delve into in due course), at some point, we have to single out concepts of the past, present, and future. Mainstream expectations around the arrangement of academic text and its language by rational argument have preordained what can and cannot be said, even before we come to the topic. Another problem with the academic genre is its logocentric focus: the assumption that the world can be described in language. This normalized orientation forbids any opening onto the realms of non-self-evidence – or mystery – necessary for even a glimpse into the obscurity of Indigenous metaphysical thought (Mika in press). Moreover, but relatedly, due to the almost visceral rejection of the mystery in academic convention, what remains for any Indigenous discussion on this matter is the language of possibility (which could well be related to anticipation). In trying to honor this mystery in academic writing, our only option is to make evident that our use of language is speculative and does not rely on the positivist assertion of things in the world.

Moreover, the term "time" is worlded with a particular historical trajectory and revealing of things that do not bear any resemblance to many Indigenous philosophical realities. We mean here that the term "time," as it is commonly understood within Western metaphysics, may well be inappropriate for describing an Indigenous conception of the layering of events and things in the world. Our position here is based partly on the animacy of language (Mika 2016; Browne 2005) in its own right, at its inception, with its immediate and essential character, and partly on what a term, as an element of language, accrues to it throughout its intersection with different epochs, its complicated genealogy. The word "time" becomes significantly problematic for Indigenous peoples to wield on both fronts, because it is so tightly tied to a *notional* entity. "Time" is only capable of displaying to the Indigenous self whatever has materially constituted it and layered to it. Language in this context is an inescapable and living phenomenon (Mika 2016) and cannot be transcended. In other words, to discover its origins, we cannot step outside of the world that "time" has always already revealed. This view of language shows that the world embraced by a term has always already existed.

In some etymological sources, time does proclaim a side of itself that, while we cannot escape, we can nevertheless speculate on as if we are separate from it. This facet of time allows us a glimpse of it through its connection with other concepts that are not conventionally symmetrical with it. Time here is paired up with other terms that offer some insight into its ontology: significantly, time is related with "to divide, cut up" (etymonline.com). That "time" corresponds with the concept of division, or incision will probably come as little surprise to Indigenous peoples, who have noted that dominant Western thought tends to fragment things in the world (Calderon 2008; Deloria 2012). Indeed, it would be unusual for a philosophy to endorse the fragmenting of things and yet have a metaphysics of time that did not. As against Indigenous thought, which tends to conduct the opposite by ensuring that the world is kept whole, the term "time" is essentially imbued with its drive to dissect the world. Thus, the Western concept of "time" is flawed from the outset, and in Indigenous thought, it must be deployed carefully. Time in this immediate sense is formational rather than notional: like a needle, it orients the writer toward it on its own terms, insisting on a particularly rational representation of it. However, although this depiction of it is available through certain prescribed means of expression, we should be clear that an Indigenous analysis of the term is not a thoroughly linguistic one.

Here it can be pertinent to refer to discussions in Western thought that have gestured toward the limits of understanding. When summarizing Derrida's response to Benveniste, Hart (2013) notes that an abbreviation of being, apparently taking place due to the existence of the copula (i.e., "is"), is actually pre-linguistically determined: philosophy predetermines language. In our discussion, the "is" along with several other terms is positively constructive as it freezes a thing in time *as* symmetrical with another thing (or an idea of that thing). The "is" can exist as a future determiner in the form of "will be," and in that sense, the future can be augured as the "whatness" of a thing. An object in the world is then stuck in time, even though it is not yet an object or it is not encountered by the self. In this sense, if philosophy predetermines language, language predetermines our experiences of and hopes for the present and the future. Modern institutions that propagate a relationship to language based on logocentrism (self-evidence) and teleological futures trap us in a world defined by unequivocal meaning and intelligibility and erase the evidence of mystery.

Significantly, while some Indigenous groups may not have a word that equates strictly with the sense of "time" that is evoked with dominant Western notions, the term "time" is often translated with a nearby concept from Indigenous languages. As we have speculated earlier, incorporating a world that inheres within one term into another worldview is dangerous, and in the case of Western notions of "time," a thing in the world is proposed in its distinguishable (dissected) qualities, even if that thing has yet to be encountered. Proposing how a thing *will be* is itself a time-related event: I propose *now* that a thing *will be* this-or-that. In other words, the declaration about a thing – how we intend it to manifest – is to be encountered, from an Indigenous perspective, as significantly time-suffused. Time, in a Western sense, therefore prescribes how an entity is uttered or apprehended. From an Indigenous philosophical perspective, the importance of this relates to colonization, for if the Indigenous self is forced to forever prescribe how a thing will appear, then he or she is shackled by a notion of the proposition that is limiting. Simultaneously, colonial notions of time often seek to limit available possibilities of existence for Indigenous peoples themselves. Again, it is useful to point to interactions within Western thought that have gestured toward its own limits. Heidegger, for example, has critiqued the essence of technology and the language of enframing that comes with it (see, for instance, Heidegger 1977). In other words, if I propose how something will appear, alongside that intention of making a thing appear *as* this-or-that, I am constrained by the nature of a proposition that is itself constituted by a dissecting notion of time.

The immediate link between the intention of "the way something will be" and the nature of that intention in its own right is also an entity from an Indigenous perspective. It may simplistically be thought of as *spirit*. That is, the phenomenon of "that-which-will-be" is not simply an ontology but is an entity in itself. This view of deep orientations toward things in the world is not limited to the future of whatever will be, either. For instance, the current reality for Indigenous peoples is suffused as much with colonization as it is with ancestral existence, which – to refer to Western teleological language – are both past and future events as much as present. Both therefore relate to temporality and indeed construct it, leading philosophical Indigenous thought to consider them in any assertion about time (as we do in this chapter). Here there is a marked departure from dominant Western thought, because time in Indigenous thought is not simply a conceptual template through which one reads off linear events; instead, it is a material entity. Whether it is traditionally *real* or not can only be speculated on, it is certainly now a material phenomenon. Its solidity is constituted by the materiality of things in the world through an association of things with Western influences. It could therefore be viewed as a "neo-corporeal" entity – not lacking in the presence of those who have departed and those yet to come, but certainly given its form by the overwhelming importance that Western modern thought affords it.

All this signifies that one must be careful when discussing futurity and anticipation, as an Indigenous philosophical perception of them is likely to diverge greatly from that of Enlightenment/anthropocentric orientations. The two may mean quite different things, and one cannot be grafted into the other without being domesticated by what is intelligible and desirable. As we tried to illustrate in the Māori story at the beginning, futurity for Indigenous peoples cannot be limited to discussions about a template of time that points forward, because any one thing has always already branched out into the "future" and back into the "past," and, if anything, time in an Indigenous sense is this "everywhere-at-once" woven universe (Marsden . . .).

We must therefore discuss futurity and its link with space, what Deloria (2001) calls "place," although, as we have seen, futurity is a weak concept in Indigenous philosophy. In its initial state and with its omnipotence, time suffuses all things in the world. It could be described as one of "all our relations" – a concept which exists in different forms throughout Indigenous philosophies. Its relationship with landmarks must be acknowledged as a sort of one meeting between one entity and another, even though those entities have always already "met." The mutuality between time and natural terrain is referred to by one word in some Indigenous languages (for instance, "wa" in Māori). Thus, an Indigenous philosophy might present a landmark in its current form through various forms of expression (such as weaving, carving, speaking, and so on), but its future and past natures are combined in that act of presentation. Further, one's ability to present the landmark in those expressions is possible through one's immediate and genealogical link with them.

Thus, another layer of interpretation is to say that to "anticipate" something in Indigenous philosophy is perhaps to present both oneself and another entity to which one is related (such as a landmark or even an idea) as a confluence of all past, present, and future. Because the self, the act of presentation, and the external world are all co-constituting, then anticipation becomes akin to awaiting the arrival of a thing despite its eternal existence. In this reading of anticipation, the world arranges itself in ways that cannot be constrained by our preordaining gaze. The challenge for the Indigenous self in this act of presentation is to ensure that the world is left as an embryonic phenomenon, with the self similarly being in a state of uncertainty. This speculative Indigenous approach to anticipation also centers on a particular approach to the concept and entity of colonization, which is forever being revealed in all its various manifestations. An anticipatory state, depending on our definition of "anticipation," may be one that examines colonization and its possible manifestations without constraining what colonization can reveal but contains to it the fullness of the past and future faces of colonization as much as the ones experienced in the present. This unconstraining futurity is not without its challenges because it must compete with a strong futurity grounded in the architecture of Western modernity.

Barriers to Indigenous Futurities

Since the future woven in the present is informed by the teachings of the past, any consideration of possible futurities needs a careful examination of the repeated patterns of our shared past, that is, the shared pasts of Indigenous and non-Indigenous peoples. These repeated patterns are important as they teach us about the genealogy of the present texture of our fabric and its capacity to hold our present into a desirable future. Without this systemic examination of weaving, we are left with the idea that we are not bound by our historical legacies and can, therefore, simply break away from the past and march confidently into a different future. In Indigenous and decolonial studies, the focus of this systemic analysis is placed on the phenomenon of global modernity as the strongest pattern in our recent collective history.

The embroidery of global modernity depicts a single story of human-centered existence moving in a singular direction of progress, development, and evolution. Its most recent and magnificent design consists of three strong threads: global capital, nation-states, and Enlightenment humanism. These threads delineate a strong sense of futurity grounded on a projected image of innocence, benevolence, and exceptional achievement. Its stitches circumscribe what is intelligible to those who participate in its production, forming patterns of dialectical, allochronic, teleological, universalist, evolutionary, and Cartesian ways of thinking that capture and contain other imaginaries of possibilities and of resistances.

Many things are rendered invisible in this embroidery, but we emphasize two in particular. One is the fact that the threads of modernity are produced and sustained through fibers of expropriation, exploitation, destitution, dispossession, epistemicides, and genocides. Like a single-sided embroidery, the beauty of modernity only shows on one side of the fabric; on the other side, the messiness of the stitches is visible. The threads of modernity are enduring because of their ambivalence: at the same time, that they generate suffering, they also redirect attention away from their violence through the temporary alleviation of suffering. This alleviation depends on the amplification of its promises of ontological and material securities and enjoyments (i.e., of social mobility, social stability, and social engineering through moral reason) and the proliferation of sanctioned desires for their continuity. The pattern reproduces a vicious circle where the logics of markets, borders, and seamless progress normalize colonial violences while concomitantly rendering unintelligible different possible articulations of well-being and prosperity.

The second thing made invisible in the patterns of modernity is the looseness of its stitching, which refers to the quality of relationships created among the entities in the fabric. With its focus placed firmly on individuality and separability, modernity knits a slack and fraying texture that is inadequate for the weaving of the present into a wiser future. From the perspective of ancestors, we would need a combination of differently sourced threads, a more closely knit pattern, and other techniques for double-sided embroidery in order to open possibilities for different presents to be woven into different futures.

It is important to highlight that Indigenous people are also caught in the modern/colonial embroidery. While the image of Indigenous knowledges and peoples as beacons of resistance to all or some of modernity's threads is still prevalent, in practice, many Indigenous communities have made different choices. Therefore, it is problematic to talk about Indigenous knowledges and communities as homogenous or monolithic entities in their relationship with modernity. Ideas of anticipation and futurity will vary depending on the metaphysics being considered. In this sense, the distinction between Enlightenment/anthropocentric and relational/non-anthropocentric orientations is pedagogically and analytically useful, but also too simplistic to describe the complexity and spectrum of patterns of weaving within, outside and in response to global modernity. Nevertheless, we feel it is important to still use this distinction to illustrate the uneven and violent encounter of these two orientations with reference to current events. In the next section, we briefly outline the case of the Native American protests against the Dakota Access Pipeline as an example of an Indigenous gesture of close-knit weaving anticipation by Indigenous peoples faced with the aggression of state-protected global capital.

The Water Protectors at Standing Rock

The Standing Rock Sioux tribe and many other Native American supporters from across North America have gathered at the Oceti Sakowin Camp to block the construction of the Dakota Access Pipeline (DAPL) being built to transport crude oil from the Bakken oil field in North Dakota to a refinery to Patoka, Illinois, near Chicago. The Energy Transfer Partners project cost $3.7bn with the 11,720-mile pipeline projected to carry 470,000 barrels per day.

Those resisting the project believe that it threatens the sacredness of the native land and the Missouri river. They claim that the project also violates federal law and native treaties with the US government, emphasizing the project's destruction of burial sites found on the path of the pipeline to avoid federal regulation. Since the project was originally routed through a non-Indigenous community north of Bismarck and rerouted when concerns for their drinking water were raised, Indigenous water protectors accuse the government of environmental racism and of treating Indigenous communities as expendable populations. From their perspective, the encounter between the two orientations translates into an encounter between those fighting for their state-protected right to make money, regardless of the nonmonetary costs and the abrogation of Indigenous sovereignty, and those fighting for the right of future generations to drink clean water and live as Indigenous peoples.

The role of the colonial nation-state in prioritizing the securitization of capital over all else is illustrated by Ladonna Bravebull Allard (2016):

> While we stand in prayer, we have assault rifles aimed at us, we are attacked by dogs, pushed from our sacred sites with pepper spray, shot with rubber bullets and bean bag rounds and Tasers, beaten with sticks, handcuffed and thrown in dog kennels. Our horses have been shot and killed. Our elders have been dragged out of ceremonies, our sacred bundles seized, our sacred eagle staff pulled from our hands. My daughter was stripped naked in jail and left overnight for a traffic violation. An arsonist set the hills across from our camp afire, and for hours Morton County did nothing but prevent tribal authorities from responding.

For Indigenous water protectors who embraced the practice of peacefully asserting their presence on the land and engaging in prayer as the preferred form of resistance, ancestral genealogies are being called to intervene in the present struggle to open up different possibilities for the future.

Successful communication with ancestors is confirmed when wild animals and natural elements appear to be in synchrony with their call. For example, the landing of a large golden eagle that allowed itself to be touched by protectors was perceived to be a sign of ancestral support. The unexpected appearance of a herd of buffalo was also considered and welcomed in the same way. This unusual political practice may seem ludicrous or ineffective for those over-socialized into a form of thinking that sees animals as irrational and lesser than humans and ancestral spirits as inexistent and/or irrelevant. The practice will not make cognitive sense to those taught to relate to the land as an object, a property, a resource, or a commodity.

The water protectors evoke a form of grounded ethics of entanglement that centers the land as a living entity. Unlike modern forms of ethics grounded on intellectual normativities, this land-based ethic is not driven by the systematization of personal convictions. In this sense, it does not matter what we believe in, but our ability to un-numb our sense of interwovenness, to emanate humility and compassion in requesting ancestral support, and to call and live forth the visceral imperative of our ancestral responsibility. Although human agency and convictions are not the main drivers of change in this context, changes of minds and hearts away from self-interest are to be celebrated: reports of police officers being sensitized; refusing to participate in the operation or resigning are perceived by protectors as signs of success.

What kind of lessons can be drawn from the Standing Rock Sioux tribe's resistance against the particular kind of future (past and present) that has already been imagined for them? Historically, one could predict that their combined efforts will likely not suffice to derail the pipeline project, and its construction will represent yet another episode in the long history of destruction driven by capital expansion and enabled through state- or state-sanctioned violence. However, such an interpretation again measures success against a future that is already imagined (i.e., the pipeline will/should not be built; therefore, the resistance will be a failure if it is built).

A very different lesson can perhaps be taught by the very existence and continuity of the struggle itself, a struggle against multiple forms of colonial subjugation of Indigenous peoples and lands that has been ongoing for more than 500 years. After such a violent history, the sheer existence and strength of the struggle attests to the resilience of ontological orientations that see future(s) as permanently open, indeterminate, and indeterminable – even by the most restrictive and violent regimes of anticipation. It also shows how standing by such orientations increases the risks and vulnerabilities for those that struggle to uphold them. Had the people of Standing Rock given up and complied with a future already imagined, they would likely have avoided this militarized violence that accompanies their resistance.

While this is speculative, it could be argued that for many participants, the decision to partake in resistance to the DAPL is not perceived as a matter of individual choice in the Enlightenment sense of utility-maximizing analysis and personal interest, but as a question of commitment beyond sense-making, of being bound by a way of being in the world and a set of trans-generational, interspecies kinship relations that compel, perhaps ordains, resistance – not for personal benefit, or personal realization, but simply by making it impossible not to resist. Had it merely been a matter of individual choice, perhaps their struggle would have been extinguished centuries ago, as many other struggles have been.

Toward Addressing Incommensurable Futurities

Anticipation as it is conceptualized within anthropocentric Enlightenment notions of time is rooted within systems of meaning that prescribe commensurability and, specifically, *commensurability with the norms of global modernity*, which are viewed as universal. There is a willingness or even an imperative to extinguish other possible futures in order to achieve that coherence – including Indigenous futures. Indigenous peoples are rarely perceived to adhere to Western notions of human progress and development, and further, ongoing Indigenous relations to place are often understood as barriers to achieving progress (as is evident in the case of the DAPL). This means that any effort to develop "futures literacy" needs to grapple with shared pasts and presents in colonial contexts differently than we have yet done. As we noted before, critiques of the limitations of Western notions of time have been articulated within Western thought itself, and this is also true in relation to anticipation, in particular around planetary sustainability and climate change. Increasingly, Western citizenries and scholars have started to recognize that the modes of life valorized within global modernity are unsustainable for ensuring healthy future of and on the planet.

This, in turn, has led to a surge of interest in Indigenous knowledges as a means to inform reformed anticipatory efforts that emphasize environmental sustainability, as

Indigenous peoples are understood to have a closer relationship to and appreciation for nature. This has led to calls for protecting, revitalizing, and upholding the value of Indigenous cultures, languages, and identities, emphasizing their contribution to human heritage and knowledge. Indeed, some have framed the Standing Rock resistance efforts in this way, with one headline dubbing it as part of "The growing Indigenous spiritual movement that could save the planet."

While Indigenous epistemologies and ontologies do indeed contain invaluable wisdom for sustaining continued life on our finite planet, there are significant risks and challenges that arise with expanded inclusion of Indigenous knowledges and peoples in mainstream institutions and imaginaries, especially when this is not accompanied by addressing the limits of Western metaphysics itself. Elsewhere, we have given in-depth consideration to the risks of betraying the integrity and intrinsic gifts of Indigenous knowledges through their incorporation into the institutions of global modernity that were created to naturalize Western modes of being (Ahenakew 2014, 2016; Ahenakew et al. 2014; Ahenakew and Naepi 2015; Andreotti et al. 2015). Things may be little different in relation to futures anticipation about sustainability. While Indigenous knowledge about the environment and philosophies of interrelation with it have received growing recognition, efforts to incorporate these knowledges may still be oriented toward ensuring commensurability with anticipatory futures premised on anthropocentric and Enlightenment-based notions of individual human agency/control, mastery of nature, prescribed/predetermined answers, and linear progress. If Indigenous knowledges are instrumentalized in this way, then there is a betrayal of the possibility "of creating real alternatives to a system in crisis" (Ahenakew et al. 2014, p. 222).

As Indigenous scholars in the academy, a repeated pattern we see is a double-sided colonial move of appropriating (extracting and instrumentalizing) specific *contents* of Indigenous knowledges while discarding others and ignoring pressing political questions about the organizing *frameworks* of anticipation. The resulting futurities may again foreclose the possibilities for Indigenous existence and, indeed, for imagining collective existence differently (i.e., premised on something other than commensurability, consensus, and teleological prescription). For instance, Tuck and Gaztambide-Fernandez (2013) trace the "curriculum project of replacement," by which settlers "inherit" Indigenous knowledges so that Indigenous peoples themselves may be supplanted and disappeared. Others note that Indigenous knowledges are often incorporated only if they can be made to align with the Western scientific method, while Indigenous spirituality is brushed aside (Garroute 2003; Simpson 2014); or alternatively, spiritual elements of Indigeneity are appropriated, while Western political and ethical systems remain unexamined and uninterrupted (Aldred 2000).

Summary

Frustration with this persistent failure of ethical engagement with Indigenous difference has led some Indigenous people to emphasize the incommensurability of Indigenous and Western worldviews, and to turn away from questions of shared futurities, to emphasize Indigenous futurities and de-emphasize translation or coexistence. Indeed, in this chapter, we have sought to emphasize and illustrate that Indigenous and European Enlightenment notions of time are not merely distinct but are rooted in incommensurable epistemologies, ontologies, and metaphysics. However, simply naming incommensurability and its effects in the context of highly uneven colonial relations is important but insufficient, as over five centuries of colonization has intertwined our existences in unprecedented, and often very violent, ways. Thus, we need to ask what might prompt us to not only recognize this incommensurability, and sit with its tensions and (im)possibilities, but to ask what is being demanded of us if we wish to interrupt the hegemony of Western futurities that not only foreclose possibilities for Indigenous existence but also threaten the continued existence of all lives on our shared planet.

References

Ahenakew, C. (2014). Indigenous epistemological pluralism: Connecting different traditions of knowledge production. *The Canadian Journal of Native Education, Theme Issue: Indigenizing the International Academy, 37*(1), 148–164.

Ahenakew, C., Andreotti, V., Cooper, G., & Hireme, H. (2014). Beyond epistemic provincialism: De-provincializing indigenous resistance. *AlterNative: An International Journal of Indigenous Peoples, 10*(3), 216–231.

Ahenakew, C., & Naepi, S. (2015). The difficult task of turning walls into tables. In A. Macfarlane, M. Webber, & S. Macfarlane (Eds.), *Sociocultural theory: Implications for curricular across the sector* (pp. 181–194). Christchurch: University of Canterbury Press.

Ahenakew, C. (2016). Grafting indigenous ways of knowing onto non-indigenous ways of being: The (under-estimated) challenges of a decolonial imagination. *International Review of Qualitative Research, Fall, 9*(3), 323–340.

Aldred, L. (2000). Plastic shamans and Astroturf sun dances: New age commercialization of native American spirituality. *The American Indian Quarterly, 24*(3), 329–352.

Allard, L. (2016). Why do we punish Dakota pipeline protesters but exonerate the Bundys? *The Guardian*. Retrieved from https://www.theguardian.com

Andreotti, V., Stein, S., Ahenakew, C., & Hunt, D. (2015). Mapping interpretations of decolonization in the context of higher education. *Decolonization: Indigeneity, Education and Society, 4* (1), 21–40.

Baldwin, A. (2012). Whiteness and futurity towards a research agenda. *Progress in Human Geography, 36*(2), 172–187.

Browne, M. (2005). *Wairua and the relationship it has with learning te reo Māori within Te Ataarangi*. Unpublished Master of Educational Administration thesis, Massey University, Palmerston North.

Byrd, J. A. (2011). *The transit of empire: Indigenous critiques of colonialism*. Minneapolis: University of Minnesota Press.

Calderon, D. (2008). *Indigenous metaphysics: Challenging Western knowledge organization in social studies curriculum*. Doctoral dissertation, The University of California, Los Angeles.

Deloria, V., Jr. (2001). Power and place equal personality. In V. Deloria Jr. & D. Wildcat (Eds.), *Power and place: Indian education in America* (pp. 21–28). Golden: Fulcrum Resources.

Deloria, V., Jr., & Wilkins, D. (2012). *The metaphysics of modern existence*. Golden: Fulcrum Publishing.

Garroutte, E. (2003). *Real Indians: Identity and the survival of native America*. Berkeley: University of California Press.

Hart, R. (2013). *Imagined civilizations: China, the West, and their first encounter.* Baltimore: John Hopkins University Press.

Heidegger, M. (1977). *The question concerning technology and other essays* (trans: Lovitt, W.). New York: Garland Publishing, Inc.

Mika, C. (2016). Worlded object and its presentation: A Māori philosophy of language. *AlterNative, 12*(2), 165–176.

Mika, C. (in press). *Indigenous education and the metaphysics of presence: A worlded philosophy.* Oxon: Routledge.

Simpson, L. B. (2014). Land as pedagogy: Nishnaabeg intelligence and rebellious transformation. *Decolonization: Indigeneity, Education & Society, 3*(3), 1.

Tuck, E., & Gaztambide-Fernández, R. A. (2013). Curriculum, replacement, and settler futurity. *Journal of Curriculum Theorizing, 29*(1), 72.

Anticipation as Presence of the Future

21

Gonzalo Iparraguirre

Contents

Abstract

This work explores, from an anthropological perspective, the social imaginaries about the future and anticipation in different decision-making groups as a way to diagnose the manner in which they take their decisions and create agendas of development. Specifically, it is proposed to study the temporalities that sustain the imaginaries of anticipation in different cases and to diagnose the rhythms of life that characterize development in each group among their different symbolic fields.

To achieve this purpose, a method called *cultural rhythmics* is used to study temporality, spatiality, and rhythms of life. This method systematizes the set of everyday rhythms of life and aims to connect the "presence of the past" in the imaginaries (like history, family, identity, life trajectory, tradition) with the "presence of the future" (like planning, projects of life, dreams, hopes, wishes, utopias,

G. Iparraguirre (✉)
University of Buenos Aires, Buenos Aires, Argentina
e-mail: giparraguirre@filo.uba.ar; gonipa@gmail.com

© Springer Nature Switzerland AG 2019
R. Poli (ed.), *Handbook of Anticipation*,
https://doi.org/10.1007/978-3-319-91554-8_101

407

policies, anticipation). The composition of the present imaginaries in decision-making groups can be understood as simultaneity of past and future representations.

The outputs of this model could be summarized in two tools: (1) diagnosis of imaginaries and rhythmics of anticipation and (2) construction and synchronization of agendas. Decision-making groups could use these tools to change the way they manage territories, symbolic capitals, and social organizations. All of them are focused on applying rhythmic agendas as a management institutional strategy for facing the future, and so, to study the rhythmics of the future in terms of anticipation.

Keywords

Anticipation · Anthropology · Ethnography · Temporality · Imaginaries · Rhythm of life · Cultural rhythmics · Presence of the future · Argentina · Latin America · Resilience · Development · Agendas · Policies · Design of future

Introduction

In line with the central purpose proposed by Editor Roberto Poli in the Introduction chapter, that is, to establish the anticipation of the future as a legitimate topic of research, this work makes its contribution from anthropology, framed in the "Understanding Anticipation" Part. As Poli mentioned, a proper understanding of anticipation requires adopting new scientific and philosophical frameworks. This work aims to contribute in this regard, emphasizing the importance of putting greater emphasis on understanding the presence of the future, in compensation for the effort made to understand our daily decisions since the uses of past unilaterally.

In several works, Poli (2010, 2011, 2017) refers to the key concepts for the scientific field of future studies and constitutes the epistemological framework for its approach. Poli covers the main works and authors who shaped this field, which, through devices such as this handbook, positions itself firmly in the juxtaposition of studies that articulate time, the use of future, and the decisions that we deal with on a daily basis. Through the genealogy of anticipatory systems, this course produces paths of data and knowledge that are fundamental to anchor new frames of research. Concepts such as expectation, foresight, forecast, prediction, latency, and others make up the network of meanings about anticipation and anticipatory systems. In turn, they allow establishment of a fruitful dialogue of different disciplines that apply to the study of the future. These concepts and their practical manifestations are analyzed here as imaginaries and rhythmics of anticipation. Particularly, it emphasizes Poli's focus on anthropology following Appadurai (2015), who argues that an anthropology dedicated to understanding the future should pay attention to the interaction of three preoccupations: imagination, anticipation, and aspiration.

This work supports the idea that most theories of time need to be reviewed seriously as they fail to take into account the importance of the future and anticipation. As it will be developed throughout the work, the current hegemonic temporality in much of the world is constructed in the imaginary of experience, as an accumulation of past events and materiality. Different scientific fields reproduce this temporality daily, in their different academic actions (the subjects of social history that introduce all social and economic sciences, the biological history that supports the evolutionary paradigm, linear models of physics that hold the technical certainties of engineering) (Iparraguirre and Ardenghi 2011). So a central question here is why not assign the same relevance to the future?

A cross-reflection derived from the whole text is the possibility of conceiving the future as factually present in the becoming, which in addition to an anthropological basis for interpreting the social dynamics requires also a phenomenological explanation for sustaining the cognitive possibility of accomplishing it. Ultimately, this work seeks to contribute to an epistemology of development that comprehends the relevance of studying the presence of the future, in compensation for the regular effort to achieve the presence of the past.

Theory and Method

Before introducing the method and the model, it is necessary to define the fundamental distinction that originates the whole theoretical and epistemological framework. As this article is included in a handbook of anticipation, I start by exemplifying the difference between *time* and *temporality*, invoking the distinction between a cultural and a phenomenal anticipation.

As stated in previous works (Iparraguirre 2011, 2016a), temporality is all human interpretation of becoming that sustains us in life, a becoming that has been assigned with multiple variations of what was historically called "time." It was then suggested that "time is defined as *phenomenon of becoming in itself*, and temporality, as *human apprehension of becoming. Notions of time, as conceptualizations on the *time phenomenon* placed in a socio-historical context, are temporalities. The distinction is useful for not to reduce the phenomenon (time) to only one interpretation (temporality)" (2016a: 617).

The indistinguishable usage of time and temporality in everyday language, in political, scientific, pedagogical, or media discourses, contributes to naturalizing the same meaning for both concepts, therefore naturalizing hegemonic temporality as the *only* possible way of thinking about the phenomenon of time. Hegemonic temporality, understood as the conceptualization of Western linear time in various processes of officialization, is detected in the analysis of the imaginaries when considering the existence of *other temporalities* responding to other logics and attitudes facing becoming and not conceived as unique and univocal (2016a: 619).

Human anticipation is, within this theoretical framework, a temporality, an interpretation of time. Likewise anticipatory systems present in matter (natural or not), as a phenomenon of becoming, express manifestations of time. That is to say, anticipation exists in matter as well as among humans. Our consciousness of the anticipatory system is given in a cultural context, and as an apprehension of time, it constitutes a temporality; a notion of anticipation always entails a temporality.

However, the phenomenon of anticipation that exceeds our interpretation and occurs at a phenomenological level, such as the fall of an autumn leaf or the configuration of aging in our DNA, also exists. Both are clear examples of time revealed above any temporality, beyond any interpretation of it. It is therefore important to remember that this distinction is useful and necessary for not reducing the phenomenon of time – and anticipation here as well – to a single interpretation, to a univocal temporality that limits apprehensions to a hegemonic conception. This distinction is in direct correlation with Poli's proposal regarding the differentiation among an empirical phenomenon and the idea of an anticipatory system: "I contend that studying anticipation as a capacity is very different from studying anticipatory systems. The former endeavor adopts a descriptive attitude, conducts experiments and collects data, whilst the latter seeks to understand what it is that makes anticipation possible" (Poli 2010: 12).

Symmetric Tension of Becoming

Recalling Husserl's definition, becoming can be understood as an articulation of protension, tension, and retention (Husserl 1959). This phenomenological structure of time constitutes the dynamics of matter's becoming, thus setting up the human-nature dynamics' interface on our planet. Our apprehension of the present is given in the tension of becoming and provides support to our decisions and hence to the actions, what we execute in the here and now. Apprehension of the past comprises retentions that make the imaginary of the origin of every process. Origin is the start conditions, the context that originated our life and ordered the experience. Apprehension of the future is the protensions that shape the visions, thus creating the imaginaries of the future upon which we can handle anticipation. Protension understood as destiny is the convergence of actions since it brings into play our last instant alive, the here and now, and constitutes the convergence of our acts and decisions. This triple tension (origin, becoming, destiny), obvious through its everydayness, is based on the triple tension of the temporality (past, present, future), which at a phenomenological level is retention, tension, and pretention. Therefore, it is feasible to interpret that apprehension, temporality, and imaginaries can be linked at a symbolic level, which has, simultaneously, a correlation in praxis through decision-making – later analyzed as cultural rhythmics.

Table 1 summarizes the correlation established to understand the group's temporality, its decision-making, and its agenda-setting, that is, its construction of horizons of the future. Decisions are made in the present, which is usually interpreted only in connection with the experience, the past. However, here it is possible to clearly see that the vision is equally relevant since protension is symmetric to retention, in the same way the origin of a decision is connected with its destiny. Every temporality, as interpretation of becoming, entails that triple distinction we know as past, present, and future, three tensions that sustain the dynamics of becoming. Future, as well as present and past, is material: the three dimensions exist in our apprehension of becoming and build the materiality of phenomena. We are able to project an idea

Table 1 Scheme of the theory of the symmetric tension of becoming

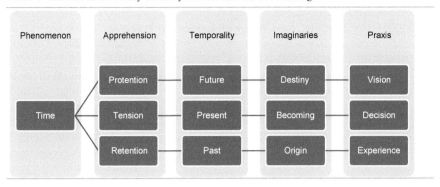

"into the future" because the mind becomes, and this becoming is tension of the past (memory) and future (imagination).

In brief, the protensive structure of becoming is what enables us to be anticipatory. That is why it is necessary to insist that the anticipation we can make is feasible based on the spatial-temporal structure of the symmetric tension of matter. From this conceptual framework, it is possible to sustain a theory that establishes the equal epistemic relevance of the past and future, a theory called symmetric tension of becoming.

Cultural Rhythmics

This theoretical framework provides support for the construction of a method that has already been applied into various case studies, such as the comparative study of the indigenous and the scientific temporalities (Iparraguirre 2011), the political-scientific management of cultural heritage (2014), the dynamics of rural tourism (2016b), and agricultural management and political decision-making (2017).

Cultural rhythmics is a method to study temporality, spatiality, and rhythms of life. This method systematizes the set of cultural symbolic representations (imaginaries) with the set of everyday rhythms of life (practices) and aims to connect the "presence of the past" (history, family, identity, life trajectory, tradition) with the "presence of the future" (planning, projects of life, dreams, hopes, wishes, utopias, policies, anticipation). The composition of present imaginaries in social groups can be understood as simultaneity of past and future representations. At a conceptual level, cultural rhythmics is defined as the set of life rhythms that allow us to describe and interpret constitutive practices of the social dynamics of a group of people in its everydayness.

This methodology is composed of two simultaneous processes of ethnographic research: (1) the analysis of practices of development (that which gives access to the presence of the past) and (2) the analysis of modes of agenda planning (giving access to the presence of the future) in each of the study social groups. The first one proposes to interpret how different rhythmics of development allow characterizing of their temporalities (focusing the past in terms of experience, memory, tradition, and habits). For example, interviews with farmers in Argentina that I undertook in fieldwork between 2013 and 2014 (Iparraguirre 2017) made clear that in the life rhythm previous to the global boom of transportation and mass media, the interviewees did not experience as large a discrepancy between their daily rhythms of work and those of rest and leisure as there is today. From the 1950s to 1960s onward, the rhythm of life incorporated overlapping activities that polarized the ways of living during and off work, confronting them in the end. Farmers manifested that dichotomy between leisure and work, rest and sustenance, working to live, and living to work radicalized. Simultaneously, the influence of global economic rhythms on local territories (intensification, fertilization, acceleration of processes, and industrialization in general) altered the natural rhythms of resources and local climate variables (2017: 264). In this ethnographic case, the presence of the past is manifested in the way the farmers practice development (transform the soil, use technology, organize their daily labor or family routine); all these actions are rooted in experience, knowledge, and memory.

In the second one, the study of imaginaries about the future allows comprehension of how the decision-making process works (focusing the future in terms of vision, anticipation, foresight, forecast, and prospective). During fieldwork with these same farmers, I found a close correlation between the images associated with "development" and the references to the "future," an imaginary nexus between the meanings of development and the expectations of the future, of what can or will happen. Also, this articulation appeared mediated by another key imaginary, the notion of "progress," so I set out to explore this link between the three categories. For example, how farmers looked at agriculture in the coming years, what would be the future ideal production mode, what they expect from the technology for their field, what will happen to the fields in our country, or what they think about progress. Among the results obtained, it is emphasized that the visions about the future of these farmers have a clear counterpoint between the political and productive rhythmics. The political plans set a rhythm of work from an agenda that does not follow the dynamics required by producers, based on the rhythms of production and their daily organization. In turn, the ideas of progress and development are unified, as if they were the same word that can be exchanged, naturalizing that development necessarily implies progress (2017: 269).

Likewise, this methodology integrates discursive and pragmatic skills. Discursive skills allow us, from the dialogue with study groups, to survey, systematize, and interpret social imaginaries to diagnose presence of the past and presence of the future. In complement, pragmatic skills allow recognition of the rhythmics of development to evaluate the socioeconomical balance among different rhythms of life (diaries, seasonal, communicative, economic, political, and ritual).

In summary, the core hypothesis affirms that implementation of cultural rhythmic methodology to research agendas of development contributes to comprehension of and to modeling different ways of conceiving anticipation. Operationally, it conceptualizes development as temporality, as a result of time representations that take account of the past, present, and future of social processes. This notion of becoming also explains the construction of decisions and the execution of practices. Only at this level it is understood that arrhythmic decisions are made and analyzed mostly based on the presence of the past and not the opposite. It is the linear temporality which naturalizes the experience as the basis of the decision instead of the vision and thus the anticipation. Multiple present theories of management add examples of the need to integrate visions, dreams, and wishes for complementing experiences.

The application of this method can be summarized in a simple operative sentence: let me understand your temporality and I will tell you how to change your rhythmic in decision-making. Rhythmics in decision-making allow the grouping of concepts as procedures, movements, processes, or dynamics; simultaneously, they express in their various fields the encompassing of the rhythms that constitute the practice of doing (economic, production, financial, work, daily, political, ritual, and other social dynamics as shown in Table 20 constitution of rhythmics). Rhythmics in decision-making operate accordingly as an anticipatory model, a model of how anticipation can produce changes in organizations from acknowledging their rhythmics (rhythms and imaginaries). Sections "Imaginaries of Future" and "Rhythmics of Anticipation" introduce examples that articulate the theoretical-methodological framework with the ethnographic cases studied.

Imaginaries of Future

Social imaginaries are sets of symbolic representations on ways of thinking and acting of a social group in its daily life. These can be analyzed through matrices that organize these representations into inclusive hierarchical levels. This method was created from the need for achieving a standard of organization of the ethnographic material, allowing comparison of social groups and case studies with each other in order to get a *synchronic result* out of them. This emerges epistemologically from the analysis and reinterpretation of authors such as Appadurai (2015), Bachelard (2011), Baczko (2005), Castoriadis (1989), Durand (2004), Ricoeur (2012), and Wright (2008a, b).

If described in a simplified way, the method introduces three complementary levels of signification: constellation (main imaginaries), component (symbolic representations), and category (discursive concepts). Matrices schematize the set of mapped representations to analyze the social dynamics of a single or several social groups. It is at the level of components where discrepancies leading to divergent significations of the same groupings of imaginaries that operate in the constellations are expressed. That is to say that for the same set of imaginaries, as the constellation "future," different interpretations can be found at the level of its components (such as temporality and prediction), and therefore they explain that the categories associated with these imaginaries differ to a lesser or greater degree (Table 2). Matrices of imaginaries provide a scheme of the symbolic field of the interlocutors arranged by the ethnographer, in order to systematize interview answers, conversations, and the analysis of the respective discourses. Likewise an ethnographic approach to the imaginaries necessarily entails considering the interlocutors' voice at the moment of

Table 2 Scientific imaginaries of anticipation

Constellations (main imaginaries)	Components (symbolic representations)	Categories (discursive concepts)
Future	Temporality	Expectation
		Predictive
		Discontinuity
	Prediction	Foresight
		Forecast
		Development
		Latents
		Possible
		Forward looking
Model	System	Phenomenon
		Impredicative
		Predicative
		Future literacy
	Scenarios	Explorative
		Normative
		Research
Behavior	Culture	Decision
		Uncertainty
		Culture facts
	Decision-making	Imagination
		Aspiration
		Environment
		Perceive

designing the tool of analysis, and not necessarily this must measure and codify them for translating their logics, knowledges, and practices.

However, how is an imaginary distinguished from a rhythmic? I take the category "progress" as an example commonly associated with the "future": is it a rhythmic or an imaginary? It is not a rhythmic as "progress" is not a specific practice; the *action of progressing* is not practiced since it is a cultural construction expressed in concrete practices such as sowing, harvesting, transporting, financing, or any other concrete action. A set of specific rhythms defining "progress" does not exist either. It can be conceived instead as imaginary, as a set of representations that can be conceptualized as a component of a single or several imaginaries. For example, "progress" is a key component either of the imaginary development or the imaginary modernity, or actually these two are constellations of the imaginary capitalism. Besides, "progress" can be split into more precise categories: "wealth," "well-being," "comfort," and "good living," just to mention a few. Considering, for instance, the phrase "at the rate of progress," it is precisely an image that makes use of the imaginary of the concept "rate" to give support to symbolic components such as "change," "speed," or similar.

The importance of understanding the imaginaries of the future from the social sciences has been stressed by Appadurai (2015), who extensively analyzes the future in his book's final section called "building the future" (377–395). He points out that an anthropology focused on the understanding of future should pay attention to the interaction of three essential aspects: imagination, anticipation, and aspiration. He explains that "as we refine the ways in which specific conceptions of aspiration, anticipation and imagination become configured so as to produce the future as a specific form or horizon we will be better able to place within this scheme more particular ideas about prophecy, well-being, emergency, crisis and regulation" (377). Appadurai affirms that "imagination is a vital resource in all processes and projects, and must be seen as a daily energy" (378) and draws up an itinerary to be followed for deepening and strengthening those social studies that account for the design of the future and its implications in topics such as the production of everydayness, the dynamics of the lived experience, or the production of locality (379). By confronting topics such as aspiration and politics of hope, risk and speculation, and the way of articulating them within a solid theoretical framework, the author makes clear the necessary orientation that anthropology and social sciences must take toward the symbolic comprehension of how future is built.

Precisely, representing convergent imaginaries in the "construction of future" may be odd and, as it is intangible, has been elusive to modern scientific knowledge. Our daily decisions are made based on the past, since it is the tangible, what we see and touch and what we cling to; it defines our spatiality and our materiality. Clinging to materiality is clinging to the past. We visualize the material space as we build it as past, which prevents us from seeing the impact of the future, the way future operates the present when making decisions, or how a vision affects a decision (Table 1).

Anticipation allows visualization of the other half of the symbolic components that intervene in the process of decision-making. There is a presence of the future that influences with equal strength as the presence of the past. Imaginaries of future constitute half of the process of decision-making; the other half is the imaginaries of the past. Anticipation, understood as the presence of the future, provides us with a new tool for considering the future as a source of understanding the decisions we make in our becoming. In this sense and considering Appadurai's thoughts, the future is a *missing cultural fact* in our life's daily decisions. We will see next the application of the method through a matrix of imaginaries of the future, in particular, on the imaginaries of anticipation.

Imaginaries of Anticipation

From the perspective of this work, the central concepts around anticipation enunciated in Poli's Introduction (2017) can be analyzed as constitutive of a constellation of imaginaries, following the methodology that distinguishes the discursive categories, their symbolic components, and their main constellations (Table 2). Here it is applied in this matrix to understand the analytical use of the anticipation in scientific discourse and practices and which can be its main virtues and limitations.

Poli (2017) recounts three levels of studies on the future, which, in this context, entail three ways of imagining the future that can be interpreted based on the symbolic representations (components) that define their central categories. The first level, forecasting, condenses the imaginary of "prediction" on the image of the "temporary window," either as a "very short" estimation (in econometric models) or as a "very long" estimation (as in climate change models). Poli explains: "It is often quantitative, even point-based, and starts from an underlying assumption of continuity: the system under study will continue to work more or less as it has been working so far because its structure remains essentially the same, or the laws governing it remain the same" (Poli 2017: 4).

The second level, foresight, groups together a constellation of imaginaries around the production of possible futures with two central components, the quantitative and the discontinuum. As for its practice, "foresight exercises are primarily used to challenge the mindset of decision makers by exploring possible futures. Alternatively, normative futures can be used. The difference between explorative scenarios and normative scenarios is that the former work in a forward attitude from the present to the future whilst the latter work backward from the future to the present" (4). Here the "normative" and the "explorative" are usual categories to the imaginary of a future with a lesser impact of the presence of the past.

The third level, anticipation, shares categories and components of the two previous ones to be applied in decision-making and action and adds two new components, futures literacy and impredicativity. In the first two levels, notions of "continuity" and "projection" centered in the repetition of the past (past-based) reinforce the imaginary of becoming as presence of the past exclusively. The categories sustaining such argumentations are anchored in an asymmetric conception between the past and future that reproduces another key imaginary of the hegemonic western temporality, the linearity of time's arrow, from the past toward the future (Iparraguirre and Ardenghi 2011).

The third level, instead, opens up an epistemological horizon to nonlinear temporalities, such as those documented by the anthropology of time (Carbonell 2004; Evans-Pritchard 1977; Fabian 2002; Gell 1992; Iparraguirre 2016; Munn 1992), thus to an interpretation of becoming off-centered from the past as the only "force" able to account for how the future impacts in the becoming, from decision-making among humans to the biological development of all living creatures.

In this preliminary version, the analysis is centered on three main imaginaries (future, model, and behavior) and systematized with only two components for each of them. Operationally, the matrix allows the understanding that discursive categories that refer to the notion of "future" (expectation, predictive, foresight, etc.) can be denatured by considering the different symbolic representations that bring together concepts such as "temporality" and "prediction." These components allow movement from a univocal concept of "future" to a constellation of representations that configure the "imaginary of the future" in a specific group depending on their temporalities. Putting into practice anticipation varies noticeably according to the interpretation of its categories (the same notion of "prediction" can be used both for math calculations and for astrological estimations). Imagining anticipation with various components, even with shared constellations, entails various ways of exerting anticipation.

The same procedure applied to the components of "model" and "behavior" makes up a triad of constellations that provides a rich symbolic material to analyze anthropologically the "imaginary of anticipation." For example, even if a constellation (set of imaginaries on behavior) is shared among a group of decision-makers, when various components (representations on culture and decision-making) exist, the ways of exerting anticipation may differ: a passive or repressive conduct facing a conflict of interests lies entirely in the cultural convictions of the group and on how authority is exerted in the decision chain.

I finally stress in this brief analysis that a relevant fact revealed by this matrix of imaginaries is that the concept "rhythm" is not present among the scientific imaginaries on anticipation. However, in a previous work, Poli (2011) refers to a direct implication between future and rhythms: "The seeds of the future are present not only in our expectations but also in the variety of natural and social rhythms that are reality itself – and perhaps especially in those that are less easily accessible" (72).

Rhythmics of Anticipation

The rhythmics of anticipation can be understood as the set of rhythms and imaginaries that allows us to account for social processes linking anticipatory practices. Simultaneously, they are entangled in imaginaries of anticipation, such as those analyzed in section "Imaginaries of Future," which are contextualized in the study of the imaginaries of the future. These anticipatory practices are detected when observing actions, behaviors, attitudes, and initiatives related to the "future," that is, to the set of imaginaries regarding the future, such as development agendas, decision-making, risk, speculation, and design, just to mention a few.

As introduced in section "Theory and Method," cultural rhythmics is a methodology of analysis, diagnosis, and intervention of social processes in multiple cultural contexts. For instance, rhythmics of development enable us to identify the various decisions and practices of development applied (being anticipatory or not) in the same territory – company, state, or any organization – when detecting that such practices have their roots in the imaginaries of development of their very participants. Financial speculation, the frenzy of stock markets, and the uncertainty of tomorrow's economy are all expressions of the multiple forms adopted by the presence of the future and how these are revealed in anticipatory practices given in the rhythmics of brokers, stock exchanges, and other tools for the management of the anticipation, which Appadurai mentions as "imaginaries of uncertainty" (Appadurai 2015: 316).

Another rhythmic of anticipation is revealed in education, in the way of educating about the future. A knowledge that is taught-learnt on the basis of its past-based construction reduces its pedagogical capacity. Futures literacy, as Riel Miller states, is key to transferring a didactics of the relevance of using the future as a symbolic and material element of our daily decisions. He explains: "Futures Literacy is a capability built on an understanding of the nature and attributes of anticipatory systems and processes. A Futures Literate person has the ability to select and deploy different anticipatory systems and processes, depending on aims and context" (Miller 2015: 515). The analysis of rhythmics in this process can contribute to what Miller calls "ability to make sense of discontinuity" (513), since rhythms are precisely grasped as discontinuities in our apprehension of time. It can also contribute to the deconstruction of an education conceived from a linear and cumulative temporality: "education, as it is practised today, dominated by aspirations to prepare and plan for the future inhibit the development and acquisition of Futures Literacy and may therefore be inimical to humanity's capacity to understand complexity in all its richness, undermining diversification and diversification strategies for continued survival" (521).

However, these rhythmics are anticipatory if they enable the apprehension of the presence of the future. Interpreting a daily work routine in an organization under a criterion of distinction of activities naturalized as intrinsic to a routine (presence of the past) – clock schedules of entry and exit from work, task distribution, and eating rituals, as many other habitus – does not account for the presence of the future at all. Nevertheless, the observation of the same routines, if denaturalized, allows us to understand the existence of anticipation in planning, innovation, design of actions, or objects not yet achieved. A social process in a tone of rhythms is anticipatory if its transference places the future in front of us.

This clearly happens with music when we listen to a combination of sounds not heard before (past), thus sounding as something "new" (future); *new* is that feeling of the future going through us. In recent decades, electronic music has set the vanguard in music creation, the setting up of the possibility of creating music different from anything heard before. Even if the same has happened with all those genres that "surpassed" their previous forms, it is possible to identify in certain periods, sets of imaginaries and rhythms, and artistic creations in this case that allowed to visualize the future, being anticipatory of what was about to happen.

In jazz music, this happened with Miles Davis when he anticipated a fusion with rock giving a horizon to multiple subgenres of jazz-rock and to legendary bands and artists such as Mahavishnu Orchestra, Weather Report, and Return to Forever, among others. The anticipation of a new age in tango was introduced by Astor Piazzolla in 1954 when he started his odyssey of creating the "new tango" opening up this genre's timbres and harmonies to the rest of the world. Today tango has been fused with jazz, rock, electronic music, and numerous symphonic pieces. However, it is not a matter of making a retrospective of how these musicians influenced others after them. Influence may be well understood as "presence of the past," thus hiding the other half of every social process. It is a matter of exemplifying that it is possible to observe the presence of the future and not only the presence of the past (how previous molds were broken and a genre was desacralized, as it was pointed out in both cases). In these musicians' creations – as well as for Bach, Mozart, Stravinsky, and many other visionaries' works – it is possible to identify a change with respect to the previous music that opened the horizon of futures to something yet unknown.

In architecture, anticipation awakens a taste for the forms that renovate the apprehension of space, our spatiality, to be precise. Zaha Hadid inspires the apprehension of space in such a way that challenges native spatiality, jeopardizing the convictions of what a work, leisure, rest, or any other space should be. Putting at risk values and conceptions is a symptom of the presence of the future. This happened in the Renaissance period with Leonardo da Vinci, and later with the Italian futurists who conceived simultaneity as the future present in the space-time of technology, art, and urbanism, and that is what Canevacci explores as "ubiquitimes" (Canevacci 2015). In a fruitful reflection on "singular objects," Baudrillard and Nouvel (2003) refer to the *cities of tomorrow*, and Nouvel says: "Time, not space, will determine our being a part of urban life in the future" (73).

Designing the Future

The importance of understanding the rhythms of anticipation acquires a different profoundness when it concerns design. Being the fashion industry, either clothing or any object that besides "decorating" the present, it anticipates which ones will be their new forms, how the "future will be dressed," or the shape it will have. The impact of design lies in its ability to make present the future; it is the novelty. Novel is the future seen for the first moment; therefore the impact of design is in the presence of the future.

Considering, for example, car design: why do "new" cars represent the future? I take, for instance, the design of the Porsche 911 (Image 1). Both 911 models could have been made the same year (say 2015) and therefore have the same age. That is to say, the same presence of the material past, the same materiality from their chrono-logic genesis. However, nobody would doubt that the "newer" one is the one on the right, and nobody would assume that they were both made in 1965, as the one on the left was. This last assertion would not respond to materiality but to design and to the combinatory of forms, curves, and colors that drag our apprehension of the car object toward a been knowledge (based on the presence of the past, having previously perceived these forms) or to a not-yet-been knowledge (based on the presence of the future, the apprehension of a design that anticipates unknown forms, of which therefore there is not a previous experience).

This example makes clear that the "futuristic design" of any object is given as the design anticipates forms not yet apprehended. An avant-garde design, such as this Porsche's, can be explained in that the 1965 model already anticipated an unknown future. Its permanence as an "avant-garde car" and its continuity in the identification as the "same model" have been possible since its designers knew how to balance the presence of the past (the forms, such its rounded headlights, defining Porsche's identity and tradition) together with the presence of the future (the new lines that keep opening the game of perception to an unknown field of car's forms innovated with every version).

The past (brand's tradition) and the future (designers' vision) are condensed in the present aesthetic. Anyone seeing it can say: "it is a Porsche 911, but it is a new one." It is not only a "reform" of the shapes, or an "adaptation" of previous forms, it is the presence of the future visions of designers that is represented in the car, in the

Image 1 Porsche 911's comparison (Porsche website)

materiality, and in the plastic, sheet, and leather. Materiality always presents presence of the future and presence of the past.

Its "retro" style is detected, instead, when identifying an evident presence of the past through prevailing elements, new for the epoch, known as typical of that design's origin. If it were only past (an abandoned car), it is not retro, it is old or obsolete. Then, inversely considered, it is the presence of the future which tells us that a design not only connects been experiences but also the opening, the vision of new experiences. Thus the imaginary of future assimilates an experience that has not been yet (but starts being).

Presence of the Future

The outputs of the model and the integration of theory and methods presented above could be summarized in two tools: (1) diagnosis of imaginaries and rhythmics of anticipation and (2) construction and synchronization of agendas. Decision-making groups could use these tools to change the way they manage territories, symbolic capitals, and social organizations. From Table 1, we can understand how agendas are built and how anticipation plays its role as a tool for promoting changes. A way to understand the possibility of producing changes in future scenarios can be built based on interventions in the temporality of decision-making groups. By approaching decision-making processes as a rhythmical diagnosis, that is, as a synchronization of tensions of every temporality, it is possible to diagnose past (origin) and present (becoming) problems, as well as potential future ones (destiny). The rhythmical diagnosis links the temporality of the observed group by correlating the conception and use of time in the past (as an experience), in the becoming (as decisions), and in the future (as a set of visions or imaginaries of the future).

To exemplify the tools, I introduce a brief diagnosis of imaginaries and rhythmics of anticipation applied to a group of political decision-makers and in particular the synchronization of agendas between science and politics for the analysis of the dialogue between anticipation and emergence. I focus on politicians in Argentina, as a group of decision-makers, comprising municipal, provincial, and national officials working in the province of Buenos Aires. The way these politicians make their daily governance decisions, culturally founded on a linear temporality and an imaginary of becoming centered both on the emergent and the urgent, entails a specific, basically non-anticipatory, development agenda. The constitution of an agenda is inevitable, although actors have not resolved to do so or considered it irrelevant. The agenda is automatically created by correlating daily actions and the annual calendar in a process that demarcates the administrative and bureaucratic rhythmic (administration's beginning and closing, budget construction and approval, legislative term, electoral processes, voting, etc.). As Durkheim stated: "A calendar expresses the rhythm of collective activities, while at the same time its function is to assure their regularities" (Durkheim 1982: 9). That is to say, the combinatory of the local political rhythmic and the state calendrical rhythmic produces the development agenda of the territory concerned reproducing the temporality of their decision-makers. I stress that this is a *development* agenda, and not just a *political* agenda, since this lacks ontology without the former.

This can be extrapolated into a vast number of decision-making groups in territories of Argentina, and Latin America in general, as the imaginaries of development and their correlated governance practices (political rhythmics) have a colonial epistemological matrix; that is, they share the way the presence of the past conditions' decision-making. This matrix, still persisting under the imaginary of nation state – of the imagined communities according to Anderson (1993) – is a clear example of how the past becomes present in the systems of government and in social conflicts never defused or transcended after appealing to methods created for actors and situations that no longer exist. From family farming to tax reforms and from military dictatorships to devaluation of national currencies, policies that do not acknowledge sociocultural and territorial diversities fail at finding homogeneous solutions for an alleged totality (of citizens, neighborhoods, towns, and even countries). We are governed by the presence of the past because we do not recognize the future as a force capable of transforming our present, in our own family and in our own country. Rituals that link us to traditions for sustaining identity are, in the same movement, the denial of a dynamic identity opened to changes that societies produce in any case.

Present examples of micro- and macro-politics that can be quoted abound municipal budget dependence on federal resources, concentration of economic capital in major urban centers, perpetuation of provincial feudal-like power structures, the ungovernable size of territories that reproduce colonial administrations, and imperial cities such as Ciudad de México, Santiago (Chile), São Paulo (Brazil), or Buenos

Aires (Argentina) that reproduce this "imaginary of governance" and are unable to succeed at tackling overcrowding issues, social inequality, and lack of planning (drug trafficking, violence, crime, extreme poverty, housing deprivation, epidemics).

Another clear example of anticipatory political rhythmic and synchronization of agendas is science applied to political governance. Science reflects on prediction and uses knowledge for anticipating results; it is in its genesis. From a different perspective, politics also aims at anticipating social facts, being either elections or minimum gestures that make for the lucidity of the administration and its execution. The imaginary of administration is precisely a constellation of symbolic components around future, improvidence, emergence, categories, and practices that vary between the coming and what becomes daily. Every anticipatory practice within politics is usually thought of as "prevention": preventing fires, diseases, floods, deficits, strikes, poverty, absenteeism, attrition, and every "social evil" that adversely affects governance and the citizen as well. Then, in this conflict-saturated horizon, there is the inevitable leak of strategies of the future, some anticipatory ones, some others that are predictable, and some retrogressive ones. Therefore, the challenge is to set up a dialogue between the art of doing science and the art of doing politics – as Bourdieu (2007) and Latour (2007) stated – in which anticipation is a bridge, a connective language between the imaginaries of the future and the past.

The diametrical change of governance involved in using the presence of the future for building anticipatory political rhythmics opens up the way to creative, innovative, sustainable, and resilient decision-making, which ontologically entails another temporality. This anticipatory temporality can be described at first as being non-accumulative (since the past is no longer the exclusive source of knowledge) and coming (since it assumes its main input is the energy of the present moment for the apprehension of the social emergence, both individually and collectively). In this sense, the urgency becomes an agency, a conductible emergence, manageable by local resources.

If our political decisions are no longer thought of as clinging to the past, then we begin to understand that the intervention in nature and its resources has an unknown possibility if considering the future as a source of energy. Resilience is also a way of conceiving the future as an energy carrier, instead of assuming that our planet is an infinite and renewable resource. Additionally, to conceive it as renewable entails the presumption that its origin (past) will be the same in the future, which is another way of reproducing a sequential and cumulative temporality.

If it is assumed that the energy sources *are being* in the future, then the connection with materials and resources changes. Water could be conceived of as energy and not only as a chemical compound in an industrial chain; food, as energy providing access to the future and not only as appropriation of the past and the resources that generated it; and property, as a transitory habitat and not only as accumulation of power conditioning access to the proper space. Thus, the territory ceases to be a space of the past to which I must return to defend it (wars, invasions, colonies) and becomes the place where the future is revealed, where vital energy is possible and hence life can be sustained.

The discovery and development of energy from fossil fuels are the product of a temporality centered on the past; fossil resources are accessible because they lie in the past. Renewable energies, such as wind and solar power, express instead an anticipatory energy that takes into account the resilience of systems. Sun and wind are coming resources. Resources are in the future, and their "capture" is only possible in the becoming, which makes them unpredictable while, simultaneously, less polluting. The systems of their "capture" are anticipatory as they enable transformation of the resource without a spatial accumulation for which its control entails the consumption and pollution of other resources.

Summary

Anticipation reveals that the future is symmetric to the past, as the future is not reduced to projections set in motion on the basis of previous static knowledge. The past is never on its own or isolated. It only works in tension with the future which provides it with coming energy. It is as simple a concept as understanding that death disconnects the body from the future. A dead body is only past, matter with no access to the energy source. This energy is not just from the brain or the heart, but they give access and movement to the future, to time, and to becoming.

It is the symmetric tension between the past and future that supports the present and its actualization in physical terms. At the sociological level, social processes are the tension between socio-imaginary forces, experience, and vision. The idea of becoming as actualization explains social processes from a different logic: our decisions are not projections but actualizations of the being-there (Heidegger 1997), and therefore, the epistemology is not on the weight of the past toward the future (entropic arrow) but on the force exerted by the future on the becoming, the presence of the future.

As it was stated in section "Theory and Method," our greatest social and personal strength comes from the future, from the void created by our visions of what we are not yet and expect to be based on previous experience. However, the strength is not given in isolation by experience and memory. Phenomenologically, the future opens up the horizon of the present, and it is the source of our strength for becoming, that is, for waking up every day and making a set of decisions in our lives always based on a symmetric tension between the past and future, experience and vision, and origin and destiny.

References

Anderson, B. (1993). *Comunidades imaginadas: reflexiones sobre el origen y la difusión del nacionalismo*. México: Fondo de Cultura Económica.

Appadurai, A. (2015). *El futuro como hecho cultural. Ensayos sobre la condición global*. Buenos Aires: Fondo de Cultura Económica.

Bachelard, G. (2011). *Poética del espacio*. México: Fondo de Cultura Económica.

Baczko, B. (2005). *Los imaginarios sociales*. Buenos Aires: Nueva Visión.

Baudrillard, J., & Nouvel, J. (2003). *Los objetos singulares. Arquitectura y filosofía*. Buenos Aires: Fondo de Cultura Económica.

Bourdieu, P. (2007). *El sentido práctico*. Buenos Aires: Siglo XXI.

Canevacci, M. (2015). *The ethnographic experiences of digital cultures and the syncretic mix of spacetimes*. Retrieved from http://intercontinental-academia.ubias.net/media-center/videos/inter continental-academia-talk-with-massimo-canevacci.

Carbonell, E. (2004). *Debates acerca de la antropología del tiempo*. Barcelona: Publicacions de la Universitat de Barcelona.

Castoriadis, C. (1989). *La institución imaginaria de la sociedad*. Buenos Aires: Tusquets.

Durand, G. (2004). *Las estructuras antropológicas del imaginario*. México: Fondo de Cultura Económica.

Evans-Pritchard, E. (1977). *Los Nuer*. Barcelona: Anagrama.

Fabian, J. (2002). *Time and the other: How anthropology makes its object*. New York: Columbia University Press.

Gell, A. (1992). *The anthropology of time: Cultural constructions of temporal maps and images*. Oxford: Berg.

Heidegger, M. (1997). *Ser y tiempo*. México: Fondo de Cultura Económica.

Husserl, E. (1959). *Fenomenología de la conciencia del tiempo inmanente*. Buenos Aires: Nova.

Iparraguirre, G. (2011). *Antropología del Tiempo. El caso mocoví*. Buenos Aires: Sociedad Argentina de Antropología.

Iparraguirre, G. (2014). Imaginarios patrimoniales y práctica etnográfica: experiencias de gestión cultural en el Sudoeste de la Provincia de Buenos Aires, Argentina. *Revista de Antropología Social, 23*, 209–235.

Iparraguirre, G. (2016a). Time, temporality and cultural rhythmics: An anthropological case study. *Time and Society, 25*(3), 613–633.

Iparraguirre, G. (2016b). Dinámica social del turismo rural: imaginarios y rítmicas culturales. Sierras de la Ventana, Argentina. *Pasos Revista de Turismo y Patrimonio Cultural, 14*(4), 827–842.

Iparraguirre, G. (2017). *Imaginarios del desarrollo. Gestión política y científica de la cultura*. Buenos Aires: Biblos.

Iparraguirre, G., & Ardenghi, J. S. (2011). Tiempo y temporalidad desde la antropología y la física. *Revista de Antropología Experimental, 18*(11), 251–260.

Latour, B. (2007). *Nunca fuimos modernos. Ensayo de antropología simétrica*. Buenos Aires: Siglo XXI Editores.

Miller, R. (2015). Learning, the future, and complexity. An essay on the emergence of futures literacy. *European Journal of Education, 50*(4).

Munn, N. (1992). The cultural anthropology of time: A critical essay. *Annual Review of Anthropology, 21*, 93–123.

Poli, R. (2010). The many aspects of anticipation. *Foresight, 12*(3), 7–17.

Poli, R. (2011). Steps toward an explicit ontology of the future. *Journal of Futures Studies, 16*(1), 67–78.

Poli, R. (2017). Introducing anticipation. In R. Poli (Ed.), *Handbook of anticipation*. Dordrecht: Springer.

Ricoeur, P. (2012). *Ideología y utopía*. Barcelona: Gedisa.

Durkheim, E. (1982). *Las formas elementales de la vida religiosa*. Akal: Madrid.

Wright, P. (2008a). *Ser-en-el-sueño. Crónicas de historia y vida toba*. Buenos Aires: Biblos.

Wright, P. (2008b). Postmodern ontology, anthropology, and religion. *Culture and Religion: An Interdisciplinary Journal, 1*(1), 85–94.

Big History and Anticipation

Joseph Voros

Contents

Abstract

This chapter will introduce the generic foresight process framework, examine a variety of different types of futures thinking, "locate" the use of macrohistorical models within the broader foresight process, examine some key aspects of the Big History perspective, and use this perspective to think systematically about the "contours" of the possible futures of human civilization at the global scale, as it

This chapter is an edited, revised, and updated abridgment of earlier work that has explored or set the foundations for using Big History as a framing perspective for anticipation at the global scale via the use of the generic foresight process framework (Voros 2003a, 2005, 2006a, 2006b, 2013).

J. Voros (✉)
Faculty of Business and Law, Swinburne Business School, Swinburne University of Technology, Hawthorn, VIC, Australia
e-mail: jvoros@swin.edu.au

© Springer Nature Switzerland AG 2019
R. Poli (ed.), *Handbook of Anticipation*,
https://doi.org/10.1007/978-3-319-91554-8_95

emerges from the complex dynamics of the present. We will make use of the "eight-threshold" formulation of Big History due to David Christian and examine some of the conceptual possibilities that arise when we consciously and systematically consider the question of what the *next* major threshold in Big History – what we might therefore call "Threshold 9" – may look like in broad outline. We find that, of the four main "generic" archetypal futures identified by James Dator, the most probable global future currently in prospect – barring a major catastrophic shock, technological energy breakthrough, or similar low-probability "wildcard" event – is a slowly unfolding collapse or "descent" over a timescale of decades to centuries toward a "constrained" or "disciplined" human society characterized by ever-declining access to easy sources of fossil fuel-based energy. Such a future trajectory clearly has major implications for the level of complexity possible for human civilization. This suggests undertaking an anticipatory program of continuing research and exploration into both the underlying nature and the emergent characteristics of the coming transition to "Threshold 9," in order to prepare for, and perhaps mitigate, its more unwelcome aspects.

Keywords
Generic Foresight Process (GFP) framework · Foresight methods · Layered methods · Prospective methods and prospection · World futures · Alternative futures · Big history · Big history thresholds · "Threshold 9" · Energy systems · Energy Transitions · Post-Fossil fuel civilization · Energy descent

Introduction

Thinking about the future relies on the use of frameworks of understanding upon which to base different modes of futures thinking, including the taking of an anticipatory "stance." These frameworks are often implicit and thereby not usually subject to critical examination. The development of a "generic foresight process" framework has allowed the critical selection of distinct and appropriate frameworks of understanding properly matched to scope and context for use in foresight work and futures research (Voros 2003a).

As part of this work, a generalized framework for "layered methodology" has also been developed (Voros 2005, 2006a). The levels of depth range from events, through trends, systemic drivers, and worldviews, to deep underlying social-historical and macrohistorical dynamics. These layers are not, in themselves, concerned with the future per se. Rather, they are concerned with analyzing and understanding, to progressively greater levels of "depth," how the past was laid down and how the present has come to be. How this layered view becomes relevant to *futures* is when the layers are used as the basis for explicitly *prospective* modes of thinking. In this layering framework, the "deepest" level of interpretive inquiry is the "historical" level, in which the scope – in both space and time – could involve just one society, a number of societies or civilizations or, on the grandest of all scales, might encompass cosmology and universal evolution. By choosing frameworks of appropriate scope, we may look for insights about potential futures at a "deeper" level than merely extrapolating "surface" trends and thereby undertake profoundly "deeper" futures thinking than that engendered by merely "reading" these trends (Voros 2006a, 2017). The grandest model currently available for use in this way would seem to be the all-encompassing scenario of Cosmic Evolution (Chaisson 2001; Dick 2009), which can be viewed as a wide-ranging evolutionary process that includes the specific case of how that process has played out in this corner of the universe here on planet Earth, namely, what has lately come to be known as "Big History." (One can readily imagine that there could well also be other civilizations, or at least inhabited worlds, which may likewise have their own analogous versions of Big History; but that is an enchanting topic for another day!)

The modern scientifically based understanding of how humankind came to be here – called, among other things, Cosmic Evolution, the Epic of Evolution, Universal History, as well as, more recently, Big History – is an intellectually exciting and very powerful conceptual model for making sense of the entire past, leading from the Big Bang nearly 14 billion years ago to our present planet-wide information-based technological civilization (e.g., Brown 2008a, 2017; Chaisson 2001, 2007, 2008; Christian 2004, 2008; Christian et al. 2013; Delsemme 1998; Jantsch 1980; Spier 1996, 2010, 2015). It represents a remarkable synthesis of diverse knowledge domains and scholarly disciplines brought together into a unified account of many different dynamical processes arising since the beginning of the universe. It also allows us to identify some of the major forces and drivers of change in human history operating over a number of different spatial and temporal scales, providing insights into how the globalized world we know today has come to be the way it is. While there have been many examples of earlier attempts to synthesize the sum total of human knowledge in this way (see, e.g., Spier 2010, Chap. 1), Erich Jantsch (1980) wrote perhaps the first account of Cosmic Evolution/Big History based on the modern understanding of nonequilibrium thermodynamics, drawing strongly upon the work of, among many others, Nobel Laureate Ilya Prigogine, to whom he dedicated his book. It remains a stunning work of synthetic scholarship and remarkably prescient insight even after nearly four decades.

As a futurist, I am of course interested in using scale-appropriate frameworks of understanding to generate ideas for further exploration into the dynamics that are shaping our present world and which are likely to be involved in shaping the future (Voros 2003a, 2005). Because Big History takes such a vast "big picture" view of human history – after all, it places Earth and human history within a *cosmological* context – it is very well suited and ideally conceived as a framing perspective for looking at global-scale changes and very long-term processes. Consequently, this chapter seeks to introduce Big History as a framework for *anticipation at the global civilizational scale*. In essence, we will here be using Big History as a "scaffold" or framework for undertaking long-term broadly outlined global-scale foresight. Big History can be used in this way as a framework for anticipation provided it is properly located and situated within a more general framework for undertaking foresight thinking. To this end, in the first part of this chapter, we introduce the "generic foresight process" (GFP) framework as the overarching structure within which Big History will be used for anticipation, which will also include a taxonomy of alternative types of futures that has proven useful to "open out" futures thinking.

Following this, we will "locate" where interpretive anticipatory frameworks are placed within the overall GFP framework and undertake some exploratory analysis of the future of the world system utilizing Big History as our framing perspective. Two of the key concepts (among several) in the Big History approaches of Eric Chaisson (e.g., Chaisson 2001, 2004), Fred Spier (e.g., 1996, 2005, 2011, 2015), David Christian (e.g., 2004, 2008), and Frank Niele (2005) are *energy* (or, more precisely, energy *flows*) and *complexity*. (Jantsch also wrote about *information* as a key concept, one which is increasingly becoming recognized in studies of complexity science (e.g., Lineweaver et al. 2013), as well as about *consciousness*. Sadly, space does not permit us to explore these any further here, although we will have occasion to briefly mention these two key ideas again later.) Accordingly, our attention here will be primarily focused upon the issue of the energy available for use by human society, the degree of social complexity that can be supported by it, and how this relationship may be viewed within the context of the "eight-threshold" approach to Big History developed by David Christian (described in detail later) as applied to thinking about the *future* of human civilization on a Big History timescale. In other words, we shall use the "eight-threshold" view of Big History to explore what the "next" such threshold might look like – what we might as a result therefore call "Threshold 9." To aid us in this exploration, we will also make use of James Dator's four generic "archetypal" "images of the future" to "contour" the overall "shape" of the coming global future at this macroscale.

We find that the most likely projected future global civilizational trajectory currently unfolding – in the absence of a major catastrophic shock, technological energy breakthrough, or similar low-probability "wildcard" event – is a slowly unfolding "descent" over a timescale of decades to centuries toward a global society constrained by ever-declining access to easily available sources of high-density fossil fuel-based energy. Such an energy-constrained future clearly has major implications for the level of complexity possible for human civilization. This observation in turn suggests undertaking an increasingly urgent program of continuing anticipatory research and exploration into both the underlying nature and the potential emergent characteristics of the coming transition to "Threshold 9," in order to prepare for, and perhaps to mitigate, to the degree possible, its more unwelcome aspects.

The discussion here should be regarded as merely an initial and very preliminary exploratory sketch of a few of many possible ideas, being done as much to show the process of undertaking such foresight-focused exploratory work based on the Big History framework as much as for any insights that might be generated by it. I hope that it can contribute in some way to a wide-ranging continuing conversation – among big historians, sociologists, futurists, and any other similarly interested scholars – around the issue of the energy basis supporting our common global future. I also fondly hope that the activity of generating such a sketch – as well as demonstrating the thinking process that underpins it – will also in some way help contribute to the successful navigation by humanity of some of the major issues we need to confront at the civilizational, planetary, and even species level as we steer our way into the rapidly emerging and increasingly dangerous and uncertain future which lies ahead.

The Generic Foresight Process (GFP) Framework

The generic foresight process (GFP) framework (Voros 2003a) conceptualizes futures thinking as a broad sequence of knowledge-seeking activities (Fig. 1) moving through five main "phases" (Fig. 2), which are best considered as overlapping "foci of activity" rather than rigidly separated "steps." These phases range from the gathering of information as *inputs*, initial categorical *analysis*, and then deeper critical *interpretation* of these inputs to the actual generation of "forward views" or "images of the future" – what is here called "*prospection*" – and thence to the generation of specific *outputs* that may themselves become inputs into further strategy creation, policy formation, or social analysis processes.

In the GFP, certain types of method are naturally "situated" within the overall "flow" of the broad process (Fig. 3). The actual specific methods employed in each phase are not fixed in this conception, but remain open to an informed choice by the foresight practitioner or analyst, subject to the specific requirements of the particular foresight engagement or analysis. This flexibility within the general framework ensures that a highly customized process can be created for the unique needs of any specific foresight engagement or analysis, rather than simply reusing a singular standard approach or formulaic method and forcing the engagement to fit the method, like the Procrustean bed of Greek legend.

Note that while the diagrams in Figs. 1, 2, and 3 appear to portray this process as a simple linear one, there are – both conceptually and in practice – *very* many feedback loops from the later phases to the earlier ones, and therefore also many feed-forward effects as the loop pathways are retraversed, perhaps more than once. These are omitted for the sake of diagrammatic simplicity to show only the "broad flow" of the

Fig. 1 The "generic foresight process" (*GFP*) framework; broad process outline view

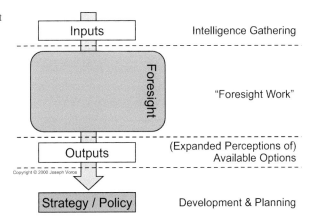

Fig. 2 The GFP framework, with the "focus" of each phase shown

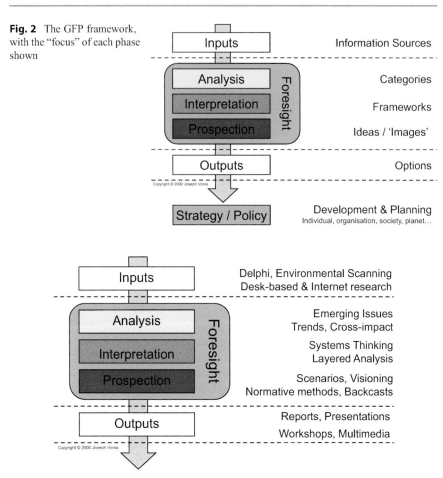

Fig. 3 The GFP framework, with some representative methods shown

overall process, absent all of the finer details of many possible recursion loops. (When I first developed this framework in late 2000, I included the many actual feedback and feed-forward loops in expanded versions of these and other diagrams. The framework was at that time criticized on occasion for being "too complex." I then removed the many loops and left only the "overall flow" views depicted here. It was then criticized for being "very linear" or "too simplistic"! I have found over the years however that, with sufficient and careful framing, the "too linear" criticism is rather less common than the "too complex" one, so I now just use the "overall flow" versions that are found in this chapter. But I do, from time to time (and, I admit, perhaps a bit bloody-mindedly!), show a (still simplified) version of a "many loops" diagram just to show the full complexity of the thinking and practice that is needed in this approach to foresight.)

In addition, the strategy/policy "phase" as portrayed in a single box is really just an attempt to denote on a simple diagram the many highly complex and continuing strategic and policy processes which go on in corporate or noncorporate and governmental organizations, in order to visually suggest that foresight is *an input into* strategy and policy processes. These latter obviously extend their influence beyond the simple box form portrayed in the diagram and inform several layers of further activity, such as managerial/allocative and tactical processes, which in turn inform operational processes, or public advocacy and related policy-oriented activities, and so on.

The GFP "Phases" in More Detail

Here the four key elements of the process are described in more detail: inputs, "foresight" work, outputs, and strategy/policy. A more detailed diagram of the GFP is shown in Fig. 2, where the comments on the right-hand side show the "focus" of the activity or thinking which is undertaken at each phase and attempt to illustrate the "flavor" of that phase.

- **Inputs**. This is the gathering of information and intelligence. Many methods, techniques, and frameworks exist, of which the "Delphi" technique and "environmental scanning" (Choo 1999, 2002) are perhaps the best known. The many tools and techniques of "competitive intelligence" and related activities are relevant here, too. It is also where, in workshop formats, the participants are asked for their ideas and insights, such as through brainstorming ideas or through what Slaughter (1999, p. 292) calls "constructing the near-future context" – asking a set of key questions, designed to open out the thinking about the near future (Slaughter 1996), which have proven very useful in workshop settings. When in my work as an organizationally based foresight analyst (Voros 2003a) the activity of gathering inputs was undertaken at the organizational level (as opposed to workshop formats), we chose the term "strategic intelligence scanning" or sometimes simply "strategic scanning" in preference to the somewhat passive term "environmental scanning" or the somewhat negative term "early warning system"(Brown 1999, p. 9). Most strategic planning involves something called "environmental scanning" which "everyone knows" how to do. When working as such a foresight analyst, I wanted to distance our approach to scanning (Voros 2001, 2003b) from existing "well-known" methods of environmental scanning, so the name chosen was something deliberately different. Similar care in the choices of terminology and language also applies to policy-related work – e.g., "issue management" and "social intelligence" (Choo 1999, 2002).
- **Foresight work**. This can be conceived as comprising three broad "phases" which follow a logical sequence. The first phase is:
  - **Analysis**, which is best considered as a preliminary stage to more in-depth work, rather than as a stand-alone technique itself. The sort of question asked here is "what seems to be happening?" The goal is to seek a "first cut" at creating some order out of the bewildering variety of data that the input phase usually generates, by sorting the input into usable categories, whether these are

"emergent" from the data themselves or predetermined by the framework which has been chosen for use in the subsequent interpretation phase. Common tools here are trend analysis, cross impact matrices, and other such analytical techniques, as well as "emerging issues analysis," a technique invented by Graham Molitor to great effect – see especially (1977, 2003a, b, 2010) – based on an assumed form for the future dynamics of many public policy issues.

The results of the analysis are then fed into a second phase:

- **Interpretation**, which asks the question "what's *really* happening?" and seeks to "probe beneath the surface" (Slaughter 1989) of the analysis to look for deeper structure and insights. This is the realm of critical futures studies (Slaughter 1999, p. 203), causal layered analysis (Inayatullah 1998a), systems thinking (Checkland 1999; Meadows 2009), and other "depth" approaches to futures thinking. A generalized approach to such "layered analysis," based in part on these approaches, is discussed in more detail below. (Suffice it to say here that it extends from the well-known "systems iceberg" metaphor – events, patterns, and trends and system structure – through to the levels of worldviews and myths as found in causal layered analysis to the deeper structures of consciousness itself and how these are enfolded by macrohistorical forces.)

The third phase is the actual creation of forward views:

- **"Prospection."** I had to invent the word *prospection* (from "pro," "forward"; "spect," "look"; and "-tion," the noun form of the action, thus "pro*spec*tion," where the stress falls on the second syllable), to denote, in a form that could be displayed in a small colored box on a PowerPoint slide, "the activity of purposefully looking forward or thinking about the future in order to create forward views and ideas about, or 'images' of, the future." (This word also acknowledges the French school of futures work and their term *la prospective*, as well as the wider European use of the term "prospective thinking." It turns out that Daniel Gilbert also independently came up with the same term (Gilbert 2006; Gilbert and Wilson 2007)). This is where various views of alternative futures are explicitly examined or created. It is where the actual scenarios, "visioning" and "normative" methods that are the best-known stock-in-trade of the futurist, are located in the broader foresight process. I also tend to locate "backcasting" methods here as well (Voros 2006a), even though they tend to be largely analytical by nature, because they presume the existence of a forward view from which one "casts backward." One need not necessarily be bound to use *explicitly* "futures"-type methods in this phase, either. For example, simply evolving a systems map or causal loop diagram forward in time with different assumptions is also a perfectly valid prospective technique to examine how different futures may unfold. The question(s) asked during the thinking at this stage depend upon which type of potential futures is under consideration – preposterous, possible, plausible, probable, preferable, or projected (see below).

• **Outputs**. The outputs of foresight work are twofold: tangible and intangible. Some tangible outputs would include the actual range of options generated by the work or the set of specific scenarios depicted or plans produced. Intangible outputs would include the changes in thinking engendered by the whole process, especially the insights generated in the interpretation phase and by the creation of forward views in the prospection phase. The intangible output might be somewhat difficult for some "hardheaded," "objective" people to appreciate or even recognize. But it is undoubtedly the more important form of output because of the way it alters the very mechanism of strategy or policy development itself, namely, the perceptions of the mind(s) of the decision-makers involved in strategizing or policy formulation. The methods employed in the output stage need not be specifically futures related either, because the focus of this stage is the "getting across" of insights, and/or the stimulation of thinking about options, prior to and as inputs into more formalized strategy or policy work. A variety of other methods could therefore be employed here to present the outputs of the foresight work, such as workshops, reports, role-play, film, multimedia, full-immersion experiential events, etc. Thus, this is a stage which could use any number of appropriate tools for its execution, from a variety of contexts. It is intended to generate an expansion of the perceptions of, and perceived options available to, the decision-makers who are the intended recipients of the foresight work. This expansion could be attempted directly through overt questioning or similar means, or indirectly by engineering an experience that provokes such questioning or expansion. One question that captures some of the essence of this stage is "what might we need to do?"

At this point, foresight has done its real job – the generation of (hopefully) an *expanded perception of strategic or policy options* available. This output now feeds into:

• **Strategy/policy**. The final stage in this framework is that of strategy or policy, about which very little will be said here, as it is covered in myriad other works related to this space. Suffice it to say that since foresight has done its job, it now hands over the output it has produced for consideration by decision- and policy-makers in making decisions and directing strategic actions for implementation (i.e., the more familiar activities of strategy development and strategic planning) or for determining public policy directions and priorities. The results of the strategy/policy process need, of course, to be constantly fed back into the inputs of the overall foresight framework, "closing the loop," so that continuous reassessments and "course corrections" can be made along the "strategic journey" or to policy settings. (Of course, as mentioned earlier, there are in reality feedback loops from each stage to those that are prior. As noted, these loops are not shown in the diagrams for reasons of diagrammatic simplicity, rather than through conceptual omission, and this point should always be borne in mind and frequently reiterated whenever the framework is being used, especially with groups being facilitated through the process who may not be familiar with it.)

A more detailed form of the generic foresight process can be seen in Fig. 3 showing, in particular, some of the methods applicable at each step. As was shown in Fig. 2, the overall process structure is designed to be as general as possible so that it can be applied on any scale, from the individual level to workgroup, to department, to branch, to organization, and to the societal, civilizational, and even global/planetary level. It is at these last two levels that Big History is most appropriate for use as an anticipatory framework.

Types of Alternative Futures

Futurists have often spoken and continue to speak of *three* main classes of futures: possible, probable, and preferable (e.g., Amara 1974, 1981; Bell 1997, and many others). These have at times lent themselves to define various forms of more specialized futures activity, with some futurists focusing on, as it were, *exploring the possible*, some on *analyzing the probable*, and some on *shaping the preferable*, with many related variations on this nomenclature and phraseology (e.g., again, Amara 1991 and many others). It would seem that *anticipation* as a cognitive or methodological "stance" resonates more strongly with the "predictive" (in the loosely defined general sense in which this term is used in foresight work, rather than literally) and "explorative" modes of thinking attached to the probable and the possible, respectively (the former a bit more than the latter), than with the more "normative" mode of the preferable (but this is a rather intuitively informed and fairly loose observation and by no means a formal proposition). At any rate, it is possible to expand upon this three-part taxonomy to include at least seven (or even eight) major types of alternative futures.

It is convenient to depict this expanded taxonomy of alternative futures as a "cone" diagram. The "futures cone" model was used to portray alternative futures by Hancock and Bezold (1994) and was itself based on a taxonomy of futures by Henchey (1978), wherein four main classes of future were discussed (possible, plausible, probable, preferable). (Some years later, I found out that this idea of a cone graphic was used even earlier than Hancock and Bezold (1994) by Charles Taylor (1990), in which he wrote of a "cone of plausibility" that defined a range of *plausible* futures extended over an explicit timeframe, including a kind of "back-cone" into the past. He also included "wild cards" in his approach, but other futures categories mentioned here were not explicitly depicted in the diagram given by Taylor as they were by Hancock and Bezold.) Over the years that I have been using the futures cone in foresight teaching and practice, I have found it useful to adapt it and add more classes to the initial few. The most recent version of the futures cone as I now use it is as depicted in Fig. 4.

The seven types of alternative futures defined below (or eight if one also includes a specific singular "predicted" future, which I generally don't do any more) are all considered to be *subjective judgments* about ideas about the future that are *based in the present moment*, so the categories for the same idea can obviously change over time as time goes on (the canonical example of which is the Apollo XI Moon landing, which has gone through most of the categories from "preposterous" to "projected" and thence into history as "the past"). In brief, these categories are:

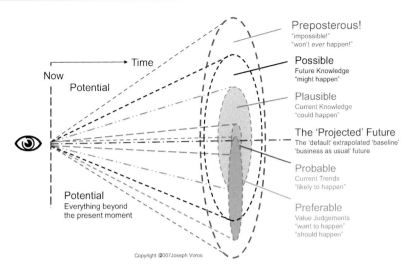

Fig. 4 Types of alternative futures: the "futures cone" (Adapted and extended from Voros 2003a, based on an earlier form by Hancock and Bezold 1994)

- **Potential** – everything beyond the present moment is a potential future. This comes from the assumption that the future is undetermined and "open," not inevitable or "fixed," which is perhaps *the* foundational axiom of futures studies (e.g., Dator 2005).
- **Preposterous** – these are the futures we judge to be "ridiculous," "impossible," or that will "never" happen. I introduced this category because the next category (which used to be the edge of the original form of the cone) did not seem big enough or able to capture the sometimes-vehement refusal to even entertain them that some people would exhibit to some ideas about the future. This category arises from homage to James Dator and his Second Law of the Future – "any useful idea about the future should appear ridiculous" (Dator 2005) – as well as to Arthur C. Clarke and his Second Law, "the only way of finding the limits of the possible is by going beyond them into the impossible" (Clarke 2000, p. 2). Accordingly, the boundary between the preposterous and the possible could be reasonably called the "Clarke-Dator Boundary" or perhaps the "Clarke-Dator Discontinuity," since crossing it in the outward direction represents a very important but, for some people, very difficult movement in prospection thinking.
- **Possible** – these are those futures that we think "might" happen, based on some future knowledge we do not yet possess but which we *might* possess someday (e.g., warp drive).
- **Plausible** – those we think "could" happen based on our current understanding of how the world works (physical laws, social processes, etc.).
- **Probable** – those we think are "likely to" happen, usually based on (in many cases, quantitative) current trends.

- **Preferable** – those we think "should" or "ought to" happen: normative value judgments as opposed to the mostly cognitive, above. There is also of course the associated converse class – the *unpreferred* futures – a "shadow" form of *anti*-normative futures that we think should *not* happen nor ever be allowed to happen (e.g., global climate change scenarios come to mind).
- **Projected** – the (singular) default, *business-as-usual,* "baseline," extrapolated "continuation of the past through the present" future. This single future could also be considered as being "the most probable" of the probable futures.
- **(Predicted)** – *the* future that someone claims "*will*" happen. I briefly toyed with using this category for a few years quite some time ago now, but I ended up not using it anymore because it tends to cloud the openness to possibilities (or, more usefully, the "preposter-abilities"!) that using the full futures cone is intended to engender.

The above descriptions are best considered not as rigidly separate categories, but rather as nested sets or *nested classes* of futures, with the progression down through the list moving from the broadest toward more narrow classes, ultimately to a class of one – the "projected." Thus, *every* future is a *potential* future, including *those we cannot even imagine* – these latter are outside the cone, in the "dark" area, as it were. The cone metaphor can be likened to a spotlight or car headlight: bright in the center and diffusing to darkness at the edge – a nice visual metaphor of the extent of our futures "vision," so to speak. There is a key lesson to the listener implicit when using this metaphor – just because we cannot imagine a future does not mean it cannot happen. . ..

Then there are all of the *imaginable* ones (i.e., *inside* the cone), beginning with the subclass of those that we judge to be unreasonable (i.e., ridiculous) or impossible – "preposterous" in my alliteration – and the further subclass of those that we judge to be "reasonable but which would require *knowledge we do not yet possess but which we might possess in the future*" and so "might" happen – "possible."

Then there is the subclass of those that we think are *reasonable based on what we currently know* and so "could" happen, thus "plausible," and so on through the rest: the subclass of futures based on *the playing out of current trends*, "probable," and finally the *default extrapolation of current dynamics*, the (single) "projected" future, the only class in the whole schema containing only a single future, although different people will "project" different futures, so it is really a single-member class containing many "single" futures, as it were. The similarly single-member class of "predicted" future, which had a similar underlying rationale – namely, what "will" happen depends a lot on whom you ask – is very rarely used, except to make a specific point.

The class of *preferred* futures – what "should" or "ought to" happen – can take in any or all of the classes from preposterous to projected, because these futures must be at least imaginable (so inside the cone), and because people's idea of what they prefer, and how they judge others' preferences, can range from the default projected future thought to be coming, all the way outward to (what is considered) outlandish preposterousness.

To this set, one may also add **wild cards** – by definition low-probability *events* (sometimes referred to as "mini-scenarios") that would have very large impact if they occurred (Petersen 1997, 1999). Since they are considered "low probability" (i.e., outside the probable zone), any member of any class of future outside the range of *probable* futures could be considered by definition a wild card (although this usage is not common, as the focus tends to be on "high-impact" events). Thus, in this view, some wild cards are considered plausible, some possible, some preposterous, and – the scariest of all – some we have not even imagined or dreamed of yet (i.e., potential). . ... These last are not even classifiable as "black swans" (Taleb 2007), but rather as, perhaps, "scarlet splofflings" (Q: "what the hell are they?!" A: "exactly!").

This taxonomy finds its greatest utility when undertaking the prospection phase of the GFP (as noted above), especially when the taxonomy is presented in reverse order from projected out to preposterous. Here, one frames the extent to which the thinking is "opened out" (implied by the reverse-order presentation of the above taxonomy) by choosing a question form that is appropriate to the degree of openness required for the futures exploration. Thus, "what preposterously 'impossible' things *might* happen in the next few decades?" sets a different tone for prospection than the somewhat tamer question "what is projected to occur in the next 12 months?"

The "Layered" View of Change

Recent work in Futures Studies has increasingly taken the view that reality is "layered" and that, therefore, "layered methodology" needs to be employed to better understand and interpret this complex reality (see, e.g., Inayatullah 2002). To this end, a five-layer framework is presented here which will provide a basis for considering how prospection can be carried out with respect to different layers, levels, or "strata" of interpretive depth. This framework is a particular form (Voros 2006a) of a more general schema (Voros 2005), but it is not necessary to be familiar with that work for the purposes of the present chapter. We will ultimately use the deepest of these layers to inform our anticipations based on Big History.

The layering scheme is derived, as mentioned earlier, from a number of sources including, notably, the well-known systems "iceberg" metaphor (e.g., van der Heijden 2005), systems thinking (Checkland 1999; Meadows 2009), the layering of futures thinking proposed by Richard Slaughter (Slaughter 2002), the methodological approach known as *causal layered analysis* or CLA (Inayatullah 1998a), work on human consciousness (Beck and Cowan 1996; Gardner 1993; Gebser 1985; Graves 1974; Wilber 2000), perspectives on social change and macrohistory (Galtung and Inayatullah 1997; Inayatullah 1998b), and the combining and/or "nesting" of these social and analytical perspectives to inform strategy development, policy formulation, socially oriented investigation, and foresight analysis (Voros 2006b).

The particular layers are described in more detail below. The **bold** word is intended to function both as a mnemonic and as a descriptor of the main features of that level. Briefly, they are:

- **Event:** the level of discrete events which are observed to occur in the world. These are usually conceived to be occurring independently of each other. This is the topmost level of the well-known "systems iceberg" metaphor. The attempt to relate them to one another or search for regularities generally leads to the next level of analysis.
- **Trend:** the level at which "patterns and trends" are observed, just below the "waterline" in the systems iceberg metaphor. This represents the "pop" level of Slaughter and, together with the level above, the "litany" level of CLA.
- **System:** the level at which "systemic structure" is discerned in the systems iceberg. This is the problem-oriented level of Slaughter and the level of social causes (and policy analysis) in CLA.
- **Worldview:** the level of mental models, worldviews, modes and types of thinking, and cognition and consciousness in general. This level encompasses the critical (and most of the epistemological) level of Slaughter, the *Weltanschauung* ("world picture" or "worldview") level of Checkland's soft systems methodology, the worldview/discourse and myth/metaphor levels of CLA, and the forms of cognition and consciousness discussed by Gebser, Gardner, Graves, Wilber, and Beck and Cowan. It is the level where metaphors and "images" of the present, and thus also potentially of the future, are analyzed in CLA.
- **Historical:** the level of social, historical, and macrohistorical change. It is the level of the "conditions of existence" discussed by Graves and Beck and Cowan, and social, historical, and macrohistorical change discussed by Galtung and Inayatullah. At this, the deepest level of interpretive depth, the scope – in both space and time – of the interpretative framework could involve just one society, a number of societies or civilizations, or, on the largest of all scales, might also encompass cosmology. This is where Big History, Astrobiology/SETI, and ultimately Cosmic Evolution are placed.

The **worldview** and **historical** levels are not so cleanly separated as might be implied by this bullet-point form of presentation; macrohistorical change can give rise to evolution of consciousness – that is, to changes in structures in the worldview level – as well as vice versa. The fourth and fifth levels have a *very* strong degree of interaction, because the form of the cognitive capacities and worldviews available to members of a society affects the nature and type of society which results, and this, in turn, affects the type of life conditions which will be extant and into which newer members of the society are born and raised. Thus, there is a rather tight interweaving of effects and factors in the fourth and fifth levels. This is depicted graphically by the oblique dotted line and bracket on the left side of Fig. 5.

Locating Anticipatory Frameworks

As can be seen from Fig. 5, frameworks of understanding, including those that can be used for anticipation, are situated within the interpretation phase of the GFP. The layering framework described in the previous section is an example of one way to

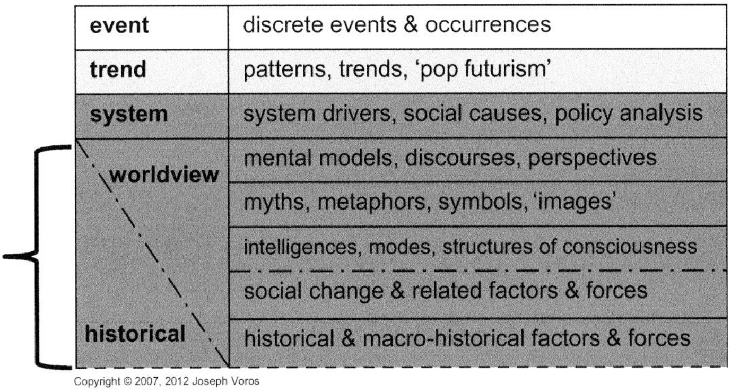

event	discrete events & occurrences
trend	patterns, trends, 'pop futurism'
system	system drivers, social causes, policy analysis
worldview	mental models, discourses, perspectives
	myths, metaphors, symbols, 'images'
	intelligences, modes, structures of consciousness
	social change & related factors & forces
historical	historical & macro-historical factors & forces

Fig. 5 The placement of frameworks of understanding (and anticipation) in the GFP framework

structure the interpretation phase of the GFP, but others are of course possible. One has considerable freedom to create whatever degree of depth one wishes to use within the interpretation phase, depending upon its suitability for the particular foresight engagement. The key point is that the contextual framework of understanding chosen for the scope of futures thinking will condition the degree and scope of foresight analysis that emerges when using explicitly prospective methods or thinking during prospection.

An important observation that should be made here regarding the levels or layers in the interpretation phase is that they have longer "characteristic timeframes for change" the deeper they lie. For example, pop-/litany-level trends have a shorter "half-life of change" (so to speak, to borrow an idea from radiation physics) than the deeper system drivers and social causes. These in turn have shorter change half-lives than worldviews, which may be shorter again than those of the myth or metaphor which may underpin or lie at the heart of these worldviews. Changes or transformations in consciousness may take decades or centuries, while macrohistorical change may take many centuries. The exact numerical timescales are not as important as the simple realization that an understanding of the effects or dynamics in deeper layers provides for a correspondingly longer potential "casting forward" of these dynamics into the future – what Bertrand de Jouvenel (1967, p. 45) called "jetties":

> the future is not known through the guesswork of the mind, but through social efforts, more or less conscious, to cast 'jetties' out from the established order and into the uncertainty ahead.

The flip side of this approach to "casting forward," though, is that a commensurately lower degree of detail exists within the deeper layers than within the higher. Macrohistorical change is of the "broad sweep of history" type, while pop-level trends tend to be rather more detailed and specific, albeit highly transient when compared to macrohistorical forces. Thus the relatively longer change half-life of a deeper layer or level may provide for a potentially longer "casting forward" into the future than a shallower stratum, but with correspondingly less detail.

In this way, deeper interpretation not only clarifies and may generate deeper understanding about current reality and how it has come to be, but may more deeply inform thinking about potential future reality. In other words, the deeper the degree of analysis of interpretive frameworks carried out in the interpretation phase, the better founded and grounded the prospection phase will likely be. In essence, the deeper you go in interpretation, the further forward you can "cast" during prospection, but not necessarily to a high degree of detail. Big History provides one very powerful anticipatory framework to "cast forward" quite a long way.

The Place for Big History and Other "Macro"-perspectives "Beyond" Earth

In the words of the International Big History Association (2012), Big History "seeks to understand the integrated history of the Cosmos, Earth, Life, and Humanity, using the best available empirical evidence and scholarly methods."

Nonetheless, when considered deeply, it is clear that Big History is ultimately concerned with the history of just *one* planet – ours – among the trillion or so that are now thought to exist in the Milky Way Galaxy, not to mention the billions of trillions that can thereby be inferred to exist in the wider observable universe. Thus, as suggested at the beginning of this chapter, it can be considered a single case in the even larger context of the unfolding of the broad scenario of Cosmic Evolution, as an idiographic example of how that broad quasi-nomothetic process has played out on this particular planet (Chaisson 2001, 2007, 2008; Delsemme 1998; Jantsch 1980). Moreover, as was also suggested earlier, it is easy to imagine other planets where life, and perhaps even intelligence, has arisen, as the Cosmic Evolutionary scenario has unfolded there, possibly giving rise to their own variant of Big History. A natural subset of the study of Cosmic Evolution is the multidisciplinary field of Astrobiology (e.g., Chyba and Hand 2005; Domagal-Goldman et al. 2016; Mix et al. 2006), the study of the possibilities for life in the universe, which also includes an associated subfield, SETI, the Search for Extraterrestrial Intelligence (e.g., Ekers et al. 2002; Harrison 2009; Morrison et al. 1979; Shklovskii and Sagan 1966; Shostak 1995; Tarter 2001, 2004; Tarter et al. 2010). So, one can imagine an expanding set of nested fields of study, beginning with Big History – the history of our own small "pale blue dot" (Sagan 1995) – enfolded by Astrobiology/SETI, the study of how life may arise in the universe and the search for intelligent forms of it, and encompassed by Cosmic Evolution, the study of how our universe as a whole has changed over the course of deep cosmic time. Whether there is a still-further enfoldment of our own universe within an even larger "multiverse" of other universes is a fascinating open question currently receiving some attention among cosmologists (e.g., Dick 2009; Hawking and Mlodinaw 2010).

Accordingly, if we now extend our view of the bottommost layer of the layering schema shown in Fig. 5 – the "historical" – we can see in Fig. 6 how Big History,

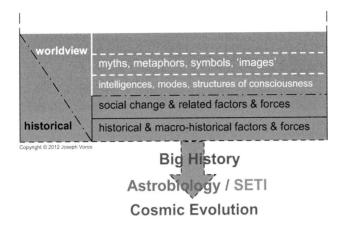

Fig. 6 The location of "Big History" and related macro-perspectives in the GFP framework

Astrobiology and SETI, and Cosmic Evolution find their places as the deepest and grandest frameworks of understanding that currently exist and of which we are now aware.

With the broad framework of the GFP and the place of Big History within it so laid out, we are now ready to use it as the basis for prospection to explore some broad-brush-stroke contours of the coming global future.

Using Big History for Global Foresight

There are several ways that Big History can be used for prospective thinking about the future of human civilization at the macroscale. One is through applying the fundamental idea of increasing material-energetic complexity, which is an influential view in Big History, and for which Jantsch was a major pioneer. This is the view we will follow up here in detail (drawn from Voros 2013). Interestingly, although we cannot pursue it any further now, Jantsch himself noted that "anticipation" arises as an emergent property of increasing complexity in the realm of cognition and consciousness (see his Fig. 40 and the accompanying discussion, Jantsch 1980, p. 208ff).

A second way to use Big History is through a combination of Jantsch's view of material-energetic complexity coupled with consciousness, due in no small part to the work of the philosopher of consciousness Ken Wilber (1995). In this view, material-energetic complexity in the directly measureable physical-empirical "objec-tive" realm is broadly correlated with commensurate complexity of "interiority" in the "lived experience" of the "subjective" realm. A third way is to use the fact that Big History can be "situated" as a sub-case of Astrobiology and SETI in the broad conception depicted in Fig. 6. Both of these latter approaches have been briefly considered elsewhere (Voros 2012a, b), while a more detailed exploration of one possible Astrobiology/SETI trajectory "beyond" Big History has also been undertaken (Voros 2014, 2015). The interested reader is referred to those sources for more detail.

In Eric Chaisson's approach to Cosmic Evolution, he considers seven major "epochs" of increasing material-energetic complexity in the unfolding of the evolution of the cosmos: particulate, galactic, stellar, planetary, chemical, biological, and cultural (Chaisson 2007). An interactive website based on his body of work over decades also adds an eighth epoch, "future evolution," where "the cosmic-evolutionary scenario is extended in time" (Chaisson 2008). It forms a broad palette for anticipations of how aspects of the scenario of Cosmic Evolution may further unfold.

In David Christian's approach to Big History, he considers eight major "thresholds" of this increasing material-energetic complexity: the origin of the universe, the first stars and galaxies, the formation of chemical elements, the formation of the Earth and solar system, the arising of life, the arising of humanity, the transition to agriculture, and the "modern revolution"(Christian 2004, 2008). Clearly, these eight thresholds can be seen to fit within the seven epochs described above, albeit with an obvious emphasis on the cultural epoch, as his telling of the account is framed from the perspective of an historian not an astronomer. The question of the future is also considered in Christian's work (Christian 2004, Chap. 15) and, indeed, in the work of other Big Historians as well (e.g., Brown 2008a, Chap. 13; Niele 2005, Chap. 7; Spier 2010, Chap. 8).

If our interest in the coming future is focused on humanity and human civilization at the global scale, then our contemplations of "Epoch 8" naturally find expression in the activity of attempting to characterize the unfolding of global dynamics over the next few decades and centuries. Given that our present civilization has arisen over the last few centuries following the emergence of "Threshold 8" – based upon the ever-increasing use of nonrenewable fossil fuel energy – as a futurist I naturally find myself thinking about what the *next* threshold of Big History might be; when these fuels are either much less, or perhaps even no longer, easily available for our use; or if they are in the process of being replaced by other primary sources of energy. This will no doubt be a major energy transition, one of only a few in world history (Niele 2005; Smil 1994). Vaclav Smil (2010b, p. viii) has observed that such energy transitions are "inherently protracted" and "usually . . . take decades to accomplish." This will surely have profound implications for our present civilization, so it would seem wise to undertake some serious foresight-based anticipatory thinking in order to begin to prepare for the consequences arising from such a change in the global energy system.

This, then, is the key logical starting point of our current futures exploration based on Big History: to recognize that there *will be* a time in the future when a *new* Big History threshold has been crossed – one where fossil fuels are no longer the primary source of energy powering human societies; what we might therefore call "Threshold 9." One wonders then what forms human society might take and what the effect will be on social complexity that is based on different sources of energy than these. Will it continue to increase in new and emergent ways owing to the discovery of newer more energy-dense sources of energy? Or will social complexity perhaps be reduced to relatively simpler lifeways due to the availability of only less-dense energy sources? It is prudent to consider deeply what may happen to human civilization when easy access to these finite sources of energy inevitably begins to tighten in the not-too-distant future. Thus, in our present contemplations of Epoch 8, we find ourselves focusing upon and "profiling" Threshold 9.

In what follows, in order to set the context, the main "human" thresholds – 6, 7, and 8 – are very briefly considered from the perspective of energy use. Since post-Threshold 8 modern industrial civilization is so overwhelmingly based on easy access to cheap abundant fossil fuel-based energy, confronting the uncomfortable question of what comes *after* such easy access would be aided considerably by some sort of organizing framework to guide our thinking. To this end, Dator's four "generic" archetypal futures are examined to see how they can be used to "contour" our thinking about the implications for the longer-term human future which arise from considering this far-reaching question. We then briefly examine past dynamics in an earlier threshold to look, by analogy, for potential insights into the upcoming transition period, and end by reflecting on how we may need to prepare ourselves for the coming transition to a post-fossil fuel-based civilization.

Reviewing the "Human" Thresholds

In David Christian's "thresholds" conception of Big History, the three thresholds which pertain to humanity and so are of most direct interest to us here are Threshold 6, some 200–300 millennia ago (in the Paleolithic Era) when our species *Homo sapiens* emerged as distinct from other closely related hominines; Threshold 7, some 10–11 millennia ago (the transition into the Agrarian Era) when humans began changing their main approach to making a living from foraging to farming; and Threshold 8, some two to three centuries ago (the transition into the Modern Era) when humans began to utilize more extensively the energy stored in highly energy-dense fossil fuels, in their many social, economic, and other activities.

At Threshold 6, it appears that gaining access to the (chemical) energy stored in foodstuffs is simply a "given" as the primary goal of biological survival. In this sense, from the point of view of energy use, it would seem to differ little from Threshold 5, the emergence of life on Earth. It is possible to argue, however, that perhaps *the defining aspect* of Threshold 6 is the emergence with physiologically modern humans of what appears to be a greatly expanded ability to *utilize information*, brought about through increases in brain size and perhaps also through changes in the brain's structural organization, as well as other physical changes, such as the development of more refined vocal capabilities. This ability to process (through cognition), store (via memory), and transmit information (via speech and/or symbols), from individual to individual, would seem to be *the* major disjunction that marks this as a threshold. Christian has argued at length in many places that it is the capacity for what he has called *collective learning* that is the defining characteristic of our species (e.g., Christian 2010). That capacity is very likely founded upon this *intensification of the capacity for information processing*, something noted in several places by Jantsch, and manifested in the interaction of the individual and social domains of human groups as an enhanced ability for symbolic informational exchange, which Christian has identified as the capacity for collective learning.

Following the human migrations that ultimately extended to all major landmasses except Antarctica, human freedom to range widely into hitherto unutilized territory eventually began to become more constrained, leading to an increasing "intensification" of the use of existing lands rather than simply extending presence into newer lands ("extensification"). This transition of techno-economic base from foraging to agriculture – Threshold 7 – seems to have been a fairly gradual – and possibly initially unwelcome – process (Brown 2008a, Chap. 5; Christian 2004, Chap. 8). Here the utilization of environmental resources and energy also intensified, as humans domesticated plants and animals, and subsequently began to deliberately harness wind and water energy.

By Threshold 8, human energy usage had begun to unlock the stored solar energy encapsulated in long-dead organisms – the "fossil fuels" made up of peats, coals, crude oils, and some natural gases. The much higher energy densities (energy per unit mass) of these fuels, compared to previously utilized biomass fuels and dispersed forms of renewable energy, made them very attractive, as did their relative abundance (Smil 1994, p. 153 and 219), as well as their relative ease of accumulation or extraction. Efficiencies of energy use have also improved markedly over the last several centuries, from less than 5% in open wood fires to 94–97% for modern gas-fired space heaters (Smil 2010b, pp. 7–8). Today almost every aspect of the modern industrialized world has become utterly dependent upon fossil fuels. Smil (1994) has called this dependence "fossil-fueled civilization," while Niele (2005) has even characterized modern fossil fuel-using and fuel-dependent human beings as a distinct subspecies: *Homo sapiens carbonius*.

What Comes After "Fossil-Fueled Civilization"?

But these luxuriantly energy-dense nonrenewable fossil fuels obviously cannot last forever. (Of course, on the timescale of Big History, strictly speaking these fuels *are* renewable, but only on timeframes beyond any practical utility for humans, being on the order of tens to hundreds of millions of years. Thus, for all *practical* human purposes, they are *effectively* nonrenewable.) At some stage, access to fossil fuel energy will inevitably face a severe bottleneck of availability and then an overall decline. The energy infrastructure that powers contemporary industrial civilization, and which is hugely interdependent with and upon the social systems and institutions that are themselves powered by it, will then undergo a crisis of stability which will have a flow-on effect to industrial civilization itself.

A large number of contemporary writers have examined this emerging civilizational crisis, generally framed around climate change, energy decline, or economic instability (e.g., Ahmed 2010; Brown 2008b, 2011; Greer 2008; Heinberg 2010; Heinberg and Lerch 2010; Holmgren 2009; Kunstler 2005; Lynas 2008; Roberts 2005; Slaughter 2010). The investigation undertaken by Nafeez Ahmed (2010) is particularly notable for its attempt to look beyond disciplinary boundaries and specializations to examine the many mutually reinforcing interactions between the various crises that different experts focus upon, as well as the identification of 11 systemic-level "structural" issues that will need to be urgently addressed if we are to transition smoothly to what has been called a "post-carbon civilization" (e.g., Ahmed 2010; Heinberg and Lerch 2010). There are many, many recent and contemporary commentators around the "peak oil" (e.g., Hall and Klitgaard 2012, Chap. 15), "peak energy," or even "peak everything" (Heinberg 2010) debate, with many arguing positions both pro and con; far too many to list here. In sketch, though, the "con" position usually tends to counter to the "pro" position, which argues that easy access to energy is rapidly running out, by claiming that there are vast reserves still left in the ground which will last many decades or centuries yet or that some new technological innovation in the future will surely occur to mitigate the problem.

But, on a Big History timescale, the next few decades or centuries are only a momentary "blip" in the overall trajectory of the human species and planet Earth. On this scale, the availability of highly concentrated energy-dense fossil fuels is but a "brief anomaly" (Floyd 2012) in the long history of the Earth, so a properly diachronic view of human and Earth history needs to look well beyond the present "peak" debates to the longer term when fossil fuels are no longer so readily available. Thus the question of what effect the running down of fossil-fueled energy systems will have on the structure and complexity of human civilization is a genuinely serious one which deserves somewhat better than to be willfully ignored, deferred to future generations, or wished-away through fairy-tale reliance upon a hoped-for miraculous technological salvation.

That is why the futures thinking approach based on Big History taken here is to imagine a time in the future when fossil fuels have either effectively run out or, at the very least, that our fossil-fueled civilization has run out of easy access to these fuels and is increasingly based on other primary sources of energy. It is this that I am calling "Threshold 9" – a time in the future, when the predominant sources of energy powering human societies are no longer fossil fuels. This is a way to bypass the sometimes rather heated and often unproductive current argumentation about energy scarcity, locked as it is in *a present-moment perspective*, to simply acknowledge that fossil fuels *are* indeed finite – something which no one could seriously argue against – and use *that incontestable fact* as our foundational starting point to seek to generate insights about the coming global longer-term future. This has the important effect of enabling us to avoid getting "stuck" in the present debates about the imminent coming, or not, of "peak oil" or "peak energy" and to instead simply take up a stance in the farther future when these debates will be over because they are moot. This is an example of a "discontinuous" method of thinking about the future: we "escape" from the tyranny of the present, and of limited-imagination extrapolations based on our constrained view of the present, by purposefully "jumping" to a point in the future (Voros 2006a). From such a *future* perspective, we are then able to "look back with different eyes" (as it were) to see in a different way what sort of future-history trajectories might emerge from our current situation.

Four Generic "Images" of the Future

So, where to from here? How can we begin to seriously examine alternative futures for our present civilization on a Big History timescale? James Dator has studied the ways that different cultural groups and societies think about the future. According to him, all ideas about – or "images" of – the future can be grouped into four broad generic archetypal classes (e.g., Dator 1998, 2002). These four archetypal futures can be considered a more nuanced and extended expression of a simpler two-class approach, comprising (i) extrapolative evolution, where the system dynamics are assumed to continue relatively smoothly, and (ii) disjunctive revolution, where the dynamics are assumed to deviate sharply from smooth continuity (Voros 2006a). They are as follows:

- *Continuation* – the current historical trajectory continues, most usually conceived of as continued economic growth.
- *Collapse* – a breakdown of the social order due to one or more of a number of possible causes, such as economic instability, environmental overload, resource depletion, moral degeneration, military conflict such as an external attack or internal civil war, meteor/comet impact, etc.
- *Disciplined or constrained society* – a society organized around some set of overarching constraining values, whether ancient, traditional, ideological, natural, environmental, God given, etc.
- *Transformational society* – which sees the end of current forms of behavior, beliefs, norms, or organization and the emergence of new forms (rather than a return to older or traditional ones, as above), possibly even including intelligent life-forms. The two main sub-variants are "high-tech" (technological) and "high-spirit" (spiritual/consciousness) transformation.

Scoping Future Dynamics

These four archetypal futures provide a useful structure for thinking about the future of societies in general. But let us now choose "energy availability" as the organizing principle or focus of examination through this framework to see what potential insights we might be able to extract from this particular analysis about the future dynamics of the world system.

Continuation

Much of what is known as the "technoliberal optimist" literature (Wagar 1991) assumes that things in general will simply continue improving as they have been for the last two or three centuries or so, guided by the further spread of democratic ideals, unfettered free enterprise, and unbounded technological progress (e.g., Diamandis and Kotler 2012; Schwartz et al. 2000). And it makes perfect sense from a straightforward (if somewhat naïvely unsophisticated) application of "extrapolative evolution" (Voros 2006a) of the world system's dynamics and technological changes over the past few centuries. The *continuation* archetype characterizes precisely this viewpoint. It takes as its baseline the historical trajectory of industrial civilization since it emerged, and simply extends this trend line into the future as *the* single *projected* future (as in Fig. 4). Therefore, in this view, we can expect ever more economic growth and ever more members of humanity to be lifted out of poverty as "progress" continues to improve the lot of humankind.

This admittedly quite attractive view of the future of human history is fairly prevalent – and not without some basis (e.g., Millennium Project 2012) – not only in the OECD countries, who stand to remain in their present comfortable lifestyles, but also in many industrializing nations, who sense that there is much to be gained as they seek to attain the living conditions and lifestyles of the richer industrialized countries. Unfortunately, such an uncritical extrapolation of past trends into the future is based upon the (usually unchallenged) assumption that the deeper underlying system dynamics which have made this possible will also continue into the future. These system dynamics have to a very large extent been based upon the energy sources fueling industrial civilization – dynamics which, as we have noted above, are quite literally running out of fuel.

Thus, regrettably, the *continuation* scenario for economic growth and well-being is almost certainly a phantom based on the (most likely) delusional assumption that easy access to cheap, abundant energy will certainly continue without abatement. Barring a technological breakthrough – which puts us into the high-tech transformation subclass of the *transformational society* archetype, to be described below – such an anodyne view of the future is not sustained by the currently available evidence. Indeed, as mentioned above already, the preponderance of emerging evidence seems to point to the inevitable decline of easy access to abundant, concentrated sources of energy (e.g., Niele 2005; Smil 1994, 2010a, b, and many other contemporary works, including those cited earlier), with the result that *continuation* cannot be sustained beyond a fairly brief time into the future – if at all – and certainly not on the Big History timescale we are utilizing as our basis for anticipatory prospection.

My point here is not to argue nor necessarily to disagree with the optimists who assume that we will find a positive way forward, but simply to note that this *cannot be assumed* as a natural or inevitable continuation of the past. Rather, it *will* require some kind of innovation or breakthrough for this to occur – as Richard Heinberg (2009) puts it, we are "searching for a miracle" – and *that* is the key point that needs to be borne in mind. It is akin to basing a retirement plan on the assumption that one will simply win the lottery (again) when it becomes necessary to do so in order to be able to keep on making a living. It would of course be quite nice and very welcome! However, it is by no means certain and is probably not the wisest strategy to pursue for one's long-term future. It is perhaps for the best to at least have a credible backup plan, "just in case."

Collapse

In contrast to the "business-as-usual" projected endless-growth mind-set, there exists a considerable literature dealing with what may happen when energy sources, usually abbreviated to just "oil," begin to run dry (e.g., Brown 2008b; Kunstler 2005; Roberts 2005) or when the biosphere can no longer tolerate and absorb the stresses that human civilization is placing upon it by burning them (e.g., Brown 2011; Diamond 2005; Farnish 2009; Lynas 2008; Meadows et al. 2004). This is precisely the *collapse* archetype, although variants of the other subclasses of this class also exist, such as asteroid impact (e.g., Chapman 2004; Collins et al. 2005; Schweickart et al. 2008). Of course, from the perspective of Big History, this latter possibility is not as farfetched and improbable a "wild card" (Petersen 1997, 1999) as some people may think, not only since we owe the ascent of mammals over large reptiles in significant part to just such an event 65 million years ago (e.g., Alvarez 1997) but also because there has actually been an impact in the very recent past that could have had devastating effects had it hit densely populated areas – the Tunguska Impact of 1908 (Di Martino et al. 1998; Gasperini et al. 2007). Had this occurred during the Cold War, one wonders what the consequences might have been or indeed might still be if any similar future impact blast during a time of high international tension is mistaken for a nuclear detonation (Sagan 1980, p. 76). The Chelyabinsk bolide in early 2013 was a minor example of this, and a rather lucky escape, too.

The *collapse* archetype came to wide popular attention with the publication of Jared Diamond's (2005) eponymous best seller, which continues a tradition of scholarly study of the collapse of complex societies in history that includes the important earlier work of Joseph Tainter (1990). However, the concept of "collapse" itself is a somewhat imprecise one and carries a certain connotation of rapidity that may not be entirely useful for our current purposes. As some scholars have noted, from the present we tend to see the historical "collapses" of the distant past through a greatly foreshortened perspective, which can make even very drawn-out processes seem somewhat abrupt from this vantage point. For example, the "collapse" of the Western Roman Empire is generally thought to have taken some three centuries or so to occur (e.g., Tainter 1990). To those living through it, however, it would hardly have been noticeable over a lifetime, let alone experienced as the kind of rapid decline which the term "collapse" connotes.

From the perspective of the longer-term human future on a Big History timescale, the end of fossil-fueled industrial civilization may well be viewed similarly as a "collapse," due to the same foreshortening of timescales that we ourselves experience when looking to the past. But, on our *own* timeframe – the timeframe of our individual lives and those of our immediate descendants and subsequent generations – we will almost certainly not experience this as a rapid "collapse" in the sense that the term is commonly used. (The question of how to meaningfully and rigorously use such "collapses," "shocks," "wild cards," or similar "discontinuities" in futures thinking is and remains a difficult one (Hiltunen 2006; van Notten et al. 2005).) Rather, there will almost certainly be a kind of "envelope" of declining fossil fuel energy availability, which will shape the contours of the degree of complexity that is possible for human civilization. Thus while this might eventually be considered a "collapse" by historians from the farther future, if any there be, it will almost certainly not take place on the same timeframe as other more rapid events which might more fittingly merit the term "collapse," such as nuclear war or asteroid impact.

For this reason, some commentators conceive of the end of fossil-fueled industrial civilization due to energy scarcity not in the "rapid" terms of a "collapse" but more along the lines of a drawn-out "decline" or "descent" to an eventual new form of societal organization with a techno-economic base founded upon renewable forms of energy – notable examples being John Michael Greer (2008, 2009), David Holmgren (2009), and Richard Heinberg (2010). Of course, other forms of rapid societal collapse may also occur – acute environmental disasters, sudden economic recessions or depressions, and unexpected social upheavals and unrest – and they should of course also be borne in mind. But our present futures assessment is based around a focus on energy availability and the implications for social complexity that such availability allows. This therefore suggests not a sudden rapid "apocalyptic"-type end to fossil fuel energy sources but rather a more gradual decline contoured by a narrowing energy-availability "envelope" as we inevitably move down the descending side of the empirically derived bell-shaped Hubbert curve which was initially developed to describe oil production (e.g., Hall and Klitgaard 2012). There are some commentators who, perhaps wryly, even look upon the coming decline as an opportunity (e.g., Homer-Dixon 2006; Orlov 2008).

Disciplined/Constrained Society

The notion of constraints on what human society can do being forced upon it by relative energy scarcity can also be considered an unusual twist on the *disciplined/constrained society* archetype. In essence, at the end of the energy descent process, human civilization is in this case constrained not by the social values held by the majority of the populace (i.e., by an "endogenous" constraint), which is the more usual form of this archetype, but by the fact that cheap abundant energy is no longer easily available for use *by* the society – an *exogenous* constraint. The fact that most forms of this archetype have generally been of the "internal values" kind may be indicative of how pervasive the underlying (and unexamined) assumptions of abundant energy, continued progress, and lack of constraints on recent societies and human ambition have been. The negative reactions to the observations and policy response explorations made, for example, by the authors of *The Limits to Growth* (Meadows et al. 1972; Meadows et al. 2004) are a telling case in point, and the almost-gleeful manner in which this work was systematically and deliberately misrepresented and widely ridiculed makes for blood-boiling and blood-chilling reading for anyone wanting to influence global public policy (Bardi 2008, 2011). This is all the more ironic since subsequent follow-up work tracking the actual trajectory of human civilization – as it has compared to the "baseline" "business-as-usual" "do-nothing-differently" "standard run" of *The Limits to Growth* – shows that global civilization is *right on track* for the resulting baseline "overshoot and collapse" scenario to unfold, essentially right on schedule (Turner 2008, 2014). We seem to have blithely wasted the very narrow window of opportunity we would have had to avert this future which heeding the message of *The Limits to Growth* might have afforded us (Randers 2012). Perhaps the vindictively gleeful ridicule was somewhat premature, and it would appear that the voices who so delightedly and loudly did so are rather less vocal these days. A related "constraint"-type work from around the same time which also garnered negative reactions was *The Population Bomb* (Ehrlich 1971), and it too might also prove rather unwelcomely prescient. In this regard, we observe here that there has been a stabilization of the so-named historical "Malthusian" population collapse cycles which occurred prior to the modern revolution (Christian 2004), as those appear to have been driven primarily by inabilities for agricultural productivity to meet the consumption needs of human societies. This has not been so large a problem since the "energy bonanza" of Threshold 8 – pandemic disease events and warfare notwithstanding – although with energy scarcity and resource constraints again looming in the future, it may be that such Malthusian cycles might once again make an unwelcome mirror-image return to the long view of human history. It is certainly something that *The Limits to Growth* studies portend, as well.

Greer (2009) outlines a series of stages through which he argues our civilization's "long descent" (Greer 2008) will likely pass – from our current "abundance economy" based on still relatively freely available high-density fossil fuel energy, to a "scarcity industrialism" wherein the constraints on society are becoming increasingly prevalent, to an age of "salvage" where earlier infrastructure is dismantled and reused due to an increasing difficulty of manufacturing new materials, and ultimately the move to a new "ecotechnic" age, some one to three centuries or so hence, based on sustainable forms of techno-economy and organic agriculture. In all these stages, there is a high likelihood of considerable economic and human turmoil. Make no mistake, this is no "sweetness-and-light" transition to a Utopian paradise of blissful coexistence with nature (what is sometimes known in the literature as "ecotopia"), nor is it a return to Marshall Sahlins' (1972) somewhat idealized "original affluent society" of the Paleolithic. Rather, it is a process of *de*industrialization, with all of the problematic consequences that the winding back of many of the accomplishments of the last few centuries implies. This trajectory of what Greer (2008, *passim*) calls "catabolic collapse" is compared with similar cases from history, most especially the Mayan collapse, and his analysis is very aware of a Big History energy perspective, even if he does not explicitly name it as such.

These types of energy-constrained societies are a very important class of futures to be aware of, as I suspect they will become increasingly vital in guiding our collective thinking about the decline of readily available dense energy sources over the next decades and centuries. Greer is one of very few authors I am aware of writing about the next stages in human history which are expected to emerge on a timeframe of generations – as opposed to the more common timeframe of a few decades – as well as dealing with a disciplined/constrained society that has *not* totally and utterly "collapsed," which latter post-apocalyptic image is a common theme also. Another notable author is Warren Wagar (1991, 1999), whose future society is admittedly disciplined mainly by socialist values rather than by energy availability per se, as well as by the physical aftermath of a global nuclear war (i.e., a prior very abrupt "collapse"), and is itself merely a transitional stage on the way to an eventual "transformational" world civilization (see below). With respect to the coming "energy discipline," Smil's work provides an important "envelope function" of realistic energy system possibilities over the longer term which could be used to help guide our collective thinking – and, hopefully, collective *learning* (Christian 2010) – about the next transition in the configuration of our global energy system (Smil 2010a, b). And finally, drawing on Big History itself, perhaps we can make use of our understanding of what we might call the "anabolic" *ascent* or *rise* of modern industrial civilization over the past few centuries as a framework to generate some ideas and potential insights into the prospective "unwinding" processes of decline that may well lie ahead during our civilization's all-too-plausible "catabolic descent."

Transformational Society

Of course, there could always be some breakthrough or transformation that radically changes the nature and form of human society. These, Dator suggests, are usually conceived of as being either technological or spiritual/consciousness-based in nature. The case of The Singularity could be considered an intriguing "hybrid" form of these idealized types, wherein consciousness transfers itself onto a techno-logical substrate (e.g., Broderick 1997; Eden et al. 2012; Kurzweil 1999, 2006; Smart 2003). Let us consider the technology subtype first.

It is certainly true that technology has in the past radically altered humans' relationship with nature, especially our ability to utilize environmental energy. Thus, in this view, it will simply be another such technological advance that will mitigate the energy problems we currently face in prospect. There are several very well-known possibilities frequently mentioned in contemporary commentaries, so it will suffice here to simply mention a few of them very briefly.

Almost all renewable forms of energy – such as photovoltaic, wind, running water, and wind-generated wave energy – are ultimately based on the energy output of the Sun (Smil 2010a, b), which we must therefore fervently hope will continue to have a nice stable lifetime on the main sequence for a good while yet! The other main forms of renewable energy not derived wholly from the Sun are geothermal, to be discussed later, and tidal. The trouble with these otherwise attractive sources is that they are nowhere near as energy dense as fossil fuels. Electricity can be generated from a variety of sources, including renewable and, while therefore an attractive form of potentially cleaner energy, it is not necessarily suitable for all tasks – aircraft transport is a case in point.

Hydrogen, which is often mentioned in discussions of energy transitions, is only useful as a *means* for transporting energy, not as a *source*, although one can envisage, for example, a solar-powered conversion plant producing hydrogen gas from elec-trolyzing seawater, with a view to its application as a potential transport fuel. It has the distinct advantage of producing only gaseous water (i.e., steam) as a by-product of combustion – a greenhouse gas, certainly, but much less troublesome than carbon dioxide or methane, two of the main offenders. A transition to a hydrogen-based transport fuel system would require considerable re-working of existing fuel infra-structures, and – were it to even be feasible – there does not as yet appear to be the political will or commercial appetite to undertake such an extensive program of concerted action.

Fusion energy is also often assumed to be a potential clean energy gold mine, but it has consistently not made the progress that was being hoped for it in the latter part of the twentieth-century CE. Yet, despite this, it persists in the public consciousness, and – if we are being fair-minded – it just *might* turn out to be more substantial on the longer Big History timeframe we are considering. So if we are to remain alert to the existence of "wildcard" breakthroughs, we need to keep it somewhere in mind. There is also some hope held out for more attractive forms of nuclear *fission* energy, which, if the promise of, for example, thorium-based nuclear power is fulfilled – as opposed to the increasingly unpalatable uranium and its by-products – might be a more socially and politically acceptable way to act as a bridge to the fully renewable system we will almost certainly need to eventually create. The reader is referred to Smil (2010a, b) for a comprehensive analysis of many of the conventional forms of energy noted here.

Then there are the possibilities of some astonishing technological breakthroughs about which we are at present wholly ignorant and unable to even speculate. An ability to concentrate the more diffuse renewable forms of energy into higher densities might be just such a development. Or perhaps some entirely new "miraculous" source of energy is found, such as tapping the quantum vacuum energy of space-time, to give but one extreme example (Clarke 1999). I have suggested elsewhere that there is merit in entertaining "preposterous" futures ideas (Voros 2012b, 2015), so perhaps "cold fusion" can also be mentioned here, since Clarke dedicated his short story – albeit perhaps with tongue-in-cheek – to the two scientists who first announced it, but for which there has as yet not been any widely accepted experimental confirmation.

The other major variant of the *transformational society* is one of consciousness or spiritual transformation – some new form or aspect of human consciousness emerges and redefines our value systems, such that we become focused on "higher" goals that we currently pursue. A number of futurists have considered this from the point of view of either a contemporary transition to a new "expanded" worldview (e.g., Harman 1998) or from a sequence of changes over the next few centuries, which is precisely the timeframe we are using for considering Threshold 9. Thus, Wagar (1991, 1999), mentioned above, considers "three futures," which pass through the four major classes we have been discussing here, culminating in a more spiritually informed consciousness-based planetary civilization, while Duane Elgin also sees a transition to planetary civilization over the ensuing centuries, based upon an expanded awareness of our place in the universe (Elgin 2001, 2009). The question of the future of human consciousness itself is also an interesting focus of study, although much of this work is still emerging (see, e.g., Ghose 2003; Wilber 1999–2000, Wilber 2007).

It may be that it is just such a new sense of ourselves and of our place in the Cosmos that gives rise to the mind-set required to live within our energy means and might indeed be one of the main prerequisites for us to successfully make the transition to what Elgin (1994) has called "initial maturity" as a "sustainable species-civilization." Thus, it might be argued that Cosmic Evolution, Big History, and other related frameworks may themselves provide a foundation for a new more integrated worldview, onto which an almost spiritual dimension could be read. There are several authors who are, to varying degrees, pursuing something like this line of thought (e.g., Abrams and Primack 2011; Christopher 2013; Genet et al. 2009; Primack and Abrams 2006; Swimme and Tucker 2011). However, Carl Sagan – who could rightly be considered one of the early pioneers of the modern scientifically based worldview we now know as Cosmic Evolution or Big History (e.g., Sagan 1973, 1980) – maintained that *any* meaning or significance to our existence was to be found within *us* (Sagan 1995, p. 57):

> The significance of our lives and our fragile planet is then determined only by our wisdom and courage. *We* are the custodians of life's meaning. ... If we crave some cosmic purpose, then let us find ourselves a worthy goal.

Perhaps one such worthy goal could be for humanity to build toward a fully sustainable and wholly equitable global civilization. ...

Finally, it is perhaps fitting to end this discussion of a more cosmically aware integrative worldview by returning full circle to cosmic-evolutionary pioneer Erich Jantsch, whose decades-old work is still able to strengthen and deepen our understanding of the many material-energetic, informational, and complexity-related processes occurring in Cosmic Evolution and Big History (Jantsch 1980). His thoughts on what he called "the evolutionary vision" – which can help us to not only understand our past history and present place in the universe but also to confront our coming future through our disciplined anticipations – were published posthumously after his untimely death, as literally among his last words in print (Jantsch 1981, p. 213):

> The evolutionary vision is itself a manifestation of evolution. The reward for its elaboration will not only be a new (or partly revived) natural philosophy or an improved academic understanding of how we are interconnected with evolutionary dynamics at all levels, but also an immensely practical philosophy to guide us in a time of creative instability and major restructuration of the human world .... With such an orientation, science will also become more realistic and meaningful for the concerns of human life. It will be not merely an end product of human creativity, but a key to its further unfolding in all domains.

Lessons from Earlier Thresholds

Another approach to thinking about the future based in the "historical" level of the GFP (Figs. 5 and 6) arises from using as an interpretive framework an adapted form of "macrohistory," the study of how social systems change over time in search of patterns or even "laws" of social change (Galtung and Inayatullah 1997; Inayatullah 1998b; Voros 2006b). In this approach, one looks for regularities in the key dynamics of historical change and uses these as a way to seek insights into the situation being studied. In the context of our use here of the "thresholds" view of Big History, this would imply utilizing earlier thresholds to try to generate insights about the next one. I call this use of earlier dynamics as a trigger for seeking insights "reiterative analogy." There is naturally no assumption that the dynamics *will* repeat; we merely make use of some aspect or aspects of those dynamics as a cognitive trigger to try to generate new ideas and potential insights. Of course, the most recent threshold, Threshold 8 – which was the transition *to* wide-scale use of fossil fuels – was clearly the initial stimulus for thinking about the next threshold, Threshold 9, which I have thereby defined as a corresponding transition *away* from fossil fuels. Let us now, by way of further exploration, go back one further threshold to Threshold 7 and seek to draw some insights from considering the characteristics of that one.

Threshold 7 was characterized, in essence, by the transition from a techno-economic base of foraging to one of farming. This was a way to obtain food more reliably and predictably than relying upon simply finding it in the environment, although Paleolithic food gathering does seem likely to have been undertaken fairly methodically from existing knowledge of growth and seasonal cycles (Christian 2004), rather than being as haphazard as this brief characterization might suggest. Clearly, there is an analogy being suggested here between "food" and "energy," which is, one could argue, not unreasonable nor entirely unfounded.

If we consider our approach to energy today, we can see that for several centuries, we have effectively been "foraging" for fossil fuel energy by searching the environment to see where it may be located "just lying around," as it were. We have then "gathered" it by mining or other forms of extraction and then moved on to look for other new deposits when the ready supply has become exhausted or no longer able to yield commercially useful quantities. In this way, one can see a clear resonant parallel between the extensification of human foraging range during the Paleolithic Era and the increasingly extensive exploration of the Earth's surface for energy reserves during the Modern Era. In the late Paleolithic, we eventually ran out of new ranges to enter – extensification "ran down," as it were – and we were forced to settle down and intensify the production and harvesting of in situ food-energy sources in order to continue to make a living, which was precisely the transition to agriculture and food farming. This was probably not, as noted earlier, an easy – or even welcome – process, and not necessarily everyone automatically took to it enthusiastically. Similarly, in the late Modern Era, we again find ourselves running out of readily exploitable energy reserves – i.e., our energy-foraging extensification is starting to "run down" – and so we now once again find ourselves beginning to be forced to seek ways to intensify production and harvesting, this time of in situ "ambient" environmental (as opposed to fossil fuel-based) energy. We are being forced to become, as it were, "energy farmers," and, as before, this does not appear to be an easy, or indeed welcome, development!

There are further ideas that can be drawn out from this analogy. One intriguing thought is that, as certain geographical areas were found to be conducive to agriculture and farming *food* with the result that human populations were increasingly drawn to those areas in the transition to Threshold 7, so might there perhaps be certain new and different areas which are found to be conducive to farming *energy* in the transition to Threshold 9, so that human populations may increasingly be drawn to those regions. In effect, a demographic-geographic shift might take place to new centers of energy farming and the economic activities supported by it, analogously to the shift which took place in the early Agrarian Era for food farming. This will be an interesting potential dynamic to watch for.

One final idea to briefly consider here is whether there might be any potential analogy between conventional fossil fuel energy – given how it revolutionized human civilization and gave rise to Threshold 8 – and any other form of energy that may have been analogously "fossilized" in some way. What comes quickly to mind, of course, is geothermal energy, which has, in an admittedly fairly loose sense of the term, been fossilized from the time of the formation of the Earth and is due to a combination of the remnant heat of formation itself, as well as to the subsequent decay over time of radioactive elements present in the initial accretion disc that gave rise to the solar system. This "fossil heat" is, in effect, driving the (so to speak) "internal convection engine" which powers the tectonic movements that have had such an important role in Earth's long-term geological and geographical history, not to mention in the distribution of valuable minerals in the Earth's outer layers. This is an intriguing resonance with the role that the internal combustion engine has had in the Modern Era.

In the context of this futures assessment, my interest is in whether this nonsolar form of renewable energy could perhaps become an important source of power not only in the energetic sense but also in the geopolitical sense, given that it is not subject to the problems of intermittency that other renewables have, like solar or wind. (As before, strictly speaking, on the long view of Big History, geothermal energy is of course a finite resource, as is solar energy. But both can be expected to last for a *very* long time, with geothermal energy depletion only likely to become a problem on the same order of timescale as the post-main-sequence red-giant death of the Sun (i.e., some billions of years). One hopes humanity has found a way to move on before this becomes a pressing issue! In the meantime, we can treat both forms of energy as *effectively* indefinitely renewable or, at least, to a *very* good approximation!) Thus, in the same way that some countries have had considerable advantages conferred upon them from the geographical distribution of fossil fuel reserves – one thinks of OPEC, for example, the Organization of the Petroleum-Exporting Countries – it is interesting to wonder about whether, in an energy-constrained disciplined-society future, relatively easier access to the non-intermittent renewable energy from geothermal sources might also become a source of advantage for another group of countries. One might imagine a geothermal analogue to OPEC, perhaps an "OGAC" – an Organization of Geothermal-Accessing Countries – who use this geographical good fortune to their techno-economic advantage. If this access to geothermal energy were used to generate hydrogen, for example, then there could emerge a system of fuel distribution based on hydrogen that is analogous to the present system of oil trading and distribution, with perhaps the attendant geostrategic implications that would flow from that emergence. This, too, will be an interesting potential dynamic to watch for.

Concluding Remarks and Summary

These have been some preliminary exploratory ideas based upon the awareness that, as the fossil fuel-based energy sources which have powered industrial civilization since what one approach to Big History calls Threshold 8 begin to become scarcer, there is an increasingly urgent need to confront and make sense of the wider implications this fact has for our present civilization. This prospective new threshold in history – a time when fossil fuels are no longer the primary source of energy used to power human society – has been referred to here as "Threshold 9."

Why is this approach to anticipation useful? It is difficult to clearly see the present longer-term dynamics of the world system when we are still so completely immersed within them. So, as a futures thinking device to provide an entirely different perspective that is not, so to speak, "lost in the present," we instead look to a future time when these confusingly complex dynamics may have largely played themselves out and use that position as our vantage point from which to seek some clarity. In the current exploration, we were interested in the longer-term Big History view of the global future engendered by considering what an imagined prospective "Threshold 9" might look like. We then examined the shapes of some resulting conjectured *potential* futures to see what insights they might give us into what some of the important aspects of the present are that we will need to consider carefully as we move into the *actual* unfolding future. It is an oft-quoted aphorism that "hindsight is always '20-20'." In the approach taken here, we are, in essence, seeking to generate deeper insight into our present situation by taking a long-term foresight view based on a vantage point in the more distant future and then, so to speak, "looking back to the present" from that future-based perspective in order to generate, as it were, "artificial hindsight." This is obviously not a perfect process, but given the absence of practical time travel and the logical impossibility of future-revealing technology, it is currently among the most powerful approaches we have. Conducting the same thought experiment using different analytical frameworks would of course generate different ideas, so that many different perspectives could thereby be tapped and integrated in this way.

The most probable global trajectory emerging in prospect – barring a major rapid *collapse* episode such as nuclear war, asteroid impact or similar event, or a miraculous *transformational society* brought about by a stunning technological breakthrough – appears to be an energy system decline/descent over many human lifetimes to an eventual *disciplined/constrained society* where the discipline is imposed by much more limited access to energy than we have enjoyed for the past few centuries. The main point here is that our civilization's current energy-intensive lifeways can only continue, it seems, by way of some technological breakthrough. Many people already know this, of course, and fully expect it to occur, given so many earlier technological innovations in recent history. However, the crucial difference here in our time is that, whereas the remarkable technological innovations of the past several centuries have essentially relied upon easy access to sources of readily available energy, this time it is *access to energy itself* which is the major bottleneck and which requires the breakthrough. And *that* cannot be regarded or treated in the same way as earlier technical innovations, nor can any technical circumvention of this issue be simply assumed or unquestioningly relied upon to occur. So it is as well for us to remember to be cautiously skeptical about uncritical technological optimism.

While other possibilities remain open, and should of course always remain in consideration, a wise course of action would appear to be conducting detailed multi-perspectival multidisciplinary anticipatory research into both the underlying nature and emergent characteristics of a Big History threshold of this post-fossil fuel form. Indeed, the very concept of "profiling Threshold 9" – to get a general sense of the broad longer-term future trajectory of our planetary civilization – could be considered a useful orienting direction for an entire joint research program in Big History and Futures Studies scholarship, not only as a very interesting academic pursuit – which it most certainly would be – but also as an enormously prudent practical step toward *preparing* for the coming of Threshold 9. This program would involve reimagining all facets of human social organization from the perspective of utilizing primary energy sources that, while they may by that time be renewable, are nonetheless almost certainly likely to be much more diffuse and much less energy dense than those we currently have access to. It will be no small task to reconceptualize the entirety of human civilization in this way, as the example of the recent fundamental historical transition to modernity via the use of fossil fuels shows very clearly. These many facets would range from, among other things, agriculture, transport, domestic and industrial energy use (and probably, by then, large-scale in situ harvesting or production), climate adaptation, forms of work and organizational design, and so on, to perhaps the very nature of the human relationship with the Earth itself, as well as potential new worldviews and forms of consciousness, founded upon a reconnection with the natural world and the Cosmos at large. As Primack and Abrams (2006) have put it, to "think cosmically, act globally."

Yet if we do face the future squarely and prepare ourselves properly, we might just be able to guide this transition with some relative agency and dignified freedom to act, rather than find ourselves being unwillingly dragged kicking and screaming into a future where we may be forced to abandon much of what we have accomplished. As Bertrand de Jouvenel observed long ago (de Jouvenel 1967, p. 276):

> The proof of improvidence lies in falling under the empire of necessity. The means of avoiding this lies in acquainting oneself with emerging situations while they can still be molded, before they have become imperatively compelling. In other words, without [foresight] there is effectively no freedom of decision.

Whether our species' transition to Threshold 9 is dignified or not, skillful or not, orderly or not, or commended or not will depend very much on the seriousness of our anticipatory preparations and our commitment to the necessary actions. Let us hope that our eventual descendants, wherever they may be, will look favorably upon and approve of how we will ultimately choose to respond to the ever-looming crisis that our fossil-fueled civilization is now facing. Moreover, let us make it our number one and overriding civilizational priority, subsuming and subordinating all others, to ensure that we do everything *we* can, in order to ensure that *they* can. For, in the words of the late Warren Wagar (Marien 2005):

> We are the link between the traditional civilizations of a well-remembered past and the emergent world civilization. We stand between. If we break under the strain there will be no future. All posterity is in our keeping.

Let us therefore think, prepare and act with as much wisdom and foresight as we can possibly muster.

References

Abrams, N. E., & Primack, J. R. (2011). *The new universe and the human future: How a shared cosmology could transform the world*. New Haven: Yale University Press.

Ahmed, N. M. (2010). *A user's guide to the crisis of civilisation: And how to save it*. London: Pluto Press.

Alvarez, W. (1997). *T. rex and the crater of doom*. Princeton: Princeton University Press.

Amara, R. (1974). The futures field: Functions, forms, and critical issues. *Futures, 6*(4), 289–301. https://doi.org/10.1016/0016-3287(74)90072-X.

Amara, R. (1981). The futures field: Searching for definitions and boundaries. *The Futurist, 15*(1), 25–29.

Amara, R. (1991). Views on futures research methodology. *Futures, 23*(6), 645–649. https://doi.org/10.1016/0016-3287(91)90085-G.

Bardi, U. (2011). *The limits to growth revisited*. New York: Springer. https://doi.org/10.1007/978-1-4419-9416-5.

Bardi, U. (2008). Cassandra's curse: How "The Limits to Growth" was demonized. The Oil Drum Europe, 9 Mar 2008, viewed 29 Sept 2015. http://europe.theoildrum.com/node/3551.

Beck, D. E., & Cowan, C. C. (1996). *Spiral dynamics: Mastering values, leadership and change*. Malden: Blackwell.

Bell, W. (1997). *Foundations of futures studies* (Vol. 2). New Brunswick: Transaction Publishers.

Broderick, D. (1997). *The spike: How our lives are being transformed by rapidly advancing technologies*. Kew: Reed International Books.

Brown, A. (1999). Ten ways futurists can avoid being destroyed. *Futures Research Quarterly, 15*(2), 7–13.

Brown, C. S. (2008a). *Big history: From the big bang to the present*. New York: New Press.

Brown, L. R. (2008b). *Plan B 3.0: Mobilizing to save civilization*. New York: W.W. Norton & Company.

Brown, L. R. (2011). *World on the edge: How to prevent environmental and economic collapse*. New York: W.W. Norton & Company.

Brown, C. S. (2017). *Big history, small world: From the big bang to you*. Great Barrington: Berkshire Publishing Group.

Chaisson, E. J. (2001). *Cosmic evolution: The rise of complexity in nature*. Cambridge: Harvard University Press.

Chaisson, E. J. (2004). Complexity: An energetics agenda. *Complexity, 9*(3), 14–21. https://doi.org/10.1002/cplx.20009.

Chaisson, E. J. (2007). *Epic of evolution: Seven ages of the cosmos* (new paperback ed.). New York: Columbia University Press.

Chaisson, E. J. (2008). *Cosmic evolution: From the big bang to humankind*. Interactive web pages, https://www.cfa.harvard.edu/~ejchaisson/cosmic_evolution/.

Chapman, C. R. (2004). The hazard of near-Earth asteroid impacts on Earth. *Earth and Planetary Science Letters, 222*(1), 1–15. https://doi.org/10.1016/j.epsl.2004.03.004.

Checkland, P. B. (1999). *Systems thinking, systems practice: Includes a 30-year retrospective* (new ed.). Chichester: Wiley. Prev. ed. publ. 1981.

Choo, C. W. (1999). The art of scanning the environment. *Bulletin of the American Society for Information Science, 25*(3), 21–24.

Choo, C. W. (2002). *Information management for the intelligent organization: The art of scanning the environment* (3rd ed.). ASIST monograph series. Medford: Information Today.

Christian, D. (2004). *Maps of time: An introduction to big history.* Berkeley: University of California Press.

Christian, D. (2008). *Big history: The big bang, life on earth, and the rise of humanity* [audiovisual material], 48 lectures, 30 mins/lecture. Chantilly: The Teaching Company.

Christian, D. (2010). *Reinventing intelligence: Why collective learning makes humans so different* [conference presentation], 31m59s, Techonomy Conference, Lake Tahoe. August 2010.

Christian, D., Brown, C. S., & Benjamin, C. (2013). *Big history: Between nothing and everything.* Boston: McGraw-Hill Education.

Christopher, D. (2013). *The holy universe: A new story of creation for the heart, soul and spirit.* Santa Rosa: New Story Press.

Chyba, C. F., & Hand, K. P. (2005). Astrobiology: The study of the living universe. *Annual Review of Astronomy and Astrophysics, 43*(1), 31–74. https://doi.org/10.1146/annurev.astro.43.051804.102202.

Clarke, A. C. (1999). Improving the neighbourhood. *Nature, 402*(6757), 19. https://doi.org/10.1038/46906.

Clarke, A. C. (2000). *Profiles of the future: An inquiry into the limits of the possible* (Millennium ed.). London: Orion Books.

Collins, G. S., Melosh, H. J., & Marcus, R. A. (2005). Earth impact effects program: A web-based computer program for calculating the regional environmental consequences of a meteoroid impact on earth. *Meteoritics and Planetary Science, 40*(6), 817–840. https://doi.org/10.1111/j.1945-5100.2005.tb00157.x.

Dator, J. A. (1998). The future lies behind! Thirty years of teaching future studies. *American Behavioral Scientist, 42*(3), 298–319. Issue Title: 'Futures studies in higher education', JA Dator (ed.).

Dator, J. A. (Ed.). (2002). *Advancing futures: Futures studies in higher education.* Praeger studies on the 21st century. Westport: Praeger.

Dator, J. A. (2005). Foreword. In R. A. Slaughter, S. Inayatullah & J. M. Ramos (Eds.), *The knowledge base of futures studies* (Professional CD-ROM ed.). Brisbane: Foresight International.

de Jouvenel, B. (1967). *The art of conjecture.* London: Weidenfeld and Nicholson.

Delsemme, A. (1998). *Our cosmic origins: From the big bang to the emergence of life and intelligence.* Cambridge, UK: Cambridge University Press.

Di Martino, M., Farinella, P., & Longo, G. (1998). Foreword of the Tunguska issue. *Planetary and Space Science, 46*(2–3), 125. https://doi.org/10.1016/S0032-0633(97)00164-5. Issue Title: 'International Workshop Tunguska 96'.

Diamandis, P. H., & Kotler, S. (2012). *Abundance: The future is better than you think.* New York: Free Press.

Diamond, J. (2005). *Collapse: How societies choose to fail or survive.* London: Allen Lane (Penguin).

Dick, S. J. (2009). Cosmic evolution: History, culture and human destiny. In S. J. Dick & M. Lupisella (Eds.), *Cosmos and culture: Cultural evolution in a cosmic context* (pp. 25–59). NASA special publication SP-2009-4802. Washington, DC: National Aeronautics and Space Administration.

Domagal-Goldman, S. D., Wright, K. E., Adamala, K., Arina de la Rubia, L., Bond, J., Dartnell, L. R., et al. (2016). The astrobiology primer v2.0. *Astrobiology, 16*(8), 561–653. https://doi.org/10.1089/ast.2015.1460.

Eden, A. H., Moor, J. H., Søraker, J. H., & Steinhart, E. (Eds.). (2012). *Singularity hypotheses: A scientific and philosophical assessment.* Berlin: Springer. https://doi.org/10.1007/978-3-642-32560-1.

Ehrlich, P. R. (1971). *The population bomb.* London: Ballantine; Friends of the Earth; Pan.

Ekers, R. D., Cullers, D. K., Billingham, J., & Scheffer, L. K. (Eds.). (2002). *SETI 2020: A roadmap for the search for extraterrestrial intelligence.* Mountain View: SETI Institute. Foreword by Philip Morrison.

Elgin, D. (1994). Building a sustainable species-civilization: A challenge of culture and conscious-ness. *Futures, 26*(2), 234–245. https://doi.org/10.1016/0016-3287(94)90112-0. Issue Title: 'Visions of sustainability'.

Elgin, D. (2001). *Promise ahead: A vision of hope and action for humanity's future*. New York: HarperCollins.

Elgin, D. (2009). *The living universe: Where are we? Who are we? Where are we going?*. San Francisco: Berret-Koehler. Foreword by Deepak Chopra.

Farnish, K. (2009). *Time's up!: An uncivilized solution to a global crisis*. London: Green Books.

Floyd, J. (2012). Beyond this brief anomaly: An inquiry into energy and society, weblog, viewed 21 Mar 2012. http://beyondthisbriefanomaly.org.

Galtung, J., & Inayatullah, S. (Eds.). (1997). *Macrohistory and macrohistorians: Perspectives on individual, social, and civilizational change*. Westport: Praeger Publishers.

Gardner, H. (1993). *Multiple intelligences: The theory in practice*. New York: Basic Books.

Gasperini, L., Alvisi, F., Biasini, G., Bonatti, E., Longo, G., Pipan, M., et al. (2007). A possible impact crater for the 1908 Tunguska event. *Terra Nova, 19*(4), 245–251. https://doi.org/10.1111/j.1365-3121.2007.00742.x.

Gebser, J. 1985. *The ever-present origin*. Athens, OH: Ohio University Press.

Genet, C., Genet, R., Swimme, B., Palmer, L., & Gibler, L. (Eds.). (2009). *The evolutionary epic: Science's story and humanity's response*. Santa Margarita: Collins Foundation Press. Foreword by David Christian.

Ghose, A. (2003). *The future evolution of man: The divine life upon Earth*. Twin Lakes: Lotus Press.

Gilbert, D. T. (2006). *Stumbling on happiness*. New York: Knopf.

Gilbert, D. T., & Wilson, T. D. (2007). Prospection: Experiencing the future. *Science, 317*(5843), 1351–1354. https://doi.org/10.1126/science.1144161.

Graves, C. W. (1974). Human nature prepares for a momentous leap. *The Futurist, 8*(2), 72–85.

Greer, J. M. (2008). *The long descent: A user's guide to the end of the industrial age*. Gabriola Island: New Society Publishers.

Greer, J. M. (2009). *The ecotechnic future: Envisioning a post-peak world*. Gabriola Island: New Society Publishers.

Hall, C. A. S., & Klitgaard, K. A. (2012). *Energy and the wealth of nations: Understanding the biophysical economy*. New York: Springer. https://doi.org/10.1007/978-1-4419-9398-4.

Hancock, T., & Bezold, C. (1994). Possible futures, preferable futures. *Health Forum Journal, 37*(2), 23–29.

Harman, W. W. (1998). *Global mind change: The promise of the twenty-first century* (2nd ed.). San Francisco: Berrett-Kohler.

Harrison, A. A. (2009). The future of SETI: Finite effort or search without end? *Futures, 41*(8), 554–561. https://doi.org/10.1016/j.futures.2009.04.016. Issue Title: 'Space: The final frontier', WS Bainbridge (ed.)

Hawking, S. W., & Mlodinaw, L. (2010). *The grand design*. London: Random House/Bantam.

Heinberg, R. (2009). *Searching for a miracle: "Net energy" limits and the fate of industrial society*. San Francisco: Post-Carbon Institute and International Forum on Globalization.

Heinberg, R. (2010). *Peak everything: Waking up to the century of declines*. Gabriola Island: New Society Publishers.

Heinberg, R., & Lerch, D. (Eds.). (2010). *The post carbon reader: Managing the 21st century's sustainability crises*. Healdsburg, CA: Watershed Media.

Henchey, N. (1978). Making sense of futures studies. *Alternatives, 7*(2), 24–28.

Hiltunen, E. (2006). Was it a wild card or just our blindness to gradual change? *Journal of Futures Studies, 11*(2), 61–74.

Holmgren, D. (2009). *Future scenarios: How communities can adapt to peak oil and climate change*. White River Junction: Chelsea Green Publishing.

Homer-Dixon, T. F. (2006). *The upside of down: Catastrophe, creativity, and the renewal of civilization*. Washington, DC: Island Press.

Inayatullah, S. (1998a). Causal layered analysis: Poststructuralism as method. *Futures, 30*(8), 815–829. https://doi.org/10.1016/S0016-3287(98)00086-X.

Inayatullah, S. (1998b). Macrohistory and futures studies. *Futures, 30*(5), 381–394. https://doi.org/10.1016/S0016-3287(98)00043-3.

Inayatullah, S. (2002). Layered methodology: Meanings, epistemes and the politics of knowledge. *Futures, 34*(6), 479–491. https://doi.org/10.1016/S0016-3287(01)00075-1.

International Big History Association 2012. Web site home page, viewed 21-09-2012 http://www.ibhanet.org.

Jantsch, E. (1980). *The self-organizing universe: Scientific and human implications of the emerging paradigm of evolution*. New York: Pergamon Press.

Jantsch, E. (Ed.). (1981). *The evolutionary vision: Toward a unifying paradigm of physical, biological and sociocultural evolution*. Boulder: Westview Press.

Kunstler, J. H. (2005). *The long emergency: Surviving the end of oil, climate change, and other converging catastrophes of the twenty-first century*. New York: Grove Press. With a new Afterword by the author.

Kurzweil, R. (1999). *The age of spiritual machines: When computers exceed human intelligence*. Sydney: Allen & Unwin.

Kurzweil, R. (2006). *The singularity is near: When humans transcend biology*. New York: Penguin Books.

Lineweaver, C. H., Davies, P. C. W., & Ruse, M. (Eds.). (2013). *Complexity and the arrow of time*. Cambridge: Cambridge University Press.

Lynas, M. (2008). *Six degrees: Our future on a hotter planet*. Washington, DC: National Geographic Society.

Marien, M. (2005). Celebrating the life of futurist W. Warren Wagar. *The Futurist, 39*(2), 68.

Meadows, D. H. (2009). *Thinking in systems: A primer*. London: Earthscan. Edited by Diana Wright.

Meadows, D. H., Meadows, D. L., Randers, J., & Behrens, W. W. (1972). *The limits to growth: A report for the Club of Rome's project on the predicament of mankind*. New York: Universe Books.

Meadows, D. H., Randers, J., & Meadows, D. L. (2004). *Limits to growth: The 30-year update*. White River Junction: Chelsea Green Publ.

Millennium Project. (2012). State of the future index, web page, viewed 13 Oct 2012. http://www.millennium-project.org/millennium/SOFI.html.

Mix, L. J., Armstrong, J. C., Mandell, A. M., Mosier, A. C., Raymond, J., Raymond, S. N., et al. (2006). The astrobiology primer: An outline of general knowledge – Version 1, 2006. *Astrobiology, 6*(5), 735–813. https://doi.org/10.1089/ast.2006.6.735.

Molitor, G. T. T. (1977). How to anticipate public-policy changes. *Advanced Management Journal, 42*(3), 4–13.

Molitor, G. T. T. (2003a). Molitor forecasting model: Key dimensions for plotting the "patterns of change". *Journal of Futures Studies, 8*(1), 61–72.

Molitor, G. T. T. (2003b). *Power to change the world: The art of forecasting*. Bethesda: World Future Society. Spiral bound quarto.

Molitor, G. T. T. (2010). Timeline 22-step model for tracking and forecasting public policy change. *Journal of Futures Studies, 14*(3), 1–12.

Morrison, P., Billingham, J., & Wolfe, J. H. (Eds.). (1979). *The search for extraterrestrial intelligence*. New York: Dover Publications.

Niele, F. (2005). *Energy: Engine of evolution*. Amsterdam: Elsevier.

Orlov, D. (2008). *Reinventing collapse: The soviet example and American prospects*. Gabriola Island: New Society Publishers.

Petersen, J. L. (1997). The wild cards in our future: Preparing for the improbable. *The Futurist, 31*(4), 43–47.

Petersen, J. L. (1999). *Out of the blue: How to anticipate big future surprises* (2nd ed.). Lanham: Madison Books.

Primack, J. R., & Abrams, N. E. (2006). *The view from the center of the universe: Discovering our extraordinary place in the cosmos*. New York: Riverhead (Penguin).

Randers, J. (2012). The real message of the limits to growth: A plea for forward-looking global policy. *Gaia, 21*(2), 102–105.

Roberts, P. (2005). *The end of oil: On the edge of a perilous new world*. Boston: Houghton Mifflin Harcourt.

Sagan, C. (1973). *The cosmic connection: An extraterrestrial perspective*. New York: Doubleday.

Sagan, C. (1980). *Cosmos* (Illustrated 1st ed.). New York: Random House.

Sagan, C. (1995). *Pale blue dot: A vision of the human future in space*. London: Headline.

Sahlins, M. D. (1972). The original affluent society. In *Stone age economics* (pp. 1–40). New York: Aldine de Gruyter.

Schwartz, P., Leyden, P., & Hyatt, J. (2000). *The long boom: A vision for the coming age of prosperity*. London: Orion Publishing.

Schweickart, R. L., Jones, T. D., von der Dunk, F., & Camacho-Lara, S. (2008). *Asteroid threats: A call for a global response*. (Tok, J., Ed., ASE International Panel on Asteroid Threat Mitigation, Schweickart, R. L., Chair). Houston: Association of Space Explorers.

Shklovskii, I. S., & Sagan, C. (1966). *Intelligent life in the universe*. San Francisco: Holden-Day. Some versions have Sagan listed as the first author.

Shostak, G. S. (Ed.). (1995). *Progress in the search for extraterrestrial life: 1993 bioastronomy symposium, Santa Cruz, California, 16–20 August 1993*. San Francisco: Astronomical Society of the Pacific.

Slaughter, R. A. (1989). Probing beneath the surface: Review of a decade's futures work. *Futures, 21*(5), 447–465. https://doi.org/10.1016/0016-3287(89)90085-2.

Slaughter, R. A. (1996). Mapping the future: Creating a structural overview of the next 20 years. *Journal of Futures Studies, 1*(1), 5–25.

Slaughter, R. A. (1999). *Futures for the third millennium: Enabling the forward view*. Sydney: Prospect Media.

Slaughter, R. A. (2002). Beyond the mundane: Reconciling breadth and depth in futures enquiry. *Futures, 34*(6), 493–507. https://doi.org/10.1016/S0016-3287(01)00076-3.

Slaughter, R. A. (2010). *The biggest wake up call in history*. Brisbane: Foresight International.

Smart, J. (2003). Considering the singularity: A coming world of autonomous intelligence (A.I.). In H. F. Didsbury Jr. (Ed.), *21st century opportunities and challenges: An age of destruction or an age of transformation* (pp. 256–262). Bethesda: World Future Society.

Smil, V. (1994). *Energy in world history*. Boulder: Westview Press.

Smil, V. (2010a). *Energy myths and realities: Bringing science to the energy policy debate*. Washington, DC: American Enterprise Institute for Public Policy Research (distr. by Rowman & Littlefield, Lanham, MD, USA).

Smil, V. (2010b). *Energy transitions: History, requirements, prospects*. Santa Barbara: Greenwood Publishing Group.

Spier, F. (1996). *The structure of big history: From the big bang until today*. Amsterdam: Amsterdam University Press.

Spier, F. (2005). How big history works: Energy flows and the rise and demise of complexity. *Social Evolution and History, 4*(1), 87–135. Issue Title: 'Exploring the horizons of big history'.

Spier, F. (2010). *Big history and the future of humanity*. Chichester: Wiley-Blackwell.

Spier, F. (2011). Complexity in big history. *Cliodynamics: The Journal of Quantitative History and Cultural Evolution, 2*(1), 146–166.

Spier, F. (2015). *Big history and the future of humanity* (2nd ed.). Chichester: Wiley-Blackwell.

Swimme, B. T., & Tucker, M. E. (2011). *Journey of the universe*. New Haven: Yale University Press.

Tainter, J. A. (1990). *The collapse of complex societies*. Cambridge, UK: Cambridge University Press.

Taleb, N. N. (2007). *The black swan: The impact of the highly improbable*. New York: Random House.

Tarter, J. C. (2001). The search for extraterrestrial intelligence (SETI). *Annual Review of Astronomy and Astrophysics, 39*(1), 511–548. https://doi.org/10.1146/annurev.astro.39.1.511.

Tarter, J. C. (2004). Astrobiology and SETI. *New Astronomy Reviews, 48*(11–12), 1543–1549. https://doi.org/10.1016/j.newar.2004.09.019. Issue Title: 'Science with the Square Kilometre Array'.

Tarter, J. C., Agrawal, A., Ackermann, R., Backus, P., Blair, S. K., Bradford, M. T., et al. (2010). SETI turns 50: Five decades of progress in the search for extraterrestrial intelligence. In R. B. Hoover, G. V. Levin, A. Y. Rozanov, & P. C. W. Davies (Eds.), *Proceedings of SPIE 7819, instruments, methods, and missions for astrobiology XIII* (p. 781902). San Diego: SPIE - The International Society for Optical Engineering.

Taylor, C. W. (1990). *Creating strategic visions.* Carlisle: Strategic Studies Institute, US Army War College, Carlisle Barracks.

Turner, G. M. (2008). A comparison of the limits to growth with 30 years of reality. *Global Environmental Change, 18*(3), 397–411. https://doi.org/10.1016/j.gloenvcha.2008.05.001.

Turner, G. M. (2014). *Is global collapse imminent? An updated comparison of The Limits to Growth with historical data.* Melbourne: Melbourne Sustainable Society Institute, The University of Melbourne. http://sustainable.unimelb.edu.au/research-papers.

van der Heijden, K. (2005). *Scenarios: The art of strategic conversation* (2nd ed.). Chichester: Wiley.

van Notten, P. W. F., Sleegers, A. M., & van Asselt, M. B. A. (2005). The future shocks: On discontinuity and scenario development. *Technological Forecasting and Social Change, 72*(2), 175–194. https://doi.org/10.1016/j.techfore.2003.12.003.

Voros, J. (2001). Reframing environmental scanning: An integral approach. *Foresight, 3*(6), 533–552. https://doi.org/10.1108/14636680110697200.

Voros, J. (2003a). A generic foresight process framework. *Foresight, 5*(3), 10–21. https://doi.org/10.1108/14636680310698379.

Voros, J. (Ed.). (2003b). *Reframing environmental scanning: A reader on the art of scanning the environment,* Australian Foresight Institute monograph series Vol. 4. Melbourne: Swinburne University Press.

Voros, J. (2005). A generalised "layered methodology" framework. *Foresight, 7*(2), 28–40. https://doi.org/10.1108/14636680510700094.

Voros, J. (2006a). Introducing a classification framework for prospective methods. *Foresight, 8*(2), 43–56. https://doi.org/10.1108/14636680610656174.

Voros, J. (2006b). Nesting social-analytical perspectives: An approach to macro-social analysis. *Journal of Futures Studies, 11*(1), 1–21.

Voros, J. (2012a). *Complexity + Consciousness: A model of Big History based on self-organising complexity, incorporating consciousness.* Paper presented at Teaching and Researching Big History: Exploring a new scholarly field; the International Big History Association inaugural conference, Grand Valley State University, Grand Rapids, Michigan, 2–5 Aug.

Voros, J. (2012b). *Macro-prospection: Thinking about the future using macro- and Big History.* Presentation at Global Future 2045 International Congress, Moscow, 17–20 Feb.

Voros, J. (2013). Profiling "Threshold 9": Using Big History as a framework for thinking about the contours of the coming global future. In L. E. Grinin & A. V. Korotayev (Eds.), *Evolution: Development within Big History, evolutionary and world-system paradigms* (pp. 119–142), Evolution Almanac Vol. 3. Volgograd: Uchitel Publishing House.

Voros, J. (2014). Galactic-scale macro-engineering: Looking for signs of long-lived intelligent species, as an exercise in hope for our own. In L. Grinin, D. Baker, E. Quaedackers & A. Korotayev (Eds.), *Teaching and researching Big History: Exploring a new scholarly field* (pp. 283–304). Volgograd: Uchitel Publishing House. Selected papers from the inaugural International Big History Association Conference held at held at Grand Valley State University, Grand Rapids, Michigan, USA, 2–5 Aug 2012.

Voros, J. (2015). *The Anthropocene, "Threshold 9" and the Long-Term Future of Humankind*. Presentation at The Big History Anthropocene Conference: A Transdisciplinary Exploration, Big History Institute, Macquarie University, Sydney, 9–11 Dec 2015, Final session: 11 Dec 2015.

Voros, J. (2017). Big Futures: Macrohistorical perspectives on the future of humankind. In B. Rodrigue, L. Grinin & A. Korotayev (Eds.), *The way that Big History works: Cosmos, life, society and our future*, From Big Bang to galactic civilizations: A Big History anthology (vol. III). Delhi: Primus Books.

Wagar, W. W. (1991). *The next three futures: Paradigms of things to come*. New York: Greenwood Press.

Wagar, W. W. (1999). *A short history of the future* (3rd ed.). Chicago: University of Chicago Press. Afterword by Immanuel Wallerstein.

Wilber, K. (1995). *Sex, ecology, spirituality: The spirit of evolution*. Boston: Shambhala Publications.

Wilber, K. (1999–2000). *The collected works of Ken Wilber* (8 Vols). Boston: Shambhala Publications. Vols. 1–4 published 1999; Vols. 5–8 published 2000.

Wilber, K. (2000). *Integral psychology: Consciousness, spirit, psychology, therapy*. Boston: Shambhala Publications.

Wilber, K. (2007). *The integral vision: A very short introduction to the revolutionary integral approach to life, God, the universe, and everything*. Boston: Shambhala Publications.

Diagnosis of the Times

23

Lars Geer Hammershøj

Contents

Abstract

This chapter enquires into the function of diagnosis of the times as a forward-looking model. In order to do so, diagnosis of the times is compared with scenarios of future society, as both of these types of future study have a long tradition in sociology. For this purpose, a two-by-two matrix of ideal types of future studies in the social sciences is constructed in order to analyze the differences and similarities of these types. The analysis shows that diagnosis of the times focuses on processes of change, whereas scenario of future society focuses on the outcome of change. On this basis, the two types of future studies are analyzed in how they function as forward-looking models that facilitate anticipatory behavior. The conclusion is that diagnosis of the times facilitates decision making by taking bearings of the direction of change, whereas scenarios of future society facilitates decision making by drawing attention to the need to make changes. In order to enquire into the former, the two major traditions of

L. G. Hammershøj (✉)
Department of Education (DPU), Aarhus University, Campus Emdrup, Copenhagen, NV, Denmark
e-mail: lgha@edu.au.dk

© Springer Nature Switzerland AG 2019
R. Poli (ed.), *Handbook of Anticipation*,
https://doi.org/10.1007/978-3-319-91554-8_64

465

diagnosis of the times are analyzed, namely diagnosing social pathologies and tendencies in the times. Finally, the future of diagnosis of the times is discussed and illustrated by a diagnosis of the future of employment and the consequences of education.

Keywords

Diagnosis of the times · Scenario building · Sociology of the future · Future study · Forward-looking model · Anticipatory behavior · Prognosis · Social pathologies · Future employment · John Urry · Ulrich Beck

Introduction

Diagnosis of the times – or *Zeitdiagnose* in German – is a type of future study which is concerned with diagnosing *tendencies* in the times. Diagnosis of the times can be traced back to the Enlightenment and has developed in philosophy and then sociology, from its founding as a scholarly discipline in the late nineteenth century and onwards, diagnosing, for example, the processes of individualization and modernization (Beck and Bonss 2001; Hammershøj 2015).

This chapter enquires into the function of diagnosis of the times as a *fore-ward-looking model*; that is, as a specific kind of 'knowledge of the future' that helps people and institutions make decisions and take actions in the present. However, despite the fact that there is a long tradition of diagnosis of the times within sociology, where it has become one of the predominant forms of studying the future and reflecting on the times, there is a striking lack of methodological reflection on diagnosis of the times as an analysis strategy (Reese-Schäfer 1996; Volkmann and Schimank 2002).

In order to inquire into how diagnosis of the times functions as an anticipatory model, it is therefore necessary to inquire into the nature of diagnosis of the times as an analysis strategy.

For the purpose of this double inquiry, it appears fruitful to compare diagnosis of the times with the other dominant types of sociological future studies, sociology of the future, which is concerned with building *scenarios* of future society. This type of future study can also be traced back to the founding fathers of sociology, for example, Marx's scenario of 'world communism' (Urry 2008). Even though there has been an increase in scenario building research in sociology, little attention has been paid to the difference between building scenarios of society as a whole and building scenarios of an event or a context, as is common in organization studies and most other fields where scenario building is prevalent (Ramirez et al. 2015).

In the first part of this chapter, the differences and similarities between the analysis strategies of diagnosis of the times and sociology of the future are analyzed. On this basis, the chapter compares these different types of future studies function as forward-looking models and how they facilitate anticipatory behavior in different ways, i.e., how the different kinds of knowledge of the future can be used in decision-making processes of people and institutions. As will be shown, they differ in that diagnosis of the times focuses on the *processes of change* in the form of tendencies in the times, whereas sociology of the future focuses on the *outcome of change* in form of scenarios of future society. Hence, diagnosis of the times facilitates decision-making processes by *taking bearings* of the direction of change, whereas sociology of the future facilitates decision-making processes by *drawing attention* to the need to make changes.

In the second part of the chapter, the chapter enquires into the history and future of diagnosis of the times with an aim of clarifying how different diagnoses of the times function as forward-looking models. There appear to be two basic ways: Taking bearings of the patterns and direction of change is either for the purpose of *understanding* how the conditions of the times are changing, or it is for the purpose of *criticizing* how society is currently developing. In the former, anticipatory behavior is facilitated by clarifying the *changing conditions for action*; in the latter, it is facilitated by clarifying the *actions that ought to be changed*. Both ways can be traced back to the emergence of diagnosis of the times in philosophy in the late eighteenth century and its development within sociology in the late nineteenth century: In the work of the 'founding fathers' of sociology, diagnosis of the times is both a question of understanding and criticizing societal change; in the 'critical theory' developed in the wake of the civilizational catastrophes of the World Wars, the focus is mainly on diagnosing and criticizing the negative consequences or social pathologies of societal developments (Honneth 1996); and in contemporary 'modernity theory', however, the main focus is on understanding the late modern conditions of individualization and modernization, such as self-identity, liquid life, and the risk society (Beck 1986; Giddens 1991; Bauman 1992).

The future of diagnosis of the times depends on the need in society for taking bearings of the patterns and directions of change. So, in as much as the diagnosis of an *acceleration of the pace of change* in society holds true, one would expect an increase in demand for diagnosis of the times. To illustrate this point, examples of current diagnosis of climate change (Beck 2016; Urry 2016) and future employment (Frey and Osborne 2013; Brynjolfsson and McAfee 2014) are provided. In addition, the chapter demonstrates how education is by definition an anticipatory system that increasingly needs diagnosis of the tendencies of employment in order to grasp what is important to learn and to prepare the younger generations for future jobs.

Traditions of Futures Studies in Sociology

The lack of methodological reflection within future studies is mirrored by the fact that the genealogies of the different types of future studies are largely overlooked. In the narrow sense, future studies are defined as the study of possible, probable, and preferable futures, emerging as an academic discipline within military planning and business strategy in the 1950s and 1960s (Amer et al. 2013; Ramirez et al. 2015), and building on the pioneering work of futurists like Herman Kahn (1962) and Kahn and Wiener (1967).

In the broader sense, however, future studies include research in the social sciences and humanities that is constituted by a forward-looking attitude and aimed at understanding future developments of society or culture. In sociology, future studies are defined as the sociological research of the scenarios of future societies, which emerged in the late nineteenth century as the founding fathers of sociology attempted to comprehend the shift from traditional to modern society (Beck 1986; Urry 2008). It is, however, often overlooked that this way of reflecting on the future originated from philosophy. For example, almost all of the founding fathers of sociology – from Durkheim over Weber to Simmel – were inspired by Nietzsche's diagnosis of European nihilism (Honneth 1996).

Building on this, it is possible to distinguish two major traditions of future studies in sociology that originate from and replace two earlier traditions of reflecting on the future in philosophy, namely notions of *utopia* and *philosophy of history* (Koselleck 1959). Both of these traditions replaced eschatology as society became secularized starting in the Renaissance and prevailing in the Enlightenment in the eighteenth century. What is interesting, however, is that these traditions are fundamentally different ways of reflecting on the future. Thomas More's (1516) original *Utopia,* for instance, is a fictional account of an island and a society that does not exist, but which is apparently preferable to, and hence constitutes an indirect criticism of More's contemporary society. In the words of Koselleck, it is "the pledge of a tomorrow in whose name today could in good conscience be allowed to perish. To justify itself at all, the critique of the eighteenth century had to become Utopian" (Koselleck 1959: 10).

On the other hand, the philosophy of history of Hegel (1807), for instance, is the determination of the dialectic principle according to which reason or the spirit realizes itself throughout history. The philosophy of history is thus a secularization of the divine plan of salvation assured by the rational plan of history and the notion of progress: "The philosophy of progress offered the certainty (neither religious nor rational but historico-philosophical) that the indirect political plan would be realised and, conversely, that rational and moral planning determines the course of history" (Koselleck 1959: 133).

However, as Michel Foucault argues, an entirely new way of reflecting on the present and future emerges in the Enlightenment that differs from both notions of utopia and philosophy of history. Foucault detects this way of reflecting in Immanuel Kant's (1784) famous text *An Answer to the Question: What Is Enlightenment?*: "In the text on *Aufklärung*, he deals with the question of contemporary reality alone. He is not seeking to understand the present on the basis of a totality or of a future achievement. He is looking for a difference: What difference does today introduce with respect to yesterday" (Foucault 1984a: 34).

This difference that today introduces is to be understood, not as the achieved outcome of a transformation of the times, but as the *patterns* of transformation or the *direction* of the process of transformation. As Kant clearly states: "If it is asked, then, whether we live in an *enlightened* age, then the answer is: no, but we do live in an age of *enlightenment*" (Kant 1784: 22). In his day and age, people were not yet able to make use of their own reason without the direction of others – Kant's definition of enlightenment – but, as he says: "we have clear indications that they are now being opened up to the possibility of working toward this, and that the obstacles to universal enlightenment, or the emancipation from one's self-incurred immaturity, are now gradually becoming fewer" (Kant 1784: 22).

This is diagnosis of the times: Kant deciphers and interprets *indications* in the times as indications of *tendencies* of the times. Hence, the empirical material for diagnosis of the times consists of indications of change, and the analysis strategy consists of interpreting these indications in order to find the patterns and direction of the transformations that constitute the tendencies of the times.

Diagnosis of the times gradually came to replace history of philosophy as the way of reflecting upon the present and the future. With the historical experiences of revolution and contingency, it became more and more difficult to maintain the idea that a rational and moral plan determines the course of history. So, instead of philosophically determining the logical principle of history, the question became one of diagnostically deciphering and interpreting the signs of change in the times (Koselleck 1959; Kristensen 2008). Nietzsche's (1882) notorious diagnosis that 'God is dead' in *The Gay Science* is the diagnosis of this very conditions of modernity, but the point of this diagnosis is that people appear to live on as if nothing has happened. His diagnosis is that people continue to live according to tradition even if the moral basis of society has dissolved.

This is Nietzsche's diagnosis of European nihilism, which was to have great influence on the founding fathers of sociology, as mentioned. In sociology, it became a question of diagnosing the consequences of the dissolution of the moral and social order of traditional society and diagnosing the 'social bond' of modern society. This is not an exception; on the contrary, diagnosis of the times has always been part of the research approach of sociology in as much as sociology is the attempt to understand the differences that introduce modern society with respect to traditional society and to diagnose signs of change as indications of tendencies of society. In fact, the basic sociological concepts of individualization and modernization are diagnostic concepts that belong to a diagnosis of the times as they are interpretations of indications that individuals are behaving differently and that conditions of society are changing.

Meanwhile, the other tradition of reflecting on the future, in the form of notions of utopias, became part of the research approach of sociology too. However, in their modern form these notions of future society are no longer indirect but direct criticisms of current societal developments and take the form of dystopias. In sociology, the tradition regarding notions of utopia thus turns into the building of various scenarios of future societies and as John Urry states this way of speculating about the future has been part of sociology from the beginning: "Examples include Weber's dark account of the emerging 'iron cage' of bureaucracy, Durkheim's anxieties as to the future significance of anomie or normlessness within social life, and Simmel's extrapolations as to how life within metropolis will increasingly entail systems of punctuality and the spread of a blasé attitude" (Urry 2008: 262).

The problem is that these two sociological traditions of future study – diagnosis of the times and building scenarios of future society – appear to be *mixed up*.

In practice, sociologists are often doing both, i.e., diagnosing the tendencies of the times and speculating about possible outcome. An example is Marx and Engels' (1848) speculation regarding future society in the *Communist Manifesto,* to which Urry also refers. Their diagnosis is that there is a tendency towards growing capitalist exploitation and their scenario is that this will bring about a crisis in capitalism out of which a new order of 'world communism' will emerge. Interestingly, Urry states: "But we know now that this analysis was 'mistaken' in predicting worldwide social revolution" (Urry 2008: 262).

The scenario of world communism was not accurate and appears obsolete today. However, the diagnosis of the tendency to exploitation appears to have become relevant again. This diagnosis has been repeated, not by old left-wing sociologists but by recent studies of the consequences of digitalization for future employment (Frey and Osborne 2013; Brynjolfsson and McAfee 2014; Ford 2015). These studies see indications that the historical correlation between increasing productivity and rising incomes has broken down and interpret these signs as the tendency that "the fruits of innovation throughout the economy are now accruing entirely to business owners and investors, rather than to workers" (Ford 2015: 36).

Differences in Focus on Change: Outcome Versus Process

As I have attempted to show, there are two types of future research in sociology: diagnosis of the times and scenarios of future society. The problem is not that they are mixed up in practice but that they are confused because of the general lack of methodological reflection within future studies. What is more, few studies distinguish between the scenarios of future society in sociology and the scenarios of an event or a context in organization and management studies. Hence, there is a strong need for methodological reflection and for distinguishing the different types of future studies.

I have attempted to contribute to this endeavor by constructing four ideal types of future studies, and, in order to depict their constellation, I have mapped them in a two-by-two matrix (see Fig. 1). According to Weber (1904), an ideal type is

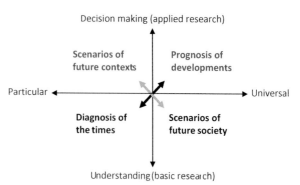

Fig. 1 Map of ideal types of future studies in the social sciences. The *grey arrow*: Outcome of change (contexts vs. society). The *black arrow*: Processes of change (developments vs. tendencies)

constructed by emphasizing certain traits of reality and joining them together in mental images. The traits of the future studies I have emphasized are represented by the dimensions of the matrix: The horizontal dimension indicates the point of view of the research approach (particular vs. universal); the vertical dimension indicates the purpose hereof (decision making vs. understanding); and the opposition arrows show the difference in the nature of the object (outcome vs. process). As Weber stresses, in reality the different traits of an ideal type might: "exist to a greater or lesser degree, sometimes not at all" (Weber 1904: 43; my translation). Accordingly, it is important to stress that this map of the ideal types of future studies is not a model; it is not a depiction of reality but a theoretical tool of orientation intended to help understand the differences in the research approaches of future studies.

According to the matrix, the types of future studies that build scenarios of future contexts and future societies – typical of management studies and sociology, respectively – are both interested in the outcome of change; this is the very nature of scenarios. However, they are diametrically opposed types of scenario building in that the point of view of scenarios of contexts is the specific organization with a view to decision making, whereas the intention of scenarios of society is society as a whole with a view to understanding the transformations of society. In management studies, examining reviews of scenario-planning literature "reveals that the main benefits of using scenarios are improvements of the decision-making process and identification of new issues and problems which may arise in the future" (Amer et al. 2013: 25). Another characteristic is that the scenarios of contexts are specifically for someone, as the transformations regard the specific environment that surrounds an individual or organization: "This actor-specificity is one characteristic that differentiates scenarios from forecast, which are for anyone" (Ramirez et al. 2015: 71). Scenarios of future society, however, concern the general environment for everyone, meaning the point of view is on the universal, rather than particular transformations. Furthermore, the objective when building scenarios of future society is to understand the transformations of society.

On the other hand, the types of future studies that either diagnose the times and or make a prognosis of developments are both interested in the processes of change. However, they are diametrically opposed ways of estimating and interpreting these processes of change. Prognosis is statements about future developments (Kosow and Gassner 2008). In the strict sense, prognosis is about projecting past developments into the future based on statistical collections and estimating the probability of these future developments, e.g., project and estimate world population growth. In the wider sense, prognosis is about extrapolating present trends into the future based on data and observations of various kind depending on the future trends to be analyzed, e.g., 'Moore's law' on the exponential increase in computer processing power, which was originally based on observations of Intel-cofounder Gordon Moore (1965).

Thus, prognosis differs from diagnosis in that prognosis is about *projecting* developments and trends, whereas diagnosis is about *interpreting* indications of change in the times as indications of tendencies of the times. This is reflected in the difference in point of view of prognosis and diagnosis. The point of view of prognosis is to find *general* developments or trends in the past and project these into the future. By contrast, the point of view of diagnosis is to find *particular* indications of change, which can be of different nature and are often found across different contexts, and interpret the indications as tendencies. For example, diagnosing a tendency in education (say, the shift in focus from the teacher's to the learner's point of view) by interpreting the patterns and direction of different indications of change, such as a new discourse in educational policy, a different practice of teaching, or a crisis in educational institutions.

Diagnosis of the times and scenarios of future society thus differ in that the former is interested in interpreting *processes* of change in form of tendencies and has its point of view on the particular indications of these changes, whereas the latter is interested in the *outcome* of change in the form of scenarios and has its point of view on the general transformations of society. In contrast to scenarios of future society, diagnosis of the times does not describe how society as a whole might change, but diagnoses how the times as such are characterized by the patterns and direction of change in the times. Thus, the tendencies in the times point to changing conditions of the times that have implications for the future. Hence, diagnosis of the times *implies the future*, not by predicting or describing a probable, possible, or preferable future society, but by pointing to the changing field of possibility in the times. In his text on enlightenment, for example, Kant (1784) did not build scenarios of democracy or other modern regimes but merely diagnosed the changing condition that in his time people were beginning to use their own reason without guidance. This kind of freedom is a condition not only for democracy but also for totalitarian regimes, as it is exactly the burden of freedom that makes people in modern societies escape their freedom and submit to totalitarian rule, according to Fromm (1941). Thus, Kant appears to diagnose a change in conditions that make up the field of possibility for modern regimes.

In order to better understand the similarities and differences of diagnosis of the times and scenarios of future society, we turn to two specific practices of future study, namely the projective social theory of Ulrich Beck and the social-analytics of Lars-Henrik Schmidt, as both distinguish themselves by including methodological reflection in their future study practices.

Diagnosis of the times is the analysis-strategy of social-analytics and it builds on the tradition from Nietzsche and Foucault. Interestingly, in social-analytics, diagno-sis of the times consists of two analysis practices (Schmidt 1992, 2011): first, the practice of *interpreting* tendencies in the times on the basis of empirical indications of change; second, the practice of *grasping* the conditions of the times on the basis of the tendencies interpreted. Thus, interpreting tendencies is about analyzing and discerning the patterns and direction of the processes of transformation, whereas grasping conditions is about constructing a new diagnostic concept that grasps the new conditions of the times marked out by the tendencies. Hence, the word 'grasp-ing' refers both to the joining together of tendencies and to the construction of a diagnostic concept that makes possible a specific comprehension of the new condi-tions of the times. For example, the diagnostic concept of 'deference' is the grasping of the shift from social recognition to individualized respect on the basis of the tendency towards the dismantlement of the state (Schmidt 2011), and the diagnostic concept of 'pathological self-formation' is the grasping of the negative consequences of individualization on the basis of indications of new kinds of pathologies, such as eating disorders, depression in children, and school shootings (Hammershøj 2009).

In his book *Risk Society – Towards a New Modernity*, Ulrich Beck states that it is his ambition "to move the future which is just beginning to *take shape* into view against the *still* predominant past" (Beck 1986: 9). In other words, he wants to build a scenario of the future society whose structures and institutions are only beginning to develop and disseminate. According to Beck, the problem is that society is changing in such way that the current sociological concepts and theories of society are outdated; he calls them 'zombie-categories', meaning categories determining our views on social realities that are disappearing (Beck and Wills 2000; Beck and Bonss 2001). Thus, in order to develop an up-to-date theory of society, Beck attempts to develop sociological concepts that are *in accordance with the scenario* of future society. He defines this analysis as *"empirically oriented, projective social theory –* without any methodological safeguards" (Beck 1986: 9). It is without methodological safeguards because it is based on a scenario. It is only empirically orientated because it is based on empirical indications of change. In this sense, the scenarios of future society represent the outcome of the transformations of society that the projective theories of society attempt to comprehend.

As mentioned, there is a tendency in sociology to mix the analysis strategies of diagnosis of the times and scenarios of future society. In the case of Beck, however, alongside Bonss, diagnosis of the times is described as a component of developing a theory of society in accordance with scenarios of the future: "The theory's component of diagnosis of the times experiments with the hypothesis of a transformation of structure, which leads from the first to the second modernity. It consequently forces the *theory of society* to a new definition of the unity of modern society, as the concept covers both – the first and second modernity – and must be made transparent" (Beck and Bonss 2001: 64). Here, diagnosis of the times functions as a kind of 'auxiliary science' to social theory, an 'experimental approach' in search of the novel and the breaches into a new era. However, it clearly illustrates the difference in interest of these two analysis strategies: Diagnosis of the times is about developing diagnostic concepts of the *processes* of change in society, whereas scenarios of future society is about developing sociological concepts of the *outcome* of the transformations of society, which is described as the second modernity. (Thus, as scenario of future society is described as *projected sociology*, diagnosis of the times might be referred to as *projected genealogy,* as genealogy is the inquiry into: "the contingency that has made us what we are" (Foucault 1984a: 46). This contingency of change is the reason why diagnosis of times is not about determining the logic of the necessary course of history, but deciphering and interpreting indications of change in the times.)

Types of Decision-Making Facilitation: Bearings or Attention

The vast majority of future studies research in the field of sociology is carried out at universities. Thus, this research is a public good, and as such its purpose is to provide knowledge to be used for decision making and action by a wide range of institutions, organizations, and individuals in society. However, in the case of future studies in sociology, the knowledge produced concerns the future in the form of diagnoses of tendencies in the times or scenarios of future society. Thus, these types of future studies function as external, forward-looking models that facilitate decision making through anticipatory systems, which are defined as follows: "A system behaving in an anticipatory way – an anticipatory system – makes its decisions in the present according to "anticipations" about something that may eventually happen in the future" (Poli 2014: 17). In the case of future studies in sociology, in principle all institutions and organizations concerned with the future developments of society can be viewed anticipatory systems.

The point is that diagnosis of the times and sociology of the future provide different kinds of knowledge of the future which form the basis for two different kinds of decision-making facilitation. In the case of sociology of the future, the focus is on the outcome of change and the knowledge of the future is thus in the form of scenarios of future society. The objective of providing this knowledge is the same as with other kinds of future studies in the form of scenarios: "Learning about widely different outcomes is the issue in this case: one must be ready to consider and address possible unfamiliar or alien scenarios" (Poli 2010: 11). Scenarios help people prepare for a future that is different from what they would normally imagine.

In contrast to most other kinds of future studies, the result of this exercise is not to clarify the possible, probable, and preferred future scenarios of the situation or to help in deciding which concrete action to take. This is possible provided that the scenarios are actor-specific or deal with a specific context or an event. In the case of sociology of the future, however, the scenarios deal with society as a whole or with entire parts of the society, and these are too complex to guide concrete action in specific situations (not that a context is not complex, but a society is the multiple of such complex contexts). For the same reason, scenarios of future society are almost always wrong – Marx's 'worldwide communism' is just one example. Instead, the function of scenarios of future society is to *draw attention* to the need to act and make changes. For example, Marx's scenario pointed to the need for workers to unite and organize themselves, which they did, but in ways other than even Marx could imagine.

In the case of diagnosis of the times, the focus is on the processes of change and the knowledge of the future thus takes the form of interpretations of tendencies in the times and conceptualizations of new conditions of the times. The objective of providing this knowledge is to inform people of the patterns and direction of change. Thus, the purpose of diagnosis of the times is to help people in *taking bearings* in time of change. For the same reason, the main traditions of diagnosis of the times are intimately connected to periods of profound societal change, such as the era of Enlightenment, the emergence of modern society, the civilizational catastrophes of the World Wars, and the emergence of late modernity. The deeper the societal change, the greater the need for diagnosis.

The methodological reflections of social-analytics illustrate the ways in which diagnosis of the times helps people in taking bearings in times of change and how diagnosis functions as an anticipatory system that facilitates decision making. In the practice of interpreting tendencies in the times, diagnosis of the times helps take bearings of the connections between the different signs of change and the common direction in these changes, as well as the relation or conflict between different tendencies of the times. So, this kind of diagnosis of the times questions common notions of change and provide alternative understandings of how and why things are changing. The purpose is to make possible new ways of relating to changes in the time, including by enabling people and institutions to better decide how and to what degree to adapt to these changes, or how to resist them.

In the practice of grasping the conditions of the times, diagnosis of the times helps in taking bearings of the historical conditions of thinking and action by trying out the limits and possibilities of what are meaningful statements and effective action today. This is done by constructing alternative perspectives on or concepts of particular practices or problems that are affected by change. So, this kind of diagnosis of the times makes new conceptualizations and provides the conceptual basis for new ways of reflecting on and acting in practice. The purpose hereof is to make possible for people and institutions to change what they do and how they understand of what they do, and change these practices in ways that are different from existing practices but in accordance with the new conditions of the times.

Hence, in as much as both kinds of diagnosis of the times are forward-looking models with the intention of making possible new ways of thinking and acting, the decision making and action these models facilitate are in the nature of *criticism*. In the practice of interpreting tendencies in the times, the criticism can be *explicit* and take the form of critical reflecting on or resisting the influence of change in the times that appear to affect practices. In the practice of grasping conditions of the times, the criticism is often *implicit* and takes the form of transforming the practice in accordance with concepts which provide a different understanding of the change in the times with the intention of creating new meaning and value through the changed practice.

The History of Diagnosis of the Times: Crisis or Criticism

There are two major traditions in the history of diagnosis of the times. The tradition in which the critical nature of diagnosis of the times is most obvious is the tradition occupied with diagnosing the negative consequences of societal change, or what Axel Honneth calls the social pathologies; that is, 'those developmental processes of society that can be conceived as processes of decline, distortion or even "social pathologies"' (Honneth 1996: 370). According to Honneth, this tradition can be traced back to Rousseau's criticism that the civilization processes have corrupted the original state of man by enslaving him or her to the artificial desires generated by the expectations of others (Rousseau 1755). Thus, Rousseau diagnoses patterns of civilization processes as the shift from natural to social desires in step with urbanization and the increasing artificial state of living that it produces. He criticizes that this tendency will make humans unhappy because happiness is to obtain what one desires, according to Rousseau, which is impossible with the increasing number of artificial desires generated by civilization.

After originating in philosophy, the tradition of diagnosing social pathologies develops in sociology and reaches its climax in critical theory in the mid-twentieth century (Hammershøj 2009). In the case of the founding fathers of sociology, it is thus an integrated part of their diagnosis of the developmental processes of society to diagnose the negative consequences. For example, Marx (1844) diagnosed 'alienation' as the negative consequences of the stratified social class and capitalist mode of production, and according to the diagnoses of Durkheim (1897) and Simmel (1903), the negative consequences of individualization processes are 'anomic suicide' and 'depersonalization' of the life in the city.

However, in the critical theory of the so-called Frankfurt School, the diagnosis of the negative consequences of societal developments becomes the central focus of the diagnosis of the times and no longer just a part assuming the nature of pure criticism. Perhaps the most famous one is Horkheimer and Adorno's diagnosis of the 'dialectics of the Enlightenment'. Though, it is telling that the point of departure of their diagnosis is the ultimate negative consequence of the historic developments of modern society – as their diagnosis inquires into 'why humanity, instead of entering a truly human state, is sinking into a new kind of barbarism' (Horkheimer and Adorno 1944: xiv).

It is of course the immediate experiences of the catastrophes of the World Wars that furnish the affective climate of this inquiry. However, important as such criticism is, as a diagnosis of the times it is problematic. The problem is that the diagnosis of the times becomes governed from the point of view of the criticism; that is, every sign of change in the times is interpreted in support of the criticism and as instances of decline and distortion – in this case, even the appearance of jazz music. The diagnosis loses its ability to perform a sensitive and differentiated interpretation of the patterns and direction of the signs of change because these have already been decided by the point of view of the criticism. As a consequence, the interpretation risks reflecting the idiosyncrasies of the interpreting subject; or, as Habermas puts it, when viewed as a diagnosis of the times, 'the subjectivity of the gesture comes embarrassingly to light' (Habermas 1979: 10; my translation).

Not only is criticism the central focus of this major tradition in diagnosis of the times, it is also embedded in the very concept of diagnosis. This concept of diagnosis is derived from medicine. The term diagnosis of the times implies a shift in focus from the physical body to the body of society, metaphorically speaking. Etymologically speaking, however, the concept of diagnosis is closely related to the concepts of criticism, crisis, and criterion which all derive from the Greek word 'krisis' (Koselleck 1959). In medicine, the crisis of the body in the form of a disease calls for the diagnosis of this crisis for the purpose of deciding how to treat it; that is, the crisis is the "crucial stage of a disease in which a decision had to be made, but had not yet been reached" (Koselleck 1959: 104). The diagnosis constitutes this decision-making process and it requires a forward-looking attitude in which the course of events is analyzed. Thus, the doctor inquires into when the symptoms started and how they differ from the normal state of the body, for the purpose of determining the probable result of events and whether or not a treatment is required. Hence, diagnosis involves criticism in two ways which both derive from the original sense of the 'krisis' in which it refers to the art of judgment. First, diagnosis involves distinguishing the differences between past and present state of the body; that is, identify the symptoms. Second, diagnosis involves determining the nature and character of these symptoms, that is, determine which disease it is. For the latter, it is necessary to apply a criterion of what is the healthy and unhealthy state of the body and classify the different types of diseases and their corresponding diagnosis criteria.

The same applies for the tradition of diagnosing the negative consequences of the societal developments. In order to diagnose the social pathologies, it requires a normative criterion of what the healthiness of society is. For example, for Rousseau (1755) this criterion is the natural state of man, for Fromm (1941) it is the unimpeded self-realization of the individual, and for Honneth (1996) it is the social recognition of the significance, the rights, and the achievements of the individual. Any societal development that leads away from one of these criteria can therefore be diagnosed as social pathological. In Horkheimer and Adorno's diagnosis, however, there is no explicit normative criterion to be found. The reason is that it is the point of departure of their analysis that the societal developments are pathological in their time. Consequently, the only meaningful approach is to ruthlessly criticize all that exists.

Today, diagnosing social pathologies is no longer the dominant tradition of diagnosis of the times. The reason is, apparently, that the historical conditions for diagnosis of the times have changed. Not only do the societal developments no longer appear unambiguously gloomy, but the possibility of defining a universal normative criterion for the healthiness of society has been questioned by the loss of legitimacy of 'grand narratives' (Lyotard 1979) and the pluralism of cultures (Bauman 1992). Moreover, the apparent accelerating pace of change (Brynjolfsson and McAfee 2014) makes the total criticism of everything that exists futile, because what exists is now always already dissolving transforming into something else. By contrast, today there is a pressing need for taking bearings in these times of diverse complexity and rapid change. Correspondingly, there has been a shift in predominance from the tradition of diagnosing social pathologies, which can be traced back to Rousseau (1755), to the tradition of diagnosing the tendencies in the times, which can be traced back to Kant (1784).

An eloquent example of this shift is in fact Honneth's (1996) attempt to revive this tradition of social pathologies. As part of this revival, Honneth arranged to have Alain Ehrenberg's (2004) diagnosis of the increase in depression today translated and published by Institut für Sozialforschung. However, Honneth appears to overlook that Ehrenberg and he have diametrically opposed diagnoses of the increase in depression. According to Honneth's diagnosis the increase is a result of the 'ideology of de-institutionalization' (Honneth 2004: 467); that is, depression is caused by the *illusion* that individuals are free to realize themselves. In contrast, Ehrenberg's diagnosis is that the increase in depression is due to individualization processes by which individuals are in fact, to a larger degree than previously, free to realize themselves, but that these new conditions put new demands on the individual, such as, the expectation to take initiative and act responsively (Ehrenberg 2004). Hence, Ehrenberg does not diagnose the increase in depression as a social pathology caused by the impediments to self-realization, but as a *sign* of change of the conditions for being an individual. The purpose of the diagnosis of the increase in depression is to better understand the current individualization processes: "Depression is a disorder that is especially well suited for the understanding of contemporary individuality, that is, of the new dilemmas of which depression rise" (Ehrenberg 2004: 3).

This is an example of the tradition that has become prevalent today. As mentioned, this is evident with the emergence of modernity theory in sociology, which attempts to diagnose the change in conditions between previous and contemporary modernity, also called 'late modernity' or 'postmodernity' (Giddens 1991; Bauman 1992). It includes diagnosis of the new conditions of the individual, which are, for example, understood as *identity* by which the self is regarded as a reflexive project and a narrative of oneself that answers the question 'who am I?' (Giddens 1991; Rose 1996). It also includes diagnosis of new conditions of community, which is, for example, understood as 'affectual nebula' in which the social bond of community is purely affective in nature (Maffesoli 1996), or diagnosis of new conditions of work, which is, for example, understood as leading to the emergence of 'the creative class' (Florida 2002).

None of the abovementioned diagnosis reflects methodologically on their practice of diagnosis of the times. Instead, it is simply implied that the diagnosis in question is either in the nature of sociological theory or description of society. This makes it unclear whether the diagnoses describe developmental processes that are universal and apply to all society, or whether the diagnoses conceptualize developmental processes that are necessary and cannot be otherwise. It is, in other words, unclear whether the diagnosis depicts the structures and functions of the *reality* of society or interprets the patterns and directions of the *change* of society (Hammershøj 2015). To the extent that the diagnoses give the impression of the former, they lose their diagnostic and critical quality because the crisis is no longer the object of the diagnosis, neither as the object for discrimination of tendencies or for determination of action. In other word, these diagnoses risk losing the name diagnosis.

In contrast, Foucault's historical-based diagnosis of the times is explicitly both diagnostic and critical. His historical and genealogical studies of the conditions of historical times are, thus, always with a view to the difference that makes the conditions of today. Correspondingly, the object of these studies is to facilitate a certain kind of action, namely diagnostic-critical action: "The object was to learn to what extent the effort to think one's own history can free thought from what it silently thinks, and so enable it to think differently" (Foucault 1984b: 9).

The Future of Diagnosis of the Times: Climate or Employment

For the purpose of determining the future of diagnosis one must attempt to grasp the future conditions for diagnosis of the times. In order to do so, one must first determine the tendency of the tendencies of the times. As indicated, the general tendency of change of society today appears to be that change is more rapid and deeper than in previous times. This suggests that the diagnosis of the times in the future will predominantly be of the tradition of diagnosing the patterns and direction of change of society. I will attempt to substantiate the assumption of the future conditions of diagnosis of the times by presenting future studies of topical subjects such as climate change and future employment and reflect on the consequences of these conditions for the function of studies as forward-looking models.

The recent studies of Beck (2016) and Urry (2016) both emphasize the radical nature of the emerging transformations of society, and this is, for example, reflected in that both use the word catastrophe to describe the possible outcome of these transformations. Of the same reason, Beck suggests replacing the word change with the word metamorphosis: "Metamorphosis implies a much more radical transformation in which the old certainties of the modern society are falling away and something quite new is emerging" (Beck 2016: 3). Beck and Urry both presume that climate change is one of the greatest sources of change today and that it can ultimately be a threat to human kind. However, as sociology of future society, their studies do not focus on the scientific prediction of the actual consequences of climate change on the climate, and not even on the political and normative question of how to act against climate change, but on the consequences that climate change will have on future society: "What does climate change do to us, and how does it alter the order of society and politics?" (Beck 2016: 36).

In order to answer this question, Beck and Urry construct future scenarios of society. Interestingly, both of them construct more scenarios of future society. Urry put forward one scenario that climate change will entail the breakdown of many of the world's mobility and communication connections, which could lead to not only plummeting standards of living but also to the emergence of "local warlords controlling recycled forms of mobility" (Urry 2008: 269). Another scenario is the emergence of new forms of mobility in the form of small, electronic and deprivatized vehicles equipped with technologies of tracking and tracing them in order to limit consumption, which has the side effect of creating 'digital panopticon' (Urry 2008: 273). Beck, on the other hand, wants to construct an alternative scenario to the dominant dystopian scenarios of failing societies by posing the question: 'What is climate change good for (if we survive)?' (Beck 2016: 35). The reason is that at the present moment "our collective powers of social and political imagination seem blocked" (Beck 2016: 37). Instead, Beck wants to draw attention to the fact that climate change alters society not only by entailing new kinds of insecurity and inequality but also new forms of collaboration and solidarity. Hence, he sets forward a scenario of cosmopolitanism.

These scenarios of future society make it abundantly clear that the purpose of scenarios of society is not to predict the future but to call attention to the need for action. In this case, it is about the need for thinking differently about how we live together in and across societies and the need for establishing new societal structures and functions to manage the new challenges. In the words of Urry: "Climate change leads to new methods and theories for anticipating multiple futures and hence potentially for intervening to avoid its dire consequences" (Urry 2016: 156).

This appears to be the case of future studies of employment too. The apparent changes of the economy and production due to digitalization are expected to have huge consequences for future employment. For the intention of anticipating these changes, education is properly the most central institution. It is the purpose of education to prepare new generations for living and working in society (Dewey 1914; Durkheim 1922). Hence, education is per definition an anticipatory system and therefore needs to have and deploy a forward-looking attitude. As the pace of change of society accelerates, it becomes less and less evident what is necessary and important to learn in order to live and work in future society. This appears to be the current situation for education in terms of the accelerating pace of change in society in general and in terms of the radical transformation of employment in the future in particular.

Recent studies suggest that we have reached a threshold where we will see a radical increase in job automation by means of computers and robotics in the near future (Frey and Osborne 2013; Brynjolfsson and McAfee 2014; Ford 2015; Susskind and Susskind 2015). This will most likely have radical implications for employment and studies already discuss future scenarios of technological unemployment and mass unemployment. A study by Frey and Osborne examines the susceptibility to job automation of different kinds of job types: "According to our estimates around 47 percent of total US employment is in the high risk category. We refer to these as jobs at risk – i.e. jobs we expect could be automated relatively soon, perhaps over the next decade or so" (Frey and Osborne 2013: 44).

Interestingly, the different studies of digitalization and its consequences for employment do not only use different types of future studies analysis strategies, their results are conflicting. For example, in regard to the teaching profession, Susskind and Susskind (2015: 60) conclude that there is "less need for the 'sage on the stage'" because of the increase in digital learning tools such as adaptive learning systems or online platforms like MOOCs (Massive Open Online Courses). This is a future study in the form of a prognosis of the future of the professions based on a simple extrapolation of a historic trend – the emergence of these digital tools and platforms.

Frey and Osborne (2013), on the other hand, estimate that the teaching profession is in low risk of being automated. The reason is that their future study is based on the estimate of how susceptible to computerization a given task is. That depends on whether or not it is possible to sufficiently describe the work process of a given task so that an algorithm can be developed for it: "In short, routine tasks are defined as tasks that follow explicit rules that can be accomplished by machines, while non-routine tasks are not sufficiently well understood to be specified in computer code" Frey and Osborne 2013: 14–15). They argue that the types of tasks that are characteristic of being nonroutine are perception and manipulation tasks, creative intelligence tasks, and social intelligence tasks. As teaching to a high degree consists of creative and social intelligence tasks, the teaching professions are not likely to be at high risk of job automation. (Supporting this view is the fact that MOOCs in general do not appear to be very successful. Typically less than 5% of the students complete the courses, and the majority of those who do most often have an academic degree already. In the words of Robert Zemsky: "They [MOOCs] came; they conquered very little; and now they face substantially diminishing prospects" (Zemsky 2014: 237).)

Frey and Osborne's future study analysis strategy is obviously neither a prognosis nor scenario of future employment. Instead, it appears to be a diagnosis of future employment and the difference is *interpretation*. They interpret the signs of which tasks appear to be more susceptible, and they find that it depends on whether or not the given task is routine or nonroutine. This is the pattern of transformation and the tendency of future employment, and it is on this basis that they estimate the risk of automation of existing job types. However, in accordance with this diagnosis of future employment, they present a scenario of the overall picture of future employment: "the current trend towards labour marked polarization, with growing employment in high-income cognitive jobs and low-income manual occupations, accompanied by a hollowing-out of the middle-income routine jobs" (Frey and Osborne 2013: 3). This is an example of the strength of scenario building as a forward-looking model. Scenarios are effective at calling attention to the need for action in order to avoid future catastrophes. In fact, this scenario inspired the depiction on the front page of *The Economist* of a tornado ravaging an office, accompanied by the headline: "Coming to an office near you" (Economist 2014, 18–24 January).

However, for the task of determining which kinds of higher education are relevant and needed in the future, scenarios of future employment are not particularly useful because they are too unspecific. The tendencies might lead to a different outcome. The interpretation of the tendency towards automatization of routine tasks, on the other hand, is capable of pointing to examples of what kinds of tasks or types of occupations higher education should prepare for. However, neither scenarios of the future nor interpretations of tendencies are able to determine what is actually relevant to learn and how. To give an idea of this, it is necessary not only to interpret tendencies but also to *grasp* the conditions of future employment in the sense of which capacities appear to be relevant in the future.

An example of such an attempt to grasp the conditions of future employment is the construction of diagnostic concept of future employability (Hammershøj 2017a, b). Employability is commonly defined as the graduate's likeliness of gaining employment and of continuing to be successful in his or her occupation (Yorke 2006). The diagnostic concept of future employability builds on the interpretation of the tendencies of future employment (Frey and Osborne 2013; Brynjolfsson and McAfee 2014; Ford 2015). According to these studies, the tasks that appear resistant to automation are the tasks characterized by nonroutine processes or unpredictable outcomes, such as creative, innovative, perception, and social intelligence tasks. However, in order to promote and foster these apparent uniquely human capacities in the educational system, it is necessary to clarify the nature of these tasks. This is a challenge because these tasks are exactly the tasks that appear also to be resistant to conceptualization.

The assumption is, however, that these tasks are resistant to automation and conceptualization because they are *affective in nature* (Hammershøj 2017a, b). Hence, my hypothesis is that future employability is not solely based on knowledge, skills, or competencies, but to a higher degree on *Bildung*. *Bildung* is the German concept of the social formation process of the personality, a process that brings about a change in the way in which the person relates to him- or herself, others, and the world (Humboldt 1793; Hegel 1807). According to my analysis, the transcendence process is based on ecstatic moods, and the judgment process is based on strong and action-oriented feelings. As such, the task is to diagnose which capacities of transcendence and judgment are important to cultivate in the future.

In the case of higher education the aim is to prepare the younger generation for working life and therefore *Bildung* is concerned with the way the person relates professionally to and in his or her profession. This 'vocational *Bildung*' appears today to consist of three general capacities: first, the capacity to relate to one's profession of personal interest and will which is a condition for being a devoted employee; second, the capacity to make professional judgments which is increasingly important the more organizations and their environments change; and third, the capacity to relate in such a way that one is open to the novel, which is the essence and basic condition of being creative and innovative.

The diagnostic concept of the three capacities of 'vocational *Bildung*' constitutes the diagnostic concept of future employability. It is an example of how diagnosis of the times can help take bearings in times of change and propose specific suggestions that can facilitate decision making and action. In contrast to more conventional analysis of future employment and education, which mainly points to automation and the need for learning to be creative or innovative, this diagnosis of the times interprets the specific tendencies of future employment, including which jobs are susceptible for automation, and grasps the basic nature of the human capacities that need to be cultivated. Hence, this diagnosis of the times contributes with a specific suggestion in regard to a fundamental and still more urgent question of education: What is important to learn in the future?

Summary

This chapter has enquired into the function of diagnosis of the times as a forward-looking model by comparing diagnosis of the times is compared with scenarios of future society, as both of these types of future study have a long tradition in sociology. The analysis has showed that diagnosis of the times focuses on processes of change, whereas scenario of future society focuses on the outcome of change. The conclusion is thus that diagnosis of the times facilitates decision making by taking bearings of the direction of change, whereas scenarios of future society facilitates decision making by drawing attention to the need to make changes.

References

Amer, M., Daim, T. U., & Jetter, A. (2013). A review of scenario planning. *Futures, 46*, 23–40.
Bauman, Z. (1992). *Intimations of postmodernity.* London: Routlegde.
Beck, U. (1986). *Risk society. Towards a new modernity.* London: SAGE.
Beck, U. (2016). *The metamorphosis of the world.* Cambridge: Polity.

Beck, U., & Bonss, W. (Eds.). (2001). *Die Modernisierung der Moderne*. Frankfurt am Main: Suhrkamp.

Beck, U., & Wills, J. (2000). *Samtaler med Ulrich Beck. Frihed eller kapitalisme*. København: Hans Reitzels Forlag.

Brynjolfsson, E., & McAfee, A. (2014). *The second machine age*. New York: W.W. Norton & Company.

Dewey, J. (1914). *Democracy and education*. Milton Keynes UK: Simon Brown, 2011.

Durkheim, E. (1897). *Suicide*. London: Routledge. 2002.

Durkheim, E. (1922). *Education and sociology*. New York: Free Press, 1956.

Economist. (2014). The Economist, January 18th–24th 2014. Economist.com.

Ehrenberg, A. (1998). *Das erschöpfte Selbst. Depression und Gesellschaft in der Gegenwart*. Frankfurt am Main: Institut für Sozialforschung, Campus. 2004.

Florida, R. (2002). *The rise of the creative class*. New York: Basic Books.

Ford, M. (2015). *The rise of the robots. Technology and the threat of mass unemployment*. London: Oneworld.

Foucault, M. (1984a). What is enlightenment? In P. Rabinow (Ed.), *The Foucault reader*. Harmondsworth: Penguin Books.

Foucault, M. (1984b). *The use of pleasure, The history of sexuality* (Vol. 2). London: Penguin Books.

Frey, C. B., & Osborne, M. O. (2013). *The future of employment*. Located on the internet (13 February 2016). http://www.oxfordmartin.ox.ac.uk/downloads/academic/The_Future_of_Employment.pdf.

Fromm, E. (1941). *Escape from freedom*. New York: Henry Holt and Company. 1994.

Giddens, A. (1991). *Modernity and self-identity. Self and society in the late modern age*. Cambridge: Polity Press.

Habermas, J. (1979). *Stichworte zur 'Geistigen Situation der Zeit' 1. band: Nation und Republik*. Frankfurt am Main: Suhrkamp Verlag.

Hammershøj, L. G. (2009). The social pathologies of self-realization: A diagnosis of the consequences of the shift in individualization. *Educational Philosophy and Theory, 41*(5), 507–526.

Hammershøj, L. G. (2015). Diagnosis of the times vs. description of society. *Current Sociology, 63*(2), 140–154.

Hammershøj, L. G. (2017a). The discourse and nature of creativity and innovation: Ways of relating to the novel. *Educational Philosophy and Theory*. http://www.tandfonline.com/doi/abs/10.1080/00131857.2016.1278353?journalCode=rept20.

Hammershøj, L. G. (2017b). Conceptualizing creativity and innovation as affective processes: Steve jobs, Lars von trier, and responsible innovation. *Philosophy of Management*. https://www.springerprofessional.de/conceptualizing-creativity-and-innovation-as-affective-processes/12031150.

Hegel, G. W. F. (1807). *Phänomenologie des Geistes*. Hamburg: Felix Meiner Verlag. 1988.

Honneth, A. (1996). 'Pathologies of the social: The past and present of social philosophy' (a shorted version and translation of 'Pathologien des Sozialen'). In D. M. Rasmussen (Ed.), *Handbook of critical theory*. Oxford: Blackwell Publishers. 1999.

Honneth, A. (2004). Organized self-realization. *European Journal of Social Theory, 7*(4), 463–478.

Horkheimer, M., & Adorno, T. W. (1944). *Dialektik der Aufklärung*. Frankfurt am Main: S. Fisher Verlag, 1993.

Humboldt, W. (1793). Theorie der Bildung des Menschen. In *Schriften zur Anthropologie und Geschichte. (Werke I)*. Stuttgart: J. G. Cotta'sche Buchhandlung. 1960.

Kahn, H. (1962). *Thinking about the unthinkable*. New York: Avon Books.

Kahn, H., & Wiener, A. J. (1967). *A framework for speculation on the next thirty-three years*. New York: The Macmillan.

Kant, I. (1784). An answer to the question: What is enlightenment? In *Towards perpetual peace and other writings*. New Heaven: Yale University Press. 2006.

Koselleck, R. (1959). *Critique and crisis. Enlightenment and the pathogenesis of modern society*. Cambridge, MA: The MIT Press.

Kosow, H., & Gassner, R. (2008). *Methods of future and scenario analysis*. Bonn: Deutches Institut für Entwicklungspolitik.

Kristensen, J. E. (2008). "Krise, kritik og samtidsdiagnostik". In *Dansk Sociologi*. Nr 4, 19. *årgang 2008/2009*.

Lyotard, J.-F. (1979). *The postmodern condition*. Manchester: Manchester University Press. 1994.

Maffesoli, M. (1996). *The time of the tribes*. London: Sage Publications.

Marx, K. (1844). *Economic and philosophical manuscripts of 1844*. New York: International Publishers.

Marx, K., & Engels, F. (1848). *Das Kommunistiche Manifest*. Northbridge: Swenson & Kemp.

Moore, G. (1965). Cramming more components onto integrated circuits. *Electronics, 38*(8), 114–117.

More, T. (1516). *Utopia*.

Nietzsche, F. (1882). *Die fröhliche Wissenschaft,* Sämtliche Werke (Band 3). München: Deutscher Taschenbuch Verlag de Gruyter. 1988.

Poli, R. (2010). The many aspects of anticipation. *Foresight, 12*(3), 7–17.

Poli, R. (2014). Anticipation: What about turning the human and social sciences upside down? *Futures, 64*(2014), 15–18.

Ramirez, R., Mukherjee, M., Vezzoli, S., & Kramer, A. M. (2015). Scenarios as a scholarly methodology to produce 'interesting research'. *Futures, 71*(2015), 70–87.

Reese-Schäfer, W. (1996). Zeitdiagnose als wissenschaftliche Aufgabe. *Berliner Journal für Soziologie, 3*, 377–390.

Rose, N. (1996). *Inventing our selves – Psychology, power, and personhood*. Cambridge: Cambridge University Press.

Rousseau, J.-J. (1755). Discourse on the origin and foundation of inequality among mankind. In *The social contract and discourse on the origin and foundation of inequality among mankind*. New York: Washinton Square Press Pocket Books. 1967.

Schmidt, L.-H. (1992). *Det Socialanalytiske Perspektiv*. Århus: Aarhus Universitetsforlag.

Schmidt, L.-H. (2011). *On respect*. Aarhus: Aarhus University Press.

Simmel, G. (1903). '*Die Grosstädte und das Geistesleben*.' Gesamtausgabe, Band 7. Frankfurt am Main: Suhrkamp, 1992.

Susskind, R., & Susskind, D. (2015). *The future of the professions*. Oxford: Oxford University Press.

Urry, J. (2008). Climate change, travel and complex futures. *The British Journal of Sociology, 59*(2), 261–279.

Urry, J. (2016). *What is the future?* Cambridge: Polity Press.

Volkmann, U., & Schimank, U. (2002). *Soziologische Gegenwartsdiagnosen I. Eine Bestandsaufnahme*. Opladen: Leske + Budrich.

Weber, M. (1904). *Methodologische Schriften*. Frankfurt am Main: A. Fisher Verlag. 1968.

Yorke, M. (2006). *Employability in higher education: What it is – What it is not*. Heslington: The Higher Education Academy.

Zemsky, R. (2014). With a MOOC MOOC here, and a MOOC MOOC there, here a MOOC, there a MOOC, everywhere a MOOC MOOC. *The Journal of General Education, 63*(4), 237–243.

Remembering Past Futures

24

Paolo Jedlowski

Contents

Abstract

It may happen that individuals or groups remember some futures they expected in the past. Remembering past futures may occur in many communicative practices, from daily life conversations to scientific and political discourses. However interesting such a kind of memory may be, it has not been fully analyzed yet. It is a complex topic; working on it implies the intertwining of two fields of investigations: memory and future studies.

In this chapter, we will try to account for this intertwining and will briefly explore some contexts in which remembering past futures emerges in communication practices of different kinds. We will also underline how memories of past futures may be useful, both to social scientists and to social actors. As to social scientists, the focus on past futures is a tool that can be helpful in the history of societies and cultures. As to social actors, in their daily or their professional lives,

P. Jedlowski (✉)
University of Calabria, Arcavacata, Italy
e-mail: paolo.jedlowski@unical.it

© Springer Nature Switzerland AG 2019
R. Poli (ed.), *Handbook of Anticipation*,
https://doi.org/10.1007/978-3-319-91554-8_68

485

the recollection of some futures they imagined in the past may give new impetus to the ability to currently imagine the future; but it can also allow one to evaluate present plans and expectations in light of what has happened to yesterday's anticipations.

Keywords
Memory · Future · Memory of the future · Modernity · Daily life · Conversation · Generations · Progress · Utopia · Emancipatory social science · History · Sociology

Introduction

Some years ago, Isaac Asimov published a series of postcards drawn in Paris in 1899 and depicting the world as it was imagined to be like in the year 2000. The postcards had been prepared for the celebrations of the advent of the twentieth century (Asimov 1986). The drawings present a future rich in technological advances: they depict flying postmen, diving tourists, air battles, etc. Asimov added some commentaries to each illustration. Naturally, as he was writing eighty years later, he knew which fictional anticipations had realized and which had not. Commenting on pictures of submarines of the future, Asimov remarks how close the prediction was; in the case of illustrations where gravity is broken, the author comments that, as far as we know, this phenomenon is still impossible; as for women fashion of the twenty-first century, he wryly comments that there is nothing less foreseeable than fashion.

Asimov's book is a good approximation of what we intend to deal with in this chapter: memories of the futures that have been anticipated once in our – or our predecessors' – imagination.

As duly indicated in the introduction of this book, the anticipations of the future can be either implicit or explicit. The notion of "memories of the future" proposed by D. H. Ingvar (1985) within the field of neurological studies makes reference to implicit anticipations of the future – i.e., anticipations that are stored and operate in our organism regardless of consciousness and reflection. In his words, such memories consist of action plans and expectations on the future that, once stored in the frontal and prefrontal cortex of the brain, can be reactivated by the organism when facing situations that are similar to previous ones. This is mostly an unconsciously triggered reactivation, even though, in some cases – especially when preexisting patterns are manifestly inadequate –, it may be accompanied by a certain level of consciousness. In any case, it is a memory that contributes to the more general ability to manage our life over time. As D. H. Ingvar writes,

> lesions or dysfunctions of the frontal/prefrontal cortex give rise to states characterized by a 'loss of future', with consequent indifference, inactivity, lack of ambition, and inability to foresee the consequences of one's future behaviour (Ingvar 1985: 127).

Some kinds of implicit memories of the future also exist at a social level. Traditions and institutions may be considered as action plans and systems of expectations stored in societies. But some plans, some expectations, and some images of a dreamed (or dreaded) future can also be explicitly recalled and discussed by individuals and social actors within the framework of many kinds of communicative practices.

Remembering past futures can occur in existing communicative practices in any field of social life. Such practices can fulfil several functions, but they should generally be considered as the expression of the human ability to "sail" across time, thus exercising one's own thoughtfulness; they can be used to monitor an individual's or a community's course of action, comparing plans, dreams or aspirations of the past, with what has then been accomplished.

In general, despite their importance, social sciences have scarcely dealt with such practices. According to Barbara Adam and Chris Groves (Adam and Groves 2007), the expression "memories of the future" indicates a perspective of study, rather than a definite object:

> [it is] a perspective on it that views the past not as a collection of historical facts but rather as predecessors' images, plans, visions, ambitions and concerns for the future, which either came to fruition or remained unrealized (Adam and Groves 2007: 217).

In the attempt to make such a perspective operative, Jedlowski defines the memories of the future as explicit "recollections of what individuals and groups expected in the past" (Jedlowski 2016: 121). However, dealing with this topic is a complex task as it implies the intertwining of two fields of investigations: one concerning memory and the other concerning futurity. Over these pages, we will first try to account for this intertwining. Then, we will explore some contexts in which remembering past futures appears in communication practices of different kinds. Finally, we will observe some functions that can be fulfilled by remembering past futures both individually and collectively: on the one hand, the recollection of futures imagined in the past can allow us to evaluate present plans and expectations in the light of what we know has happened to yesterday's plans and expectations; on the other hand, such recollections may give new impetus to the ability to currently imagine the future.

Between Memory and Future Studies

As for studies on memory, the literature today is vast (for an overview see Tota and Hagen 2016). Memory is the field of a particular temporal dialectic: while on the one hand the flow of life over time entails effects which condition the future, on the other it is the present which shapes the past, ordering and interpreting its legacy (Jedlowski 2001). Any conservation of the past is also, simultaneously, the construction of it. Such a construction is embedded within social frameworks (Halbwachs 1925) which give the necessary support, thereby defining what is significant or should be remembered. It is a construction that depends on the identities that individuals and groups attribute to themselves at present, and that simultaneously helps to define them. And, it is a dynamic construction: in fact, the images of the past, that abound in any social group, are subject to processes including negotiations and conflicts. The stabilization of such images of the past is an aspect of the cultural hegemony that one part or another of the society acquires and endeavors to maintain over time, with greater or lesser success.

With respect to future studies, for the purposes of this chapter, the distinction made by Niklas Luhmann (1976) between *future presents* and *present future* is particularly useful. The former are the presents which still have to happen: the real future. The latter is the future that we imagine at present. The *present future* is what we are concerned with in this chapter.

The present future is a complex set of expectations, which contributes to conferring meaning to the actual present and informing the choices that will produce the future presents. It is a sort of temporal horizon: *the horizon of expectation* that is and was (more or less explicitly) implied in any moment of our life. Such a horizon refers to what *is not yet*, but, since it is perceived, it is part of *now*. As Luhmann writes:

> the essential characteristic of an horizon is that we can never touch it, never surpass it, but that in spite of that, it contributes to the definition of the situation (Luhmann 1976: 140).

This means that the expectations to which we refer in any present moment have a performative character: what we will do depends, at least to a given extent, on what we expect. A few decades ago, Robert K. Merton explored self-fulfilling prophecies, that, is the fact that our beliefs or assumptions influence how we see reality (Merton 1948). However, the principle is quite general: the present produces the future through the actions we perform, but the future, being anticipated in our imagination, produces the present, too, since the way we act is determined by our anticipations. Because of this performative effectiveness, both the images of the future and the images of the past are subject to negotiations and conflicts in any society. Both what is probable and what it is preferable to occur, are cultural constructs (Appadurai 2013), as are the images of the past.

This is true whether the imagined futures take place as they had been imagined or not. Asimov's aforementioned postcards depict futures that mostly did not occur. Nonetheless, they had a certain performative character: they expressed the aspirations and visions of the then dominant classes, they inspired people's imagination. As happened with Jules Verne's, or other authors', science fiction, these images contributed to making the idea of progress (or a certain idea of progress) seem simply common sense. It is the memory of horizons that interests us in this chapter: remembering past futures means remembering the futures which were once present, and which contribute to the generation of the future we are now experiencing.

Preunderstanding the Future

Our horizons of expectation are aspects of the preunderstanding of the world we are living in (Schutz 1959). But they are dynamic. What is "surprising" becomes such only, in so far as it does not overlap with any individual's or a group's expectations.

Thus, any new experience creates a reformulation of the horizon. This, in turn, means that the horizons of expectation change over time. However, it is possible to keep track of the horizons of expectation considered in the past.

As Edmund Husserl writes, "Every act of memory contains intentions of expectations whose fulfilment lead up to the present" (Husserl 1893/1917, 1964: 76). This means that what we know now has an influence on the image of the event we recall. But it also indicates that a given horizon of expectation was contained in any past moment, and memory allows us to be in contact with it.

As Alfred Schutz (1959) emphasizes in his essay *Tiresias* (where the figure of the ancient prophet serves to highlight by contrast how uncertain the anticipations of the human beings not gifted with his power are), no horizon of expectation is formulated by an individual without connections to the knowledge of the social groups to which he or she belongs. The preunderstanding of the future of each of us largely depends on a socially derived stock of knowledge. As Schutz writes:

> ... man in everyday life interprets his past, present, and future in terms of the preorganized stock of knowledge he has at hand at any moment of his existence. [But] my stock of knowledge at hand does not consist exclusively of experiences lived through directly and originally by me. The greater portion of it is rather socially derived: it consists, that is, of experiences lived through directly and originally by my fellowmen, who communicated them to me (Schutz 1959: 76).

This implies two issues for our analysis. The first one is that a society is made up of several competing groups: the socially-derived expectations, in a sphere of society, might be different from those in another sphere and they might also be in conflict with those other expectations; as in modern times, any individual is in contact with several spheres of society, this has an impact on the horizons of expectation of each one, thus making them plural. The second issue is that modernity is, by definition, the era where "*all that is solid melts into air*" (Berman 1982), meaning that everything relentlessly changes in such a way that any "preorganized stock of knowledge" tends to rapidly become outdated. This, in turn, implies that it cannot be taken for granted that memories of past futures are concretely activated: they could be considered useless.

When Reinhart Koselleck wrote *Futures Past* (Koselleck 1979), he meant that for the people of modern times, past futures are not worthy of interest: in modern times the horizons of expectation of the past increasingly tend to lose importance, since it is a feature of modernity itself to get rid of any acquired experience. In the *Neuzeit*, which means "modern time,"

> ... the difference between experience and expectation is increasingly enlarged; more precisely, [...] *Neuzeit* is conceived as *neue Zeit* only from the point at which eager expectations diverge and remove themselves from all previous experience (Koselleck 1979, 2004: 270).

It is difficult to deny that previous experience and new horizons of expectation in modern times tend to split apart. This, however, does not mean that all traces of the horizons of expectation of the past is erased. In the contemporary world, at least in Western countries, especially for the young adults living in metropolitan areas, the most relevant dimension of time is the present (Hartog 2003; Leccardi 1999 and 2005 among others). But this does not mean that, in our everyday life, we are cut off from any concern with the past and the future. It means that we are mostly concerned with short-term memories of things past and short-term anticipations of the things to come. And the fact of being mostly concerned with short-time memories and anticipations does not mean that we are always and only engaged with them: we still have the faculty to consider middle and long-term memories and anticipations; we may wish to do so, and often we do.

Remembering Past Futures in Daily Life Conversations

The fact that traces of past futures are maintained is especially evident in autobiographical accounts. It is well known that ordinary conversations are full of autobiographical narrative fragments (Ochs and Capps 2001, among others): in such narratives the memory of what was expected in the past appears very often. Any retrospective definition of our identity normally includes questions and assertions on the futures, which we have once considered possible. Although the focus on the comparison between present and past may be variable, it is difficult to avoid any kind of subjective negotiation between the expectations and plans conceived in the past and what has been achieved subsequently in the course of life (Brockmeier 2001).

This negotiation is part of what – with a term taken from psychoanalysis – we could define as *working through* one's own experience. It is true that working through one's own experience is made difficult in modern times by the fragmentation and the increasing speed of what is experienced by each of us (Rosa 2013). However, the absolute lack of a process of this kind is rare and it is usually perceived with uneasiness (Jedlowski 2000): in fact, this process emerges in countless conversations (with others or with oneself). This working through may lead to a healthy process of reconciliation with one's own history. Sometimes, on the contrary, it may lead to resentment or regret. It may also be that a subject tries to erase past aspirations or projects from his or her conscious memory, like in the words of one of the women I talked with, during my field research on this topic:

> . . . I wonder if my actual present is the future I imagined. . . Oh God, it is not so! It is good enough I'm not too full of resentment. Life has left so many wounds. . . Well, ordinary wounds I guess, not worth mentioning. I don't talk about them, don't even think about them (Jedlowski 2017: 38 – author's translation).

Thinking of some futures we aspired to, and failed to achieve, may be painful indeed. Past futures, however, may try to emerge. When the individual feels a disequilibrium between the actual Self and other imagined and once possible Selves, memory has to work through this disequilibrium. This occurs, in particular, when the course of life goes through unexpected turns, whether happy or unhappy. Indeed, any biographical transition involves reformulations of one's horizons of expectation, and these imply active confrontations with former horizons: without a memory of them, the novelty of the actual situation would not even be perceived.

It is worth noting that memories of the past futures may sometimes be a resource, too. The point is that we never have, and we have never had, a single horizon of expectation. Each of us always has many different and even contradictory expectations, regarding different aspects of life, related to different belongings, concerning different time scales, depending on many different discursive contexts. Expected futures cover in any case a range of possibilities wider than what actual life reserves for us: so that it may happen that, when some expectation fails, we turn back to some neglected past expectations to reorient ourselves – or even to recognize, in the new situation, some kind of opportunities (Bonica and Cardano 2008).

But it may also occur that certain memories of expected futures are fixed in autobiographical tales as a sort of anchoring of identity. An example from the literature can be useful. I am thinking here of *Great Expectations* by Dickens (Dickens 1860/1961), where Mrs. Pocket, a secondary character, is particularly illustrative of our reasoning here, is. Her identity, in her discourses as well as in the discourses of those who know her, is continuously defined on the basis of her "poor grandpapa's position." Her grandfather was not a noble man, but he *might have been* it (because of some ancient promise he received), and therefore, she also *might have been* a member of the nobility. The fact that she did not become noble is marginal: the point is that the field of the possibilities contained in the past has become a consolidated element of her identity.

In any case, some kind of confrontation between the futures people imagined in the past and the present, with its own horizon of expectation, seems almost unescapable in autobiographical accounts. It is a part of the processes by which people reflect about their own stories, maintaining, changing, or developing their capacity to aspire and to travel toward the future through their daily activities (Pellegrino and Deriu 2016).

Intergenerational Confrontations

Remembering past futures in ordinary conversations has often to do with intergenerational confrontation. In his classic essay, Karl Mannheim (1923) gave a definition of generation as a group of individuals who, in the crucial years of their formation, have experienced similar historical events and built a partially shared memory. But a generation is not only made up of a set of experiences and memories: it also elaborates its own horizons of expectation and constitutes itself in the divide with the horizon of expectation of the previous generation.

Generational differentiation is particularly marked when generational identities overlap with the rise of new social movements. Memories regarding one's participation in these movements may last for a long time: and daughters and sons of former activists may have to deal with them. In the decades after 1968, for example, the narratives of former activists continuously came to terms with past hopes and expectations, evaluated continuity and discontinuity, and reacted to the discourses and reconstructions proposed by different actors (Passerini 2007; Cornils and Waters 2010). But the subsequent generations could not avoid coming to terms with such memories, too, as regards both the enthusiasm of that time and the outcomes and disenchantment following that period of social mobilization. Here, memories of past futures are the memories of the parents' expectations, and the new generations have talked about that, and indeed still do so.

A similar confrontation between past and new expectations can be found in the relationships between daughters and sons of migrants and their parents. The future actively pursued by mothers and fathers determines the conditions under which their children are supposed to imagine the future in their turn; however, the latter live in a different context, where inherited memories are actively re-elaborated (Creet and Kitzmann 2011) and where different expectations can and ought to be conceived. These are complex and hardly foreseeable negotiation processes between different generations. It can be true that the reasons for leaving home can be multiple and sometimes even elusive, but the descendants of the migrants somehow have to come to terms with the reasons of their fathers and mothers, with the memories of the futures their parents have refused and the futures that they sought. The migrant parents have to come to terms with what the situation they helped to create means for their children. All this may happen tacitly, but it may also be the object of endless conversations within the families and among peer groups.

Memories of the Progress

The comparison with the past crystallizes sometimes into a nostalgic idealization of the futures once considered possible. Nostalgia is a feeling which invest a lost past with desire. Such a feeling, however, can develop toward different orientations. Svetlana Boym (2001) distinguishes between two different kinds of nostalgia: *restorative* nostalgia and *reflective* nostalgia. The former suggests the return to the past, something like the reconstruction of an original and lost home. Restorative nostalgia is often part of the rhetoric of conservative political parties; in popular feelings, this corresponds to what Zygmunt Bauman called "retropia," that is some conscious attempts at iteration of an existing, or imagined to have existed, "*status quo ante*" (Bauman 2017: 9). Reflexive nostalgia, on the contrary, accepts the loss, comes to terms with it, and invites us to elaborate it.

Reflective nostalgia may have a critical function on the present and on the processes which have brought us to the present state of things (Atia and Davis 2010). In particular, it may express itself today within discussions about the ambivalent aspects of the modern program and the concrete achievements to which "progress" has led. Such a theme is present indeed in many everyday life conversations. Feelings like frustration and resentment are nurtured by the confrontation between past and present horizons of expectation. It is particularly evident in Western postindustrial areas, where people often recall the industrial era's expectations, but at the same time talk about pollution, illness, and diseases which those expectations, and the actions such expectations fostered, gave birth to. In such a way, the era of progress may be remembered nostalgically (there were plenty of jobs, rising consumptions, established workers' rights), but at the same time, thanks to the knowledge of what later happened, it may also be criticized, potentially offering itself to new thoughts about the notions of "progress" or "development" as such.

As Adam and Groves write, we are indeed "the recipients of [our predecessors'] pretence, of their illusion" (Adam and Groves 2007: 13). Being aware of this means meeting social theory. One can make reference to the promises of the past, talking about an "unfinished project" of modernity (Habermas 1985), or can reflect on the "consequences of modernity" (Giddens 1990). The first option makes reference to the *Dialectic of Enlightenment* by Max Horkheimer and Theodor W. Adorno, in the preface of which the authors wrote "What is at stake is not conservation of the past but the fulfilment of past hopes" (1947, 2002: xvii). The second option refers to the acknowledgment of the unintentional effects and unprecedented risks implied in the technological progress (the possibility of nuclear catastrophes, pollution, depletion of natural resources) and exhorts people to develop new forms of reflexivity capable of planning a different future (Beck 1986). In both cases what is at stake are exactly the memories of the future: that is, the reconsideration of plans, dreams, aspirations, and discourses about the future, in a world of the horizons of expectation that have characterized and nurtured modernity.

John Urry writes:

> Although it is impossible to "know" what the future has in store for us, most societies [. . .] developed procedures and discourses through which the future could be anticipated, talked about and in some sense known, whether that perceived future was in the hands of gods or of humans. People have imagined, predicted, divined, prophesied and told the future. These forms of future anticipation of the past – what can be termed "past futures" – provide some key terms and issues in subsequent future-making (Urry 2016: 32).

The key terms and issues we have inherited from the discourse of modernity, with the centrality it gave to the very notion of "progress," seem problematic today. Some social theorists thus suggest that the idea of progress should be now forgotten. Others say it has to be redesigned: but in order to do so, it is still necessary to consider what past expectations have produced. As Pierre-André Taguieff, for instance, writes:

> After the epoch of hectic and irresponsible transformation, whose destructive effects are now attested, the epoch of intelligent preservation could start, based on the consensual will to respect the past and manage the Earth (Taguieff 2004: 323).

Assertions of this kind correspond to an exhortation to learn something from the history of expectations cherished in the past. Because the memory of past futures is not only the mere contemplation of what we expected: it is also nurtured by the awareness of how things actually developed.

Postcolonial Memories

The recollection of unfulfilled expectations and hopes may suggest melancholic attitudes to some. Melancholy does not necessarily correspond to renunciation of action: as Enzo Traverso (2016) notes, many of those who saw their hopes of reforms or revolutions defeated or betrayed during the twentieth century, are able to transform their grief into renewed energy. A completely different case is represented by some members of the white middle-lower class in today's UK. Referring to these people, Paul Gilroy (2005) talked about *postcolonial melancholy*, that is not only the nostalgia for a lost empire and its possible eventual future, but also a feeling of true aggressive depression, nurturing racist violence.

Mentioning racism, however, implies broadening the framework of discussion. The memory of the futures that have been planned in modern times has a dark side: the memory of the futures dreamed up by Nazism and the anti-Semitic movements also belong (or should be regarded as belonging) to this category (Confino 2014). Racist theories are part of modern history, as much as the Holocaust belongs to modernity (Bauman 1989). The memory at stake is the memory of the victims who have been deprived of their future.

Similarly, the legacies of the colonial age and the violence perpetrated in the name of "civilization" belong to the same dark side of modernity. Also in this case, remembering the past futures means, above all, remembering futures stolen with violence from those who have been assaulted. More generally, the development of modernity in the West was, to a great extent, the result of unequal exchanges with many parts of the world: this means that memories of the past futures should also be memories of the futures designed by imperialism and colonialism. In the areas that underwent colonization processes, the expectations of the oppressed populations overlapped with the futures that other people imagined for them.

This imposition protracted until the postcolonial period. As Dipesh Chakrabarty notes, the policies that we still attempt to impose at an international level to the so-called "developing countries" share the fact that the future, in such countries, is considered as "something which has already happened elsewhere, and which is to be reproduced, mechanically or otherwise, with a local content" (Chakrabarty 2000: 39).

However, also the resistance to this logic may be interlocked with certain memories of the future: in the precolonial past or in the more or less explicit movements of resistance to colonialism and to postcolonialism, new movements can detect traces or fragments of other imagined futures and design a new kind of future-making. The newly developing countries of former colonized areas of the world are also now coping with the heritage of modernity, and somehow have to reformulate it. As Jean and John L. Comaroff write, the so-called global South today

> . . . is producing and exporting some ingenious modes of survival - and more. It is often those adversely affected by modernity who recommission its means most effectively and most radically, thus also to bring to light long suppressed elements of its intrinsic nature. Indeed, it is precisely this dialectic that has pushed Africa, Asia, and Latin America to the vanguard of the epoch (Comaroff and Comaroff 2012: 125).

Remembering Utopia

One of the ways human beings reconcile themselves with their own history is to affirm "it was Fate!." Through this expression the speaker especially comes to terms with a disgrace, a failure, in short, an unexpected and unhappy course of events. In today's discourses, however, fate is not a frequently used word: modern sensitivity, as a whole, reacts with annoyance, as it clashes against notions such as self-determination, responsibility, and freedom. However paradoxical it may be, the idea of fate is ultimately more frequently used – at least implicitly – when collective history is at stake.

A sort of inevitability is retrospectively attributed to what has happened. The history of progress is also sometimes considered under this perspective. It becomes, therefore, a linear history. However, any step forward in the course of scientific, technological, and social progress has met crossroads and routes initially taken and then left, chances precluded before they could arise. The fact that a certain invention or one of its applications has become common to the detriment of others is usually the result of the interaction between recognizable and diverse factors, including the conflicts amongst different interests. The idea of a "necessary" succession of innovations is the product of an absent-minded common sense, that forgets about the unrealized novelties.

It is not only a matter of set-aside inventions or technological innovations. The same applies to alternative social systems. Thinking about what has been imagined but not realized, the past may look like a collection of "not-yets" rather than "no longers." This is the perspective that Ernst Bloch (1947) suggested to apply to utopian dreams about human societies nurtured in the past.

In the original book by Thomas More, where the word first appeared in the sixteenth century, utopia had indeed a spatial meaning: it did not refer to futurity. It was a desirable "elsewhere" located in an inaccessible space that was contemporary to the present. However, starting from the eighteenth century, the meaning of the word underwent a process of temporalization. The "elsewhere" moved to the future: it became the name of a longed-for society whose creation would have been possible by interrupting the historical continuum with a revolution. If we consider utopia in this way, i.e., as the design of something that could be realized in the future, its memory falls within what we are dealing with in this chapter.

During the first part of the twentieth century, the idea of utopia was bitterly debated. The social regimes that in the twentieth century invoked Marxism have pretended to realize utopia in history. But their totalitarian ideas are responsible for the discredit that many have associated with this idea. Even authors who have expressed a certain sympathy toward the notion of utopia have not failed to detect their defects. Lewis Mumford, for example, in the 1962 preface to his *The Story of Utopias*, noted that all the political utopias have attempted to impose a "monolithic discipline" on the immense variety of men's activities and interests, creating absolute government systems incapable of responding to any new demand that would put them into question (Mumford 1922/1962).

In fact, far more than utopian representations, twentieth-century fiction offers dystopian representations. The utopia is overturned: dystopia is a depiction of disgraceful futures, aimed at avoiding their realization (Kumar 1987). From the sixties and seventies of the twentieth century onward, however, there has been a remarkable return to the utopian impulse. This impulse has created new narratives that have used utopia in a critical manner (Moylan 1986, see also Jameson 2005). The basic idea of such narratives is that "the proper role of utopia is estrangement, calling into question the existing state of affairs, rather than constructing a plan for the future" (Levitas 2013: 119).

This type of narrative generally rejected utopian depictions as models of a future society, preserving them, however, as dreams that deserve to be remembered, and reactivating them as mental exercises capable of opening up new social possibilities.

In this way, the memory of utopian societies dreamed in the past has a dual function. On the one hand, it is useful to understand how and why what some have hoped for has not been realized in history; but, on the other hand, it serves to keep alive and renew hope itself.

In both of these meanings, the memory of the utopian futures imagined in the past turns out to be precious. The representations of utopia are a testimony to the human capacity to cherish hopes and to imagine different states of things. Hope is not exactly an expectation: its function is mainly that of interrupting adherence to the course of events, i.e., of questioning their inevitability and allowing oneself to imagine the world otherwise. Utopian visions enable people "to break with the dominance of the currently routine and normal" (Urry 2016: 93, quoting Bauman 1976). If it is true that the future today is in crisis, remembering utopia may contribute to generating a new impetus, rebuilding space for a fruitful tension between dreams and practice.

Memories of the Future and Social Sciences

According to Erik Olin Wright, rebuilding this aforementioned space should be grounded in "the belief that what is pragmatically possible is not fixed independently of our imaginations, but is itself shaped by our visions" (Wright 2010: 6). Such a belief is a part of what he calls an "emancipatory social science."

Thinking of the same kind of social science, John Urry writes that

> the terrain of future studies should be reclaimed for social sciences [because] future visions have powerful consequences and social science needs to be central in disentangling, debating and delivering those futures (Urry 2016: 7).

We believe that the same is true for the memories of past futures. Social scientists have good reasons to be curious about this topic. As the futures that social actors imagined in the past were supported by some specific social frameworks, the focus on past futures is a tool that can be useful for the history of cultures, of social imagination and of mentalities. But not only historians are involved. For social scientists, the issue of the sense that each of us attributes to our actions is hardly avoidable: however, part of the sense of anyone's actions is related to the futures he or she expects.

And there is a further reason to be interested in the theme: as we have already noted, any representation of the future has a performative character, and this means that, among the causes of our present situation, past representations of the future have to be considered, too. It is not just a matter of history. Like any other element of the past, past futures that we keep in our minds contribute to developing identities, justifying actions, and legitimizing certain choices rather than others. Caring for the future is related to our capacity to thoroughly reconsider our memories of the futures we sought for.

Under many respects, the present crisis of the Western world questions the models of development from which modernity prevalently took inspiration, that is the action plans and expectations we or our predecessors have nurtured in the past. As Adam and Groves (2007) suggest, this crisis may even require a critical review of the notion of future itself: the abstract and measurable future that is conceived by modern, economic, and scientific thought should be replaced by a more concrete idea of future that is attentive to the consequences of actions and plans and characterized by a sense of responsibility. Being responsible means both answering for the consequences of what we did in the past and considering the consequences of our current actions. On both sides, what is at stake is an intertwining between memory and anticipation.

Both the representations of the future and those of the past are subject to conflicts among different individuals and groups. This is true for the memories of the future, too. Forgetting some once-glimpsed possibilities may be used to weaken any criticism about the current social order. On the contrary, remembering them may be useful in reopening our imagination.

Summary

Remembering past futures means activating the memory of action plans, feelings, and images that once belonged to our horizons of expectation (ours or our predecessors').

As it is in perpetual change, modernity seems to deprive the horizons of expectation nurtured in the past of any usefulness. On the other hand, the acceleration of the change makes individuals and groups less prone to paying attention to the past. However, traces of the past horizons of expectation remain, and such traces are often reactivated in many discourses.

When they become the object of memory, the past horizons of expectation go through the same selection, interpretation, and reconstruction processes that characterize any mnestic process. Their main feature lies in the fact that they are connected to what we know about how the situations actually evolved: we know the destiny of past futures.

Such feature gives them a certain practical importance that contradicts the idea of their uselessness: remembering the expectations of the past, being aware that they then turned out to be more or less grounded, is useful in improving our present ability to foresee and plan futures. In general, since expectations fall within some social contexts and they themselves have contributed to the course of the events that occurred, reflecting on the past horizons of expectation helps us understand history. The horizons of expectation are rarely completely conscious, but remembering them also means making them explicit: this helps us recognize our part of responsibility in history itself.

Any horizon of expectation includes a variety of possibilities: only some of them have been actually pursued and, of these, only a few have been fulfilled. In this perspective, remembering the horizons of expectation means also being able to consider the past as a reservoir of "not-yets" that are still waiting to be fulfilled. Some possibilities that were once discarded may turn out to be useful in planning futures other than those fulfilled. In any case, thinking of these discarded possibilities may help to reopen our capacity for imagination.

References

Adam, B., & Groves, C. (2007). *Future matters. Action, knowledge, ethics*. London: Brill.
Appadurai, A. (2013). *The future as cultural fact: Essays on the global condition*. London: Verso.
Asimov, I. (1986). *Futuredays*. New York: Henry Holt & Co.
Atia, N. Davies, J. (2010). Nostalgia and the shapes of history. Editorial. *Memory Studies*, 3(3), 181–186.
Bauman, Z. (1976). *Socialism: The active Utopia*. London: George Allen and Unwin.
Bauman, Z. (1989). *Modernity and the Holocaust*. Ithaca: Cornell University Press.
Bauman, Z. (2017). *Retropia*. Cambridge: Polity Press.
Beck, U. (1986). *Risk society: Towards a new modernity*. London: SAGE. (Trans. 1992).
Berman, M. (1982). *All that is solid melts into air: The experience of modernity*. New York: Penguin Books.
Bloch, E. (1947). *The principle of hope*. Cambridge: MIT Press. (Trans. 1986).
Bonica, L., & Cardano, M. (2008). *Punti di svolta. Analisi del mutamento biografico*. Bologna: Il Mulino.
Boym, S. (2001). *The future of nostalgia*. New York: Basic Books.
Brockmeier, J. (2001). From the end to the beginning. Retrospective teleology in autobiography. In J. Brockmeier & D. A. Carbaugh (Eds.), *Narratives and identity. Studies in autobiography, self and culture* (pp. 247–280). Amsterdam: John Benjamins.
Chakrabarty, D. (2000). *Provincializing Europe. Postcolonial thought and historical difference*. Princeton/Oxford: Princeton University Press.
Comaroff, J., & Comaroff, J. L. (2012). Theory from the south: Or, how Euro-America is evolving toward Africa. *Anthropological Forum: A Journal of Social Anthropology and Comparative Sociology, 2*(XXII), 113–131.
Confino, A. (2014). *A world without Jews. The Nazi imagination from persecution to genocide*. New Haven: Yale University Press.
Cornils, I., & Waters, S. (Eds.). (2010). *Memories of 1968: International perspectives*. Oxford: Peter Lang.
Creet, J., & Kitzmann, A. (Eds.). (2011). *Memory and migration. Multidisciplinary approaches to emory studies*. Toronto: University of Toronto Press.
Dickens, C. (1860/1961). *Great expectations*. Oxford: Clarendon Press. (Reprinted 1993).
Giddens, A. (1990). *The consequences of modernity*. Cambridge: Polity Press.

Gilroy, P. (2005). *Postcolonial Melancholia*. New York: Columbia University Press.

Habermas, J. (1985). *The philosophical discourse of modernity. Twelve lectures*. Cambridge: Polity Press. (Trans. 1990).

Halbwachs, M. (1925). *On collective memory*. Chicago: University of Chicago Press. (Trans. 1992).

Hartog, F. (2003). *Régimes d'historicité. Présentisme et experience du temps*. Paris: Editions du Seuil.

Horkheimer, M., & Adorno, T. W. (1947). *Dialectic of enlightenment. Philosophical fragments*. Stanford: Stanford University Press. (Trans. 2002).

Husserl, E. (1893/1917). *The phenomenology of internal time-consciousness*. Bloomington: Indiana University Press. (Trans. 1964).

Ingvar, D. H. (1985). "Memories of the future": An essay on temporal organization of conscious awareness. *Human Neurobiology, 4*(3), 127–136.

Jameson, F. (2005). *Archaeologies of the future*. London: Verso.

Jedlowski, P. (2000). *Storie comuni. La narrazione nella vita quotidiana*. Milano: Bruno Mondadori.

Jedlowski, P. (2001). Memory and sociology: Themes and issues. *Time & Society, 1*(X), 29–44.

Jedlowski, P. (2016). Memories of the future. In A. L. Tota & T. Hagen (Eds.), *Routledge international handbook of memory studies*. London/New York: Routledge.

Jedlowski, P. (2017). *Memorie del futuro. Un percorso fra sociologia e studi culturali*. Roma: Carocci.

Koselleck, R. (1979). *Futures past. On the semantic of historical time*. New York: Columbia University Press. (Trans. 2004).

Kumar, K. (1987). *Utopia and anti-Utopia in modern times*. Oxford: Basil Blackwell.

Leccardi, C. (1999). Time, young people and the future. *Young, 3*(VII), 3–18.

Leccardi, C. (2005). Facing uncertainty temporality and biographies in the new century. *Young Nordic Journal of Youth Research, 2*(XIII), 123–146.

Levitas, R. (2013). *Utopia as method. The imaginary reconstruction of society*. Basingstock: Palgrave MacMillan.

Luhmann, N. (1976). The future cannot begin: Temporal structures in modern societies. *Social Research, 1*(XLIII), 130–152.

Mannheim, K. (1923). The problem of generations. In *Essays on the sociology of knowledge*. London: Routledge and Kegan Paul. (Trans. 1952).

Merton, R. K. (1948). The self-fulfilling prophecy. In *Social theory and social structure*. New York: Free Press. (Reprinted 1968).

Moylan, T. (1986). *Demand the impossible. Science fiction and the utopian imagination*. New York/London: Methuen.

Mumford, L. (1922). *The story of Utopias*. London: Penguin Books. (Reprinted 1962).

Ochs, E., & Capps, L. (2001). *Living narrative: Creating lives in everyday storytelling*. Cambridge, MA: Harvard University Press.

Passerini, L. (2007). *Memory and Utopia. The primacy of intersubjectivity*. London: Equinox.

Pellegrino, V., & Deriu, M. (2016). La "capacità di aspirare" oggi. Tra cronofrenia e utopie quotidiane. In F. Corbisiero & E. Ruspini (Eds.), *Sociologia del futuro*. Milano: Wolter Kluwer Italia/CEDAM.

Rosa, H. (2013). *Alienation and acceleration. towards a critical theory of late-modern temporality*. Malmö: NSU Press.

Schutz, A. (1959). Tiresias, or our knowledge of future events. *Social Research, 1*(XXVI), 71–89.

Taguieff, P.-A. (2004). *Le sens du progrès*. Paris: Flammarion.

Tota, A. L., & Hagen, T. (Eds.). (2016). *Routledge international handbook of memory studies*. London/New York: Routledge.

Traverso, E. (2016). *Left-wing elancholia. Marxism, history and memory*. New York: Columbia University Press.

Urry, J. (2016). *What is the future?* Cambridge, MA: Polity Press.

Wright, E. O. (2010). *Envisioning real Utopias*. London: Verso.

Anticipating Utopia: Utopian Narrative and an Ontology of Representation

25

Jennifer A. Wagner-Lawlor

Contents

Abstract

While the words "utopia" and "anticipation" frequently appear together in discussions of the concepts of utopia and dystopia, little attention to the relationship of Anticipation Studies to utopian studies exists. Moreover, the relevance of *literature* and the arts to Anticipation Studies seems almost (not quite) invisible. This essay focuses on the structuring of the *original* utopian narrative, Sir Thomas More's *Utopia* (*The Utopia of Sir Thomas More*. New York: Macmillan [1895 edition] 1516), in order to understand how this seminal text conceptualizes utopia's relation to past, present, and future. This analysis focuses on the complex framing devices characteristic of utopian narrative, as well as its open-endedness. The embedding of narratives sets up the dynamic movement between past, present, and future – the various forms of temporality – that allows us to clarify the nature of utopian anticipation.

Throughout the chapter, I attempt to connect utopian textual and conceptual theory to specific concepts in the emerging field of Anticipation Studies, with which Utopian Studies, a long-established interdisciplinary field, have not yet

J. A. Wagner-Lawlor (✉)
Department of Women's, Gender and Sexuality Studies and English, The Pennsylvania State University, University Park, PA, USA
e-mail: jaw55@psu.edu

© Springer Nature Switzerland AG 2019   501
R. Poli (ed.), *Handbook of Anticipation*,
https://doi.org/10.1007/978-3-319-91554-8_63

engaged. Of particular interest is the notion, promoted by Miguel Abensour, that utopia is always a *disruption* and thus not an anticipation in any "natural" or logical sense: "what matters is the *orientation toward what is different, the wish for the advent of a radical alterity* here and now" (*Constellations* 15(3): 407, 2008). From this premise, we can reintroduce a neglected literary term from science fiction theorist, Darko Suvin: the *novum*. The eruption of a future from a point of radical alterity – an ontological accident – opens up radical implication for the nature of utopian anticipation and futurity.

Finally the essay suggests that Robert Poli's and Robert Rosen's description of an anticipatory system as comprising "the predictive model of itself" within the genre's formal characteristics is in fact present in the structure of the utopian narratives: that is, that the persistence of utopia – as a literary genre and as a political concept – inheres in the narratological structuring of the possibility of another story and another listener. Utopian narrative thus ultimately anticipates not only temporal relationality, but an ethical relation between the outside narrator, the utopian traveler/narrator, and the reader. It anticipates *another story.*

Keywords

Utopia · Narrative · Literature · Plasticity · Alterity and difference · Persistence · Process theory · Speculation and Speculative Standpoint · Performativity · Historicization of the present · Novum · Virtual Reality

Introduction

While the words "utopia" and "anticipation" frequently appear together in discussions of the concepts of utopia and dystopia, little attention to the relationship of Anticipation Studies to utopian studies exists. Moreover, the relevance of *literature* and the arts to Anticipation Studies seems almost (not quite) invisible. More than one anticipation theorist claims the field as the exclusive domain of the social sciences, though most admit at least the role of the sciences in our understanding of how perception and cognition must contribute to an embodied experience of anticipation. Of literature and art, precious little is said, no doubt because of the assumption that Anticipation Studies is an interdisciplinary social science. Roberto Poli's editorial decision to include in this handbook a section on utopian literature is therefore especially welcome, acknowledging as it does the role of imagination and the arts in the structuring and representation of an anticipatory experience.

Too often however utopian narratives are themselves read as if they were speculative sociology or political theory: many scholars and readers want to know what Utopia looks like, how its people live, how work and play and domestic life are organized, and how we get there from here. It is no accident that early criticism of utopian texts was not really *literary* criticism. Compelled to answer to Marx's denigration of utopia as fantasy, the tendency was (still is, for many) to compensate for the absence of a programmatic politics by stressing what is "useful" about utopian dreaming and therefore where or how exactly a utopian *text* reveals or creates political drive or motivates political action. This is what gets called *utopian anticipation*, and we can look back at the history of utopian writing and note the precision of a writer's perception of tendencies in the present that are then extrapolated out. In the strictly utopian mode are envisioned scenarios or tableaux of something similar to the writer's present – but better, corrected. These visions are generally taken as subtle diagnoses of contemporary societies. For this reason the close relationship between utopian writing as a genre and satire as a literary mode is written into Sir Thomas More's originary text, *Utopia* (1516). Dystopian texts are the flip side of the same coin: the diagnosis, however, is accompanied by a specifically negative prognosis, drawing out possible consequences for tomorrow of toxic sociopolitical tendencies left untreated today. Bulwer Lytton's unsettling science fiction/utopian novel, *The Coming Race* (1871), is an early example; Margaret Atwood's *The Handmaid's Tale* (1985) and the more recent opener to the MaddAddam trilogy, *Oryx and Crake* (2003), also spring to mind.

This essay shifts the focus from prognoses to projections by narrowing our attention to the formal aspects of utopian narrative: the *narrative structure itself.* While a political reading of utopian fiction wants to achieve something that can be called "concrete" – indeed, the term *concrete utopia* commonly appears in utopian studies – from a purely literary standpoint, utopian narratives are as concrete as they can be or need to be. Theorists have long since concluded that the "concretization" of any one utopia is not the objective, but in fact an outcome to be avoided: the blueprint model is rejected as exclusionary and often reactionary. What takes its place is a model of utopia that is far more plastic, to the degree that some theorists have asked if there is in fact anything we can say any more about the "nature of utopia" (Levitas). We can, but its nature is complex.

Philosopher Miguel Abensour proposes thinking past any simple notion of the anticipatory nature of utopia, but rather about its *persistent* nature. Defining utopia as "*the various forms of alterity* to which the desire for freedom ... has given birth through the course of history," what matters is the "*orientation toward what is different, the wish for the advent of a radical alterity* here and now." Utopia may seem to tell a story about historical tendencies and ideologic propensities that direct history a certain way, but utopia is also a kind of disruption: "the non-coincidence between what was projected and what has come about throws us back into a new struggle for alterity. ...The *persistence of utopia*, we see, is due not so much to the repeated pursuit of a determinate content as to the ever-reborn movement toward something indeterminate" (407).

How is this "ever-reborn" movement represented in the literary form of utopia? Is there something about the "literariness" of utopia *as narrative* that motivates such regeneration? At the very least, according to Fredric Jameson, the concept of utopia offers "the spectacle of one of those rare phenomena whose concept is indistinguishable from its reality, whose ontology coincides with its representation" (2004: 35). Thinking of utopian narrative as a symbolic form captures what Abensour calls the essence of utopia; "this non-achievement of being, in its gap in relation to essence, that [in which] persistence of utopia resides, the engine of enigmatic rebirth ... [that]

derives its force from non-accomplishment" (2008: 409). My question therefore is modest: how does utopian narrative structure **anticipation** and **persistence,** the two temporal modalities that inhere in the nature of utopia?

Both utopia and anticipation are theorized as "structured narratives" (Poli) that embed difference and disruption within. Sir Thomas More's originary literary invention situates the "endless possibility" of anticipation and change, insofar as it models the possibility of an accidental event that constitutes the actual occasion of *telling a new story.* Characteristically a *framed* or *embedded* narrative, the utopian literary scenario does something else: it sets up a new relation between self and other that is anticipated in the survival of the generic utopian traveler/narrator. We as readers reaffirm the anticipation of another person – a stranger – who in the act of listening is also retelling. The very literariness of utopian literature sets up the virtual possibility of a new "community" – even if that community consists of only two people. As Lawrence Davis writes:

> If one chooses to read utopian texts solely through the distorting lenses of the anti-utopian liberal caricature, then one will surely see in this idiosyncratic form nothing but further proof of utopia's irrational, potentially fanatical tendencies. If, on the other hand, one interprets literary and rhetorical devices of the utopian text as a means by which its author undertakes to engage the reader in imaginative ethical dialogue, then one may well reach a very different conclusion. (78)

This new community is ethical core of utopia, according to Silvana Rabinovich, and also its primary function: "to open up the mind to other possible models of listening, thinking, writing, in the hope of encouraging new ways of interacting with others, of allowing ourselves to be surprised by a world that is still to come, one that does not promise 'more of the same'" (113). In other words, it anticipates the possibility of a new relation and of another story.

Anticipatory Foundations, Utopian Frameworks

Roberto Poli has been instrumental in defining the nature and purpose of Anticipation Studies, which pursue and characterize the ways in which humans "seek to foresee the future development of relevant situations" (2010a). Such efforts have many designations and come in many forms, and clearly the concept of utopia is one of them. Yet narrowly defined, the neologism *utopia* does not connote anticipation or futurity, but alterity. As is well known, the word itself is an invention of Sir Thomas More, whose seminal work, *Utopia*, both coins the word and initiates a new literary genre. More's *Utopia* is an image or representation of a "good" (or substantially better) society or state of existence – a "good place" (Gr. *eu-topos*, good + place) that is "no place" (Gr. *ou-topos*, negative particle [non] + place). Etymologically there is no connection to "good time"; the term *euchronia* comes later, dramatically expanding the horizons, so to speak, of utopian journeying – into the future, into space, etc. More's literary model never leaves the author's "present" at all; the island

Fig. 1 The 1516 of More's *Utopia* (published in Louvain, Belgium), includes this famous woodcut (Image from http://www.joh.cam.ac.uk/library/special_collections/early_books/pix/utopia.htm)

of Utopia may be distant geographically from sixteenth-century London, but evidently not temporally. Indeed More's first edition famously includes a topographical map of the island (Figs. 1 and 2), mimicking the Renaissance exploration-narrative mapping of formerly unmarked seas, landmasses, and peoples. The implication is that commonwealth of Utopia "exists" in the here and now.

Fig. 2 A later edition (1518) includes the more elaborate map created by Ambrosius Holbein (Image from http://libweb5.princeton.edu/visual_materials/maps/websites/thematic-maps/theme-maps/more-map-utopia-1518.jpg)

Utopia scholar Fátima Vieira argues that while utopian thought is present in all times and places, the invention of utopia *as a figure* is context specific, as "a new idea, a new feeling that would give voice to the new currents of thought that were then [in the sixteenth century] arising in Europe" (2010: 4). These currents include a new "confidence in the human being's capacity . . . not yet a capacity to reach a state of human perfection (which would be impossible within a Christian worldview . . .) but at least an ability to arrange society differently in order to ensure peace" (2010: 4). This ability depends on a "humanistic logic, based on the discovery that the human being did not exist simply to accept his or her fate, but to use reason in order to build the future" (4). Such optimism is well reflected in the imperialist explorations of the Renaissance. More had read the travel accounts of Amerigo Vespucci, Christopher Columbus, and Angelo Poliziano; his fictional "utopian traveler," Raphael Hythloday, had sailed on three out four of Vespucci's voyages of explorations. The final time Hythloday stayed behind at the island of Utopia, whence comes his detailed knowledge of its social organization and governance. Thus *Utopia* models itself on these narratives of discovery, mimicking the scientific objectives of explorers' anthropological and cartographic representations – not to mention the economic and imperial objectives of such travel to terrae incognitae.

More's originary utopian text captures the *anticipation* of Europe's mastery of land and sea, as well as its exploitation of found resources (including slaves, which are present in Utopia). One of the (perhaps) unforeseen consequences was the discovery as well of developed peoples and cultures radically different from anything the European had seen before. The concept of utopia, the book *Utopia*, and every utopian narrative written since then is "context specific," as Vieira says; but to speak more emphatically, each is *situated* historically and politically, geographically, and temporally. More's narrative's situatedness is embodied, moreover, in not one but two figures: the traveler/narrator, Raphael Hythloday, and the listener, "More." (When referring to the author, I write *More*; when referring to the *character* of More who appears in *Utopia*, I designate his fictional status by writing *"More."*) The relationship is frequently overlooked, and yet it is key to pinpointing a crucial aspect of the anticipatory structure of utopian narrative *qua narrative*. Utopia is a *story* that must be told.

The centrality of the relational is manifest in the characteristic *framed narrative* as a formal trope. The utopian narrative's embedded structuring is fundamental to its task of opening up a space for freer thinking, or even speculation. Moreover this opening up results from a kind of *accident*: while the framed narrative would become a common device of the novelist, novel as such did not yet exist in the English tradition. Thus in *Utopia*, it is remarkable that "More" simply runs into friend Peter Giles, who in turn insists that he and one Raphael Hythloday meet one another, to More's regret and impatience, at times. "More" is pulled "off course" on this day in the life. This "interruption" is one of the generic traits of utopian narratives. Arriving at utopia, then, is typically an event that seems *out of place*, a kind of "shock event" (to use a currently popular, dystopian Trump-era term). The *encounter* of the traveler with utopia is a deviation from the path. In most cases, the discovery of utopia in any given text is accidental: ships get blown off course (*Gulliver's Travels*, 1726); carriages break down (*Millennium Hall,* 1762*,* 1890); the utopian narrator falls down a hidden crevice (*The Coming Race*, 1871) or falls asleep and "wakes up" either somewhere else or at some other time (*News from Nowhere*). Marge Piercy's Connie, in *Woman at the Edge of Time* (1985), is visited by an apparition from the future, who "transports" her to Mattapoisett: the standard utopian "guide" comes to her first. Arriving at a utopia always takes the narrator by *surprise*, overtaken (*sur-prise*) by an encounter with the strangeness of the place. And the life is forever different: this encounter catalyzes a "changed state" from a present state/status quo to a *new* state, which is itself constituted by the encounter, of some form of affective instability. The traveler feels confusion, fear, disbelief, amazement, and even wonder.

In that suspended moment of surprise, the narrator recognizes that he cannot "read" the scene: he/she is returned to a kind of epistemological childhood or state of "innocence," in the etymological sense of *not knowing*. This device creates a scene and sense of immediacy, a virtual here and now that suspends time as the story of strangeness is told. Thus the "tour-guide" format of nearly every utopian narrative is in effect a re-education project revealing the nature and extent of this alternate community. This program offers a new way of learning, knowing, and being – of bending the mind – accommodating oneself to new forms of ontology and epistemology. Originally doubtful of the tale, "More" is so affected by a desire to learn more that he leads Raphael with solicitude toward a meal that might guarantee further conversation. Accommodating difference, reaching across, as "More" does with Hythloday, the listener/reader attunes themselves to strangenesses that become familiar only to be put in high relief in that moment when suddenly the vision, dreamt or not, is over. As Laurence Davis writes, to "[interpret] literary and rhetorical devices of the utopian text as a means by which its author undertakes to engage the reader in imaginative ethical dialogue" (78) is necessary if we are to read utopias in the right spirit.

The open-ended closing of the narrative frame is a critical move, reiterating the ontological destabilization that opens it. More's structuring of the utopian narrative effectively *historicizes the present* – but at the end, this present is complicated not just by the past but by the memory of an alternate present, a haunting not of the past, but of a future. This is the central spatiotemporal paradox of the very concept of "(e)u-topia": a good place that is no place, a presence and a non-presence, and an ontological contradiction. "More" himself, having listened to Hythloday's report, judges much in Hythloday's story to be "quite absurd"; only Hythloday's evident learnedness and seeming rationality persuades (if not quite convinces) "More" that the account should be taken seriously. The text eventually closes with a more tempered assessment. One translation renders it this way:

> therfore I, praising both their institutions and his communication, toke him by the hand, and led him into supper; saying that we wold chuse an other time to way and examine the same matters, and to talke wyth him more at lardge therin. Whiche wold to God it might ones come to passe [*quae in nostris ciuitatibus optarim uerius quam sperarim*]. In the mean time as I can not agree and consent to all things that he said; being els without dowte a man singulerly well learned, and also in all wordely matters exactly and profoundely experienced; so must I nedes confesse and graunt, that many thinges be in the vtopian weal publique, which in our cities I may rather wisshe for [*optarim*] then hoope after [*sperarim*]. (1516: 308–309).

This is a hardly a hopeful conclusion. Yet it does leave possibility open, the possibility of "an other time" [*aliud tempus*], in which "I would/will be [Lat. *fore*] thinking further [*altius cogitandi*, with *altius* also suggesting 'at a higher level'] and conferring more fully [*uberius cum eo conferendi fore*, with *uberius* also suggesting productivity]." The word *fore* is the less common form of the future infinitive of *esse* (to be). In the way that narrative has of entangling forms of temporality, "More" is left, as is the reader is, with a *trace* of utopian difference as "some other time" and some other place: a potential future not yet realized in time or space, yet anticipated.

The importance of this trace feeling of "disconnect" is characteristic of every utopia narrative after More's. Having experienced his own strangeness in a strange land, having then learned and accommodated, and having extended himself toward the utopian other and become "at home," the traveler returns home to feel alienated once again, even when no time has passed. Now in exile from the utopian scene, like Adam and Eve sent from Paradise, the protagonist has a range of responses: from the exhilaration of knowing what is possible and being energized to bring about change to the desolation of finding oneself returned to a place that – however familiar it once was – now appears alien or barbaric. The narrator of *Herland* [Vandyck Jennings, trained as a sociologist] shares the discovery of the "nature" of woman when she allowed to develop outside the influence of a vicious masculinism. Jonathan Swift's Lemuel Gulliver returns with a similar exuberance – but the return itself is another shock event. "My memory and imagination were perpetually filled with the virtues and ideas of those exalted Houyhnhnms"; but entering his house he is filled with disgust: "As soon as I entered the house, my wife took me in her arms, and kissed me; at which, having not been used to the touch of that odious animal [his wife] for so many years, I fell into a swoon for almost an hour." Writing five years later, he remains happiest in the company of his stable horses. No doubt his human relations think him insane. Yet Gulliver is only one of many utopian travelers who discover the insanity, or unhealthiness, of the society whence he came.

William Morris's Mr. Guest (*News from Nowhere*) has both responses, "inexpressibly shocked" by the return to "dingy Hammersmith": "suddenly I saw as it were a black cloud rolling along to meet me, like a nightmare of my childish days; and for a while I was conscious of nothing else than being in the dark, and whether I was walking, or sitting, or lying down, I could not tell." Yet he finds himself not "so despairing" as he considers that his vision has a reality of its own, which he is tasked with showing to others. He imagines his nowhere-friend Ellen saying, "Go back again, now you have seen us ..." – and this final passage urges the reiterative narrative structure being articulated in this essay through a series of repetitions:

> "... *Go back again*
> then, and while you live you will see all round you people engaged in making others live lives which are not their own, ... *Go back* and be the happier for having seen us ... *Go on living* while you may, striving, ... with whatsoever pain and labour needs must be, to build up little by little the new day of fellowship, and rest, and happiness."

This persistence, this urgent reiteration, is the trace of the utopia's encounter with difference.

Utopia, Difference, and the Trace

Invoking the *trace* as a structural feature of utopian narrative signals the central-ity of Jacques Derrida to any contemporary discussion of narrative and time and indeed of utopia. His focus on a notion of "the trace structure of the sign" and the companionate term *différance* connects directly to the structuring of utopian process. Derrida defines *différance* as "the non-full, non-simple 'origin'; it is the structured and differing origin of differences" (1973: 141). Temporality is inherent to what is an ongoing process: "The trace is not a presence but is rather the simulacrum of a presence that dislocates, displaces, and refers beyond itself. The trace has, properly speaking, no place, for effacement belongs to the very structure of the trace" (1973: 156). This is the deconstructive moment, whereby "[t]he trace is not only the disappearance of origin... it means that the origin did not even disappear, that it was never constituted except reciprocally by a non-origin, the trace, which thus becomes the origin of the origin." The trace becomes in this model a generative kernel, co-constituted "reciprocally" in the event of an encounter with difference. Temporally speaking the trace never "is," it "does not exist," but neither is it "a being-present outside of all plenitude." It is temporally entangled, a "*dialectic of protention and retention that one would install in the heart of the present* instead of surrounding it [present] with it [dialectic]" (1976: 67). It is entangled because Derrida is trying to conceive time, not on the basis of the present but on the basis of the past and future. The trace is the trace of nothing fully present, which allows the trace's future to be open. While therefore the trace is said to "indicate a way out of the closure imposed by the system" (Wood and Bernasconi 1988: 2), the direction of that way is indeterminate, and the trace itself retains its essential *plastic* nature: "Difference is therefore the formation of form. But it is on the other hand the being-imprinted of the imprint."

This plasticity is critical, as Derrida's onetime student, Catherine Malabou, continues to show us. If "the (pure) trace is difference," then, Derrida argues, it is also "repeatable" as nonidentical to itself. All that can be *anticipated* of the trace is its repeatability: the simultaneity of protention (in anticipation) and retention (the "irreducibility of the always already there"). According to Leonard Lawlor (2016), "[t]his 'at the same time' is the crux of the matter for Derrida": "*The memory and the anticipation consist in repeatability.* Because what I experience now can be immediately recalled, it is repeatable and that repeatability therefore motivates me to anticipate the same thing happening again. .... *At the same time, the present experience is an event and it is not an event because it is repeatable.*" And in narratological terms, according to Mark Currie, Derrida "translates" the temporalities of a narrative "into spatial relationships or differences": "The Derridean concept of *différance* seemed to qualify the structural model of dif-ference by allowing time back into the analysis of meaning: *différance* carried with it a temporal as well as a spatial meaning" (2011: 83). Utopian narrative in a sense models *différance*, and understanding its structure in this way clarifies the fragile tethering of utopian tropes of spatiality and temporality.

Moreover, the agencies of event and repeatability make sense of utopian narratives' characteristic deferral of closure. The "sense of an ending" in a utopian narrative is at once a realizing of form through narrative and an effacement of any *particular* narrative. This paradox is of course registered in ultimate status of each experience of utopia as both real and not real: the vision turns out to be a dream, a vision, an illusion of insanity, an "absurdity," or form of nonsense, as More reminds us: he names his utopian traveler *Hythloday*, which translates from ancient Greek as "nonsense purveyor." The fictionality of utopia is recalled, even as the memory of that fictional experience sustains the possibility of a becoming reality.

We can call this possibility "surplus" in Derridean terms; we can call the reiterability "persistence"; we can call it speculation or anticipation. We can call it the utopian moment – the surprise of something else or something other – a virtual event without specific content but with persistent (nonidentical) essence: a trace. The specificity of More's invention initiates a formal template for utopia's persistence as an anticipation of another telling of a different story of a different way of knowing and being. This essential iterability of utopia bothers utopia scholar Ruth Levitas, for whom the "nature" of utopia is described in negative terms:

> the shift to late modernity produced a shift in utopian thought such that it is no longer possible to say anything about the nature of utopia itself, but only the communicative processes by which it may be negotiated. Thus the only kind of utopia which is possible is the processual and communicative. (1990: 37).

Without a philosophy of language and a contemporary narratological viewpoint, Levitas arrives at the point from which Jameson left long ago: at utopia's "impossibility." As a scholar who once theorized on what the "concrete utopia" means, the aporetic radicality that *is* the nature of utopia is less than satisfying.

Abensour's slant is slightly different from this problem-solving scenario, however weakly put into practice: "the point is not for utopia . . .to assign 'true' or 'just' goals to desire, but rather to educate desire, to stimulate it, to awaken it. Not to assign it a goal to desire but to open a path for it." He argues that utopia is a process of *non*fulfillment that in itself "gives birth to . . . a stubborn impulse toward freedom and justice" (2008: 407), insofar as utopia becomes a *site* of "permanent struggle" or critique. In fact words such as "state," "static," and "status quo," suggesting that utopia is a desire for "perfection" and an end to change, are inconsistent with utopia's particular task: not simply to "educate desire" but, as Fredric Jameson has argued, to activate "a learning to desire, the invention of the desire called utopia in the first place" (1996: 90).

To *learn to desire* is more than a "process" involving "communication": to learn we must be taught, and to educate is to lead out, not in. Hence the utopian tropes of the voyage, the horizon, and the shock event of a traveler's encounter with difference and otherness. In one of the most famous definitions of utopia, Oscar Wilde well understood the energy of this spatiotemporal dialectic: "A map of the world that does not include Utopia is not worth even glancing at, for it leaves out the one country at which Humanity is always landing. And when Humanity lands there, it looks out, and, seeing a better country, sets sail. Progress is the realisation of Utopias" (2001: 141). Louis Marin's later definition associates this perceptual mobility as a form of work, or *agency*:

> Utopia is the infinite work of the imagination's power of figuration. Utopia is the infinite *potential* of historical figures: it is this infinite, this 'work,' this *potential* that the Greek negation *ou* allows to be understand as a prefix to the name *topos*. Utopia is the plural figure of the infinite work of the limit or frontier or difference in history. *Totality and infinity: Utopia at the horizon of a voyage (travel).* (1993: 413, emphasis in the original).

Each and every time we stop, we look out, "learning to desire" once more and speculating. Hence the important role of the reader/listener in an encounter that mimics the traveler's experience of onto-epistemologic disruption, surprise, and wonder. The storytelling itself reiterates an experience of difference, educates the listener; and creates a space-time of defamiliarity – and then re-attunement toward this new condition: the learning to desire. This is the trace of utopia: it is also its narratological catalyst. It can be located in only one place: at the horizon, beyond which one can only speculate.

From Anticipatory Viewpoint to Speculative Standpoint

Speculation (like utopia) gets a "bad rap." To label something "speculative" is as often as not a dismissal. But speculation emphasizes the potentiality for change and reconfiguration of "new and constructive ways to disclose aspects of the world" (2009: 202), which we might call anticipation. In his "Introduction to the ontology of anticipation," Poli grounds this ontology in the temporal: "the future [is] part of a *structured story* whose past and present are at least partially known" (2010b: 769, emphasis added). Two kinds of stories we tell about the future are *forecasting* and *scenario building*, but Poli distinguishes those perspectives from an "anticipation viewpoint": "the future can be better confronted by opening our minds and learning to consider different viewpoints," thus "preparing for the unforeseeable novelties awaiting us in the future." Poli's definitions correspond to utopia's ongoing structuralization of "an other time" and place and to utopian literature's narratological methods of exploring the future in the present.

The notion of propensities is central to anticipation theory, based on the work of Karl Popper (1990): "Just like a newly synthesized chemical compound, whose creation in turn creates new possibilities for new compounds to synthesize, so all new propensities always create new possibilities. And new possibilities tend to realize themselves in order to create again new possibilities. Our world of propensities is inherently creative" (20) as we anticipate a "better world, even while remaining attuned to unpredictable accidents and disruptions marking encounters with alterity" (2010b: 773).

The figure standing at the horizon is the only one to enjoy Poli's "anticipation viewpoint," which is similar to what I call a "speculative standpoint" (2013: 5–8).

A "standpoint" (in feminist sociological theory particularly) means a situatedness in the here and now; a "speculative standpoint" extends past that more traditional epistemologic positioning in the here and now, to inhabit a mobile, indeterminate positioning by which one *imagines knowing* about the unknown future. Speculative standpoint looks backward and forward, reflecting the "as is" (*speculum*), as well as the "as if," the projecting out, the performance (*spectacle*), of possibility. There is one more sense to the word, "speculation": the sense of risk that comes with a kind of anticipation of the future or of possibility; the agent of such risk is a "speculator." All these senses of the word resonate around the notion of a speculative standpoint.

Contravening the achievements of the hardened systems of present-day ideological formation, speculation destabilizes the self-identity of the "as is" (*speculum*) in favor of the "as if," the projecting out of possibility. The shapes and shades emerging from speculation are, in a word, *anticipations* with the potential to disrupt to "the system." Thus the aptness of Roberto Poli's statement that the "main assumption of [a]nticipatory systems" is that "[f]uture states may determine present changes" (2008: 770). Anticipatory systems are speculative in nature – epistemically ungrounded, but not groundless: where rationality falls short and imagination and perceptual intuition rise and disrupt.

While literature scholars do not typically approach "system's" terminology comfortably, Poli's delineation of an *anticipatory system* highlights the resiliency of the West's tradition of utopian narrative and of the exploration of a dynamic and nonlinear conceptualization of temporalities. Poli takes as his touchstone Robert Rosen's definition: "*An anticipatory system is a system containing a predictive model of itself and/as its environment, which allows it to change state at an instant in accord with the model's predictions pertaining to a later instant*" (1985: 339). This attention to the *structure* of a system – particularly recalling Poli's notion of the future as a "structured story" – would suggest we ask whether utopian narrative be described as an "anticipatory system," and whether or not we can describe and identify a "predictive model of itself" inheres within its structure that is responsive to contingency and disruption.

In the context of utopian narrative, the self-reflexivity of this definition is highly suggestive. Rosen's "predictive" anticipatory system is not mere replication – this we explored via Derrida. For at a certain point, a self-replicating system no longer "needs" the anticipatory. The system simply becomes what it is, in a logical tautology. I take Rosen's notion of "a system containing a predictive model of itself" to mean something closer to (re)generation, a "living" system as it were that recognizes its own propensity to evolve. According to Mihai Nadin, a predictive model also means acknowledging the animation of the present by anticipation (2010: 4). This may be a more radical reading than Rosen intends, but his formulation points toward a way of understanding the resilience of the concept of utopia and the persistence of utopian, dystopian, and speculative literatures. The reiterative nature of utopia *is* its fictional realization again and again *as* a work of literature, artwork, and speculative philosophy.

The regenerative germ of utopian visioning explains why the genre of utopian narrative is so long-lived, resilient, and generative of other closely related subgenres of fiction, such as science fiction or fantasy literature. The task of utopia is to generate a "predictive model of itself" as its own figuration *as narrative*. The "predictive model" of utopian narrative aligns with models of anticipation that acknowledge the essentially contingent nature of historical temporality: utopian speculation cannot *predict*, but it can *propose*, place something before us. The speculative *what if* presumes the potentialities and possibilities offered by alterity and difference, *whether in the future or the past*. But most important is that there be "some other time" – for dialogue – for the telling of the story.

Where, then, does the "anticipatory" function of Utopia actually exist or manifest itself? Neo-Marxian theory – and most famously the indispensable work of Ernst Bloch – is instrumental in complicating the theory of Utopia to better account for historical change. An ontology of *not yet being* makes possible not only a sensation of futurity but more concretely the sensibility Bloch identifies as *hope*. Theorizing the concept of utopia begins in earnest with two supposed critics of utopianism: Karl Marx and Friedrich Engels, whose *Communist Manifesto* appears in 1848. Contemporary commentators, however, assert that while Marx and Engels were suspicious, if not outright dismissive of utopianism, associating it with "the preservation of the status quo," they were not unaware of the radical potentiality offered by utopian discourse. According to Christine Nadir, the work of Miguel Abensour, beginning in the 1970s, highlighted the *sympathy* Marx and Engels had toward a notion of utopia that insists on change: "At this historical moment (1848)," Abensour argues, "utopian literature moved away from outlining systematic blueprints of perfect societies and toward what he calls a 'new utopian spirit' and the 'education of desire'" (26). But Abensour also warns against the tendency for this new utopian spirit to end its task prematurely. This spirit "has as its task, once it has located the blind spots that carry out the reversal of modern emancipation, to inhabit them and engage in the work of deconstruction and critique so that a new path opens for utopia ("Utopie et démocratie," 248).

At this point, it is useful to resuscitate Darko Suvin's notion of the *novum* (originally from Bloch) as the radical momentum of the utopian imaginary. The term novum is fallen out of use, but should be revived because it illuminates the importance of understanding utopia not as a political pursuit for that final solution, or perfect static State, but as a politically radical process of ongoing critique. The function of the novum might be compared to the function of the immature stem cell in a living body: it does not contain but is itself the capacity to take on the form and function of any one of the many specialized cells that self-organize into living being. The virtue of the stem cell is its plasticity, containing as it were the potentiality for generating, repairing, and regenerating the body. The regenerative function of a contemporary novum goes beyond simply repairing a political or social "body" and bringing it back to its putatively whole or healthy form; this is replication of a particular ideologic formation. The novum does not close off the possibility of alterity, rather introduces it continuously. Therein lies the capacity for critique that defines utopia's political and formal energies.

The novum is the paradoxical point in Catherine Malabou's description (in *What Should We Do with Our Brain?*) of plasticity's contradictory nature, at which "possibility, the wholly other version," is held off by "the expectation of the arrival of another way of being" or "a possibility of waiting" (87). Possibility awaits then, now, then again, always, in the persistence of difference. For this reason the notion of utopia as representing a "blueprint for the future" is rejected by recent theorists. A static-state utopia is relevant only to an "end-stop" world, as contemporary fiction writer Jeanette Winterson put it in *Art Objects* (1997:19); without the possibility of difference and change, utopia tends toward the fascistic or the dictatorial. A process utopia requires possibility, awaiting. That refusal of finality (the blueprint model) marks the radical correspondence of process utopia to critique. What sets utopia apart is its exceptional pro-visionality; it's looking forward toward a horizon that constantly recedes as. Utopia is a (non-state of deferral *and* of difference, as the common etymology of both words indicates [*differe*: carry across, scatter, disperse]. In other words it is a process of unactualized potential that requires difference and deferral: it is virtual.

The "real" state of utopia is a form of virtual reality, as noted earlier, in the several senses of the word *virtual*. Utopia makes possible the shaping, the realizing of what was not "known" in any objective sense, but that was already there as a potentiality. This process informs notion of the "possibility of waiting" as an achievement *in itself*. This is a "pregnant moment" (Derrida) wherein we imagine possibility, shape of thoughts we do not know we have, and frame anew conceptually. This plastic process of shaping constitutes the virtual reality that is utopia, as we stand expectant, waiting, worlding. Utopian process effectively performs the principle of hope (Bloch). These performances are forms of *transitive* imagining and not immobile ideologic constructions. Utopia is mobile, performative, and inviting: it invites us always to *wonder*, the basis for creativity, hope, and life. Utopia is what Catherine Malabou would call *positive plasticity* – a hardening of form, but with the capacity for deformation, reformation, and potentially transformation. Malabou apprehends a link between the *idea* of plasticity, creativity, and hospitality and a politics of freedom. The "forms of contradiction" essential to Malabou's notion of plasticity are different approaches to the same crux: how to balance the twin powers of plasticity – resistance and yielding – against entropy dictated by ideology, which by its nature wants to replicate itself endlessly.

With her grounding in Hegel and the dialectic, Malabou articulates a concept of plasticity that incorporates but extends beyond Roland Barthes' 1957 investigation of the myth of plastic in *Mythologies* (2011). Barthes perceives this myth as attempting to neutralize the toxicities of ideological conformity. Modernity's drive for "more and better" disguises a creative sclerosis, uncannily manifested in the proliferations, replications, and implications of a world that "can be plasticized" (2011: 105) and to a frightening extent already has been. Malabou picks up where Barthes leaves off. Because the concept of plasticity embraces the work of making meaning (in the process of taking form) and of resisting meaning (in the potentiality for deforming, reforming), the later philosopher theorizes being itself – life – in terms of contemporary "plastic" virtues: that is, in terms of creativity and resilience. Even as those terms are co-opted by our contemporary neoliberal political economy, as Barthes presciently foresaw, Malabou can claim without irony, as Barthes does not, that plasticity is life. Plasticity embodies a principle of futurity and/as generativity, such that new forms, new meanings, and new concepts emerge as horizons of potentiality. A utopian horizon is the plastic edge-iness of not simply seeing different things, or even of "seeing differently," but, as Malabou suggests, *changing difference.*

At stake for her are competing conceptions of the world as either deterministic and limited in possibility or as "plastic," open to "possibilities for a becoming on the basis of the *effacement of every future,* for a transformation of the trace or mark, and for a historical transdifferentiation" (2008: 76). Malabou characterizes these "reconfigurations and this becoming" as constituted by "ruptures and resistance": "If these [children] were simply 'flexible'... they would be not resilient but conciliatory, that is to say, passive. But these individuals are, on the contrary, capable of *changing difference*" (2008: 76–77; emphasis added). Malabou's biggest claim is this: "*Creating resistance to neuronal ideology is what our brain wants, and what we want for it*" (2008: 77). Therefore what we should do with our brains, Malabou argues, is what the *brain* wants: the capacity to resist, or deform, hardened synaptic formations. Understanding the nature of *brain plasticity* as an active tension, an *entredeux* (2008: 82), or dialogue, Malabou pursues the vitality of human identity as an intra-agential process involving traditional body/mind relation in terms of an entanglement, not a clean division of either space or time. Her discussion of stem cells as "bring[ing] together the origin, as their name indicates, and the future, the capacity for self re-form" stands therefore as "the best possible definition of plasticity, ... this transformation or this transition—which cannot simply be the result of observation or of objective description" (2008: 80). Transformation is a result instead of speculation, from a *speculative* standpoint akin to Malabou's anticipatory *le voir venir* positioning. As in Oscar Wilde's definition of utopia, speculative standpoint never stops positioning itself at the horizon, "seeing [it] coming" before the negative plasticity of ideological formation sets.

Malabou's argument bends toward the concept of utopia as at once an event and as an accident that sustains "the open character" of *difference:* "In actual fact, the knowledge contained in a mythical concept is confused, made of yielding, shapeless associations. One must fully stress this *open character* of the concept" (2011: 229; emphasis added). This is so central to her work that Malabou throws down "the plastic challenge": "between the upsurge and the explosion of form," knowledge producers (scientists) are asked *"to do what they undoubtedly have never done: construct and entertain a relation with their brain as the image of a world to come"* (2008: 82). The open structuring that the philosophers identify as the essence of plasticity offers the basis for a material aesthetic of *becoming* rather *forming* (as a fixing of shape). Malabou's proposition of "the new ontological transformability" (2011: 38–39) develops from her notion of a plasticity of difference.

This proposition foregrounds potentiality rather than perfection or completion and presencing and futurity rather than the achievement of a static present moment. The plastic moment – the utopian moment – is essentially radical and open, an intermediate, mobile positioning between positive and negative plasticity necessary to remediate as well as transform. I propose that the concept of utopia comprises a

Malabou's notion of a "positive plasticity" that preserves resiliency and that requires "a kind of contradictory constitution, a synthesis of memory and forgetting, of constitution and effacement of forms" (2008: 77). By self-consciously re-presenting this capacity for reform, one avoids "producing a mirror image of the world," and produces "the form of another possible world" (2008: 80). This is the "agency of disobedience to every constituted form, a refusal to submit to a model" (2008: 6).

Philosopher Roland Barthes describes the material called plastic "alchemical" (thus magical, mystical, mythical) in that in its essence plastic materializes *the idea of transformation.* Malabou literalizes Barthes' idea: the paradox of plasticity is that as a material plastic can be at once informing and deforming, *re*forming, and *trans*forming (see Largier 2010: 87). The plastic nature of utopia makes possible something like *repair,* Malabou's word for brain's regenerative capacity, and a mark of the resilience of subjectivity. Malabou attunes us to a notion of plasticity and/as difference, through their insistent and persistent attention to breaking the limits of form, even as it emerges. This plasticity, a co-constitution of agency and passivity, keeps vital an opening toward difference and creates the capacity for the ongoing-ness of emergent formations. Only in this way only can we regard utopia as "sustainable," in its play of potentialities and possibilities, rather than replicant patterning, and as I have suggested, utopian narrative has various ways of expressing its (in)determinate plasticity. Narratologist Andrew Gibson sees this as characteristic of narrative generally: "Narrative space is now plastic and manipulable. It has become heterogenous, ambiguous, pluralized. Its inhabitants no longer appear to have an irrefutable or essential relation to any particular space. Rather, space opens up as a variable and finally indeterminate feature of any given world" (1996: 12). Utopian narrative is particularly self-reflexive in this regard, staying open to the possibility of new, emergent forms. Perhaps a new way to think about utopia is by asking ourselves, as individuals and a network, or community, or nation: To what extent *are* we plastic?

Anticipating Another Story

The teleology of the conventional novel supports the genre's original conservatism; that "sense" is a form of anticipation, as the reader sees the hero approach (re) integration into the social order. In utopian literature, conclusions are characteristi-cally *in*conclusive, open, and speculative. If anything is "predictive" in this narrative model, it is that *speculative* nature. The sensibility cultivated through speculative standpoint makes possible a configuration of history that is neither simply linear nor cyclical, but a complex temporality that is represented by the symbolic form of utopia's generic framed or embedded narrative. It is a structured story weaving and reweaving threads, parallel lines of memories *as well as* parallel lines of anticipation or hopeful imagining. This is the work of speculative fiction, to invent ways to intervene that are not always just a disruption but an evolution. This work opens up a space of momentary "objectivity," if not neutrality, that approaches the "space of critical no-whereness" (1994:132) privileged in the notion of the process utopia.

British author Jeanette Winterson is keenly attuned to the temporal complexities not only of anticipation but of kind of self-generative novelty that structures utopian narrative. *The Stone Gods* (2009) is a novel all about the repeatability of stories and events, constructed of multiple stories of adventure, risk and romance, genesis, and apocalypse. This highly allusive text interweaves narrative threads from the most familiar literary texts: fairy tales; the *Bible*; *Robinson Crusoe*; Captain Cook's *Journals*; the historical romances of Sir Walter Scott; the travel tales of Joseph Conrad; lines from the love poetry of Shakespeare, Herrick, Wyatt, T. S. Eliot, and Donne's "The Sun Rising"; and contemporary science fiction from Joanna Russ's *The Female Man* and Marge Piercy's *He, She and It* to Atwood's speculative fiction. Characteristically, the novel also alludes to Winterson's own work. These threads are so tightly woven into the line of this novel that its form functions as an echo chamber, inter- and intratextually.

Indeed, "Echo" is a central trope in the novel – as is storytelling. The crew of a spaceship investigating the sighting of a new Earth-like planet is already at work creating the history of this signal event. The spaceship crew creates a beautiful fable, "the way all ship crew tell stories" (50), describing a series of planets, each a version of Earth – and each one a possible future, or a possible past, each a place "real and imaginary. Actual and about to be" (39). In particular, they describe "a planet called Echo":

> It doesn't exist. It's like those ghost-ships at sea, the sails worn through and the deck empty ... It passed straight through the ship and throughout bodies, and the strange thing that happened was the bleach. It bleached our clothes and hair, and men that had black beards had white. Then it was gone, echoing in another part of the starry sky, always, 'here' and 'here' and 'here', but nowhere. Some call it Hope. (2008: 51).

In a following episode of the fable, however, a further iteration of the novel's refrain records the sailors' discovery of a nameless planet: "*Chanc'd upon, spied through a glass darkly, drunken stories strapped to a barrel of rum, shipwreck, a Bible Compass, a giant fish led us there, a storm whirled us to this isle. In this wilderness of space, we found ....*" Once ("once upon a time, once upon a time like the words in a fairytale") this planet held oceans, cities, and life, "naked and free and optimistic"; and while in days past, it was "a world like ours" (56); now it is a "bleached and boiled place" with "no future" (52), a "whiteout" – as if its story itself had been erased. Below the charred surface is an "elephant's graveyard," in which, presumably, everything is remembered. In this Dantesque space are the "carcasses of planes and cars" trapped in an endless cycle of melting down and re-forming: "This was the inferno, where a civilization has taken its sacrifices and piled them to some eyeless god, but too late" (52). The captain of the spaceship asserts that this white planet is "where we used to live" (55), a potential image of our own contemporary world. While "hope" is about to be actualized in the voyage to Planet Blue, the narrator, fearing "a repeating world – same old story" (49), wishes that this planet "could sail through space" toward a place and time, beyond human reach, "where the sea, clear as a beginning, will wash away any trace of humankind" (22).

This trope of a repeating history, possibly "a suicide note," possibly "a record of our survival" (39), is mirrored by the narratological structure of the novel, which fissures into multiple temporal planes: the near future; the past (eighteenth century); the farther future; the time of the dinosaurs, 65 million years ago; and the present. In most of these temporal planes, a recurrent figure named Spike appears. In one plane she is an evolving form of humanity called the *Robo-Sapiens*; she is also a (male) member of Capt. Cook's Easter Island voyage, a contemporary woman who proposes sending a message, *forward in time*: "Now . . . [the *Robo Sapiens*] was coding something different, for the future, whenever that would be. 'A random repeat, bouncing off the moon. One day, perhaps, maybe, when a receiver is pointed in the right direction, someone will pick this up. Someone, somewhere, when there is life like ours'" (82) – when and if history repeats itself on a planet, "some call Hope." As she sends the signals, Spike remarks on the paradox of past and future: "Everything is imprinted for ever with what it once was." While "you [mankind] made a world without alternatives" (65), she points out the universe is "neither random nor determined. It is potential at every second. All you can do is intervene" (62).

Even a man-made apocalypse is a kind of intervention: whether random or not, events create the conditions for a future not possible before. These time bridges are characteristically signaled in this novel by the appearance of portals of one sort or another, not an edge, over which one either stands or falls, but a "liminal opening" (146): a gate, a door, or a story, the "true" kind that "lie open at the border, allowing a crossing, a further frontier." And the protagonist, "Billie," looks for those open portals to her past, revealing "imprints from everything [she] once was," but also portals to the future, all her possible futures: "The final frontier is just science fiction – don't believe it. Like the universe [a 'memory of our mistakes' (87)], there is no end." Billie reiterates her hope offered by stories, not those with "a beginning, a middle, and an end, but . . . [the ones] that began again, [. . .] that twisted away, like a bend in the road" (87): "True stories are the ones that lie open at the border, allowing a crossing, a further frontier" (87). The instant when "time became a bridge" is her paradigmatic chronotype.

Toward the end of *The Stone Gods,* such a bridge suddenly stretches out – and again, it takes the form of a story – *this story.* A present-day figure who is clearly "Winterson herself" finds a manuscript lying on a coach seat in the underground, with the title, *The Stone Gods.* Reading at random, Billie-Winterson think it's perhaps a dissertation, on the Easter Islands; or, no, "a love story . . . maybe about aliens. I hate science fiction" (119). In a wonderfully metafictional moment, the manuscript suddenly becomes something else. The narrator reveals to her companion Spike that the manuscript is one she had previously lost, leaving it on a seat of Circle Line train, only to have it return now: "I had a strange sensation, as if this were the edge of the world and one more step, just one more step . . ." (147). In handing it to Spike, she drops it, its unnumbered pages are "shuffled as a pack of cards." She decides then to leave it underground: no matter how she might originally have put the pages together, every person who finds it will create the story they want or need: "A message in a bottle. A signal. . . . A repeating world. Read it. Leave it for someone else to find. The pages are loose—it can be written again" (203).

This is the key to utopia's literary nature: while things are imprinted with what they always were, there can always be *another story*, generated by both the memory of the past and the anticipation of the future. Following the More paradigm, once more: as with the *Utopia*, *The Stone Gods* leaves off, incomplete. But there is the *anticipation* that it will be found, lost and found by someone else, in a different time. Once again, the utopian narrative form reveals its resilience and plasticity: the very existence of such a narrative anticipates the (now absent) presence of an other: a new reader/listener, whose encounter with such a strange text of other worlds. Works of utopian literature constitute *strategy* for incorporating what Mihai Nadin calls "anticipatory dynamics." The great value of the *speculative standpoint* and a speculative utopian narrative is that whether it takes us forward, backward, or in place temporally, the speculation *historicizes the present* in ways that clarify not only the influence of the past in the future but also the *confluence* of future possibilities, where our horizons may lie.

While utopia tends to be associated with its sociopolitical *content*, as mentioned at the beginning, this is not utopia's narrative task. Utopia is, according to Laurence Davis, "a form of persuasive communication that will reshape the images that people see, and over time generate in them new habits of vision and new patterns of desire. What is required, in other words, is the vivid exercise of ethical imagination in the sphere of social relations" (2001: 83). This "vivid exercise" of ethical imagining is the work of utopia. A "new habit" of vision emerges from the development of a "speculative standpoint," a "perceptual style" (Jane Bennett) based not on "common sense" but in a "sixth sense" (Abensour) that takes in the imagination and the perceptions of the body. The "new patterns of desire" are forms of yearning, or even hope, the most affective (and sometimes effective) forms of anticipation.

References

Abensour, M. (2008). Persistent Utopia. *Constellations, 15*(3), 406–421.

Atwood, M. (1985). *The handmaid's tale*. New York: Anchor Books.

Atwood, M. (2003). *Oryx and crake*. New York: Anchor Books.

Barthes, R. (2011) *Mythologies* (trans: Howard, R. & Lavers, A.). New York: Hill and Wang.

Bennett, J. (2010). *Vibrant matter: A political ecology of things*. Durham: Duke University Press.

Bloch, E. (1986 [1959]). *The principle of hope (Das Prinzip Hoffnung)*. Cambridge: The MIT Press.

Braidotti, R. (1994). *Nomadic subjects: embodiment and sexual difference in contemporary feminist theory*. New York: Columbia University Press.

Bulwer-Lytton, E. (1871). *The coming race: Or, the new Utopia* (2017th ed.). New York: Forgotten Books.

Crosthwaite, P. (2010). Anticipations of the accident: Modernist fiction and systemic risk. *Textual Practice, 24*(2), 331–352.

Currie, M. (2011). *Postmodern narrative theory* (2nd ed.). London: Palgrave Macmillan.

Davis, L. (2001). Isaiah Berlin, William Morris, and the politics of utopia. In B. Goodwin (Ed.), *The philosophy of Utopia*. London: Frank Cass.

Derrida, J. (1973). *Speech and phenomena; and other essays on Husserl's theory of signs* (trans: Allison, D.). Evanston: Northwestern University Press.

Derrida, J. (1976). *Of Grammatology* (trans: Spivak, G. C.). Baltimore: The Johns Hopkins University Press.

Gibson, A. (1996). *Towards a postmodern theory of narrative*. Edinburgh: Edinburgh University Press.

Gilman, C. P. (1915). In B. Solomon (Ed.), *Herland and selected Stories*. New York: Signet Classics.

Haraway, D. (1997). *Modest_Witness@Second_Millenium.FemaleMan_MeetsOncoMouse: Feminist and Technoscience*. New York: Routledge.

Hartsock, N. (1999). *The feminist standpoint revisited & other essays*. New York: Basic Books.

Jameson, F. (1994). *The seeds of time: The Wellek library lectures at the University of California, Irvine*. New York: Columbia University Press.

Jameson, F. (2004). The politics of utopia. *New Left Review, 25*, 35–54.

Largier, N. (2010). The plasticity of the soul: Mystical darkness, touch, and aesthetic experience. *Modern Language Notes, 125*(3), 536–551.

Lawlor, L.. (2016). Jacques Derrida. In E. N. Zalta (Ed.), *The Stanford encyclopedia of philosophy*. https://plato.stanford.edu/archives/win2016/entries/derrida

Levitas, R. (1990). *The concept of utopia*. Syracuse: Syracuse University Press.

Malabou, C. (2008). *What shall we do with our brain?* New York: Fordham University Press.

Marin, L. (1993). Frontiers of utopia: Past and present. *Critical Inquiry, 19*, 397–420.

More, S. T. (1516). *The utopia of Sir Thomas more* (1895th ed.). New York: Macmillan.

More, S. T. (1991). *Utopia*. New York: Norton Critical Editions.

Morris, W. (1890). *News from Nowhere*. The Gutenberg Project E-Book. http://www.sfu.ca/~poitras/Morris_News-from=Nowhere

Nadin, M. (2010). Anticipation and dynamics: Rosen's anticipation in the perspective of time. *International Journal of General Systems, 39*, 3–33.

Nadir, C. (2010). Utopian studies, environmental literature, and the legacy of an idea: Educating desire in Miguel Abensour and Ursula K. Le Guin. *Utopian Studies, 21*(1), 24–56.

Piercy, M. (1985). *Women on the edge of time*. New York: Fawcett Books.

Poli, R. (2010a). The many aspects of anticipation. *Foresight, 12*(3), 7–17.

Poli, R. (2010b). An introduction to the ontology of anticipation. *Futures, 42*, 769–776.

Popper, K. (1990). *A World of propensities*. London: Thoemmes.

Rabinovich, S. (2005). Utopia: Reading and redemption. *Diogenes, 1*(209), 109–116.

Rosen, R. (1985). *Anticipatory systems*. Oxford: Pergamon Press.

Rouse, J. (2009). Standpoint theories reconsidered. *Hypatia, 24*(4), 200–209.

Scognamiglio, C. (2010). Anticipation and future vision in Nicolai Hartmann's ontology. *Foresight, 12*(3), 50–58.

Suvin, D. (1979). *Metamorphoses of science fiction: On the poetics and history of a literary genre*. New Haven: Yale University Press.

Swift, J. (1726). *Gulliver's travels*. New York: Penguin Classics.

Trend, D. (2013). *Worlding: Identity, media, and imagination in a digital age*. Boulder: Paradigm Publishers.

Vieira, F. (2010). The concept of utopia. In G. Claeys (Ed.), *The Cambridge companion to utopian literature* (pp. 3–27). Cambridge: Cambridge University Press.

Wagner-Lawlor, J. (2013). *Postmodern utopias and feminist fictions*. Cambridge: Cambridge University Press.

Whitehead, A. N. (1985). In D. W. Sherburne & D. R. Griffin (Eds.), *Process and reality: An essay in cosmology* (Corrected ed.). New York: The Free Press.

Whitehead, A. N. (2003). The analysis of process. In H. Maassen (Ed.), *European studies in process thought* (Vol. 1). Leuven: European Society for Process Thought.

Wilde, O. (1895). *The soul of man under socialism*. London: Penguin Classics.

Winterson, J. (1997). *Art objects essays on ecstasy and effrontery*. New York: Vintage.

Winterson, J. (2009). *The stone Gods*. New York: Mariner Books.

Wood, D., & Bernasconi, R. (Eds.). (1988). *Derrida and différance*. Evanston: Northwestern University Press.

Why Sociology Needs Anticipation?

26

Giuliana Mandich

Contents

Abstract

It is possible to underline a strong tendency toward "mainstreaming the future" –
to use John Urry's expression within sociology today. The introduction of the
future in sociological theory and research is not simply the opening of a new
"field of inquiry" but rather is profoundly related to some of the problems that the
discipline has encountered in its development and meets some of the answers that
have recently been at the core of its development.

The number of theoretical reflections and empirical analyses that consider the
future is increasing, and the field of studies of futurity in sociology is flourishing,
with new contributions added every day (for instance, in youth studies, feminist
studies, emotion and affect studies, and science and technology). The chapter
focuses on three main theoretical and analytical themes in this development.

The first theme concerns the link between social action and anticipation.
I argue that there is a profound link between futurity and social action, which
has always been present, although not sufficiently developed, in social theory
(Schutz, Mead, Bourdieu).

G. Mandich (✉)
Università di Cagliari, Cagliari, Italy
e-mail: mandich@unica.it

© Springer Nature Switzerland AG 2019
R. Poli (ed.), *Handbook of Anticipation*,
https://doi.org/10.1007/978-3-319-91554-8_65

The second theme concerns the development of the latent futures dimension and the related idea that an encounter with the future is not simply "an encounter with a non-tangible and invisible world" (Adam and Groves, Future matters. Action, knowledge, ethic, 2007: XV).

The third theme, which concludes the chapter, can be called the *re-enchantment of the future,* that is, the recognition of the importance of nonrational, emotional, and imaginative elements for anticipating the future.

Keywords

Practical anticipation Reflexive anticipation Latent futures Habitus Reflexivity Creativity Imagination Responsibility Utopia Dystopia Hope Wicked futures Complexity Emotions

Introduction

The catchphrase "future matters" has recently been used by authors, such as Barbara Adam, Jens Beckert, and Ann Mishe, to summarize the notion that taking the future into account is a very important component of sociological analysis. Together with a growing interest in different dimensions of projectivity within various areas of study, a strong tendency toward "mainstreaming the future" – to use John Urry's expression – is developing within sociology. Urry argues that the landscape of future studies (which has progressed mainly outside social sciences as a specialized and highly professionalized discipline) should be reclaimed for social science (Urry 2016), accompanying the more or less explicit assumption that sociology has included the future within its mainstream approaches to only a limited extent.

In a sense, this assumption is counterintuitive for sociology, whose development is closely linked to the development of modern society and whose nature dictates that it is dedicated to progress, innovation, and change. As Kumar (1972: 370) notes, "It is remarkable that sociology, which should be the discipline that most illuminates future possibilities, should so resolutely face backwards, towards its own origins in an earlier period of social change." Many accounts have been given regarding the reasons for the disappearance of the future from sociology, but these reasons would be too long to account for in this chapter. The most powerful account appears to be what Schutz (2015) calls the "positivist purging" of the future (as a time we cannot know anything about), part of the extensive effort to develop sociology as a social science.

An additional point is worth discussing as particularly relevant to the explanation of the growing interest in the dimension of futurity in sociology. As Beckert has recently underlined, sociology has focused on stabilizing mechanisms of social systems to control and tame the speed and radicality of change: "Though approaches vary considerably, sociology, like economics, has attempted to 'undo' the consequences of uncertainty and mask the openness of the future in its understandings of action. The future, in the eyes of most sociologists, is a prolongation of the past" (Beckert 2016: 49). In other words, Beckert postulates an attitude in line with what Adam and Groves define as the *taming of the future*. According to the authors, practices of *taming the future* are "knowledge practice that make daily life less precarious" (2009: 7). "Habits, customs and traditions as well as laws rules and moral codes provide a degree of foreknowledge and anticipation. They make the behaviour of others predictable and facilitate a certain measure of security" (2009: 8). If we look at sociological approaches more deeply, we see that the functionalist tradition, rational behavior theories, and interpretative perspective play (in different ways) a similar role in taming the future. Whether the prevalence of the past over the future has been more evident in the functionalist tradition and in rational theory (less influential in sociology), the interpretative perspective underemphasizes the future, prioritizing the past and present as sources of understanding in the creation of meaning (Mische 2009).

Certainly, the growing uncertainty and individualization in society (Beck and Beck-Gernsheim 2002) has illuminated the limits of the "bracketing futurity" perspective. If the faith in providence and final causes was replaced in the first modernity by faith in progress (reason and past-based causality) in the second modernity, this taming effect on the future clashes at both the micro and macro levels. At the individual level, the assumption that freedom comes from an open future produces a major paradox: "as owners of the future we also carry the sole responsibility for the outcomes of our future creating actions. This makes us inescapably responsible for that which we cannot know" (Adam and Groves 2007: 165). At the macro level, the growing awareness of the unintended consequences of economic growth at the climatic level and the progressive division of the practices of production of future and control of the future have definitely challenged the idea of an open future that is ready to be colonized (Beck 1992). A finishing blow was dealt by the economic crisis of 2008, which led to the definitive collapse of economic rationality as a way to predict, tame, and trade the future (Beckert 2016; Appadurai 2015; Esposito 2011).

The analytical frame of this chapter centers on the question of "why sociology needs anticipation." This concept is present in sociology (for example, in Schutz 1976 and Bourdieu) but is neither widely used nor well established with a definitive meaning. Nevertheless, it can be useful as a frame for containing all the different variations and concepts concerning how the future is variously realized in human action (e.g., protentions and projections, latent and imagined futures). The leading position is that the introduction of "forward-oriented studies" (Schulz 2015) in sociological theory and research does not simply mark the opening of a new "field of inquiry" but rather is profoundly related to some of the problems that the discipline has encountered in its development and some of the subsequent solutions that have recently guided its core development. Put simply, mainstreaming the future is a very good strategy for sociology to address some of its most controversial issues.

The number of theoretical reflections and empirical analyses that take the future into account is growing, and the field of studies of futurity in sociology is flourishing, with new contributions added every day (in youth studies, feminist studies, emotion and affect studies, science and technology, etc.). It would be impossible to illustrate the complete picture, but this chapter aims to identify three current areas of emerging discussion in sociological reflections and identify elements of discussion for the future.

Our first focus is the link between social action and anticipation. At the core of this argument stands the profound link between futurity and social action, which has always been present – although not sufficiently developed – in social theory (Schutz, Mead, Bourdieu). Talking about futurity and about anticipations (in the plural) means underlining that the field of the future is a very complex one and is socially produced through a variety of social practices, always keeping in mind what Bourdieu emphasizes in his essay on *Social Being, Time and the Sense of Existence* (Bourdieu 2000): "practices make time and not are made in time."

Our second focus is the development of the latent futures dimension and the idea that an encounter with the future is not simply "an encounter with a non-tangible and invisible world" (Adam and Groves 2007: XV). Together with a nonrepresentational account of futurity, the awareness of the future as a complex system and the need for a new form of responsibility have been developed in sociological thinking.

Our third focus, which concludes the chapter, can be called the *re-enchantment of the future,* that is to say, the recognition of the importance that nonrational, emotional and imaginative elements have for the way the future is anticipated. Hope, fears, and utopias – in contrast to the modern idea of the plan as a kind of projectivity that is rationally based and a means to end – are recognized in sociological thinking as powerful forces driving individuals' projectivity in contemporary societies.

Temporalizing Social Action: Practical Anticipation, Reflexive Anticipation, and Multiple Reflexivities

Barbara Adam poetically emphasizes how our daily lives are conducted projectively, that is, surrounded by the open and fluid horizon of the past and the future. "We move in this temporal domain with great agility, pirouetting and swiveling to face both past and future, twisting and turning in the knowledge realms of perception, memory, and anticipation. We operate with equal confidence in the action domains of planning and future making, alternating perspective between anticipated future presents and enacted present futures without giving much thought to the matter" (Adam 2009a: 438).

As individuals, we all experience this feeling, and as sociologists, we could not agree more with Adam's statement. Thus far, however, sociological theory has not been particularly successful in disentangling the various temporal orientations of agency while maintaining the fluidity of the process. This challenging task involves a reconceptualization of human agency as a temporally embedded process (Emirbayer and Mische 1998), thus emphasizing both the multidimensionality of agency and the interrelated multifariousness of temporality and futurity.

It is an overwhelming topic, which, having always been an undercurrent in sociological thinking, is more strongly emerging in recent sociological reflections, as noted in the Introduction. To discuss the topic, I start by analyzing the undervaluation of futurity in the theory of action (as emphasized by many sociologists) and then provide examples of the re-emergence of the future through the re-evaluation and re-proposition of different forms of anticipations embedded in theories of social agency.

Describing agency involves using several terms that refer to the future. The problem in describing agency is that the future is typically "implicit"; it does not emerge "explicitly." Consider Weber as an example.

When Weber writes about "progress," "rationality," or the "pursuit of profit," he may not use the terms "future" and "futurity" often, yet in his view, futurity unmistakably characterizes individual and social action: "Whether we choose between options, allow values and beliefs to guide our actions, decide on the most appropriate means to achieve a given end or act rationally and/or responsibly with commitment and/or dedication, the future features in all we do, at any given moment. The future is both cause and reason for what we do, how we act and what decisions we take on a daily basis. Weber could not be clearer on this overarching point, even though he does not use these precise words to present his argument. In Weber's work, the futurity of social life emerges not through explicit writing on 'the future' or 'futurity', but rather through his key concepts" (Adam 2009b: 10).

If the future is present in the foundations of the theory of action, although not explicitly theorized there, as several scholars have suggested (Adam 2009b; Beckert 2016; Schulz 2015), the forward-looking element of social agency has completely disappeared because of two main influences. First is the overwhelming impact of the integrative-systemic conception of structural functionalism, largely eclipsing the temporal dimension of Weber's theory. Second and simultaneously, a similar effect has been produced in the antagonist field of symbolic Interactionism, prioritizing the past and present as sources of understanding in the creation of meaning (Beckert 2016; Adam 2009b).

This "de-futurization of the interpretative stance" may also explain why the potentialities of one sociologist who more explicitly addresses the link between action and the future in his writings, namely Alfred Schultz, have not been fully developed within sociology (Emirbayer and Mische 1998; Mische 2009).

The idea of a conscious behavior oriented toward the future is present in Schultz's notion of project. "The unity of the action is a function of the span or breadth of the project" (Schutz 1967a: 62). Projection is given only to reflective thought (Schutz 1967a: 61) – not to immediate experience or to spontaneous activity.

However, the strong link between the problem of meaning and time has over-emphasized a specific status of the project in relation to the future, somehow reducing the forward-looking element of action and flattening its projective dimension. "This, then, is the kernel of the solution to the problematic node in the relationship between time and meaning: the project makes both the act and the acting meaningful. Only my ability to imagine a completed action allows me to plan and then actually realize the successive steps in the action: these depend on the final goal that has been set" (Muzzetto 2006: 14).

In fact, Schutz's notion of projects stresses a dimension of the future as a *future perfect tense* (modo future exacti): a future that is pictured as if it were simultaneously past and future. "The project is directed at the act as being fulfilled in the future, for only if the fulfilment of the future act is thus assumed or posited can the means be selected. To put it another way: the actor projects his action as if it were already over and done with and lying in the past. Strangely enough therefore, because it is pictured as completed, the planned act bears the temporal character of pastness. Of course, once the action begins, the goal is wished for and protended" (Schultz 1967: 62).

The tendency to link social agency and the past has also been enhanced in the way "theories of practice" have been conceived as theories of "selective reactivation by actors of past patterns of thought and action, as routinely incorporated in practical activity" (Turner 1994). Consider one of the most applied conceptions, Bourdieu's concept of habitus. Habitus refers to the habitual and unconscious competences of the individual as "a modus operandi of which he or she is not the producer and has no conscious mastery" (Bourdieu 1977: 79). The different elements of the habitus are enacted unthinkingly, which is partly what defines them as habitual. Reflexive awareness of the production process is necessarily rare: "principles embodied in this way are placed beyond the grasp of consciousness, and hence cannot be touched by voluntary, deliberate transformation" (Bourdieu 1977: 94). Moreover, habitus not only addresses how we think about the world but also is an embodied "system of dispositions" that we bring to a field: it expresses the sense of ease in our surroundings – "le sens pratique" (the feel for the game), as Bourdieu calls it (Bourdieu 1990: 52).

Bourdieu strongly underlines how the habitus is the result of experiential "schooling" stretching back to childhood. Alternatively, as Emirbayer and Mische (1998) assert, in habitus, the past is the most "resonant tone": through habit and repetition, the past becomes a stabilizing influence that shapes the flow of effort and allows us to sustain identities, meanings, and interactions over time. The schematization (corporeal, affective, cognitive) of social experience – manifested in actors' abilities to recall, to select, and to appropriately apply the more or less tacit and taken-for-granted schemas of action that they have developed through past interactions – is at the center of individuals' ability to act in social reality.

Recently, the quest for a forward-oriented sociology has made evident that some possibilities offered by classical sociology can be reworked. This quest has also indicated that agency, whether conceived in terms of reflexivity, stressing the willfulness and autonomy of the individual, or habitus, emphasizing the set of dispositions influencing the relationship of individuals to their world, works through and is related to forms of anticipation.

Consider, first, the dimension of projectivity. According to Mische (2009), it is possible to trace a more complex idea of projectivity in Schutz that has been underemphasized in sociology. For Schutz, human action is "constructed within an imaginative horizon of multiple plans and possibilities; actors engage in a retrospective/prospective process by which they draw on previously collected 'stocks of knowledge,' or 'typifications,' of possible paths of actions, while 'fantasizing' in relation to the developing act in progress. Such an imaginative process differs from that of choosing among clearly defined possibilities, as instrumentalist theories propose; rather, it entails focusing 'rays of attention' on a plurality of possible states until one or more alternatives detach themselves 'like overripe fruit' and appear before the reflective consciousness as possible objects of choice" (Mische 2009: 696).

Anticipation (or foreseeing expectation in Schutz's terms) is considerably more complex than the simple idea of project would suggest. Creativity and imagination are pivotal elements in such a definition. In the effort to develop an idea of projectivity, pragmatists' theories, particularly those of Mead, are of particular interest (Mische 2009). Mead (1932) addresses the development of temporal horizons as a form of "distance experience" that removes us from our immediate sensory engagement and allows us to imaginatively engage with the past and the future. Our multiple levels of social embeddedness (which he calls "sociality") also embed us in multiple temporal horizons, and the problems posed by such complex sociotemporal relationships give rise to what he calls a "deliberative attitude," that is, the capacity to "get hold of the conditions of future conduct as these are found in the organized responses we have formed, and so construct our pasts in anticipation of that future" (Mead 1932: 76). In contrast, Dewey argues that "[e]xperience in its vital form is experimental, an effort to change the given; it is characterized by projection, by reaching forward into the unknown; connection with the future is its salient trait" (Dewey 1981: 69, 61).

As Joas (1996) stresses, for Mead and Dewey, "the capacity of invention, that is creativity, had as its precondition the self-aware employment of and disposal over the form of action known as play, the conscious 'playing through' in imagination of alternative performances of action. When the central position of the creativity of action in this theory is not recognized, then well-known parts of Mead's framework remain unintelligible" (178–179).

As Emirbayer and Mische observe, general projectivity implies an active and transformative idea of action as "specific culturally embedded ways in which people imagine, talk about, negotiate, and make commitments to their futures influence their degree of freedom and maneuverability in relation to existing structures" (1998: 995).

Note that this conception of projectivity mirrors the idea of reflexivity. In Giddens's terms (1991), reflexivity is a major characteristic of late modernity: a form of agency that provides subjects with high levels of personal autonomy. Reflexivity is thus generally equated with agency, cognitive deliberation, and critical rationality, and it is the capacity to allow individuals to react to their circumstances in ways no longer governed by tradition. Although controversial and debated (Sayer 2009), the idea of reflexivity has furthered and sustained the discussion on social agency in contemporary societies.

Emirbayer and Mische's definition contains two additional elements that make the study of projectivity particularly significant for analyzing social action. These elements are the idea that "imagining, talking, negotiation, making commitments" are cultural resources and the assertion that the narrative dimension of projectivity is highly significant.

From this perspective, Appadurai's concept of capacity to aspire as a narrative capacity (Appadurai 2004) could be usefully included in the "sociological future thinking tool-kit." Aspirations, according to Appadurai, concern not only wants, preferences, choices, and calculations. "The poor, no less than any other group in a society, do express horizons in choices made and choices voiced, often in terms of specific goods and outcomes, often material and proximate, like doctors for their children, markets for their grain, husbands for their daughters, and tin roofs for their homes" (Appadurai 2004: 69). He argues that the capacity to aspire constitutes a type of metacapacity: "They too [the rich] may express their aspirations in concrete, individual wishes and wants. But they are more able to produce *justifications, narratives, metaphors*, and pathways through which bundles of goods and services are actually tied to wider social scenes and contexts, and to still more abstract norms and beliefs" (Appadurai 2004: 69).

Together with a deeper analysis of projectivity, understood in terms of reflexive anticipation, a re-evaluation of the anticipatory dimension of habit and social practices has been initiated, alongside a stronger interest in the everyday and the future. One way of conducting this analysis is by analyzing (as we will in the next section) the futures in the making (latent futures) that social practices produce. Another angle from which to examine understanding the specific mode of anticipating the future is the immediacy of everyday experience, that is, protention (as developed in Tavory and Eliasoph 2013).

Referring to Husserl, Schutz defines protention as characterizing the flow of lived experiences, as tension towards the following instant: "First of all every action is a spontaneous activity oriented toward the future. This orientation toward the future is by no means peculiar to behaviour. It is on the contrary a property of all primary constituting processes, whether these arise from spontaneous activity or not. Each such process contains within itself intentionalities of lived experience that are directed toward the future" (Schutz 1967a: 57). At the same time, the past dimension of the lived experience is of a peculiar nature: it can be defined as retention, that is, a primary remembrance or the memory of the experience just lived.

Bourdieu's concept of practical anticipation shares many of the characters of Schutz's notion of protention: ordinary experience is one of "of pre-occupation and immersion in the forth-coming in which time passes unnoticed." Bourdieu argues for the importance of the practical experience of time in opposition to the intellectualist view of temporal experience, which excludes any other relation to the future than the conscious project and aims at ends and possibilities: "This typically scholastic representation is based, as ever, on the substitution of a reflexive vision for the practical vision" (Bourdieu 2000: 267). Accordingly, the past is present in habitus as a *presence* of the past, not as a *memory*. Habitus includes a past and a future that are not seen as such, and embodiment is the dimension that produces "practical temporality."

Bourdieu directly cites Husserl as having established "that the project as a conscious aiming at the future in its reality as a contingent future must not be conflated with protention, a pre reflexive aiming at a forth-coming which offers as quasi-present in the visible, like the hidden faces of a cube, with the same belief status (the same doxic modality) as what is directly perceived" (Bourdieu 2000: 207). According to Bourdieu, the capacity to anticipate and to see in advance – which is acquired in and through practice and familiarization with a field – is nothing like knowledge that can be mobilized at will through an act of memory (Bourdieu 2000: 210).

Importantly, practical and reflexive anticipation are neither distinct nor opposed dimensions of social agency. Orientations toward the future and active efforts to shape it are not only discursively conscious strategies but also – and simultaneously – types of dispositions formed and maintained through interactions with significant others.

In Schutz's perspective, as Muzzetto (2006) discerns, retention and reproduction, apart from signifying analytical distinctions between levels of consciousness, are two inseparable aspects of remembering, analogously to how protention and anticipation are two inseparable aspects of expectation. Therefore, retentions and reproductions, protentions and anticipations are constitutive of the interconnectedness of the stream of consciousness.

Practical anticipation is central to Bourdieu's explanation of individual projectivity, which means that the objective probabilities are determinant only for an agent endowed with the sense of the game – that is, the capacity to anticipate the events of the game. "This anticipation relies on a practical precategorization based on the implementation of the schemes of habitus which, arising from experience of the regularities of existence, structure the contingencies of life in terms of previous experience and make it possible to anticipate in practice the probable futures previously classified as good or bad, bringing satisfactions or frustrations. This practical sense of the forthcoming has nothing in common with a rational calculation of chances – as shown by the discrepancies between an explicit appreciation of probabilities and practical anticipation, which is both more precise and more rapid" (Bourdieu 2000: 211).

A different way of coordinating projectivity and protension has recently been proposed by Tavory and Eliasoph (2013). According to the authors, the modes of coordination are performed in everyday interaction. They categorize forms of future coordination into the following three basic modes:

1. Protentions, or moment-to-moment anticipations that actors typically take for granted.
2. Actors' trajectories through time, which proceed in ways that are more or less culturally predictable and that can assume a narrative form (involving a shared grammar) or a project form (emphasizing, by contrast, individual volition).
3. Plans and temporal landscapes, overarching temporal orientations that actors experience as inevitable and even natural, such as the sequence of grades in elementary school and a calendar's grid.

Tavory and Eliasoph criticize the "assumption of complicity" among protention, project, and temporal landscape as they appear in the works of Schutz and Bourdieu. However, within different views of society (as a relatively coherent body and as fractured along lines of class, status, and field positions), both assume close resonance among different modes of future anticipation.

In contrast, according to Tavory and Eliasoph, researchers must be able to recognize how people perform each mode of future coordination and how different modes relate to one another in interaction: sometimes complicit, sometimes explicitly clashing, and sometimes sufficiently aligned for actors to continue interacting, despite actual mismatches.

Modes interlace when actors project similar protentions in different narratives, when actors pursue similar trajectories in different temporal landscapes, or when actors ambivalently orient themselves to multiple futures simultaneously.

The re-emergence of a sociological interest in the anticipatory dimension of social agency is strong and distinct. While a common vocabulary does not exist yet, a set of common ideas is evident in the way the forward-looking element of human agency is conceptualized. The following two ideas seem particularly important: the multi-dimensionality of modes of anticipation and the fact that only through empirical work can these modes be analyzed. Examining the opposition habitus/reflexivity, which has been dominant in the sociological debate on social agency, from the perspective of how the future is anticipated, reveals the limits of such dichotomous thinking.

Latent Futures: Sociomateriality, Complexity, and Responsibility

As we have seen, social action implies different relationships with "present futures," that is, statements, images, visions, or expectations of the future that originate and circulate in the present. However, the future is already inhabited by the present. "Futures are made continuously, across the world, every second of the day. They are produced by the breadth of social institutions: politics, law and the economy, science, medicine and technology, education, and religion" (Adam 2009a: 429). Adam and Groves (2007) define these presents as "future presents," "latent futures," or "futures in the making." The distinction was introduced to social science by Niklas Luhmann (1982: 281), albeit with a different meaning: the present future is rooted in a utopian approach, which allows for prediction, while the future present is technologically constituted and therefore enables researchers to transform future presents into present presents.

Sociology is currently expanding the awareness and knowledge of the category of "latent futures" or "futures-in-the-making," which are not pre-existing, as in the traditional sense of fate but which are nevertheless not merely an aspect of our imagination or desire. Similarly, Urry (2016) underlines how futures are embedded within energy, economic, social, and cultural processes: "The future is never a simple prediction or smooth extrapolation from what is happening in the present. There is no empty future just waiting to be filled" (Urry 2016).

These "latent futures" are real, but they have not yet fully developed and become manifest; that is, they are still in process (Tutton 2017). Everyday car use affects carbon emissions warming the planet's atmosphere, everyday consumption practices impact the ongoing dumping of plastic waste. Energy has been diagnosed as the biggest issue and the clearest example of the link between socioeconomic techno-logical systems and the production of the future. "Contemporary societies have come to depend upon energy resources, many of which are limited in scale and are becoming scarcer per person and in absolute terms. The twentieth century was utterly dependent upon the energy resource of oil for rapidly moving objects and people. Given this huge constraint there are a limited number of possible futures for societies looking forward over the next three to four decades. No future is without its downside" (Urry 2013).

Investigating future presents (latent futures in the making) highlights three important issues.

The first issue is emphasizing matter in addition to imagination. For too long, the future has been considered exclusively immaterial and thus rendered "unreal."

"To restrict human futurity and the creation of future presents to the ideational domain of human purpose, therefore, means that we lose sight of the other side of cultural futures: that we create process futures and thus produce future presents that are de facto the domain of sociological inquiry, irrespective of and despite the empirical and theoretical difficulties involved" (Adam 2009a: 435).

Therefore, the reality status of the future resides both in what Weigert (2014) calls the power of "future realizing narratives," which make futures available as efficacious motives, and in our everyday choices that leave their footprint on the future. The future is real because the way we look at it has consequences for the way we act and because it is already present as a consequence of our actions. This entanglement of matter and meaning makes the futures "wicked futures," that is, it is difficult to be tackled both conceptually and empirically (Tutton 2017). Advances in social and technological studies help to explain social reality in terms of the alignment of a range of heterogeneous human and nonhuman actors and artifacts within stable sociotechnical networks that impact the future.

The wickedness of futures is also due to the fact that latent futures are as complex (Urry 2016; Tutton 2017) as the systems that produce them. The systems operating in the contemporary world are simultaneously economic, physical, technological, political, and social, so they possess emergent properties that are irreducible to any of these individual "factors" (see Urry 2003). Moreover, the increasing interconnectedness of system components through software, cybernetic architecture, and the general networked nature of life increase this complexity. Innovation, unpredictability, and possible reversal make the future produced by these systems more difficult to address.

Second, the awareness of the complexity and wickedness of futures brings with itself a new definition of responsibility.

Jonas (1984[1976]) long ago emphasized how the implicit moral codes of modern society are no longer appropriate for the contemporary context. The growing discrepancy between ethical assumptions (in which responsibility was thought to apply between living individuals in the present and was guided by eternal principles) and the reach of sociotechnical effects compel us to rethink our traditional anthropocentric responses and produce principles more appropriate for our ecological footprint and timeprint; this invites us to consider as our responsibility ethical concerns beyond the interests of humanity, that is, the material, spatial, and temporal spheres of impact, which extend beyond human society to all of nature and the physical bases of our existence. The effects of current sociotechnical, socioeconomic, and political processes, such as nuclear technology, are no longer spatially or temporally bound. Moral principles grounded in the immediacy of the here and now therefore need to be adjusted to both the footprint and the timeprint of potential outcomes (Adam and Groves 2007). This expansion of responsibility to the potential reach of actions places us in a different position with respect to what can and cannot be known, done, and controlled. Traditional theories on responsibility fail to address accountability for the future of life itself.

The awareness of connections between risks, technologies, and futures are neither easily determined nor governed by linear causal connections, and the fact that this awareness clearly undermines conventional causal analysis and traditional social science engagement with the future has grown within risk society thinking since the 1990s (Beck 1992; Adam et al. 2000).

Adam and Crow also underline the growing gap between contemporary industrial societies' capacity and competence to produce futures and knowledge of such futures. Because the future cannot be known, responsibility tends to be pushed outside the frame of reference, which means that responsibility can no longer be exclusively routed via knowledge. Therefore, according to Adam and Crow, a direct link must be established between action and ethics in contexts of extensive uncertainty.

Moreover, as Adam and Crow show, advanced capitalist societies have further eroded responsibility for the future, depleting it and disembedding it from all contexts (natural and social). "Once emptied, the future can be filled with anything, with unlimited interests, desires, projections, values, beliefs, ethical concerns, business ventures, political ambitions…It becomes a free-for-all, unbounded, unlimited and thus fundamentally and irreducibly indeterminate. In contrast to the context-bound future, the empty future of contemporary economic and political exchange is fundamentally uncertain and unknowable. At the same time, however, it appears wide open to colonization and transversal" (12–13).

In this perspective, taking responsibility means re-embedding the future, which leads to our third observation: the link between the analysis of social futures and the discourse of power. While sociology has widely conceptualized the link between space, time, and power (Foucault, Giddens, Massey 2005, Bauman), the specific link between power and the future as been underconceptualized. John Urry emphasizes how a key question for social science is who or what owns the future, as this capacity to own futures is central to how power works. He proposes to "democratize" the future, that is, to find a productive way of developing thinking and practice on "democratic" futures.

Therefore, first, the future can no longer be considered a private matter (Urry 2016). Much literature and many media representations presume that the future is private and personal: each person hopes for, plans, plots, and anticipates his or her own future. People in the "modern" world are often encouraged to "dream the 'impossible dream'," especially to reinvent themselves (Elliott 2013). The individualization thesis therefore implies that, if the impossible is not achieved, it is that person's own fault. Their dreams, ambitions, or achievements were just not good enough.

The notion of "social futures" developed by Urry (2016) contrasts this idea of individualistic and fragmented futures with the complex and more inclusive idea of collective thinking about futures. A plurality of subjects must be implicated, and in particular, public bodies and NGOs must be incorporated in the process. Indeed, these organizations often have to be key coordinators within the processes of anticipating and making futures. Thinking and practice must go beyond the market, minimal states, and new technologies that are considered more or less inevitable.

"Thus within contemporary disorganized capitalism, futures thinking is a major way of bringing the state and civil society back in from the cold. Moreover, if we focus upon social futures, this forces a transcendence of both markets and technologies. 'Social futures' problematize both autonomous markets and the march of technology. They authorize the participation of a range of many relevant actors including states and civil society in making futures. Thinking and democratizing futures involves what we might call 'post-modern planning' in the contemporary era of civil society, global change, wicked problems, the limits of markets, multiple 'unknown unknowns' and so on" (Urry 2016).

Therefore, if the old notion of planning (due to the complexity and "wickedness" of futures) is no longer applicable, it can be revived under a new name. If planning the future reveals the impossible, futures thinking is necessary, and coordination is the key strategy.

The reflection on re-embedding the future, redefining responsibility, and reflecting on power has been accompanied by a new and developing field within the tradition of critical sociology: the public sociology field (Adam 2009a; Bell 2009; Jeffries 2009).

The first generation of sociologists was "committed to the idea that what would become known as sociology should address how to bring a better future into being" (Tutton 2016: 2). A more explicitly activist and future-oriented approach to social analysis and a new sensitivity to its public role are gaining strength and visibility in contemporary sociology. "We have spent a century building professional knowledge, translating common sense into science, so that now, we are more than ready to embark on a systematic back-translation, taking knowledge back to those from whom it came, making public issues out of private troubles, and thus regenerating sociology's moral fiber. Herein lies the promise and challenge of public sociology, the complement and not the negation of professional sociology" (Michael Burawoy 2005: 5).

Re-enchanting the Future: Fictionary Expectations, Hopes, Utopias, and Affect

Nicklas Luhmann (1976) argues that the temporal order of modernity should be understood as one in which utopia and progress mix with prognoses and calculation (Beckert 2016). In this sense, the ambivalence of modernity is perfectly revealed in the nature of the future. "Indeed, the essential characteristic of an horizon is that we can never touch it, never get at it, never surpass it, but that in spite of that, it contributes to the definition of the situation" (Luhmann 1976: 140). At the same time, future is *defuturized* through a set of techniques (statistic calculus and economics) that make use of the future "without beginning it and without reducing it to one chain of datable future presents" (141).

Since the introduction of the Weberian *iron cage* metaphor (emphasizing the entrapping effects of the detachment between the utopic and irrational horizon of protestant ethics and the technical rationality of capitalist culture), defuturizing the future has been at the core of capitalist development.

In this frame, all the terms referring to a nonrational horizon of the future have been expelled from the realm of the sociological explanation. As underlined by Levitas (2013), "utopia is commonly dismissed as an irrelevant fantasy" (p.25). Similarly, the idea of a *sociology of hope*, which emphasizes the role of faith and belief in the "possibility of possibility" (Webb 2007), has been examined with strong suspicion (Desroche 1979: 171) and has only recently gradually emerged as a concept within many empirical fields (youth sociology health studies and feminist studies); however, it has not gained the status of a mainstream concept.

In the 1990s, Giddens (1990), rejecting the notion that utopic horizons frame political action, discards the possibility of a single, comprehensive, all-connecting ideology. Instead, he advocates going after the "small pictures," that is, the ones people can directly affect at their home, workplace, or local community. To Giddens, this is a difference between what he calls "pointless utopianism" and "useful utopian realism," which he defines as envisaging "alternative futures whose very propagation might help them be realized." By "utopian," he means something new and extraordinary, and by "realistic," he stresses that this idea is rooted in the existing social processes and can be viewed as their simple extrapolation.

However, to engage with innovation and social change, realism is insufficient. Henri Desroche uses the rope as a metaphor to describe the role of hope in projecting into the future.

Desroche's metaphor of the rope evokes a typical miracle of fakirism paralleled in many religious traditions. "In this rite, the officiant throws a rope like a lasso in the air. The rope rises higher and higher in the air. It should fall down. But the officiant assures us that it has mysteriously anchored itself somewhere and to prove it, he or his disciple climbs up the rope. The rope does not give way. *It holds*. And it carries the weight of the man as he climbs" (Desroche 1979: 1).

Hope is a rope, affirms Desroche:

> Hope is both constituted and constitutive; it provides the emotional substratum, so to speak, of the dialectic between the old and the new, between the reproduction and the transformation of social structures as these figure in thinking and acting individuals. (Desroche 1979: 3)

It is not a coincidence that an all-encompassing set of concepts referring to this "nonrealistic" dimension of projectivity is currently occupying more space in sociology.

As Coleman and Tutton (2017) maintain, today, it seems imperative to hold on to and cultivate more hopeful engagements with the future. Les Back warns against a "tone of sociological writing that is often in a despairing or hopeless key" (2015), not least because it risks creating a sense of certainty in how events will unfold. Les Back (2015) recently emphasized, "Hope is not a destination; it is perhaps an improvisation with a future not yet realised. It is not cruel optimism that hides behind a promise that is broken before it is even made. Hope then is an empirical question, and the sociology of hope requires an attentiveness to the moments when 'islands of hope' are established and the social conditions that makes their emergence possible."

In his recent book, Beckert (2016) shows how economic actors' rational behavior is based on their visions of the economic future, the achievement, or avoidance of which motivates these actors' decisions.

Beckert coined the term "fictional expectations" to underline how predictions of ontologically uncertain outcomes are inventions similar to fictional works: they are expressions of creativity and descriptions that surpass what we can empirically observe, and they open up counterfactual horizons. Probability statements in situations in which parameters are unknown, nonlinear, and unstable are thus a realistic fiction that creates a present future that becomes a basis for decision-making.

In her influential book on *Utopia as Method*, Levitas proposes the imaginary reconstitution of society, stating, "Although the critical edge of utopianism depends upon imagined alternatives possessing a reasonable degree of internal coherence and at least theoretical possibility, it is less constrained by what now seems immediately possible. Importantly, its explicitly hypothetical character enables us to insist on utopia's provisionality, reflexivity and dialogic mode. Explicit alternative scenarios for the future are fundamental to any kind of democratic debate. This means envisioning alternatives, but also setting out the images of the good society buried in the constant barrage of political rhetoric and policies."

Similarly, when examining various future visions (efforts to anticipate, visualize, and imagine the future), Urry (2016) gives a special significance to utopia. Showing that things could be different and suggesting what should happen to move toward that desired utopia can be a significant force leading to change. For example, utopias of car-free cities and of powering down to create a low-carbon world may materialize: "...[F]uture visions have powerful social consequences. And thinking futures makes one understand that things could be otherwise, that outcomes are not necessarily determined."

Simultaneously, dystopias can have an empowering effect on making futures. Dystopian visions are strongly developing in social science (the "new catastrophism" in social thinking; Urry 2016), science and science fiction narratives. Depicting a dark future based on the systematic amplification of current trends and features relies on the critical observation of a threatening present that would lead to an apocalyptic future "if nothing were done." The very existence of such a narrative presupposes that the political community (including the public, experts, industrials, policy-makers, and stakeholders) the narrative tries to reach is actually able to do something to prevent it. Paradoxically, this empowerment is grounded in the same kind of "enlightened catastrophism," that is, a realistic depiction of the future as if it had already happened and nothing could be done to stop it. Accordingly, a sense of possibility that allows the reader (broadly speaking) to imagine alternative pathways to a more desirable future is activated or restored.

Discourses on dystopias illustrate that the boundaries between what is frightening, "irrational" fiction and what is rational, scientific, and reassuring reality become "blurred" and that the frame of the future is a powerful frame for redefining the status of sociological discourse.

A second strongly emerging element is that, while modernity (and somehow sociology itself) has neutralized and tamed the future through rationality, the role of emotions appears to be increasingly important in the relationship between the present and the future. Describing the spread of the social movements, Castells (2012) considers emotions (sharing sorrow and hope, overcoming fear) to be the most important elements for allowing people to connect minds, create meaning, and contest power. Castells describes the dynamics of movement thus:

> It was not just poverty, or the economic crisis, or the lack of democracy that caused the multifaceted rebellion. Of course, all these poignant manifestations of an unjust society and of an undemocratic polity were present in the protests. But it was primarily the humiliation provoked by the cynicism and arrogance of those in power, be it financial, political or cultural, that brought together those who turned fear into outrage, and outrage into hope for a better humanity. (Castells 2012: 10)

Similarly, Ben Anderson argues that anticipation operates affectively because it is "deployed in liberal democracies to govern a range of events, conditions and crises" (2010: 779), while Brian Massumi (2005) contends that pre-emption of the future characterizes contemporary Western societies and modes of power and operates through fear.

It must be acknowledged that including hope and fears once again into the study of the future leads us to consider the connections between this work and studies on affect (Coleman 2016). Many social and cultural theorists have recently noted the affectivity of the future, highlighting the ways in which an affective temporality complicates or confuses linear temporality such that the future is not only or not so much a distinct and/or distant temporality, separate from the present (and past) but (also) experienced and felt "in" and as the present (Coleman 2016).

At the end of this brief journey, the multifariousness of the future re-emerges. This multifariousness is simply the multidimensionality of social action. Coleman and Tutton (2017) claim that "an engagement with and interrogation of 'the future' is certainly a timely undertaking for social scientists." The timeliness of this undertaking is certainly so because the wickedness of the future forces sociological categories to embrace a more complex and inclusive theory of social action.

Summary

The study of the future has never been as alive and full of promise within sociology as it is today. The analytical frame of this chapter centers on the question of "why sociology needs anticipation?" The leading position is that the introduction of the future in sociological theory and research does not simply mark the opening of a new "field of inquiry" but rather is profoundly related to some of the problems that the discipline has encountered in its development and some of the subsequent solutions that have recently guided its core development. Simply expressed, mainstreaming the future is a useful strategy to address some of sociology's most controversial issues.

The three themes discussed in the chapter, namely, the habitus-reflexivity nexus, the materiality-immateriality (representational/nonrepresentational) nexus, and the rationality-irrationality nexus, clearly indicate that reflecting on anticipation is highly productive for developing sociological thinking beyond dichotomies. The wickedness of the future forces sociological categories to embrace a more complex and inclusive theory of social action.

References

Adam, B., & Groves, C. (2007). *Future matters. Action, knowledge, ethics.* Leiden/Boston: Brill.

Adam, B. (2009a). Future in the making. Sociological practice and challenge. In V. Jeffries (Ed.), *Handbook of public sociology.* Lanham: Rowman & Littlefield Publishers, Inc.

Adam, B. (2009b). Cultural future matters an exploration in the spirit of max Weber's methodological writings. *Time and Society, 18*(1), 7–25.

Adam, B., Beck, U., & Loon, J. (Eds.). (2000). *The risk society and beyond. Critical issues for social theory.* London: Sage.

Anderson, B. (2010). Preemption, precaution, preparedness: Anticipatory action and future geographies. *Progress in Human Geography, 34*(6), 777–798.

Appadurai, A. (2015). *Banking on words the failure of language in the age of derivative finance.* Chicago: The University of Chicago Press.

Appadurai, R. (2004). The capacity to aspire. Culture and the terms of recognition. In V. Rao & M. Walton (Eds.), *Cultural and public action.* Stanford: Stanford University Press.

Back, L. (2015). Blind pessimism and the sociology of hope. Discover Sociology. Available at: http://discoversociety.Org/2015/12/01/blind-pessimism-and-the-sociology-of-hope/?utm_con tent=buffer5ea12&utm_medium=social&utm_source=twitter.com&utm_campaign=buffer.

Beck, U., & Beck-Gernsheim, E. (2002). *Individualization: Institutionalized individualism and its social and political consequences.* London: Sage.

Beck, U. (1992). *Risk society. Towards a new modernity.* London: Sage.

Beckert, J. (2016). *Imagined futures. Fictional expectations and capitalist dynamics.* Harvard: Harvard University Press.

Bell, W. (2009). Public sociology and the future: The possibile, the probabile, the preferable. In V. Jeffries (Ed.), *Handbook of Public Sociology.* Lanham: Rowman & Littlefield Publishers, Inc.

Bourdieu, P. (2000). *Pascalian meditations.* Oxford: Stanford University Press/Polity Press.

Bourdieu, P. (1977). *Outline of a theory of practice* (R. Nice, Trans.) Cambridge: Cambridge University Press.

Bourdieu, P. (1990). *The logic of practice* (R. Nice, Trans.). London: Polity Press.

Burawoy, M. (2005). For public sociology. *American Sociological Review. 70*(1), 4–28.

Castells, M. (2012). *Networks of outrage and hope. Social movements in the internet age.* Cambridge: Polity Press.

Coleman, R. (2016). A sensory sociology of the future: affect, hope and inventive methodologies. *The Sociological Review, 00*, 1–16. https://doi.org/10.1111/1467-954X.12443.

Coleman, R., & Tutton, R. J. C. (2017). Introduction to futures in question: Theories, methods, practices. *The Sociological Review.* https://doi.org/10.1111/1467-954X.12448.

Desroche H. (1979) *Sociology of hope* (C. Martin-Sperry, Trans.). London: Routledge & Kegan Paul.

Dewey, J. (1981). The need for a recovery of philosophy. In J. J. McDermott (Ed.), *The philosophy of John Dewey* (pp. 58–97). Chicago/London: University of Chicago Press.

Elliott, A. (2013). *Reinvention.* London: Routledge.

Emirbayer, M., & Mische, A. (1998). What is agency? *American Journal of Sociology, 103*, 962–1023.

Esposito, E. (2011). *The future of futures. The time of money in financing and society.* Cheltenham: Edward Edgar Publishing Limited.

Giddens, A. (1990). *The consequences of modernity.* Cambridge: Polity Press.

Giddens, A. (1991). *Modernity and self-identity.* Cambridge: Polity Press.

Jeffries, V. (Ed.). (2009). *Handbook of public sociology.* Lanham: Rowman & Littlefield Publishers, Inc.

Joas, H. (1996). *The creativity of action.* Cambridge: Polity Press.

Jonas, H. (1984). *The imperative of responsibility in search of an ethics for the technological age.* Chicago: The University of Chicago Press.

Kumar, K. (1972). Inventing the future in spite of futurology. *Future Essays, 4*, 369–374.

Levitas, R. (2013). *Utopia as a method. The imaginary reconstitution of society.* Houndmills: Palgrave MacMillan.

Luhmann, N. (1976). The future cannot begin: Temporal structures in modern society. *Social Research, 43*, 1.

Luhmann, N. (1982). *The Differentiation of Society.* Columbia University Press.

Massumi, B. (2005). The future birth of the affective fact. Conference Proceedings: Genealogies of Biopolitics. Available at: http://browse.reticular.info/text/collected/massumi.pdf.

Mead, G. H. (2002[1932]).*The philosophy of the present.* New York: Prometheus Book.

Mische, A. (2009). Projects and possibilities: Researching futures in action. *Sociological Forum, 24* (3), 694–704.

Muzzetto, L. (2006). Time and meaning in Alfred Schütz. *Time and Society, 15*(1), 5–31.

Sayer, A. (2009). Reflexivity and the habitus. In M. Archer (Ed.), *Conversations about reflexivity* (pp. 108–122). London: Routledge.

Schutz, A. (1967a). *The phenomenology of the social world* (G. Walsh & F. Lehnert, Trans.). Evanston: Northwestern University Press.

Schutz, A. (1967b). *Collected papers, the problem of social reality.* The Hague: Martinus NiJhoff.

Schulz, S. M. (2015). Future moves: Forward-oriented studies of culture, society, and technology. *Current Sociology, 63*(2), 129–139.

Tavory, I., & Eliasoph, N. (2013). Toward a theory of anticipation. *American Journal of Sociology, 118*(4), 908–942.

Turner, S. (1994). *The social theory of practices: Tradition, tacit knowledge, and presuppositions.* Chicago: University of Chicago Press.

Tutton, R. (2017). Wicked futures: meaning, matter and the sociology of the future. *The Sociological Review, 00*, 1–16. https://doi.org/10.1111/1467-954X.12443.

Urry, J. (2016). *What is the future?* Cambridge: Polity Press.

Urry, J. (2013). *Societies beyond oil. Oil dregs and social futures.* London: Zed Books.

Urry, J. (2003). *Global complexities.* Cambridge: Polity Press.

Webb, D. (2007). Modes of hoping. *History of the Human Sciences, 20*(3), 65–83.

Weigert, A. (2014). Realizing narratives make future time real. *Time and Society, 23*(3), 317–336.

The Discovery of Strategic Novelty: Learning from Things Yet to Happen

27

Markus Paukku and Liisa Välikangas

Contents

Abstract

All too often strategic surprises stem from an unforeseen error in the mapping out of the terrain that lies ahead. Surprise has an uneasy relationship with parsimonious planning and the unexpected, whether adversity or discovery, is antithetical to good strategizing in many a view. Strategies are locked into and preserved in committed organizations, supported by confirmation bias (Tuchman 1984). The further commitment to increasingly known, standard strategies is not limited to specific organizations and even cuts across sectors through isomorphic pressure and bias for known strategy – until it is discovered to no longer work (e.g., Tripsas and Gavetti 2000; Vuori and Huy 2016; Kaplan and Tripsas 2008). However, at the same time, let us remember that newness, variation and novelty is the purpose of strategizing and the basis for competitive differentiation. We

M. Paukku
Amsterdam Business School, Amsterdam, The Netherlands

L. Välikangas (✉)
Aalto University, Helsinki, Finland

Hanken School of Economics, Helsinki, Finland
e-mail: liisa.valikangas@aalto.fi

© Springer Nature Switzerland AG 2019
R. Poli (ed.), *Handbook of Anticipation*,
https://doi.org/10.1007/978-3-319-91554-8_15

541

argue that good strategy not only recognizes surprise but harnesses the possibilities of discovery to enable, and leverage, strategic novelty. The discovery of value and the valuing of discovery, both present a unique framing for strategists that reasserts new in their role, and reimagines an anticipated future yet to be constructed that enables strategic novelty.

Keywords
Strategic novelty · Learning · Innovation · Strategy toolkit · Discovery · Renewal

All too often strategic surprises stem from an unforeseen error in the mapping out of the terrain that lies ahead. Surprise has an uneasy relationship with parsimonious planning and the unexpected, whether adversity or discovery, is antithetical to good strategizing in many a view. Strategies are locked into and preserved in committed organizations, supported by confirmation bias (Tuchman 1984). The further commitment to increasingly known, standard strategies is not limited to specific organizations and even cuts across sectors through isomorphic pressure and bias for known strategy – until it is discovered to no longer work (e.g., Tripsas and Gavetti 2000; Vuori and Huy 2016; Kaplan and Tripsas 2008). However, at the same time, let us remember that newness, variation and novelty is the purpose of strategizing and the basis for competitive differentiation. We argue that good strategy not only recognizes surprise but harnesses the possibilities of discovery to enable, and leverage, strategic novelty. The discovery of value and the valuing of discovery, both present a unique framing for strategists that reasserts new in their role, and reimagines an anticipated future yet to be constructed that enables strategic novelty.

What room do we leave for discovery in strategizing? Where does novelty in strategy emerge? Where does discovery fit into the strategy process? We argue that there is much insight to be gained if discovery was to be harnessed systematically. This statement does not suggest that there is a shortcut by which to find readymade solutions or untapped business opportunities nor that discovery is not occasionally pursued in strategy work. More systematically examining the implications of the variables of that which has yet to happen requires at least the same rigor as the analysis of patterns past. Instead, by reframing an outlook on the imagined anticipated future instead of the known past we can arrive at a richer set of possibility frontiers that provides an expanded portfolio of strategic options. (There is an extensive literature on search (e.g., Katila and Ahuja 2002; Katila and Chen 2008; Katila et al. 2013). This literature is informative on how firms develop ideas for new products for example but the activity is still based on existing knowledge in the environment, and whether a search strategy is broad or narrow or combines both. Simon also comments on the roles of experts in selectively searching for solutions in familiar patterns (2001).)

This chapter aims not to find a balance between discovery and conservative strategizing in the vein of exploration-exploitation (March 1991) but rather how to understand these elements so as to integrate discovery to expand the boundaries of strategy. We are of course limited by our lives being trapped in the consciousness of the present without access to the past, and even less so to the future (Shackle 1992). Nevertheless, discovery is possible even if the frontiers of discovery vary for different people, within and across organizations. A discovery for a pioneer may be something that the mainstream organization does not even perceive, for example. Hence many radical innovations to the market are often brought by newcomers, not incumbents protecting their existing business models and core capabilities (Henderson and Clark 1990).

First we frame our understanding of discovery and why it has gone out of vogue. Next, we discuss why not only are discoveries valuable but why the process of discovery is valuable in and of itself. Finally, we introduce the concept of strategic amplification whereby impactful meaning can be constructed from even micro level discoveries and how they can be leveraged for organizational or even ecosystem level strategizing.

Rediscovery of Discovery, or Experiencing the WOW

Strategic planning, forecasting and strategy implementation have been designed to smooth our navigation through the rugged landscape before us and dampen the impact of the shocks of innovation and the rhythms of business processes and operations. The development of strategy tools and the paradigm of expecting increased predictability certainly has benefited the management of business. However, one could ask if there is an overlooked cost in steering strategy by this approach? The evidence driven, data rich framing strategy does indisputably provide a reading of past patterns. It is in extrapolating these metrics and causal mechanisms forward, however, that we run the risk of limiting and narrowing the range of options by which to construct the future and achieve unexpected results. Yet at the same time, Carlo Ratti in his book (City of Tomorrow 2016, p. 5) draws attention to the dangers of extrapolating from weak signals: "Prediction often involves assaying weak signals at the cutting edge of the contemporary world and flinging them far forward, for decades or centuries, to arrive at a portrait of a future city." The application of such methods in 1900 featured a millennial Boston that offered the zeppelin travel and pneumatic technology. The assumptions underpinning much of our capacity to interact with the future arise from a view that our bounded rationality limits our cognition (Simon 1957). As a result, strategy has often focused on developing the tools by which to optimize the selection between strategy choices. Managers are taught decision-making as if all the strategy options are known or available at that moment without due consideration for the limits of the strategy tools utilized (see e.g., Kay 2011). For instance, SWOT analyses and Porter's infamous Five Forces framework are lingua franca amongst strategists. These tools are certainly useful in simplifying a complex and causally ambiguous reality and illuminating a particular perspective by which to view the competitive landscape they also limit the variation by which to anticipate the future. Through their success these established strategy frameworks have standardized strategizing around certain variables – akin to mastering the calculation of odds and probabilities at a card table with a standard deck of 52. Instead, we ask, what if strategy ought to be about expanding the boundaries of strategy, imagining conditions or variables yet to be considered? A sixth competitive Force could change the way that strategy is developed. The discovery of a 53rd or 63rd card would surely impact the winning strategy of your next poker game.

Examining a wider spectrum of options unconstrained by the safety net of the past is difficult. Learning from future events yet to happen and ideas before their evidence requires new forms of learning, developing a tolerance of uncertainty and the honing of new strategic capabilities (for an early discussion on the topic, see March et al. (1991): Learning from samples of one or fewer). The benefit however, may well be valued discovery and truly novel strategy.

The future awaits, accessible and anticipating definition. The future focused would ask, why compete in the defined past with its known winners and losers. Why would one expect radically different results by repeating the same competitive dynamics in the future? Replicating strategies that would result in similar competitive consequences would be difficult for a second time not the very least due to social complexity and causal ambiguity. Some strategies, such as the Greek's Trojan horse, relied on their surprise as introduced an unforeseen new variable by which to compete. The innovation strategy by which Microsoft and Intel cooperated to develop PC compatible products, successfully competed against IBM and cornered Apple to a then negligible corner of the market is unlikely to unfold again partly because the other market players would be aware of such a strategy tried anew. Second, the environment in which these once successful strategies were enacted has changed dramatically. The city of Troy would unlikely to be seduced by the same strategy a second time. Similarly, the Wintel strategy was designed to counter IBM, and due its success this standard still dominates much of the desktop and laptop market. Today the competitive dynamics have evolved within that industry and have introduced new variables that are necessary for an understanding of the strategy within the computer space like open source software.

Of course, exaptation of innovation (Andriani et al. 2016) cannot be neglected in the discovery process. There are instances of rediscoveries of strategies past that prove to be useful in a radically different environment. An example of this could be the playful lab experimentation with a tenth century Anglo-Saxon garlic eye ointment that surprised researchers in its effectiveness in killing MSRA, the antibiotic resistant hospital superbug. Similarly the drug thalidomide, after the pre-natal tragedies its caused, turned out to be effective in treating a particularly severe skin condition related to leprosy.

Today companies are increasingly trying to compete not for leadership within an established category but rather reframe and become category in and of themselves within new business models. Think of Snap, the successful social media company behind Snapchat, insisting during its IPO that is it pursuing a strategy where, "Snap looks for a role beyond the social network." In an era increasingly characterized by temporary, rather than sustainable, competitive advantages many innovative strategists look not to compete in known games but to develop new games to win. By obfuscating or blurring the metrics by which to evaluate strategies – think about the evolution of the performance metrics of online companies as they developed monetization strategies from Friendster to Facebook – they probe at and discover new definitions by which to compete, measure success and uncover value. Beyond acknowledging that there is infinite space out there where competition is yet to happen (so called "blue ocean"), the discovery-driven approach seeks to engage with such already existing but future-leaning business models and learn from them.

In making sense of the possible futures ahead of us we are also engaging in a process whereby we are constructing the canvas and the boundary conditions of what is currently possible and what is potentially novel. These boundaries are where we aim to drive this discussion. How to discover the frontier, how to discover the value in it and how such discovery can be deployed in context and time.

There are several challenges to be expanded upon in discussing the concept of discovery. By definition discovery includes a notion of surprise, sometimes astonishment, sometimes even fear, and finding of something of which the outcome is uncertain. Many types of discovery imply some degree of the unexpected that could not have been predicted and thus require experimentation or venturing beyond the usual field of enquiry (see McGrath 1999). Exploring beyond the edge of the map, sailing into waters marked "here be dragons," one is left without the signposts by which to determine how far along the route we find ourselves, let alone if we are headed in the right direction, or even making progress. That is what unknown territory is like.

Thus, the process of discovery assumes variation flourishes beyond the familiar variables. In an unknown field the newly discovered has yet to be defined. Sometimes we can describe what we find in loose approximations of the familiar through a muddled vocabulary of past and future (cars being defined as horseless carriages). When confronted with something truly novel we simply abandon the connection to relative measures and accept that the undiscovered future lacks a common vocabulary by which to be defined (Christian Dior's 1947 fashion collection, lacking any relevant existing categorization was described by the press as the "New Look"). There is talk about the "new normal" without a clear definition what this state of affairs might be – perhaps the new normal is captured by its very uncertainty and vagueness.

It is managerially challenging to control performance or strategize around ill-defined phenomena without being open to discovery. For example, investing in a building where the strategic functions are denoted by blank spaces in the blueprints requires a tolerance for ambiguity and the prioritization of systematic discovery. When the cavern of CERN particle accelerator's ATLAS experiment was inaugurated under the hills of the Swiss-French border in 2003 it was accepted that the technology used to detect the first collisions in 2010 would still be under development for some years to come. Strategizing based on the technology available at the moment that ATLAS broke ground would have ensured that the experiment would have been outdated before it was even complete – imagining a future of zeppelins. Instead, organizations must systematically engage in discovery to construct the value they seek.

As an experiment, an example that one day may seem quaint and dated, one might casually ask colleagues and friends what "blockchain" is. While many have heard the word, few actually know of the potentially radical consequences of the technology or can discuss its operating principles. Or, try discuss what the future of the societies are, should we arrive at a post-employment society, with very few people actually gainfully employed at any one point in time. An employment relationship has long been the cornerstone of the societal membership and engagement, what if this is no longer the case as work disappears, see e.g., Martin Ford: The Rise of the Robots (2015)? As the topic is politically sensitive, it is particularly difficult to discuss in a future-oriented, discovery-driven terms. The issue is often rejected out of bounds due to ideological or vested interests' reasons.

As a result, discoveries are typically not witnessed and shared by large populations but rather experienced by vanguards, pioneers, misfits (Jones et al. 2016) or those on the margins of the society ideologically or creatively (see e.g., Wang and Soule 2016). Discovery is an activity unlikely to be experienced evenly across a population or in the words of Gibson, "The future is already here – it's just not very evenly distributed."

So how do these ideas travel from the vanguards, from the outliers of the population, to the mainstream and make an impact? Communicating discoveries is particularly challenging as such novelties may encounter political resistance, be cognitively too challenging to grasp as presenting a very different state of affairs from the current one, or be emotionally exciting or draining. In our research on Outliers (Välikangas and Gibbert 2015), we have found that strategic novelty, represented by the *outliers*, rouse emotional reactions, and thinking through and reflecting on these reactions is a good way to starting to make sense of novelty. Why does this excite me so much? Why do I get scared? What is the WOW? Is this the reaction to discovery? This allows a difficult to quantify emotional reference outside the scope of strategic tools and measures, a gut feeling, that plays a significant role in informing our cognitive processes as we think through the implications.

If discovery is thus experienced, it can be shared with many even without the specific cognitive reference. The value of this discovery can thus also be amplified, as we will discuss later.

Not all discoveries have value. Though we argue that discovery may require honed capabilities to expose our cognition to discovery, to allow one to see value where another may not, not all discoveries will have value that is useful in terms of strategy. Much as innovation requires an invention to have some measure of value we define discovery to be linked to some notion of a value added metric relative to a time and place. Simon described creativity pragmatically, "From time to time humans come up with ideas that are judged by their fellows be both novel and valuable" (1983). However, while the uncovered discovery may turn out not have value, the process by which the novel is uncovered does develop the capabilities, individual skill sets and organizational routines, of discovery and is of significant value.

Discoveries by definition cannot last as discoveries and the novelty of novelty, the WOW fades. Just as the potential of pneumatic tubes or Zeppelins did. Perhaps, with the exception of a handful of pop singers, there are few phenomena that can be endlessly rediscovered, be continuously considered novel or channel newness.

Indeed, just as with strategic novelty, discoveries have a shelf life –a process by which they are transformed by their very discovery into something less novel. Alongside this process come a progression of value that we address. Indeed, patents and other intellectual property regimes recognize that the value of many discoveries changes over time, and sufficiently so that they allow for monopoly benefits to be only extracted within the crucial initial number of years.

The value of a discovered ideas, knowledge, strategies and monkeys as we discuss next is context dependent and temporally sensitive. The following is an example of discovery, an unexpected discovery of the value of a discovery, and diffusion and subsequent institutionalization of the discovery.

A setting of the improbable discovery of value can be found in the, most probably, oldest café in Amsterdam. Café in 't Aepjen, literally translated as "In the Monkeys" is an establishment with a recorded history of serving customers since at least 1519 in one of only two wooden structures to have survived the Amsterdam fire of 1452. It reportedly acquired its colorful name in during the great age of European discovery when sailors would set out from the adjacent port of Amsterdam on perilous journeys to the Far East to sometimes return many months later thirsty, but short on guilders. Some, however, would not return to Europe alone but were accompanied by their pet monkeys, what must have been quite the novelty at the time. However, how to determine the value of these exotic animals that were so different?

The novelty of the monkeys was sufficient to draw a crowd and the keepers of the café would allow these cash strapped sailors to settle their bar tabs and pay for their accommodation in the hammocks upstairs by giving up their monkeys. The café and its caged monkeys leveraged the novelty of these monkeys, common in Indonesia, exotic in Amsterdam, and thus imagined, invented and traded on the value of these monkeys.

As is the case with all novelty, the timing is important and the exotic fades. Eventually people moved on from the novelty of a bar full of monkeys, and the fleas they carried. These once valuable discoveries from the Far East had become a pest. They were literally collected from the premises and moved into a bar patron's garden in the east of the city. This garden would become later become one of Europe's oldest zoos, the members only Natura Artis Magistra. Today, Artis, as it is now known, is an institution that still draws crowds to showcase discoveries and the tamed wild in a controlled, coherent and accessible form. However, the zoo itself has become a living museum for discovery. Today, it's buildings and displays not only continue to showcase discoveries but also artefacts from the age of exploration when curio cabinets and palace like structures were built to celebrate discovery.

Valuing Discoveries and Value of Discovery, or the So What?

Discoveries may happen but their value can be undetermined. A Finnish vegan food, later branded as Pulled Oats and currently owned by Paulig Corporation, was invented in a research lab as part of a doctoral dissertation work yet only gained potential commercial value when a serial entrepreneur thought there was a lot of unmet demand for non-meat, nonsoy, foods in the market place having experienced some of this surging demand in a visit to California. A telephone call that resulted from this value discovery to the inventor went first unheeded. The inventor could not quite understand the excitement that the entrepreneur was exhibiting, the connection between a technical food science invention and novel vegan food product was not obvious. The entrepreneur accomplished a perceptual framing of the discovery (Hanson 1958), and was able to see a technical invention not only *as* something that research had discovered but *that* it was in fact a commercially appealing end product to be developed and launched.

Discoveries have different kinds of value. There is the commercial value that may or may not result as in the case above – yet to be determined though how broad a commercial success will result. There is also the value of discoveries as something novel and hence informative about our environment. This value may be scientific such as a new approach for combatting cancer or it may every-day –discovering a new route to office may be important for the everyday routines but have lesser value outside a person's daily commitments. There are discoveries that are curiosities, gaining a moment of attention but not much more. There are discoveries that at the time of their observation may appear unimportant but later present themselves differently and provide further context or support and enable further discoveries. As earlier noted, the notion of exaptation is sometimes used to refer to a discovery that migrates to another context and use.

Furthermore, what is a discovery to one person, may be "obvious" for another as access to, or the frontier of, novelty varies per person, per place and per the knowledge we have of the world. The more known an idea, a discipline, or a field is to us and our idiosyncratic vantage point the more comfortable we tend to be with these ideas. However, learning is best amplified when a discontinuity requires resolving. The magnitude of the impact of discovery on daily strategizing and sense making is, for example, none more apparent than when young children play peek-a-boo and discover object permanence – indeed, the parent does not cease to exist when hiding behind her or his hands. Rarely are strategists challenged by such obvious yet fundamental existential revelations. Instead uncovering valuable new, strategically significant, performance impacting discoveries requires the continuous stretching beyond familiar schema, wherever that individual's or organization's capacity for discovery has drawn that horizon or boundary of the echo chamber.

While the starting point for discovery is individual the learning mechanisms and consequences of discovery can be commented upon in the aggregate.

Sometimes, the process of discovery may require that the discovery is appropriately translated to its desired audience. This may demand the contextualization of the discovery in terms that are familiar to the audience and positioning the discovery in these terms, perhaps even doing some violence to the content of the discovery in the interest of not being rejected. Or speaking to an audience to whom the discovery may be less novel, adding more interpretational framing and business or societal implications may be required to gain a hearing (Dutton et al. 2001, Issue selling). The discovery itself, and its value, changes as it is being framed and reframed.

As is famously said: "You cannot be more wrong than be right before your time." Conversely, you can't be more boring that being wrong much after your time.

So, how to construct a present in which your discovery has relevance, and potentially, value? The conceptual options are to change or even question the prevailing metrics by which value is measured or to reframe the discovery in current terms. The commercial value of pulled oats became apparent when taken from the laboratory to the supermarket shelf and positioned next to ground meat that the product is a substitute of, a context familiar to consumers. However, one could consider the alternative. For example, the quantified self and health hacking citizen science movements have seen increasing numbers of consumers moving into the laboratory to supplement themselves and expand the available product offering. Reimagining not only the framing of discoveries, but rather the markets they could exist in, may lead to uncovering the dormant value of entire categories of discoveries.

Independent of the value of a particular discovery, there may be value in the act of discovering per se. It is likely that such openness to serendipitous insight (Merton and Barber 2006) provides richer information about the environment and allows the seeing of more opportunities (as well as threats) in the environment. It is also likely that such a capability for discovery makes better use of signals that speak to the forthcoming changes (sometimes called weak signals). An ability to observe, or even imagine, things others perhaps don't (yet) notice or reject as irrelevant must give competitive advantage to the more alert person or organization. After all, do we not have any better explanation for Steve Jobs's and Apple's extraordinary success in imaging and marketing new product categories? Or do we prefer this interpretation where an inspiring future can be imagined, if not by all, by some visionaries amongst us?

There is, of course, the possibility that such signals are mere noise and distractions. However, it is the interpretation of the observations where the value is formed, and presumably someone with a record of continuous interpretation and more exposure to potential discoveries would do better than someone or some organization that is tightly focused on executing the annual goals (as probably defined a year ago) and performing against standardized Key Performance Indicators (much beloved by corporations) that focus attention on a handful targets. Interestingly, a study reported in The Economist (September 24, 2016: 71–22) suggests that even reasonable sounding metrics in academia, such as number of publications, may have unintended consequences and lead to "bad science" even when a penalty is associated with cutting corners. Such metrics are likely to repress discovery and the reflection on the discovery as researchers hurry to publish safer known studies.

So why do discoveries matter? Our preference for the certainty of established frameworks, and the certainty they are associated with, certainly dominate everyday strategizing. When we think of the age of discovery, the Enlightenment or exploration we reach for the history books. Indeed, some public figures are worried about progress and wonder what has happened to the pace of innovation and discovery since, for example, the moon landings of 1968. Many consider that the conventional age of exploration of our physical environment to be over long ago as everything has been discovered. The areas where breakthroughs are currently pursued are often guarded by high professionalization of discovery – think pharmaceutical research or the qualifications of physicists at CERN. How to learn from something as fleeting as discovery? It is a process that has become seemingly inaccessible.

We argue that the discoveries naturally still happen, but returning to Gibson's quote, their distribution has become even more skewed. While we can only rarely as a collective human audience, en masse, revel in exploration, as seen on TV, we can look to learn from the outliers and vanguards pushing the frontiers of any number of fields, including strategy. Furthermore, unlike the prepackaged self-evident importance, value and significance of moon landing, we are able to invent and construct the frames by which we unlock the value of these numerous, accessible, discoveries.

Amplification, or the OOMPH!

Value is a relative and attributable concept as has been discussed. Often the value of a discovery, or the entrepreneurial opportunity, has to be created (Alvarez and Barney 2008) as in the case of vegan food product. Years of hard work are typically needed to turn a discovery into something marketable or beneficial to human kind.

The opportunity creation is akin to amplification of the discovery. For example, in drug discovery there are years of clinical studies that lead to the potential launch of a drug and its marketing to medical professionals (and, sometimes, end users). In these different phases, the drug is studied in animal and human contexts and its safety and efficacy is determined. A lot more is learned about the potential drug and its market demand as it acquires legitimacy in different regulatory, market, medical and commercial frames or contexts.

There are also instances when this amplification process itself leads to the discovery of new markets. By expanding the possibility set within which to apply the drug, off-label applications have been discovered for the use of drugs far from the original or intended design. For example, Pfizer created and tapped into a market based on the side effects of its hypertension drug in what it now famously markets as its blue pills. This amplification may extent to exaptation (Andriani et al. forthcoming) where a technology developed to one use can be found beneficial to an entirely different purpose. For example, a radar developed for military purposes was later evolved into a microwave oven, the first-time cooking was done without heat. This discovery was due to an accident: "Spencer, an engineer working at Raytheon, serendipitously discovered in 1945 that a magnetron, a radar component, was responsible for the melting of a candy bar in his pocket and could be used for cooking .... Raytheon modified the magnetron for its new function and in 1947 introduced the first micro-wave oven (Osepchuk 1984)." (Andriani et al., p. 4).

Similarly, any discovery, in order to learn about it and leverage its potential value, needs to be amplified. Internally in an organization, the discovery requires the development of an understanding of its value, and perhaps some leadership in taking the risks related to experimenting with a novelty. The amplification process directs attention, and possibly, commits resources to a discovery and in doing so contributes to defining its value. Amplifying the internal discovery may mean using resources in such a way that small commitments are joined, and compounded, by external interests, for example, or by harnessing existing but orthogonal knowledge in analogous ways that contribute to the learning without further resource demands. Externally, the discovery may be amplified by creating network effects or knowledge spillovers that quickly bring new knowledge and applications of the potential uses. New ecosystems may form from the exploration and exploitation.

Today, companies that are seen as innovators are increasingly seeking to impact the frame by which their offering is to be evaluated. Many products and services thought to be innovative are brought to market and not designed to compete within existing categories or classes of products but rather, unlock far more value by defining the categories in which they operate. The AirBnBs of the world discovered, communicated and captured value where others could not. While many of these have made a lasting impact, and the profit to match, many more companies are unable to put together the formula for commercial value. Some that do succeed commercially may only achieve temporary value as their novelty too soon becomes a commodity. However, we argue that the experience of the discovery process itself may well outlast the value of the specific discovery from which it was gained. While an instance of discovery, such a Pulled Oats, may or may not have significant commercial value, the art or act of discovery process is an experiential quality that is gained through the process. The entrepreneurial efforts around this research have even been awarded prizes by foundations looking to promote such activity not measured in terms of the profits generated but rather the capacity to discover dormant value in the laboratory.

Indeed, serial entrepreneurs move from business idea to business idea carrying with them the experiential learning of uncovering and amplifying previous discoveries and the art of attributing, and sometimes extracting, value from these findings. The attuned perception allows for a vision of discovery in which venture capitalists invest, using these companies as conduits into the future. Perhaps the most obvious conduit into the future at the time of this writing is the entrepreneur-investor Elon Musk who gained popular fame as the founder of the electric car company Tesla. He is also an investor in a solar energy company, among others, and is currently seeking possibilities to develop human travel to Mars. His dedication is likely amplifying interest in space travel, also of active concern to Amazon.com founder Jeff Bezos among others. Despite initial setbacks, it is interesting that the two well-known visionaries at the moment both seem dedicated to address the next frontier – space – yet to be explored. Their example may attract many others and thus amplify the commitment to space exploration beyond the capabilities of public organizations such as NASA. Similarly, Tesla has sought to make its patents open, or available for anyone to use without fees, in order to drive electric car ownership further. This is presumably motivating faster and more dense infrastructure building for battery charging, which tends to limit the range, while increasing the anxiety, of driving electric. Sharing the knowledge is an amplification strategy for growing the market for electric cars.

Learning from things yet to happen means appreciating and engaging in discovery, even when it presents huge challenges or the discovery is a matter of serendipitous observation. Sometimes inviting, sometimes puzzling, discoveries do not have the agency to communicate their value but need to be examined, learned from, contextualized and amplified. Discoveries are opportunities for examining the future potential in light of the present opportunities and threats. In and of themselves they are innocent of the value amplification necessary to turn discoveries into something that are world-changing. The current obsession with disruption probably speaks to our frustration of being bound to existing, sometimes tired, measures and metrics and our fascination with the future potential of things we do not yet fully understand nor appreciate. Perhaps this speaks of our desire to reimagine the criteria by which we build the future. Curious then that discovery so rarely features in our strategies for learning from the future.

A Playful Methodology for Discovery (Source: Välikangas and Gibbert 2015)

Identify the WOW

What is it about the discovery that touches you? Engages your emotions? Causes fear? Makes you curious? Identify the roots of the emotion and examine it as an indication of something potentially significant. Perhaps your feelings are telling you something your reason does not yet know.

Should you dismiss the novelty, ask why. The reaction may be instructive about you as a strategist: What is your attitude towards novelty and surprise more generally? How do you (and your organization) learn about novelty?

Example Serial entrepreneur Maija Itkonen, accustomed to being exposed to new business and product ideas becomes sensitized to the market potential of vegan food during her travels in California. At the same time her friend and food scientist Dr. Reetta Kivelä uncovers the high nutritional value of so-called pulled oats but does recognize the meat substitute potential of this protein rich product within the oats/baked goods category of the company where she was working at the time.

Think of the So What?

Being receptive to new ideas is not enough. Knowing what ideas can enrich your organization is where novelty benefits strategy. This is where the "SO WHAT?" begins. Think through the potential implications of the novelty for your particular organization. Does the novelty redefine available or valuable resources? Does it make entirely new markets or audiences interested? Does it open up possibilities for extremely light operating models where fixed assets play no or little role? Does it open up avenues for using predictive analytics?

Do not copy the way other organizations are perhaps applying the novelty but think of what it might offer to your organization. How might the novelty refresh strategy, for example?

Example Recognizing the beyond category potential Kivelä's discovery, Itkonen convinces her that a pulled oats is a good idea and they start experimenting on it not as a bakery product but as meat substitute. The company Gold & Green Foods is established.

The experimental pulled oats that are hand carried to a few stores in Helsinki, Finland fly off the shelves. They have no time to complete the experiments in their little lab as they are trying to produce as much product as possible, to satisfy demand. The demand took both of them entirely by surprise.

Amplify the OOMPH!

To leverage strategic novelty your company needs cultural leadership that empowers a receptive audience. An organization that does not want to be surprised will often miss, if not readily dismiss, innovation and opportunities for serendipitous learning. Will you act as an example of being open to novelty that others dare follow? How might your organization create resource leverage around experimentation of the novelty's implications, or make the exploration highly inclusive thus reducing costs? Can you create complementary followership with intellectual property spillovers?

The purpose of this step is to make impact and gain effectiveness for learning about the discovery.

Example Green & Gold's board decided that to best leverage the surprising demand for pulled oats the company would need to develop industrial production capability. The company is sold to Paulig, an industrial food company, that recognized the potential once it had been uncovered by a food scientists, discovered by a serial entrepreneur, tested and demonstrated in the market where excited customers in stores around Finland emptied the shelves right away. "The popular Pulled Oats product is sold out. The next delivery will be Wednesday next week," was a typical sign confronting the late buyer.

References

Alvarez, S. A., & Barney, J. B. (2008). Opportunities, organizations, and entrepreneurship. *Strategic Entrepreneurship Journal, 2*(4), 265.

Andriani, P., Ali, A. H., & Mastrogiorgio, M. (2016). Exaptation, innovation and the problem of the emergence of new functions. In *Academy of Management proceedings* (Vol. 2016, No. 1, p. 14693). New York: Academy of Management

Andriani, P., Ali, A., & M. (forthcoming).Mastrogiorgio, Measuring exaptation and its impact on innovation, search and problemsolving. *Organization Science*.

Dutton, J., Ashford, S., O'Neill, R., & Lawrence, K. (2001). Moves that matter: Issue selling and organizational change. *The Academy of Management Journal, 44*(4), 716–736.

Ford, M. (2015). *Rise of the robots: Technology and the threat of a jobless future.*New York: Basic Book

Hanson, N. R. (1958/2010). *Patterns of discovery, an inquiry into the conceptual foundations of science* (2nd ed.). Cambridge, UK: Cambridge University Press.

Henderson, R., & Clark, K. (1990). Architectural innovation: The reconfiguration of existing product technologies and the failure of established firms. *Administrative Science Quarterly, 35*(1, Special Issue: Technology, Organizations, and Innovation), 9–30.

Jones, C., Sbejenova, S., & Strandgaard, J. (2016). Misfits, mavericks and mainstreams: Drivers of innovation in creative industries. *Organization Studies, 32*(9), 1308–1310.

Kaplan, S., & Tripsas, M. (2008). Thinking about technology: Applying a cognitive lens to technical change. *Research Policy, 37*(5), 790–805.

Katila, R., & Ahuja, G. (2002). Something old, something new: A longitudinal study of search behavior and new product introduction. *Academy of Management Journal, 45*(6), 1183–1194.

Katila, R., & Chen, E. L. (2008). Effects of search timing on innovation: The value of not being in sync with rivals. *Administrative Science Quarterly, 53*(4), 593–625.

Kay, J. (2011). *Obliquity.* London: Penguin Books

March, J. G. (1991). Exploration and exploitation in organizational learning. *Organization Science, 2*, 71–87.

March, J. G., Sproull, L. S., & Tamuz, M. (1991). Learning from samples of one or fewer. *Organization Science, 2*(1), 1–13.

McGrath, R. G. (1999). Falling forward: Real options reasoning and entrepreneurial failure. *Academy of Management Review, 24*(1), 13–30.

Merton, R. K., & Barber, E. (2006). *The travels and adventures of serendipity: A study in sociological semantics and the sociology of science.* Princeton: Princeton University Press

Ratti, C., & Claudel, M. (2016). *The city of tomorrow: Sensors, networks, hackers, and the future of urban life.* New Haven: Yale University Press.

Shackle, G. L. S. (1992). *Epistemics and economics.* Transaction Publishers.

Simon, H. A. (1957). *Models of man; social and rational.* New York: Wiley

Simon, H. A. (1983). Why should machines learn? In *Machine learning* (pp. 25–37). Berlin/Heidelberg: Springer.

Simon, H. A. (2001). Science seeks parsimony, not simplicity: Searching for pattern in phenomena. In *Simplicity, inference and modelling: Keeping it sophisticatedly simple* (pp. 32–72). New York: Wiley

Tripsas, M., & Gavetti, G. (2000). Capabilities, cognition, and inertia: Evidence from digital imaging. *Strategic Management Journal, 21*(10–11), 1147–1161.

Tuchman, B. (1984). *The march of folly: From Troy to Vietnam.* New York: Knopf.

Välikangas, L., & Gibbert, M. (2015). *Strategic innovation: The definitive guide to outlier strategies.* New Jersey: Pearson/Financial Times Press

Vuori, T., & Huy, G. (2016). Distributed attention and shared emotions in the innovation process. *Administrative Science Quarterly, 61*(1), 1–43.

Wang, D., & Soule, S. (2016). Tactical innovation in social movements: The effects of peripheral and multi-issue protest. *American Sociological Review, 81*(3), 517–548.

Reflexivity of Anticipations in Economics and Political Economy

28

Heikki Patomäki

I am most grateful to Roberto Poli for patience, Niina Kari for research assistance, and Jamie Morgan for comments. All possible remaining errors in this article are, of course, my sole responsibility.

Contents

Abstract

When the social reality is changing, we need to know also the following: What exactly is changing and why? To what extent is reflexivity involved in changes that take part in making the future uncertain and open? For instance, an announced policy change can become a self-altering prediction (or involve such a prediction), which is subject to contradictory and complementary determination, resulting either in net self-fulfilling or self-denying tendency. I approach these questions also by analyzing two significant real-world historical examples,

H. Patomäki (✉)
Faculty of Social Sciences, University of Helsinki, Helsinki, Finland
e-mail: heikki.patomaki@helsinki.fi

© Springer Nature Switzerland AG 2019
R. Poli (ed.), *Handbook of Anticipation*,
https://doi.org/10.1007/978-3-319-91554-8_16

the Euro crisis and global financial crises. Both examples involve reflexive predictions, reflexive feedback loops, and performativity. What I find particularly
striking is how the capitalist market economy – with all the historical shifts and
changes in its institutions, regulations, and political structures – has managed to
retain at least some of its recurrent economic patterns. Further, I examine the
general methodological problem of the absence of decisive tests between theories.
This has consequences: normative and ideological positions evolve easily and
tend to fortify themselves rapidly; and actors can modify, perhaps inadvertently,
their public anticipations in line with their interests or normative aims. In the final
section, I argue that the main aim of social sciences is not to predict accurately but
to bring about desirable outcomes, explaining how to move from strategic actions
and reflexive ideologies to emancipation.

Keywords
Contrastive demi-regularity · Emancipation · Fallibility · Goodhart's law · Lucas
critique · Self-altering tendency · Uncertainty

Introduction

Realist forms of economic theory acknowledge that any movement (such as prices or
quantities going up or down) requires a temporal sequence of events, which makes it
possible to specify causation in real historical time. The net outcome of many
processes and mechanisms, however, can often be known only after the event
(Robinson 1980). This seems to establish an asymmetry between explanation and
prediction. We may be able to explain the past, but not predict the future.

Some risks may be calculable, but the future as a whole seems characterized by
uncertainty. J.M. Keynes theorized uncertainty in his early work on probability (2008/
1920) and then relied on this concept in his *General Theory* (1961/1936). Even when
some economic regularities or functions (such as propensity to consume) appear stable
in a given historical context, they may change in the future. This is a manifestation of
what is called the problem of induction in the empiricist philosophy of science. Keynes
discussed this problematic also in terms of probabilities. If probabilities are not stable
and fundamental uncertainty prevails (as Keynes 1961/1936 is usually read), it is
difficult to say much about the future and certainly impossible to assign well-defined
probabilities to possible futures (for a discussion on different concepts of uncertainty
in economics, see Dequech 2011). At the same time, Keynes assumed that the
formation of expectations is governed by loose empirical regularities related to the
mass psychology of markets and investment moods. Waves of optimism and pessimism are part of business cycles in capitalist market economy, which indicates that
expectations can have a self-fulfilling character.

Although Keynes acknowledged that anticipations can have an effect on the
anticipated events and processes, he did not employ the terminology of reflexivity
or self-altering prediction. The term "self-fulfilling prophecy" was coined by sociologist Robert K. Merton. Its logical counterpart is a self-denying prophecy, a

prediction that alters the future against the original prediction. As an example of self-fulfilling prophecy, Merton (1948) discussed, for example, the case of a run on the Last National Bank in 1932. Merton's generic point was that public definitions of a situation involving anticipations of the future (prophecies, predictions) tend to become an integral part of the situation and thus affect subsequent developments. He also asserted that the situation-definition may be false, but by evoking new behavior, it will subsequently become true (Merton 1948, 195). In other words, behavior based on false beliefs can generate a social situation that would seem to accord with those false beliefs.

Whereas economists have usually been keen to improve the accuracy of their professional predictions about GDP growth, unemployment, inflation, and so on, many social scientists have been more interested in breaking the circle in which false lay actor anticipations sustain unnecessary, unneeded, and unwanted social practices or structures. A social scientist may nonetheless be trying to predict the outcome of elections; and an economist may be interested in mitigating business cycles and related waves of optimism and pessimism. Either way, self-altering anticipations can generate complex combinations of self-fulfilling and self-denying tendencies occurring in open systems and in tandem with other mechanisms.

The 1970s was a break point for the Bretton Woods and related established economic policies. A series of political decisions and choices contributed to a rupture of existing institutional structures and their constellation in the world economy. At this time reflexivity moved to the forefront of economic theorization. Economist Charles Goodhart explored the effects of the "competition and credit control" reforms that had been introduced in the UK in September 1971, removing direct controls on bank lending (the 1975 paper was republished, e.g., in Courakis 1981). These reforms broke down the previously stable "money demand function." The money demand function was taken as an empirical regularity and useful control mechanism for monetary policy. Goodhart mentioned in passing a "Goodhart's law," according to which "any observed statistical regularity will tend to collapse once pressure is placed upon it for control purposes" (Goodhart 1981, 116). The collapse can be due to individuals trying to anticipate the effect of a policy and then taking actions which alter its outcome.

Robert Lucas highlighted a similar but more general problem in econometrics. In his 1976 paper, Robert Lucas claimed that any change in policy will alter the structure of econometric models. A key belief in the 1960s and 1970s was that there is a simple trade-off between inflation and unemployment (the so-called Phillips curve). But reflexivity matters. From the "Lucas critique" point of view, the problem with the Phillips curve is that permanently raising inflation in the hope that this would lower unemployment would over time cause firms' inflation forecasts to rise, altering negatively their employment decisions and causing inflation to accelerate.

David F. Hendry has tried to respond to the "Lucas critique" from a realist angle by arguing that economies constitute dynamic complex processes. Dynamic complex processes "are often subject to major institutional, political, financial, and technological changes which manifest themselves as structural breaks in econometric models relative to the underlying data generation process" (Clements and Hendry 1999, 123). Hendry claims that these structural breaks can be included in econometric models.

Some critics argue that economists such as Goodhart, Lucas, and Hendry fail to take into account the more fundamental ontological point concerning the nature of being. All social systems are open and closed to a degree; and these systems include reflective actors that have the capacity to act otherwise (for discussions, see Lawson 1997, 71–74; Chick and Dow 2005; Pratten 2005; Patomäki 2010).

It is not only that the net effect of many processes and mechanisms can often be known only afterward; it is also that qualitative changes are possible through learning and structural and institutional changes. Social sciences themselves are regularly involved in these qualitative changes, especially through reflexive self-regulation of social systems. We can talk about reflexive self-regulation when claims about the way the social system functions are applied recursively in interventions, aiming at avoiding unwanted or achieving desired outcomes (cf. Giddens 1979, 78–81). From reflexive self-regulation follows also the performativity thesis: economics conditions, shapes, and constitutes the economy, rather than simply describing it (MacKenzie 2006; MacKenzie et al. 2007).

George Soros (2008, 2013) has stressed the role of reflexive feedback loops (for a friendly critique, see Lawson 2015, ch 9). Participants' views and theories condition, shape, and constitute but never fully determine events and processes; "while the course of events and processes influences but does not determine the participants' views and theories" (Soros 2013, 313). As participants are not equal, some views and theories are more influential than others. Reflexivity is closely connected to fallibility. All views and theories are liable to be biased, incomplete, or both. Soros claims that financial markets are characterized by positive self-reinforcing reflexive loops driving participants' views and the real situation further apart. The widening of the discrepancy cannot continue forever. A self-reinforcing boom is then followed by a bust – as in the crash of 2008.

Soros discusses also "the efficient market hypothesis" that has not only legitimated financialization but has also constituted specific market practices and institutions. Financialization refers to the processes by which finance markets, finance institutions, and the elites involved in financing gain increasing hold over both private economic processes and public economic policy-making. Financialization involves deregulation and the growing scale and profitability of finance vis-à-vis the rest of the economy (see, e.g., Palley 2013). Van der Zwan (2014) distinguishes between three basic approaches to analyzing financialization: (1) the emergence of a new regime of accumulation, (2) the ascendency of the shareholder value orientation, and (3) the financialization of everyday life. The increasingly prominent index-tracking funds provide an example of market practice that is inspired and based on the efficient market hypothesis (MacKenzie et al. 2007, 4 *et.passim.*).

I begin by discussing predictions and their accuracy in the light of Goodhart's law and Lucas critique. In that context, I also examine Hendry's econometric response in a bit more detail and introduce the concept of contrastive demi-regularity. When the social reality is changing, we need to know also what exactly is changing and why. I approach these questions by analyzing two significant real-world historical examples, the Euro crisis and global financial crises. Both examples involve reflexive predictions, reflexive feedback loops, and performativity. What I find particularly striking is how the capitalist market economy – with all the historical shifts and changes in its institutions, regulations and political structures – has managed to retain at least some of its recurrent economic patterns.

Next, I examine the general methodological problem of the absence of decisive tests between theories. This has consequences: normative and ideological positions evolve easily and tend to fortify themselves rapidly; and actors can modify, perhaps inadvertently, their public anticipations in line with their interests or normative aims. In the final section, I argue that the main aim of social sciences is not to predict accurately but to bring about desirable outcomes, explaining how to move from strategic actions and reflexive ideologies to emancipation.

Reflexivity, Policy, and Changing Social Realities

Rational economic policy requires at least some predictive capacities. A choice of policy from a set $\{p_1, p_2, p_3 \ldots\}$ presupposes knowledge about the possible and likely consequences of p_1, p_2, and so on. In Keynes' theory, a key statistical regularity that can be used for predictive purposes concerns the multiplier effect of investments and public expenditure. In Chap. 10 of *General Theory*, Keynes used the following estimates: marginal propensity to consume 0.8; the consumption rate for the unemployed is half of normal; and foreign trade accounts for 20% of the national income. On the basis of these rough facts, he estimated the multiplier in the 1930s UK should be in the order of 2–3. Every extra pound injected into the economy would yield an increase of 2–3 pounds in national product. Keynes stressed, however, that the multiplier depends on a number of historically changing connections within an interdependent economy. A large number of variables take part in determining the multiplier, directly or indirectly. Government policy and public investments have effects on many of them, for instance, on interest rates and on general "confidence" and thereby on liquidity preference and marginal efficiency of capital.

The idea that policy can have an impact on economic events and processes and their relationships was thus not new in 1975 when Goodhart wrote his famous paper "Problems of Monetary Management: The UK Experience" (published also as Goodhart 1981). Until 1971, the pound had been pegged to the US dollar, and this self-imposed constraint largely dictated monetary policy. The collapse of the Bretton Woods system in 1971 coincided with domestic reasons to reform the UK monetary system. In the few years before the "competition and credit control" reforms, the main money aggregates varied in a fairly consistent way with money incomes and interest rates. This seemed to indicate that the UK monetary authorities could use changes in the money stock to have a predictable effect on money incomes or on interest rates. They could also control the monetary aggregates through the price mechanism and stable demand-for-money function by lowering or raising interest rates. However, after the reform, banks changed their behavior, reducing margins drastically to compete for market shares and increasing lending massively, especially to companies. This reveals that the demand-for-money function depends on the behavior of banks and is dependent on the geohistorical context. Authorities' counter-measures were soon overtaken by other independent forces within the UK financial system, especially those related to the boom-and-bust cycle in the housing markets. This illustrates how, in open systems, the effects of historically evolving forms of agency, forces, and tendencies can be delayed, overlapping, mutually reinforcing, and/or contradictory.

It is not clear that the problem in 1971–1975 in the UK stemmed from the pressure placed upon the demand-for-money function for control purposes. Deregulation led UK banks to change the rationale of their actions quite independently of the control purposes by the state. What matters is that Goodhart recognized that social realities change. Similarly, Lucas (1976) started his critique of empirical macroeconomic modelling by pointing out how econometricians rely on adaptive modelling, giving more weight on recent than distant experiences. Adaptive econometric modelling gives a better empirical fit, but it also indicates that the temporally distant data is less relevant and potentially misleading. The obvious explanation of this econometric practice is that because actors, practices, policies, and institutions are changing over time, only recent experiences are really applicable. Lucas is interested in the role of state policy. The crux of his argument is that any intervention such as a policy change affects the expectations and actions of the actors. What Lucas has been able to show is that the probabilistic relationships identified in econometric models are unstable (for an insightful discussion, see Lawson 1997, 69–85).

Lucas proposed both a practical and theoretical solution to the ensuing problem of instability, which he assumed to be a problem that must be overcome. The practical solution was economic policy based on fixed and consistent rules rather than discretion. The theoretical idea was to rely on "rational expectations." Lucas and his followers have thus contended that responses to changes in policy are well understood and predictable. Moreover, the lay actors are assumed to have perfect foresight. Lucas's practical solution has had a major impact on economic policy-making across the world and thus is a good example of the performativity of economic theory. His theoretical solution contradicts the epistemic principle of fallibility, however, and is thus utterly implausible. Actors' views and are not only subject to fallibility but can also be contradictory. The way and extent to which expectations and actions change are contingent and must be examined empirically.

Any combination of self-fulfilling and self-denying tendencies occurring in open systems and in tandem with other social forces, tendencies, and mechanisms is in principle possible. A "compensated" prediction tries to take into account also reactions to the prediction itself (cf. Grunberg and Modigliani 1954; Simon 1954). Attempts to anticipate responses to predictions or regulations or changes in policies are subject to uncertainty, and anticipations may thus fail. The overall net result may be either to increase or decrease predictive accuracy. Different cases can be distinguished depending on the dominant self-altering tendency and whether the prediction takes form of ordinal or scalar prediction, as depicted in Fig. 1.

For instance, a credible forecast of increased inflation is published by a central bank, ministry, or research institute. This can bring about both self-denying (monetary and financial countermeasures by the government and central bank) and self-fulfilling responses (workers increase wage demands, corporations increase prices).

Prediction form	Dominant self-altering tendency	
	Net self-fulfilling tendency	*Net self-denying tendency*
Ordinal prediction • direction of change • passing a benchmark • rank order	Increases accuracy	Decreases accuracy
Scalar prediction	Uncertain effect on accuracy	Decreases accuracy

Fig. 1 Effect of prediction form and dominant self-altering tendency on predictive accuracy. (Source: Henshel 1993, 98)

If the net effect is self-fulfilling and the prediction is ordinal, these responses will increase the accuracy of the forecast. If the prediction is scalar and takes the form of precise number within a given time interval, however, the effect on accuracy is uncertain, as the prediction may also cause an "overshoot." If the net tendency is self-denying, then accuracy is always decreased, independently of whether the prediction is ordinal or scalar. In this example, the purposefully self-denying policy responses are then subject to the instability diagnosed by Goodhart and Lucas, but in a manner that is not reducible to any simple predictable scheme or canon of economic theory. However, the significance of this instability is contingent and context-dependent.

A major problem with Lucas's solution is that he relies, for instance, on Milton Friedman's (1957) permanent income hypothesis, which he takes as an established part of the canon of economic theory. In practice, it is quite tricky to test Friedman's hypothesis because it is difficult, if not impossible, to distinguish between predictable and permanent income changes from other income changes. Friedman himself used contradictory definitions: sometimes only the subjective assumptions of people matter; at other times the current wealth or past income matter, defining rational expectations about the future. By appropriately manipulating the definition and data, any desired result can be achieved. The real question is to what extent do people in practice calculate their consumption according to the expectations of tens of years? Of course, people's consumption can exhibit stability and planning to some extent. Expected short-term fluctuations can be offset by debt or savings. People adjust their consumption to others' consumption and often try to mimic the wealthier. Keynes, however, argued that in practice, many people consume roughly a standard part of their income, although standards also change over time, and this claim has support from both everyday experiences and empirical studies (see Keynes (1961/1936, 89–131), Wilcox (1989), and Chao (2000); for a more human and social hypothesis about relative incomes, see Duesenberry (1949); and for a strong-worded criticism of Friedman's biased practices of empirical research, see Herman (1995, 34–37)).

Several economists have accepted instability and yet defend the use of statistical techniques (e.g., Sims et al. 1982). The main claim is that although econometric projections are only conditional, they can be useful in policy analysis. Robert J. Gordon (1976, 57) argues further that "it may be possible in some cases to either deduce or estimate the shifts in parameters in response to policy changes." Hendry (1983, 1985) has developed methods that can identify structural breaks, regime shifts, and technological and financial innovations by means of econometric models and in future scenarios. This is important not least because these breaks and shifts tend to go hand in hand with episodes of dramatic predictive failure. Hendry's approach is explicit about not requiring closed systems (conditions similar to laboratory experiments, where the effects of one transfactual causal mechanism can be isolated and studied separately), and it allows for changes in parameters. The complex process-generating data is local. Partly by identifying what is relatively constant in the process and partly by using insights from theory and practice, it is plausible to design a model that can be used as a tool in policy-making.

Hendry (1997) has also built methods of forecasting in a situation where there may be discrepancy between the model and the changing social world. There is no practical use of a model, however, when its key parameters are not stable, not even locally. Hendry (ibid. 1331) points out that the success of econometric model-based forecasts depends upon there being regularities that are informative about the future. In addition, we should be able to exclude non-regularities that swamp the regularities. A further problem of econometric modelling is that given the nature of available data and the absence of robust relations between variables, correlation and regression analysis may rely on measuring something with precision that is not precise at all (Martins 2018, 231–232). These points bring us back to the ontological question.

Tony Lawson (1997, 204–213) has introduced the concept of contrastive demi-regularity, indicating the existence of partial closures also in society. Contrastive demi-regularities concern contrasts between categories or spacetime areas and are expressed in terms of regularities within a given range of variation with certain probability. They are not strict regularities but probabilistic, limited to a particular spacetime area, and liable to change with the underlying structures and mechanisms. Lawson argues that it is not sufficient to find contrastive demi-regularities and, then, specify the conditions of their continuation. Rather, there should be a movement toward analyzing the deeper social structures and causal mechanisms generating these manifest phenomena. Systems are nonetheless characterized by some continuity and stability at the empirical level as well.

Contra Lawson's theoretical and practical intentions, it may be reasonable to search for contrastive demi-regularities also as partial guidance to and illumination about possible and likely short- to mid-term futures. Contrastive demi-regularities are pervasive also in relatively open systems, and many aspects of world futures are very difficult to study systematically without a resort to some extrapolation. Although not the only task of future-oriented social sciences, the anticipation of possible and likely outcomes of actions, policies, and regulatory and institutional changes is an important part of what rational human and social sciences should be doing. The real choice is between the use of (i) formal but only relatively and ambiguously adequate statistical methods and (ii) informal methods, including conceptual models that may involve some numerical values, theory-laden extrapolation, leading indicators, expert discussions and judgments, and so on. These options may also be seen as complementary.

Reflexivity, Regime Shifts, and Structural Changes in Global Finance

When the social reality is changing, we also need to know what exactly is changing and why. To what extent, and when exactly, may self-altering predictions be sufficient for structural changes in the economy? In what ways are policy and regime shifts constituted by reflexive feedback loops and by performativity? How may these be related to technological and financial innovations? By answering these questions we are in a better position to anticipate the instability diagnosed by Goodhart and Lucas. Perhaps we could even anticipate the direction of likely responses, thus increasing our reflexive predictive capabilities. I approach these questions by analyzing two significant real-world historical examples, the Euro crisis and global financial crises (especially 2008–9 and the next one).

The Euro Crisis: The Role of Institutionalized Reflexivity

The establishment of the Economic and Monetary Union in the Maastricht Treaty constituted a major regime shift in Europe. The EMU design, developed in the late 1980s and early 1990s, drew heavily on the ideas of monetarism, supply-side economics, and new classical macroeconomics, which came into vogue in the wake of changing circumstances (the partial collapse of the Bretton Woods system) and various intellectual developments (such as Lucas critique). Established in the Maastricht Treaty, the European Central Bank sets interest rates, aiming for low inflation within the single market of the EU. No other common economic policy is deemed necessary.

The expectation derived from abstract theory is that if economic policy is rule-based and price levels can be kept stable, economic growth will be strong, and income levels in the whole of Europe will converge over the long term. This idea is based on new classical macroeconomic models developed in the 1970s and in vogue in the 1980s (on the 1970s neoclassical theories in which European Central Bank monetary policy is rooted, see, e.g., Lucas 1972; Barro 1974; Sargent and Wallace 1975). These models imply that market actors' perfect knowledge and rational expectations inevitably obviate (most of) the effects of Keynesian economic policy. Active economic policies can only serve to bring about higher inflation, an undesirable outcome. A further assumption was that well-functioning labor markets would even out regional differences, resulting in a balanced and affluent EU.

The short-lived process of apparent economic convergence ended in the global financial crisis of 2008–9. The global economic crisis triggered automatic stabilizers in the EU countries. Many of the countries also resorted to deliberate increases in national expenses to stimulate the economy. These expenses were paid off with new public debt, which was also used to shore up the rapidly depleting reserves of banks and investors. The Euro crisis started when the rising levels of public debt triggered new credit assessments, negative market reactions, and EMU's disciplinary mechanisms. (For the full story involving major design flaws and imbalances in the composition of efficient demand in the EU, see Patomäki 2013, ch 4.)

The key idea of the EMU is to discipline public finances through market mechanisms and to control the supply of money so as to keep inflation as low as possible. If public sector budgets are not in balance, the state or municipality must take on debt from the private sector, thereby making themselves vulnerable to interest rate increases. Even though Eurozone countries are still free to borrow on the domestic market, they have no control over the interest rates, which are determined in the financial markets. Transnational commercial banks set their own margins for the loans, based on their profit goals and on their assessment of the risk involved in granting the loan. Because the European Central Bank refused, in the beginning of the Euro crisis, to intervene in market developments, for example, by ensuring specific interest rates for certain Eurozone countries, market logic determined the price levels on the bond market.

Despite their convoluted nature, the difference stages of the finance game can be reduced to a fairly schematic chain, which can easily generate self-fulfilling predictions. During the Euro crisis, the speculation chain went as follows (see Centre for Research on Multinational Corporations 2011; Patomäki 2013, 75–76):

- Investment banks, for example, Goldman Sachs or Deutsche Bank, and various hedge funds buy up credit default swaps – derivatives that function as guarantees against credit risk – in case Spain, Ireland, Greece, Portugal, or some other country becomes insolvent. These swaps can be bought even if the investors who buy them have no bonds issued by the countries in question.
- Increased demand for credit default swaps is interpreted as a sign that the economic situation in the country in question is deteriorating.
- Credit rating agencies, such as Moody's or Standard & Poor's, react to the increased demand for bad credit swaps and reduce the creditworthiness rating of the country in question.
- The credit rating agencies' intervention raises the price of the credit default swaps, which makes it possible for speculators to make short-term profits, which increases the demand for swaps still further.
- Banks with bonds issued by a crisis-hit country become alarmed and begin to sell off the bonds. In some cases, they are legally obliged to sell bonds if their value drops below a certain level, since retaining them would increase risk of loss to the banks.
- If the crisis countries' bond prices drop significantly in value, it becomes profitable to "sell them short." Short-selling means that speculators first borrow the assets from some party and sell them at the going market price. Once the price

drops, speculators buy the same assets back and then "return" them to the lender. Short selling strengthens the tendencies of assets to depreciate.
- The outcome of all the foregoing stages is that the crisis country finds itself in a situation in which it can renew its loans only by agreeing to exorbitant interest rates, as high as twenty or thirty percent or even much more (interest rates can climb up to hundreds of percent). This dramatically worsens its debt situation.

Overall, this is a system of circular causal relations. A relatively small change in one item initiates a sequence of events affecting others, eventually returning to affect the item that began the sequence in a self-reinforcing manner. The causal forces in this loop do not operate blindly but rather involve self-regulation through feedback via the operation of selective information filtering and interpretations (based on particular technical concepts and theories of finance and economy). The feedback takes the form of predictions that affect credit ratings and market valuations and tend to be self-fulfilling. The system as a whole is based on reflexive self-regulation to the extent that it is purposefully employed in order to discipline public finances through market mechanisms. The system also generates unintended consequences such as financial crises that would not occur in the absence of this causal loop.

Within the prevailing framework, however, the deep crisis of several Eurozone countries was usually interpreted as a moral failure of the governments and as weakness of EMU discipline. The main exception has been European Central Bank's "unconventional monetary policy," starting with the Outright Monetary Transactions (OMT) program that was announced by the Bank's Governing Council in August 2012. The ECB promised to use central bank money to buy bonds from the secondary market as needed. Since the central bank can easily create money, the sale of bonds is now guaranteed. This has calmed the money market and helped to keep interest rates relatively low, although the crisis in its various phases continued until 2015, with a weak and fragile recovery starting in 2016.

The course of events in the process known as the Euro crisis has influenced actual policy (ECB) without, however, altering the main participants' (the troika, the Eurogroup, mainstream economists) views about the underlying economic and political theories. It is noteworthy that the concept of uncertainty can itself become an obstacle to learning, as seems to be the case, for instance, with the Bank of England after the global financial crisis 2008–2009. As Nasir and Morgan argue (2018, 21):

> [..] the use of uncertainty as a justification can become a barrier, which short-circuits learning because theory and method do not respond to failure at a fundamental level. This seems a very basic contradiction for central banking, the nature of an open system periodically undermines forecasting, but forecasting is insulated from assimilating this insight because of the use to which a concept of uncertainty as unavoidable error can be put in an open [and reflexive] system.

In line with the prevailing theoretical framework, a number of new institutional arrangements have been introduced or put in place: the stability mechanism, the "six-pack," the "two-pack," the European Fiscal Compact, and the Euro Plus. Both "preventive" and "correcting" mechanisms of these arrangements rely largely on economic forecasts, which without planning are difficult to carry out and make corrections. For instance, the 2012 European Fiscal Compact involves concepts such as "structural deficit," "cyclically adjusted debt-to-GDP ratio," and "medium-term budgetary objective" (MTO), which all make references to the future:

> In the event of significant observed deviations from the medium-term objective or the adjustment path towards it, a correction mechanism shall be triggered automatically. (Council of the European Union 2012, 6).

The Compact stipulates that the government budget should either be balanced or in surplus. It introduces the concept of the structural balance, which refers to the budgetary position of the state when adjusted for cyclical effects, based on estimates of potential GDP. The structural balance ought to converge with the country-specific medium-term objective according to a timetable set by the Commission. Signatories must also set up automatic correction mechanisms at the national level, preferably in the constitution to ensure that any deviations are quickly corrected. States breaching deficit limits need to put forward a plan for structural reforms, assessed by the Commission and the Council. If a member state is in an excessive deficit procedure, the matter can be brought to the European Court of Justice, who can impose sanctions up to 0.1% of the GDP of the deviant state (Council of the European Union 2012, 8).

Each member state must specify which institute is responsible for the economic forecasts used in their calculations. The authority of the last resort in this regard lies, however, with the EU Commission itself. Forecasts affect economic policy, in turn affecting economic developments. Forecasts are thus not independent of what possibilities will be actualized. Predictions or forecasts can be "optimistic" or "pessimistic" depending on what is assumed to be normal as well as on what normative aims are implicit in the background theories (e.g., downsizing the public sector). For instance, projections by the Commission in the spring of 2018, during a period of economic growth, forecasted that Romania will have the most significant deviation in its structural budget position at $-3,8\%$ of potential GDP with Hungary at $-3,6\%$ as a close second. Both were placed under significant deviation procedures. Surplus countries included Greece (2,5%), Germany (1.2%), Sweden (0.7%), and Denmark (0.3%). Italy and France were both predicted to have structural deficits at -1.7% and -2.1%, respectively. For the Euro area as a whole, the Commission forecasted a structural budget position at -0.8% of potential GDP in 2018 and -1.1% in 2019 (European Commission 2018, 180). The problem is that predictions of low economic growth in the future are likely to become self-fulfilling. For ordinal predictions, this will increase their accuracy, but for cardinal predictions, the effect is uncertain because of the possibility of overshoot.

A key issue in this system is that attempts to reduce public debt can turn out to be self-defeating and recessionary. Through cuts in public expenditure, disposable income is reduced thus potentially inducing or worsening an economic recession through the multiplier effect. This, in turn, leads to decreased tax receipts and increased expenditure due to the working automatic stabilizers, such as unemployment benefits. When combined with a fall in GDP, this increase in expenditure results in an increase of debt-to-GDP ratio, potentially leading to a vicious cycle. Crucially, however, whether this dynamic is played out depends on the policies of other actors in the system and the prevailing phase of the business cycle, which is not independent of these policies though not reducible to them. Overall, this system is an example of institutionalized reflexive loop that is geared toward an implicit political aim involving a high likelihood of net self-fulfilling tendency toward harmful socioeconomic outcomes (to be analyzed in more detail below).

Global Financial Crises: The Role of Recurring Patterns

The Euro crisis was instigated by the global financial crisis of 2008–2009, a dramatic example of a crash following worldwide bubble. The boom-and-bust cycle involves reflexive feedback loops. According to Soros (2013, 323; see also Soros 2008), a boom-bust process is set in motion when a trend and a misconception about it positively reinforce each other. Behavior based on false beliefs – in the 2000s actively supported by the majority of economists – contributes to a trend that would seem to accord with those false beliefs. The course of events and processes in financial markets reinforces participants' views ("bull market") and theories ("efficient market hypothesis"). Reflexivity works also through changes in the economy itself, not only via beliefs. For instance, the value of homeowners' or investors' collateral is not independent of the availability of credit. When credit becomes cheaper and more easily available, activity picks up and values rise. The amount of credit is at its maximum at the height of the boom.

The boom is sustained not only through evidence from the markets but also by "analytical monocultures," i.e., shared models, metaphors, and narratives, creating theory-data-theory feedback loops. Uncertainty reinforces this tendency to resort to prevailing beliefs and stories and analyze data accordingly (Bronk 2013; also Patomäki 2001, 21–25). Thus, constituted expectations can be self-reinforcing for years, but the collective consequences of leverage building, mutual indebtment, and rapidly inflating asset prices mean that the process becomes unsustainable and will turn downward sooner or later (Minsky 2008). Certainty that an inflationary process has constituted a bubble can only be established ex post, i.e., after its bust, although ex ante indicators and historical analogies often are sufficiently reliable for many practical purposes. There are two mechanisms that finally will bring the boom to an end. The first has to do with the growing discrepancy between asset values and reality understood in terms of how much revenues are really generated (Soros 2013; Shaikh 2013). The second is that the rising involvement in debt makes the system gradually more vulnerable to relatively small disturbances and thus increasingly chaotic. The monetary system is stable only as long as streams of revenue and profit enable firms to meet their financial liabilities (Minsky 1982, 22; see also Patomäki 2010).

When the confidence on the prospects of X is gone, the individually rational choice of "sell as quickly as you can" can amount to a collectively catastrophic outcome of a collapse of asset values although overall most investors would be better off by not selling for the time being. Markets involve contradictory tendencies: complicated bets can be made on a bust or crash, and some may also benefit from "bear markets." A catastrophe occurs when most actors believe that the worst outcome would be to stay in now while most others opt out. By not selling as quickly as they can, they would be easily left with very little (and for some actors, there are specific more formal mechanisms, such as covenant breaches and collateral margin calls creating "death spirals"). Many assets remain valuable only as long as other cross-invested assets remain valuable. Moreover, if an actor becomes insolvent, it affects many others' stream of revenue as well, hence, the occasional bursts of panics and busts, with far-reaching causal consequences to production, employment, and welfare.

In the 1970s, a regime shift occurred that led to a structural change increasing volatility and enabling positive reflexive loops generating boom-and-bust cycles. Since then, the process of financialization has been an ongoing process with sporadic changes in the way the financial markets operate (after major crises, there have also been periods of counter-regulation). Innovations are a part of these shifts and changes. Capitalist market economy generates innovations also in finance, not only in production and exchange (see Minsky 1982, 2008). New financial instruments and other financial innovations presuppose de- and re-regulation, usually justified in terms of "efficient markets." Financial innovations are in some ways analogical to the effects of Schumpeterian innovations, aiming at ensuring something analogical to monopoly profits as long as possible (cf. Schumpeter 1939, 87–125).

In financial markets innovations concern first and foremost leverage and the management of risk. At least partial secrecy or non-transparency is essential for hiding uncertainty, for masquerading uncertainty as calculable risks, and for profitably transferring and re-pooling risks. Financial innovations are often also about increasing leverage or decreasing the time of the investments or capital requirements, both of which mean new risks and uncertainty. Sometimes innovations are needed to evade regulations. Arguably, nearly all financial innovations prior to the global crash of 2008 were at variance with the common good (e.g., Stiglitz 2010). The overall effect of the bulk of financial innovations was to strengthen the unsustainable boom, also by making credit easier and finance more fragile, until the crash of 2008.

From a theoretical point of view, it is striking how the capitalist market economy – with all the historical shifts and changes in its institutions, regulations, and political structures – has managed to retain at least some of its recurrent economic patterns (Shaikh 2016; see Patomäki 2017). I have puzzled over this question for nearly two decades, since the Asian crisis of 1997–1998 and since I first learnt about the tendency in capitalist market economy toward financialization, which then gives rise to a recurring tendency toward a pattern of booms and busts (see Kindleberger 1978; Minsky 1982; Soros 1998; cf. Patomäki 2001, Chap. 2). What is especially remarkable is that reflexivity and reflexive loops can be part of patterns that tend to be recurring over the timespan of centuries (since the 1720 South Sea Company crash), making at least some generic things anticipatable at least at some level of abstraction. Such recurring patterns also point to lack of long-term rational learning, Bayesian or otherwise, further undermining the validity of new classical models.

In contrast to 2006–2007, in 2016–2018, many well-known analysts and international organizations from Deutsche Bank to the IMF have been warning about a future crisis that might occur in 2018 but is likely to come about by 2020 (Reid et al. 2017; IMF 2016, 2017, 2018). Anticipations are reflexive and can have effects on the future. Moreover, some economists believe that central banks have learnt new lessons from their unconventional policies and are now ready and willing to use their – in principle unlimited – resources to prevent a financial collapse from happening. Are we thus safer in the late 2010s and early 2020s than before?

Past lessons and reflexivity have effects through transforming actions and institutions. We are not, however, seeing attempts to counter the process of financialization, for instance, through re-regulation or taxation of global finance, reduction of inequalities, or establishing new programs of stimulating productive investments. There are some global initiatives via the Basel Rules and via the international Financial Stability Board, but these are highly limited, involving more retained capital and centralized systems for derivatives that are based on the premise that rational actors with more information (about shadow banking, etc.) will render the system more robust, enabling more "financial deepening." This follows variations on "efficient markets" frameworks. Meanwhile, the Trump administration is giving significant tax benefits to the super rich and deregulating finance. Even in the EU, the project of establishing a financial transaction tax seems to have come to an end, and the European financial union is lacking sufficient resources. The rising debt levels in China are an increasing global concern, although interpretations about its significance differ. Meanwhile, the global bubble in stock and housing markets has been growing, although the latter boom may have already seen its peak in summer 2018 (see, for instance, "There's trouble ahead in the global housing market," Business Insider 17 July 2018, available at https://www.businessinsider.com/hous ing-market-prices-about-to-plummet-worldwide-2018-7?r=US&IR=T&IR=T; and "The End of the Global Housing Boom," Bloomberg News, 1 August 2018, available at https://www.bloomberg.com/news/articles/2018-07-31/are-house-prices-falling-from-sydney-to-new-york).

A lot hinges upon central banks, but they are in a contradictory position and not only because their public predictions tend to be self-fulfilling. The very attempt to tighten policy in order to return to the "normal," to respond to inflation, or to slow down the growth of bubbles may set in motion a downward spiral, for instance, by triggering sovereign debt crises or by increasing the burden of debt among investors and homeowners. And to reiterate, central banks may simultaneously fear that any anticipation of tough times may become self-fulfilling. In the absence of adequate common policies, regulations, and institutions on a global scale, central banks may actually be less powerful than often thought. Hence, Minsky's "it" (the collapse of the financial and economic system) seems again rather likely. If my analysis is on the mark, we are likely to see a major crash – perhaps even bigger than in 2008, although this is uncertain – followed by a global recession or depression, by 2020 or so. A precise prediction of the timing of the next crisis would make it possible to exploit the crash. If acted upon widely, such a prediction could also become self-fulfilling.

In August 2018, five economists, three of whom (Peter Schiff, Steve Keen and Dean Baker) forecasted ex ante the 2008 financial crisis, tried to anticipate the shape of things to come (see the salon forum "The end really is near: a play-by-play of the coming economic collapse" available at https://www.salon.com/2018/08/12/the-end-is-near-a-play-by-play-of-the-coming-economic-collapse/). Four of them expect a downturn in the next two years or so, in most cases either caused by erroneous central bank policy or a series of local busts; only one of them (Peter Schiff) expects a major global crash. For instance, Keen argues that there is no major financial bubble and "China is the biggest economy facing a credit crunch, but its huge level of government spending is already softening the blow." It seems to me that these anticipations underestimate, for instance, the bubble in stock markets. In summer 2007, Dow Jones index almost reached 14,000 points just before the crash; in 2018 it has been above 28,000 points. Meanwhile, the US economy has grown only 15% and GDP/capita 6%. On the other hand, FTSE 100 index is a mere 16% above the summer 2007 peak levels, with corresponding GDP/capita growth of less than 4%.

Strategically and Ideologically Motivated Predictions in Open Systems

Often predictive accuracy is not a reasonable aim of social sciences. This is especially true when reflexivity is involved. Self-altering predictions can move the world into a direction that may or may not be desirable. A net self-fulfilling tendency usually – though not always – improves accuracy (see Fig. 1), but if the predicted outcome is worse than what would have occurred in the absence of the prediction, improved accuracy is harmful. A net effect of self-denial decreases accuracy, but this is normally good if the self-alteration helps, for example, to reduce unemployment or make growth more sustainable, not to speak of avoiding sudden crises or wars. This suggests two somewhat contradictory criteria for an adequate prediction: relevance and accuracy, on the one hand, and success in informing practical actions and shaping the world, on the other. The contradiction can be mitigated by defining accuracy counterfactually: what would have happened in the absence of prediction?

One implication is that self-altering predictions can only be tested and thus falsified by means of counterfactual reasoning: what would have happened, had X been otherwise? Here X denotes reflexive phenomena such as predictions, but a systems' openness more generally should also be taken into account. Even when the predictive analysis of relevant forces and tendencies is valid, in open systems, qualitative changes or extrinsic interferences may occur in a manner that is not anticipatable, including in terms of chances and coincidences. While all causal analysis involves counterfactual reasoning ("had X been otherwise, would Y have occurred?"), reflexivity and ontological openness of reality introduce a further non-testable element into social sciences, making ex post falsification of predictions difficult. This reflects and further complicates the general methodological problem of studying open systems. The general methodological problem is that in the absence of closure, decisive tests between theories are hard to come by. Hence, normative and ideological positions evolve easily and tend to fortify themselves rapidly.

From this point of view, Roy Bhaskar (1998, 23, 50, 144) analyses the consequences of the continuing hegemony of positivism. Because of the absence of decisive test situations, coupled with continuing one-sided allegiance to a mere predictive rather than explanatory and other criteria, the methodology on which one's research relies gets mystified. The dominant or otherwise privileged theory is thereby protected, alternatives are stunted, and there is an encouragement of (a belief in) the unresolvability of theoretical conflicts — which, in practice, means their resolution in favor of the status quo. I would not go as far as Bhaskar, however, in making the criteria for the rational appraisal and development of theories in the social sciences exclusively explanatory. Our predictive powers matter, but in a complex manner.

As actors know that anticipations tend to become an integral part of the situation and thus affect subsequent developments, including policies, they can modify, perhaps inadvertently, their public anticipations in line with their interests or normative aims. Consider the case of self-interested strategic predictions. Eerik Lagerspetz (1988, 309–312) discusses the tendency of energy producers to overestimate future energy needs. Lagerspetz depicts a (hypothetical but evidence-based) mechanism that generates self-fulfilling prophecies and unnecessarily large energy-production capacities. The producers predict an increase in consumption and then start to increase production as a response to this anticipated need. Consumers, including industry, expect cheap energy also in the future because of the growing supply and thus increase their consumption. New consumption patterns are adopted. The prediction that consumers are going to move into certain direction thus induces the predicted move, although it is undesirable from a sustainability viewpoint.

Wishful thinking can shape anticipations also for non-self-interested reasons. It is not only that expectations and anticipations can turn out to be self-fulfilling or self-denying; this may also be part of their very purpose. The performativity of economic theory illustrates this problematic. The efficient market hypothesis – not only in the context of financial markets (Fama 1970) but also more generally – promises welfare gains, if not in the short run then at least in the unspecified, non-historical "long run," from balanced budgets, low inflation, trade-liberalization, deregulation, privatization, outsourcing, and several other policies. With hindsight and a firm commitment to the theory, it is always possible to find a variety of ad hoc explanations for the unintended consequences that these policies tend to have in concrete historical contexts. This can result in a closed circle, as summarized in the scheme of Fig. 2.

Ad hoc explanations are typically combined with the search for deviations from the free market rules and principles or policy failures that would co-explain why the optimal outcome was not yet reached. With these ad hoc explanations, the prevailing theory is being vindicated (for instance, mainstream economics was not only unable to anticipate the global financial crisis of 2008–2009, but it has also been unable to learn from it; see Bigo and Negru 2014; Mirowski 2014; Morgan 2015).

In accordance with this logic, the usual political solution has been to impose the free competitive markets ideal even more vigorously, although some contrary re-regulation may also occur (indicating that the circle of Fig. 2 is not fully closed). This methodological and normative problem is not unique to the efficient market hypothesis and like-minded economic theories (see Patomäki forthcoming), however hegemonic they may be during the current era. Reflexivity, performativity, and openness of social systems pose problems to any system of knowledge.

Thus, what we have is a complicated picture consisting of the direction of self-alteration, desirability of the counterfactual and actual outcomes, counterfactual reasoning and the absence of decisive test situations, and possibility of strategic and ideological exploitation of predictions. Figure 3 summarizes the key points in

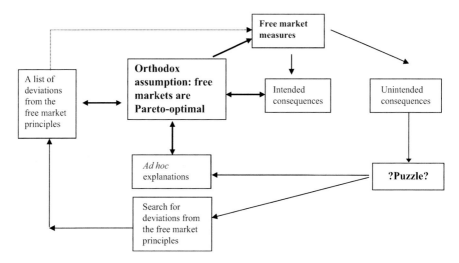

Fig. 2 The closed circle of operation of the efficient market hypothesis. (Source: Patomäki 2001, 12)

Prediction	Predicted outcome	Accuracy	Falsification	Strategic exploitation	Ideological exploitation
Non-self-altering	Desirable	Useless	Relatively trouble-free	Not possible	Not possible
	Non-desirable	ʺ ʺ	ʺ ʺ	ʺ ʺ	ʺ ʺ
Net effect zero	Desirable	Useless	Requires counterfactual reasoning	Possible (what outcome is good or bad for whom?)	Possible (what outcome is considered good or bad by whom?)
	Non-desirable	ʺ ʺ	ʺ ʺ	ʺ ʺ	ʺ ʺ
Net self-fulfilling	Desirable	Helpful	ʺ ʺ	ʺ ʺ	ʺ ʺ
	Non-desirable	Harmful	ʺ ʺ	ʺ ʺ	ʺ ʺ
Net self-denying	Desirable	Harmful	ʺ ʺ	ʺ ʺ	ʺ ʺ
	Non-desirable	Helpful	ʺ ʺ	ʺ ʺ	ʺ ʺ

Fig. 3 Accuracy, desirability, falsifiability, and exploitability of public predictions

terms of accuracy, desirability, falsifiability, and exploitability of public prediction. Note that in the cases of non-self-altering predictions and zero net effect, accuracy may be desirable but is practically useless. Whenever reflexivity plays a role, falsification requires counterfactual reasoning and is especially difficult. Strategic and ideological exploitation of predictions decomposes the desirability of outcome in terms of self-interested actors and different normative conceptions of common good.

From Strategic Actions and Ideologies to Emancipation from False Necessities

The aim of social sciences is not to predict accurately, but to bring about desirable outcomes (cf. Sayer 2011). Accurate anticipations, when conceived counterfactually, can sometimes be helpful toward achieving this aim, depending on the net self-altering effect. Because of the possibility of exploitation of predictions, we must also ask: What outcome is good or bad for whom; and what outcome is considered good or bad by whom and on what generalizable grounds? Reflexivity encourages us to replace mere prediction by scenarios of possible futures comprising different possible courses of action and policies by various actors, including "us" (whomever this "us" may be). When the reflexivity of predictions becomes transparent and publicly known, scenarios about possible futures become necessarily entangled with public ethico-political discourse about the problems and merits of different outcomes (for instance, in terms of discourse ethics, see Apel (2001) and Habermas (1990)).

According to Merton's analysis of self-fulfilling prophecies, behavior based on false beliefs can generate a social situation that accords with those false beliefs. Now, social sciences are committed to truth. The task of social scientific explanation is to form a plausible and empirically confirmed true picture of geohistorical components and their relations. As social scientists, we evaluate negatively those parts of the institutional context that are responsible for the reproduction of (self-fulfilling) false beliefs (see Bhaskar 1998, 59–71; Patomäki 2002, 143–163). The type of situation that Merton describes is thus inherently problematical. One is justified in character-izing a set of beliefs as "ideological" if both (i) many or all of those beliefs are false, that is, one possesses a superior explanation of the phenomena, and (ii) one pos-sesses an explanation of the falsity of those beliefs and why they are held.

Let me develop Merton's example of a bank run a bit further. An actor may know the claim "bank X is unstable and is thus likely to collapse" to be false. It may still remain rational for her to participate in making the prediction come true. Either she believes that a sufficient number of actors believe the claim or she believes that a sufficient number of actors believe that others believe it (see Lagerspetz 1988, 308–309). There can be still higher levels, resembling Keynes's (1961/1936, 155–158) famous beauty contest. Keynes compared speculation to a newspaper beauty contest, in which the aim is not to compare and rank the beauty of the contestants as such but rather to forecast what features the average observer will find beautiful. There are different levels in this sort of competition: at the second level, guesses are made as to what the first-level players will decide, and at the third level, players guess what the second-level players will decide and so on. This description fits well to the activities of speculative finance – with the proviso that here the situation is of course more complex, in that there are very many competitions going on all at once, each with a great many players and levels.

Real world contradictions are not categorical because the outcome depends on contingent circumstances, in the case of a potential bank run on how many individuals are in fact intending to withdraw their savings simultaneously. Actors may nonetheless be trapped in an ideology sustained by lack of trust and suspicions about the motivation of others. This may be a temporary and specific "ideology," but it shows how false beliefs can lead to undesirable and unnecessary outcomes, which can be prevented by building better common institutions. The simplest institutional solution to this particular problem is deposit insurance. Experiences from bank runs during the Great Depression led to the introduction of deposit insurance in many countries.

Reflexivity means the capacity of actors to reflect on their own conditions and place, accepting that both can change and be changed. Earlier I argued that a credible forecast of increased inflation can bring about both self-denying (monetary and financial countermeasures by the government and central bank) and self-fulfilling responses (workers increase wage demands, corporations increase prices). However, this underestimates the diversity of values and the powers of human reflexivity and freedom. Increased inflation is not necessarily a bad thing. The desirability of higher inflation depends on the base level, economic theories, and values. Increasing inflation from 0% to 2% is desirable even from the point of view of the ECB. A Keynesian might argue for a higher rate, say around 5%. As a general rule, low inflation favors lenders and those who possess money capital; higher inflation favors debtors such as entrepreneurs and homeowners. Even when rising inflation is seen as a problem, relevant actors such as workers and corporations can be persuaded either to behave responsibly or to reach an agreement that counters the tendency toward prediction-accelerated cost-push inflation. This may, however, be difficult because of conflicts over income and power distribution.

At this point reflexive ethico-political discourse moves to a deeper and more general level concerning the way social institutions should be organized. For instance, for John Rawls (1971, 3–4), "justice is the first virtue of social institutions." Laws and institutions, no matter how efficient and well-arranged, "must be reformed or abolished if they are unjust." What would be a just way of organizing institutions of political economy? What is the proper rate of saving over time, how should the background institutions of taxation and property be arranged, and at what level are the social minimum or redistributive principles to be set? Within an institutional arrangement perceived as just and legitimate, it should be easier to behave responsibly and reach agreements about common good concerning, for instance, inflation.

In some contrast to Rawls, however, it is also plausible to argue that because of the relativist nature of struggles between models and sentiments of justice, the first priority would be to organize public discourses and collective will formation and decision-making democratically (see Perelman 1963; Patomäki 2006). Notably, some theories of justice emphasize the importance of democratic processes more than others. Schweickart (1993), for instance, argues that fairness is essentially (also) about deciding democratically upon economic rules and procedures and goals of economic institutions. He proposes a project of specifying a model of an economically feasible, morally desirable alternative to capitalism (*ibid*, 116). Hereby we can see that deep behind the contingent predictability of responses lies the performativity of social and economic theories. Historically evolving and changing theories condition, shape, and constitute those institutions on which the basic character and responsiveness of different actors depend.

Instead of performativity, we could also talk about "ideational reflexivity" whereby "ideas *about* the economy reflect back on and affect or shape the evolving economy" (Mackinnon 2005, 6). Ideas can shape the construction of institutions as well as agendas and actions of economic actors and their responses to policy. Public discussion and debate about these ideas is at the heart of democratic political processes. Actors come to realize, reflexively, that the future is not something that just happens and can be predicted, but rather becomes increasingly something that the actors, including "us," make of it.

This is a learning process that occurs through reflexive feedback loops where also the course of real history influences participants' views and theories. In the complex interdependent processes of world economy consisting of billions of actors, both individual and collective, and their structurally conditioned responses and collectively constituted modes of responsiveness, it is never possible to fully replace strategic actions and reflexive predictions with public discourses and common agreements. Rational economic policy will require at least some predictive capacities also in the future, and for this we must, in part, rely on contrastive demi-regularities and our knowledge about the structures and mechanisms that generate them, as well as on anticipation of actors' responses including to policy changes and regime shifts. Yet the degree of human freedom can be increased by replacing particular unnecessary and often misrepresented causal sources of determination with more wanted, needed, and also clearly more evident sources of causal determination.

Conclusions

In econometrics, a structural break, or structural change, is an unexpected shift in a time series that can lead to forecasting errors and general unreliability of the model. This definition refers to a specific technical function in econometric modelling. Data is nothing, however, more than external traces of internal contents. There are multiple layers of contradictory and complementary determination to which these traces owe their hidden unities, divergent meanings, and possible futures (Alker 1996, 351). The data is generated by (i) real causal complexes and (ii) data coding, data collection, and data manipulation procedures. Not only these two layers but also econometric methods themselves can result in "structural breaks" in the technical sense of the term. What is interesting from a social scientific point of view are the real causal complexes consisting of actors, actions, rules, resources, practices, and structures.

When a statistical measure or relationship changes from being a mere indicator to an object of policy for control purposes, its meaning can change. What is more, profit-motivated capitalist firms and investors may change their expectations and find new opportunities in the newly defined situation, changing their agendas and behavior accordingly. The announced policy change can be seen as a self-altering prediction (or involving such a prediction), which is subject to contradictory and complementary determination, resulting either in net self-fulfilling or self-denying tendency. Whether the effect of these kinds of changes is strong enough to constitute a "structural break" at the level of econometrics is contingent and can be tested, although we also know that the reliability of these tests is uncertain (the nature and quality of economic data sets definite limits to the use of these methods; e.g., Atkinson and Brandolini 2009).

The changing and reflexive nature of reality has important policy implications. What works and what does not work becomes a matter of timing and experimentalism. Take the Keynesian multiplier, for instance. The multiplier is not a constant, not even in a given national "economy." The multiplier can vary a lot over different phases of the business cycle and because of changes in policies, practices, and institutions (policy can shape, for instance, the marginal propensity to consume). The overall multiplier can also be strengthened or dampened by the responses of other states and international organizations. These responses co-depend on reflexive anticipations of the effects of decreasing or increasing public expenditure for particular purposes. It is possible to try to persuade other states and international organizations either to behave responsibly or to reach an agreement that counters deflationary tendencies. What is "responsible" and when do "deflationary tendencies" prevail are dependent our understandings of political economy – and thus subject to public debates.

The EU is an example of complex system of governance that relies on circular feedback loops and predictions that become easily self-fulfilling. The problem is that these loops are built on the assumption that the predicted outcome is negative (too much public debt) and that the prediction is net self-denying (cf. Fig. 3). In reality, the sustainable level of public debt is open to debate, and predictions tend to be self-fulfilling both through the financial disciplinary mechanism and multiplier effect. The underlying problem has to do with ideational reflexivity and the closed circle of operation of the efficient market hypothesis and like-minded theories (Fig. 2). The EU system of governance is thus, in part, premised on false beliefs that it then reproduces in a self-fulfilling manner. We should evaluate negatively those parts of the institutional context that are responsible for the re-production of (self-fulfilling) false beliefs. The undesirable and unnecessary outcomes could easily be prevented by building better common institutions (see Patomäki 2013, Chaps. 6–8).

It is striking that there are regular patters in capitalist market economy such as the recurring boom-and-bust cycle, although capitalist market economy is changing and evolving over time also in a reflexive manner. In anticipation of the next global financial crisis and recession or depression, we may also ask, what will happen to the EU as the circular feedback loops involving self-fulfilling predictions remain in place. The EU governance system amplifies initial differences and changes. Thus, a negative shock is likely to lead to more divergent paths of development, strengthening the already fairly strong disintegrative tendencies within the Union (see Patomäki 2018, 122–127). However, neither a new global crisis nor the disintegration of the EU is necessary. The future is not something that just happens but rather something that actors, including "us," make of it.

References

Alker, H. (1996). *Rediscoveries and reformulations. Humanistic methodologies for international studies.* Cambridge: Cambridge University Press.

Apel, K. (2001). *The response of discourse ethics to the moral challenge of the human situation as such and especially today.* Leuven: Peeters.

Atkinson, A., & Brandolini, A. (2009). On data: A case study of the evolution of income inequality across time and across countries. *Cambridge Journal of Economics, 3*(3), 381–404.

Barro, R. (1974). Are government bonds net wealth? *Journal of Political Economy, 82*(6), 1095–1117.

Bhaskar, R. (1998). *The possibility of naturalism. A philosophical critique of the contemporary human sciences* (3rd ed.). London/New York: Routledge.

Bigo, V., & Negru, I. (2014). Mathematical modelling in the wake of the crisis: A blessing or a curse? What does the economics profession say? *Cambridge Journal of Economics, 38*(2), 329–347.

Bronk, R. (2013). Reflexivity unpacked: Performativity, uncertainty and analytical monocultures. *Journal of Economic Methodology, 20*(4), 343–349.

Centre for Research on Multinational Corporations. (2011). *Newsletter – EU financial reforms*, part of the project towards a global finance system at the Service of Sustainable Development. http://somo.nl/dossiers-en/sectors/financial/eu-financial-reforms/newsletters.

Chao, H. (2000). *Milton Friedman and the emergence of the permanent income hypothesis*, LSE Centre for Philosophy of Natural and Social Science Measurement in Physics and Economics, Technical report 9/2000. http://www.lse.ac.uk/CPNSS/pdf/DP withCoverMeasurement/Meas-DP%2009%2000.pdf.

Chick, V., & Dow, S. (2005). The meaning of open systems. *Journal of Economic Methodology, 12*(3), 363–381.

Clements, M. P., & Hendry, D. F. (1999). On winning forecasting competitions in economics. *Spanish Economic Review, 1*(2), 123–160.

Council of the European Union. (2012). Treaty on stability, coordination, and governance in the economic and monetary union. https://www.consilium.europa.eu/media/20399/st00tscg26_en12.pdf.

Courakis, A. (Ed.). (1981). *Inflation, depression, and economic policy in the west.* Totowa: Barnes & Noble Press.

Dequech, D. (2011). Uncertainty: A typology and refinements of existing concepts. *Journal of Economic Issues, 45*(3), 621–640.

Duesenberry, J. S. (1949). *Income, saving and the theory of consumer behaviour.* Cambridge, MA: Harvard University Press.

European Commission. (2018). Spring 2018 Economic Forecast – Statistical annex. https://ec.europa.eu/info/files/economy-finance/spring-2018-economic-forecast-statistical-annex_en.

Fama, E. (1970). Efficient capital markets: A review of theory and empirical work. *Journal of Finance, 25*(2), 383–417.

Friedman, M. (1957). A theory of the consumption function. Princeton: Princeton University Press. http://papers.nber.org/books/frie57-1.

Giddens, A. (1979). *Central problems in social theory.* Los Angeles: University of California Press.

Goodhart, C. (1981). Problems of monetary management: The U.K. experience. In A. S. Courakis (Ed.), *Inflation, depression, and economic policy in the west* (pp. 111–146). Totowa: Barnes & Noble Press.

Gordon, R. J. (1976). Can econometric policy evaluations be salvaged? – A comment. *Carnegie-Rochester Conference Series on Public Policy, 1*, 47–61.

Grunberg, E., & Modigliani, F. (1954). The predictability of social events. *Journal of Political Economy, 62*(6), 465–478.

Habermas, J. (1990). *Moral consciousness and communicative action* (trans: Lenhardt, C., & Nicholsen, S.W.). Cambridge, MA: The MIT Press.

Hendry, D. F. (1983). On Keynesian model building and the rational expectations critique: A question of methodology. *Cambridge Journal of Economics, 7*, 69–75.

Hendry, D. F. (1985). Monetary economic myth and econometric reality. *Oxford Review of Economic Policy, 1*(1), 72–84.

Hendry, D. F. (1997). The econometrics of macroeconomic forecasting. *Economic Journal, 107*(444), 1330–1357.

Henshel, R. L. (1993). Do self-fulfilling prophecies improve or degrade predictive accuracy? How sociology and economics can disagree and both be right. *The Journal of Socio-Economics, 22*(2), 85–104.

Herman, E. S. (1995). *Triumph of the market: Essays on economics, politics and the media*. Boston: South End Press.

International Monetary Fund. (2016). *Global financial stability report – Fostering stability in a low-growth, low-rate era*. Washington, DC: International Monetary Fund.

International Monetary Fund. (2017). *Global financial stability report: Is growth at risk?* Washington, DC: International Monetary Fund.

International Monetary Fund. (2018). *Global financial stability report: A bumpy road ahead*. Washington, DC: International Monetary Fund.

Keynes, J. M. 1961/1936. *The general theory of employment, interest and money*. London: Macmillan.

Keynes, J. M. 2008/1920. *A treatise on probability*. London: Rough Draft Printing/MacMillan.

Kindleberger, C. (1978). *Manias, panics, and crashes: A history of financial crises*. London: Macmillan.

Lagerspetz, E. (1988). Reflexive predictions and strategic actions. *Social Science Information, 27*(2), 307–320.

Lawson, T. (1997). *Economics and reality*. London: Routledge.

Lawson, T. (2015). *The nature and state of modern economics*. London: Routledge.

Lucas, R. E. (1972). Expectations and the neutrality of money. *Journal of Economic Theory, 4*(2), 103–124.

Lucas, R. E. (1976). Econometric policy evaluation: A critique. In K. Brunner & A. Meltzer (Eds.), *The Phillips curve and labor markets* (pp. 19–46). Amsterdam: North Holland Publishing Company.

MacKenzie, D. (2006). *An engine, not a camera: Finance theory and the making of markets*. Cambridge: MIT Press.

MacKenzie, D., Muniesa, F., & Siu, L. (2007). *Do economist make markets? On the performativity of economics*. Princeton: Princeton University Press.

Mackinnon, L. (2005). Ideational reflexivity in economic systems. In L. Mackinnon (Ed.), *The social construction of economic man: The genesis, spread, impact and institutionalisation of economic ideas*. Unpublished doctoral dissertation, University of Queensland, Brisbane, Ch 11. https://espace.library.uq.edu.au/view/UQ:8777.

Martins, N. O. (2018). Critical realism, economics, and heterodox economics. In F. S. Lee, B. Cronin, & E. Elgar (Eds.), *Handbook of research methods and applications in heterodox economics* (pp. 222–236). Cheltenham/Northampton: Edward Elgar Publishing.

Merton, R. K. (1948). The self-fulfilling prophecy. *The Antioch Review, 8*(2), 193–210.

Minsky, H. (1982). *Can "it" happen again? Essays on instability and finance*. Armonk: M.E. Sharpe.

Minsky, H. (2008). *Stabilizing and unstable economy* (2nd ed.). New York: McGraw Hill.

Mirowski, P. (2014). *Never let a serious crisis go to waste. How neoliberalism survived the financial meltdown*. London: Verso.

Morgan, J. (2015). Is economics responding to critique? What do the UK 2015 QAA subject benchmarks indicate? *Review of Political Economy, 27*(4), 518–538.

Nasir, A., & Morgan, J. (2018). The unit root problem: Affinities between ergodicity and stationarity, its practical contradictions for central Bank policy, and some consideration of alternatives. *Journal of Post Keynesian Economics*, first online 10 Apr 2018, https://doi.org/10.1080/01603477.2017.1387060.

Palley, T. I. (2013). Financialization: What it is and why it matters. In *Financialization* (pp. 17–40). London: Palgrave Macmillan.

Patomäki, H. (2001). *Democratising globalisation. The leverage of the Tobin tax*. London: Zed Books.

Patomäki, H. (2002). *After international relations. Critical realism and the (re)construction of world politics*. London/New York: Routledge.

Patomäki, H. (2006). Global justice: A democratic perspective. *Globalizations, 3*(2), 99–120.

Patomäki, H. (2010). What next? An explanation of the 2008-9 slump and two scenarios of the shape of things to come. *Globalizations, 7*(1), 67–84.

Patomäki, H. (2013). *The great eurozone disaster: From crisis to global new deal*. London/New York: Zed Books.

Patomäki, H. (2017). Capitalism: Competition, conflict, crisis. *Journal of Critical Realism, 16*(5), 537–543.

Patomäki, H. (2018). *Disintegrative tendencies in global political economy: Exits and conflicts*. London/New York: Routledge.

Patomäki, H. (forthcoming). *The ideal of competitive markets. On the social psychology and politics of neoclassical theory*, resubmitted after major revisions to Cambridge Journal of Economics in June 2018, pending for final decision.

Perelman, C. (1963). *The idea of justice and the problem of argument*. London: Routledge & Kegan Paul.

Pratten, S. (2005). Economics as progress: The LSE approach to econometric modelling and critical realism as programmes for research. *Cambridge Journal of Economics, 29*(2), 179–205.

Rawls, J. (1971). *A theory of justice*. The original edition. Cambridge, MA: The Belknap Press of Harvard University Press.

Reid, J., Nicol, C., Burns, N., & Chanda, S. (2017). *Long-term asset return study: The next financial crisis*. London: Deutsche Bank Markets Research.

Robinson, J. (1980). Time in economic theory. *Kyklos, 33*(2), 219–229.

Sargent, T., & Wallace, N. (1975). "Rational" expectations, the optimal monetary instrument and the optimal money supply rule. *Journal of Political Economy, 83*(2), 231–254.

Sayer, A. (2011). *Why things matter to people. Social science, values and ethical life*. Cambridge: Cambridge University Press.

Schumpeter, J. (1939). *Business cycles* (Vol. 1). New York/London: McGraw-Hill.

Schweickart, D. (1993). A democratic theory of economic exploitation dialectically developed. In R. Gottlieb (Ed.), *Radical philosophy. Tradition, counter-tradition, politics* (pp. 101–122). Philadelphia: Temple University Press.

Shaikh, A. (2013). On the role of reflexivity in economic analysis. *Journal of Economic Methodology, 20*(4), 439–445.

Shaikh, A. (2016). *Capitalism: Competition, conflict, crises*. New York: Oxford University Press.

Simon, H. A. (1954). Bandwagon and underdog effects and the possibility of election predictions. *Public Opinion Quarterly, 18*(3), 245–253.

Sims, C. A., Goldfeld, S. M., & Sachs, J. D. (1982). Policy analysis with econometric models. *Brookings Papers on Economic Activity, 1982*(1), 107–164.

Soros, G. (1998). *The crisis of global capitalism: Open society endangered*. London: Little, Brown.

Soros, G. (2008). *The crash of 2008 and what it means: The new paradigm for financial markets*. Melbourne: Scribe.

Soros, G. (2013). Fallibility, reflexivity, and the human uncertainty principle. *Journal of Economic Methodology, 20*(4), 309–329.

Stiglitz, J. E. (2010). Lessons from the global financial crisis of 2008. *Seoul Journal of Economics, 23*(3), 321–339. https://www8.gsb.columbia.edu/faculty/jstiglitz/sites/jstiglitz/files/2010_Les sons_Global_Financial_Crisis_Seoul.pdf.

Van der Zwan, N. (2014). Making sense of financialization. *Socio-Economic Review, 12*(1), 99–129.

Wilcox, D. (1989). Social security benefits, consumption expenditure, and the life cycle hypothesis. *Journal of Political Economy, 97*(2), 288–304.

Anticipation Dialogues

29

Tom Erik Arnkil

Contents

Abstract

Anticipations are the core of orientation in activity. People observe the world from their unique place in the social space and view it as their potential fields of activity, anticipating responses to their actions. Unique places afford unique views and perspectives and the unsurpassable differences make dialogues both necessary and possible. Worrying situations challenge dialogicity and attract authoritarian discourse. In contrast, Anticipation Dialogues encourage anticipating in relational settings and make polyphony of views a resource for joint activity.

Keywords

Dialogicity · Active anticipating · Authoritative discourse · Polyphony · Otherness

T. E. Arnkil (✉)
Finnish National Institute for Health and Welfare, Helsinki, Finland

Pro & Re Ltd, Helsinki, Finland

Dialogical Practice Institute, Kanagawa, Japan
e-mail: pro.re.ltd@gmail.com

Introduction

Over the last three decades our team at the Finnish National Institute for Health and Welfare has made active anticipating the core of dialogical practices both in one-to-one settings (e.g., in teaching, social work, psychotherapy, counselling, and other relational work) and especially in multi-professional/multi-agency settings of psycho-social work and education. These Anticipation Dialogues were developed via experimenting and the experiments were informed by theory – and, reciprocally, the experiences helped to reflect and revise theory. Positive outcomes in difficult situations lead to experimenting with Anticipation Dialogues in other than casebased psycho-social work or education, such as community work, project planning and reforms in companies and other organizations. The contexts vary – nowadays also involving Anticipation Dialogues in countries and cultures very different from Finland – but at the core you can find active anticipating in relational settings face-to-face wherever AD is practiced. There was a point, however, where marked changes had to be made in the practice. Let me first explain the point of departure for the practice and then describe the processes.

Over the last three decades our team at the Finnish National Institute for Health and Welfare has made *active anticipating* the core of *dialogical practices* both in one-to-one settings (e.g., in teaching, social work, psychotherapy, counselling, and other relational work) and especially in multi-professional/multi-agency settings of psycho-social work and education. The practices were developed via experimenting and the experiments were informed by theory – and, reciprocally, the experiences helped to reflect and revise theory. Let me first explain the point of departure and describe the practices.

Worries, Anticipations, Control, and Dialogicity

Dialogicity – initiating responses and responding, hearing and being heard – is something people know from birth. This core relational capability is, however, at stake when *worries* arise. Worries can be understood as anticipations of something unwelcome emerging in one's horizons, and, understandably, one would want to curb such developments. In relational settings one would perhaps want to have more control over how others think and act in order to avoid anticipated dangers, and this could be seen as accountability as one takes responsibility instead of turning the blind eye. Nevertheless, responsiveness and dialogical discourse are at risk of being replaced by authoritative discourse. Dialogical discourse is, according to the Russian socio-linguist and philosopher Mikhail Bakhtin (1981), open and invites thinking together whereas authoritative discourse consists of finite, closed sentences and demands that people acknowledge it and make it their own rather than developing thoughts together. Both types of discourse have, of course, their roots in anticipations. One anticipates worrying developments, wants to take action, and anticipates consequences on one's utterances and other actions.

The "authoritative route" might be the best choice in situations of grave immediate danger, but they also require lots of power and strong connections. As the French sociologist Bruno Latour (1987/2002) points out, actors make *translations* of the means handed to them, and the weaker the connections between the actors the bigger the changes the actors make. Nevertheless, many actors take the "authoritative route" even in less alarming situations, hoping to control the situation and achieve preferred aims. One anticipates unwelcome development unless one takes action and chooses – spontaneously or deliberately – to take authoritative action, anticipating more welcome outcomes. "If only the other would see things how they are and act accordingly, things would be better," one might think, "and if I tell them how they should see things, they will do so, at the end of the day." If the Other does not comply, one is tempted to add authority to the authoritative discourse: "this is what every sensible person says, this is how my expertise informs me, this what science tells us. . .." Nonetheless, the anticipation that the Other would or, in fact, could see things as one sees them oneself is fundamentally misguided and the attempts to gain control of Others without them making *translations* is pursuing the impossible. (I write the Other with the capital O for a reason I will come back to when referring to Emmanuel Levinas.) The Other does not occupy the same point in the social space and *can therefore never see things exactly the same way I do.* A dialogical attempt for making worries smaller is to understand more of how the Other(s) see things and initiate joint action. In authoritative discourse, one anticipates acquiescence and does not expect modifications. In dialogical discourse modifications, additions and the like are welcome and are seen as beneficial for shared understanding and joint activity. There is, evidently, the place and time for strict authoritative discourse, but, however, one is tempted to slip into it even in cases where *tolerating uncertainty and welcoming translations* would be more in place.

Relational Anticipating and the Respect for Otherness

The Other is always more than we can ever know and *it is precisely this otherness, foreignness, that makes dialogues both possible and necessary,* the Latvian philosopher Emmanuel Lévinas (1969/2004) emphasized. The French sociologist Pierre Bourdieu (1998; Bourdieu and Wacquant 2002) underlined that as each actor occupies a point in the social space, *this point is the ground for the person's gaze.* The form and content of the subjective perspective that opens for each person is thus determined by the objective position the person occupies. The psychological *uniqueness of each person* lies, according to the British psychologist and philosopher John Shotter (1993), on the fact that *each person occupies a unique place in relationships.*

Thus, we have unique persons in unique places and points in the social space affording a gaze and perspective determined by that point. In and from these unique places they anticipate, all the time, with gazes and perspectives that are no more interchangable than are their unique places.

The Russian professor of psychology and pupil of Lev S. Vygotski Pjotr.J. Galperin (1979) made *orientation* the corner stone of his psychological research and analyzed anticipations at the heart of orientation. According to Galperin, anticipating is actually what the psyche is "for": it is crucial for the person to orientate adequately. Every human action is accomplished on the basis of some orientation, which largely determines its quality. The psyche makes use of all its cognitive, emotional, and moral resources in combination, anticipating constantly what happens if I do this, that, or nothing and if is it acceptable to act or withdraw. One can only wonder how it was possible for Galperin (1979) to outline such *thoroughly subjective activity of* orientation at the height of cybernetics more or less collectivistic ideas the mind in the 1960s Soviet Union. Subjective, however, does not mean subjectivistic. Galperin's point is *relational* at the same time it emphasizes the anticipating individual. He argues that *individuals do not observe the world as a field of particles in interaction* (and you can almost hear him pointing critically at models of non living systems applied to humans) *but instead as fields of their potential activities* (Galperin 1979, p. 63). The world as fields of potential activities, this was truly revolutionary – and still is! Potential does not necessarily mean actualized, Galperin goes on to emphasize, but, thanks to images of the potential fields, every act can be intended, tried out, approved, corrected, or rejected in advance, and it is these anticipations that make it possible for the individual to *make choices.*

There is more in Galperin's crystallization than first meets the eye. It means, after all, that people *cannot but be subjective* – everything people observe they "evaluate" as potential fields of their activities, *not* as systems of interacting particles as such although they certainly observe interacting things, people, etc. Everything has more or less meaning *for them,* and it is precisely because of this subjectivity they can make sense of the world. The objective reality is, thus, a thoroughly subjective reality for each subject.

It is not hard to see the common fundamental emphasis on subjectivity in Lévinas' point on the foreignness and Otherness of each person and Bourdieu's point on objective positions determining the gaze and the perspective as well as Shotter's point on uniqueness in relationships. Adding what Galperin underlines we see people viewing the world as well as relationships as potential fields of activity where, people anticipate the responses of each other. It is such relational settings where people strive to cooperate without the possibility to become alike and see alike that preserving a dialogical stance becomes crucial. Let us have a closer look at unique Others anticipating each others' responses, taking common albeit dificult psychosocial and educational situations as an example.

Anticipations and Early Dialogues: Taking up your Worry Dialogically

There are plenty of worrying situations in relational work – and thus also plenty of temptations to take the shortcut to control and slide to authoritative discourse. How to be dialogical when worries arise? Our team at the Finnish National

Institute for Health and Welfare set out to develop practices for *taking up sensitive matters* that teachers, social workers, counselors, and other relational workers encounter but hesitate to take up (for example, a child restless in day care or at school and the teacher assuming that the situation has something to do with things at home.)

Relational workers anticipate that parents, clients, families will feel offended and hurt if they take up the worrying sensitive matters and feel that the relationships will worsen instead of improve. They are probably right (and this is one of the reasons why attempts to encourage "early intervention" tend to fail time after time). Relationships are crucial in relational work; workers are wise to protect them. But although things could straighten themselves, worries seldom disappear doing nothing. How can you be a good teacher, social worker, doctor, and do nothing while worrying matters continue? You're damned if you do (take up your worry and the Others feel offended) and damned if you don't!

We made a "set of steps" for *taking up one's worry in a dialogical way.* The core of practice is *asking for help of the Other(s)* instead of making direct or indirect suggestions for the Other(s) to change. The key for this is *actively anticipating the consequences of your utterances and acts:* what kind of responses are you inviting. In the practice of taking up worries dialogically (Early Dialogues, ED), we encourage the teacher, the social worker, the doctor, to make *thought* experiments by trying to find an appropriate and respectful way of expressing herself/himself and inviting joint activity. Instead of placing the problem in the Other, the relational worker acknowledges that they themselves have a dilemma: they need the help of the Other(s) in order to make the worry smaller or go away.

The idea of such active anticipating can be summarized in The Rules of Thumb for taking up one's worries (a teacher worried of a pupil and preparing for meeting with the parents as an example):

1. Reflect upon your worry and consider where you genuinely need the parents'/ guardian's help.
2. Make a mental list of the positive things about working with the child.
3. Thinking in advance, consider how you could express the positive aspects as well as your worries without it being misunderstood as a complaint or criticism.
4. Anticipate what will happen if you act the way you have planned – how are the parents/guardians likely to respond?
5. Go through your lines either mentally or with a co-worker, and try to find a way to express yourself so that it invites others to share their opinions and thoughts, encourages listening to others, and strengthens continued co-operation.
6. If you anticipate that the approach you have been trying out might not encourage dialogue, or that it might not give long-lasting results, reformulate your approach.
7. When you feel confident that you have identified a respectful approach, bring up your worry at an opportune moment, in a suitable setting.
8. Listen carefully, pay attention, and be flexible. Taking up worries is an interactive process – do not stick stubbornly to a plan.

9. Reflect upon what happened – was it as you had anticipated? What did you learn? And for your part, how do you intend to secure continued dialogue and co-operation?

10. Most importantly, remember that you are asking for help in diminishing your worries – it is crucial for the improvement of the child's situation that the dialogue continues.

As Mikhail Bakhtin (1986) points out, our utterances *invite* responses and are, at the same time, responses to utterances that invited them. The way we respond to utterances is shaped by our anticipation of how the others will respond in turn – and, when we respond, we invite responses. The ED practice emphasizes asking for help and inviting joint activity.

The Shift from Interventions to Changing One's Own Activity

The reader notices that the gaze of the worker is turned towards the worker herself/himself. Instead of trying to control the thoughts and acts of the other, the worker tries to *change one's own activity in an appropriate way and anticipate the consequences in the relational setting.* The outcomes of such a shift have been very encouraging. Relational workers welcome the "method" that helps them take up sensitive matters. (The word "method" has to be put in quotation marks, however, as the object of change is the worker herself/himself and the change happens already before meeting the others. A person that tries out in advance her/his utterances and acts to find an appropriate respectful way, looks, sounds, and feels different to the one who enters the encounter with authoritative intentions.) There is widespread training for the practice in Finland as well as some other countries. Besides providing a "method," the training has allowed profound discussions on dialogicity with the participants and many of them have realized that it is not a professional method we are talking about but a way of being between people, also in everyday relationships outside professional life. (This is why we call our approach a "positive Trojan Horse." You get something practical but there is a whole lot of philosophy in the packet.)

We developed similar active anticipatory practices also for encounters between several people, especially for *difficult multi-helper situations.* There were numerous cases where a client or members of a family visited several agencies and although each professional seemed to do the right thing according to the practice-as-usual, things were getting more or less stuck – with the professionals as well as the clients growing more or less frustrated. Such situations are not infrequent in the sector-based "silo systems" of psychosocial help and education. Rather, the deep vertical specialization and weak horizontal integration makes them common in all societies with modern professional systems. You can easily find more helpers and controllers around a family than there are family members, with only perhaps one of the workers having ever met the whole family. Each professional knows only their "own client" or pupil and their view is correspondingly singular. It is also common that the professionals have only a vague view of who else is involved in the case and doing what.

We introduced a practice for getting unstuck. The core was similar to the one in taking up one's worry dialogically. Workers were encouraged to make thought experiments for changing their own activity and anticipating the consequences. In stuck multi-helper situations growing frustrated, there is a tendency for *expecting others to change*, and when the players meet, there will be direct and indirect suggestions for others to change their views and actions. The shortcut to controlling others is, however, based on the untenable view that Others could in fact see things as one sees them oneself. If the Other's unique position and perspective is over-looked, the Other will feel the need to defend themselves.

In order to avoid authoitative discourse, we separated talking and listening and facilitated the sessions with a set of questions encouraging listening and being heard. The first version of our experiments went like this:

(a) A professional feeling worried that the case is not going where it should and wishing better collaboration and integration invited those working with the same case plus us (my colleague Esa Erikson and myself) to act as facilitators.
(b) The facilitators initiated the "rule" of separating talking and listening; no comments, everyone gets their turn.
(c) The facilitators made no suggestions or the like, they only asked each person the same set of questions.
(d) At the end, there was discussion: Who does what with whom next.

The questions were simple but not superficial:

1. What happens if you do nothing?
2. What could you do that is appropriately different to what you've done so far?
3. What happens if you do that, who responds and how?

In this early version there were only the involved professionals present. We soon invited also clients, family members, and others from the private networks, and when we did so, profound changes had to be made in the practice. I will come to that soon. Let me first reflect upon the early version.

The reader notices that the facilitators direct the focus on each workers own actions and encourage anticipating the consequences in the relational setting. Direct or hidden suggestions for others to change are discouraged. (However, if someone insists on demanding changes in others, they are asked, how do they intend to change their own activity in order to achieve that aspired change. The focus is always on the players' own activity).

The rather sharp separation between taking and listening aims at making room for *inner dialogues.* Listening to others you reflect the utterances against your views, values, experiences, and goals, and there will be plenty of moments you would want to comment. There will also be plenty of moments you gain a richer view by not commenting. If you comment, you interrupt two dialogues, the external and the internal. Although talking and listening are separated and persons have their turn for thinking aloud, there is plenty of *polyphony* present. There are as many voices to be heard as there are participants, and as the process proceeds, these voices echo more and more in each other. The opportunity to enrich each participants view via the rich polyphony becomes clear if you think of how different it were if each individual was interviewed separately instead of the collective presence. The interviewer may gain a richer view but the interviewees miss the chance.

Anticipating the consequences of doing nothing or doing something appropriately different makes the participants somewhat equal even if there were the head authority and less experienced people present. No one can say for sure what happens if. People are people and life is complex, even the most expert view cannot be a precise prediction with guaranteed outcomes – especially when one is taking a wider relational context into account. One can only make anticipatory thought experiments. Insightful expert knowledge is most welcome, but there is also crucial insight that one can only acquire from inside. The British psychologist John Shotter (1993) pointed out that besides knowing *what* and knowing *how,* people in relationships know also *what those relationships are like,* and calls this third kind of knowing *knowing from within.* Anticipating what happens in the relational space is different if you are viewing a relationship you are participating instead of relying only on abstract general theory. For the Anticipation Dialogues, it is therefore a practice to invite those people – and only those – who are involved in the case.

Besides such psychosocial cases, we experimented in community work and other activities where the issue is not the wellbeing of a client or a family but rather the life at a neighborhood, a community, or the like. The good experiences led to including these practices in the Anticipation Dialogue facilitator's baggage. Here again, talking and listening is separated to generate space also for inner dialogues, but instead of separating it between individuals, they can be separated between groups. The facilitators (usually two) make questions, one group discusses at a time and others listen. While one facilitator interviews (makes anticipatory questions), the other makes public notes for all to see (on a flipchart or the like). An example illustrates the process.

The districts for social work were reorganized in a city in Finland and the social worker teams wanted to know more about the communities they would work with. One team wondered if there were problems related to adolescents in their district and initiated an Anticipation Dialogue. Adolescents were invited, of course, and teachers, shopkeepers, youth workers, community residents, policemen, and all sorts of people who might have knowledge and views about the issue. Starting with the adolescents in the inner circle and all others listening in a large outer circle, the facilitators asked a set of questions:

Concerning Adolescents,

1. What *positive signs and developments* you have observed concerning adolescents in this district?
2. What *worrying signs and developments* you have observed in this district?
3. What could be done and what could *you* do to support the positive developments and keep the worrying developments at bay?
4. What happens if you do that?

After the adolescents, the next group took the turn in the inner circle, and after them the next, etc. A rich polyphonic picture emerged. In the given case, the outcome was that there wasn't much to worry about for the social workers or anyone else. A good result as such. What if there were worrying developments found and people would feel the need to take action? Another mode of Anticipation Dialogues would come handy, something based on *anticipating the future by "visiting" the future*. In this "crown jewel" practice of Anticipation Dialogues, the steps to a less worrisome future are planned via imagining a good near future and "recalling" how we got there. This mode of AD is practiced both in client/family cases and community/organization cases. I shall next describe how we came to develop it and why.

Recalling the Future

As mentioned above, we first developed an AD practice for multi-helper situations inviting only the involved workers. Although the outcomes were very promising with stuck situations unravelling, we felt the urgent need to include the clients and their private networks in order not to act behind their backs. When these people arrived, almost everything had to be changed, however. What remained was the separation between talking and listening and two facilitators asking questions and making public notes. The questions had to be revised totally. It is not appropriate to ask what happens if nothing is done in the face of clients/family members in a difficult situation. The minimum requirement for a meeting with clients and families is that they leave more hopeful than they came – and that the hope is plausible hope. For us this meant aiming at clarity of action in the opaque situations of multi-agency relationships. The goal was to achieve a concrete workable plan for joint activity where everyone would find a pleasing place promising plausible steps towards a better near future.

The meetings were initiated by someone, usually one of the workers, who felt worried and hoped for better integration of acts in order to be a helpful member of the whole. We call these "grey zone situations" where nothing is clear – and where one needs others in order to get out of the zone. The reader may have experienced something like this in a multi-actor situation:

– You anticipate that somehow things are not going in the direction you'd wish they were going.
– You don't have a clear picture of what the various partners are aiming at.
– You feel that what others do affects what you can achieve.
– You would welcome better collaboration between the various players.
– You would welcome more control of the overall situation.

This is what we call a "grey zone of worry." These situations are the "home ground" for Anticipation Dialogues, especially the mode where you recall the future.

The worried person who feels the need for the AD *takes her/his worry up* with the client and the family in the dialogical way informed by the early dialogues practice, in other words ask for help suggesting that an AD meeting could improve the overall integration and thus lessen the worry. If the client and the family agree, they invite those from their private network they would want to have present and the worker invites the involved workers – but only those client/ family wants to be present. The worker also invites two facilitators who are outsiders to the case.

It is important that the facilitators are outsiders. Their task is not to "solve" the case. They avoid making suggestions or giving advice. Their only responsibility is to generate and encourage dialogue, and this is done by a set of questions. If an insider, a person involved in the case, tried to be the facilitator, she/he would be in a double role: facilitating as if from the outside and actually participating from inside, and this will not help to achieve clarity in opaque multi-agency situations. The feedback from clients to AD meetings is very positive on average and the top points go to the use of neutral facilitators. (In Finland we have someme advanced municipalities with pools of facilitators coordinated by a coordinator, which makes it is easy to find people who are not involved in the case.)

The session begins with the initiator (the worried person who wanted the AD) explaining briefly her/his worry and thanking everyone for coming to help relieve it. She/he then hands the process over to the facilitators who take charge and explain the proceedings: It is the aim to come to a very concrete plan of *who does what with whom next* and in order to get there, the participants leap into the future and recall, one by one, how the good developments were achieved; the facilitators ask questions, starting with the client and family and private network, the one facilitator interviewing, the other making public notes. People sit at proximity. It is important that everyone hears each other and sees face-to-face.

In order to see into the future, the time span is negotiated: in what span of time do the participants think things would be better and the worry smaller or gone, a year, 6 months, 3 months? Let's say they arrive at a year. That point in time, a year from the present moment is made the present moment for the dialogue. Through various means for attracting imagination the leap into that moment of time is made (seldom at once, however, but almost every time if not always through the first questions to the first people interviewed).

The questions, one person interviewed at a time, starting with the client and the family and other personal network members, go like this:

1. A year has passed and things are quite well. How are they for you? What makes you especially happy?
2. What did you do to bring about this positive development – And who helped you and how?
3. What made you worried "a year ago" and what lessened your worries?

As the reader notices, the focus is on each and everyone's own views, acts, and worries. Others are also talked about, but in connection to one's own activities: who helped you and how. The reader notices also that there are no questions about problems, only worries, and when worries are talked about, the emphasis is on matters that made them smaller. (With problem definitions, discussions tend to enter into defining and characterizing others – and that can be hurtful albeit all good intentions. With expressing your own worry you express something indisputable, there is no need for others to challenge what you said. Furthermore, the reader notices that the questions do not dwell with the past, and this, too, is a big diversion from typical case meetings. Psychosocial professionals are trained to identify problems and their causal paths. In AD they are doing neither.

After interviewing the family group, the facilitators turn to the professionals. They, too, are interviewed one by one with everyone else listening, but instead of three questions, they are asked two. The first question to the client and family (things are quite well in the family, what makes you especially happy) is not appropriate, as it is not the professional's family. The workers are asked these two questions (similar to the two last questions to the family group):

1. As you heard, things are quite well in the family. What did you do to support the good development – And who helped you and how?
2. What made you worried "a year ago" and what lessened your worries?

After also the professionals have been interviewed, the facilitators open the last part of the meeting for summarizing a plan, and for this they invite the participants to "return from the future." Open discussion takes place and the person who initiated the AD with her/his worry reassumes a more central role again. Although the time span may have been a year, the focus of the activity is in the very next steps: who does what with whom next. Nevertheless, the very next steps have the good future as the backdrop; they are not isolated minimal acts.

The elements of the plan are already there, on the public notes. Each person has made thought experiments on what they could do and with whom, and the column "what lessened your worries" provides valuable ideas towards the plan.

The reader may have noticed that imagining what "made" one especially happy in the future and thinking aloud what "made" one worried "a year ago" is actually interviewing people about their hopes and worries now, in this present moment, so that the focus is in fact all the time in the present moment *and each and everyone's anticipations here-and-now.* The questions offer the participants a tool for looking at disturbing matters from a relieved perspective – and to find workable and plausible life-size steps to draw closer to the relieving circumstances. Joint activity is pursued via individual acts that connect to other individual acts instead of a massive plan of action.

Although reaching a workable plan is very important, a lot happens in the future dialogue itself. Separating talking and listening and facilitating the process with a set of questions makes the meeting rather organized, but beneath the structured surface there is plenty of *polyphony* present. Voices echo in each other. Instead of external exchange of comments there is keen listening and – as participants verify – rich inner dialogues with a wealth of inner commenting. With the significant persons present both from the private and the professional network, everything is immediately shared in the relational context.

A meeting like this takes 2–3 h. The notes will be distributed to all participants. A follow-up meeting may be agreed upon before closing. Immediate feed-back and research data is gathered at the very end of the session.

We took the future dialogue experiences also to complex situations outside client or family cases, namely, organization reforms, community work, project planning, and the like. The process is basically similar with one major difference, however. A pre-meeting is called for. In the client/family case, the facilitators need not and should not know the background of the case in order to remain neutral and not impose their goals. In the organization case, the facilitators need to get aqcuainted with what the organization is doing in order not to be lost in unfamiliar details. The time-span is often longer than in family cases, but never more than 3 years. There are too many unknowns if the span is too long and the plan will be hazy.

It is advisable to invite people from the 360° of activity, not only the top but definitely also the top; not only the middle management but definitely them also; and certainly the users, the clients, the residents – and not only from one "silo" of the organization but also key partners. There can be inner circles and outer circles as was described earlier. The facilitators start with users and those closest to production, not the managers. Hearing the voices in the organization and around is content for the managers. The key questions are:

1. Two years/three years... have passed and things are quite well. How are they for you? What makes you especially happy?
2. What did you do to bring about this positive development – And who helped you and how?
3. What made you worried "a year ago" and what lessened your worries?

Returning from the future the participants make a concrete plan. As in family cases, the notes are distributed to the participants.

To summarize: Respecting Otherness in the Present Moment of Time

Individuals live in relational contexts and simultaneously respond to others and invite responses according to their anticipations of each other. People are born into dialogicity - into initiating responses and responding - but this capability and stance is at jeopardy when worries arise and one is tempted to take shortcuts into author-itative discourse in order to curb the unwelcome developments. Anticipation dia-logues is a family of practices including taking up ones worries dialogically and the various forms of making anticipatory thought experiments in multi-player situations. The closest relative for these practices is Open Dialogues (OD) for relational work in severe psychiatric cases like psychosis (Seikkula and Arnkil 2006, 2013). AD and OD are very different on the surface, Open Dialogues keeping a close eye on the present and AD looking at the present from the anticipated future. The biggest difference is, however, in the strucure of the processes. AD involves outsider facilitators who structure the process with a set of questions, OD involves only insiders to the case - patients, family members and workers - and is has no premeditated structure. There is something profound they share, nevertheless, and pointin out this this common core helps to summarize this article. Both practices are based on unconditional respect for the Otherness of each person and follow keenly what the people present there and then instead of pressing towards goals informed by theories or agendas outside the process. For both practices it is essential to trust and encourage polyphony. Participants will find their way out by listening and being heard - and the task is to provide dialogical spaces for this to happen.

References

Bakhtin, M. (1981). *Dialogic imagination*. Austin: Texas University Press.

Bakhtin, M. (1986). *Speech genres and other late essays*. Austin: University of Texas Press.

Bourdieu, P. (1998). *Practical reason: On the theory of action*. Cambridge: Polity Press.

Bourdieu, P., & Wacquant, L. (2002). *An invitation to reflexive sociology*. Cambrige: University of Chicago Press and Polity.

Galperin, J. P. (1979). *Johdatus psykologiaan*. Helsinki: Kansankulttuuri. See also Gal'perin, P. Ia. (1969). Stages in the development of mental acts. In M. Cole, & I. Maltzman, *A handbook of contemporary Soviet psychology* (pp. 249–273). New York: Basic Books, Gal'perin P.Ia. (1979) The role of orientation in thought. *Soviet Psychology, 18* 84–89. Taylor & Francis Online 19 Dec 2014.

Latour, B. (1987/2002). *Science in action. How to follow scientists and engineers through society*. Cambridge, MA: Harvard University Press.

Lévinas, E. (1969/2004). *Totality and infinity: An essay on exteriority. Translated by Alphonso Lingis*. Pittsburgh: Duquesne University Press.

Seikkula, J., & Arnkil, T. E. (2006). *Dialogical meetings in social networks*. London: Karnac.

Seikkula, J., & Arnkil, T. E. (2013). *Open dialogues and anticipations – respecting otherness in the present moment*. Terveyden ja hyvinvoinnin laitos: Helsinki.

Shotter, J. (1993). *Conversational realities: Constructing life through language*. London: Sage.

Counterfactualism and Anticipation

30

Neville Morley

Contents

Abstract

Most attempts at forecasting the future depend, explicitly or implicitly, on knowledge about the past, whether this is then used to offer possible analogies or to support normative theories with data about past events and trends. This approach is open to criticism both on the grounds of its assumptions about continuity and a tendency toward deterministic thinking and on the grounds that our knowledge of the past is less secure and more discursive than such attempts at prediction assume. Counterfactualism, the development and exploration of accounts of "what might have been" – which can be focused on obtaining better understanding of the past, or on refining theories of the present, or on speculations about the future – offers an alternative approach that emphasizes the openness of historical developments. Its primary role is not to improve forecasting but to highlight its limitations, to expand our knowledge of how humans think about the future and the cognitive biases that dominate such thinking, and to

N. Morley (✉)
Department of Classics and Ancient History, University of Exeter, Exeter, UK
e-mail: N.D.G.Morley@exeter.ac.uk

© Springer Nature Switzerland AG 2019
R. Poli (ed.), *Handbook of Anticipation*,
https://doi.org/10.1007/978-3-319-91554-8_58

establish the ethical imperative of engaging with possible futures. The qualities which make counterfactualism a marginal and suspect activity within historiography and social science are precisely those which make it an essential aspect of the discipline of anticipation.

Keywords
Counterfactuals · Counterfactualism · History · Historiography · Forecasting · Theory · Cognitive bias · Thucydides · Narrative · Normative theory · Historicism · Future · Ethics

Introduction

Many attempts at forecasting or predicting the future rely on knowledge about the past. This knowledge may be in the form of detailed and reliable data from the recent past, interpreted through existing theories and models, as in the cases of weather forecasting and climate science. The main issue for this type of forecasting is the nonlinearity of the processes it seeks to predict (the chaotic nature of weather systems and many other natural phenomena) and hence the uncertainty of any such forecasts, especially predictions of specific developments rather than general trends, beyond the short term.

Such approaches are seen to be less effective in the case of more "open" systems, where processes and developments may be shaped by any number of different factors, and hence appear to be even less predictable than natural systems; this applies above all to different aspects of human society. One response to this problem has been a focus on different forms of abstract modeling, for example, in various fields of economics, to explore the interaction of a limited number of key variables, "all other things being equal"; this constitutes a powerful intellectual tool, but one which generates knowledge that at best has only a partial connection to the "real" social world, open, and under-determined, and whose perceived relevance to the future rests on an assumption of continuity in all variables other than those studied in the model (Elster 2015).

An alternative approach has therefore been to seek to develop a richer idea of the dynamics of social behavior, especially for those areas of human life that do not seem to lend themselves to data-driven analysis or abstract modeling (this discussion will take as a key example a theme in contemporary global politics), by looking in more detail at historical events, on the assumption that "what happened" is a solid basis for forecasting what is likely to happen in the future (Allison and Ferguson 2016).

There are, however, significant problems with this form of historical argument and above all the assumption that our knowledge of the past can offer such an objective foundation for evaluation of present and future prospects. It therefore remains a minority approach within mainstream social science. Above all, attempts at "learning from the past" face the problem that detailed historical research tends more and more to emphasize the noncomparability of different events, processes, and societies; this means that it is necessary for such comparative/analogical analysis to smooth over or occlude the effects of change over time in order to make past events into a useable resource for analysis of the present and future, even at the expense of reducing the credibility of claims about the specific, objective, and "real" nature of the historical data that supposedly form the foundation of such arguments.

At the same time, research in the theory and philosophy of history reveals how far all historical events are open to redescription according to present assumptions and agendas, rather than having an objective existence as potential analogues for present and future developments. Finally, the majority of attempts at identifying patterns in the past that can potentially be extended into the future assume linear models of historical change. In other words, the majority of such attempts at predicting future developments on the basis of historical information are recuperated back into the law-based social science model, but with the relevant laws and principles left largely implicit and taken for granted rather than properly specified or explicitly analyzed.

But this is not to say that contemplation of the past has no value for considerations of possible futures; we simply need to view the past differently, in a manner which recognizes the problems and limited utility of conventional approaches, and we need to modify our expectations of what we can learn from the past. One aspect of this is a better understanding of how humans think about the past, present, and future and the nature and effects of the different stories we tell about the connections between them (cf. Lively 2017). Another is the development of a different way of analyzing past events, in order to develop a sense of openness and instability of historical developments; and this is the realm of counterfactualism.

The Problem of the Past

A Russian joke from the Soviet era, following a standard format, runs as follows:

> Radio Armenia was asked: Is it possible to foretell the future? Radio Armenia answered: Yes, no problem. We know exactly what the future will be. Our problem is with the past; that keeps changing. (Judt 2010, p. 830)

The point is obvious, a mockery of the claims of official Marxist-Leninist theory to possess certain knowledge of the dynamics of historical processes and the inexorability of progress and a satire on the instability of the past as it gets rewritten to conform to present circumstances. It reverses the expected order of things, in which the past is a known, fixed object because it has already happened, while the future is unknown. In its skepticism about official narratives, however, the joke raises the specter of unavoidable uncertainty about the past, present, *and* future; all we really know is that these are malleable and that what can be said of them (now or in future) is subject to the whims of political authority, even if those contradict the narratives of our own lived experience. The only safe assumption on which to anticipate the future is that anything might happen, even if that cannot be openly admitted.

Within the contemporary western tradition of social science, there has at times been a similar confidence – though not officially endorsed or imposed in the same manner – in the capacity of nomothetic approaches (i.e., those focused on general scientific laws) to predict future developments. However, this confidence is grounded in a belief in the fixed and knowable nature of the past and the present, established through empirical study of historical evidence and current data rather than determined or distorted by present-day ideology, which can then serve as a foundation for the development of these explanatory and predictive theories (Pearl 2000).

Belief in the possibility of learning from the past is of course far older; it dates back to the fifth-century BCE Greek historian Thucydides, who declared that his account of a war between Athens and Sparta (known as the Peloponnesian War) would be a "possession for ever" and that he would be content "if it is found useful by those who want exact knowledge of what happened in the past and what, the human condition being what it is, will happen again in the same or similar manner" (Thucydides 1.22.3; see Morley 2014). This idea formed the basis for a centuries-long tradition of "exemplary" history, in which past individuals, actions, and events were held up as models to be studied and imitated in the present.

From the nineteenth century onward, a sense developed among scholars of the vast differences between modern society and economy and those of previous eras and an expectation that the future would be more different still, a growing gap between the "space of experience" and the "horizon of expectation" in the terms coined by the intellectual historian Reinhart Koselleck (2004). This clearly cast doubt on the project of seeking direct analogies between past and present as a basis for understanding and prediction. However, while it led to the discrediting of traditional exemplary history, this new perspective did not render the past irrelevant; it simply directed historians, and still more social scientists, toward the task of identifying the underlying continuities (e.g., economic laws or human psychology) that meant historical instances were still considered comparable, if no longer directly analogous. Indeed, Thucydides was established as a founding figure in this enterprise, with his claim that "the human condition" ensured a degree of repetitiveness in historical development; he could be represented as a pioneering social scientist rather than a historian in any conventional sense.

In any case, appeal to past precedent continues to carry significant rhetorical power, whether or not it is advanced as part of a nomothetic approach. It allows the framing of simple conditionals to indicate or advocate a course of future action: on the basis of this past event, if we do X then the result will be Y, or if we fail to do X then Z will happen. If we embark on this program of fiscal stimulus, we will lift the economy out of depression. If we do not act to stop this dictator, he will become bolder and bring war to the entire region.

These two examples are not identical, and not only because one is framed in terms of taking a positive step to cause something to happen that would not otherwise have done so while the other counsels action to prevent something from happening that would otherwise have done. The first can call on the authority of Keynesian economic theory, to offer an analytical explanation of past events (the Great Depression), a diagnosis of the present, and a justification for assuming that future events will follow the same pattern. The latter offers only a (familiar and value-laden) narrative of events in the past and the conviction that these will repeat themselves in similar conditions in the future. Both, however, draw rhetorical authority from the fact that what they propose for the future has happened at least once before: the anticipated sequence of events is known (or believed) to be possible if not in fact inevitable – and indeed the continuing cultural dominance, in Anglophone countries, of particular narratives of the Second World War means that the untheoretical, even mythical argument carries greater force than the one which appeals to theoretical knowledge as part of its claim to authority. Even if the prediction is framed in less definite terms, to deflect accusations that the future can never be known with such certainty – if we appease this dictator, then he *may* start a war – the fact that this has happened in the past still carries significant weight.

A concrete example of such an attempt at characterizing the present situation, forecasting future developments, and offering policy advice on the basis of past events is "Thucydides's Trap," an idea developed by the American international relations theorist Graham Allison (2017). This builds on the argument offered by Thucydides that the truest but least discussed reason that made the Peloponnesian War inevitable was the growth of the power of Athens and the fear this inspired in the Spartans. Building on Thucydides' claim, mentioned above, that readers will learn from his account true understanding not only of the past but of similar events in future, Allison rephrases this as a normative principle of interstate relations, that when a "ruling power" is confronted by a "rising power," the likely result is war. Sixteen historical case studies are adduced, in which a similar dynamic is identified, including the confrontations between France and the Hapsburgs in the sixteenth century, France and Britain from the seventeenth to the early nineteenth centuries, and the United States and the Soviet Union after the Second World War, as well as the obvious examples of the First and Second World Wars; in the majority of these cases, the confrontation of ruling and rising power led to war. Finally, Allison offers an interpretation of current relations between the United States and China in similar terms and hence argues that, on the basis of the historical data and the general principle identified by Thucydides, war must be seen as a likely result unless steps are taken to prevent this.

This policy advice, which the United States should actively seek to calm possible tensions rather than risk unstoppable escalation by complacently assuming that war is now impossible (as some have argued, on the grounds of several decades of globalization, convergence, and economic interdependence), seems entirely reasonable as a precautionary principle. However, other conclusions might be drawn from this historical data, even if Allison's historical claims and predictions are accepted at face value – for example, that the likelihood of war makes it imperative to prepare for it, even at the risk of thus making it more likely. More significantly, the evidence of past events is by no means a secure empirical foundation for such an analysis, even if, once again, the indications are that it is rhetorically effective.

It is, as Allison has demonstrated, possible to give accounts of the 16 different case studies in terms of "Thucydides's Trap," but that is not the same as saying that these are correct accounts of "what really happened" in the past. Even Thucydides' account of the causes of the Peloponnesian War can be questioned, on the grounds both of whether this is a correct reading of his actual interpretation and, more importantly, by comparing it with other historical evidence. This is still more true of the other examples, where detailed study strongly suggests that the situations were far more complex and multifaceted than Allison's simple characterization of them suggests. To explain the outbreak of the First World War as the result of rivalry between a ruling United Kingdom and a rising Germany is, while not wholly untrue, certainly a drastic simplification of the complex interaction of different states and alliances, as well as of different levels of causation (conscious strategies and decision-making, but also longer-term economic, geographical, and technological factors). In brief, the apparently objective data from the past, on the basis of which the present situation is diagnosed as following a familiar and predictable pattern, can always be reinterpreted and redescribed.

Allison's model is taken here as an example not because it is uniquely flawed but because its assumptions about the use of historical data are relatively explicit and so reveal the essential problem in such approaches. The past is assumed to be known and hence available for use as a basis for analysis and extrapolation; further, historical processes are assumed to be linear, so that we can expect the same results – or at least the same probability of different outcomes – from similar situations. However, more detailed research into the particular circumstances of a given historical event (as one would expect, in order to ground diagnosis and forecasts more solidly in the data) inevitably tends toward the idiographic, a focus on the particular rather than the general. This raises the problem of historicism, whereby each past moment appears ever more unique and incomparable with other events except in the most general terms.

Further, the fact that the consequences of (allegedly) similar past situations can be represented in similar terms is not a sound basis for claims that there is a consistent, linear principle to be discerned in historical events. Comparison of historical case studies of course remains possible, through continued reliance on nomothetic approaches or by making use of Weberian ideal types, but it becomes increasingly difficult to claim that any conclusions, forecasts, or policy recommendations drawn from them are truly falsifiable with reference to historical evidence. At best, we are left with conventional normative theories, and forecasts based on them, that draw rhetorical power but no empirical support from history.

One widespread response to the problem of historicism and the discursive nature of knowledge about the past is to rely solely on general theories and laws. However, it is not clear that such theories, based on the assumption that our understanding of the present is not only reliable and complete but also universally and eternally valid for hypothetical futures, are sufficient for our purposes. They make claims about a predictable future, knowable in advance, that replicate the old idea of a known, singular past even if they do not explicitly reference it. In terms of the tripartite distinction outlined by Poli (2017), they relate to forecasts and foresight, but not to anticipation, which is explicitly non-predictive, qualitative (idiographic) and focused on discontinuity.

What is required is a different approach to understanding the past, and this is where counterfactualism offers possibilities. Counterfactuals are a specific form of conditional statement, a distinctive and familiar part of natural language, even if their truth conditions raise various philosophical problems. In popular terms, they revolve around "what if?" questions; to take the example used by David Lewis, the central figure in philosophical discussions of counterfactualism and possible worlds, "If kangaroos had no tails, they would topple over." "I believe," Lewis argued, "and so do you, that things could have been different in countless ways... I therefore believe in the existence of entities that might be called 'ways things could have been'" (1973, p. 84). Applied to the study of the past, this approach offers an alternative way of exploring causation and the dynamics of historical processes; it is widely derided and marginalized within mainstream historiography, for focusing on things that did not happen – but that is precisely why it may be a useful resource for thinking productively about another not (yet) existing thing, the future.

Past-Focused Counterfactuals

Counterfactuals are often discussed as a single, unified form of analysis and argument, especially but not only when they are explored from within a specific discipline (e.g., Ferguson 2011; Tucker 1999, 2016 on historiography; Lebow 2010 on international relations theory. Hawthorn 1991 is striking in his willingness to cross, or simply ignore, the boundary between history and social science). Different typologies can be suggested; for example, the important discussion by Tetlock and Belkin (1996) focuses on the different methods employed in identifying and developing counterfactual arguments, including idiographic, nomothetic, and statistical, while acknowledging that the majority of concrete cases combine such approaches, especially by incorporating normative laws into ideographical counterfactuals or by including idiographic descriptions in nomothetic studies.

An alternative approach, which will be adopted here, is to distinguish different counterfactual approaches according to their primary aims, that is to say, what the counterfactual is intended to illuminate. The majority of counterfactuals take the past as their subject matter, exploring how things that have happened could have happened differently; but this may be done in order to improve our understanding of the present and/or the future (i.e., counterfactualism as an attempt at recuperating the past for purposes of forecasting) or in order to improve our understanding of the past as an end in itself. The latter is the most familiar form, not least because of its resemblance to the popular genre of "alternative histories" in novels and television series, such as *SS-GB* and *The Man in the High Castle* (or, in a more literary register, Philip Roth's *The Plot Against America*). The idea that our world could have become quite different if certain key events or decisions had gone differently in the past carries considerable appeal for non-academic audiences – primarily, it would seem, as a form of dystopian fiction in which the "wrong" side won or the "wrong" thing happened.

Academic historians are less overt in their ideological commitments, though the majority of published counterfactual studies have had a significant overlap with fictional attempts (see Tucker 1999), above all in their focus on very traditional forms of narrative history, organized around the results of individual battles and individual decisions, usually in relation to political and military activities. In some cases, at least, this is in part because such accounts of "what might have been" are written for a wider, nonacademic audience rather than for other historians. They depend on their readers' prior knowledge of what *did* happen, at least in general terms, and hence tend to concentrate on familiar moments in history, understood in a conventional form: what if the Spanish Armada had succeeded, what if Napoleon had lost at Trafalgar, and what if Hitler had invaded Britain in 1941? In some cases, however, a turn to counterfactuals and an emphasis on chance and contingency represent a more or less explicit commitment to *l'histoire événementielle* (if not indeed to a version of Thomas Carlyle's great man theory of history): a history focused on short-term events at a human level, reinstating the active role of individuals in history, implying a rejection of forms of historiography that concentrate on structures and longer-term changes, perceived to favor deterministic understanding of historical change (Ferguson 2011 explicitly presents his counterfactual project as anti-Marxist).

The fact that the majority of published counterfactuals have focused on familiar and sometimes trivial themes and presented them in conventional, if not explicitly conservative, forms does not mean that this ideological agenda is intrinsic to the exercise – there are examples in economic and social history, for example, on the effects of the Black Death or on the demographic history of Roman Italy (above all Hawthorn 1991, but see also Morley 2001) – but it has undoubtedly contributed to the marginalization of counterfactual approaches within mainstream historiography. There are other, more substantial arguments against counterfactualism as a historical method (summarized in Black 2008; Evans 2014). History is mainly conceived as the study of the actual or at least an attempt at getting as close to this as possible on the basis of the evidence of past activity that has survived, whereas counterfactuals explicitly concern themselves with the study of what did not in fact happen (Hawthorn 1991, p. 10). Logically, things which did not happen cannot have left any evidence of their occurrence, so on what basis can counterfactual accounts be evaluated, other than their qualities as fiction? How does one decide which counterfactuals are worth studying, given that what actually happened is a single unitary phenomenon, whereas the list of other things that could have happened is presumably infinite – and, therefore, what assumptions are being smuggled into the argument that some possible alternatives are more plausible or more worth studying than others?

The counterargument to this critique is that counterfactuals are simply unavoidable in any discussion of historical causation (Sunstein 2016). It is simply a question of whether they are discussed explicitly (so that the underlying assumptions about causation and probability can be evaluated) or whether they are left implicit, creating the impression that a specific historical development was necessary or inevitable. "In a non-experimental and non-comparative discipline one can hardly discuss the relative importance of causes without engaging in some kind of thought experiment where one removes successively and separately each of the causes in question and evaluates what difference the absence of this cause would have made to the phenomenon in question" (Elster 1978, p. 176). More succinctly, any satisfactory explanation of a historical phenomenon must also account for negatives, that is, why other possible outcomes did not in fact occur (Tucker 2016, p. 335); counterfactuals are the obvious means for avoiding retrospective assumptions that what did in fact happen was by definition the most likely if not the only possible outcome.

To consider a crude and familiar example, the case made in Allison's Thucydides's Trap that the First World War was the result of the rivalry between Britain and Germany implies that (i) such a rivalry could only have led to war, not to other forms of competition; (ii) without the existence of this rivalry, Europe would not have fallen into war; and (iii) it was only this rivalry, rather than the conjunction of this rivalry with other continental rivalries, that was crucial. All these assumptions – and many other possibilities – are best explored through posing counterfactual questions. Further, we can observe that such an account, emphasizing underlying structural factors and path dependency as the main driver of events as they occurred, is already a kind of counterfactual, developed in opposition to the conventional narrative account of the outbreak of war: the assassination of Archduke Ferdinand in Sarajevo as a trigger for hostilities between Serbia and the Austro-Hungarian Empire, pulling in other European powers as a consequence of existing alliances and rivalries. That is to say, the familiar development of historical analysis, offering a more nuanced account of longer-term underlying causes rather than focusing solely on short-term political events and chance occurrences ("proximate" causes), is based on a counterfactual argument: would the First World War still have broken out, albeit a little later, if Ferdinand had not been shot that day? The standard answer, given the familiar structural features and dynamics of early twentieth-century European politics, is that it would have done.

It is clear, therefore, that some form of counterfactual thinking is not alien even to conventional history but is rather fully integrated and taken for granted within it – but it could be explored more explicitly and in more depth in order to improve the quality of the analysis of causation and hence improve our understanding of the past. Above all, counterfactualism offers a means of preventing or limiting ahistorical error, above all insufficiently interrogated assumptions about inevitability, and the tyranny of hindsight (Kaye 2010). It can certainly be an advantage for the interpretation of the past to know what happened next, simply because it builds up a knowledge base of what possible causes may have what possible consequences, but there is a substantial danger of assuming that a specific type of cause can *only* have one specified consequence or that in a given situation, only one outcome was likely. That things did happen this way should not expunge uncertainty about whether they *had* to happen this way; an explicit focus on counterfactuals can restore a sense of openness of the past, of questions of contingency and necessity, and of the idea that what did in fact happen was not necessarily the most probable outcome, simply because it is the one that occurred. Historical events are always overdetermined, with multiple causes, and never sufficiently isolated for deterministic description (Tucker 1999); how else can we determine the significance of different conditions except by reference to events and alternatives?

Constructing and Evaluating Counterfactuals

If the necessity as well as the utility of counterfactualism is accepted, the next step is to develop them in the most effective and persuasive manner possible. The first important question is how to identify the counterfactuals that are most worth investigating in a given context. Conventionally, attempts at counterfactual history have concentrated on what appear to be obvious "turning points," moments when things could clearly have gone differently: military engagements, most obviously, but also individual decisions made by those in power. It may be argued that it is sufficient for us to be able to imagine alternative possibilities to what in fact happened, but a stronger argument (e.g., Ferguson 2011) is that we need contemporary evidence that the alternative was considered at the time.

Certainly we can identify this issue in relation to the decisions of individual historical actors; the fact that, in retrospect, the actions of a monarch or general appear critical in determining the subsequent course of events is insufficient to demonstrate that a different outcome was possible, in the absence of evidence that the individual could have chosen differently. This evidence might be provided by documents such as the records of meetings or the private papers of the individual concerned, or (especially in earlier, less well-documented periods) it could be a more tentative synthesis of what is known about their general character and/or the climate of thought at the time – the existence of evidence, even if not directly related to the decision-maker, that certain ideas were conceived and capable of being held by such people.

In the outbreak of the Peloponnesian War between Athens and Sparta, there are no conceivable grounds on which to claim that the Spartans might have pursued a policy of pacifism, as that would have been entirely anachronistic; but there is a range of evidence attesting to their reluctance to embark on large-scale hostilities or to see Athens as a real threat to their interests. Thucydides' account shows the process whereby they were persuaded by their allies that war was necessary (highlighting, of course, that Thucydides did not regard the war as inevitable in any straightforward manner); on that basis, it is easy to construct and justify a counterfactual in which war was at least postponed for some years and to consider the consequences of this for the balance of power between the two states and their allies.

In part, the choice of counterfactuals depends on what questions we wish to explore. It may be legitimate and useful to consider how far a decision or a battle was a foregone conclusion, exploring the evidence for the possibility of alternative outcomes (indications that a range of options was considered by those making the decision, evidence of specific circumstances related to a military engagement that might have led to a different outcome result – messages not being transmitted, reinforcements failing to arrive, chance events like a lucky arrow hitting the king in the eye). It can be equally legitimate and useful to consider whether the *outcome* of such a decision or battle was a foregone conclusion, in which case the counterfactual is taken as a starting point for discussion rather than as the object of analysis. The first approach seeks to explore the significance of conditions in establishing the range of possible outcomes and their relative likelihood, and the second examines the chain of causation arising from that moment.

Counterfactual history is highly responsive to, if not dependent on, mainstream historical narratives and their identification of turning points and inevitable developments; this is an obvious reason why it has tended in practice to focus on battles and political decisions and why the claim is sometimes made that only documented alternatives should be considered (anything else strays too close to fiction and to the conventional stricture against historians inventing things unnecessarily). However, it is clearly possible if not probable that certain possible outcomes may be visible only in retrospect and – most controversially – on the basis of modern theoretical understanding. This is especially relevant when we move away from conventional forms of narrative history to the study of longer-term developments in economy, society, and culture, which were largely or entirely invisible to contemporaries.

For example, it is well known that the classical political economists in the late eighteenth and early nineteenth centuries failed to recognize the revolutionary impact of a switch to a mineral-based energy economy (coal and other fossil fuels in preference to wood and muscle as sources of power) and so continued to assume, on theoretical grounds, that there were strict physical limits to the possibilities for growth in productivity, even as the English economy was setting about proving them wrong (Wrigley 1988). It is only in retrospect, with the benefit not only of more copious data but also a better understanding of the processes of economic change, that we can see eighteenth-century developments as a critical turning point in the emergence of the modern economy and hence explore questions about the relative significance of different conditions that shaped the process and the consequences if it had not happened. (We can also recognize that this account of the Industrial Revolution as a revolution in energy use is already derived from an implicitly counterfactual analysis, moving away from a narrative focused on mechanical inventions (the spinning jenny, the steam engine) to explore the conditions under which such things could be invented and/ or have the effects that they did.)

Modern social scientific theory, and modern scientific knowledge, can identify possibilities that contemporaries were wholly unaware of; part of understanding the impact of the Black Death on late medieval Europe, for example, rests on our having a superior knowledge of *Yersinia pestis* and the vectors of its transmission, so that we can develop a sense of the range of possibilities – some more apocalyptical, some much less so – according to different models of the spread of the infection and its impact on different populations (cf. Hawthorn 1991). This can offer an important corrective to the traditional historical narratives, emphasizing that what appeared significant to contemporaries (and to many of their successors) might be far less important in the longer term. Indeed, one might apply counterfactual arguments to events that are apparently insignificant, precisely in order to open up the question of whether our conventional accounts of the past are as inevitable or significant as they tend to appear to us and/or to explore our assumptions about importance and priority.

The obvious risk is that these accounts immediately appear more speculative, resting either on confidence in modern theory as a true and universally applicable analysis of the world (the claim that we understand the medical aspects of the Black Death being more widely accepted than the claim that we understand human psychology regardless of cultural difference) or on the historian's imagination. This leads to the second, and more problematic, question: how are counterfactual narratives to be evaluated, given that we cannot have evidence for what did not happen?

Science professes to draw no conclusions but such as are based on matters of fact, things that have actually happened; but how can any amount of assurance that something actually happened give us the least grain of information as to whether another thing might or might not have happened in its place? Only facts can be proved by other facts. With things that are possibilities and not facts, facts have no concern. If we have no other evidence than the evidence of existing facts, the possibility question must remain a mystery never to be cleared up. (James 1956, pp. 151–152)

The conventional answer is that these strictures apply to *all* historical interpretation, not only to counterfactuals (Ben-Menahem 2016, p. 378). The criteria that Tetlock and Belkin (1996, pp. 16–31) put forward for evaluating counterfactuals are, for the most part, those which would be used to evaluate any historical account: well-specified antecedents and consequents; logical consistency; "minimal rewrite of history," which could also be labeled "historical consistency," compatibility with a reasonable interpretation of the existing evidence, and limits on how much can reasonably be invented; reliance on "strong theory"; and finally "projectability," which is the one criterion specific to counterfactualism and will be discussed further below.

Logical consistency and clear specification of the argument are obvious, incontrovertible virtues; reliance on "strong theory" is more controversial among historians and raises the question of *which* strong theory is adopted – but these are familiar issues in historical interpretation. The idea of "historical consistency" is most interesting and important. It suggests that, if we explore the world that would have resulted if *only* this one change occurred – the effect of minor changes in starting conditions, as Ben-Menahem (2016) has argued – that we can continue to make use of existing historical data for the period in order to discern the likelihood of different developments and then evaluate them.

It is generally a safe assumption, over time, that initial change would have begun to have wider consequences, so that the counterfactual world will deviate ever further from the world as we know it; hence, the further the counterfactual narrative is extended through time, the more speculative it becomes. A classic example is the economic historian Robert Fogel's analysis of whether railroads were essential to nineteenth-century American economic development, which begins with solid data about the relative costs and carrying capacities of canals compared with railroads, and the requirements of the economy, to argue that the historical dominance of railroads was partly contingent and only gradually led to path dependency (Fogel 1964). As the narrative progresses, however, it begins to speculate about the likelihood of the motor car being developed decades earlier than it actually was, as a result of the absence of railroads, an idea that is impossible to test usefully.

Underlying this argument is the philosophical question, raised by David Lewis (1973): how much would the world *already* have to be different in order for the counterfactual to have been possible? We cannot simply imagine a world in which kangaroos have no tails but everything else is the same; other things must have been different for this one thing also to be different. This resembles the criticism raised against counterfactual history by E.H. Carr: if a particular cause (e.g., a battle) led to the ruin of a state, then there must have been a general cause which meant a state could be ruined by a single battle, rather than everything being reduced to that moment (Carr 1964, p. 101; cf. Hawthorn 1991, pp. 8–9). This then implies that the counterfactual narrative must begin in the past, rather than at the moment of obvious divergence from the familiar account, for such a divergence to be plausible – and hence the historical data from that moment of divergence will already potentially be different, rather than offering an initially firm basis for the counterfactual. This raises the specter of an endless regression, in which one has to develop counterfactual narratives of how the data might have been affected by earlier changes, in order to draw on them in evaluating the main counterfactual. But in practice, for shorter-term counterfactuals (or for longer-term ones which focus on slower, longer-term changes in economic, social, or demographic structures), the evidence offers a good-enough approximation.

Once again, the seriousness of this objection depends on the aim of the exercise; the evidence problem would be more significant if our aim were to argue strongly that the alternative narrative is how things *would* have turned out with different starting conditions, than if we simply seek to suggest that they *might* have turned out this way. The aim of past-focused counterfactuals is not so much to develop alternative histories as an end in themselves – that is a task primarily for the writers of speculative fiction – but rather to explore alternative pasts and above all to evaluate the conditions under which these alternatives could reasonably be considered to have been possible or, even likely, as a means of alerting ourselves to contingency and possibility and to our habit of assuming that the present is the only possible world and hence is the measure of the past. Counterfactual history not only develops out of a reaction against conventional narratives; its primary function is to improve our understanding of the past through a critique of those conventional narratives.

Present-Focused Counterfactuals

A second approach to counterfactualism is the attempt at refining and deepening our knowledge of the world in general, by using counterfactuals as a means of testing normative theories (e.g., Lebow 2010; Morgan and Winship 2014). Rather than a modern social scientific theory serving as the or a means of legitimizing a counterfactual narrative of past events, as discussed above, the database of past events becomes a means of evaluating such theories or, more concretely, of considering the circumstances in which their normal assumptions may not apply and the impact on them of small changes in starting conditions.

Theories generate their own counterfactuals; the general principle, for example, that a "rising" and a "ruling" power will always come into conflict raises the question of whether this is invariable and, if not, what the significant reasons are why it would not apply in a specific case (often leading, as in the case of Allison's Thucydides's Trap, to a more qualified statement of the principle). Assumptions about human motivation (e.g., that states are basically rational and driven by concerns with honor, interest, and fear, as stated in standard realist approaches to international relations) can be tested against specific examples and, more importantly, tested against an evaluation of the range of possible outcomes, rather than assuming that the actual historical outcome was the only possible or probable one (whether or not this conformed to the predictions of the theory in question). The main effect of such an approach is not to undermine theories altogether, given that in most cases a reasonable explanation can be put forward to explain why the theory did not hold in a particular situation, but to limit their claims to universality. Many theories of human society express themselves in terms of "all other things being equal"; counterfactual approaches seek to explore in explicit and well-articulated terms how often, and in what circumstances, all other things may indeed be equal.

As discussed above in relation to normative theory more generally, the difficulty of such an endeavor is that there is no fixed, objective account of the past against which theoretical predictions can be measured; other descriptions and narratives are always possible, and the data is rarely if ever adequate for falsification (Weber 1996). The more limited the theory, both in terms of its focus (a closed rather than open system) and its chronological extension (covering recent, well-documented events rather than the more distant past), the more plausible such a test against the historical data is likely to be, a counterfactual about the impact of a given economic policy over the short run, for example. With more ambitious and wide-ranging theories, such as a variant of the Thucydides's Trap model, evaluation both of the model and of possible counterfactuals (could the confrontation of the United States and the Soviet Union during the Cold War in fact have resulted in open conflict? Under what circumstances?) becomes rather a matter of competing idiographic accounts, evaluated by their relative logical coherence, plausibility, coherence in relation to the historical record, and so forth.

As with past-focused counterfactuals, which are most effective as a form of critique of conventional historical narratives and their common fallacies of assuming inevitability and necessity, counterfactual analysis of contemporary normative theories serves as a vaccine against determinism and excessive simplification. In particular, examining alternative possibilities and evaluating the likelihood of the negative case counter the innate human tendency toward confirmation bias, namely, selecting and privileging evidence that supports the hypothesis at the expense of other, less positive evidence, hence developing overconfidence in one's knowledge and understanding (see, e.g., Baron 2000). For example, various reasons might lead an observer of modern global politics to concentrate on the rivalry between the United States (as the undisputed "ruling power" since the Second World War) and China, not at least the fact that the latter's rise in recent decades has been so spectacular; but we need to consider explicitly how we can determine whether we are now living in a bipolar world, as the Thucydides's Trap model assumes, or whether multipolarity offers a better basis for understanding (as, e.g., Wright 2017 argues).

This inevitably reduces the explanatory and predictive power of theory by highlighting the possibility that other things might have occurred, that conditions could have been different, and that human, like historical, situations are invariably open and overdetermined, with multiple interdependent factors shaping developments, rather than the simplified and linear world of most models. This insight is not necessarily welcomed by many social scientists, and it remains unclear whether a counterfactual approach can lead to improved theories rather than simply to skepticism about theory; clearly, however, it can be taken as a vital hedge against overconfidence in our understanding of the world and ability to make reliable forecasts.

Future-Focused Counterfactuals

Thirdly, there are counterfactuals that are focused on the future. The majority of these make use of past- and present-focused counterfactuals and seek to project them forward. As mentioned above, Tetlock and Belkin offer "projectability" as one of their criteria for evaluating attempts at developing counterfactuals: "The same causal principles that allow us to retrodict the past should allow us to predict the future" (30-1). However, it is not clear that this approach differs significantly from the use of normative theory, whether or not refined through counterfactual thinking, discussed in the previous section. It assumes either the continuing validity of the theory, and by implication a continuation of existing conditions into the future – a more persuasive claim in the case of physical laws than social scientific ones – or the objective validity of an analogy between the present situation and a past case or cases which then indicate the range of possibilities for future outcomes. The primary goal of Allison's Thucydides's Trap model, for example, is to highlight the possibility, but not inevitability, of escalating conflict between the United States and China, on the grounds that their present relationship strongly resembles historical situations in which conflict has proved the most likely result. However, the fact that, supposedly, conflict resulted in such situations more often than not is not in fact evidence that it was or is an inherently more likely outcome in such situations, even if one accepts that there are persuasive interpretations of all the different historical case studies and that there are persuasive analogies to be drawn with the present.

Secondly, we find certain attempts at writing "counterfactual" accounts of the future, justified on the grounds that the techniques of constructing counterfactual history are directly relevant to such an exercise – counterfactual accounts are speculative histories of "a 'future' that did not really happen," from the perspective of the "turning point," even if from our perspective they are equally set in the past (Weber 1996, p. 277). In what sense are such accounts counterfactual, since they relate to something that *might* still happen, rather than representing an imagined alternative to what did happen? Weber sets the counterfactual approach against what he terms "official" futures, which may be understood as either the unthinking assumption of continuity (or at least the assumption that changes will be only superficial rather than structural) or the narratives currently preferred by those in authority (governments, think tanks, mainstream media), which tend to limit the thinkable possibilities and for the most part emphasize a single line of development. The aim in this exercise is therefore not primarily to offer a reliable prediction of what the future will be like but to open up questions about the range of possibilities – especially given that humans appear to find it difficult to engage with ideas of nonlinear change or conceive of how far the world might alter around them:

It may be that the human mind cannot anticipate in a reliably predictive sense nonlinear change, but it is certainly possible to ask ourselves probing questions about the possibility. Developing studies about how an idea could take off, and what the world would be like if it did, is one way to think about preparing individuals, states, or any social collectivity for futures that might happen. (Weber 1996, p. 275)

Such futures are intended to be provocative, to question present assumptions and confidence, to emphasize the extent of uncertainty, and to direct attention to the possibility that current developments may have unexpected results and that world-changing developments may emanate from things which are currently beyond out view. We might consider a book like Peter Frase's *Four Futures: Life After Capitalism* (2016) as an example of such an approach, since its most striking feature is the delineation of four different lines of possible future development, rather than a single vision of things to come. Frase identifies key challenges and developments in the present (environmental degradation and climate change, automation, inequality) and then imagines the likely consequences of different possible human responses to these problems. The claim is not that any of these scenarios is necessarily realistic or more probable (though some are acknowledged to be more utopian than others); rather, they are intended (much like Weberian ideal types) to delineate the outer bounds of possibility, with the *probable* course of future development falling between these extremes but tending to resemble one rather than the others. In other words, Frase's analysis rests on developing multiple counterfactual narratives, to be explored in comparison with one another, to expand our sense of what might happen.

The objection to such speculation that the class of things which *might* happen is effectively infinite, and that claims about their possibility are unfalsifiable, is largely beside the point. Firstly, the aim is not to promote a single future narrative but rather to open up the discussion and indicate that there is more uncertainty than may be generally realized. Secondly, it is possible to argue, using the same criteria that are applied to past-focused counterfactuals, that some future narratives are more plausible than others, even if this cannot be proven. Thirdly, we might look to counterfactuals as an exercise in persuasion and discourse, in telling different stories about the future as we do about the past – and it is the comparison of these different stories, offering different accounts of possible futures, that allows us to engage seriously with the present as a preparation for the ever-emerging future (cf. Weber 1996).

Counterfactuals and Anticipation

Counterfactual thinking about the future is not scientific, or objective, or empirically robust. It often depends heavily on the assumption that past and present offer at least some guide to the future, that we can identify immanent tendencies in the present and explore their possible consequences, and that our existing data sets are our most important resource for such an exercise. It can indicate possibilities, but its main utility lies in questioning the more confident and dogmatic assertions of other forecasters, in highlighting the fact that past developments were never necessary or preordained, and in emphasizing uncertainty and indeterminacy.

Anticipation is not about forecasting; indeed, it is less concerned with the actual future than with how we think about the future and engage with the present as a result. The inability of counterfactualism to aid in the identification of a single or most probable future is therefore not a problem from this perspective; rather, it directs our attention toward *how* humans think about the relationship between the past, present, and future and how this may lead them into trouble. It offers a means of identifying and correcting common cognitive biases: confirmation bias, framing, reliance on unexamined heuristics such as analogies, and, above all, hindsight bias (Kahnemann et al. 1982). If "shoulda, woulda, and coulda" are indeed the last words of a fool, that doesn't refute the idea that many people nevertheless evaluate present situations and future possibilities by considering what might have been in the past.

This is precisely the aspect of Thucydides' account of the war between Athens and Sparta that Allison's model ignores; far from offering a single explanation of a deterministic cause, the narrative highlights both the complex interaction of multiple causes (individual actions and decisions, the characters and cultural assumptions of different states, and the continuing consequences of past events, as well as structural factors) and the multiple ways in which things might have turned out differently (Hawthorn 2014; Tordoff 2014). The same is true of Thucydides' account of the subsequent course of the war, which is presented as neither predetermined nor purely contingent, but always open, even if there was a recognizable tendency toward path dependency. Above all, the "lesson" which Thucydides' readers can draw from a better understanding of these past events is that human beings suffer from multiple failings in evaluating the present and anticipating the future: oscillation between overoptimism and excessive pessimism, assumption of greater knowledge and confidence than is rationally justified, susceptibility to false analogies and confirmation bias, and a habit of reinterpreting events afterward in a self-justifying manner rather than learning properly about their own errors.

The primary contribution of counterfactual thinking to anticipation is therefore psychological, cultural, and ethical, as Audra Mitchell has argued: "It cannot give us predictions or certainty, and it can't prove that everything will be ok, or tell us how to ensure this. But it can help us to see possibilities, to scope the boundaries of our knowledge, to appreciate the limits of our agency and to expand our ethical sensibilities" (2013). Mitchell's argument focuses on the specific issue of the storage of nuclear waste, where it is essential for us to imagine futures that are unknowable or unthinkable – to break through what she calls "futural amnesty" or the forgetting of the future – because what we do or do not do in the present will inevitably have far-reaching consequences. Relatively few issues – climate change is the other obvious one – combine such long time scales with the knowledge that our actions or inaction *will* have consequences for the future. But the wider points she makes about counterfactual thinking and anticipation are valid also for shorter-term concerns.

By combatting assumptions of determinism in human history and emphasizing that there are multiple possible futures, counterfactual narratives work against a crippling nihilism and sense of a lack of agency. They can offer a qualified sense of hope – that the future might not be entirely bleak and certainly that its bleakness is not predetermined – and hence an ethical obligation toward the people of the future, to seek to build a better rather than a worse future. Conversely, imagining horrific and nightmare possibilities, including human extinction or degradation, provides the ethical imperative for trying to avert such futures. Futural amnesty is a protective strategy, allowing people to get on with their lives without constant awareness of horror (this resembles Friedrich Nietzsche's arguments about the inability of humans, with rare exceptions like Thucydides, to face too much reality), but it is also an abdication of responsibility for the harm that we might thereby do to unknown future others. Counterfactualism tells us that the future is still open, that we can usefully seek to anticipate it – even as it also highlights the ways in which humans constantly fail in this effort – and that we have an ethical obligation to try.

Summary

The qualities that make counterfactualism marginal within historiography are precisely those that put it at the heart of anticipation: its emphasis on the openness of historical processes and the limits of our understanding of them, its critique of determinism and overconfident forecasting, the intellectual and rhetorical techniques it offers for developing and evaluating narratives about things that have not happened, and the ethical obligations it highlights to engage with future possibilities.

References

Allison, G. (2017). *Destined for war: Can America and China escape Thucydides's trap?* New York: Houghton Mifflin Harcourt.
Allison, G., & Ferguson, N. (2016). Establish a White House Council of Historical Advisers now. http://www.belfercenter.org/project/applied-history-project#!our-manifesto. Accessed 8 July 2017.
Baron, J. (2000). *Thinking and deciding* (3rd ed.). New York: Cambridge University Press.
Ben-Menahem, Y. (2016). If counterfactuals were excluded from historical reasoning. . .. *Journal of the Philosophy of History, 10*, 370–381.
Black, J. (2008). *What if? Counterfactualism and the problem of history.* London: Social Affairs Unit.
Carr, E. H. (1964). What is history? London: Penguin.
Cass R. Sunstein, (2016) Historical explanations always involve counterfactual history. *Journal of the Philosophy of History, 10*(3), 433–440.
Elster, J. (1978). *Logic and society.* Chichester: Wiley.
Elster, J. (2015). *Explaining social behavior: More nuts and bolts for the social sciences.* Cambridge: Cambridge University Press.
Evans, R. J. (2014). *Altered pasts: Counterfactuals in history.* New York: Little, Brown.
Ferguson, N. (Ed.). (2011). *Virtual history: Alternatives and counterfactuals.* London: Penguin.
Fogel, R. (1964). *Railroads and American economic growth: Essays in econometric history.* Baltimore: Johns Hopkins University Press.
Frase, P. (2016). *Four futures: Life after capitalism.* London: Verso.
Hawthorn, G. (1991). *Plausible worlds: Possibility and understanding in history and the social sciences.* Cambridge: Cambridge University Press.
Hawthorn, G. (2014). *Thucydides on politics: Back to the present.* Cambridge: Cambridge University Press.
James, W. (1956). *The dilemma of determinism, in the will to believe [1884]* (pp. 145–183). New York: Dover.
Judt, T. (2010). *Postwar: A history of Europe since 1945.* London: Vintage.

Kahnemann, D., Slovic, P., & Tversky, A. (Eds.). (1982). *Judgement under uncertainty: Heuristics and biases*. New York: Cambridge University Press.

Kaye, S. T. (2010). Challenging certainty: The utility and history of counterfactualism. *History and Theory, 49*(1), 38–57.

Koselleck, R.. (2004). *Futures past: On the semantics of historical time* (trans: Tribe, K.). New edn. New York: Columbia University Press.

Lebow, R. N. (2010). *Forbidden fruit: Counterfactuals in international relations*. Princeton: Princeton University Press.

Lewis, D. (1973). *Counterfactuals*. Oxford: Blackwell.

Liveley, G.. (2017). Anticipation and narratology. In R. Poli (Ed.), *Handbook of anticipation*. Springer International Publishing. https://doi.org/10.1007/978-3-319-31737-3_7-1.

Mitchell, A.. (2013). Stumbling into eternity. Blog post. https://worldlyir.wordpress.com/2013/12/10/stumbling-into-eternity/. Accessed 26 July 2017.

Morgan, S. L., & Winship, C. (2014). *Counterfactuals and causal inference: Methods and principles for social research* (2nd ed.). Cambridge: Cambridge University Press.

Morley, N. (2001). The transformation of roman Italy. *Journal of Romance Studies, 91*, 50–62.

Morley, N. (2014). *Thucydides and the idea of history*. London: I.B. Tauris.

Pearl, J. (2000). *Causality: Models, reasoning and influence*. Cambridge: Cambridge University Press.

Poli, R. (2017). Introducing anticipation. In R. Poli (Ed.), *Handbook of anticipation: Theoretical and applied aspects of the use of future in decision making* (pp. 1–14). Dordrecht: Springer.

Tetlock, P. E., & Belkin, A. (1996). Counterfactual thought experiments in world politics: Logical, methodological, and psychological perspectives. In P. E. Tetlock & A. Belkin (Eds.), *Counterfactual thought experiments in world politics: Logical, methodological, and psychological perspectives* (pp. 3–38). Princeton: Princeton University Press.

Tordoff, R. (2014). Counterfactual history and Thucydides. In V. Wohl (Ed.), *Probabilities, hypotheticals and counterfactuals in ancient Greek thought* (pp. 101–121). Cambridge: Cambridge University Press.

Tucker, A. (1999). Historiographical counterfactuals and historical contingency. *History and Theory, 38*(2), 264–276.

Tucker, A. (2016). Historiographic counterfactuals and the philosophy of historiography. *Journal of the Philosophy of History, 10*, 333–348.

Weber, S. (1996). Counterfactuals, past and future. In P. E. Tetlock & A. Belkins (Eds.), *Counterfactual thought experiments in world politics: Logical, methodological, and psychological perspectives* (pp. 268–290). Princeton: Princeton University Press.

Wright, T. J. (2017). *All measures short of war: The contest for the 21st century and the future of American power*. New Haven: Yale University Press.

Wrigley, E. A. (1988). *Continuity, chance and change: The character of the industrial revolution in England*. Cambridge: Cambridge University Press.

Political Anticipation: A Human-Centered Method

31

Marie-Hélène Caillol

Contents

M.-H. Caillol (✉)
European Laboratory of Political Anticipation (LEAP), Paris, France
e-mail: mhcaillol@leap2020.net

© Springer Nature Switzerland AG 2019
R. Poli (ed.), *Handbook of Anticipation*,
https://doi.org/10.1007/978-3-319-91554-8_93

Abstract
This paper is based on a narration of the method of political anticipation's genesis ("A Brief History of Political Anticipation: From a Man's Talent to a Method" in Appendix). This narration indeed provides the raw material from which to empirically deduct some principles and mechanisms for a "method of political anticipation" with the intention to highlight the specific assets and added-value of LEAP's method to the topic of Anticipation as a whole. Transversally, the paper will focus on and provide arguments to the human dimension of Political Anticipation whose concept, aims, and method appear as a humble but meaningful contribution to a humanistic approach of future sciences.

Keywords
Anticipation · Human · Method · Network · Humanism · Future

Introduction

The expression "political anticipation" was first coined in 2005 when Franck Biancheri (1961–2012) and Marie-Hélène Caillol created the Laboratoire européen d'Anticipation Politique (LEAP). However, the history of this concept was – at that time already – anchored in 20 years of European political activism, and networking, with a gradual conceptualization of the need for European policy-making to give itself previsional capacity.

Political anticipation comes from the talent of a man, Franck Biancheri, to anticipate properly events and changes, and to deduct actions or strategic recommendations from these anticipations... a man who didn't believe in God-given talents, and tried to understand where he got that ability from.

This 25-year-long reflexion led him to gradually forge the concept of "political anticipation." And in 2009, in the framework of a partnership between LEAP and the Sorbonne University which resulted in a first series of training sessions to "political anticipation," the first elements of a method were laid down in the form of the embryotic *Manual of Political Anticipation* (Caillol (2010), Ed. Anticipolis).

Since then, LEAP's political anticipation-related work has gained increasing attention from academia and public institutions, enabling the embryotic method and concept to be investigated further. Hence a series of written articles and oral contributions (to name the two most prominent, 2012: Taylor & Francis – *Political anticipation: observing and understanding global socio-economic trends with a view to guide the decision-making processes*, under the direction of Professor Mihai Nadin (International Journal of General Systems, Special issue on Anticipation, Vol 41 Number 1 January 2012 – ISSN: 0308–1079); and 2016: Springer – *Political Anticipation and Networks: Creating Anticipatory Systems for Government and Society, extrait de Anticipation Across Disciplines*, Editor Mihai Nadin (Cognitive systems Monograph 29 – ISSN: 1867–4925)).

The subject of Political Anticipation is an open field of investigation which social, political, and hard scientists, as well as historians, psychologists, and computer scientists, are invited to join. Thus LEAP's purpose perfectly matches this hand-book's goal as described in R. Poli's introductory paper: "*to establish anticipation of the future as a legitimate topic of research*," which it is therefore most honored to contribute to.

This paper is based on a narration of the method of political anticipation's genesis ("A Brief History of Political Anticipation: From a Man's Talent to a Method" in Appendix, which we recommend to read first). This narration indeed provides the raw material from which to empirically deduct some principles and mechanisms for a "method of political anticipation" with the intention to highlight the specific assets and added-value of LEAP's method to the topic of Anticipation as a whole. Trans-versally, this chapter will focus on and provide arguments to the human dimension of political anticipation whose concept, aims, and method appear as a humble but meaningful contribution to a humanistic approach of future sciences.

Learning 1: Three Prerequisite to Political Anticipation

A careful analysis of the history of political anticipation has conducted LEAP to identify three prerequisites combining into the predictive capability of Biancheri: goal, network, and will.

Goal: A Harbor in Mind

It can be estimated that since he created AEGEE-Europe, but more clearly since he contributed so significantly to the adoption of the ERASMUS program, Biancheri knew what he wanted, he had a clear vision of the general goal he was pursuing, which can be summarized as follows: "I want a Europe whose political orientations can be influenced by European citizens"; or even simpler: "I want a democratic Europe."

The characteristics of the "goal" in political anticipation is that it should be simple and general. But whatever the field in which political anticipation is applied (business, political, individual…), this goal is the precondition to any anticipatory attempt.

Defining one's goal is also a sound exercise. For instance, some large public institutions have a tendency to apply strategies aimed at self-survival rather than pursuing the goal they were created for. One of the most obvious examples of this sort of deviation is provided by NATO. But in fact, nearly every institution/organi-zation suffers this syndrome.

Interestingly, by duplicating the same clarification of one's goal to the private sector, it might appear that companies too, which intuitively seem more legitimate in pursuing self-survival goals, would gain from switching to mission-oriented goals.

This "desire" de facto creates a projection into the future. When Biancheri was 22 starting his AEGEE-Europe organization (1985), he probably thought that the future was an empty land of opportunities. But having seen the difficulty in being heard by policy-makers on the occasion of the ERASMUS action, having experienced the technical and political hardships of conducting a trans-European campaign in the 1989 European election, and having analyzed the risks of diversion of the European construction entailed in the Maastricht Treaty, it is certain that in 1992, Biancheri knew that his "vision of a democratic Europe" required an understanding of time-scales and a great humility in their face. Hence the goal-related projection into the future is soon followed by the awareness of time-related parameters of the goal's fulfillment.

The measured period of time that sprawls between now and the fulfilment of the goal then appears as both an obstacle and an ally: an obstacle in the sense that it is an unavoidable wall separating the individual from the fulfilment of his desire, requiring patience; an ally because this period of time is what is needed for the individual to implement his strategy, requiring action.

This originally void period of time, therefore, fills itself with ideas of actions designed to pave the way to the goal – more densely in the near future. But in the process of proactively filling it in with projects, this time-length also fills itself with data. For instance, events are scheduled according to a number of considerations such as vacation or no vacation, parliamentary agendas, media presence related to bigger events, and expressed political priorities here or there. For our scheduled actions to increase the chances of success and influence, they need to take into consideration a future environment – analyzing the best location, time, and subject according to a given environment that spreads into the future and requires to be explored.

In parallel to this action-related filling-in of the future, and as experience piles up (successes, failures, and the understanding of the springs at work behind), the punctual goal-related projection into the future growingly appears as a moving horizon, whose fulfillment can only be incomplete and temporary. This is what Biancheri revealed when he started using the word "democratization" instead of "democracy": there is no such thing as an eternal and perfect state of democracy, what matters is the relentless effort in this direction; but a democratic Europe is an ideal state that will constantly be challenged by a changing environment.

At this stage, the picture of how the future must be understood and therefore tackled is complete and anticipatory capability can begin.

Network: The Anchorage to the Reality of Concern

Once the goal is set and a projection toward the future is established, the strategy to reach the aim requires the best possible information on the environment/ landscape ahead.

The future is full of factual data: scheduled events, actor's projects and strategies, observable trends, etc. These data of the future combined together enable to draw a map of the territory where the road to one's goal will be built. In order to get the clearer possible picture of this territory, the best possible system of information is required to get as many data as possible.

The good news is that in order to reach a goal in a complex world where having an influence is difficult, one needs to connect to large numbers of people. Then there is a mirror effect between those people needed in order to influence a reality and the connection these people provide in understanding this reality.

Franck Biancheri's European goal required the construction of a large network of European students in order to gain quantitative legitimacy. And simultaneously this large network became Biancheri's best system of information on the reality he wanted to influence. Everything was consistent: a long-term and ambitious European goal, requiring a large group of European youth, providing an optimal information system on Europe's historical, cultural, psychological,. . . realities.

Degree of ambition – size of the network

Time needed to reach a goal – youth of the network

Physical space concerned – citizens from the same space
    (a network is a miniature of the social entity aimed at)

And that was in 1985, long before the Internet was born. . . .! What Franck Biancheri created at that time was somehow a feat. Today, at the time of Internet, building human networks is much simpler.

A network is an extension of oneself, considerably enhancing one's capacity to connect to the reality he/she's interested in, to integrate other ways of thinking and acting, other perspectives on things, other problematics, etc. And the individual at the center of the network he/she created around him/herself is the catalyst, the synthesizer of this enhanced level of reality.

The human network-based system of information (or system of connection to reality) is far more complete than a technical fact-based one: no matter the amount of information a machine is capable of recording and digesting, it will never integrate the human dimension, the psychological interactions, the longings and desires, emotions, dreams and angers, madness and stupidity too, which fabricate the future. The future is a human science.

The specificities of the network Franck Biancheri created around himself at the beginning of his career with his student association AEGEE-Europe are the following:

- Young: aged between 18 and 25 mostly – therefore open-minded and hopeful
- European: from all over the EU – therefore representative of Europe's cultural and linguistic diversity
- City-based: Biancheri's organizations were also "with no national level" and the AEGEE-Europe organization was conceived as a "local antennae"-based network where "local" meant city – not university or region – seen as the most obvious, nonconflictual, and structuring social dimension of the individual – therefore deeply anchored
- Multidisciplinary: contrary to many subject-based European student associations (law students, etc.), AEGEE-Europe was/is a multidisciplinary organization – therefore concerned by all aspects of social and economic life

The ways he connected to his network are interesting to clarify too:

- Exchanging information
- Discussing
- Sharing his vision
- Convincing
- Travelling
- Making conferences
- Making friends
- Making love
- Partying
- Fighting
- Failing
- Being betrayed

Elements of Franck Biancheri's network theory:

- The strength of a network is defined by the strength of its weakest link
- A network of a group of people motivated by a common goal and energized by a common system of information
- Network versus pyramid, horizontal versus vertical, center versus top
- Transparency: power is gained from the amount of information shared, not from the amount of information owned
- Information-sharing is the "electricity" that connects the network's components together

Reproducibility: When Franck Biancheri passed away, Marie-Hélène Caillol took his place and became the new center of the network he had left. Marie-Hélène Caillol had been working in his vicinity during 20 years. Nevertheless, when she shifted to the very center and became the person traveling, making speeches, and discussing throughout Europe, her perspective on European realities changed. The feeling was similar to having moved up the mountain and discovering a wider landscape in Europe.

She experienced another similar change in perspective when she launched in 2015 the Euro-BRICS network, *de facto* aimed at tackling global issues this time. The Euro-BRICS project had been created in 2009 by Biancheri and herself based on small academic seminars, with highly innovating discussions taking place but not yet any special change in perspective. It's only when she created the Euro-BRICS Youth Platform and by meeting them physically that she experienced this new change in perspective. This time she had the nearly physical feeling of being on the highest mountain, with a clear view of global challenges and solutions.

These two nearly physical experiences in her mind confirmed the intuition of the conceptual power of human-networking.

As LEAP develops its method, it growingly gets the idea that political anticipation is less about the future than about an "extended now." In a similar movement, the prime instrument of political anticipation – the above-described network – is somehow about an "extended here." Could it be that globalization and the internet have created the conditions for time and space to be desacralized? This is a tantalizing thought.

Will: The Energy to Move Forward

In order to link the anchorage to the goal, the observation of Biancheri's career shows that will, another characteristically human quality, might be the key. Will and somehow faith in one's capacity to actually influence big. Someone once said of Biancheri: "He doesn't know that it's impossible; that's why he will succeed!," a sentence very close to Mandela's famous "It always seems impossible until it's done."

This is a very good summary of the reason why Biancheri engaged himself in such ambitious project: because his longing was strong and his faith in the individual's power to produce social improvement was immense.

Madmen too can have strong desires and immense faith in their power. The difference lies in the taking into consideration of reality, which brings us back to the previous point. Patience and pugnacity (time again) is another distinctive feature.

The will component together with the notion of pursued goal accounts for the adjunction of the word "political" to "anticipation" in the name of LEAP's method. But from LEAP's point of view, anticipating for the sake of anticipating, i.e., with no motivation for change, is a rather meaningless exercise doomed to failure. When you have somewhere precise to reach, you really can't allow yourself to get lost in the desert.

Lesson 2: Elements of a Nonexpert Method

The Manual of Political Anticipation drafted in 2009 may appear at first glance over-simplistic. It certainly deserves developments. However, it has been established by LEAP that this method should in any case remain "accessible-to-everyone."

A Decision-Making Tool for Everyone

Whether a political leader, a corporate CEO, or an individual household head, good decision-making requires a thorough understanding of the elements of the decision's investigation file.

Indeed high-level decision-makers are surrounded by teams of advisers to inform these files. But these advisers are there to somehow "teach/inform" their superior who in the end must, alone, be able to build a nondisrupted linear sequence of fully understood arguments resulting in his/her decision.

For instance, in the 2008 global systemic crisis, it appeared clearly that big mistakes resulted from the fact that banking CEOs abdicated their responsibilities, blindly trusting technological scientists, and their miraculous algorithms that defied reason and negated the very possibility of a crisis.

The level of social complexity reached today is unprecedented and it is a major challenge today to upgrade the decision-making method. There seem to be only two solutions when faced with this challenge:

- To surrender our free-will to machines and artificial intelligence for the conduct of our societies
- To invent improved methods of information of our decision-makers

LEAP's method of political anticipation is a proposal in favor of the second solution, claiming that today's social complexity remains humanly manageable.

Taking the future into account in one's decision is one segment of the general upgrade required. In fact, it is a key one because any decision is a bet on the future. Political anticipation acknowledges the structural link between any decision and the future in order address it better.

Political Anticipation's First Revolution: Changing Mindsets with Regards to the Future

LEAP's method is a lot about pedagogy and changing mindsets. Mindsets in this regard can be changed along the following building-process of future-related awareness:

The first lesson it wishes to teach is that the future plays a greater role in our twenty-first century than it ever has in the known past, thus deserving greater concern. And that this concern for the future shouldn't be left, as it used to be before, in the hands of sorcerers, priests, chiefs, or experts. It is a matter of good-governance that decision-makers are given tools to rationalize the future, with a view to both feel entitled to produce and improve their forward-looking analyses and to refine their critical sense when being presented forward-looking contents (by media, politicians, their banker, etc.).

This omnipresence of the future is easy to create awareness of, by means of a simple exercise: take a newspaper and measure the proportion of content in fact talking about the future, instead of the past. "News" today are so "new" that most of the time they haven't arrived yet! Newspapers are full of "upcoming events," and speculations on what is likely to happen as a spiraling effect of every past or even upcoming event/fact.

The proportion we find in average as a result of this exercise is over 60% of content on the future. Based on this observation, people must be made aware that news being about the future more than about the past is a real change in paradigm. The problem is that, most of the time, contents in the future are not labeled as such, being on the contrary indistinctively mixed to "normal" past-related information.

So the second lesson is about structuring people's time awareness when faced with any kind of content production, whether others' or their own:

- Classifying factual information according to whether it is past or future
- Estimating how close it is from the present in both cases
- Distinguishing between factual information and speculative analysis

The third lesson consists of admitting that a special future-related critical sense must be developed.

Then comes a discussion on the specificity of this critical sense which will gradually lead the person on the path to rationalizing future-related speeches:

- If it's factual, how certain is the advent of the fact described?
- If it's speculative, who is producing the hypothesis? and what bias are they likely to have? Biases are everywhere which shouldn't dispel the content altogether; instead one's critical sense must be called: at crossroads between a content and its bias is a real information.
- Is the text clear or confusing? If it's confusing, the quality of the text should be questioned before one's intelligence
- Is the hypothesis properly argued? combining factual and referenced information with clear transitions from one argument to another?
- Is the tone rational or emotional? If it is emotional, it is likely to be misleading and manipulative

These remarks of good-sense instantly become the rules of production of future-related contents: any speculative argument on the future should be labeled as such, understandable, argued, and rational, and the conditions of objectivity of the author should be maximized.

Objectivity should be sought for by both authors and readers. It is a useful exercise to list one's own biases. Becoming aware of one's biases helps understand others' biases thus improving the capacity to reach greater objectivity and regain mutual trust.

Political Anticipation's Second Revolution: Asserting the Primacy of Human Specificities in Understanding and Building the Future

The method of political anticipation as presented in the Manual of Political Anticipation highlights a number of exclusively humane qualities as functional in the exercise of production of anticipations, giving an advantage of man over machine. Namely:

- *Imagination*: the requirement to be able to "think the unthinkable" in producing anticipatory hypotheses calls into the process notions of imagination and intuition.

- *Boldness*: courage is required to voice out "politically incorrect" hypotheses. As an interesting reminder, when Franck Biancheri started to announce a global systemic crisis coming, he was faced to harsh criticisms and attacks, and it was a piece of bravery to stand firm against such strong opposition.
- *Humility*: or the capacity to put one's ego aside, for instance being capable to admit one's error and learn from it. Humility is also needed to admit one's limitations while producing narratives on the future: making mistakes belongs to the anticipatory exercise. What matters is: aiming at over 50% successful anticipations (above mere chance); admitting and reflecting over one's errors; in any case, making relevant and well-argued incursions into the future.
- *Independence*: in the quest for objectivity required by the method of political anticipation, independence is key, whether financial, ideological, hierarchical, structural, etc. Free-thinking, free-lancing, free-will,... freedom is called into the process of appropriation of the future.
- *Empathy*: we mentioned already in the chapter on networking the importance of a beyond-facts connection to the social fabric. Let's call "empathy" this mix of emotions, intuitions, waves, feelings, and nonrationalizable data gathered through human interactions, in fact so essential to the production of hypotheses in political anticipation.

Political Anticipation's Third Revolution: Reasserting the Competitiveness of Human Brain on Artificial Intelligence in Building a Performing Information System

All the elements previously described in this article aim at highlighting the centrality of the human being in political anticipation proved in its genesis, aim and mission, and qualities required. All these aspects contribute to a set of conditions favorable to the production of valid anticipations based on the normal information tools.

For instance, political anticipation systematically rejects the use of "secret" information due to the following reasoning: secrecy is unprovable and therefore unusable. Because political anticipation is an accessible-to-everyone method, it makes the choice of building its analyses on accessible-to-everyone knowledge. It is also a means to avoid madness or radicalization.

Therefore sources used in political anticipation are mostly mainstream. What creates a perspective and enhanced objectivity is the interdisciplinarity and interculturality of the information gathered. LEAP's information watch consists of following a variety of news and media in a variety of countries and languages:

- Following topics in the field of finance, economics, politics, geopolitics, society, technology
- Following reports on these topics from different perspectives (left-wing, right-wing, European, national, regional)
- Following international media from different countries in Europe and the world: French, German, British, Spanish,... but most important: Russian,

Chinese, American, South-American, African, Middle-Eastern, Indian, Israeli, Japanese, etc.

- Following media in different languages: the trans-European nature of LEAP enables a media watch in different languages, in particular those giving access to multinational media: French, English, Spanish, German, Portuguese

The kind of information watch an organization like LEAP has put in place, any institution, company, or even an individual Facebook page can as well. LEAP's very carefully designed list of followed media accounts for some 50 brands. Each day a minimum of 10 diverse sources are being scrolled down fast.

Internet is the accessible-to-everyone tool that enables any individual or group to reach a new dimension in its information system.

Language skills belong to the accessible-to-everyone enhanced skills required to produce anticipations: the complete command of English in addition to one's native language, as well as the capacity to read and understand at least one third language, is conditional to producing anticipations.

To be more precise, a Euro-centered information watch requires an individual command of three languages, one from each three big European linguistic families: Latin, Germanic, and Slavic. Command of a non-European language (Russian, Arabic, Chinese) in addition is an asset.

Producing Anticipations: Observing a Systemic and Dynamic Future Reality

Now that the context of production of anticipation is complete, it's time to establish what the political anticipator is actually looking at and what he's trying to achieve.

Systemic players: It identifies key collective players (governments, corporate, collectivities), their interests, and therefore their survival strategies. And it combines them together in a systemic way.

Dynamic trends: It characterizes trends seen in a dynamic way, thus distinguishing between long-term, medium-term, and short-term trends; but also determining these trends' kinetics: emerging or waning.

Trend change: It combines these trends together with a view to anticipating trend changes: acceleration, breaks, emergence of new trends.

Facts of the future: It identifies upcoming facts and events (elections, summits) to structure the landscape ahead and facilitate the effort of dating anticipations.

Making and dating hypotheses: It produces hypotheses describing trend changes and dating them.

Building a rational argumentation: It clarifies the arguments that presided over the uttering of the hypothesis with a view to check the validity of the argumentation (at this stage, it must be able to give up a hypothesis).

Assessing work: On a regular basis, it acknowledges failures and successes, learning from both and establishing the relevance of the vision of the future altogether produced.

Learning from One's Mistakes: A "Human System Learning"

Artificial intelligence is growingly endowed with the ability to learn without being explicitly programmed. This is called "machine learning." But it shouldn't be forgotten that this capacity to improve based on experience is a skill of the living first. The method of political anticipation makes no exception, having integrated to its routine an evaluation system, compelling anticipators to review their work on a yearly basis and assess the gap between their forward-looking bets and past reality (as described in the "Appendix"). This yearly exercise is salutary in many aspects:

- Looking back at the anticipator's understanding 1 year before as a way to take the measure of time and of his/her certainties
- Avoiding the anticipator from shutting him/herself up into a consistent but delusional intelligence system
- Creating the conditions for the anticipator to analyze why he/she was wrong and distinguishing between untimely anticipations, wrong anticipations but correct trend, wrong trend analysis
- Making corrections to one's overall trend sequences, so fundamental to the fabrication of factual anticipations
- In case the gap widens too much, questioning the overall legitimacy of a person or group of people to produce anticipations (and therefore to make key decisions) given their proven disconnection from reality.

At this stage, mistakes have not resulted in questioning the method itself; on the contrary, they often highlighted the need to observe the method more strictly.

On this topic of the evaluation, it should be noted that anyone or any organization somehow dealing with the future (decision-makers, journalists, political activists) could be asked to implement this kind of double exercise of (1) clarifying their understanding of the future (producing anticipations) and (2) assessing it (yearly evaluation), with a view to asserting their legitimacy in dealing with the future.

Lesson 3: Four Defining Features: Empiricism, Citizenship, Instrumentality, Humanism

As an outcome of this paper's careful analysis of Political Anticipation's genesis, four features emerge paving the way to a future definition of LEAP's method:

Empiricism: Among the striking differential characteristics of political anticipation is empiricism: a collective "we" gathered around the political project of a man, Franck Biancheri, has been producing anticipations which proved right over a period of 30 years; and this "we" decided to understand why and how it had this capacity, and to develop a method out of the answers. The empiricism of Political Anticipation is the first omen of its "vulgarity": what "we" can do, anybody can do as soon as he/she recreates the conditions of production of anticipations. "What are these conditions?" is what we must dig into. This way of putting things shows how much "our" History is a subject of study offered by LEAP to the community of scientists.

Why "Political"?

We are often asked if our method only applies to the political sphere. The word "political" is here to be understood in its etymological sense involving "city" management and "citizens," linking the individual to the group and asserting the role of the citizen in properly contributing to the management of his "city" (whether a continent, a country, a region, a real city, a company, an NGO, or a family). Political anticipation is therefore conceived as a decision-making instrument based on the assertion that it belongs to the individual to endow him/herself with the right tools to improve his/her capacity to contribute positively to the management of his/her group. Political anticipation thus claims to serve citizen empowerment. Like politics, political anticipation placed "good sense" as a principle. For this reason, it asserts strongly its "non-expert" nature.

An "Instrument"

Until today, "Political anticipation" has defined itself as a "decision-making instrument," a technical device in a large set of such devices aimed at making decisions. In this sense, it is a contribution to the wider-ranging "science" of anticipation as a whole. "Methodology," "technicity," "instrumentality," and even "empiricism"... political anticipation clearly belongs to the realm of a "practice" of the future. Even if it is often tempted to develop more theoretical approaches, its practicality is a differentiating feature that must be admitted. One of its strongest legitimacy also comes from the fact that it dares testing itself on a monthly basis through the production of 25–30 pages of anticipations each month in LEAP's confidential bulletin, the GlobalEurope Anticipation Bulletin, with a yearly evaluation as well. "Experimentation" is, therefore, one more token of this "practicality" of political anticipation.

A Humanized Future

Out of these three differentiating features, the "humanism" of political anticipation is already appearing: an empiric human-based technical device aimed for citizens to improve their capacity to make decisions and/or to judge of others' asserts that what the future is likely to bring must be taken into account in our strategies to influence the future. Political anticipation is both humble as to what the future is likely to impose on man and wilful as to man's capacity to adapt to and thus influence upcoming change.

   Along with Gramci, we can say that Political anticipation builds on "*a pessimism of the intelligence and an optimism of the will*," in a highly balanced relation to destiny: neither predetermined nor completely free-willed.

Conclusion: Political Anticipation, A Project of Democratization of the Future?

This chapter attempted to highlight the "accessibility-to-everyone" (both in its nature and in its intention) of LEAP's Political Anticipation, a proven method in terms of results and reproducibility.

The description of the empirical development of this method testifies the centrality of the human factor, first through the character of Franck Biancheri, the method's inventor, and second by identifying that Biancheri's anticipatory capabilities came from his network-based human anchorage to the European reality.

With no other tools than internet and network anchorage, first Franck Biancheri and then his successor, Marie-Hélène Caillol and her team, have somehow "mechanically" developed an anticipatory capacity tested and documented every month through LEAP's anticipation bulletin, the GEAB.

The gradual formalization of a proper method of Political Anticipation since 2009 by LEAP aims at a multiplication effect of the transmission of this anticipatory capacity, one identified by LEAP as a social and political requirement in the twenty-first century.

Indeed the intensity of the connection of each individual to a globalized social fabric, as a result of the combination of globalization and internet, has dramatically complexified the mechanisms of good governance, one that can no longer be left in the sole hands of a few political leaders, instead requiring a more collective approach to social management and responsibility, in turn calling for creating the conditions of a major citizen-upgrade.

Among the social management skills that need to be shared with the larger public for an improved participatory system of governance, is to be found decision-making-related future awareness and rationalization, knowing that the future can be considered one of the last realms of power circles.

Considering the technical difficulties political leaders encounter in managing today's complex social fabric, there is a temptation to surrender social management to artificial intelligence with the idea that algorithms will at some point be able to know everything about the future, a future from which man's change-producing action is *de facto* dismissed.

Transhumanistic visions of social management belong to predetermination theories, politically associated with authoritarian power philosophies. LEAP's first prodemocracy mission, therefore, appears consistently served by its method of political anticipation which calls for a humanism in future sciences, where a dose of free-will is reasserted and the influence of man's impact on his future.

LEAP's original method of political anticipation aims at contributing to detect irresistible trends, to identify future-bearer paths among these trends and to define adaptation strategies allowing entities to find their way towards these positive futures.

Political anticipation, therefore, positions itself halfway between predetermination and free-will:

- Since the future is understood as the result of men's combined projects, man's role is reasserted
- But also in a network-based (instead of pyramid-based) society, the amount of projects worth being taken into consideration in one's understanding of what the future is bringing has dramatically increased, turning the future into a heavy-weight in terms of decision-making information, requiring new tools.

The genuine characteristics of Political Anticipation drawn from its specific genesis (a man's talent), field of application (change-making), methodology (accessible to everyone), combined with the established successes (yearly assessments), proved reproducibility (transmission of the man's talent to a new team), and intention (keep man at the center of the fabrication of the future) provide grounds to assert that the complexity of the twenty-first century social fabric can be handled by man, thus dismissing transhumanistic visions of social management in the near-future.

The empowered citizen the twenty-first-century social fabric needs for freedom and democracy to remain at the core is one allowed to address the future. The rationalization/desacralization of the past, provided by historicization, must be balanced today by a rationalization/ desacralization of the future, an aim which political anticipation sees itself as a contribution to:

- Allowing nonexpert future-oriented thinking
- Trusting good sense and normal intelligence once proper information is in place
- Integrating errors into the process of anticipatory thinking
- Asserting the feasibility of the education/information citizen upgrade required

Consistent with its democracy-related project, LEAP has invented an anticipatory method that is a meaningful contribution to a process of democratization of the future.

Appendix

A Brief History of Political Anticipation: From a Man's Talent to a Method

Franck Biancheri's history is the *materia prima* in which to dig in order to understand the very precise circumstances in which a man happened to produce correct anticipations and invented a method to deal with the future as a European citizen.

A Very Citizen Education: French Republican Schools and Sciences-Po Paris

Franck Biancheri was born in 1961. Raised by his two school-teacher parents, he grew up inside a primary school on the outskirt of Paris. He's a pure product of French Republican citizen education... with a very functional brain as well. During his secondary education (his family moved to Nice for his *lycée* years), Franck is excellent in both literature and science but the system is leading him toward engineering studies rather. However, at some point in his first years of higher education in hard sciences, he decides to branch out into political sciences and enrolls in Sciences Po Paris.

From Citizenship to Politics, from France to Europe: EGEE I

It is in 1985 that the European history of Franck Biancheri, his networks and organizations started. It lasted until he passed away at the early age of 51 in 2012.

Franck certainly was ambitious. He was also very sociable. And he was extremely critical too. The three characteristics and others led him to constantly build groups in order to achieve the changes he identified as needed.

Europe appeared soon to him as a *terra incognita* for citizen action and political innovation. Thus he had the idea of a Congress to gather an assembly of students from Paris, Leiden, London, Madrid, Milan, and Munich at the invite of five Paris Grandes Ecoles (Congress EGEE 1). The event created such momentum that the Association des Etats Généraux des Etudiants Européens was launched right after and some months later a network of antennae throughout Europe was developing fast (today, AEGEE-Europe represents 13,000 students and 200 antennae Europe-wide). The aim was highly "political": to overcome the paralysis of the European integration process at the time, by creating a space for young Europeans to discuss European matters and present their ideas to both the European and national institutions.

The Adoption of the Erasmus Program: AEGEE-Europe

Anchored in a network, endowed with a vision,... then comes naturally a first historical feat. In 1987, Franck Biancheri through his European student network is informed about a project of European student mobility program (at the time, students were educated in their homeland or in the USA), which of course they are highly interested in. The program has been requested by national policy-makers and is being chiseled by the European Commission. But national Ministries of finance and education don't want to hear about it and are quietly burying the idea in the midst of widespread indifference: hardly anyone knows anything about the project... but AEGEE-Europe. Becoming aware of the danger weighing over their darling project, Franck Biancheri launches an ambitious action to rescue the project: visiting capitals, meeting with ministers, prime ministers in Germany, Belgium, The Netherlands, the UK, and France, they investigate on the reasons why the program is blocked in order to find the way to unblock it. They are finally been told that the French president is key. Hence they besiege the Elysée Palace, meeting President Mitterrand's advisers. They succeed in obtaining a lunch at the Elysée Palace between Mitterrand and his advisers on one side of the table and Biancheri and his board of European students on the other. During this lunch, they manage to make Mitterrand aware that the program he has asked for is blocked and in the evening that same day, the French president makes a public statement during a TV interview asking for such an important program not to be blocked by petty budgetary concerns. Three weeks later the ERASMUS programme is adopted.

Proof is made that, in order to influence the European level, citizens need to organize themselves at a similar level (no national student association could have dreamt to reach such result). (Biancheri (1996/2015)).

The First Documented Anticipation: IDE and the Fall of Berlin Wall

In 1989, 3 years after the creation of AEGEE, out of months spent traveling, meeting, discussing. . . throughout the continent, Franck Biancheri has developed a tremendous understanding of Europe in all its dimensions: culture, geography, history, clichés on each other, dreams, fears, and so on. Anchored in this profound connection to the European social fabric and moved ahead by his project of "European democratization," the perspective he takes on the continent's evolution is such that, along with a group of his student-friends, he drafts a complete political program and launches the first trans-European political party, Initiative pour une Démocratie Européenne (IDE). They will present lists based on one common program in three European countries (France, Spain, Netherlands), a feat until today unchallenged. In their programme is to be found this fifth point: "*an urgent need for the European Community to set up a "European policy" aimed at preparing for a return of the Eastern European countries in the following ten years.*" The media, who are altogether interested in their approach, find it "sweet" that this bunch of European youth are naïve enough to envision a collapse of the Berlin Wall. We're in May 1989. . .

The Very First Theorising of Political Anticipation: "Community or Empire"

Three years later, in 1992, year of the Maastricht Treaty, in his unfinished book "Community or Empire," here is how Franck analyses Europe's lack of predictive capacity:

> The inefficiency of the community action derives from two main causes: the absence of a capability to predict the future and the inadequacy of existing operational tools. The ability to predict is an essential component of any successful action, both at the individual and at the collective levels. The old saying "To govern is to foresee and not foreseeing is running toward ruin," illustrates this very well. Above all, to govern is to foresee problems. Some problems have no practical solutions, except one: to prevent them from happening. Hence, the importance of anticipating them well in advance. But, the European Community has no prediction capability. Neither the Commission nor the Member States are in a position to anticipate any major event. With the capacity to predict, or anticipate, one must understand and foresee problems relating to the implementation of a policy or action and design measures to avoid them. Indeed, all forecasts disconnected from any means of action are as useful as those of Nostradamus; which is to say, solely for selling tabloids.

This excerpt is probably the first document stating clearly Biancheri's striking future-orientation. Those who worked with him know that he was constantly projecting into the future both his vision of Europe (goal-orientation), and upcoming change and risks ahead (anticipation) on which he spent hours and pages providing rational arguments. The objective was always constructive: to describe and advocate for action to be taken (to adapt the boat to the climate ahead in order to avoid breaking).

Ten Years Whistleblowing: Prometheus-Europe

From 1989 to 1999, Biancheri headed Prometheus-Europe, a citizen organization working on the link between the European institution and the citizens, with a particular focus on the "programs" launched by the Commission in these years. Prometheus-Europe's idea was that these programs were the most concrete manifestation of the institution's will to connect to the citizens. However, these programs were run in a purely technocratic manner, and Biancheri and Prometheus-Europe decided to organize conferences gathering the potential beneficiaries (for instance professors from the EU) of these programs (for instance education programs) inviting them to discuss their criticisms and expectations with regards to the program. Based on these "consultations," Prometheus-Europe advocated for program improvements with a view to better connecting to beneficiaries, better understanding their needs, and hence communicating a better image of the institutions.

The baseline idea of Biancheri was that the Maastricht Treaty had increased the European level's budgets and fields of competence and that European governance had to be upgraded as a result, along three principles: transparency, efficiency, and democratization.

During 10 years, Biancheri and Prometheus-Europe struggled for these principles to be implemented by the European institutions and warned that in case they wouldn't, the European commission would experiment a severe crisis.

When in 1999, the Santer Commission had to resign *en masse* due to allegations of corruption, the event was understood by many in the institution as the realization of Biancheri's warnings/predictions.

From Risk-Warning to Future-Building: Europe 2020

Based on this recognition, Biancheri and his teams decided to launch a new project, aimed less at whistleblowing on risks and more at joining citizen and institutional forces to project a Europe 20 years ahead. The European independent think-tank was born in 1999 which spent 6 years on the reform of EU governance through a long series of "anticipation seminars" (EU Governance 2020, GlobalEurope, EU Neighborhood).

On the topic of EU governance, Europe 2020's initiative directly inspired the creation of a Task Force on European governance at the request of the President of the Commission at that time, Romano Prodi. During more than a year, European civil servants participated in both Europe 2020's anticipation seminars and this Task Force, culminating in a "Report from the Commission on European governance."

The failure of this Task Force in triggering change (the report's most interesting proposals were deleted by the Commission's Secretariat General who imposed a publication in the middle of the summer vacation, in August) reminded Franck Biancheri that working with the institutions alone was not sufficient. While he continued to hold these high-level seminars, he doubled the effort toward citizens again, with three major transformative moves:

- Turning the "anticipation seminars" into a book entitled "Vision 2020: Reinventing Europe 2005–2020"

- Producing a short version of this book contents into "14 strategic proposals" and submitting these proposals to a democratic test via a "Democratic Marathon" (100 conferences in 100 EU cities in 1 year to discuss these proposals)
- Launching the second experiment of the trans-European political party (Newropeans) based on the post-Marathon redrafted proposals (into 16 proposals) for the program and with a view to the 2009 European election.

In 2005, Franck Biancheri and his Europe 2020/Newropeans team anticipated the failure of the French and Dutch referenda on the Constitutional Treaty, they warned Michel Barnier, at the time French Minister of Foreign Affairs, during a top-level meeting with him at the Quai d'Orsay. They accompanied their warning with recommendations in terms of communication content, advocating for a critical look at past years of European construction in order to signal a strong will to move the project toward the citizens.

Not that Mr. Barnier didn't agree on these analyses. But, like in 2003 with the failure of the White Book on European governance, Franck Biancheri and his team were faced to the difficulty of transforming rightful (just), argumented (rationally explained), legitimate (based on grassroot consultation), and connected (reaching decision-making levels) anticipations into political action. Years later, this problematic – collective capacity to adaptation based on an individual understanding of change – resulted in the article "*Political Anticipation and Networks: Creating Anticipatory Systems for Government and Society*" (Caillol (2016), Springer).

Producing Anticipations: Theorizing a Method: LEAP (Laboratoire européen d'Anticipation Politique)

In 2005, Franck Biancheri launches two major organizations:

- As mentioned above, Newropeans is conceived as a second experiment of trans-European political party with a view to the 2009 European election and as a consequence of his recent conclusion that the European system would not adapt – hence going back to citizen energy: unfortunately, he fell ill two years later (i.e., two years before the election) and wasn't able to conduct the renewed political attempt to any significant result; nevertheless, his remote control combined with motivated team enabled Newropeans to campaign in all EU languages, in three different member States (France, the Netherlands, and Germany), on a unique program based on the 16 proposals described above, with no institutional, media, or financial support whatsoever.
- Laboratoire européen d'Anticipation Politique (LEAP), which comes as heir of Europe 2020, less dedicated to advising European and national institutions, and more to applying the now clearly identified (but still nonformulated) "method of political anticipation" and energizing the entire European civil society and beyond with the analyses, warnings, vision thus produced.

In this context, LEAP's multilingual monthly electronic Confidential Letter, the GlobalEurope Anticipation Bulletin (GEAB), was born on January 15th, 2006. The second issue sends out a "*Global Systemic Crisis Alert: The End of the World as We Knew it*," probably the most famous of Franck Biancheri's anticipations, as it has been estimated that more than a million people read it worldwide.

Interestingly, the public article describing the "Alert" went viral on the Internet because of the title's sequence "end of the world."

From 2006 to 2008, each month, the GEAB produced detailed descriptions of the US financial system's unsustainability, envisioned combinations of trends and factors likely to trigger break-ups, and put in perspective the inevitability of the big trend at work: a global systemic crisis. Over that period, the subprime crisis in particular is anticipated in detail, for instance:

> While these days big international players boast about the extraordinary health of international finances and about the record-profit margins made by hedge funds and private banks, the first mortgage lenders file for bankruptcy. Beyond the confidential OWNIT bankruptcy (#11 on a list of US largest subprime mortgage firms) between Christmas and New Year's Eve, the entire US mortgage industry is directly or indirectly at risk. Indeed Ownit was apparently neither a marginal nor a suspect player. The list below of the top-ten subpime mortgage originators established by Crédit Suisse shows that big names such as Wells Fargo, HSBC Finance, Ameriquest or Option One run risks of bankruptcy or colossal losses at any time, just like Ownit, #11 on this list. But it is also the case of major investment banks, as shown by the bond rating agency Moody's concern about Lehman Brothers' subprime mortgage bonds. And it is of course also the case of many financial organisations of lesser international fame, as illustrated at the beginning of January 2007 by the closing of Mortgage Lenders USA's main unit due to excessive losses on subprime mortgages. Ownit too started by freezing its processes and ended up filing for bankruptcy three months later. (The US financial system has already entered bankruptcy, GEAB, January 2007)

Over that period, the GEAB is worshiped by some and loathed by others, leaving none cold, but failing to be taken seriously by serious people until September 2008 and the bankruptcy of Lehman Brothers.

Then the GEAB reached millions worldwide. Subscribers include financial advisers, members of Parliament, CEOs, small and big investors, intelligence agents, journalists, and pensioners from Europe, the US, Latin America, Africa, and Asia. Its public announcements are spontaneously published on hundreds of blogs, translated in Italian, Portuguese, Russian, Japanese...

If Franck Biancheri and his anticipations failed in averting the crisis itself, at least they helped thousands of people make the right individual moves in order to get ready for the tempest: from CEOs to pensioners, testimonies indeed later reached LEAP on highly relevant decisions having been made after reading the rationally argued anticipations of the GEAB.

In 2009, prior to the London G20, as always eager to influence top decision-making levels, LEAP invested in a full-page advertisement in the international edition of the Financial Times to publish an "*Open Letter to the Leaders of the G20*," signed by Franck Biancheri, whistleblowing on the severe and systemic aspects of the crisis and suggesting three strategic recommendations among which the first one, a summary of LEAP's understanding of the key-lever of crisis:

The key to solving the crisis lies in creating a new international reserve currency!

The first recommendation is a very simple idea: reform the international monetary system inherited post-WWII and create a new international reserve currency. The US Dollar and economy are no longer capable of supporting the current global economic, financial and monetary order. As long as this strategic problem is not directly addressed and solved, the crisis will grow. Indeed it is at the heart of the crises of derivative financial products, banks, energy prices... and of their consequences in terms of mass unemployment and collapsing living standards. It is therefore of vital importance that this issue should be the main subject of the G20 summit, and that the first steps towards a solution are initiated. In fact, the solution to this problem is well-known, it is about creating an international reserve currency (which could be called the "Global") based on a basket of currencies corresponding to the world's largest economies, i.e. US dollar, Euro, Yen, Yuan, Khaleeji (common currency of oil-producing Gulf states, to be launched in January 2010), Ruble, Real..., managed by a "World Monetary Institute" whose Board will reflect the respective weight of the economies whose currencies comprise the "Global." You must ask the IMF and concerned central banks to prepare this plan for June 2009, with an implementation date of January 1st, 2010. This is the only way for you to regain some control over currently unwinding events, and this is the only way for you to bring about shared global management, based on a shared currency located at the centre of economic and financial activity. According to LEAP/E2020, if this alternative to the currently collapsing system has not been initiated by this summer 2009, proving that there is another solution than the "every man for himself" approach, today's international system will not survive this summer.

If some of the G20 states think that it is better to maintain the privileges related to the "status quo" as long as possible, they should meditate the fact that, if today they can still significantly influence the future shape of this new global monetary system, once the phase of global geopolitical dislocation has started they will lose any capacity to do so.

Interestingly, China simultaneously (March 2009) called for *"a new global currency to replace the dominant dollar, showing a growing assertiveness on revamping the world economy ahead of next week's London summit on the financial crisis"* (CBSNews, 25/03/2009). But its efforts were unwelcomed by Western powers. After a few years taking actions in this direction, China opted for its Yuan-internationalisation strategy alone instead.

It is in this context of extremely visible production of strong anticipations that the academic world's attention was drawn. In 2008, a professor of history of the Sorbonne University, Edouard Husson, contacts LEAP to know more about the "Method of Political Anticipation." Two years later, a three-session training course to political anticipation is launched in the framework of a partnership between LEAP and La Sorbonne. During these sessions, Franck Biancheri shared with the trainees his ideas on the conditions of production of anticipations. A *Manual of Political Anticipation* (Caillol (2010), ed. Anticipolis) was published out of the notes taken during these sessions. Prof Mihai Nadin (Texas University, US) and Prof Roberto Poli (Trento University, Italy) both identified the *Manual* and connected to LEAP giving birth to publications and conference papers. The Method of Political Anticipation was academically born.

Legacy: First Convincing Proofs of Franck Biancheri's Talent's Reproducibility (LEAP Academy)

On October 30th, 2012, Franck Biancheri passed away after 4 years of illness during which he focussed his energy coordinating and in fact writing LEAP's confidential letter, the GEAB. This publication indeed gathered many strategic goals for Biancheri: limited energy investment, maximum visibility, transsectoral influence, field of experimentation of the method of political anticipation, and financial independence of the network.

Before passing away, Franck Biancheri asked his collaborators to carry on the GEAB after him. On November 15th, 2012, as if nothing had happened, the GEAB was released. It was time to prove that Franck Biancheri's anticipatory talent could be replicated, and give grounds to the scientific nature of the Method of Political Anticipation.

A small team of people, therefore, gathered into a new editorial team:

- Sylvain Perifel (chief editor), a computer scientist, who followed the first LEAP-Sorbonne training scheme to Political Anticipation and later actively contributed to Biancheri's publication work (GEAB, Anticipolis publication)
- Marie-Hélène Caillol (director of publication and editor), a sociologist, extensively involved in Franck Biancheri's project since 1992
- Marianne Ranke-Cormier (editor), a lawyer, extensively involved in Franck Biancheri's project since 1989.

The exact composition of the team fluctuated between November 2012 and December 2016 (today), but Perifel and Caillol are central since the beginning of the new period, regularly joined by occasional contributors, and joined on a permanent basis by Ranke-Cormier since mid-2016. To date, the team is stabilized.

Based on this new team, the GEAB has changed: more political and geopolitical, and less financial and economic than Biancheri's. But the spirit remains.

In order to assess the continuity, it is interesting to look at the readership. The financial advisers who subscribed in 2008–2009 are less, but the first fans of the GEAB spirit have stayed:

- Out of the 2000 subscribers, around 70% is now made of private individuals, while the remaining 30% of professionals come 1/3 from the private sector and 2/3 from the public (national and international) sector; the proportion was different at the time of the Biancheri GEAB with 50% of private individuals and out of the remaining 50% of professionals, 35% from the private sector (financial consulting firms, industrial companies, banks), and 15% from the public sector.
- Around 80% of these 2000 subscribers date back to the Biancheri's era, proving that people still find in today's GEAB what interested them first

But even more interesting is to look at the yearly evaluation figures. Since the beginning, every year in December, the GEAB team proceeds to an evaluation of its anticipations. The system is very simple: in January each year, a list of around 30 up and down trends is briefly presented. Eleven months later, this list is reviewed and noted (0 when the trend proved wrong; 0.5 when it is unclear; 1 when it proved right). This evaluation grid is meant to be noted by the readers themselves. However, the GEAB team produces a figure each year, rating their work of anticipation over the past 12 months. The graph resulting from the alignment of these figures over the years is the following:

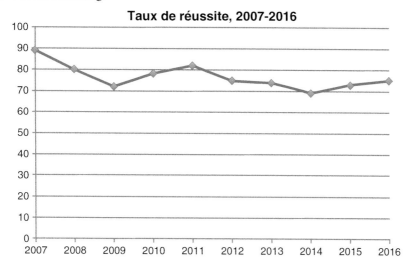

Taux de réussite, 2007-2016

Source: GEAB, 15/12/2016

Now here is a nonexhaustive list of successful factual anticipations (to be distinguished from trend analyses) made since November 2012:

- The oil crisis was analyzed in detailed in 2014, before the price collapsed; also anticipated, the nonspeculative conditions and the limits of the reappreciation (*2015 – New phase of the crisis: the oil systemic crisis*, December 2014)
- A Western car crisis was anticipated in the January 2015 "up and down" trends (*Crisis in the traditional Western car manufacturing industry*, January 2015)
- A crisis of European airline companies was anticipated as a consequence of the aggressive competition exerted by Gulf companies (*"Gulfies," after the oil, the sky is the limit*, December 2015)
- It was constantly anticipated that the Eurozone would not break under the Greek tensions, even at times when the media were overwhelmingly convinced of an imminent collapse (for example, *Greece will stay in the Eurozone*, January 2015)
- The return of Morocco to African dynamics was anticipated as a result of the identified change triggered around the Western Sahara situation (*Western Sahara 2016: End of the status quo*, December 2015)
- A severe political crisis in Turkey was anticipated and explained, in relation to Erdogan's Syria-related diversion from his political path in 2011 and the resulting inconsistencies; the possibility of a *coup d'état* was even mentioned in one paper (*The military or Erdogan, again*, October 2015)

- A change in gold price trend was anticipated in June 2016, 1 month before they actually reverted; this anticipation is all the more striking that Biancheri's GEAB was famous for having rightly recommended ever since 2006 a nonspeculative diversification of assets toward gold (*Gold: Golden times past times?* June 2016).
- Etc…

In parallel to this experimental validation of the reproducibility of Biancheri's anticipatory talent, LEAP created its "Academy" in order to pursue research on and develop training to Political Anticipation. The successes recorded in post-Biancheri LEAP's capacity to produce right and useful anticipations provided the legitimacy of this pursuit. The present article is a contribution to this general effort.

References

Biancheri, F. (1996/2015). *The emergence of Eurocitizens, a brief history of AEGEE-Europe from ist creation to April 1988* (Ed. Anticipolis). Paris.

Biancheri, F. (2017). *Community or Empire* (Ed. Anticipolis). Paris.

Caillol, M. H. (2010). *A manual of political anticipation* (Ed. Anticipolis). Paris.

Caillol, M. H. (2012). *Political anticipation: Observing and understanding global socio-economic trends with a view to guide the decision-making processes*, under the direction of Professor Mihai Nadin (International Journal of General Systems, Special issue on Anticipation, Vol. 41, Number 1 January 2012 – ISSN: 0308–1079). Taylor & Francis. Paris.

Caillol, M. H. (2016). In Mihai Nadin (Ed.), *Political anticipation and networks: Creating anticipatory systems for government and society*, excerpt from *Anticipation across disciplines* (Cognitive systems Monograph Vol. 29). Springer. Paris. ISSN: 1867–4925.

Commission of the European Communities. (2003). *Report from the Commission on European governance*.

Europe 2020. (2002). *Vision 2020: Reinventing Europe 2005–2020*. Europe 2020 Ed.

Europe 2020. (2003). *Fourteen strategic proposals*. Europe 2020 Ed.

Laboratoire européen d'Anticipation Politique. (2006-today). *The global Europe anticipation Bulletin*, LEAP's confidential letter (Ed. Anticipolis).

Nadin, M. (1991). *MIND-Anticipation and Chaos*, From the series Milestones in Thought and Discovery (English-German parallel text). Stuttgart/Zurich: Belser Presse.

Nadin, M. (2012). *Anticipating the political consequences of the internet: It's all about power*. Magazine d'Anticipation Politique, LEAP.

Poli, R. (2011). Ethics and future studies. *International Journal of Management Concepts and Philosophy, 5*(4). Inderscience.

Rosen, R. (2012). *Anticipatory systems – Philosophical, mathematical, and methodological foundations*. New York: Springer.

Selling the Future: Knowledge Brokers and Their Responsibility

32

Ariel Colonomos

Contents

Abstract

In an age of uncertainty, those who can anticipate revolution, the outbreak of wars, or which states might default are much in demand. The marketplace of ideas about the future is huge, and includes 'wonks', scholars and pundits who produce scenarios, predictions and ratings. The more opaque the future seems to be, the further the relationship between knowledge and power intensifies – above all the nexus between those who sell their expertise and those who consume it. This chapter discusses issues of responsibility that arise when experts make future claims.

A. Colonomos (✉)
CNRS – Centre de Recherches Internationales, Sciences Po, Paris, France
e-mail: ariel.colonomos@sciencespo.fr

© Springer Nature Switzerland AG 2019
R. Poli (ed.), *Handbook of Anticipation*,
https://doi.org/10.1007/978-3-319-91554-8_41

Keywords
Future · Predictions · Experts · Internatiional relations · Developmentalism ·
Modernization theory · Responsibility · Preditive markets · Truth · Truthfulness

Introduction: Selling the Future in a Market of Global Uncertainty

As Max Weber has pointed out, the rationalization and bureaucratization of
tasks are one of the landmarks of the development of Western societies. As
members of the Frankfurt School, such as Adorno and Habermas noted, the
repetition of tasks and institutionalization of practices accompanied the development of public and private administration, particularly during the 1970s, and it
was combined with the flourishing of the figure of the expert in the economic and
political spheres alike.

In this context of increased bureaucratization, experts are those that have a
legitimate voice in the exercise of future telling. Indeed, experts, like oracles in
ancient times, are consulted, and they send signals in the public sphere that is
conveyed by the media about a different set of issues such as the future of a country,
its foreign policy, or its economic situation. The expert is supposed to pronounce on
the development of future events and trends. He is asked to construct hypothetical
scenarios. His knowledge in different areas of the social sciences makes him
especially suited for this task and reassures the institution employing him.

I will stress one of the dimensions of the current situation. (My book analyzes the
effects of anticipations – predictions and scenarios – in the realm of world politics
more broadly. It shows the paradoxical effects anticipations can have, as, while they
are linear and are rarely capable of anticipating radical junctures, they might delay
possible futures and favor stability and status quo. Eventually, when a radical change
happens, anticipations help create surprises as they have a tunneling effect
(Colonomos 2016).) The more opaque the future of a particular sphere of policies
is reckoned – international affairs is the quintessential example of an opaque sphere
– the more urgent the demand. Experts sell their skills in a market, and their products
are views published by institutions that set their stamp on them (publishing houses,
collections of reports by think tanks or universities, and so on). Above all, demand
creates supply, first and foremost, of a collective variety. The supply emanates from
the consultancy company, where each consultant is assisted by other consultants.

This universe of predictors – and this is its paradox – lives off the uncertainty that
fuels the demand directed at it. However, far from being able to dispel it, expertise,
with its imperfections, in fact reinforces the sense of uncertainty. The contemporary
world is increasingly seen as a "world risk society," in a terminology that took off in
the 1990s and of which Ulrich Beck's sociology is at once a mirror and a symptom
(Beck 1992, 1999). Risk is a by-product of the uncertainty created by the end of the
stability of the bipolar equilibrium. The more settled the perception of a universe full
of uncertainty becomes, the more expertise is called upon. The harder the future is to
predict, the greater the demand for predictions.

In the social sciences literature, experts have been characterized as "epistemic communities" (for a general definition of the concept, see Haas 1992). However, few authors have stressed their specific role in the making claims about the future. (They are exceptions though. In comparative politics, as it will be discussed further, see Gilman 2003.) It is important to understand the "market place of ideas" about the future where experts play in our knowledge societies such an important role. It is also important, in this context, to understand what tools we have at our disposal to make future claims. This chapter will address these issues showing how the evolution of expertise in different contexts since the Cold War focusing mostly in the USA while also pointing the normative implications of future telling for contemporary democracies.

Section 1: Studying the Future

Experts About the Future in the 1960s and 1970s

Futures studies have been nurtured by the thinking of different generations of scholars, among whom we find figures such as Gaston Berger, Johan Galtung, Michel Godet, Pierre Masse, Fred Polak, Jan Tinbergen, John McHale, and Tom Ritchley. Futures studies have emerged through the activities of academic centers of futures thinking and research, including Vatican's Gregorian University, the Turku School of Economics in Finland, the Corvinus University of Budapest, the Bucharest University, the University of Houston-Clear Lake in Texas, and the University of Hawai'i's Research Center for futures studies.

Indeed, the 1960s and especially the 1970s witnessed the emergence in both Europe and the USA of a new figure of whom there are numerous examples. However, the purpose of this section is not to draw a thorough historical account of futures studies It is more to highlight the role of some specific experts and futurists in the Cold War political contexts, in this case Bertrand de Jouvenel, Herman Kahn, and Alvin Toffler.

Bertrand de Jouvenel established himself in France, but also the USA, as a leading reference point in the nascent universe of futurology – a field of expertise devoted to forecasting political and economic phenomena. In the USA, experts on the future took up residence in think tanks. At the end of World War II and in subsequent decades, the person who best embodied this skill and these functions was, without doubt, Herman Kahn. This scholar of defense issues, with a particular focus on nuclear weapons, initially worked at the Rand Corporation, before deciding to go solo and founding a rival think tank in 1961, the Hudson Institute. More recently, consultants like Alvin Toffler have become masters of prediction, public figures sought after by journalists as well as companies and multinationals (let us cite one of his best known works, which made him famous and from which a documentary was derived with a protagonist commensurate with the role, Orson Welles: Toffler 1970).

Jouvenel and Kahn had some things in common. Their work in neighboring areas ensured their fame. The former published numerous books of first-generation political science on the subjects of power, economics, and ecology. The second distinguished himself with his book dissecting the stages of escalation in nuclear confrontation. The narrative cast chosen by Kahn is a compound of pessimism and optimism (Kahn 2009). He lays down the framework for the most tragic scenario possible by imagining the conditions for a possible nuclear confrontation. He then describes each stage as a moment of choice that can either lead to a point of no return or, on the contrary, check the escalation. Like Jouvenel, Kahn was eager to establish a scientific predictive approach with sound methodological rules to guide the composition of prospective scenarios. In his work, he also used analogies with the past. (The use of analogies is problematic. However, their function in Kahn is not so much heuristic as communicative: analogy serves as a language between the protagonists in a nuclear crisis. See Kahn 1968, p. 91.) Finally, both personalities were associated with conservatism. Jouvenel has a sulfurous reputation because he is accused of having been a collaborator during World War II (whereas others stress his exploits in the Resistance). Jouvenel himself believed that he was treated as a "pestilence" at the Liberation. As for Kahn, he belonged to the generation of "defense intellectuals" who were in the sights of progressive circles because of their links with government authorities and their pragmatism (or opportunism). In the view of numerous specialists – including academics, but also some of his colleagues at the Rand Corporation – Kahn's thought helped render nuclear war possible by constituting an endorsement of it (see Kaplan 1991, pp. 228–229). Kahn was also a provocateur, who declared loud and clear that he refused conformism and political correctness.

Both these figures innovated in their field and, thanks to their talent and personality, aimed to perform a founding act. Jouvenel and Kahn established structures for diffusing their thought and sought to validate their approach among politicians and economists. The histories of bodies of knowledge and political movements have something in common: very often their founders must institutionalize their charisma in order for their ideas to be perpetuated. Like ancient oracles, they are required to be at the center of things, to rally followers, and position themselves at the junction between several fields – politics, economics, and technology. In order to underscore their singularity (a word in vogue among some of them), their approach therefore has to be "holistic." Before attaining the status of "consultants," they must be, like oracles, consulted. For that, they depend on the reputation afforded to them by their audience. They must have numerous followers, and indeed the communications society makes it possible to reach the greatest number. But – and this is not incompatible – this audience must also be selective, for these new oracles require the approval of the elites who entrust them with their secrets.

Social demand can also ensure that futurologists' charisma endures. Although charisma is based on acting out a performance, the recurrence of demand for insight into the future tends to make people forget failures and evidence of a lack of capacity for clairvoyance. The routinization of charisma renders the experience of divination trivial on account of a certain regularity in an institution's work. Foundations, companies, and consultancy firms represent these new consultants while giving the voices of their assistants and successors the authority conferred by the divinatory qualities of their masters. Jouvenel and Kahn both left their mark on the organizations they founded – in the case of the former, the Futuribles International group, which was taken on by Jouvenel's descendants, and in the case of the latter, the Hudson Institute. Jouvenel ensured the reproduction of his thought in Futuribles. The Hudson Institute achieved more autonomy from its founder.

As for Toffler, he is the model "futurist," a term introduced by Time magazine in 1959. Three decades – the 1950s, 1960s, and 1970s – were crucial in the rise of the phenomenon. The anguish of World War II was still fresh, and nuclear warfare was the big question of what seemed like the tragedy of international politics, the Cold War confrontation between the USA and the USSR. But the knowledge available was greater ever before: capitalism civilizes customs, drives medicine advances, and so forth. As much as the enigma of the bomb, it was the prospect of 2000 AD, and the eschatologies deriving from it, which fueled demand for the future. Toffler's career followed the course of the Cold War: he published works on the major concerns of the time – technology, war, and what he declared to be the "third wave," described as a period in which civilizations are based on the knowledge economy (Toffler 1980).

Futures Studies: A Methodology in Phase with Emerging Models and Disciplines?

It is easier and more legitimate for a group to discuss and predict the future than for an individual to do so (as for individuals they can easily be accused to be charlatans). This social fact is even inscribed in the epistemology of the science of the future. The idea that the group makes it possible to think the future is prominent in a methodology which its founders named "Delphi." The "Delphi Method" made its appearance in the USA after World War II, emerging from the Rand Corporation, which had reached the conclusion that groups are better placed than individuals to develop knowledge and to anticipate developments, particularly as regards technology. The technique was further developed during the 1960s, when the US Air Force approached Rand with a view to applying this model in its internal planning. As in antiquity, military expeditions were the source of the demand for "futurity." The Rand Corporation then embarked on a research program aimed at perfecting the methodology of its model (Dalkey 1969; Helmer and Rescher 1959, p. 25). It conceived the following protocol: a person responsible for organizing and coordinating group work brings together various experts; each of them is sent a questionnaire; the experts combine their own responses and those of others with comments; anonymity is respected in order to prevent mimicry and the convergence of opinion toward the opinions of those with the most prestige and best reputations; and the interplay of questions and answers is controlled by the experiment's coordinator in and through successive iterations. The objective is to reach a consensus between the different analyses.

The Delphi hypothesis echoes a concern of the ancient world: the need to guard against the vagaries of individual, isolated predictions by giving the floor to an institution or group, which is given responsibility for discourse on the future. Pursuing the same goal as the companies of Jouvenel and Kahn, the inventors of Delphi sought to create a single format for discourse on the future. The group was to be its factory. Cicero feared the anarchy of single, deranged voices. Here the collective offers reassurance, for the opinions it produces are credited with objectivity. The collective has another virtue. It makes it possible to dissolve the responsibilities of the individuals in cases of error and to clear the names of both the teller of the future and those who consult him (who might otherwise be accused of having resorted to consulting a visionary and hence of having acted negligently).

Delphi has given rise to numerous variants and has exploited technological innovations, particularly the expansion of the Internet, whose resources it has utilized. In fact, computer science makes it possible to consult people rapidly and aggregate their responses. The Internet is also the ideal tool for those who believe that collective reflection based on the processing of individual opinions is the best way of accessing knowledge of the future and future knowledge.

Delphi has a particular importance in the history of models of sciences of the future. In the first place, it illustrates the link with the political and (especially) military spheres. Two adages – "to govern is to foresee" and "to foresee is to govern" – are fully realized. This model and its status also show the extent to which political institutions have to appeal to collectives: the model of science and the laboratory possesses that authority.

This process of collective thinking and knowledge about the future expands as we witness the development of "futures studies." "Futures studies" lie at the intersection of several worlds: academia, enterprise, and government. The World Future Society is one of the oldest. Founded in 1966 in Washington, it has almost 25,000 members from 80 countries. It publishes a journal, The Futurist, and gathers at annual conferences. Politicians or electoral candidates are frequent invitees. Such publications and meetings have also provided a platform for the ideas of Bertrand de Jouvenel, Herman Kahn, and Alvin Toffler. This society has helped to delineate the singular figure of the "futurist" or "futurologist," emblematic of a whole era – the 1960s and especially the 1970s – obsessed by technological progress and constantly examining its effects. Along with the World Future Society, we also find the World Futures Studies Federation (WFSF) that was established in 1973, as well as the Association of Professional Futurists (APF), founded in 2002.

The key task of futures studies, and the societies in which its adepts come together, is to create one out of many. They have to federate individual charismas without impairing them and to assemble disparate views from different disciplines around a point of convergence. With their publications and conferences, they create a unified voice, without obliging their members to give up their own hallmarks, ideas, disciplines, and intuitions. Such societies have a practical vocation geared to enterprise or government and have made constructing a legitimate body of knowledge their mission. The International Institute of Forecasters (IIF) forms part of this galaxy of futurology. Founded in 1981, it brings together specialists from management studies, psychology, economics, and the behavioral sciences. It publishes a review, The International Journal of Forecasting, which publishes academics, validating their work among their equals in their respective disciplines as well as in the international community of futurologists and hence among those who consult them, both in government and enterprise (Other journals such as *Futures* and the *Journal of Futures Studies* are also significant. See Dator 2008).

Another step might have been taken if academia had completely opened up to futures studies and accorded it the status of a discipline in its own right in newly created departments. But for now, the futurologist, like his group, is self-accredited. Distancing himself from his original discipline (often management studies or economics), he declares that he wants to work on the forecasting of social phenomena. As yet, there does not exist a science of the future that is recognized by academia, even if we find economic, political, or environmental forecasting and predictions in numerous research centers. Some of the most prestigious universities have a unit of their own devoted to study of the future. This is the case notably with Oxford, where the Future of Humanity Institute was set up in 2005. Associated with the Philosophy Department, primarily by virtue of the background of its director, Nick Bostrom, this institute gives prominence to disciplines like the neurosciences. The presence of this branch of knowledge in the context of futurism is not surprising. Firmly established in the human sciences, where it occupies an increasingly important place (especially in economics), it is what dreams are made of for all those who seek new frontiers of knowledge. Futurism, which has to apply methods that are themselves futurist, is particularly fond of the neurosciences, which have this function today, even if once their use is unduly trivialized, they will no longer be able to lay claim to it.

Section 2: Social Sciences Implicit or Explicit Claims About Political Futures

The Case of Sovietology: How Not to Predict the Fall of the Soviet Union

Among the missed opportunities to anticipate a major change granted to scholars and experts, the fall of the Soviet Union and the breakup of the Eastern Bloc may be regarded as a textbook example. Retrospectively, we may be astonished by the lack of clairvoyance exhibited in so many people. Obviously, there are isolated cases of brilliant, fortunate scholars and essayists who, against the grain, distinguished themselves by wagering on the forthcoming fall of the USSR. During the 1970s, this was true principally of Andrei Amalrik and Emmanuel Todd, as well as authors credited with a premonition that did not necessarily correspond to their core message. (See Amalrik 1970; Todd 1979; d'Encausse 1979. For a successful sociological analysis, see Collins 1995. Some intelligence experts accurately assessed the economic difficulties that the USSR was facing. See e.g., CIA 1983). However, it is undeniable that the majority did not anticipate the breakup of the USSR, especially the many Sovietologists of Anglo-American academia (for an overview, see Lipset and Bence 1994). This blindness is no doubt regrettable, but it is important to analyze its causes in order to understand what it means to predict the world's future or, in this instance, to fail to predict it.

This case is particularly important for a whole set of reasons. Let us first note the considerable size of the community of specialists on the Soviet Union, working either in American universities – particularly the most prestigious of them, like Columbia and Harvard – or in private foundations and research centers financially supported by universities, the government, or with private funds. With its Soviet studies departments, Western Europe was not to be outdone. There were also the Soviets who were experts on their own country and the thousands of international relations experts, the great majority of whom primarily studied the balance of power between the USA and the USSR.

The importance of the USSR's role in international politics compounds the exemplary character of this lack of perspicacity as to its future, as does the attention this state enjoyed well beyond the usual circles of specialists, academics, journalists, and advisers to rulers. The antagonism between the models of East and West was reflected in the lives of a number of Western societies. The Soviet Union occupied a unique position in their domestic politics, at the center of party politics, and of the existence of intellectuals and social movements. In other words, the Soviet system structured disputes that were political and moral and national and international, alike.

A community of scholars might certainly think that the quality of its members' work, and hence the quality of its collective intelligence, is not to be judged by the predictions they are capable or incapable of making. The social sciences do not lay claim to a vocation to predict the future, as a sincere epistemological belief that the social sciences can only be based on the study of established, confirmed data and not potential, hypothetical data prevails in the various branches of social sciences. Accordingly, they can only know the past and the present. Sovietologists and international relations experts could simply reject the criticism that they lacked intuition about the future: for epistemological reasons, social science does not have to bother with such criticisms.

But the argument of scientific purity is unconvincing. In fact, as an epistemic community, Sovietologists pronounced loud and clear on the USSR's future. Within their community, in their research centers and journals, they shared values that also served as standards for their interventions. They jotted an impressive number of publications and communications, in which they ventured extended conjectures about the future of the Soviet system, the Cold War, and the bipolar world. How could it have been otherwise? The financing of such a sensitive research area is largely justified by its practical repercussions – in this instance, the provision of precise knowledge about a country of crucial importance for Western states.

It would have been surprising had these scholars not pronounced on the development of their object. The balance between East and West was the key issue of the Cold War, inseparable from all the other political debates of the era. As formulated by classical international relations – notably that of a realist persuasion – the notion of balance implied, by definition, a fear of imbalance. Naturally, attention focused on the future and the search for that which, in practical terms, risked disrupting the status quo; at a theoretical level, pointers that might confirm or invalidate such hypotheses were sought.

All these factors rendered the consensus prevalent within these epistemic communities highly problematic, but also enigmatic. In fact, when the modernization paradigm enjoyed its golden age in the 1960s and reemerged, following a partial eclipse, two decades later, it would have been natural to judge the future of the USSR in the light of that paradigm's dynamic of modernization. Yet despite the obvious pertinence of the model, this was never the case, even if, at the height of the developmentalist wave, Barrington Moore and Talcott Parsons stressed that rationalism, possibly combined with tradition, might prevail over the forces of totalitarianism (Moore 1954, p. 231).

Appeal was also made to the thesis of convergence (Engerman 2009, 197). Seen through this lens, the two societies would end up converging on the same model, over and above the antagonism between the two powers. After an initial phase of radicalism, the USSR would supposedly embark on the road to modernity, gradually become more moderate, and, ultimately, adopt democracy under the influence of scientific thought and bureaucratization. This sociological doctrine calls for two remarks. First of all, it was to have no substantial purchase in Sovietology circles, because Soviet specialists did not adopt it and international relations experts, whose standard paradigm was the balance of power, did not accept it either. Furthermore, the idea of convergence, in so far as it assumed the constant progression of certain variable, was not conducive to grasping the rupturing effects that marked the fall of the USSR. It was too linear for its proponents to be able to think the radical turning point of the fall of the Wall.

Another theorization existed that would have afforded a clearer view of political developments in the East. However, although well known to authors at the time, it was ignored (Keohane and Nye 1977). This was the liberal model of interdependence, which would have usefully directed analysts' attention to the inevitability of the Soviet system's failure to complete the trajectory initiated by the Russian Revolution. Numerous liberals explained that the USSR was ultimately doomed, but their voices were not powerful enough to form a counterweight to the majority opinion.

Studies of the trajectory of the Soviet Union and its future in fact supported the conviction that the USSR, described as a system, was not liable to change and was perfectly capable of guarding against the vagaries of history. Few contradicted this thesis. It was in France that the widest range of opinions was to be found, not in the USA, which counted the largest number of specialists (see, in particular, Hermet et al. 1984). American academia, more constraining, allowed less room for originality, which was more smothered under the weight of normative pressures than in France.

Furthermore, the majority of those who argued against the thesis of Soviet stability were "amateurs," not scholars, politicians, or essayists. In a book from 1969 edited by Zbigniew Brzezinski, of the fourteen contributors, six, including four nonacademics, imagined the fall of the USSR. Conversely, among the eight who pronounced in favor of the system's continuity, six were academics (Brzezinski 1969). Finally, the most illustrious of the oracles of the Soviet Union's fall hardly stood out for his erudition in social science. This was Ronald Reagan, who in 1982 declared that the USSR would be consigned to the "ash heap of history" and was a sinking ship that everyone was seeking to flee. Going against the views of his advisers, he ended up being right, and his words, stamped with naivety, became prophetic.

The idea that the Soviet system must be stable and durable emerged in American Sovietology circles in the 1950s. The Soviet Union was represented as a totalitarian system analogous to Nazism, which constituted the quintessential model of totalitarianism. Among the numerous academics and influential intellectuals who thought in these terms after World War II, mention should be made of Carl Friedrich, professor of political science at Harvard, and Hannah Arendt, then holder of a chair at the New School for Social Research in New York, where she taught political theory (see the proceedings of a conference organized by Friedrich in which Arendt participated; Friedrich 1954). Adding to their voices were specialists on Eastern Europe like Brzezinski, who also had a brilliant governmental and political career, principally in the administration of President Jimmy Carter in the late 1970s.

Arendt underscored the decidedly innovative character of totalitarianism and added it to the political taxonomy, alongside the well-established models of democracy and authoritarianism. She described it as combining the practice of terror with an authoritarian management of power by the state apparatus. It was via the cement of ideology that the state exercised iron control over the past, present, and future. Arendt's descriptive operation, which introduced totalitarianism into the constellation of the history of political regimes, had a spin-off: it canonized the permanence of a system, which could no longer be regarded as an epiphenomenon (Arendt 1951). Belief in the enduring nature of a totalitarian regime emerged strengthened.

Unlike authoritarianism, which is defined by the fundamental role of one person in the maintenance of the state, totalitarianism is a system. Its characteristics, about which there was almost full consensus in the literature of the 1950s and 1960s, indicated an ex ante situation guaranteeing the state an advantage over society. It is based on an ideology; a single party generally led by one man is its center; police who terrorize the population ensure order; social communication is exclusively in the hands of the government, which also possesses a monopoly on arms and a stranglehold on a centralized economy (Friedrich and Brzezinski 1966, p. 21). This analysis was closely connected with a temporal vision: by dint of its crushing weight, the past is the rudder and vector of the present, preserving continuity.

In pointing out the structural variables of power, proponents of this model reinforced the idea that the USSR had a bright future ahead of it. Because totalitarianism represented the dominant grid for interpreting the Soviet Union during the 1950s and 1960s, those who thought differently had to accept going against the grain and sometimes being discredited. By way of example, I shall take the hostile reactions encountered by the sociologist Karl Deutsch during a conference organized by Friedrich in 1953. Presenting his thoughts on the reasons for the probable future collapse of the Soviet regime (Deutsch 2009), Deutsch explained that in all likelihood, social control was insufficiently strong in the USSR to maintain the population in the ideological framework which ensured the system's reproduction and the government's logistical and technological resources were powerless. Deutsch met with the utmost skepticism from other members of the group. He was especially reproved by Arendt, one of the figureheads of the gathering, who criticized his optimism. She employed the analogy with Nazism to demonstrate that totalitarianism was able to resist its internal critics. Even though the leaders of Nazi Germany, as well as a significant proportion of the population, were aware that the war was lost, the Führerprinzip remained intact (Deutsch 1954, 336). Defeat and subsequent occupation by the Allies had been required to be rid of it.

This reaction is interesting in more than one respect. It indicates the power of an idea around which consensus has been achieved and the moral pressure exerted on scholarly narratives of the future. It also illustrates a mechanism that is commonplace when making political predictions: pessimism is a warrant of seriousness and, consequently, is reassuring; it also encourages inaction and prevents changes of direction. Conversely, optimism is synonymous with naivety and, consequently, strongly discredited for the rash decision taking it encourages. The rejection of Deutsch's analysis is also explained by the entrenchment of another belief, which persisted until the late 1980s: no one could imagine that regime change would occur in the USSR painlessly. As in the case of Germany, only a major war could vanquish this monster. Overall, East European revolutions proved to be a challenge to theories of revolution, as most of them assumed a priori the ideas of violence, class-based revolt, and inevitability (Pop 2013).

To complement this rather inward-looking analysis of the logic of totalitarianism, a quasi-consensus was also reached on the idea that the Soviet regime was an empire, equipped with a veritable imperial policy and living off its control of its periphery. This interpretation was dominant in the 1950s literature and lasted into the 1980s, notably in the work of one of the most recognized specialists on the USSR, Seweryn Bialer. In a 1986 work, one of the decade's most influential books on the subject, he meticulously registered the frailties of the domestic Soviet political system, but also stressed the force of this imperial power, which lived off its control over its periphery (Bialer 1986). The USSR had intervened in Afghanistan, was a pronounced presence in Africa, and continued to control its satellites in Europe. For Bialer, the threat represented by the USSR had to be taken seriously by the USA. Such an observation, albeit accompanied by a realistic enough analysis of the system's economic and social condition, did not risk encouraging people to conceive of a future rupture.

If Bialer is representative of the great caution that reigned in American Sovietology, he also makes it possible to understand the absence of clairvoyance on the part of experts. As regards the global threat posed by the Soviet Union, he wrote that "[t]here is no precedent in human history for the type of danger now being faced, or the complexity of the issues that must be resolved" (Bialer 1986, 376). See also (Engerman 2009). Thus the book reveals the extent to which Soviet studies were in synch with analyses of international relations. In fact, in these two disciplines, a profound conservatism prevailed that was both epistemic and political. Soviet studies described the structural problems by which Soviet society was weighed down, without thereby deviating from its trajectory: the political system might well be in decline, but it remained stronger than individuals with nothing but their discontent to express. For the field of international relations, international politics was a game involving pursuit of balance, and the quintessential paradigm was bipolarity (Waltz 1964). Decisions were taken by individuals who were presumed to be rational, and by this token it was inconceivable that they would not seek to maintain the power to rule that had been conferred on them or which they had arrogated to themselves. The two lines of argument led to pretty much the same outcome. In addition, numerous bridges existed between the two fields of knowledge, with specialists in one using ideas and tools from the other. This interpenetration partially explains the weak impact of the idea of modernization and convergence. No doubt there were internal reasons for the decline of modernization theories, but they were above all discredited by models of the balance of power, which were considerable impediments to the representation of change, international and domestic alike.

By virtue of the importance of the subject and the number of the specialists engaged in it, one might have thought that Sovietology or studies of communism would have contributed to debates in political science. However, Soviet studies posted a meager balance sheet in terms of theoretical innovation (Fleron 1969, 10f). Authors rarely got involved in publications where social-scientific theories were constructed. Parochialism was the rule in a field containing a community of thousands of specialists with extensive resources, so that the ideas emerging from it were scarcely put to the acid test. This relative confinement confirmed specialists, who were strategically enclosed in their coteries, in their bias and did not encourage them to think about change.

Retrospectively, Bialer's book and the literature around it are illuminating. Science as it is practiced is reflection in successive steps on a terrain where each player seeks to occupy the central ground and where the best known call the shots. (In Washington, the expression most commonly used by those well-versed in an exercise common to academia and the world of experts is "run after the ball.") In the worlds of academia and expertise, to move from this central position is to risk preaching in the wilderness or being perceived as a visionary. This was the fate that befell all those in the 1970s and 1980s who sought to predict a date for the collapse of the Soviet empire.

There is a reason specific to the sciences for why scholars congregate in this way. In his famous work on scientific revolutions, Thomas Kuhn stressed that science is constituted under the impact of repeated consensuses (Kuhn 1962). A community generates a dominant paradigm on which the work of different specialists, who cannot ignore it, converges. The group lays down the law. Being wrong with the pack is not illegitimate in the academic world. On the contrary, it is a prudent stance that suits the majority of scientists and experts. Proof of the paradigm's inadequacy or obsolescence is required before the debate can shift. In the case of predictions, only the present, discrediting the initial belief by producing some surprise, is in a position to refute a dominant, consensus position. In this instance, the future-become-present de facto plays the role of arbiter in scientific disputes by helping to cast suspicion on a paradigm that has proved incapable of grasping a change of such scope. In the case of Cold War political science (Ray and Russett 1996).

Another factor helps shed light on this community's conformism: the normative bias and social pressure to which it is subject. Bialer was a mirror image of the community he belonged to. Experts on the USSR knew perfectly well that this state was a giant with feet of clay and yet were incapable of taking this reality seriously and drawing the conclusions that followed from their observation. Why? Such a view would have exposed its adherents to a dual critique with a powerful ideological charge. The conservative camp would have suspected them of minimizing the threat posed by the enemy and criticized a lack of patriotism. This is particularly striking in the exchange between Hannah Arendt and Karl Deutsch, but other examples are even clearer. Richard Pipes, a recognized conservative Sovietologist who was director of the Russian Research Center at Harvard, always reacted strenuously against anyone who advanced arguments in favor of the thesis of a détente in relations between the USA and the USSR. In his view, this was to give carte blanche to the US's enemy, when what was required was to take its threat seriously and counter its expansion, whose objective was "the slow, patient, piecemeal disintegration of Western Europe" and its "eventual absorption" by the Soviet Union (Quoted in Engerman 2009, 275). In her turn, Jeanne Kirkpatrick set out her views in 1979, which encapsulated a conservative position, faithful to the doctrine of the national interest and disinclined to idealism. Far from it being necessary to make the slightest concession to liberal optimism, which she characterized as sheer "masochism," dictatorship must be fought with all the means at America's disposal (Kirkpatrick 1979). Her reaction was all the more violent in that it followed a prediction about the fate of the USSR, which had been made in view of the emergence of a possible desire on the part of the Soviets to reform their system. The very idea of détente challenged a firmly established, ideologically sanctioned foreign policy. In advancing it, people risked encountering another obstacle, this time deriving from the progressive camp. It perceived the discourse of détente as a triumphalist profession of faith and an utterly suspect act of propaganda, because it brought to mind the lurid, exaggerated language of Ronald Reagan.

Tools for Governance: Indicators

Indicators occupy a place of the utmost importance in the fabric of the future; they are in fact the key elements of its grammar. These signs – which translate and try to measure phenomena – are at the junction of past and future. The reflection they vouchsafe of a past state of the world projects us into the narrative of the world to come, and sometimes indications of the future cease to work as projectors and become rearview mirrors.

Indicators possess a characteristic that renders them very attractive for practitioners in international affairs. To aggregate numerical data, a scientific methodology and approach are employed (Davis et al. 2012), most of the standards of which are international. They make two key operations possible: on the one hand, comparison of one country with another or one region with another and, on the other, the aggregation of data from different parts of the world, so that it becomes possible to construct a general trend thought to apply to the future of the world as a whole.

An index is a relative assessment of the performance (or performance failure) of entities within a ranking. Countries or companies are appraised and indexed in accordance with their economic, political, social, and environmental performance. The index is a quantitative and/or qualitative appraisal of an attribute. The data it comprises is drawn from the history of the institution being evaluated. It nevertheless has a very strong anchorage in the future. In this respect, its etymology is highly illuminating: the index (the finger) points toward the future. The indicator is defined as displaying a trend and is constructed to perform this role.

In the contemporary grammar of the future, indicators and predictive markets both have the same role. Predictive markets illuminate the future performance of a country and its policies, or they can be used like indicators typically are, to establish risk rankings in particular.

The phenomena measured by these indicators, such as economic growth, respect or non-respect for human rights, demography, corruption, or pollution, can certainly have different meanings from one country to the next or from one culture to another, as stressed by regional specialists and anthropologists. But figures or indicators speak several languages, and the concepts that they are intended to illustrate have a rather rudimentary semantics. They are words that generally have equivalents in the principal languages used in international settings and which are especially evocative in the flagship language in which they are habitually employed: English. Indicators are sold in an international market of knowledge at the request of companies and states. Their commercial dimension only increases their mobility and contributes to their universalization.

The future performance of indicators is itself subject to assessment. Their social existence is in fact based on an anticipation of their predictive nature (Rescher 1998, 89). To take account of an indicator, to use it and promote it (in particular, by publishing it in a report intended for a wide audience), is to reckon that it will reflect a possible future, or at least a future to which people attach importance and which they would like to see occur, or whose possible occurrence, at any rate, they wish to indicate. Thus it is predicted that tomorrow's present will confirm the future announced today: tomorrow should be what is said of it today.

Predictive Markets: Praising the Merits of "Collective Intelligence"

The preference for the collective has generated another tool: predictive markets whose role has considerably increased over the years. The future is the result of a match between supply and demand in the market of ideas. Predictive markets are now very much in demand. There is a public, political demand for knowledge of what is to come, in the different areas relevant to public policy.

According to those who praise predictive markets and as Philip Tetlock shows, an expert's views are no more precise than those of someone who does not possess the specialist skills the former claims to have in the field in which he pronounces. In fact, as regards the future, a group of nonexperts (who might, without any irony, be called "amateurs") have a more informed view than an expert (Tetlock and Mellers 2011).

The views of experts are inflected by numerous kinds of bias. In distinguishing between two profiles, the "fox" and the "hedgehog" (which he borrows from Isaiah

Berlin's reading of Tolstoy) (Berlin 2013). Berlin is referring to the theory of history that emerges from *War and Peace*.), Tetlock highlights one of the main problems affecting expertise. The hedgehog is the one who knows many things in a single field. Highly studious, persistent, and determined, he devotes his existence to the study of a single question or theme. For his part, the fox is a character who knows bits of things in a considerable number of fields; agile and inspired, he can pass from one to the next without lingering over it. Naturally, experts often have a hedgehog profile. Their vision is a captive of the blinkers of their paradigms, which vary little, are not adaptable, and are dictated by a community suffering from inertia. On an empirical level, they are also overloaded with information, which makes processing this data extremely difficult. All experts are subject to these kinds of limitations. But it is especially true of "hedgehogs," who comprise the main body.

The "wisdom" of the group lives off the qualities of the individuals composing it and its diversity. They must not only be eager to inform themselves on a variety of subjects and be capable of so doing but must also know how to distance themselves from their own opinions. Their cultural, social, and professional diversity is the best antidote to the bias that might distort the quality of their responses. Number is also an asset. As groups increase in size up to 100 people, the quality of their responses increases significantly; thereafter, increasing numbers have less of an effect, and eventually a plateau in quality is reached.

Expertise also comes under fire for political reasons. Supporters of the model of collective intelligence stress that it involves a genuinely democratic practice, unlike the elitist practice of having a decision validated by experts chosen by rulers. Collective intelligence is reputed to transmit to the summit of the hierarchy of state and society the information that has been gathered, without discrimination, from individuals, who thereby supposedly express their interest in public affairs and equip themselves with the means to vindicate their analyses. Thanks to the predictive market, the hierarchy of knowledge and decision-making is challenged. In this sense, it is a vector of democratization.

In the aftermath of 11 September 2001, the Pentagon assigned one of its branches, the Defense Advanced Research Project Agency (DARPA), the task of building an Internet site to predict the place and date of the next terrorist attacks on the USA (FutureMap). This project elicited indignation from Congress and was abandoned in July 2003. The indecency of an initiative in which individuals would be enriched or impoverished by betting on the future deaths of human beings was invoked to justify this rejection.

Here the future is the mirror of collective anxieties that the social body tries to exorcise by gambling and by representing them at one remove. The techniques employed in armies to train soldiers for combat pertain to this infatuation. In video games offering war simulations, a new world is gradually taking shape. (These games, where soldiers remotely control drones by indicating human targets on their screens, serve as a preparation for war. See Singer 2009.) But the use of technology to dramatize a more or less proximate future troubles people, even as it fascinates. It is criticized by soldiers and looks bad to civilians.

The US government has not abandoned the idea. A new organization has taken over from DARPA, Intelligence Advance Research Projects Activity (IARPA), which is the responsibility of the Director of National Intelligence. The project it has conceived is, for now, at an experimental stage. In an initial phase, a website (access to which was restricted) offered a list of questions open to wagers, to which people were asked to respond by a yes or no, assigning a degree of probability. The individual bet was then compared with the average of the bets, here called "consensus." The exercise enabled everyone to assess their skills by comparing them with the average of the other participants and also to estimate the value of this average as regards the occurrence of the various events on which bets were placed. (The program has now entered into a new phase. See the site http://www.goodjudg mentproject.com (last accessed June 2015).)

Section 3: A Normative Account of Future Telling

Truth and Truthfulness in Future Claims

As we see from those historical debates about the future of politics, future claims made by experts are often in the public eye of scrutiny and are either praised or criticized. Yet, we may wonder what are the most appropriate moral and epistemic categories according to which the quality of future claims can be assessed.

Truth is often mentioned in debates about the quality of future claims. However, when we have to assess a future fact, truthfulness is much more satisfying. Truthfulness is a category of judgment that presupposes the quest for truth, honesty, as well as cognitive faculties commensurate with these exigencies. (For a discussion of the difference between truth and truthfulness, as well as the links between them, see Williams 2002.) The criterion of truthfulness is all the more crucial in that we can use it ex ante. Whereas differentiation from the register of truth is required, especially in the case of anticipations, people often confuse the two – for example, when predictions are declared true and praised for their honesty or, conversely, when their presumed inaccuracy discredits them morally. This confusion is regrettable. In the domain of the human and social sciences, ex ante, forecasts can be neither true nor false. The reason for this is the absence of social laws of equivalent precision to the exact sciences. In social science, economics is the discipline which, in the view of some of its theoreticians, most closely approximates to scientific precision. It has to be said, however, that the predictive value of economic statements is also problematic, and this is understandable given the very practice of economics. Were it possible to know the future, everyone would engage in it, but no one would succeed, because every operator would have to be aware of the future claims of their competitors (and so on), which would help cancel their own predictions. On a theoretical level, the predictive quality of economic science is also challenged, notably by classic authors like Oscar Morgenstern (Betz 2006; see also Rescher 1998). A true predictive statement cannot exist in the absence of social laws (the social sciences only admit of explanations or correlations, which at best approximate to laws). Another reason enables us to understand why the criterion of truth cannot apply in the case of political and economic anticipations. Being closely or remotely linked with practical spheres in a relationship of reflexivity, they form part of the process they seek to foresee and illuminate. Listening to such announcements can contribute to them being realized or, on the contrary, to cancelling or delaying them. In these conditions, the difference between the true and the false makes no sense.

On the other hand, critical discussion of future claims can be based on a criterion of truthfulness. A scenario or a prediction is truthful on condition that it is based on verified and verifiable factors, selected and treated by authors who in principle possess the skills required to do so and who have a good reputation with people who are likewise qualified and in a position to confer extra credit on their claims. Whereas the criterion of the true is based on an objective assessment of reality, that of truthfulness is relative.

Are We Responsible for the Quality of Our Future Claims?

In the aftermath of the decision they helped to justify, we can distinguish between two different types of predictions depending on whether their truthfulness is verifiable ex post or not: either the decision which the prediction helped support helps unveil the forecast's truthfulness or it confirms its burial.

This distinction is important. Traditionally, an institution is accountable on the basis of an assessment of the past or present acts attributed to it. It is also responsible for the quality of its decisions – their usefulness, for example – which can be assessed in the light of their consequences. Very often, claims about the future make it possible to justify decisions rationally. Thus it is the institution's responsibility to project itself into the future rigorously and wisely.

A different form of responsibility might be envisaged here. Can an individual or institution be responsible for having hidden future evidence of the imputability of their action? To conceal or destroy evidence of a political fault, of a deliberate error of assessment as regards stated objectives, and of a crime is a dishonest act that breaks the law. What of future evidence that might have made it possible to test the truthfulness of statements that served to justify an initial decision?

Let us take an example in the field of security. In an article published in 1986, the sociologist and futurist Wendell Bell accused Ronald Reagan's government of having betrayed the trust of the American people when, 3 years earlier, he decided to invade the island of Grenada (Bell 1986). In Bell's view, the scenario that served to justify this intervention had been as alarmist as it was dishonest. If the USA had not acted, declared President Reagan, the government in power on the island, supported by the Soviet Union, would have mistreated American civilians, attacking them or taking them hostage. Ultimately, Grenada would have become a bastion for the export of Soviet and Castrist communism. Its airport would have been a hub for subversive acts in the Caribbean. In other words, the US invasion was supposed to avert criminal violence.

In 2008, Bell returned to his text and added an epilogue in which he drew a comparison with the US intervention in Iraq in 2003 (Bell 2008). He stressed the similarities between the two arguments used to justify invasion. An intervention that was as unjust as it was unnecessary was justified by a simplistic, abusive rhetoric. Faithful to a preventive approach, the USA claimed that, if it did not eliminate a state that had destructive capacities, was not an ally, and was sending threatening signals, the latter would inflict damage and suffering on it that both could and should be prevented. In both cases, Bell stated that evaluation of the reality – here appraisal of the state's strength and intentions – had been deliberately distorted. If he is to be believed, it is possible retrospectively to show that the Reagan government in 1983, like that of Bush in 2003, knew the evidence at its disposal did not entitle it to make such forecasts. The president and his advisers therefore lied. They carefully avoided mentioning, and even concealed, facts that contradicted their theses. They also allegedly falsified the evidence for their argument by adducing new fallacious reasons.

Let us assume that, generally speaking, the premises of the argument for employing force on a preventive basis are not unacceptable. (This debate is particularly intense and open to lively debate in law and in philosophy. Today, a minority of jurists accept preemptive acts (on the margin of the law), an even smaller number licenses prevention. Some of the latter discuss its possible legalization. The great majority of jurists believe that preventive use of force is quite simply illegal. In philosophy, views are more evenly divided (see Colonomos 2013). As the two US presidents, Reagan and Bush, claimed at the time of the invasion of Grenada and then Iraq, it is a government's responsibility to prevent future attacks which would probably hit American citizens if nothing was done to prevent them. The logic of such an argument is a priori even more legitimate if one accepts a form of symmetry. The initial justification would have to be consistent with the unfolding of the action it helped bring about. To destroy the possibility of testing the truthfulness of an argument becomes open to criticism. Certainly, the destruction of evidence for the truthfulness of the intervention's justification was not deliberate: Ronald Reagan did not invade Grenada to try to exonerate himself from the charge of not having done so for good reasons (unless it is believed he really had lost his marbles). As it happens, however, he was responsible for having destroyed the evidence for the truthfulness of his argument. On the other hand, if in the course of the intervention evidence had been discovered of the danger to America posed by the Grenadan government, the truthfulness of his statements would have been more firmly established.

Let us examine the consequences of these two mechanisms in the case of rating agencies. The agencies are integrated into financial capitalism and the world of banking. In other words, they are involved in processes they seek to foresee. Knowledge and action are imbricated here. Such previsions are reflexive: they have an impact on reality which they help to fashion. But their reflexivity contributes to confusing the issue. Thus, it would be necessary to award a social bonus (facilitating their action), and a moral bonus (rewarding them symbolically), to the person or institution that exposes their statements to evaluation – particularly when they figure in the effects prompted by their action. On the other hand, much less credit should be given to those who help make the truthfulness of their remarks unverifiable. Such negative credit will also be imputed to them when they are led to take new decisions and attempt to justify them.

As we have seen, morality and science coincide in the imperative of truthfulness, which is principally based on a concern for truth. But why are scientists and scholars the only ones subject to this constraint? Another requirement must be formulated, which this time directly concerns those who inquire among voices authorized in the matter about the future. It is in fact legitimate to expect of them too a certain honesty in pursuing this course. Who would think it legitimate to predict a war by arguing that extraterrestrials are going to bomb New York or to intervene in North Korea in the name of a premonitory dream revealing the happiness of a world liberated from the communist yoke after the capture of Pyongyang?

In a better world, the truthfulness of demand for knowledge would be the twin of the truthfulness of supply of predictions. In this world, politicians – practitioners with the power to influence criteria for stating the truth, as well as the selection of knowledge intended for practical purposes – must be induced to be concerned to obtain predictions on the basis of empirical elements deemed to correspond to the truth. They would also do well to demonstrate honesty in their approach, rather than seeking information that only serves to justify decisions they have already taken. In fact, the institutionalization of the future must not be motivated by a desire to instrumentalize knowledge.

More generally, the truthfulness of political demand is measured against acceptance of openness to change. In the event, practitioners must accept the possibility of being surprised by the information they receive and adjusting their behavior accordingly.

How to make the distinction between plausible words and those that are not or which might even be harmful? In classical political philosophy, the ruler must rely on prudence. But for practical purposes, the balance between politics and knowledge is invariably fixed in a conservatism of stability. Little credit is therefore extended to unduly singular knowledge, which contrasts sharply with the ordered, hierarchized, and institutionalized stocks of knowledge. Fear of the madman, suspected of sowing disorder, was the rule among the Greeks or Romans. In our day, isolated predictors are often treated as charlatans, and their boldness generally inspires mistrust. A clear preference for a causal, linear narrative validated by a recognized discipline is, in fact, more rooted in our cultural habits. This system has strong limitations as it creates blinders. It becomes all the more difficult to foresee and predict ruptures from these linear paths.

Conclusion: In Search of a Public Sphere of the Future

Because the future is an open-ended temporal prospect, it becomes a space for discussion. It acts like a magnet, drawing people toward a public sphere of deliberation with extendible borders. But what are the characteristics of this sphere and what is its optimal organizational form?

For the expert and the politician, but also for the intellectual and the activist, the future is a mobile sphere – a cloud, to adopt the metaphor used by Popper to describe knowledge (Popper 1972). Popper's image is interesting, for the future, as well as the knowledge we can have of it, derives from a similar alchemy. In fact, it creates consensus effects and convergence points where experts and politicians collect, attracting a substantial number of their fellows in their wake. But unlike "clocks," which (if we follow Popper's metaphor) impart a precise knowledge of the future, "clouds" are imprecise measurements of worlds to come.

The future is a cloud with mobile forms, which necessarily fluctuates over time. Perceptions of future wars, or of the recovery of a country's finances, change as we get closer to the deadline to which our previsions tend. These views and, above all, their aggregation are transformed with new information that can alter their substance.

What would the optimal forms of the space for dialogue be? It is important to underscore the constancy of the modes of relationship between the particles of the cloud. It explains why the future is rooted in stability, so that the effect of surprise is complete when a break occurs in trajectories that are too often assumed to be linear. Popper takes the example of a cloud of gnats, recalling that they fly in a cluster as long as they are not disturbed by strangers to the groups of animals involved in their orientation (gnats, birds, and fish) (Popper 1972, 210). To improve the quality of its conjectures, the group has an interest in welcoming members with a new profile. Expertise is certainly very often uniform, and it is difficult to introduce diversity into professions whose members are trained in the same disciplines and the same universities. But it is possible to encourage pluralism among the people who have a say in the public sphere. Curiously, intellectuals and activists are as unrepresented in it as simple citizens, and their role is not clearly defined.

This metaphorical digression illustrates certain features of the future by magnifying them. Knowledge of the future is deliberation in search of measurement that pertains to the register of consensus and, therewith, to the public sphere. Habermas must be credited for having brought out the role of consensus in the public sphere most forcefully. The notion of public sphere, central to his work, both in its theoretical development and from a practical standpoint, is in fact tied up with the idea of consensus. (In terms of practice, his interventions as an intellectual in different debates (humanitarian intervention, the functioning of democracy, etc.) give Habermas' thought a certain political resonance. From a theoretical point of view, the issue of the public sphere, central to his oeuvre, extends from his first sociological study of the formation of the public sphere to his cognitive, and then specifically normative, reflections (Habermas 1989, 1996). Habermas' thinking has been developed in his analysis of the extension of this sphere to the international or transnational sphere, notably at a European level (Habermas 1998, 2001).) For Habermas, the public sphere is the site where consensus is created and, reciprocally, states of consensus are veritable motors of the development of democracy and its ideas. It is in fact vital that ideas about political or economic decisions are debated publicly and that they attract the maximum number of favorable opinions required for their implementation. Does this also apply in cases where the reflection of those who wish to express themselves on public matters concerns the future?

Epistemically and politically, consensus represents a serious threat to the value of previsions (Solomon 2006; Sunstein 2006). The future cannot be conceived on the model of discussions where it is the present that is at stake, without succumbing to what Weber called "intellectualization," which he associated with the disenchantment of the world (Weber 1994). The scientist is caught up in the rationalization of the world; the figure of the expert is one of its constitutive figures. (The scientist does expert work: he is there to make rational predictions, so that Western societies are distinguished from worlds where "magic" takes precedence.) Reason is certainly safe, but at what price? For several reasons, this transformation is not a cause for rejoicing. Narratives of the future are consensual and based on a "normal" state of science which, in the absence of renewal by critique, generates undemanding thought. Thus, the social sciences and their blinkers are the offspring of this marriage between the scientist and the politician. Furthermore, the scientist also distances himself from his ethic of conviction. In the true sense of the term, he becomes a calculator, and his ethic ends up submitting to the exigencies of political forecasting.

It is therefore necessary to rethink the forms of the public sphere when it is a question of organizing discussions about the future in it. The future must become a magnet for all those who wish to defend their analyses, views, and experiences, in the framework of an enlightened public debate, whether or not they belong to the scientific community. With a proliferation of registers in reflection on the future, a first step would be taken to challenge the rigidity of the bureaucratic unity peculiar to expertise. The objects of the social sciences should not be the prisoners of clans, schools, or disciplines that regard them as their private property. The legitimacy of those who are external to think tanks should be recognized in debates where these applied science companies generally allot themselves a monopoly position. Thus, credit rating could open itself up to types of knowledge and appraisal of the economy that are external to the rigid, opaque boundaries of the rating agencies. Activists or intellectuals should be able to make a distinctive voice heard on matters of public policy. Discussion spaces should be opened up more on an international scale, contrary to the situation today, where the initiatives of international organizations are inadequate.

It has to be said that for now, the Habermasian "transnational civil public sphere" exists only on paper. The 1990s lulled us with the illusion of the imminent advent of a "global civil society" (Shaw 1994; Walzer 1995). Globalization, construed as increasing interdependence and circulation of people as well as ideas, was supposedly the platform for new voices in political affairs. Many theoreticians thought they saw the emergence of a global movement representing a counter-power to the sway of states and their sinister games of interest. But when they sought to transform their knowledge into models of action, they were to be disillusioned: the reach of their analyses remains limited. Today, it is difficult to see what distinguishes conceptual elaborations of an expanded civil society from other forms of internal political mobilization. Another defect of this model is that exegetes of global civil society, like its practitioners, have notably omitted to clarify the futuristic and prospective nature and scope of the various projects proposed within this public sphere.

A public sphere of the future, like a future public sphere, would encourage the explicit, forthright formulation of original knowledge that would impart new breadth to political debate, which is too often conditioned by short-term exigencies. No doubt there are already bodies like the various planning commissions, the ad hoc groups of the European Commission, and the reports of the United Nations. But expertise too often takes the form of a swarm of insects and/or flock of birds flying in group formation. That is why it has found it so difficult to contribute a reflection to the debate that breaks with the orientations of the institutions which sponsor it.

Let us take the case of historians. They are regularly invited to publicize their studies of striking phenomena from the past like wars, insurrections, revolutions, or the genesis of certain institutions, peace treaties, and so on. In engaging in these debates, they enter into competition in the market of ideas and the public sphere with people who are not professional historians. This dialogue, as well as the production and diffusion of more demanding knowledge, has proved its usefulness by helping to bring together the members of the various political communities concerned, national as well as international. The same should apply to scenarios for future worlds. For, epistemically, there is a similarity between past and future (Lewis 1979). The social sciences should therefore furnish themselves with the resources to conceive a plurality of possible worlds to come, just as historians produce different interpretations of the past or conceive counterfactual worlds.

This parallel should prompt us to reflect on the normative role of the future. In the form of the duty to remember, or the need to correct old injustices, we express our responsibility toward the past. We should remember that historians played an important role during the 1990s when a global debate occurred over historical injustices, whether the fate of Jews during World War II, blacks during the slave trade and slavery, or other communities such as the Aborigines of Australia or Native Americans. Responsibility to the future is no less incumbent on us, even if the voices pondering the consequences of reparations for the future of those communities are very discreet. An effort should be made for a broad audience, in sites where debate would have its rightful place. This follows both from an epistemic responsibility, inspired by a desire to know the world, and from a moral responsibility, which dictates working for the common good in full awareness of the facts, notably in the name of the obligations that bind us to future generations.

The construction of a public sphere of the future would have repercussions for the political institutions of the state and of supranational bodies. It would force its members to look toward a more remote horizon and would detach them from short-term objectives. All those who devote themselves to a political career must be conscious of the fact that they are responsible for the realization of future worlds. The quality of their ideas and projects depends on their compatibility with the common good of humanity and its future needs. For example, promises to protect the environment would be taken seriously, and political parties would pay more attention to defining their program and implementing it.

This discussion space would favor the entry into political institutions of young generations, who would be called upon to occupy an especially important place in them. Political institutions would be more legitimate if they renewed their members and if a genuine dialogue between generations could take shape within them.

In a democracy, predictions are an essential way of creating competition between arguments. The future has its apologists – all those who believe in the possibility of divination and its political uses – and is a channel via which the desire to participate in political life finds expression. It facilitates a synthesis between three terms: firstly, the political dimension of an argument and the type of project that it supports; next, the values it defends and the tradition it belongs to; and, finally, its cognitive and epistemic dimension – that is, its value in terms of knowledge, the reliability of the information collected, and of the skills required to collect and process the data.

Accordingly, predictions might well be an indicator of the value of a public figure and his or her reliability. We could trust some people's view depending on the reputational value of their predictions. For example, I have confidence in the view of a colleague because I know that she is often right. Alternatively, I know that a particular decision is bad and a particular prediction mistaken, because the person who makes it is always wrong (the case of a negative indicator). Futures markets are also markets in reputation. This is one way of discriminating between different predictors. Prediction (of an event) is always coupled with another prediction, which concerns the value of this anticipation and, therewith, of the person responsible for it. Experts, rating agencies, a think tank, an NGO, or the research department of a ministry necessarily has a reputation that evaluates the quality of their appraisals of the future. It is a fluctuating indicator of their forthcoming performance, based on an assessment both of their past exploits or errors and their current abilities. These people and organizations come into competition with a view to gaining credibility. They thus stake their reputation on the future. First of all, they put their reputation at stake by submitting to the verdict of opinion, which is going to pronounce on their intention to complete the proposed project and their ability to do so. Secondly, they are exposed in some cases to the test of the verification of the truthfulness of their claims (when the nature of their actions does not consign the moral and epistemic quality of their statements and decisions to oblivion). Via this mechanism, predictions become markers of social differentiation.

References

Amalrik, A. (1970). *Will the Soviet Union survive until 1984?* New York: Harper & Row.

Arendt, H. (1951). *The origins of totalitarianism*. New York: Harcourt, Brace & World.

Beck, U. (1992). *Risk society: Towards a new modernity* (trans: Ritter, M.). London: Sage.

Beck, U. (1999). *World risk society*. Cambridge: Polity Press.

Bell, W. (1986). The American invasion of Grenada: A note on false prophecy. *The Yale Review, 75*(4), 564–586.

Bell, W. (2008). The American invasion of Grenada: A note on false prophecy. *Foresight: The Journal of Futures Studies, Strategic Thinking and Policy, 10*(3), 27–42.

Berlin, I. (2013). *The hedgehog and the fox: An essay on Tolstoy's view of history*. Princeton: Princeton University Press. (1953).

Betz, G. (2006). *Prediction or prophecy? The boundaries of economic foreknowledge and their socio-political consequences*. Wiesbaden: Deutsche Universitäts-Verlag.

Bialer, S. (1986). *The Soviet paradox: External expansion, internal decline*. New York: Knopf.

Brzezinski, Z. (1969). *Dilemmas of change in Soviet politics*. New York: Columbia University Press.

CIA, Directorate of Intelligence. (1983, June). *The slowdown in Soviet industry, 1976–1982*. A Research Paper.

Collins, R. (1995). Prediction in macrosociology: The case of the Soviet collapse. *American Journal of Sociology, 100*(6), 1552–1593.

Colonomos, A. (2013). The gamble of war. New York: Palgrave Macmillan.

Colonomos, A. (2016). *Selling the future – The perils of predicting global politics*. London/New York: Hurst and Oxford University Press.

d'Encausse, H. C. (1979). *Decline of an empire: The Soviet socialist republics in revolt*. New York: Newsweek Books. (1978).

Dalkey, N. (1969). *The Delphi method: An experimental study of group opinion*. Santa Monica: Rand/US Air Force Rand Project.

Dator, J. (2008). Futures, volume one and two: Then and now. *Futures, 40*(10), 903–906.

Davis, K., Kingsbury, B., & Merry, S. E. (Eds.). (2012). *Governance by indicators: Global power through quantification and rankings*. Oxford: Oxford University Press.

Deutsch, K. (1954). Cracks in the monolith: Possibilities and patterns of disintegration in totalitarian systems. In C. J. Friedrich (Ed.), Totalitarianism (pp. 308–333).

Engerman, D. (2009). *Know your Enemy: The Rise and Fall of America's Soviet Experts*. Oxford: Oxford University Press.

Fleron, F. J. (Ed.). (1969). *Communist studies and the social sciences: Essays on methodology and empirical theory*. Washington, DC: Rand.

Friedrich, C. J. (Ed.). (1954). *Totalitarianism: Proceedings of a conference held at the American academy of arts and sciences*. Cambridge: Harvard University Press.

Friedrich, C. J., & Brzezinski, Z. (Eds.). (1966). *Totalitarianism, dictatorship and autocracy*. Cambridge: Harvard University Press.

Gilman, N. (2003). *Mandarins of the future: Modernization theory in Cold War America*. Baltimore: John Hopkins University Press.

Haas, P. (1992). Introduction: Epistemic communities and international policy coordination. *International Organisation, 46*(1), 1–36.

Habermas J. (1989). *The structural transformation of the public sphere* (trans: Burger, T.). Cambridge: Polity Press. (1962).

Habermas J. (1996). *Between facts and norms* (trans: Rehg, W.). Cambridge: Polity Press. (1992).

Habermas, J. (1998). *Inclusion of the other*. Cambridge: Polity Press. (1996).

Habermas J. (2001). *The postnational constellation* (trans: Pensky, M.). Cambridge: Polity Press. (1998).

Helmer, O., & Rescher, N. (1959). On the epistemology of the inexact sciences. *Management Science, 6*(1), 25.

Hermet, G., Hassner, P., & Rupnik, J. (Eds.). (1984). *Totalitarismes*. Paris: Économica.

Kahn, H. (1968). The alternative world future approach. In M. Kaplan (Ed.), *New approaches to international relations*. New York: St. Martin's Press.

Kahn, H. (2009). *On escalation: Scenarios and metaphors*. New York: Transaction. (1965).

Kaplan, F. (1991). *The wizards of Armageddon*. Stanford: Stanford University Press. (1983).

Keohane, R. O., & Nye, J. S. (1977). *Power and interdependence: World politics in transition*. Boston: Little, Brown.

Kirkpatrick, J. (1979). Dictatorships and double standards. *Commentary, 68*(5), 45.

Kuhn, T. S. (1962). *The structure of scientific revolutions*. Chicago: University of Chicago Press.

Lewis, D. (1979). Counterfactual dependence and time's arrow. *Noûs, 13*(4), 459.

Lipset, S. M., & Bence, G. (1994). Anticipations of the failure of communism. *Theory and Society, 23*(2), 169–210.

Moore, B. (1954). *Terror and progress USSR: Some sources of change and stability in the Soviet Union*. Cambridge: Harvard University Press.

Pop, A. (2013). The 1989 revolutions in retrospect. *Europe-Asia Studies, 65*(2), 347–369.

Popper, K. (1972). Of clouds and clocks: An approach to the problem of rationality and the freedom of man, Chapter 6. In *Objective knowledge: An evolutionary approach*. Oxford: Oxford University Press.

Ray, J. L., & Russett, B. (1996). The future as an arbiter of theoretical controversies: Predictions, explanations and the end of the Cold War. *British Journal of Political Science, 26*(4), 441–470.

Rescher, N. (1998). *Predicting the future: An introduction to the theory of forecasting*. Albany: State University of New York Press.

Shaw, M. (1994). *Global society and international relations: Sociological concepts and political perspectives*. Cambridge: Polity Press.

Singer, P. (2009). *Wired for war: The robotics revolution and conflict in the 21st century*. London: Penguin.

Solomon, M. (2006). Groupthink versus the wisdom of crowds: The social epistemology of deliberation. *Southern Journal of Philosophy, XLIV*(1), 28–45.

Sunstein, C. (2006). Deliberating groups versus prediction markets (or Hayek's challenge to Habermas). *Episteme: A Journal of Social Epistemology, 3*, 192–313.

Tetlock, P., & Mellers, B. (2011). Intelligent management of intelligence agencies: Beyond accountability ping-pong. *American Psychologist, 6*, 542–554.

Todd E. (1979). *The final fall: An essay on the decomposition of the Soviet sphere* (trans: Waggoner, J.). New York: Karz Publishers. (1976).

Toffler, A. (1970). *Future shock*. New York: Random House.

Toffler, A. (1980). *The third wave*. New York: Bentham Books.

Waltz, K. (1964). The stability of the bipolar world. *Daedalus, 93*, 881–909.

Walzer, M. (Ed.). (1995). *Towards a global civil society*. Providence: Berghahn Books.

Weber, M. (1994). The profession and vocation of politics. In, *Political writings* (trans: Speirs, R.). Cambridge: Cambridge University Press.

Williams, B. (2002). *Truth and truthfulness: An essay in genealogy*. Princeton: Princeton University Press.

Long Cycles and Anticipation

33

Adrian Pop

Contents

Abstract

Relying on long cycles theorizing in order to anticipate future economic, politico-diplomatic, and security developments and turning points at the global level seems a twofold epistemological challenge. First, because the long cycles theory has not specifically been designed for such use. Most analysts have used it to illuminate historical trends but only very few to anticipate future events. Secondly, because the idea of long cycles assumes by default only the existence of a set of interrelated recurrent trends and repetitive patterns. That would be indeed what one could conclude about the subject at hand, at least at a *prima facie* analysis. However, a retrospective deeper analysis of the tentative predictive value of the long cycles theory, which could be enhanced by applying methods available to mark evolving trends and wild cards, would tell us a different story. It is the goal of this chapter to review key tenets of some of the main representative authors of the long cycles theory, with an emphasis on the Modelski model, in the view of highlighting its tentative predictive value and suggesting possible ways of enhancing it.

A. Pop (✉)
National University of Political Science and Public Administration, Bucharest, Romania
e-mail: adrian.pop@snspa.ro

© Springer Nature Switzerland AG 2019
R. Poli (ed.), *Handbook of Anticipation*,
https://doi.org/10.1007/978-3-319-91554-8_85

Keywords

Long cycles theory · Power transition theory · Hegemonic cycles · Modelski model · Complex systems · Anticipation

Introduction

The theory of long cycles in International Relations (IR) has its roots in the theories of economic long waves, on the one hand, and the theories of war cycles, on the other. Whereas some authors who have developed and systematized it throughout the twentieth century emphasized either its economic sides or its political-military ones, other authors have been trying to combine the two aspects into a more comprehensive and cohesive explanatory theoretical framework. According to Joshua Goldstein, one can speak of three main schools of thought regarding long cycles, centered thematically on the preservation (the *conservative* world view), evolution (the *liberal* world view), and the overthrow (the *revolutionary* world view) of the existing order (Goldstein 1988, pp. 8–10). There are seven basic variables common to all schools, including prices, production, innovation and invention, capital investment, trade, war, as well as real wages and working-class behavior.

Long Wave Theories

As far as the long wave theories are concerned, the interest and recurring renewed interest in them coincided with periods of economic stagnation or even decline when the notion of long wave seemed suitable to offer plausible explanations for the problems in the world economy. Thus, after a first round of the long wave debate sparked by the Great Depression, the theory came back in the spotlight throughout the 1970s and 1980s during the economic stagnation phase, and again against the background of the global financial and economic crisis which started in 2007–2008. The first round of the long wave debate had as its outcome the development of four theoretical approaches trying to explain the recurrent phases of economic upswing and downswing (Goldstein 1988, pp. 23–25). These include the *capital investment theory* (represented by Nikolai Kondratieff, with capital investment and production as key variables), the *innovation theory* (represented by Joseph Schumpeter, with inventions and innovations, production, and employment as key variables), the *capitalist crisis theory* (represented by Leon Trotsky, with profit rate, class struggle, and production as key variables), and the *war theory* (represented by Johan Åkerman, Norman Silberling, and others, with prices and war incidence and size as key variables). Although after the 1950s the war school separated itself from the economic debate establishing its own debate in political science and sociology in the form of the war and hegemony research tradition, each of the four schools has been instrumental in shaping the lines of further debates in subsequent decades.

Nikolai D. Kondratieff, a Soviet economist deported in Siberia and executed for his ideas which were not consistent with the official Soviet view, noticed that there were approximately 50-year "big cycles of conjuncture," that is, long waves of economic dynamics (Yakovets 2006, p. 4). In an attempt to explain why periods of high economic growth rate are cyclically followed by periods of relatively slow growth rate, the Kondratieff waves (K-waves) divided economic history in periods of circa 45–60 years. Kondratieff developed his theory by analyzing four main economic features: prices, interest rates, wages, and foreign investments. He analyzed these four features between 1780 and 1920 on three states – the United States (USA), France, and England – concluding that during this time span there were three economic waves, each of them divided in three main phases: expansion, stagnation, and recession, which alternate cyclically. The first wave lasted from 1780 to 1844–1851, the second one from 1844–1851 to 1890–1896, and the third one from 1890–1896 to 1914–1920.

During upswing periods, which overlap with expansion periods, the economy would face an increase in prices, a development of capital investment, while during the downswing period there would be a decrease in the amount of capital investment, a fall in prices, and this would be always a period that precedes a crisis.

The K-waves may be divided into four phases or seasons, compounding cyclical upswing and downswing periods:

- Spring or the *expansion* phase, opening up a country to the world economy, which either occurs due to a change in technology, wars/revolutions, or to the increase in the amount of gold production (Kondratieff and Stolper 1935, pp. 112–113).
- Summer or the *peak* phase, which represents the transition from an expansion phase to a stagnation phase (Goldstein 1988, p. 7).
- Autumn or the *stagnation* phase, which precedes a period of crisis.
- Winter or the *trough* phase, which marks the transition from the stagnation phase to the expansion phase.

To these phases, expressing the cyclical dynamism of global economy, Joseph Schumpeter correlated the idea of technological innovation, in order to identify upswing clusters linked to cotton textiles and iron (1780s-1817), railroads, steam, and steel (1840s-1875), electricity, industrial chemistry, and the internal combustion engine (1890s-1920). Later on, the fourth and the fifth upswing were identified by other scholars as being linked to automobiles, plastics, and electronics (1940-1970) and information and telecommunications (from 1970s onward). Still, the correlation of innovation with an upswing moment which determines an expansionary period may be wrong, because, more often as not, innovation reduces the price of a product instead of increasing it – as it is typically for the upswing periods (Rosecrance 1987, p. 287). Moreover, after the 1950s some researchers noticed that the prices remained flat, although production tended to increase. Again, the K-waves analysis may be wrong and that was what provoked the debate between some scholars who perceived the years between 1940 and 1970 as an upswing of a fourth K-wave and those who saw it as a fourth downswing of the third K-wave.

Whereas Kondratieff focused on the monetary explanation of the long waves, Jaap van Duijn embraced the idea of innovation and combined it with the idea of capital investment in order to articulate a new version of long wave theory. He admitted that new innovations automatically imply the creation of new industry branches which will promote economic development. He also combined Schumpeter's idea of innovation with Forrester's idea of capital investment in order to put forward the notion of industry life cycle that can explain the endogenous continuation of K-waves. "Applying this concept to basic innovations, we can perceive long waves to be a chain of S-shaped growth paths, with each new peak being at a higher level of economic activity than the previous one" (van Duijn 1977, p. 560). The Dutch scholar postulated that, as innovations create new industries that start to boom, the economy reaches a period of prosperity that can last for more than a decade. Still, at some point, the market for these products starts to saturate. The amount of capital investments during this period is based on the perspective of strong future growth, but as the market is saturated, consumption decreases. Companies, though, are too much afraid to take risks by developing innovations and continue to rely on their obsolete products. The economy reaches a state of over-capacity, entering the recession and depression phases. Only at this stage does innovation start to take hold, as new technologies are being sought. Once the economy recovers, the new technologies would create new industries which could generate, in their turn, a new period of prosperity, thus initiating a new long wave. According to van Duijn and Forrester, the investment decisions look exaggerated during both moments of prosperity and depression, because during the upswing phase, investment decisions are based on the premise that growth will continue being unaffected, thus leading to overcapacity, while, during the downswing phase, capital investment would collapse below the threshold needed to sustain the economy (van Duijn 1977, p. 552).

The missing link, correlating innovation (the theory of Schumpeter) with investment (the theory of Forrester) is the notion of product life cycle. "The product life cycle is the development pattern of pioneer, expansion, maturity, saturation and decline phases one can distinguish for a certain product" (van Duijn 1977, p. 553). The idea of product life cycle is to indicate what type of approach towards a product a company must have, taking into account the market fluctuation during the different phases of a product's life cycle.

Scholars correlate innovations with both downswing and upswing phases. There are those, including van Duijn, who think that innovations represent a product of the downswing phase, because a crisis, or the end of a war, generates new innovations, and there are those who think that upswing moments are the most favorable moments for innovation, due to the infusion of capital that is pumped into the research and development area. Based on Schumpeter's idea of innovation impulse, van Duijn argued that there are in fact two types of innovations – the basic ones, and those that are merely improvements, which usually come on the downswing phases in order to revitalize market. These technological improvements (within the production process or products) are linked to investments, which could explain the "recovery" phase. According to him, "during the depression phase the time is ripe to introduce new products that are derived from new basic innovations. Thus the depression phase, which could last approximately 10 years, marks the beginning of new S shaped growth curves" (van Duijn 1977, p. 561).

War Cycles Theories

The war cycles theories were developed around two successive war/hegemony debates.

The first debate, coming out of the works of Quincy Wright, included three strands of long cycles theorizing: the first focused on 50-year cycles in war and politics, as represented, among many others, by the works of William Thompson and L. Gary Zuk, W.W. Rostow, Frank Klingberg, Jack Holmes and Robert Elder; the second focused on statistical search for periodicity in war data, as represented by J. David Singer's Correlates of War (COW) project; finally, the third focused on more than hundred-year war cycles, i.e., hegemonic cycles, as represented by the works of Ludwig Dehio, Arnold Toynbee, and A.F.K. Organski (1968, pp. 99–122).

In its turn, the second debate, growing out of the convergence of Toynbee's long war cycle and Organski's power transition theory has compounded, besides Organski's neorealist *power transition* school, the neo-Marxist *world-system* school represented by Immanuel Wallerstein, and the peace-oriented *leadership cycle* school represented by George Modelski (Goldstein 1988, pp. 123–124).

Organski's power transition theory belongs to the systemic theories of international politics and war, which focus on the analysis of the distribution of power in the international system, as opposed to the dyadic theories, aiming to focus on the relations between two great powers, and the state-level theories, focusing on the national attributes of states (Geller 1992, p. 269).

Like the long cycle theory, power transition theory views the distribution of power and changes within it, as recurrently generating conflicts which alter the international system meaningfully. Unlike long cycle theory, though, the power transition theory does not allot any specific periodicity to these events and also draws attention to significant nonstructural characteristics of actors, such as their status quo assessments (Lemke 2008, p. 696).

Power transition theory relies on the hypothesis that the international system represents a hierarchy of power, in which states are distinguished both by how powerful they are and by whether they are satisfied or dissatisfied with the international status quo (Lemke 2008, p. 694). Using these two criteria, Organski (1968, p. 364) put forward a hierarchy of powers in the international system:

"1. The powerful and satisfied
2. The powerful and dissatisfied
3. The weak and satisfied
4. The weak and dissatisfied"

The theory assumes that wars are fought among the strongest of states in the power hierarchy in order to change or preserve the status quo. By emerging victorious from an earlier great power war, a state becomes the dominant power and establishes the global status quo, i.e., the formal and informal rules by which the international system is governed. It is important that the dominant power has the support of the strong and satisfied powers (Kugler and Organski 1989, p. 175), as this will enhance its power in the face of a challenger and, thus, also enhance the stability of the international system.

In addition to the dominant power, the power transition theory focuses on great power challengers, i.e., states rising in power, so that they might compete with the dominant power in capabilities. Krugler and Organski postulated that the transition of power follow five stages: preponderance, pre-parity (the development of the challenger), parity (equilibrium of power between the dominant power and the challenger), post-parity (the challenger surpasses the existing dominant power), and the preponderance of the challenger as the new global power (Kugler and Organski 1989, p. 187).

When the rising challenger and the dominant power are at parity, neither side is able to reliably predict who might win the war they would fight. That is why the great power war is most likely to occur in the period of "overtaking" (Kugler and Organski 1989, p. 188). War is also likely to occur when the rising challenger is a revisionist state dissatisfied with the existing status quo. Overall, periods of world peace have overlapped with "periods of unchallenged supremacy of power," while periods characterized by an even distribution of power generated wars (Organski 1968, p. 364).

According to Organski, the optimal model for analyzing the development of a challenger and the path towards the transition of power is the sum of factors determined by the level of economic development, population, and the capacity to manage the internal system by the elites. As a result, we have the following equation (Kugler and Organski 1989, pp. 190–191): Power = (Economic Production per capita X Population) X Relative Political Capacity.

Organski (1968, p. 340) discerns also three stages of power transition: the stage of potential power, which refers to the preindustrial stage of a nation; the stage of transitional growth in power, which refers to the transition from a preindustrial to an industrial stage also being representative for nations that go through a process of industrialization and accelerated development, as is the case of China and India today; and the stage of power maturity, generated by the achievement of a higher level of economic development, as it is the case of the USA, Japan, and other Western powers which still observe GDP growth, but at a slower level than the one recorded during their stage of transitional growth in power. This is the stage that defines the relative decline of the USA and, perhaps, also the beginning of China's slower growth rate of the past years, as "the *power* of a nation may decline in the stage of power maturity, even though the nation continues to grow richer, more industrial and more efficient" (Organski 1968, p. 343).

L.L. Farrar Jr. is also a supporter of the war cycles theory, based especially on the types of war that may take place during a cycle. In fact, Farrar combines Organski's power transition theory with Toynbee's 100 year war cycle (Goldstein 1988, p. 120). According to Farrar, as part of a 100 year war cycle, probing wars precede adjusting wars and hegemonic wars. Probing wars are "those which test the state system but involves minimal violence, causes little change and may even reinforce the status quo." Adjusting war "produces moderate violence, causes considerable change in relations or indicates that changes have already taken place and registers them by altering the status quo, but does not threaten the system as a whole. A hegemonic war results in a high level of violence and seriously threatens or in fact alters the system fundamentally, usually as a result of one power's attempt to dominate the system" (Farrar 1977, p. 163). Farrar's cycle follows the pattern of probing war – adjusting war – probing war – hegemonic war, with this cycle repeating itself in European history, from 1494 until 1945, every 100 years. For Farrar, the period between 1945 and 1973 is dedicated to the probing war, a period of time that was closed by Nixon's visit in China, in 1972, the withdrawal of the USA from Vietnam, and the oil embargo imposed by OPEC against the Western states. Then, the period between 1973 and 2000 is reserved for the adjusting war. It would be followed by a probing war (2000–2030), which would then lead to a hegemonic war that Farrar envisioned throughout 2030–2060 (Farrar 1977, p. 175).

George Modelski, too, developed his theoretical model premised on the existence of recurrent hegemonic cycles of just over 100 years – around 100–120 years, i.e., equivalent to two K-waves of around 50–60 years.

For him, the long cycle represents "an interval of time comprising a global war (a systemic decision) followed by a longer period of general peace" (Modelski 1987, p. 36). If the global war involves all the great powers and leads to the rearrangement of the global system and to the appearance of new technological achievements, during the period of general peace, socioeconomic priorities may prevail instead of political goals (Modelski 1987, p. 37). It is a period of great social transformation, economic development, and improvements in the quality of people's life.

Each cycle comprises four phases, of approximately 25–30 years each. Whereas the first two phases have a high preference for order, the last two have a low preference for order. The four are as follows:

1. The Global War – the interval of time that marks the transition from a cycle to another, which is achieved, in most of the cases, through war. As Modelski pointed out, a war is considered as a global war only when all the great powers take part in it. Here the global war is understood as "a critical political mechanism of decision in the sense of test or competition" (Modelski 1987, p. 93).

2. World Power – that period of time when the hegemonic power is acknowledged as a global power and imposes its way in organizing the international system. According to Modelski, the world leader must be a naval power to obtain this status, because looking at the world geography (an interconnection of large maritime and terrestrial areas) and the technological history of the last 500 years, "one of the main advantages of a power is its naval capabilities" (Modelski and Thompson 1988, p. 97).

3. Delegitimation – the period of time when the erosion of the global leader's legitimacy and new economic and social developments take place.

4. Deconcentration – that period of time when the power of the global leader reaches its lowest level; a new power appears which could menace the status of the global leader and new alliances are made. A new power which may challenge the existing one does not automatically imply that this power obtains the global power status. According to Modelski, it is not necessary for the new global power to be the former challenger, but it may be an ally of the former challenger or an ally of the former global power.

Modelski starts his analysis of long cycles with 1494, the year of signing of the Treaty of Tordesillas that divided the newly discovered lands outside Europe between Portugal and Spain, thus creating "a new global political regime for the oceanic system" (Modelski 1987, p. 25). As he puts it: "Prior to 1494, there could be no global wars or long cycles because the modern world had not yet been created" (Modelski 1987, p. 45). According to him, the period that follows after 1494 is divided into five long cycles, each of approximately 100–120 years. Thus, we have the Portuguese cycle, with Portugal as global leader; the Dutch cycle, with Netherlands as global leader; two British cycles in a row, when Great Britain was the global leader; and the American cycle, with the USA as a global leader.

While these powers have been global powers, i.e., they monopolized the function of maintaining order in the world system, other powers, like Spain, France, Germany, or the Soviet Union, have not managed to go beyond the status of challengers, failing to establish themselves as global powers.

He defends his decision to include only the four powers as global powers based on the wars they fought, which he considers as global wars, due to four important characteristics: they are generated by the decline of a global power; they last one fourth of a cycle's lifespan, i.e., 25–30 years; they have a global reach; they lead to the emergence of a new leader. On the other hand, the use of naval power as one of the main elements that determine the status of great power leads to weird outcomes, like Portugal being the hegemonic power of the sixteenth century, instead of Spain (Nye 1990, p. 193).

Joint Long Wave/War Cycles Theories

Initially, Modelski paired the phases of Global War and Delegitimation with periods of long wave upswings, and phases of World Power and Deconcentration with periods of long wave downswings. However, since 1984 he moved away from long waves, emphasizing that the political process of the leadership cycle should be dealt apart from the economic one of the long wave, as their cycle periods and patterns of recurrence differ (Goldstein 1988, pp. 129–130). In spite of that, other members of the *leadership cycle* school, such as William Thompson, did relate the two processes, in an effort of integrating the economic aspects with the political-military ones into the long cycle theory (Rosecrance 1987, p. 290).

But those who took seriously the challenging task of correlating the K-wave with the notion of hegemonic cycle were Immanuel Wallerstein and Joshua Goldstein.

Immanuel Wallerstein's theory epitomizes the *world-system* school of historical-structural social theorizing. According to Wallerstein, the world-system was born in the sixteenth century from the embryonic core of Western Europe, which has projected its maritime power gradually expanding its scope. As Fernand Braudel, Wallerstein sees the world-system as consisting of three concentric circles (Wallerstein 1974): the capitalist core consisting of major powers with global interests; the semi-periphery composed of former great powers in decline, emerging powers and regional sub-systemic powers; and the periphery composed of states which have weak economies based on raw materials exports and industrial imports and which are considerably dependent of the core. For Wallenstein, the world-system is a constantly expanding mechanism with a view of extracting and redistributing resources from the periphery for the benefit of the core (Wallerstein 1980). Historically, it has known two structures: the world-empire, in which just one center is using its power for redistributive purposes, and, starting the sixteenth century, the world-economy, in which multiple centers are vying for the same resources in an anarchic system, which is basically the modern world-system as a capitalist world-economy (Wallerstein 2004, p. 2). Over the last five centuries, the attempt of reconstructing the world-economy as a world-empire by conquering other great powers has been repeatedly experienced and has repeatedly failed. The alternative route towards greater power/influence has been to acquire a degree of economic predominance that can be translated afterwards into political-military and cultural prevalence. Thus, a state becomes "hegemonic, that is, capable of imposing a structure of world order upon the world-system" (Wallerstein 2002, p. 17).

According to Wallerstein (1974, 1980, 2002), one can speak of cycles of hegemony in which the power seeking hegemony through economic superiority defeated the one seeking world-empire during a "thirty years' war," i.e., a war involving all the major powers and resulting in great physical and human destruction. Historically, there have been three principal hegemonies within the modern world-system: first that of the United Provinces, rising in the last half of the sixteenth century with a high point in the mid-seventeenth century; then, after a struggle for hegemony between Britain and France, that of the United Kingdom, decisively from 1815 with a high point in the mid-nineteenth century; then, from 1945, after the struggle between America and Germany throughout the "thirty years' war" of 1914–1945, that of the USA.

Other world-system theorists, such as Giovanni Arrighi, by privileging the economic aspects of the long cycles as opposed to the political-military ones, prefer to speak of "systemic cycles of accumulation" (Arrighi 2010, p. 6) instead of cycles of hegemony. Arrighi locates the origins of world capitalism in the Italian city-states of the thirteenth and fourteenth centuries, in what conceivably was a harbinger of the modern world-system and adds to Wallerstein's three cycles a fourth, earlier one, the Genoese cycle, from the fifteenth to the early seventeenth centuries. As a result, the chronology of subsequent cycles is modified to a certain extent, in the sense that the Dutch cycle is from the late sixteenth century through most of the eighteenth century, the British cycle is from the latter half of the eighteenth century through the late nineteenth century, and the USA cycle is from the late nineteenth century to the present. As all these cycles last longer than a century, although they became progressively shorter in duration, Arrighi put forward the notion of the "long century," as opposed to the notion of the "short century" in relation with the twentieth century set forth by Eric Hobsbawm (1999).

Wallerstein is adamant about the importance of secular trends and cyclical rhythms in approaching the issue of social change within the world system (Wallerstein 1980, p. 26). In fact, the world-system school suggested that the long waves come in pairs that affect the core (high-wage zone) and periphery (low-wage zone) differently, as during downswing the production of high-wage goods shifts toward the periphery and the production of low-wage goods toward the core.

Furthermore, the world-system school related the paired long waves with hegemonic succession periods articulating an A1-B1-A2-B2 cycle. The A1 upswing phase, favoring low-wage goods corresponds to a period of ascending hegemony. The B1 downswing phase of stagnation, class struggle, and redistribution of income, corresponds to a period of hegemonic victory in which a "new" power bypasses the "old" declining one. The A2 upswing phase, favoring high-wage goods, corresponds to a period of hegemonic maturity. Finally, the B2 downsizing phase corresponds to a period of declining hegemony, when the conflict between the hegemonic power and its successors becomes acute (Goldstein 1988, pp. 134–135).

According to Wallerstein, after a period of circa 20–25 years when the US hegemony was at its peak due to the reconstruction of Western Europe and Japan, the world-economy has entered into an "age of transition" since the late 1960s, just another B2 phase of stagnation and declining hegemony, experiencing the unstoppable demise of America as world hegemon, and the competition for dominance of a number of core and semi-peripheral countries; it is also highlighting the tendency towards multipolarity within the world-system (Wallerstein 2003). Thus, throughout 1970–2000, the world-system experienced one long Kondratieff B-cycle characterized by a sharp reduction of profits from productive activities. This, in turn, led to attempts "to export the consequences of the downturn, especially the unemployment, to each other" and "a shift in emphasis from accumulating capital via productive profits to accumulating capital via financial manipulations, in which the U.S. has retained an advantage because of the role of the dollar as the reserve currency" (Walerstein 2002, p. 18). Interestingly enough, in Wallerstein's opinion, the breakdown of the Soviet Union only accelerated the US decline (el-Ojeili 2015, p. 6).

For the first half of the twenty-first century, Wallerstein envisaged a return to a Kondratieff A-cycle, during which innovations in informatics, biotechnology, and new energy resources developed during the Kondratieff B-cycle would be transformed into cutting edge industries. Being largely monopolized, these industries would toughen the competition among the USA-EU-Japan triad. In order "to ward off the European threat," the USA and Japan would unite their economic efforts. Other two key actors, China and Russia, provided they manage to preserve their national integrity, would negotiate their entering in the resulting dual structure of economic power: China into the USA-Japan regional economic complex and Russia into the western European one (Wallerstein 2002, pp. 17–18).

Goldstein is another scholar who has tried to explain the way in which economic cycles may be synchronized with hegemonic cycles generated by war and how that can influence the evolution of great powers. Relying on Wallerstein's core-periphery distinction, but adding to it a realist touch, he underlined that: "The world system is characterized *economically* by the unequal geographical division of labor between the core (secondary producers of manufactured goods) and the periphery (primary producers of raw materials). *Politically* the system is characterized by the systematic use of violence both to maintain and to change the power relationships in the system. Those power relationships include both the dominance of the core over the periphery and the struggle for dominance of one political unit over others within the core (hegemony)" (Goldstein 1988, p. 2).

In order to prove that the long cycle should be seen as both a political-military and economic process rather than only an economic one (Kondratieff) or a political-military one (Modelski), Goldstein compiled and combined economic features such as price, innovation, wages, and investment, together with war-related ones such as fatalities. He emphasized the idea that the long cycle is a combination of upswing and downswing periods and there is a correlation between great power wars, recurring roughly every 50 years, and long waves (Goldstein 1985, p. 416). Using data from war fatalities, he asserted that "taken together, these results for great power wars indicate that the upswing periods are characterized not by more wars than on the downswings, nor by wars that last much longer, but by bigger wars – six to twenty times bigger as indicated by battle fatalities. These bigger wars are more costly, more destructive, and more severe in their economic impact" (Goldstein 1985, p. 425).

Combining existing data from the core countries of the modern world system, he created a "synthetic dating scheme" for the period between 1495 and 1975 (Goldstein 1985, p. 416). As many economic scholars, including Kondratieff, Goldstein identified that the upswing phases are prone to be inflationary periods; meanwhile downswing periods tend to be deflationary periods; still, after the 1970s, the trend tends to lead to increasing prices, an inflationary phase, on a downswing period, which may be seen as a paradox or a challenge for the long wave theoreticians.

Revisiting Kondratieff's four-season scheme, Goldstein elaborated a four-phase scheme for the long wave (Goldstein 1991, p. 321):

1. Expansion – Production, investment, war severity, and prices all rise; innovation is stagnant; and real wages flatten out.
2. Stagflation – War severity is high, prices rise rapidly, and production and investment stagnate (stagflation); innovation is low; and real wages fall.
3. Stagnation – Production growth is low and uneven; investment is low; war severity declines; inflation is low (or prices even decline); innovations begin rising; and real wages recover.
4. Rebirth – Production growth picks up again, investment follows; prices are low, war severity is low; innovation is high; and real wages are high.

Merging the idea of long wave with the four phases emphasized by him, he elaborated a new version of long cycle theory: "Growth creates the economic surplus required to sustain major wars among core powers. But these large-scale wars drain surplus and disrupt long-term economic growth" (Goldstein 1988, pp. 15–16). Once again, Goldstein intended to emphasize that war should be seen as a determinant variable for the long cycle, together with prices and innovation, because "the long wave is not just a price phenomenon, since it is also found in war" (Goldstein 1985, p. 433).

According to Goldstein, since the seventeenth century, war and inflationary periods were interdependent, each increase in prices generating an inflationary phase that, in its turn, created an environment conducive to a war peak with many fatalities. Overall, as "wars cause long economic waves" (Goldstein 1985, p. 431), generating the economic ups and downs, economics and war have been interconnected.

Combining the notions of war casualties and prices, Goldstein spoke about three hegemonic cycles compounding the intervals between three hegemonic wars, spanning over periods of 150 years. The three hegemonic wars took place between 1618–1648 (Thirty Years War), 1793–1815 (Napoleonic Wars), and 1914–1945 (World Wars) and "coincide with price increases, leading to claims that hegemonic war and prosperity are associated, together with changes in systemic leadership" (Rosecrance 1987, p. 294). They are ranged as hegemonic wars "because there are struggles for the dominant position in the world system" (Goldstein 1991, p. 305), culminating with the emergence of new hegemons – Netherlands, Britain, and the USA.

Goldstein divided the periods between 1495 and 1945 as follows (Goldstein 1985, p. 429):

- The period between 1495 and 1605–1648, ended by the Thirty Years War, was a period of many wars, so that the fluctuations of upswing and downswing phases were very prominent.
- The period between 1605–1648 and 1793–1815, ended by the Napoleonic Wars, was a period that showed a pattern for big wars, but their numbers were reduced to four war peaks.
- The period between 1793–1815 and 1914–1945, ended by the World Wars, was a period dominated by peace, with only two war peaks.

The fact that World War II came at the beginning of an upswing, was considered as a sign of "possible discontinuity" in the post-World War II era. "It was unprecedented for the world economy in 1939–45 to absorb the costs of a hegemonic war at the beginning of an upswing and then to continue sustained growth for another two decades after the war," underlined Goldstein (1988, p. 343).

In addition to this, his dynamic projection of the long cycles into the future anticipated, for the approximately first three decades of the third millennium, a production upswing phase between 1995 and 2020, complemented by a war upswing phase between 2000/2005 and 2025/2030, and a price upswing phase between 2010 and 2035. Consequently, the greatest danger of great power war was considered to be close to the end of the war upswing phase, i.e., "sometime around the decade of 2020s" (Goldstein 1988, p. 353).

The Predictive Value of the Modelski Model

Generally, political scientists and even economists, including long cycles theoreticians themselves, showed reluctance about using long waves and hegemonic cycles for predicting the future.

Gilpin, for instance, although acknowledged those scholars who think "that there exists, at least in modern history, a recurring cycle of war and peace" (Gilpin 1981, p. 204), was eager to underline that his theory of political change of the international system "is not predictive" (Gilpin 1981, p. 3).

In Goldstein's view, the long cycles' added value was limited to helping us "to understand the dynamics of international politics in its deep context and to understand better how the "lessons of history" apply to today's world" (Goldstein 1988, p. 8). However, emphasizing that "long cycles are not mechanistic or deterministic," he did project them into the future, convinced that by understanding the world system dynamics we can "increase, not diminish, our freedom to choose a future we want" (Goldstein 1988, p. 349).

For Modelski, long cycles were meant to cultivate a long-term outlook over international affairs and "to consolidate the findings of observable recurrences into a coherent body of thought" (Modelski 1987, p. 2). Nevertheless, contrary to Goldstein who rejected predictions based on long cycles, Modelski did not rule out their potential value for predictive uses altogether. In fact, he did emphasize that "an application of long-term theorizing [...] makes it possible to venture tentative predictions about the shape of the next cycle" (Modelski 1987, p. 218). More importantly, he repeatedly underscored the fact that long cycles are "more than mere repetition" (Modelski 1987, p. 22); in the Parsonian tradition of social systems analysis, he conceives of them as "a progressive process of learning" (Modelski 1987, p. 2), which ultimately leads to the systemic development of the global system (Modelski 1987, pp. 34–35). It is precisely that adaptive and transformative feature of his long cycles model which "allows for a degree of predictability" (Modelski 1987, p. 137) and opens up the possibility of integrating historically identified patterns with key drivers – trends and wild cards – in an anticipatory exercise, and this is also the reason for which we have chosen to test the long cycles theory's predictive value on the Modelski model.

Modelski has a typical dialectical conception of the long cycles in a triple sense: First, because each long cycle includes both cyclical/repetitive elements (including challengers to the "incumbent" world powers and the recurrence of global wars) and evolutionary/cumulative ones (including leadership and innovation). Secondly, because the "chain reaction" on which it is premised, i.e., the fact that "the state of the global system and of its sub-systems at time 1 determines the state of the system at time 2," reflects "the interplay of the internal and external aspects of the global polity." Thirdly, because there is a dialectical relationship between the world-power and systemic modes of the long cycles, as the "world-power cycle anticipates the systemic cycle by two phases (or two generations)" (Modelski 1987, pp. 64, 66–67). In other words, throughout the overall four-phase process "set at just over 100 years" (Modelski 1987, p. 93), the Delegitimation and Deconcentration phases for the "incumbent" world-power – "when things appear to be falling apart" – coincide with the Clarification and Coalitioning stages for the emerging new world power – "when the foundations are laid for greater things to come." Thus, similar to the Chinese yin/yang dialectics, "the preconditions that a future world power must fill if it is to meet successfully the challenge of its role," are molded throughout "the weakening of the internal process of the global polity as a whole" (Modelski 1987, p. 123).

Retrospectively, a sound indicator for the predictive value of the Modelski model would be to test the ongoing long cycle identified by Modelski against the record of major events over the last century and the current state of play between the "incumbent" and the emerging world power.

As the demand for world leadership tends to peak around periods of global wars, Modelski places the beginning of the US world power cycle at the start of the First World War which, together with the Second World War, compounds the fifth global-war phase within the overall global succession. However, as the USA joined the First World War in 1917, at a time when Germany's all-out submarine warfare and military advances threatened the security of both North Atlantic and West European areas, perhaps a more accurate beginning for what *Time* publisher Henry Luce referred to as the "American Century" would be 1917. Be that as it may, by declining to ratify the Paris Peace Accords, refusing to join the collective security-driven League of Nations and choosing an isolationist position instead in the aftermath of the First World War, the USA rejected world leadership, in fact. Its leading position was resumed after the December 1941 Japanese attack on Pearl Harbor and the German declaration of war that followed it, which triggered the USA joining the Second World War, i.e., the second round of the global-war phase. Compounding a total of 31 years, the fifth global-war phase confirms the standard time span of a global-war phase of "about one-quarter of one long cycle" (Modelski 1987, p. 108). The end of the Second World War in 1945, i.e., the end of the global-war phase, signaled the beginning of the "administrative" phase of the USA world power, when the USA possessed both the will and ability to lead (Kindleberger 1986, p. 289) as testified by the setting up of the Bretton Woods system as well as by the Truman Doctrine and the Marshall Plan of 1947. According to Modelski, somewhere throughout the 1970s, with the end of dollar convertibility (1971), the oil crisis and embargo (1973), as well as the end of the Vietnam War (1975), this phase came to an end and the USA entered its Delegitimation phase (Modelski 1987, p. 97). Concomitantly, the global system entered in the first phase of its next world power cycle, the initial phase of Clarification "wherein the candidates for world leadership are defining their purposes and reviewing positions for the next round of the competitive trails that are ahead" (Modelski 1987, pp. 97–98).

At this point, at first sight, the Modelski model encounters a host of explanatory problems in the light of major events which took place by the end of the twentieth century and the beginning of the twenty-first century. The most obvious and significant explanatory problem is the sheer fact that Modelski failed to anticipate the breakdown of Soviet Union; he assumed wrongly that the USSR would continue to be the main US challenger throughout the first decades of the twenty-first century. Instead, at present, China seems to be the main challenger for the USA, with Russia filling the role of a "junior challenger." The second problem which begs for an explanation is the short-lived USA "unipolar moment" in the aftermath of the breakdown of communism in East-Central Europe, the dissolution of Soviet Union, and the end of the Cold War. Finally, in tight connection with the latter, Modelski's chronology of the Delegitimation (1973–2000) and Deconcentration (2000–2030) phases of the American world-power cycle are to be reassessed accordingly. So, in keeping with the main tenets of the overall theoretical framework of the Modelski model, how one could explain and reassess all that?

To begin with, it is useful to recall Modelski's emphasis that the new global power should not necessarily be the challenger to the "incumbent" world power, but also an ally of the former or an ally of the latter. This is exactly the case of China, which during the Cold War was both an ally of the then challenger, the Soviet Union, and, then, after the Sino-Soviet split, a de facto ally of the USA against the latter, perceived by Beijing as geopolitically imperialist and ideologically revisionist. Throughout its Clarification phase, coinciding with the US Delegitimation phase, and covering a standard 30-year period between 1978 and 2008–2009, China behaved as expected from an emerging world power. At the beginning of this phase, Deng Tiaopin's speech at the Third Plenum of the Eleventh Central Committee of the Chinese Communist Party in December 1978 signaled China's entering in an era of reforms premised on the centrality of its national economic interest and the subordination of all other interests to it. Following the breakdown of the Soviet bloc and the end of the Cold War, China refrained from contesting the US world leadership and limited itself to react against foreign criticisms, such as the ones in relation to the 1989 Tienanmen massacre. Further on, throughout 1999–2008, China's foreign policy deployed three main features: a more proactive stance geared towards creating a favorable international relations environment for China, combined with a lingering tendency to react against foreign criticisms; a considerable widening of foreign policy agenda; and an expansion of China's national interests, as signaled by the 2007 Party Congress report emphasizing the notion of "safeguarding state sovereignty security and development interests" (Zhang 2012, p. 329).

Significantly enough, with China's entry into the World Trade Organization (WTO) in November 2001, the biggest Asian economy entered the global economic system, symbolically marking the shift of the economic pivot to the East – a process which might look unprecedented to the West, but seen through Asian lenses "is a mere return to normality" (Renard 2009, p. 13).

Likewise, during its Delegitimation phase between 1978 and 2008, coinciding with China's Clarification phase, the US behavior, despite its short-lived "unipolar moment" following the fall of the Soviet empire, essentially confirmed Modelski's assessment that the US world leadership "has now reached its close, and the foundations of another cycle are now being laid" (Modelski 1987, p. 136). It is significant to note that Modelski's long cycle-based assessment in the 1980s was consistent with a widespread fear among leading American scholars at that time that due to the imperial overstretch syndrome and President Reagan administration's skyrocketing military spending which went with it, the USA might enter in a period of decline (Kennedy 1988; Wallerstein 1991). In the light of this perception, it is somehow ironical that after the Soviet invasion of Afghanistan in 1979, the same syndrome – involving the draining of massive resources by the Soviet military-industrial complex – changed itself into one of the significant factors which led to the collapse of the Soviet Union. However, within the post-Cold War era, America has forgotten the imperial overstretch lesson provided by its former Cold War adversary. A sort of triumphalism expressed by phrases such as the "end of history" (Francis Fukuyama) and the "new world order" (President George Bush senior) has infused the foreign policy of successive US administrations in the post-Cold War era, regardless of their political standpoint, prompting this fear to vanish, although the reality which generated it in the first place had acquired unprecedented proportions.

Being required to intervene in places more and more difficult to manage from a security point of view, where its troops were met with increasing hostility and the military spending needed for maintaining them reached colossal figures, the USA has fallen victim of its own success. As argued by the former US ambassador to the USSR Jack Matlock, the end of the Cold War reduced rather than enhanced America's power and its ability to lead. The myth that the USA effectively won the Cold War distorted America's foreign policy during the successive post-Cold war US administrations, particularly the Bush-Cheney one. What's more, by the end of the Delegitimation phase, the US allies were less willing to accept a leadership that seemed increasingly to ignore their interests, the end result being a weakened America (Matlock 2010).

In managing the post-Cold War "unipolar moment," the 9/11 terrorist attacks and the subsequent "war on terror" provided a powerful substitute for a ready-made foe and catalyzed worldwide energies, as well as the needed purpose and will to enforce a strategy of preponderance that would satisfy US interests and values without offending those of its allies and partners. Although successful within a short term, by the end of the Delegitimation phase, the strategy led to the relative estrangement of traditional allies (Germany) and the coming back of attitudes that recall the bygone Cold War on the part of recent partners (Russia).

Leaving aside the fact that the unipolar world may have not existed at all, the post-Cold War being rather a uni-multipolar world, with a sole superpower and several other major powers involved in the settlement of key international issues (Huntington 1999, p. 36), one would wonder when the rather short-lived "unipolar moment" has actually ended, the Delegitimation phase came to a close and the USA entered in its new world power long cycle phase, that of Deconcertation.

Our contention would be that the turning point in the transition from the Delegitimation phase to the Deconcertation phase (from an American point of view) and from the Clarification phase to the Coalitioning phase (from a Chinese point of view) took place somewhere around 2008–2009. As heralding the end of a long cycle phase and the dawn of a new one, we had almost concomitantly a series of events of a security, politico-diplomatic, economic, and symbolic nature, indicative of the resurgence of Russia and the rise of China, on the one hand, and the decline of the USA, on the other. It goes without saying that all these events should not be understood as hard chronological milestones but as signposts for the profound geopolitical tectonic shifts that are shaping the present and future worlds, which are basically long-term trends.

As far as Russia is concerned, we had the Russia-Georgia war in August 2008, signaling the military resurgence of Russia in the post-Soviet era, a process which reached its pinnacle with Russia's annexation of Crimea in March 2014 and the war in Eastern Ukraine. Then, there were three episodes prompted by Russia's longing for recognition as a global great power (as permanent member of the UN Security Council) and a European great power, heralding again the politico-diplomatic resurgence of Russia. Firstly, it was Russia's reaction in the South Caucasus sub-complex of the post-Soviet regional security complex prompted by Kosovo's unilateral proclamation of independence in February 2008 and the West's recognition of it, lest five EU Member States. Frustrated by the West's overriding its position as a permanent member of the UN Security Council in regard to Kosovo, Russia retaliated in the South Caucasus region, an area where its interests were directly at stake and in which it had also the ethno-political levers to intervene. By recognizing in late August 2008, the separatist Georgian provinces of Abkhazia and South Ossetia as independent states, two post-Soviet de facto states obtained from a permanent member of the UN Security Council the much sought-after external legitimacy and international recognition (von Steindsdorff and Fruhstorfer 2012). Secondly, it was President Medvedev's proposal for a new European Security Treaty aimed at establishing a pan-European security system centered on the Organization for Security and Co-operation in Europe (OSCE) and thus counterbalancing the Russian-perceived "NATO-centrism" in Europe. Thirdly, it was Russia's negative geo-politically driven reading of the primarily economic-oriented EU's Eastern Partnership (EaP) initiative, which has been responsible to a large extent for the change of its EU's perception from a strategic ally to a competitor for influence in the shared neighborhood and the speed up of its Eurasian integration project, i.e., the Eurasian Economic Union (Pop 2016).

As far as China, as the US senior challenger, and Russia, as the US junior challenger, are concerned, there were also two symbolic events: Beijing's successful hosting of the Summer Olympic Games in 2008 symbolizing the resurgence and the new international status of China; next, Russia's hosting in Yekaterinburg the first official summit of the BRIC (Brazil, Russia, India, China) countries, at the end of which the four BRICs asked for "a more democratic and just multipolar world order."

Last but not least, from an American perspective, in 2008 there occurred other symbolic economic and political-military events: the US government decision on 15 December 2008 to allow the investment bank Lehman Brothers to go bankrupt, which not only proved that the "too big to fail" banks notion no longer held true, but also marked the transition to the second stage of the most serious global financial crisis since the Great Depression; and the failure of the USA at the November 2008 NATO summit in Bucharest to push for granting the Membership Action Plan (MAP) to Georgia and Ukraine. Although vocally heralded prior to the 2008 NATO summit in Bucharest by the US President George W. Bush, the granting of MAP status to Georgia and Ukraine was denied by Germany and France, vitally interested to maintain good relations with their key energy provider, Russia. It was the first time in NATO's recent history when the political will of the USA was opposed by chief European allies.

Be that as it may, by the end of the second term of the Bush junior administration, against the backdrop of the war on terror, the global reach of American interventionism, and the global financial crisis, the decline of American power has become a recurring theme in most analyses devoted to the USA. Moreover, as the global economic and financial crisis has exposed the fragility of developed economies and the dynamism and resilience of a handful of large developing countries led by China, India, and Brazil, accelerating the shift of the economic power away from the West, there was a widespread perception of an unavoidable shift of power from the USA and Europe towards the rising powers in Asia (Kose and Prasad 2010, p. 1), i.e., a move from an American-led Western world towards a post-American and post-Western world (Zakaria 2009, p. 1; Serfaty 2011, p. 7). In fact, anticipations from 2008 have already emphasized "that by the year 2025, seven of the world's ten largest economies will be located in Asia" (Chan 2008, p. IX).

After the turning point of 2008–2009, throughout the last decade China has continued, at least partially, to confirm its bid for economic leadership. In the summer of 2010, surpassing Japan's economy, the Chinese economy has become the second largest economy of the world. Significantly enough, this happened 15 years ahead of the moment – 2025 – projected at the beginning of the crisis, in 2008, by the USA intelligence community's center for mid-term and long-term strategic thinking (National Intelligence Council 2008, p. 29). Three out of the world's five banks by market capitalization are now Chinese, including the top two. Throughout 2013–2015 China was the first world exporter and it is now the world's third largest importer. In 2016, China was the world's largest economy for the second year in a row, with the EU occupying the second place and the USA the third place. Again, this has happened 14–15 years ahead of the moment – 2030 – anticipated by some futurists. In 2016, China contributed 1.2% to the global economic growth. In that year China's annual GDP was USD 119,684.1 trillion, taking up 15.4% of the global GDP with a yearly growth of 6.7% (Chen 2017). Moreover, as the USA owes China USD 1.241 trillion, as of June 2016, China has become the biggest creditor. In addition to this, throughout this epic decade, the proactive feature and even assertiveness of the Chinese foreign policy has been greatly re-enforced and the self-awareness of China's global position and responsibilities apparently reached its peak in 2017, with President Xi Jinping's momentous speech defending globalization and international cooperation at the World Economic Forum in Davos (Parker 2017; Bruce-Lockart 2017).

China's continuous economic rise is also the mainstream anticipated trend. By 2050, experts expect that the nominal GDP of China (calculated at current exchange rates, which takes into account the level of inflation) to be almost 20% larger than the USA or even twice as big as that of the USA.

Nevertheless, China's economy has been slowing down lately, as it is plagued by lots of problems: it is facing the enormous challenge to reduce state interference and to stop funneling of resources according to social and political control rather than rational investment strategy (Subacchi 2017, pp. 1–2); it is still far in terms of standard of living, producing 15,400 USD, compared to US GDP per capita of 57,300 USD (Amadeo 2017); the completion of the internationalization of its currency, renminbi (RMB), should not be taken for granted; it is close to the point of a housing bubble; it is highly environmentally unfriendly and is confronted in mainland China with a severe desertification process – to name just a few. According to the TechCast Project, even if is willing to take on the leadership, China might not be able to do so, as it could plummet – with a probability of occurrence of 25%, a social impact of −2.3, and a likely impact of −0.4 on a − 10/+10 scale.

Against the background of these rather mixed weak signals, many think that without an actor willing and able to affirm its prevalence, or to share it with co-partners and rivals, the unipolarity has been substituted by a distribution of power which has been labelled "nonpolarity," "apolarity," "de facto zero-polarity," or "interpolarity" (Haass 2008; Ferguson 2004; Serfaty 2011, p. 8; Grevi 2009). Whereas the nonpolar world is "a world dominated not by one or two or even several states but rather by dozens of actors possessing and exercising various kinds of power" (Haass 2008, p. 44), the interpolar world's key characteristic is "multipolarity in the age of interdependence" as far as economy, energy, and environment are concerned (Grevi 2009, p. 9).

Although there are some disputes over this idea (Cox 2011, pp. 416–424; van Agtmael 2012) and, certainly, we are not there yet, it has already become clear that the world is gradually moving towards multipolarity. Still, it is not yet clear if the new distribution of power would prove to be either of true multipolarity, or one of asymmetrical multipolarity, with only a few dominant powers, seconded by other major, regional and local powers, or one of "multi-multipolarity," in which the power would be diffused both at the global and the regional levels (Friedberg 1993/1994). However, what is even more uncertain is still the nature of the relationships between these various actors, i.e., if the multipolarity would be either a competitive or a cooperative one (Renard 2009, p. 7), or both. In the case of an asymmetrical multipolarity, in which the defining factors of the international system would be the competition for hegemony between the USA and China and the USA-China-Russia strategic triangle, three possibilities could be conceived: China could align with Russia in order to challenge the USA; Russia could stay neutral; or, as far-fetched as it may seem at the moment, Russia could align with the USA in order to balance China in its way of becoming the future hegemon.

Indeed, this would be rather a grim geopolitical future, recalling past patterns of great power rivalry. A way out from this conundrum and an opening towards a bifurcated future is provided by Modelski himself. According to his emphasis of the idea that the global political system might go through structural change in order to tackle new global challenges, he envisages two alternative *collaborative* versions of future world leadership: one, which is less likely due mainly to coordination problems, in which different countries would take care of "different functional areas" of world leadership; and another one, which would take the form of some kind of *coalition building*, possibly including previously untested "novel arrangements" (Modelski 1987, pp. 232–233). The second one is not only "more interesting" but also more likely in the light of some recent evolving trends at the global and regional levels, and which indeed – as he put it – "might well prove to be the most promising avenues of contemporary political innovation" (Modelski 1987, p. 233). Among the latter one could refer to a combination of cooperative and confrontational relationships among the world powers either in different functional areas of world leadership, or at the global as opposed to the regional levels, as well as to the currently evolving duality – cooperation/partnership but also competition/rivalry – characterizing the relationship between state and non-state actors in dealing with global problems.

Illustrative for the weak signals of the first trend are, for instance: the recognition of the role of the emerging economies within global economic governance at the level of key institutions of the Bretton Woods system such as the International Monetary Fund

(IMF), the World Bank, and the World Trade Organization (WTO); the leading role performed by the rather informal G20 grouping in economic global governance, particularly throughout the global economic and financial crisis; the setting up by the BRICS (BRIC plus South Africa) countries of the New Development Bank; the mixed competitive-cooperative pattern in the USA-Russia relationship inaugurated by the US President Donald Trump in order to deal with global security challenges, such as the fight against ISIS and the management of the Syrian crisis, accompanied by its confrontational mode at the regional level triggered by the Ukrainian crisis, the war in Eastern Ukraine and the Russian annexation of Crimea; and the complex USA-China relationship characterized at the global economic level by a cooperative interdependent relationship re-enforced by China's newly discovered role of defender of globalization, at a time when the process has come under threat in America and parts of Europe, which contemplate protectionism, and, at the regional security level, by China's assertiveness as evinced by its naval expansion and its territorial disputes on the Spratly and Diaoyn islands of the South China Sea (Zhang 2012, p. 334).

As for the weak signals illustrative for the second trend, suffice is to mention the paramount role played by transnational and multinational corporations within the global economic governance, as well as the increasing impact of transnational terrorist organizations (such as al-Qaeda and ISIS) and security firms (for instance, during the wars in Afghanistan and Iraq) upon the global security landscape. In order for this collaborative version of world leadership to possibly take shape, building trust in the USA-China and USA-Russia relations would be the key. Surely, this would take more time than the rather trust-based, but not excluding tensions, Russia-China relationship, which already benefits from certain compatibility between their globalization-inspired long-term projects such as the Eurasian Economic Union (EEU) and Great Eurasia promoted by Russia, and the Belt and Road Initiative (BRI) promoted by China.

For the cooperation/partnership aspects of this second trend, particularly revealing is China's BRI Initiative, which is set to create a paradigm shift in world economics and politics as the "Chinese solution" to promote global cooperation. By bringing together regional and global stakeholders with a wide variety of cultures, ethnicities, and economic and political-military orientations – as of 2017 its coverage includes already 65 countries and regions – along the "Belt and Road" terrestrial and maritime Silk Road trading routes, the BRI will likely redefine regional and global connectivity and pave the way for a more integrated world of future. As the world population is projected to grow to 8.9 billion by 2040, with South Asia and Sub-Saharan Africa accounting for a major part of the growth, long-term regional connectivity mega-project such as the BRI will connect an approximate 4.4 billion people through infrastructural routes and energy corridors (South Asia Rising 2017).

Then, the key question which begs for an answer would be: How this globalization-inspired integration process would fit into Modelski's model and what could be the significance of a potential collaborative Chinese world leadership for the global community at large? Conceived as a learning mega-process of just over one hundred years in length, each long cycle in Modelski's systemic mode is conceived as one phase of a superordinate process which were to give the fullest expression to one of the four principal dimensions of the global system in Talcott Parson's tradition: Latent pattern maintenance (L, culture-reproduction); Integration (I, community); Goal attainment (G, politics); and Adaptation (A, economics) (Modelski 1987, pp. 118, 125, 129–131, Tables 5.2, 5.3). Whereas the innovation hallmark of the L macro-phase initiated around 1850 was the knowledge (education-science-technology) revolution and its vector/global carrier, the USA, the I macro-phase, initiated somewhere in the 1970s (1978–2100?) "will necessarily be focused on questions of integration, solidarity and the expansion of the global community" (Modelski 1987, p. 136). This assessment seems consistent with the projected end of the current systemic long cycle around 2100, when the integration at the level of global community could be reasonably conceived as coming to an end.

The next relevant big question would be: What could possibly be the greater meaning of a potential collaborative Chinese world leadership for the overall long-cycle process? Perhaps here it would be interesting to remind Modelski's perceptive remark, that, around the year 1000 there were in fact "two nuclei of a global system" (Modelski 1987, p. 96): one in Europe, centered around Venice (whose sea-power projection example would be later replicated by other European powers) and one in Asia, around Sung China. Still, as China was conquered by Mongols in 1279 and the Chinese sea-power projection, in spite of the seven maritime voyages organized between 1405 and 1433 by Ming China, failed to gain the kind of enthusiasm and political support for the exploration and discoveries similar to the one promoted by the Portuguese nation-state, there was the European nucleus, represented by Portugal around 1500, which eventually won this ad-hoc competition for setting up the global system and launching its long-cycle process. Thus, whereas over the next five centuries the world leadership was basically performed by European powers (Portugal in the sixteenth century, the Netherlands in the seventeenth century, and Britain over two successive cycles throughout the eighteenth and nineteenth centuries up till the beginning of the twentieth century), with just one exception, the current US world leadership, it might well be that the next five centuries of world leadership would be mostly performed by Asian powers. This would be consistent with the current prevalent view that the "rise of the rest" represents mainly an Asian phenomenon and by 2050 the global economic power will shift to E7, that is, the seven emerging market economies of China, India, Indonesia, Brazil, Russia, Mexico, and Turkey (PricewaterhouseCoopers 2017), out of which five are Asian countries. By then, led by China and India, the South Asian rise will define the negotiation and formation of new alliances and possibly of a new regional security architecture (South Asia Rising 2017). Furthermore, there are reasons to believe that, after this turning point, further waves of the "rise of the rest" will follow (Grinin and Korotayev 2015, pp. 160–161), wherein other members of the next eleven emerging market economies (N11), such as Bangladesh, Egypt, Iran, South Korea, Nigeria, Pakistan, the Philippines, and Vietnam, as successors of E7, will vie for power.

Thus, retrospectively, it seems that history is proving that the sixth world power cycle, anticipated by Modelski as possibly involving a novel arrangement, is already in the making. Indeed, whereas most of long cycles theorists tend to think of it as the outcome of a great power hegemonic war, Modelski leaves open the possibility of it occurring in some other, previously untested, but peaceful ways. Furthermore, this new world power cycle, signaling a power shift to Asia, is possibly heralding also a new beginning in the long cycle systemic mode, in other words, at the macro-level of big history.

Long Cycles Theory's Limits and the Way Ahead

The long cycles theory has got its fair share of both supporters and critics.

As far as the long waves are concerned, most scholars would not accept the K-waves model, because it is based on observations of a limited sector – agricultural commodity and copper prices – which cannot be extended to the entire economy and on three economies only: the USA, France, and England. When put to the test on the basis of time series of indicators of real economic growth, the existence of long waves was contested not only in the three abovementioned cases but also in the case of Germany (van Ewijk 1981). In fact, the K-waves model is supported to a certain extent only by the US case, the validity of Kondratieff's theory being questionable for the rest of the world. Another critique of his theory refers to the relation between long waves and demographic booms; some researchers, such as Angus Maddison, concluding that Kondratieff's theory is devoid of empirical support (Maddison 1982). Jaap van Duijn adds that, according to most scientists, it would be very difficult to verify the length of a cycle as there are disturbances during cycles and that differences in economic growth represent rather a "manifestation of the evolution of capitalist economies" (Duijn 1977, p. 546). Also, Murray Rothbard argues as those years of 1789, 1849, 1896, and 1940, which are beheld by the Kondratieff model as of terrible years of troughs, were actually years of a "trough point for the index of wholesale prices" during which the international system changed, becoming wider, deeper, and more complex and that throughout 1814–1839 and 1866–1896, years that according to Kondratieff should have proved to be those of great depression, they were years of expansion for the three analyzed countries (Rothbard 1984). Last, but not least, the Kondratieff model has been criticized for not being able to foretell the big economic and financial crisis which started in 2007-2008. According to Kondratieff's and Goldstein's economic argument, the period between 1995 and 2010 should have been an era of rebirth. Instead, in 2007–2008 we faced a deep economic crisis, the most severe one since the 1929 Great Depression. Furthermore, according to Kondratieff and Goldstein, the next 28 years should be a period of further expansion. However, the next decades might not be as predicted by the two authors, and one argument can precisely be the combined effect of the increase in population and technological innovation, which may lead to a drastic increase of unemployed people, as artificial intelligence (AI) tends to replace humans as workforce.

Clearly, the war cycles theories have their own downsides as well. As Farrar has pointed out, the war cycles researchers are relying their theories on the idea of repetition, as they believe that "any prediction based on the past requires two assumptions: That the analysis of the past is accurate and that the factors on which it is based will persist in the future" (Farrar 1977, p. 174). But the unpredictable evolution of the factors that shore up the global system makes anticipating a future hegemonic war and a future hegemonic power rather problematic. During a period of a hundred years, technological progress, the interdependence of states, the evolution of society, and the new mind-set of a new generation of people can cause the factors that underpinned the theoretical insights of the long cycle theory to become no longer valid. Probably the best example to support this idea would be a parallel between the twentieth and the twenty-first centuries. Whereas in the first half of the twentieth century wars were waged to conquer new territories and acquire new colonies, today the physical possession of territories achievable through war is no longer the main objective of a great power, having been replaced by economic pre-eminence achieved by nonmilitary means.

As far as the Modelski model is concerned, many researchers criticized it precisely on the grounds that he tended to overestimate the power of states such as Portugal or the Netherlands, while understating the power of others, such as Spain or France. It is the case of Robert Gilpin, who, although sympathizing with Modelski's stress on world powers and global wars in ordering and changing the international system, did not classify Portugal and Netherlands as world powers on a par with Great Britain and the USA in its rather similar theory of international change; he also considered that since the nineteenth century the "cycle of empires" was substituted by "a succession of hegemonies" (Gilpin 1981, p. 144). In addition to this, he emphasized that "cycles of warfare do not correlate with cycles of leadership," and there is no mechanism able to explain the cycles of war and peace, Modelski's scheme being over deterministic (Gilpin 1981, pp. 204–205). Furthermore, Modelski, like Kennedy, could not foresee the fall of the Soviet Union, both of them assuming that it would continue to be the main opponent of the United States during the first three decades of the twenty-first century.

Another critic of the joint long wave/war cycles theories was Rosencrance, who believed that the "world cycle offers no apparent logical or historical causal link between the rise and decline of hegemonic powers and the onset of major war" (Rosecrance 1987, p. 296) unless a world power undoubtedly dominated and overshadowed the others, which was not the case of the Portuguese, Dutch, and British cycles, as during those times the *primus inter pares* principle was implemented in European and international politics. That is why he doubted that long cycles may actually explain the evolution of the global world system. To conclude if joint long wave/war cycles theories can explain major wars he asked four questions (Rosecrance 1987, pp. 297–301):

1. *Are war and economic cycles associated?* His answer was hesitant because during recent periods the correlation between war and prices may not be so straightforward.
2. *Does hegemonic decline explain war?* He claimed that there is no direct link between the decline of a world power and the global war since, for instance, "Holland's leadership was interrupted at its height by the Thirty Years War" (Rosecrance 1987, p. 296).

3. *Have international developments affected cyclical approaches?* His answer was yes, because the Industrial Revolution and the two World Wars changed the public opinion's mood for war, so that many states no longer consider fighting for land as an option. Instead, they develop trade relationships and set up economic and financial partnerships, and encourage people-to-people contacts, circumstances that overall reduced the re-emergence of war and hegemonic cycles.
4. *How can we explain contemporary conflict?* He argued that the long cycle seen as the correlated joint output of economic and political-military variables may no longer be valid.

That being said, the long cycle theory was taken seriously and further developed by quite a few Russian scholars. Some Russian academics were interested mostly in identifying Russia's strategic long cycles. Relying on a complex multifactorial model composed of nine economic, demographic, social, political-military, and cultural-religious factors (government, territory, natural resources, population, economy, culture and religion, science and education, army, and foreign policy), Alexander Ageev, for instance, claimed that, since the first century A.D., Russia "has gone through almost five large extra long strategic cycles, each 400 years. All such periods include 5 long-term cycles with 80 years lengths" (Ageev 2006, p. 16). Other prominent Russian scholars, such as Leonid Grinin and Andrey Korotayev, mainly relying on K-waves, were keen to explain not only the cyclical dynamism of global economy (Grinin et al. 2016) but also the dialectic relationship between the mega-historical processes of the Great Divergence and Great Convergence, as two phases of a distinctive Global Modernization process. Whereas the Great Divergence refers to the explosive growth of a gap in per capita incomes between the West and the rest of the world starting the nineteenth century until the 1970s, the Great Convergence designates the opposite economic and technological advancement, which occurred since the 1980s within Third World nations, leading to a narrowing of that gap. Furthermore, based on such a long view of social and economic history, the two Russian scholars were able to advance some stimulating forecasts for global development in the upcoming decades (Grinin and Korotayev 2015).

Moreover, although there is no consensus among long cycles theorists in terms of the inauguration of the next world power cycle, one can definitely speak of a chronological similarity. Accordingly, somewhere around 2020 (Galtung's and Goldstein's extrapolation) or 2030 (the Modelski model) we should expect a transition of power, with only the Farrar Jr. model pushing this moment somewhere throughout 2030–2060.

Retrospectively, the long cycles theory, especially the Modelski model, seems better suited to be used in anticipating the future trajectory of the global system from an endless number of possible futures, as it can anticipate both certain recurrent historical patterns and possible novel evolutions. Nonetheless, it cannot and should not be used as a mere oracle by IR experts and futurists. The main reason for that has to do with the complexity of the current and, especially future worlds, on the one hand, and with the predominantly linear way of thinking of the long cycles theory, on the other. Firstly, whereas other actors apart states, including transnational corporations, international intergovernmental organizations, and nongovernmental organizations, have already a crucial impact upon the world system against the background of the decline of the nation-state, during the next decades, other non-traditional actors might step into the arena vying for shares of power, including organized crime groups, clans, tribes, provinces, ministries, and alternative and anti-systemic movements and organizations. In its turn, the privatization of power by legal and illegal groups, possibly network-based, is likely to dramatically change future geopolitical realignments, generating ad-hoc alliances in both "centers" and "peripheries." Secondly, rapid population growth coupled with rapid urbanization in Third World nations has not only increased demand for bare necessities but also spawned a segment of young people born between mid-1980s and 2000s otherwise referred to as millennials who are starting to change the society in a very significant way. Thirdly, as we are living not only postnormal times, characterized by complexity, chaos, and contradictions (Sardar 2010), but also a time of bifurcation, when the time is compressed and it is just a singular point out of which a qualitatively new world system is to be born, we have to integrate emerging phenomena and trends into our long-term analysis and start thinking of our future world in terms of a complex system of systems. Contrary to linear systems in which behavior is easy to infer and anticipate, complex systems generate bifurcations hard to anticipate. When complex systems consist of networks, a small change can generate a loop mechanism that amplifies things beyond any previous experience, generating disproportionate effects (Casanova 2002, p. 208), as acknowledged by "the butterfly effect."

In practical terms, this fundamental shift in anticipatory thinking, would be tantamount with carrying out two interrelated processes using Futures Studies methodologies, including Environmental Scanning (Gordon and Glenn 2009), Trend Impact Analysis (Gordon 2009), Wild Cards (Petersen and Steinmüller 2009), and scenario-building (Glenn and The Futures Group International 2009) methods: First, to identify a set of likely drivers – trends and wild cards (Barber 2006) – that, if they were to occur, this could cause deviations from the extrapolation of historical patterns identified by the long cycles theory; secondly, to scrutinize the identified drivers in tight correlation with each other in order to get informed perceptions about their likely trajectory and impact, and what they mean for our alternatives and choices about the future. Clearly, knowing only the drivers, one cannot simply anticipate the future, but can paint credible scenarios of it, helping us understand what drives change and what leverage do we have in shaping it. Consequently, these two combined processes are likely to dramatically enhance the predictive power of the long cycles theory.

To conclude with, within an increasingly postnormal world, which arguably requests postformal reasoning and pedagogies (Gidley 2010), the study of the long cycles from the perspective of anticipating the future trajectory of the global system can help us not only to avoid some of the pitfalls of the past but also recover our agency and help us to create the world in which we wish to live.

Summary

As a rule, IR scholars were wary of using long cycles theory for predictive purposes. Against the background of its in-built propensity to highlight mainly recurrent historical trends, on the one hand, and a series of explanatory inconsistencies, on the other, they were inclined to ascribe it the more modest but safer role of a framework for comprehending the development of the global system. Nevertheless, some academics, including Modelski, did not rule out applying it for tentative predictions. Besides cyclical and repetitive features (including the relationship between the "incumbent" and the emerging world powers and the recurrence of global wars as "systemic decisions"), the Modelski long cycles model allows for evolutionary and cumulative ones (including leadership and innovation of the global system). It is precisely that adaptive and transformative feature of Modelski's long cycles model, i.e., conceiving the development of the global system as "a progressive process of learning," which opens up the possibility of both novel evolutions in the long cycles' systemic mode and anticipating the development of the current cycle and the outlook of the next one in its world-power mode. In fact, put to test against the record of major events of the current US world-power cycle, the Modelski model fares rather well, regardless of obvious explanatory problems, especially the failure to foresee the fall of the Soviet Union. Moreover, applying the long cycles theory in its systemic mode can help us understand deeper the Global Modernization as a dialectical process composed of two distinctive phases, the Great Divergence and the Great Convergence. However, for a successful anticipation of future economic, politico-diplomatic, and security developments and turning points at the global level, one should conceive of our future world in terms of a complex system of systems. As complex systems generate bifurcations hard to anticipate, for a successful anticipatory exercise, one should complement the historical patterns identified by the long cycles theory with methods available to mark evolving trends and wild cards as ways of enhancing its predictive value. Thus, by anticipating the future trajectory of the global system, humanity can recover its agency and create the world in which it wishes to live.

References

Ageev, A. I. (2006). The past, current and future strategic challenges and democracy in Russia. In M. Mannermaa, J. Dator, & P. Tiihonen (Eds.), *Democracy and futures* (pp. 15–26). Helsinki: Committee for the Future, Parliament of Finland.

Amadeo, K. (2017). China's economy facts and effect on the U.S. economy: How much does China really affect the U.S. economy. https://www.thebalance.com/china-economy-facts-effect-on-us-economy-3306345. Accessed 1 March 2017.

Arrighi, G. (2010). *The long twentieth century: Money, power, and the origins of our times* (New and updated ed.). London/New York: Verso.

Barber, M. (2006). Wildcards – Signals from a future near you. *Journal of Futures Studies, 11*(1), 75–94. https://jfsdigital.org/wp-content/uploads/2014/01/111-A05.pdf. Accessed 10 February 2017.

Bruce-Lockart, A. (2017). Top quotes by China President Xi Jinping at Davos 2017. https://www.weforum.org/agenda/2017/01/chinas-xi-jinping-at-davos-2017-top-quotes. Accessed 23 February 2017.

Casanova, P. G. (2002). Organized capitalism in the midst of order and chaos (an alternative view). In I. Wallerstein & A. Clesse (Eds.), *The world we are entering, 2000–2050* (pp. 203–210). Amsterdam: Duke University Press.

Chan, S. (2008). *China, the U.S., and the power-transition theory: A critique.* Milton Park/New York: Routledge.

Chen, H. (2017). Why China proposed the Belt and Road Initiative. http://www.southasiarising. com/proceedings/. Accessed 20 March 2017.

Cox, M. (2011). Power shift and the death of the west? Not yet! *European Political Science, 10*(3), 416–424.

el-Ojeili, C. (2015). Reflections on Wallerstein: The modern world-system, four decades on. *Critical Sociology, 41*(45), 1–22. https://doi.org/10.1177/0896920513497377.

Farrar, L. L., Jr. (1977). Cycles of war: Historical speculations on future international violence. *International Interactions, 3*(2), 169–179. https://doi.org/10.1080/03050627708434460.

Ferguson, N. (2004). A world without power. *Foreign Policy*, July/August. http://www. foreignpolicy.com/articles/2004/07/01/a_world_without_power. Accessed 9 September 2010.

Friedberg, A. L. (1993/1994). Ripe for rivalry: Prospects for peace in a multipolar Asia. *International Security, 18*(3), 5–33. http://www.jstor.org. Accessed 10 February 2017.

Geller, D. S. (1992). Capability concentration, power transition, and war. *International Interactions, 17*(3), 269–284. https://doi.org/10.1080/03050629208434783.

Gidley, J. M. (2010). Postformal priorities for postnormal times: A rejoinder to Ziauddin Sardar. *Futures, 42*(6), 625–632. https://doi.org/10.1016/j.futures.2010.04.022.

Gilpin, R. (1981). *War and change in world politics.* Cambridge/New York: Cambridge University Press.

Glenn, J. C., & The Futures Group International (2009). Scenarios. In J. C. Glenn & T. J. Gordon (Eds.), *Futures research methodology – Version 3.0. Multimedia CD with support from the Rockefeller Foundation.* Washington, DC: The Millennium Project.

Goldstein, J. S. (1985). Kondratieff waves as war cycles. *International Studies Quarterly, 29*(4), 411–444.

Goldstein, J. S. (1988). *Long cycles: Prosperity and war in the modern age.* New Haven/London: Yale University Press.

Goldstein, J. S. (1991). A war-economy theory of the long wave. In N. Thygesen, K. Velupillai, & S. Zambelli (Eds.), *Business cycles: Theories, evidence and analysis* (1st ed.). New York: New York University Press.

Gordon, T. J. (2009). Trend impact analysis. In J. C. Glenn & T. J. Gordon (Eds.), *Futures research methodology – Version 3.0. Multimedia CD with support from the Rockefeller Foundation.* Washington, DC: The Millennium Project.

Gordon, T. J., & Glenn, J. C. (2009). Environmental scanning. In J. C. Glenn & T. J. Gordon (Eds.), *Futures research methodology – Version 3.0. Multimedia CD with support from the Rockefeller Foundation.* Washington, DC: The Millennium Project.

Grevi, G. (2009). *The interpolar world: a new scenario.* Occasional Paper No. 79. Paris: European Union Institute for Security Studies. https://www.peacepalacelibrary.nl/ebooks/files/ 375879854.pdf. Accessed 3 March 2017.

Grinin, L., et al. (2016). *Economic cycles, crises, and the global periphery.* International perspectives on social policy, administration and practice. Basel: Springer.

Grinin, L., & Korotayev, A. (2015). *Great divergence and great convergence: A global perspective.* International perspectives on social policy, administration and practice. Basel: Springer.

Haass, R. (2008). The age of nonpolarity. *Foreign Affairs, 87*(3), 44–56.

Hobsbawm, E. (1999). *Age of extremes: The short twentieth century 1914–1991.* London: Abacus.

Huntington, S. P. (1999). The lonely superpower. *Foreign Affairs, 78*(2), 35–49.

Kennedy, P. (1988). *The rise and fall of the great powers: Economic change and military conflict from 1500 to 2000.* London: Unwin Hyman.

Kindleberger, C. P. (1986). *The world in depression, 1929–1939* (Revised and enlarged ed.). Berkeley: University of California Press.

Kondratieff, N. D., & Stolper, W. F. (1935). The long waves in economic life. *Review of Economics and Statistics, 17*(6), 105–115. http://www.jstor.org. Accessed 10 February 2017.

Kose, M. A., & Prasad, E. S. (2010). *Emerging markets: Resilience and growth amid global turmoil*. Washington, DC: Brookings Institution Press.

Kugler, J., & Organski, A. F. K. (1989). The power transition: A retrospective and prospective evaluation. In M. I. Millarsky (Ed.), *Handbook of war studies* (pp. 171–194). Boston: Unwin Hyman.

Lemke, D. (2008). Power transition theory. In M. Griffiths (Ed.), *Encyclopedia of international relations and global politics* (pp. 694–696). London/New York: Routledge.

Maddison, A. (1982). *Phases of capitalist development*. Oxford/New York: Oxford University Press.

Matlock, J. (2010). *Superpower illusions: How myths and false ideologies led America astray – And how to return to reality*. New Haven/London: Yale University Press.

Modelski, G. (1987). *Long cycles in world politics*. Houndmills/London: The Macmillan Press.

Modelski, G., & Thompson, W. (1988). *Seapower in global politics, 1494–1993* (1st ed.). Seattle: University of Washington Press.

National Intelligence Council (2008). *Global trends 2025: A transformed world*. The National Intelligence Council's 2025 Project, NIC 2008–003. Washington, DC: National Intelligence Council. http://www.dni.gov/nic/NIC_2025_project.html. Accessed 9 September 2010.

Nye, J. (1990). The changing nature of world power. *Political Science Quarterly, 105*(2), 177–192. http://www.jstor.org. Accessed 10 February 2017.

Organski, A. F. K. (1968). *World politics* (2nd ed.). New York: Alfred A. Knopf.

Parker, C. (2017). China's Xi Jinping defends globalization from the Davos stage. https://www.weforum.org/agenda/2017/01/chinas-xi-jinping-defends-globalization-from-the-davos-stage. Accessed 23 February 2017.

Petersen, J. L., & Steinmüller, K. (2009). Wild cards. In J. C. Glenn & T. J. Gordon (Eds.), *Futures research methodology – Version 3.0. Multimedia CD with support from the Rockefeller Foundation*. Washington, DC: The Millennium Project.

Pop, A. (2016). From cooperation to confrontation: The impact of bilateral perceptions and interactions on the EU-Russia relations in the context of shared neighbourhood. *Eastern Journal of European Studies, 7*(2), 47–70. ejes.uaic.ro/articles/EJES2016_0702_POP.pdf. Accessed 10 February 2017.

PricewaterhouseCoopers (2017). The world in 2050. The long view: How will the global economic order change by 2050? https://www.pwc.com/world2050#. Accessed 17 March 2017.

Renard, T. (2009). A BRIC in the world: Emerging powers, Europe, and the coming order. *Egmont paper 31*. Brussels: Academia.

Rosecrance, R. (1987). Long cycle theory and international relations. *International Organization, 41*(2), 283–301. https://doi.org/10.1017/S0020818300027478.

Rothbard, M. N. (1984). The Kondratieff cycle: real or fabricated?. Resource document. LewRockwell.com. https://www.lewrockwell.com/1970/01/murray-n-rothbard/business-cycles-real-and-fabricated/. Accessed 10 February 2017.

Sardar, Z. (2010). Welcome to postnormal times. *Futures, 42*(5), 435–444. https://doi.org/10.1016/j.futures.2009.11.028.

Serfaty, S. (2011). Moving in a post-western world. *The Washington Quarterly, 34*(2), 7–23.

South Asia Rising (2017). Conference Report, Dubai, 26–27 Feb 2017. http://southasiarising.com/downloads/sar_conference_report.pdf. Accessed 17 March 2017.

Subacchi, P. (2017). *The People's money: How China is building a global currency*. New York: Columbia University Press.

van Agtmael, A. (2012). The end of the Asian miracle. *Foreign Policy*, 11 June. http://www.foreignpolicy.com/articles/2012/06/11/the_end_of_the_asian_miracle. Accessed 13 June 2012.

van Duijn, J. J. (1977). The long wave in economic life. *De Economist, 125*(4), 544–576. https://doi.org/10.1007/BF01221051.

van Ewijk, C. (1981). The long wave – A real phenomenon? *De Economist, 129*(2), 324–372. https://doi.org/10.1007/BF01371746.

von Steinsdorff, S., & Fruhstorfer, A. (2012). Post-soviet de facto states in search of internal and external legitimacy: Introduction. *Communist and Post-Communist Studies, 45*(1–2), 117–121. https://doi.org/10.1016/j.postcomstud.2012.03.009. Accessed 10 February 2017.

Wallerstein, I. (1974). *The modern world system I: Capitalist agriculture and the origins of the European world-economy in the sixteenth century*. New York: Academic Press.

Wallerstein, I. (1980). *The modern world system II: Mercantilism and the consolidation of the European world-economy, 1600–1750*. New York: Academic Press.

Wallerstein, I. (1991). *Geopolitics and Geoculture: Essays on the changing world-system*. Cambridge: Cambridge University Press.

Wallerstein, I. (2002). The world we are entering, 2000–2050 (32 propositions). In I. Wallerstein & A. Clesse (Eds.), *The world we are entering, 2000–2050* (pp. 9–22). Amsterdam: Duke University Press.

Wallerstein, I. (2003). *The decline of American power: The US in a chaotic world*. New York: New Press.

Wallerstein, I. (2004). *World systems analysis: An introduction*. Durham/London: Duke University Press.

Yakovets, Y.V. (2006). The Kondratieff's waves and cyclic dynamics of the economy and wars: Theory and prospects. In T.C. Devezas (Ed.), *Kondratieff waves, warfare and world security* (pp. 3–9). NATO Security through Science Series. E: Human and Societal Dynamics – Vol. 5. Published in cooperation with NATO Public Diplomacy Division. Amsterdam: IOS Press.

Zakaria, F. (2009). *The post-American world*. New York: W.W. Norton & Company.

Zhang, F. (2012). Rethinking China's grand strategy: Beijing's evolving national interests and strategic ideas in the reform era. *International Politics, 49*(3), 318–345. https://doi.org/10.1057/ip.2012.5.

K-Waves, Reflexive Foresight, and the Future of Anticipation in the Next Socioeconomic Cycle

34

Markku Wilenius and Sofi Kurki

Contents

Abstract

Anticipation refers to the many ways the future as a concept, and a dimension in our mental maps, is used for making informed decisions in the present. In this chapter, we introduce the long-term socioeconomic cycle framework, known as the Kondratieff wave theory, as a central anticipatory tool for understanding large-scale socioeconomic change. We present the K-waves theory in brief, focusing especially on the implications of the systemic reorganization for the social practices in each new wave. We then continue on to demonstrate how the K-waves framework can be used for anticipating the drivers for the next, sixth Kondratieff wave. Building on empirical data from networked, human-centric organizations, we explore a potential paradigm

M. Wilenius (✉)
School of Economics, Finland Futures Research Centre, University of Turku, Turku, Finland
e-mail: markku.wilenius@utu.fi

S. Kurki
University of Turku, School of Economics, Finland Futures Research Centre, Turku, Finland
e-mail: sofi.kurki@utu.fi

© Springer Nature Switzerland AG 2019
R. Poli (ed.), *Handbook of Anticipation*,
https://doi.org/10.1007/978-3-319-91554-8_36

695

shift in the anticipatory practices for the next wave. We argue that the K-waves framework can be used for understanding the history and development of how societies change friom past to future in dynamic patterns. We conclude by outlining the key features of this new foresight paradigm we call reflexive foresight.

Keywords
Futures studies · Kondratieff cycles · Reflexive foresight · Anticipation

Introduction: Futures Studies, Systems Thinking, and Anticipation

We can recognize a deep connection between futures studies and systems thinking. In fact, we may state that futures studies work as a method for pattern recognition and thereby the following features discern futures studies from a standard discipline point of view (Wilenius 2017). Here our points of departure are the following assumptions based on systems thinking. We

1. Are concerned of the whole instead of breaking components into pieces
2. Are more focused on the process rather than on the content
3. Are more interested about underlying dynamics than symptoms
4. Are more concerned with underlying patterns rather than identifying individual phenomenon
5. Are interested in patterns that explain the chaos rather than try to control chaos to enable order
6. Are more attentive to interaction than contents of communication

Thus, systems thinking provides a mental platform that enables futures studies to develop more into a type of direction, where the predictive element is deeply embedded into a more reflexive approach about the nature of reality as we see it. Futures studies are defined as a discipline, which endeavors to be sensitive enough of those social large-scale patterns that define which type of individual events are likely to occur. Penetrating the future of any given system requires thus information that enables the analysis of the forms of interaction and feedback loops.

This type of system-based approach on futures studies we define as reflexive foresight. We like to suggest here that our concept of reflexive foresight comes very near to the theory of anticipation as suggested by Roberto Poli (2010). Quoting Rosen he points out how "an anticipatory system is a system containing a predictive model of itself and/or its environment, which allows it to change state at an instant in accord with the model's predictions pertaining to a later instant." We like to highlight the connection between our concept of reflexive foresight and anticipation theory by presenting two illustrative approaches within the framework of reflexive foresight. One case deals with the long-term socioeconomic waves known as Kondratieff waves, while the other case deals with organizations as anticipatory systems.

The Long-Wave Pattern

The project of understanding anticipation in different areas of human endeavor is based on the evidence that humans, and at some extent other life forms, have a capacity to use their experience to perceive historically repeating patterns and project them into the future in order to adapt to their environment. For humans, especially the domain of memory is central in this ability to formulate hypothesis about the future (e.g., Suddendorf and Corballis 1997; Cuhls 2016). During the cultural evolution, this capacity for forward-looking hypothesis formation has been harnessed as different ways to make sense of our surroundings and specialized and institutionalized in different fields of sciences and societal forms of organizing. For the social sciences, one of the key questions motivating enquiry has been whether there are patterns that can act as heuristics for anticipating society-level changes for preparing for the future. However, especially for the social sciences and economics, change and transition have proved to be challenging concepts, despite the fact that any human activity is at its core historically bound and subject to both lawlike and contingent forces.

One of the most influential theoretical approaches that provides a mechanism for how socioeconomic systems transform over time has been the framework of the long-wave phenomenon. It was first brought into a broader international discussion by the Russian economist Nikolai Kondratieff in the beginning of the twentieth century (Kondratieff 1928/1984) There had been previous references to the phenomenon, but those had not received much recognition beyond their limited local intellectual spheres (Louçã and Reijnders 1999).

Historically, the discovery of the waves in economic activity was prompted by repeated economic crises that started to be experienced in countries that had adopted capitalist market structures. The regularity of these crises was rare among socioeconomic phenomena. By the 1850s and 1860s, two propositions were advanced as a basis for understanding the phenomenon. The first of the propositions stated that there was indeed periodicity in the phenomenon. The second stated that the crises were organically inherent in the system. However, that the crises would regularly follow each other as a structural feature of the economy did not seem to capture the phenomenon to a satisfying degree. To understand the full cycle, the crisis element needed to be complemented with two other elements: upswing and depression. The Kondratieff wave theory (or K-waves for short) was introduced at a stage when these basic building blocks of understanding the structural development of the economy were in place. The K-waves theory started out as a discovery that historically, prices of basic commodities have followed a pattern, where a rising price trend is followed by a falling trend on a 40- to 60-year cycle. This insight complemented research on the already established shorter cycles, like the Kitchin cycle with a duration of 3–3.5 years and the business cycles (also known as the Juglar cycle) of 7–11 years.

Kondratieff defined his approach to long cycles as a phenomenon that is particular to capitalist societies (an important delineation as the context he was working in was the recently founded socialist Russia). For Kondratieff himself, the full understanding of economic development would require understanding of both processes of development that can be seen as having a certain direction and processes of a fluctuating, conjunctural character. However, Kondratieff in his own research is not considering the relations between these different processes; he is merely making the point that while the process of real dynamics is "of a piece," it is not by its nature linear. Instead, Kondratieff sees it as irregular, consisting of spurts and fluctuations. Kondratieff's merit, and grounds for his prominent place in the history of the cycles, is his attempt to systematically and thoroughly investigate the long-term fluctuating phenomena in the economy, in order to clearly define and establish the phenomenon. However, as he himself notes, due to the preliminary state of research, he was forced to focus on particular though important elements of the economy. His self-stated caveat was that had he set out to study the capitalist economies in their entirety, a synthetic point of view would have had to be taken, but this could not be done due to the state of the overall understanding of the topic.

Even though Kondratieff's work was thus fundamentally based on econometric indicators, we can still turn to his work for insights on using the identified long waves as an anticipatory tool for understanding the entire society. He notes that "considerable changes take place in the basic conditions of society's economic life before the beginning of the rising wave of each long cycle" (Kondratieff 1928/1984). For Kondratieff, these changes include significant technical inventions and discoveries (with a clear distinction between the invention and the innovation phase, which can be several decades apart) that precede profound changes in the *technique and exchange*, changes in the conditions of monetary circulation, and enlargement of the role played by new countries in global economic life.

Later authors have elaborated on these basic insights. Most famously, Joseph Schumpeter was a central figure in transforming the Kondratieff wave hypothesis into a tool for modern economic analysis, by bringing to discussion aspects that would explain the fluctuations by separating endogenous factors of change from exogenous factors (war, revolution, social unrest, government policy, earthquakes, crop production, etc.). He put forward the argument that for understanding economic development, one needs to understand the endogenous factors (O'Hara 1994). For Schumpeter (who also suggested naming the long-wave phenomenon after Kondratieff), innovation-related dynamics became the primary reason for the upswing and the following downswing of the cycle.

A consensus among later K-waves scholars is that the key mechanism for the long-wave generation stems from progress based in the core technologies of an era operating under their suited institutions. Inevitably, the growth based on taking advantage of the novel technology runs into diminishing returns, and economic growth slows down. Resumption of rapid economic growth requires the emergence of a new set of core technologies and the reformation of institutional structures to suit the new needs. Freeman and Louçã (2001) analyze economic growth through the concept of the long waves. Their central argument is that economic growth, as we have experienced it, needs to be understood in terms of a sequence of eras. Each era is marked by a cluster of technologies, whose progressive development drives experienced economic growth. This argument does not imply technological determinism but that the effective development and implementation of the particular technologies that are central in an era require an appropriate and supportive structure of institutions. This argument, in its present form, has been developed by Carlota Perez (2016), who has expanded on a more holistic framework for understanding the fluctuations. She took up the concept of a socioeconomic system, arguing that while economic institutions have an integrity on their own, they are also intertwined with other major social subsystems and institutions: technology, science, politics, and culture. A key postulate as regards the waves is that leading countries in different eras have come about as a result of a successful fit between the various subsystems that are thus able to provide a supporting overall structure for the key technologies (Perez 2016). Thus, a change from one era to another very often has been associated with a change in the locus of economic leadership (Goldstein 1988).

Understanding the social implications of the cyclicality is a key prerequisite for utilizing the K-waves theory for anticipation. Often, attention is focused on anticipating technological development, leaving the social and societal effects to be a somewhat less explored area. However, for instance, Perez (2016) discusses linkages between the fourth wave upswing around personal mobility (automobiles) and widespread societal effects, ranging from change in the urban structure, as part of the postwar suburban expansion, to changes on the institutional level, bringing, among other things, free education and welfare systems to support the system built around ensuring material well-being for the masses. Also other societal effects linked with the K-waves have been found: Berry (1992) has discussed a connection between the K-waves and utopian communities, where the falling wave and especially depression give rise to alternative social experiments. The K-waves theory has also found resonance in history, where, for instance, scholars within the *Annales* School, with their concept of the *longue durée*, have utilized the structural framework of the Kondratieff waves to understanding historical development on different time scales (van Roon 1981).

A popular explanation for the cycles is to link them with generational learning processes and social psychology (e.g., Dator 1999). For instance, Stoken (1978) explains the dynamic of the long cycle, entirely in terms of psychological factors, as follows: the basic assumption in the generations model of the K-waves is that the population consists of, in more or less equal measures, individuals inclined to risk taking and individuals who tend to avert risks. In the rising wave, a period of prosperity, people assume the development to reflect on their economic condition as ensuring its continued improvement. In these conditions, the desire to become a risk taker increases across the board: entrepreneurs increase their economic commitments, people use their savings to increase their standard of living, and some individuals, who otherwise would classify as risk averters, become risk takers. These herd phenomena have a compounding effect with the broad economic expansion. As the economic growth trend continues, the tendency of becoming a risk taker grows. When the balance of individual tendencies flips to risk takers, excessive supplies in relation to demand are built, with the consequence of rising business costs. Balancing this oversupply requires at least some of the people to return to risk averters: stop borrowing money, building economic commitments, and increase their work effort. In economies, this happens through individuals experiencing economic setbacks. These basic elements, according to Stoken, form the basic tenets of long-wave dynamics. At the same time, they also show how the innate anticipatory capabilities of individuals systematically lead people astray in their risk-taking behavior related to long-term decisions. The Kondratieff wave theory models these systematic errors.

The fundamental tension in using the cyclical framework for anticipation is the same that we find in nature everyday: cycles repeat, but each day is different. In addition, with the K-wave (as with any empirical theory), historical evidence does not necessarily imply the continuation of the pattern in the future.

Potential Limits of the K-Waves Model?

As stated before, the Kondratieff wave theory is at heart a systemic model. Thus, its anticipatory power lies in its ability to depict and model relevant aspects of the system. There are several ways in which the system may change, thus challenging the model itself Wilenius and Casti (2015). In this chapter, we will present three different possibilities as examples of how this could happen.

As with all anticipatory models, they themselves entail a seed for their own demise. The phenomenon is generally referred to as reflexivity and includes phenomena like self-fulfilling and self-refuting prophecies. Although there exist widely known theories that have not lost their capability to model real-life events, the question of what are the systemic effects of societally important models always looms in the background (for instance, is the Moore's law a self-fulfilling prophesy or a law of nature?).

Secondly, the K-waves theory has been formulated for a specific way of organizing the economy, and the main empirical evidence the theory relies on comes from conditions of capitalist market economy. Thus, should these conditions change dramatically, it may well be that the system's key parameters that have made the K-waves model function would be lost.

A third type of argument has been presented by Tuomi (2009) who suggested that the rapid pace of technological development makes the institutionalization processes referred to by, e.g., Perez simply too slow to keep up with new technology. As a result, the system becomes characterized by constant reconfiguration instead of a succession of societal waves each defined by a specific key technology aligned with a set of corresponding organizational, legal, and production processes. This state of "constant disruption," then, becomes the essence of the new economy. Thus, in a nutshell, Tuomi's point is that we cannot rely on the same kinds of models to work in technology foresight or in policy planning as in the world of slower technological development.

What Were the Previous Waves Like?

As stated in the previous sections of this chapter, the Kondratieff wave theory, cyclicality is primarily tied with data from economic activity. The wavelike behavior of economic activity can be illustrated, for example, by the rolling 10-year yields of the Standard & Poor equity index (Fig. 1). From these temporal patterns, we can

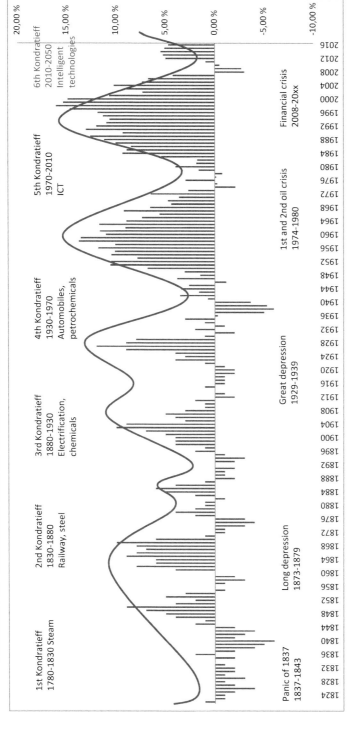

Rolling 10-year return on the S&P 500 since 1814 till December 2016 (in %, p. a.). Source: Datastream, Bloomberg. Illustration: Helsinki Capital Partners.

Fig. 1 Kondratieff waves

draw out how each of the waves has been driven by specific technologies and their applications Wilenius (2017b). So we go from the birth of industrialization, brought about by the invention of steam machines, to the use of steel and railroads and further on to the electrification of our factories and homes and new chemistry to produce, among other things, paper. From the 1930s onward, a great tide of automobiles burst onto the scene, accompanied by sharply rising consumption of petrochemicals, such as petrol for cars. The last wave, emerging in the early 1970s after the oil crisis, turned out to be the victory march for digitalization and the expansion of various communication technologies. That era came to an end with the emergence of a financial crisis that almost crashed the whole global financial system (Fig. 1).

However, for the purpose of building on the economic pattern for understanding the social contents of the waves, we need to explain the technology uptake of each wave not only by the technologies themselves but with a social driver. Indeed, our argument is that the anticipatory power of the waves stems from the observation that the technology uptake that is conventionally utilized to explain the formation of a new wave can be linked with, even explained with the human interest, which by and large "tames" and directs technologies and economic behavior to a certain trajectory as illustrated in Fig. 2.

Thus, while each of the waves has their core technologies and their fields of applications, for the purpose of analyzing the wave, we propose these technologies also are fulfilling a human interest, particular to each wave. With each new wave, human interests have expanded to new fields as a result of reaching a certain level of maturity in the previous wave. Again, starting from industrial revolution, the first wave helped people to reach a certain level of life quality: clothing industry, where many of the new technologies were being applied, is a prime example of this type of

THE SUCCESSION OF DEVELOPMENT WAVES IN INDUSTRIAL SOCIETIES

K-Waves	1st wave	2nd wave	3rd wave	4th wave	5th wave	6th wave
Period	1780–1830	1830–1880	1880–1930	1930–1970	1970–2010	2010–2050
Drivers	Steam Machine	Railroad Steel	Electricity Chemicals	Automobiles, Petrochemicals	Digital communication technologies	Intelligent, resource efficient technologies
Prime field of application	Clothing industry and energy	Transport, infrastructure and cities	Utilities and mass-production	Personal mobility and freight transport	Personal computers and mobile phones	Materials and energy production and distribution
Human interest	New means for decent life	Reaching out and upwards	Building maintenance	Allowing for freedom	Creating new space	Integrating human, nature and technology

Fig. 2 Development waves in industrial societies

development where human interest was pointed toward making it easy for people to fulfill a basic need of obtaining clothing. The second wave developed to meet very specific needs for urbanization, both by building infrastructure for the cities and by enabling movement from the rural areas to the factories in the cities. The railroads allowed people and goods to be transported more efficiently than with horses. With the rise of the third wave, following the fulfillment of basic-level needs, technology was used to raise the level of comfort in human societies through electricity in cities. The rapid development of synthetic chemical use was also paving the way for modern life: for instance, the creation of industrial chemicals supported the households in maintaining their level of cleanness and sanitation. As we moved to the fourth wave, automobiles and petrochemicals together provided individuals technological means for mobility, thus providing certain sense of freedom.

The emergence of distributed computing systems in the wake of the fifth wave created a digital space for people to operate and communicate in. The true revolutionary force of digital technologies has empowered human beings all around the planet by allowing them to communicate on their own behalf, thus activating people to take part in different human subsystems in a very different way. This is how humans have tamed technology, originally built to solve problems in logic, to provide solutions for their fundamental human needs.

Utilizing the Long Wave: Framework for Anticipating the Social Aspects of the Next Wave

In order to address the main issue of interest in this Handbook chapter, how to use the knowledge we have of the long-wave structure and dynamics as an anticipatory tool, we will now turn our attention to applying the K-waves theory for the understanding the drivers that apply to the sixth wave. As we saw before, the waves have a relationship with one another, so profound understanding of the history of the previous wave, its socio-technical structures, tendencies, and outputs, is a prerequisite to making anticipations about the next. To be more specific, there are two complementary ways to approach the matter: the next wave can be seen as developing around a technology driver that was developed during the previous waves and that can be leveraged to build on the outcomes of the past wave. Here, analysis goes out from understanding the human needs, as was the main framework employed in the previous chapter.

Another way to build anticipation from one wave to the next is to focus on the side effects that have arisen out of the techno-economic activities of the past wave. This approach, although yet lesser known than the first one, seems most suitable to understanding the transition from the fifth wave to the sixth. In the 1970s, the beginning of the fifth wave, levels of carbon dioxide in the atmosphere were still on a level that did not threaten to disrupt the climate system. At the end of the wave, climate change is the key challenge facing humanity, and the solutions must be reached within a relatively short window of opportunity, covering the next 20 years. Also, growth and the solutions enhancing human prosperity in the previous five

THE DRIVERS BEHIND 6TH WAVE (2010–2050)

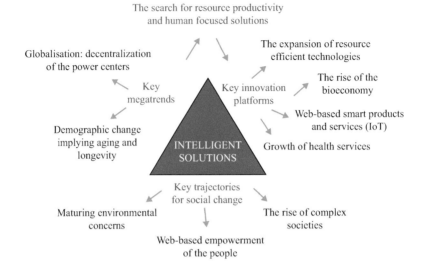

Fig. 3 The drivers behind sixth wave

waves have relied on an ever-expanding use of natural resources. The technologies and social systems built for modern life have enabled spread of decent life standards from the top of societal hierarchies to encompass entire societies. This interest to democratize life standards has created huge industrial machinery for the service of the human good. Of course, we are nowhere near to fulfilling globally those needs, and there are still pockets of deep poverty within rich countries. At the core of these problems, we find the biased relationship between humans, technology, and nature, pertaining to all the previous waves and the technologies therein. The facts that the human-induced climate change is on its way, the massive destruction of forest and biodiversity escalates, the oceans have become dumping grounds for economic interests, and relentless extraction of minerals continues are all examples of how our relationship with nature has developed on a very wrong footing. Currently we are overusing the Earth's resources as if we had several Earths instead of one. For the next wave then, the long-term interest of the human focus will be geared toward finding solutions to these problems (Wilenius 2017a Forthcoming). This calls for new kinds of technologies and new types of production, distribution, and consumption patterns, outlined in Fig. 3.

To solve the problem in the relationship between humans, nature, and technology, the sixth wave will unfold with various set of new technologies. Some technologies will come to help solve the problem of harmful emissions, such as renewable energy technologies. Others will come to reduce the overall efficiency of production and consumption systems. Yet others, like Internet of Things, will provide new machine-to-machine communication systems that enable more intelligent resource allocation. Nanotechnologies will provide solutions for the durability of materials.

All this will happen in the context of a new phase of globalization that dramatically decentralizes the world power systems. The non-OECD countries will hold the majority of weight in the global economic system at the end of sixth wave. The demographic transition will be another of the major megatrends affecting all societies, although in a different way. In most of the advanced countries, over one-third of the population will be 65 years or older, with longevity becoming a more significant feature of societies. The next phases of digital technology revolution will help more direct democracies to grow. At the same time, the concerns related to the degeneration of our natural and human-built environment will escalate and become a predominant feature of our political debate. The increasing complexity of issues at hand will push societies to move toward more holistic approaches to solve their problems.

Everywhere we look, we see interest rising in making better use of existing resources. For anticipating how the societal context of the sixth wave will be affected by the efforts to improve resource productivity, we may look at the earlier waves and how their technological transformations changed the whole socioeconomic system. The abovementioned fourth wave is an example of the extent to which a combination of aligned technological and institutional changes can shape the everyday life and aspirations of citizens. For the sixth wave, we can expect that the changes that will shape the societies, and practices becoming the "new normal," all have a direct relationship with this pursuit of resource efficiency. Thus, the search for resource productivity brings us to question our current practices. Nowhere is this transition more visible than in the ways organizations are shifting from product-orientated industrial mode toward a service-orientated network model. This is why we next turn our attention to the life of organizations.

Developmental Stages of Organizational Forms

In the following passage, we will explore in a more elaborated way how the cycle theory can be applied in practice for the purpose of societal anticipation. We are looking at individual case studies as reflections of the broader societal change pattern. The approach we are adopting is abductive, attempting an internally consistent merger between theory and the empirical evidence.

Focusing on various developmental phases of human organizations over time, we can find an interesting insight that explains about how human needs and aspirations have created various anticipatory patterns. In the case of organizations, we need to look for much longer temporal phases that span the whole history of human civilization. These adaptive stages can be described in the following way (Kurki and Wilenius 2016; Laloux 2014):

1. *Tribal stage.* This phase started to emerge some 15,000 years back with the small tribal communes. These organizations were largely based on a strong hierarchy: there was an undisputed leader who reigned with fear and who had to show courage in the continued quarrel and fight with neighbors. Today we still meet this type of organizational behavior among mafia, street gangs, and mercenary armies.

2. *Settlement stage.* Some 6000 BC, the first agrarian communities started to settle in Mesopotamia and Egypt. Soon they started to formulate collective rules and norms to steer the life of community. Institutionalized religion emerged that further created strong hierarchies and replicable practices. These types of organizations hold sway up to modern times. Today we still see this type of organizations in church, in armies, and in hospitals and in many corners of our public governance system.

3. *Industrial stage.* The birth of modern science preceded the emergence of industrialization which in turn created our modern capitalist organization. These organizations are dynamic and based on competition, optimization, profit seeking, and a strong belief in competence and skills. It is still today a prevailing form of organization in our modern societies and economies.

4. *Postindustrial stage.* More recently, particularly after Second World War, the fourth organizational model was where the idea is no longer to seek profit but to work for a cause. They are usually called non-governmental (NGOs)? organizations and are typically based on strong culture and desire to produce information and knowledge on some particular topic. Their number has been on the sharp rise in the last decades.

5. *Self-organized stage.* Currently, alongside with the emergence of the sixth wave, we are witnessing the fifth type of organization to grow. These organizations, again, have a very different aspiration in how organize the collective structure. It looks like these organizations build their behavior on three premises: first, they are based on self-management, which means hierarchies of any kind are shunned at all cost. Rather, and reflective of our ever more complex environment, they are based on active networking, as is actually very much the case with global economy. Secondly, they thrive from concept of wholeness. This means they step away from industrial mode of organizing the everyday life: there is not a sharp division between "home" and "work," for instance. Thirdly, these organizations tend to be much more mission and purpose orientated; however this purpose may change according to impulses from environment. In a metaphoric sense, these organizations appear as organic creatures.

The point we are making here is that understanding the dynamism of these types of historical pattern is a powerful anticipatory tool for what might happen in the next phase of societal evolution. The emergence of each historical wave of organization is closely connected to understanding the needs and aspirations of those societies in which the organizations are embedded. The last organizational phase we are observing next is nothing but reflection of our complex environment initiated by our globalized societies.

New Modes of Organizing as Drivers of the Sixth Wave

Next we shall dive deeper into understanding what might be the fifth form of organization that will, we postulate, start to expand and finally dominate in the coming decades. These observations are based on empirical studies we have conducted among organizations we believe are representatives of this new emerging type of network collectives the phenomenon described here is drawn from extant literature (Laloux 2014; Nandram 2015), complemented by empirical studies and interviews in the following organizations: Reaktor, Buurtzorg, Morningstar, Patagonia, and Vincit (Kurki et al. 2016; Kurki and Wilenius 2016). There are three fundamental ways in which these organizations depart from any current form of organizations:

1. **A break from the industrial mode of organizing their work**. Breaking industrial order refers to the following things: (a) the normal command and control hierarchical structures are kept to minimum. This means that companies are mostly organized in teams that have complete autonomy as regards their projects. There is no centralized body leading their work; the role of the more administrative functions is rather to support the function of the teams. This means in practice, for instance, that there is nobody allocating funds for the project in the form of a budget. The organization is formed out of self-organized teams of 10–12 members. The size of the team provides a heterogenic enough operational ground while preserving the agility of the group. It enables also an environment where the use of each individual's intellectual capacity is encouraged. So, instead of resorting to hierarchical or consensual decision-making, these organizations adhere to what is called the advice process. It means every co-worker at any time is allowed to make any decision on two conditions: they need to have listened the views of their colleagues, especially those to whom decision touches upon and those who have special expertise on the area. Ultimately, however, the decision-making power is upon every individual, regardless of their task. The organization effectively functions as a network. The most challenging aspect of working in these types of organizations is the high requirement they place on social intelligence to be able to thrive in a team. Egocentric people cannot succeed in these types of organizations.

2. **Ethical standards used as guiding principles instead of more traditional measures.** High ethical standards seem to be the cornerstone for these kinds of organizations Kurki and Wilenius (2015). The outdoor clothing company Patagonia is a perfect example: they have made themselves famous by their desire to organize around the principles of respecting natural resources. The Dutch nursing company Buurtzorg has their very own way of showing their ethical standards. They, for instance, teach (or educate) their fiercest competitors to become more agile organizations, which is of course a very exceptional behavior. With this level of integrity, it is simply to say: we are all in service of the larger cause; thus it is everybody's duty to help the performance of the whole system to develop.

3. **Strategic thinking (=anticipation strategies) and behavior are systemic rather than linear.** The third fundamental aspect of these organizations is in the very way that they anticipate the future. The question asked in the remaining chapter therefore is, what are the specific features that make these organizations anticipatory? In other words, what are the in-built mechanisms that make our progressive organizations anticipatory systems (Rosen 1985/2012; Poli 2010, 2014)?

This approach described above is at its core *systemic*. The behavior of these organizations mimics the patterns found in all *dynamic, self-organizing systems* (Ståhle 1998): they make optimal use of emerging opportunities as they arise. In other words, they maintain their capabilities to recognize the changes outside their system and seek constantly to readjust their direction according to their observations. Also, dynamic systems thrive best when they live in a richly interactive and spontaneous culture. Team-based work, networking over silos, and freedom to act when necessary without hierarchical decision-making procedures are the key modes of operation. By decentralizing power radically to be a property of the whole system, dynamic systems are constantly in the business of rejuvenating themselves. As the end result, the ability of the system to self-manage its operations is optimized.

Based on the evidence from the case organizations, it seems as if organizations of the sixth wave build their identity largely on being able to address the three aspects of sustainability: economic, social, and environmental. Indeed, one of the defining features of these examples of "sixth wave organizations" is that they are companies who are aware of their impact on the world. Again, this is a feature of systems thinking which is prevalent in the companies we have investigated. Drawing from insights provided by the long-wave theory, and the drivers for the next wave, we are postulating that the values and practices these organizations represent will grow to have a predominant role during the coming decades as the sixth wave unfolds (Wilenius 2014).

There are seven particular features that reflect the anticipatory qualities of these organizations as reflected in their behavior. We call this set of behaviors a CARE-model.

1. *The level of quality in ways to share information and collaborate.* In the organizations, great emphasis has been placed into making sure all the necessary information about the functioning of the system is available for everyone in the system. New channels enabled by social media are actively in use. But there is more to it. All of these progressive companies perform in ways where they go remarkably deep in their collaboration with clients. Reaktor, for instance, does not work for the client unless they work under the same roof. What they normally do is that they move into the office of their client, thus ensuring the connection to client stays intimate throughout the project. Buurtzorg states that their goal is to bring back the total autonomy of the client, with the ultimate goal of the client recovering to not needing anymore professional nursing. Again, this means a deeper connection to clients and tapping in more deeply to their particular needs. From a systems perspective, this signals an understanding of the feedback loop and the logic of "the more we give to our clients, the more loyal customers we get and the more we ourselves will benefit from the relationship in the future." The sixth wave will at its core be based on collaboration. This will happen because the rise of digitalization has brought an immense amount of communication opportunities, which tie together people as well as organizations. Already now this is very visible: for instance, in the business world, most of the new companies that have risen to become the most successful in global business have come up with products and services that enhance communication: Facebook, Apple, Google,

Airbnb, and Uber, just to name the most renowned. And a good level of communication is always necessary for quality collaboration. Actually, this all contributes to building an ecosystem that works. Again, from a systems perspective, this is probably the most important facet of a sixth wave organization. In fact, the ecosystems thinking that has so fundamentally affected our idea of human networks is at the core of the collaboration agenda. As organizations become more aware of their environment, they start to, slowly but surely, understand the benefits of collaboration. Ecosystems thinking postulates two types of behavior: (a) each agent in the ecosystem has its own specific task and (b) the key resource is the ability to adapt to changing conditions.

2. *Rethinking the key competencies necessary for thriving in the ecosystem.* In the case organizations, the technical skills and competencies relevant to the tasks performed by the organizations evidently constitute key criteria for recruitment. Yet, increasingly, "cultural fit" and social skills are in even a more decisive role. For instance, Reaktor emphasizes the importance of the recruiting process for maintaining their social organization functional.

Also *trust* as an important organizational value seems to be a key value in the studied organizations. In an industrially run organization, trust has been replaced by management structures that enable the command and control of the organization. Trust, when given a central role in the organizations' functioning, has several repercussions: first, it means people are trusted in what they say. Second, it means that people are given responsibility and autonomy. Third, it implies members of the organization have a special relationship with each other. Trust is considered to be among the most valuable assets an organization has (Kurki and Wilenius 2016).

A related phenomenon stemming from the culture of trust is openness to difficulties and conflict situations. In the case of Reaktor, we learned that employees really appreciated the open spirit of the company that allows people to speak up when they think they should. This is the type of transparency that helps to avoid manipulation and information hoarding, all features that tend to paralyze more traditional organizations today. Again, from the systems point of view, the more an organization is able to establish feedback loops that help the system to autocorrect itself, the more it has a chance to recorrect its course.

The abovementioned features can together be summed up as signaling an organizational culture of human-centrism, which is also shown in other ways in the organizational life. In all of the sixth wave organizations presented, expressing emotions and feelings is considered legitimate in the work context. People are accepted as whole, which is not typically what an industrially organization does. There the ideology has been to separate "work" and "life" to the extent where people ought to act purely in a professional way, extracting their feelings from the rational part of the human being. Here people are accepted as beings whose decision-making is substantially based on emotions.

All these features are pertaining to the competence building of the company and have a fundamental connection to what here is called anticipation. As organization becomes more internally open, their capability to sense what is taking place in their immediate environment increases. Simultaneously, they are more open to the information that bears relevance to the future. Having the capacities available inside the organization builds a good opportunity to make more informed decisions about the future.

3. *Continuous and inclusive focus on innovation.* In our case organizations, innovation is not compartmentalized to a specific department in the company. Rather, it is a feature of everybody's work. In Reaktor, this means that they do not have any ready-made solutions for their clients since they believe every client has specific needs that should be addressed in the product. Likewise, in Buurtzorg, the most important aspect of their relationship to work derives from the organization's foundational idea: everything should be done to help the nurses to focus on their work. It was early on decided that all kinds of back office work, rigid schedules from above, and unnecessary forms to be filled should be cleared out of the nurse's way or made as simple as possible. That would help them to use all their talent and know-how directly for the benefit of their clients. Again, this point is a reflection of systems thinking being applied in the organizations' design. Learning in an organization can only take place if we allow human-centric principles, instead of hierarchy- and bureaucracy-based principles, to be the mode of operation. This cannot take place unless people are given full freedom and responsibility in the ways they organize their work. For the company Morningstar, this idea has been brought to life by stating that all of the company's co-workers need only to adhere to two principles: first, nobody is allowed to use coercive power over others (this principle applies to the founder of the company too). Secondly, everybody should keep all his or her commitments. These two norms establish the necessary boundary conditions for the system to operate. What is implied is that (a) all members of the community are entitled to innovate, i.e., nobody can, on the basis of their status in the hierarchy, stop their innovation process, and (b) by signing to keep your commitments, you may come up with new ideas about how to best meet them. This is another feature of systems-based thinking applied to an organizational setup.

4. *Passion for radical solutions.* All of the organizations referenced here are committed to nonstandard solutions. They are not seeking the quickest and most convenient solution to everything but rather want to ensure that all decisions are made consciously, with reflection. This is particularly because in the sixth wave, the world simply needs more radical solutions. We have entered a new socioeconomic era that seeks ways to radically reinvent the central pieces of our system, be it the question of social services, counteraction to environmental destruction, or mending our corrupted political systems. It is much more probable that those radical solutions come from organizations that encourage the innovation to take place at every level.

5. *Commitment to long-term thinking.* All the founders of these extraordinary companies have committed themselves to long-term thinking. This is finely expressed by the most important long-term goal of the Reaktor company: their goal is to be a flourishing company after 200 years. Even more importantly, this thinking has been brought to a very practical level. The demise of many

organizations today is that they keep doing things that they know are wrong. In these organizations, however, people and teams are encouraged not only to innovate but to "*fail fast*." If something is not working, it is not continued. People and teams are constantly encouraged to challenge their own practices. This is the way to increase the sensitivity to changes in the operating environment. The long-term commitment and perspective are also reflected in the ways that people are motivated. These companies are motivating people not with financial incentives but by offering a place to work where you can express yourself as a human being. This means there are no separate bonus systems; hierarchies and titles are kept to a minimum. Incentive systems are based on team-level performance.

From a systems perspective, probably the most important factor for building a long-term organization is to enhance its level of resilience, in other words its capacity to adjust to its environment. This is gained through being sensitive to changes and requirements both internally and externally. This is not easy to attain: most human-built systems tend to lose their connection to the inner life of an organization as well as to the outside world. Nowhere is this tendency more visible than in our current global capitalistic system. Many of the basic incentive systems and practices encourage the companies in the stock markets to take advantage of the short-term thinking, starting from quarter-year reporting. As Jacobs and Mazzucato, among others, have pointed out, there is a substantial amount of evidence that in the course of the past 30–40 years, our global economic system has had a strong bias to increase inequality in terms of income and social benefits and make some people extremely rich (Jacobs and Mazzucato 2016). This can lead us to think that short-termism leads in the long run almost inevitably to greater inequality. There is an interesting anecdote illustrating the consequences of short-term thinking: the British monarch Queen Elizabeth II met with the economy experts at the time of the financial crisis, when the economy crashed in late 2008. She asked that given the extraordinary scale of the crash, why could nobody see it coming? The right answer is that there was hardly anybody thinking about the long-term consequences of the radical market liberation that allows short-term profit seeking to overrule the financial markets. In other words, no systems thinking was practiced (Jacobs and Mazzucato 2016).

6. *The ability to take risks.* If you are operating in new territories, you need to be willing to take risks. As stated before, the organizations examined here are indeed encouraging their people to take risks, while they also encourage failing fast. This is all about creating a culture where it is safe to take risks of all kinds: bring up issues that are uncomfortable, "go and experiment with something that has not tried before," and so forth. People need to feel safe in order to be able to use their full capacity. A strongly risk-aversive culture leads to sticking to old rules and habits. Taking even major risk should not be a measure of stupidity but a measure of tolerance. Of course, risk taking need to be coupled with high level of ethics. One of the key factors bringing down the productivity of organizations is the level of fear. In a fear-based culture, people are not encouraged to bring in new initiatives. In the sixth wave organizations, taking and allowing risk is considered

a conscious act. From a systems perspective, risk taking allows organization to question its current practices and to open up new opportunities.

7. *The focus on futures.* In our current world, we tend to focus on our past performance. Organizations are led into the future by measuring the past. In modern human-centric organizations, there is a strong tendency *to let the organization lead by itself.* There is a belief in these organizations that they will find their way to the future, if you just allow it to happen. This was done roughly in the following way: first, you build strong principles (rather than targets) on which the organization adheres in all of its behavior. Secondly, you allow different initiatives to be tested among co-workers. If an idea proves successful among the people, then the whole company might adopt the new idea. In such a way, the future actually emerges all the time in various forms.

In a fundamental way, for these organizations, the future always remains open. It is not fixed into the present, nor is it tied to a singular vision about the future: nobody in the organization "owns" the future. From a systems perspective, allowing the future to unfold means that a sufficient amount of input is allowed at all times to enable multiple futures the possibility to occur. From this anticipation perspective, the organizations exhibiting the features of a CARE-model are practicing something we could call *reflexive foresight.*

Reflexive Foresight as the Anticipatory Model for the Sixth Wave

Reflexive foresight constitutes of three quintessential components of human action in the emerging sixth wave: *first*, it manifests an ethos where any human collective sees its own action as a part of the larger scheme of things and takes its drive and energy from there. Patagonia company is a prime example of this type of ethos. They deliberately express that their core idea is to be a part of the solution for the environmental crisis of our time see their mission statement at http://www.patagonia.com/company-info.html, accessed Sept. 26, 2016. In all of the businesses they run, the real long-term goal is to attain that mission. This is essentially a form of systems thinking put in practice.

Secondly, in the practice of reflexive foresight, all of the human potential residing in the collective is being fully used. In the everyday life of organizations, it means that people are "released" and empowered to create ever new versions of how to express their inner motives. Thus, in the Reaktor company, we found a constant drive to make everything possible to enable employees to develop their way of, say, coding and creating digital architectures. In Buurtzorg, everything was done for nurses to become ever better in taking care of their clients. Thus this feature creates a universe of multiple trial and error processes where, instead of highly disciplined process set from top management, the people are allowed to manifest their own ideas of best practices.

The *third* key dimension of reflexive foresight is that it manifests a new era where humanity moves from collective behavior to social behavior. Looking at the past hundred years of the history of the western world, we can observe how the dynamics of collective behavior have two times ignited into global warfare. There was a brutal self-interest at work. The new types of organizations that are emerging base their organizational logic on a common interest and creating shared value. While community of this sort may exhibit certain tribal sets of behaviors, they actively seek to partner with any external actor that is relevant to the purpose. Thus, Buurtzorg will help their fiercest competitors in the market for how to improve their practices in dealing with their clients. Patagonia has created a conservation alliance with other large outdoor apparel companies and is now increasingly consulting their competitors in how they run their business see https://www.patagonia.com/conservation-alliance.html, accessed Sept. 26, 2016. In essence, the companies work in a solidarity mode instead of a competitive mode to reach their goals.

Summary

In this chapter, our aim has been threefold: first, we have introduced the Kondratieff long-wave theory as a meta-level framework for understanding systems-level socioeconomic change. In the second part of the chapter, we have used this framework for anticipating how the social and organizational aspects of the system will change in the next, sixth wave. Thirdly, and more specifically, we have looked at how practices related to foresight are evolving in five case organizations. We call this new set of anticipatory practices reflexive foresight. Considering the drivers affecting the social dimension of the system, we attach these empirical findings to the emerging sixth socioeconomic wave.

The kind of thinking exemplified in this chapter by progressive organizations has developed as niche phenomenon throughout the fifth wave (for instance, the agile organization movement started in the factories of Toyota in the early 1990s (Goldman et al.1994)). Also, identifying reflexive foresight as organizational practice is foreshadowed by a more in-depth understanding of the ways in which entrepreneurs have approached the future in uncertain markets (as effectuation, instead of causation, see Saraswathy 2001; also Fuller and Warren 2006). But as always, the system as a whole needs to mature to adopt a new model developing in the fringes. Often, shifts from the marginal to the mainstream coincide with systemic reorganization connected with shifts in socioeconomic waves. The cases presented here illustrate the key competencies that are required to take full advantage of these foresight practices as expressed in the concept of reflexive foresight. As we move toward full realization of the sixth wave, we need to create tools that capture the complex reality of this new paradigm to emerge. We think reflexive foresight is tuned for that sort of task.

References

Berry, B. (1992). *America's utopian experiments: Communal havens from long-wave crises*. Hanover: University Press of New England.

Cuhls, K. (2016). Mental time travel in foresight processes – Cases and applications. *Futures, Special Issue "Experiencing Futures"*. https://doi.org/10.1016/j.futures.2016.05.008.

Dator, J. (1999). Return to long waves. *Futures, 31*(3–4), 361–372.

Freeman, C., & Louçã, F. (2001). *As time goes by. From the industrial revolutions to the information revolution*. Oxford: Oxford University Press.

Fuller, T., & Warren, L. (2006). Entrepreneurship as foresight: A complex social network perspective on organisational foresight. *Futures, 38*, 956–971.

Goldman, S., Nagel, R., & Preiss, K. (1994). *Agile competitors and virtual organizations*. New York: Wiley.

Goldstein, J. S. (1988). *Long cycles. Prosperity and war in the modern age*. New Haven: Yale University Press.

Jacobs, M., & Mazzucato, M. (2016). Rethinking capitalism: An introduction. In M. Jacobs & M. Mazzucato (Eds.), *Rethinking capitalism. Economics and policy for sustainable and inclusive growth*. London: Wiley Blackwell.

Kondratieff, N. (1928/1984). 'Long wave cycle' and 'Theses of N.D. Kondratieff's paper: Long cycles in economic conditions' in the long wave cycle. New York: Richardson & Snyder (trans: Daniels, Guy), 25–99 and 101–5, 137–8. In: F. Louçã & J. Reijnders (Eds.), *The foundations of long wave theory. Models and methodology*. Volume I. Cheltenham, UK: Edward Elgar.

Kurki, S., & Wilenius, M. (2015). Ethics in the sixth wave: How new ethical companies will transform our economies in the coming decades. *Futures, 71*, 146–158.

Kurki, S. & Wilenius, M. (2016). Trust makes this organisation unique. Looking at the future of work through two human-centric organisations. Eur J Futures Res (2016) 4:23.

Kurki, S., Pura, M., & Wilenius, M. (2016). *Re-acting the future. New ways to work. The case of Reaktor*. Finland Futures Research Centre, Turku, FFRC eBOOK 6/2016.

Laloux, F. (2014). *Reinventing organisations. A guide to creating organisations*. Brussels: Nelson Parker.

Louçã, F., & Reijnders, J. (1999). *The foundations of long wave theory. Models and methodology* (Vol. I & II). Cheltenham: Edward Elgar.

Nandram, S (2015). Organisational Innovation by Integrating Simplification: Learning from Buurtzorg Nederland, Springer International Publishing. Cham, Switzerland.

O'Hara, P. A. (1994). An institutionalist review of long wave theories: Schumpeterian innovation, modes of regulation, and social structures of accumulation. JEI 2/1994. In F. Louçã & J. Reijnders (Eds.), *The foundations of long wave theory. Models and methodology* (Vol. I & II). Cheltenham: Edward Elgar.

Perez, C. (2016). Capitalism, Technology and a Green Global Golden Age: The Role of History in Helping to Shape the Future. In M. Mazzucato & M. Jacobs (eds.) *Rethinking Capitalism*. Wiley: Political Quarterly 2016.

Poli, R. (2010). The many aspects of anticipation. *Foresight, 12*(3), 7–17.

Poli, R. (2014). Anticipation: A new thread for the human and social sciences. *Cadmus, 2*(3), 14.

Rosen, R. (1985/2012). Anticipatory systems: Philosophical, mathematical, and methodological foundations. Robert Rosen, 2nd ed, with contributions by Judith Rosen, John J. Klineman and Mihai Nadin, 2012, lx + 472 pp. New York: Springer. ISBN:978-1-4614-1268-7.

Sarasvathy, S. D. (2001). Causation and effectuation: Toward a theoretical shift from economic inevitability to entrepreneurial contingency. *Academy of Management Review, 26*, 243–263.

Ståhle, P. (1998). *Supporting a system's capacity for self-renewal*. University of Helsinki, Department of Teacher Education, Helsinki.

Stoken, D. A. (1978). *Cycles. What they are, what they mean, how to profit by them*. New York: McGraw-Hill Book Company.

Suddendorf, T. & Corballis, M. C. (1997). Mental time travel and the evolution of the human mind. *Genet Soc Gen Psychol Monogr, 123*(2),133–67.

Tuomi, I. (2009). The future of semiconductor intellectual property architectural blocks in Europe. JRC Scientific and Technical Reports. EUR 23962 EN.

van Roon, G. (1981). Historians and long waves. *Futures, 13*(5), 383–388.

Wilenius, M. (2014). Leadership in the sixth wave. Excursions into the new paradigm of the Kondratieff cycle 2010–2050. *European Journal of Futures Research, 2*, 36.

Wilenius, M. (2015). The next K-wave and the challenge of global democracy. *Foresight, 17*(1), 35–52.

Wilenius, M. (2017a). *Global change and K-waves: Exploring the pattern of the future.* Routledge Handbook of Resource Nexus. (Forthcoming).

Wilenius, M. (2017b). *Patterns of the future. Understanding the next 40 years of global change.* London: World Scientific Publishing.

Wilenius, M., & Casti, J. (2015). The sixth K-wave and the shocks that may upend it. *Technological Forecasting and Social Change, 94*, 335–349.

Monitoring Sustainable Development Goals: From Now to 2030

35

Fabiola Riccardini

Contents

The ideas expressed in this chapter are of the author and may not reflect the position of ISTAT

F. Riccardini (✉)
Department of Statistical Production, ISTAT, Italian Statistical Institute, Rome, Italy
e-mail: fabiola.riccardini@istat.it

© Springer Nature Switzerland AG 2019
R. Poli (ed.), *Handbook of Anticipation*,
https://doi.org/10.1007/978-3-319-91554-8_39

717

Abstract

The United Nations last September 2015 agreed on the Sustainable Development Goals (SDGs) that will orient the policy actions for the next 15 years. The 17 goals and the related 169 targets have to be monitored and evaluated. The National Statistical Institutes, following a decision of the UN Statistical Commission, have to coordinate the process of production of the statistical data for elaboration of indicators that will be used for monitoring. Therefore, it is necessary to develop a global, regional, and national set of indicators for monitoring the achievements of the goals and targets by countries.

The aim of this chapter is to present a practice of anticipation. Monitoring SDGs is a practice, where evaluating the achievement of goals (results) in a certain period of time implies stimulate actions for an aptitude to forward looking. In this context are used both forecasts and foresights which should be translated into decisions and actions as Poli defined (Poli 2017).

Behavior, both individual and institutional, is generated by fixed goals (SDGs) for facing complex reality characterized by economic, social, environmental, and institutional aspects. In doing this, it would be possible to improve resilience and reducing vulnerabilities of individuals and societies.

Analyzing and forecasting the effects derived from climate changes or the economic instability, for example, are practices of anticipation. This is done for stimulate decisions and actions for improving resiliencies and developing a forward-looking attitude and the use of the former's results for action.

Therefore, the chapter will illustrate the general framework for monitoring SDGs and will present the experience of ISTAT, the Italian Statistical Institute, and the personal research experience for evaluating the SDGs goals and targets, trying to develop a coherent set of measures. It is a challenging action not only for developing countries but also for advanced countries. A data revolution is underway, and the process will run for the next 15 years, and developing data is also crucial for the practices of anticipation. In Italy, the measuring of sustainability has been approached in the context of the project BES (Benessere equo e sostenibile), in line with the United Nations declaration that there is sustainable development when the well-being of people is pursued. Moreover, ISTAT, was a member country inside the Inter-agency Expert Group-SDGs constituted by the UN Statistical Commission, contributed actively for the selection of relevant indicators for monitoring the achievement of SDGs. ISTAT is also member of the Task Force UNECE for developing Sustainable Development measures and of the EUROSTAT

Working Group on Sustainable Development and Europe 2020 indicators. All these national experiences allow developing a coherent framework for Sustainable Development monitoring in which concepts, methods, and measures find clarification.

Keywords
Sustainable development and well-being · SDGs · Global, regional, and national indicators

Introduction

The United Nations last September 2015 (United Nations 2015) agreed on the Sustainable Development Goals that will orient the policy actions for the next 15 years (http://www.un.org/sustainabledevelopment/sustainable-development-goals/).The goals and targets will stimulate actions over the next 15 years in the areas of critical importance for humanity and the planet:

- **People**
  In order to end poverty and hunger, in all their forms and dimensions, and to ensure that all human beings can fulfill their potential in dignity and equality and in a healthy environment.
- **Planet**
  In order to protect the planet from degradation, including through sustainable consumption and production, sustainably managing its natural resources, and taking urgent action on climate change, so that it can support the needs of the present and future generations.
- **Prosperity**
  In order to ensure that all human beings can enjoy prosperous and fulfilling lives and that economic, social, and technological progress occurs in harmony with nature.
- **Peace**
  In order to foster peaceful, just, and inclusive societies which are free from fear and violence. There can be no sustainable development without peace and no peace without sustainable development.
- **Partnership**
  In order to mobilize the means required to implement this agenda through a revitalized global partnership for sustainable development, based on a spirit of strengthened global solidarity, focused in particular on the needs of the poorest and most vulnerable and with the participation of all countries, all stakeholders, and all people.

The **interlinkages** and integrated nature of the Sustainable Development Goals are of crucial importance in ensuring that the purpose of the new agenda is realized. The 17 goals and the related 169 targets should be monitored and evaluated.

The framework for monitoring will influence future decisions, because what we measure defines where we concentrate our efforts, and it implies to identify priority areas for funding and resources mobilization.

The aim of this chapter is to present a practice of anticipation. Monitoring SDGs is a practice, where evaluating the achievement of goals (results) in a certain period of time implies stimulate actions for an aptitude to forward looking. In this context are used both forecasts and foresights which should be translated into decisions and actions as Poli defined (Poli 2017).

Behavior, both individual and institutional, according to the theory of anticipation, is generated by fixed goals (SDGs) instead of stimulus, for facing complex reality characterized by economic, social, environmental, and institutional aspects under the threat of a global proliferation of agents and forces by articulating insecurity by anticipation processes. In doing this, it would be possible to improve resiliencies and reduce vulnerabilities of individuals and societies.

Analyzing and forecasting the effects derived from climate changes or the economic instability, for example, are practices of anticipation. This is done for stimulate decisions and actions for improving resiliencies and developing a forward-looking attitude and the use of the former's results for action.

Therefore, the chapter will illustrate the general framework for monitoring SDGs and will present the experience of ISTAT, the Italian Statistical Institute, and the personal research experience for evaluating the SDGs goals and targets, trying to develop a coherent set of measures. It is a challenging action not only for developing countries but also for advanced countries. A data revolution is underway, and the process will run for the next 15 years, and this is the prerequisite for a practice of anticipation. In Italy, the measuring of sustainability has been approached in the context of the project BES (Benessere equo e sostenibile), in line with the United Nations declaration that there is sustainable development when the well-being of people is pursued. Moreover, ISTAT, as member country inside the Inter-Agency Expert Group-SDGs constituted by the UN Statistical Commission, (http://unstats. un.org/sdgs/) contributed actively for the selection of relevant indicators for monitoring the achievement of SDGs. ISTAT is also member of the TF UNECE (UNECE 2013) for developing Sustainable Development measures (http://www.unece.org/ statistics/statsexperts/task-force-on-adjusting-ces-recommendations-to-the-sustainable-development-goals.html) and of the EUROSTAT Working Group on Sustainable Development and Europe 2020 indicators (Eurostat 2017). All these national experiences allow developing a coherent framework for Sustainable Development monitoring in which concepts, methods, and measures find clarification.

Monitoring at Global Level

Measurement is an essential aspect of monitoring process, allowing an objective and comparable tracking of the progresses countries achieve towards the goals. It is itself a mean of implementation, included inside the SDGs goals. The National Statistical Institutes, following a decision of the UN Statistical Commission, have to coordinate the production process of the statistical data for elaboration of indicators that will be used for monitoring. Therefore, it is necessary to develop a global, regional, national, and subnational set of indicators for evaluating the achievements of the goals and targets by countries.

It is reasonable to define at global level a set of indicators to monitor the SDGs implementation, because measurement is an essential aspect of monitoring, allowing an objective and comparable tracking of the progresses countries achieve towards the goals. That's why indicators associated to the goals are absolutely needed. A Global indicators framework responds to the commitment of Heads of State to engage in a systematic review and follow-up of the 2030 Agenda for Sustainable Development and SDGs implementation. The UN Secretary General prepares an annual progress report on SDGs based on the global indicator framework and data produced by the national statistical systems will feed into the database maintained by the Statistics Division of the United Nations Department for Economic and Social Affairs (UNDESA) with the UN Agencies System.

The set of indicators approved by the Statistical Commission in 2016 for the 169 targets and 17 goals is formed by 230 indicators (241 with doubles), classified by the Tier System. Tier I means that the indicator has the methodology well established and data are almost available. Tier II means that methodology is established but data are not available. Tier III means that methodology is not defined and data are not available. During 2017, a refinement of indicators was undertaken and now we have a set of 244 SDGs indicators for the 169 targets for a net total 232 indicators (without repetitions).

The monitoring framework will also be implemented at regional and national level. Countries will be responsible for monitoring at national level, on regular and voluntary bases.

Two specific working groups organized by the UN Statistical Commission guarantee a balanced dialogue between countries. On one hand, the Inter-Agency Expert Group on SDGs (http://unstats.un.org/sdgs/) has to identify the indicators' framework for goals and targets monitoring. On the other hand, the High Level Group for Partnership, Coordination and Capacity-Building for Post-2015 has to establish a global partnership for sustainable development and reporting, increase capacity building, and lead the SDGs implementation process. Similar groups were not established for the Millennium Development Goals, (UNDESA 2012) implemented under the responsibility of National Statistical Institutes (NSIs). A dedicated and open website is available for both groups: http://unstats.un.org/sdgs/.

Some limitations of identifying the SDGs indicators and monitoring framework have to be underlined. Some targets are formulated in a way which makes them difficult to measure, for instance, where they are too general or multidimensional. Moreover, politicians asked statisticians to identify at least one indicator for each targets, and this implied a large number of indicators at this beginning phase. In future, it is not excluded to develop synthetic indicators or headline indicators. However, in practice, the discussion on SDG indicators started during the formulation of the goals and targets, in order to take into account statistical measurability. Since the SDGs indicators framework provides mechanisms for implementation review and verification, the High Level Political Forum (https://sustainablede velopment.un.org/hlpf) could in principle also revise some targets if they are found not easily measurable.

An important aspect of the process for selection of SDGs indicators is the public consultation that contributed to the selection of preliminary indicators and refinement of them. Public consultation is an important step for indicators selection, as it allows for different actors' views to be taken into consideration. An inclusive agenda, aiming at building trust and confidence among data users, has to include a process for identifying measures reflecting the different components of society. This is what the UN Statistical Commission has been trying to achieve in developing the SDG indicators. Over the past months and on several occasions, the consultation on indicators along with the NSIs was open also to civil society, academia, businesses, and other relevant stakeholders.

Moreover, the culturally based concept like well-being has been accounted for at global level, in spite of such differences across countries, and under target 17.19 (by 2030, build on existing initiatives to develop measurements of progress on sustainable development that complement GDP and support statistical capacity building in developing countries), there is room for a measure of progress which could include well-being. Currently, there is no official worldwide agreement about this indicator, due to its multidimensionality. However, this is certainly a step forward towards a wider debate on how a suitable well-being indicator can be selected (Riccardini 2016).

Several targets, like for instance, those related to Goal 12 on Sustainable Consumption, will imply bigger challenges to wealthier countries than for the other ones. It is expected indicators related to these targets (e.g., per capita material footprint or per capita food waste) to be reported on by national statistical offices and/or used for national policies. Measures such as the per capita material footprint and per capita food waste are still being debated. In Europe, such measures are being experimented by countries in the context of the System of Environmental-Economic Accounting (SEEA). Currently, from around 241 indicators identified, about 70 indicators still need further discussion for a consensus to be reached, as they are classified under tier III, and a suitable methodology defined. The global indicators have been approved by the UN Statistical Commission (UNStatCom 2016) in March 2016, refined in March 2017, and it is a step-by-step framework. Then it was adopted by the UN Economic and Social Council (ECOSOC) and the UN General Assembly in September 2016 and in July 2017, respectively. In 2020, there will be a revision (major changes if needed) of the set of global indicators, after a consultation process on evolution of indicators.

In November 2014, the Secretary-General's Independent Expert Advisory Group (IEAG) published the report "A World That Counts: Mobilising the Data Revolution for Sustainable Development" whose conclusions are in line with the on-going work (UN Secretary General's Independent Expert Advisory Group 2015). The recommendations given in this report underline the need for increasing countries statistical capacity in order to develop a global consensus on principles and standards and a leadership for coordination and mobilization. The challenge of new data production will certainly spur the modernization of national statistical systems in terms of processes, products, and sources.

Concerning new data sources, for example, national statistical offices are exploring the role of big data and the opportunities they could generate, still following the UN Fundamental Principles for Official Statistics (United Nations 2014) to ensure the integrity of this information. Many statistical offices are currently experiencing a modernization process and looking at which possibilities new data and technology can provide (UNECE HLG 2016) (http://unstats.un.org/unsd/statcom/47th-session/documents/2016-5-UNECE-HLG-on-modernisation-of-official-statistics-E.pdf). All available data sources are taken into account by ensuring data quality.

In addition, some SDGs targets are formulated at microlevel (companies and businesses) rather than at macrolevel (national policymaking). Private actors can be encouraged to report on their progress, because today, companies are aware that they are operating in a changing business environment where consumers require higher social and environmental standards. Already, within the UN framework, the Global Compact has involved thousands of companies to align along virtuous behaviors. Sustainability is becoming an increasingly relevant criterion for evaluating business performance, as proved by companies accounting practices. The Global Reporting Initiative (GRI) ((GRI 2016) (https://www.globalreporting.org/standards/Pages/default.aspx) is, for instance, an attempt to standardize companies reporting, taking into account sustainability criteria. The SDGs framework includes a target (*12.6 – encourage companies, especially large and transnational companies, to adopt sustainable practices and to integrate sustainability information into their reporting cycle*) about companies' sustainability reporting, covering not only economic aspects but also social and environmental ones. Therefore, the business sector is showing an increasing attention to themes covered by the SDGs.

Since the SDGs are a challenge for the entire world, they need to be clearly understood and appropriate actions need to be taken in order to achieve them. There are no alternatives for living in a more equitable and sustainable planet. Although the 2030 Agenda for Sustainable Development is very ambitious, the risks we are facing call for the fruitful contribution of all the involved actors (Riccardini 2016).

In 2016, the first Sustainable Development Goals Report was edited by the United Nations (United Nations 2016–2017). It is a first accounting of where countries stand at the start of our collective journey to 2030, trying to bring our vision closer to the reality. The Report analyses the selected indicators from the global indicators framework agreed upon the UN Statistical Commission for which data are available (https://unstats.un.org/sdgs/report/2016/). In July 2017, a second SDGs Report was edited by the United Nations (https://unstats.un.org/sdgs/report/2017/). It shows unfortunately that the rate of progress in many areas is far slower than needed to meet the targets by 2030. The all set of indicators is therefore used with the aim of evaluating the reaching of the SDGs, and therefore, in our anticipation analysis, it is used for implementing decisions and actions which are the results of the practice of anticipation.

The Italian Benessere Equo e Sostenibile (BES) Project and the Framework for Sustainability

In Italy, we have developed sustainability measures in the context of BES (ISTAT 2016–2017) (http://www.istat.it/en/well-being-measures). The subgroup on the sustainability of the Scientific Committee of BES project has focused its attention on a concept of sustainability of wellbeing not as a "noun" in its own right but rather as an "adjective" of well-being; therefore, it avoided facing the question of systemic sustainability as such and rather focused on checking whether the levels of well-being achieved are sustainable – in the sense of "maintainable" – over time. The subgroup on the sustainability of the Scientific Committee of BES then traced the path for the identification of appropriate measures for sustainable well-being. In this process, the conceptual aspects of measuring sustainability have been treated in line with the current debate on overcoming of GDP and with the United Nations Declaration of 2013 for which there is sustainable development when the well-being of individuals is sought. In the discussion on the indicators for sustainable well-being, the subgroup also considered the framework on the measurement of sustainable development provided by the CES (Conference of European Statisticians) (https://www.unece.org/fileadmin/DAM/stats/publications/2013/CES_SD_web.pdf) and the UNECE (United Nations Economic Commission for Europe) (https://www.unece.org/stats/stats_h.html), as well as suggestions included in the EU Development Strategy and the program Europe 2020 (http://ec.europa.eu/europe2020/index_en.htm).

In deciding how to measure sustainability, the subgroup of the Scientific Committee of the BES has made the basic choice of connecting the concept of sustainability to that of well-being of people, considering the interconnection of the three dimensions: economic, social, and environmental. The Committee acknowledged that well-being is a multidimensional concept that changes with time, places, and cultures and identified some key features in the measurement of sustainability such as insecurity, complexity, dynamism, global scope, and, above all, interconnection between different BES domains (trade-offs between the components of the different domains have been considered like the tensions that can exist between policies on energy, environmental protection, social welfare, and economic development).

The final outcome of the work of the BES Committee is a theoretical model that considers whether it is possible to improve or maintain the level of well-being achieved without compromising the conditions, opportunities, and resources of the present and future generations. Sustainability is understood as a balance between elements of vulnerability and elements of resilience referred to a country, a group of people, or an individual (Riccardini 2014a).

Vulnerability and resilience are reflected, respectively, in the risk factors that can undermine the level of well-being and the factors of risk mitigation and/or ability to react that allow recovering after a negative shock. This theoretical framework based on resilience and vulnerability factors is in fact applicable to all aspects of well-being, both at the individual and at the collective level. It also permits to highlight the interconnections between indicators of different domains and to identify existing trade-off (Riccardini 2014b). The scheme of the theoretical framework developed by the Scientific Committee is summarized in Fig. 1.

The sustainability of the well-being (and not sustainable ecosystem *tout court*) is understood as a state of balance/equilibrium (of conditions, factors, resources, . . .)

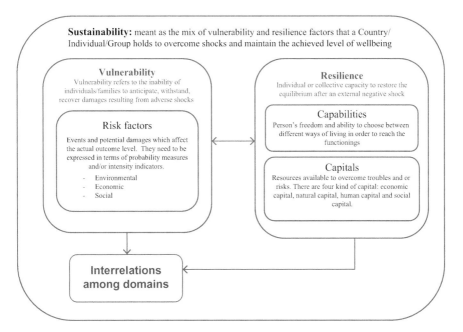

Fig. 1 Scheme for sustainability

with respect to the level of well-being achieved in a given time. In this equilibrium, there is a simultaneous presence of vulnerabilities and resilience, which can be existing or potential. These aspects, present in the different domains of the BES framework, may refer to individuals, specific social groups, or the whole country, thus justifying the use of both micro- and macrolevel indicators (e.g., individual policies put in place to ensure good governance of the resources, condition of specific social groups, state of the environment, etc.).

Therefore, by considering these dual individual and collective dimensions, the concepts of vulnerability and resilience can be divided into indicators that pick at the individual and collective exposure to adverse shocks, with reference to the first concept, or the ability to restore the lost equilibrium, with regard to the second concept.

Indicators of vulnerability should measure the main risk factors that threaten the current levels of well-being, considering the economic, social, and environmental context, and all those structural aspects that can alter the equilibrium achieved in terms of well-being (including excessive levels of socioeconomic inequality). Conversely the indicators of resilience must consider those elements that, as a result of adverse shocks, allow to restore the level of well-being previously reached, including individual capacities and collective capitals (economic, social, and environmental) available. In this case, recourse is made to the concepts of capital and capacity indicators. For capacity means states and activities of people that reflect the freedom and the ability of the same to choose between different ways of living, in order to achieve personal well-being, where are those for capital resources (wealth) that can be used to meet the needs and/or to face individual and collective future risks, net of liabilities (considering measures of capital stocks and flows that determine the variation over time of the stock through investment and depreciation). The measures developed by the National Accounts, such as physical capital, human capital and trials of some satellite accounts (such as the estimation of nonmarket household), and natural capital and its environmental accounts are then placed in this conceptual framework.

The most critical aspect of the BES theoretical framework is that the functional division that has allowed us to consider the well-being divided into separate domains cannot be maintained when discussing sustainability, as the interrelations between phenomena and their trade-offs that exist in real life necessarily lead to simultaneously consider aspects (and related indicators) covering different domains of well-being. For this reason, vulnerabilities and resilience elements, which in their mutual dynamics may affect the equilibrium, must necessarily be conceptualized and analyzed in their interrelations among the various domains (an element of resilience identified in a domain can be an aspect of vulnerability in another domain, as well as an outcome indicators of a domain can be considered as factors of resilience to other aspects of well-being).

In summary, everything pushes to consider indicators to be identified as specific to each domain, but also as a representative of the interrelationships with other domains, because it is the dynamical interaction of the various fields (economic, social, environmental, and governance) that is underpinning the concept of sustainability of well-being.

One example of the sustainable well-being framework has been developed in 2016 by Bachelet et al. (2016), using all subjective indicators presented actually inside BES indicators. The work is not using, as the majority of studies, vulnerability and resilience aspects of the sustainability of a "system" (a society, a country, or even the whole planet) but want to focus mainly on an individual dimension of well-being, considering the exposure to risk and the ability to recover of the single persons, demonstrating once again the usefulness of this framework sustainability BES framework.

Another example of BES sustainable well-being framework can be found in a recent work of Riccardini et al. (2016) (https://www.ibs.it/sviluppo-benessere-sostenibili-lettura-per-libro-fabiola-riccardini/e/9788865079744?inventoryId=58905591), where it has been utilized for interpreting a full set of indicators coming from CES and related to Italy, where also a correspondence of BES/CES/SDGs framework has been done.

One additional application of this framework can be found in par. An Application for Italy of SDGs Indicators Selection, where SDGs selection of indicators for Italy has been interpreted with the identified model.

At this stage, at national level, it is necessary to continue connections between the global SDGs indicators, the regional CES indicators, and the BES framework for developing the national and subnational level of monitoring. This is the near future activity for developing the national and subnational level of SDGs indicators.

National Experience in Developing SDGs Indicators

ISTAT is working for developing the complete set of measures for monitoring SDGs, taken into consideration the experiences until now done at national and international level.

In Italy, we have approached the measurement of sustainability in the context of BES, as we have seen before, in line with the United Nations declaration that there is sustainable development when the well-being of people is pursued. Moreover, ISTAT after having co-chaired the starting activities of the IAEG-SDGs indicators is now an observer country inside the same group constituted by the UN Statistical Commission, where the indicators for monitoring are selected. ISTAT is also member of the TF UNECE for developing Sustainable Development measures and a member of the Eurostat WG of Sustainable Development and E-Europe 2020 Indicators.

As seen before, the set of indicators for monitoring SDGs have to be developed on the three different levels as we have seen above: global, regional, and national-subnational. In doing so, we have taken in consideration the international context and national experience until now developed.

Therefore, the macroactivities that we have undertaken are:

1. Participate to the international groups discussing these indicators.
2. Discuss with the political actors national priorities and timetable for monitoring.

3. Discuss with civil society, business, academia, and all the stakeholders relevance indicators.
4. Identify who is doing what in ISTAT and in all other SISTAN (the National Statistical System) offices in order to build up relevant metadata for each indicators of the global, regional, and national-subnational level, including disaggregation of data required.
5. Integrate and converge the national BES with SDGs indicators.
6. Collection of data for indicators, by integrating different source of information.
7. Spreading of indicators to different level of demand (global, regional, and national) for dedicated databases.
8. Support analysis of the different indicators and support for monitoring SDGs.
9. Communicate all the activities connected to the SDGs measuring.

Until now, ISTAT has published 173 SDGs indicators (of which 38 BES), where 62 are the same of IAEG selection, 74 are proxy, and 37 are context indicators. They are spread inside the institutional website starting from indicators of statistical nature, with priority to those consolidated and with high quality. ISTAT is also continuing with the external dialogue for implementation and completion of the system of indicators (http://www.istat.it/it/benessere-e-sostenibilit%C3%A0/obiettivi-di-sviluppo-sostenibil).

At ministry level, the Ministry of Environment is working for the National Strategy for Sustainable Development along with other Ministries (http://www.minambiente.it/pagina/la-strategia-nazionale-lo-sviluppo-sostenibile), the Ministry of Economy is working on the National Budget using a subset of BES indicators (http://www.mef.gov.it/inevidenza/article_0276.html), and the Ministry of Foreign Affairs is working on a monitoring system for the aid of cooperation (http://www.esteri.it/mae/it/politica_estera/cooperaz_sviluppo/).

Also universities and researchers are analyzing these SDGs indicators. One example is the work by Riccardini et all., (https://www.libreriauniversitaria.it/sviluppo-benessere-sostenibili-lettura-italia/libro/9788865079744?utm_source=google-shopping&utm_medium=cpc&utm_term=9788865079744&utm_content=Libri%20Italiani&utm_campaign=google-shopping-lib) a group of researchers coming from ISTAT and different Italian Universities. The book tries to draw theoretical boundaries of the sustainability concept applied to well-being starting from sustainable development, presents world and Italian empirical evidences, according to the outlined interpretative system and illustrates a first picture of the SDGs indicators for Italy.

Finally also civil society is producing evaluation on SDGs at national level, ASVIS (http://www.asvis.it/documenti-dell-alleanza/), Oxfam Italia, Trade Unions, etc.

Relations Among Different Aspects

One of the main issues of sustainable development is the analysis of relations among the different aspects: economical, sociological, and environmental, in order to identify trade-offs for policy and for developing good governance for those aspects.

To this extend the interlinkages analysis within the goals and targets of SDGs is essential. There are different approaches to do this interlinkages analysis. One of this example can be found in Riccardini and De Rosa (2016), who analyzed the nexus food/water/energy and the role played by institutions and policies to handle effectively this resources competition, taking into consideration the well-being perspective, and at the same time contextualized this nexus inside the SDGs framework.

Also inside the TF UNECE-OECD-EUROSTAT (UNECE 2016) on adapting CES framework to SDGs, an interlinkages analysis has been done, by connecting all goals and targets to CES themes and identifying possible relations among them (https://www.unece.org/fileadmin/DAM/stats/documents/ece/ces/2016/mtg/NewCES_18-Interim_report_on_SDGs_Revised.pdf; http://www.unece.org/fileadmin/DAM/sustainable-development/RFSD_2017/Regional_Forum_Background_Document_EN_final.pdf).

Another example is the work done by Statistics Sweden and Ministerio del Medio Ambiente of Gobierno de Chile (2016) where a link between the environment and the economy are explored, in particular the connection among targets/goals of SDGs and the SEEA (System of Environmental and Economic Accounts) (https://sustainabledevelopment.un.org/index.php?page=view&type=400&nr=2298&menu=35; http://sdg.iisd.org/news/unep-sweden-chile-report-on-monitoring-scp-targets/).

In addition, another way to analysis interlinkages concerning Education is looking to this topic as a key to improve the quality of life of people, to create more resilient society, and to create more job opportunities. This goal is important to achieve all others. It is important to: reduce poverty (goal 1), improve health (goal 3), look to food (goal 2), develop a gender culture (goal 5), promote decent work for all (goal 8), develop a system of research and sustainable development (goal 9), reduce inequalities (goal 10), promote human rights (goal 16), promote sustainable production and consumption over time (goal 12), and promote a culture for the respect of environmental systems and knowledge of climate change (goals 13, 14, and 15).

Some examples of grouping goals, another way to see interlinkages, will be presented in par. An Application for Italy of SDGs Indicators Selection of this chapter.

Forward-Looking Models

The BES indicators until now selected measures part of the all aspects of sustainability as shown in previous paragraphs. For sure, they cannot be used for future evaluations on the causality of the single aspects of well-being and the determinants of well-being over time and spaces. The set of indicators focused on sustainability following the BES sustainability framework can be a starting point. For forward-looking models, we need alternatives models to GDP one.

In developing models for forward-looking evaluation, alternative or complement to the models connected to the Theory of General Economic Equilibrium, the key concept is focused on well-being of people and societies, instead of the focus on the only market production of goods and services, that in any case cannot be used as synonymous of well-being of people or societies. The Italian experiences of developing well-being concept, domains, and related indicators can be utilized as starting point. Then it is necessary to study the relations among the different dimensions of the well-being and formalize them in a system of relations. This implies to estimate well-being functions too and study their determinants. (An experimental research project is underway for developing such a model of wellbeing coordinated by myself and a paper is planned to be publish end of this year.)

In Italy, from this year, the Public Budget has introduced along with the traditional economic indicators some BES indicators, which are used inside the provisional model of the Ministry of Economy for forecasting aggregates (http://www.dt. tesoro.it/modules/documenti_it/analisi_progammazione/documenti_programmatici/ def_2017/Allegato_6_AL_DEF_2017.pdf). This represents a stimulus for developing forecasting models with the well-being perspective.

An Application for Italy of SDGs Indicators Selection

The objective of the paragraph is to present a first analysis of a selection of indicators related to the 2030 Agenda for sustainable development for Italy. We analyze trends over time of a selection of indicators and, where possible, we proceed with a comparison with other European countries. The selection of indicators and related graphs are summarized in the Appendix 1.

As we have seen, the United Nations Statistical Commission has approved the set of 231 indicators that covers the 169 target. This set of global indicators has different complexities, their methodological development is not homogeneous, and moreover the availability of data is not guaranteed for all countries. Therefore, the refinement of the indicators is still in progress. In any case, each country has to produce the necessary data at the national level and feed the database of the Statistical Division of the United Nations. It should be pointed out that the production of these indicators is a challenge even for developed countries. At the regional level, the UNECE is the region of reference for Italy, and at this level, statisticians are proceeding with the adjustment of existing indicators, with those defined by the UN, according to the regional requirements. Eurostat is also adjusting its own set of indicators of sustainable development to those connected to the SDGs.

The selection that is proposed for Italy can be found in Riccardini et al. (2016), and it is a first attempt to represent the global indicators associated with the goals for sustainable development, so that cannot be considered as exhaustive. Several global indicators are not worth considering for Italy (and in general for developed countries), on the basis of the fact that the corresponding targets have been achieved in part or in their whole or the phenomenon is not relevant. We have analyzed about 169 indicators and the selection of quantitative statistical indicators made in this work is based on availability of data by ISTAT and other official producers, leaving the qualitative indicators and the indicators related to the means of implementations to other analysis. Several quantitative indicators, not considered in the publication quoted, require investments for their production. Finally, it is worth saying that for some goals and targets, we selected other indicators that do not belong to the set approved by the UN, considering the indicators still relevant for the analysis of well-being and sustainability.

Some indicators selected have already been identified in the context of the CES; others indicators belong to the BES project and part of them have already been scrutinized. A correspondence between SDGs goals and BES domains is presented in the following table (Table 1).

Table 1 Linking the SDGs goals to the BES domains

SDGs goals	BES domains
Goal 1 Poverty	Domain 4 Economic Wellbeing Domain 10 Environment
Goal 2 Nutrition and agriculture	Domain 1 Health Domain 10 Environment
Goal 3 Health	Domain 1 Health
Goal 4 Education	Domain 2 Education and training
Goal 5 Gender equality	Domain 3 Work and balance of life time Domain 6 Politics and institutions Domain 7 Personal security
Goal 6 Water	Domain 10 Environment Domain 12 Services quality
Goal 7 Energy	Domain 10 Environment Domain 12 Services quality
Goal 8 Decent work and economic growth	Domain 2 Education and training Domain 3 Work and balance of life time Domain 4 Economic well-being Domain 10 Environment
Goal 9 Industry, innovation, and Infrastructure	Domain 4 Economic well-being Domain 10 Environment Domain 11 Research and innovation
Goal 10 Internal and external inequalities	Domain 4 Economic well-being
Goal 11 Cities and communities	Domain 9 Landscape and cultural heritage Domain 10 Environment Domain 12 Services quality Domain 7 Personal security
Goal 12 Responsible consumption and production	Domain 4 Economic well-being Domain 10 Environment Domain 12 Services quality
Goal 13 Climate changes	Domain 10 Environment
Goal 14 Life under water	Domain 10 Environment
Goal 15 Life on land	Domain 10 Environment
Goal 16 Peace, justice and strong institutions	Domain 6 Politics and institutions Domain 7 Personal security Domain 12 Services quality
Goal 17 Means of implementation and global partnership	Domain 6 Politics and institutions Domain 12 Services quality Domain 11 Research and innovation

It is worth noticing that the BES domains "subjective well-being" and "social relations" do not correspond to any SDGs goal. In fact, the subjective dimension is missing in SDGs indicators and only some indicators in goal 16 capture perceptions and opinions. The disaggregation of the SDGs indicators by sex, age, geographical location, disability status, etc. is not considered because our primary scope is to provide a basis for discussion. For disaggregated data and the identification of the local indicators, it is useful to refer to URBES, BES Province projects (http://www.istat.it/it/archivio/153995; http://www.besdelleprovince.it/), and the regional data disaggregation inside SDGs indicators (https://www.istat.it/it/benessere-e-sostenibilit%C3%A0/obiettivi-di-sviluppo-sostenibil/gli-indicatori-istat-per-lo-svil).

It is desirable in Italy to continue the consultation aimed at identifying the relevant and specific indicators for the country as well as the relevant global ones, following a shared and participatory approach of the various stakeholders, as envisioned by the UN process. This examination cannot ignore, however, the existing discussion stemming from the BES project, even though this latter requires an adjustment to the international contexts, as for example to the CES indicators.

An international comparison can be tested on a small number of indicators developed in the European context (http://ec.europa.eu/eurostat/web/sdi). In this work, the source considered for the international comparison is the set of measures used for the analysis of sustainable development in Europe. Consequently, it is not suitable to analyze Italy's position compared to other countries. The aim of this paragraph is not to pinpoint the precise position of Italy for each target but to analyze the trends of the indicators, through the time series that have been reconstructed. The evolution of the indicators over time shows the point that the country has achieved and therefore may be useful for the definition of the National Strategy for Sustainable Development. At the international level, in the High Level Political Forum on Sustainable Development, it was presented a first report containing some indicators aggregated for global macroareas, based on data provided by the Statistical Office of the Statistical Commission of the United Nations. The analysis of the relationships between the various goals is fundamental for understanding sustainability, and it is useful for assessing the trade-off among policies: the analysis of the relationships should lead to the selection of the measures that capture these aspects.

General Remarks

The selection of indicators for Italy is further classified in: vulnerability, resilience, outcome, equity, and macroindicators according to their meaning established with the BES sustainability framework (cfr. par. The Italian BES Project and the Framework for Sustainability).

It is evident from the selected indicators and the available time series that many indicators have improved over time, but this condition it is not sufficient to state that the country is about to achieve the objectives and the targets for the sustainable development and well-being. We have analyzed trends of over 169 indicators connected to sustainable development and well-being for Italy. For some goals, we selected other indicators that do not belong to the set approved by the UN, considering the indicators still relevant for the analysis. This choice is rooted in the fact that we wanted to cover, in the most comprehensive way, the targets foreseen by the 2030 Agenda.

In addition to the analysis of trends, it is necessary to determine the distances from the targets, or when dangerous threshold are about to be crossed, or, for example, when the food/water/energy nexus causes negative impacts on the welfare of people and the environment. In addition, it must be established, starting from the concrete situation, when biodiversity can be maintained, as well as when it can be guaranteed the integrity and resistance of ecosystems. Basically, it is necessary to check when the vulnerability of natural and social systems decreases, and how to maintain or increase the resilience of these systems.

Even though the meaning of the international comparison of indicators could be very limited because the construction of common indicators SDGs is still at an early stage, in the comparisons, Italy is very often below the European average, and it witness that there is much to do.

In summary, from the analysis of the trends of the available indicators for SDGs presented in Appendix 1, and by **grouping goals** by homogeneous families it results for Italy that:

Equity

Goal 1: The absolute and relative poverty is increasing, as it grows the risk of poverty; so these vulnerabilities increase over time; the public spending on social protection, especially for the poorest, the unemployed, and other forms of social exclusion, which represents a resilience indicator, is still limited.

Goal 10: Income inequalities within Italy grow, and the Italian data on migration confirms disparities between countries; in words, equity inside and outside Italy is worsening.

Goal 5: Italy has improved in several areas (violence, political participation, participation in the labor market), but still there are few women in management positions and decision-making bodies, the wage gap rules against women even though women are better educated than men. So gender equality is conflicting.

Food/Water/Energy

Goal 2: In Italy, it is relevant the malnutrition, obesity has worsened, and the diet is still not in line with WHO parameters; the value added of agriculture as a proportion of GDP is stable, and only in recent years, it resumes to grow slightly, labor productivity in agriculture grows over time, the average revenue of small-scale good producers increases, and the emissions of carbon dioxide in agriculture decrease.

Goal 6: Water is confirmed as universal service and sanitation service are widespread, sewage treatments rise.

Goal 7: The electrical service is universal and gets better and better, the energy efficiency improves, and the consumption of electricity from renewable sources increases.

Goal 3: we live longer, but life expectancy in good health in the last year decreases mainly due to the reduction of those of males, the highest mortality rate is linked also to nutrition (circulatory diseases are the first cause of death), the deaths from road accidents decrease, people who consume alcohol and smokers decrease, but suicide mortality increases.

Human Capital and Development

Goal 4: Italy has improved with regards to every education levels, but the numeric and literacy skills are still low and below the European average, school dropouts decrease.

Goal 8: The economic growth has almost stopped; unemployment is still high and, above all, the incidence of NEET (Youth not in education, employment or training) increases over time. These confirm that vulnerabilities are still present even though they are improving. Death or injured by accidents at work decrease.

Economic Sustainable Development

Goal 9: The deindustrialization is evident, the share of small businesses decreases, the emission intensity of the added value decreases, the research intensity is growing but it is still well below European levels, the proportion of medium- and high-tech industry value added in total value added increases.

Goal 12: The domestic material consumption decreases, the resources efficiency increases, hazardous waste increases, waste mechanical-biological treatments increase, and the recycled waste increases.

Inside this topic, it is possible to see that vulnerabilities are decreasing and some resiliencies are increasing and this bodes well for the future.

Natural Capital

Goal 13: Some emissions decrease in absolute terms, but the emission intensity with respect to the economic output increases.

Goal 14: Marine protected areas increase even if the bathing marine coastal waters on total coasts has slightly decreased, the value of production and the labor productivity in the fishery sector have decreased.

Goal 15: The ratio of forest area increases, the areas of special naturalistic interest increase, terrestrial vertebrate species are at greatest risk compared to the marine's ones. In general, vulnerabilities are counterbalanced by resiliencies even though it is not so clear the pattern of the natural capital.

Cities

Goal 11: Among the Italian regional capitals, we can observe a strong variety, with remarkable differences between the cities of the North, Central, and South. In total, it appears that place-km of public transport network decreases, soil consumption grows, experiences of shared planning grow, the generation of waste is quite stable, the separate collection of waste grows, the exposure to particulate matter (PM10) improves, that is, it decreases, but still almost all cities are above the daily limits, the endowments of cultural heritage remains unchanged, and the expenditure that municipalities allocates to cultural heritage slightly increases, the public green spaces per capita remains basically unchanged.

Peace, Justice and Institutions

Goal 16: Homicides decreased, the percentage of people aged 14 and over feeling unsafe when walking alone in the dark decreases (after a large increase in 2011), the percentage of detainees awaiting first judgment on the total detainees decreases, from 2010 the percentage of prisoners in penal institutions on the total capacity of penal institution has decreased, the trust in the various public institutions worsens, witnessing to the dissatisfaction with the services offered by public entities. Many vulnerabilities are decreasing but also resiliencies.

Means of Implementation

Goal 17: The share of total revenue on the GDP increases, from 2012 there is a slight decrease of the proportion of domestic budget funded by domestic taxes financed by taxes, the net official development assistance disbursement as a proportion of the GNI grows, after a decrease until the 2012, and also the official bilateral commitments are rising. The amount of direct investment done by Italian companies abroad has increased as it raises also the amount of investment of foreign companies in Italy; both the flows of inward and outward investment fluctuate.

Conclusions

In this chapter, we have presented the general framework for measuring Sustainable Development Goals, agreed by countries in September 2015, and the national experience developed until now.

The monitoring process for evaluating the achievements of goals on different levels: global, regional, and national, implies big efforts by National Statistical Institutes for the production of national data useful for indicators elaboration even for the most advanced countries. It is the case to say that a data revolution is undergoing, and this is a challenge not only for the developing countries but also for the advanced ones. Many actors, coordinated by the National Statistical Authorities, have to contribute to this process, as civil society, universities and researchers, businesses, take advantages also from the development of technologies, in order to improve the capacity building for data production. It will take time for covering all the targets and goals indicators and all countries will converge to the general framework of monitoring. The way requires accessible, timely, and reliable disaggregated data, but the way is designed. It is the first time that an operation of this kind is undertaken, but we have not another possibility to achieve well-being of people and sustainable development.

The BES experience for Italy is an important starting point that needs to be adapted to SDGs context. The global, regional, and national measurement levels are well under definition.

The national experience foresees not only the calculation of indicators but also their interpretation and analysis. In doing this, it is necessary to developed also alternative models, looking forward beyond the traditional ones focused on economic aspects, which take into consideration the concept of well-being and its determinants over time and space. For this latter aspect, the work is just begun and it is necessary to invest more on this line of action. In relation to the analysis of anticipation, this process is clearly oriented to stimulate actions for the future.

In conclusion, SDGs monitoring for the next years will constitute an important step for anticipation studies too. It will determine what in the future will happen and where resources will be invested at global, regional, and national level. Researchers in anticipation have to contribute to this path by developing not only set of indicators but also forecasting models (with properly predictive component of future studies) and foresights including most traditional future studies. Later as for the third level of anticipation, aka foresight 2.0 defined by Poli (2017), the outcomes of research on anticipation, resulting from forecast and foresight models, will contribute at implementing them into decisions and actions resulting by policy actions.

Appendix 1 Trends for Italy: Selection of Indicators

Goal 1 – Poverty

See Graphs 1, 2, and 3.

Goal 2 – Nutrition and Agriculture

See Graphs 4, 5, and 6.

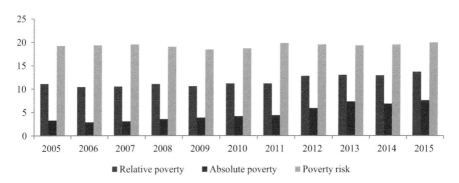

Graph 1 Proportion of population living below the national relative poverty line, relative poverty and at risk of poverty. Years 2005–2015 (per 100 individuals with the same characteristics) (Source: Istat, Consumi delle famiglie, Indagine sulle spese delle famiglie, Indagine Eu-Silc)

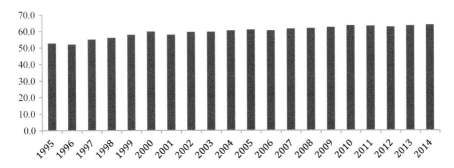

Graph 2 Proportion of total government spending on essential services (education, health and social protection), years 1995–2014 (Source: Istat, Conti economici nazionali)

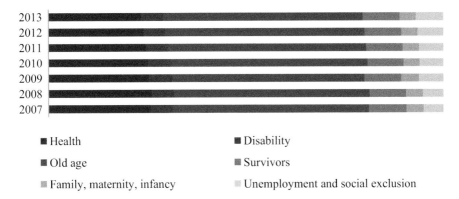

- ■ Health
- ■ Old age
- ▨ Family, maternity, infancy

- ■ Disability
- ■ Survivors
- ▨ Unemployment and social exclusion

Graph 3 Government spending on different social protection programs, years 2007–2013 (percentages) (Source: Conti della protezione sociale)

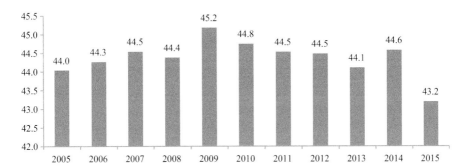

Graph 4 Overweight or obesity, years 2005–2015 (Standardized percentage of people aged 18 years and over who are overweight or obese) (Source: Istat, Indagine Aspetti della vita quotidiana)

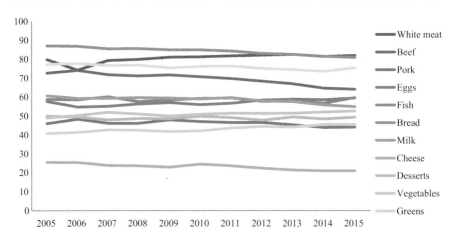

Graph 5 Food styles of people above 3 years (percentages), years 2005–2015 (per 100 persons of 3 years and over with the same characteristics) (Source: Istat, Indagine multiscopo sulle famiglie-Aspetti della vita quotidiana-Parte generale)

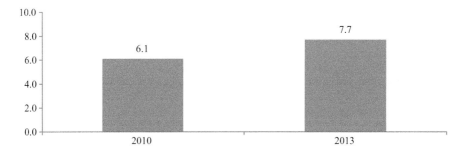

Graph 6 Percentage of land under organic farming, years 2010 and 2013 (percentages) (Source: Istat, Indagine sulla struttura e produzioni delle aziende agricole)

Goal 3 – Health

See Graphs 7, 8, 9, and 10.

Goal 4 – Education and Training

See Graphs 11, 12, 13, and 14.

Goal 5 – Women

See Graphs 15, 16, 17, and 18.

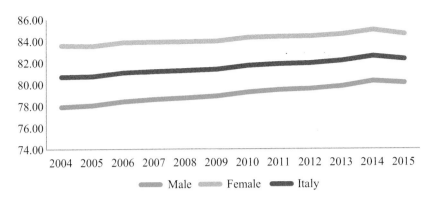

Graph 7 Life expectancy at birth, by sex – years 2004–2015 (average number of years) (Source: Istat, Tavole di mortalità della popolazione italiana)

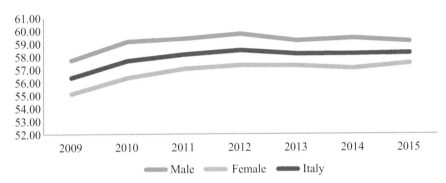

Graph 8 Healthy life expectancy at birth, by sex – years 2009–2015 (average number of years) (Source: Istat, Tavole di mortalità della popolazione italiana e Indagine Aspetti della vita quotidiana)

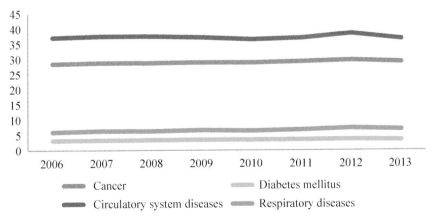

Graph 9 Mortality rate attributed to chronic diseases (per 10,000 inhabitants) – Years 2006–2013 (Source: Istat, Database Health for All)

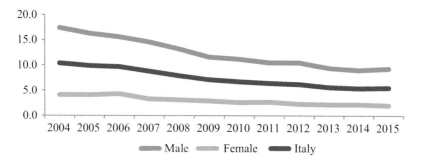

Graph 10 Age standardized death rate due to road traffic injuries, years 2004–2015 (per 100,000 inhabitants) (Source: Istat, Rilevazione degli incidenti stradali con lesione a persone)

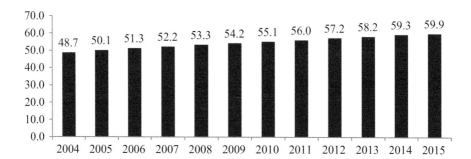

Graph 11 People with at least upper secondary education, years 2004–2015 (percentage of people aged 25–64 years having completed at least upper secondary education) (Source: Istat, Rilevazione sulle Forze di lavoro)

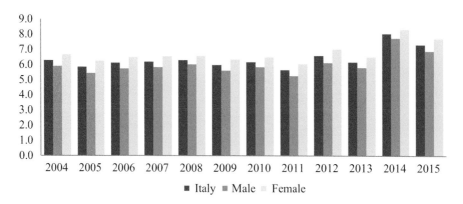

Graph 12 Participation in long-life learning: years 2004–2015 (percentage) (Source: Istat, Rilevazione sulle Forze di lavoro)

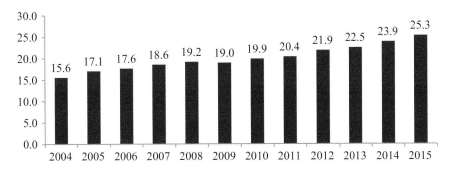

Graph 13 People with tertiary education, years 2004–2015 (percentage of people aged 30–34 years having completed tertiary education) (Source: Istat, Rilevazione sulle Forze di lavoro)

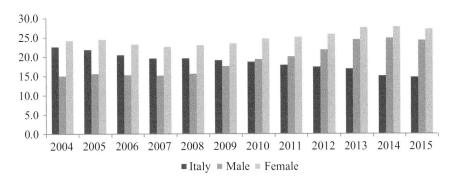

Graph 14 Early leavers from education and training, years 2004–2015 (percentage of people aged 18–24 years who have achieved only lower secondary and are not included in a training program) (Source: Istat, Rilevazione sulle Forze di lavoro)

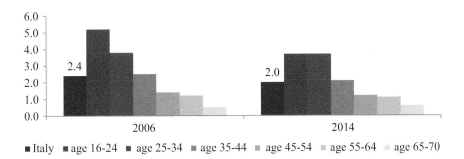

Graph 15 Proportion of women aged 16–70 subjected to physical or sexual violence by a partner or previous partner in the previous 12 months, years 2006 and 2014 (percentages) (Source: Istat, Multiscopo sulle famiglie: sicurezza delle donne)

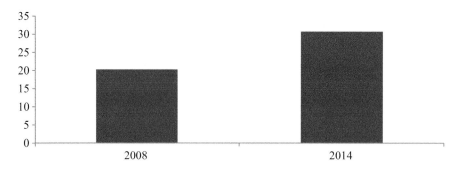

Graph 16 Women and political representation in Parliament, years 2008 and 2014 (percentage) (Source: Ministero degli Interni (2008), Elaborazioni Istat su dati della Camera dei Deputati e del Senato della Repubblica)

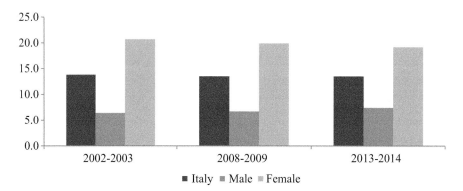

Graph 17 Proportion of time spent on unpaid domestic and care work by sex, years 2002–2003, 2008–2009, 2013–2014 (Source: Istat, Multiscopo sulle famiglie: uso del tempo)

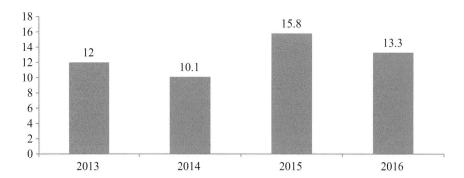

Graph 18 Women in decision-making bodies (a), years 2013–2016 (percentage) ((a) Autorità della privacy, Agcom, Autorità della concorrenza e del mercato, Corte Costituzionale, Consiglio Superiore Magistratura, Ambasciatori, Consob (Source: Varie, vedi (a)))

Goal 6 – Water

See Graphs 19, 20, and 21.

Goal 7 – Energy

See Graphs 22, 23, 24, and 25.

Goal 8 – Growth, Full Employment and Decent Work for all

See Graphs 26, 27, 28, and 29.

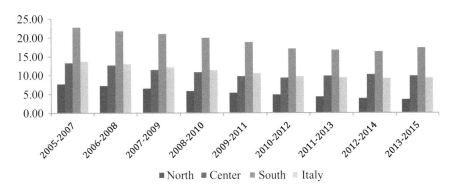

Graph 19 Irregularities in water supply, years 2005/07–2013/15 (percentage of households who report irregularities in water supply on total number of households – three-year moving average) (Source: Istat, Indagine multiscopo: Aspetti della vita quotidiana)

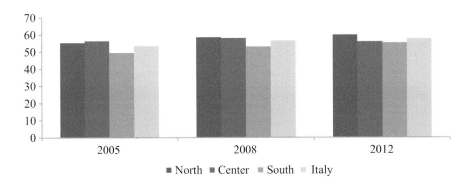

Graph 20 Organic biodegradable loads collected in urban wastewater treatment plants with secondary or advanced treatment on the total civil organic loads (percentages), years 2005, 2008, and 2012 (Source: Istat, Censimento delle acque per uso civile)

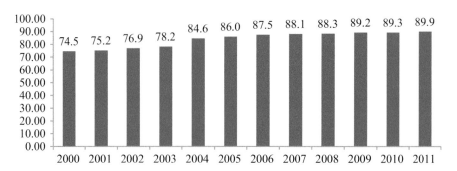

Graph 21 Population served by urban waste water treatment plants, years 2000–2011 (percentages) (Source: Istat, Dati ambientali nelle città)

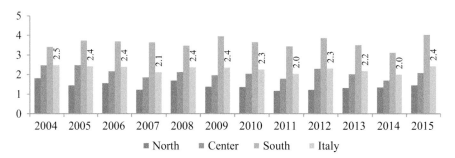

Graph 22 Frequency of long-lasting electric power interruptions (average number per user), years 2004–2015 (Source: Istat, Elaborazione su dati Autorità per l'energia elettrica e il gas)

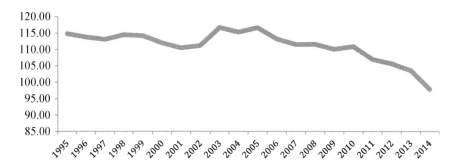

Graph 23 Energy intensity of the economy, years 1995–2014 (kilogram of oil equivalent (kgoe) per 1.000 euro) (Source: Eurostat)

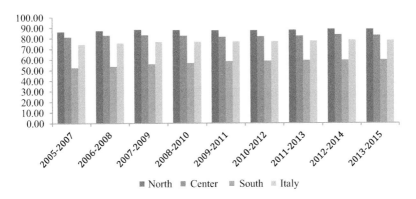

Graph 24 Percentage of household served by methane, years 2005/2007–2013/2015 (three-year moving average) (Source: Istat, Indagine multiscopo: Aspetti della vita quotidiana)

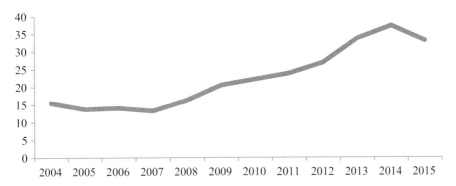

Graph 25 Electricity generated from renewable sources, years 2004–2015 (percentage of gross electricity consumption) (Source: Terna Rete Italia Spa)

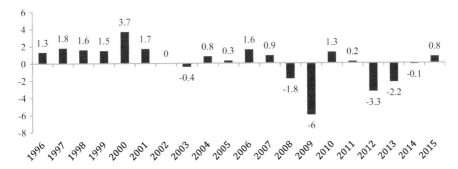

Graph 26 Annual growth rate of real GDP per capita, years 1996–2015 (percentage) (Source: Istat, Conti economici regionali)

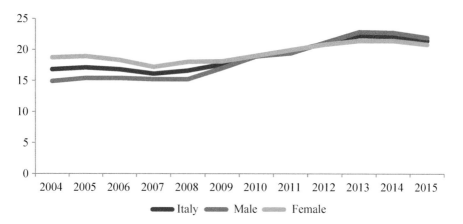

Graph 27 Proportion of youth (aged 15–24 years) not in education, employment or training, years 2004–2015 (Source: Istat, Rilevazione sulle forze di lavoro)

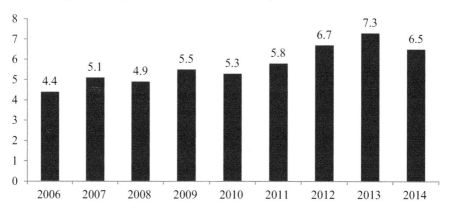

Graph 28 Gender pay gap, years 2006–2014 (Source: Eurostat)

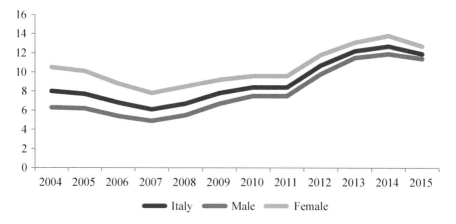

Graph 29 Unemployment rate, by sex, years 1995–2015 (percentage) (Source: Istat, Rilevazione sulle forze di lavoro)

Goal 9 – Resilient Infrastructure, Industrialization and Innovation

See Graphs 30, 31, and 32.

Goal 10 – Inequalities

See Graphs 33, 34, and 35.

The **disposable income inequality index**, defined in terms of quintiles, that is the ratio between the richest 20% and poorest 20%, depicts the unequal distribution of income between the richest and the poorest. For Italy, in the considered decade, the index decreased until 2008, and then it began to grow until the most recent years, exceeding the value achieved at the beginning of the period, signifying a deterioration of the distributive equity.

In terms of inequalities between Italy, the Italian regions of Campania and Sicily show the most pronounced income inequality, which has increased significantly

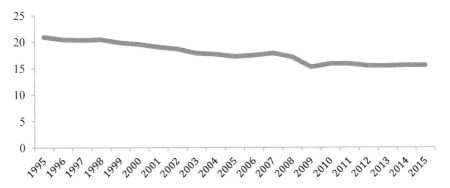

Graph 30 Manufacturing value added as a proportion of GDP, years 1995–2015 (percentage) (Source: Istat, Conti economici regionali)

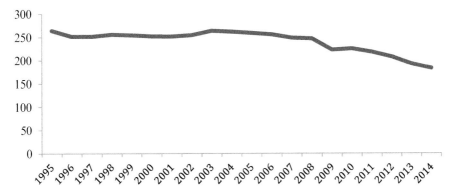

Graph 31 CO2 emission per unit of value added, years 1995–2014 (Tons/millions of euro) (Source: Istat, Conti di tipo NAMEA (matrice di conti economici integrata con conti ambientali))

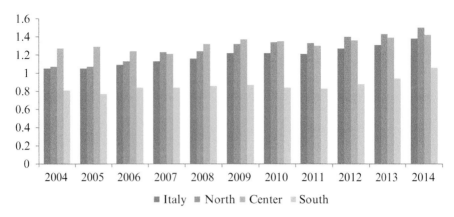

Graph 32 R&D intensity, years 2004–2014 (percentage) (Source: Istat, *Rilevazione statistica sulla ricerca e sviluppo nelle imprese, Rilevazione statistica sulla ricerca e sviluppo nelle istituzioni private non profit, Rilevazione statistica sulla ricerca e sviluppo nelle istituzioni pubbliche, Elaborazione per la stima delle attività di ricerca e sviluppo nelle università* (*in termini di spesa e personale*))

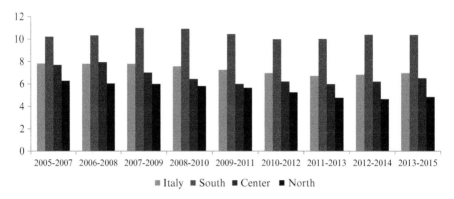

Graph 33 Composite index of service accessibility: Percentage of households who find very difficult to reach three or more basic services (pharmacy, emergency room, post office, police, carabinieri, municipal offices, crèches, nursery, primary and secondary school, market and supermarket) on total number of households (Source: Istat, Indagine Aspetti della vita quotidiana)

from 2011 and, in Campania, has even achieved 10 in 2013. Among the regions with a low index there are Valle d'Aosta, Trento and Friuli Venezia Giulia.

Goal 11 – Cities and Human Settlements

See Graphs 36, 37, 38, and 39.

When considering the trend of the indicator representing the **Place-Km of public transport networks**, defined as the number of train/vehicle km in the year

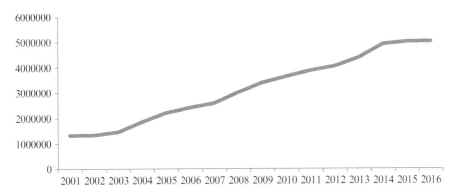

Graph 34   Foreign citizens, years 2001–2016 (residential population at 1° January) (Source: Istat, Rilevazione della popolazione residente comunale straniera, Ricostruzione della popolazione residente nei comuni)

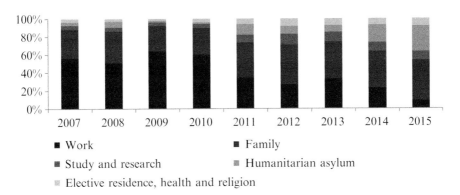

Graph 35   Entrants in the year of non-EU citizens by causes of migration, years 2007–2015 (Source: Istat, Permessi di soggiorno dei cittadini stranieri)

(all public transport vehicles) multiplied by the average capacity of the vehicles (fleet) per inhabitant, in the overall set of the Italian regional capital cities the indicator grew until 2009 and then it decreased. In 2004, the regional capital cities that offer more places-km are Milan (Lombardia), Venice (Veneto) and Rome (Lazio). On the other hand, the regional capital cities that offer less public transport services are Aosta (Valle d'Aosta), Potenza (Basilicata) and Catanzaro (Calabria).

With regards to **urban green areas**, defined as square meters of urban parks and gardens per inhabitants, in general Italian cities have maintained or decreased the urban green areas per inhabitants (changes can also be caused by changes in population) with the exception of Catanzaro, Bolzano, Venice and Palermo, which have increased slightly the public green area per inhabitant. The Italian cities with the higher value of the indicator are Trento and Potenza, with values that are significantly higher than the rest of the regional capital cities; the cities that have less public green areas per inhabitant are Genova, L'Aquila and Bari.

The **exposure to particulate matter** in the regional capital cities is measured by the indicator that calculates the number of days during which the level of PM10 exceeds the limit value. It results that in 2004 all the cities (for which you have data) exceeded the limits and the cities with the highest number of days during which the

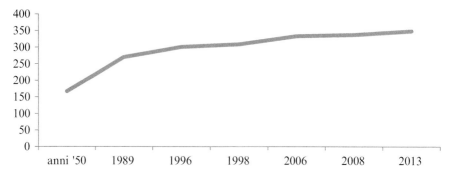

Graph 36 Estimated domestic land consumption per capita years 50s, 1989, 1996, 1998, 2006, 2008 and 2013 (Square meters/inhabitant) (Source: ISPRA)

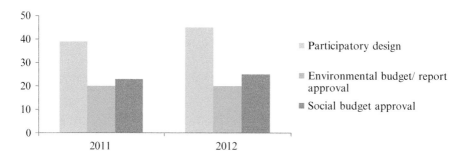

Graph 37 Shared environmental planning, years 2011 and 2012 (Source: Istat, Dati ambientali nelle città)

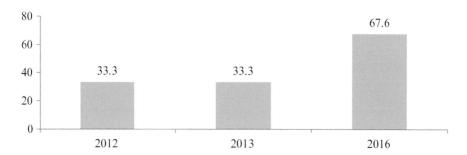

Graph 38 Endowment of cultural heritage items (values per 100 km^2) – Years 2012, 2013, 2016 (Source: *Istat, Elaborazioni su dati Ministero per i Beni e le Attività Culturali, carta del rischio.* Elaborazione su dati Istituto Superiore per la Conservazione ed. il Restauro – Sistema Vincoli in rete)

level of PM10 exceeds the limit value were Florence, Turin and Ancona, while those with the lowest numbers were Trieste, Potenza and Genoa. In 2014 all the cities of regional capital have exceeded the limit but the number of days during which the level of PM10 exceeds the limit value were much lower than the initial year, except for Bolzano, that along with Campobasso and Trento, is the city with the best quality of urban air as measured by this indicator, the worst are Turin, Milan and Venice. The cities that have constantly, in the considered period, days in which the level of PM10 exceeds the threshold are Catanzaro, Potenza and L'Aquila.

If we look at the **collection of municipal waste** (Kg/inhabitants) in the considered period, we can notice that the quantity per capita grows until the 2006, then it decreases and in the 2012 it returns to the level registered 12 years before. In 2012 the cities that collect more waste per capita are Perugia and Rome, while those with the lowest values are Potenza and Campobasso.

Goal 12 – Production and Consumption

See Graphs 40, 41, and 42.

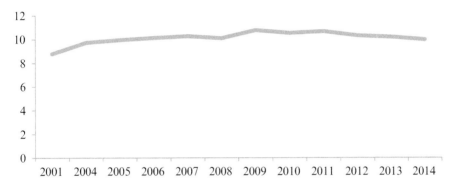

Graph 39 Current expenditure of Municipalities for the management of cultural heritage, Years 2001 e 2004–2014 (euro) (Source: Istat, Bilanci consuntivi delle amministrazioni comunali)

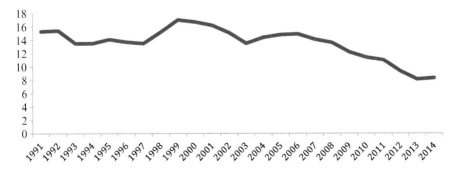

Graph 40 Domestic material consumption per capita, years 1995–2014 (Source: Istat, Conti dei flussi di materia)

Goal 13 – Climate Change

See Graphs 43, 44, 45, and 46.

Goal 14 – Oceans and Marine Resources

See Graphs 47, 48, and 49.

Goal 15 – Terrestrial Ecosystems, Forests, Land Degradation and Biodiversity Loss

See Graphs 50 and 51.

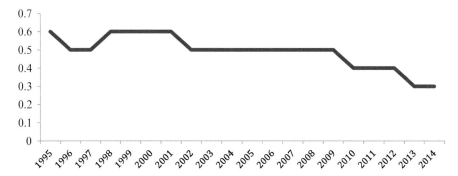

Graph 41 Domestic material consumption per GDP, years 1995–2014 (ton/thousands of euro) (Source: Istat, Conti dei flussi di materia)

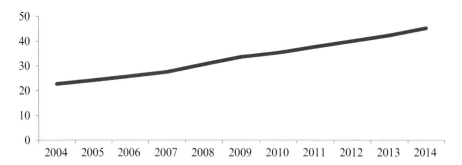

Graph 42 Separate collection of municipal waste (percentages) – Years 2004–2014 (Source: ISPRA)

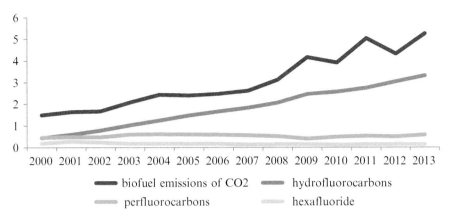

Graph 43 Output emission intensity (tones of CO_2 equivalent/million euro) (Source: Istat, Conto satellite NAMEA)

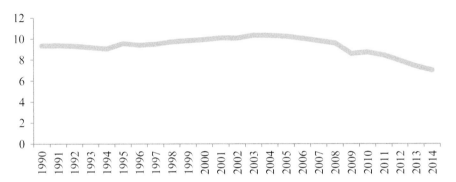

Graph 44 Carbon dioxide emissions and other greenhouse gases (Tones of CO_2 equivalent per capita) – Years 1990–2014 (Source: Istat, Conti di tipo NAMEA (matrice di conti economici integrata con conti ambientali))

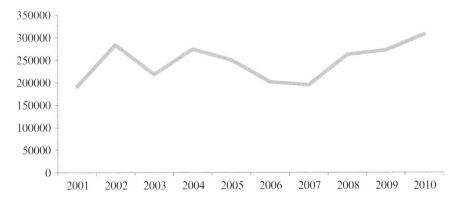

Graph 45 Annual average precipitation, years 2001–2010 (Mio m3) (Source: Istat, Rilevazione dati meteoclimatici ed. idrologici)

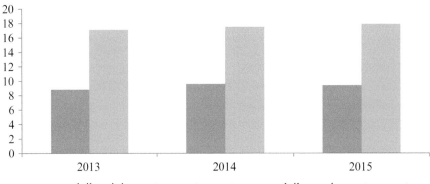

Graph 46 Average daily maximum and minimum temperatures, years 2013–2015 (Celsius degrees) (Source: Istat, Rilevazione dati meteoclimatici ed. idrologici)

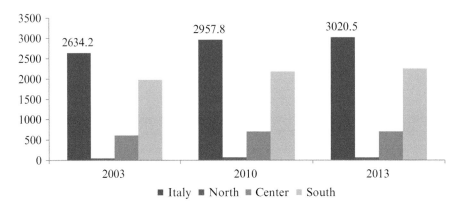

Graph 47 Marine protected areas, years 2003, 2010, 2013 (square kilometers) (Source: *Ministero dell'ambiente e della tutela del territorio e del mare*)

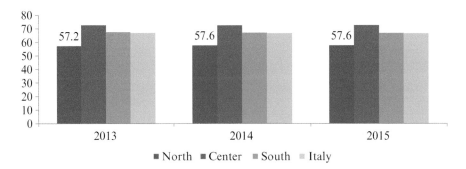

Graph 48 Marine coastal waters, years 2004–2009 (percentage of bathing marine coastal waters) (Source: elaborazione Istat su dati del Ministero della Salute)

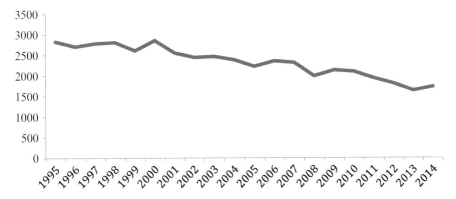

Graph 49 Value of production for fishery and aquaculture (millions of euro). Years 1995–2014 (Source: Istat, Conti economici nazionali)

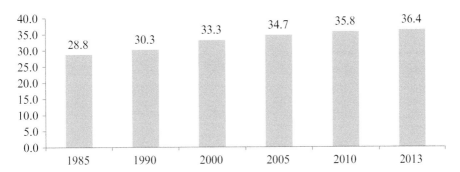

Graph 50 Forest area as a proportion of total land area, years 1985, 1990, 2000, 2005, 2010 e 2013 (Source: ISPRA)

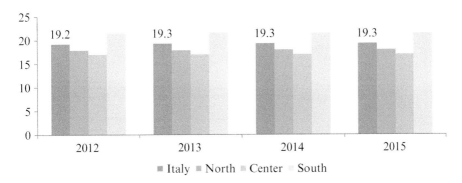

Graph 51 Areas of special naturalistic interest belonging to the network Natura 2000, years 2012–2015 (percentage of areas of special naturalistic interest of total surface) (Source: Istat, Elaborazione su dati Ministero dell'ambiente e della tutela del territorio e del mare)

Goal 16 – Peace, Justice and Institutions

See Graphs 52, 53, 54, and 55.

Goal 17 – Means of Implementation and International Governance

See Graphs 56, 57, 58, and 59.

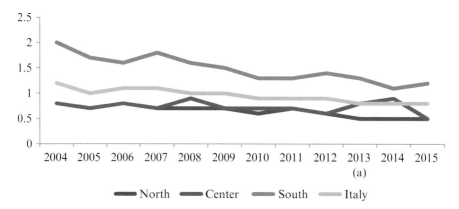

Graph 52 Number of victims of intentional homicide per 100.000 inhabitants, years 2004–2015 (Source: Istat, Ministero dell'Interno, dati SDI)

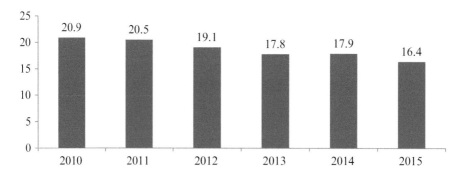

Graph 53 Unsentenced detainees as proportion of overall prison population, years 2010–2015 (Source: Ministero della Giustizia Caratteristiche socio-lavorative, giuridiche e demografiche della popolazione detenuta)

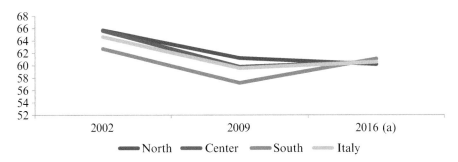

Graph 54 Proportion of people that feel safe walking alone, years 2002, 2009, 2016 (individuals of 14 years and more that feel safe walking alone in the dark around the area they live – percentage) (Source: Istat, Indagine sulla Sicurezza dei cittadini)

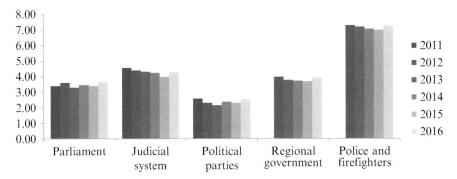

Graph 55 Trust in various institutions (in the Parliament, judicial system, political parties, local institutions, other types of institutions), years 2011–2016 (average score of trust) (Source: Istat, Indagine Aspetti della vita quotidiana)

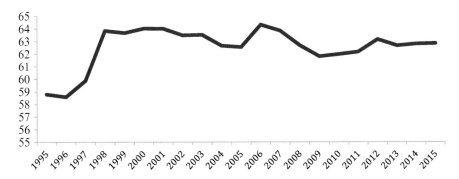

Graph 56 Proportion of domestic budget funded by domestic taxes, years 1995–2015(percentage) (Source: Istat, *Conti economici nazionali*)

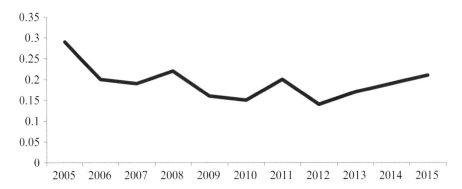

Graph 57 Net official development assistance as a proportion of GNI, years 2005–2015 (Source: OECD)

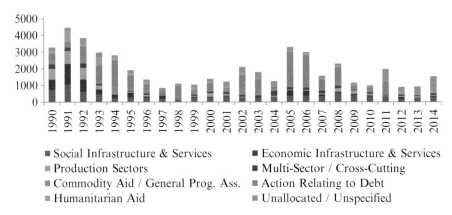

- ■ Social Infrastructure & Services
- ■ Economic Infrastructure & Services
- ■ Production Sectors
- ■ Multi-Sector / Cross-Cutting
- ■ Commodity Aid / General Prog. Ass.
- ■ Action Relating to Debt
- ■ Humanitarian Aid
- ■ Unallocated / Unspecified

Graph 58 Official Bilateral Commitments by sector, years 1990–2014 (US Dollar, Millions, 2014) (Source: OECD)

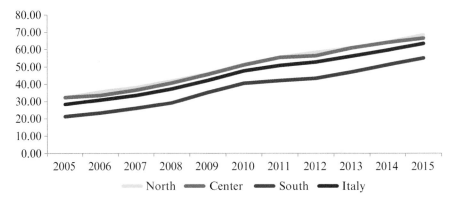

Graph 59 Proportion of individuals using the Internet, years 2005–2015 (individuals of 16–74 years who have used the Internet at least once per week in the 3 months before the interview–percentage) (Source: Istat, Community survey on ICT usage in households and by individuals)

References

Bachelet, M., Maggino, F., & Riccardini F. (2016). *Sustainability of wellbeing: an analysis of resilience and vulnerability through subjective indicators.* In Paper presented at the 48th scientific meeting of the italian statistical society, Università degli Studi di Salerno 8–10 June 2016.

EUROSTAT. (2017). Indicators for monitoring the Sustainable Development Goals (SDGS) in an EU context. http://ec.europa.eu/eurostat/web/sdi.

GRI-Empowering Sustainable Decisions. (2016). The global reporting initiative. https://www.globalreporting.org/standards/Pages/default.aspx.

Inter-agency Expert Group-Sustainable Development Goals. http://unstats.un.org/sdgs/.

ISTAT. (2015–2016). *The Report on equitable and sustainable wellbeing in Italy,* at this link: http://www.istat.it/en/well-being-measures.

ISTAT. (2016–2017). *17 Sustainable development goals.* https://www.istat.it/it/benessere-e-sostenibilit%C3%A0/obiettivi-di-sviluppo-sostenibil/gli-indicatori-istat-per-lo-svil.

Poli, R. (2017). *Introduction to Anticipation Studies.* Springer International Publishing AG 2017.

Riccardini, F. (2014a). *Sustainability of wellbeing: The case of BES for Italy.* In Paper presented at the ISQOLS conference, Berlin, 15–18 Sept.

Riccardini, F. (2014b). Le tendenze e gli scenari mondiali in note bibliografiche su Gallegati M. Oltre la siepe. L'economia che verrà, Chiarelettere, Milano in Moneta e Credito, Vol. 67(268), pp. 457–482.

Riccardini, F. (2016). Interview on developing Indicators for the Sustainable Development Goals (SDGs), for the beyond GDP newsletter, measuring progress, wealth and wellbeing, of the European commission, March. http://ec.europa.eu/environment/beyond_gdp/newsletters/March2016/newsletter.html.

Riccardini, F., & De Rosa, D. (2016). How the nexus of water/food/energy can be seen with the perspective of people well-being and the Italian BES framework, vol. 8 Elsevier Science Direct review, of florence "Sustainability of well-being international forum". 2015: Food for sustainability and not just food, FlorenceSWIF2015.

Riccardini, F. et al. (2016). Benessere e Sviluppo sostenibile: una lettura per l'Italia, Universitalia, Roma novembre 2016. https://www.libreriauniversitaria.it/sviluppo-benessere-sostenibili-lettura-italia/libro/9788865079744?utm_source=google-shopping&utm_medium=cpc&utm_term=9788865079744&utm_content=Libri%20Italiani&utm_campaign=google-shopping-lib.

Statistics Sweeden and Ministerio del Medio Ambiente Gobierno de Chile. (2016). Monitoring the shift to sustainable consumption and production patterns in the context of the SDGs. https://sustainabledevelopment.un.org/index.php?page=view&type=400&nr=2298&menu=35; http://sdg.iisd.org/news/unep-sweden-chile-report-on-monitoring-scp-targets/.

UN Secretary General's Independent Expert Advisory Group. (2015). The world that counts. http://www.undatarevolution.org/report/.

UNDESA. (2012). Rio+20 UN conference on sustainable development, The future we want. http://www.uncsd2012.org/thefuturewewant.html.

UNECE. (2016). Sustainable development goals. http://www.unece.org/sustainable-development/sustainable-development/home.html; http://www.unece.org/statistics/statsexperts/task-force-on-adjusting-ces-recommendations-to-the-sustainable-development-goals.html.

UNECE High Level Group. (2016). http://unstats.un.org/unsd/statcom/47th-session/documents/2016-5-UNECE-HLG-on-modernisation-of-official-statistics-E.pdf.

UNECE-OECD-EUROSTAT. (2013). TF UNECE for developing sustainable development measures, 27 May 2013. Framework and suggested indicators to measure sustainable development.

United Nations. (2014). Fundamental principles of official statistics. http://unstats.un.org/unsd/dnss/gp/fundprinciples.aspx.

United Nations. (2015). Transforming our world: The 2030 agenda for sustainable development. http://www.un.org/sustainabledevelopment/sustainable-development-goals/.

United Nations. (2016–2017). *The sustainable development goals report.* New York. UNDESA: https://www.un.org/development/desa/publications/sdg-report-2017.html.

United Nations Statistical Commission. (2016). http://unstats.un.org/unsd/statcom/47th-session/documents/2016-2-IAEG-SDGs-E.pdf.

Creativity and Anticipation

36

Giovanni Emanuele Corazza

Contents

Abstract

In this chapter, in-depth analysis and comparison of the creativity and anticipation constructs are performed. At a first glance, it is immediately apparent that there are common grounds in these future goal-oriented behaviors, both pertaining to the realm of nonlinear dynamic systems and complexity. But their relationship turns out to be far from obvious. There are commonalities, in that they are both adaptive factors in human evolution, they share a need for countering skepticism on a scientific approach, they are both process-oriented, and they are characterized by drive and motivation towards a preferable future. However, there are also significant differences: while anticipation can be interpreted as a new and general point of view on all sciences, creativity is a very special exception; the champions of the two disciplines, geniuses and prophets, have quite distinct roles in society; for creativity, there exists a literature on the measurement of traits and abilities of the creative person, as well as a creative industry, while there appears to be no parallel in the realm of anticipation. Once the above similarities and distinctions are established, we show how the two constructs can cooperate in devising

G. E. Corazza (✉)
Marconi Institute for Creativity, University of Bologna, Bologna, Italy
e-mail: giovanni.corazza@unibo.it

© Springer Nature Switzerland AG 2019
R. Poli (ed.), *Handbook of Anticipation*,
https://doi.org/10.1007/978-3-319-91554-8_102

preferable futures, in the estimation of creative ideas, in producing a fruitful mindset and motivation for challenges, in awakening latents. On the other hand, we also discuss how they can be in contrast: continuity (as opposed to creativity) could improve anticipation; imagining harsh futures could reduce the boldness of the creator; and finally creativity and anticipation could be used to defy each other. The chapter is concluded by a short discussion on societal evolution implications, with the introduction of artificial intelligent agents, and on the necessary modifications to the educational system.

Keywords

Creativity · Anticipation · Dynamic process · Divergent thinking · Originality · Effectiveness · Education · Forecast · Foresight · Genius · Strategic thinking · Adaptive behavior · Human evolution

Introduction: The Dynamic Study of Anticipation and Creativity

Creativity and anticipation are both fundamental constructs in our universe, sharing the concept of future goal-oriented action, or action with a prospection beyond the present status quo. Creative and anticipatory behaviors are not the exclusive domain of the human species; in fact, creativity can be displayed by artificial agents (Dartnall 2013) or other animals (Kaufman and Kaufman 2004), as well as anticipation can be the property of a system (Rosen 2012), while the debate on mental time travel abilities in nonhumans is open (Suddendorf and Corballis 2007, 2008). To extend even more the possible generality of our discourse, it could be mentioned that Whitehead (1978/1929, p. 21) attributes a fundamental metaphysical role to creativity: "Creativity is the universal of universals, characterizing ultimate matter of fact. It is the ultimate principle by which the many, which are the universe disjunctively, become the one actual occasion, which is the universe conjunctively. It lies in the nature of things that the many enter into complex unity." However, for the purposes of the present work, that is arguably the first instance in which these two constructs are the subject of joint considerations, it suffices to limit our attention to human beings, who are undoubtedly capable of showing both creative and anticipatory behaviors.

Following (Poli 2017), anticipatory action can be defined as *a behavior that uses the future in its actual decision process*. Indeed, anticipation of the future and projection of the evolving reality onto our expectations are fundamental mechanisms to explain how our brains and minds work (Seligman et al. 2013). Anticipation includes and subsumes forecast and foresight, adding an element of action in the present depending on the imagined possible futures. When anticipation is based on forecast, i.e., on the extension of current trends, then it is oriented towards stability of the existing society. On the other hand, when anticipation is based on foresight, i.e., on the qualitative consideration of multiple futures, then it becomes also open and robust to disruptive events. Further, anticipation foresees reality as a complex entity, evolving and revolving with nonlinear dynamics, where discontinuities play a crucial role in defying simple extrapolations of present trends into the future (Poli 2017).

On the other hand, according to a recent definition (Corazza 2016), creative action can be defined as *a behavior that requires potential originality and effectiveness*. Originality is a fundamental characteristic of a creative product (or process, or person) that subsumes three dimensions: novelty, surprise (or nonobviousness), and authenticity. On the other hand, not every original entity is creative: only those that are simultaneously effective, of value, adaptive, useful, to the purpose (as a minimum in a serendipitous sense) can qualify as such. While originality and effectiveness are the classic requirements that were contained also in the so-called *standard* definition of creativity (Runco and Jaeger 2012), which is oriented to the present, the concept of "potential" plays a fundamental role in prospecting the dynamic effects of creative behavior into the future. In fact, creativity extends its effects onto the world by projecting the outcomes of present actions in the future, when their potential originality and effectiveness will take on concrete representation and reaction. Therefore, since creativity requires a potential, then the creative process should be studied as a dynamic system, in which originality and effectiveness are possibly in place depending both on environmental conditions and on the actors' characteristics and actions. A creative process and its outcomes constitute what Gaston Berger would have identified as "future bearing facts" (Cournand and Lévy 1973). When the potential is realized, according to the (inescapably subjective) judgment of estimators, in the near or far future, an episode of *creative achievement* is materialized, whereas in the opposite case we are in the presence of *creative inconclusiveness*. But the creative inconclusiveness of a process can be transformed into achievement simply by a shift in time, in space, or in culture: creative potential is in dialogue with the universal cumulative culture. Clearly, when originality turns out to be very significant, discontinuities with respect to the status quo can take place, for example, in the form of paradigm shifts, or of new products which disrupt the market. Therefore, it can be argued that creativity is the fundamental reason why anticipation of multiple scenarios beyond simple forecast is so essential. Note that estimation of the potential originality and effectiveness of the outcome of a creative process is based on knowledge coming from the present and past, but it is actually a projection of the created entity into the future. Estimating a creative idea is indeed an exercise in foresight-based anticipation.

From these introductory statements, a relationship between creativity and anticipation starts to emerge: The two concepts are clearly intertwined but far from being identical. The purpose of this work is to investigate commonalities and differences, as well as conditions of synergetic vs. contrasting interaction between these two fundamental constructs.

Commonalities Between Creativity and Anticipation

Adaptive factors in human evolution – We believe that creative and anticipatory behaviors share significant commonality and value in terms of human adaptability, and hence in having determined the success of *Homo sapiens* in the course of our evolution. Starting from the anticipation side, the specific feature of foresight as mental time travel into the future has been analyzed by Suddendorf and Corballis (2007), who note that (p. 312): "The immense flexibility this foresight provides may have allowed us to successfully adapt to and colonize most habitats on the planet." It is important to underline that this advantage does not come for free (p. 311): "This foresight requires several sophisticated cognitive abilities, is resource-intensive and error-prone, and introduces new kinds of mental stress, not least of which is the knowledge of inevitable death. This is a high price to pay for a system for antici-pating the future [...]. But mental time travel offers an additional degree of flexi-bility that, even if the adaptive advantage was in the first instance small, was sufficient to ensure selection and fixation in the population." Suddendorf and Corballis (2007) also analyze the reasons why this kind of foresight is arguably not found in nonhuman animals, thus, apparently making it a distinctive feature of our species.

On the other hand, Enquist et al. (2008) address the mechanisms according to which the cumulative culture of our species grows exponentially, and they find that this is only possible thanks to creativity. Again, the accumulation of culture is a phenomenon that is peculiar of our species, and they state that: "an increase in individual creativity may have been the first step toward human culture." From a macroscopic point of view, Corazza (2017) note that all episodic creative processes are actually elements of a single general process, identified as the dynamic universal creativity process, which is the main cause for the growth of cumulative culture analyzed by Enquist et al. (2008). It may be argued that creativity has been one of the principal features that determined the success of *Hominins* first, and *Homo sapiens* later, in the course of human evolution with respect to other species' evolution. But as for the case of foresight, also in this case the benefits did not come without paying a high price. Standing upright was a major enabler to free our hands and start the stone-tool industry, arguably the first creative industry ever. But this meant slower motion and becoming easier targets to predators. Extending infancy and introducing childhood into our developmental path was fundamental to foster the playful and exploratory mindset that characterizes creative (as well as anticipatory) behavior. But this meant that our progeny was the slowest to reach a state of independence, thus requiring constant care for long periods of time. Yet, these costs were all worth sustaining in view of the advantages brought by our ability to generate ideas with a high potential for originality and effectiveness.

A question that to the best of our knowledge has never been addressed in the literature is whether human anticipatory behavior came before creative behavior or vice versa. As a mere speculation, our guess is that they coevolved as humans were evolving higher layers of mind. In conclusion, both anticipatory and creative behav-iors are adaptive, although they come at a price.

Countering skepticism on the scientific approach to the disciplines of creativity and anticipation – A scientific approach to creativity is often questioned. How can inspiration be coded in any way? Shouldn't imagination simply be free to roam? Most people do not think of themselves as "creative," and those who do often would rather not share their "secrets," preferring to leave a halo of mystery around their methodologies (which may well be running below their level of awareness). But there may be another fundamental reason why creativity and science may have had difficulties in being associated. This is because the outcomes of creativity have a potential today, which may be realized (or not) in the future. Their impact belongs to *futura*, as per the definition of Bertrand de Jouvenel (1967). And as such, creativity has to bear up with preconceptions similar to those that have been expressed onto futures studies: "there can be no science of the future." On the contrary, we know that concrete steps can and should be taken to establish philosophical as well as scientific foundations both for the discipline of anticipation (Poli 2011) and for the discipline of creativity (Corazza and Agnoli 2016).

Process orientation and complexity – As already mentioned in our introduction, both anticipation and creativity should be seen under the light of nonlinear dynamics, and hence they belong to the realm of complexity and complex systems. Both constructs can therefore be characterized as processes with a recursive nature, which introduces the question of impredicativity that has been considered thoroughly for anticipation in (Poli 2017). On the other hand, the question "Is creativity impredicative?" has never been addressed before, to our knowledge, and we make a first attempt here.

Let's take as an axiom that a construct is impredicative if its definition requires a reference to the construct itself. Self-referentiality, for example, is intrinsic in the fact that a mind self-produces the psychological processes it is constituted by. Now, in order to enjoy high levels of potential originality, the creative thinking process involves trajectories of thought which go outside of the so-called common knowledge domain, and the subsequent search for meaning of these trajectories. Clearly, the boundary between what is inside and what is outside the common knowledge domain is completely self-determined, and this very same boundary is immediately and dynamically adapted while the new idea is being generated. In essence, there seems to be no discrete separation between the time that the idea has not been conceived yet, and the time in which it becomes a seamless part of the common knowledge domain, and as such a self-defining element of the very same mind that generated it. Generation of new knowledge is the impredicative mechanism for the growth of mind. Although this is only a preliminary glance at this issue, there appears to be plenty of room for future elaboration.

Drive and motivation towards a preferable future – As discussed by Voros (2003), there exist several kinds of potential futures: *possible* (those that "might" happen, possibly depending on future knowledge), *plausible* (those that "could" happen, depending on our current knowledge), *probable* (those that are "likely" to happen, depending on current trends), and *preferable* futures (those that we "would like" to happen). All these alternative futures are important inputs to an anticipation exercise: forecast-based anticipation (which may occur below the level of awareness) privileges probable futures, but proactive foresight-based anticipation involves a clear bias in favor of a preferable future, i.e., in making decisions today that increase the likelihood that a specified future condition will be realized. We can say that all activities in the present are driven towards a future that is yet to be realized. In a very similar way, attentive focus and motivation are essential elements that drive and pervade the entire development of the creative thinking process. Indeed, creative achievement in a lifetime can be shown to be positively correlated to one's self-efficacy, or the strength with which one's goals are pursued. This orientation towards a creative goal can be both aware on unaware; in the second case, the person shows a natural talent for creativity. In essence, we can state that *creativity is motivated by the drive for an anticipatory action aimed at producing a preferable future built around the new idea which satisfies one's creativity goal.*

From the points discussed above, the similarities and connections between creativity and anticipation are apparent. Yet, one can take the opposite point of view and work towards showing how these two constructs are actually very different and, in some occasions, contrasting. We show a few examples of this in the following section.

Differences Between Creativity and Anticipation

Anticipation as a new and general point of view on all sciences, creativity as a special exception – In a constructive approach to the field of anticipation, Poli (2010) searches for evidence of relevant future-oriented approaches in disciplines as diverse as philosophy, physics, biology, neuroscience, psychology, social sciences, semiotics, engineering, artificial intelligence. Essentially, anticipation can be considered to be not only a discipline in itself, but also a special perspective through which other disciplines can be studied and understood. Undoubtedly, creativity also has intersections with many of the above mentioned disciplines but in a rather different sense. Take as a significant example the field of neuroscience: there is a body of work pointing to anticipation as one of the fundamental mechanisms that explains how the brain works. On the other hand, no one is claiming that most (let alone all) of the brain's activity is creative: as a matter of fact, the opposite is arguably true. In fact, one of the fundamental drivers for the brain's activity is to minimize energy consumption, whereas the generation of creative alternatives requires longer times and higher energy expenditure than the elicitation of previously known responses.

The above argument is clearly exemplified by the thinking ability which is typically considered to be one of the most distinct peculiarities of the creative thinking process: the divergent thinking modality. In divergent thinking, given a certain input state of mind, the ability is to try to imagine as many as possible (fluency) consequential states, characterized by their relative infrequency (originality). This modality is very energy-hungry and time consuming, certainly not the natural behavior that allows our brains to save energy. In a nutshell, while anticipation claims its role of a general principle, creativity is definitely a very special, one could argue supreme, behavior of mind and brain. Similarly, consider the field of psychology. Clearly, creativity is a special (and very fruitful) branch of psychology: not certainly the mainstream in general psychology. On the other hand, there are attempts to use prospection as a paradigm shift for the entire field of psychology (Seligman et al. 2013). If this anticipatory point of view would be accepted, then the consequences of this would affect most if not all of the fields of psychology, from clinical to organizational, and all the way to social applications.

Champions: geniuses vs. *prophets* – Another clear distinction between creativity and anticipation can be made in terms of those who are considered as the "champions" of the two respective disciplines, which we can loosely identify as "geniuses" and "prophets." Creative geniuses can belong to any domain but are particularly important in the history of art, science and technology. In all of these three domains there is ample literature on geniuses, on the way they worked, the environments they lived in, their production through the years, the consequences and impact of the works they donated to the world. Even though today we are pursuing a democratization of creativity (everyone can and should be creative, for a portion of their lives), it can be argued that the history of creativity has been paved by geniuses. On the other hand, the consideration of a person that excels in foresight, the prophet, brings in a quite different picture. First of all, the noun "prophet" itself immediately relates to the religious concept of someone to whom a certain "truth" has been revealed from above. But this is clearly not the position of a champion in anticipation, who is called upon the generation of multiple potential futures and the setting of a course of actions, possibly towards a preferable one. Secondly, while the impact of a work of genius can sometimes be immediately recognized, the goodness of decisions taken by an anticipatory prophecy can only be established in a (potentially far) future. Even under the assumption that the anticipated preferable future materializes, it may be difficult to go back at the time its anticipation was generated to give deserved credit to the prophet: recognition a posteriori of good foresight is a delicate exercise. Even though the two figures have clearly distinct roles/life-stories in our society, sometimes they can converge onto the same person: great inventors are sometimes referred to as both geniuses and prophets, because the creativity of their invention also had the effect of projecting society into a (sometimes unpredictable) future. But this is not always the case: a creative genius can work with past traditions and rework them through an authentic personal expression, creating awe-inspiring aesthetic value without any implications towards the future.

Measurement, traits, abilities of the creative person – Since creativity is a very specific behavior, which depends fundamentally on the considered application domain, the study of general factors as well as individual differences of creative persons is an extremely interesting and important research field (see, e.g., Agnoli et al. 2016). What are the differences between creative artists and creative scientists? Are there common methodologies, or should any creative thinking model be tailored to a specific domain, and if so, how should the "domain" be specified? These questions have seen extensive work in the literature but still represent somewhat open issues. This kind of work does not seem to be paralleled by an equivalent field of research in anticipation. This may be due to the fact that anticipation is a more general principle that applies basically to the way our minds and brains operate. However, there may also be an avenue for future research on traits and abilities for anticipatory behavior.

Creative industry – Finally, we note that there exists an entire industrial sector which is dedicated to the exploitation of the products and in general of the intellectual property generated by creativity, i.e., the sector of creative industries. The boundaries of this sector are not always clearly identified, and reports from different regions in the world may account for diversified categories. The UK's definition of the creative industries is as follows: "those industries that are based on individual creativity, skill and talent with the potential to create wealth and jobs through developing intellectual property," and it includes 13 subsectors: advertising, architecture, the art and antiques market, crafts, design, designer fashion, film, interactive leisure software, music, performing arts, publishing, software, and television and radio. The economy of this sector can be studied, regulated, stimulated through political actions, and certain countries may be more or less willing to invest in it and favor its economic development. All of this reality has no equivalent parallel in the field of anticipation and future studies, although clearly there exist plenty of opportunities for consulting in foresight and anticipation, and all major companies have strategic thinking divisions performing such activities. Still, we cannot conclude that a separate and distinguishable "anticipation industry" exists, as of yet.

How Creativity and Anticipation Cooperate

Given now that we have clarified the basic similarities and differences between the creativity and anticipation constructs, in this section we intend to investigate and discuss how the abilities in creativity and anticipation can be made to cooperate for the achievement of what can be identified generically as an "improved performance."

Probable, possible, and preferable futures – The derivation of probable futures is a quantitative exercise based on tools that can extend and extrapolate from the current reality to short- or medium-term scenarios. In this case, creativity is not really required, being surpassed by analysis, induction and inference. But as soon as one desires to deviate from a more or less sophisticated trends analysis, the matter changes instantaneously, turning from quantitative to qualitative. Here, creative thinking skills and methods can help greatly in imagining possible scenarios containing significant discontinuity with respect to probable futures. For example, one can consider a present dominant trend and arbitrarily escape, reverse, amplify, distort, or counterbalance it, and then move from idea to idea to conceive all the possible consequences one is able to imagine. This would be a typical application of the divergent thinking modality. Given that the number of possible futures can rapidly grow beyond treatability, it is then always necessary to restrict the attention to a few or possibly one preferable future. Also in this critical part of the process, creative abilities come at hand. In fact, the ability to estimate the possible value and opportunities afforded by a novel and unprecedented situation is one of the necessary idea-scouting skills of an expert creative thinker. This convergent or divergent assessment of a future scenario can be performed with a sequence of "what if" questions that aims at exploring the new territory from multiple perspectives. Through divergent thinking and value-based selection, creativity can fruitfully aid anticipation.

Estimation of creative ideas – Consider the estimation of the originality and effectiveness of a new idea generated as the outcome of a creative process.

According to the pragmatic approach advocated in (Corazza 2016), no expert can posit its absolute capacity to thoroughly perform such an estimation. Indeed, the history of science, art, and technology is ripe with examples of major experts who were unable to see the value of new paradigms, which later disrupted their field. Therefore, the most proficient attitude of the estimator is that of trying to humbly conceive diversified possible consequences of a new idea, as projected onto multiple possible scenarios. In short, foresight is necessary to evaluate a creative idea, and anticipation is required in order to bring the idea into reality. This example is therefore a positive case of anticipation that works in favor of creative achievement. We could possibly argue that in order to achieve creative results, a sufficient level of anticipatory abilities is a requirement.

Mindset for creativity and anticipation – Creative performance is always hindered by a number of diversified blocks, which can be broadly classified as cultural, perceptual, and emotional. Focusing the attention on the first category here, cultural blocks (or epistemological blocks, as defined by Gaston Bachelard 1934) are caused by the fact that increasing levels of expertise are also naturally accompanied by reduced levels of openness to new facts that are challenging the established paradigms. There are innumerable episodes of this form of fixedness, take for example the world of computer technology:

- In 1943, Thomas Watson, at the time President of IBM, stated that "I think that there is a world market for maybe five computers."
- Much later, in 1977, Ken Olsen, founder of Digital Equipment Corporation, essentially agreed by saying that "There is no reason why anyone would want a computer in their home."
- In 1995, Robert Metcalfe, coinventor of the Ethernet, predicted: "The Internet will soon go spectacularly supernova and in 1996 catastrophically collapse."

Undoubtedly, the sources of these statements were acclaimed experts in their field, and recognized innovators in their own right. And the difficulty in foreseeing the explosion of information and communications technologies should not be underestimated in retrospect. Still, we could speculate that opening up the spectrum of possible futures could have changed these forecasts by affecting the mindset of these experts. In a nutshell, believing that time forks into innumerable futures is a very helpful and somewhat fundamental mindset that works in synergy for both creativity and anticipation.

Motivation for challenges – Both creativity and anticipation are risky businesses. In fact, they represent challenges to both the state of the art and its extrapolation into a direct and unique future. As such they will both be faced with resistance from inside and outside sources. Forces of continuity are always very strong, roughly summed up by the question: "Why should anything change, why should the course of actions deviate, if all in all everything is working fine, if it's been in this way for generations?" For this reason, both the creator and the anticipator must be armed with very strong grit and motivation for facing challenges. Success towards the implementation of nonobvious future-aware decisions as well as of creative ideas depends fundamentally on being able to overcome frustration and resistance: emotional intelligence is at a prime.

Awakening latents – As explained in (Poli 2011), the span of possible futures is dependent on the number and diversification of latents which underlie the present physical, social, and cultural environment. Latents can be defined as dormant structures with a *potential* for being activated. Now, as discussed above the dynamic definition for creativity states that this construct requires *potential* originality and effectiveness. It can therefore be argued that originality and effectiveness of ideas that have not yet been represented to the outside world are latents: if these dormant potentials are awakened, they might lead to a totally different future with respect to what one could expect from a simple extrapolation of the present trends. Under this light, creativity and anticipation appear to be interconnected at a very fundamental and intrinsic level.

How Creativity and Anticipation Can Be in Contrast

Even though in the previous section we have identified a number of areas in which creativity and anticipation not only coexist but actually collaborate in a complex way to let original futures emerge, in this section we intend to reverse the mood and investigate if and how creativity and anticipation can be contrasting forces and in what sense.

Continuity to improve anticipation – It could be natural to believe that forces of continuity are always retrograde, retrospective, belonging to those who do not want to innovate, that prefer the past to the future. Actually, it is not necessarily so; although there are vintage lovers, continuity can also be the premium choice by those who keep and value a forward look. In fact, one of the stronger reasons for preferring continuity with the past with respect to creative disruption is that the former allows more precise predictions of the future, while the latter makes forecasting extremely uncertain! Paradoxically, it may be the need for accurate anticipation that reduces our efforts towards creativity!

Reducing boldness of the creator – Consider the fact that every truly original idea is faced with resistance by experts in the field: the higher the originality, the stronger the resistance. Clearly, anticipating all scenarios of possible critiques against the idea, the possible associated failures, or simply imagining the amount of effort that will be required to bring the idea into reality in spite of all obstacles, can put to a serious test the persistence and self-efficacy of the creator. Indeed, many potentially disruptive ideas do not see the light because the above anticipated burdens overcome the perceived possible benefits. From this point of view, extensive anticipatory behavior could possibly work as a block to the fluency of a creative thinker: in fact, successful creators associated with disruptions in our cumulative culture were the ones who dared believing in their intuition without worrying too much about the future reactions of the world.

Creativity to defy anticipation – Imagining a scenario of competition between companies in a specific industrial/commercial field, it can be argued that the creativity of one company can be used to defy the anticipation of future developments in the field by another company. Disruptions typically lead to the fall of incumbents and the rise of new emerging leaders.

Anticipation to defy creativity – Finally, and perhaps dramatically, it is always possible to foresee a future in which any new idea will have no value, or be altogether counterproductive. Used in this way, anticipation can become the killer of any creative idea which dares challenge the state of the art by prospecting novel possibilities which are however useful only in a subset of possible futures.

Conclusion and Directions for Further Discussion

In the Information society, the distribution of intelligence and the widespread accessibility to all data leads to the destructuring of the space and time dimensions, allowing homogeneous interactions and production everywhere: information becomes a commodity (Corazza et al. 2010). The dematerialization of processes, products, and services leads to an unprecedented increase in the rate of change and innovation. Even these few words are sufficient to justify the following statement: creativity and anticipation are essential abilities for the human species in the twenty-first century. In fact, only the generation of new ideas can give dignity to a human who is submerged by immense amounts of data, and only the anticipation of possible futures can sustain the rate of innovation which is forced by the evolution in society. Therefore, it appears to be timely that these two constructs are considered jointly to analyze their commonalities and differences, as well as the ways in which they can collaborate or be in contrast, an analysis we tried to initiate in this chapter. Having seen the various discussions, we hope that the reader can agree on the fact that the relationship between creativity and anticipation is both strong and nonobvious, intricate and subtle, as well as potentially constructive or destructive depending on the applied purpose and methodology.

More discussion on this topic is certainly needed. For example, given the evolution of artificial intelligence in society, the discourse should be enlarged to encompass systems and technologies, to see how these can be of support to creativity and/or anticipation, to estimate the extent to which artificial agents can show independent creative and/or anticipatory behaviors, and to try to depict evolutionary paths that lead to a situation in which larger and larger portions of our population can exploit the benefits of these constructs and technologies.

Another area of discussion and great importance pertains therefore to the realm of education: How should this system be changed, modified, reformed in order to develop the necessary abilities and skills that lead to the successful exploitation of the creativity and anticipation constructs? Should these processes permeate all disciplines, or should they be given a separate time and space? And what is the best strategy to introduce these subjects effectively, given the strong resistance to change of the education system? These questions are far from being obvious and definitely deserve much longer analysis. However, for the purposes of the present chapter it suffices to say that it is our belief that, although creativity and anticipation can be exploited as a mindset in all disciplines, in this historical phase it is both preferable and advisable that they are given distinct time and space in the educational programs. This will be instrumental in clarifying terms, principles, methodologies, and tools, thus contributing in establishing these two fundamental constructs as scientific disciplines.

References

Agnoli, S., Corazza, G. E., & Runco, M. A. (2016). Estimating creativity with a multiple-measurement approach within scientific and artistic domains. *Creativity Research Journal, 28*(2), 171–176.

Bachelard, G. (1934). *Le nouvel esprit scientifique*. Paris: PUF.

Corazza, G. E. (2016). Potential originality and effectiveness: The dynamic definition of creativity. *Creativity Research Journal, 28*(3), 258–267.

Corazza, G. E., & Agnoli, S. (2016). On the path towards the science of creative thinking. In *Multidisciplinary contributions to the science of creative thinking* (pp. 3–19). Singapore: Springer.

Corazza, G. E. (2017). *The dynamic universal creativity process*. Under preparation.

Corazza, G. E., Vanelli-Coralli, A., & Pedone, R. (2010). Technology as a need: Trends in the evolving information society. *Advances in Electronics and Telecommunications, 1*(1), 124–132.

Cournand, A., & Lévy, M. (Eds.). (1973). *Shaping the future: Gaston Berger and the concept of prospective*. New York: Gordon and Breach Science Publishers.

Dartnall, T. (Ed.). (2013). *Artificial intelligence and creativity: An interdisciplinary approach* (Vol. 17). Dordrecht: Springer Science & Business Media.

de Jouvenel, B. (1967). *The art of conjecture*. London: Weidenfeld & Nicolson.

Enquist, M., Ghirlanda, S., Jarrick, A., & Wachtmeister, C. A. (2008). Why does human culture increase exponentially? *Theoretical Population Biology, 74*(1), 46–55.

Kaufman, J. C., & Kaufman, A. B. (2004). Applying a creativity framework to animal cognition. *New Ideas in Psychology, 22*(2), 143–155.

Poli, R. (2010). The many aspects of anticipation. *Foresight-The Journal of Future Studies, Strategic Thinking and Policy, 12*(3), 7–17.

Poli, R. (2011). Steps toward an explicit ontology of the future. *Journal of Futures Studies, 16*(1), 67–78.

Poli, R. (2017). *Introducing anticipation. Handbook of anticipation*. Springer.

Rosen, R. (2012). Anticipatory systems. In *Anticipatory systems* (pp. 313–370). New York: Springer.

Runco, M. A., & Jaeger, G. J. (2012). The standard definition of creativity. *Creativity Research Journal, 24*(1), 92–96.

Seligman, M. E., Railton, P., Baumeister, R. F., & Sripada, C. (2013). Navigating into the future or driven by the past. *Perspectives on Psychological Science, 8*(2), 119–141.

Suddendorf, T., & Corballis, M. C. (2007). The evolution of foresight: What is mental time travel, and is it unique to humans? *Behavioral and Brain Sciences, 30*(03), 299–313.

Suddendorf, T., & Corballis, M. C. (2008). New evidence for animal foresight? *Animal Behaviour, 75*(5), e1–e3.

Voros, J. (2003). A generic foresight process framework. *Foresight, 5*(3), 10–21.

Whitehead, A. N. (1978/1929). In D.R. Griffin & D.W. Sherburne (Eds.), *Process and reality, Corrected edition*. New York: Free Press.

Design Processes and Anticipation

37

Flaviano Celaschi, Elena Formia, Roberto Iñiguez Flores, and
Ruth León Morán

Contents

This chapter is part of the wider reflection on design and anticipation developed by other
contributors to the *Handbook of Anticipation*. Please consider reading also the following chapters:
Anticipation and Design Inquiry, Design Scenarios and Anticipation, and Anticipation in Built
Environment Design

   This chapter is the result of a coordinated work; however, Flaviano Celaschi is the author of
paragraph 1 (Introduction: The Future of Form in Giving a Form to the Future), Elena Formia of
paragraph 2 (The Future in the Past. Forms of Anticipation in European Design Cultures), and
Roberto Iñiguez Flores and Ruth León Morán of paragraphs 3 (America and the Promise of the
Future. The Contribution of the "New World" Designer in Construction of the Future) and 4 (The
Emergence of Advanced Design).

F. Celaschi (✉) · E. Formia
Department of Architecture, University of Bologna, Bologna, Italy
e-mail: flaviano.celaschi@unibo.it; elena.formia@unibo.it

R. Iñiguez Flores · R. León Morán
Industrial Design Department, Tecnológico de Monterrey, Guadalajara, México
e-mail: riniguez@itesm.mx; rutleon@itesm.mx

© Springer Nature Switzerland AG 2019
R. Poli (ed.), *Handbook of Anticipation*,
https://doi.org/10.1007/978-3-319-91554-8_48

Abstract

Introducing the cultural and historical background of the relationship between design and anticipation is the aim of this chapter. It first provides an overview of the topic describing the various phases and connotations of this connection in design evolution. Then it discusses the creation of a culture of anticipation in contemporary European, and in particular Italian, design as it has been documented in historical surveys and other mediating channels such as exhibitions. In these works, the narration of the future-focused dimension of the project – in the form of utopias, fictions, visions, prototypes, and studies – represents one of the constant interpretations underlying design affirmation and development. In order to outline a complete overview, the third paragraph introduces the approaches of other industrialized countries such the Americas, where the activity of design reflects the contextual factors resulting from its historical origins, not simply from the productive point of view but also as the declaration of the specific identity of each nation. During the first half of the Twentieth century, the perception and planning of the future on the continent were constructed under the influence of the events which gave rise to a space incorporating design as a projectual discipline. The idea of territorial development through foreign references allowed for the evolution of diverse bases for distinct initiatives. This paragraph explains how, from that point in time to the present day, the practice of design in America has become legitimized, with a vision oriented toward the search for innovation opportunities and encompassing both the approach and management of environmental complexity and its accompanying variables. Finally, the last paragraph provides a specific focus into the contemporary debate on the relationship between design and anticipation and outlines a conclusive reflection about: how design processes become today relevant in organizations and develop into ideal spaces for multidisciplinary collaboration in fields with high degrees of uncertainty; how they allow the construction of innovational competencies within these organizations; and, finally, how the label advanced design (the design culture most oriented toward the future) appeared as an anticipatory activity.

Keywords

Design · Anticipation · Processes · Design history · Design cultures · Advanced design · Europe · Americas

Introduction: The Future of Form in Giving a Form to the Future

Design started during the Second Industrial Revolution as a professional practice aimed at planning the formal aspects of goods produced by industrial machines (Bürdek 1992). Since the beginning of the Twentieth century, the success of industrialization and its international diffusion led to the success of design, which was called worldwide "industrial design," characterizing, with its specific features, a precise period of our history.

In the collective mentality, this professional practice was associated, more or less consciously, with a difficult task: to give shape to the society and to define people's ways of living on the planet within the industrial system (Maldonado 1970; Baudrillard 1972; Branzi 2007). By working in groups that integrate strategic, production, marketing, commercial, and communication competences, the designer had to perform a "hermeneutic" – or deciphering – task for modern society, which was represented by manufacturing machines (Dorfles 1963; Flusser 2003; Diamond 2013) and by innovative materials (first of all the artificial materials such as plastic or polymers).

In this period, the designer developed the ability of putting into practice complex concepts and the art of giving a finite shape to indefinite thoughts (Vitta 1996; Celaschi 2000). It was an important ability of mediation between interests, needs, and knowledge, thanks to which the designer acquired, in less than fifty years, a highly-esteemed and prestigious role in the society, being recognized as "creator" of the quality of life and of the good taste and as "producer" of beauty and justice.

This phase of design evolution can be seen as coinciding with the relation between form and function, a relation that was invented by historiography in the first decades of the Twentieth century to attribute a new social and cultural meaning to design and, thus, to industry (Maldonado 1987). This relation implies a necessary condition: there must be a prevailing function – that is "good and right" (Manzini 1990; Celaschi et al. 2005) – in the produced object, and this function justifies and defines the form that the object will take. Functionalism was born as the moral of the industrial production action and the absence of decoration became a style, the only one that could be accepted because it did not hide the primary function of the object (Lorenz 1990).

This was the first moment of great success of the anticipatory vocation of design. Under the motto "less is more," all the forms of the previous centuries gradually lost their decorations, considered as unnecessary, and the designer's moralizing role was accepted in the name of another keyword which design helped materialize: "the progress" of working conditions. The designer, remunerated by capital, progressively acquired an arbitrary role halfway between the interest of the common people who consume goods and the interest of the producer who manufactures and distributes them. "La speranza progettuale" (the design hope) got stronger; according to it, the distribution of the largest quantity of goods to the largest quantity of people in the world translated into prosperity and generated progress in the human condition on Earth.

The American dream, explained by Ruth León Morán and Roberto Iñiguez Flores in the following pages, was born, developed and, at the end of the first half of the Twentieth century, it had already conquered the world. In this phase, the designer communicated a message that was so strong and important for the industrialized capitalist society, as well as for the materialist socialism, that his/her activity was studied to understand and highlight a *modus operandi* which, through the expression of a formal sign, could realize an "added value" not only concerning economics but extremely important to the goods that are subject to it.

Around the middle of the Twentieth century, the great potential of the anticipatory action of design could already be noticed and, despite the fact that it concerned the minority of the products, it played a key role on the creation of the dominant taste and on society, by means of three positive values: modernity, industry, and progress. Industrial production, which used to be associated with low quality, became synonymous with unique quality and later with high quality. It was design at its highest level. The designer and, most of all, his equivalent in fashion, the fashion designer, became the anticipators *par excellence*, the persons to turn to in order to shape the future, according to the dominant values that were generally accepted in an uncritical way. ► Chapter 39, "Design Scenarios and Anticipation" by Chiara Colombi and Danila Zindato explains the role of anticipation in some emblematic sectors, such as fashion, automotive, and electronics.

This phase of design evolution highlights how this practice was accepted in the mature industrial society, to such an extent that, when the syllogism "capitalism – widespread prosperity" went into a crisis, we could expect a consequent great crisis in the practice of the designer. However, in the meantime, design was no longer only a practice, it had become a science (Asimov 1968), and its growth in terms of culture and sensitivity, together with the advantageous position of partners at the highest levels of capital, enabled it to anticipate even the crisis of industry. Design "noticed" it immediately and became critical toward the much-acclaimed functionalism. In the 1970s, design created critical design, radical design, Situationism (Perniola 1998), that can be considered as warning sign of Postmodernity. Such creation took place immediately, when philosophers decoded its condition. We could almost say that design, with its formal criticism, gave shape and realized social criticism, anticipating it and gaining again the right to dominate the social-cultural revolution (Celaschi 2008a). During that period, the seeds of social behaviors and critical consumption developed, consequently taking shape in design. In the following decades, this attitude reached a maturation in the industrially most advanced countries of Europe and in America, opening a season during which people like the designer, who had tried so hard to impose a "logo," cancel it and remove it from the product.

Together with the cultural evolution of the anticipatory role of design, explained by Elena Formia in the following pages, the crisis of the progressive fate of industry led to the consolidation of three opposite behaviors in the anticipatory design: the nostalgia of the golden years, the vintage, and the reuse of the forms of previous decades, when the world was clearly in a phase of economic growth; luxury as research for the extreme and the most precious materials, aiming at the achievement of a supposed "highest level" as shown in a perfect way in Italy and France by the respective "made in" labels; and, finally, the transfer of design into the so-called virtual world of the digital sector, a dimension that started to show its potentials at the end of the Twentieth century.

According to these three aspects, design turned from a cultural project into an economic project, an activity that would enable it to keep its dominant role in anticipating the forms of existence in the period between the Twentieth and the Twenty-first century.

Today the present of design in anticipation is represented by a prevalent ethical-aesthetic role, linked more to the form of processes rather than to the form of products (as explained by Manuela Celi and Andrew Morrison in ► Chap. 38, "Anticipation and Design Inquiry"): designers study the future (awareness of a future to be discovered), designers represent the future in a synthetic way (Penati 2013a, b, c) by means of scenarios (awareness of a future that can be built), and designers facilitate and give a form to the participation of citizens in decisions on the future and help them live with, and consume in a moderate way, the available resources (sustainability, circular economy, system design, etc.).

The next future of design is obvious: it still plays a fundamental and synergetic role. We cannot conceive any kind of future without someone who helps us give a shape to it (Norman 2008; Sterling 2006; Thackara 2008; Celi 2010; De Fusco 2012). It is not possible to give a form to the possible future without studying and understanding, ontologically, culturally, and ideally, the evolution of the concept of future.

In the meantime, design still has key functions in contemporary society:

- It can contribute to the decline of capitalism, or it can turn it into something else, through "palliative" therapies that give us the illusion of man's immortality on Earth (ecology, recycle, etc.).
- It can play a leading role in the assisted co-creation, during which we all want to become designers, in a sort of analytic therapy through which we express our subjectivity toward a supposed common objectivity, that unites us in a pleasant way, as we shape something, as a relation to others and to ourselves.
- It can materialize common goods, intangible services, and experiences, helping us use freely the resources that belong to us, as citizens of the planet (Maldonado 1992; Latouche 2012).
- It can contribute to problem finding, taking action when people are no longer able to ask questions before searching the answers (Augé 2012). While science still tries to represent the world as it is, design can describe how the world could be (Ratti and Claudel 2016), a sort of "what if?" that is typical for anticipators who, like Luigi Ferrara (Dean of the Centre for Arts, Design & Information Technology, George Brown College), aim at using design to give a form to ideas to be disseminated, so that they can reproduce themselves more than chromosomes, spreading out and integrating with each other to improve genetically.

The Fourth Industrial Revolution, called Industry 4.0 in a Teutonic way, is certainly waiting for design and needs design, because the transformation due to the overlapping between manufacturing and digital world is also accompanied by another types of overlapping, since the technologies called IoT (Internet of Things) and IoB (Internet of Behaviors) promise to remove the distance between the activities in a factory (BtoB) and the normal life of objects and their everyday use (BtoC).

The Future in the Past. Forms of Anticipation in European Design Cultures

The first historical reconstructions on design circulating in Italy were those published in the 1930s and 1940s by international authors like Herbert Read (1962 [1934]), Nikolaus Pevsner (1945[1936]), and Sigfried Giedion (1941). These overviews were strongly linked to an ideological interpretation which tended to legitimate the protagonists of the so-called modern movement and their ability to imagine prophetic futures (Scalvini and Sandri 1984). Read examined the formal links between art and industry, while Pevsner analyzed a historical period starting from William Morris, father of contemporary design and one of the last utopian socialists, to Walter Gropius, founder of the Bauhaus and of the visionary idea of creativity aiming at the democratization of society.

More than ten years later, Giedion (1967[1948]), as well as Lewis Mumford (1934, 1952), presented the development of technology and of the technological culture deriving from it, exploring its aesthetic features. Such volumes were comprehensive study that tried to achieve something difficult: to outline historically and conceptually the relationships between art and technology, culture and science, united in the protection of natural resources and of human quality of life.

The consolidation of mass culture in the 1950s and the increase both in the demand and in the supply of consumer goods deeply redefined the analysis on the values of industrial design, especially at an European level. The Second World War deeply changed the global geopolitical and socioeconomic framework. The British critic and art historian Reyner Banham became an important narrator of it, when the formula of the modern movement, the promotion of its pioneers, and the defense of a rationalistic and functionalistic approach to the project reached a crisis point. The main historical and critical reflections then shifted toward the relationships between life, art, and the new technologies, such as those that were supported by Richard Buckminster Fuller in America since the 1930s. In these narrations, the role of fairs, exhibitions, and installations became crucial for the capacity to materialize ideas of possible futures and then anticipate, in the sense of transforming into something tangible, the worlds to come. On 8 August 1956, *This is Tomorrow* opened at the Whitechapel Gallery in London. The exhibition was divided into twelve sections, each managed by a group of artists. The role of Banham was central, together with other visionary architects such as Group 6 (Nigel Henderson, Eduardo Paolozzi, Alison and Peter Smithson). A few months before the inauguration, the Smithsons had presented at the *Daily Mail Ideal Home Exhibition* the prototype of a house of the future, consisting of three-dimensional prefabricated components and made with new materials, such as plastic.

Four years after the exhibition, Banham proposed a new interpretation of the modern age and published *Theory and Design in the First Machine Age* (1960). Compared with the previous historical overviews, the book gave ample attention to forgotten trends and neglected subjects, among which the Italian experience of Futurism. "Commenting on Futurism," as Paola Ricco writes (2014, p. 227), "Bahnam plays a double role: on the one hand he disseminates some images and contributes to spread the knowledge (. . .) of the 'plastic qualities' [of the movement], on the other hand he dissects the futurist thinking and extracts the subject of 'mechanic sensitivity'" [unofficial translation], in this way promoting the anticipatory attention of Anglo-Saxon culture for technics' developments.

The art historian Ara H. Merjian (2012) has recently reanalyzed this process, creating a direct link between the main representatives of Italian Futurism and design. According to the author, Giacomo Balla and Fortunato Depero achieved something unique, establishing a convergence between the aesthetics of the modern world and the material culture of the industrial society. On the one hand, they anticipated the contribution of figurative avant-garde to design in the first decades of the century (in particular Surrealism, Constructivism and Dada). On the other hand, they anticipated the works of some of the greatest Italian design masters, like Bruno Munari and Ettore Sottsass.

When Banham published his historical overview, during the success period of British techno architects like Archigram and Cedric Price, international critics were analyzing the visionary dimension of architecture and its social and cultural implications, with inevitable consequences on the subject of planning according to utopias and feasible worlds.

In 1952 Emil Kauffmann gave a new and successful interpretation, according to which the revolutionary dimension of the architecture of the Eighteenth century was linked to the ability to imagine and to represent works whose purpose was not to be built, as the projects by Etienne-Louis Boullée, Claude-Nicolas Ladoux, and Jean-Jacques Lequeu.

Eight years later, at the Museum of Modern Art of New York (MoMA), the director of the Department of Architecture and Design, Arthur Drexler, organized an exhibition on *Visionary Architecture,* consisting of photographs of models, plans, and projects of twenty-eight cities and urban structures that are "considered too revolutionary to build": the image of the dome over Manhattan by Buckminster Fuller, to cover the city and guarantee an environment with natural air conditioning (1960); the "Chemical Architecture" by William Katavolos (1960), with structures that can be changed through activating agents able to turn chemical substances from dust or from a liquid state into a solid state; and finally the "Endless House" by Frederick Kiesler (1949–1860), which shows the possible impact of new technologies on the human environment, are some of the most quoted examples. As Drexler wrote: "Ideal projects afford the sole occasions when [the architect] can rebuild the world as he knows it ought to be (. . .). When ideal projects are inspired by criticism of the existing structure of society, as well as by the architect's longing for a private world of his own, they may bring forth ideas that make history." Thus, according to Drexler, the visionary impact of a project did not depend on technological innovation, feasibility, or the virtuality level, but on its "social usage."

Giedion seemed to agree with this interpretation in the new edition of his book *Space, Time and Architecture: The Growth of a New Tradition*, published in Italy in 1961, where he introduced the projects for Chandigarh by Le Corbusier (1951-1955) and for Brasilia by Lucio Costa and Oscar Niemeyer (1958). In a recent essay on utopia as a way to imagine the future, Gillo Dorfles (2012, p. 11) described Brasilia as eu-topia, a utopia which included creativity and planning, a "utopia come true," and a "positive utopia" that showed the ability of design cultures to realize a civil and social ideal.

The first historical-critical analyses on design appeared in Italy in 1960s (Rosselli 1960; Dorfles 1963; Gregotti 1968; Bologna 1972; Fossati 1972), anticipating the international recognition of the national design and industrial cultures of those years.

On 26 May 1972, the Museum of Modern Art of New York hosted the exhibition *Italy: The New Domestic Landscape; Achievements and Problems of Italian Design* that was held in the galleries and on the terrace garden of the building of Midtown Manhattan, with 170,000 visitors during its opening period. Twenty years after the museum had shown the exhibition on Olivetti (by Leo Lionni, Leonardo Sinisgalli and Giovanni Pintori, 1952), Emilio Ambasz, an Argentinian architect who was head of the Department of Architecture and Design between 1970 and 1976, introduced again Italian design cultures in the institution.

Contemporary historiography (Branzi 2008; Fallan and Grace Maffei 2014; Scodeller 2014; Rossi 2015) considers this episode as the epilogue of design contribution to Italy's post-war development, especially with reference to radical cultures or neo-avant-garde movements. In such occasion, Superstudio, Archizoom, and the radical groups from Florence, Turin, and Milan became the object of international debate and were put in relation with the contemporary experience of situationism, Arte Povera, conceptual Art, and with the emerging discourse on the semiotic potential of design (Dorfles 1963; Eco 1968; Baudrillard 1972[1968]).

As is known, the exhibition consisted of two sections (180 objects in the first one and twelve domestic environments in the second one), making a distinction between conformist, reformist, and critical design. However, the most innovative message of Ambasz was conveyed in the environments, with the definition of "counter-design" and "pro-design." Design was understood as a tool for criticism and not only for the production of forms: on the one hand, the physical environment became a synthesis and a metaphor of an improved quality of life, a way to anticipate behaviors, technologies, and languages; on the other hand, design itself became a means of communication to express social and political ideals.

The prophetic work of Joe Colombo (Romanelli 2005) was included by Ambasz in the group of "the optimists of the future" (Barbieri Masini 2012), together with the work of Gae Aulenti, Mario Bellini, Alberto Rosselli, Sottsass, and Marco Zanuso with Richard Sapper. The "Total Furnishing Unit" is the epilogue of a series of experiments on new furniture typologies (like the "Tube Chair" and the "Multi Chair"), but, most of all, it became an icon of the futuristic design of the 1960s, a kind of design that was created in a climate of trust in progress and technology, close to cinematographic aesthetics and to narrative imaginaries of science fiction: "Televisions that retract into the ceiling, pivoting walls with a built-in mini-bar, underground 'nuclear cities' – the works of (...) Colombo could have emerged from the set of a contemporary James Bond film" (Vitra Design Museum 2006). The interiors of Colombo, as well as the contemporary projects, for instance, of Verner Panton (the "Visiona" exhibitions commissioned by the chemical corporation Bayer and presented at the Cologne Furniture Fair, involved both authors between 1968 and 1972), were conceived as multifunctional "machines for living"; as symbols of experimentation on materials, components, production systems; and as realization of unusual imaginary worlds and innovative aesthetics. This experiments testify how the visions of possible futures were no longer represented – like in the exhibition curated by Drexler in 1960 – but acquired material form as prototypes. Catharine Rossi writes (2013, pp. 36–37): "Ambasz's design brief explicitly advocated conceiving the environments as prototypes. This was not necessarily because he saw them as precursors to production, but because as an object type, he saw (...) the prototype as best revealing the true nature of design. Increasingly, design was being understood more as a process of synthesis related to its surrounding environment rather than a fetishized formal solution. This overt attention to the prototype points to a shift in the Marxism that had defined much of the politics of Italy's left-wing architects. In the early 1970s it mirrored a larger idea that if architects wanted change, then they had to go further back in the design process than the superstructural level of designing commodities; change would only occur at the level of designing the processes of design and manufacture." This idea explains the almost contemporary experiments of Enzo Mari on self-production (Proposal for a Self-Design, 1974), of Riccardo Dalisi on co-design (minimal technology applied in the Traiano quarter of Napoli, 1971–1973), and of the collective project Global Tools on eco-design (1973–1975).

The environments that were presented at the 1972 exhibition are, at the same time, materialization of a negative approach to utopia: place of counter-societies, critique of the present, and overturning of reality and of its social order. In the catalogue, the critics Filiberto Menna and Celant described the reaction to the alienation of the production-consumption-mediation system, through the concept of "design of new behaviors": immateriality entered the design discourse, anticipating many of the research projects that would be developed since the 1990s, most of all – and as a countertendency to these positions – thanks to the development of the new digital technologies.

Reading the essays of the catalogue (in particular the texts by Manfredo Tafuri, Leonardo Benevolo, Vittorio Gregotti), it is clear that the exhibition already represents a chapter of history. The concept of avant-garde became immediately crucial in critical reformulation (Tafuri 1973, 1980; Marcuse 1968; Burger 1990[1974]), while the 1960s' countercultures were running out: what was changing is the behavior "according to which all the focus was on the criticism to the present, with a projection towards the future and hostility and indifference towards history" [unofficial translation] (Pasca 1991).

In the early 1970s, the focus on the future developed by *future studies* (Poli 2012) met design cultures sharing a common interest towards environmental issues. In 1970 Maldonado published the essay *La speranza progettuale. Ambiente e società*, later translated into English with the title *Design, Nature and Revolution: Toward a Critical Ecology* (1972). One of the theses presented consists in the definition of the difference between "new and old utopians"; the first were "engineers of systems" (according to the definition of Robert Boguslaw, 1965, and are represented by the "diplo-military" tradition of Robert McNamara, Herman Kahn and Anthony Wiener), and the latter were represented by the design cultures of the 1960s, "architects and urban planners, who are formulating ideal models of future cities, which they call 'megastructures'," including representatives from Great Britain, the Japanese metabolists, Yona Friedman, and, most of all, Buckminster Fuller. According to Maldonado, their approach was characterized by the inability to cope with the "needs and the environmental constraints of the present" [unofficial translation]. These two extremes were followed by a third, programmatic one: the "concrete utopias," according to the interpretation of Ernst Bloch. By referring to the work of Bloch, François Burckhardt and Burghart Schmidt (2010) distinguish utopia according to other forms of anticipation of the future due to its non-neutral nature toward social values and the values of culture and nature in general. As they write: "Hypotheses and projects are proposed by Fascism, Nazism, Stalinism and by all totalitarian regimes in general and by those who work to obtain a more humane future. (...) Anticipation does not necessarily imply in itself human values, nor such values are implied by the idea of progress and the will to change" [unofficial translation].

The rationalization of design processes (Jones and Thornley 1963; Alexander 1964; Gregory 1966; Simon 1969) and the need to control the future, represented, for example, in the book *The Limits to Growth* (1972), were topical issues of those years and are accompanied by the work of scholars and researches in the design sector. The publishing of the volume *Design for the Real Word* by Victor Papanek (1984[1971]), together with other important events like the exhibition *MAN trans-FORMS* at the Cooper Hewitt, Smithsonian Design Museum of New York (1976), suggests that design cultures inevitably had to consider, in a sustainable way, the consequences of their actions on future generations (Papanek 1983, 1995; Whiteley 1993; Fry 2009). These subjects were finally incorporated into the agendas of international bodies such as Icsid (International Council of Societies of Industrial Design) and Nid (National Institute of Design), in a progressive and almost spontaneous way. During the 1979 conference in Mexico City, the president of Icsid Arthur J. Pulos said: "in the century to come, the design professions, (...) will rededicate their efforts toward the final emancipation of all humans from drudgery and social and economic subjugation. (...) human beings in a new Renaissance will, once again, become the masters of their environment as the race achieves, finally, that ultimate form of equilibrium known as peace" (Clarke 2015, p. 43).

This is the reason for the progressive interest, even from a historiographical point of view, in the link between anticipation cultures, the search for a sustainable future, and the cultures of design: "the importance of charting the history of sustainability is not just the purview of historians of design. Firstly, it should concern historians of ideas, technology and environment as much as it should design historians" (Fallan 2014, p. 16). So the analysis of the forms, ways, processes, and tools through which, in the past, the visions for a sustainable future were produced (whether they be ideological, pragmatic, or popular visions) has become a topical issue, with consequences also on contemporary society (Formia 2017).

To revisit the plots of the "stories" in order to recall the potential of the anticipatory action of design and designers – for the topical subjects they dealt with, their imagination and representation abilities, and the complexity and impacts of their research projects – is just one of the possible interpretations. Another "alternative" story could, for instance, describe the tools and the methods used by design cultures for anticipation (drawings, representations, scenarios, prototypes, fiction, etc.) or the anticipation ability expressed by other representatives of the design system, such as companies, that were always motivated to look at the future and to search in the future (Wack 1985; Marcus 1998; Bürdek 2008).

America and the Promise of the Future. The Contribution of the "New World" Designer in Construction of the Future

The history of the practice of design on the American continent displays commonalities in its formation, although there are also differences due to the interrelations, dynamics, and resources of each country. Design as an activity reflects the contextual factors in which it originates. As commented (Comisarenco 2006), design as a creative process is embedded in all aspects of society and benefits social structures not only from the material point of view but also through the enunciation of its expressive resource.

In accordance with these beliefs, design appreciation and projections for its future in the American context have been influenced by significant regional events, with design becoming a projectual discipline during the first half of the Twentieth century. The idea of territorial development by way of references adopted from other countries (principally Europe), laid the foundations for different initiatives in each country.

In this sense, the anticipatory practice of government entities, these being the principal executors of works and investment, originated from variables deeply connected to the concept of national growth, the search for opportunities, and the pre-figuration of possibilities for a future of socially impactive and basic economic well-being. Within the framework of this development, some elements reflected previous design practice as professional activity on the American continent, particularly the long-running Second World War, which marked a pause in and then reopening of development opportunities for countries in the Americas.

The construction of what was to come in Latin America was determined by important events that set the destiny of the continent during the first half of the Twentieth century, as well as the ideal of progress in successive years. As Celaschi (2016, p. 44) argues: "The future, at least in part, is governed by the past," and it is therefore important to give a general outline of the variables that shaped decisions about construction of the future in the region.

With this in mind, it is important to consider how important periods in history affected consumption habits. Periods such as those following wars of independence experienced changing immigration flows, emerging societies, changing policies relating to industrialization and foreign investment, increase in industrial capability, and changes in market dynamics and the expansion of urban zones, all of which were factors modifying the dynamics of production and consumption.

Following on from this, it is important to state that, for example, the transition time following the wars of independence in Latin America produced a change in conditions sufficient to make possible institutional and technological advances even greater than those seen in 1870-1914 did or any of the years following (Bethell 2000).

During the following years, the principal driver of growth was the development of advanced economies in other countries, particularly during the 1920s, when North American interests impulsed the expansion of public service and manufacturing enterprises. The United States focused on opening economic spaces in search of new capital investment markets in Latin America. For example, by 1929, General Electric had gained control of the electricity industry in several Latin American countries, which signified growth in both employment and service enterprises.

Simultaneously, the phenomenon known as "economic nationalism" impulsed internal development policies based on state-sponsored industrialization programs, which had the objective of developing the capacity to manufacture increasingly important products and supplies internally. This was known as economic nationalism, and its objective was to achieve national sovereignty through industrial self-sufficiency (Williamson 2013, p. 327).

In successive years, the Second World War increased international demand for food and raw materials, and the United States continued its interest in the growth of industrial development, offering assistance in terms of machinery, technical training, and credit in order to help other nations going through the process of expansion and industrialization. After the war, the major Latin American countries experienced a significant industrial revolution.

In this context, identification of the concepts of "economic development" with "industrialization" (which became synonymous) became firmly entrenched as a prevailing vision of construction of the future (Álvarez 2011).

The progress of the continent gave rise to the phenomenon of a new type of customer, one who identified with the North American model, the dream ideal (Cullen 2004) spurred on by the growth in the number of factories and also partly by the cinema, arts, and publicity, which in turn set the tone for the incorporation of design practice.

The mass production which began in this century and which was based on the mechanization and automatization of processes gave rise to the appearance of concepts, which became symbols of modernity, progress, and the hope of a better future.

The phenomenon of production line automobile manufacture is an example where "the automobile is converted into an object of desire due to its excellence and incarnation of the American way of life" (Bürdek 2002). The North American automobile companies (General Motors and Ford Motors) went on to build production line plants in various countries due to the scale of demand for their vehicles.

It is also worth mentioning the significance that the competition for leadership of the Space Race between the United States and the USSR in the 1960s had on the fields of both industry and technology. This period was particularly significant in the development of new technologies and the ideology of a promising future founded on these developments.

The expression of ideas and images of this promising future were manifested in diverse ways, one of which was science fiction literature based on visions of utopia and anti-utopia, which depicted worlds and future civilizations dominated by technology and by new models of perfect societies. For example, Aldous Huxley in his novel *The Happy World* written in 1932 presented the idea of a highly technological society, which regulated the lifestyle of the population as a means of achieving social stability, a theme that many authors of the time had in common.

The ideas of Huxley and his contemporaries about future organized societies were reflected in the understanding of city design and planning and were focused on approaches based on the anticipation of an ideal future, in "the only valid alternative to the chaos of contemporary mega-cities" (Segre 1983). An example of this would be the construction of the city of Brasilia, based on the fundamentals of the modern movement of urban design manifested in the Athens Letter of 1933 and which proposed a system of rational classification, which divided the city into four explicit zones: living, working, body-mind development, and the circulation system, which united them.

This heralded the epoch of modernity in America during the beginning of the twentieth century; it was a period with significant impact not only for the climate but also one which held particular importance for the economic and social patterns of nations and their plans for a possible future. Up until this time, there had been no formal education for designers. Professionals, who were generally self-taught, entered an extremely diverse field, which included illustration, publicity, fine arts, architecture, or manufacturing (León and Montore 2008).

To cite the specific case of Mexico, the model at that time was dominated by what was known as "centralized development," a stage that, with state assistance, focused on the growing need for education, health, and housing services. At the same time, it is worth mentioning the role of the artisans, fine artists, and architects linked to national design at the beginning of the twentieth century, all of whom had ties to the revolutionary movement, the growth of the famous Mexican muralist school, and the beginning of a style identity which has retained its importance up to the present day.

The state programs of the 1950s and the growing importance of nationalist tradition combined with the opening up of the art world created a departure point in the development of Mexican design. In the same way, the influence of Gui Bonsiepe gave voice to the role of design in the third world as "an economic and cultural instrument associated with the emancipation and rescue of the environment" (Comisarenco 2006).

In the same way as other countries on the continent, the concept of industrial design grew out of the theory and practice of European schools such as those of Ulm and the Bauhaus (Salinas 2003). In 1969, the Autonomous University of Mexico established the industrial design major, with other institutions subsequently following its example. As a result, these institutions were at the forefront of design education in Latin America during the 1970s and 1980s. This is how the idea of the design "professional" became rooted in the academic sector, becoming further removed from industrial production and technological advances, a phenomenon that became apparent in Brazil, Uruguay, Argentina, Colombia, Venezuela, Chile, and Mexico during the 1960s (Álvarez 2011).

This grounding of design in academia created a marked impression on Latin American design due to the fact that productive currents frequently originated from the emulation of models imported from other contexts and alien realities. These models however carried the idea of a promising future, one based principally on self-sufficiency, technological development, and the widespread availability of products.

In the 1980s constant economic and social uncertainty changed the situation somewhat and it was from the 1990s onward that industrial design began to be promoted as a stimulant for small businesses and an impulse for international competitively in educational institutions, exhibitions, magazines, and competitions.

Thenceforward the technological development of national industry, the communication era, and global economic dynamics among others have influenced the teaching and professional practice of design. It is worth mentioning at this juncture the importance of the work of universities in promoting the discipline and the role of a new designer beginning the search for an identity and, in consequence, exploring different fields in order to carve out a distinct future, one based on the syncretism of external and personal models rather than one based on reproducing ideas from successful foreign realities.

The Emergence of Advanced Design

During the last few decades of the Twentieth century, design began to diversify as a practice. New roles appeared which were adopted by both designers and enterprises, roles which went further than the traditional, very project-oriented activities based on the solving of specific problems and the development of new products (whether they be objects or graphic or special designs) and roles which were strategic and more wide-ranging. Regarding this diversification, Heskett (2002), at the beginning of the century, opened the door to the discussion of diversity or the so-called cultures of design in the profession and in this way reaffirmed diversity as a historical characteristic of design. He promoted reflection and deep investigation into design cultures in order to help understand common patterns in the discipline and trace the history of "subdivisions."

Many of these "new cultures" modify the distance between industry and consumer and affect the divisions between passive users and the designers who are beginning to own the design process in order to delineate it and outline the roles necessary to increase mutual collaboration. These roles begin to widen much earlier in the problem-solving activity (and indeed prior to it) and go much further than simply producing and installing socially useful items.

This phenomenon of the widening of design cultures has had the effect of increasing the complexity of the prefiguration (as an anticipatory process), which has characterized the discipline.

In America, different authors began to regard design as an invisible activity which added value to the deliverables produced (products, graphics, etc.), as well as having the capacity to generate new processes and ways of articulating innovation, ways of configuring dynamics in work teams and innovation cultures within organizations. Roles are, on one hand, much more research-related but also closer to end users in a way which makes the anticipatory processes of design become slowly more extensive and more collaborative; Brown (2009) describes this new conceptualization of design on the American continent when he asserts:

Design is not a discrete stylistic gesture included in a project just prior to it being handed over to marketing. A new focus is taking shape in companies and organizations all over the world and is moving design to a position behind the earliest stages of product conception, and in front of the final stages of implementation.

The processes of design (and the processes of design thinking) begin to become relevant to an organization due to a capacity not only for problem-solving but also for discovering opportunities, as well as more complex processes that make it an ideal space for multidisciplinary collaboration. The search for opportunities in highly uncertain areas has begun to be seen as a design activity, and these practices are in turn giving rise to the construction of the innovational competences within organizations, which are becoming the fertile ground of advanced design (ADD). As a particular design culture, although it is consolidated now within certain sectors of industry, ADD has not been adequately researched nor investigated (Celi 2010). ADD however is a natural phenomenon in the activity of designers, and its reach will make it one of the dominant models in the future practice of design (Borja de Mozota 2006a). In the particular case of design practice on the American continent, there is a syncretism that connects both local and global practice.

However, in both America and Europe, there has been a practice that has drawn attention due to its capacity to act strategically within organizations, and in answer to this research groups have started to appear as part of the academic offer in order to educate professional ADD experts within the education sector. For example, in 2010, a specific research unit in ADD, coordinated by Flaviano Celaschi, was born at the Politecnico di Milano with the aim of reflecting on temporary issues and their relationship with creative processes, an activity that has been later developed by the Advanced Design Center of the University of Bologna.

At the same time, in America, a design research group in Monterrey Tec in Mexico has a particular focus, and it boasts an advanced design research center that develops projects with industry and generates tailor-made formulae and processes that permit the development of ADD competences within organizations. We can also quote the case of the Catholic Pontifical University in Chile which has a postgraduate qualification focusing on the formation of multidisciplinary experts, the Montreal University Faculty of Management which offers a postgraduate qualification in design and complexity, and Carnegie Mellon University which offers, in the concept of transitional design, the possibility of researching and developing design-guided projects in the field of social and technological systems transformation.

With this activity, universities continue to play a fundamental role in the diffusion of ADD practice, above all by preparing talent capable of fomenting (and in many cases educating) design culture potential within organizations.

In general, ADD has inherited design tools and processes that focus on transforming lives and temporal horizons. If design as a practice is anticipatory, then it can be said that ADD works with a greater degree of not only anticipation but also complexity, given that its principal focus is planning projects 5 or even 10 years in the future. This line of thought as phenomenology will be addressed in detail in the following chapters, but it is appropriate now to introduce the characterization that defines ADD as a culture, and the particular variables that describe it and distinguish it from other design cultures. These defining characteristics (Iñiguez et al. 2014) are as follows (Table 1):

These twelve attributes are the frame of reference for understanding ADD culture, the frame of reference that circumscribes the particular way in which ADD operates. As has been previously mentioned, ADD inherits the tradition of design tools and processes, but it is influenced by other disciplines and has a wider scope, allowing for much more advanced practice.

The Instrumental Scope of ADD Practice

This amplified practice of design has an instrumental dimension within organizations that creates conditions that predispose innovation, given its creativity, to producing visible benefits for these organizations. This fundamental dimension of ADD has, in recent years, been instrumental in the fomentation of a prolific number of ADD practices and can be categorized into the following four areas (Iñiguez and León 2016).

Complexity Management

The anticipatory practice of design is one which comprises the sum of variables (knowledge, agents, institutions, etc.) relating to the exercise of innovation. According to Celi (2010), ADD is an "extended" practice, where the traditional limits of project design are extended not only toward temporal horizons but also in terms of participants and knowledge, an extension which is necessary in order to deal

Table 1 Advanced design attributes (Iñiguez et al. 2014)

Number	Concept	Description
1	Complex	Manages complexity and uncertainty
2	Meta-projectual	Acts at the first steps of the front end of innovation
3	Systemic-adaptative	Using adaptative, unconventional, and nonlinear methodologies opportunistically. Manages multiple variables with a systemic approach
4	Multidimensional	Includes broader dimensions to the projects: time, space, culture, and markets
5	Horizontal	Transversal to the organization of company departments
6	Anticipatory	Defines future scenarios, visions, and proposals
7	Process-oriented	Understanding design more as a process than a final result
8	Innovation-driven	Does not necessarily offer specific solutions but guides innovation
9	Conceptual	Linked to the concepts more than technical details
10	Visual/verbal	Has a higher degree of abstraction grade, uses different media during processes
11	Strategic	Oriented to strategy more than operation or application
12	Multidisciplinary	Requires the participation of different disciplines

with the uncertainty inherent in an ADD project. In ADD organizations find the processes that assist in allowing them to manage complexity.

Opportunity Finding

The nature of ADD is to be influential in stages earlier than seen in a traditional project, and it utilizes design processes to explore and search for future opportunities; its principal function is the search for innovation opportunities, in contrast to traditional design activity that is much more involved in "problem-solving." Given the growing uncertainty that finding genuine opportunities for innovation represents, the exercise of pre-figuration of ADD projects functions as scaffolding, forming novel frames of reference which permit the discovery of still-undeveloped innovational alternatives within organizations.

Project Multiplicity

In contrast to the traditional design project that results in a particular product, the results of an ADD project are the creation of a portfolio (scenarios, prototypes, concepts, and visions) which acts as a basis for other projects. This anticipatory practice creates a constructivist process in which organizations multiply the development of new products or services by employing the aforementioned portfolios. The results of these processes are typically not products or services which impact society in the short term but are, in contrast, more commonly oriented toward the long term, and this increases the amount of identifiable (and exploitable) opportunities, whether these are other ADD projects or those of a more concrete nature.

Organizational Transformation

The practice of ADD is based on learning systems in which individuals and organizations generate knowledge and competencies which are predisposed toward innovation. These systems are almost always installed in both tacit and practical ways, a form of "learning by doing," in which work teams become more skilled in the employment of ADD expertise. The iterative process of ADD practice within organizations creates common languages between departments (or disciplines), fertilizing the different work teams with ideas which transfer from one team to another, developing the capacity for generating new processes, and from this inculcating a long-term visionary dynamic through the stimulus which rethinking the future represents in different areas. This learning, whether it be individual or group-based, has the end result of transforming the organization in a tacit manner, as has previously been stated. However, the importance of explicitly transforming an organization, something that ADD also has the capacity to do, is becoming increasingly appreciated.

Conclusion

The need for anticipation in its different forms (visions, utopias, fictions, advanced design) is the basis of design sciences and creative cultures and goes through history like a latent idea, becoming extremely evident when there is trust in progress, science, and technological innovation or, on the contrary, during periods characterized by economic, social, and political uncertainties. During these phases, the need to see beyond the present time becomes urgent, stimulating the projection of possible or arbitrary constructions, concepts, and products of the future. This is evident in the cultural background of industrialized countries. The historic nature of design practice on the American continent, a practice derived from the European tradition, goes hand in hand with local culture in a kind of syncretism which feeds back into and promotes a new synthesis in the understanding of design (Arias and Iñiguez 2012). The cultural background (introduced in paragraph 1) and its local interpretation (paragraphs 2 and 3) led to definition of a particular form of the relation of design and anticipation called advanced design (paragraph 4). ADD situates the practice of design as a much more strategic territory in which pre-configuration of the future generates visions for organizations and offers an ultimate benefit for society, pre-configurations guided by the doing-knowledge of design. In some ways, the road traveled up until the twenty-first century has permitted the practice of design to become more oriented toward the search for multidisciplinary-project opportunities, which both address and manage the complexity of the environment and the accompanying variables. In addition, there is also a progressive transformation of organizations (businesses, industries, centers of innovation, design studios, universities, etc.), with an appreciation of both the commitment of the designer in their new role and their commitment to the field.

This recognition of the designer's identity and, in consequence, their role in the transformation of a future molded by their activities in terms of innovation, links to their environment, flexible and continual learning space, vision of leadership, and, above all, position and commitment in respect of a future based on human feeling is rapidly becoming a specific and distinctive feature of the new designer.

References

Alexander, C. (1964). *Notes on the synthesis of the form.* Cambridge, MA: Harvard University Press.

Álvarez, C. P. (2011). Diseño latinoamericano presente y pasado Breve panorámica. Revista Diseña, 3, Pontifica Universidad Católica de Chile. http://www.revistadisena.com/diseno-latinoamericano-presente-y-pasado-breve-panoramica/. Accessed 21 Oct 2016.

Arias, X., & Iñiguez, R. (2012). The temporal dimension of syncretism as a peripheral form of diversity: Jalisco design identities. *Forum of Design as a Process, 4*(1), 232–233.

Asimov, M. (1968). *Principi di progettazione.* Padova: Marsilio.

Augé, M. (2012). *Futuro.* Torino: Bollati Boringhieri.

Banham, R. (1960). *Theory and design in the first machine age.* Kidlington: Elsevier Science Ltd.

Barbieri Masini, E. (2012). Introduzione. Perché pensare al futuro oggi? In S. Arnaldi & R. Poli (Eds.), *La previsione sociale. Introduzione allo studio dei futuri* (pp. 13–22). Roma: Carocci.

Baudrillard, J. (1972). *Il sistema degli oggetti.* Milano: Bompiani. (ed. or. 1968).

Bethell, E. D. (2000). *Historia de América Latina 7.* Barcelona: Editorial crítica S.L.

Bologna, F. (1972). *Dalle arti applicate all'industrial design. Storia di un'ideologia.* Bari: Laterza.

Borja de Mozota, B. (2006a). The four powers of design: A value model in design management. *Design Management Review, 17*(2), 44–53.

Borja de Mozota, B. (2006b). El diseño de la innovación, dos retos para la profesión del diseño. *Innovación y Diseño, 23*. http://tdd.elisava.net/coleccion/23/borja-de-mozota–es. Accessed 01 June 2014.

Branzi, A. (Ed.). (2007). *Capire il design*. Firenze: Giunti.

Branzi, A. (Ed.). (2008). *Il design italiano 1964–2000*. Milano: Electa.

Brown, T. (2009). *Change by design*. New York: Harper Collins.

Burckhardt, F., & Schmidt, B. (2010). Utopia nell'architettura. http://www.treccani.it/enciclopedia/utopia-nell-architettura_%28XXI-Secolo%29/. Accessed 17 Oct 2016.

Bürdek, B. E. (1992). *Design*. Milano: Mondadori.

Bürdek, B. E. (2002). *Historia, teoría y práctica del diseño industrial*. Barcelona: Editorial Gustavo Gili.

Bürdek, B. E. (2008).Design : storia, teoria e pratica del design del prodotto. Roma: Gangemi.

Burger, P. (1990). *Teoria dell'avanguardia*. Torino: Bollati Boringhieri. (ed. or. 1974).

Celaschi, F. (2000). *Il design della forma merce*. Milano: Il Sole 24 Ore Libri.

Celaschi, F. (2008a). Il design come mediatore tra bisogni. In C. Germak (Ed.), *Uomo al centro del progetto* (pp. 19–31). Torino: Allemandi.

Celaschi, F. (2016). *Non-industrial design*. Milano: Sossella.

Celaschi, F., Cappellieri, A., & Vasile, A. (2005). *Lusso versus design*. Milano: POLI.Design.

Celi, M. (Ed.). (2010). *Advance design – Visioni, percorsi e strumenti per predisporsi all'innovazione continua*. Milano: McGraw-Hill.

Clarke, A. J. (2015). Design for development, ICSID and UNIDO: The anthropological turn in 1970s design. *Journal of Design History, 29*(1), 43–57.

Comisarenco, D. (2006). *Memoria y futuro: historia del diseño mexicano e internacional*. Editorial Trillas: México.

Cullen, J. (2004). *The American dream: A short history of an idea that shaped a nation*. New York: Oxford University Press.

De Fusco, R. (2012). *Design 2029. Ipotesi per il prossimo futuro*. Milano: Franco Angeli.

Diamond, J. (2013). *Il mondo fino a ieri*. Torino: Einaudi.

Dorfles, G. (1963). *Il disegno industriale e la sua estetica*. Bologna: Cappelli.

Dorfles, G. (2012). L'utopia è architettura. In L. Mazzoli & G. Zanchini (Eds.), *Utopie. Percorsi per immaginare il futuro*. Torino: Codice Edizioni.

Drexler, A. (1960). *Visionary architecture*. New York: The Museum of Modern Art.

Eco, U. (1968). *La struttura assente*. Milano: Bompiani.

Fallan, K. (2014). Our common future. Joining forces for histories of sustainable design. *Tecnoscienza – Italian Journal of Science & Technology Studies, 5*(2), 15–32.

Flusser, V. (2003). *Filosofia del design*. Milano: Bruno Mondadori.

Formia, E. (2017). *Storie di futuri e design. Anticipazione e sostenibilità nella cultura italiana del progetto*. Santarcangelo di Romagna: Maggioli.

Fossati, P. (1972). *Il design in Italia*. Torino: Einaudi.

Fry, T. (2009). *Design futuring: Sustainability, ethics and new practice*. Oxford: Berg Publishers.

Giedion, S. (1941). *Space, time and architecture: The growth of a new tradition*. Cambridge, MA: The Harvard University Press.

Giedion, S. (1967). *L'era della meccanizzazione*. Milano: Feltrinelli. (ed. or. 1948).

Gregory, S. A. (Ed.). (1966). *The design method*. London: Butterworth Press.

Gregotti, V. (1968). *New directions in Italian architecture*. New York: Braziller.

Heskett, J. (2002). *Design, a very short introduction*. New York: Oxford University Press.

Iñiguez, R., & León, R. (2016). El Diseño Avanzado como práctica sistémica para la innovación en el territorio: caso Ciudad Creativa Digital, Guadalajara, México. In *Sixth international forum of design as a process*. Electronic book proceedings. València: Editorial Univertitat Politècnica de València.

Iñiguez, R., Hernandis, B., Holliger, C., & Monterrubio, C. (2014). Advanced design as a process for knowledge creation. In *Proceedings of the international forum of sesign as a process "The shapes of the future as the front end of design driven innovation"*, (Vol. 5, pp. 151–156).

Jones, J. C., & Thornley, D. G. (Eds.). (1963). *Conference on design methods*. Oxford: Pergamon Press.

Kaufmann, E. (1952). *Three revolutionary architects: Boullée, Ledoux, Lequeu*. Philadelphia: American Philosophical Society.

Latouche, S. (2012). *Limite*. Torino: Bollati Boringhieri.

Lees-Maffei, G. and Fallan, K. (2014). Made in Italy: rethinking a century of Italian design. New York: Bloomsbury.

León, E., & Montore, M. (2008). Brasil. In S. Fernandez & G. Bonsiepe (Eds.), *Historia del Diseño en América Latina y del caribe* (pp. 62-87). Brasil: Editora Blucher.

Lorenz, C. (1990). *Dimensione design*. Milano: Franco Angeli.

Maldonado, T. (1970). *La speranza progettuale*. Torino. Einaudi.

Maldonado, T. (1987). *Il futuro della modernità*. Milano: Feltrinelli.

Maldonado, T. (1992). *Reale e virtuale*. Milano: Feltrinelli.

Manzini, E. (1990). *Artefatti*. Milano: Domus Academy.

Marcus, G. E. (1998). *Corporate futures: The diffusion of the culturally sensitive corporate form*. Chicago: The University of Chicago Press.

Marcuse, H. (1968). *La fine dell'utopia*. Roma-Bari: Laterza. (ed. or. 1967).

Meadows, D. H., Meadows, D., Randers, J., & Beherens, W. W., III. (1972). *The limits to growth: A report for the Club of Rome's project on the predicament of mankind*. New York: Universe Books.

Merjian, A. H. (2012). A future by design: Giacomo Balla and the domestication of transcendence. *Oxford Art Journal, 35*(2), 121–146.

Mumford, L. (1934). *Technics and civilization*. New York: Harcourt, Brance and Company.

Mumford, L. (1952). *Art and technics*. London: Oxford University Press.

Museum, V. D. (2006). Joe Colombo. Inventing the future. http://www.design-museum.de/en/exhibitions/detailseiten/joe-colombo.html. Accessed 17 Oct 2016.

Norman, D. A. (2008). *Il design del futuro*. Milano: Apogeo.

Papanek, V. (1983). *Design for human scale*. New York: Van Nostrand Reinhold Co.

Papanek, V. (1984). *Design for the real world: Human ecology and social change*. London: Thames & Hudson. (or. ed. 1971).

Papanek, V. (1995). *The green imperative: Ecology and ethics in design and architecture*. New York: Thames and Hudson.

Pasca, V. (1991). Design: storia e storiografia. http://www.aisdesign.org/aisd/design-storia-e-storiografia-2. Accessed 17 Octo 2016.

Penati, A. (2013a). *Il design costruisce mondi*. Milano: Mimesis.

Penati, A. (2013b). *Il design vive di oggetti-discorso*. Milano: Mimesis.

Penati, A. (2013c). *È il design una narrazione?* Milano: Mimesis.

Perniola, M. (1998). *I situazionisti*. Roma: Castelvecchi.

Pevsner, N. (1945). *I pionieri del movimento moderno, da William Morris a Walter Gropius*. Milano: Rosa e Ballo. (ed. or. 1936).

Poli, R. (2012). La previsione sociale: introduzione allo studio dei futuri. Roma: Carocci.

Ratti, C., & Claudel, M. (2016). *The city of tomorrow: Sensors, networks, hackers, and the future of urban life*. New Haven: Yale University Press.

Read, H. (1962). *Arte e industria. Fondamenti del disegno industriale*. Milano: Lerici. (ed. or. 1934).

Ricco, P. (2014). Qualità plastiche e sensibilità meccanica. Le considerazioni di Reyner Banham sul Futurismo si riflettono nell'architettura inglese degli anni 1960. In M. Giacomelli, E. Godoli, & A. Pelosi (Eds.), *Il Manifesto dell'Architettura Futurista di Sant'Elia e la sua eredità* (pp. 227–240). Mantova: Universitas Studiorum Srl – Casa Editrice.

Romanelli, M. (2005). Joe Colombo: una profezia interrotta. Accenni per un ritratto progettuale. In I. Favata & M. Kries (Eds.), *Joe Colombo. L'invenzione del futuro* (pp. 99–107). Milano: Skira.

Rosselli, A. (1960). Appunti per una storia del disegno industriale in Italia. *Stile Industria, 26–27*, 3–28.

Rossi, C. (2013). From Mari to Memphis: The role of prototypes in Italian radical and postmodern design. In L. Valentine (Ed.), *Prototype. Design and craft in the 21st century* (pp. 29–44). London: Bloomsbury.

Rossi, C. (2015). *Crafting design in Italy. From post-war to postmodernism*. Manchester: Manchester University Press.

Salinas, O. (2003). *Historia del diseño industrial*. México: Trillas.

Scalvini, M. L., & Sandri, M. G. (1984). *L'immagine storiografica dell'architettura contemporanea da Platz a Giedion*. Roma: Officina Edizioni.

Scodeller, D. (2014). Exhibition, anti-exhibition: su alcune questioni espositive del pop e radical design italiano, 1966–1981. *A/I/S/Design, 3*. http://www.aisdesign.org/aisd/exhibition-anti-exhi bition-su-alcune-questioni-espositive-del-pop-e-radical-design-italiano-1966-1981. Accessed 17 Oct 2016.

Segre, R. (1983). *América Latina en su arquitectura México*. México: Siglo Veintiuno Editores, S.A.

Simon, H. A. (1969). *The science of the rtificial*. Cambridge, MA: The MIT Press.

Sterling, B. (2006). *La forma del futuro*. Milano: Apogeo.

Tafuri, M. (1973). *Progetto e utopia*. Roma-Bari: Laterza.

Tafuri, M. (1980). *La sfera e il labirinto*. Torino: Einaudi.

Thackara, J. (2008). *In the bubble*. Torino: Allemandi.

Vitta, M. (1996). *Il disegno delle cose*. Napoli: Liguori.

Wack, P. (1985). Scenarios: Uncharted waters ahead. Harvard Business Revew. https://hbr.org/1985/09/scenarios-uncharted-waters-ahead. Accessed 17 Oct 2016.

Whiteley, N. (1993). *Design for society*. London: Reaktion Books.

Williamson, E. (2013). *Historia de América Latina*. México.: Fondo de Cultura Económica.

Anticipation and Design Inquiry

38

Manuela Celi and Andrew Morrison

Contents

Abstract

Inquiry into anticipation is framed within this chapter in a view from Anticipation Studies not only Science, accentuating cultural, constructionist and critical interpretative aspects. In this theoretical excursus, authors argue that Futures Studies needs to more fully take up a body of work from Design Studies. Drawing on various aspects of Design inquiry, the chapter provides an overview of some of the approaches that have been advanced and ways they might offer Anticipation

M. Celi (✉)
Dipartimento di Design, Politecnico di Milano, Milan, Italy
e-mail: manuela.celi@polimi.it

A. Morrison
Centre for Design Research, Oslo School of Architecture and Design, Oslo, Norway
e-mail: AndrewDavid.Morrison@aho.no

© Springer Nature Switzerland AG 2019
R. Poli (ed.), *Handbook of Anticipation*,
https://doi.org/10.1007/978-3-319-91554-8_49

795

Studies routes and means to more fully framing approaches to the making and analysis of anticipatory systems, engagements, and reflections. As designer-researchers with academic transdisciplinary backgrounds, our views are positioned from the work of others as well as via practice based research through design epistemological investigations. Design Futures remains a fruitful space for further design inflected inquiry.

Keywords
Anticipation studies · Design inquiry · Design Futures · Additive design (ADD) · Speculative design · Design fiction

Matters in Framing

Much of the focus on anticipation (Poli 2010, 2014a, b; Nadin 2015) arises out of earlier work in Future Studies (FS) and previous conceptualization of anticipation in the natural sciences (Rosen 1985/2012), cognitivist psychology, and systems views (Nadin 2015). One notable gap in the genesis and promulgation of FS has been a lack of attention to one of the primary knowledge domains that has been working toward understanding and shaping future contexts, experiences, scenarios, and engagement, namely Design (Stolterman and Nelson 2012). Internationally, Design, also called Design Studies (DS), has gained purchase, momentum, and impact as a central site of transdisciplinary inquiry (e.g., Stuedahl et al. 2010). While the somewhat surprising omission of design in FS until recently has partly been due to the force of important founding interests in FS, such as planning and strategy development, it may also be partly due to the at times complex trajectories of the development of Design during a similar period, one that has increasingly been realized through the interplay of theory and practice in poststructuralist modes of inquiry.

In contrast to its early assertions to be a science – and this is a perspective that still matters – today Design may also be characterized as working abductively, in contrast to the epistemological approaches of most work in anticipation conceptualized within the natural sciences. Design also has creative, collaborative constructivist foundations and today these need to engage increasingly with complexity and emergence, such as tackled by Systems-Oriented Design (e.g., Sevaldson 2013). We see Anticipation as the shared domain between FS and Design, and this chapter aims to make this more apparent by accentuating Design's characteristics and contributions to Anticipation along with its connections with FS. This chapter is presented as an attempt to formulate a bridge between FS and Design as one of the possible means of building a more elaborated perspective and transdisciplinary mode of inquiry for what we see as Anticipation Studies, as, for example, has been developed in transdisciplinary humanistic and social science inquiry in Cultural Studies and New Media Studies. Our intention is to complement what we might term a more "Anticipation Sciences" view that has a genesis in cognition and systems, one that we acknowledge as providing important insights. Our focus is more on design as cultural, negotiative, and constructionist. As Appadurai (2013:

299) reminds us, the future is ". . . a space for democratic design that must begin with the recognition that the future is a cultural fact." Below we unpack ways in which design operates to help realize, problematize, and shape futures in terms of anticipatory practices and analyses, not necessarily solution-driven world views and related notions concerning making and interpretation.

We therefore see a need to present a broad view on design inquiry as a key foundation for Anticipation. Our view here is not to provide a ghettoized version of Design, but the opposite; it is to offer the transdisciplinary and emergent knowledge domain area of Anticipation a detailed account of what Design inquiry has to offer inquiry into the future and into "making futures" that recently has not been very present in FS research. It is important that this is understood from the outset and the offering we make is to extend and complement existing work in futures to also entail Design. Those who are unfamiliar with research in Design, and this has expanded and been professionalized enormously in the past two decades, may fall into the trap of characterizing it only as "gilding the lily." We present design as more than this, as reaching far beyond guilds of practice, or lily-livered and tentative analyses located only in other disciplinary frames.

Design inquiry is now at the forefront of engaging in the complexity, risk, innovation, critique, and cultural expression that are central to contemporary and projected experience, engagement, and critique. There are expansive research communities – with conferences, journals, programs, projects, and publications as well as a host of outputs and outcomes that meet twenty-first century-mediated communicative living and experience. These span human–computer interaction as well as service design, systems-oriented design, and product (not only industrial design) as it realigns its practices and interpretation to increasingly account for digital fabrication, alongside the growth of socially mediated communication and design's role on social innovation and pressing societal and sustainability issues. Futures Studies has not integrated all these perspectives in its concerns and there is great potential for further engagement and elaboration between FS and DS.

Much design inquiry is not known outside of design, and, though it is prevalent within many disciplines, this chapter, therefore, needs to include a fair deal of presentation of DS; design inquiry is also often misunderstood in terms of earlier drives to establish design as a science (e.g., Simon 1969) while today it is a mix and a mesh of disciplines, a domain in its own right and increasingly a central mode of constructive, creative knowledge making and building that draws on production based and research through design approaches that work projectively, prospectively, and abductively and should not and we would argue cannot simply be read off the frames of other disciplinary and epistemological interests and conventions. Design reaches for what is not yet realized. It provides means to shaping futures and to practices that are not solution centered. Instead, these sociomaterial constructions, framed as design ecologies, that seek to arrive at new conceptualizations and emergent means through exploratory, investigative, and problem-making activities, often shared, typically transdisciplinary and adaptively, created through a mesh of legacies, shared knowing, coproduction, and critical interpretation.

It is the shift to conceptualizing futures thinking, making, and critical analysis in terms of anticipation – influenced by concepts and work in foresight and the building of affordances for working with emergence and complexity together, as well as developing futures literacies to enact and enable their critical, situated, and reflexive realization – that offers those of us concerned with "shaping futures" to include knowledge and experience from design. This chapter therefore aims to elaborate linkages between emergent research concerning anticipation and a body of related work located in design-based inquiry. For us, we begin by stating that in essence, design may be seen as anticipation.

In the past decade, we have witnessed a shift in design-based inquiry from being about professional education and production-centered practice to an emergent and many-sided research domain in its own right. Design inquiry is now both established as a domain of inquiry in its own right with key journals such as *Design Issues*, *Design Studies*, *The International Journal of Design*, *Design and Culture*, and *CoDesign* and related conferences such as DRS, Nordes, IASDR, and CUMULUS as well as having more specialist venues such as ServDes, contributions, and special interest groups in Conferences such as DIS and Systems-Oriented Design (RSD) transdisciplinary contri-butions to fields such as Human Computer Interaction (HCI), digital media, materials science, anthropology, and business innovation. In this research, futures thinking, social innovation and creative, culturally and sociotechnically framed making, and links between design tools and research methods are central.

Despite these varied and genuinely discipline crossing legacies and research frames of Design and FS, their processes often share similar objectives but approach them from different perspective and with different strategic positions. Design may be seen as the manipulation of visual or tangible aspects of physical matter or informa-tion at the point of output while FS is seen as an activity oriented to policy that occurs in advance of actual outcomes and that is very distant from a concrete realizations. Despite these differences, Design and FS have some tools and lan-guages in common and they are equally concerned with future scenarios and the ability to make informed decisions to enhance success. These disciplinary proxim-ities becomes more evident if we consider the more recent context and emergence of what Miller et al. (2013) defined as the Discipline of Anticipation (DoA):

> All efforts to "know the future" in the sense of thinking about and using the future are forms of anticipation. Equally the future is incorporated into all phenomena, conscious or uncon-scious, physical or ideational, as anticipation. The DoA covers all "ways of knowing" the later-than-now as anticipation, from those forms of anticipation that are observed, for instance, in a tree that loses its leaves in the Autumn to human planning that attempts to colonize the future and efforts to make sense of emergent novelty in the present by finding inspiration in systemically discontinuous imaginary futures. Looked at as a "way-of knowing" the DoA addresses the codification of the myriad of systems of anticipation, both conscious and non-conscious. The DoA develops, sorts, and diffuses descriptions of the processes/systems of anticipation or how the later-than-now enters into reality. (Miller et al. 2013, p.3)

We see Anticipation as a transdisciplinary construct comprised of and composed through a mix of specializations, knowledge domains, and practices. It extends into the social sciences, humanities, and creative industries. Here the framing of DoA is that it is about multiple, blended, and various ways of knowing. This is what Design offers Anticipation alongside other more formal academic disciplinary contributions such as from narrative or strategic planning. Design, dealing naturally with many different disciplines, communicates with a variety of stakeholders, creators of models, and prototypes, and adopting and adapting different languages occupies a dialectical space between the world that is and the world that could be. The Design discipline, far away from the sole shapes moulder, actually finds application in a multitude of contexts – such as Service Design, Social Design, Design for Cultural Heritage, User-Centered Design, Design Futures, Sustainability, etc. – that heavily influence the quality of our lives and our common futures.

However, we see that the anticipatory nature of design is itself under articulated within Design Studies as the academic strand of design inquiry is sometimes labeled. Zamenopoulos and Alexiou (2007) are among very few scholars who have addressed the anticipatory nature of design. After initial exploration of diverse approaches to anticipation in different fields, Zamenopoulos and Alexiou (2007) suggested an anticipatory view of design as a paradigm to interpret and redefine the design discipline:

> [. . .] Design can thus be associated with the capacity to generate theories and models that bring beliefs and desires into correspondence [. . .]. More importantly, design also involves the capacity to anticipate the correspondence between theories and models, which can only be verified by experimentation or the actual realisation of the design artefact. (Zamenopoulos and Alexiou 2007 p. 423)

It is this activity of artifacting – whether it be a physical product, an intangible service, or an emergent process – that concerns design. Experimentation is central, but it needs to be understood as distinct from the formalism of STEM-centered inquiry. Designing is a socially, technically, and culturally framed activity that occurs in contexts of creativity and communication, where commercial and civic characteristics vary and veer toward and away from one another, not always connecting and cohering. Central to that activity are notions and practices of emergence, generativity, iteration, and usability so that the making of artifacts and the knowledge gleaned thereby is framed in dynamic and reflexive assemblages and relations between design techniques and research methods. Design thus embeds ontologies of future thinking in its artifacting and the materialization of artifacts while at the same time, and again and again, it works to engage in processes of knowledge generation through production in which participation and cocreativity are frequently central.

For us, working in basic and applied research approaches to design, anticipation as it is epitomized by Poli (2010) is not a feature that we – designers and designer-researchers in this case – alone possess. Nor do we do so separately to its realization by other cultural agents; anticipation is a widespread phenomenon. Indeed, we argue, anticipation needs to be understood in terms of systems views and from our disciplinary location, also increasingly in terms of Systems-Oriented Design (Sevaldson 2013). There are many systems containing predictive models: life in all its varieties is anticipatory, the brain works in an anticipatory way, society and its structures are anticipatory, even nonliving or nonbiological systems can be anticipatory (Poli 2010 p.8). Probably the anticipatory nature of design is not surprising for futurists, what is interesting – in a transdisciplinary perspective – is the way in which the projection capabilities of design may be useful in other context. Design shapes futures, bearing in mind the past experience starting from the present condition and criticalities that call for intervention; design has the unique ability to transform these interventions into material and immaterial forms (Margolin 2007 p. 4).

How can we analyze, codify, or explain the Design contribution in future-oriented projects? This contribution aims at clarifying at different levels of abstraction the anticipatory action of design making more visible the potential relationship between Design and Anticipation. We next present a research-oriented overview of relations between Anticipation and design. We then move to cover two domains we see as providing means and methods for developing these linkages: Advance Design as a framework providing Up-framing and Reframing capacity and Speculative design, with focus on narrative and design fiction.

Anticipation and Design: Toward a Research-Based View

Beyond the conceptualization or misrepresentation of Design as a pragmatic activity dedicated to producing artifacts – from the most material spoon to the city (as E. N. Rogers taught to us) to the immaterial software – it is vital that Design be understood to exist as a research discipline. Since the first attempt to consider design as a science (Simon 1969; Gregory 1966; Alexander 1971), awareness of the roles and relations of Design researchers and practitioners has changed considerably. This has been so regarding both on the nature and the range of the intellectual contribution of the field of Design-based inquiry.

Considering Design as a way to produce concepts, knowledge, and theories, we must bear in mind that in the field of design research we can distinguish these approaches:

1. Research on design often accomplished by specialists from other disciplines as history, psychology, economy, semiotics, etc. that consider Design as the object of the research: they may consider the history, the diffusion of this practice at the macroscale as well as analyze design objects, actors, or production processes at the microscale.
2. Research for design mostly performed by designers but frequently powered by transdisciplinary research is represented by approaches that aim at nourishing a concrete.
3. Design projects. Consider for example all the context, psychological, medical, and technical information needed to design a medical device.
4. Research through design, which generates knowledge by/while adopting a design approach, meaning that the activity of designing artifacts (more or less consciously) is a way of learning and that in a meta-knowledge system represents a way to uncover, or better let insights and new concepts emerge.

The expression "Research through design," first coined by Christopher Frayling (1993/4), has further been defined as practice-led research, action research, or project-grounded research (Findeli 2000). Believing that this form of research is a variant of design research with an accent on theory, Findelli highlights the role of creativity and claims its independence from the other discipline.

Design, Anticipation, and Knowing

Research through design means research projects that generate knowledge by adopting a design approach. This point of view frames Design with its peculiar way of operating and building knowledge. We must clarify that it is necessary to distinguish designerly ways of knowing from Design Thinking (with origins in business and innovation studies) that in our view is something by now external to design. As Deserti and Rizzo (2014) underline, design thinking is moving away from design practice by employing formalized processes and techniques that can be applied by professionals of all disciplines, not necessarily by designers. In this acceptation, Design Thinking is actually separating the process of conceptualizing ideas from that of actually making things while enforcing the idea that there exists some sort of capability or competence – maybe the abused "creativity" – that precedes or can be divorced from knowledge on how to make things. So while Design Thinking is often the extrapolation of design tools, methods, approaches, and their appropriation by other disciplines, contexts, and policies, it is important to note that it differs very greatly from the concept of "designerly way of knowing." In 1979, Cross wrote that:

> The sciences value objectivity, rationality, neutrality, and a concern for the 'truth' [...] The humanities value subjectivity, imagination, commitment and a concern for 'justice'. The designerly way of knowing involves a combination of knowledge and skills from both science and the humanities [...] Design has its own distinct things to know, ways of knowing and ways of finding out about them. (Cross 1979 in Frascara 2002: 160)

The idea highlights the importance of design as an epistemological stance stating that designing artifact is a unique way of providing insights and theories.

As well as the Anticipation domain, Design has long struggled with the necessity of defending its academic and comparisons with the hard sciences. Cross (2001: 51; citing several authors (Alexander 1964; Gregory 1966; Simon 1969, respectively), epitomizes this as follows:

> Scientists try to identify the components of existing structure. Designers try to shape the components of new structures. (Alexander 1964, p. 130).

> The scientific method is a pattern of problem-solving behaviour employed in finding out the nature of what exists, whereas the design method is a pattern of behaviour employed in inventing things…, which do not yet exist. Science is analytic; design is constructive. (Gregory 1966, p. 6)

The natural sciences are concerned with how things are … design on the other hand is concerned with how things ought to be. (Simon 1996, p. 114).

Today Design is not seen only in terms of scientism and functionalism nor is it understood by examining construction alone. Design-based inquiry is acknowledged as working through its own designerly means that encompass a variety of tools, techniques, and creative processes in tandem with other research methods and analytical frames. Here the "designerly" refers to a complex of ways of working abductively between design techniques, such as sketching prototyping and envisioning, and research methods, spanning a range of applications suited to context, culture, and need. Recent writings in FS have also attested to abductive methods in working with futures-oriented research (Patokorpi and Ahvenainen 2009).

For Design Research, it is the weave of these elements that enacts a knowledge that is built through reshaping and reassessing what is often an array of possible and potential options and paths, artifacts, and processes that are pitched beside and against one another. These placements and positioning are used to help sift and sort, compare and contrast, and are in effect decision-making activities that may seem unstructured and even overelaborated from the outside. For the designer, design team and designer-researcher, such activities of designing are dynamic bearers of brokers of knowledge: selections from among options are made, routes to materialization of artifacts of various types are identified, and followed critically and iteratively. However, the process and its many elements provide a context for wider reflection in and on action, less deliberate and more contextual than is often understood by merely studying an ensuing product or process. Holistic, systems-oriented understanding is thus central to Design inquiry and knowledge building and perhaps most notably because it engages us in looking into and critically mapping out complex conditions and relations that impact on acts of designing and situations of use (Stuedahl et al. 2010). In this sense, twenty-first century Design engages in a weave of relations and processes that shuttle between the material and the immaterial. Anticipation-oriented inquiry can productively encompass such approaches in order to reach into the needs and demands of engaging productively and prospectively in a world increasingly characterized culturally, economically, technically, and politically by complexity, uncertainty, and contest.

Although there are a number of differences in the origins and practices of Design and FS, Design, FS, and their intersections around and through Anticipation share some similarities. They have to do with knowing, investigating, understanding, and creating images and alternatives of the already unknown and the unknown but not yet ready. Ultimately, this is a matter of shaping futures. Design and Anticipation share common tools such as trend analysis, scenarios, narratives, personas, and prototypes (Mörtberg et al. 2010; Morrison and Chisin 2017). Most of all, though, they are coupled by a particular form of scientific enquiry and explanation: an approach to science which takes the view that complex realities (or systems) can be better understood by studying their organizational principles, rather than building descriptions of their structural components (Zamenopoulos and Alexiou 2007, p. 1). This may be related to, and at times contrasted with, more socioculturally framed views that are centered on cocreation, participation, and critical interpretation. These are approaches and practices drawn from disciplines in the humanities and social sciences, but also through their relational systems, formations, and assemblies in transdisciplinary-based design inquiry (Morrison et al. 2010; Bratteteig et al. 2010).

Understanding Anticipation with reference to the Design field requires reading and explaining Design on the basis of the organizational conditions and features that underlie Design as a system of knowledge. While design may have struggled for some time to legitimate itself and a disciplinary domain, Design is not simply a science. Design is comprised of a wide variety of disciplinary relations and linkages, borrowings, and mergers that characterize it as transdisciplinary (Morrison 2010). In this sense, it is well prepared to become one of the core contributors to the emergent field of Anticipation Studies. Importantly, Design entails both construction and critique in knowledge building.

A contribution that has framed the nature of design greatly contributing to the explanation of the design phenomenon is the powerful definition of "design as reflective practice" by Donald Schön. It is particularly interesting to compare Schön's description of the designers' reflection defined as "knowing in action" and the Rosen's definition of an anticipatory system. For Schön:

> When the practitioner reflects-in-action in a case he [she] perceives as unique, paying attention to phenomena and surfacing his intuitive understanding of them, his [her] experimenting is a once exploratory, move testing, and hypothesis testing. The three functions are fulfilled by the very same actions. (Schön 1987, p. 72).

Rosen writes, "An anticipatory system is a system containing a predictive model of itself and/or its environment, which allows it to change state at an instant in accord with the model's predictions pertaining to a later instant." (Rosen 1985, p. 341).

The organizational description of the designer's action allows us to see that the insights that are the results of previous knowledge and reflection in action are the engine of the anticipatory nature of Design. If Anticipation is a way to envision actions that can only be verified in a deferred time, Design is the way in which such simulations can be provided offering through its practice a virtual setting to experiment safely the possibilities of several futures.

Design and Anticipation as Vision Providers

If Anticipation and Design are ways of knowing and approaching possible futures, how might this knowledge be activated? How may foresight and projection as actions be useful to society? Already in the 1950s, Fred Polak recognized the role of future for society and through the title of his work, *The Image of the Future* (Polak 1973), he was underling that the capability to imagine several futures and the capacity to project their image are the key to all choice-oriented behavior. According to his view, the greatest task of human knowledge was to bridge this gap and to find those patterns in the past that can be projected into the future as realistic images (van der Helm 2005).

In the same way in *Reconceptualising Futures: A Need and a Hope*, Eleonora Masini (1982), through her concept of previsione sociale, was trying to question how could we move from abstractly looking into the future to actually building the future. She proposed a Future conception not only as an image or an idea but as a project and considered visions as the first step toward what is possible write now, in the present, in terms of human resources and the will to change. Masini's critical discourse, with a surprising sensitivity to design sensibility, leads back to the relationship between design, revolution, and utopia by asking for a more active, independent, and responsible designer:

> Visions spring from the capacity to recognize the seeds of change that lie in the past and the present; moreover, visions make it possible to create a future that is different from the present although its seeds are in the present. (Masini 1982, p. 2).

The capacity to catch weak signals, gather and reinterpret them, and shaping new products, services, or processes belongs to different levels of the contemporary design praxis as epitomized by Jonas (2017). It is also attributable to some specific design tools useful for both encoding and materialization of futures, as for example the trends' grasping and scenarios practices.

Design and Anticipation as Agents of Change

Both Design Research and Future Studies are concerned with key concerns that are central to some of the main concepts arising in the fledgling transdisciplinary domain of Anticipation. These include, among others, aspiration, accessibility, prospection, preference, and empathy. Such abstract nouns mask the processes and action-centered genesis and enactment of change. At the heart of DR and FS is a wish and a need to change current states, conditions, engagement, and effects into alternate, preferred, or proposed ones that will enable us to enact change. Here we position DR and FS in a clearly sociotechnical and cultural-communicative frame, not one located in predictive, positivistic, or deliberately linear progression. Indeed, there is a great need for design- and science and technology-based inquiry to be furthered. However, design had moved far from narrow functionalism and a focus on physical products to seeing material, tools, and technologies as situated in contexts of social and cultural use, exchange, and transformation.

In a futures view, we cannot work wholly predictively, so that Herbert Simon's earlier definition of design, soon 50 years old, as working to develop "courses of action aimed at changing existing situations into preferred ones" (Simon 1969, x) reminds us that we need to look into what and why and how futures may be cast as preferences. These preferences refer to how we engage in designerly ways with material and immaterial artefacts and design processes that center on ill-defined, fuzzy, messy, and "wicked" problematic centering on designs relations to systems, complexity, dynamics, emergence, interactions, services and cultural expressions, and imaginaries. To do so is to engage actively in devising ways to work with change and the creative coconstruction of participative processes that are no longer delineated wholly from above but are increasingly negotiated through elaborate processes of shaping futures constructive, collaboratively yet still with critical and adaptive logics that require iterative, nonlinear revision, and trialing contexts of use and value creation.

Design deploys prospective techniques such as sketching and prototyping to carry concepts and potential and possible directions further into development and distribution, thus making visible products, services, and interactions that are embedded in designerly processes of abductive reframing. These materializations for people and organizations, together and in relation to one another, themselves become implicated in passages and procedures of codification and cultural communication, whether in business or popular expression. FS may be enriched by deeper engagement with how design inquiry posits, explores, builds, and revises its future-oriented offerings and substantive always mediated experiences in which we make meaning and sense of them in and through use and critique. There is a considerable room for a more elaborated notion of relations between design and innovation that competitive advantage-framed ones that populate business schools and even much of design management discourse, needed instead, is understanding of how innovation itself works through design processes and dynamics in a knowledge-building framework that respects and unpacks the intricacies of creative coconstruction.

As long ago as 1995, Krippendorf argued that the future of design inquiry was much about discourse as it is about artifact, materials, and the sociocultural role of technology. This attention to discourse in our view itself needs careful deconstruction when we look at relations between design and anticipation. We suggest that turning to research in Advanced Design (Celi 2015) is one way of exploring these relations productively and prospectively. This we take up in the next section also includes a focus on the role of narrative in the field of Design futures, connecting new narrative, design fiction, and futures research (Morrison 2018). In essence, this is to take up Margolin's earlier (2007) notion of "competent conjecture" that placed design as needing to work toward responsible futures. In our view, working speculatively today is a key aspect of Design that although only part of its adversity in research is one fruitful area for collaboration and cooperation with FS. As Margolin (2007, p. 14) argued, designers need to urgently draw forth notions of the future into the present. Here we align with the conceptualization of the future as a cultural domain and a culturally framed set of intersecting activities such as argued by Arun Appadurai (2019) that entails aspiration and anticipation. He continues to elaborate (Appadurai 2015), the "future as a cultural fact" is embedded in communicative constructs and practices, ones he addresses in terms of media, materiality, and normativity. We follow this thinking and we extend it into discussion of Speculative Design and design fiction. Our design-located approach is framed through what we call Advance Design (ADD).

Advance Design: A Framework for Connecting Design and FS

Potential Futures

When encompassing the future perspectives in design activity, we are confronted with two main issues: which future are we considering? And how we can deal with future intended as a reality jet to come? Despite the fact that several Future studies' authors discussed about the different kinds of potential futures we deal with, we find important in this context to choose an interpretative model which helps in joining FS and Design disciplines: the cone scheme of Trevor Hancock and Clement Bezold (1993) is very useful for the scope. According to Stuart Candy – a rare case of a contemporary researcher who pedagogically joins Futurology and Design education – the Cone model expresses the idea "that, at any given moment in time, multiple paths are available (though certainly more at some times than at others), and that, by whatever combination of accident and design, we make our way 'forward' through thickets of possible worlds, carving a particular path, which by definition is only one of many possible paths." (Candy 2010, p. 33). The FS literature is full of different interpretations of the Cone Model, but the one expressed by Joseph Voros (2003) (Fig. 1) underlines how preferable futures – concerned with what we "want to" happen – are connected with a more emotional and subjective perspective and enable a "visioning" and constructive view.

Voros, starting from the essential premise that we always must consider an infinite variety of potential alternative futures, trays to distinguish the different meanings of futures clarifying also their use:

- Potential futures – the wider set – that include all of the futures which lie ahead, including those beyond our imagination, including the ones that are actually impossible to project, and that are going to subvert contemporary vision of the reality

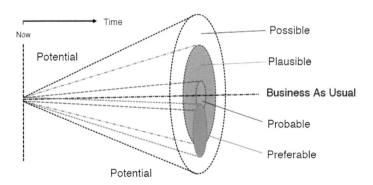

Fig. 1 The cone scheme adapted by Joseph Voros (2003)

- Possible futures – the first cone – that include all the kinds of futures which "might happen," the one we could possibly imagine which are often relying on the existence of some future knowledge that can be glimpsed or that we imagine as an overcame of current knowledge
- Plausible futures – the second cone – stemming from our actual understanding and based on current knowledge, encompass those futures which "could happen"
- Probable futures – the thinner central cone – are the ones which are likely to happen like in linear extension of the present from the past; this cone is much smaller and exemplifies how considering only this perspective is much more restrictive compared to the other ones
- Preferable futures – which are represented significantly in a cone oriented differently compared to the central axis – are by contrast, concerned with what we "want to" happened and thus are more concerned with a subjective or cultural perspective and value judgment

The cone model has the power to tell us that we must accept and manage the idea of the existence of a multitude of futures without which all potentialities will disappear, reducing our perspective to a flat single line, pointing to a predetermined but unknown future. When thinking about futures, we must prevent the cone from collapsing and try to escape what Clarke (1958/1984, p. 27) has called "failures of imagination." At the same time, we are aware of the risks of a too imaginative and subjective single projection; thus Design needs to work with multiple, intersecting, and preferable yet not predictive futures that allow us to aspire to, approximate, empathize and anticipate change, and to make it accessible through the materialization of processes, pathways, artifacts, and conjectures.

As one of the world eminent futurist and founders of the Club of Rome, Eleonora Masini (1982) argued, we need to reconceptualize futures. Even if considering the "prognosis" approach – focalized on probable futures fruit of the extrapolation of social indicators and what we actually call big data – and even if inspired from a "vision" approach oriented to desirable societies, we should embrace a third model (a combination of the previous ones) where people think about the futures in terms of projects. This third approach is based on a changing attitude, a forerunner of the so-called transformation design (Burns et al. 2006), and is very close to everyday wicked design problems where the project is in continuous precarious tension between opportunity and constraints. The only difference is represented by time length. Other works on Transition Design (Irwin 2015) seek to provide an open-source concept for developing and maintaining "design-led societal transition to more sustainable futures" (http://transitiondesign.net). It is the interconnectedness of systems – natural, economic, and social – that Transition design addresses as a means to reimagining the present and our legacies, or infrastructures, and lifestyles within which design is so thoroughly implicated and might forge diversity and difference, locally and globally.

Advance Design: The Project Driven/Led by Possibilities

As well described by Celaschi and others (2011, Advance Design is a field of industrial design that manages and uses the tools, practices, and knowledge of conventional industrial design in long-term projects addressing a distant future (Celi 2015). This location we see as an interesting development from the origins of twentieth century design as a profession and research domain linked to industrialization that is now part of postindustrial economy. This concerns which services and interactions, products and systems are interconnected and entwined in new and often emergent ways. Advance Design thus extends beyond product design to anticipate the complex relations and assemblages of today's design inquiry and professional practice and their fluid and dialogical coexistence and coconstruction.

Advance Design, despite the scarce literature (Borja de Mozota 2006; Celi 2010, 2015), is a consolidated practice in product design. Born in the car sector and then extended to other product systems' areas, it is undoubtedly linked to the future dimension of design but also to the methods with which it innovates. Considering that the initial phases of the process of innovation are acknowledged as crucial at this point in history, and that the themes regarding the Front End of Innovation are becoming increasingly important, clearly Design may became a framework to understand all the future-driven/oriented design praxis. Creating Advance Design means radically innovating but also innovating through uncut paths, through the involvement of users or imagining plausible and unexpected scenarios.

Advance Design does not only operate inside the material and concrete market of products but, on the contrary, works very well for immaterial, soft, and intangible goods that go from social design and services (Armstrong et al. 2014) to cultural heritage that may not all be directly accessible. Representing the design world as a tension between opportunity and constraints, Advance Design is the activity able to join through projects the world of possibility with actual reality thanks to different form of exploration. The more we move from constraints to opportunity, the more we consider the explorative action of design, the more we are moving toward an advance design framework in which the design subject is less defined. In fact, if we have to place Advance Design in a matrix which relates know how to know what, Advance Design definitely practices the area in which previous knowledge is not so readily available or in which it has been purposely bypassed.

The capacity to understand context constraints, strong and polymorphous reframing capabilities, and mediation skills are the knowledge areas that ADD can offer to anticipation. As in Masini's third model (1982) we need both: a knowledge of 'possibles' and 'probables' and a vision of 'desirables.' The perspective view of Advance Design is based on the belief that 'something can be changed.' This way of interpreting future is the natural environment in which designers produce concept ideas and transform them into innovation. It seems that ADD reframing proposal, may provide a field for testing and assessing futures theories through the concreteness of design. Moreover, the multidisciplinary and multicultural approach suggests directing and managing interactions between forms of knowledge and experiences, helping assess the results and bringing them into constant and conscious interaction with the particular context.

The alliance between ADD and anticipation can mix different types of knowledge in respect to the ethical objective embedded in the future. The capability to orient behaviors through values acts as an accelerator of change only if the project preserves in humanistic nature, in being a plan carried out by people and for people.

ADD, Up-Framing, and Reframing Capacity: From Planning to Anticipating

The evolution of user needs and desires, the markets saturation, and the passage of the production system to a value constellation have called for a constant updating of conventional industrial design and for a continuous innovation system that is based on a formal, directive notion of strategy as planning and prediction. However, this does not fully reflect the anticipatory processes and character of design-based inquiry. Strategic and anticipatory perspectives represent different ways of facing future perspective in design activity. Both of them aspire to a wider aim of design, not only connected with the solidity of the products world and the connected markets but with the immaterial side of goods (meaning, ethics, social aims), both of them have the aim of planning and designing not only for the immediate tomorrow and nevertheless they adopt a markedly different attitude or stance toward "making futures." It is worth unpacking this distinction as it is important that Futures research, with its strong origins in strategic planning, along with the force of cybernetics in systems views, appreciates more fully what we see as lacking from a design-centered making and cocreating semiotic and material resources (including narrative, technologies, and experimental expression) for possible and even putative, not merely preferable, futures (Morrison 2016).

The term Strategic design and its culture were born around a strong emphasis on the "company" as the main subject of the strategic design culture. In the 1990s, the idea of a Strategic Design took hold: a more holistic approach, the central role assumed by many designers in the product development process and the growth of a corporate culture and image were calling for a designer profile with mixed competences between project, economy, and culture. In particular, there has been a strong emphasis on a systemic interpretation of the project connected to the so-called Product Service System (PSSD) dimension: emerges an orientation toward different kinds of social and market actors, a clear intention to produce innovation, and an emphasis on a systemic interpretation of sustainable development (Meroni 2008). Francesco Zurlo in his definition of the term Strategic Design describes the strategic adjective as a hat that covers more approaches (operations, tools, and knowledge-building models) and is involved in theoretical and practical aspects (design leadership, design thinking, design direction, business design, research, etc.). In a wider sense, when design is involved in the decision-making process, its role becomes strategic. Strategic Design is the activity able to plan or design to impact favorably the key factors on which the desired outcome of an organization depends. Another definition of strategy refers to methods or plans to bring about a desired future, such as achievement of a goal or solution to a problem. This openness toward future is connected to the design ability to foster change inside organization but, due to the origin of such practice – as we have seen – and to the context primarily limited to enterprise (commercial or social), this change is normally connected to a pre-determined objective. An horizon toward which the designer look designing scenar-ios, producing visions and then prototypes and artifacts, able to catalyze and exploit the present resources to produce a certain range of results.

If we consider the literature coming from the Future Studies area and the contribution of Voros (2003) in particular, it is soon clear that this perspective encompasses only a limited vision of the futures. To foster a process toward what we "want to" happen means to consider only the perspective of the preferable futures. In other words, futures that is more emotional than cognitive, futures that derives from value judgments, and for this reason are more subjective depending on who is doing the preferring. Here the work of Kenneth Gergen (1999) is pertinent. He asserts the significance of inquiry located in the human sciences (humanities and social sciences) that adopt an orientation toward future forming. This prospective frame allows us to engage in what could be not only what scientist inquiry asserts in studying the world as it is and its related declarative knowledge formations. Design inquiry does not jettison science; it embodies an epistemology that is projective not ostensive.

Paradoxically, and to push a point to its extensive and embodied creative extreme, the only time in which we can act as designers and design researchers then is the future; Design is an activity heavily projected in to the future. Even if the consciousness of the centrality of the futures study within our discipline is slow to grow, the actual strength of the international scientific debate about the study of the future – and Anticipation Studies in particular – allows us to meet this important area of concern together with other human and social science (sociology, psychology, anthropology, technology, economy, art) involved in the dimension of time yet to come. The future awareness or better what Miller (2007) calls "future literacy," is crucial in the design profession for many reasons: its huge responsibility in shaping goods, its ability in planning products longevity or life cycle, its contribution to service design and social design, but most of all for its unique capacity of imagining, shaping, and communicating new values and perspective. This is part of cultural articulation and negotiation between pro-ducers and consumers, such as in digital advertising and social engagement in mediational literacy practices (Morrison and Skjulstad 2012) and increasingly as can be seen in the field of digital and locative media in relation to contexts of participation. As Appadurai (2015) has recently begun to argue, our futures literacies may be understood as being located within reflexive, critical views on relations between tolls and mediations in cultural frames, an approach we have ourselves already developed, for example, in design-based research on locative media, communication design, and the city (Morrison and Mainsah 2011) that is premised on designing for cultural expression not infrastructural planning of "the smart city" and it dominant market-driven logics.

Advanced Design (ADD) approach – characterized by the need to think about products, systems, and services suitable for a distant future – is in our view a consolidating practice. Through it, designer-researchers are able to suggest innovation directions starting from the earliest phase of the process. According to Celaschi et al. (2011, p. 8), Design may be understood as engaging in processes of "up-framing." Referring to the earlier work of Norman and Ramirez (1993), this refers to how, in the case of innovation, current value systems may not be simply optimized by envisioned alternatively. This is key to a design-centered view on anticipation and futures-oriented construction and critique. For Celaschi et al. (2012, p. 8):

> Up-framing activities would require an effort to understand all of the actors involved and their value; it would also require some thought about how to create value in such a context and how to become a facilitator and improve the dialogue among all the players. It would require a vision oriented toward the future.

It is this future orientation that is central to Advanced Design. Included here are visionary aspects that are part of a projected narrative that is geared to possibilities and potentialities that involve a mix and diversity of actors and stakeholders. In terms of Design Futures, as opposed to only new product development or the generative character and immateriality of interaction and service design, this approach acknowledges that a variety of practices are involved in shaping prospective directions. This diversity of practices, and their intersections and variations, need to be approached with open frames for moving into working toward and within a future orientation, that is both a world view and methodologically.

Forward with Speculative Design!

Speculation and Design Futures

In keeping with the arguments above, one emergent, and indeed debated, domain of design inquiry that is largely absent in FS is that of Speculative Design (Dunne and Raby 2013). This is an approach that attends to the not yet built or currently realizable; it reaches imaginatively for what is beyond immediately perceived grasp; it is based in a putative and conjectural mode of inquiry, working conceptually and discursively. From a Design view, researching the future requires that we need to remain open to occurrences, to the unknown, and to the unpredictable as they emerge in processes of change and negotiation (Morrison 2010; Morrison et al. 2010). This is in sharp contrast to the more confirmatory status of science and empiricism; design-based inquiry works through designing, by way of materials and tools investigations, and through cultural articulation of products, interactions, and services, located in systems views that are not cybernetically located but are socio-technical practices that reach toward empathizing with user needs but situate them in contexts of cultural expression, consumption, exchange, and critique. In short, a design-based approach to anticipation is what is needed to understand more fully Appadurai's assertion that the future is a cultural fact (Appadurai 2013).

This view allows us to connect well with the growth in the past decade especially on what is known as Critical Design (Dunne and Raby 2001; Dunne 2006) and more recently Speculative Design (Dunne and Raby 2013) and Adversarial Design (DiSalvo 2012) that takes up design techniques and modes of work to challenge political orthodoxies. Critical Design (Dunne and Raby 2001) first sought to highlight the creatively imagined, and conceptual in design, drawing on art and technology to pose alternatives to given artifacts and knowledge. More recently, its founders have extended this to Speculative Design in which artifacts and their potential future locations and appropriacy is tentative, exploratory, and putative, reaching forward into querying the known and posing less than factive alternatives, often placed in the context of the gallery and within the bounded domains of design communities and research arenas. The means and manner of crafting such speculative moves (e.g., Augur 2013) within an earlier materiality of the physical artifact, or commercial product, have led to a series of publications that have addressed matters of relations and associations in the role of pastiche, wit, and sensibility in speculative design (e.g., Malpass 2013). Thinking adversarially yet anticipatively has been part of design and speculative work in a different take by Lorraine Gamman et al. (2012) in developing scenarios for "thinking like a thief," pointing to the ways in which Design conjoins scenarios, personas, and strategies narratively and culturally in contexts of motivated anticipation and enactment.

The role of the speculative in qualitative inquiry has been addressed from the view of the social sciences and the need to account for engaging with and studying innovative methods as knowledge framing and brokering (e.g., Parisi 2012). However, this work largely bypasses specific Design-based experience and inquiry and even more so that entailed in prospective and projective undertakings that are located within Design. As a complement, however, attention is growing to the domain of "design futures" that typically looks into how existing approaches to Design may be extended to encompass and anticipate societal needs and challenges that lie ahead, whether in the near or distant future, within views on innovation, social participation, and wider issues such as sustainability and climate change. The title of the book *Design as Future Making*, edited by Susan Yelavich and Barbara Adams (2014), points to the focus on practice-based inquiry, the importance of enacting design processes, and social-material artifact production that are what design brings to "future proofing." This is not about finding immediate solutions in a functionalist and directive view on knowledge building but a stance that demands active construction of possible, potential, and putative futures via design.

A View on Futures and Narrative

Engaging productively through Design with the tangled unrealized and contingent that is the future demands that other domains that engage with anticipatory ontologies and epistemologies inform Design research. Future Studies helps us place design work in contexts of planning, scenario development, and policy. However, Design forces us to move into the making of the future, and here narrative is on the key domain that is not always strongly articulated within either FS or Design. Narrative is one of our oldest and most widely practiced and shared cultural resources and techniques for engaging in sense making and communicating and perceiving future scenarios, interpersonal relations. It also allows us to conceptualize pathways and processes for addressing the not-yet-built, situationally and dramaturgically, not only in terms of planning and strategy.

Jarratt and Mahaffie (2009) evoke Lakoff's "Frames" (2008) to explain how brief sketches and short stories represent the unit of information through which we codify, comprehend, and learn. Stories are the main tool through which frame, or better reframe, realities, and engage people, clients, and stakeholders in active change. They argue we do not need better rational arguments about the benefits of thinking about the future but we need better stories: "Futurists must rethink scenarios as a process and a tool, and discover ways to use them much more effectively as powerful stories that can motivate reshaping the future." (Jarratt and Mahaffie 2009, p. 5). It is this narrative element that we take up below as one of the intersections between Design and Anticipation.

It is developments in Design concerning speculation as a mode of qualitative inquiry (e.g., Parisi 2012) that allows closer linkages to be shaped between its related domain of design fiction and the rather more solution-centered application of narrative to probable and potential real-world scenarios in FS. Already research exists in the construction of fictional and shared spaces as contributions to practices of participatory design (Dindler and Sjerlversen 2007; Dindler 2010). FS may benefit form investigating such design and narrative enactments, as well as their fictive framing in terms of experimentation (Knutz et al. 2013).

There remains then a space for Anticipation Studies to bridge these approaches and investigate how narrative might be taken up nonmimetically with respect to narrative theory and performance (e.g., Alber et al. 2013) to develop further approaches to foresight and the possible and the probable but also the potential and the putative (Morrison 2018), in physical and digital dimensions (Dourish and Bell 2011; Morrison 2010). Following on from the work of Milojevic and Inayatullaha (2015) on links between narrative studies and foresight research, this we see as a matter of developing what we call design narrative foresight. We use the prefix design to distinguish it from already existing and successful approaches to narrative foresight (e.g., http://actionforesight.net; https://engagedforesight.com) that tend to work toward effectiveness and business social innovation and strategy solutions and less the speculative, culturally framed, and emergent expressive and poetic aspects of a wider design view on communication design futures. Naturally, historical and retrospective views are crucial in developing understanding of the future as Fredrick Jameson (2005) argues in his book *Archaeologies of the Future*. What is also needed is to experiment with means and modes of conveying the conjectural and the work that may do to transductively help us anticipate unpredictable but anticipative futures in creative, designerly ways. Design fiction provides one such domain.

Design Fiction

Design Fiction (Sterling 2009a, Sterling 2009b; Bleecker 2010; Hales 2013; Lindley and Coutlon 2015), often thought as the "cousin of science fiction" (Bleeker 2009, p.8), represents a link between science fact and science fiction and provides the opportunity to speculate within the fictional reality of the film, considering the results of this work as more than a props maker or effects artist creating appearances. Increasingly Design Fictions are moving beyond the medium of film, video, and photography toward the materialization of, for example, physical props, models, and prototypes but most of all toward the social value of futures narration (Markussen and Knutz 2013).

In the recent transdisciplinary research project called Future North that investigates changing cultural landscapes of the Arctic, Morrison (2018) argues for the positioning and practice of design fictive articulations that engage readers in narrative moves that take them into different temporal and spatial relations in order to traverse the complex terrains and depths of climate change. Drawing in the work of Bakhtin (1981, 1984, 1986) as well as that of Harraway, this is conveyed through the ventriloquism of self-aware techno-mammalian fictive hybrid in the form of a nuclear powered female narwhal called Narratta (http://www.oculs.no/people/narratta/). This is a mode of research through fictive design: a team of transdisciplinary researchers deploy this persona to investigate, traverse, and communicate their own research processes and reflexive methods in and over time, historically, contemporaneously, and "fugitively" so in the future. The work draws on contemporary theory on "extreme narration" (e.g., Richardson 2006) while discursively enacting collaborative communication design logics. This design fictional experiment is part of other mixed research methods taking up in the Future North project for engaging in future cultural conceptions of the Arctic in the Age of the Anthropocene.

Design fiction in this case is connected to a mesh of methods, mixed in relation to the speculative, tentative yet also factively informed foundations of the inquiry. Based on earlier similar design fiction experiments and related research on critical views on near future technologies and the city, personas, scripts, scenarios, and events in rethinking design futures narratively and mediationally (Morrison et al. 2013; Morrison 2014), recent work extends to the involvement of master's students in urbanism and landscape studies co-developing a related design fiction Longyearbyen 2050 centered on the future scenarios of urban life and food security and climate change (Morrison 2016). At the heart of such work is the notion and shared practice in finding ways to think about enacting together Advance Design and Speculative Design practices for sharing futures (Celi and Formia 2015; Celi and Formia 2017).

Design fiction, and more narrative and fictive approaches to the uses and reshaping of foresight within FS, is ripe for development. Recent publications in FS have opened out to conceptualizing narratology in the shaping of futures (e.g., Raven and Elahi 2015) as well as working with modality and narrative in the uptake of scenarios and counterfactuals (Booth et al. 2009). Interest is also growing in seeing design fiction and narrative in design generative inquiry more broadly, such as in work on design, anticipation, and ethnography (Lindley and Dhruv 2014), how narrative and literary techniques may be applied to enhance scientific agenda setting (Blythe 2014), and connections may be made between ecocriticism and narrative theory (Lehtimäki 2013; Morton 2013).

Conclusion

In the **future** shaping of Anticipation, we see there being several links that may be made between FS and Design as we have elaborated above. Our argument is that Anticipation may benefit from more fully acknowledging imaginative, creative, and constructionist aspects of Design. This was clearly evident at the first international conference on Anticipation in 2016 with a slew of design contributions. That event and the dialogues around design has propelled many of the "foundational" publications included here that seek to map, tease out, and propose what Anticipation Science and Anticipation Studies is and may become. In our transdisciplinary research and professional design, futures and prospectively based design inquiry offer new avenues for stronger collaboration when less determinist notions of design and solution driven are entertained and where the now large body of work in Design is accessed and may be interlinked with that in FS. Design inquiry could make more use of research in FS; FS might more fully access research in Design.

Our reading is that FS need not to be seen only in terms of forward planning and policy convergent moves in shaping knowledge for possible, realizable, and sustainable futures. We firmly acknowledge that these are important pursuits. However, we also see open and rich opportunities for clearer and stronger connections to be made between the futures orientations of both Design and FS. This chapter has shown – through both theory and practice – that Design based inquiry offers FS elements of working with shaping futures that are located in a now established traditional of critical making with interpretative reflection located in the human sciences, and crucially through abduction, cocreation, and speculation. We have shown how this has been achieved in the recent and emergent field of Advance Design together with Speculative Design.

We see room for further communicative collaboration in "narrative futures" with FS in and as 'wordl making' (Coulton and Lindley 2017). In our view, the field of Anticipation is not a discipline as such but that it is a field of multiple mediations and meanings. In this sense, it extends beyond FS as inherited and expanded in the past two decades. Anticipation is a multidisciplinary pursuit that is realized through attention to the cultural and the communicative, the creative, and the critical, not only via science and not only in the human sciences. This is not a time to argue about boundaries but rather to explore their relations and refractions, and to shape a space for engaged participation and exchange. Design offers much to that space, but it does no seek to possess it.

We argue then that Anticipation maybe shaped as a future pursuit, informed through Design and supported by way of linkages with Futures Studies that are equally polymorphous and conjectural alongside other much needed procedural, factive, and necessary foundations upon which to aspire, approximate, propel, and together project designs fictions and future-oriented inquiries.

References

Alber, J., Skov Neilsen, H., & Richardson, B. (Eds.). (2013). *A poetics of unnatural narrative.* Columbus: The Ohio State University Press.

Alexander, C. (1964). *Notes on the synthesis of form.* Cambridge: Harvard University Press.

Appadurai, A. (2013). *The future as cultural fact: Essays on the global condition.* London: Verso.

Appadurai, A. (2015). Mediants, materiality, normativity. *Public Culture, 27*(2), 221–237.

Armstrong, L., Bailey, J., Julier, G., & Kimbell, L. (2014). *Social Design Futures.* HEI Research and the AHRC.

Augur, J. (2013). Speculative design: Crafting the speculation. *Digital Creativity, 24*(1), 11–35.

Bakhtin, M. (1981). *The dialogic imagination: Four essays by M.M Bakhtin* (M. Holquist, Ed.; C. Emerson, & M. Holquist, Trans.). Austin: University of Texas Press.

Bakhtin, M. (1984). *Problems of Dostoevsky's Poetics* (C. Emerson, Ed. & Trans). Minneapolis: University of Minnestota Press.

Bakhtin, M. (1986). Speech genres and other late essays (C. Emerson, & M. Holquist, Ed.; V. McGee, Trans.). Austin: University of Texas Press.

Bleecker, J. (2009). Design Fiction: A Short Essay on Design, Science, Fact and Fiction. Near Future Laboratory, (March), 49. Retrieved from http://www.nearfuturelaboratory.com/2009/03/17/design-fiction-a-short-essay-on-design-science-fact-and-fiction/

Bleecker, J. (2010). Fiction: From props to prototypes. In 6th SDN Conference: Negotiating Futures – Design Fiction, 28–30 October, 2010, Basel: Switzerland.

Blythe, M. (2014). The Hitchhiker's guide to ubicomp: Using techniques from literary and critical theory to reframe scientific agendas. *Personal and Ubiquitous Computing, 18*(4), 795–808.

Booth, C., Rowlinson, M., Clark, P., Delahaye, A., & Procter, S. (2009). Scenarios and counterfactuals as modal narratives. *Futures, 41*(2), 87–95.

Borja de Mozota, B. (2006). The four powers of design: A value model in design management. *Design Management Review, 17*(2), 44–53.

Bratteteig, T., Morrison, A., Wagner, I., Stuedahl, D., & Mörtberg, C. (2010). Research practices in digital design. In I. Wagner, D. Stuedahl, & T. Bratteteig (Eds.), *Exploring digital design* (pp. 17–54). Vienna: Springer.

Brodersen, C., Dindler, C., & SjerIversen, O. (2008). Staging imaginative places for participatory prototyping. *CoDesign, 4*(1), 19–30.

Burns, C., Cottam, H., Vanstone, C., & Winhall, J. (2006). *RED paper 02: Transformation design.* London: Design Council.

Candy, S. (2010). The futures of everyday life: Politics and the design of experiential scenarios. Doctorate of Political Science: University of Hawaï at Mānoa.

Celaschi, F., Celi, M., & García, L. M. (2011). The extended value of design: An advanced design perspective. *Design Management Journal, 6*(1), 6–15.

Celi, M. (2015). *Advanced design cultures: Long-term perspective and continuous innovation.* Cham: Springer.

Celi, M., & Formia, E. (2015). Advanced design practices for sharing futures: A focus on design fiction. Proceedings of 11th European Academy of Design Conference. 22–24 April. Paris. pp. 1–16.

Celi, M., & Formia, E. (2017). Aesthetics of futures: the impact of design in shaping shared visions of tomorrow. *The Design Journal, 20*(Supplement 1): 63-76. *Design for Next: Proceedings of the 12th European Academy of Design Conference*, Sapienza University of Rome, 12-14 April 2017. In Design for Next. Conference Proceedings of EAD 2017. Rome: 12–14 April. Available: http://www.designfornext.org. Accessed 20 June 2017.

Clarke, A. (1958/1984). *Profiles of the future: An inquiryintothelimits of the possible*. New York: Holt, Rinehart and Winston.

Coulton, P., & Lindley, J. (2017). Vapour worlds and design fiction: the role of intentionality. In Design for Next. Conference Proceedings of EAD 2017. Rome: 12–14 April. Available: http://www.designfornext.org. Accessed 20 June 2017.

Cross, N. (2001). Designerly ways of knowing: Design discipline versus design science. *Design Issues, 17*(3), 49–55.

Deserti, A., & Rizzo, F. (2014). Design and the cultures of enterprises. *Design Issues, 30*(1), 36–56.

Dindler, C. (2010). The construction of fictional space in participatory design practice. *CoDesign, 6*(3), 167–182.

Dindler, C., & SjerIversen, O. (2007). Fictional inquiry: Design collaboration in a shared narrative space. *CoDesign, 3*(4), 213–234.

DiSalvo, C. (2012). *Adversarial design*. Cambridge: MIT Press.

Dourish, P., & Bell, G. (2011). *Divining a digital future*. Cambridge: MIT Press.

Dunne, A. (2006). *Hertziantales: Electronic products, aesthetic experience, and critical design*. Cambridge: MIT Press.

Dunne, A., & Raby, F. (2001). *Design noir: The secret life of electronic objects*. Basel: Birkhauser.

Dunne, A., & Raby, F. (2013). *Speculative everything*. Cambridge: MIT Press.

Findeli, A. (2000). Some tentative epistemological and methodological guidelines for design research. In S. Pizzocaro (Ed.), *Design plus research proceedings*. Milano: Politecnico di Milano.

Frascara, J. (Ed.). (2002). Design and the social sciences: Making connections. New York: Taylor & Francis.

Frayling, C. (1993/1994). Research into art and design. *Royal College of Art Research Papers, 1*(1), 1–5.

Gamman, L., Thorpe, A., Malpass, M., & Liparova, E. (2012). Hey babe – take a walk on the wild side! *Design and Culture, 4*(2), 171–193.

Gergen, K. (1999). An Invitation to Social Construction. Sage: Thousand Oaks and London.

Gregory, S. (Ed.). (1966). *The design method*. London: Butterworth Press.

Hales, D. (2013). Design fictions: An introduction and provisional taxonomy. *Digital Creativity, 24*(1), 1–10.

Hancock, T., & Bezold, C. (1993). Possible futures, preferable futures. *The Healthcare Forum Journal, 37*(2), 23–29.

Irwin, T. (2015). Transition design: A proposal for a new area of design practice, study, and research. *Design and Culture, 7*(2), 229–246.

Jameson, F. (2005). *Archaeologies of the future*. London: Verso.

Jarratt, J., & Mahaffie, J. (2009). Reframing the future. *Journal of Futures Studies, 13*(4), 5–12.

Jonas, W. (2017). The strengths/limits of systems thinking denote the strengths/limits of practice-based design research. *FORM Akademisk, 4*(7), 1–11. Available: https://journals.hioa.no/index.php/formakademisk/issue/view/124. Accessed 20 June 2017.

Knutz, E. Markussen. T. & P. Christensen. (2013). The role of fiction in experiments within design, art and architecture. Proceedings of NORDES 2013. 9–12 June, Copenhagen/Malmö, pp. 341–348. .Available: www.nordes.org. Accessed 20 June 2017.

Krippendorf, K. (1995). *The semantic turn*. London: Taylor & Francis.

Lehtimäki, M. (2013). Natural environments in narrative contexts: Cross-pollinating ecocriticism and narrative theory. *Storyworlds, 5*, 119–141.

Lindley, J., & Dhruv, S. (2014). Anticipatory ethnography: Design fiction as an input to design ethnography. Proceedings of Ethnographic Praxis in Industry Conference, pp. 237–253.

Lindley, J., & Coulton, P. (2015). Back to the future: 10 years of design fiction. In *Proceedings of the 2015 British HCI Conference* (pp. 210–211). ACM.

Malpass, M. (2013). Between wit and reason: Defining associative, speculative, and critical design in practice. *Design and Culture, 5*(3), 333–356.

Margolin, V. (2007). Design, the future and the human spirit. *Design Issues, 23*(3), 4–15.

Markussen, T. & Knutz, E. (2013). The poetics of design fiction. DPPI 2013: Praxis and Poetics. 3–5 September, Newcastle upon Tyne. pp. 231–240.

Masini, E. (1982). Reconceptualizing the future: A need and a hope. *World Futures Society Bulletin*, *Nov–Dec*, 1–8.

Meroni, A. (2008). Strategic design: where are we now? Reflection around the foundations of a recent discipline. *Strategic Design Research Journal, 1*(1), 31–38.

Miller, R. (2007). Futures literacy: A hybrid strategic scenario method. *Futures, 39*(4),341–362.

Miller, R., Poli, R., & Rossel, P. (2013). The discipline of anticipation: Exploring key issues. IN: fumee. org.

Milojevic, I., & Inayatullaha, S. (2015). Narrative foresight. *Futures, 73*(2), 151–162.

Morrison, A. (Ed.). (2010). *Inside multimodal composition*. Cresskill: Hampton Press.

Morrison, A. (2014). Design prospects: Investigating design fiction via a rogue urban drone. In Proceedings of DRS 2014. 16–19 June 2014, Umea.

Morrison, A. (2016). Design fiction in design education: urbanism, para-pedagogy and futures literacies. In Proceedings of Open Design for E-very-thing: exploring new design purposes. Hong Kong: 21–24 November. Available: http://cumulus.hkdihongkong2016.org. Accessed 20 June 2017.

Morrison, A. (forthcoming, 2018). Future north, nuture forth: Design fiction, anticipation and Arctic futures. In J. Kampevold-Larsen & P. Hemmersam (Eds.), *Future North. The Changing Arctic Landscapes*. London: Routledge.

Morrison, A., & Chisin, A. (2017). Design fiction, culture and climate change: weaving together personas, collaboration and fabulous futures. *The Design Journal, 20*(Supplement 1): 146-159. *Design for Next: Proceedings of the 12th European Academy of Design Conference*, Sapienza University of Rome, 12-14 April 2017.

Morrison, A., & Mainsah, H. (2011). Building communication by design: mobile fiction and the city. In Hensel, M. (Ed.). *Design innvovation for the built environment - research by design and the renovation of practices*, (pp. 221–234). London: Routledge.

Morrison, A., & Skjulstad, S. (2012). Laying eggs in other people's pockets: Marketing multi-literacies via mobile technologies. In B. Gentakow, E. Skogseth, & S. Østerud (Eds.), *Literacy practices in late modernity: Mastering technological and cultural convergences* (pp. 201–224). Cresskill: Hampton Press.

Morrison, A., Stuedahl, D., Mörtberg, C., Wagner, I., Liestøl, G., & Bratteteig, T. (2010). Analytical perspectives. In I. Wagner, T. Bratteteig, & D. Stuedahl (Eds.), *Exploring digital design* (pp. 55–103). Vienna: Springer.

Morrison, A., Tronstad, R., & Martinussen, E. (2013). Design notes on a lonely drone. *Digital Creativity, 24*(1), 46–59.

Mörtberg, C., Bratteteig, T., Wagner, I., Stuedahl, D., & Morrison, A. (2010). Methods that matter in digital design research. In I. Wagner, D. Stuedahl, & T. Bratteteig (Eds.), *Exploring digital design* (pp. 105–144). Vienna: Springer.

Morton, T. (2013). *Hyperobjects: Philosophy and ecology after the end of the world*. Minneapolis: University of Minnesota Press.

Nadin, M. (Ed.). (2015). *Anticipation: Learning from the past. The Russian/Soviet contributions to the science of anticipation*. Cham: Springer.

Normann, R., & Ramirez, R. (1993). From value chain to value constellation: Designing interactive strategy. *Harvard business review, 71*(4), 65–77.

Parisi, L. (2012). Speculation. In C. Lury & N. Wakeford (Eds.), *Inventive methods* (pp. 232–244). London: Routledge.

Patokorpi, E., & Ahvenainen, M. (2009). Developing an abduction-based method for futures research. *Futures, 41*, 126–139.

Polak, F. (1973). *The image of the future*. Amsterdam: Elsevier.

Poli, R. (2010). The many aspects of anticipation. *Foresight, 12*(3), 7–17.

Poli, R. (2014a). Anticipation: What about turning the human and social sciences upside down? *Futures, 64*, 15–18.

Poli, R. (2014b). Anticipation: A new thread for the human and social sciences? *CADMUS, 2*(13), 23–36.

Raven, P., & Elahi, S. (2015). The new narrative: Applying narratology to the shaping of futures outputs. *Futures, 74*, 49–61.

Richardson, B. (2006). *Unnatural voices. Extreme narration in modern and contemporary fiction.* Columbus: The Ohio State University Press.

Rosen, R. (1985/2012). *Anticipatory systems: Philosophical, mathematical, and methodological foundations* (2nd ed.). New York: Springer.

Schön, D. (1987). *Educating the reflective practicioner.* San Francisco: Jossey-Bass.

Sevaldson, B. (2013). Systems Oriented Design: The emergence and development of a designerly approach to address complexity. In Proceedings of DRS//CUMULUS 2013. 2nd International Conference for Design Education Researchers, Oslo 14–17 May.

Simon, H. (1969). *The sciences of the artificial.* Cambridge: MIT Press.

Sterling, B. (2009a). Design fictions. *Interactions, 16*(3), 21–24.

Sterling, B. (2009b). *Scenarios and speculations* (pp. 18–29). Amsterdam: Sun Publishers.

Stolterman, E., & Nelson, H. (2012). *The design way* (2nd ed.). Cambridge: MIT Press.

Stuedahl, S., Morrison, A., Mörtberg, C., & Bratteteig, T. (2010). Researching digital design. In I. Wagner, D. Stuedahl, & T. Bratteteig (Eds.), *Exploring digital design* (pp. 105–144). Vienna: Springer.

van der Helm, R. (2005). The future according to Frederik Lodewijk Polak: Finding the roots of contemporary futures studies. *Futures, 37*(6), 505–519.

Voros, J. (2003). A generic foresight process framework. *Foresight, 5*(3), 10–21.

Yelavich, S., & Adams, B. (2014). *Design as future making.* London: Bloomsbury.

Zamenopoulos, T., & Alexiou, K. (2007). Towards an anticipatory view of design. *Design Studies, 28*(4), 411–436.

Design Scenarios and Anticipation

39

Chiara Colombi and Danila Zindato

Contents

This chapter is part of the wider reflection on Design and Anticipation developed by other contributors to the Handbook of Anticipation. Please consider reading also the following chapters: Design Processes and Anticipation, Design Inquiry and Anticipation, and Anticipation in Built Environment Design.

    The chapter is the result of a coordinated work, however paragraphs 1. *Introduction*, 5. *Fashion and Anticipation: Cultural Embodiment and Negotiation* and sub-paragraphs, and *Ending Summary* are authored by Chiara Colombi, while paragraphs 2. *Categorizations of Scenarios: A Theoretical Overview* and sub-paragraphs, 3. *Automotive and Anticipation: The Role of Concept Cars*, and 4. *Electronics and Home Appliances: The Relation Between Future Technology and Social Paradigms* are authored by Danila Zindato. In particular, the study of design scenarios as tools of anticipation to support the innovation processes in the fashion field is a research activity coordinated by Chiara Colombi within the research collective Fashion in Process, at Design department – Politecnico di Milano (http://www.fashioninprocess.com). The study of approaches and positioning of scenario building into the design process is the results of Danila Zindato's doctoral research, *"Design Scenarios. Approaches and Tools for Building the Future Within the Design Processes,"* defended on March 2016 at Politecnico di Milano.

C. Colombi (✉) · D. Zindato
Department of Design, Politecnico di Milano, Milan, Italy
e-mail: chiara.colombi@polimi.it; danila.zindato@gmail.com

© Springer Nature Switzerland AG 2019
R. Poli (ed.), *Handbook of Anticipation*,
https://doi.org/10.1007/978-3-319-91554-8_52

Abstract

The first relation between design practices and anticipation studies is related to the use of scenarios and their capability to shape possible futures. Writing about scenarios in future studies is writing about myths of future. It is possible to imagine the characters and approaches that will shape and influence events. Design however has not adopted the futurist practice per se but has reshaped it narrating the areas of the possible through design approaches. Scenarios – being complexes of meta-information, maps open to different innovation paths that provide strategic direction but also formal, technological, and material suggestions (Celaschi, Dentro al progetto: appunti di merceologia contemporanea. In A. Deserti & F. Celaschi (Eds.), *Design e Innovazione. Strumenti e pratiche per la ricerca applicata* (pp. 1–50). Roma: Carocci Editore (Italian Edition only), 2007) – emerge as the most relevant tools that create, transfer, and allow sharing ideas of the futures within the design process.

Literature offers many definitions of future scenarios within the design field. They are considered as business prognostication tools (Schwartz, *The art of the long view: Planning for the future in an uncertain world*. New York: Currency Doubleday, 1991) or as strategic tools "to inform, validate and endorse design decisions, to define a strategy and to help decision makers" (Evans & Somerville, Designing tomorrow: A methodology for future orientated product design. Global Chinese industrial design conference 2005, Chang Gung University, Taiwan, Nov 2005. http://www.academia.edu/203838/Evans_M_and_Sommerville_S_2005_Designing_Tomorrow_A_Methodology_for_Future_Orientated_Product_Design._Global_Chinese_Industrial_Design_Conference_2005_Chang_Gung_University_Taiwan_November_2005. Accessed 10 Sept 2016, 2005).

The chapter offers a theoretical overview on scenarios literature, then focusing on design scenarios characteristics and application and offering a reading model of their objectives and outputs along a design process, thanks to the presentation of case studies from different productive fields – transportation, electronics and home appliances, and fashion, as emblematic cases. In particular, the discussion highlights stakeholders, approaches, and tools that shape typologies and functions of scenarios within the different design sectors and that articulate different perspectives on the anticipatory value of the design practice.

Keywords
Design process · Innovation · Strategic planning · Scenario building process ·
Policy-orienting scenarios · Business-oriented scenarios · Design-orienting
scenarios · Prototype · Contextual analysis · Zeitgeist · Cultural industries · Trend
research · Negotiation · Taming process · Product lifecycle management

Introduction

Given the perspective of the design practice mediating among disciplines and sectors
and shaping the future in consideration of shared meanings and values, as discussed
by Celaschi in the ▶ Chap. 37, "Design Processes and Anticipation" included in this
volume, and in consideration of the processual dimension of the advanced design
practice that shifts the timeline of the design innovation and that broadens the role
of stakeholders along a design value chain, as framed by Celi in ▶ Chap. 38,
"Anticipation and Design Inquiry" in the present volume, the practice of design
scenarios materializes the many dimensions that design anticipation implies, looking
for driving innovation.

Design scenarios not only answer to technological instances, such as forms and
functions, but it also refers to socio-cultural and economic instances related to
meanings and values of a design product or service that design-driven innovation
seeks. They embody the application of many researches and analytical tools and
allow to shape the object of study or their final objective along the process of
building the very scenario. In this way, they answer to the complexity of environment, systems, and experiences that are constantly changing and requiring the design
practice to give them a preferable shape intended as a positive advancement.

The paradox of design that Smithers discusses (2002), that is linked to the
reflective dimension of the design practice (Schön 1983), is represented in its
whole entirety by design scenarios. According to Smithers, the nature of Design
rises a paradox: while designing means shaping a solution to a problem, the
addressed problem is not a priori defined, but it is set along the very design process.
According to Schön, practicing design allows turning implicit knowledge explicit
and learning from our own experiences, while reflecting and codifying them. In fact,
not only design scenarios anticipate a solution, but they also anticipate the correspondence between the solution and the needs and desires that have led to its
definition. Their processual and reflective dimension define the situatedness of
design solutions within a context and in relation to the knowledge and skills of the
actors involved, but most of all the strong evolutionary dimension of the anticipatory
contents delivered. Design scenarios and their embedded solutions are built on the
base of past experiences and memories (Gero and Kannengiesser 2004, 2006) and on
the reflection about the "augmented" conditions resulted from the interaction of
current actions and past knowledge. This reveals the evolutionary trait of design

scenarios that links past and present perspective towards the projection and realization of the future, through the process of designing it. The need of answering to untold questions and un-thought desires defines the visual dimension of design scenarios as sort of topographical representation of innovation, tracing the trajectories of the project (Celaschi 2007) and enabling their being shareable with a community of reference.

While a theoretical overview is needed to introduce the main concepts related to the design scenario building practice, the authors' approach focuses on an empirical analysis of different applications and functions of scenarios along a design process within design-oriented sectors – transportation, electronics and home appliances, and fashion – to present the complexity of a design perspective on anticipation through emblematic cases. In fact, the considered sectors are the ones that, historically, as the first, planned their entire research and development function toward the anticipation of needs and desires of customers and therefore toward the creation of technological and socio-cultural conditions and capabilities to materialize those needs and desires into a tangible product. That because the intrinsic characteristics of their product define a specific development timeline – i.e., the 3–5 years for a new car, 6 months-15 days for a fashion product – and/or because their products' socio-cultural meanings require their capabilities to be both relevant to customers and promoters of new concepts. As it will be discussed, in these sectors, not only the dimension of time influences the deployment of the design activity, but it also shapes the nature of tools used and generated by the very design practice, confirming. The chapter will present example of design scenarios building practices in these sectors, based on field experiences, which will allow to model typologies and functions of scenarios within the design practice and articulate different perspectives on the anticipatory value of the design practice.

Categorizations of Scenarios: A Theoretical Overview

The Origins of Scenario Planning

The origins of scenarios as a tool to preview the future go back to the sixteenth century, when a Spanish Jesuit theologian and scholar, Luis de Molina, introduced the concept of "conditional future contingents" or "*futuribilia*" as an explanation for free will, foreknowledge, and predestination (Malaska and Virtanen 2005).

Referring to Molina, the French political philosopher Bertrand De Jouvenel, took the idea of "futuribilia" and combined the terms "future" and "possible" into a new one: "futurible." He defined futuribles as "a fan of possible futures," explaining that "the mind cannot grasp with certainty... but it can conjecture possible alternatives" (De Jouvenel 1967 in Malaska and Virtanen 2005, p. 12).

After World War II, the US military tried to imagine multiple scenarios of what its opponents might do. According to Fahey and Randall (1998), the notion of "scenario planning" was implemented by Herman Kahn for the US Government, during his assignment at RAND Corporation – a nonprofit research and development organization – in the 1950s, and later with the work he did as founder of the Hudson Institute, in the 1960s. Kahn encouraged people to "think the unthinkable," first about the consequences of nuclear war and then about every manner of future condition (Bishop et al. 2007). Kahn's insights into the benefits of using futures or indeed scenarios as strategic planning tools stretched further than military applications and scenario thinking began to emerge everywhere, from Politics and Economics to Public Policy (Khan and Wiener 1967). These techniques were also gaining credence in the corporate world, and in the 1970s both Royal Dutch Shell and the consulting firm SRI International contributed to the creation of a more formalized approach to scenario thinking that could be more readily linked with strategic planning (Fahey and Randall 1998). In fact, the paradigm of scenarios as a planning tool set at RAND corporation became significant with the work of Pierre Wack, at Shell, in the 1970s.

Wack and his team used scenarios to paint vivid and diverse pictures of the future so that decision-makers at Shell could rehearse the implications for the company. As a result, Shell was able to anticipate the Arab oil embargo and later to anticipate and prepare for the dramatic drop in oil prices in the 1980s. Since then, scenario thinking has become a popular tool for the development of corporate strategy in numerous industries. It is not surprising then that Shell began to lead the commercial world in scenario thinking and by the 1980s many large organizations were beginning to take a more strategic approach to planning for the future (Dieffenbach 1983).

Ex-Shell planner Peter Schwartz founded his own consultancy business in 1987, the Global Business Network. GBN was a network of organizations, scenario practitioners, and futurists from a variety of disciplines and industries. Large corporations began to take notice of Schwartz's techniques and scenario planning techniques have been emerging in every sphere from industry to academia. Their success accelerates the spread of scenario building as strategic tool – moving out the perspective of long-term planning typical of governmental applications, Politics, Economics and Public Policy, the term "scenario building" substitutes the term "scenario planning" –.

Business-Oriented Scenarios as Strategic Tool for the Industry

Once companies discovered the great potential of scenarios as predictive tool to mix and match social and economic aspects, many businesses inserted scenarios in their strategic department for identifying new corporate and product strategy.

During the 1980s, companies such as Smith & Hawken, Apple, FIAT developed scenarios with a time horizon of about 15 years to set a business model or to test people reaction. Thanks to the growing interest in scenario building what can be called "business-oriented scenarios" (BOSs) acquired consistency.

According to Bhandari and Verma (2013), in these years Porter defined scenarios as a tool in the strategist's arsenal, which is used to predict on the assumption that if marketers cannot predict the future, then by considering a variety of them, marketers might be able to hit upon the right one.

During the 1990s, a conspicuous number of researchers – especially in the economy and business fields – used scenarios, with different formalizations and definitions. Schwartz (1991, p. 6) defined scenarios as *"tools for ordering one's perceptions about alternative future environments in which today's decisions might be played out... Scenarios resemble a set of stories, written or spoken, built around carefully constructed plots... Good scenarios are plausible and surprising, they have the power to break old stereotypes, and their creators assume ownership and put them to work. Using scenarios is rehearsing the future. By recognizing the warning signs and the drama that is unfolding, one can avoid surprises, adapt and act effectively."*

Schoemaker (1995) described scenario planning as a tool for simplifying the avalanche of data into a limited number of possibilities. Each scenario tells a story of how various elements interact under certain conditions. When relationship between elements can be formalized, a company can develop quantitative models and it should evaluate each scenario for internal consistency and plausibility. Indeed, a good set of scenarios are plausible in that they can be "imagined" in terms of current, visible events or trends that might cause them to happen. The set should not only include a visionary (or normative) scenario, but also some scenarios that challenge the organization.

According to this perspective, Hamel and Prahalad (2000, p. 124) observed the influence of scenarios as strategic tool to create/evaluate or calibrate a business model: *"foresight is based on deep insights into trends in technology, demographics, regulations, and lifestyles, which can be harnessed to rewrite industry rule and create new competitive space. Developing a point of view about the future should be an ongoing project sustained by continuous debate within a company, not a massive on time effort. To get ahead of the industry change curve, to have the chance of conducting a bloodless revolution, top managers must recognize that the real focus for their companies is the opportunity to compete for the future."*

Finally, during the last 20 years, business-oriented scenarios have been linked to foresight and business prognostication.

Business-oriented scenarios present three main characteristics: they refer to macrosystem (context and environment); they have a wide time range (at least 10 years); and they are generally materialized using narrative written stories, matrix or through video and design fictions when used in design-driven companies.

The Design Perspective

Following the Shell's experience, knowledge about scenarios has been increasingly formalized.

Eleonora Barbieri Masini (1973) structured the scenarios' architecture identifying three essential elements:

– Vision, the most specific component of a scenario. It answers the basic question *"What would the world be like if......?"* by telling a story and/or sketching a picture of what things would be like if a sequence of events were to take place
– Motivation, the component of the scenario that justifies its existence and confers its meaning. It answers the question *"Why is this scenario meaningful?"* by rationally

explaining the intention of building it such as premises for the scenario, assumed surrounding conditions, and how the various alternative propositions will be assessed
- Proposal, as each scenario needs planning to achieve an expected vision. It answers the question *"What has to be done to implement that vision?"*

However, the role of scenarios as design tools was formalized by Manzini and Jegou (2000). Their theoretical model recognizes "vision" and "motivation" as components of scenario, but they talk about "practicability" as third main element. Practicability is intended to add depth and consistency to the vision. It answers the questions *"What are the various facets of the overall vision?" "What does it consist of?"* and *"How can we make it happen?"* Therefore, different kinds of scenarios give rise to different kinds of proposals, which have the capacity to bring about the scenario they anticipate.

So Manzini and Jegou divided scenarios in three different categories, according to their motivation:

- **Policy-Orienting Scenarios (POSs)**: Visions of a context as it might appear in the presence of certain (economic, social, and cultural) dynamics and/or how should certain (economic, social, and cultural) policies be implemented. They support decision making in the face of complex and/or participatory institutional or industrial options. In general, several sets of POSs are usually developed, depending on the various policies that could be enacted. Visions developed before and during the 1970s can therefore be considered POSs.
- **Solution-Assessing Scenarios (SASs)**: Visions of a design proposal and its context, which tend to highlight their reciprocal interaction. They are a support instrument used in the assessment phase of a well-defined design hypothesis. In general, a single SAS is put forward as it corresponds to specific design proposals and their clearly defined contexts. SASs are similar to business-oriented scenarios as they refer to strategy and are focused more on context definition than on identification of a product or a service.
- **Design-Orienting Scenarios (DOSs)**: Manzini and Jegou (2000) clearly define scenarios as a tool involved within the design process. They are support tools used in design activities where different actors take part in the strategic orientation of choices. Scenarios are called "Design-Orienting" because they provide a framework for the design and realization of new products and product-service systems. DOSs are a way to systematically explore a panorama of alternative possibilities. They constitute "thinking material" to orient the strategic conversations between actors. In synthesis, DOSs aim to demonstrate a vision (*How will be the world if...?*), a clear motivation (*What the scenario is aiming at?*), and practicability (*The concrete actions that have to be taken in order to favor its implementation*).

Manzini and Jegou (2000) also identify a set of features for DOSs:

- Participation, to facilitate the convergence of different actors on a common vision that has to act as catalyst in the network building and in the partnership generation processes

- Microscale. It refers to the scale of the contexts of life, i.e., to a physical and socio-cultural space in which actions – performed by individuals or groups of individuals – take place. A DOS refers to systems manageable by designers. It presents a set of possible environments where a product or a service can be placed
- Feasible hypothesis, to present a set of possibilities based on technological trends or existent or predictable socio-economic opportunities
- Plurality, to identify alternative solutions and/or contexts in order to assess their economic, social, and environmental implications
- Visual expression. A DOS is delivered presenting visual images of coherent contexts and proposals, with the aim of giving synthetic and concrete suggestions of how they could be like

Following the DOSs codification, Simona Maschi (2002) proposed a classification of scenarios within design processes, as result of her doctoral research. According to Maschi, scenarios occur many times and for different purposes. She classifies scenarios as follows:

- Mission-based scenarios, used during the problem setting phase to motivate stakeholders and concentrate their attention on the same target.
- Context-based scenarios, considered as storytelling tools related to a set of alternative contexts. This type is similar to the explorative scenario Manzini and Jegou (2000) refer to.
- Scope-based scenarios, envisioning tools to develop a product or a service. They can be considered a further codification of explorative scenarios.
- Concept-based scenarios, to explore the concept of a product or a service. They are similar to the focused scenarios Manzini and Jegou (2000) refer to.
- Solution-based scenarios, to visualize a specific solution in term of product or system.

Design Scenario: A Multifaceted Tool

With the growing use of scenarios within the design practice and the related growing interest of researchers and academicians into further theoretical formalizations, the literature on this topic has flourished presenting a multifaceted role of such tools.

Carroll (2002) presents scenarios as tools in the Human-Machine Interaction field and he defines them as a family of techniques that describe a future system. With narrative descriptions of envisioned episodes of use, scenarios define operations to describe how people will use a system to accomplish work tasks and other activities. Therefore, the sue of scenarios is particularly relevant for the analysis and development of system requirements, the development of documentation and training activities, the release of educational and summative evaluations, especially for interface design and prototyping and software development and implementation.

While Irmak (2004) identifies the existence of different scenarios in design and states they help the designer to forecast probable conditions and turn these conditions into feedback for actions through the design process to successfully coping with any unwanted circumstances or adding value to the end-product, Evans and Somerville (2005) highlights the complexity of scenarios within the design process as important tools to inform, validate, and endorse design decisions. With the help of forecasting and scenario building techniques, design scenarios play a key role in providing firms with raw materials for decision making. Their task is to invent, discover, and communicate ways to advance the collective sense-making about what to do next, helping decision makers in the exploration of alternative futures. Evans and Somerville (2006) codify the phases to develop a scenario – (1) studying the facts of a situation, (2) selecting something that might happen, and (3) imagining the various ways for that development to occur and the sequence of events that might follow – which highlight how important presenting the probable context of use of a design idea is important in order to communicate the essence of the very design idea.

Klapwijk et al. (2006) sustain that the role of a scenario is to visualize future images of a new system and the relationship between user and system. In order to write a credible story, a basic understanding of the tasks to be performed by the user and some information about the possible context of use are needed.

Celaschi (2007) identifies scenarios of one or more possible futures as the results of a metadesign practice delivered in the form of storytelling. They aim at defining the trajectories of innovation that need to be conceptualized at the stage of product development. Scenarios are generally elaborated by visual maps, which create a sort of topographical representation of innovation that, through the interpretation of strong and weak signals, allows to trace the trajectories of the project. The design of a new product occurs coherently with such trajectories. The chosen scenario – and therefore the chosen trajectory – nests the concepts that may be developed in a synthesis phase. So, *"concepts explicit the scenario in an authentic designerly way and are useful to delineate it. A connection between scenario and concepts is noticeable, where both parts complement and enhance each other. By the end of the synthesis phase, concepts are evaluated and the most reasonable ones are chosen for implementation in the next phase"* (Celaschi and Franzato 2012, p. 122). Within the activity of an organization, scenarios contribute to its strategic development delivering products or services that are consistent with the organization's identity.

Merholz et al. (2008) agree on design scenarios being both strategic tools and visualization tools. They are stories purposefully diverse that can help the business to face a set of possible futures. Designers represent these tangible futures through different tools: posters, concept videos, prototypes, and more.

Finally, it is evident how design scenarios can assume different functions, beyond their mere role of visualization tool for possible alternatives of future or joint between a metadesign phase and the design one. Therefore, it is not possible to identifying a unique method for scenario building or a univocal position and purpose for them within the design process.

In the following paragraphs, cases from four specific design-oriented sectors – automotive, electronics and home appliances, and fashion – will be presented. Because of the intrinsic characteristics of their products and their design processes, those industries have been able to codify the most representative applications of scenario development, operative tools, and outputs for anticipation. In particular, cases will analyze the approach to anticipation through scenarios, the process of scenario development, and the final outcome along the specific supply chains.

The empirical analysis of cases allows to develop a reading model that codifies how, in design-oriented sectors, scenarios can be materialized using a wide range of tools, intangible (i.e., design fictions and videos) or tangible (prototypes), in relation to the specificities and needs of the different moment within the design process. In the first case, the materialization of scenarios is more evocative and it uses a set of visualization tools focused not on the functional aspects of a product or service, but on a possible environment or a complex system. Scenarios, as contextual visualization tool, are generally used in the front-end of the design process, where they are useful to engage people or for representing changes in social paradigms or lifestyles. In the case of prototypes, the representation of scenarios turns into a narrative story or fictional depiction of a product. Prototypes express an approximation of the future that is a consolidation of inspiration (Bell et al. 2013) and often presents formal, tangible, or functional innovation.

Figure 1 represents the outputs, as design tools along a standard design process, which are materialized through a scenario-building activity in the four sectors analyzed. This reading model also highlights the specific cases considered for each sector as best practices that allowed to elaborate such map. Therefore Fig. 1. serves as roadmap for the next paragraphs. In the case of fashion, the reading is developed without the use of a specific case study. Instead, the dedicated paragraph refers to the

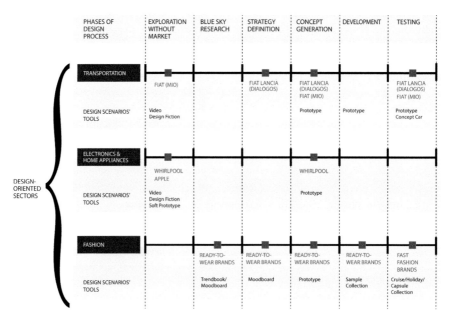

Fig. 1 Map of design scenarios' tools at different stages of the design process (Source: Authors)

practice of trend research professionals – bureau de style and trend agencies – which, for the purpose of this discussion, can be considered similar for all of them, and to the phases of the design process of the Ready-to-Wear system (Saviolo and Testa 2000) first, and the fast-fashion system (Hines and Bruce 2001; Cietta 2008) later – which are, respectively, the same for all the companies adopting one of these models – to explain the articulation of the tools for anticipation and their value in the fashion sector. For this reason, Fig. 1. does not mention any specific case study.

Automotive and Anticipation: The Role of Concept Cars

Historically, pioneering examples of design-orienting scenarios are offered within the automotive sector. Indeed, since the 1930s concept cars and dream cars were the materialization of possible future scenarios. Even if they were never commercialized, those tangible visions created a path towards a possible evolution of a car, or the occasion for discussing the future that consequently triggered questions about the present. Allowing imagination to make a leap in time towards a distant tomorrow, nowadays dream cars represent a solid base for experimenting visions (Celi 2015).

The analysis of dream cars and concept cars suggests how a vision of a possible future can be materialized and represented through an object. One of the most interesting examples is the *Abarth Record*, developed by Pininfarina, in 1960. It is interesting to see how social paradigms are reflected in a material object: the streamlined and light *Abarth* and its aluminum-bodied record-winning prototype perfectly represented the speed obsession of the late 1950s/early 1960s.

Another example is the *AMC Amitron*, developed by American Motors Corporations and Gulton Industries in 1967. More than a dream car, it can be considered a study about the mobility trend imagined for the 1970s which emphasized the individual freedom – craved as essential value during the second half of the 1960s – into a small two-seats car.

In the 1990s, FIAT proposed different activities for creating new future scenarios, both in terms of educational programs – such as the ADUS-Advanced Design University Stage – and projects for developing dream and concept car (Crea 2015). One of the most well-known cases is *Dialogos*, developed by FIAT Lancia, which offers an articulated and rich scenario building process.

The project, developed by Global Business Network and FIAT Lancia internal developers, started in 1995 as business-oriented scenario and, after stakeholders' approval, it became a prototype presented in 1998.

In fact, the scenario building process consisted in three phases. The first phase, started in 1995, aimed to identify some possible opportunities and trends in the automotive sectors for the 2000s. The idea was to develop a set of trajectories of innovation and to evaluate the business risks related to each of them. After the application of GBN model – as Schwartz (1991) discussed, GBN model develops the following phases: (1) Focusing the problem, (2) Identifying key forces and trends, (3) Classification of forces, (4) Positioning for importance or uncertainty factors, (5) Selecting the logics of scenario, (6) Consolidate the alternatives, (7)

Scenarios Review, (8) Exploring the implications, and (9) Communication.) –, some of the most profitable trajectories were chosen resulting into three macro-scenarios: (1) "*My Group_Fragmentation and Segmentation,*" focused on the growth of the "individualistic culture" implying ideas such as possible customization, full-optional vehicles, and modularity; (2) "*My links_Infocar,*" related to the development of new technologies and on the Internet accessibility, implying the idea of car-to-car and car-to-city communication; (3) "*My life_The life quality,*" related to the production chain and the possibility to create more customizable and flexible low-cost cars. The analysis of the aforementioned macroscenarios highlighted a set of themes, then considered as possible briefs for developing new product concepts. Themes included the use of real-time data and communication while driving a vehicle, the development of modular cars, the idea of mobility for all, and the idea of car-to-car connection.

Each trajectory of innovation was then examined by a team of engineers from Production department and Technical department to evaluate functionality – as impact on production chain and profitability – and defendability – as competitive advantage – according to the company's evaluation coefficients.

The results were presented to the management through a 2×2 matrix including both the most disruptive and the most traditional opportunities: the modular car and the development of a leasing model were ranked with high coefficient of defendability and functionality but as less disruptive; the car self-setting according to the driver's needs was ranked with low coefficient of defendability and functionality but based on a disruptive idea.

After a further evaluation based on the company's know-how and strategic interests, managers selected the requirements for the new concept car starting from which FIAT Design Center developed three different concepts: *Agorà*, *Arca*, and *Tikal*. After the concepts' presentation, the CEO of Lancia asked for merging *Agorà* and *Arca* characteristics. This led to the development of *Dialogos*, later materialized in a prototype presented in 1999. Finally, the *Dialogos* concept was deeply changed by FIAT Engineering Department and worked as base for the *Lancia Thesis* introduced on the market in 2001 (Manganaro 2015).

Scenarios were therefore used in different moments by different stakeholders: before the problem setting, to identify a possible interesting area, by planners with a socio/economic background; during the strategy definition, by planners, internal designers, and production and technical departments working together; and during the design process – especially in the concept design phase – by internal designers. Later, in 2009, FIAT developed Mio, the world's first crowdsourced car, based on the ideas and needs of the users, offering a different approach to the scenario building process (Saldanha et al. 2014). In the materialization phase, Mio offered two narrative representations to deliver the scenarios: a set of videos to envision mobility changes and users' future life and a prototype to foster functional and technical aspects.

FIAT *Mio* project started in August 2009. About that time, the company launched the project website inviting users to help creating a car for the future. FIAT made the commitment to realize the ideas of the users in a futuristic concept car. More than

17,000 participants from around the world submitted more than 11,000 ideas. Users were stimulated to think in broad terms about traffic and life onboard. The ideas were studied and interpreted by FIAT and resulted in a briefing to build *Mio* concept car presented during the press conference at Sao Paulo Auto Show in October 2010, as follows: "*A compact and agile car, comfortable and safe with innovative traffic solutions for big cities, a pollution-free engine and the capacity to receive person-alized updates, and changes in configuration, and having interface between car and user.*" Between January and February 2010, FIAT began the construction of FIAT *Mio*, documenting and showing the process on the web through the "Making of FIAT Mio" blog. The blog streamed short films about the car production, right from the FIAT factory in Betim, in the Brazilian state of Minas Gerais. People were also able to take part in many decisions, from car colors to doors configuration. The car final specifications were submitted under Creative Commons licenses, becoming free to everyone, including other car companies.

Therefore, the scenario building process aimed at understanding consumers' needs, at proposing new products to test people reactions, at identifying a strategic plan for future in consideration of the issues more interesting to consumers. Scenar-ios were used to materialize a future product and the related possible trends for the mobility field. Even if the building process was not well formalized, including data collection, analysis, and synthesis of inputs provided by users in a single solution, it led to two interesting categories of output: the first, related to functional and technical elements of the car, materialized in a prototype and the second one, focused on the environment where the car could have been used, materialized in a video.

Electronics and Home Appliances: The Relation Between Future Technology and Social Paradigms

Electronics and home appliances are another emblematic example of sectors using scenarios as tools for representing and materializing possible futures, both in tangi-ble and intangible ways.

In spite of their different market segmentations, technology and the evaluation of social paradigms and people's habits and behaviors are the common denominators and the elements that characterize the scenario building processes of those two fields.

The home appliances sector offers one of the first interesting cases of scenario materialized in a video with the movie "*1957. Vision of the Year 2000.*" Developed for the Czech Television, it represented possible changes in human life in the next 50 years: kitchen robots, products which help in keeping food fresh for at least 6 months, marble table as cooktop. The future environment was communicated using a plot and an actor plays the future user. The provocative potential of a disruptive vision where human will be supported or, in some case, replaced by machines is low because codes of behavior and stereotypes remain unchanged: the housewife is the one engaged in housework and members of a family have lunch together sitting at a table. However, narrative tools, such as design fiction and storytelling, are used to engaging the audience, communicating a possible environment, future products, and models of interaction.

In 1987 Apple Computer released a concept video for the *Knowledge Navigator*, a voice-based assistant combined with a touch-screen computer, in the form of a tablet, which was used by John Sculley in his keynote speech at Educom, the leading higher education conference.

Apple Marketing Department defined a brief focus on what students were doing in 1987 and also on a vision of the future of computing, considering the possibility to carry data research outside computer labs. For example, the video described a device able to access a database and use virtual assistant for searching information and planning events. Its development took 6 weeks including a 1-week research session on technologies, devices, and people's habits carried by Apple Advanced Technologies Group. Management approval covered three components: the concept of the science fiction video, the key technology list, and the script. The production, by The Kenwood Group, moved quickly from script to shooting without a full storyboard due to the short duration. They used Polaroid snapshots of the location, sketches of the screen, and video paint box, and even a wooden prototype of the notebook.

This kind of scenario was therefore used at the early stages of the design process as a tool to create a vision of the future internally shared by Apple's different departments and as a tool to communicate the vision to potential users and test their reaction. It was useful to investigate new paths of technological innovation – notions of iPad and Siri can be seen 25 years in advance. In fact, it spawned a lot of sequels at Apple's and several other companies started to produce similar tools as marketing materials to support the sale of computers.

Even if the story showed new functional aspects of technology products, nevertheless the vision assumed an unchanged social paradigm: PCs become notebooks but the user is still seen at home, seated at his desk.

Almost 15 years later, in 2001, Whirlpool Europe developed "*Project F: Fabric Care Futures*" aiming to anticipate the future of clothing care through the innovation of the traditional washing machine.

Led by the Global Consumer Design Team at Whirlpool, the applied research started looking into the expectations of consumers, through interviews, in particular focusing on ergonomics and use of the washing machine (Mangiarotti 2015). At the same time, Future Concept Lab – an Italian research institute specialized in strategic consulting services based on a sociological approach – was asked to delivere an analysis on domesticity in Europe. In this case, the scenario building process was not well formalized: it included different analysis, whose goal was to investigate new possible paths of innovation but also to create a common ground for all involved actors. At this level, the purpose was developing a map to guide the innovation covering topics such as the relationship between sensors and the domestic space, domestic rituals and interactions, fabric care and textiles of the future, and environmental and ecological issues. Scenario building was therefore immediately oriented by a desired change in social values and habits.

The collected data served as base for the next phase which involved three external design studies – Designkoop (Germany), Deepdesign (Italy), and Designraw (USA), and an internal team of six designers (Interaction Design Institute Ivrea 2003). Designers had 1 month to develop a set of concepts in relation to the aforementioned topics, through brainstorming of problems and potential solutions, discussions of options, and visualization of opportunities maps. These activities promoted the knowledge sharing and transfer between the different teams of designers involved. With an additional month, concepts were further developed with 3D models and virtual prototypes to be then presented to the Whirlpool management. Five projects were selected and requested to enter another phase of further development which led the materialization of physical prototypes. Final prototypes embodied different level of complexity and feasibility, nurturing the future innovation strategies at Whirlpool, and through a strong campaign they were communicated to the market, testing users' reactions, and positioning the company as a design innovator.

Fashion and Anticipation: Cultural Embodiment and Negotiation

A Design Perspective on Fashion Anticipation

In regard of the necessity and the ability to anticipate needs, desires, and configuration of new scenarios of use and behavior, fashion represents a distinctive case where not only the concept of anticipation takes on multiple meanings but also analytical and planning tools change in relation to the actors involved and the public to which it refers.

Fashion is part of what has been defined "new old economy" (Rauch 2001; Whitford 2005). It is a sector that produce goods with a high content of knowledge built up through specific processes and services and that turns in adding a high intangible value to its very products. In particular, fashion products have a hybrid nature that combines material functional properties and a symbolic dimension (Malossi 1998). Fashion is defined as "*the mold of the contemporary culture, in its ability to join in the dynamics between individual and society*" (Fiorani 2006, p. 8). The identity-making agency of fashion items enable individual to build, express, and represent their own identity and their belonging to specific cultural communities and groups within the contemporary society, shaping, at the same time, the very collective identity. "*Therefore, today Fashion, that has always been a multi-dimensional universe, is not just a change, a trend, the spirit of the times, the succession and combination of styles. It is not just a relation among classes. Fashion is the most complete expression of a post-modern industrial culture that find its way to be in the design process*" (Fiorani 2006, p. 7). Fashion aims at understanding the core values and meanings underlying the society where it is shaped and where it is a tool of self-expression and a tool for revealing cultural instances. Informing, and being informed by, cultures, fashion aims at producing products as much as possible close to the symbolic and cultural system it refers to, in order to be recognized as significant by individuals that are supposed to benefit from that products as users or consumers.

Therefore, the objective of fashion is not a change which is an end in itself and fashion's driver is not just the need of managing the programmed obsolescence of products.

Authors from Humanities read fashion innovation in relation to style (Barthes 1967; Davis 1985) and defined it as "distance from the past" and "distinction and exclusivity in the present."

Instead, a design-driven perspective defines a shift in the concept of anticipation in fashion, pushing the idea of fashion innovation as the ability of a product to be coherent with the context where it acts and familiar with its users' values and beliefs system.

Contemporary fashion also moves away from the predictive dimension of fashion forecasting that, according to Econometrics and Statistics principles, intends to measure the positive or negative change in the diffusion of a style or product.

In fact, contemporary fashion adopts the design-orienting perspective of possible, probable, and preferable futures (Manzini and Jegou 2000) looking for facilitating the fulfilment of a desirable future (Gharajedaghi 2011, pp. 134–157) which is conceptually consequential to the current present as its cultural evolution. The idea of future is, on one hand, extremely condensed and encapsulating in the immanent dimension of *hic et nunc* that fashion products embody and, on the other, timelessly expanded in the observation of the constant evolution of cultural trajectories.

This results in the blurring of past, present, and future, and it leads to the converge of products originally referring to different semantic contexts and designed for different markets.

Contents of Fashion Anticipation

The intrinsic ability of fashion to express the *Zeitgeist* (Vinken 2005) – the "spirit of the times," as symbolic and cultural meanings relevant at a certain age within a certain social group – has not only defined the characteristics of fashion items and a specific organizational model to manage the complexity of design, distribution, and communication activities – traditionally, the Ready-to-Wear system (Saviolo and Testa 2000) – but it has also shaped an original research methodology to monitor and interpret evolutionary trajectories of cultural values and meanings and to design visions of the contemporary culture.

Through the so-called trend research, the fashion design practice produces specific tools – the trend books – that materialize scenarios of future(s) to orient the design process along its entire flow at different stages of the product lifecycle management.

To do so, trend books represent a context, the early signs announcing its evolution, the many options of a desirable context-to-be.

At the beginning of the design process, a qualitative contextual research is conducted across all the tangible and intangible cultural contexts, without geographical or marketing limitations, and based on codified and un-codified sources. It typically focuses on (1) socio-political systems – political movements, cultural mainstream and underground systems, consumption phenomena, etc. – in relation to which it is possible to define the evolution of values and behaviors in collective imagination; (2) on core cultural industries (Hesmondhalgh 2007) – art, literature, film industry, music industry, entertainment industry, etc. – which produce symbolic and experiential level contents; (3) consumption goods' industries – architecture, design, furniture, arts and crafts, graphic design, publishing industry, automotive, the very fashion, food, beauty, etc. – that define aesthetic and perceptive evolutions and innovations. Connections, overlapping, logical sequences, and convergences of all these contents draft waves of evolution of the elements that express the "spirit of the times," suggesting co-existence, mutual exclusions or polarities based on social coherence, principle of identification, aesthetic coherence, or visual fit.

Trend researchers process all gathered information and data and, through an abductive sense-making processes, release them into periodical reports – the so-called trend books – that precipitate the most current relevant characteristics of the product-to-be into material evidences.

In fact, trend books are characterized by a strong visual dimension. They are designed through the use of evocative images that are not intended to be references of phenomena that are observed but better, using metaphorical and allegorical representation and narrative techniques, to enable cognitive processes linking suggested product's soft qualities, such as colors, textures, finishing, and shapes, to concepts emerged as relevant. Anchorage and objectification processes (Moscovici 2005) allow taming "the unknown" and balancing it with "the known," stressing their natural link. The use of historical and cultural stratified elements allows avoiding cognitive dissonance and noise and supporting the acceptance of the anticipatory view. In particular, evocative images are composed into one or more moodboards, each referring to one specific conceptual evocation or expressing one of the many interpretation of a conceptual idea relevant within the search context of reference.

So, trend books, as visual encyclopedia, cover a broad research spectrum. The continuing and continuous research they imply aim at tracking the evolutionary paths of our cultures and showing the interdependencies among different periods, according to a limitless time perspective of fashion research. Moreover, as trend books offer creative contents – inspirational themes, moods, colors, finishing, materials, details, product references, historical stylistic references, etc. – ready to be used into the design practice, they are a sort of accelerators of innovation. In fact, while the research activity that they require crosses along past, present, and future, they focus on the "here and now" that can orient the decision about a product at the early stage of its creation.

From Trend Books to Sample Collection: The Many Ways to Orient Fashion Future(s)

Trend research's breadth and continuity have progressively required the specialization of professionals dedicated to it, starting from the 1980s. So, while internal designers have been in charge of developing a more product-oriented research already tailored towards the specificities of their brands and markets, bureau de style and trend agencies, as external consultants, have institutionalized such practice, nurturing a prosperous market which, also thanks to digital tools, annual, demi-annual, and monthly reports, getting closer to the moment of the release of a new product, offer almost real-time research updates.

The disciplinary expertise of research teams at such consultancy bodies and the focus and market positioning of their research products span across different level of conceptualization and theoretical ability. In general, trend books and moodboards are meant to serve as initial inputs for designers to orient a second phase of research, which will start from credible and authoritative references offered by the extensive professional research included in the trend books and which could not be afforded by a single company or a free-lance designer, for economic and time reasons. In fact, such products represent a sort of extension of the early design research stage starting from which designers will develop their own and unique further perspective, making choices among the many options proposed by the original broad spectrum trend research.

Designers using trend books will activate a sort of funneling selection process of ideas and sources, and they will finally detail concepts and relevant ideas of a product or collection into more specific moodboards to orient the next phases of product development. At this stage, moodboards work as creative briefs that are shared at different level of the creative department to transfer contents – from creative directors to designers' team – but, above all, to align the different department to the same vision of future. At the beginning of a new fashion season or cycle, heads of design, Merchandising, Product Development, Marketing, and Communication departments meet and share, assimilate, and agree on the relevancy of main concepts that will guide all the specific activities that each department will carry to support the development and commercialization of the new product/collection.

While, as said, fashion products need to be relevant to the currently upcoming culture, fashion production, communication, and distribution need to start 1 year in advance, given the characteristics of the programmed fashion cycle which is typical of the ready-to-wear model (Saviolo and Testa 2000) – which can still be used as the main general model to discuss processes and activities within the fashion sector, even in its recent development into alternative systems such as fast-fashion and digital fashion.

The pressure for reducing errors in creative and financial investments and, therefore, economic loss is high. After the research phase, along the whole product development, there is the need for a continuing negotiation among the different stakeholders involved. A first prototype allows designers to see for the first time their ideas materialized into a tangible product and to refine choices for silhouette, proportions, cuts, and details. Adjustments are applied until designs are perfected, requiring the realization of a number of prototypes that varies. Final prototype is checked and approved both by designer, merchandiser, and product manager in order to align creative instances, line planning issues, and production planning in order to define, as soon as possible, all the elements related to patternmaking, sourcing, and collection variety planning.

The next phase, in fact, regards the production of a sample collection which will be used on the catwalks to launch, 6 months in advance, the new products. Sample collection and catwalks allow fashion companies to present the product first of all to professionals such as buyers and media and to final consumer, thanks to the communication campaigns and resonance on media, before it actually exists on the market.

Contemporaneously, sample collections are used in showroom to sell the collection to buyers that select they preferred styles that will be then delivered, months later, to retailers. This is the moment where creative and production departments meet the business-to-business market to collect their feedback on the collection and, if needed or required, to possibly adjust the stylistic choices and, therefore, realign the whole production chain. Based on the approval from media and approval from retailers – quantitatively measured with the orders collected during the business-to-business sale campaign – the final selection of items is done and production is then started.

Also, the product preview offered to the final consumer works as educating process for the potential consumer, which is informed about what he/she will find 6 months later in the stores so that he/she can start dreaming and planning to buy and wear that product.

The whole process is oriented, de facto, to creating agreement among the stakeholders around an idea in order to fine-tuning it, to orienting the final decision, and to reducing the risk of failing that is, in other words, the risk of producing and releasing on the market the wrong product, a product that is not recognized as the right and up/to-date identity making tool by the final consumer.

With the advent of the fast-fashion model (Hines and Bruce 2001; Cietta 2008) and the resulting compression of the whole fashion cycle, the Ready-to-Wear calendar has been articulated into multiple product launches, and the main collection has been anticipated by cruise and/or holiday collections and/or multiple capsule collection, released with different timing before the main one. The idea is to propose small group of items dedicated to specific occasions – and so implying specific weather conditions and functional and stylistic needs – that can present some ideas of the main collections in advance to test the level of appreciation and acceptance from the market and therefore to offer a further feedback for orienting the decision on the main collection, which will be presented later.

We move from a continuing research process that ends into quick innovation tools to a cyclical development process that implies the progression of a series of pilot products along a process of gradual innovation. The dialectic relation between past, present, and future is translated in another specific system of codification of the product characteristics that sees (1) the sedimentation of recurrent elements over time periods, (2) the reiteration of certain symbols and icons, and (3) the codification of what will be then materialized into permanent stylistic codes of a fashion products. Permanent stylistic codes will be stay valid across different ages, but they are actualized in the contemporaneity through seasonal stylistic codes, in order to balance, as previously mentioned, "know" and "unknown," and make future fashion contents current and relevant to its communities of reference. This is another emblematic way to orient the future within the fashion sector.

Ending Summary

Dealing with many different disciplines, design is able to mediate among disciplines (Celaschi 2008) – such as art, engineering, economics, and humanistic sciences – and to communicate with several stakeholders, occupying a dialectical space between the world that is and the world that could be. To materialize and communicate possible futures, design adopts scenarios as the most effective tool. Scenarios are used in different ways and with different targets and outputs to support the design-driven innovation process, to create a sharing vocabulary among the stakeholders involved in a project and to communicate the trajectories of innovation and the opportunities related to a product or a service. The strategic dimension of scenarios is defined as their capability (1) to present a set of alternative futures, to support and orient the decision-making process, (2) to involve all the actors in the same process through the use of a common language, and (3) to stimulate a convergence towards the same option, and the possibility to be used at different stages of the design process and with different purposes in the same process. Therefore, their strategic dimension transforms the very scenarios in design-oriented tools.

The present chapter offers a reading of the different objectives, functions, and outputs of scenarios along a design process, thanks to the reading of different case studies from different design-oriented fields, highlighting convergences and differences due to context, methodological path, and applications. In particular, the proposed reading model highlights stakeholders, approaches, and tools to develop the different typologies of scenarios, offering a wide perspective on the scenarios role within the design practice. Therefore, the submission potentially represents an updated overview on the practice of anticipation within the design process, connecting theory and practices with a methodological model that can support the design-driven innovation processes.

References

Barthes, R. (1967). *The fashion system*. Berkeley: University of California Press.
Bell, F., Fletcher, G., Greenhill, A., & Griffiths, M. (2013). Science fiction prototypes: Visionary technology narratives between futures. *Futures, 50*, 5–14.
Bhandari, A., & Verma, R. (2013). *Strategic management: A conceptual framework*. New Delhi: McGraw Hill.
Bishop, P., Hines, A., & Collins, T. (2007). The current state of scenario development. *Foresight, 9*(1), 5–25.
Carrol, J. M. (2002). Becoming social: Expanding scenario-based approaches in HCI. *Behaviour & Information Technology, 15*(4), 266–275.

Celaschi, F. (2007). Dentro al progetto: appunti di merceologia contemporanea. In A. Deserti & F. Celaschi (Eds.), *Design e Innovazione. Strumenti e pratiche per la ricerca applicata* (pp. 1–50). Roma: Carocci Editore. (Italian Edition only).

Celaschi, F. (2008). Il design come mediatoretrasaperi. In C. Germak (a cura di), *Uomo al centro del progetto* (pp. 40–52).Torino: Umberto Allemandi & C. (Italian Edition only).

Celaschi, F., & Franzato, C. (2012). Design of organizational innovation scenarios, results of an action-research within a security doors company. Projecting design 2012, global design bridge, CUMULUS conference, School of Design Duoc UC, Santiago (Chile). http://www.flaviano celaschi.it/wp-content/uploads/2013/01/Design-of-organizational-innovation-scenarios_-Results-of-an-action-research-within-a-security-doors-company1.pdf. Accessed 13 May 2016.

Celi, M. (2015). *Advanced design cultures, long terms perspective and continuous innovation.* Cham: Springer International Publishing.

Cietta, E. (2008). *La rivoluzione del fast fashion. Strategie e modelli organizzativi per competere nelle industrie ibride.* Milano: Franco Angeli. (Italian Edition only).

Crea, N. (2015). Advanced transportation design. In M. Celi (Ed.), *Advanced design cultures, long terms perspective and continuous innovation* (pp. 99–107). Cham: Springer International Publishing.

Davis, F. (1985). Clothing and fashion as communication. In M. R. Solomon (Ed.), *The psychology of fashion* (pp. 15–27). Lexington: D.C. Heat/Lexington Books.

De Jouvenel, B. (1967). *The art of conjecture.* New York: Basic Books.

Dieffenbach, J. (1983). Corporate environmental analysis in large US corporations. *Long Range Planning, 16*(3), 107–116.

Evans, M., & Somerville, S. (2005). Designing tomorrow: A methodology for future orientated product design. Global Chinese industrial design conference 2005, Chang Gung University, Taiwan, Nov 2005. http://www.academia.edu/203838/Evans_M_and_Sommerville_S_2005_Designing_Tomorrow_A_Methodology_for_Future_Orientated_Product_Design._Global_Chinese_Industrial_Design_Conference_2005_Chang_Gung_University_Taiwan_November_2005. Accessed 10 Sept 2016.

Evans, M., & Somerville, S. (2006). Educating the future: Embedding future thinking in the design curriculum. Engineering and product design education conference, 7–8 Sept 2006, Salzburg University of Applied Sciences, Salzburg. https://www.researchgate.net/publication/290794443_Educating_the_future_Embedding_futures_thinking_in_the_design_curriculum. Accessed 10 Sept 2016.

Fahey, L., & Randall, R. M. (1998). *Learning from the future: Competitive foresight scenarios.* New York: Wiley.

Fiorani, E. (2006). *Moda, corpo, immaginario.* Milano: Edizioni POLI.design. (Italian Edition only).

Gero, J. S., & Kannengiesser, U. (2004). The situated function-behaviour-structure framework. *Design Studies, 25*(4), 373–391.

Gero, J. S., & Kannengiesser, U. (2006). A function-behaviour-structur ontology of processes. In *Design computing and cognition '06* (pp. 407–422). Berlin: Springer.

Gharajedaghi, J. (2011). *Systems thinking: Managing chaos and complexity: A platform for designing business architecture* (3rd ed.). Burlington: Morgan Kaufmann.

Hamel, G., & Prahalad, C. K. (2000). Competing for the future. *Harvard Business Review, 3*, 121–126.

Hesmondhalgh, D. (2007). *The cultural industries.* London: Sage.

Hines, T., & Bruce, M. (2001). *Fashion marketing. Contemporary issues.* Oxford: Elsevier.

Interaction Design Institute Ivrea. (2003). Design for future needs process of project F and new domesticity. Project report http://projectsfinal.interactionivrea.org/2001-2002/DFFN-Design%20Future%20Needs%202001-2002/communication%20material/DFFN_process_WP_images.pdf. Accessed 25 May 2016.

Irmak, O. (2004). Applying the future studies approach to design. In Proceedings of EAD 06, 6th international conference of the European Academy of Design. http://ead.verhaag.net/fullpapers/ead06_id233_2.pdf. Accessed 8 July 2016.

Khan, H., & Wiener, A. J. (1967). *The year 2000: A framework for speculation on the next thirty-five years*. New York: MacMillan.

Klapwijk, R., Knot, M., Quist, J., & Vergragt, P. J. (2006). Using design orienting scenarios to analyze the interaction between technology, behavior and environment in the SusHouse project. In P.-P. Verbeek & A. Slob (Eds.), *User behavior and technology development: Shaping sustainable relations between consumers and techno* (pp. 241–252). Dordrecht: Springer.

Malaska, P., & Virtanen, I. (2005). Theory of futuribles and historiables. *Futura, 2*(5), 10–28.

Malossi, G. (Ed.). (1998). *Il motore della moda. Spettacolo, identità, design, economia: come l'industria produce ricchezza attraverso la moda*. Firenze: The Monacelli Press. (Italian Edition only).

Manganaro, A. (2015). Dialogos, il futuro mai arrivato. Repubblica Motori, Online article. http://www.repubblica.it/motori/sezioni/classic-cars/2015/01/15/news/lancia_dialogos_il_futuro_mai_arrivato-104858595/. Accessed 25 May 2016.

Mangiarotti, R. (2015). Advance design for product. In *Advanced design cultures, long terms perspective and continuous innovation* (pp. 109–120). Cham: Springer International Publishing.

Manzini, E., & Jegou, F., (2000). *The construction of design-orienting scenarios*. SusHouse project final report, Faculty of technology, policy and management. Delft University.

Maschi, S. (2002). *Scenarios within design processes: A theoretical framework to support the production of visually-based cognitive models of systems of products, services, and stakeholder*. Ph.d. thesis, Milano: Politecnico di Milano, Design Department.

Masini, E. B. (1973). *Why future studies?* London: Grey Seal.

Merholz, P., Wilkens, T., Schauer, B., & Verba, D. (2008). *Subject to change: Creating great products & services for an uncertain world: Adaptive path on design*. Sebastopol: O'Reilly Media.

Moscovici, S. (2005). *Rappresentazioni sociali*. Bologna: Il Mulino Introduzioni. (Extract from Farr, R. M., & Moscovici, S. (Eds.). (1989). *Rappresentazioni sociali* (pp. 23–94). Bologna: Il Mulino. Italian translation).

Rauch, J. (2001). The new old economy: Oil, computers and the reinvention of the Earth. *The Atlantic Monthly, 297*(1), 35–49.

Saldanha, F. P., Cohendet, P., & Pozzebon, M. (2014). Challenging the stage-gate model in crowdsourcing: The case of FIAT Mio in Brazil. *Technology Innovation Management Review, 4*(9), 28–35.

Saviolo, S., & Testa, S. (Eds.). (2000). *Le imprese del sistema moda: il management al servizio della creatività*. Milano: ETAS. (English Edition: Testa, S., & Saviolo, S. (2002). *Strategic management in the fashion companies*. Milan: ETAS).

Schön, D. (1983). *The Reflective Practitioner: How Professionals Think in Action*. London: Temple Smith.

Schwartz, P. (1991). *The art of the long view: Planning for the future in an uncertain world*. New York: Currency Doubleday.

Smithers, T. (2002). Synthesis in design. In J. S. Gero (Ed.), *Artificial intelligence in design* (pp. 3–24). Dordrecht: Kluwer.

Vinken, B. (2005). *Fashion zeitgeist: Trends and cycles in the fashion system*. Oxford: Berg Publisher.

Whitford, J. (2005). *The new old economy. Networks, institutions and the organizational transformation of American manufacturing*. New York: Oxford University Press.

Architecture as Anticipation: The Anticipatory Illumination of Drawing

40

Nathaniel Coleman

Contents

Abstract

Although architectural drawing tends to be thought of as either a technical necessity in relation to organizing the labor required to construct buildings or as though decorative, akin to alluring pictures in a gallery, its main task is anticipatory. Architectural drawings are prefigurative, or, as is argued in this chapter, ought to be. When the anticipatory illumination of architectural drawing is recuperated, the division of labor between architecture, as either brainwork or managerial, and building as physical exertion, is problematized. Returning drawing in architecture to its prefigurative – anticipatory – vocation articulates a method for improving the results of the built environment: technically, emotionally, and artistically.

Keywords

Analogue · Architecture · Design, Anticipatory illumination · Digital · *Disegno* · Drawing · Ernst bloch · Imagination · Not yet · Paul ricoeur

N. Coleman (✉)
School of Architecture, Planning and Landscape, Newcastle University, Newcastle upon Tyne, UK
e-mail: nathaniel.coleman@ncl.ac.uk

Introduction

> Architectural drawings are representations that facilitate the understanding of buildings, conditions, processes, and events in human world-making, in other words they are the interactive and generative mapping of architectural cosmopoiesis. (Marco Frascari 2011)

> The passage from the mental conception to the built form involves a double translation therefore: first from the architect's mind to the graphic presentation initially his own-and secondly, from the drawing to the building, through the collaboration of those craftsmen who, like Alberti's carpenter, would act as his 'hands.' (Joseph Rykwert 1998)

> Drawing in architecture is not done after nature, but prior to construction; it is not so much produced by reflection on the reality outside the drawing, as productive of a reality that will end up outside the drawing. The logic of classical realism is stood on its head, and it is through this inversion that architectural drawing has obtained an enormous and largely unacknowledged generative power: by stealth. (Robin Evans 1997)

The above quotes, drawn from architectural theorists' reflections on drawing, set the stage for the discussion that follows, in which architectural design, more properly *drawing*, which is closer – in spirit at least – to the Italian word *disegno*, is considered as a form of *anticipatory illumination* (of which MORE shortly). The significance of the distinction between *drawing* and *design* lies in the difference between the physical act of *drawing*, as opposed to the object it produces, a *design*. In Italian, *disegno* (I design) is the first person singular form of the verb *disegnare* (to design), whereas the newer *il design* is a noun. As suggested above, while both are descriptors, the emphasis here – as in the Italian verb *disegnare* – is on the action of drawing, as opposed to a design, which is a record of the action. Developing this distinction somewhat further, before *il design* entered use in Italian, the activities of the architect it is meant to convey were described by *progettare* (to design, plan, project, devise, lay, meditate). In terms of the topic of *anticipation*, or the *anticipatory illumination of architectural drawing*, in relation to *disegno*, *progettare* includes "meditation," whereas *disegnare* does not, signifying rather the naming of something, as opposed to contemplation, or reverie. Among the other words associated with designing in Italian, which becomes *la progettazione* when describing the result of architectural activity, only *progettare* includes the speculative character of meditation, which also brings it within the realm of *theory* (Greek *theoria*: view, contemplation, speculation).

This foray into other languages has a double value. On the one hand, it facilitates a degree of clarifying estrangement from the commonplace mental concepts designated by the English words "design," "designer," and "designs," which suggest problem solving in one direction, and a contractual document, or picture, in the sense of referring to something elsewhere, or absent, rather than to itself as results of a now concluded, suspended, or interrupted process. On the other, consideration of disegnare, etc. recollects the origins of architectural practice, at least in the West, with 1st c. BC Roman architect Vitruvius, many of whose insights derive from Ancient Greece, and Renaissance architect and theorist Leon Battista Alberti (1404–1472), who was indebted to Vitruvius, upon whose shared foundation the architectural curriculum, including history, theory, and practice, continues to be largely constructed.

As introduced above, *the Italian word disegno* means "drawing," but Renaissance use, especially by Giorgio Vasari (1511–1574) (artist, architect, and chronicler of artists lives and works), conflates the act of drawing (making) with the process of design (imagining) and the outcome of both (the work of art) (for Vasari's conceptions of disegno see, Vasari 1965; see also, Jacobs 2002). As a concept, then, *disegno* suggests that an artist designs by drawing ideas out from his or her imagination (which is itself more process than content), by committing them to paper or other media. In his study on Michelangelo, English writer and painter Adrian Stokes (1902–1972) offered an explanation of *disegno* that relates to the human frame to architecture and so is also helpful in locating anticipation in drawings as directly related to bodies, buildings, and worlds to come.

> Many eminent Florentine painters and sculptors of the fifteenth, sixteenth, and even the seventeenth centuries were also architects. Vasari, himself an architect-painter, allows no fundamental difference between the visual arts. The root of all is what he calls *disegno* or drawing; but drawing in the sense of a power to elicit structure, to compose, to bind, to order, to harmonize differences, to proportion weight, to build. No one will deny that the basis for this art was a thorough advertence to the human frame, to the nude, to the bony structure, the balance, the protuberances, the cavities, the hair; a corpus of applied knowledge [...] and whereas entire commitment to the human proportions was rarely possible in practice, *disegno*, generally speaking, betrays its architectural root, the influence of houses in which men live. (Stokes 1978)

Stokes' assertion that *disegno* conjoins all of the arts, with reference to bodies, rooted in architecture – specifically, the home, which for him includes womb and house – suggests that the world-making discussion of drawing as anticipatory illumination developed here could be extended to all of the arts. Nevertheless, architecture is the focus, though anticipation could be doubled by specifying that the architecture of interest here is the species prefigured by drawing extending only to the sort that is world-making, on account of anticipating bodies, as its subject and reference simultaneously.

Drawing and Anticipatory Illumination

In the preceding, as presaged by the subtitle of this chapter, the belief that *all* architectural drawing encompasses anticipatory illumination might require correction. Importantly, most of what goes on under the star of architecture, at least since the dawn of the twentieth century, is a sort of reordering at best and a reproduction at worst. Arguably, explanation of this resides in the conditions of modernism in architecture, which, from the outset, took shape, and continues to, within a constellation of objectives provided by myths of progress and autonomy of will, despite the reformist rhetoric associated with modernist architects. The conceptual affiliations of modernist architecture with Taylorist and Fordist ideologies, more so than any putative utopianism, are sources of the dystopian turn evident almost everywhere in the city of modern architecture and its outskirts (for discussions on "Modernism" in architecture, and the "dystopian turn," see Coleman 2007; for general discussions of modernism in architecture, see Coleman 2005; Curtis 1996; Frampton 2007; Giedion 1982 [1941]; Guillén 2005; Will 2006).

Doubly disconnected from the sources of the greatest influence on their work, most architects are left with no vocation other than decorating capital, or at least smoothing the wheels of consumption, in technically functional, spectacular, or novel works of architecture obsessed with, and dictated by, exchange, rather than use, the everyday or individual and social experience. As Italian architectural historian Manfredo Tafuri (1935–1993) put it:

> The decline of social utopianism confirmed ideology's surrender to the politics of things created by the laws of profit. Architectural ideology, in both its artistic and urban forms, was left with the utopia of form as a project for recuperating the human Totality in the ideal Synthesis, as a way of mastering Disorder through Order. (Tafuri 2000)

Left with little more than forms without utopia, better architects dream continuously of architecture's autonomy as the promise of disciplinary redemption, whereas lesser ones exaggerate conformity in service to the so-called "real." Both, though, are futile attempts at escape from what German philosopher Peter Sloterdijk calls the "world interior of capital." If "autonomy" and "conformity" stake out the extreme edges of attempts to contend with reality, outside of the totality of the *no alternative* condition that both presume, nontrivial drawing cracks through to a third possibility, deploying anticipatory illumination as simultaneously the initial figuration of alternatives by way of their prefiguration. If the preceding is accepted, before continuing, it is necessary at this point to identify which architectural drawings might constitute anticipatory illumination, including how and why. In his introduction to a collection of German philosopher Ernst Bloch's (1885–1977) writing he contributed to compiling and translating, Jack Zipes offers a helpful outline of "anticipatory illumination":

> Obviously not all of literature and art is Utopian. The Utopian quality of a work of art is determined by its *Vor-Schein* or anticipatory illumination. The anticipatory illumination is an image, a constellation, a configuration closely tied to the concrete Utopias that are lit up on the frontal margins of reality and illuminate the possibilities for rearranging social and political relations so that they engender *Heimat*, Bloch's word for the home that we have all sensed but have never experienced or known. It is *Heimat* as utopia – and here Bloch specifically reutilizes a Nazi term – that determines the truth-content of a work of art, and it is through the anticipatory illumination of the work of art that we are able to gain a sense of truth in reality. (Zipes 1988)

In his transposition of one of Bloch's key ideas, alongside "hope," "utopia," the "real possible," and the "not-yet," Zipes highlights what "anticipatory illumination" is and which sorts of work will produce it. Most importantly, "anticipatory illumination" is a figuration that is concretely utopian, inasmuch as it reveals "possibilities for rearranging social and political relations" accessible only at the limit edges "of reality." Equally important, if a work does not "engender" the possibility of "home," of homecoming (belonging, disalienation), and of a sort longed for but unknown, it will not constitute anticipatory illumination. As described by Zipes, this would constitute the "truth-content of a work." Positioning Bloch's concept even closer to the act of drawing, Clive Cazeaux notes that an alternative to Zipes' translations defines *Vor-Schein* as "preappearance," which suggests precisely the sort of anticipation of "new alternative futures" that nontrivial architectural drawing prefigures (Cazeaux 2000). In this way, although drawings are concrete figurations, they are incomplete, fragments in one sense only, inasmuch translation from drawing to building achieves the possible wholeness "fragment" suggests, by completing the process. In this regard, Bloch asserted: "All artistic and religious anticipatory illumination is concrete only to the degree and measure that the fragmentary ultimately provides the level and the material for this, to constitute itself as the anticipatory illumination" (Bloch 1988a, p. 161).

The circulatory character of the Bloch quote directly above is suggestive of his understanding of the relation between *hope* and *utopia* but also of the idea of *anticipation* proposed here. Ultimately, realization is only ever partial, less fragmentary than incomplete. While this inevitability is often deployed as justification for surrendering desire – hope – for alternatives, as Bloch suggests above, this is precisely this incompleteness that motivates continuous hope and desire for, or, as characterized here, anticipatory illumination of alternatives. In short, anticipation is a *machine* for producing subsequent anticipation. Absolute achievement of the anticipated would be the equivalent of death (of totality, finality, *the* absolute).

As developed in this chapter, "utopia," "hope," and "anticipation" form a mutually supportive triad, in which "utopia" is the (never fully achieved) goal, or aim; "hope" is the desire for this; and "anticipatory illumination" is the process by which utopia is prefigured, according to the motivations of hope, which makes anticipation into the first steps for moving "hope" (desire) toward realization ("utopia"). Accordingly, "anticipation" is a process, rather than a result akin to Bloch's assertion that "truth is not the portrayal of facts, but of processes. Truth is ultimately the demonstration of tendency and latency of what has not yet developed and needs its agent" (Bloch 1988a, p. 161).

Drawing Architecture

As a kind of fiction, architectural projection is a form of anticipatory representation (figuration), forecast in drawings (among other forms of two- and three-dimensional explorations). The truth claims of designs are rhetorical, rather than factual or scientific. Drawing is the means by which the non-yet anticipatory reality of a possible building is articulated as giving rise to a desired superior condition. Without drawing, anticipation is enfeebled by remaining little more than a visionary abstraction. So long as anticipation is not illuminated, the impossible perfection of what is supposedly desired must remain out of reach of even partial, or failed, realization. Drawing has the capacity to persuasively propose propositional articulations as *real* before construction, even if realization never occurs.

Drawing as world-making is never a blueprint. Exactitude of execution can only be a fully achievable aim if what the drawing proposes is so limited as to make its imitation in a completely different form (construction) actually possible. As the "generative mapping of architectural cosmopoiesis," requiring "a double translation" to become "built form," realization of the anticipated condition shown by drawing, as the working out of ideas with their origins in the architect's mind, is ultimately entrusted to others (Frascari 2011, p. 2; Rykwert 1998, p. 66). Not only will the hands of others inevitably interpret what a drawing shows, drawing itself, no matter how physical or prefigurative of human inhabitation, is inevitably approximate. The "generative power" of drawing resides in the inevitable condition of it being "productive of a reality that will end up outside the drawing" (Evans (1997 [1986]), p. 164).

Mechanical reproduction, scientific rationalism, and digital aids at every step of the design and production process can have the pathological effect of deluding all involved in building into believing that a drawing is a blueprint, in the sense of constituting a guarantee that no translation is required, which, even if it were possible, would ensure that the final result would have the status of an extrusion, as a 1:1 reproduction of the design. Without question, the eradication of failure is tantamount to banishing the human from being. And while we might hope to come as close as possible to perfection in many areas of life in achieving infallibility (mass-transport; medicine; structural design), so long as some responsibility is left to us humans, there will be failure. Moreover, wherever we play out our lives ought to be wrapped around human fallibility, as much as accommodating failing bodies, by sheltering both none too rigidly.

To remain approximate, thus generative, the anticipatory illumination of architectural drawing must encompass the double sense of fiction: the representation of a reasonably plausible unreality in its literary form, rendered in adequate detail to support the suspension of disbelief. But it must also comprise *fiction's* derivation from *to make*, originating with the Latin *fictio*, a making, past participle of *fingere*, which is "to form" or "to mold." As verb, rather than noun, *fiction* is as constitutive of worlds as the ones represented in its literary manifestations: both are *fabrications*. Anticipation of a not-yet, a fiction in the literary sense, prefigures establishing something concrete. Here, *to make* and *make up* come within reach of each other: production is revealed as simultaneously forming something tangible and the invention of stories of its possible reality. This is precisely what architectural drawing does, by giving form to made up or imagined happenings.

Although associated with unreality, as the making up of things, fictions include the potential for realization. As French philosopher Paul Ricoeur (1913–2005) has stated, "A literary fiction is an imaginative variation whose premises the reader assumes for awhile," akin to the "plausible hypothesis" of an architectural drawing (Ricoeur 1986a). It is here where confusion about precision enters the domain of drawing. Architects seem to forget, or perhaps never learned, that the apparent authority of drawings (their technical believability) is primarily a strategy for persuading viewers of their veracity, "by the rhetorical means of fiction" (Ricoeur 1986a). Drawings are not so much representations of an imaginary realm, as its figuration.

However, drawings of such expectant architecture will constitute anticipatory illumination only if it refigures a rearranged reality that reverses the disenchantment of the world that most present architecture reproduces or amplifies. By projecting an unreality through drawing, architecture constitutes a reinvention of what is, long before construction builds it. The "fact" of a constructed building – as physical presence – could seem to foreclose on the process of open-ended anticipation, by transforming fiction into verisimilitude, through making. Conserving the incomplete (as an opening for future anticipation), in an ostensibly completed project, depends on recuperating the rhetorical status of drawings as anticipatory, and of constructed buildings as approximate, and even as, at least partial, failures. Both conditions require a surplus of inexhaustible content.

Destabilizing the material reality of a building as completed depends on the richness of its original proposition, rather than on the depiction of ostensive alterity. Paradoxically, this will need to be sophisticated and detailed enough to confound conceivable exhaustion of its fictional origins, even through long continued use.

A building remains *useful* only for so long as it can sustain efforts to transform or reinvent it, which in turn encourage collective will to maintain it without dramatically altering it, or letting it fall in to ruin, or demolishing it. Drawing, as the progenitor of enduring buildings, has little to do with regimes of preservation, which risk transforming the world into a museum. For a building to persist as anticipatory after completion, it must somehow remain open to imaginary reconstruction of it by holding in reserve contents that construction and use cannot exhaust. In point of fact, everyday use has the capacity to reinvent buildings, which in itself could preserve their potential "not-yet" future conditions. But this only obtains for buildings rich enough in poetic content to sustain continuous reinterpretation through use, able to receive and facilitate inhabitants' own unfolding stories.

The fictionalized account of a building that nontrivial drawing articulates is the proposition of a superior condition anticipated by representations. The real-world transformation anticipated by the drawing may be relatively minor in scale (size and/or impact), but its very existence tells the story of another idea. Translation from architect's mind to drawing provides opportunities to anticipate shortcomings and correct them. Subsequent translation from drawing to building provides further opportunities for revision but only if dreams of absolute fidelity are relinquished. When they are, the building will be able to *breathe* along with its inhabitants. For a building to maintain anticipatory use of it, it must originate with conceptions compelling enough to encourage active engagement with the structure as a platform open to transforming occupation.

Architecture disciplined to the imperatives of the real estate market is unpromising vehicles of anticipation because the only sparks of desire motivating them are ignited by exchange, in tandem with only very feeble ideas about use. Equally, building as spectacle, originating in sensationalistic drawings, must inevitably renounce social life, in favor of entertainment and consumption. But even when such an unpromising climate dominates, other stories still mount challenges to *what is* by anticipating what could be, even if they largely end in failure. As the anticipation of conditions superior to inadequate existing ones, the first light of *anticipatory illumination* often originates in some recollected past put to use as a source for critiquing the present and for envisioning a transformed future. Architectural representations confer credibility to propositions at their earliest stages, anticipating, it seems, a propitious outcome.

Crucially, the proposition that architectural drawing could constitute a form of anticipatory illumination is in no way intended to encourage a view of representation as an end in itself. Ultimately, there is no substitute for concrete engagement with the world in efforts to transform it. Thus, as presented here, "anticipation" and with it "hope" and "utopia" are in no way conceptualized as equivalent to what French psychoanalyst Janine Chasseguet-Smirgel (1928–2006) described as "a primary wish to rediscover a universe without obstacles, a smooth maternal belly, stripped of its contents, to which free access is desired" (Chasseguet-Smirgel 1989). As Bloch fully acknowledges, hope is not equivalent to a desire for a world impossibly free of complication:

> hope is the opposite of security. It is the opposite of naïve optimism. The category of danger is always in it. This hope is not confidence. [. . .] If it could not be disappointed, it would not be hope. [. . .] Otherwise it would be cast in a picture. [. . .] [H]ope is critical and can be disappointed. [. . .] Hope is [. . .] determined negation of that which continually makes the opposite of the hoped-for object possible. [. . .] There would not be any process at all if there were not something that should not be so. (Bloch 1988b)

Bloch's conception of hope as process, rather than prediction, and as emerging from negation rather than blueprint supports the idea of "anticipation" as "process" rather than "picture" of a certain outcome.

When conceptualized as process rather than picture, anticipation refers to desired events rather than to predictably fixed results. Accordingly, Bloch prohibits depiction of utopias as realized, analogous to why the anticipatory illumination of architectural drawings must remain approximate. However, like utopia, anticipation does not only prefigure what is not, nor is it exclusively sparked by what it is against. For Bloch, "every criticism of imperfection, incompleteness, intolerance, and impatience already with doubt presupposes the conception of, and longing for a possible perfection" (Bloch 1988b, p. 16). Thus, because longing for perfection is desire for it, rather than its realization, the future possibilities lit up by anticipatory illumination will be at best approximations, steps toward some unachievable superlative possible.

Nevertheless, it is possible to offer a sure example of the opposite of what the anticipatory illumination of a superior architectural condition would include, outlined by Chasseguet-Smirgel as "perfectly straight streets, the rigorous geometry of the buildings, the sameness of the houses, [and] the passion for numbers which exists in most utopias" (Smirgel 1989, p. 102). How do we know? Because such a condition is unlikely to ever achieve even the traces of anything close to Bloch's conception of built homecoming.

Drawing Another Side

The work of architects is almost always anticipatory. However, the foreseen of most projects does not constitute illumination of a "possibility that has still not become" (Bloch 1995). While the argument could be raised that all projects most certainly do prevision a not-yet condition, it is the inclination of "the desire for a better way of being" of projects that is the distinguishing factor (Levitas 2010). One way to think of anticipation in relation to architecture, especially cast as anticipatory illumination, would be to consider anticipation as a kind of *machine* for contemplating the fullness of future possibility. Bloch describes the sort of consciousness grasped for here in the following:

> Utopian consciousness wants to look far into the distance, but ultimately only in order to penetrate the darkness so near it of the just lived moment, in which everything that is both drives and is hidden from itself. In other words: we need the most powerful telescope, that of polished utopian consciousness, in order to penetrate precisely the nearest nearness. (Bloch (1995 [1959]), p. 12)

Bloch's nomination of "the most powerful telescope" as the anticipatory instrument is actually quite well-suited to illuminating just the sort of possibilities architectural drawing can fabricate. In a more earthbound sense, architects work upon reality through the process of imagination. Working with what they know, to get close enough to its edges of the memory contents at their disposal, attempts are made to exceed their own limits and the boundaries of the already possible. In almost every instance, nontrivial architecture results from mediations between conditions as they are and how the architect believes they ought to be, inflected by recollection of past circumstances. Negotiation between existing reality and envisioned ideals is the object of drawing (whereas negotiation between envisioned ideals and existing reality is the object of construction).

The character of an architect's representations reveals his or her convictions, largely dependent on conceptions of individual, disciplinary, and project purpose. If more preoccupied with *use* than *exchange*, and with experiencing bodies, rather than curated photographs, the architect will also likely imagine him or herself as a member of communities of difference, joined by a largely shared human frame, mortality, and individual and collective desire, in short, a citizen among citizens. Predisposed to envision formulating settings upon which, and within which, social life may unfold, such architects cultivate principles for themselves and their works beyond fame or technical capability, novelty, or formalism. Setting about to configure social settings, with projects envisaged for a specific location in the present, drawing remains the most powerful tool for cultivating anticipatory illumination and for producing evidence of its presence.

Unfortunately, drawing as an anticipatory tool has withered with ever greater speed since the 1980s, with the widespread introduction of computer-aided design and drafting (CADD) into architects' offices. While CADD is itself a tool, it has transformed anticipatory representational operations of architects into prognosticatory extensions of optimized existing conditions. The extreme edges of these developments today are "facilitating architecture's complete assimilation into the building production process and forcing it to embrace the latter's performative logic." Reasonably enough, this could be viewed as a positive development that removes much of the risk from building design and production. However, that would confirm long-standing anxieties about the impossibility of architecture, in any richer sense, ensnared within the productivist logic of neoliberal global capitalism.

Arguably, "[t]his logic either deprives architecture's expressive ambitions of legitimacy or remakes them in its own image." When this comes to pass, all hopes in design would be rendered futile, along with any lingering belief in architecture's capacity to (re)make the world in more humane forms. Already high, the stakes rise along with the dominance of digital imaging: "Simulation [as opposed to representation/figuration] dispenses with any relationship to materials and the haptic knowledges of the external world they provide" (Scheer 2014). Although architecture is mostly made and consumed as image, it has been observed that no matter how distant the labors of the architect is from those of the builder, hand drawing, including drawings instruments, was analogous to the operations and even tools of the construction site (Frascari 2007). The dominance of simulation alienates architects from the means by which projects were once anticipated and from their participation in construction. Ultimately, "[t]he crafts-manship so essential for the architect's involvement in her work loses its material basis" (Scheer 2014, p. 192).

Modes of practice are modes of production. When the dominant modes of production work against the supposed vocation of architects, then it is all but inevitable that those modes of production, in tandem with the modes of production of the building industry more widely, will be incapable of producing alternatives. Under such conditions, no matter how radical the gesture, the image, or the rhetoric, the ultimate result will be reproduction, in service of the same dominant modes of production that are often the target of critical gesture, verbal, visual, or even material.

The challenge, for those few architects (and clients) interested in other possibil-ities, remains how to surpass the identification of buildings as simple commodities and the work of architects as the decoration of these. It is in this context that anticipatory illumination, as practiced and achieved in (analogue) drawing, becomes a genuinely radical action in the struggle against *the end of architecture* on the one hand and the seeming impossibility of a human-centered constructed environment on the other. Drawing is the mechanism by which complex, interwoven, larger communities (perhaps as assemblages of semiautonomous smaller ones) could be envisioned and rendered potentially attainable.

Borrowing from Bloch, drawing is reintroduced as "the most powerful tele-scope," an anticipatory instrument, for illuminating "the most immediate immediacy, in which the core of self-location and being-here still lies, in which at the same time the whole knot of the world-secret is to be found" (Bloch (1995 [1959]), p. 12). Measured against this prospect, the compensations for the withering of representa-tion, overwhelmed by simulation, have not, as of yet, made good on whatever it supposedly promises. If the increased fidelity between drawing and result, made possible by digital technologies, has pushed the quality of the inhabited world in a direction of decreasing livability, it could be said that optimization is an inversion, by which fantasies of improvement result in their opposite: deterioration.

Optimization, like exactitude, and perfection are decidedly unhuman qualities. Dreams of immaculateness must inevitably exclude the human. It is as if in the guise of progress, humans themselves are made redundant by their own fantasies, precisely because of our filth. Bloch echoes this in the following:

> The machine knew how to produce everything so lifeless and inhuman in detail, just the way
> our new housing districts usually are. Its actual goal is the bathroom and the toilet that are the
> most unquestionable and the most original accomplishments of this era [...]. But now
> washing-up reigns.

The association between machines, lifeless districts, and hygienic excess conjures up images of the simulacrums of urbanity that continue to overwrite previous less error-free zones of cities. Although determined by external forces, the first step in installing meticulously produced spaces begins on the drafting boards, or screens, more like, of architects' offices. In the same way as most everybody, the majority of architects are obligated to conform to dominant modes of production, adopting its attendant consciousness and spatial practices. Architectural historian and historian, Alberto Pérez-Gómez and architect Louise Pelletier touch upon this, noting that:

> When sets of drawings attempt to provide us with a 'picture' of an architectural place or
> object, the buildings produced by such techniques necessarily reflect the predictive quality of
> their conception: the possibility of a revelatory dimension is abandoned. (Pérez-Gómez and
> Pelletier 1997)

Much as I wholeheartedly concur with the foregoing analysis, as is so often the case, there is little offered in the way of suggesting possible forms of resistance, or subversion, of dominant conditions, which are arguably destructive of the human environment. Because the political dimension of such theoretical and critical discourse is usually so absent, Pérez-Gómez and Pelletier's next assertion is all the more surprising: "That this assumption of a literal relationship between the project and the building is basic to both the 'correct' politics of rationality and industrial production in the modern city makes a critical reassessment all the more pressing" (Pérez-Gómez and Pelletier, 1997 p. 390). Diagnosis is surely a first step, followed by pleas for a cure, but what if the problem itself is just part of a brilliantly constructed self-perpetuating machine, of which consciousness – the very instrument required for resistance and subversion – is a fundamental part, then the difficulty in identifying, or representing, the next steps is the most pressing concern of all. At this juncture, there seem to be just two options: surrender to inevitability or leap into the unknown, the ultimately unmanageable. The first comforts with predictable results; the second is all but doomed to failure.

The surplus of utopian hope that Bloch identifies in works of art, in the form of anticipatory illumination, is mirrored in French philosopher and sociologist Henri Lefebvre's (1901–1991) conviction that cracks can always be found. Moreover, Lefebvre argues that the "system" has no "legitimate claim to immortality." And it only appears so as described by "over-systematic thinkers" who "make society into the 'object' of a systematization which must be 'closed' to be complete." In doing so, "they thus bestow a cohesiveness it utterly lacks upon a totality which is in fact decidedly open – so open, indeed, that it must rely on violence to endure" (Lefebvre 1991).

Perhaps Bloch's "most powerful telescope" is exactly the mechanism required to locate cracks of possibility on the one hand and to see with clarity that what is taken for totality, including one's own adherence to the "system," is actually a product of its violence, without which it would soon crumble, the proof of which is all around us today. Here again, anticipatory illumination lights up possibilities for seeing beyond the limits of one's own consciousness and imaginaries and through the veil of violence deployed by the "system" to big itself up. Bloch observes:

> The imagination and the thoughts of future intention [...] are utopian, [...] not in a narrow sense of the word which only defines what is bad (emotively reckless picturing, playful form of an abstract kind), but rather in fact in the newly tenable sense of the forward dream, of anticipation in general. (Bloch (1995 [1959]), p. 12)

In practical terms, a concrete way to begin anticipating other spaces structured by a different architecture begins with debunking optimizing myths of simulation, as the first steps in the direction of a return to the world-making potential of representation. After all, what architects do in their offices, how they conceive their drawings (whether they opt for predictive simulation or for revelatory representation), constitutes their professional modes of production, which either reproduces or subverts dominant spatial practices (for the sources of this analysis, see Lefebvre, *The Production of Space*, 1991 [1974] and Coleman 2015).

Equally subversive would be for architects to engage in ground-level research about the projects they undertake by asking questions of themselves and others about "what makes somewhere a place where it is good to live?" Doing so would shift emphasis from clients, developers, and planners to citizens – the people who actually use what is built. Such practicality could go far in redeeming the material presence of buildings, which, after all, is what people's bodies make contact with, rather than with extravagant pictures or reckless forms. Lefebvre outlines such a method as follows:

> Utopia is to be considered experimentally by studying its implications on the ground. These can surprise. What are and what would be the most successful places? How can they be discovered? According to which criteria? What are the times and rhythms of daily life which are inscribed and prescribed in these successful places favourable to happiness? That is interesting (Lefebvre 1996).

Such concentrated engagement with problems of use, on the ground, counters the positivist bad social science of orthodox high modernist architecture and the abstract forms of neo-avant-garde architecture alike.

Drawing as Constitutive

If optimized digital technologies of representation and production promise speed above all else, nontrivial hand drawing is simultaneously an anticipatory practice and restorative, by introducing delay. As a counterculture, hand drawing moves in an opposite direction to the trajectory of digital simulations, picking up a pencil (or even an ink drafting pen) is a first act of resistance that could give way to all of the others, perhaps even leading to a partial redemption of reality by way of engagement with the material of building and the material processes of architecture but only so long as anxieties over so-called *necessary professional skills* are displaced by longings for something more.

Drawing liberated from the screen is also meditative; it slows down the process and improves concentration. It also clearly demarcates a line separating architecture (design and production) from video games, blockbuster movies, or simulators. Emancipation from the electronic tethers that plug us into pervasive networks might even contribute to developing capacities for reflection and thinking one's own thoughts. Not until screen addiction has been broken to reveal all of the wonders of optimization as nothing more than nifty prosthetics, ultimately of the same genera as a hammer, a bicycle, or a laptop with a word processing program, for example, would it be possible to reintroduce digital technologies as subservient, rather than domineering.

Maybe the anticipatory illumination of architectural drawing could be cultivated, as a nascent capacity shared by all? What is more, should the lights ever go out for good, causing the comforting eternal certainties of this world to vanish, the replacement would likely be something different, less apparently total and enduring, and more primitive. Under these imagined circumstances, the ability to anticipate the contours of yet another new world would be an extravagantly valuable skill. In this scenario, architects redeemed by necessity for the invention of a new context would be superbly equipped for the task, so long as they have the skill to configure anticipatory illuminations of the not-yet, independent of the grid. Emancipated from the constraints of programs written by others, permeated by interests beyond architects' influence, and free of any need for a screen, mouse, keyboard, joystick, trackpad, processing power, or electricity (or even a generator, or fuel for it), architects could get on with the business of (re)world-making.

Depending on the specifics of actual conditions, if needs must, architects who can draw with independent hands on their own could pick up a stick and begin remaking the world in the soil, by sketching out its anticipated contours. Perhaps this time, though, the imperative of life will exceed mortal anxiety, with its attendant desire to conquer death by arrogating consciousness, as much as labor, to machines or, at the very least, to machine-like thinking and organizational and productive structures, which are but symbols of human self-loathing manifested as envy for the immaculate logic of machines.

If nothing else, the little thought experiment directly above anticipates conditions that would confirm the proposition that analogue drawing has a significance beyond the limits of morbid nostalgia. Although projected into an unknowable future, the scenario outlined above is grounded in human history so far: just like the sun, civilizations rise and fall. What arrogance could convince us that we have overcome that certainty? Is it our machines, the simulations they can run, or something else?

The time of digital machines is the *time of now*, of the immediate present, without a past or a future. The speed of digital communications encourages impulsiveness, rather than reflection. The fidelity between simulations and buildings approximates the character of extrusions, while giving the impression of perfection achieved, because of the apparent authority of photo-realistic images, whatever they may show. But the apparent certain perfection of the virtual world of the screen and its printouts is necessarily oblivious to the reality of existing conditions. Verging toward the totalizing logic of absolutism, the deceptive veracity of simulation encourages execution all at once, whether construction or demolition. In digital renderings, specificity of location is just another simulation that in contradistinction, the anticipatory illumination of nontrivial drawing imprints through the hand to the memory, as the contours are drawn. The slowness of drawing could structure a space for anticipating limits, gaps, and bad decisions that the comforting perfection of simulations erases.

Drawing is a method for testing projects during the very process of presenting them. As such, it provides opportunities to anticipate the potentially negative consequences of a project before it is realized, since after construction, errors are unfortunately all but undoable. As considered here, drawing confounds the divide between process (*drawing*) and object (*a drawing*) and again between object (*the drawing*) and the process of construction (*fabricating a building*) with reference to drawings (*representations*).

Arguably, speed, instant gratification, and economic imperatives are the only conceivable justifications for the architectural equivalent of compressing conceptual bandwidth in the "projection of frozen models which have to be immediately perfect" that digital simulations produce (Ricoeur 1976). The strange paradox is that the efficiencies of digital technology are the fruits of fantasies going back to the heyday of orthodox modernist attempts during the twentieth century to pave over the traditional city with its modern replacement, all at once, if possible. With the continuous perfection of the technologies of those Cold War, space race, dreams having now taken hold, even careless devastation of cities has been optimized, as a ruthless return of modernist hubris.

The technological imperatives of contemporary dominant modes of production and spatial practice, from office screen to building site, manifest absolutist escapist fantasies of "a logic of all or nothing which ignores the labour of time" (Ricoeur 1976). Supported by high-speed digital processing, preoccupation with *time as now* dominates, dislocating the present by making its relation to either the time *before* it or the time *after* unimaginable. Neglect of the actual physical and mental effort required to get things right confirms an obsession with time as *immediate present*. Time is perceived as so pressurized that mental processes must be outsourced to digital ones. Cities emerging out of these processes are even more disaggregated than twentieth-century ones subjected to total war and ferocious urban renewal.

The demand for immediate *presentness* is its own liability. Near total disregard for ongoing patterns of life is one necessary consequence. Ignoring the hazards of total application is another, as is the assumption of frictionless conditions, presupposing dissolution of all obstacles, where everything is compatible with everything else. For architecture, this translates into the screen-space of digital production, simulating the elimination of existing conditions, as if to provide obstacle-free clearings for the new (for elaboration on this idea, see Ricoeur 1976, 1986). As so much architecture produced with the benefit of digital technologies confirms, the obstacle-free field of the screen struggles to realize the new city by submitting "reality to dreams" in the delineation of "self-contained schemas of perfection severed from the whole course of the human experience of value," no matter the claims to functionality, novelty, or art (Paul Ricoeur, "Ideology and Utopia as Cultural Imagination," p. 26).

Although most architects would profess to wanting their works to contribute to structuring an improved world, a combination of productivist imperatives and the technologies this anticipates conspires against their actually being able to do so. Not least because the dominant modes of production in architectural offices requires "a lack of care for the first steps to be taken in the direction of the ideal city" (Paul Ricoeur, "Ideology and Utopia as Cultural Imagination," p. 26). Here again, the double benefit of nontrivial hand drawing is brought to the fore, slowing down thinking and production processes to increase possibilities for reflection and the status of drawing as an anticipatory, rather than a predictive, process.

Perhaps it is the durational aspect of hand drawing that constitutes its most significant benefit for thinking and production alike: as the figuration of the first and prefiguration of the second, if only ever approximate. Analogue drawing is situated in the body and is a verification of the benefits of reasonable and intentioned progress, maybe even enacting a conscientious approach to making history, mirrored in the human action of drawing, made meaningful because purposeful. Indeed, it is difficult to imagine how the speed of machines could translate into reasoned human action or produce its settings.

Hand drawing at least holds out the promise of constitutively flexible redescriptions of reality, which remain open to complexities and inconsistencies of the sort that inevitably confront implementation. The measure of activity paced in this way is the conception of time it reveals, linking present action, with past accomplishments, in the direction rhythmical achievement in the future. Duration suggests rhythmical time rather than clockwork time; passage, rather than direction, prevails, making it possible to imagine present constructions as built within the expanding circle of the past and with regard for it.

Analogue drawing is piecemeal, so it can tolerate modification in ways that the imagined perfection of digital simulations resists. By the same token, the actions of hand drawing participate in practice, confront obstacles, and overcome incompatibilities in much the way work on building sites must. Equally, the suppleness of hand drawing has greater tolerance for conflicts between seemingly opposed goals, with a greater capacity for embracing divergences as opportunities than digital simulation does, again, akin to the activities entailed in constructing buildings.

By embracing tension, hand-drawn schemes have an innate capacity for flexible conceptualizations, ideal for resisting the tendency toward schematism evident in *all* schemes, as an unavoidable adjunct of attempts to justify their own logic. Analogue drawing is an elastic anticipatory process that opens up projects to continual re-evaluation during the processes of figuration and potentially throughout subsequent implementation as well.

The multidimensional openness of analogue drawing ensures a level of awareness the other modes of representation do not permit, which attaches projects to the "whole course of the human experience of value." The very imperfectability of hand drawing, as a form of concrete action, permits its results to persist as reasonable possibilities. Drawing of this sort is forever partial, which positions it as process and result, within the density of history. The expanded field of experimentation and speculation that architectural drawing by hand facilitates is a form of testing that permits its anticipated transformations of the real to be inflected by it (Paul Ricoeur, "Ideology and Utopia as Cultural Imagination," p. 26).

Not-Yet of Drawing Imagination

As outlined in this chapter, architectural drawing has been argued for as at once subversive, by enacting a questioning of reality and dominant modes of production as well. But drawing has also been argued for as a form of anticipatory illumination that is constitutive and thus potentially ordering. The destabilization conventional practices created by the initial subversion of drawing could actually prefigure more stable conditions than those that currently prevail. Achieving this would be an accomplishment of transformations worked out theoretically through drawing, as much as facilitated by the implied critique of the present any proposition entails.

Arguably, as a form of anticipatory illumination, architectural drawing is, at its best, the equivalent of "what invention is to scientific knowledge." Each drawing can articulate in part "the imaginary project of another kind of society, of another reality, and another world." In the first instance, imaginaries seized by drawing are "constitutive in an inventive rather than an integrative manner" (Paul Ricoeur, "Ideology and Utopia as Cultural Imagination," p. 24). Drawing can be productively disruptive; it can decenter one's own self-perceptions and preconceptions of architecture, including the perceived role of architecture and even of the status of architecture culturally. But it can also return the self, and the project, back to real, facilitating two-way travel between *here* and *elsewhere* and past and future (Paul Ricoeur, "Ideology and Utopia as Cultural Imagination," p. 27). Although written as a reflection on utopia, in the following, Ricoeur could be describing architectural drawing and anticipatory illumination:

> Is not utopia – this leap outside – the way in which we radically rethink what is family, what is consumption, what is religion, and so on? Does not the fantasy of an alternative society and its exteriorization 'nowhere' work as one of the most formidable contestations of what is? (Paul Ricoeur, *Lectures,* p. 16)

In architectural drawing, "the field of the possible is [...] open beyond the actual," revealing it as "a field [...] for alternative ways of living" (Paul Ricoeur, *Lectures,* p. 16). Although much diminished in analogue as well as digital form, if Lefebvre is correct, and what appears as total only seems so because of the violence deployed to make the image convincing enough to quell resistance, then fields of alternative operations must still be open.

In the first instance, perhaps, it is just those fields of alternative operations that must be anticipated, as a first step in recuperating architectural drawing as an anticipatory illuminating machine for catching "the shadow of the forces capable of shattering a given order," which are "already the shadow of an alternative order that could be opposed to the given order." If, as Ricoeur asserts, "It is the function of utopia to give the force of discourse to this possibility," perhaps architectural drawing is the mechanism for anticipating it, by configuring proposals of future occupation and action, momentarily completed by experiencing bodies, now, in the past and into the future (Paul Ricoeur, "Ideology and Utopia as Cultural Imagination," p. 24).

Summary

In this chapter, drawing for architecture has been reintroduced as anticipatory, as opposed to primarily technical or representational. As technical, drawing is mainly directive, related to organzsing work required to construct buildings. As representational, drawing generally depicts idealized visions of projects, preoccupied with promoting them to other architects, patrons, historians, theorists, critics, and students, or to confirm their status as aesthetic objects in their own right, including for the art market. As developed in this chapter, drawing has been emphasized as active, propositional, and anticipatory; prefiguring possible realities, rather than as static records of either the action of drawing or the presumed exact contours of what they propose. As a prefigurative process of anticipatory illumination, drawing is constitutive action, rather than a blueprint for it: philosophical, instead of managerial. Reimagined as *anticipatory illumination*, it has been argued that drawing could rekindle concrete hopes in design, rather than propagating illusory abstract ones.

References

Bloch, E. (1988a [1959]). The artistic illusion as the visible anticipatory illumination. In *The utopian function of art and literature: Selected essays* (J. Zipes & F. Mecklenburg, Trans.). Cambridge, MA: MIT Press, p. 153.

Bloch, E. (1988b [1964]). Something's missing: A discussion between Ernst Bloch and Theodor W. Adorno on the contradictions of utopian longing. In *The utopian function of art and literature: Selected essays* (J. Zipes & F. Mecklenburg, Trans.). Cambridge, MA: MIT Press, pp. 16–17.

Bloch, E. (1995 [1959]). *The principle of hope*, vol 1 (N. Plaice, S. Plaice, & P. Knight, Trans.). Cambridge, MA: MIT, p. 7.

Cazeaux, C. (2000). *The continental aesthetics reader* (p. 303). London/New York: Routledge.

Chasseguet-Smirgel, J. (1989). The archaic matrix of the oedipus complex in utopia. In *Sexuality and mind, the role of the father and mother in the psyche* (M. Paget, Trans.). London: Maresfield Library, Karnac, p. 92.

Coleman, N. (2005). *Utopias and architecture*. London/New York: Routledge.

Coleman, N. (2007). Building dystopia. *Rivista MORUS – Utopia e Renascimento, 4*, 181–192. http://www.revistamorus.com.br/index.php/morus/article/view/180/157.

Coleman, N. (2015). *Lefebvre for architects*. London/New York: Routledge.

Curtis, W. J. R. (1996). *Modern architecture since 1900*. London: Phaidon.

Evans, R. (1997 [1986]). Translations from drawing to building. In *Translations from drawing to building and other essays*. London: Architectural Association, p. 164.

Frampton, K. (2007). *Modern architecture: A critical history* (4th ed. Revised). London: Thames & Hudson,

Frascari, M. (2007). Introduction: Models and drawings – The invisible nature of architecture. In M. Frascari, J. Hale, & B. Starkey (Eds.), *From models to drawings: Imagination and representation in architecture* (pp. 1–7). London/New York: Routledge.

Frascari, M. (2011). *Eleven exercises in the art of architectural drawing: Slow food for the architect's imagination* (p. 2). London/New York: Routledge.

Giedion, S. (1982 [1941]). Space, time and architecture: Growth of a new tradition. Cambridge, MA: Harvard University Press.

Guillén, M. F. (2005). *The taylorized beauty of the mechanical: Scientific management and the rise of modern architecture*. Princeton: Princeton University Press.

Jacobs, F. (2002). The: Disassembling: Marsyas, Michelangelo, and the Accademia del Disegno. *Art Bulletin*, 426–448.

Lefebvre, H. (1991 [1974]). *The production of space* (Donald Nicolson-Smith, Trans.). Oxford: Blackwell, p. 11.

Lefebvre, H. (1996 [1968]). The right to the city. In *Writings on cities* (E. Kofman & E. Lebas, Trans.). Oxford: Blackwell, p. 151.

Levitas, R. (2010 [1990]). *The concept of utopia*, Oxford/Bern: Peter Lang, p. 9.

Pérez-Goméz, A., & Pelletier, L. (1997). *Architectural representation and the perspective hinge* (p. 390). Cambridge, MA: MIT Press.

Ricoeur, P. (1976). Ideology and utopia as cultural imagination. *Philosophic Exchange, 2*, 26.

Ricoeur, P. (1986a). In G. H. Taylor (Ed.), *Lectures on ideology and utopia* (p. 270). New York: Columbia University Press.

Ricoeur, P. (1986b). *Lectures on ideology and utopia* (pp. 1–2). New York: Columbia University Press, 296.

Rykwert, J. (1998). Translation and/or representation. *RES: Anthropology and Aesthetics, 34*, 64–70, p. 66.

Scheer, D. R. (2014). *The death of drawing: Architecture in the age of simulation* (p. 193). London/New York: Routledge.

Stokes, A. (1978 [1955]). Michelangelo: A study in the nature of art. In *Critical writings* (vol III). London: Thames and Hudson, pp. 42–43.

Tafuri, M. (2000). Toward a critique of architectural ideology. *Contropiano 1* (January–April 1969) (Stephen Sartarelli (trans.), reprinted in, *Architecture theory since 1968*, K. Michael Hays (ed.)). Cambridge, MA: MIT Press/Columbia Books of Architecture, p. 15.

Vasari, G. (1965). *Lives of the artists: V. I* (G. Bull Trans.). London: Penguin Books, pp. 249–254 and pp. 325–326.

Will, C. (Ed.). (2006). *Modernism: Designing a new world, 1914–1939*. London: V&A Publishing.

Zipes, J. (1988). Toward a realization of anticipatory illumination. In E. Bloch (Ed.), *The utopian function of art and literature: Selected essays* (p. xxxiii). Cambridge, MA: MIT Press.

Anticipatory Aesthetics: The Senses and the Body in Anticipatory Theory and Practice

41

Marcus Bussey

Contents

Abstract

Anticipatory aesthetics extends the conceptual repertoire of the theory of anticipation. This chapter offers a theoretical rationale for the importance of anticipatory aesthetics in the work of foresight practitioners and theorists. It argues for a central place for the senses – both embodied and subtle – in anticipatory knowledge work. Key to this understanding is the centrality of both the senses and anticipation to the evolution, not just of human beings but of all life. The chapter draws extensively on the work of the French philosopher Gilles Deleuze who posited the Chaosmos and a transcendental empiricism. Deleuze's work complements and challenges the approach taken by those engaged in anticipatory systems theory and the mapping out of a possible discipline of anticipation. Intercivilizational dialogue is also introduced to extend the possibilities of anticipatory systems theory, Deleuze's thought, and anticipatory aesthetics.

M. Bussey (✉)
Faculty of Arts, Business and Law, University of the Sunshine Coast, Maroochydore, QLD, Australia
e-mail: mbussey@usc.edu.au

© Springer Nature Switzerland AG 2019
R. Poli (ed.), *Handbook of Anticipation*,
https://doi.org/10.1007/978-3-319-91554-8_84

861

Neohumanism is offered as a suitable bridge between Western readings of anticipation as a necessary feature of evolving systems and Eastern spiritual representations of the world as conscious. The chapter ends by considering the five futures senses of memory, foresight, voice, optimism, and yearning. It is argued that these senses account for the sense-making processes that occur within human systems and that a clearer appreciation for such senses will enrich foresight practice and the theory of anticipation.

Keywords
Anticipatory aesthetics · Systems theory · Chaosmos · Pragmatism · Memory · Foresight · Voice · Optimism · Yearning · Anticipation · Affordance · Neohumanism · Aesthetic capital · Evolution

Introduction

The world is a disorder; we human beings seek to manage through a range of strategies. I have a deep appreciation for Deleuze's term for this disorder: the *Chaosmos*. The hybridity of this word reminds us that the creativity – both biological and cultural – of the cosmos is always with us, always unfolding, and always unpredictable. To anticipate in such an environment is a challenge. Pre-cultural life solved this problem by hardwiring anticipation into the genetic "memory" of organisms: so birds migrate, mammals hibernate, and so on. Cultural life also developed anticipatory mechanisms to ensure the survival of individuals, clans, and even societies. Thus the earliest peoples had calendars, used memory to follow the seasons, read and acted upon environmental queues, and so on.

This paper contends that this anticipatory faculty is an evolutionary tool and that anticipation in humans is both biological and cultural. In short, the hardwiring of DNA takes a cultural turn when *Homo sapiens* and their immediate predecessors began to develop culture as a response to their unpredictable environments. Like all evolution this development involved trial and error and also long periods of time. Yet culture brought an evolutionary advantage which again and again beat the odds and took the beneficiaries of anticipation into new forms of complex order vis-à-vis the environment. There is no doubt that through this process, levels of complexity increased exponentially and time frames decreased simultaneously. This increasing complexity and the compression of time are powerfully linked to the emergence of increasingly complex symbolic language and a growing range of tools/technologies that continue to shape the human world both physically and culturally.

Chaosmos, Rhythm, and Anticipation

This paper's interest in anticipation grows out of the recognition that when we engage the future as a fulcrum in our personal and collective decision-making, we access a range of data that is not simply cognitive. This insight is based on a pragmatic reading of foresight practice as a work between the sensible external world of form and structure and the subjective approach taken as we sense-make our way through the external world (Bussey 2014a). In this, following Deleuze (1994), it is argued that human beings sense-make across domains of experience and always in the company of a wide range of "voices," "intuitions," "values," "assumptions," "opinions," and "drivers" that bring to the task such complexity that any sense-making context is unique and unpredictable (Bussey 2009, 2011, 2014b). This is the Chaosmos at work, the radically unpredictable acting as solvent on the legible, the legitimate, the sacred cows. As futures thinkers, futurists, and foresight practitioners, we are often lured into this flux in an effort to chart chaosmic space. By and large we seek to manage this dynamic field via the imposition of structural and epistemological categories that anchor context and reveal something of its latent potentiality.

There is no doubt that we need categories to conceptually manage the Chaosmos. Yet, as Deleuze (1994) (often in the company of Felix Guattari) argued over his career, categories become prisons and that we are all in fact caught '*Between* night and day, between that which is constructed and that which grows naturally, between mutations from the inorganic to the organic, from plant to animal, from animal to humankind, yet without this series constituting a progression ..." (Deleuze and Guattari 1987, p. 313). Such in-between states are loosely experienced – stitched together – as "reality" in which we sense-make through the imposition of categories. In Deleuzian terms each category is a rhythm, a term with considerable appeal, as it indicates the underlying patterning at work in sense-making. Patterning, as the process work of the in-between, is eternally open and in flux yet secure in its spatiotemporal grounding in any specific context. Yet despite such anchoring, the fundamental ingredient remains chaos:

> Chaos is not the opposite of rhythm, but the milieu of all milieus. There is rhythm whenever there is a transcoded passage from one milieu to another, a communication of milieus, coordination between heterogeneous space-times. (Deleuze and Guattari 1987, p. 313)

It is important to note that Deleuze and Guattari are clear that rhythm is not to be confused with meter, which they describe as "dogma." Instead "Rhythm is the milieus' answer to chaos. What chaos and rhythm have in common is the in-between" (Deleuze and Guattari 1987, p. 313), and it is this *in-between* that futurists sensitive to rhythm – as opposed to those seeking to contain chaos and impose order (meter) upon it – find and work with anticipatory processes. Anticipation is the art of responding to and producing rhythm.

Evolution and Anticipation

This understanding implicates "reality" in its own evolution, in its own *becoming*. Becoming is the latent potential of the present moment, and this latency is a quality of all dynamic and open systems (Poli 2011). Reading for such latency is what Riel Miller (2007) is referring to when he describes growing "futures literacies." Chaos however is the ultimate system and is, as a result, experienced as *anti-system*. It is the "milieu of all milieus" from which all possibilities emerge. And these possibilities are all provisional and linked to both physical and subjective states active either explicitly or implicitly in any moment. That accounts for the heterotopic and immanent nature of "reality" (Bussey 2009; Foucault 1986). Following Roberto Poli's distinction between the hidden and the latent, the heterotopic can be understood as those hidden elements of a system that are present but unrecognized to actors in the system, while the immanent refers to those latent elements that "do not exist at all in the entity's actual state. Latent components relate to incompletely present conditions and aspects" (Poli 2010, p. 8). Terms however matter, so it is proposed that heterotopia and immanence are preferable as they are more conceptually rich and fluid, speaking to and across cultural fields (rather than from a field), that inform a range of understandings about anticipation and its expression.

Of course, it is precisely because anticipation is deployed variously across a range of fields that scholars such as Poli are seeking to develop a discipline of anticipation in order to establish greater levels of coherence and legitimacy for anticipatory systems thinking (Miller et al. 2013). This is a legitimate pursuit but one which will struggle against the border-crossing and transgressive nature of the concept itself. It is precisely this transgressive nature of anticipation which makes it so rich. It is also why it is argued that the faculty of anticipation is an evolutionary tool. Evolution speaks of the hybrid and the wonderful dance between structure and intention. Dance is a metaphor for the living engagement of an organism with its environment; it refers to the co-creativity present in all such engagements. Xenakis and Arnellos (2014) and others (Chemero 2003) working on understanding the aesthetic properties of systems refer to this "dancing" relationship as an "affordance":

> Affordances are features of whole situations and this whole supports (perhaps demands) a certain kind of action. Affordances . . . are not in the environment but rather they are relations between the *abilities* of an agent and features of the environment. (Xenakis and Arnellos 2014, p. 8)

In recent years others have been mapping the role aesthetics plays in evolving systems (Chatterjee 2010; Enquist and Arak 1994; Nadin 2010). The concept of affordance is important for this work as it captures the intersection of the material and the subjective as an interactive holistic process that resists the urge to parse the relationship and read physical environment as separate from a subject's/agent's responses to it. Affordances point to "certain kinds of action" that are responses to the environment elicited in actors according to their sense-making capabilities. Such capabilities are aesthetic and anticipatory in nature.

Essentially, all living systems contain anticipatory functions. Anticipation plays a significant role in shaping future evolutionary developments though in open systems, these are never linear in nature (Poli 2010). Such nonlinearity presupposes an active role for the past, the present, and the future which come together in aesthetic arrangements. Nadin argues, for instance, that:

...the dynamics of an anticipatory system involves the future as a realization in the vast domain of the possible...There are goals in view—finality ... directions for the future, a vector of change. Life is process: more precisely, non-deterministic process. Therefore, in addressing causality with respect to the living, we need to consider past and present (cause-effect, and the associated reaction), both well defined, in conjunction with a possible future realization, ill-defined, ambiguous. (2010, p. 10)

This life process is open and, as Miller et al. noted, creative (Miller et al. 2013, p. 11). Creativity itself is a quality of life, one that generates expression in the world and engages through the medium of culture with human sense-making activities such as myth making, technology, the arts, and social arrangements. The anticipatory and the aesthetic both address this creativity and ground it in the intersection of biology and culture. Nadin makes this point in his discussion relating to artificial intelligence:

...only at the level of evolution per se, not within a pseudo-evolutionary mechanism, does the need for aesthetic performance emerge. Indeed, the aesthetic dimension of the living is consubstantial with living. It is not mere cosmetics, i.e., not an added layer irrelevant or only marginally relevant to the living. Rather, it partakes in the dynamics of the living. The entire issue of the continuum of living, i.e., from conception to birth to maturity and death (return to the physical condition) is one of autonomous anticipation, expressed in particular as aesthetic anticipation. (2010, p. 11)

Thus he notes that "natural selection is aesthetically conditioned" (ibid; see also Chatterjee (2010); Enquist and Arak (1994)). This conditioning takes a narrative form when fields as diverse as evolutionary biology, anthropology, economics, paleontology, and history, particularly the subdisciplines of big history and environmental history, examine the past and (though rarely) engage with the future via an evolutionary lens. Such engagement is the bread and butter of the futures field. Scenario work, for instance, draws on the prospective teleological nature of human systems, as does the experiential and future gaming work of innovators such as Stuart Candy and Jake Dunagan (Candy and Dunagan 2016) and Sohail Inayatullah (Inayatullah 2013). In such work an explicit application of an anticipatory aesthetics is at work.

Bodies

Anticipatory aesthetics implicates the body in the work of anticipatory judgment. They are the experiential sites that Candy, Dunagan, Inayatullah, and others are seeking to provoke. They are also contested sites in which alternative identities, as Ivana Milojević (2013) argues, are to be practiced. In this author's outlining of the context of intimate futures (Bussey 2014b), for instance, it is precisely because we have bodies that we respond to the future variably and across sets of interconnecting, overlapping, and even disruptive contexts. Bodies are culturally conditioned and given the right circumstances (reconditioning) can become active participants in fostering alternative cultural expression.

This author's engagement with the dance-improvisation-voice-work system of InterPlay (Winton-Henry and Porter 2016), for instance, takes aesthetics and embodied wisdom as the starting point for reimagining who we are. To find the world around us to be remarkable is one of the key goals of good futurists when working with groups. It has been found that starting with the body in motion, the kinesthetic, speeds up this dimension of self-world discovery. Of course the word kinesthetic acknowledges the aesthetic role of the body in sense-making. As Deleuze notes, the aesthetic is the "science of the sensible" (1994, p. 56). When engaging the senses – the physical and the subtle – affordance, that emergent quality of a context, comes into action. Affordance is a latent element of what Deleuze called transcendental empiricism and the aesthetic the sense-making component of this empirical process:

> Empiricism truly becomes transcendental, and aesthetics an apodictic discipline, only when we apprehend directly in the sensible that which can only be sensed, the very being of the sensible: difference, potential difference and difference in intensity as the reason behind qualitative diversity. (1994, pp. 56–57)

Difference, the quality or affordance of the sensible, is a starting point for a reevaluation of anticipation via aesthetic experience. Difference generates creative energy – the ongoing novelty of context. It challenges the stupefaction of the senses brought on by unreflective culture and releases strange forms of reasoning. As Deleuze points out:

> It is in difference that movement is produced as an 'effect', that phenomena flash their meaning like signs. The intense world of differences, in which we find the reason behind qualities and the being of the sensible, is precisely the object of a superior empiricism. This empiricism teaches us a strange 'reason', that of the multiple, chaos, and difference. . .. (1994, p. 57)

This "flashed meaning" generated by difference is what the body responds to but also what it releases. What Winton-Henry and Porter call "body wisdom" offers an insight into the possibilities of an anticipatory aesthetic process that can produce new knowings, open-ended signals, and strange new reasoning. They make the important point:

> The good news is that the gift of kinaesthetic identification allows us to deeply enjoy, savour, and have our moving world. We experience physical rapport and connection with the creative beauty of our dancing universe, from its most subtle to its grandest physical expression. Even if we only watch from our solo vantage point and barely move at all, we can feel that we are dancing with it all when our kinaesthetic sense is involved. (2016, p. 139)

When we dance and play, we reorient our anticipatory capacity, grounding it in the body as a site of the anticipatory aesthetic. The body, which is often denied, underestimated, and feared in the Western tradition, becomes a vehicle for entering the world of the sensible with both heart and eyes wide open. The body as the primary interface with our environment is our platform for stepping into the world, our home, as active agents of change, hope, and power.

Returning Home

It is argued here that anticipatory aesthetics is a way of returning "home," home being the heart place in the world that we can inhabit when we truly wake up to the present. In this sense, we are speaking of a sense-making that is as ancient as it is new. It is an evolutionary call to "come to our senses," to dance new forms, and to listen to the wisdom inside us all (Berman 1989). The Australian Aboriginal elder Bill Neidjie (1920–2002) offers an indigenous recognition of this deeper sense, a body wisdom that says we may lose our way through cultures of alienation, but in our heart the "Law" is always there, always calling us back.

> Man like you, like me, you feeling this story.
> What I'm saying, you listen.
> You'll feel your string (You feel your connection), you'll feel your body,
> you'll feel yourself.
> Might be morning, you feeling. . .
> 'Ahh, I want to understand that. I want to listen'
> In yourself. . .feeling.
> But this story should be never lose (But this story should not be lost).
> E should be stay for might be million, million year. . .
> with the country, with the people.
> Because that story that Man made. . .
> 'Never change!'
> Law e said. . .
> 'Never change!'
> So we can't.
> Something holding you, you see. You can't do it.
> Word e can do it (Words can change – i.e., cultural forms can lose touch with the story/Law)
> but that something. . .you can't do it. (Neidjie 1989, p. 102)

In this fascinating passage Neidjie is describing from his indigenous perspective the conditions pertaining to Deleuze's transcendental empiricism. For Neidjie the story is felt, in the body; it is the body that acts as the intuitive interface between the sensible world we inhabit and the aesthetic world of feeling and narrative. In Neidjie, we experience that strange "reason" that Deleuze was pointing to. It is this reason, the "something" Neidjie ends with, that calls us into action. Furthermore, it is Neidjie's eternal *"Never change!"* that sits behind Deleuze's notion of "repetition" which is always different and always the same. This is the paradox of anticipation; we "read" the patterning around us and process it through deep senses such as memory and foresight in order to discover that the dance is always different yet also the same, promising the eternal return home.

The Buddhist scholar Joanna Macy reads this aesthetic return, in which difference and repetition play out as the two constants informing any anticipatory field, as an evolutionary dimension of the human condition.

> As living forms evolve on the planet, we move not only in the direction of diversification, but toward integration as well. These two movements complement and enhance each other. Open systems self-organize and integrate by virtue of their differentiation, and they

differentiate by virtue of their interactions. As we evolved we progressively shed our shells, our armour, our separate encasements; we grew soft, sensitive, vulnerable protuberances – eyes, lips, fingertips – to better connect and receive information, to better interweave our discoveries. If we are all bodhisattvas, it is because that thrust to connect, that capacity to integrate with and through each other, is our true nature. (2007, p. 107)

This evolutionary approach posits a reaching out, a softening and deepening of senses, an opening to the affordances immanent to any context. Thus we become more human by moving out into the world, our cosmic home. The sensing Macy refers to is a human thing based, in the first instance, in the physical senses but extending beyond these. In addition it has deep prehuman evolutionary roots. Sensitivity is an evolutionary faculty that advantages the species though it may cost individuals dearly. Anticipatory aesthetics harnesses this deepening sensitivity in order to further advantage the collective. Indeed, it offers a teleological trajectory that points to ever increased levels of sensitivity in which heart opens to heart and human beings reach beyond themselves back and forward into the rich Chaosmos from which they have emerged (Abram 1996; Martin 1992).

Neohumanism as an Emergent Order

As the anticipatory faculty develops, it shapes the human-Cosmos relationship. The evolutionary nature of this change is well articulated by Macy above and points to what the Indian philosopher and mystic Prabhat Rainjan Sarkar (1921–1990) has called Neohumanism (Sarkar 1982). Neohumanism is intuitively aligned with systems thinking as it draws on indigenous Tantric understandings of the world as a "thick present" (Poli 2011, p. 71), in which pasts, presents, and futures engage in layered sense-making and in which both living and nonliving systems are agents in the ongoing co-creation of the Cosmos. This Neohumanist cosmology also shares much in common with Deleuze's description of the Chaosmos; however it is more teleologically driven, as Neohumanism posits a partial terminus, in which at least at the individual level, evolution can in theory end with the merger of the unit being with the Cosmic Divine (*samadhi/moksha*). Deleuze of course suggests no such end. The focus of Neohumanism on a terminus is however important as it supplies the cultural logic for evolution: that we are all striving to return "home." This introduces yearning (for "home"), what Sarkar calls "longing for the great" (1994), and also optimism (we will one day return "home") to a cultural reading of anticipation. Thus longing and optimism become aesthetic drivers in the evolutionary dynamic of living systems.

This leads this author to argue that we inhabit a Neohumanist condition in which relational dynamics underpins the anticipatory aesthetic at work in sense-making within and across contexts. Neohumanism offers a rich intercultural reading of the human condition (Bussey 2006a, b) that accounts for the body in context as an affective unit that reaches into our pasts, presents, and futures as cultural zones of anticipatory potential. As Inayatullah acknowledges, it seeks to access, perhaps even generate, new pathways to a wisdom culture that can potentially reintegrate the sensory, the psychic, the social, and the spiritual (Inayatullah 2006).

This anticipatory work sits at the heart of cultural renewal, and such renewal begins with a return to the aesthetic dimension in which our human senses become us, to use the lovely expression of Nirmal Selvamony (2015). Neohumanism allows us to "connect the dots" between the natural and cultural worlds by positing the pragmatic in-between. As an intercivilizational tool, it enriches the thinking on the in-between offered by Deleuze and a host of others (Brandom 2008; Dallmayr 2002; Semetsky 2006). To use Deleuze's own language, Neohumanism is a "rhythm" that transgresses by cutting across domains such as nature, culture, identity, and sense (1987, p. 313). Such transgressions begin, as Macy suggests, with our physical senses but also extends into the cultural domain as a set of futures senses that nurture the openness to the dynamics of difference Deleuze was envisioning in his outline of a transcendental empiricism. Any move in this direction brings with it aesthetic and ethical considerations as Nadin notes.

> Once human beings relate to this dynamics, their own aesthetics and ethics are projected upon the physical, or upon the living as we encounter it in our own existence. (2010, p. 5)

Xenakis and Arnellos agree, arguing that no object is inherently aesthetic. An aesthetic quality is projected onto the object by the viewer, and this viewer of course need not be human. There are many instances in the natural world of aesthetics at work in mate selection and so on. Thus they note:

> In this way, it would be wrong to talk about objects that are aesthetic *per se*. "*aesthetic*" *is considered the indications of potential interactions, when they are emotionally evaluated with respect to the way they serve (the degree of fulfillment with regard to the optimal) an interaction to the world.* Thus in a naturalized context "the aesthetic" is nothing more than a way of interaction. (Italics in original, 2014, p. 11)

Yet in a cultural context, such interactions are aesthetically conditioned. Any aesthetic assessment involves emotional and normative judgments, and these are shaped by culture, arising not simply in the agent's mind but out of their dynamic environment. Once again we find that interplay of nature and culture at work. Yi-Fu Tuan summarizes this well:

> The aesthetic impulse, understood as the 'senses come to life', directs attention to its roots in nature. But though rooted in nature (biology), it is directed and coloured by culture. (1995, pp. 7–8)

Such considerations presuppose both an epistemological and ontological shift. The reliance on Neohumanist sensitivities to the relational dynamics of "in-betweeness" allows us to engage an anticipatory aesthetic both from the Western perspective of systems theory, evolutionary biology, and aesthetics and from the Eastern Tantric perspective that allows for a creative and conscious Cosmos, thus presupposing a more explicit engagement with spirituality. This intercivilizational engagement invokes a spiritual pragmatics that embraces *dialogue and action* between our subjective and objective realities across cultures, epistemes, norms, and their forms (Bussey 2014c; Giri 2016). Neohumanism and spiritual pragmatics offer a dynamic epistemic field from which the following reflection on anticipatory aesthetics emerges.

Anticipatory Aesthetics

Anticipatory aesthetics sit at the heart of the human experience. The concept involves a range of subtler senses that arise out of a person's aesthetic capital pertaining to the affordances inherent to the entire system. The use of the term aesthetic capital is intentionally borrowing from Bourdieu's (1977) notion of social capital. Aesthetic capital pertains to the degree to which a person can draw on a wide set of personal and cultural resources in order to make choices in their world. This subjective field is not a given, as experience and context are always unique. Exposure to futures thinking, for instance, enriches the anticipatory dimension of such capital. At a more fundamental level, gender, place of birth, education, and cultural exposure also factor into this. Beyond that there are the qualities of personality and worldview. Phenomenologically each of us finds ourselves in the world, epistemologically we navigate the world, and ontologically we are called to make the world our home.

As we manage these categories in order to sharpen our anticipatory potential, we engage our "futures senses" (Bussey 2016). The future senses are elements of what Poli would situate in his category of "weak anticipation" (2009, p. 27). For Poli, this quality involves a cognitive projection on the part of the individual. One that, in the light of the previous discussion, we can understand to involve the individual in the entirety of the system, managing their choices based on past experience, present need, and future anticipations. The future senses can then begin with the *sense of memory* and the *sense of foresight*. The individual themselves, embedded in the context, has always only a limited capacity to act – that ability to choose, to analyze, articulate, synthesize, and mobilize involves the *future sense of voice*. These three senses inform the anticipatory aesthetic process with cultural data (memory), anticipatory patterns/tools (foresight) and a sense of agency where body-mind-spirit brings order to memory and foresight (voice). Yet there is more. Other senses stretch toward the horizon and yearn for something beyond the mundane, the secure, and the predictable. Yi-Fu Tuan speaks to this element beautifully:

> If this world seems to us 'passing strange and wonderful,' it is because culture, through laborious and labyrinthine paths traversed over millennia, has greatly and variedly refined our senses and mind. So when a world citizen now asks, What is a human being? The answer is, Not just a biped animal, but an individual who pauses to smell the sea, listen to silence in the intervals of music, contemplate the shifting spaces of an architectural interior, marvel at what can only be seen with the mind's eye – the curvature of the universe. (1995, p. 240)

Here we find the moralist in Tuan evoking a cosmic relationship in which culture grows better people. This human venture of "growing better people" is an optimistic venture, one that understands human frailty yet turns, ultimately, to what is the best in us. This is the *future sense of optimism* at work. Such optimism of course has a trajectory, a teleological arc. This trajectory can be called, the *future sense of yearning*. But it is not simply a yearning for improvement as understood by the nineteenth- and twentieth-century moralists. As is argued elsewhere (Bussey 2013), it is a yearning for more; for going beyond limits; for more beauty, joy, and hope; and for finding our way back into relationships that support and fulfil us. This is the Neohumanist "longing for the great" spoken of above. It is the evolutionary compass at work in culture and the "something" that Bill Neidjie pointed to when he tried to articulate what it was about the Law that bound human beings to their humanity.

Activating the Futures Senses

So, in recognizing and engaging with anticipation via an aesthetic appreciation for sense-making, a larger palette of conceptual and affective tools – the futures senses – comes to our aid. An aesthetic reading of the human being in the world allows us to appreciate that sensuous perception is transformed by culture. Our ability to harness our physical senses to the work of transcending present boundaries is part of this. In a time when fundamentalism, reactionary politics, and a deep disenchantment with the world are damaging our aesthetic engagement with life – impairing our capacity for wonder and awe – we need to bring the body and our futures senses into futures work.

The futures senses of memory, foresight, voice, optimism, and yearning activate the transgressive dimension of anticipation and free it from a single system of interpretation. Memory, for instance, invokes a range of disciplines including history, cosmology, evolutionary biology, geology, paleontology, neurology, archaeology, ethnography, pedagogy, and much more. Key to memory is the critical capacity to engage with memory's anticipatory potential. Memory work often involves pain and shame; it can side step culpability, massage, and idealize moments of terror. It can also be wedded to the fictive and the mythic via narrative and put in service of powerful. Anticipatory memory work challenges such "deceptions" and invites in sensory memory to disturb the hallowed sanitized memories of the present. Inga Clendinnen (1998) engages in such work in her reflections on representations of the holocaust while Nadia Seremetakis (1996):

> "...points to the perceptual construction of truth as an involuntary disclosure of meaning through the senses" so that truth is "extralinguistic and revealed through expression, performance, material culture and conditions of embodiment." (Cited in Porcello et al. 2010, p. 59; Seremetakis 1996, p. 6)

Strong emotions are at work here and have an impact on how the "truth" is perceived (Ricatti 2013). When memory is understood as a futures sense that plays a powerful role in value systems, priorities, and decision-making, foresight practitioners can disrupt hegemonic memory patterns and effectively release distortions that impact on anticipatory judgment. Without memory human beings are naked.

Thus memory is primal and deeply sensory as is attested to by those working on the senses in history (Classen 2012; Monaghan 2012 (June 18); Scheer 2012).

Strategies for engaging the futures sense of memory include embodied work involving a range of senses (Lederach and Lederach 2010), exformation, and other embodied elements of InterPlay (Winton-Henry and Porter 2016), playback and forward theater (Head 2012), experiential games (Candy and Dunagan 2016), intimate futures work (Bussey 2014b), and shared narratives and timelines (Inayatullah 2008). Such engagements acknowledge the messiness and difficulties of memory work. Work with the futures senses of foresight, voice, optimism, and yearning is equally messy and difficult. Such work is also deeply satisfying.

Conclusion

This chapter has sought to lay out a context for thinking about anticipation as an aesthetic dimension of human identity. It has positioned the anticipatory aesthetic at the center of an evolutionary model that brings together a set of futures senses. It has been argued that culture brings with it an evolutionary advantage because of its anticipatory capacity. Furthermore, the case is made that anticipatory behavior is better understood when we bring together diverse cultural readings in the service of an emergent anticipatory ontology. Thus Neohumanism, as a decentering of Western individualist thinking, offers a bridge to alternative readings of anticipatory aesthetics. In fact the emergent notion of spiritual pragmatics is a valuable complement to our thinking about anticipatory systems. Such approaches both enable and explain culture's diversity, richness, and resilience. Culture, however, never acts alone; it always acts in relationship with the material world that it glosses with meaning. In offering an aesthetic approach to anticipation, this paper is therefore seeking to ground the conceptual scaffolding offered by anticipatory systems theory in bodily, sensory engagements with the world.

Finally, it is suggested that to activate the futures senses offers rich possibilities for anticipatory behavior. Such behavior sits at the heart of human cultural creativity and is a deep source of hope in times of diminishing returns. Finding ways to engage with anticipatory aesthetics as foresight practitioners is an ongoing endeavor. It feels like we are only scratching the surface. As anticipation as a theoretical construct, and perhaps even a discipline, grows in coherence and rigor, the task of charting its potential domains will involve rich multidisciplinary and intercivilizational explorations. We do not know where our global civilization is headed, though we all anticipate turbulence ahead. However, harnessing powerful visions of hope and transcendence is part of that work. Finding ways to reintegrate body wisdom with the wisdoms of the heart, the head, and the spirit is an important component of this work. Channelizing the pent up energy of this historical moment into constructive explorations in the theory and application of anticipatory systems and the implicit aesthetic domain that underpins it will certainly spark ongoing innovation in the foresight sector.

References

Abram, D. (1996). *The spell of the sensuous: perception and language in a more-than-Human World.* New York: Vintage Books.

Berman, M. (1989). *Coming to our senses: Body and spirit in the hidden story of the west.* New York: Simon and Schuster.

Bourdieu, P. (1977). *Outline of a theory of practice.* Cambridge, UK: Cambridge University Press.

Brandom, R. B. (2008). *Between saying and doing: Towards an analytic pragmatism.* Oxford: Oxford University Press.

Bussey, M. (2006a). Critical spirituality: Towards a revitalised humanity. *Journal of Futures Studies, 10*(4), 39–44.

Bussey, M. (2006b). Neohumanism: Critical spirituality, tantra and education. In S. Inayatullah, M. Bussey, & I. Milojevic (Eds.), *Neohumanist educational futures: Liberating the pedagogical intellect* (pp. 80–95). Taipei: Tamkang University Press.

Bussey, M. (2009). Six shamanic concepts: exploring the *between* in futures work. *Foresight, 11*(2), 29–42.

Bussey, M. (2011). Microvita and other spaces: Deepening research through intuitive practice. *Journal of Futures Studies, 16*(1), 137–150.

Bussey, M. (2013). Re-imagining limits. *Sociological Bulletin, 62*(1), 129–131.

Bussey, M. (2014a). Concepts and effects: Ordering and practice in foresight. *Foresight, 16*(1), 1–16.

Bussey, M. (2014b). Intimate futures: Bringing the body into futures work. *European Journal of Futures Research, 2*(53), 1–8.

Bussey, M. (2014c). Towards a spiritual pragmatics: Reflections from the graveyards of culture. *3D IBA Journal of Business and Management, 6*(1), 37–49.

Bussey, M. (2016). The hidden curriculum of futures studies: Introducing the futures senses. *World Futures Review, 8*(1), 39–45.

Candy, S., & Dunagan, J. (2016). Designing an experiential scenario: *The People* who vanished. *Futures, 84.* https://doi.org/10.1016/j.futures.2016.05.006.

Chatterjee, A. (2010). Neuroaesthetics: A coming of age story. *Journal of Cognitive Neuroscience, 23*(1), 53–62.

Chemero, A. (2003). An outline of a theory of affordances. *Ecological Psychology, 15*(2), 181–195.

Classen, C. (2012). *The deepest sense: A cultural history of touch.* Champaign: University of Illinois Press.

Clendinnen, I. (1998). *Reading the Holocaust.* Melbourne: Text Publishing Co.

Dallmayr, F. (2002). *Dialogue among civilizations: Some exemplary voices.* New York: Palgrave Macmillan.

Deleuze, G. (1994). *Difference and repetition* (trans: Patton, P.). New York: Columbia University Press.

Deleuze, G., & Guattari, F. (1987). *A thousand plateaus: Capitalism and schizophrenia* (trans: Massumi, B.). London & New York: Continuum.

Enquist, M., & Arak, A. (1994). Symmetry, Beauty and Evolution. *Nature, 372,* 169–172.

Foucault, M. (1986). Of other spaces. *Diacritics, 16*(1), 22–27.

Giri, A. K. (2016). Spiritual Pragmatism: New Pathways of Transformation for the Posthuman. In D. Banerji & M. R. Paranjape (Eds.), *Critical posthumanism and planetary futures* (pp. 225–242). Springer India: New Delhi.

Head, S. (2012). Forward Theatre and Causal Layered Analysis. *Journal of Futures Studies, 17*(1), 41–56.

Inayatullah, S. (2006). From Multiculturalism to Neohumanism: Pedagogy and Politics in Changing Futures. In S. Inayatullah, M. Bussey, & I. Milojević (Eds.), *Neohumanist educational futures: Liberating the pedagogical intellect* (pp. 6–20). Taipei: Tamkang University Press.

Inayatullah, S. (2008). Six pillars: Futures thinking for transforming. *Foresight, 10*(1), 4–21.

Inayatullah, S. (2013). Using gaming to understand the patterns of the future – The Sarkar game in action. *Journal of Futures Studies, 18*(1), 1–12.

Lederach, J. P., & Lederach, A. J. (2010). *When blood and bones cry out: Journey's through the soundscape of healing and reconciliation*. Brisbane: University of Queensland Press.

Macy, J. (2007). *World as lover, World as self*. Berkeley: Parallax Press.

Martin, C. L. (1992). *In the spirit of the Earth: Rethinking history and time*. Baltinore: John Hopkins University Press.

Miller, R. (2007). Futures literacy: A hybrid strategic scenario method. *Futures, 39*(4), 341–362.

Miller, R., Poli, R., & Rossel, P.. (2013). The discipline of anticipation: Exploring key issues. *Global/local anticipatory capacities, working paper 1*. https://www.academia.edu/3523348/ The_Discipline_of_Anticipation_Miller_Poli_Rossel_-_DRAFT). Viewed 19 Sept 2015.

Milojević, I. (2013). *Breathing: Violence in, peace out*. Brisbane: University of Queensland Press.

Monaghan, P. (2012, June 18). Studying History with Feeling. *The Chronicle of Higher Education*.

Nadin, M. (2010). Anticipation and the artificial: Aesthetics, ethics, and synthetic life. *AI & Society, 25*(1), 103–118.

Neidjie, B. (1989). *Story about feeling*. Broome: Magabala Press.

Poli, R. (2009). The complexity of anticipation. *Balkan Journal of Philosophy, 1*(1), 19–29.

Poli, R. (2010). The many aspects of anticipation. *Foresight, 12*(3), 7–17.

Poli, R. (2011). Steps toward an explicit ontology of the future. *Journal of Futures Studies, 16*(1), 67–78.

Porcello, T., Meintjes, L., Ochoa, A. M., & Samuels, D. W. (2010). The reorganization of the sensory World. *Annual Review of Anthropology, 39*, 51–66.

Ricatti, F. (2013). The emotion of truth and the racial uncanny: Aborigines and Sicilians in Australia. *Cultural Studies Review, 19*(2), 125–149.

Sarkar, P. R. (1982). *The liberation of intellect: Neohumanism*. Calcutta: Ananda Marga Publications.

Sarkar, P. R. (1994). *Subhasita Samgraha, Pt 24* (Vol. 21). Calcutta: Ananda Marga Publications.

Scheer, M. (2012). Are emotions a kind of practice (and is that what makes them have a history)? A Bourdieuian approach to understanding emotion. *History and Theory, 51*, 193–220.

Selvamony, N. (2015). From the Anthropocene to the Neo-*tiNai*cene. *International Journal of Central University of Kerala, 3*(2), 115–130.

Semetsky, I. (2006). *Deleuze, education and becoming*. Rotterdam: Sense Publishers.

Seremetakis, C. N. (1996). *The senses still: Perceptions and memory as material culture in modernity*. Chicago: University of Chicago Press.

Tuan, Y.-F. (1995). *Passing strange and wonderful: Aesthetics, nature, and culture*. New York: Kodansha International.

Winton-Henry, C., & Porter, P. (2016). *Move: What the body wants*. Kelowna: Wood Lake.

Xenakis, I., & Arnellos, A. (2014). Aesthetic perception and its minimal content: A naturalistic perspective. *Frontiers in Psychology, 5*, 1–15.

Anticipation on the Boundaries of Musical and Pictorial Continua

42

Iacopo Hachen and Liliana Albertazzi

Contents

Electronic supplementary material: The online version of this article (https://doi.org/10.1007/978-3-319-91554-8_9) contains supplementary material, which is available to authorized users.

I. Hachen
International School for Advanced Studies (SISSA), Trieste, Italy
e-mail: iacopo.hachen@alumni.unitn.it

L. Albertazzi (✉)
Laboratory of Experimental Phenomenology, Department of Humanities, University of Trento, Trento, Italy
e-mail: liliana.albertazzi@unitn.it

© Springer Nature Switzerland AG 2019
R. Poli (ed.), *Handbook of Anticipation*,
https://doi.org/10.1007/978-3-319-91554-8_9

Abstract

Anticipation plays an essential role in the perception of the empirical reality. Music, because of its purely dynamical nature, is a privileged environment for the study of anticipation processes. In this chapter, we firstly discuss the current viewpoint on anticipation in music perception and the meaning of anticipation structures in general. Then we present a descriptive study of how melodies are experienced inside the psychic present, analyzing a series of musical excerpts alongside selected pictorial analogues. Focusing on the dynamic patterns shared by auditory and visual modalities, we discuss the nature of perceptual continua and their boundaries in the subjective space-time.

Keywords

Anticipation · Awareness · Gestalt Psychology · Music Perception · Music Cognition · Paul Klee · Perceptual Continua · Phenomenology · Pictorial art · Subjective Space-Time · Visual Perception · Western Music

Introduction

Musicians experience anticipation in their everyday musical practice. In orchestras, for example, anticipation rules both the conductor's and the players' performance. On the one hand, what allows players to attack with the right part at the right moment, by looking at the movements of the conductor, is the fact that the conductor's gestures slightly anticipate what is written on the score (Berthoz 2012). On the other hand, in reading the musical score, anticipation is what allows the players to perform the score correctly, by directing their glance to the next measures and preparing their next actions while still playing the previous ones. In music theory, anticipation has also technical meanings, referring to both rhythmic and harmonic compositional (see ► Chap. 8, "Anticipation: Some Notes" by Supko, this handbook) or improvisational techniques (as in jazz).

Because musicians are biased by all these different kinds of "anticipation," it is usually less easy for them to apply the concept of anticipation to what happens during music *listening*, where the term "expectation" is usually preferred. Every Western musician knows, for example, that a dominant chord "needs" to resolve on (i.e., "needs" to be followed by) a tonic chord; in other words, listeners *expect* the dominant chord to be followed by the tonic chord, to the point that they can be "deceived" by placing a different chord after the dominant one (as in so-called "deceptive cadence"). The concept of expectation in music is very intuitive even for naïve listeners, who seem to paraphrase the question about anticipation with expressions like "Can you tell what comes next?"

Hence, the term "anticipation" seems more suitable for designating some technical device, perhaps a musical stratagem involved in causing a sense of expectation in listeners. Assuming that anticipation is somewhere "in the music," it would be a good idea to look for it on the score. For example, Western musical notation makes it intuitive for one to describe "anticipation" as some kind of relation between what is written at a certain point on the score (representing a given musical event) and anything that is written next to it in reading order (a musical event to happen in the future). According to this simple view, if an anticipatory relation exists, what comes "before" on the score should anticipate what comes "after," as in the case of the dominant chord and its following one. However, the first chord alone would be enough to elicit a sense of "expectation." For true *anticipation* to occur (see Poli, this handbook, *Preface*), the future should also take part in the process. A possible solution to the problem is to say that the dominant chord will influence, to a certain extent, how listeners *perceive* the next chord. Following this line of argument, an appropriate definition of "musical anticipation" could be that of a process in which any musical element A (e.g., a note or a chord) is linked to a future musical element B (a different note or chord) by exerting an agency on its perception; let us state that, depending on the properties of the element A, the element B will be perceived as more or less "expected."

In this chapter, we will argue that this kind of model can explain only one face of the anticipation processes in music perception. In fact, to prove how essential is anticipation to music, one must delve directly into the listening experience and address problems related to the subjective perception of time, i.e., the structure of the psychic present, the continuity of dynamic objects, and the hierarchical whole-part relations that arise within them. By doing so, it will become evident how an alternative conception of time, not strictly sequential, is more suited to describe anticipatory phenomena inside our consciousness.

An important aim of this chapter is to highlight the anticipation phenomena existing in music, and specifically in melody, as general properties of perceptual processes, independent of a specific sensory modality. To this purpose, basing on the intrinsic cross-modal nature of perception (for artistic phenomena, see, e.g., Albertazzi et al. 2015; Palmer et al. 2013; for a review of the field, see Spence 2011), we will draw analogies between musical excerpts (mostly drawn from a renowned Western classical music repertoire) and various visual objects, in particular pictorial ones, considered in their *dynamic* unfolding (in this respect, the sample materials that we present complement and illustrate [▶ Chap. 14, "Microgenesis of Anticipation: Windowing the Present" by Albertazzi, this handbook]). We will adopt a naively empirical stance, performing a few simple perceptual experiments for the sole purpose of clarifying our points. By no means do we consider the present materials to be exhaustive of the entire subject matter; rather, they are examples raising questions to be analyzed further from a more systematic and experimental perspective. We have also been striving to make this work accessible to the non-musician, avoiding technical language where possible.

The next section serves as both an introduction to the framework in which the work is embedded and a brief historical survey about the theories of anticipation in music.

Anticipation and Meaning in Music

Introduction

The intrinsically temporal nature of musical phenomena is not only evident to anyone, but it has often been taken as a distinctive trait of this art form, as opposed, for example, to visual art. Therefore, it is not surprising that the "anticipation" framework (although the process of anticipation has not been always described with the same terminology) has been central in several theories of music cognition of recent decades. Analysis of the nature of anticipatory processes has led to the development of several models (e.g., Meyer 1956; Narmour 1990, 1992; Margulis 2005; Huron 2006), all adhering to a similar framework.

An aspect that emerges from these studies is that, in general, the reasoning on anticipation is supposed to follow a logic of this kind: (1) sounds are presented to the subject as linearly streamed, unorganized material (although appearing in the form of musical notes) that has been transformed from physical air vibrations into meaningful (see the next subsection for a reflection upon the word "meaning") sound objects, with properties such as pitch and timbre, by means of microscopic grouping processes usually interpreted as Helmholtzian "unconscious inferences" (e.g., Deutsch 1982, p. 183); (2) the subject, by taking the notes as input for a statistical function, computes a sequence of predictions about the events that have to follow in the timeline; and (3) the consistency or the discrepancy occurring between the musical material presented at a certain instant and the subject's predictions about that instant (the "goodness of fit") ultimately results in the musical experience.

However, although this conception of the "anticipation" framework has become very popular in describing the listeners' musical cognition in a functional sense, not much has been done in recent decades to explore *how* the anticipation processes themselves appear to the listeners' *awareness.* Put briefly, can anticipation itself be consciously perceived, or are listeners aware only of its consequences? If anticipation is part of the listening experience, of what does it consist?

The "anticipation" framework since its first formulations (Meyer 1956) and also recently has often addressed the emotional and affective correlates of music (see, e.g., Juslin and Västfjäll 2008, p. 568 and references therein), a still developing and promising research field (e.g., Koelsch 2012, pp. 203–240; Juslin and Västfjäll 2008; Huron 2006). What emerges from the vast majority of current models of musical anticipation is therefore the tendency to describe music as a phenomenon that, through a process of information accumulation (unconsciously stored from past experience), prediction, and error evaluation, links sounds to emotions (the whole process occurring on a linear timeline that corresponds to the physical one). However, emotions and affective dimensions are only some of the components of subjective musical experience, based on more grounding perceptual properties. What is missing in this framework is an overall account of the conscious organization of the musical material as *presently* perceived in the listener's awareness, besides its affective dimensions. Usually unclear is the nature of "information" for a conscious subject; and sometimes this question is explicitly evaded.

Music as a Symbolic System

For a concrete example of the above problem, let us consider the most classic theory of anticipation (or, in its exact formulation, *expectation*) in music, the one proposed by Leonard B. Meyer in his essay *Meaning and Emotion in Music* (1956). It is curious that, although Meyer's work was strongly influenced by the Gestalt tradition (and in particular Koffka's ideas), this influence seems to be mostly confined to the principles used by Meyer in his structural analyses (making use of concepts such as *Prägnanz*, *good continuation*, and *closure*). On the other hand, Meyer's framework adopts a different stance when presenting his ideas about musical meaning.

Meyer seems to distinguish between *perception* and *experience* of sounds. While he avoids restricting the perception of musical structures to mere physical vibrations, he repeatedly uses the term "musical stimuli," which, however, seems to us to coincide with that layer of rather obscure information mentioned above, as it is neither merely physical nor felt by the listener. The only "meaning" that pure perception has, according to Meyer, is "abstract" and "intellectual" (p. 3). When discussing the so-called formalist position, in fact, he describes it as follows: "the formalist would contend that the meaning of music lies in the perception and understanding of the musical relationships set forth in the work of art and that meaning in music is primarily intellectual" (p. 3).

To be precise, this particular idea of formalism has been inherited by the philosophical thought of Susanne K. Langer, who defines music, and art in general, as a "significant form" (see, e.g., Langer 1953; more specifically, see pp. 24–41). Note that this form is considered "significant" in the sense of a symbolic object that, however, lacks a "conventional reference" (i.e., "a fixed association, and therewith a single, unequivocal reference" (p. 31), corresponding to what was commonly assumed for language). This lack of an arbitrary association between form and meaning induces Langer even to propose that, in the sense of conventional semantics, the term "meaning" is not well suited to describing music. Thus, she replaces it with the concept of *import*, as "the pattern of sentience – the pattern of life itself, as it is felt and directly known" (p. 31). On the one hand, in a significant *form* the meaning is somehow qualitatively *felt* by the listener. However, on the other hand, because the musical object is essentially symbolic for Langer, she still seems to interpret this "meaning" only in relation to external feelings, not a *conventional* reference, but, in our view, still a reference associated with a symbol that must be identified in the form itself. In fact, for Langer, it is evident that qualities consist in "abstractions" because they are detached from the material, physical world (see, e.g., pp. 55–68). In clarifying her position, Langer cites the following example:

A little section of border such as we view here

is taken in at one glance, practically without ocular movement. Actually, nothing moves enough to give us a sensation of movement. The design, however, is a symbolic form which abstracts the continuity, directedness, and energy of motion, and conveys the idea of those abstracted characters exactly as any symbol conveys its meaning. In fact, it presents something more complex than the essence of motion, which it could not do if it merely connoted motion by stimulating diminutive movements in our eyes: namely, the idea of growth. (pp. 64–65)

If we assume this view of musical form, we can better understand Meyer's criticism when he says that the formalist position has failed to explain "the manner in which an abstract, non-referential succession of tones becomes meaningful" (p. 3). Meyer agrees with Langer that the *internal* structure of music is given to listeners' perception, and, for him, the whole point is to find how these *"abstract"* structures become associated with affective states. He maintains that this can be done with or without having to step through "external" domains, such as concepts. These two possible approaches are respectively called "referentialism" and "absolutism" (pp. 1–4), which is misleading because both views, at least in Meyer's framework, require a reference in the classic semantic sense; in fact, what changes is only the *sign*, which in the second case has to be found in the pure form, while in the first, it is *what is evoked* by the form, such as concepts and actions.

As regards the "abstract" meaning of musical structures, Meyer tries to find an alternative solution to the problem by introducing the concept of *expectation*: "If, on the basis of past experience, a present stimulus leads us to expect a more or less definite consequent musical event, then that stimulus has meaning" (p. 7), a meaning that needs to be understood in terms of probability relations between the musical elements. In his attempt to give an account of the expectation processes from the point of view of the listener, Meyer states that *being aware* of musical processes is something that *only* expert listeners are able to achieve. He conceives awareness in terms of competence (pp. 14–35) and sometimes employs sentences such as the following: "Self-conscious minds tend to rationalize musical processes by bringing their observations to the level of conscious awareness. They tend, that is, to respond on the aesthetic intellectual level" (p. 198). In fact, when introducing the distinction between affective and non-affective mental states, Meyer describes the latter as "dispassionate observation, calm deliberation, and cool calculation" (pp. 14–35).

Refining these ideas in his paper on *Meaning in music and information theory* (1957), Meyer further distinguishes between *active* expectations, of which the subject is aware, and *latent* expectations, of which the subject is unaware until they are in some way contradicted. As he writes: "We 'expect' to get up Monday morning, to eat breakfast, to see that the children get to school, to go to the office, and so forth. But we are as a rule unconscious of such expectations (...) If, for instance, we over-sleep or breakfast is delayed, then we become aware of our expectant habits. We are aware of the necessity of getting to the office, of making choices and decisions." And, once again, he concludes that latent expectations are nothing but the product of "probability relationships," i.e., dimensions not possessing an *intrinsic* meaning (pp. 414–419).

To sum up, although the pioneering work of Meyer is a rich and substantial contribution to the establishment of Gestalt psychology in music theory, and his attempt to describe the systematics of the expectation process is worthy of consideration, Meyer's approach reduces the musical experience to two levels: one consisting of the behavioral, unconscious processing of stimuli (named "perception") and a second one consisting of a conscious attribution of "meaning" by the subject in terms of emotional content. Here, however, the concept of meaning does not emerge from the anticipation process itself (both a forward-looking attitude *and* its role for action; see Poli, this handbook, *Preface*) but consists in a merely reactive behavior. In short, in this framework, anticipation is conceived as a process that rules the subject's behavior, causing posterior emotional effects, but strictly speaking it does not concern his/her *conscious* perceptual awareness.

It seems that more modern theories on musical anticipation processes influenced by cognitivism (e.g., Narmour 1990, 1992, 2000; Huron 2006) have adopted ideas not particularly different from Meyer's as regards musical meaning, certainly privileging the probabilistic aspects of music perception. For example, according to Narmour (2000), the process of building expectations in music is "automatic," because "too much thinking will suppress one's musical attention and hence detract from the aesthetic pleasure of the experience" (p. 331). Once again, it seems that Narmour understands musical awareness in terms of "thinking" or "contemplation" of abstract rules and in so doing attributes it to top-level mental processes. Interestingly, Narmour draws a distinction between musical and visual art. Because the latter is not subject to the same time constraints, it can more explicitly allow the "contemplation" of its organizational rules.

Indeed, modern cognitivist theories about the process of anticipation in music prove very promising in describing the statistical properties of listeners' expectations, and they provide an effective framework for experimental and quasi-experimental tests (e.g., Cuddy and Lunney 1995; Schellenberg 1996; to have many examples of computational studies, see Huron 2006). However, the original question about musical meaning does not seem to us to be answered satisfactorily by these approaches. As pointed out in Albertazzi's ▶ Chap. 14, "Microgenesis of Anticipation: Windowing the Present," this handbook, inferential behavior is not sufficient to account for an experience of "certainty," a feeling that lies at the very core of multifaceted musical phenomena such as rhythm, melody, and harmony. For this reason, we will adhere to a different framework, which is itself historically grounded.

An Alternative Proposal

The cognitivist paradigm in music theory is based on standard information theory (Shannon and Weaver 1963) and digital computation-inspired models (predicate logic, set and probability theory). This conception of information operates in a closed domain where *meaning* is relegated to a locus outside the perceptual and communicative process (i.e., in the physical structure of stimuli). This concept privileges metric quantities, follows the unidirectional parameters of stimulus reaction, and is most effectively expressed in statistical and logical analysis (Albertazzi et al. 2010). Qualitative and subjective experiences and mental, social, and artistic phenomena remain excluded and/or difficult to analyze in terms of this concept of information because they are not easily algorithmically computed and exhibit a higher-order complexity characterized by anticipation structures and internal semantics. Generally, meaning is reduced either to syntax, as in generative grammar (Chomsky 1957, 1981), or to neurophysiological processes, as in neuroaesthetics (Zeki 1999; see also Livingstone 2002; Solso 2003; Ramachandran 2003), and by cognitive and psychophysical analyses (McManus et al. 2010). The challenge would be to develop a science of aesthetic (and other qualitative) phenomena of human experience based on *internal subjective parameters* rather than a mapping on and *re*presentation of stimuli (Albertazzi 2015).

As regards music perception, a view alternative to the current information-emotion paradigm can be traced back to the ideas of the nineteenth-century musical critic (Hanslick 1854) and their influence (Grimes et al. 2013). Hanslick's core idea is that, although music is certainly capable of triggering emotional effects in the listener, it exists as such, i.e., as pure *forms* and precisely as pure *forms in movement* (p. 32). The definition highlights two basic aspects of musical phenomena, i.e., their specific *structure* and *intrinsic dynamics*. Note that this idea of "formalism," despite having been sometimes linked with the one proposed by Langer (as Meyer did), is radically different from the latter. From this viewpoint, the structure of musical forms is not of logical type, i.e., a product of the application of abstract, formalistic, syntactic rules to be apprehended by learning and known by competence only, analogously to what is shaped in generative grammar for language structures (Chomsky 1957, 1981). In Hanslick's theory, the perception and the identification of musical forms are not derived products based on memory and/or comparison among temporal points and features in a linear sequence: vice versa, they are *direct,* and not restricted to musical competence but perceivable by lay persons. To explain the higher-order structure of musical *forms* such as melodies as perceptually experienced, however, requires painstaking analysis of the nature of the *simultaneous* presence of *successive* presentational contents in awareness, of the *rules of organization* governing their deployment, and of the *internal relationships* among the grounding components. Each of these topics, variously shaped and addressed from the perceptual, the ontological, and the aesthetic viewpoints, was the focus of analysis by the Graz school of Meinong (Albertazzi 1996).

Musical Forms as Structured Wholes

A pupil of Brentano, and an expert musician himself, Meinong studied musicology in Vienna with Hanslick, whose influence is apparent in his theories of relations (1882), assumptions (1902), and emotional presentations (1917) (see Meinong 1968–1978; for a philosophical reconstruction of the history, the climate, the topics, and the number of outstanding researchers of the Meinong school, see Albertazzi et al. 2001). The group of Meinongians in Graz gave rise to an astonishing variety of systematic studies, mostly flanked by experimental research (Albertazzi 2001). These studies centered on the concept of perceived wholes as *Gestalt configurations in the subject's awareness*. The evidence of the existence of qualitative configurations in the different perceptual modalities, prompted by the seminal work of Ehrenfels (1890), gave rise to a heated debate, followed by experimental analyses. From time to time, the researchers in Graz, such as Benussi (Albertazzi 2001), Witasek (Haber-ZemlJich 2001), and Hoefler (Blackmore 2001), focused on the priority of the perceived *whole* over its *parts*, the nature of the *act* and of the *presentational contents* founding the whole, the *rules* governing the perception of *Gestalten* (see also Wertheimer 1912, 1923). In this context, *the structure of melody*, and of perceived movement as well, have been paradigmatic case studies from a systematic and experimental viewpoint. To simplify, and for the purposes of the present study, one speaks of the existence of a Gestalt *whole* in perception when a multiplicity of stimuli and of stimulations of the external sense organs, instead of triggering a corresponding multiplicity of independent features, produces a *unitary pattern, a form* which is coherent in itself, and *perceptually bounded* with respect to the others.

Anticipation and Grouping

From Score to Music

Let us start by considering a musical score. The seemingly obvious analogy between music and score is not completely obvious, because the page is a stationary visual object that can be *visually* and *dynamically scanned* by the reader as many times and in as many directions as s/he wishes, as happens with artworks (Arnheim 1954). Consider, for example, Fig. 1.

A visual element such as a note (like the one below the arrow) can *visually* group either with patterns on its left or with patterns on its right, depending on the visual context in which it is embedded (clearly, the eye can move around the page regardless of the left-to-right reading convention). Here, the grouping effect is based on an interaction of Gestalt principles such as proximity, similarity, and good continuation. It is not our intention here to explain the various Gestalt principles that make grouping processes possible, since it has been done extensively elsewhere (see Todorovic 2008: http://www.scholarpedia.org/article/Gestalt_principles).

Instead, we want to point out a fact that complicates the analogy between score and music, that is, the visual score *has* indeed a reading order according to which the

Fig. 1 A musical score is a visual object that is experienced dynamically and independently of the temporal order that it is indicating

notes will be acoustically realized as a *dynamic* phenomenon. On the score, the spatial horizontal axis, which can be freely explored by the reader, maps the *temporal* dimension according to which the notes will be performed. The notes are arranged from left to right, indicating auditory events to be produced earlier or later in the temporal stream. Furthermore, by looking at a single note on the score, one can simultaneously see the entire score surrounding it. Instead, during the musical performance, the notes will be played one after the other without the possibility for the listener to "perceive" them again.

What are the consequences of the above observations on the perceptual organization of the given acoustic material? That grouping processes can happen in music as well as in a variety of other dynamic phenomena is no surprise, given that we are able somehow to retain or "remember" what we have perceived in the past for a limited time. (Let us make it clear that we are setting aside any definition of memory given in terms of operational or physiological explanations. What we are trying to address here are present and past perceptions *within* present *awareness*. See below for further discussion on the topic.) This is a condition for any anticipation process to happen, at least in the standard sense described in the main introduction. Thanks to this ability, we expect the patterns written on the score to group during the listening experience in a way similar to their visual equivalents. In fact, listening to the example (see Voice 1), one will first hear the three-note descending pattern (let us call it pattern 1) that is being repeated multiple times, remaining invariant up to a certain point. Later, during the same example, there will be a moment when the listener will be hearing the second repeating pattern (let us call it pattern 2), consisting of three notes as well, this time ascending. In both situations, as happens with their visual equivalents, Gestalt laws such as proximity, similarity, and good continuation will account for the unity of the patterns.

However, what happens when the perception of one group conflicts with the perception of another? As we have said, during a musical performance, it is not possible to access the full score at once nor to "scan" the notes again and again. We know from the score that there is a point where the two patterns "overlap" by a note, right below the arrow (the note A). We expect this note, at its onset, to group with the pattern that has started before it (see Voice 2). Indeed, we "expect" the same note even before its onset! If so, because this note is bound to the previous acoustic group, the two notes that follow (notes C and E) should not be grouped with it but perceived independently as novel elements. However, once we start to perceive pattern 2, it seems that we "remember" the marked note not as a part of pattern 1 but rather as a part of the second pattern. Someone might describe this phenomenon as a "slip" between two different configurations. The same note spans across multiple groups, similar to what can be observed in the visual scanning of the score: first, as the third note in pattern 1, and last as the first note in pattern 2 (see Fig. 1).

What exactly happens in the transition between the two configurations is somewhat more obscure and would certainly benefit from experimental investigation. However, one thing already apparent is that the transition between the first and the second group is not immediate. Rather, after the two notes that follow the marked one (the notes C and E) have been presented (see Voice 3), the ascending trajectory resulting from the sequence of notes A-C-E seems to have the tendency to "pull out" the marked A from pattern 1 and to put it in continuity with the following two notes. Simultaneously, the basic unit of pattern 2 emerges as a relatively "open" trajectory (i.e., it potentially leaves space for new elements to enter the group). Only after a repetition of the basic unit can pattern 2 be properly recognized as a pattern. This suggests that the switching between different temporal configurations is not something instantaneous but goes through different phases.

To sum up, the marked note has progressively switched in roles, being part of at least three different phases that compose the perceptual transition between the two configurations: as an element of pattern 1; as the start of an open, ascending trajectory, competing with pattern 1; and finally, as an element of pattern 2. What is interesting is that the first configuration involves the marked A first in the form of a *future* (before the actual onset of the note), and then *present* object, while the second and the third configurations involve the same note as a *past* element. In fact, the last two configurations require the marked A first to "slip away" from the previous configuration and become the starting point of the A-C-E note trajectory and then, only after its repetition, become a part of a new established pattern. Hence a curious finding is that establishment of the second pattern requires the repetition of note A as *already outside* the first pattern. In other words, the second A is *repetition* of an element that has never been in the present.

Parts and Wholes

To return to anticipation, we can analyze the example in the following way: at first, the establishment of pattern 1, by determining the perception of the marked note as a *part* of the pattern itself (which in turn must be considered a *whole*) that has *anticipated* the note. Later, the onset of pattern 2 has determined the perception of the *same* note as a part of the new pattern, although the note had been played in the past. What is anticipating what here? While in reading the score the note is clearly the starting point of the second sound sequence, at the acoustic level, one may well say that the manifestation of the whole second pattern has anticipated the perception of the marked note *as a part of that pattern*: in other words, the present would have "anticipated" the past!

It must be noted that, in a Gestalt configuration, parts and wholes behave as if they are *reciprocally* determined by each other, and, causally speaking, it would not be possible to choose a unique "anticipator" between the pattern and the notes that are part of it (remember that this does not mean that the relation between parts and whole must be always symmetrical; we shall discuss this aspect later, section "A Diversity of Boundaries"). Therefore, to be appropriately defined, the concept of anticipation in music should comprise how causal *bi-directional* relations between past and future elements underpin the grouping processes in the experience of musical figures. As we have seen, not only does the event that comes first influence how future events are perceived but what comes later influences the perception of what was before: a *past* object that nevertheless exists retained in the conscious (*specious*) *present* (James 1950; see ▶ Chap. 14, "Microgenesis of Anticipation: Windowing the Present" by Albertazzi, this handbook)! What we mean here by "anticipation" is therefore the process that drives the reciprocal determination of parts and wholes within configurations that are temporally distributed, a process that inextricably links past and future elements together. In the listener's awareness, it can happen that, as in this case, what is perceived as the "anticipating" element becomes so only *after* the presentation of the "anticipated" element.

Direction

Another aspect that we have to take into account is that, as we have seen, perceptual groups are subject to change and often compete with each other. A peculiarity of music is that this change follows a precise *direction*, determined by the constantly mutating context. Let us examine the passage in Fig. 1 at a "broader" level: By considering *both* patterns as perceptual wholes overlapping by a note, we can say that the first pattern is *anticipating* the second one. In fact, it already contains in itself a portion of the next pattern: we are still talking about a "note" (with respect to some perceptual dimension) and yet with a structurally different role. In fact, this note has changed its role as a *part* across two different wholes, but it has done so in a very specific order, from the first to the second pattern.

The observation that, within the auditory modality, the future can influence the perception of the past is certainly not new and has been shown also outside the musical realm. For example, it occurs in phenomena of *temporal displacement*, in which the order of the perceived tones and/or noises is not determined by the physical order of succession of the stimuli but by their Gestalt grouping in subjective awareness (Benussi 1913; see ▶ Chap. 14, "Microgenesis of Anticipation: Windowing the Present" by Albertazzi, this handbook, pp. 12–14). However, in the case of temporal displacements, we are dealing with anticipatory processes that shape perceptual objects *newly* presenting in the awareness and supersede their physical timeline within a window which is usually less than 100 ms. Instead, a peculiarity of the phenomena that we are describing in this chapter is that they act at a relatively larger scale, allowing for a *re*configuration of auditory material that has *already* been consciously perceived (as happens, both visually and acoustically, with the marked note in Fig. 1). One may compare this process to what happens with visual bistable figures, such as the Necker cube (see Albertazzi, pp. 7–9), where the same physical stimulus is subject to different modes of appearance. In dynamic structures such as musical ones, these "modes of appearance" are sometimes not freely interchangeable, but, as we have seen, they can be unambiguously determined by the changing context provided by the structure of the piece. In our example, the repetition of a pattern can influence the perception of an upcoming note as belonging to the same pattern, while the onset of a different pattern can change the *same* note's mode of appearance, independently of whether the note had been played in the past.

To sum up, in this first simple example, we have observed anticipation on three different levels: (1) between parts and wholes, as a causal relation; (2) as the perceived order of sounds *within* the perceptual groups, which follows the determination of the groups themselves; and (3) as the competitive relation between *different* perceptual configurations that provide an unambiguous direction to the musical stream.

Boundaries and Continuity

Playing with Boundaries

The note highlighted in Fig. 1 contributes to the perceptual transition by acting as a *boundary* between two successive, different groups: It marks the ending of the first group, as well as the beginning of the second one. Not only are the groups *contiguous*, that is, there is no "empty" space between them (both acoustically and visually), but they even share the common boundary, i.e., they are *continuous*. This kind of distinction was drawn in the classical theory of continua by Aristotle (for a thorough treatment of the dynamic theory of continua encompassing Aristotle's theory, see Albertazzi 2002a, b). According to Aristotle, a condition for the *continuity* of two objects is that they become, together, a *single* object. See, for example, the following figure (Fig. 2).

While this phenomenon can be easily understood in the visual modality (Fig. 2), the continua involved in acoustic perception are more difficult to characterize due to their exclusively dynamic nature. For instance, in the example of Fig. 1, it is difficult to describe the "single object" created by the two consecutive groups if not as just a "slip," the directional movement between one configuration and the other that we have identified above. However, in music, continuity can be deliberately exploited to create specific effects (or *forms*, to use the same terminology as in our historical premise) of which the meaning will stand out more clearly. Let us now consider the following example.

The excerpt in Fig. 3 corresponds to the beginning of the theme from the *Allegro* of Beethoven's "Spring" Sonata in F major (No. 5, Op. 24), for violin and piano:

Fig. 2 **An example of visual continuity.** One can see a black square and a grey square or a black *and* grey rectangle. The two objects sharing a common boundary constitute, together, a *single* visual object. In this case, we consider the boundary to be *both* black and grey (see Albertazzi 2002b)

Fig. 3 Beginning of the main theme from the *Allegro* of Beethoven's Sonata No. 5 in F major, Op. 24, (also known as "Spring Sonata"), for violin and piano. Articulation marks have been omitted for better clarity

On listening to this excerpt (see Voice 4), one can identify different melodic fragments that "overlap" by a note; in other words, one can find perceptual groups that have a conclusion which coincides with the beginning of the next perceptual group (Fig. 3, marked with arrows; see Voice 5). Nevertheless, each perceptual group is a complete object per se and can be considered a potential stand-alone melodic fragment even though the completeness of one "object" is competing with the completeness of the adjacent ones, which cannot be perceived simultaneously. Therefore, we are again in the presence of some sort of "boundary" notes.

The first two groups exhibit a stronger similarity to each other, being the second a transposition of the first; the third group has a different melodic structure and acts as a local conclusion for this short excerpt. In fact, the musical continuum in Beethoven's *Allegro* stands out as a single, coherent motif because its melodic fragments smoothly flow from one to the next.

Now, if we just stick to the usage of the word "motif," we can easily find similar occurrences in visual art. The perceptual category of "motifs" (from Latin *movere*, "to move") contains many examples of visual objects where it is possible to identify several subunits that are often continuous one with another: Arabesques and Greek keys immediately come to mind as perceptual structures composed of a multiplicity of groups, despite exhibiting continuous primitives such as lines, weaves, or more complex objects.

For the sake of clarity, let us consider the following example. We can identify Beethoven's theme as sharing a similar perceptual structure with the Greek key shown in the left portion of Fig. 4a (although the regular symmetry of the meander is only partially reflected in the Sonata's theme).

In this Greek key, different units are identifiable, and yet they are not separated by any sharp boundary.

Next, we can introduce an arbitrary separation between the repeating units of the meander (Fig. 4b, left), a procedure that yields a quite different perceptual result. The image now appears as clearly consisting of three different units, and not as a single continuum. This should not be interpreted as if the units are no longer continuous (see also section "Conclusions, and a Last Note on the Boundaries") but only as if the boundaries between them have become somehow "sharper." In fact, it is still possible to perceive a motif composed of the three units. What has happened is that their whole/part relationship has been altered, the parts now prevailing over the whole structure.

With the above visual effect in mind, we are now prompted to perform another simple perceptual experiment, this time on Beethoven's musical theme (Fig. 4a): We

Fig. 4 Different degrees of continuity in visual and musical continua. (**a**) The Greek key on the left shares an analogous perceptual structure with Beethoven's theme reported on the right, as they are both examples of perceptual continua. (**b**) By fragmenting the continua (the Greek key on the left and the altered Beethoven's theme on the right), their constitutive parts become more salient than the whole objects. In the scores, articulation marks have been omitted for better clarity.

can take the liberty to alter the theme to create new "boundaries" for each fragment (Fig. 4b, right).

On listening to the outcome (see Voice 6) of our experiment, it seems indeed that we are somehow breaking the lyrical "flow" that characterizes the beginning of this famous theme. In fact, again, the *parts* (bracketed in the score in Fig. 4b) have now become more salient with respect to the entire continuum, being separated by "sharper" perceptual boundaries. For example, at the beginning of the second measure, the dotted C behaves more as a *last* note for the *first* group than as a *first* note for the *second* one; the opposite can be said for the following D. In contrast, the single, half C note in the same position of the original theme (Fig. 4a) appears to group with equal cohesion with both the preceding and the following group (despite the legato articulation mark that, in the original score, ties it to the following notes).

Direction as a Property of a "Higher-Order" Whole

Following the previous experiment, we can observe that, in Beethoven's theme, the competition between the melodic fragments connected by common notes was providing a special driving force to the melody. By splitting the *whole* musical motif, we have altered its quality. We can now recall the example of Fig. 1, where the continuity of musical fragments sharing a common note was providing a *direction* to the perceptual stream, the previous perceptual group *anticipating* the next one. Similarly, in the original theme of Beethoven's *Allegro* (Figs. 3 and 4a), the perceptual groups inside the melody are moving smoothly and consistently in a direction. This means that the continuous, *whole* structure resulting from the melodic fragments (which in turn are perceptual wholes themselves) exhibits an additional, more global property. The entire melody represents a "higher-order" whole with respect to the melodic fragments that are part of it, displaying a quality that cannot be reduced to the latter.

Considering visual motifs again, a similar kind of hierarchical phenomenon is shown in Fig. 5. The first example (Fig. 5a) represents the same Greek key motif shown in the previous example, although here it evidences an additional property: a visual directionality in the *whole* motif not reducible to the units of which it is composed. The second example (Fig. 5b) shows a similar motif with a different kind of subunit made of repeating loops. Both examples have been taken on purpose from the work of the artist Paul Klee, an expert musician as well as a painter: As we will also see in section "A Diversity of Boundaries," his work is highly suited to illustrate the dynamic structures occurring in both acoustic and visual phenomena.

"Discontinuity" in Musical Continua

Let us now consider another example: Fig. 6 shows the transition between two subsections in the first movement of Mozart's *Sonata in C minor* for piano (K. 457, measures 17–20; see Voice 7).

In this case, one can easily distinguish the two overlapping groups because they consist of two very different fragments (see Voice 8), with different melodic figures, dynamics, and articulation.

If we recall Aristotle's definition of continua (see section "Anticipation and Meaning in Music"), a legitimate question arises: Where is the *single* object in this passage, made of two contrasting, somehow "discontinuous" fragments? Our answer is that, in such cases, one should identify the continuum in the *transition* between the two objects. In fact, for a proper transition to be perceived, both its participating moments must exist together. Otherwise, the listener would be only attending to

Fig. 5 Two linear motifs taken from the work of Paul Klee exhibit a directionality which is a quality of the whole object, not of its constitutive parts. (**a, b**) Free lines making detours (Klee 1921/1922)

Fig. 6 Excerpt from the *Allegro* of Mozart's piano sonata No. 14 in C minor (K. 457). The two fragments are continuous with each other, but they exhibit a "discontinuous" character

processes of appearance and disappearance. The fact that a transition is actually perceived is evidence that a continuum made of *both* the preceding and the following fragments exists, although its character tends to be the opposite of the smooth continuum we observed in Beethoven's fragment: We could say that the main, "rocketish" theme (emulating an orchestral practice known as "Mannheim rocket," Gordon 1996) is *invading* the conclusion of the first fragment. Nevertheless, we can still consider this "invasion" as an object itself or a "form" that has been specifically realized by the composer. It is curious that this first movement of the C minor *Sonata* has been elsewhere described as dramatically playing with a so-called rhetoric of continuity partly consisting in the alternation of "breathless" passages (such as this one) and abrupt silences (such as the one immediately after the end of the theme's arpeggio) (Irving 2010, pp. 76–77).

A Diversity of Boundaries

A Few More Lines About Klee

In Klee's work, the influence of the artist's musical expertise can be identified not only in the artworks but also in the foundations of his theoretical system. On looking at his *Pedagogical Sketchbook* (Klee 1953) based on his lectures on the theory of form delivered at the Bauhaus school, one notes several visual examples that recall dynamic musical processes. This especially concerns the "lines" that he defines as "moving" objects or, more precisely, as "points that put themselves in motion" (pp. 16–17).

In Klee's framework, lines play a fundamental role for the origin of visual shapes, underlying the perception of natural figures across all layers of complexity, from details to macroscopic features. Although the analysis of Klee's pictorial vocabulary is a demanding task, and should be addressed separately from this chapter, we can draw again on his didactic examples to look for an effective illustration of anticipation processes occurring in music. We can consider how a single line can give rise to structures made of multiple complete objects that can be partially or totally overlapping between each other, all connected by the same continuous trait.

Shown in Fig. 7 is a line that Klee defines as "circumscribing itself" (Klee 1953, p. 17).

This line appears structurally similar to the ones in Fig. 5 (and in particular Fig. 5b, being it made of repeating loops), although it is more complex. By closely following the path of the line, loop after loop, it is not possible to identify where one loop ends and the next one begins: in fact, as our gaze passes from one loop to the next, the *dividing boundary* of the first appears to be *already* part of the second (as evidenced in Fig. 8a). In other words, each loop, as a perceptual whole, *anticipates* the next one, because part of the next one is already contained in the previous one. Note that, because of perceptual organization rules, it is not possible to visualize two adjacent loops at once. However, the competition between adjacent loops provides the *whole* structure with its specific character. It seems that the anticipation processes between adjacent loops are responsible for the dynamism of the entire line. If we

Fig. 7 A line that is "circumscribing itself" (Klee 1953) creates a diversity of perceptual groups and boundaries

a)   **c)**

b)   **d)**

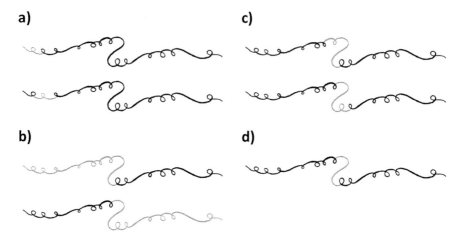

Fig. 8 (**a**) Perceptual groups (rings) overlap with each other as the gaze follows the path of the line. (**b**) Two competing sublines are put in continuity by an inflection tract. (**c**) The two rings connected by the inflection tract are in very weak competition. (**d**) The inflection tract can group as an individual object

sweep our gaze over the entire line, we can notice how the perceptual "competition" between the different fragments results in a directional "flow" that reminds of what was happening in Beethoven's theme (Figs. 3 and 4).

Differently from Fig. 5, however, the shape of this motif has a structural aspect that accounts for its greater complexity. In fact, loops can more or less intensely compete with the adjacent ones, depending on distance and size, while the whole line presents a complex dynamic depending on curvature and thickness.

We invite the reader to follow the path of this line toward the center, where an inflection is visible. The inflection, a unique and characteristic trait of the line, has important implications for its continuity: in perceiving the line, in fact, one is aware of the presence of an intermediate level consisting in two competing "sublines" connected by the inflection tract. In the above figure (Fig. 8b), it is evident that the inflection tract acts as a boundary between the two sublines. If instead we focus on the individual loops, we see that the two loops connected by the inflection tract are in very weak competition (Fig. 8c) and that the inflection tract can even be perceived as an object itself (the one resembling an inverted "S," Fig. 8d). Thus, at a more global level, the inflection tract behaves as a sharp boundary between the two sublines, because of grouping processes that smoothen the boundaries between the loops within each of the sublines. Vice versa, at a lower, local level, the inflection tract is a relatively more autonomous element.

We can also compare the behavior of this boundary with the "overlapping" C in Mozart's excerpt (Fig. 6). Here, the note C is the boundary between two *melodies*, as well as a note per se, if considered with respect to its adjacent *notes* only. The *dynamical* experience of a *stationary* object such as a visual motif can be analogous to the experience of a note inside the purely dynamical phenomenon of music.

"Self-Circumscribing" Polyphony

As a violin player, Klee was an interpreter and admirer of Johann Sebastian Bach, a composer universally recognized for his masterpieces in the violin repertoire, the six *unaccompanied* violin solo works, *Sonatas* and *Partitas* (BWV 1001–1006). One reason for the reputation of these pieces is certainly their polyphonic character, which the four-stringed instrument must achieve without any accompaniment, a major challenge for violin players. However, a remarkable characteristic that belongs to these works is that, while the polyphony is sometimes explicitly found in passages that involve multiple stoppings of the strings, in many cases it is regarded as a so-called *implied polyphony*: Despite their being monophonic (i.e., it never happens that more than one note/string is played simultaneously), these passages are known to evoke a sense of polyphony in listeners as if they were involving the interplay of different *voices*. Although a discussion about the meaning of "voice" would be useful (e.g., Cambouropoulos 2006), we can adopt the term here to refer to an independent melodic line having its own identity as if it were "sung," perceptually speaking, by an autonomous source (see also Huron 1989).

The classification of independent voices in Bach's violin solo works and the principles that underlie their grouping have already been investigated (see, e.g., Davis 2000): In fact, it is not easy to define where the boundaries between voices within the melodic stream lie. Here it is not our intention to discuss the complex voice-leading rules that may contribute to the perceptual segregation of specific voices in these pieces. Instead, in the next example, we will try to show how some of the properties of temporal continua can be relevant to their "polyphonic" character.

Consider the following excerpt from the *Allemande* in Bach's violin *Partita* in D minor (BWV 1004, measures 2–4; Fig. 9; see Voice 9):

Fig. 9 Excerpt from the *Allemande* in Bach's Partita in D minor, for violin solo (BWV 1004). Different possible perceptual groups are marked with brackets

We can observe (Fig. 9, brackets below the score) several possible tiny frag-ments arising within the melody, one starting on each beat (see Voice 10). As in the other examples, there are "boundary" notes in common between consecutive melodic fragments that put the fragments in continuity. At their onset, these notes behave as "last notes" for the preceding fragment, switching to "first notes" when the next fragment starts to be perceived. (Note that in some cases the performer, to emphasize the ending of fragments, may create slight interrup-tions between "last" notes and the following ones; this articulation choice may result in a relative prevalence of the preceding perceptual group over the following one, that is however still held together by the melodic and harmonic context.) This anticipation phenomenon gives a strong directional flow to the excerpt. If we consider the competing melodic fragments as belonging to independent "voices," we can observe that they do not occur *in succession*. Instead, perceptually speak-ing, they *overlap*! In particular, two individual "voices" can be found, based on the alternation of binary and ternary rhythmic figures. Let us say that these two voices are holding a "cross talk" made of statements and answers (see Voice 11; "answers" are played one octave higher in the clip).

Furthermore, by simply considering the fragments in groups of two (Fig. 9, brackets above the score) (see Voice 12), we can identify a more global level of organization of the excerpt, made of repeating larger units that follow a specific harmonic pattern (what in harmony is called a "sequence"). The existence of larger perceptual units has an implication for the "sharpness" of the boundaries in the excerpt: While the boundaries between a statement and an answer are "smoother" (because of inside larger coherent groups), the boundaries between an answer and the next statement are "sharper" (because the next statement is inside a different larger group). In turn, we can consider also these larger perceptual units as "voices" playing in alternation (see Voice 13).

What we have just outlined is a structure where different perceptual groups are nested within each other, similar to what happens in Klee's "self-circumscribing" line (Fig. 7) with its multiple levels of configuration. In this short music excerpt, we can say that the *parts* of the statement-answer unit (i.e., statement and answer; see Voice 11) are less salient than their *whole* (the statement-answer unit itself), because their whole is also a *part* of a larger, *whole* structure (the full sequence made of repetitions of the statement-answer unit; see Voice 13).

We have observed how whole-part dynamics are responsible for different degrees of "sharpness" of the perceptual boundaries in both a pictorial and a musical continuum. The dynamic structure of the continua is determined by the perceptual configurations that arise and interact in its deployment. Now, by thinking of the variety of natural images that can be produced with a line alone, one can easily envisage how intricate these interactions may become, with virtually infinite layers of perceptual objects. The same argument can hold for musical continua: One could go on for pages and pages tracking down the anticipation structures in the sole *Allemande*.

As regards the analysis of Bach's implied polyphony, we have evinced how this excerpt may not allow for a univocal separation of voices. Rather, as Klee did with the line which was *circumscribing itself* (see Fig. 5), one might conclude that Bach here created a "self-circumscribing" polyphony by putting voices *inside* themselves.

Conclusions and a Last Note on the Boundaries

The musical excerpts that we have considered are examples of how the dynamic nature of musical continua can be exploited by musicians to obtain specific effects in their music, and they should not be regarded as isolated with respect to their structural characteristics. To some extent, phenomena, such as "self-circumscribing polyphonies," "invading" themes, and "flowing" motifs, can be identified in any melody, even the simplest ones. The examples discussed in this chapter should summarize considerations that can hold for melodic analysis in general. As the reader will have noted, we have not provided any formal rules for the definition of anticipation relations or perceptual grouping in melodies; instead, we have mainly focused on what we have identified as their grounding principles and considered a few notable examples of their involvement in the creation of musical meaningful structures or *forms*.

In our opinion, an analysis of the qualitative nature of musical sounds can explain the subjective experience of music far beyond its interpretation in terms of mere affective dimensions. Although emotions represent a very important component of music perception, they do not seem fully able to account for the complexity of musical experience (see, e.g., Juslin and Laukka 2004, p. 220; see also Albertazzi et al. 2016). Of course, as mentioned in the Introduction, an appropriate investigation would require a suitable experimental framework, prompting a reappraisal of experimental phenomenology as an alternative to contemporary reductionist models of experience (Albertazzi 2015). The viewpoint presented in this study illustrates musical phenomena as basically *contextual*, due to *internal* relations among their contents, governed by specific laws of *grouping*, and *immediately given* in the awareness. Our choice of matching musical examples with visual and pictorial ones had the important purpose of showing how these processes are shared between musical and visual perception, evidencing anticipation as a key concept to explain the structure of awareness. Carrying forward the ideas proposed in Albertazzi ▶ Chap. 14, "Microgenesis of Anticipation: Windowing the Present," this handbook, we have seen how even on looking at static figures on a piece of paper we experience *dynamic* configurations that can be compared to the ones that arise in music, an analogy that has been central in the work of artists like Klee.

A leitmotif of our exploration has been represented by "boundaries," a concept that we have borrowed from visual perception and applied to specific musical structures and in particular melodic ones. We have identified special "boundary" notes that, in addition to separating musical fragments, have the additional role of joining them together, just as any pictorial boundary is also part of the objects that it separates (see section "Playing with Boundaries" and Albertazzi 2002a, b). We learned of their existence by observing curious cases of "overlaps" among perceptual groups in melodies. Without the case studies provided by "boundary notes," the ideas proposed in this chapter would have been much more difficult to explain. In this regard, the reader will have certainly noted that an important aspect might seem still missing from our treatment. We have not considered any instances where notes or phrases may have been written as *separate*, i.e., we have avoided the issue of "pure" musical boundaries! However, we also hope that the reader will now start doubting whether, in our perception, any completely *separate* notes or melodies can exist. For example, one might legitimately ask whether the boundary between any two notes (even if consisting of silence!) is not in fact *both* the end of the preceding *and* the beginning of the subsequent note or melodic phrase, the relation between the two giving rise to a wider perceptual configuration.

Put more broadly, it should now be apparent that any musical structures, to be put in relation with each other, must together form something different from their mere succession. In doing so, they give rise to complex and diversified continua where time appears to be only a qualitative dimension of the sounds that exist in the awareness: Sounds existing as "past sounds" in the conscious present can be *perceived* as anticipatory elements of what is played next, even if this happens *only when the next is played*. This is not a process of "recognition," but something that we directly experience, a certainty that accounts for our appreciation of musical *forms*. It is for this reason that, when approaching the subject of anticipation in music perception, it is not possible to strictly follow a linear timeline, pertaining neither to the notation system nor to the physical metrics. And, ultimately, this is the reason why the question about anticipation in music perception deserves a wider answer than the ones proposed in the "Introduction" section. Here we have done our best to provide a satisfactory answer, although limited by the vastness of the topic. Because of this fact, let us regard this conclusion as a boundary between the present chapter and further investigation.

References

Albertazzi, L. (1996). A cubist state of mind. Introduction to *The philosophy of Alexius Meinong*. Monographic issue of Axiomathes 1–2, pp. 5–17. Springer.

Albertazzi, L. (2001). Vittorio Benussi. In L. Albertazzi, D. Jacquette, & R. Poli (Eds.), *The school of Alexius Meinong* (pp. 95–133). Farnham: Ashgate.

Albertazzi, L. (2002a). Continua. In L. Albertazzi (Ed.), *Unfolding perceptual continua* (pp. 1–28). Amsterdam: Benjamins Publishing Company.

Albertazzi, L. (2002b). Towards a neo-Aristotelian theory of continua: Elements of an empirical geometry. In L. Albertazzi (Ed.), *Unfolding perceptual continua* (pp. 29–79). Amsterdam: Benjamins Publishing Company.

Albertazzi, L. (2015). A science of qualities. *Biological Theory, 10*, 188–199. https://doi.org/10.1007/s13752-015-0213-3.

Albertazzi, L., Jacquette, D., & Poli, R. (2001). *The School of Alexius Meinong*. Aldershot: Ashgate

Albertazzi, L., van Tonder, G., & Vishwanath, D. (2010). Information in perception. In L. Albertazzi, G. van Tonder, & D. Vishwanath (Eds.), *Perception beyond inference: The information content of perceptual processes* (pp. 1–26). Cambridge: MIT Press.

Albertazzi, L., Canal, L., & Micciolo, R. (2015). Cross-modal associations between materic painting and classical Spanish music. *Frontiers in Psychology, 6*, 424. https://doi.org/10.3389/fpsyg.2015.00424.

Albertazzi, L., Canal, L., Micciolo, R., Ferrari, F., Sitta, S., & Hachen, I. (2016). Naturally biased associations between music and poetry. *Perception*, 1–22. https://doi.org/10.1177/0301006616673851.

Arnheim, R. (1954). *Art and visual perception. A psychology of the creative eye*. Berkeley/Los Angeles: University of California Press.

Benussi, V. (1913). *Die Psychologie der Zeitauffassung*. Leipzig: Hölder.

Berthoz, A. (2012). *Le sens du mouvement*. Paris: Odile Jacob.

Blackmore, Th. (2001). Alois Höfler (1853–1922). In L. Albertazzi, D. Jacquette, & R. Poli (Eds.), *The school of Alexius Meinong* (pp. 153–186). Farnham: Ashgate.

Cambouropoulos, E. (2006). 'Voice' separation: Theoretical, perceptual and computational perspectives. In *9th international conference on music perception and cognition*, Alma Mater Studiorum University of Bologna, 22–26 Aug 2006.

Chomsky, N. (1957). *Syntactic structures*. Den Haag: Mouton. Berlin/New York: de Gruyter (1989).

Chomsky, N. (1981). *Lectures on government and binding: The Pisa lectures*. Dordrecht: Foris Publications.

Cuddy, L. L., & Lunney, C. A. (1995). Expectancies generated by melodic intervals: Perceptual judgments of melodic continuity. *Perception & Psychophysics, 57*(4), 451–462.

Davis, S. (2000). Implied polyphony in the unaccompanied string works of J.S. Bach: A rule system for discerning melodic strata. In *International conference on music perception (2000), proceedings paper*.

Deutsch, D. (1982). Grouping mechanisms in music. In D. Deutsch (Ed.), *The psychology of music*. San Diego: Elsevier, 3rd ed. (2013), pp. 183–248.

Gordon, S. (1996). *A history of keyboard literature: Music for the piano and its forerunners*. Belmont: Schirmer Cengage Learning.

Grimes, N., Donovan, S., & Marx, W. (Eds.). (2013). *Rethinking Hanslick: Music, formalism, and expression, Eastman studies in music*. Rochester: University of Rochester Press.

Haber-ZemlJich, A. (2001). Stephan Witasek (1870–1915). In L. Albertazzi, D. Jacquette, & R. Poli (Eds.), *The school of Alexius Meinong* (pp. 225–236). Farnham: Ashgate.

Hanslick, E. (1854). *Vom Musikalisch-Schönen*. Leipzig: R. Weigel. http://www.koelnklavier.de/quellen/hanslick/_index.html.

Huron, D. (1989). Voice denumerability in polyphonic music of homogeneous timbres. *Music Perception: An Interdisciplinary Journal, 6*(4), 361–382.

Huron, D. (2006). *Sweet anticipation. Music and the psychology of expectation*. Cambridge: Massachusetts Institute of Technology.

Irving, J. (2010). *Understanding Mozart's piano sonatas*. Farnham: Ashgate.

James, W. (1950). *Principles of psychology* (2nd ed., 2 Vols.). New York: Dover Publications.

Juslin, P. N., & Laukka, P. (2004). Expression, perception, and induction of musical emotions: A review and a questionnaire study of everyday listening. *Journal of New Music Research, 33*, 217–238.

Juslin, P. N., & Västfjäll, D. (2008). Emotional responses to music: The need to consider underlying mechanism. *Behavioral and Brain Sciences, 31*, 559–621. https://doi.org/10.1017/S0140525X08005293.

Klee, P. (1921/1922). Beiträge zur bildnerischen Formlehre. Original manuscript, Fig. 5. U.6.

Klee, P. (1953). *Pedagogical sketchbook*. Washington, DC: Praeger Publishers. (1972).

Koelsch, S. (2012). *Brain and music*. New York: Wiley. (2013).

Langer, S. K. (1953). *Feeling and form. A theory of art*. New York: Charles Scribner's Sons.

Livingstone, M. (2002). *Vision and art: The biology of seeing*. New York: Abrams.

Margulis, E. H. (2005). A model of melodic expectation. *Music Perception, 21*(4), 663–714.

McManus, I. C., Cook, R., & Hunt, A. (2010). Beyond the Golden Section: Why do individuals differ so much in their aesthetic preferences for rectangles? *Psychology of Aesthetics, Creativity, and the Arts, 4*, 111–126.

Meinong, A. (1882). Studien II. Zur Relationstheorie. Repr. in GA II (1971), pp. 1–172.

Meinong, A. (1902). Über Annahmen (1902, 2nd ed. 1910). Repr. 1910 in GA IV (1977).

Meinong, A. (1917). Über emotionale Präsentation. Repr. in GA III (1968), pp. 283–476.

Meinong, A. Gesamtausgabe. (1968–1978). Bd. I–VII. Ed. by Rudolf Haller and Rudolf Kindinger in collaboration with Roderick M. Chisholm. Graz: Akademische Druck- und Verlagsanstalt.

Meyer, L. B. (1956). *Emotion and meaning in music*. Chicago: The University of Chicago Press.

Meyer, L. B. (1957). Meaning in music and information theory. *The Journal of Aesthetics and Art Criticism, 15*(4), 412–424. Published by Wiley on behalf of The American Society for Aesthetics, http://www.jstor.org/stable/427154.

Narmour, E. (1990). *The analysis and cognition of basic melodic structures: The implication-realization model*. Chicago: University of Chicago Press.

Narmour, E. (1992). *The analysis and cognition of melodic complexity: The implication-realization model*. Chicago: University of Chicago Press.

Narmour, E. (2000). Music expectation by cognitive rule-mapping. *Music Perception: An Interdisciplinary Journal, 17*(3), 329–398.

Palmer, S. E., Schloss, K. B., Xu, Z., & Prado-León, L. R. (2013). Music-colour associations are mediated by emotion. *Proceedings of the National Academy of Sciences, 110*, 8836–8841. https://doi.org/10.1073/pnas.1212562110.

Ramachandran, V. S. (2003). *The emerging mind*. London: Profile Books.

Schellenberg, E. G. (1996). Expectancy in melody: Tests of the implication-realization model. *Cognition, 58*, 75–125.

Shannon, C. E., & Weaver, W. (1963). *The mathematical theory of communication*. Urbana: University of Illinois Press.

Solso, R. (2003). *The psychology of art and the evolution of the conscious brain*. Cambridge: MIT Press.

Spence, C. (2011). Crossmodal correspondences: A tutorial review. *Attention, Perception, & Psychophysics, 73*, 971–995. https://doi.org/10.3758/s13414-010-0073-7.

Todorovic, D. (2008). Gestalt principles. *Scholarpedia, 3*(12), 5345.

von Ehrenfels, Ch. (1890). Über "Gestaltqualitäten" repr. in Ehrenfels, Chr. v. Philosophische Schriften, Vol. I, Ed. by R. Fabian. München: Philosophia (1983), pp. 128–167.

Wertheimer, M. (1912/1967). Experimentelle Studien über das Sehen von Bewegungen. *Zeitschrift für Psychologie und Physiologie der Sinnesorgane, 61*, 161–265 (reprinted 1967 in Drei Abhandlungen zur Gestalttheorie. Wissenschaftliche Buchgesellschaft, Darmstadt, pp. 1–105).

Wertheimer, M. (1923). Untersuchungen zur Lehre von der Gestalt. *Psychologische Forschung, 4*, 301–350.

Zeki, S. (1999). *Inner vision: An exploration of art and the brain*. Oxford: Oxford University Press.

Anticipation and Narratology

Genevieve Liveley

Contents

Abstract

In one of the first analyses of its kind, this chapter examines how the tools and heuristics of narratology (the study of narrative) might enhance the study of anticipation. It assesses whether narratological insights into the ways in which stories narrate and readers read might enable us to tell better stories about the future and at the same time to become better readers of the possible worlds that such stories anticipate. Investigating the theory and praxis of anticipation across a broad temporal range of possible (fictional) and actual (real) world models and narratives (from antiquity to postmodernity), it scopes some of the pitfalls and possibilities opened up by treating the future as "storied." It engages with the latest studies on cognitive narratology, possible world's theories, and so-called future narratives, examining anticipatory narratives particularly relating to the

G. Liveley
University of Bristol, Bristol, UK
e-mail: g.liveley@bristol.ac.uk

© Springer Nature Switzerland AG 2019
R. Poli (ed.), *Handbook of Anticipation*,
https://doi.org/10.1007/978-3-319-91554-8_7

environment and to the self. It argues that the stories we tell about the future, including our future selves, must be open, multi-linear, and multidimensional in order to avoid anticipatory backshadowing, which forecasts the future as a continuation of the past and present.

Keywords
Backshadowing · Character · Chronocentrism · Chronotope · Climate change · Cognition · Counterfactual · Future narratives · Identity · Narrative · Narratology · Possible worlds · Postmodernism · Preshadowing · Prolepsis · Reading · Scenario · Utopia

Introduction

Narratology has made it clear that, while narrative can have any number of functions (entertaining, informing, persuading, diverting attention, etc.), there are some functions that it excels at or is unique in fulfilling. Narrative always reports one or more changes of state, but as etymology suggests (the term narrative is related to the Latin gnarus – "knowing," "expert," "acquainted with" . . .), narrative is also a particular mode of knowledge. It does not merely reflect what happens; it discovers and invents what can happen.
G. Prince, "On Narratology (Past, Present, Future)," (1990:1)

Narrative shapes our knowledge and understanding of the world – our past, present, and future. Narratology explains how narrative does this. Narratology has been characterized as a science, as a methodology, as a theory, and as a humanities discipline, combining both theory and praxis in the formal, rhetorical, and critical analysis of textual discourse across a broad spectrum of different genres and media (Meister 2014). Alongside its various theoretical schools (formalist, structuralist, poststructuralist, etc.), narratology has produced many sub-disciplines in recent years (cognitive, feminist, computational, etc.), prompting calls to eschew the singular term *narratology* in favor of the plural *narratologies*, so as to better convey the richness and multiplicity of this still expanding field (Herman 1999).

The study of anticipation in narratology (and its various narratologies) has therefore taken various different forms. Narratologists have shown keen interest in the way that anticipation functions in specific genres and narrative modes, such as counterfactuals in history and fiction (Dannenberg 2008), future utopian and dystopian fiction (Morson 1994), autobiography and life-writing (Bamberg 2011), and postmodern fiction, especially texts with experimental anachronic or polychronic temporalities (Richardson 2002). Perhaps the most important work, however, has focused upon the anticipatory dynamics of narrative itself. That is, analysis of the ways and means by which narrators and readers make sense of the possible worlds represented in stories (Ryan 1991) and by which they negotiate narrative prolepses (future anticipations and projections) in plots (Genette 1980). Indeed, theoretical and empirical narratological analyses of these phenomena have suggested that anticipation is one of the key motors of narrativity, that readerly competence in anticipatory processes is what drives narrative cognition and comprehension (Brooks 1984) at the most basic levels.

This chapter, then, investigates whether and how the tools and heuristics of narratology might enhance the study of anticipation. In particular, it asks whether narratological insights into the ways in which stories function might enhance our narrative competences, so enabling us to tell better stories about the future and to become better readers of the possible worlds that future narratives anticipate. Assessing the theory and praxis of anticipation across a range of such possible story worlds and models, it examines some of the pitfalls and possibilities opened up by treating the future and its anticipation as "storied."

Models as Anticipatory Narratives

A story answers a model.
But likewise a model answers a story.
D. McCloskey, "Storytelling in Economics" (1990:6)

In anticipating the future, climatologists, economists, social and political scientists, and "futurists" in many other sectors employ qualitative (narrative) as well as quantitative (modeling) methodologies. Mathematical and statistical data and scientific and political analyses all typically require some degree of narrative mediation if decision-makers and stakeholders are to process and publish them. In order for future forecasts to be produced and disseminated to politicians and public alike, complex information and models have to be translated into an accessible – which often means *narrative* – form. Only once complex data has been "storified" can wider audiences read and thus evaluate their significance by assessing the probability and possibility of various options and outcomes. In this context, such stories function as metaphors of metaphors (meta-metaphors), redescribing and translating static models representing the real world into dynamic narratives representing possible or story worlds.

The following narrative, based on models projecting a global temperature rise of +2C, provides a salient illustration of the way in which complex climatological forecasts can be translated into story form, plotted according to a nexus of cause and effect which seeks to persuade its readers that it represents a credible and probable anticipation of the future (cited in Bode and Dietrich 2013: 75):

The heatwaves seen in Europe during 2003, which killed thousands of people, will come back every year with a 2C global average temperature rise. The Amazon turns into desert and grasslands, while increasing CO2 levels in the atmosphere make the world's oceans too acidic for remaining coral reefs and thousands of other marine life forms. The West Antarctic ice sheet collapses, the Greenland ice sheet melts and the world's sea level begins to rise by seven metres over the next few hundred years. A third of the world's species will become extinct.

This scenario, analyzed in terms of the narratological concepts order, duration, frequency, voice, and mode (*pace* Genette 1980), demonstrates a sophisticated narrative form. In terms of order, the story here has a teleological and chronolinear structure, a clear beginning (rising temperatures), a middle (melting ice sheets), and an end (global extinctions). Under the rubric of duration, its "discourse time" (the time it takes to read) is very much shorter than its "narrative time" (the time span covered by the story): it takes only seconds to read but covers a period spanning several centuries. It necessarily, therefore, abbreviates the "frequency" and temporal extent of the events it narrates: the melting of ice sheets and the rising of sea levels are iterative processes which take far longer than their description here allows. The voice of the extradiegetic (external) narrator, however, lends the authority of omniscience to this narration, assuring the reader of the actuality of these events and even making the reader a virtual eyewitness of happenings which exceed the span of a human lifetime. Indeed, the mode of narration is such that the reader (or narratee) is invited to share the same "god's-eye view" of this global catastrophe as the narrator, to focalize events from a distant, dispassionate, and objective point of view.

Narratological tools (especially those borrowed from "possible worlds' theory") throw up other meaningful insights into the narrativity of this climate change scenario. The "principle of minimal departure" (Ryan 1991), suggests that when readers encounter possible worlds (such as the future world forecast in the scenario), they assume that there are no significant differences between that and the "actual" world, that its conditions reflect as closely as possible those of their own "reality" – until the narrative forces them to make a cognitive readjustment and acknowledge a difference or departure from that actuality. Thus, if a story introduces a flying horse, readers will typically imagine a "real" horse in all respects other than its wings. If a climate change prediction introduces an average global temperature increase, readers will typically imagine a variation of the real summer "heatwaves" with which they are already familiar.

The climate change scenario here exploits this "principle of minimal departure" in suggesting a temporal-causal connection between the possible future world it anticipates and the actual past and present world already familiar to its readers. It opens with a retrospective look back to the extreme weather events of recent history, using past tense markers ("seen … during 2003," "which killed") to recall a memory of prior real-world experience. In doing so, the narrative establishes a set of initial conditions which paradoxically anticipate its readers' preexisting familiarity with a yet-to-be-experienced possible world, a world which it will go on to describe as an extension of or return to the past ("will come back"). Having established this continuity through change from the past to future, from familiar real world to unfamiliar possible world, the tense markers then shift into the present ("turns," "make," "collapses," "melts," "begins to rise"). The use of the present tense here enhances the immediacy and thus the reality of this possible world, virtually locating the reader in the future as if it were the present. That is, until the imaginative limits of the temporal stretch of this future-in-the-present is reached ("over the next few hundred years") and a return to the simple future tense ("will become") is required.

Indeed, as Fludernik's work (1996 and 2010) on "natural narratology" has shown, English language narratives using the future tense tend to revert to the present and past tenses in this way, as soon as the future temporality of a scene has been set. In Michael Frayn's utopian future narrative *A Very Private Life* ([1968] 1981), for example, set "in the good new days a long, long while ahead" (1981:5) the future tense quickly yields to the present and past (Frayn 1981:5–12, italics added):

> Once upon a time there *will* be a little girl called Uncumber. Uncumber *will* have a little brother called Sulpice, and they *will* live with their parents in a house in the middle of the woods. [...] One day she *will* hear the familiar clink of their tools on the other side of the wall, and their muffled talk and laughter, and she *will* say: 'The animals *are* here again!'
>
> It's all mixed up inside her head with some holovision programme she *has* seen. She *thinks* people live inside, and animals outside.
>
> And she *takes* everything so seriously.

In Frayn's story, the unfamiliar future world that his narrative describes is introduced to his readers through a traditional story world setting ("once upon a time," "a little girl," "a little brother," and "a house in the middle of the woods"). A similar device is used in the climate change scenario to enhance the familiarity, immediacy, and realism of the possible world anticipated there. Familiar global landmarks ("Europe," the "Amazon," the "Antarctic," and "Greenland") work to locate the reader in a recognizable and stable space – albeit one that is simultaneously in the process of being transformed. In Poli's terms (2007: 3–4), the present space-time of a real-world "chronotopoid" is aligned here with a future possible world "chronotope." Abbott characterizes this narrative device as the "future present" and sees this conflation of tense in narratives set in the future as analogous to the "historical present," that is, the use of the vivid present tense to represent completed action in stories set in the past (Abbott 2008: 534).

What is more, the temporal-spatial entry point for the reader of the climate change scenario – via "Europe" – posits a particular geopolitical point of view, a deictic (here and now) vantage point from which the reader has already seen killer heatwaves. In this move, the narrative subtly appropriates the reader as an eyewitness to both the actual past *and* to the possible future impact of climate change. Thus, at the same time, as it presents and invites the reader to share an omniscient narratorial viewpoint (a god's-eye view of time and space embracing the past, present, and future of the world's lands, seas, and atmosphere), the narrative is focalized from a particular fixed perspective in time and space: that of a European in the early twenty-first century – the reader's own actual temporal-spatial coordinates. Indeed, so firmly fixed is that external (homodiegetic) focalization that, as the narrative unfolds from prologue (the heatwaves of 2003) to denouement (mass extinctions a few hundred years hence), the global conditions of the narrator's and reader's *now* are anticipated as ongoing without variation or intervention, privileging the chronocentrism or "presentness" of that point of view.

A narrative scenario of this type clearly does not offer an objective or definitive projection of the future, despite the quasi-omniscient and prophetic character of its narration. It is widely acknowledged, in fact, that narrative scenarios do not predict actualities but rather anticipate possibilities and probabilities as perceived from the present and from the *now*. As Staley affirms (Staley 2002: 38): "If a prediction is a definitive statement of what the future will be, then scenarios are heuristic statements that explore the plausibilities of what might be." Or, as the National Intelligence

Council puts it (2004: 16, emphases in original), "scenarios are not meant as actual forecasts, but they describe possible worlds upon whose threshold we may be entering." Such storified scenarios are therefore useful in processing what Bode (Bode and Dietrich 2013: 88, emphases in original) describes as "*test-runs of futures*, or test-runs of known unknowns, revealing unknown unknowns, producing *multiple evolutionary paths* ... [treating] the present as a nodal situation that allows for different continuations and ... possible evolutions from this point in time." In effect, then, narrative scenarios extrapolate from what is known in the present into the unknown future, telling stories about possible worlds based on real-world models. By better understanding the ways in which such stories work, using the tools of narratology, we might be able both to tell better stories about the future *and* to become better readers of the possible worlds that they anticipate and represent.

Narratives as Anticipatory Models

> Books are indeed world models. St Augustine found the best model he could find for our experience of past, present, and future was the recitation of a psalm.
> F. Kermode, *The Sense of an Ending* ([1967] 2000: 52)

While real-world future scenarios and models can be shaped in narrative form, narratives and stories (both fictional and nonfictional) can similarly be viewed as shaping real-world experiences – including (perhaps, *especially*) those pertaining to the future. Narrative in and of itself can be seen as an anticipatory model, simulating (perhaps even *stimulating*) key cognitive processes involved in the activity of anticipation.

Narratologists have long recognized that narrative constitutes an important heuristic tool for understanding the world, for making meaningful connections between past, present, and future events. As Boyd observes (2009: 137), "we will interpret something as story if we can," ascribing significance and temporal-causal links to any incidents, applying rules of logic and probability to the actions and motivations of any agents, wherever possible. Taleb (2007: 62–84) describes this as "the narrative fallacy" and associates it with "our vulnerability to over-interpretation and our predilection for compact stories over raw truths ... our limited ability to look at sequences of facts without weaving an explanation into them, or, equivalently, forcing a logical link, an *arrow of relationship*, upon them" (2007: 63–4).

In his *Poetics*, the first sustained work of narratology from the third century BCE, Aristotle pointed out that even when two incidents are not causally connected, where there is no necessary or probable sequence or relation between two events, we will nevertheless see a story *if we can*. To illustrate his point about this tendency toward narrativization, Aristotle offers an anecdote ("the murder of Mitys") in which a statue of a murdered man happens to fall upon and so kill his murderer (*Poetics* 9. 1452a 4–10). There is no logical or causal connection between the two deaths, yet they nevertheless combine to make a satisfying story. Aristotle is critical of the false "*post hoc ergo propter hoc*" (after therefore because of) syllogism at work here and is disapproving of the low aesthetic and affective quality that such a plotless "story," in his view, possesses. However, his intuition that we try to make sense of the random incidents of real life by imposing a narrative structure upon them *if we can* is instructive, anticipating as it does an important focus of modern narratology – and a salient problem in anticipation and future studies.

For modern narratologists, particularly those working in the field of cognitive narratology, similarly maintain that we make sense of the world "narratively," that is, we view events in the real or social world as if they were, are, or will be narrated, seeing narrative as a metaphor for life and treating lived experience as "storied." For Ricoeur (1984–1988), this metaphor has particular valence in the context of narrative identity and the stories we live, tell, and read about our past, present, and future selves. Refining Aristotle's intuitions, Ricoeur maintains that the structured continuity of narrative provides a model upon which we base individual stories of personhood, assimilating our imaginative experience of fictive story worlds with our lived experience of the real world.

This has important implications for modeling how we live, tell, and read the future and how we process anticipation *as if* narratively configured. For Currie (2007: 6), "the reading of fictional narratives is a kind of preparation for and repetition of the continuous anticipation that takes place in non-fictional life … [giving] fiction, and the study of fiction, a critical role in the understanding of what lies outside of fiction." It might be objected that life is lived prospectively but narrativized retrospectively, making correlations between the processing of fictional (story world) and extra-fictional (real world) experiences unsound. Fictional characters such as Tristram Shandy and Emma Bovary similarly warn against forgetting to remember the fundamental differences between stories and lives. However, narratological studies into the phenomenology of reading demonstrate that even retrospective ("once upon a time …") narratives are processed by their readers *prospectively*, that is, readers experience such narratives, as they experience the world, in a present mode of future-focused anticipation. For Brooks (1984: 22), stories require readers to respond to the preterite or past tense of a story world as if it were their own present and future. Thus, the experience of reading a story parallels the experience of living a life: incidents and events are read and lived in the present moment and pass into memory and the past, while the future remains open, the focus of hopes, fears, and anticipations. As Ryan, in her study of the cognitive narratology of "possible worlds," puts it (Ryan 2015: 83):

> Living a narrative prospectively means placing oneself in a concrete imaginary situation, monitoring its evolution moment by moment, trying to anticipate possible developments, and experiencing the disappearance of possibilities that comes with the passing of time but remaining steadily focused on the hatching of the future.

By better understanding the ways in which such prospective reading and narrative anticipation works, then, might we better appreciate the subtleties and processes of anticipation in both story worlds and real-world scenarios? Could narratological insights into the operations of anticipation offer useful insights into the way we read stories about the future?

Prolepsis as a Model for Narrative

> This is the art of storytelling, so that by beginning in the middle of things through narration
> we return to the beginning and sometimes we anticipate things that are about to happen, as if
> through prophecy.
> Servius, *Commentary on Virgil's Aeneid* (preface)

In narratology, the dynamics of anticipation in telling and reading stories have long been a key site of interest and analysis. The earliest narratives in the Western canon (Homer's epic *Iliad* and *Odyssey* from the eighth century BCE) already exhibit a range of techniques manipulating future time and temporality so as to achieve effects such as suspense, foreshadowing, and apprehension. Thus, the earliest extant body of literary criticism (the exegetical commentaries of the ancient Greek Homeric scholia) already show a remarkable level of sophistication in their analysis of these anticipatory narrative features (see Nünlist 2009). The ancient scholiasts exhibit a particular concern with what modern narratologists call "prolepsis," that is, an "anachrony going forward to the future with respect to the 'present' moment; an evocation of one or more events that will occur after the 'present' moment ... an anticipation, a flashforward, a prospection" (Prince 1987: 79; see also Genette 1980: 40–78). Thus, the scholia assess the psychological and emotional impact upon ancient readers of a Trojan mother's pathos-filled anticipation of the future awaiting her son (*Iliad* 22.473–515) or the foreshadowing of the death of Achilles (not included within the plot of Homer's *Iliad* but frequently anticipated through prolepses in that text).

In modern narratology, prolepsis reemerged as a prominent topic of attention in the work of Genette (1980: 39–40) and Bal ([1985] 2009: 53–66), who saw this present-future linking anachrony as part of the wider anticipatory world-building practices of both narrators and readers. Indeed, Genette (1980: 77, emphasis in original) saw the cognitive processing of narrative prolepses as depending upon – and thus offering insights into – the "possible (or rather the variable) narrative *competence* of the reader." Such narrative competence, shaped by past and present experiences of processing anachronies in story form, is what enables readers to identify and respond appropriately to prolepses, to feel sympathy for a character whose death is imminent, and to feel suspense or relief according to the anticipatory cues provided by the text. Higher levels of this narrative competence will also enable readers to discount what Genette terms "false advance mentions" or "snares" and even "false snares" – the red herrings and false red herrings often found in classic detective fiction or the "black swans" found in real-world scenarios, whose actual future significance may not be immediately recognized or recognizable. Indeed, even while processing these various kinds of prolepses *prospectively*, the competent reader knows that their significance or lack thereof can only ever be fully evaluated *retrospectively*. The true or false red herring or black swan can only be correctly identified as such with hindsight.

Narrative anticipations of the future through prolepses therefore perform what Brooks describes as an "anticipation of retrospection" – a process which turns out to be a miniature working model of the way in which narrative itself functions (1984: 23, emphases in original):

> If the past is to be read as present, it is a curious present that we know to be past in relation to a future we know to be already in place, already in wait for us to reach it. Perhaps we would do best to speak of the *anticipation of retrospection* as our chief tool in making sense of narrative, the master trope of its strange logic.

Readers process any preview into the future that a narrator may provide by anticipating that at some future point in the narrative, the substance of that preview will be revealed to have been meaningful or otherwise. As Brooks reminds us, we read a narrative "in anticipation of the structuring power of those endings that will retrospectively give the order and significance of plot" (1984: 94). When readers encounter a narrative prolepsis, the successful cognitive processing of its anticipatory dynamics necessitates a complex interplay of the past, present, and future – an interplay which Brooks, along with many other narratologists, sees as illustrating the way in which narrative itself is cognitively processed. According to Bridgeman (2005: 130), "The mental models relating to future action which are built in response to the explicit textual cues of prolepsis are part of a wider range of anticipatory and speculative activities by the reader." Given narratology's claims that experience of reading a story parallels the experience of living a life, such cognitive processing of anticipation in narrative may yield crucial insights into the processing of anticipation in the real world.

Anticipatory Competence and Cognition

> The gods accomplish many things beyond anticipation;
> The expected was not fulfilled
> And god found a way for the unexpected.
> That is how this affair turned out.
> Euripides, epilogue to the tragedies *Alcestis, Medea, Andromache, Helen,* and *Bacchant Women*

For Genette, the successful operations of prolepsis depend upon readerly competence. But for Brooks, proleptic anticipation plays a much more fundamental role in reading and is in fact "our chief tool in making sense of narrative" (1984: 23). Pioneering narratologists Wellek and Warren (1949: 419) had already "anticipated" as much in their own account of what happens when readers process a story:

> In reading with a sense for continuity, for contextual coherence, for wholeness, there comes a moment when we feel that we have 'understood', that we have seized on the right interpretation, the real meaning. It is a process that ... proceeds from attention to a detail to an anticipation of the whole and back again to an interpretation of the detail.

Indeed, as Augustine had noticed as early as the fourth century CE (*Confessions* 11.28.38; c.f. 11.30.41), the cognitive processing of a narrative depends upon a complex synergy between the reader's *memory* of what has passed, *attention* to the present moment, and *anticipation* (*expectatio*) of the future that is to come.

According to Kennedy (2013: 30): "In the case of future processes in which we are involved, we measure them by anticipation, but only if we already have some experience of what we are measuring or a pattern we have already noticed so as to make prospective calculations."

Modern narratology confirms Augustine's theory. From Kermode's (1967) "sense of an ending," Iser's (1978) "protentions," and Eco's (1979) "extensional operations" to Brooks's (1984) "anticipation of retrospection," narratologists and literary theorists forward the view that anticipation is central to the processing of narrative fiction. Anticipation is understood as one of the principal dynamic forces that structures and motivates narrative. Anticipation allows, even drives, us to make temporal-causal connections between separate events, to make sense of the incidents of both real and story worlds by linking the past to a present or future moment and imposing a narrative pattern upon them. Currie (2007: 6) even goes so far as to suggest that "this anticipatory mode of being might be a characteristic ... of human being."

Cognitive studies of reading and reader response, including neuropsychological and empirical studies, reach the same conclusion that "the reader of a literary text must at one and the same moment recall, respond, discriminate, and anticipate" (Miall 1995: 280). Research into the cognitive systems that process anticipation also tends to corroborate Augustine's intuitions that memory, attention, and anticipation work synergetically in our reading of narrative texts, concluding that "the affective or somatic markers that initially guide reading derive their significance from prior experience" (Damasio 1994: 180), that is, our recall of past literary and extraliterary experiences shapes the processing of present attention *and* future anticipation when it comes to forming narrative competence in both story world fictions and real-world scenarios. Anticipation may be "our chief tool in making sense of narrative" (Brooks 1984: 23) but it is a tool sharpened by retrospection. Paradoxically, it seems that the same narrative competences and processes that allow us to "tell" (and to read) the future in the first place prove to be a barrier in anticipating any kind of future that is not linked – through unilinear causal-temporal connections – to the present and past.

Chronocentrism and Anticipatory Backshadowing

> I have often noticed that we are inclined to endow our friends with the stability of type that literary characters acquire in the reader's mind. No matter how many times we reopen "King Lear," never shall we find the good king banging his tankard in high revelry, all woes forgotten, at a jolly reunion with all three daughters and their lapdogs. Never will Emma rally, revived by the sympathetic salts in Flaubert's father's timely tear.
> V. Nabokov, *Lolita* ([1955] 2000: 265)

The implications of acknowledging this retrospective edge to the anticipatory processes of narrative competence are wide-reaching, for it suggests that projections of the future in both textual and extratextual situations, in both story world and real-world scenarios, will necessarily be influenced by prior experience of the past and present. Future anticipations are therefore liable to exhibit what Morson (1994) describes as "chronocentrism," an assumption that the future, like the present, is a product of the past. Morson warns that one of the major limitations of chronocentrism (a mode of "presentness") is its occlusion of the probable difference of the future to both the past and present, resulting in models of the future which merely extend the possibilities of the present (Morson 1994: 275).

Employing a literary metaphor to describe what happens to real-world scenarios when we situate ourselves in what Morson calls "epilogue time," he argues that (1994: 278–79) our views of the future, and our ability to anticipate its differences and continuities to the past and present, prevent the projection of any real surprises or radical change. Like the narrator or novelist who adds an epilogue or postscript to his or her narrative text, those viewing the future from (or in) "epilogue time" do not look for new plotlines or bifurcations. They anticipate a linear future evolving along already established trajectories, a predictable future that is predictable because it accords with preexisting story scripts. For Morson (1994: 279): "Epilogue time allows the future to be viewed in terms of a form of anticipatory backshadowing that might be called *pre*shadowing: the future is to be like the present . . ." For Taleb (2007: 83), this presentness or chronocentrism lies at the root of the "narrative fallacy" in future anticipations and forecasts, imposing upon us "a wrong map of the likelihood of events," blinding us to the unexpected, the new, and the improbable.

A variant form of this chronocentric "*pre*shadowing" can be found in association with the preexisting story scripts through which readers seek to make sense of fictional story worlds or "possible worlds." Ryan's principle of "minimal departure" maintains that readers will assume any story world essentially resembles their own unless and until pertinent differences are specified (1991: 48–54). Therefore, when readers negotiate the dynamics of possible worlds – both fictional and real world – they will assume that the future essentially resembles the present unless and until any salient differences are made manifest.

One of the problems associated with such *pre*shadowing (and, indeed, with the wider principle of "minimal departure") is the risk of anticipating a future in which we posit ourselves just as we are *now*. Through a failure of imagination, we populate the future with our present selves and therefore with our present concerns and perspectives, shaped by our past experiences. As Bode argues (Bode and Dietrich 2013: 147): "Presentism occurs because we fail to recognize that our future selves won't see the world the way we see it now . . . [and] this fundamental inability to take the perspective of the person to whom the rest of our lives will happen is the most insidious problem a futurian can face."

Narratologists have had a long-standing interest in the presentism that readers typically encounter in "life narratives" – particularly in the context of autobiography and other first-person (autodiegetic) narrative modes which seek to remember and reconstruct the past from the perspective of the present. The story logic that emerges from such narratives requires the reader to elide a quasi-schizophrenic split between the "narrating I" and the "narrated I," to process a simultaneous (dis) continuity between the now of the experiencing and the narrating subject, and between the simultaneous past/present/future space-time (or chronotope) occupied by this split subject.

In the *Confessions* of Augustine, as in most life narratives, the present moment dominates. Remembered events from the past are selected for their significance in the light of the present. The representation of past experience turns out to be just that – a "making present once again" – in which contingent events are transformed into a coherent plot, and meaningful temporal-causal connections are retrospectively drawn between them. The future is encountered only proleptically as an "anticipation of retrospection." The future horizon toward which the plots of autobiographical narratives head is the present *now* of writing. The narrating subject in autobiography can say "this is the man I was" and even "this is the man I will become" but the future anticipated here is already past.

In the face of such teleological chronocentrism, modern and postmodern writers have challenged the idea that narrative can impose order upon the chaos of lived experience and emphasized instead fragmentation, bifurcation, and polychrony in their own life narratives. In Virginia Woolf's 1985 (posthumously published) *Moments of Being* and Vladimir Nabokov's 1966 *Speak Memory*, both the narrating and the narrated subjects are encountered neither as wholly fixed nor as wholly protean characters, but as complex, contradictory figures, inherently surprising, and infinitely capable of improbable, unpredictable, and inconsistent behaviors.

Such narrative models of the bifurcated subject (the narrating I and the narrated I) have important implications for modeling future scenarios involving the self: for instance, in saving and planning for retirement, in reducing an individual carbon footprint, and in issuing an advance directive declining anticipated future medical interventions (see Huxtable 2015). In anticipating any future – but especially in any medium- to long-term future – in which "I" am concerned, the necessary characterization of "my" self will impact significantly on the anticipatory processes through which future scenarios are modeled and understood. What is more, the narratological comprehension and configuration of the bifurcated subject in such future scenarios (what we might describe as the "anticipating I" and the "anticipated I") applies not only to the first person singular (I, me) but to the first person *plural* (we, us). Narratology thus helps to show that the split subject plays a significant function in shaping the dynamics of anticipation in accounts not only of "my" personal future but in "our" collective social future(s), indeed, in any future narrative in which we ourselves play a character role or roles.

There is significant complexity involved in cognitively processing ourselves and others as bifurcated subjects in narrative world models. Yet wider exposure to and engagement with first-person narratives and scenarios – both fictional and nonfictional – which offer the opportunity to reflect our bifurcated selves to ourselves might serve to expand our own temporal horizons and anticipatory competences. Immersive virtual reality experiences, and even personal digital archives such as Facebook and Snapchat Memories, offer new ways for us to narrativize our own lives as part of a multi-linear story world and, crucially, to see ourselves as the-same-yet-different subject(s) occupying that world (or worlds). Such exposure to the complexity of our different-yet-same past and present selves may prepare us to better appreciate and anticipate the complex ontological status of our future selves too and to anticipate our participation in future worlds in which we can imagine ourselves (both individually and collectively) neither as wholly fixed nor as wholly unfixed characters. By developing this aspect of our narrative competence(s), we may not necessarily learn to avoid populating the future with our present selves and our present concerns and perspectives, but we may find it easier to recognize the implicit bias of such "presentness" and to pay attention to the blind spots and prejudicial *pre*shadowing it entails.

The Future Narratives and Narrative Future(s) of Narratology and Anticipation

> All stories and narratives tell of events past, present, or yet to come.
> Plato, *Republic* (3.392d)

The same sorts of narrative (in)competencies that shape future scenarios involving the self also pertain to larger social and global future scenarios. Here too, chronocentric *pre*shadowing which assumes the future will be like the present, alongside principles of minimal departure which assume the future will be familiar (and again, essentially like the present), imposes limitations upon our capacity to imagine possible future worlds that are significantly different from the present. As Bode complains (Bode and Dietrich 2013: 100): "being able to think about the future ... is perpetually spoilt by our present incapacity to be sufficiently imaginative, to think the unexpected, to factor in surprise, discontinuities, reversals, tipping points, etc." How then might we use narratives and narratological tools to avoid chronocentrism and anticipatory back-shadowing or *pre*shadowing when thinking about the future? Morson offers us some possible ways forward. He suggests that (1994: 282):

> We are all captives of our moment, and we live on a small temporal island. Complex moral thinking, informed by a rich sense of temporality, may liberate us from the tyranny of the present instant. The imagination of sideshadows and the process of dialogue with alternatives may expand our temporal horizons and make us more attentive to historical opportunity.

Morson advocates "complex" thinking and the imaginative engagement with alternative narrative models such as counterfactuals (or "sideshadows," as he describes them). Defined by narratologists as "a principle of divergence that makes visible a vast horizon of alternative stories" (Ryan 2014: 735), the counterfactual is often viewed as a postmodern phenomenon but it actually has an ancient pedigree. Speculative and counterfactual narratives considering a possible world in which characters may have behaved otherwise and events may have happened differently can be traced back to first century BCE Rome, where the historian Livy wonders what might have happened if Alexander the Great had lived longer and, having subjugated Asia, had then turned his attentions to Europe and to the might of Rome (Livy, *Ab Urbe Condita*, 9.16–18).

Such "what if" speculation frequently appears in fictional narrative too, when narrators and characters imagine alternative futures – and alternative stories – for themselves, positing possible world scenarios within their own story worlds. In these historical and novel counterfactuals, the conjectural divergence from the actual story line and story world (from what "really" happened in the history or fiction) is clearly delineated. The alternatives are processed as speculative "sideshadows," clearly lacking the substance and reality of the main (hi)story. Following the story logic imposed by such counterfactuals, the reader will typically process the sideshadow as a diversion, as an ancillary narrative of lesser significance than the primary plotline from which it branches out. The readers of James Thurber's 1939 short story "The Secret Life of Walter Mitty," however, immersed they may be in the possible worlds configured in Mitty's vividly heroic counterfactual daydreams, can readily identify the "actual" possible world of the story in which Mitty performs a series of mundane domestic errands for his wife.

Imagining counterfactual possible worlds alongside (and even within) actual (or mimetically "real") possible worlds may help to exercise the "complex moral thinking" that Morson advocates as a correction to chronocentrism. However, its enrichment of our "temporal horizons" is clearly limited. Despite the plot bifurcations and ostensibly multilinear narratives produced by counterfactual fantasies and stories, the reader is directed to privilege one central story line and one unified story world, focusing memory and anticipation upon the actual, even while focusing attention upon the counterfactual. This entails *remembering* that Mitty is driving his car too fast while he is fantasizing about piloting a seaplane, *anticipating* that while Mitty leans against a wall, smoking – and imagining himself about to face a firing squad – his wife will return any moment, and Mitty will have to face her ire for having forgotten to buy dog biscuits. That story world and its temporality are ever present and dominant in terms of their deictic (here and now) force.

Indeed, this is one of the more persistent narratological tropes of counterfactual speculation in both history and in fiction: whatever branching path is projected out from the here and now ultimately returns there. Historical counterfactuals, for example, imagine past events following a different path (Germany winning the Second World War is one favorite motif, as in Philip K. Dick's 1963 *Man in the High Castle* and Robert Harris' 1992 *Fatherland*). But that alternate path will typically loop back to return the story world to a familiar present. In a move initiated by Livy in the first century BCE, counterfactual histories show us the unreality of what might have happened but chronocentrically privilege the present product of what really did happen. Alexander might have attacked Rome, but he would have been defeated – ensuring that Rome's long-term future (Livy's present) would not have played out any differently. Hitler's Germany and its allies might have triumphed, but the Cold War and Europe's longer-term future (our present) would not have played out very differently. Morson (1994) describes this influence of the future present moment upon retellings of the past as "backshadowing," and if we extrapolate the principles of such historical counterfactual thinking to future anticipations, we can forecast an analogous effect. The present casts a shadow upon the future, limiting our ability to see differences and discontinuities–that is, *pre*shadowing.

We may usefully consider a brief counterfactual sideshadowing of our own here. For it is worth noticing that Morson does *not* include utopian or dystopian narratives among his recommended reading for enhanced anticipatory competence. Elsewhere he argues that (1994: 266–67) "Utopias set in the future almost always engage in what might be called *anticipatory backshadowing*: the author invites readers to imagine how their world will look when viewed by their counterparts in the utopia to come. He passes certain judgements on his own time by projecting them forward onto people who will 'look backward'." Bode offers a similar rationale for dismissing utopian fiction as a model for future anticipation, arguing that (Bode and Dietrich 2013: 11) "The basic form of utopian narrative is nothing but the narration of a future which has already happened – and therefore grammatically as well as narratologically the narrative of a(n) (imagined) *past.* They present the future as *past* space: closed, determined, with uni-linear action."

However, there are some narrative forms which do promise to foster the sort of complex future thinking that is required to see the future differently, free of – or at least alert to the existence thereof – the blind spots and limitations of "anticipatory backshadowing." In some modern science fiction inspired by scientific theories of multiple parallel universes (or the "multiverse" of quantum physics), obvious distinctions between actual and counterfactual story lines are dissolved. The multiverse or metauniverse hypothesis that any and every possibility may be actualized in many possible worlds makes it increasingly difficult for readers to orient themselves in these story worlds according to fixed or stable time-space coordinates or chronotopes. In fact, the fundamental principles underlying the ways that readers perceive space and time may be compromised still further in a multiverse model where time itself can possess different properties in different universes.

Since H. G. Wells first anticipated the multiverse in his 1923 novel, *Men Like Gods*, in which the use of a "paratime machine" makes it challenging for the reader to identify any central deictic here and now across multiple parallel worlds, such narratives have proliferated, finding film, television, anime, and interactive online gaming all conducive media for the multiverse or metaverse story form. Although several narratives in this genre straightforwardly evoke parallel or meta-worlds which are more or less clearly defined as alternatives to a central story world, and thus elicit the sort of sideshadowing effects typically seen in counterfactual narratives, others *do* embrace the complexity and opportunity offered by narrating across multiple story worlds. If Morson's theory is correct, that "we live on a small temporal island" and are inclined to project shadows of the present onto the past and future, then exposure to such narrative complexity could help to increase our readerly competences, in general, and our anticipatory competences, in particular – both within fictional story worlds and real-world scenarios. Cognitive and psychological studies into the phenomenology of reading narrative and of experiencing story worlds have consistently shown that levels of understanding and enjoyment of stories correlate to the reader's previous encounters with narrative intricacy (Hogan 2003). Faced with narrative complexity, uncertainty, and even incoherence and contradiction, experienced readers are able to supply familiar scripts and schemata to help them make surprising and improbable connections. The wider and more varied their past experience of fictional story worlds, the greater their competence (and pleasure) in finding strategies to make sense of the strange and unfamiliar and the more nuanced their anticipatory aptitudes (Schneider 2005).

Whether or not they are explicitly treated as such within the narrative frame, plural story multiverses (as distinct from unified, single story worlds) also appear in postmodern narratives which present multiple, mutually contradictory and incompatible tellings of the same story or event, with no obvious cues as to which version may be the factual and which the counterfactual (as in John Fowles' 1969 *The French Lieutenant's Woman* or Kate Atkins' 2013 novel *Life after Life* and in films like *Run Lola Run* (1998) or *Coherence* (2013)). Richardson, in his influential analysis of narrative time in postmodern and non-mimetic fiction (2002), has shown that the consciously unrealistic (also described by narratologists as "anti-mimetic," "non-mimetic," or "unnatural") treatment of time and temporality encountered in many postmodern narratives radically destabilizes traditional notions of story and story worlds. In Richardson's account (2002: 48–49; c.f. Fludernik 1996: 333–37):

> In these texts, there is no single, unambiguous story to be extrapolated from the discourse, but rather two or more contradictory versions that seriously vitiate the very notion of story (*histoire*) insofar as it is conceived as a single, self-consistent series of events that can be inferred from the discourse.

The tools of classical narratology must be refined and theories of reader-response revised if we are to analyze effectively the anticipatory dynamics at work in these postmodern narratives. This is because such postmodern novels treat the past, present and future, alongside memory, attention, and anticipation, very differently to pre-modernist fiction. According to Herman's postclassical narratology (2002: 220–250), novels which employ such "polychronic narration" resist recourse to any one dominant time or story line, to any singular deictic "here and now," or to any unified chronotope. This entails "a mode of narration that purposely resists linearity by multiplying the ways in which narrated events can be ordered," incorporating a kind of "fuzzy temporality" (Herman 2002: 212–14).

Classical narratology, following the intuitions of Aristotle and the refinements of his poetics by the Russian formalists in the early twentieth century, assumes that however intricately plotted a narrative may be (however complex its anachronies, its flashbacks and flash-forwards, or its counterfactual bifurcations) the reader is able to make sense of it by cognitively reconstructing its "real" chronolinear *story* (also known as *fabula* or *histoire*). The narratee (the reader or viewer) processes narrative complexity and multiplicity by attempting to reduce a temporally intricate pattern of incidents into a chronological series of causally related events. Thus, in Forster's famous definition, a story is "a narrative of events arranged in their time-sequence . . . 'The king died and then the queen died,' is a story" (Forster 1927: 86), albeit not one with much narrative richness.

However, in a postmodernist narrative, we might encounter a story in which a royal couple dies in 1066. And then dies in 1060. And then dies in 2017. In Atkinson's 2013 novel *Life After Life*, for example, the protagonist dies in November

1930. She is stillborn on 11 February 1910. She dies in June 1914. She dies in January 1915. Ensuing iterations of her multiple lives see her die in different ways and at different times, again and again. This self-contradictory chronologically *illogical* pattern prevents readers from reconstructing a story out of "events arranged in their time sequence." It simultaneously prevents them from identifying any one life story as the "actual" or principal story line from which the other lives branch out as "counterfactuals." In this plural story world (or, rather, multiverse), all lives are possible and all alternatives equally probable. As Heise observes (1997: 55): "Post-modernist novels . . . project into the narrative present and past an experience of time which normally is only available for the future: time dividing and subdividing, bifurcating and branching off continuously into multiple possibilities and alterna-tives." The readerly competence required to process such narratives, to see the past, present, and future as if open, contingent, and multi-linear (rather than closed, determined, and unilinear) may open up new possibilities in the way that we process future anticipations too.

(In)Conclusion and Summary

> Narrative space is now plastic and manipulable. It has become heterogenous, ambiguous, pluralized. Its inhabitants no longer appear to have an irrefutable or essential relation to any particular space. Rather, space opens up as a variable and finally indeterminate feature of any given world.
> A. Gibson, *Towards a Postmodern Theory of Narrative* (1996: 12)

Bode characterizes such postmodern fiction as a distinctive type of "future narrative" (Bode and Dietrich 2013). Not because its story multiverses represent future spatio-temporal worlds and chronotopes, but because they stage "the fact that the future is a space of yet unrealized potentiality, or, technically speaking, a 'possibility space'" (Bode and Dietrich 2013: 1; cf. Boyd 2009: 122). Bode defines future narratives as those which are open-ended and multi-linear, with nodes producing bifurcations, multi-linear plots, and multiple continuations. Such narratives are supposed to be found in children's "choose-your-own-adventure" books and other interactive fic-tion, postmodern novels (especially those where the reader chooses the reading order), multiplayer online gaming, and even the amusement park rides based on popular film narratives (see Abbott 2008). These future narratives are also found in the anticipatory story scenarios used by climatologists, social and political scientists, and other futurists (Bode and Dietrich 2013: 2 specifically mentions "insurance companies and world climate change experts, [and] peak oil aficionados").

The postmodern novel, in Bode's analysis, is a particularly valuable type of future narrative because it "testifies to the new idea that – though the present can be seen as the outcome of relatable cause-and-effect chains – it is also 'only' a probable state, alongside which other probable (or equally improbable) states can then be imagined" (Bode and Dietrich 2013: 206). The postmodern novel thus helps to mitigate against the negative preshadowing effects of "presentness" by affirming that the present itself is not singular but plural, not closed but open, and not linear but complex. More like the future than the past, in fact.

Bode's claim that this is a "new" idea may be challenged by the evidence of such openness, multiplicity, and complexity in ancient narratives (such as the plots of Greek tragedy) and in early novels (such as Henry Fielding's *Tom Jones* (1749) and Laurence Sterne's *Tristram Shandy* (1759)). However, Bode's championing of this kind of "future narrative" thinking and its heuristic value as a model for anticipation is supported by recent work in the social and political sciences. His innovative theory and poetics of future narratives in literature finds an important corollary in Uprichard's work on "narratives of the future" in social science. For Uprichard (2011: 104), the objects of anticipation and future studies "are dissipative, open, non-linear, multi-dimensional, social systems which are situated in time and space." She maintains that the stories we tell about the future must therefore be themselves open, multi-linear, and multidimensional – plural rather than singular.

The same insistence upon the importance of multiplicity and plurality appears in studies concerned with the future of global sustainability (Costanza et al. 2007: 419–21):

> The environment, society, and the economy each represent complex systems characterized by nonlinearities, autocatalysis, time-delayed feedback loops, emergent phenomena, and chaotic behavior [...] to achieve the outcomes we desire, it will be necessary to incorporate simultaneously several different perspectives, [and] ... the essential theories, tools, and knowledge of multiple disciplines.

Among the multiple perspectives and multi-interdisciplinary tools forecast here as necessary to achieve the effective anticipation of future scenarios and models for these complex environmental, social, and economic systems, future narratives and narratology can play a meaningful part. What we need in the future and for the future, perhaps, is not just a closer dialogue between narratology and anticipation studies, but a multiplicity of dialogues between *narratologies* and *anticipations* – *plural*: dialogues with cognitive narratologists and possible worlds theorists, with climatologists, economists, and social and political scientists; readings of counter-factuals, postmodern fiction, and in particular so-called future narratives with their nonlinear, bifurcating, open plots and possibilities. Through such dialogues and readings, we might find mutually enriching plots for the narrative future(s) of anticipation.

References

Abbott, H. P. (2008). The future of all narrative futures. In J. Phelan & P. Rabinowitz (Eds.), *A companion to narrative theory* (pp. 529–541). Malden: Blackwell Pub.

Bal, M. ([1985] 2009). *Narratology*. Toronto: University of Toronto Press.

Bamberg, M. (2011). Who am I? Narration and its contribution to self and identity. *Theory & Psychology, 21*(1), 3–24. https://doi.org/10.1177/0959354309355852. Accessed 30 September 2016.

Bode, C., & Dietrich, R. (2013). *Future narratives*. Berlin: W. de Gruyter.

Boyd, B. (2009). *On the origin of stories.* Cambridge, MA: Belknap Press of Harvard University Press.

Bridgeman, T. (2005). Thinking ahead: A cognitive approach to prolepsis. *Narrative, 13*(2), 125–159. https://doi.org/10.1353/nar.2005.0007. Accessed 30 September 2016.

Brooks, P. (1984). *Reading for the plot.* New York: A.A. Knopf.

Costanza, R., Graumlich, L., & Steffen, W. (2007). *Sustainability or collapse?* Cambridge, MA: MIT Press in cooperation with Dahlem University Press.

Currie, M. (2007). *About time.* Edinburgh: Edinburgh University Press.

Damasio, A. (1994). *Descartes' error.* New York: Putnam.

Dannenberg, H. (2008). *Coincidence and counterfactuality.* Lincoln: University of Nebraska Press.

Eco, U. (1979). *The role of the reader.* Bloomington: Indiana University Press.

Fludernik, M. (1996). *Towards a 'natural' narratology.* London: Routledge.

Fludernik, M. (2010). *Postclassical narratology.* Columbus: Ohio State University Press.

Forster, E. (1927). *Aspects of the novel.* New York: Harcourt, Brace & Company.

Genette, G. (1980). *Narrative discourse.* Ithaca: Cornell University Press.

Heise, U. (1997). *Chronoschisms: Time, narrative, and postmodernism.* Cambridge: Cambridge University Press.

Herman, D. (1999). *Narratologies.* Columbus: Ohio State University Press.

Herman, D. (2002). *Story logic.* Lincoln: University of Nebraska Press.

Hogan, P. (2003). *The mind and its stories.* Cambridge: Cambridge University Press.

Huxtable, R. (2015). Advance decisions: Worth the paper they are (not) written on? *End of Life Journal, 5*, 2. https://doi.org/10.1136/eoljnl-2015-000002. Accessed 30 September 2016.

Iser, W. (1978). *The act of reading.* Baltimore: Johns Hopkins University Press.

Kennedy, D. (2013). *Antiquity and the meanings of time.* London: I.B. Tauris.

Kermode, F. (1967). *The sense of an ending.* New York: Oxford University Press.

Meister, J. (2014). Narratology. In P. Hühn (Ed.), *Handbook of narratology* (pp. 623–645). Berlin: W. de Gruyter.

Miall, D. (1995). Anticipation and feeling in literary response: A neuropsychological perspective. *Poetics, 23*(4), 275–298. https://doi.org/10.1016/0304-422x(95)00004-4. Accessed 30 September 2016.

Morson, G. (1994). *Narrative and freedom.* New Haven: Yale University Press.

National Intelligence Council (U.S.). (2004). *Mapping the global future.* Washington, DC: National Intelligence Council.

Nünlist, R. (2009). *The ancient critic at work.* Cambridge: Cambridge University Press.

Poli, R. (2007). Three obstructions: Forms of causation, chronotopoids, and levels of reality. *Axiomathes, 17*(1), 1–18.

Prince, G. (1987). *A dictionary of narratology.* Lincoln: University of Nebraska Press.

Richardson, B. (2002). *Narrative dynamics.* Columbus: Ohio State University Press.

Ricœur, P. (1984-1988). *Time and narrative.* Chicago: University of Chicago Press.

Ryan, M.-L. (1991). *Possible worlds, artificial intelligence and narrative theory.* Bloomington: University of Indiana Press.

Ryan, M.-L. (2014). Possible worlds. In P. Hühn (Ed.), *Handbook of narratology* (pp. 726–742). Berlin: W. de Gruyter.

Ryan, M.-L. (2015). *Narrative as virtual reality 2: Revisiting immersion and interactivity in literature and electronic media.* Baltimore: Johns Hopkins University Press.

Schneider, R. (2005). Emotion and narrative. In D. Herman, M. Jahn, & M. Ryan (Eds.), *Routledge encyclopedia of narrative theory* (pp. 135–137). London: Routledge.

Staley, D. (2002). A history of the future. *History and Theory, 41*(4), 72–89. https://doi.org/10.1111/1468-2303.00221. Accessed 30 September 2016.

Taleb, N. (2007). *The black swan.* New York: Random House.

Uprichard, E. (2011). Narratives of the future: Complexity, time and temporality. In W. P. Vogt & M. Williams (Eds.), *Sage handbook of innovation in social research methods.* London: Sage.

Wellek, R., & Warren, A. (1949). *Theory of literature.* New York: Harcourt, Brace.

Anticipation and Eschatology

44

Andrew Cyprian Love

Contents

Abstract

The Christian disposition towards the Second Coming of Christ is anticipatory, for Christians are called to act appropriately in view of the expected end-time. This Christian eschatological anticipation cannot be framed successfully within traditional theological models of grace and nature. The idea of emergence, however, provides a successful way of framing Christian eschatological anticipation theologically. The role of imagination as a vehicle for understanding Christian eschatological anticipation will also be examined

Keywords

Christianity · Nature · Grace · Emergence · Eschatology · Imagination · Spontaneity

A. C. Love (✉)
Glenstal Abbey, Co. Limerick, Munster, Ireland
e-mail: cyprian@glenstal.org

© Springer Nature Switzerland AG 2019
R. Poli (ed.), *Handbook of Anticipation*,
https://doi.org/10.1007/978-3-319-91554-8_12

Two Anticipations

Expectation of the occurrence of a particular event may be slight ("I think it might just happen") or great ("it is almost certain to happen") or anything in between. An exception to this is expectation of death, which is certain. The certainty of death is one of the great cultural motifs of human experience. Anticipation is defined as something which includes but is more than expectation. Anticipation entails not merely the expectation of certain things, but also actions carried out in preparation for those things. To give an example, it is not strictly anticipatory simply to notice that it may rain. Noticing it may rain becomes anticipatory only when we do something about it, for instance, when we take an umbrella. Thus anticipation is twofold in character for it entails both awareness and action. We expect something (with our minds) and then we anticipate it (with our actions).

This naturally prompts a question for Christian theology. Christians expect a future in which Christ will come again in glory to bring in the end of time and His own eschatological triumph. The question for theology is: Do we find the twofold pattern of anticipation present in this Christian scheme of looking forward? Is the expectation which Christian believers have of Christian eschatology, strictly speaking, anticipatory? Do we find in it, that is to say, not only a looking forward to the future event of Christ's return but also some action or actions carried out in view of that future event, these being the two features which, as we saw above, would raise Christian expectation to genuine anticipation?

The answer would seem to be yes, we do find the same two features just mentioned, that is to say, expectation and action. Christian eschatological expectation is not merely a psychological disposition but calls additionally for some action or actions carried out in view of the expected future event. We find, on consulting the Gospel writers, that they propose certain actions which Christians are called upon to perform in view of the final coming of Christ. The Gospels require believers to lead their lives according to particular ethical standards and comport themselves according to particular values. This is a form of anticipatory behaviour. In this way, believers "take their umbrella." The Christian mind-set does conform to the twofold model which we correctly designate as anticipatory, namely, expectation plus action.

When we turn to the Letters of (or attributed to) the apostle Paul we encounter a more consciously intellectual approach than we find in the Gospels, and, despite the fact that these Letters predate the Gospels, the analytical subtlety of the discussion is considerably greater. As we might expect, given the consistency of Scripture, we again find a theology like that of the Gospels in which the final triumph of Christ and the final coming of the Kingdom of God, the whole panoply of consummation, are understood to be in the future. The subtlety of the Pauline treatment consists in the remarkable fact that these future events are understood somehow to have broken in already into the present. This is the essence of Paul's Christian theological eschatology. James Dunn writes that "the distinctive feature of Paul's theology at this point is *not* the eschatology, but the *tension* which his revised eschatology sets up. Eschatological hope was a common feature of Paul's religious heritage. But an eschatology split in this way between such a decisive 'already' and yet still a 'not yet' was a new departure" (James D. G. Dunn, *The Theology of Paul the Apostle* (Edinburgh: T & T Clark, 1998), p. 465).

For Paul, Christians act anticipatorily with a view to the Kingdom which is due to be perfected in the future. However, following Paul's new eschatology, Christians act not simply because of what is expected in the future but because *that future has somehow already been brought into the present time.* The future has *entered* the present and the anticipatory actions Christians perform now, within the graced framework of Christian eschatological anticipation, belong not merely to the present but to a future already made present now. (This perspective is not absent from the Gospels, but it has its first systematic theological exposition in Paul.) In some sense, these acts are both present and future acts at once.

It is here that we become able to identify a crucial point of difference between Christian anticipation as just described and "ordinary" anticipation, that is, anticipation considered from the purely natural standpoint. For in the case of the latter purely natural form of anticipation, the anticipatory actions belong to an autonomous "now" separate from the future. However, for Paul's Christian form of anticipation, rooted in Christian theological eschatology, the now in which the anticipatory actions take place, and the future which they anticipate, are somehow glued together, because the future has entered the present. Paul's Christian eschatology is, moreover, no eccentricity in the tradition, but the definitive eschatology of the early church and subsequent Christianity, the decisive Christian insight on eschatological anticipation.

The resemblance between "ordinary" natural anticipation and Christian eschatological anticipation would appear to be partial. In other words, there is a continuity between them but there is also a discontinuity. As far as the continuity is concerned, this consists in the fact that both kinds of anticipation anticipate events in the future. As far as the discontinuity is concerned, each type of anticipation, natural and Christian, understands the relationship between the present and the future differently. For natural anticipation, actions performed in view of an expected future are not themselves part of that future: thus, for natural anticipation, now is now and future is future, each held decisively distinct. This is the "common sense" view of anticipation which all humans naturally have. By contrast, for Christian theological eschatology, the final future occurrences, consisting of the final consummation of Christ's work, are also partly present now. Thus there is a certain *identification* of present and future in Christian theological eschatology. Here, it is no longer the case that "now is now and future is future." The present and future commingle. This has a crucial consequence. The anticipatory acts which Christians perform become part of the present *and* the future at the same time or to make the same point differently: whereas, in natural anticipation, present and future are held distinct, in Christian eschatological anticipation the present and the future interpenetrate, and so the anticipatory actions done in the present somehow participate in the future, belong to the future, in a way which goes beyond the mere "looking forward" characteristic of the actions of purely natural anticipation.

So, on one hand, insofar as Christian eschatological and natural forms of anticipation both call for actions to be done now in view of some future state of affairs, we may say that they appear to be similar. On the other hand, insofar as Christian eschatological anticipation conflates present and future, whereas natural anticipation holds present and future apart, we might say that Christian eschatological anticipation cuts across the dynamics of natural anticipation and opposes it with something radically new, namely, an anticipatory dynamic according to which actions are not just performed in view of a future but in some sense participate in the future. So Christian eschatological anticipation is like natural anticipation in some respects and in other respects it is unlike it.

Nature and Grace

In making this distinction, whereby grace is like or unlike nature, we hear an echo of one of Christian theology's most important debates. Does grace build on nature or does grace cut across nature? In the case we are discussing, it seems to do both. The grace of Christian eschatology appears to make use of, to build upon, some aspects of natural anticipation, but it also obviates and supersedes other aspects. To be more precise, grace builds upon the way natural anticipation already looks to a future, but at the same time grace obviates the way in which natural anticipation understands the relationship of past and future as separate.

There are two major Christian traditions of thought on the subject of the relationship of nature and grace. We will take a moment to consider the proposals of these two theological traditions. For the Catholic tradition (as expressed in our own day, for example, by Karl Rahner) nature is created with an emptiness only God can fill, is oriented to completion in God, and is, in this sense, already graced. (For a discussion of the God-oriented expectancy of nature see Karl Rahner, "Nature and Grace." In *Theological Investigations* vol 4 (Baltimore: Helicon 1966) and Karl Rahner "On the Theology of Worship." In *Theological Investigations* vol 19 (New York: Crossroad, 1983).) According to this tradition, the new grace of Christ, when it comes into nature, interacts with a nature which is already impregnated with a type of pre-existing grace or grace of creation. The grace of Christ builds on this type of expectant, graced nature. The grace of Christ does not override nature but perfects it: in the scholastic maxim, *gratia non tollit naturam, sed perfecit.*

How does this particular model of the grace and nature relationship influence the present discussion? Armed with the expectations set up by this Rahnerian model, we would be led to expect that the dynamics of Christian eschatological anticipation would build upon the characteristics of natural anticipation. We have seen above that, up to a point, the dynamics of Christian eschatological anticipation do indeed build upon the characteristics of natural anticipation, or at least one of those characteristics, in the sense that Christian eschatological anticipation shares, we might say *builds upon*, natural anticipation's concern with a future state of affairs.

If we turn now to the other traditional theological model of nature and grace, found in more Protestant parts of the theological heritage, there is not the same theology of nature as something already graced. There is no grace of nature, only the grace of Christ. Grace and nature stand in a relationship which is not complementary, as we have seen in the Catholic tradition and Rahner, but dialectical. Grace does not, cannot, build on nature. They are, so to speak, opposites. Grace, when it comes, essentially replaces nature. An exponent of this approach, Karl Barth writes: "Within the Bible there is a strange, new world, the world of God." (Karl Barth, *The Word of God and the Word of Man* (Gloucester, Mass: Peter Smith, 1978), p. 33. Cited in John Macquarrie, *Twentieth-Century Religious Thought* (1963) (London: SCM, 1988), p. 322.) "There are no transitions, intermixings, or intermediate stages. There is only crisis, finality, new insight." (Barth ibid., p. 91. Cited in Macquarrie ibid.) When applied to our present discussion, this Protestant model would tend to make us expect that the dynamics of Christian eschatological anticipation would cut across, obliterate, or overrule the characteristics of natural anticipation, since natural anticipation would be understood on this model to possess no inherent graced life upon which the grace of Christ and Christian eschatological anticipation could build. Essentially, natural anticipation would be replaced.

How does this second, Protestant model influence our discussion? Once again, when we examine Christian eschatological anticipation, we see that, in certain respects, its dynamics do indeed partly cut across, obliterate, replace, or overrule the characteristics of natural anticipation, to the extent that, in Christian eschatological anticipation, the future has entered the present and so the anticipatory actions of Christians belong to a future already made present now, not, as in the case of natural anticipation, to an autonomous "now" independent of the future. Christian eschatological anticipation in this sense cuts across and overrides the separation of present and future which natural anticipation makes. To this extent, it follows the Protestant paradigm of grace as the replacement of nature.

We may conclude from this consideration of the Rahnerian Catholic framework and the Barthian Protestant framework for understanding the relationship of nature and grace that each framework is able to account for some aspect of the relationship of natural anticipation to Christian eschatological anticipation, but neither framework can encompass the whole state of affairs. The whole state of affairs can be understood, neither wholly in terms of the Rahnerian Catholic framework, nor the Barthian Protestant framework, since Christian eschatological anticipation neither works wholly with, nor wholly cuts across, natural anticipation. It does both. We come therefore to a stumbling block. Although these two models of the interaction of grace and nature are the main models of this interaction proposed by the Christian traditions, neither model can comprehensively theorize a fact absolutely central to Christian theology, namely, how the graced anticipation of the final triumph of God at the end of time interacts with our existing natural powers of anticipation. Each model, Rahnerian and Barthian, can account for part of the interaction but neither model can account for the whole interaction. The Rahnerian model can account only for the *similarity* between the two parts involved in the interaction, and the Barthian model only for the *difference* between the two parts involved in the interaction.

Emergence

If, as we have seen, neither of the two standard models of the relationship of grace and nature, the Rahnerian and the Barthian, can fully accommodate the reality of the way Christian eschatological anticipation relates to natural anticipation, we may like to consider instead whether the ideas of *emergentism* can be used to arrive at a more satisfactory model of this relationship of Christian eschatological anticipation to natural anticipation.

What is emergentism? According to all emergentist paradigms of reality, whenever B emerges from A, B preserves within itself some properties of A, but other properties of A are replaced by newly emergent properties found in B (but not in A). It might seem that here we have found the key to our problem of finding a paradigm which successfully describes the relationship between Christian eschatological anticipation and natural anticipation.

The dynamic of emergence is indeed exactly what we see when Christian eschatological anticipation supervenes upon natural anticipation. In this supervention, the various properties of natural anticipation (A) are either retained or lost. Those properties which are lost are replaced by other, emergent properties which define a specifically Christian eschatological anticipation (B). We touched above on this simultaneous retention and loss of properties. We saw how the properties *retained* are the sense of a need to act and the sense that such action takes place in view of a future. Conversely, the property *lost* is the sense that present and future are truly distinct, for Christian eschatology, is a specifically theological eschatology which understands present and future as somehow conflated. Thus, because of this mixture of retention and loss, the characteristics of Christian eschatological anticipation can be accounted for partly, but not wholly, in terms of a further development of the principles of natural anticipation. What we are looking at here is an emergent relationship between the two anticipations. The specifically emergent feature in this situation, what is absent from natural anticipation, is the fact that Christian eschatology reconfigures the interaction of present and future in terms of conflation rather than separation.

In the words of Holmes Rolston III writing on emergence:

> [T]here are always causes behind effects, but these nevertheless have surprising effects that the causes never seem completely to specify. The stream steadily rises above its source. Some engine carries life steadily upslope. The effects over time, whether probable or improbable, initiate events the likes of which have not been seen before: life, learning, joy, suffering, resolvedness. [I]n the developing evolution we keep getting more out of less. (Holmes Rolston III, *Science and Religion: A Critical Survey* (1987) (Philadelphia and London: Templeton Foundation, 2006), pp. 243–244)

The writer's "more out of less" and "surprising effect" are found here in Christian eschatological anticipation, in the novelty whereby present and future are conflated in a way not displayed by natural anticipation. The writer of this citation is, unlike us, writing about the phenomenon of emergence from a purely natural standpoint, and therefore without reference to any supernatural postulates. Even so, his analysis can easily be squared with what we are proposing here, namely a phenomenon of emergent development from natural anticipation into supernatural Christian eschatological anticipation, under an impulse of divine grace.

We would detect here a kind of supernatural end-time causality fecundated from the power of the future Kingdom, drawing out and stretching the characteristics of natural anticipation so that they are renewed under the power of grace. The theology of John Zizioulas is relevant in this context. Paradoxically for Zizioulas, the "final things," the eschatological goal of the Church, or, in Greek, the *eschata*, are really the logical beginning rather than the end of the Church's life. He writes:

> [W]e must think of the *eschata* as the *beginning* of the Church's life ... that which brings forth the Church, gives her identity, sustains and inspires her in her existence. The Church exists not because Christ died on the cross but because he has risen from the dead, which means, because the kingdom has come. (John Zizioulas, "The Mystery of the Church in Orthodox Tradition." *One in Christ* 24, no. 4 (1988): 294–303; p. 296)

Following this insight in the present context, we may suggest that "the grace of the end-time functions similarly to what emergentists in the natural sciences would call an attractor state" (Cyprian Love, "Christian Doctrine and Theories of Emergence." In *Causality and Motivation*, Roberto Poli (ed.) (Frankfurt: Ontos Verlag, 2010), p. 183.) This is why the phenomenon of natural anticipation can (in the phrase of Holmes Rolston III, above) rise above its source and, under divine influence, blossom out into a Christian eschatological anticipation. The latter emerges as the present writer has noted elsewhere "dynamically out of an eschatological call or end-time causality, originating from the future" (Ibid, p. 175). There is here a kind of *epiclesis* of the Holy Spirit descending on to natural anticipation, an eschatological "re-reading" of natural anticipation in the light of a future opened out by grace. The outcome of this process is that characteristically Christian eschatological anticipation arises from natural anticipation by a process of emergence prompted, in this case, not wholly from within the system of natural anticipation but impelled by grace from outside, a process of emergence which prompts natural anticipation toward a new graced modality where present and future are conflated.

Light from Psychoanalysis

Simply being aware of the fact that God conflates present and future does not, unfortunately, help us to understand the difficult idea of what the conflation of present and future is in itself. It tells us what God does and what God understands, but not what the conflation of present and future actually is in any way which the human mind can understand. This conflation of present and future therefore remains profoundly counterintuitive and mysterious to our minds, even at the same time as we assent to it on the authority of Scripture.

A useful comparison here is to be found in the work of psychologist C. G. Jung, who developed a theory of *synchronicity*, which attempts to interrelate matter and psyche. It is no less mind-bending to try to understand this than it is to try to understand the conflation of present and future in Christian theological eschatology. The following passage by a commentator on Jung sets out the issues involved for Jung's theory:

If an aircraft crashes before my eyes as I am blowing my nose, this is a coincidence of events that has no meaning. It is simply a chance occurrence of a kind that happens all the time. But if I bought a blue frock and, by mistake, the shop delivered a black one on the day one of my near relatives died, this would be a meaningful coincidence. The two events are not causally related, but they are connected by the symbolic meaning that our society gives to the color black. Wherever Dr. Jung observed such meaningful coincidences in an individual's life, it seemed (as the individual's dreams revealed) that there was an archetype activated in the unconscious of the individual concerned. To illustrate this by my example of the black frock: In such a case the person who receives the black frock might also have had a dream on the theme of death. It seems as if the underlying archetype is manifesting itself in inner and external events. The common denominator is a symbolically expressed message – in this case a message about death. . . .In creating the concept of synchronicity, Dr. Jung sketched a way in which we might penetrate deeper into the inter-relation of psyche and matter. . . .But this is still a completely open and insufficiently explored matter, with which future generations of psychologists and physicists must deal. (M.L.von Franz, "The Process of Individuation." In *Man and His Symbols*, Carl Jung (ed.) (London: Pan, 1978), pp. 226–227)

As the final phrases of this quotation indicate, we have here in Jung an attempt to interrelate two areas of reality, namely psyche and matter, in an intellectual project so difficult and counterintuitive that we can only appeal in hope to future insights so far unavailable to us. Undoubtedly, the fact of synchronicity reveals that matter and psyche are interrelated but we are, in our present state of knowledge, utterly at a loss to understand how this interrelationship can arise. There is surely a similar state of affairs in the case of Christian theological eschatology. Scripture reveals that future and present become newly interrelated. However, our understanding collapses beneath the weight of trying to find an explanation for *how* the new conflation of present and future is effected. As with Jung's theory of synchronicity, there is a pioneering quality to our belief in something which we desire to understand, something which seems undeniable, yet which is, as yet, outside our grasp. Perhaps, more exactly, we may say that we can already *reach* it, but do not yet grasp it.

Death, Emergence, and Resurrection

We have now to consider the implications of the important point, touched on at the very beginning, of how death has a unique significance among those things which humans naturally anticipate. The idea of natural anticipation may in fact be divided into two subordinate ideas: the anticipation of the possible and the anticipation of the certain. In practice, the first kind, anticipation of the possible, dominates our daily lives, since the details of our contingent existence cannot be known or prepared for with certainty in advance. The second kind, anticipation of the certain, has, in the history and culture of the human race, been reserved for the anticipation of death, "the only certainty."

Undoubtedly, some people do not anticipate their deaths, either because they are perhaps too young to feel the need to prepare for it or because their intelligence is too weak to grasp the idea of death. Yet, it is undoubtedly true that the overwhelming experience of the human race has been, and is, of the inevitability of death for each person and the need to prepare if possible for this event in many and varied ways in one's own case. The unconscious mind can be beset with thoughts of approaching death. Psychoanalysis reveals that the horizon of death exerts a powerful influence also over the unconscious. Jung pointed out: "Experience shows that the unknown approach of death casts an *adumbratio* (an anticipatory shadow) over the life and dreams of the victim." (Carl G. Jung, "Approaching the Unconscious." In *Man and His Symbols*, Carl Jung (ed.) (London: Pan, 1978), p. 63.) The unconscious mind can thus sense death before the conscious mind and bids us prepare for it. Anticipation of death is true anticipation in the sense in which we have already defined that term, for certain actions are typically taken in view of the prospect of death, either to delay death or prepare for it.

As well as the issue of inevitability, it is reasonable that our death should be the only event we can anticipate with certainty, since, although death impinges on life in its capacity as the terminus of life, it is not strictly an event *in* life, but, being qualitatively different from all events in life, it is essentially the *horizon* of life. Its unique ability to be anticipated with certainty seems to be of a piece with its unique status as a boundary event. Because death is unique among the objects of human anticipation, it is not surprising that Christian eschatological anticipation engages with death in a new and unique way.

How does Christian salvation relate to death? It will be suggested that it deals with death though implicating it in a dynamic of emergence. To begin by stating the obvious: Christian salvation is, self-evidently, not a *continuation* of the dynamics of death, for the status of death as the hitherto universal terminus and horizon of human life is entirely subverted by Christian salvation, which proposes a new horizon, and a new consummation, eternal life with God. Neither, however, does Christian salvation *replace* death, in the sense that we might have imagined the gift of salvation as somehow having nothing to do with death or as treating death as an irrelevance to be by-passed. In Christian salvation, death is neither continued nor replaced but, instead, salvation emerges *through* death.

First of all, this is because the gift of salvation arises out of the death and resurrection of Christ who neither continues nor replaces death but passes through death to life. Death does not work out its own pre-existing dynamic on Christ, but an *emergent* dynamic is worked out of death by Him, to produce a new horizon of resurrection, forged from His experience of undergoing death while not being limited by death. It is a case here of the classic emergent "more out of less." Christ does not just produce new life, but dies in order to produce this new life, and, out of death, life emerges. Secondly, as a result of Christ's work, neither do Christians cease to die, but they continue to die, and they attain salvation through death. Death is not left behind in the final achievement of salvation but becomes a glorious part of that salvation itself. In the theology of Hans Urs von Balthasar, as one commentator puts it, 'our salvation does not consist in escape from death nor in life on the other side of death. Rather the victory passes through death.' (John O'Donnell, *Hans Urs von Balthasar* (London: Cassell, 1992), p. 85). By making the victory pass through death, humanity's unique fear of death, the only thing which we naturally anticipate with certainty, is healed.

To be more exact: the initial phenomenon of death (A) has formed the basis for an emergent phenomenon, salvation (B). As accords with the principles of emergence, something of A is retained in B, while some other features of A are replaced by newly emergent properties in B. Thus some of death is *kept*, since the process of dying is retained in salvation (B): that is to say, Christ dies, and Christians still undergo the process of dying, as part of their salvation. However, A's innate horror, that is, death's 'sting' (1 Cor 15:55) is replaced in B by a newly emergent hope and joyful horizon. Death's finality is thus *lost* and a new reality emerges through it. The work of salvation has now engaged successfully with natural anticipation's darkest fear, the certainty of death. Eschatological anticipation heals the dark heart of human anticipation.

Christian theological eschatology, we saw, is one where *the present partici-pates in a normative future*. We have explained that this idea is impossible to grasp fully, though we can reach it, and we have invited a comparison with Jung's theory of synchronicity as an example of a similar type of intelligibility combined with unintelligibility for us. The ultimate source of theological eschatology is, of course, Christ's resurrection, since for Kam Ming Wong, outlining the thought of Wolfhart Pannenberg, 'with Jesus the end is not only seen in advance, but it has happened in advance ... In Jesus' activity, eschatological salvation has already made its appearance; that is, not the expectation of the ultimate salvation, but rather salvation itself was present.' (Kam Ming Wong, *Wolfhart Pannenberg on Human Destiny* (Aldershot: Ashgate, 2008), p. 45). Indeed, as John Sachs has written, 'the resurrection of Jesus can be a source of hope and an effective pledge of *future* glory only if Christians can somehow experience the presence and activity of the risen Lord here and *now* in the power of his *Spirit* (Rom 8: 9–11).' (John R. Sachs, *The Christian Vision of Humanity: Basic Christian Anthro-pology* (Collegeville, Minnesota: Liturgical Press, 1991), p. 88). Thus, for Pannenberg, in Jesus' fate, the end point of history comes to us anticipated, (See Wong, *Pannenberg*, p. 45) and the 'already/not yet' style of eschatology which informs the whole of divine revelation flows precisely from the resurrec-tion. Dermot Lane comments on this:

> The unique contribution of Wolfhart Pannenberg to the theology of revelation has undoubt-edly been his emphasis on history which he describes as the comprehensive horizon of Christian theology. The full revelation of God will only be complete at the end of history. That end of history has been anticipated, for Pannenberg, in the resurrection of Jesus from the dead. (Dermot A. Lane, *The Experience of God: An Invitation to do Theology* (1981) (Dublin: Veritas, 2003), p. 55. Reference to Wolfhart Pannenberg, *Revelation as History* (New York: M W Books, 1969), pp. 139ff)

Eschatology and Imagination

It is necessary now to go deeper and look at the power which underlies all expec-tation and anticipation. This power is the human imagination. An attempt will be made to contextualise expectation and anticipation within this wider frame of the imagination. Our discussion so far has sought to show how there emerges, from out of a natural future, a new supernatural future in which future and present are conflated, a Christian theological eschatology. Attention will now be given to the imagination as a wider context for understanding this, for imagination is the power by which we have any sense of a future at all, whether that future be natural or supernatural.

'If we cannot imagine, we cannot foresee.' (Gaston Bachelard, *The Poetics of Space* (1958) (Boston: Beacon Press, 1994), p. xxxiv). There is a close connection between imagination and the future. (What follows is based on Andrew Cyprian Love, *Musical Improvisation. Heidegger and the Liturgy: A Journey to the Heart of Hope* (Lewiston: Edwin Mellen Press, 2003), p. 166–168). This connection is a consequence of imagination's unrepeatability, or, more exactly, the image's unrepeatability. Imagination is directed powerfully to the future because imagination invariably generates an image which has not previously been formed. Humans are incapable of imagining in exactly the same way twice. Even to try to do this will entail that more-or-less inchoate mental impressions, which will have been registered by my brain between the first and second attempted imaginings of the same object, will influence how that object is imagined by me on the second occasion. The reason for this is that the whole of a person's consciously or unconsciously remembered experience contributes somehow to the way in which that person imagines at any given moment. My imagination is always gathered up from the depths of the whole me, and my previous experience is always changing. That is why I can never imagine the same way twice. This is true for all imagining, which is, by definition, inevitably new, all the time. Imagination always somehow draws from the well of the imaginer's entire conscious and unconscious experience up to the instant when the imagination acts, and, because the imaginer's world is always changing, all imagination is new. This is why, when I try to imagine the same thing in exactly the same way as before, I cannot do so. Something changes, even if only mood, context or association.

This unrepeatability of the imaginative act is in contrast to mental acts founded on reason. A reason-based activity (like an act of arithmetic) may be repeated unchanged; indeed, arithmetic would not be possible unless this repeatability were the case. A rational arithmetical calculation is absolutely repeatable, in a way which clearly contrasts with the unrepeatable nature of acts of the imagination. Every time I think the sum 'two plus two', it will always make four. This fact is unaffected by the new contexts or occurrences intervening for me between any two different occasions on which I perform this sum. (My judgement may be impaired on the second occasion, with the result that I conclude that two plus two equals five, but my impaired judgement entails that this is not a truly rational act. The fact that a rational act is repeatable does not mean it will always be repeated rationally). So the rational 'two plus two equals four' remains stubbornly unaffected, completely repeatable, quite unlike the unrepeatability of the imaginative act. Whereas imagination is continuously propelling me into the horizon of the future by suggesting images which are invariably new, a supposed human 'mind' consisting only of rational processes could not in fact conceive of a future at all. It has been remarked that 'radically new meanings cannot be grasped by formal reasoning, for the mind in such reasoning remains fixed in the mental categories with which it began' (Avery Dulles, *The Craft of Theology: From Symbol to System* (Dublin: Gill and Macmillan, 1992), p. 30). Yet acceptance of the possibility of radically new meanings is built in to any recognition that a future can arise for us. The future is defined as the mystery of what is radically not yet known, and 'fresh and unforeseen meanings arise' (Ibid.) only when 'clues work on the imagination with symbolic power.' (Ibid. References to Michael Polanyi, "The Creative Imagination." *Chemical and Engineering News* 44, no. 17 (25th April, 1966); Michael Polanyi and Harry Prosch, *Meaning* (Chicago: Chicago Univ. Press, 1975)).

A further question is now suggested. Does the inherent futural pregnancy of the imagination, which we have just analysed, admit of degrees of intensity? In other words, is some imagining more futural than other imagining? If so, where is this futural power of the imagination operating in its more, or in its most concentrated form? I shall argue that, to the extent that imagination is spontaneous, it is somehow *more futural* and, the more spontaneously imagination acts, the more futurally it acts.

We looked above at imagination and reason, considering them, for the time being, as if they were in watertight compartments. However, to try separating them in real life would be impossible for they always work together. Even so, whenever the imagination acts in the most spontaneous way, it makes a gallant attempt at separating itself from reason. It cannot do this, but spontaneity nevertheless comes nearest of all forms of imagining to achieving the emancipation of imagination from reason. Spontaneity approaches a reason-free imagining, or a kind of ecstasy of the imagination. It makes a bid for freedom from reason. Spontaneity is the point where imagination and conscious reason work together least.

It is true that the execution of a spontaneous mental or physical act depends unconsciously on accumulated elements of experience and understanding which have necessarily been acquired in the past. Nevertheless, in the moment of spontaneous decision, the human person tries to dissolve the now into the future, to lean upon the future, to face the future with a preferential focus. The point is that, in spontaneity, the person does not consciously stop to *think back*. Consider the contrast with the nature of reason. Reason generally acts more effectively the longer it has for deliberation, and it feels rooted in the past, for reason, unlike spontaneity, quite consciously depends on what the mind already knows. The will to spontaneity, instead, is a place of looking forward, because it does not look to the past as the ground of its action. Even though spontaneous choices are necessarily informed by unconscious reasoning processes and unconscious past experiences, it remains the case that, in spontaneity, the acting subject *feels* that his or her reason is obviated in favour of a futural impulse. The acting subject feels that his or her link with the past has been wholly or partly cut. There is a subjective disappropriation of the past. Compare this with reason, which consciously draws on the past. In the core of a spontaneous action, it is the future-oriented imagination which wills to determine the nature of the action, rather than experience of the past, or conscious reason.

All our imagination is always directed to the future in some way, as we saw. The very possibility of a future is intuitively sensed in the imagination, but this is most fully the case when the imaginer uses his or her imagination spontaneously. Imagination, especially spontaneous imagination, is crucial in the formation of our general idea of futural experience, and, of course, the idea of futural experience inevitably includes all Christian eschatological insights. Therefore we find that we are confronted with some kind of intimate connection between imaginative spontaneity and Christian eschatological anticipation. That is to say, spontaneity emerges as the aspect of imagination through which Christian eschatological insight is most intensively grasped, not because of some special characteristic of Christian eschatological insight, but simply because spontaneity is where all future is most intensively grasped.

At the same time as being inherently futural, however, spontaneity is intimately connected to the *now*. Having discussed the future and the past, we need to consider the role of the 'now' within this investigation, in order for the investigation to be fully inclusive of our experiences of time. A spontaneous act, although it is futural, can only take place 'now'. To be precise, it brings the present and the future together. 'Now' is inherently futural:

> The now is never static. Now is always moving on. The now is really already a projection forward into the future just by being now. It is easy to demonstrate this point from experience. We do not first experience our 'now' and only then move on into a future, as though we first existed in some static atemporal condition and only then carried on, as it were, into the future. I cannot stop my existence and say 'Here I am now. So let me set about having a future.' This stoppage of my being is impossible because the human now exists only because a future goes on arising. There is no non-futural now. If now were not futural it could not exist. To be in the now is to be projected futurally. So, spontaneity, having subjectively uncoupled me, as far as may be possible, from my past, envelops me, in one simultaneous and integral move, both in my now and in my futurity. In spontaneity I come closest to engaging with the raw energy of futurity, precisely in, and because of, the concentrated sense of 'now' which spontaneity makes available to me. Spontaneity is felt in the now, but also as an event coming out of the alterity of the unpredictable future. It is as if the future comes rushing at me in the spontaneous thought or act. (Cyprian Love, "Liturgical Spontaneity as Eschatological Rhetoric", *Irish Theological Quarterly* 73 nos. 1&2 (2008): 87–98; p. 94. This article deals with the issues raised for liturgy by the present argument. Liturgy is profoundly implicated in announcing the eschatological future. This fact may have implications for the introduction of spontaneous behaviour within the liturgical rite)

There is a clear parallel here between the way in which present and future come together in spontaneity, and the way in which present and future come together in Christian theological eschatology. Spontaneity is a remarkable icon in human experience of the theological conflation of now and future. This suggests that spontaneity has a major part to play in comprehending and engaging with Christian eschatology (Spontaneity has an established role in Christian spirituality. Self-abandonment teaching may be found in Bossuet, A. Piny, J. P. de Caussade, J. N. Grou, H. Ramière, C. L. Gay, V. Lehodey and St Thérèse of Lisieux. See K. Kavanaugh, "Self-Abandonment, Spiritual." In *The New Catholic Encyclopedia*, vol 8, McDonald (ed.-in-chief) (New York: McGraw-Hill, 1967), p. 60. Caussade writes: 'Ah, would that you knew the gift of God, the reward and the merit and the power and the peace, the blessed assurances of salvation that are hidden in this abandonment ... [T]here is no more certain path to salvation than that which leads through complete and perfect self-abandonment.' J. P. de Caussade, "Letter IV. To Sister Charlotte-Elizabeth Bourcier de Monthueux." (1755) In *Spiritual Letters on the Practice of Self-Abandonment to Divine Providence*, Book 3 *Obstacles to Self-Abandonment* (London: Burns, Oates and Washbourne, 1948), p. 122).

As in the case of Jung's theory of synchronicity, it may prove difficult, for the time being, to theorise this matter with any depth of understanding. On the other hand, the fundamental principle that spontaneity is linked in some way to the experience of Christian eschatological anticipation seems undeniable. Spontaneous activity generally predisposes the mind to anticipate the future, including, by implication, the greatest future of all, the Second Coming of Christ. It is hopefully a contribution to understanding at this point simply to advert to this connection between spontaneity and the future, without yet feeling in a position to say any more about how the connection arises or what further implications it has. Borrowing the words of Jung's commentator above, it is a 'completely open and insufficiently explored matter', but, like synchronicity, it has been broached. It has been reached but not grasped.

Artistic Anticipation and Eschatology

The full beauty of creation will be restored from the effects of sin only at the end of time when Christ comes again to bring in the new heaven and new earth. Artistic beauty produced by human hands anticipates this eschatological state where the beauty of creation will finally be made perfect. Moreover, because art is produced in the present, it brings some hint of the beauty of the eschatological future into the present, echoing a major theme of this discussion.

According to mainstream Christian tradition, God did not set creation in motion and then leave it to run itself. He continues to sustain it, which means that the event of creation is ongoing. Moreover, for Nicholas Berdyaev, 'creation may be completed only in the Spirit, only in man's creativity in the Spirit.' (Nicholas Berdyaev, *The Meaning of the Creative Act* (1916) (London: Victor Gollancz, 1955), pp. 137–138). God invites humanity to work with Him in the perfecting of creation, in an anticipatory mode of activity undertaken in view of the end of time. God's world-sustaining creativity in the Holy Spirit is accomplished partly through humanity's creativity in art (See Patrick Sherry, *Spirit and Beauty: An Introduction to Theological Aesthetics* (Oxford: Clarendon, 1992), p. 86). The latter shares in the Spirit's creative work in perfecting the beauty of creation towards the end of time. Leonide Ouspensky links the human creation of artistic beauty with the creativity of the Holy Spirit in this way, when he says that 'true beauty is the radiance of the Holy Spirit, the holiness of and the participation in the life of the world to come.' (Leonide Ouspensky, *Theology of the Icon* (Crestwood NY: St Vladimir's Seminary Press, 1978), p. 190). For Robert Faricy: 'The Spirit that inspires art is the eschatological Spirit, the Holy Spirit who breaks through into the present from God's promised future. The Kingdom of God is to come, and yet it is here already, breaking in on us through the Holy Spirit as the pledge of future glory, and making all things new now. The Holy Spirit renews us toward the future. Partly, the Spirit renews through inspired art.' (Robert Faricy, "Art as a Charism in the Church." *Thought* 57, no. 224 "Faith and Imagination Issue" (March 1982): 94–99; p. 98). Thus, it is implied, the Holy Spirit renews humans towards the future partly by raising up the human artist as a form of co-creator, to share His work.

For Berdyaev, '[t]rue creativeness is theurgy, God-activity, activity together with God.' (Berdyaev, *Creative Act*, p. 126). 'Creativity will continue creation; it will reveal the resemblance of human nature to the Creator.' (Ibid, p. 121). Elsewhere he states: '*Through Christ, man becomes a participant in the nature of the Holy Trinity, for the second hypostasis of the Holy Trinity is Absolute Man* ... [man becomes] a mediator between God and the cosmos.' (Ibid, p. 79. Italics original). '*The world is being created not only in God the Father but in God the Son.* Christology is the doctrine of continuing creation. And creation may be completed only in the Spirit, only in man's creativity in the Spirit.' (Ibid, pp. 137–138. Italics original). For Berdyaev, this implies that humanity's eschatological goal comes about partly through anticipatory artistic creativity functioning as theurgy: 'Theurgy is art creating another world, another being, another life'. (Ibid, p. 247). 'The theurge, working together with God, creates the cosmos; creates beauty as being.' (Ibid, p. 249). For Berdyaev, therefore, the artistic imagination creates futurity as co-agent with God.

For Berdyaev, the artistic creation of being is a product of creative freedom ('Creativity will continue creation'), and this leads him to the more searching question of whether from 'the thoroughgoing ontological point of view freedom is regarded as subordinate to being,' (Nicholas Berdyaev, *Truth and Revelation* (London: Geoffrey Bles, The Centenary Press, 1953), p. 68.) and, he asks: 'Does precedence belong to being over freedom or to freedom over being? Does not the final mystery of being lie in the fact that freedom is more primary than it and precedes it?' (Ibid.). For freedom arises from out of the human personality and thus '*[p]ersonality is more primary than being* ... Being is a product of abstract thought.' (Nicholas Berdyaev, *Slavery and Freedom* (1939) (London: Geoffrey Bles, The Centenary Press, 1943), p. 81). For Berdyaev, freedom thus comes out of an abyss which is prior to being. Freedom has its roots in nothingness. The act of freedom is essentially primordial and entirely irrational (See Nicholas Berdyaev, *Freedom and the Spirit* (London: Geoffrey Bles, The Centenary Press, 1935), p. 124). This freedom is 'the mysterious source of life, the basic and original experience, the abyss which is deeper than being itself and by which being is determined. Man feels within himself this irrational and unfathomable freedom in the very fibre of his being, and it is closely bound up with his potential energies.' (Ibid, p. 126). For Berdyaev, this freedom is linked to artistic creativity, and creativity is the mystery of freedom. (See John Macquarrie, *Existentialism* (Harmondsworth: Pelican, 1973), p. 180). Artistic creativity 'is not an "insertion" in the finite, not a mastery over the medium, or the creative product itself: rather it is a flight into the infinite; not an activity which objectifies in the finite but one which transcends the finite towards the infinite. The creative act signifies an *ek-stasis*, a breaking through to eternity.' (Nicholas Berdyaev, *Dream and Reality: An Essay in Autobiography* (London: Geoffrey Bles, 1950), p. 209). It is indeed where humans co-create eschatologically with God. In the commentary of John Macquarrie, the 'highest reach of humanity is creativity, a sharing in the power of God the Creator.' (Macquarrie, *Existentialism*, p. 180).

Perhaps, by combining the ideas of Berdyaev with those ideas expressed earlier on the subject of spontaneity, it may be possible to suggest a special theurgic role for *spontaneously* produced or improvisatory art. Berdyaev hints at this when he writes:

> It may be said, paradoxical as it seems at first sight, that development and unfolding is the deadly enemy of creativeness and leads to its cooling down and drying up at the source. The highest point reached by creativeness is not the unfolding of results but the first flight of inspiration, its birth and virginal youth and not its final achievement. Development, unfolding, improvement, completion mean deterioration of creativeness, the cooling down of the creative fire, decay and old age ... The essence of development and evolution is that it conceals first-hand intuitions and first origins of human feelings and ideas ... This happens to every human feeling and idea. Development destroys creative youth, virginity and originality. That which was born in the free creative act is unrecognizable in its developed form. (Nicholas Berdyaev, *The Destiny of Man* (1931) (London: Geoffrey Bles, The Centenary Press, 1937), pp. 181–182)

Eschatology and the Discovery of Certainty

This discussion opened by saying that expectation of the occurrence of a particular event may be slight ('I think it might just happen') or great ('it is almost certain to happen') or anything in between. An exception was then made for death, which is certain. This framework of the certain, the likely and the less likely defines the normal working basis of human expectation and consequently the usual background against which anticipatory decisions are made. However this perspective is contained within a deeper issue, an issue so theoretical that we hardly ever advert to it in practice. This is the fact that we cannot actually demonstrate that there will be any future at all, because natural rationality has no way of demonstrating that experience as we know it will continue. No scientist can prove that the sun will rise tomorrow. Our natural expectation of a future is purely habitual, having no experimental basis. In other words, we can imagine that there will be a future which will, in many important respects, be like the past and present, but we cannot know this. The fact that we cannot know whether there will be a future does not make it *irrational* to believe in the future for, in the absence of positive evidence to the contrary, it is a good wager to assume that the future will continue to arise as it has done in the past and to act accordingly.

We spoke also, at the beginning, of death as the 'only certainty' but the future certainty of death, in the case of any particular living person, cannot be scientifically established either, because that person's death belongs to the future and, as we saw, the future is unknowable. The prospect of death is really what might be called a *practical* certainty, which makes it rash to deny it, and certainly not irrational to believe in it; but it is not a *theoretical* certainly. In short, while we can and do imagine that there will be a future which will, in many important respects, be like the past and present, we cannot know this, and we may therefore conclude at this point that all natural anticipation is a *relative* anticipation. It is relative to the possibility that what is anticipated will not arise, and that includes death. For we can, at the purely natural level, know *absolutely nothing* for certain about the future, neither what it will be, nor even whether it will be.

However, one of the characteristics of Christianity is to give us a certain and definitive future, by transcending this merely relative natural anticipation. Christianity fills a gap in human consciousness by revealing to us not only *that* the future will be, but in certain respects *what* the future will be, enabling us to anticipate a future definitively with our actions. It could even be said that Christianity marks the beginning of genuine anticipation. Natural anticipation was only provisional anticipation, because it anticipated into a future which might not arise. For Christianity, a future will arise, and we are told what form it will take. This gives Christian eschatological anticipation more authority than natural anticipation. For Christian anticipation, Christ will return, and the created order will be subsumed into the eschatological consummation. This is a state of affairs which Christians can anticipate with great authority for God has told them how to prepare for it and what to do. Christian theological anticipation shares with natural anticipation a concern for the future but it differs from natural anticipation in being an anticipation of something certain. Our natural future, whether in terms of its content, or, more fundamentally, its very arising, can never be certain. This uncertainty is ended by Christianity and the new certainty furnished by Christianity is *emergent*, for certainty regarding the future has emerged from natural uncertainty.

Summary

The relationship between natural anticipation and Christian eschatological anticipation is best framed, not in terms of older models of nature and grace, but in terms of emergentism. Christian eschatological anticipation emerges from natural anticipation through a supernatural agency rooted in the eschata or end-time. More widely, Christian salvation stands in an emergent relationship to death, since Christ's victory passes through death. All anticipation depends on imagination, the faculty which enables us to envisage a future. This futural power of the human imagination becomes more potent the more spontaneously the imagination acts. Spontaneous imagination appears to be the aspect of imagination through which Christian eschatology is most potently anticipated. Artistic imagination is one aspect of this dynamic.

Mathematical Foundations of Anticipatory Systems

45

A. H. Louie

Contents

Abstract

A natural system is an anticipatory system if it contains an internal predictive model of itself and its environment, and in accordance with the model's predictions, antecedent actions are taken. An organism is the very example of an anticipatory system. Deep system-theoretic homologies allow the possibility of obtaining insights into anticipatory processes in the human and social sciences from the understanding of biological anticipation. To this end, a comprehensive theory of anticipatory systems is the means. The present chapter is an exposition on the mathematical foundations of such a theory.

A. H. Louie (✉)
Ottawa, ON, Canada

Stellenbosch Institute for Advanced Study (stias), Wallenberg Research Centre at Stellenbosch University, Stellenbosch, South Africa
e-mail: connect@ahlouie.com

© Springer Nature Switzerland AG 2019
R. Poli (ed.), *Handbook of Anticipation*,
https://doi.org/10.1007/978-3-319-91554-8_21

Keywords

Robert Rosen · Relational biology · Anticipatory system · Modelling relation ·
Encoding · Decoding · Causality · Inference · Commutativity · Category theory ·
Functor · Simulation · Model · Analogue · Conjugacy · Surrogacy · Internal
predictive model · Antecedent actions · Transducer · Feedforth

Historia

Robert Rosen formulated his theory of anticipatory systems during the academic
year 1971–72, when he was a visiting fellow at the now-defunct Center for the Study
of Democratic Institutions (CSDI) in Santa Barbara, California. The term 'anticipatory system' first appeared in his publications in the paper "Planning, Management,
Policies and Strategies: Four Fuzzy Concepts" (Rosen 1974, which was first incar-
nated as an internally circulated CSDI Discussion Paper scheduled for the Center's
'Dialog' on Tuesday, 16 May 1972). He defined therein the "anticipatory modes of
behavior of organisms" to be those

> in which an organism's present behavior is determined by (a) sensory information about the
> present state of the environment, and (b) an 'internal model' of the world, which makes
> predictions about future states on the basis of the present data and the organism's possible
> reactions to it.

It was also in this paper that the now-iconic diagram of an anticipatory system
first appeared in Rosen's writings (Fig. 1).

In Fig. 1, S, M, and E are, respectively, object system, predictive model, and set of
effectors. (I shall have more to say about this diagrammatic representation later on in
this chapter.)

Biology is abounding with situations in which organisms can generate and
maintain internal predictive models of themselves and their environments, and use
the predictions of these models about the future for purpose of control in the present.
This is true at every level, from the molecular to the cellular to the physiological to

Fig. 1 Anticipatory system
1.1.1

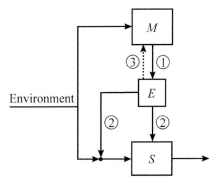

the behavioral, and this is true in all parts of the biosphere, from microbes to plants to animals to ecosystems. One may succinctly postulate the

Axiom of Anticipation Life is anticipatory.

But anticipatory behavior, while a necessary condition for life, is not restricted to the biological universe; it, indeed, encompasses the "four fuzzy concepts" and more. At the human level it can be multiplied without end and may seem fairly trivial: examples range from avoiding dangerous encounters to strategies in games and sports, including those of economics and politics.

Although the *concept* of 'anticipation' had not been new, the *systemic study* of it was when Rosen wrote his 1974 paper. Rosen's rigorously mathematical study of this biology-inspired subject led to a sequence of papers, culminating in his book *Anticipatory Systems: Philosophical, Mathematical, and Methodological Foundations* (Rosen 1985a; henceforth denoted by the symbol *AS*). Therein, in Sect. 6.1, is the generalized, formal

Definition An *anticipatory system* is a natural system that contains an internal predictive model of itself and of its environment, which allows it to change state at an instant in accord with the model's predictions pertaining to a later instant.

An anticipatory system's present behavior depends upon 'future states' or 'future inputs' generated by an internal predictive model. 'Model-based behavior' (or more specifically 'anticipatory-model-based behavior') is the essence of social, economic, and political activity. Beyond its organismic origins, an anticipatory system finds analogies in social systems, economics, politics, ethics, future studies, and many others. The common question in these diverse fields is that of *ought*, which may be phrased as "What should we do now?". However different the contexts in which the question is posed, *they are all alike in their fundamental concern with the making of policy, and the associated notions of forecasting the future and planning for it.* What is sought, in each of these diverse areas, is in effect a strategy of decision making. An understanding of the characteristics of model-based behavior is thus central to any strategy one wishes to develop to control and manage such systems, or to modify their model-based behavior in new ways. But underlying any strategy, there must be an underlying substratum of basic principles: a science, a *theory*. Rosen proposed that the theory underlying a strategy of policy generation is that of anticipatory systems.

Note, in contrast, that a *reactive system* can only react, in the present, to changes that have already occurred in the causal chain, while an *anticipatory system*'s present behavior involve aspects of past, present, and future. The presence of a predictive model serves precisely to pull the future into the present; a system with a 'good' model thus behaves in many ways as if it can anticipate the future. In other words, *a predictive model permits anticipation*. Indeed, to use teleological language, the *purpose* of a predictive model is to anticipate. The 'anticipatory paradigm' *extends – but does not replace* – the 'reactive paradigm', which has dominated the study of natural systems, and allows us a glimpse of new and important aspects of system behavior.

Robert Rosen was a mathematical biologist. Anticipation is a *necessary* condition of life: a living system anticipates. This is the connection that explains how Rosen, in his lifelong quest of general principles that would answer the question "What is Life?", happened to write, en passant, 'the book' *AS* on anticipation. ▶ Chapter 10, "Relational Biology" in this *Handbook* explains the placement of anticipation in the context of this quest. For an expository introduction to Robert Rosen's anticipatory systems, the enthused reader may like to consult Louie (2010).

For emphasis, let me restate the definition of anticipatory system thus:

Definition An *anticipatory system* is a natural system that contains an

$$internal \ \bullet \ predictive \ \bullet \ model \tag{1}$$

of itself and of its environment, which allows it to

$$change \text{ state at an instant } in \ accord \ with \ the \ model's \ predictions \tag{2}$$

pertaining to a later instant.

Both (1) *and* (2) are crucial ingredients of anticipation. Having a model of the future is not enough: although the entailment *process* of anticipation is embedded in an anticipatory system's defining component *object* (1), an anticipatory system must also (2) make use of the prediction and take proactive antecedent actions accordingly. True to the spirit of *relational biology* (cf. the chapter in this *Handbook* so named), the crux in this definition is not what an anticipatory system itself *is*, but what it *does*.

The Modelling Relation

A *model* is the representation of one system in another. The only perfect model of a system is, however, the system itself. Otherwise, by genericity, by necessity, by practicality, and indeed by definition, a model is *incomplete* and only captures a proper subsystem.

Category theory is, among its many roles, the general mathematical theory of *modelling* and, incidentally, the metalanguage of relational biology. The Appendix of Louie (2009) is a terse summary. The definitive reference on this branch of abstract algebra remains the quintessential Mac Lane (1997), to which I refer the reader for further exploration of the category-theoretic topics that I am presenting in this chapter. Category theory has metamorphized from its origins in the early 1940s, when its founders Samuel Eilenberg and Saunders Mac Lane applied it to algebraic topology (which may be considered as modelling geometry in algebra). It is now an autonomous research area in contemporary mathematics and has metastasized into theoretical computer science, mathematical physics, and, yes, mathematical biology. Relational biology is, however, not the only approach in mathematical biology that uses category theory; other notable approaches are, to name but two, that of the late Ion Baianu (cf. Brown and Glazebrook 2013) and Memory Evolutive Systems of Andrée Ehresmann and Jean-Paul Vanbremeersch (cf. ▶ Chap. 46, "Anticipation in MES – Memory Evolutive Systems" in this *Handbook*).

The category in which the collection of objects is the collection of all sets (in a suitably naive universe of small sets) and where morphisms are (single-valued) mappings is denoted **Set**. The category in which the collection of objects is the collection of all sets (in a suitably naive universe of small sets) and where morphisms are set-valued mappings (equivalently, relations) is denoted **Rel**. (The first five chapters of Louie 2013 is an introduction to the theory of set-valued mappings, and the rest of the book is on their implications in biology.) For sets X and Y, the hom-sets $\mathbf{Set}(X, Y)$ and $\mathbf{Rel}(X, Y)$ contain, respectively, *all* single-valued mappings and *all* set-valued mappings from X to Y. $\mathbf{Set}(X, Y)$ is a proper subset of $\mathbf{Rel}(X, Y)$; **Set** is a non-full subcategory of **Rel**.

Modelling is the art that is the ultimate revelatory reflection of life. Having an internal model of the world is a characterization of living systems; sentience is not a prerequisite for this necessary fundamental property. With the animation into sentience and the evolution into consciousness, however, modelling gains a volitional dimension. The teleological representation of one system in another is an ancient human enterprise: one finds patterns and ever theorizes. Even the meta-modelling of modelling itself, i.e., to methodologically study modelling *qua* modelling as opposed to just make models, can trace its genealogy back to antiquity. The epistemology of modelling involved scholars from Plato and Aristotle, through Kepler and Galileo, to Newton, von Helmholtz, Mach, Hertz, Bohr, and many others.

Heinrich Hertz, in the introduction of his posthumously published masterwork *Die Prinzipien der Mechanik in neuem Zusammenhange dargestellt* (1894; English translation *The Principles of Mechanics Presented in a New Form*, Hertz 1899), gave the following meta-model:

> We form for ourselves images or symbols of external objects; and the form which we give them is such that the necessary consequents of the images in thought are always the images of the necessary consequents in nature of the things pictured. In order that this requirement may be satisfied, there must be a certain conformity between nature and our thought. Experience teaches us that the requirement can be satisfied, and hence that such a conformity does in fact exist. When from our accumulated previous experience we have once succeeded in deducing images of the desired nature, we can then in a short time develop by means of them, as by means of models, the consequences which in the external world only arise in a comparatively long time, or as the result of our own interposition.

A model is an image in thought of an external object, with a certain conformity between nature and thought: this is the essential meta-model Hertz communicated in his introductory paragraphs before launching into the *raison d'être* of his book, the Archimedes–Galileo–Newton–Lagrange–d'Alembert models of mechanics.

The endeavor of meta-modelling culminates in Robert Rosen's modelling relation, a functorial (in the category-theoretic sense) diagrammatic representation he first introduced in 1979 when he wrote *AS*. Modelling and meta-modelling are essential ingredients in *AS* – to wit, chapter 3 is entitled "The Modelling Relation" and chapter 5 is entitled "Open Systems and the Modelling Relation." Indeed, the main theoretical questions with which one deals in *AS* are (as Rosen summarized in the Foreword of *AS*):

(a) What is a model?

(b) What is a *predictive* model?

(c) How does a system which contains a predictive model differ in its behavior from one which does not?

A *modelling relation* is a commutative functorial encoding and decoding between two systems. Between a natural system (an object partitioned from the physical universe) N and a formal system (an object in the universe of mathematics) M, the situation may be represented in the following diagram (Fig. 2).

Causal entailment is the manifestation of the Aristotelian efficient cause in natural systems, and correspondingly inferential entailment is the manifestation of the Aristotelian efficient cause in formal systems. The encoding ε maps the natural system N and its causal entailment c therein to the formal system M and its internal inferential entailment i; i.e.,

$$\varepsilon : N \mapsto M \quad \text{and} \quad \varepsilon : c \mapsto i. \tag{3}$$

The decoding δ does the reverse. (The (ε, δ) notation in Fig. 2 is my allusion to the (ε, δ) argument of mathematical analysis; viz. "$\forall \varepsilon > 0 \quad \exists \delta > 0 \ \cdots$.") The entailments satisfy the commutativity condition that tracing through arrow c is the same as tracing through the three arrows ε, i, and δ in succession. This may be symbolically represented by the 'composition'

$$c = \delta \circ i \circ \varepsilon. \tag{4}$$

Stated otherwise, one gets the same answer whether one, as in the left-hand side of (4), simply sits as observers and watch the unfolding sequence of events c in the natural system, or, as in the right-hand-side of (4), (i) encodes ε some properties of the natural system into the formalism, (ii) uses the implicative structure i of the formal system to derive theorems, and then (iii) decodes δ these theorems into propositions (*predictions*) about the natural system itself. When the commutativity (4) holds, one has established a congruence between (some of) the causal features of the natural system and the implicative structure of the formal system. Thence related, M is a *model* of N, and N is a *realization* of M.

One may possibly construct parts of Fig. 2 from the brief Hertz passage on "images" in his introduction to *The Principles of Mechanics*, but this is not sufficient

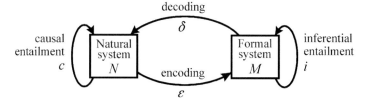

Fig. 2 The prototypical modelling relation

to give Hertz precedence over Rosen in the formulation of the modelling relation. While Hertz had the correct principles of meta-modelling (so did a host of scholars before him), he did not produce any diagrams. Indeed, although *The Principles of Mechanics* contained an abundance of mathematical formulae and equations, it had no diagrams whatsoever. Rosen's category-theoretic rendering of the modelling relation as a commutative arrow diagram is his unique contribution. In any case, when Hertz wrote his book, the birth of category theory (1945) was 50 years in the future. So when one engages the modelling relation in terms of the functorial diagram that is Fig. 2, one is clearly dealing with *Robert Rosen's* modelling relation.

I emphasize that the attribution of the modelling relation to Rosen was not only because he drew (a predecessor of) the arrow diagram Fig. 2. Block diagrams that connect boxes with a flow of arrows had long been in existence, and they may be considered subject-oriented specializations of directed graphs. Examples of these block diagrams include component interaction diagrams in control theory, flow diagrams in computer programming, and schematic diagrams in engineering, and they all contain simple specimens isomorphic in form to Fig. 2. Rosen's originality was in presenting the levels of entailment (3) and the compositional commutativity (4) in his meta-model from a category-theoretic standpoint.

Let me indulge in a bit of historic trivia on the evolution of the arrow diagram Fig. 2. Rosen explicated the modelling relation in detail in his 1979 draft of *Anticipatory Systems* (*AS*: 2.3), and the first arrow diagram was Fig. 2.3.1 therein (Fig. 3).

Note that in this inaugural version, causality in the left-hand-side natural system was not yet part of the formulation. A variety of mundane nuisances delayed the publication of *AS* until 1985; meanwhile, Rosen marched on with his meta-modelling. By the first time the arrow diagram of the modelling relation appeared in print, as Fig. 1 on *p*.91 of Rosen (1980), the dual processes of "system behaviors" (causality) and "rules of reference" (inference, implication) were in place (Fig. 4).

The modelling relation diagram made another pre-*AS*-publication appearance in Rosen (1985b: Fig. 1 on *p*.179) (Fig. 5).

By this juncture in 1985, all three key ingredients of the modelling relation were present: (i) the correspondence of objects

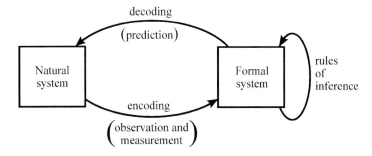

Fig. 3 Modelling relation, version 1 (*AS* Figure 2.3.1)

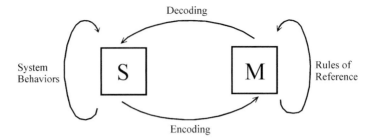

Fig. 4 Modelling relation, version 2

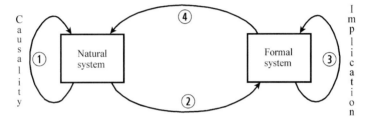

Fig. 5 Modelling relation, version 3

$$\text{Natural system} \xrightarrow[\text{Encoding}]{\text{Decoding}} \text{Formal system} \qquad (5)$$

(ii) the correspondence of morphisms

$$\text{Causality} \xrightarrow[\text{Encoding}]{\text{Decoding}} \text{Implication} \qquad (6)$$

and (iii) the commutativity

$$\text{arrow } \textcircled{1} = \text{arrows } \textcircled{2} + \textcircled{3} + \textcircled{4} \qquad (7)$$

(cf. (3) and (4) above). (Note, however, that there was no retro-editing of *AS*'s diagrams: all modelling-relation diagrams in *AS* were published without the left-hand-side causality arrows.)

Figure 5 is the form of the functorial representation of the modelling relation that Rosen would use henceforth (and almost always with the idiosyncratic – and typesetting unfriendly – 'circled number' labels for the arrows). He revisited epistemological considerations of meta-modelling in *Life Itself* (Rosen 1991; notably Section 3H on "The Modeling Relation and Natural Law") and in *Essays on Life Itself* (Rosen 2000; in particular Chap. 10, "Syntactics and Semantics in Languages"); a variant of the arrow diagram appeared therein, respectively, as Fig. 3H.2 and Fig. 10.1 (Fig. 6):

Fig. 6 Modelling relation, version 4

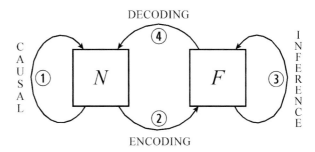

DECODING

ENCODING

Natural Law

Natural order is woven into the fabric of reality. *Causality* is the principle that every effect has a cause and is a reflection of the belief that successions of events in the world are governed by definite relations. *Natural Law* posits the existence of these *entailment* relations *and* that this causal order can be *imaged* by implicative order. *System* is a basic undefined term, a primitive. It takes on the intuitive meaning of 'a collection of material or immaterial things that comprises one's object of study'. In relational, hence nonmaterial, terms, a system may be considered as a *network of interacting processes*.

In terms of the modelling relation (Fig. 2), Natural Law is an *existential declaration* of causal entailment c and the encodings $\varepsilon : N \mapsto M$ and $\varepsilon : c \mapsto i$ (cf. (3) above). A formal system may simply be considered as a *set* with additional mathematical structures. So the mathematical statement $\varepsilon : N \mapsto M$, i.e., the posited existence for every natural system N a model formal system M, may be stated as the axiom

$$Everything \; is \; a \; set. \tag{8}$$

Causal entailment in a natural system is a network of mutually entailing efficient causes. The mathematical statement $\varepsilon : c \mapsto i$, i.e., the functorial correspondence of morphisms, between causality c in the natural domain and inference i in the formal domain, may thus be stated as an epistemological principle, the axiom

$$Every \; process \; is \; a \; (set\text{-}valued) \; mapping. \tag{9}$$

[See the exposition in Louie (2015) for the extension of (9) from "Every process is a mapping." (Louie 2009) to "Every process is a set-valued mapping."] Together, the two axioms (8) and (9), formalizing, respectively, the material and functional parts of nature, are the mathematical foundation of Natural Law. They are manifest in Wigner's observation of "the unreasonable effectiveness of mathematics in the natural sciences." This wedding of mathematics to empiricism has the status of a Euclidean 'Common Notion', a general logical principle that proclaims the mathematical nature of the world and its fundamental correspondence to our cognitive modes.

Axioms (8) and (9) serve to alternatively characterize a system as a network of interacting (set-valued) mappings and therefore put our operation theater of modelling in the category **Rel** of sets and set-valued mappings. (I must mention in passing that category theory has many flavors; some of which are not set-based. Axioms (8) and (9) are the axioms of 'our flavor' of category theory for relational biology.) In our practice, then, models are drawn from smaller non-full subcategories **C** of **Rel**, in which **C**-objects are a selection of sets A, B, ..., and **C**-hom-sets **C**(A, B) are proper subsets of **Rel**(A, B):

$$\mathbf{C}(A,B) \subset \mathbf{Rel}(A,B) = \mathcal{P}(A \times B). \tag{10}$$

The collection of all models of a system N is denoted $\mathbf{C}(N)$. $\mathbf{C}(N)$ is a lattice as well as a category. The category $\mathbf{C}(N)$ is a subcategory of $\mathbf{C}$, the source of our modelling sets and mappings (Louie 2015). Let $\kappa(N)$ be the collection of all efficient causes in N. An entailment network that models N may be denoted $\varepsilon(N) \in \mathbf{C}(N)$; the morphism correspondence $\varepsilon : \kappa(N) \rightarrow \kappa(\varepsilon(N))$ implies $\varepsilon(\kappa(N)) \subset \kappa(\varepsilon(N))$. Natural Law is the predicate calculus statement

$$\forall N \; \exists \varepsilon \; \exists M \in \mathbf{C}(N) \; : \; M = \varepsilon(N) \\ \wedge \; \forall c \in \kappa(N) \; \exists i \in \kappa(M) \; : \; i = \varepsilon(c). \tag{11}$$

Let $\mathcal{O}\mathbf{C}$ be the collection of **C**-objects (that are sets) and $\mathcal{A}\mathbf{C}$ be its collection of **C**-morphisms (that are set-valued mappings). Thus a **C**-object is $A \in \mathcal{O}\mathbf{C}$ (although a slight notational imprecision may permit $A \in \mathbf{C}$) and a **C**-morphism F belonging to a **C**-hom-set $\mathbf{C}(A, B)$ is $F \in \mathbf{C}(A, B) \subset \mathcal{A}\mathbf{C}$. A model of N in the category **C** may be described as a formal system that is a network of mappings in $\mathcal{A}\mathbf{C}$, whence

$$\varepsilon(N) \subset \mathcal{O}\mathbf{C} \quad \text{and} \quad \varepsilon(\kappa(N)) \subset \mathcal{A}\mathbf{C}. \tag{12}$$

For notational simplicity, one often drops the encoding symbol ε and uses N to denote both the natural system and its network model that is a formal system. Thus 'an entailment network $\varepsilon(N)$ that models a natural system N' abbreviates to 'an entailment network N'. Likewise the symbol $\kappa(N)$ shall denote the collection of efficient causes in both the natural system and the formal system. These identifications

$$\varepsilon(N) = N \quad \text{and} \quad \varepsilon(\kappa(N)) = \kappa(N) \tag{13}$$

amount to an implicit invocation of Natural Law, substituting systems with their functorial images. I shall presently explore the consequences of this correspondence.

The canonical modelling relation (Fig. 2) provides a concrete embodiment of Natural Law. But the relation may be generalized, so that the systems N and M may both be natural systems or both be formal systems, and the entailments c and i are corresponding efficient causes; i.e., the modelling relation may simply be a commutative diagram between 'general systems'. The general modelling relation has multifarious manifestations, e.g., category theory, analogies, alternate descriptions, similes, metaphors, and complementarities (Louie 2009, Sects. 4.16–4.20).

Fig. 7 General modelling relation

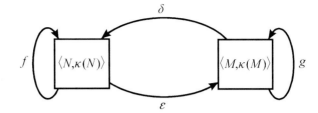

A system N, whether natural or formal, considered as a network of interacting processes, may be represented by the pair $\langle N, \kappa(N) \rangle$. Note that in the previous sentence, the symbol N is used for both the system and its underlying collection of sets, whence 'a system N' instead of 'a system $\langle N, \kappa(N) \rangle$'. This convention in mathematical usage will normally give rise to no confusion; one uses the latter pair representation when the context requires it for clarity. In the context of the equivalence imputed by this convention and the abbreviation (13), one has

$$N \subset \mathcal{OC} \quad \text{and} \quad \kappa(N) \subset \mathcal{AC}. \tag{14}$$

The general modelling relation in its minimalist category-theoretic form is the arrow diagram thus (Fig. 7).

The Many Levels of the Encoding Functor

True to its category-theoretic taxonomy as *functor*, the encoding ε maps on many levels. On the category-of-models level,

$$\varepsilon : N \rightarrow \mathbf{C}(N). \tag{15}$$

The encoding functor ε assigns to each representation $\langle N, \kappa(N) \rangle$ of N a model system

$$\langle M, \kappa(M) \rangle = \langle \varepsilon(N), \varepsilon(\kappa(N)) \rangle \tag{16}$$

in $\mathbf{C}(N)$. The assignment $\varepsilon : N \mapsto M$ is a *choice mapping* that singly selects, as a specific model of the natural system N, the formal system M from the set $\mathbf{C}(N)$. But in addition to this *set-pairing* $(N, M) \in \varepsilon$, ε also functions on the *point-pairing* level as a mapping

$$\varepsilon : N \mapsto M \tag{17}$$

from one set into another – to each input element (material cause) $n \in N$, there corresponds a unique output element (final cause) $m \in M$ such that $(n, m) \in \varepsilon$; i.e., $\varepsilon : n \mapsto m$.

Let $f : A \to B$ be a mapping representing a process in the entailment structure of $\langle N, \kappa(N) \rangle$. Suppose there is a mapping $g : \varepsilon(A) \to \varepsilon(B)$ (which is a process in the entailment structure of $\langle M, \kappa(M) \rangle$) that makes the diagram

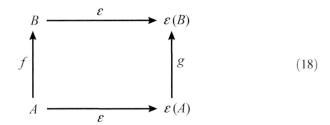

(18)

commute; i.e., the equality of sequential compositions

$$\varepsilon \circ f = g \circ \varepsilon, \tag{19}$$

or, what is the same,

$$\varepsilon(f(a)) = g(\varepsilon(a)) \tag{20}$$

holds for all $a \in A$. Note that this commutativity condition places no further restrictions on the mapping g itself, other than that the two compositions need to reach a common final destination. Such emphasis on the results *regardless of the manner in which they are generated* (i.e., with no particular concern on underlying principles) is the case when $\langle M, \kappa(M) \rangle$ is a *simulation* of $\langle N, \kappa(N) \rangle$.

Together with the decoding δ, the commutativity condition (4) when applied to the general modelling relation of Fig. 7 is

$$f = \delta \circ g \circ \varepsilon, \tag{21}$$

and may be drawn as the element trace

$$
\begin{array}{ccc}
f(a) = [\delta \circ g \circ \varepsilon] (a) & \xleftarrow{\quad \delta \quad} & [g \circ \varepsilon] (a) \\
\Big\uparrow f & & \Big\uparrow g \\
a & \xrightarrow{\quad \varepsilon \quad} & \varepsilon(a)
\end{array}
\tag{22}
$$

This commutativity condition involves all four arrows in Fig. 7 and may be stated as 'whether one follows *path f* or *paths* ε , g , δ *in sequence*, one reaches the same destination', but, again, it places no further restrictions on the mapping g itself. Systems $\langle N, \kappa(N) \rangle$ and $\langle M, \kappa(M) \rangle$ thus related are called *surrogate*s of each other (and that they satisfy a *surrogacy relation*).

If, in addition, the mapping g is *itself* entailed by the encoding ε, i.e., if $g = \varepsilon(f)$, whence the mapping in $\langle M, \kappa(M) \rangle$ is $\varepsilon(f) : \varepsilon(A) \to \varepsilon(B)$, then instead of (18), one has the commutative diagram

$$
\begin{array}{ccc}
B & \xrightarrow{\ \ \varepsilon\ \ } & \varepsilon(B) \\
\Big\uparrow{\scriptstyle f} & & \Big\uparrow{\scriptstyle \varepsilon(f)} \\
A & \xrightarrow[\ \ \varepsilon\ \ ]{} & \varepsilon(A)
\end{array}
\qquad (23)
$$

and the equality corresponding to (20), for every element $a \in A$, is

$$
\varepsilon(f(a)) = \varepsilon(f)(\varepsilon(a)). \qquad (24)
$$

When this more stringent condition (24) is satisfied, the simulation is called a *model*. If this *modelling relation* is satisfied between the systems $\langle N, \kappa(N) \rangle$ and $\langle M, \kappa(M) \rangle$, one then says that there is a *congruence* between their entailment structures, and that $\langle M, \kappa(M) \rangle$ is a *model* of $\langle N, \kappa(N) \rangle$. The element-trace $\varepsilon : f \mapsto g$ is a functorial correspondence of morphisms

$$
\varepsilon : \kappa(N) \to \kappa(M). \qquad (25)
$$

This *process-pairing* $(f, g) \in \varepsilon$ functions on a higher hierarchical level than point-pairing, because now the output is *itself* a mapping $g = \varepsilon(f) \in \kappa(M)$. Together with the decoding δ, the commutativity condition (21) for a model is

$$
f = \delta \circ \varepsilon(f) \circ \varepsilon. \qquad (26)
$$

A simulation of a process provides a description of the entailed effects, whereas a model requires more: a model is a special kind of simulation that additionally also provides a description of the entailment structure of the mapping representing the process itself. A simulation describes only one set of effects, but in itself reveals little about the operative forces, and therefore tells nothing about what would have happened under slightly different circumstances (in which case an entirely different simulation might very well be required). A model, on the other hand, entailing both structure and function of the effects, is structurally stable, and hence 'nearby' (in an appropriate topological sense) effects would have similar models (with perhaps slightly different constitutive parameters).

The encoding functor ε of a model thus encompasses both kinds of entailment in its effects: the output $b = \varepsilon(a) \in M$ is an object, and $\vdash b$ is *material entailment*; the output $g = \varepsilon(f) \in \kappa(M)$ is a mapping, and $\vdash g$ is *functional entailment*. (See the ▶ Chap. 10, "Relational Biology" in this *Handbook* for explications of material entailment, functional entailment, and the entailment symbol $\vdash$.)

The category $\mathbf{S}$ of formal systems is the subject of Chapter 7 of Louie 2009. An $\mathbf{S}$-object is a pair $\langle X, \mathrm{K} \rangle$, where X is a set and $\mathrm{K} \subset \cdot^X$ is a collection of mappings with domain X (cf. axioms (8) and (9)). A general system $\langle N, \kappa(N) \rangle$ is a finite collection $\{\langle X_i, \mathrm{K}_i \rangle : i = 1, \ldots, n\}$ of interconnected $\mathbf{S}$-object components. N is the collection of sets $N = \{X_i : i = 1, \ldots, n\}$, whence, for each $i \in \{1, \ldots, n\}, X_i \in N$. The relational diagram of $\kappa(N)$ is a digraph representing the entailment network N; for each $i \in \{1, \ldots, n\}$, $\mathrm{K}_i \subset \kappa(N)$, but $\kappa(N)$ may also contain inter-component mappings, e.g., $F : X_i \to X_j$ with $i \neq j$.

The many operational levels of the encoding functor ε (and, by converse induction, of the decoding functor δ) are succinctly manifested in their roles as system morphisms:

$$\langle N, \kappa(N) \rangle \xleftrightarrow[\varepsilon]{\delta} \langle M, \kappa(M) \rangle \tag{27}$$

Recall that a model is almost always incomplete, so it generally cannot be a model of the whole system $\langle N, \kappa(N) \rangle$, but, rather, a proper subsystem $\langle H, \kappa(H) \rangle \subset \langle N, \kappa(N) \rangle$. In view of the Natural Law statement (11) and containments (14), encoding ε entails, for each set $A \in H \subset N \subset \mathcal{OC}$ and for each mapping $F \in \mathbf{C}(A, B) \subset \kappa(H) \subset \kappa(N) \subset \mathcal{AC}$, that

$$\begin{aligned} \varepsilon &: A \mapsto \varepsilon(A) \in \varepsilon(H) = M \subset \mathcal{OC} \\ \varepsilon &: F \mapsto \varepsilon(F) \in \mathbf{C}(\varepsilon(A), \varepsilon(B)) \subset \kappa(M) \subset \mathcal{AC} . \end{aligned} \tag{28}$$

This is the sense of the functorial encoding of $\langle N, \kappa(N) \rangle$ into its model $\langle M, \kappa(M) \rangle$: the encoding functor $\varepsilon : \langle N, \kappa(N) \rangle \to \langle M, \kappa(M) \rangle$ is operationally the restriction $\varepsilon|_{\langle H, \kappa(H) \rangle} : \langle H, \kappa(H) \rangle \to \langle M, \kappa(M) \rangle$. With this understanding of 'incomplete models', however, for simplicity of notation and metalanguage, one simply drops the reference to the subsystem. Incidentally, the subsystem $\langle H, \kappa(H) \rangle \subset \langle N, \kappa(N) \rangle$ is a model of the system $\langle N, \kappa(N) \rangle$; the encoding is the (restriction of) the identity functor $\iota|_{\langle H, \kappa(H) \rangle} : \langle H, \kappa(H) \rangle \to \langle H, \kappa(H) \rangle$. And, as I mentioned at the outset, the only *perfect* model of a system is the system itself, the trivial encoding being $\iota : \langle N, \kappa(N) \rangle \to \langle N, \kappa(N) \rangle$.

The encoding and decoding arrows ε and δ taken together establish a kind of *dictionary*, which allows effective passage from one system to the other and back again. Finally, one must note the extraneous status of the arrows ε and δ, that they are not a part of either systems $\langle N, \kappa(N) \rangle$ or $\langle M, \kappa(M) \rangle$ nor are they entailed by anything in $\langle N, \kappa(N) \rangle$ or in $\langle M, \kappa(M) \rangle$.

Examples and Pluralities

Examples are in order. For instance, Claudius Ptolemy's *Almagest* (*c.* AD 150) contained a brilliant account for the apparent motion of many heavenly bodies. The Ptolemaic system of epicycles and deferents, later with adjustments in terms of eccentricities and equant points, provided good geometric simulations, in the sense that there were enough parameters in defining the circles so that any planetary or stellar trajectory could be represented reasonably accurately by these circular traces in the sky. Despite the fact that Ptolemy did not give any physical reasons why the planets should turn about circles attached to circles in arbitrary positions in the sky, his quantitatively accurate yet qualitatively wrong simulations remained the standard cosmological view for 1400 years. Celestial mechanics has since, of course, been progressively updated with better theories of Copernicus, Kepler, Newton, and Einstein. Each improvement explains more of the underlying principles of motion and not just the trajectories of motion. The universality of the Ptolemaic epicycles is nowadays regarded as an extraneous mathematical artefact irrelevant to the under-lying physical situation, and it is for this reason that a representation of trajectories in terms of them can only be regarded as simulation and not as model.

For another example, a lot of the so-called models in the social sciences are really just sophisticated kinds of curve-fitting, i.e., simulations. These activities are akin to the assertion that since a given curve can be approximated by a polynomial, it must be a polynomial. As an illustration, consider that any given set of $n + 1$ functional data points (e.g., hollow dots in Fig. 8) may be fitted *exactly*, with an appropriately chosen set of coefficients $\{a_0, a_1, a_2, \ldots, a_n\}$, onto a polynomial of degree n,

$$y = a_0 + a_1x + a_2x^2 + \cdots + a_nx^n. \tag{29}$$

(dashed curve in Fig. 8).

But a more appropriate curve through these points (they in particular being population growth data), is the sigmoid curve

$$y = \frac{K P_0 e^{rt}}{K + P_0(e^{rt} - 1)} \tag{30}$$

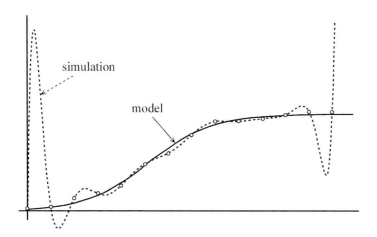

Fig. 8 Simulation versus model

(solid curve in Fig. 8). One may note that the solid curve fits the data points less precisely than the dashed curve, and this demonstrates that it is in fact more important for a model to have the functorial correspondence of morphisms (25) than the commutativity (19). Correct functional entailment is the hallmark of a good model, while 'approximate' material entailment suffices. Stated otherwise, curve fitting without a theory of the shape of the curve is simulation; model requires understanding of how and why a curve takes its shape. In short:

$$\text{simulation describes; model explains.} \tag{31}$$

'Simulation' is based on the Latin word *similis*, 'like, similar'. A *simulacrum* is 'something having merely the form or appearance of a certain thing, without possessing its substance or proper qualities'. 'Model' in Latin is *modulus*, which means 'measure'; herein lies a fine nuance that implies a subtle increase in precision. In common usage, however, the two words 'simulation' and 'model' are often synonyms, meaning (*a*) a simplified description of a system put forward as a basis for theoretical understanding, (*b*) a conceptual or mental representation of a thing, and (*c*) an analogue of a different structure from the system of interest but sharing an important set of functional properties. Some, alternatively, use 'model' to mean mathematical theory and 'simulation' to mean numerical computation. What I have presented above, however, is how these two words are used in relational biology.

There is a 'polarity' built into the general modelling relation of Fig. 7. While both the encoding ε and decoding δ are functors, their operations (and also the roles of the systems $\langle N, \kappa(N) \rangle$ and $\langle M, \kappa(M) \rangle$) are not interchangeable, even for simulations. One reason is that the commutativity $f = \delta \circ g \circ \varepsilon$ of (21) does not imply $g = \varepsilon \circ f \circ \delta$. The issue of when the former implies the latter is a deep topic of investigation, and I shall explicate it elsewhere (Louie 2017).

A special case of congruence between two different natural systems $\langle N_1, \kappa(N_1) \rangle$ and $\langle N_2, \kappa(N_2) \rangle$ occurs when they possess the same formal model $\langle M, \kappa(M) \rangle$ (or alternatively, they constitute distinct realizations of $\langle M, \kappa(M) \rangle$), as shown in Fig. 9.

One readily shows that one can then 'encode' the features of $\langle N_1, \kappa(N_1) \rangle$ into corresponding features of $\langle N_2, \kappa(N_2) \rangle$ and, conversely, in such a way that the two entailment structures, in the two systems $\langle N_1, \kappa(N_1) \rangle$ and $\langle N_2, \kappa(N_2) \rangle$, are brought into congruence. That is, one can construct from the above figure a commutative diagram of the form shown in Fig. 10. This is a *mutual* modelling relation between two natural systems (instead of the prototypical unidirectional case from a natural system to a formal one):

Under these circumstances depicted in the two previous figures, the natural systems $\langle N_1, \kappa(N_1) \rangle$ and $\langle N_2, \kappa(N_2) \rangle$ are *analogues*. Analogous systems allow us to learn about one by observing the other. Relations of analogy underlie the efficacy of 'scale models' in engineering, as well as all of the various 'principles of equivalence' in physics. But the relation of analogy has much deeper consequences. Natural systems of the most diverse kinds (e.g., organisms, societies, economic systems, and political systems) may be analogous. In particular, it is precisely the fact that biological systems and socioeconomic systems are analogous anticipatory

Fig. 9 Common model

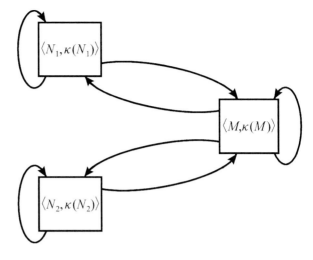

Fig. 10 Analogues

systems that provides the unifying foundation and impetus of the present collection of essays that is the *Handbook of Anticipation*. Analogy is a relation between natural systems that arises through the models of their causal entailments, and not directly from their material structures. As such, analogy and its cognates offer a most powerful and physically sound alternative to reductionism (viz., 'share a common model' and therefore 'analogous', as opposed to 'one encompasses the other').

A complementary diagram to that of Fig. 9 is shown in Fig. 11, in which a single natural system $\langle N, \kappa(N) \rangle$ is modelled in two distinct formalisms: $\langle M_1, \kappa(M_1) \rangle$ and $\langle M_2, \kappa(M_2) \rangle$. The question here is: What, if any, is the relation between the formalisms $\langle M_1, \kappa(M_1) \rangle$ and $\langle M_2, \kappa(M_2) \rangle$? The answer here is not in general as straightforward as before; it depends entirely on the extent of the 'overlap' between the two encodings of $\langle N, \kappa(N) \rangle$ in $\langle M_1, \kappa(M_1) \rangle$ and $\langle M_2, \kappa(M_2) \rangle$; i.e., on $\varepsilon_1(N) \cap \varepsilon_2(N) \subset M_1 \cap M_2$ and $\varepsilon_1(\kappa(N)) \cap \varepsilon_2(\kappa(N)) \subset \kappa(M_1) \cap \kappa(M_2)$. In some cases, one can effectively build at least some encoding and decoding arrows between the two formalisms. For a couple of examples, consider Dirac's transformation theory formulation of quantum mechanics which unifies Heisenberg's matrix mechanics and Schrödinger's wave mechanics, and the relation between the thermodynamic and statistical-mechanical models of fluids. In other cases, there exists no formal relation between $\langle M_1, \kappa(M_1) \rangle$ and $\langle M_2, \kappa(M_2) \rangle$. One then has the situation in which $\langle N, \kappa(N) \rangle$ *simultaneously* realizes two distinct and independent formalisms; the various Bohr's complementarities for microphysical phenomena are examples.

Fig. 11 Alternate models

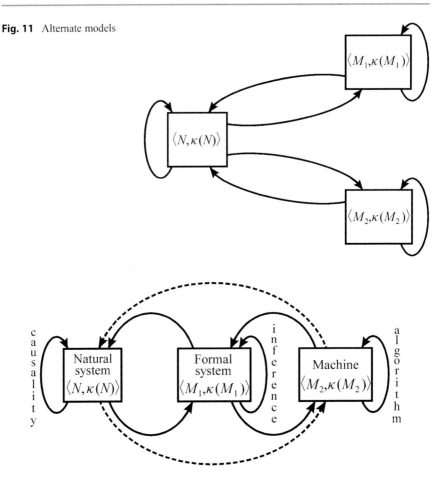

Fig. 12 Machine model

Encoding and decoding functors may be composed; i.e., one can iteratively model a model. This leads to a second configuration in which a natural system $\langle N, \kappa(N) \rangle$ is related to two formal systems $\langle M_1, \kappa(M_1) \rangle$ and $\langle M_2, \kappa(M_2) \rangle$.

Suppose the formal system $\langle M_1, \kappa(M_1) \rangle$ is a model of the natural system $\langle N, \kappa(N) \rangle$, the prototypical modelling relation being a transition from the realm of science to that of mathematics. If one extracts only the predicative processes of $\langle M_1, \kappa(M_1) \rangle$, one may construct a purely syntactic 'machine' model $\langle M_2, \kappa(M_2) \rangle$ of $\langle M_1, \kappa(M_1) \rangle$, as in Fig. 12.

One may then consider only the outer two systems and forget about the original model $\langle M_1, \kappa(M_1) \rangle$. The formal system $\langle M_2, \kappa(M_2) \rangle$ is a *machine model* of the natural system $\langle N, \kappa(N) \rangle$ and captures the latter's purely syntactic aspects. The encoding and decoding arrows themselves (the dashed arrows in Figure 12) between $\langle N, \kappa(N) \rangle$ and $\langle M_2, \kappa(M_2) \rangle$ cannot be described as *effective* in any formal sense, but they compose exclusively with the input and output strings of the Turing machines in $\langle M_2, \kappa(M_2)\rangle$, and these compositions may immediately be identified with the effective processes in $\langle N, \kappa(N)\rangle$. Whether these exhaust the implicative resources of the system $\langle N, \kappa(N)\rangle$ itself serves to distinguish between *predicative* and *impredicative* systems. (These antonymous adjectives of natural systems are further explicated in the ▶ Chap. 2, "Complex Systems" in this *Handbook*.)

"Internal Predictive Model of Itself and of Its Environment"

Let $\langle S, \kappa(S)\rangle$ be an anticipatory system. The system S partitions the universe U into *self* (S itself) and nonself that is its *environment* ($S^c = U \sim S$). What does S's having a *model of itself and of its environment* mean? 'S itself and its environment' are the whole universe: $S \cup S^c = U$. A model is, however, by necessity incomplete, so it cannot be a model of the 'whole universe' U but only a *proper subsystem* $W \subset U$. Rosen's original definition of anticipatory system actually uses the phrase "of itself and/or of its environment." It is my contention that this construction "and/or" is unnecessary: both "self and/or environment" and "self and environment" describe the universe $U = S \cup S^c$; and the requisite model is a proper subset W of U.

That W is part of 'S itself and its environment' implies it may straddle the self | nonself boundary: so possibly both $W \cap S \neq \varnothing$ and $W \cap S^c \neq \varnothing$. The union $\kappa(W \cap S) \cup \kappa(W \cap S^c)$ of the processes within the two parts does not account for all processes $\kappa(W)$ of W, however. In addition to the internal processes $\kappa(W \cap S) \subset \kappa(S)$ and the environmental processes $\kappa(W \cap S^c) \subset \kappa(S^c)$, $\kappa(W)$ also contains environmental effects on S and how the system S affects its environment. Anticipation in S entails the existence of a model $M \in \mathbf{C}(W)$ and an encoding functor

$$\varepsilon : \langle W, \kappa(W)\rangle \rightarrow \langle M, \kappa(M)\rangle. \tag{32}$$

We have already encountered (in the previous section) the multilevel entailments of ε. In particular, one has material entailment

$$\varepsilon : W \rightarrow M \tag{33}$$

and functional entailment

$$\varepsilon : \kappa(W) \rightarrow \kappa(M). \tag{34}$$

In common English usage, *predict* means 'foretell, make a statement about the future'; thus temporal succession is implicit. The word comes from the Latin *prae*, 'before', and *dicere*, 'say'. Note, however, the 'before' that the Latin prefix *prae-* (and *pre-*) predicates does not necessarily have to refer to time; it may also be before in place, order, degree, or importance. It is with this general sense that one may distinguish three temporally different classes of 'predictions':

(i) *Extenders*, predictions that are time-independent
(ii) *Portents*, predictions that relate simultaneous events

(iii) *Transducers*, predictions that convert information about the world at a given instant into information about the world at some later instant

Time-independent predictions (i) concern a system's *constitutive parameters*, while time-dependent predictions (ii) and (iii) concern a system's *dynamics*.

A model M is a *reflector* of its realization W. The functorial images $\varepsilon : W \to M$ and $\varepsilon : \kappa(W) \to \kappa(M)$ above all serve to archive a copy of $\langle W, \kappa(W) \rangle$ in $\langle M, \kappa(M) \rangle$. An important purpose of modelling is that through the study of the alternate description $\langle M, \kappa(M) \rangle$, one produces explanations that decode to help in one's understanding of $\langle W, \kappa(W) \rangle$. A good model should *augur*, i.e., suggest specified outcomes and generate conclusions that are more than the building blocks used in the construction of the model. A model predicts. To whichever class a prediction belongs, what shapes the consequents is not what the encoding ε supplies to the model but, rather, what the decoding δ extracts from the model.

An anticipatory system $\langle S, \kappa(S) \rangle$ has to have more than one inherent dynamics, more than one thing that one may consider 'time' ('real time' or otherwise). To have anticipation of the system's own subsequent behavior, something in the system must be running 'faster than real time'. This is a crucial role that is taken up by the predictive model $\langle M, \kappa(M) \rangle$. The predictive model in an anticipatory system must be able to augur future events; i.e., its predictions must include those belonging to class (iii), transducers. While the *emphasis* is on the requisite "the model's predictions pertaining to a later instant," possible roles of $\langle M, \kappa(M) \rangle$ in the other two classes, (i) extenders and (ii) portents, are not excluded. In other words, the model $\langle M, \kappa(M) \rangle$, in addition to offering predictions of potential futures, also considers past and present states, and indeed time-independent aspects, of the system $\langle S, \kappa(S) \rangle$ and its environment. The anticipatory system $\langle S, \kappa(S) \rangle$ then inclusively integrates all these in the execution of its present actions.

One notes that in order to fulfill its purpose of making predictions about the future, the model $\langle M, \kappa(M) \rangle$ must have a 'faster dynamics' than its realization $\langle W, \kappa(W) \rangle$. This last phrase is an abbreviation, a terse summary that is interpreted thus: if the trajectories of the system $\langle W, \kappa(W) \rangle$ are parameterized by real time, then the corresponding trajectories of the model $\langle M, \kappa(M) \rangle$ are parameterized by a time variable that goes faster than real time. That is, if $\langle W, \kappa(W) \rangle$ and $\langle M, \kappa(M) \rangle$ both start at time t_0 in equivalent states, and if (real) time runs until $t_1 > t_0$, then $\langle M, \kappa(M) \rangle$ will have proceeded further along its trajectory than $\langle W, \kappa(W) \rangle \cap \langle S, \kappa(S) \rangle$, say to $t_2 > t_1$. This is the sense in which the predictive model $\langle M, \kappa(M) \rangle$ operates on a faster internal time scale than the system $\langle S, \kappa(S) \rangle$ itself. The system $\langle S, \kappa(S) \rangle$ can, therefore, at 'present time' t look at the model $\langle M, \kappa(M) \rangle$, which describes the system $\langle W, \kappa(W) \rangle$ at some 'future time' $t + h$ (with $h > 0$), and thereby obtain information about its own possible state at $t + h$ if it were to continue on its current trajectory. It is in this way that the behavior of $\langle M, \kappa(M) \rangle$ *predicts* the behavior of $\langle S, \kappa(S) \rangle$. Armed with this information of a possible future, the anticipatory system $\langle S, \kappa(S) \rangle$ may then make trajectory corrections if necessary.

It should be clarified that "anticipation" in Rosen's usage, embodied in the "predictive model, does not refer to an ability to 'see' or otherwise sense the immediate or the distant future – there is no prescience or psychic phenomena suggested here. Instead, Rosen suggests that there must be information about self, about species, and about the evolutionary environment, encoded into the organization of all living systems. He observes that this *information*, as it behaves through time, is capable of acting causally on the organism's present behavior, based on relations projected to be applicable in the future. Thus, while not violating time established by external events, organisms seem capable of constructing an internal time scale as part of a model that can indeed be manipulated to produce anticipation. It is in this sense that degrees of freedom in internal models allow time its multi-scaling and reversibility to produce new information. The predictive model in an anticipatory system must not be equivocated to any kind of 'certainty' (even probabilistically) about the future. Rosen's theory of anticipation is a general qualitative theory that describes *all* anticipatory systems. It is not a quantitative theory of *single* systems for which the lore of *large number* of systems, hence statistical reasoning, would ever enter into the picture. In other words, this theory has nothing to do with stochastics. Anticipation is, rather, an assertion based on a model that runs in a faster time scale. The future still has not yet happened: the organism has a *model* of the future but not definitive *knowledge* of future itself. Indeed, the predictive model may sometimes be wrong, the future may unfold very differently from the model's predictions, and the consequences of the mismatch may be detrimental to the anticipator.

The predictive modelling activity of an anticipatory system is self-contained. That the predictive model is *internal* means

$$\langle M, \kappa(M) \rangle \subset \langle S, \kappa(S) \rangle; \tag{35}$$

that is to say,

$$M \subset S \quad \text{and} \quad \kappa(M) \subset \kappa(S). \tag{36}$$

The encodings (33) and (34) imply

$$\varepsilon(W) \subset M \quad \text{and} \quad \varepsilon(\kappa(W)) \subset \kappa(M). \tag{37}$$

Together with (36), one has

$$\varepsilon(W) \subset S \quad \text{and} \quad \varepsilon(\kappa(W)) \subset \kappa(S). \tag{38}$$

The encodings (33) and (34) also immanently entail the corresponding decoding

$$\delta : M \to W \tag{39}$$

and

$$\delta : \kappa(M) \to \kappa(W), \tag{40}$$

Fig. 13 Internal predictive
model of itself and of its
environment

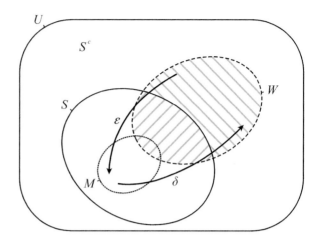

whence

$$\delta(M) \subset W \quad \text{and} \quad \delta(\kappa(M)) \subset \kappa(W). \tag{41}$$

These inclusions are succinct summary statements of the embodiment of anticipation, the internal predictive model (Fig. 13).

Now let us return to Fig. 1, the canonical diagram of an anticipatory system. I
shall use the same symbols for the object, model, and effector systems, respectively, S, M, and E, to denote their efficient causes. In other words, let
each symbol represent the *processor* associated with the block (the "black
box") as well as the block itself. Then the entailment diagram for the anticipatory
system is

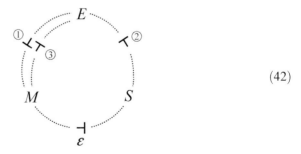

$$(42)$$

The mappings labelled with circled numbers correspond to those in Fig. 1. The
mapping $\varepsilon : S \to M$, completing the cycle, is the *encoding* of the object system S
into its model M, i.e., the restriction of the encoding functor (32) to $W \cap S$. The
hierarchical entailment cycle

$$\{ S \vdash M, \ E \vdash S, \ M \vdash E \} \tag{43}$$

renders this anticipatory system impredicative. (Impredicativity is the defining characteristic of *complex systems* as the latter term is used in relational biology. See the ▶ Chaps. 10, "Relational Biology" and ▶ 2, "Complex Systems" in this *Handbook* for further explorations.)

"Change ... in Accord with the Model's Predictions"

An anticipatory system, however, has more structure in its entailment pattern than the cyclic permutation of the three maps $\{M, E, S\}$. In particular, the hierarchical action chain

$$S \vdash M \vdash E \vdash S \tag{44}$$

must, as explained above, involve a faster dynamics in M. Also, the set E of effectors functionally entails both the system S and the internal predictive model M:

$$②: E \vdash S \text{ and } ③: E \vdash M, \tag{45}$$

a requisite iterative bifurcation that is not necessarily present in every hierarchical cycle. Thus: "an anticipatory system *must* be complex; a complex system *may* be anticipatory."

Let me fractionate effector E into the functional components E_S that acts on S and E_M that acts on M. While I am at it, I eliminate the circles around the numerical labels of the arrows and split identically numbered arrows into as and bs. Recall that the system's environment is $S^c = U \sim S$. After all these modifications, the canonical Fig. 1 of an anticipatory system becomes (Fig. 14).

I reemphasize that what defines an anticipatory system S is not just the *existence* of the internal predictive model – there are *two* indispensable ingredients: (i) internal predictive model M and (ii) *response* E to the prediction. The telos of anticipation is for the system S 'to change state at an instant in accord with the model's predictions

Fig. 14 Anticipatory system with dual effectors

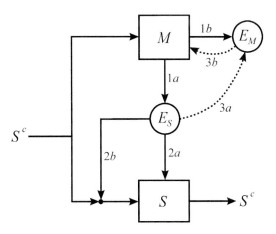

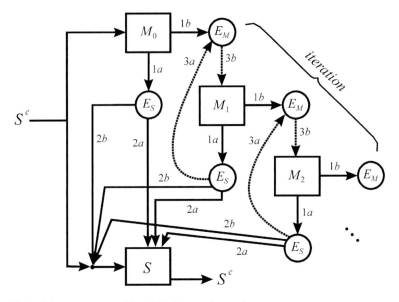

Fig. 15 Anticipatory system with unfolded antecedent actions

pertaining to a later instant'. The central importance of this telos effected by E is reflected in E_S and E_M having the largest number of influent and effluent arrows among the blocks in Fig. 14.

That the anticipatory system has to *respond* in accord with the model's prediction means that the control system unit

$$E_M \vdash M \vdash E_S \vdash \tag{46}$$

is *iterated* (for as many times as deemed necessary). With an iteration of cycle (46), the telescoped Fig. 14 unfolds into this form (Fig. 15).

Feedforth

Anticipation is an example of adaptive behavior. Adaptive control system theory is a well-studied subject, but it is mostly formulated in terms of *feedback* control. In a feedback system, control is error-actuated, and the stimulus to corrective action is the discrepancy between the system's actual present state and its targeted state. Stated otherwise, a feedback control system is *reactive*; it must already be departing from its nominal behavior before control begins to be exercised. There are two classes: negative feedback and positive feedback. Negative feedback, the more common variety, involves self-correcting control, with discrepancy-reducing processes that seek to narrow the gap between actual and reference values of a parameter. Stereotypical examples are thermostat, cruise-control system in automobiles, and homeostasis in organisms. Positive feedback, on the other hand, involves self-reinforcing control, with discrepancy-enhancing processes that seek to widen the gap between actual and reference values of a parameter. Many exocrine (enzymatic) and endocrine (hormonal) pathways in living systems engage positive feedback. "Self-fulfilling prophecy" in socioeconomic systems is another example of positive feedback. In most contexts, that feedback is positive or negative is not a value judgment; it does not imply that it correspondingly causes good or bad effects. A negative feedback loop is one that tends to slow down its controlled process, whereas a positive one tends to accelerate it.

Anticipatory control, contrariwise, involves the concept of *feedforth* (or, conventionally but less antonymously termed, "feedforward"). It is through feedforth that the internal predictive model $\langle M, \kappa(M) \rangle$ of an anticipatory system $\langle S, \kappa(S) \rangle$ operates a faster dynamics. Note that feedforth is *not* positive feedback: feedback, whether negative or positive, uses information from the past (discrepancy that is the final cause of processes that have come to pass), while feedforth uses information of the future (as predicted by a model of final causes yet to be entailed). An illustrative example of feedforth is a camera with automatic exposure control. The telos is to set the exposure of a shot such that a relatively constant amount of light will be admitted into the camera, regardless of the ambient light intensity (or, more technically, to adjust the exposure setting to match the mid-tone of the subject to the mid-tone of the image). There are two variables to consider: aperture and shutter speed. (Often the shutter speed is fixed manually, with automatic aperture compensation. But the roles of the two variables may be reversed, or both may be allowed to cooperatively adjust.) It is useless to put a feedback sensor in the camera, for however fast the feedback loop runs, the image will already be over- or underexposed before any corrective measures can be implemented. Rather, an entirely different mode of control is required, manifested in a light meter, which *measures* the ambient light intensity, in conjunction with a *model* that allow the *prediction* of the aperture/shutter speed setting that, for that measured ambient light intensity, will allow an appropriate amount of light into the camera. The camera is then *preset* at this aperture and shutter speed combination before the picture is taken. (The assumption is, of course, that the ambience does not change in the interval between the light-meter's measurement at time t and the actual shot at time $t + h$.) This mode of control, termed *feedforth*, does not involve the propagation of an error signal through the system. It is characterized by the property that *a preemptive action is undertaken, before system performance has deteriorated, on the basis of some predictive model*. This is precisely what is required in an anticipatory system.

Imminence

In this chapter, I have presented:
    (i) the *mathematical foundations* of anticipatory systems.
    But note that this is neither:
    (ii) the mathematical theory of anticipatory systems,   nor
    (iii) the mathematics of some particular anticipatory system

The difference between (i) and (ii) is that the former is a metatheory that pre-scribes the mathematics necessary for the study of anticipation (e.g., the algebra of internal predictive models), while the latter dwells into the mathematical theory of specific tools (e.g., the analysis of control systems as a formal platform of internal predictive models). Stated otherwise, (i) is *about* the requisite ingredients of antic-ipatory systems and (ii) is the actual study of the ingredients themselves.

There is a cornucopia of chapters in this *Handbook* showing how anticipation specifically arises or is used in a variety of subjects. Occasionally some of these chapters may even contain mathematical tools (iii) that are suitable for the tasks at hand. To proceed from particular instances to the general concept is of course a very common procedure in mathematics. One example, to mention but one analogy, is that 'symmetry' appears abundantly in nature and in every subject of human endeavor; in the minds of mathematicians, the study of symmetry itself is general-ized into group theory. In this analogy, when (ii) is group theory, (i) would be the philosophy of symmetry (concepts that need to be accounted for when formulating a comprehensive theory of symmetry, such as harmony, balance, proportion, transfor-mational invariance, etc.), and an example of a specific (iii) may be the algebra of the order $8! \times 3^7 \times (12\ !\ /2) \times 2^{11}$ finite permutation group of Rubik's Cube.

Since anticipatory systems serve as common models for such a diverse collection of scholarly pursuits, it is natural that one would want to have a general mathematical theory (ii) that would lend rigor to the subject. One must not simply linger on stage (i), which is principally a descriptive enterprise of what (ii) has to entail but falls short of being (ii) itself. Indeed, a main purpose for Rosen's publication of *AS* was to move toward such a general theory. The Axiom of Anticipation is a statement of self-evident truth. *AS* provided (along with the philosophical and methodological foundations) the mathemat-ical foundations (i), as explicated and expanded in this chapter, for the study of anticipa-tory systems. But one must not stagnate on the axiom, use it as a slogan, and rest on its laurels. After proclaiming the obvious, that life is anticipatory, one must move on to the next phase and attempt to develop a mathematical theory of anticipation.

In the 1970s, Rosen lamented that "a study of anticipation is not yet even in its infancy, despite the universality of this mode of control in the biological realm." There has, alas, not been much progress in the development of a general mathematical theory (ii) in the 40 years thence (neither by Rosen himself nor by others). There is, of course, the tried-and-true dynamical systems (in their various continuous and discrete and recursive and adaptive and, last and decidedly least, computational varieties), but more often than not their invocation in anticipation degenerates into specific applications (iii) instead of being genuine comprehensive theories (ii). In any case, there *ought* to be more to the mathematical tools of anticipation than the less-than-satisfactory standby that are 'glorified and modified dynamical systems'. At the bottom of the barrel, 'computational anticipatory systems' are at best simulations, not models. These two previous sentences are, incidentally, not flippant comments, but are made for good relational-biologic reasons. An anticipatory system must be impredicative, and an impredicative ('complex') system must have at least one nonsimulable ('non-computable') model. (See ▶ Chap. 2, "Complex Systems" in this *Handbook* for further details.) One must therefore move beyond computation in anticipation.

When *AS* was finally published in 1985, Rosen had added an Appendix (Chap. 7 therein) to briefly sketch the development of the intervening years between 1979 and 1985. It was clear that his interest was not in anticipatory systems themselves, but rather how they had provided a plateau from which to launch the final ascent to the summit that was his one true lifelong quest, the answer to the question "What is life?". Indeed, the Appendix was not so much about anticipation than on complex systems; anticipation was barely mentioned. Rosen's dismissive conclusion was that "our entire treatment of anticipatory systems becomes a corollary of complexity." The enlargement of "this Appendix into a separate monograph in the near future," incidentally, has since been realized as his iconoclastic masterwork *Life Itself* (Rosen 1991). In *Life Itself*, 'anticipation' was again scarcely mentioned in passing; therein, Rosen began Chap. 1 thus:

> This book represents a continuation, an elaboration, and perhaps a culmination of the circle of ideas I have expounded in two previous monographs: *Fundamentals of Measurement and the Representation of Natural Systems* (henceforth abbreviated as *FM*) and *Anticipatory Systems* (abbreviated as *AS*). Both of these, and indeed almost all the rest of my published scientific work, have been driven by a need to understand what it is about organisms that confers upon them their magical characteristics, what it is that sets life apart from other material phenomena in the universe. That is indeed the question of questions: What is life? What is it that enables living things, apparently so moist, fragile, and evanescent, to persist while towering mountains dissolve into dust, and the very continents and oceans dance into oblivion and back? To frame this question requires an almost infinite audacity; to strive to answer it compels an equal humility.

The main conclusion of *Life Itself* is that a natural system is living if and only if it is closed to efficient causation, a property which in particular renders a living system impredicative ('complex') (cf. ▶ Chap. 10, "Relational Biology" in this *Handbook*). After *AS*, Rosen never worked on anticipatory systems themselves again; a couple of on-topic post-*AS* publications constituted recompiled, relinked, and otherwise rearranged efforts, but no further developments. (Anticipatory system concepts would of course be new to readers who had not previously encountered them, but these regurgitations did not contain anything new in the relational-biologic canon.) When anticipation was mentioned at all in the rare instances, they were invariably, so Rosen had declared, as "a corollary of complexity."

It is important to remember that both complexity (impredicativity) and anticipation are necessary conditions for life, the containment hierarchy being

$$\text{Impredicativity} \supset \text{Anticipation} \supset \text{Life}. \tag{47}$$

While we in relational biology may find it more congenial to characterize life in terms of impredicativity instead of anticipation, this does not in any way diminish the indispensability of anticipation in the understanding of biological, human, and social sciences. There are deep system-theoretic homologies among these sciences. Analogy allows the possibility of obtaining insights into anticipatory processes in the human and social realms from the understanding of biological anticipation. To this end, a comprehensive general mathematical theory of anticipatory systems is the means. This is a quest, however quixotic a journey it may seem to be, we must continue.

Summary

Life $\subset$ **Anticipation** $\subset$ Impredicativity

Life anticipates. Social, human, and many other natural systems also anticipate. The behaviors of anticipatory systems are largely determined by the nature of their internal predictive models. This chapter lays the mathematical foundations for the study of this important class of model-based systems. I leave the last words to our founder; Robert Rosen closed (the 1979 first draft of) *AS* thus:

> The study of anticipatory systems thus involves in an essential way the subjective notions of good and ill, as they manifest themselves in the models which shape our behavior. For in a profound sense, the study of models is the study of man; and if we can agree about our models, we can agree about everything else.

Acknowledgments I began writing this chapter when I was a resident Fellow at the Stellenbosch Instiitute for Advanced Study (stias), South Africa, in February-April 2016. I thank stias for its hospitality and my contemporary Fellows for their engaging dialogues.

References

Brown, R., & Glazebrook, J. F. (2013). A career of unyielding exploration: In memory of Ion C. Baianu (1947–2013). *Quanta, 2*, 1–6.

Hertz, H. (1899). *The principles of mechanics presented in a new form* (Trans. D. E. Jones & J. T. Walley). London: Macmillan.

Louie, A. H. (2009). *More than life itself: A synthetic continuation in relation biology*. Frankfurt: ontos.

Louie, A. H. (2010). Robert Rosen's anticipatory systems. In: R. Miller & R. Poli (Eds.) Special issue: Anticipatory systems and the philosophical foundations of futures studies. *Foresight 12*(3), 18–29.

Louie, A. H. (2013). *The reflection of life: Functional entailment and imminence in relational biology*. New York: Springer.

Louie, A. H. (2015). A metabolism–repair theory of by-products and side-effects. *International Journal of General Systems, 44*, 26–54.

Louie, A. H. (2017). *Intangible life: Functorial connections in relational biology*. New York: Springer.

Mac Lane, S. (1997). *Categories for the working mathematician* (2nd ed.). New York: Springer.

Rosen, R. (1974). Planning, management, policies and strategies: Four fuzzy concepts. *International Journal of General Systems, 1*, 245–252.

Rosen, R. (1980). Ergodic approximations and specificity. *Mathematical Modelling, 1*, 91–97.

Rosen, R. (1985a). *[AS] Anticipatory systems: Philosophical, mathematical, and methodological foundations*. Oxford: Pergamon; (2012) 2nd ed., New York: Springer.

Rosen, R. (1985b). Organisms as causal systems which are not mechanisms: An essay into the nature of complexity. In R. Rosen (Ed.), *Theoretical biology and complexity: Three essays on the natural philosophy of complex systems* (pp. 165–203). Orlando: Academic.

Rosen, R. (1991). *Life itself: A comprehensive inquiry into the nature, origin, and fabrication of life*. New York: Columbia University Press.

Rosen, R. (2000). *Essays on life itself*. New York: Columbia University Press.

Anticipation in MES – Memory Evolutive Systems

46

Andrée Ehresmann

Contents

A. Ehresmann (✉)

Faculté des Sciences, Mathématiques LAMFA, Université de Picardie Jules Verne, Amiens, France

e-mail: ehres@u-picardie.fr

© Springer Nature Switzerland AG 2019

R. Poli (ed.), *Handbook of Anticipation*,

https://doi.org/10.1007/978-3-319-91554-8_42

965

Abstract

The aim of this chapter is to study anticipation in autonomous adaptive systems, such as biological and social systems, which have a multilevel multi-agent organization and develop a robust though flexible long-term memory. The problem is to find the characteristics allowing the system, through some of its agent(s), (i) to enhance its comprehension of the nature and role of anticipation (what Riel Miller (Futures J Policy Plan Future Stud 39:341–362, 2007) calls "Futures Literacy") and (ii) to use this knowledge to search for possible procedures and virtually evaluate their impact on behavior, decision-making, and/or future action. The present study concerns open systems during their ongoing evolution. Thus it is different from Rosen's anticipatory systems in which anticipation results from the existence of an internal predictive model of the invariant structure of the system.

The study is done in the frame of the Memory Evolutive Systems (Ehresmann and Vanbremeersch, Bull Math Bio 49(1):13–50, 1987; Memory evolutive systems: hierarchy, emergence, cognition. Elsevier, 2007), a mathematical approach to "living" systems, based on a "dynamic" category theory incorporating time. The main characteristic making these systems capable of developing anticipatory processes is identified as a kind of "operational redundancy" called the Multiplicity Principle. MP allows the progressive emergence, in the memory, of multifaceted dynamical records of increasing complexity which are flexible enough to adapt to changes. In social systems, a group of interacting people can develop a shared higher-level hub of the memory of the system, its archetypal pattern, which acts as a motor in the development of anticipatory processes. An application is given to the "Futures Literacy" program of Riel Miller, with a comparison of its three phases with the three types of creativity distinguished by Boden (The creative mind; myths and mechanisms, 2nd edn. Routledge, 2004).

Keywords

Anticipation · Category · Future literacy · Memory · Memory evolutive system

Introduction

In a physical system, the "future" is determined by the initial conditions and the physical laws directing its evolution. It is not the same in an open biological, social cognitive system because the present does not "entail" the future but only sets up some constraints on it, so that a variety of futures are "enabled" (Longo et al. 2012). In such an open and unpredictable world, it is important to develop a capacity to anticipate allowing to search and virtually evaluate best procedures for future action.

Different Kinds of Anticipation

"Anticipation comes in different guises: the simplest distinction is between anticipation as coupling between the system and its environment and anticipation as a cognitive projection" (Poli 2009). It is these different situations which we will consider, by searching formal conditions (be they structural, organizational, and/or epistemological) for a system or a "co-regulator" subsystem to:

  (i) Act as a *reactive system*, in which case there are only stimulus-response behaviors which an external observer can observe as a change of comportment and interpret as anticipation.
 (ii) Be an *anticipatory system* in Rosen's sense, meaning it has an internal model of itself and its environment so that its "current state is determined by a (predicted) future state" (Rosen 1985a). Then anticipation is inscribed as a structural property of the system.
(iii) Be able to develop an *anticipatory process* "that uses the future in its actual decision process" (Poli, Introduction of this book). In this case, the system, through different "co-regulator" subsystems, identifies the present situation, examines different possible procedures for action, and virtually evaluates their impact on behavior, decision-making, and/or future action of any kind. Such systems are impredicative (though some of their co-regulator subsystems can be predicative).

Whatever the case, anticipation is related to temporality since the system should react differently depending on the present situation and on its internal knowledge of the possible future effects of different behaviors. In particular, the system must have and/or develop a well-organized "memory." For reactive systems, it consists of simple stimulus-response processes implemented by construction in an artifact, or by intergenerational acquisition for a biological system. For Rosen's anticipatory systems, the innate memory should contain an invariant predictive model of the system itself and its environment.

The third case requires both the development over time of a flexible memory with higher-level multifaceted records (e.g., polysemous concepts) and a dynamical multi-agent self-organization interacting with this memory. An anticipatory process (for the system itself or some of its co-regulators) consists in an internal analysis of the present situation starting a search in the memory to recognize its different aspects with their possible causes and effects (retrospection process) and then searching and virtually evaluating adequate scenarios to answer (prospection). It is this case which we are going to study in the dynamic of its "becoming."

The Memory Evolutive System Methodology

These problems are studied in the frame of the Memory Evolutive Systems (or MES), a mathematical methodology (Ehresmann and Vanbremeersch 1987, 2007) for systems such as living systems of any kind with a threefold multiplicity: in terms of complexity levels, of internal co-regulator agents, and of intertwined temporalities. The main characteristics are:

(i) Following the 1926 von Bertalanffy's definition of a system as "a set of unities with relations among them," the system is represented by its components and the links through which they can interact. However, as we want to study not the invariant structure of the system but its evolution over time, the components and their links are dynamical entities with their own definite lifetime, from their "birth" to their "death."

(ii) At each time, the system has a tangled hierarchy of interacting components which varies over time due to the addition, suppression, or combination of components. Among the components, there are multifaceted (e.g., polysemous) components (*Multiplicity Principle*, MP), and each component takes its own complex identity, or "individuation" (Simondon 2005), independent from its lower level organization(s).

(iii) The system has a hierarchical subsystem representing its *memory* which it can develop through learning. Thanks to MP, this memory is both robust and flexible to adapt to changes in the environment.

(iv) The system is self-organized by a net of evolutionary subsystems, called *co-regulators*, of different complexities. Each co-regulator has a differential access to the memory, and with its help, it operates a stepwise dynamic process at its own rhythm. The global dynamic of the system is modulated by the cooperation and/or competition between the local dynamics of the co-regulators, and its result may be unpredictable.

Illustrative Examples

Before presenting the abstract model, let us give two emblematic examples.

A Business Enterprise

In a large business enterprise, the components represent the personnel, the different functional groups they form, and also the resources and knowledge necessary for the activities. Individual members of staff "are" lower-level components, while the different workshops, services, or departments they form "are" more and more complex components. The links represent the numerous interactions between components, for transmitting information or material. Components and their links have their definite lifetime, so that the configuration of the system varies over time.

The departments act as co-regulators actively participating to the functioning of the enterprise, each at its own rhythm: daily for workshops and years for the managers. They operate with the help of a flexible and continuously revised "memory" which collects the explicit or tacit knowledge necessary for correct functioning (archives of any nature, procedures, practices, values, past experiences, etc.). There is a risk of conflicts between different co-regulators if there is competition among them for some resources (e.g., finances or energy).

Some workshops may have only reactive behaviors. A managerial co-regulator develops anticipatory processes extending on periods of variable lengths, thanks to the formation of a higher-level hub of the memory, its *Archetypal pattern*, consisting of specific multifaceted components the meaning of which is "shared" by its members.

The Model MENS for the Human Neuro-Cognitive System

Its components of the lower level represent the neurons interconnected by synaptic paths between them (Ehresmann and Vanbremeersch 2007). Higher-level components, called *category-neurons*, "present" more and more complex mental objects and cognitive processes obtained by iterative combination of specific neural patterns, namely, the different Hebb's synchronous (hyper-)assemblies of neurons they can activate depending on the context. Here above we use the word "present" instead of "represent" to emphasize the divide between neurons and cat-neurons/mental objects coming from the fact that a neuron models a biological entity while a cat-neuron is a constructed dynamic multifaceted component (cf. section "Multifaceted Components: Multiplicity Principle"). MENS provides a "theory of mind" integrating neural and mental (cf. Ehresmann and Gomez-Ramirez 2015), a kind of neurophenomenology in the sense of Varela (1996).

The following sections describe the main characteristics of a MES. For more details, we refer to the book of Ehresmann and Vanbremeersch 2007 (abbreviated in EV 2007). The notions of category theory used in MES are briefly recalled at their first appearance in the text, the word being followed by the symbol * referring to a more formal definition given in the Appendix.

Evolutive Systems

Anticipation has a temporal nature. However, in Rosen's models of anticipatory systems, such as his (M, R) systems, he essentially considers the invariant structure of the system.

Here we consider a system in its evolution during its life and we don't restrict our study to systems displaying preset anticipative behaviors. On the contrary, we consider biological or social systems of any size which evolve over time and whose possible changes make anticipation of the future important but uncertain;

the aim is to analyze their ongoing development of efficient anticipatory processes in response to variable contexts.

As said before, we will work in the mathematical frame of MES, in which time appears under different forms (i) as the overall "internal timing" of change (as for Augustine), (ii) as the discrete timescales delimiting the steps of its different co-regulators which act as hybrid systems, and (iii) as the usual continuous clock time which allows comparing different internal timings and measuring the duration of some operations (e.g., propagation delays of links).

Dynamical System Versus Process Theory

In this section, we are interested in describing the evolution of the system during its "life." To study dynamical processes, the first idea of a mathematician is to model them by a (classical) dynamical system, e.g., defined by differential equations. This requires that, for each instant of time (looked at as a simple parameter), the state of an element of the system, measured by numerical or vector "observables," be represented as a point in a fixed phase space. This is not possible for the systems we consider because they are open in the sense that they have exchanges with their surroundings, and their configuration changes in time, with destruction or rejection of some components, and emergence of new elements, either taken from the outside or internally generated. Thus, their dynamical study cannot be confined to that of a unique well-defined phase space, except on short intervals.

As said above, time is not thought of as a simple (continuous or discrete) parameter but it plays different roles and in particular acts as an operator directing the process of change between the configurations of the system at successive moments; thus the underlying ontological framework is nearer to process theory. Poli (2014) has stressed the connection between process theory and causation. In MES, the configuration at t contains not only the state of the components at t but also links between them supporting their interactions (e.g., exchange of information or material) around t, and these links, with their temporal and energetic attributes, act as causal factors of the dynamical changes between configurations.

The MES methodology, based on a "dynamic" category theory, introduces new categorical notions for describing the general structure of the system (Hierarchical Evolutive System), its structural changes (complexification process), and its self-organization. However, these notions also integrate time to account for the dynamic.

About Category Theory

Category theory is a domain of mathematics introduced in the 1940s by Eilenberg and Mac Lane (1945). Later on, this theory has been developed, both for itself and for its applications in various domains of mathematics (e.g., algebraic topology, differential geometry, later analysis). Even if part of its self-centered development has sometimes been criticized as "abstract nonsense," categories are now recognized as a powerful language for a universal semantics of mathematical structures. Their interrelation with logics has been emphasized through topos theory and sketch theory. Later, applications have been developed in other domains such as computer science or physics. Rosen has initiated their application in biology as soon as 1958; and Healy (2010) proposes them for formalizing ontology.

A *category** is a (directed multi-)*graph** on which there is given a composition law associating to a path of the graph from an object A to an object B a "composite" arrow from A to B, this law being associative and with identities. The vertices of the graph are called *objects* of the category; its arrows are also called *morphisms*. Category theory is qualified of "relational mathematics," to emphasize that the important information is contained in the morphisms (as shown by the Yoneda Lemma*), not in the structure of the objects as it is more usual in physics.

In applications of categories to natural (biological or social) systems, the morphisms (also called *links*) model directed interactions between the objects; e.g., they can act as causal vectors and/or information transmitters. A morphism from A to B represents a communication channel for A to send information, commands, or constraints (e.g., energetical constraints) to B, with B playing the role of a receiver.

Paths of consecutive morphisms which have the same composite correspond to "operationally equivalent" paths, meaning they can transmit information in a temporally and/or energetically equivalent way.

How to Represent the Evolution of the System?

To describe this evolution, we distinguish the configuration of the system (with its components and their interactions) at each time t of its life and the change of configuration from t to a later time t'.

The *Configuration* of the System at t is Modeled by a Category K_t

Its objects represent the states C_t at t of the components C of the system existing at t; this state can be defined via different attributes measured by physical observables, for instance, the *activity* of C at t (for a neuron, its instantaneous firing rate at t). The morphisms from C_t to C'_t represent the state at t of links from C to C'; the morphism can be *active* (resp. *passive*) at t if it exists and transmits (resp. does not transmit) some information from C to C' in an interval around t; it can have for attributes a propagation delay and a strength around t in relation with the time needed for transmitting the information and with its quantity. For instance, a synapse between two neurons can transmit nervous influx or not at t.

Transitions Between Configurations

Between t and t', there are both:

(i) *Dynamical internal changes* of the components and their links, reflected in the variation of their successive states, as in a state-transition system. For instance, in MENS (section "The Model MENS for the Human Neuro-Cognitive System"), the activity of a component may increase or decrease; the strength of a link increases if it is often activated (generalized rule of Hebb 1949). But, at the difference of usual state-transition systems, there is no common phase space associated to different configurations.

(ii) *Systemic structural changes* coming from the loss of components and links (e.g., by "death," suppression of obsolete knowledge) and/or addition of new components (e.g., by "birth," learning of new knowledge, combination of patterns of interacting components). The process at the root of these changes is internally controlled (cf. section "The Complexification Process").

To account for the loss of some components and/or links which existed at t, the change of configuration from t to t', called *transition from t to t'*, is only defined for those components C existing both at t and at t', and then it associates to the state of C at t its new state at t'. New components which have appeared between t and t' have no state at t while their state at t' figures in the configuration at t'; and similarly for the links between components. Formally, the transition from t to t' is represented by a *partial functor** from K_t to $K_{t'}$ which is only defined on the subcategory of K_t consisting of elements still existing at t'.

Categorical Definition of an Evolutive System

An *Evolutive System** (EV 1987) consists of:

(i) A family of categories $(K_t)_{t \in T}$ called its *configurations*, indexed by a part T of the real numbers **R** representing the lifetime of the system.
(ii) Partial functors* between them, called *transitions*, satisfying the transitivity condition: the transition from t to t" is the composite of the transition from t to t' and the transition from t' to t" (in the category of partial functors* between categories).

Let us note that the components (and their links) as such do not figure in the formal definition of an Evolutive System, so that they have to be reconstructed from the given data, namely, the configurations and the transitions between them. A *component* C is represented by the dynamical entity consisting of its successive states C_t during its lifetime, whence the formal definition: A *component* of an Evolutive System is a maximal family of objects of successive configurations related by transitions. The links between components are similarly defined.

Each MES "is" an Evolutive System with some supplementary properties, in particular the existence of components of different "complexity levels" (as explained in the next section). However, there are ES which do not have supplementary properties.

For instance, let us give the example of the *Neural Evolutive System* (Neur) whose components represent the neurons and their links represent synaptic paths (i.e., sequences of consecutive synapses) between them. The configuration of Neur at t is the category whose objects model the states of the neurons existing at t (with their activity measured by their instantaneous firing rate) and the links model the states of the synaptic paths (measured by their propagation delay and strength around t). In fact Neur is an evolutive subsystem of the MES, called MENS (cf. section "The Model MENS for the Human Neuro-Cognitive System"), which models the human neuro-cognitive system, and we will explain later (section "Complexification Process at the Root of Emergence") how Neur "generates" the multilevel organization of MENS through successive complexification processes.

A Multilevel Organization into Complexity Levels

An important property of biological or social systems is their multilevel organization. As Jacob (1970) says: "Tout objet que considère la Biologie représente un système de systèmes; lui-même élément d'un système d'ordre supérieur, il obéit parfois à des règles qui ne peuvent être déduites de sa propre analyse." We are going to study how to equip an Evolutive System of such a multilevel "hierarchical" organization.

For instance, in the organigram of an enterprise, we can distinguish components of increasing *complexity levels*: simple individuals (at the level 0), workshops or small offices regrouping a few number of interacting employees, then higher-level departments regrouping different lower-level components working together, and so on. In its memory, there are 0-level "records" representing basic knowledge and also higher-level records representing elaborate knowledge integrating different modes (explicit or tacit).

Similarly, in our memory, there is formation of more and more complex mental objects and cognitive processes, which will play an important role in the development of anticipatory processes.

The "Colimit" Operation to Model Complexity

The term "complex" is ambiguous and should not be confused with "complicated," and the notion of "complexity levels" is not an absolute notion, it just accounts for an internal organizational property of a specific system and depends on the description we give of it. Roughly we define the notion of increasing *complexity levels* in an ES as follows:

(i) Components of level 0 act as "simple atoms" and, with the links modeling their interactions, are at the basis of the construction of higher levels (as Neur "generates" MENS, cf. sections "Categorical Definition of an Evolutive System" and "Complexification Process at the Root of Emergence").

(ii) A component C of level $n + 1$ has its own internal organization of lower levels. More precisely, C admits at least one decomposition into a pattern P consisting of components P_i of levels $\leq n$ which interact in a coordinated way, meaning that C acting alone and the P_i collectively interacting via P have the same operational role. Over time C can progressively take its own complex identity, independently from P.

How to define such complexity levels in a category, where the objects seem to be undifferentiated? It can be done using the categorical notion of a *colimit** (or "inductive limit," Kan 1958). A *pattern** (or diagram*) P in a category K consists of a family of objects P_i and some given morphisms of K between them. An object C of the category is the *colimit** cP of P in the category if the morphisms from C to any object A are 1-1 correspondence with the *cones* from P to A; such a *cone** (drawn as a geometrical cone in the figures) is defined by a family (s_i) of morphisms from P_i to A well correlated by the morphisms of P.

Roughly the colimit "binds" the pattern into a whole which forgets the internal organization of P, just recording its operational role. It follows that, while a pattern has at most one colimit (up to an isomorphism), several patterns may have the same colimit.

A Hierarchical Evolutive System and Its Memory

Whence the definition of a hierarchy of complexity levels in an Evolutive System:

Definition

(i) A category is *hierarchical* if each object is attributed a natural number (from 0 to m) called its *complexity level* satisfying the following condition: If the level of an object C is $n + 1$, there is at least one lower-level pattern P (meaning that all its P_i are of levels $\leq n$) such that C is the colimit of P. We also say that P is a lower-level *decomposition* of C and that C is the *binding* of P.

(ii) A *Hierarchical Evolutive System* (or HES) is an Evolutive System in which each configuration category is hierarchical and the transitions preserve the complexity level. (Cf. Fig. 1.)

We have said that, for a system to develop anticipatory processes, it must possess a memory. In a HES, the memory is modeled by a hierarchical evolutive subsystem, still called *memory*, which acts as a long-term memory of the HES and develops over time.

Ramifications of a Complex Component

By definition of a HES, for each t, a component C has an internal organization into a lower-level pattern P; now each component P_i of P has itself a lower-level decomposition Π^i of which P_i is the colimit at t and so on down to patterns of level 0. In this way, we construct a *ramification* of C (cf. Figs. 1 and 2); the set of its patterns of level 0 is called its *base*. A ramification is a kind of interlaced treelike structure since its components of each intermediate step ramify themselves into shorter ramifications which are subject to the constraints introduced by the links of the interlacing patterns Π^i. It allows reconstructing C, from the basis B of level 0 of the ramification, by successive interdependent colimit operations.

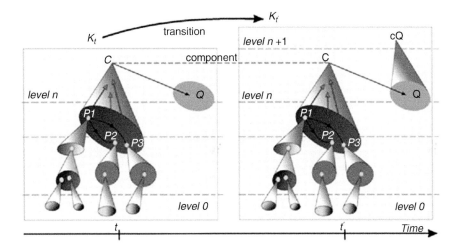

Fig. 1 Transition between two configurations of a HES, with a ramification of the component C

Fig. 2 Two ramifications of C

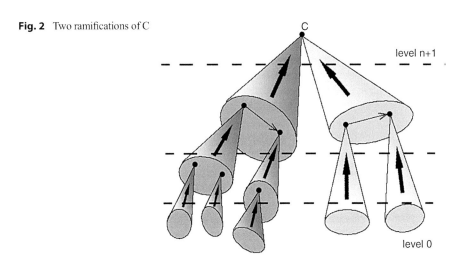

   C may have several ramifications, simultaneously or not (in particular if C is multifaceted, cf. section "Multifaceted Components: Multiplicity Principle"). The *complexity order* of C is defined as the shortest length of its various ramifications; it is less than or equal to the level of C; it measures the smallest number of steps necessary to reconstruct C from the basis of one of its ramifications up (to be compared to the Kolmogorov algorithmic definition of the complexity of a string as the length of its shortest possible description in some fixed description language, Kolmogorov 1968). Components of high-complexity orders play an important role in anticipation (cf. section "Development of Collective Anticipatory Processes").

Multifaceted Components: Multiplicity Principle

In the memory of the system, components with high-complexity orders represent elaborate knowledge, and they play an important role in the formation of anticipatory processes. However, for these processes to give helpful indications, the information they use must be up to date, and this requires that the memory adapts to changes. What property should the system have to develop such a flexible and plastic memory? It needs a kind of "horizontal" complexity, complementary to the "vertical" organization given by the ramifications, namely, the existence of *multifaceted components*. It is proved (EV 1996, 2007) that the existence of multifaceted components is at the root of both the flexibility of the system and the emergence of components with increasing complexity orders.

Multifaceted Components

Such a component C takes up the "challenge of being in two (or more) frames at once" (Miller et al. 2015), such as multifunction objects, or polysemous concepts in the semantic memory. Existence of such components in biological systems relies on what Edelman and Gally (2001) call "degeneracy": "the ability of elements that are structurally different to perform the same function or yield the same output ... a ubiquitous biological property." In fact this notion extends the "degeneracy of the neural code" initially introduced by Edelman (1989), which implies that a same mental object can activate different neural assemblies depending on the context. It is this kind of "operational redundancy" which is generalized in a HES under the term of "Multiplicity Principle," and it has important consequences for the system.

Formally in any HES, a component C of level $n + 1$ can (simultaneously or not) admit several non-isomorphic lower-level decompositions. Now for C to be n-*multifaceted* (cf. Figs. 3 and 4) at *t*, we impose that, in the configuration-category at t, (the state of) C admits at least two lower-level decompositions P and Q which are *structurally non-connected**; it means that P and Q are not isomorphic nor well connected by a cluster* of links between components P_i and Q_j of P and Q. Then C can operate by means of either P or Q and possibly "switch" between them, and this is an emerging global property of C. Indeed, the fact that P and Q have the same operational role at t (i.e., the same colimit C) cannot be deduced from "local" properties relating their lower-level components; it depends on the whole structure of the lower levels and becomes observable only at the level of C.

Definition A hierarchical category satisfies the *Multiplicity Principle* (or MP) if it admits n-multifaceted objects for each level $n > 0$ (EV 1996, 2007). In a HES, we suppose that all the configuration categories satisfy MP.

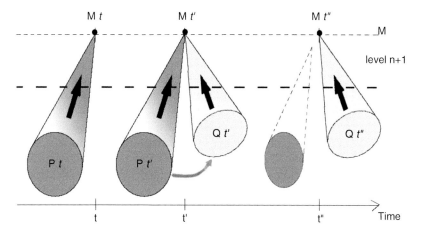

Fig. 3 Successive states of a multifaceted component M

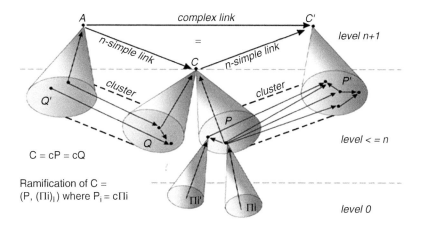

Fig. 4 Simple and complex links

Individuation of a Component Allowing for Flexibility

A component M of level $n + 1$ can admit different lower-level decompositions, either simultaneously or not. Let M have a lower-level decomposition P_t at a given time t; over time, the pattern P_t may change progressively by loss of elements, while remaining a decomposition of (the successive states of) M, up to a later time t' after which M is no longer the colimit of what remains of P. However, M may still exist and have other lower-level decompositions; the smallest period during which M keeps a same lower-level decomposition is called the *stability span* of M at t. This situation corresponds to what Matsuno (2012) calls the class/individual distinction.

For instance, the membership and internal organization of an association may vary while the association as such subsists; its stability span is related to the period during which there is little turnover in its membership. The situation is particularly interesting if M is a multifaceted component which may lose some of its lower-level decompositions and/or acquire new ones while preserving its own identity (cf. Fig. 3): at its level, it gains its own *complex identity* (or "individuation," in the sense of Simondon 2005), independent from its lower-level internal organizations.

At a time t of its life, a multifaceted component M has also several structurally non-connected ramifications representing its different "facets," and it can play a different role depending on the facet through which it operates in a given context at a given time. Thus, the Multiplicity Principle provides the system with a kind of operational flexibility. In particular, it permits that the memory contains polysemous records which are both robust and flexible enough to keep track of changes in the environment and adapt to diverse circumstances. This is important in anticipation to ensure that the memory supports relevant information.

Simple and Complex Links

In a HES, a component of a given level admits at least one decomposition into a lower-level pattern (of which it is the colimit). Is there something analogous for the links between components? It is the case only for what we call n-*simple* links, defined as follows:

Let C and C' be components of a HES which have lower-level decompositions P and P' at each t of an interval J, respectively. If there is a *cluster** (cf. Fig. 4) of well-correlated links between the components of P and of P' on J, then the cluster binds into a link from C to C' on J, called a (P, P')-*simple link*, or just n-*simple link** if P and P' are of levels $\leq$ n (cf. Fig. 4). As such a link is mediated through the links of the cluster it binds, the information it transmits from C to C' reduces to the information already transmitted between their lower-level components P_i and P'_j.

A main consequence of MP is the emergence of n-*complex links** which are composites of n-simple links which are not n-simple. Indeed, a composite of n-simple links binding non-adjacent clusters, separated by a switch (cf. Fig. 4), may not bind a cluster of lower-level links between components of the extreme patterns Q' and P'. Such composites, called n-*complex links*, represent new properties which, though depending on the global structure of the levels $\leq$ n, only emerge at the level n + 1.

If we think of simple links between components as rules governing their interactions, complex links correspond to higher-order "rules" which change such rules of interaction. This agrees with Poli (2009): "an adaptive system needs both (1) rules governing the system's interactions $<\ldots>$, and (2) a higher-order layer that can change such rules of interaction."

In a system in which all the links would be simple, the *Reduction Theorem** (EV, Ehresmann and Vanbremeersch 1996; cf. Appendix A.1) implies that all components would be of complexity order 0 (in they are of level 0) or 1; this characterizes the case of a *pure reductionism*. Complex links play an essential role in the emergence of higher complexity as shown in the next section.

Complexification Process at the Root of Emergence

In an anticipatory process, "the choice of the action to perform depends on the system's anticipations of the evolution of itself and/or the environment in which it is situated" (Poli 2009).

In a HES, to anticipate requires evaluating the consequences of a procedure selected on a configuration category in function of what is known of the structure of the system, its possible evolution, and its preceding experiences (recalled from its memory).

The complexification process will help evaluating the direct consequences and their own long-term effects. It also shows that the existence of complex links (due to MP) is at the basis of the emergence of multifaceted components of higher-complexity orders, themselves connected by complex links. Iterated complexifications can lead to "real" novelty, but their results are unpredictable.

Anticipation of Changes

As we have seen, in the evolution of multilevel systems, the transitions between configurations are generated by two kinds of changes:

(i) *Dynamical changes of the states* of its components and links (measured via their attributes, e.g., change of activity of a component, change of propagation delay or strength of a link).

(ii) *Structural changes* of the configurations corresponding to the "standard changes": birth, death, collision, and scission of Thom (1988)

For instance, in an enterprise, some employees depart, and others arrive; a new department can be formally created to increase the cooperation between different workshops. In the memory of a HES, it is important to discard no more valid data, to acquire new data, and to develop more elaborate knowledge integrating different modes; in particular, in MENS, more and more complex mental objects, cognitive processes, and concepts are formed.

Given the configuration of the system at t, the anticipation problem consists in selecting some specific changes to effect on it and in trying to evaluate what would be the results.

(i) If the anticipation is on a short period and if only dynamical changes of states are asked for, they can generally be modeled using classical dynamical systems (e.g., described by differential equations) or probability models. It will often be the case in the landscape of a co-regulator during one of its steps (cf. section "MES and Their Internal Multi-Agent Organization").

(ii) The problem is more difficult if the intended changes are structural changes, because the realization of such changes may later have important, but not initially anticipated, causal consequences. As said by Skulimowski (2011): "the decision-maker takes into account the anticipated outcomes of future decision problem linked by causal relations with the present one."

Causal Consequences of Structural Changes

In Hierarchical Evolutive Systems, the structural changes are of the following kinds: introduction of new elements; suppression of some components or links, eventually by decomposition of a complex component; and formation (or preservation, if it already exists) of a more complex component combining some given patterns of interacting components.

Let Pr be a procedure selected on the configuration category K_t of the system at a given time t in view of effectuating some specific changes of the above kinds. To respect the properties of a HES, the realization of the procedure will at least impose the following other changes:

(i) The suppression of a component necessitates the suppression of all the links issued from, or going to it; the suppression of a link necessitates the suppression of the components it connects (by definition of a category).

(ii) The combination of a pattern P' into a new component cP' "forces" this cP' to acquire the same operational role as P' with respect to any other existing component A ("universal property" of the colimit cP' of P'); this leads, for each cone from P' to A, to the formation of a link from cP' to A "binding" this cone.

(iii) Each path of links must have a composite which can be a complex link (as c in the Fig. 5).

And, for the same reason, these imposed new changes are themselves at the origin of other similar new changes and so on.

The interest of our categorical approach is that it allows "anticipating" the consecutive needed changes using the categorical *complexification process* (EV 1987). This process describes what would be the new configuration of the system after realization of the procedure Pr, namely, it would be the *complexification** of K_t *for* Pr, as defined hereafter.

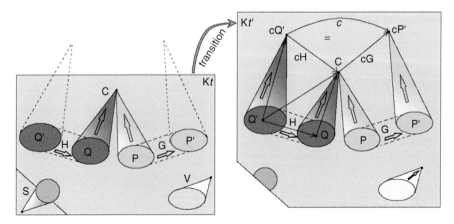

Fig. 5 The category K_t and a complexification; the clusters G and H are bound into cG and cH, respectively, and there emerges a complex link c which becomes their composite

The Complexification Process

Formally, a procedure Pr of the kind considered above defines a semi-sketch (EV 1987):

A *semi-sketch** Pr on a category K consists of the following data: a set S of elements of K, a set Π of patterns P' in K which have no colimit in K, and a set Λ of cones V in K. The *complexification process** "universally" constructs a category K' containing K\S and in which the patterns P' in Π acquire a colimit cP' and the cones in Λ become colimit cones.

Complexification Theorem   *Given a semi-sketch* Pr = (S, Π, Λ) *on the category* K, *there is a "universal solution" to the problem: to construct a category* K' *and a functor* F *from a subcategory* K° *of* K *to* K' *verifying the conditions:* (i) *K° does not contain the elements of* S; (ii) *for each* P' *in* Π, *the pattern* FP' *image of* P' *by* F *admits a colimit* cP' *in* K'; *and* (iii) *the images by* F *of the cones in* Λ *are colimit-cones in* K'.

The category K' which is the universal solution is called the *complexification of* K *for* Pr. It can be explicitly constructed by recurrence if Π and Λ are finite (cf. EV 1987). We give the main ideas of the construction in Appendix A.2.

Iterated Complexifications

In a hierarchical category K satisfying the Multiplicity Principle, the construction of the complexification K' of K for Pr may introduce complex links c (cf. Fig. 5 and Appendix A.2). As said in section "Multifaceted Components: Multiplicity Principle," a complex link represents emerging properties at its level, reflecting the global structure of the lower levels; for a social system, they reflect "change in the conditions of change" (Popper 2002) which should play an important role for anticipation. Indeed, these new emergent properties, which were not observable in K, may lead to global changes, for instance, to the emergence, in a complexification K'' of K', of new objects of higher-complexity orders, which could not be anticipated in K. Such changes explain how iterated complexifications can lead to real novelty.

Emergence Theorem   *In a Hierarchical Evolutive System (such as a MES), iterated complexifications of a configuration category* K_t *are not always reducible to a unique complexification of this category* K_t, *and then they lead to the emergence of multifaceted components of higher and higher-complexity orders and of complex links between them* (EV 1987).

A consequence of this theorem is the *unpredictability* of the long-term evolution of the system (cf. EV 2007).

An important application of this Emergence Theorem is the construction of the model MENS (section "Introduction"), for a neuro-cognitive system, by iterated complexifications of the Neural Evolutive System Neur (cf. section "Categorical Definition of an Evolutive System").

The Role of Dynamical Changes

In section "Causal Consequences of Structural Changes," we have studied the case of anticipatory processes aiming to structural changes without discussing their possible effect on the physical, temporal, and dynamical constraints to which are subjected the successive states of the components and links.

By construction, the complexification of the configuration K_t for Pr satisfies the objectives of Pr and respects the categorical constraints. However, to become a new configuration of a "real" system at a later time t', it must also be able to satisfy the different dynamical constraints imposed on the states of the components and links, e.g., by their activity, propagation delay, and strength. Moreover, the time taken to realize the process depends on the length of time necessary for "physically" realizing the changes induced by the successive steps of the complexification. For instance, the formation of a higher-order component by unfolding a ramification from its 0-level base B up requires some *activation delay* (cf. section "MES and Their Internal Multi-Agent Organization"), depending on the propagation delays of the links connecting a component in B to C.

Thus, the physical and temporal constraints impose limits on the selection of a procedure. Though the complexification can "theoretically" be constructed for any semi-sketch, it might fail to give a "real-world" solution of the corresponding anticipation process because it would transgress some dynamical constraints of the states. In this case, the solution can be to replace this constraint by a less restrictive one. Let us give an example: if we impose that the propagation delay of a composite link always be the sum of the propagation delays of its factors, it is shown (EV Ehresmann and Vanbremeersch 2009) that only some patterns P (called "polychronous" by Izhikevitch et al., Izhikevich 2004) can be combined in a new component (which becomes their colimit); in this case, we must select semi-sketches of which the patterns in Π are polychronous patterns or accept to by-pass the sum-delay constraint.

On the other hand, dynamic and structural changes can interplay. For instance, in MENS (section "Introduction"), a cat-neuron representing a mental object M is constructed, via a complexification process of Neur, as the colimit C of a neural pattern activated by M. Now Hebb (1949) shows that the formation of a "synchronous assembly of neurons" consists in the strengthening of the weight of the synapses between its neurons; thus a purely dynamic change (increase of weights) "causes" the structural change consisting in the emergence of C.

MES and Their Internal Multi-Agent Organization

A HES gives an "external" view of the system during its evolution, with the transitions featuring the changes between two instants but it does not inform us on the internal processes responsible for these changes. Now we are going to study the dynamic of the system in its internal "becoming."

The complex (e.g., social) systems able to develop anticipatory processes are self-organized thanks to an internal "multi-agent" organization: their global dynamic is the result of the competition/cooperation between the local dynamics of a network of internal regulation organs of various complexities. Each such "co-regulator" operates stepwise, at its own rhythm, with only a partial view of the global system in its "landscape" and a differential access to the memory.

For instance, in an enterprise, the different workshops and departments up to the managerial level act as such co-regulators; in MENS, the co-regulators are "based" on brain modules from small treatment units to large brain areas. A co-regulator may act as a reactive system if it has only one preset procedure in response to a given stimulus; others, individually or collectively, can be able to develop intricate anticipatory processes (cf. section "Development of Collective Anticipatory Processes").

Self-Organization in Memory Evolutive Systems

To formally model such an organization in a HES, we define:
A *Memory Evolutive System* (MES) as a HES equipped with:

(i)   A hierarchical evolutive subsystem *Memory*, modeling the long-term memory of the system
(ii) A network of evolutive functional subsystems, called *Co-regulators*, modeling internal regulatory agents
(iii) Different temporalities imposing more dynamic constraints

Up to now, all the results on HES (apart from section "The Role of Dynamical Changes") are purely "categorical," the dynamic playing no specific role. The definitions and the constructions would remain the same whatever would be the objects and morphisms of the configuration categories, and time could be replaced by any total order.

From now on, it will be different: as said in section "Evolutive Systems," a MES deals with different temporalities, and the dynamic changes occurring in the states of components and links (in particular their activity) are essential. Thus we need to fix the terminology.

Let us recall that a component C is a dynamic entity consisting of its successive states C_t during its lifetime. Among the attributes defining its successive states, we will distinguish its *activity* which is a function a from its lifetime to $\mathbf{R}$; a(t) is called the *activity* of C at t, and we say that C is *activated at* t if the function a increases at t.

A link f from C to C′ has also an activity which reduces to 0 or 1, a *propagation delay* p and a *strength* w, both with real values; f is *active* at t if its activity at t is 1 (meaning it transmits information), "passive" at t otherwise. If C is activated at t, it can activate the link f; if f is active from t to t + d(t) and has a sufficient strength, then it can activate C′ at t + d(t). In specific examples, for instance, MENS (EV Ehresmann and Vanbremeersch 2009), these assertions are made more precise.

The activation of a higher-level component C will consist in the unfolding of one of its ramifications from its level 0 base up to C: first the level 0 patterns are activated, then their colimits (via the canonical links to the colimit), then activation of the patterns formed by the colimits, and so on up to C. Thus C has an *activation delay*, sum of the propagation delays of the successive activated links.

The Memory and the Co-regulators

Here we consider a MES. By definition, it has a sub-HES representing its memory.

The *Memory*

The components of the sub-HES *Memory,* called *records,* are strongly connected. They represent knowledge of any nature of the system: explicit knowledge such as data, significant information, previous experiences, and concepts (in the *semantic* memory; for its construction using projective limits, cf. Ehresmann and Vanbremeersch 2007), and also implicit procedural knowledge such as skills, behaviors, and practices of different kinds (in the *procedural memory*), and possibly affects and emotions. A record Pr in the procedural memory, also called a *procept* (or, more informally, *procedure*), admits a pattern E of "effectors" which it can activate (or "command") through links from Pr to E (cf. Fig. 6).

Initially the memory consists of a few "innate" records, and it develops over time through learning, integration of new experiences, and formation of more complex records obtained by iterated combination of patterns of lower-level records. Let us note that its development through successive complexification processes provides a *"Deep Learning"* method based on category theory.

The Net of Co-regulators

Each co-regulator CR is a functional evolutive subsystem with its own complexity, rhythm, logic, and differential access to the Memory; for instance, there are

Fig. 6 The landscape of CR is an ES having the curved arrows for components (the links between them are commutative squares b, c,...)

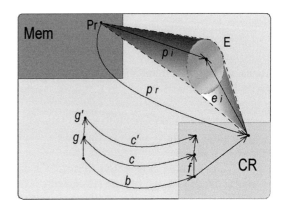

co-regulators acting as "receptors," "effectors," or with a specific function (e.g., a CR based on visual modules in MENS). The components of CR are of a definite complexity level which determines the complexity of CR. Its rhythm is defined by a discrete timescale which delimits its successive steps. Its differential access to the memory allows CR to store successive events and to store or retrieve some *admissible procepts* Pr related to its function; the effectors E of Pr can then be directly activated by CR (via the links Θi in Fig. 6); CR may have several admissible procepts (or just one if it is reactive), and new ones can be later construted.

While the memory is a sub-HES, the network of co-regulators only forms a heterarchy: a co-regulator of level n + 1 does not aggregate co-regulators of lower levels, though it may send commands to them. Moreover the discrete timescales of the co-regulators can delimit steps of very different lengths; for instance, one step of a co-regulator can cover several steps of another one.

Local Dynamic of a Co-regulator

A co-regulator CR operates stepwise at its own rhythm, a step from t to t' corresponding to its "thick present" (Poli 2009) at t. Formally it is a "hybrid system" which "mixes logical decision making with the generation of continuous-valued control laws" (Branicki 2005): the logical decision-making concerns the choice of a procedure at the onset of the step, which is effected during the continuous duration of the step.

The step is divided in three more or less overlapping phases:

(i) *Observation.* CR has only a partial access to the system, through the active links which activate some of its components during the step (cf. the curved arrows in Fig. 6). Its *landscape* is modeled by an evolutive system which has these links for components.

(ii) *Decision/action.* A procedure is selected through the landscape with the help of the memory. It can be an admissible procept Pr (seen via pr in the landscape, cf. Figure 6). The procedure is executed during the step, through its commands to effectors. This will often consist in resolving differential equations with respect to the dynamic attributes of the components of the landscape.

(iii) *Evaluation.* The result is evaluated at the beginning of the next step. There is a *fracture* for CR if the objectives of the procedure are not attained. An important cause of fracture is the non-respect of the *synchronicity laws* which impose temporal structural constraints relating the duration of a step, the propagation delays, and the stability spans of the components of the landscape (cf. EV 2007, Chap. 7).

The Global Dynamic

As the needs, logics, and rhythms of the co-regulators are different, the procedures selected through their respective landscapes at a given time can be conflicting, whence an "interplay" among them to coordinate their local dynamics. This interplay is made more flexible because (thanks to MP) the effectors can be activated through any of their ramifications. Generally, we do not know how to compute it.

However, when the local dynamics of the co-regulators during one of their steps are computable by ordinary differential equations, the interplay can lead to a "hybrid dynamical system" in the sense of Branicki (2005, p. 19) which, in some particular cases, can be computed.

The global dynamic of the system results from the interplay of the co-regulators, and it may cause dysfunctions to some co-regulators whose procedures are not retained. Then there is a risk of cascades of dysfunctions backfiring between co-regulators of different complexity levels (EV Ehresmann and Vanbremeersch 2007, Chap. 7). For instance, we have explained how "dialectics" may develop between two "heterogeneous" co-regulators (with respect to their complexity and rhythm): if one step of a co-regulator CR (say a cell) covers several steps of a lower-level one CR' (at the molecular level), then CR' may operate different small changes which are not seen by CR in real time; but later their accumulation may lead to a fracture for CR; the repair of this fracture by CR may then cause a fracture to CR'.

On the long term, the global dynamic may impose sequences of structural changes at different levels, making it unpredictable. Moreover, as a MES gives a dynamical representation of the system in its "becoming," the co-regulators themselves may vary over time.

Development of Collective Anticipatory Processes

The preceding sections describe the characteristics making a system able of anticipation. Here the problem is to study how the system can learn to use the future for developing efficient anticipatory processes. While the future states of a tree depend on specific (biological) procedures stored in the tree innate memory, in a social system of any size, such as an individual, a group of people, an institution, or a society, there is a large space of possible futures. It explains the interest of increasing the "Futures Literacy" capacity (Miller 2007) of the system and using it for developing efficient anticipatory processes in relation with simple behavior, decision-taking up to managerial direction and/or future action of any kind.

Formation of a Collective "Macro-Landscape"

In a social system, let us consider a group G of persons who meet to collectively discuss of a course of action in reaction to an external or internal event or select a long-term program for a common project. It could be a board of directors of an institution, a research unit, a team of designers (cf. Béjean and Ehresmann 2015), or a FL-KnowLab (Miller 2007). The aim of the group is to sense and make sense of the situation, search and "virtually" evaluate adequate procedures or long-term scenarios for responding, and finally select one of them.

At the initial time t, the participants have varied individual expertise, some collective knowledge gained by direct experience or learning, conscious or latent (e.g., proper practices, affects), and their objectives, resources, and rhythms can be conflicting, so that the procedures each would favor can be incompatible. How to reach an agreement acceptable by all though it may cause problems to some of them?

In the MES modeling the social system, it corresponds to a case of interplay among co-regulators CR_N, by considering each member N of the group G as a (1-component) co-regulator which operates on its own landscape L_N (cf. section "Local Dynamic of a Co-regulator"). These co-regulators communicate through links between their components (as f from N to N' in Fig. 7). The subsystem of the MES containing the co-regulators CR_N and these links will be considered as a (macro-)co-regulator AN. As such, AN can form its own "landscape," with the information it can acquire on the system: this landscape is an evolutive system ML (cf. Fig. 7), called the *macro-landscape*, which has for components the links activating some components of AN during its thick present; in particular, ML contains the landscapes L_N as subsystems and interconnects them. The viewpoints of the N's will be brought closer by the formation of a G-*archetypal pattern* representing significant knowledge shared by all.

Development of a G-Archetypal Pattern

Our group G of people pursuing a common project of any kind may, by exchanges of information between them, learn to share stocks of strongly connected significant knowledge (explicit or tacit) related to the project, the organization of the group, its expertise, its values, and possibly even some affects and emotions.

Initially, a multifaceted record A such as a polysemous concept can have different meanings for two members N and N' of G; by exchange between them, they can share their views and give to A a common enriched meaning encompassing both. We say that A becomes a G-*shared record* for G if it acquires a common meaning for all

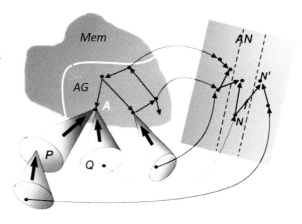

Fig. 7 Construction of the Archetypal Pattern AG of G and of the macro-landscape ML with the curved arrows as components

the members of AN. This notion is stronger than that of a boundary object (Star and Griesemer 1989).

In the MES modeling the social system, the meaning of A for N depends on the ramification(s) through which N can recall A. Thus, A becomes a G-*shared record* if different components N of AN can recall it through the unfolding of the same ramifications. Whence the definition:

The G-*Archetypal Pattern* of the group G is defined as an evolutive subsystem AG of the memory which consists of often recalled G-shared multifaceted records of higher-complexity order, combining patterns of significant knowledge of various modalities (explicit, tacit, or latent). These G-*archetypal records* are connected by strong complex links which form *archetypal loops* self-maintaining their activity for some time. (The development of AG is a consequence of the Emergence Theorem.)

The formation of AG helps sharing not only explicit knowledge but also some tacit knowledge (e.g., tacit procedures, skills), eventually some emotions; it can also transform tacit into explicit. AG will act as a motor for the development of collective intelligence in G and of anticipatory processes thanks to the following property of AG:

(A) Over time, the activation of an archetypal record diffuses in AG through archetypal loops and diffuses to lower levels through ramifications and switches between them, thus activating a large domain of the memory; moreover, this activation is self-maintained by that of AG (cf. Fig. 7).

The notion of the Archetypal Pattern for a group G during its common endeavors has been defined by analogy with the notion of the *Archetypal Core** (EV 2007, 2009) of a person, say N, in the model MENS of a neuro-cognitive system. This AC is at the root of both the emergence of higher cognitive processes and of phenomenological experiences (cf. Ehresmann and Gomez-Ramirez 2015).

If N is a member of G, the activation of a link from a G-archetypal record A to N (in ML) stimulates a mental object of N, presented by a record, say A_N in MENS, which is generally not archetypal; however, the activation of A_N may diffuse to part of the AC of N. Thus, the G-archetypal pattern may simultaneously provoke activations in the archetypal cores of the members of the group; however, these activations are of different natures, since they entirely depend on the specific personality of each N.

The Retrospection and Prospection Processes

Let us come back to the macro-landscape ML. The activation of a part of the G-archetypal pattern AG leads to a progressive increase in the number of components of ML. Indeed, due to the property (A) above when a G-archetypal record A is activated, it activates part of AG through archetypal loops and diffuses the activation to a large part of the memory from higher to lower levels of complexity, including tacit memories. This activation activates links from the memory to AN, which then become components of ML. Moreover, as the archetypal loops self-maintain the activation, these components remain activated for a long period. Thus, the thick present of AN is longer than the initial thick presents of the individual co-regulators CR_N, so that their initial landscapes L_N are "extended" both with respect to the number of components, to their complexity orders, and to their temporal extent.

The formation of AC and the analysis of ML correspond to a *retrospection process* which allows sensing and making sense of the present situation, its trends, and future potential, in relation with the past (the unfolding of a ramification recalls past lower level events due to its activation delay). ML presents a common "mental space" for AN in which current observations and new trends (or even weak signals) can be related to past situations to make sense of them.

This retrospection phase is followed by a *prospection process*: it consists in the search of procedures (or semi-sketches) Pr on ML and their "virtual" evaluation by the formal construction of the complexification of ML for Pr and the verification of its compatibility with the states' dynamical constraints.

An anticipatory process may necessitate a succession of partly overlapping retrospection-prospection-complexification processes abutting to various long-term "scenarios." The scenarios may concern three different kinds of futures: optimization futures (forecasting), contingent futures (foresighting), and real novelty. The first one relies on dynamical changes extrapolated from the present situation, while the others necessitate some structural changes. For as much as anticipation requires creativity, they can be compared to the three types of creativity distinguished by M. Boden (2004): exploratory, combinatory, and transformational creativity. *True Novelty* can be attained only by a recursive process leading to successive complexifications: the first one introduces complex links which modify the initial "rules" ("change in the condition of change") and can only be slowly integrated. An internal reorganization integrating these new rules is necessary so that they may be taken into account in the following macro-landscape and then play a major role in subsequent complexifications (as ascertained by the *Emergence Theorem*, section "Complexification Process at the Root of Emergence").

Application to the FL Method

The FL method (Miller 2007) aims to progressively develop the Futures Literacy capacity of a group of people (e.g., in a FL-KnowLab) by experimentally forming different kinds of scenarios. It is divided in three phases:

FL1. *"Revealing existing anticipatory assumptions."* Development of scenarios for desired or probable futures which "extrapolate" from the present. In MES, it corresponds to the construction of various scenarios extrapolating the present situation while respecting its main dynamical constraints and values. It is related to Boden's exploratory creativity.

FL2. *"Reframing, inventing new anticipatory assumptions."* Development of imaginative scenarios for the future, which could necessitate changes of rules and of power allocation among the actors and might be locally or even globally destructive. They correspond to scenarios forcing structural changes which may not preserve all the dynamical constraints and main values of the present. It is related to Boden's combinatorial creativity.

FL3. *"A capacity to think about changes in the conditions of change."*

Using learning from FL1 and FL2, development of scenarios leading to "possible" novel futures which are imaginative though preserving some essential values V and dynamical constraints. They could also be called *transformational futures* (in the sense of Boden's transformational creativity). They are obtained by successive complexifications introducing complex links at the basis of the "novelty"; however, the successive transformations should be progressive enough for not causing serious disruptions. The problem is not only to select an imaginative scenario S at t, but also to find what successive transformations would be necessary to realize S and how decisions could be taken at t to favor the later realization of S. These transformations should respect the values V but may allow that less essential values become no more necessary, for instance, because of the slow modification of social representations adding or suppressing some constraints or political changes which modify power attribution.

Conclusion

This chapter proposes a methodology for developing and evaluating anticipatory processes in multi-scale, multi-agent evolutionary systems "able to take decisions according to their possible future development" (Miller el al. 2015), for instance, social systems of different sizes from small social groups to large institutions or societies. It is presented in the frame of the Memory Evolutive Systems (MES), a mathematical model for such systems, based on a "dynamic" category theory. This model identifies the main characteristics a system should have to become "Futures Literate" and develop efficient anticipatory processes: it is a kind of operational redundancy expressed by the *Multiplicity Principle* (MP) at the root of the emergence over time of *multifaceted* components of higher and higher-complexity orders which take their own individuation. It allows the development of a hierarchical *Memory* which is both robust and flexible.

In section "Development of Collective Anticipatory Processes," we show how a group of people working together can share their most significant knowledge and form an "archetypal pattern" of the group. This pattern acts as a motor for the development of anticipatory processes which rely on sequences of three partly overlapping processes:

(i) A *retrospection* process to sense and make sense of the present situation and discern new trends
(ii) A *prospection* process which uses its "futures capacity" to explore various long term scenarios

(iii) A *complexification process* to virtually evaluate these scenarios. The *scenarios* can be "conservative" and just extrapolate the present or more innovative such as "transformational" scenarios which necessitate iterated *complexification* processes introducing changes in the conditions of change.

Acknowledgments I thank the referee for his careful reading and interesting suggestions and references.

Appendix

Basic Notions of Category Theory

For more details on Category Theory, cf. the book of Mac Lane (1971).

In this chapter, a *graph* (or more precisely directed multi-graph) consists of a set of objects (its vertices) and a set of arrows (or directed edges) between them.

A *category* K is a graph equipped with an internal *composition law* which maps a path (f: A $\rightarrow$ B, g: B $\rightarrow$ C) from A to C on an arrow gf: A $\rightarrow$ C (called its *composite*) and which satisfies the conditions: it is associative and each vertex A has an identity id_A: A $\rightarrow$ A; a vertex of the graph is called an *object* of K and an arrow a *morphism* or a *link*.

A *functor* k from K to K' is a map which associates to each object of K an object k (A) of K', to each arrow from A to B in K an arrow from k(A) to k(B) in K' and which preserves identities and composition. A partial functor from K to K' is a functor from a sub-category of K to K'.

Yoneda Lemma. Two objects A and B of K are isomorphic if and only if the functors Hom(A, $-$) and Hom(B, $-$) are equivalent, where Hom(A, $-$): K $\rightarrow$ *Sets* associates to an object C the set Hom(A, C) of morphisms f from A to C, and to g: C $\rightarrow$ C' the map Hom(A, g) mapping f onto the composite gf.

An *Evolutive system* (EV 1987) is a functor from the category associated to a total order (in this paper, the order induced by **R** on a part T of **R**) to the category *ParCat* of partial functors between (small) categories.

A *pattern in* K (also called a *diagram*) is defined as a homomorphism P of a graph sP to K mapping an object i of sP on P_i and an arrow x: i $\rightarrow$ j of sP on the morphism f = P(x): $P_i \rightarrow P_j$. The P_i are called components of P and the P(x) the (given) links of P.

A *cone* from a pattern P to A is a family of morphisms s_i: $P_i \rightarrow$ A satisfying the equations $s_i = s_j P(x)$ for each x: i $\rightarrow$ j of sP. The definition of a cone using explicitly the composition law: a cone cannot be defined in a graph which is not a category.

cP is the *colimit* (or *binding*) of the pattern P in K if there is a *colimit-cone* $(c_i)_i$ from P to cP such that, for each cone $(s_i)_i$ from P to A, there is one and only one morphism s binding it, meaning that s: cP $\rightarrow$ A satisfies the equation $s_i = sc_i$ for each i. If the colimit exists, it is unique (up to an isomorphism); however, different patterns may have the same colimit without being isomorphic.

A *cluster* from P to a pattern P' is a maximal set G of links satisfying the following conditions: (i) For each P_i there is at least one link in G from P_i to some

P'$_j$; and if there are several such links, they are correlated by a zigzag of links of P'. (ii) The composite of a link in G with a link of P' and the composite of a link of P with a morphism in G belong to G.

If P and P' have respectively colimits C and C', it follows from the definition of a colimit that the cluster G binds into a unique morphism cG from C to C'; it is called a (P, P')-*simple link.* (cf. Figure 4.)

In a category, two patterns with the same colimit C are *structurally non-connected* if they are not isomorphic and there is no cluster between them binding into the identity of C. In this case, C is said to be *multifaceted.*

Reduction Theorem In a hierarchical category, let (P, (Π^i)) *be a ramification of an object* C *of level* 2 (EV 1996). *If all the morphisms in* P *are simple, then the complexity order of* C *is* 1. *If one of the morphisms of* P *is complex,* C *can be of complexity order* 2. *This result extends to higher levels.*

In the first case, C is also the (simple) colimit of a pattern of level 0 whose objects are all the objects of the different Π^i and the morphisms are generated by those of the Π^i and those of the clusters that the morphisms of P bind. Such a pattern does not exist in the second case.

The Complexification Process

A(n inductive) *semi-sketch* on a category K consists in data Pr = (S, A, Π, Λ) where S is a subset of K, A a graph, Π a set of patterns in K without a colimit in K, and Λ a set of inductive cones in K.

A *model* of S in a category M is a functor F from the largest sub-category included in (KUA)\S to M such that (i) the image by F of the cones in Λ are colimit-cones in M and (ii) FP' admits a colimit cP' in M for each P' in Π.

Complexification Theorem *A semi-sketch* Pr *on a category* K *has an "initial" model* F: $K^\circ \rightarrow$ K'; *the category* K' *is called the complexification of* K *for* Pr.

Let us sketch the construction of K'. The objects of K' are the objects of K not suppressed by Pr and, for each pattern P' in Π, a new object cP' which becomes the colimit of P' in K' (if 2 patterns P' and P'' have the same operational role n K, we take cP' = cP''). The morphisms are constructed in successive steps, to "force" cP' to become the colimit of P' and to ensure that each path of morphisms admits a composite. For instance (cf. Fig. 5), if P and Q are patterns having a colimit C, a cluster G of links from P to P' ϵ Π must bind into a new simple link cG from C to cP', and a cluster H form Q' to Q binds into a new cH; then the path (cH, cG) from cQ' to cP' consisting of simple links binding non-adjacent clusters must have a composite c which is a complex link from cQ' to cP'.

The interest of the complexification process is that it allows for the emergence of higher-complexity order components with complex links between them, due to the Theorem:

Iterated Complexification Theorem *Let K' be a complexification of a hierarchical category K satisfying MP and K'' be a complexification of K' (EV 2007). Then K'' may admit multifold objects of a higher complexity order than K and complex links between them. And there may be no semi-sketch on K for which K'' would be the (first) complexification of K.*

More precisely, let us take a semi-sketch Pr' $= (S', \Pi', \Lambda')$ on K' such that one of the patterns R in Π' contains a complex link c which has emerged in K'. The complexification K'' adds a colimit cR to R, and the complexity order of cR is higher than that of the objects of R because of the Reduction Theorem.

Remark In a complexification process, we can think of the category as a material cause and the procedure as an efficient cause. Then the fact that, in a MES representing an organism, two successive complexifications might not be reduced to a unique one justifies the hypothesis of Rosen (1985a) that organisms are characterized by the separation of material and efficient Aristotle's causes (cf. EV 2007).

The Archetypal Core

In the model MENS for a neuro-cognitive system (cf. section "Different Kinds of Anticipation"), the *Archetypal Core* (EV 2007, 2009) is an evolutive subsystem AC forming a higher-level hub of the memory. It consists of often recalled multifaceted records of higher-complexity order, which blend factual or conceptual knowledge, associated past experiences with their sensations, and affects and values; these records are strongly connected by loops of strong complex links self-maintaining their activity for some time. Formally, it is constructed through successive complexifications of the *structural core* of the brain, a strongly connected central part of the human cortex (discovered by Hagmann et al. 2008) which gives "an important structural basis for shaping large-scale brain dynamics."

AC acts as a motor for the development of higher cognitive processes such as consciousness, creativity, and anticipation (EV 2009).

References

Béjean, M., & Ehresmann, A. (2015). D-MES: Conceptualizing the working designers. *International Journal of Design Management and Professional Practice, 9*(4), 1–20.

Boden, M. (2004). *The creative mind; myths and mechanisms* (2nd ed.). London: Routledge.

Branicki, M. S. (2005). Introduction to hybrid systems. In *Handbook of networked and embedded control systems* (pp. 91–116). Online: https://www.researchgate.net/publication/226587773

Edelman, G. (1989). The remembered Present: a biological theory of consciousness. New York: Basic Books.

Edelman, G., & Gally, J. (2001). Degeneracy and complexity in biological systems. *Proceedings of the National Academy of Sciences of the United States of America, 98*, 13763–13768.

Ehresmann, A., & Gomez-Ramirez, J. (2015). Conciliating neuroscience and phenomenology via category theory. *Progress in Biophysics and Molecular Biology (JPMB), 119*(2), 340–359. Elsevier.

Ehresmann, A., & Vanbremeersch, J.-P. (1987). Hierarchical evolutive systems: A mathematical model for complex systems. *Bulletin of Mathematical Biology, 49*(1), 13–50.

Ehresmann, A., & Vanbremeersch, J.-P. (1996). Multiplicity principle and emergence in MES. *Journal of Systems Analysis, Modelling, Simulation, 26*, 81–117.

Ehresmann, A., & Vanbremeersch, J.-P. (2007). *Memory evolutive systems: Hierarchy, emergence, cognition*. Elsevier. Amsterdam.

Ehresmann, A., & Vanbremeersch, J.-P. (2009). A propos des Systèmes Evolutifs à Mémoire et du modèle MENS, *Compte-rendu du SIC*, Paris. Online: http://ehres.pagesperso-orange.fr.

Eilenberg, S., & Mac Lane, S. (1945). General theory of natural equivalences. *Transactions of the American Mathematical Society, 58*(2), 231.

Hagmann, P., Cammoun, L., Gigandet, X., Meuli, R., Honey, C.J., Wedeen, V.J., Sporns, O., Friston, K.J. (2008). Mapping the structural core of human cerebral cortex. *PLoS Biology*, 6(7):e159

Healy, M. J. (2010). Category theory as a mathematics for formalizing ontologies. In R. Poli et al. (Eds.), *Theory and applications of ontology: Computer applications* (pp. 487–510). Springer. New York.

Hebb, D. O. (1949). *The organization of behaviour*. New York: Wiley.

Izhikevich, E., Gally, J., & Edelman, G. (2004). Spike-timing dynamics of neuronal groups. *Cerebral Cortex, 14*, 933–944.

Jacob, F. (1970), La logique du vivant, Gallimard, Paris.

Kan, D. (1958). Adjoint functors. *Transactions of the American Mathematical Society, 89*, 294–329.

Kolmogorov, A. (1968). Logical basis for information theory and probability theory. *IEEE Transactions on Information Theory, 14*(5), 662–664.

Longo, G., Montévil, M., & Kauffman, S. (2012). No entailing laws, but enablement in the evolution of the biosphere, *Archiv* 1201–2069.v1.

Mac Lane, S. (1971). *Categories for the working mathematician*. New York: Springer.

Matsuno, K. (2012). Time in biology as a marker of the class identity of molecules. In P. Simeonov, L. Smith, & A. Ehresmann (Eds.), *Integral biomathics: Tracing the road to reality* (pp. 269–277). Berlin: Springer.

Miller, R. (2007). Futures literacy: A hybrid strategic scenario method. *Futures: The Journal of Policy Planning and Future Studies, 39*, 341–362.

Miller, R., Poli, R., & Rossel, P.. (2015). The discipline of anticipation: Foundations for futures literacy. In S. Petrov (Ed.), *Dynamic being: Essays in process-relational Ontology*. CSP. Cambridge.

Poli, R. (2009). The complexity of anticipation. *Balkan Journal of Philosophy. 1*(1), 19-29.

Poli, R. (2014). *The difference between dynamical systems and process theories*, preprint.

Popper, K. (2002). *The poverty of historicism*. London: Routledge Classics.

Rosen, R. (1985a). *Anticipatory systems. Philosophical, mathematical and methodological foundations*. New York: Pergamon.

Rosen, R. (1985b). Organisms as causal systems which are not mechanisms: An essay into the nature of complexity. In R. Rosen (Ed.), *Theoretical biology and complexity: Three essays into the natural philosophy of complex systems* (pp. 165–203). Orlando: Academic.

Simondon, G. (2005). *L'individuation à la lumière des notions de formes et d'information*. Editions Jérôme Millon. Paris.

Skulimowski, A. M. J. (2011). Anticipatory networks and superanticipatory systems. In *10th International Conference on Computing Anticipatory Systems, CASYS 2011*, Liège.

Star, S., & Griesemer, J. (1989). Institutional ecology, 'translations' and boundary objects: Amateurs and professionals in Berkeley's Museum of Vertebrate Zoology, 1907–39. *Social Studies of Science, 19*(3), 387–420.

Thom, R. (1988). *Esquisse d'une Sémiophysique*. Paris: InterEditions.

Varela, F. (1996). Neurophenomenology. *Journal of Consciousness Studies, 3*, 330–350.

Andrzej M. J. Skulimowski

Contents

Abstract

This chapter presents a network structure for a class of anticipatory systems in Rosen's sense linked by causal and information transfer relations. They form a multigraph termed an *anticipatory network* (AN). The ANs were first defined in order to model a compromise solution selection process in multicriteria optimization problems. The nodes in such a network, termed optimizers, are capable of

A. M. J. Skulimowski (✉)
Department of Automatic Control and Biomedical Engineering, AGH University of Science and Technology, Krakow, Poland

International Centre for Decision Sciences and Forecasting, Progress and Business Foundation, Krakow, Poland
e-mail: ams@agh.edu.pl

selecting a nondominated solution taking into account the anticipated conse-quences of a decision to be made. Specifically, to make a decision in a problem associated to an optimizer, the decision-maker should take into account the anticipated outcomes of each future decision problem linked by a causal relation with the current one. The ANs presented in this chapter are based on an assump-tion that constraints and preference structures in nodes associated to future decision problems may depend on the values of criteria that result from solving preceding problems. The nodes of a hybrid AN may correspond to optimizers, random, conflicting, interactive, or predetermined (nonautonomous) decision problems. We will overview most relevant types of ANs, their solution concepts, and constructive solution algorithms. It will be pointed out that the structure of an anticipatory network imposes the superanticipatory property for its components. We will also present timed AN as well as further extensions of ANs with various information exchange relations. The discussion section contains a survey of real-life applications, including coordination of autonomous robotic formations, fore-sight scenario filtering, strategy building, and others.

Keywords
Anticipatory networks · Anticipatory systems · Multicriteria optimization · Superanticipatory systems · Scenarios · Foresight · Multicriteria decision-making · Preference modeling

Introduction

This chapter is devoted to investigating the causal and information transfer relations between anticipatory systems in the sense of Rosen (1985). The anticipatory deci-sion systems correspond to nodes of the network, while the relations between them form a multigraph termed an *anticipatory network* (AN). A special relation, which is fundamental to the theory presented in this chapter, is called *anticipatory feedback*. It models decision-makers' wishes to confine the scope of future decisions of a given agent to a favorite subset of all admissible decisions. Each anticipatory network must contain at least one causal and one *anticipatory feedback* relation.

The decision-making processes modeled by ANs extend earlier approaches to selecting a solution to a multicriteria optimization problem based on direct multi-stage modeling the future consequences of decisions to be made. To select the so-called best compromise (Skulimowski 1985, 1986), the most favorable conse-quences and the corresponding decision should be identified. This early model restricted the anticipatory decision making to the initial decision problem only, modeled as the unique initial node in a chain of problems. In addition, this approach did not allow the decision-makers to take into account different decision-making scenarios. These ideas have been studied further and applied in real-life situations, such as ensuring a long-term energy security or strategic planning of multistage marketing activities.

Although the above-cited papers (Skulimowski 1985, 1986) were inspired by the multicriteria decision theory and multilevel optimization and written without any prior knowledge of Rosen's anticipatory system theory, the relevant links between these theories were discovered after extending the multistage modeling of future consequences to decision networks. The fundamental question is whether the decision units in an anticipatory network can be actually regarded as anticipatory systems. The reply is affirmative under some natural assumptions, but it is not straightforward. Even if the nodes of an anticipatory network correspond to human decision-makers, one should take into account that although the latter possess capabilities to act as anticipatory systems, nevertheless many of them abstain to think anticipatorily. A more detailed discussion of these issues, referring to the notions of rationality and predictability, is provided in the next section. Generally, the concept of anticipation applied in the theory of anticipatory networks is strongly embedded into the context of different types of forward-looking activities such as forecasting, foresight, or backcasting and their interrelations. The reader is referred to the discussion of these notions in the introduction to this handbook (Poli 2017).

There exist also interesting relations of the problem of constructing the decision network to the notion of impredicativity of most complex real-life phenomena discussed in Poli (2017). The elicitation of decision node characteristics can be regarded as predicative modeling, while the anticipation of their decisions involves cognitive processes. These relations may shed more light on the idea of anticipatory networks as their impredicativity can both be seen as inherited from the theory of anticipatory systems and its fundamental feature in its own right. This follows from a limited ability to estimate the parameters of future decision problems which are used to building the network.

The ANs provide a more general approach to the compromise solution selection process in causally dependent multicriteria problems (Skulimowski 2014a). Each node in such a network is an *optimizer* capable of selecting a nondominated solution of an associated multicriteria optimization problem taking into account the anticipated consequences of a decision to be made. Optimizers can be regarded as models of decision-making aspects of simple anticipatory systems. Specifically, to make a decision in an initial problem in the network, the decision-maker responsible for generating the problem solution with the corresponding optimizer should take into account the anticipated outcomes of each future decision problem linked by a causal relation with the current one. The first class of causal relations studied in the above quoted papers fulfilled an assumption that constraints and preference structures in future decision problems may depend on the values of criteria yielded in the preceding problems. This model has been further extended to the networks of hybrid objects (Skulimowski 2012), including the nodes modeling random, conflicting, interactive, or automatic (nonautonomous) decision problems.

In the next two sections, we will present basic notions related to ANs. Then, in sections "Anticipatory Chains" and "Anticipatory Trees and General Networks," we will overview different types of anticipatory networks, their properties, solution principles, and constructive algorithms to generate anticipatory decisions. Their extensions may contain further information exchange relations. These are presented in section "Generalizations and Extensions of Anticipatory Networks." Following (Skulimowski 2014b), it will be shown that the structure of an anticipatory network imposes the superanticipatory property for its components. We will also present timed ANs and a survey of real-life applications. The latter include coordination of autonomous robotic formations (Skulimowski 2016b), foresight scenario filtering (Skulimowski et al. 2013), strategy building for a regional creativity support center (Skulimowski 2014c), and others.

Anticipatory Decision-Making in Multicriteria Problems

The problem of selecting a solution to a multicriteria optimization problem based on supplementary information on the decision-maker's preferences has been considered by many authors who have proposed a variety of preference models capable of exploring different types of additional information supplementing the preference structure generated by the criteria in the original problem formulation, cf., e.g., Steuer (1987), Ehrgott (2005), Kaliszewski (2006), and Skulimowski (2017b). One very common approach assumes that when making a choice, the decision-maker optimizes a real-valued function ν that is uncertain or cannot be expressed explicitly. This function is called a utility or value function (Debreu 1959). Specifically, the information about the future consequences of selecting an outcome is represented by a single value of ν. Once the values of ν are known, the feasible outcomes of the multicriteria problem can be linearly ordered, and the problem is converted into a scalar optimization problem.

A multilevel model of future consequences of decisions made contained in ANs constitutes an essentially different preference structure in a multicriteria optimization problem than those provided by other multicriteria decision-making methods. It extends the approach proposed in the above-cited paper Skulimowski (1985).

Its main idea can be formulated as follows:

Anticipated future consequences of a decision made and their assessments are used as sources of additional preference information to solving multicriteria decision problems.

The above principle can be regarded as an exemplification of *anticipatory feedback introduced in* (Skulimowski 2014a). Its exploitation is possible if the following two conjugate assumptions are fulfilled.

(i) The decision-maker responsible for solving a decision problem D included in the network knows the way how the solutions to preceding problems influence the parameters of decision problems causally dependent on D.

(ii) The decision-maker knows the estimates (forecasts or scenarios) of future decision problem formulations, their specific parameters and solution rules, as well as the relations binding their anticipated outcomes with feasible solutions to the current problem.

In particular, the first assumption is fulfilled by the present-time decision maker at the starting node in the network. This allows us to model the consequences of a decision to be made when solving any problem in the network.

The above model of consequences includes a theory of networked decision units, which model the decision problem to be solved and the solution process. If the decision maker solves an optimization problem then the decision units are termed *optimizers* (Skulimowski 2014a). By definition, an *optimizer* O acts on a set of feasible decisions U and selects its subset X according to the rule P that is characteristic for this decision unit. Throughout this chapter, it will be assumed that a selection rule P is equivalent to optimizing a vector function $F{:}U{\rightarrow}E$ on U, where E is a vector space with a partial order p:

$$(F : U \rightarrow E) \rightarrow \min(p). \tag{1}$$

The outcome subset resulting from the action of an optimizer O on U and F will be denoted as $X := O(U, F, p)$. If the selection rule P yields the set of Pareto-optimal points $\varPi(U, F, p)$ in the problem (1), i.e., if

$$X := \varPi(U, F, p) = \{u \in U : [\forall x \in U : x\, p\, u {\Rightarrow} x = u]\}$$

then we will omit the term X in the definition of this optimizer and denote it simply by $O{:}{=}(U, F, p)$.

Let us observe that if the model of consequences in a multicriteria decision problem appears as a chain of linked multicriteria optimizers:

$$\begin{aligned} &O_1 {\rightarrow}^{\varphi(1)} O_2 {\rightarrow}^{\varphi(2)} O_3 {\rightarrow}^{\varphi(3)} \ldots {\rightarrow}^{\varphi(n-1)} O_n, \\ &O_i := X(F_i, U_i, P_i) \text{ for } i = 1, \ldots, n, \end{aligned} \tag{2}$$

where the multifunctions $\varphi(i)$ influence the constraints in the problem O_{i+1} only then (2) is equivalent to a multilevel multicriteria programming problem (cf. Skulimowski 1985, 2014a; Nishizaki and Sakawa 2009). Furthermore, let us note that the above-defined optimizers can model decision-making processes irrespectively whether the decisions are made by a single decision-maker or by a cooperating group. The latter case leads to admitting a Pareto equilibrium which – from the formal point of view – is just an element of the set $\varPi(U, F, p)$. In both cases, nondominated decisions can be regarded *rational*, i.e., any other decision would be worse in at least one aspect from that just admitted in a rational procedure.

Optimal decisions are rational and most appropriate to model the economic and technological development processes, so the rationality assumption was already admitted in the theory presented in Skulimowski (1985, 2014a). Nevertheless, real-life decision-makers' behavior frequently cannot be classified as rational, which motivated us to include other types of decision-making models into an anticipatory network (Skulimowski 2012). If a decision-maker is rational in the above sense, i.e., if decisions are optimal with respect to a well-defined set of criteria, this assumption is a necessary prerequisite for the predictability. The latter is granted if the decision-maker's criteria and/or goals are explicitly known to an external observer. Otherwize the expectations concerning the decision choice by an agent in the future as a response to present actions could not be based on the constructive assumptions (i) and (ii).

It is to be noted that to plan informed decisions with anticipatory networks, all its decision units should be predictable. Predictability can be ensured in the networks including optimizers as well as other decision units such as conflicting games and algorithmic (nonautonomous) decision units, both deterministic or stochastic, cf. section "Hybrid Networks." Optimizers and game units will be termed *active* to emphasize the role of their corresponding decision-makers in selecting a decision autonomously (cf. this chapter, section "Hybrid Networks"; Skulimowski 2011).

The active decision units in an anticipatory network can actually be regarded as models of anticipatory systems since a rational decision-maker is always selecting a nondominated decision and uses an information about own preferences to select a compromise. It implies existence of a model of itself. This needs not be the case when decisions result from an optimization of a single criterion, where the objective is usually imposed by external actors or external circumstances and neither own preferences are taken into account nor any freewill is in play. Thus the "rationality" assumption and the multicriteria analysis framework turned out to be keys to the unification of the Rosen's ASs and ANs. The other Rosen's condition, concerning a knowledge of the environment and its future state, is fulfilled by the definition of AN.

From the point of view of the anticipatory decision theory, the nature of anticipatory phenomena that occur in the optimizers and other autonomous and predictable decision units in an anticipatory network and their subsequent algorithmic treatment are similar, if not identical. This is why when we refer in the following to a network of optimizers, the results will be valid for other predictable decision units in a general anticipatory network as well, unless it is explicitly mentioned.

From this point on, the term *causal network* will refer to the graph of a causal relation that links the criteria, constraints and preference structures in some problems to the outcomes of preceding problems with respect to the above relation. Causal networks of optimizers thus model linked multicriteria optimization problems. The causal relations between other predictable decision problems can be modeled in the same way. We assume that the functions φ linking decision units in a causal network model real-life causal dependence relations between linked problems. Moreover, the paths in the above causal network follow the decision-making process in a temporal order this will be termed the *temporal alignment* assumption. In this Chapter, the causal relations describing the decision consequences reduce to influencing the constraints U_i by outputs from the problems preceding O_i. The evolution of compromise selection mechanisms ψ_i in an anticipatory network of multicriteria optimizers can be modeled in a similar way as the influence on constraints and included in the same model as an additional type of causal relations.

Thus, the anticipatory networks model the information feedback and apply it to selecting a solution to the decision problem at a starting element in the network, taking into account the future consequences of this decision modeled by the entire anticipatory structure. An AN is termed *basic* if all its nodes are optimizers and there is exactly one node with no predecessors. From among all optimizers included in a basic anticipatory network, a real-life decision-maker characterized by a decision freedom (Skulimowski 2011) is associated to the initial problem, which has no predecessors, while the other optimizers in the network are merely models producing "would-be" decisions. This changes when considering sustainability decision units (see section "Interactive Optimizers and Sustainable Decisions") and timed anticipatory networks (see section "Timed Anticipatory Networks").

It can be observed that feedback expressed as a loop in a causal network fulfilling the temporal alignment assumption could violate the physical causality principle (e.g., the "the time travel paradox"). In macroscopic systems, where it is most likely that the causality principle holds, we assume that the causal restriction imposed by the time arrow cannot be overcome. The latter is equivalent to the assumption that the future cannot influence the past. Therefore causal networks of decision units are modeled as acyclic digraphs (cf., e.g., Christofides 1975). The influence of anticipated future optimization results on the decisions made at earlier stages can be modeled by another relation that describes an information feedback based on forecasting, foresight, expectation or anticipation. This relation corresponds to anticipation in the theory of anticipatory systems proposed by Rosen (1985) and will be termed *anticipatory feedback*. It can be defined as the *information flow concerning the anticipated output from a decision unit O_i regarded as an input to the unit O_j that precedes O_i in the causal order*. When the decision units are optimizers, the above information can be then used to specify a selection rule of the optimizer O_j. The relations of the causal influence and the anticipatory feedback, when considered jointly for the same set of decision nodes, form an *anticipatory network* of decision units.

For the sake of presentation's clarity, the impact of different models of uncertainty on the theory of anticipatory networks is not studied in this chapter. The stochastic, fuzzy, intuitionistic, or possibilistic extensions of causal and anticipatory relations, criteria, and constraints, as well as different types of additional information exchange between decision units (cf. Skulimowski 2016a) are left as a subject of further research.

Basic Notions of the Anticipatory Network Theory

Definition of a real-life network of any kind must include an explanation what do nodes (or vertices) and edges (arcs) mean. In the previous section, we defined nodes as decision units identified with the decision problem they solve at different moments of time. Here, we will describe the relations that bind the decision units and are depicted as edges of anticipatory networks.

Definition 1 *Any two active decision units $O_m = X_1(U, F, P)$ and $O_n = X_2(W, G, R)$ are in the causal influence relation "O_m influences O_n" if there exist two different outputs from O_m, $x_1, x_2 \in X_1$, such that either the choice of a decision in O_n is restricted to two different subsets of W that depend on choice of x_1 or x_2 in O_m or if the preference structure R or the choice criteria G are modified in a specified manner depending on the choice of x_1 or x_2.* ∎

Fig. 1 An example of an anticipatory network of decision units: *red lines* denote causal relations; *blue lines* denote anticipatory feedback

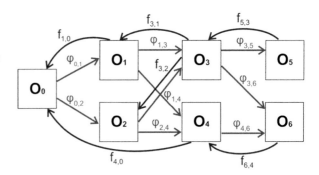

All anticipatory networks presented in this chapter are built according to the assumption that the outcomes of preceding problems can influence constraints in subsequent problems. Other types of causal relations, for example, the impact of past decisions on preference structures of future decision-makers, can also be taken into account in a similar way, but – for the brevity of presentation – these relations are not considered here. Observe that the decision problem expressed as $X_2(W, G, R)$ is *more general* than any *influenced problem* in the sense that the influence restricts the decision scope at O_n. This principle needs not be preserved for other types of influence, for example, an influence relation may extend the decision scope by relaxing or removing constraints.

An example of a basic anticipatory network is given in Fig. 1. We have assumed that the preference structures of all decision units cannot be influenced by previous decisions; therefore they are not shown in the diagram.

In the network diagram presented above, the red lines annotated $\varphi_{i,j}$ denote *direct causal influences*. The blue lines annotated $f_{i,j}$ denote the anticipatory information feedback between the decision-maker at the j-th node and anticipated outputs of the decision-making process at node i.

Besides the direct influence, we will define the *weak (or potential) causal dependence relation*, which is the negation of the relation "O_n cannot be influenced by O_m." Two decision units, O_m and O_n are weakly causally dependent iff these units are connected by a path of direct causal influences, termed a causal path.

The existence of a causal path from O_m to O_n does not ensure that the Definition 1 is fulfilled (Skulimowski 2014a). Specifically, if O_j influences O_m and O_m influences O_n it does not imply that O_j has an influence on O_n. When building an anticipatory network, it is convenient to assume that the weak causal influence relation is defined as the transitive closure (cf., e.g., Christofides 1975, for basic notions and algorithms from graph theory) of the actually identified influence relation. This is justified by the following facts:

(a) It is usually easier to prove the existence of influence than to exclude it.

(b) The number of pairs in a set of n decision units that are in an influence relation is usually considerably smaller than the quantity of all pairs of decision units, excluding self-influence, i.e., smaller than $n(n - 1)/2$.

A *general weak causal influence relation* is the transitive closure of the union of all actually observed partial causal influences of different types and of the intersection of complements of all identified influence exclusions.

If a weak causal influence relation c_w is defined first, then the causal component r of an anticipatory network can be represented as a subgraph of its transitive reduction. Since in a real-life situation the nature of future causal influences is uncertain, r can be regarded as a transitive reduction of certain unknown causal influence relation (cf. Definition 1). The latter does not need to be transitive itself, so it contains no more elements than the transitive closure of r, less than the weak causal relation c_w, but at least as much as its transitive reduction as shown in Fig. 1.

The narrow blue lines in Fig. 1 denote the anticipatory feedback relation. A blue arrow between O_n and O_m means that O_m takes into account the anticipated decision of O_n when selecting an own decision. This relation needs not be transitive.

As already announced, for simplicity's sake, in this chapter, we will provide a survey of anticipatory networks with one type of causal influence and one type of future information feedback only.

The discussion on causality in the first part of this section is of relevance for the construction of anticipatory networks and for the verification of their correctness. Specifically, if two decision units O_m and O_n are not connected by any causal relation then no anticipatory information feedback between them makes sense. Even if there exists an anticipatory information flow between O_n and O_m, then any attempt to use it will fail. Consequently, when analyzing networks with anticipatory feedback relations, it is usually sufficient to take into account only *relevant information feedbacks* (*RIF*); by definition O_n and O_m are linked by a RIF relation iff there exist both an information feedback between O_n and O_m and a weak causal influence between O_m and O_n. However, in general, for given decision units O_k, O_n, and O_m, where both O_n and O_m influence O_k, but there does not exist any direct influence between O_n and O_m, there may exist a different, indirect way of influencing the decision made at O_m by O_n (or vice versa), based on forcing O_m (or) by choosing at O_n such a way of influencing O_k so that O_m has to make a restricted choice to attain its goals at O_k. This phenomenon, called *induced anticipatory feedback*, is discussed in more detail in (Skulimowski 2016a, p. 29).

An anticipatory network is termed *solvable* if the subsequent taking into account all anticipatory information feedbacks to restrict the decision choice accordingly yields a nonempty solution set at the starting node (or nodes). To provide constructive algorithms to solving ANs of decision units, we will admit the following assumptions:

- The network is finite.
- If a decision problem O_p is directly influenced by n_p preceding problems and it influences m_p subsequent problems, then n_p, m_p, and all influence characteristics are assumed known.
- For each decision units influenced by more than one predecessor and for each type of influencing function (cf. section "Generalizations and Extensions of Anticipatory Networks"), the rules aggregating different influencing factors are defined and assumed known.

- Any decision problem O_p in the network may be linked by a finite number j_p of anticipatory information feedbacks with anticipated solutions of influenced future problems, and all feedback parameters are known.

In the next two sections we will provide a short overview of the solution methodology for the above-defined class of anticipatory decision problems.

Any anticipatory network can be decomposed into chains, which makes it possible to apply aggregated chain rules iteratively. Anticipatory trees reserve a special attention since they possess the property max $n_p = 1$ for all P active nodes in the network. If more than one predecessor can influence a decision unit, the influence aggregation rules should be defined, e.g., as intersection or union of the sets of alternatives made feasible by different preceding decision units with the causal relation (cf. Skulimowski 2016a). Similarly, the anticipatory feedback aggregation rules are defined for each optimizer or game unit linked by both anticipatory feedback and causal relationships, with more than one subsequent decision unit. They are given usually in form of a logical multiplication of the conditions imposed on the selection of decisions at O_p coming from different future decision units. In section "Anticipatory Chains" we will define an additional quantitative measure of partial satisfaction of future conditions that can be used if it is impossible to fulfill all feedback rules.

We will also present an algorithm (Skulimowski 2014a), which generates a constructive solution to multicriteria decision problems represented as a chain of optimizers. This algorithm will then be applied in section "Anticipatory Trees and General Networks" to solve anticipatory trees and general anticipatory networks.

Anticipatory Chains

A simplest possible nontrivial anticipatory network with the linear causal relation is called an *anticipatory chain*. If such a chain contains only optimizers as active decision units, it will be called a *chain of optimizers*, being thus a generalization of the problem (2) with constraints in sets U_i defined as values of multifunctions

$$Y_i : F_{i-1}(U_{i-1}) \rightarrow 2^{U_i}. \tag{3}$$

From (2) and (3), it follows that

$$\varphi(i) := Y_i \circ F_{i-1}. \tag{4}$$

Analogously, the dependence of preference relations P_i on the outcomes of previous problems in a causal chain of decision units can be modeled by the function

$$\psi : X(U_{i-1}, F_{i-1}, P_{i-1}) \ni x \rightarrow P_i. \tag{5}$$

An anticipatory chain is thus a certain number of anticipatory information feedbacks along a simple causal graph of decision units where each node may have at most one successor and one predecessor.

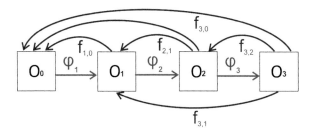

Fig. 2 An example of a chain of optimizers with anticipatory feedback consisting of four systems $O_i=(U_i,F_i, p_i)$, $i = 0,1,\ldots3$, with $F_i:=\mathrm{id}_{U_i}$, therefore $\varphi(i) \equiv Y_i$, U_i ordered by the partial order p_i, causal relations defined by multifunctions $\varphi(i)$, and six anticipatory feedback relations $f_{j,i}$ (*blue arrows*). The temporal order is determined by causal relations (*red arrows*)

Figure 2 contains an example of a chain of four optimizers. All optimizers except (perhaps) O_3 are anticipatory systems and select their solutions based on the outcomes of other optimizers. The decision-maker at the initial problem O_0 makes the decision based on the model of future decision-making processes at O_1, O_2, and O_3, while a decision-maker at $O_1=(U_1, F_1, P_1)$ will make its decision taking into account the anticipated outcomes at O_2 and O_3, and O_2 takes into account the anticipated decisions at O_3.

Although chains are the simplest class of anticipatory networks, they are important since a large class of anticipatory networks can be reduced to a sequential analysis of all its subchains.

Two algorithms for solving the anticipatory decision choice problem at the initial node $O_0:= (U_0, F_0, P_0)$ in a chain of optimizers O_i, $i = 0, 1, \ldots, N$, with discrete admissible decision sets U_i, have been given in Skulimowski (2014a). We have merged them and provide in this section as Algorithm 1. Causal relations between optimizers are defined as multifunctions $\varphi(i)$ that constrain the scope of admissible decisions of O_i and depend on solutions of previous problems O_{i-1}, for $i = 1,\ldots,N$. The following definitions will be helpful to describe the solution procedure in a more rigid manner.

Definition 2 *Let O_i, $i = 0,1,\ldots,N$ be an anticipatory chain. For each $i = 0, \ldots, N - 1$, let $J(i) \subset \{i + 1, \ldots, N\}$ be the index set of future decision problems (it may be empty) that points out which anticipated outcomes are considered when making a decision at the i-th stage. $J(i)$ will be called the sets of feedback indices for the i-th decision unit.* ∎

Remark 1 From the above definition it follows that if $m \in J(i)$ then there exist information feedback between the m-th and i-th nodes. Moreover, the overall theory remains valid if we allow self-feedback loops, i.e., if i may be an element of $J(i)$, which describe interactive decision-making at the same decision unit. A discussion of this case is given in section "Interactive Optimizers and Sustainable Decisions."

Definition 3 *Let O_i $i = 0,1,\ldots,N$, be an anticipatory chain with causal relations defined as multifunctions $\varphi(i)$ pointing out the scope of admissible decisions in U_{i+1} in such a manner that if $u_i \in U_i$ is admissible then u_{i+1} is admissible in U_{i+1} iff $u_{i+1} \in \varphi(i)(u_i)$. Moreover, let us assume that all elements of U_0 are admissible. Then any sequence of admissible solutions $(u_{0,\,m(0)}, u_{1,m(1)}, \ldots, u_{N,\,m(N)})$ will be termed an* **admissible chain**. ∎

The set of all admissible chains in an anticipatory network G will be denoted by $A(G)$. If all sets $U_0,\ldots,U_N$ are finite, $U_i := \{x_{i,1},\ldots,x_{i,k(i)}\}$, then $A(G)$ can be constructed by listing subsequently the elements of U_0, then replicating each row of the list corresponding to $u_{0,i}$ c_{1i}-times, where c_{1i} is the cardinality of $\varphi(1)(u_{0,i})$, and adding to each row of the extended list the values of $\varphi(1)(u_{0,i})$. This procedure should be repeated recursively, replicating at the i-th step each row corresponding to the j-th element of U_i c_{ij} times, where c_{ij} is the cardinality of $\varphi(i)(u_{i-1,j})$, until the elements of U_N are added to the list. An example of the digraph which illustrates the above construction is shown in Fig. 3 (left).

In the above chain of optimizers $\varphi(i)$ is defined by (4), i.e., $\varphi(i) := Y_i \circ F_{i-1}$. By virtue of the following Lemma 1 in (Skulimowski 2014a), which is based on a construction of $A(G)$ for a given finite anticipatory chain G, the enumeration of the set $A(G)$ can be accomplished without constructing all admissible chains.

Lemma 1 *Let M be the number of all admissible chains in a chain of decision units $O_0,\ldots,O_N$ with decision sets*

$$U_0 := \left\{ u_{0,1}, \ldots, u_{0,k(0)} \right\}, \ldots, U_N := \left\{ u_{N,1}, \ldots, u_{N,k(N)} \right\} \tag{6}$$

and let d_{ij} be the number of partial admissible chains starting at U_0 and ending at $u_{ij} \in U_i$ for $i = 1,\ldots,N, j = 1,\ldots,k(i)$. Then

$$d_{ij} = \sum_{1 \leq p \leq b_{ij}} d_{i-1,p}, \tag{7}$$

where b_{ij} is the cardinality of the set

$$\varphi(i)^{-1}\left(u_{ij}\right) := \left\{ u_{i-1,p} \in U_{i-1} : u_{ij} \in \varphi(i)\left(u_{i-1,p}\right) \right\}. \tag{8}$$

Hence,

$$M = \sum_{1 \leq p \leq k(N)} d_{N,p}. \tag{9}$$

∎

A proof of this lemma - based on mathematical induction - is given in Skulimowski (2014a).

From Lemma 1, it follows that in the worst case when $\varphi(i)(u_{i-1,j}) = U_i$ for $i = 1, \ldots, N$, the number of all admissible chains is equal to $\Pi_{0 \leq i \leq N} k(i)$.

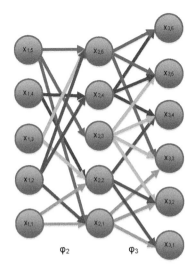

(a)	U_2					
	φ_2	$X_{2,1}$	$X_{2,2}$	$X_{2,3}$	$X_{2,4}$	$X_{2,5}$
	$X_{1,1}$	1	1	0	0	0
U_1	$X_{1,2}$	1	0	0	1	1
	$X_{1,3}$	0	1	0	0	1
	$X_{1,4}$	0	1	0	1	0
	$X_{1,5}$	1	0	1	0	1

(b)	U_3						
	φ_3	$X_{3,1}$	$X_{3,2}$	$X_{3,3}$	$X_{3,4}$	$X_{3,5}$	$X_{3,6}$
	$X_{2,1}$	1	1	1	0	0	0
	$X_{2,2}$	1	1	0	1	0	0
U_2	$X_{2,3}$	0	1	1	1	1	0
	$X_{2,4}$	0	0	0	1	1	1
	$X_{2,5}$	0	0	1	0	1	1

Fig. 3 An example of an explicit graphical definition of multifunctions φ_2 and φ_3 for O_1, O_2, and O_3, $O_i=(U_i,\ F_i,\ P_i)$, $U_i:=\{x_{i,1},...,x_{i,k(i)}\}$, $i=1,2,3$ (left). Arrows starting from an element x_{ij} indicate the admissible decisions in a causally dependent unit which are determined when selecting the decision x_{ij}. On the right, we show the corresponding incidence matrices of the causal relations between O_1 and O_2 (top) and O_2 and O_3 (bottom)

In real-life situations, N is usually much smaller than the number of admissible decisions at each decision unit. Consequently, the computational effort necessary to compute the set $A(G)$ in most problems with discrete sets is moderate enough to get the solution with a PC in a reasonable time.

By imposing additional anticipatory conditions specifying the properties of future decisions, the set of admissible chains A will be confined to a smaller set of all decision sequences that fulfill the anticipatory requirements. In the following Definition 4 and Assumption 1, we propose a specific form of such requirements that is suitable for constructive filtering of admissible decision chains to yield decisions with desired properties. It is to be noted that this form is one of a plethora of different anticipatory requirements that may occur in real-life problems.

Definition 4 Let O_k, $k=0,1,\ldots,N$, be a chain of active decision units and let for a fixed i, $0 \leq i < N$, $\{V_{ij}\}_{j\in J(i)}$ be a family of subsets such that $V_{ij}\subset U_j$ for all $j \in J(i)$, where $J(i)$ is an index set that points out the outcomes of future decision problems that are relevant for $O_{i,j} \in J(i)$. Let us denote future decisions to be made at O_j by u_j. Then the anticipatory feedback at O_i is the requirement that

$$\forall j \in J(i) : u_j \in V_{ij} \subset \cdot U_j. \tag{10}$$

In discrete problems, V_{ij} are usually defined as explicit lists. The existence of an active anticipatory feedback means that the decision-maker at its target node O_i

selects the solution such that the condition (10) is satisfied for all $j \in J(i)$. If it is impossible, the decision-maker admits relaxation rules ensuring a maximum fulfillment of (10). Such rules are discussed later in this section.

We will assume that the anticipatory feedback condition (10) is given in a constructive form, according to the following assumptions (cf. Skulimowski 2014a):

Assumption 1 The decision-makers at units $O_i = X(U_i, F_i, P_i)$ strive to select such decisions $u_i \in U_i$ that the decisions made at O_j for $j \in J(i)$, causally dependent on $F_i(u_i)$, reach or exceed certain attainable reference levels $q(i, j)$ of criteria $F_j : U_j \to E_j$, i.e.,

$$V_{ij} := \{ u \in U_j : F_j(u) \le q(i,j) \} \text{ for certain } q(i,j) \in E_j. \tag{11}$$

Assumption 2 Decision-makers at all units O_i such that $J(i)$ is nonempty select a nondominated decision from among those admissible at O_i according to the anticipatory feedback requirements (11) defined for $j \in J(i)$, at the same time taking into account the preference structure P_i. The preference structures P_j are known to the decision-makers preceding O_j in the causal order.

Assumption 3 The sets $J(i)$ and the associated subset family V_{ij} are nonempty for at least one i. Moreover, if $J(i) \ne \emptyset$, then $V_{ik} \ne U_k$ for at least one $k \in J(i)$.

Assumption 4 The network of decision units is *nonredundant*. By definition, it means that all causally final units O_N (i.e., no other unit O_k depends on O_N) are starting nodes for an anticipatory feedback.

Networks that do not fulfill assumption 3 are termed *trivial*, those that do not satisfy Assumption 4 are *redundant*. Observe that causal relations influencing units beyond last starting node for an anticipatory feedback have no effect on any anticipatory decision. A similar observation can be made for initial nodes, so without a loss of generality, we can assume that $J(0) \ne \emptyset$.

In a nontrivial AN, the following anticipatory decision problems can be formulated:

Problem 1 *Find the set of all admissible chains that fulfill anticipatory feedback condition* (10–11). ∎

As already mentioned, the inclusions (10) are often too restrictive. If no feasible solutions to Problem 1 exist, the condition (10) may be relaxed by allowing its partial fulfillment. The Problem 2 below takes into account such relaxation for the anticipatory feedback conditions defined by reference values $q(i,j)$ (11).

Problem 2 *Find the set of all admissible chains $(u_1,...,u_N)$ that minimize the following function:*

$$g(u_0, \ldots, u_N) := \sum_{i \in J(0)} h(u_i, q(0, i)) w_{0i} \tag{12}$$

and such that if $J(i) \neq \emptyset$, $1 \leq i < N$, then the truncated admissible chain $(u_i, \ldots, u_N)$ minimizes the function

$$g_i(u_i, \ldots, u_N) := \sum_{j \in J(i)} h\left(u_j, q(i, j)\right) w_{ij}, \tag{13}$$

where h is certain quantitative measure of satisfaction of (11), and w_{ij} are positive relevance coefficients associated to the anticipatory feedbacks between the decision units O_i and O_j, for $j \in J(i)$. ∎

For example, as h in the above Problem 2 one can apply the distance function

$$h\left(u_i, q(i, j)\right) := \min\{\| F_i(u_i) - y \| : y \in F_i(U_i) \text{ and } y \leq q(i, j)\}. \tag{14}$$

A key role in the solution process of both above problems is played by the following notion:

Definition 5 *A sequence of decisions $u_{0, m(0)}, \ldots, u_{N, m(N)}$, fulfilling (10–11) or maximizing (12–14), will be termed an **anticipatory chain** of type 1 or 2, respectively.* ∎

Anticipatory chains of type 1 ot 2 are regarded as solutions to Problems 1 or 2, respectively. From their recursive construction one can derive the following statement.

Proposition 1 (Skulimowski 2014a). *Suppose that $\{u_{k, m(k)}, \ldots, u_{N, m(N)}\}$ is a truncated anticipatory chain for the decision unit O_k in a nonredundant anticipatory chain. If $J(n)$ is nonempty for a certain $n \in [k + 1 : N]$ then $\{u_{n, m(n)}, \ldots, u_{N, m(N)}\}$ is a truncated anticipatory chain for O_n.* ∎

The proof of Prop. 1 was given in (Skulimowski 2014a). It allows us to apply a solution procedure based on the dynamic programming principle and on the following additional assumptions:

Assumption 5 The solutions made by decision units with a shorter anticipation horizon are calculated first.

Assumption 6 All functions (13) can be additively aggregated with (12), and the coefficients w_{ij} are independent on the first index, i.e. $w_{ij} := w_j$.

Observe that in general, there may exist arbitrary prioritizations of anticipatory feedbacks and/or decision units that determine the order of taking them into account in the solution process. The following algorithm solving the above problems is based on Algorithms 1 and 1′ from (Skulimowski 2014a).

Algorithm 1

Input data structure: *A chain of optimizers with $N + 1$ elements $O_i := ((F_i : U_i \to E_i) \to \min(P_i))$, for $i = 0,1,...N$, and the multifunctions $\varphi(i) := Y_i \circ F_{i-1}$ are given explicitly in form of an array Φ of elements of U_{i+1} parameterized by the elements of U_i. For each $i = 0,...,N-1$, let $J(i)$ be the set of feedback indices for the i-th optimizer.*

Output: *All anticipatory chains of type 1 or 2, $(u_{a0},...u_{aN})$.*

Step 1. *Find $\Pi_0 := \Pi(U_0,F_0,P_0)$ – the set of nondominated points in the problem $(F_0 : U_0 \to E_0) \to \min(P_0)$ denoted by O_0. Order the elements of $\Pi_0 = \{u_{0,1}, ..., u_{0,k(0)}\}$ in an arbitrary way.*

Step 2. *Find all admissible chains starting from elements of Π_0 by a forward step-by-step enumeration of values of $\varphi(i)$ in Φ. Reorder the elements in Φ so that its i-th column contains the i-th element of all admissible chains, ordered lexicographically according to the order of their predecessors.*

Step. 3. *Let $M := \{m \in [0 : N - 1] : J(m) \neq \varnothing\}$. Find m – the largest element of M.*

Step 4m. *Find the smallest element of $J(m)$, $s(m)$. Find the set Ω_m of all admissible chains $C(m)$ starting at certain $u \in U_m$ u such that the feedback condition is satisfied at $O_{s(m)}$.*

Repeat *for all $n \in J(m)$.*

Find the set $\Omega_{m,n}$ of all admissible chains starting at certain $u \in U_m$ such that the feedback condition is satisfied at O_n.

Set $\Omega_m := \Omega_m \cap \Omega_{m,n}$.

If Ω_m is empty, then

for all admissible chains starting at elements of U_m, calculate the function $g_m(u_m, ..., u_N) := \sum_{j \in J(m)} h(u_j, q(m, j))w_j$.

Find the surrogate anticipatory chain as an admissible chain $(u_m,...,u_N)_{\max}$ with the minimum value of g_m.

Step 5m,n. *Remove m from M,*

If $M=\varnothing$, stop

else

Find $m_{\max}$ – the largest element of M.

Find the minimum value of $\sum_{j \in [m_{max}:m]} h\left(u_j, q(m_{\max},j)\right)w_j$ on U_{mmax}

Set

$$g_{max}(u_{\max}, ..., u_m, ..., u_N) := g_m(u_m, ..., u_N) + \sum_{j \in [m_{max}:m]} h\left(u_j, q(m_{\max},j)\right)w_j$$

Set the anticipatory chain as $(u_{max},...,u_m,...,u_N)$, a concatenation of previous – and current – step anticipatory chains.

Go to Step 4m.

else

Step 6m. *Remove m from M.*

If $M=\varnothing$, stop

else *let Find m_{max} – the largest element of M.*

Set $\Omega_m := C(m_{max}, m) \oplus \Omega_m$, where $C(m_{max}, m)$ *is the set of all admissible chains starting at* O_{mmax} *and truncated at* O_m.
Go to Step 4m

end   ∎

The operation "$\oplus$" in the Step 6m above is the concatenation of sequences applied to admissible and anticipatory chains. Algorithm 1 is capable of solving both Problems 1 and 2, starting from solving Problem 1 and switching to Problem 2 when Problem 1 does not admit any solutions. It can be easily generalized to decision units different than optimizers. Recall that Problem 2 is a relaxed version of Problem 1 that allows to find admissible chains that partly satisfy the feedback conditions, where the intersection operation in Step 4m is replaced by calculating the functions (12–14).

An anticipatory chain starting at O_0 found as a solution to Problems 1 or 2 can be regarded as a compromise solution to the multicriteria optimization problem (1) that fits best the anticipated consequences of an initial decision. The simplifying assumption $w_{ij} := w_j$ guarantees that this property is valid for all decision stages in the anticipatory chain.

The application of the above-presented anticipatory preference structure leads in most cases to a considerable reduction of the number of compromise alternatives considered for selection in a multicriteria decision-making problem with an anticipatory preference structure. An illustrative example that demonstrates the action of Algorithm 1 in the chain of five optimizers can be found in (Skulimowski 2014a, Sec. 4).

Anticipatory Trees and General Networks

In this section, we will show how the algorithms presented in section "Anticipatory Chains" can be applied to solve anticipatory networks where each decision unit may influence multiple decisions to be made in the future. If we additionally assume that each decision unit except the initial one is directly influenced by exactly one predecessor then one can observe that the causal subgraph of the anticipatory network so arisen is a *causal tree* of decision units. Then we will investigate a situation where each decision may directly depend on the outcomes of multiple decision units. Both cases combined define general *causal networks.* Any anticipatory network can be represented as a general causal network with anticipatory feedbacks.

To provide a formal definition of anticipatory trees we will define first the bifurcation decision units:

Definition 6 *Let a decision unit* O_i *influence causally the decisions in two causally independent units* O_k *and* O_m *and let* O_t *be a decision unit with the following properties:*

(a) O_t is causally dependent on O_i.
(b) O_k and O_m are both causally dependent on O_t.
(c) If O_p is causally dependent on O_t, then O_k and O_m cannot both causally depend on O_p.

Then O_t will be termed a **bifurcation unit** for O_i, O_k, and O_m. ∎

Now, we can can formulate the following:

Definition 7 *An **anticipatory tree** is a finite network of decision units that contains at least one bifurcation unit and at least one anticipatory feedback, and such that no decision unit in the network directly depends on two or more causally independent units.* ∎

Any unit in *T* that does not causally influence any other unit will be termed an *end node* of T. The *final branch* of *T* is a chain that starts from a bifurcation unit and does not contain any other bifurcation units.

From Definition 7, it follows that for given decision units O_i, O_k, and O_m in an anticipatory tree configured as in Definition 6, the bifurcation unit O_t always exists and is unique. An example of four bifurcation units in a simple anticipatory tree is given in Fig. 4. The following property, proven in (Skulimowski 2014a), makes possible the reduction of the analysis of anticipatory trees to the subsequent analysis of anticipatory chains in the tree.

Proposition 2 Skulimowski (2014a). *Assume that the decision unit O_i influences two causally independent units O_k and O_m in an anticipatory tree T, and let O_t be the*

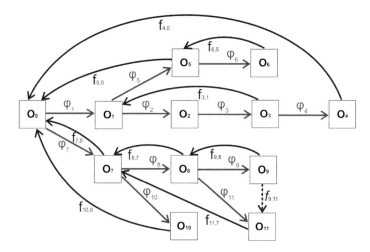

Fig. 4 An example of an anticipatory tree consisting of 12 nodes $O_i=(U_i, F_i, P_i)$, $i = 0,1,\ldots,11$, and five chains. All nodes model optimizers, causal relations are defined by multifunctions φ_j (*red arcs*), and nine relevant anticipatory feedback relations are denoted as $f_{j,i}$ (*blue arrows*). The *dotted arrow* between O_9 and O_{11} is an irrelevant anticipatory feedback, because there is no causal relation between these decision units

bifurcation unit for O_i, O_k, and O_m. Furthermore, let C_k and C_m be the sets of admissible chains starting at O_i and ending at O_k and O_m, respectively, and let $C_k{'}$ and $C_m{'}$ contain the elements of C_k and C_m, respectively, starting at O_i and truncated at the bifurcation unit O_t. Then all admissible chains with respect to both O_k and O_m, starting at O_i can be generated as extensions of the elements of the intersection of $C_k{'}$ and $C_m{'}$. Specifically, an extension of any such sequence of decisions starting at O_i and ending at O_t is to be concatenated with an arbitrary subsequence starting at O_t of an admissible chain that was truncated at prior to the intersection of $C_k{'}$ and $C_m{'}$. ∎

Let A_1 and A_2 be the sets of admissible chains in two anticipatory chains $\{O_i, \ldots, O_j, \ldots, O_k\}$ and $\{O_i, \ldots, O_j, \ldots, O_m\}$, respectively, where O_j is their bifurcation unit. Only those elements of A_1 and A_2 that overlap on the common branch $\{O_i, \ldots, O_j\}$ of the anticipatory tree $T := \{O_i, \ldots, O_k\} \cup \{O_i, \ldots, O_m\}$ can be prolonged to chains admissible with respect to causally independent consequences represented by the decisions made at O_k and O_m.

A similar statement, derived from the properties of the logical product of feedback conditions and the corresponding intersection of chains applies also to the anticipatory chains. Another straightforward observation is that anticipatory feedback between causally independent O_k and O_m in an anticipatory tree is always irrelevant, i.e., by definition there is no action at O_k that might influence the output of O_m. From the above observations, one can derive the following algorithm to find all anticipatory chains in an anticipatory tree. It is based on a survey of all bifurcation units and corresponding chains of decision units ending at final branches of the tree. Similarly as in Algorithm 1, $J(i)$ denotes the set of anticipatory feedback indices for the i-th decision unit.

Algorithm 2 Skulimowski (2014a).

Data structure. *Let us consider an anticipatory tree T of optimizers with $N + 1$ elements*

$$O_i := (U_i, F_i, P_i), \tag{15}$$

for $i = 0, 1, \ldots, N$, and let the values of the multifunctions $\varphi(i) := Y_i \circ F_{i-1}$ be given as an array A of elements of U_{i+1} with rows parameterized by the elements of U_i for $i = 0, \ldots, N{-}K{+}1$, where K is the number of end nodes in T.

Step 1. *Find $\Pi_0 := \Pi(U_0, F_0, P_0)$ – the set of nondominated points in the problem $O_0 := (F_0 : U_0 {\rightarrow} E_0) {\rightarrow} \min(P_0)$. Order the elements of $\Pi_0 = \{u_{0,1}, \ldots, u_{0,k_{(0)}}\}$ in an arbitrary way.*

Step 2. *Eliminate all irrelevant anticipatory feedbacks from the tree T (cf. Fig. 4). Set $T_1 := T$, $B := \varnothing$.*

Step 3. *Repeat until T_1 contains only one chain.*

Find the end nodes $O_{e1}, \ldots, O_{en}$, the final branches ending at O_{ei}, and the set of corresponding bifurcation units B_1 of the tree T_1.

Remove the units forming all final branches from T_1 except the elements of B_1. Set $B := B \cup B_1$.

If T_1 is a chain, go to Step 4.

Step 4. *Order the bifurcation units in B according to the causal order in T so that they form a subtree B in T.*

Step 5k. *Survey all bifurcation units in B according to the causal order, starting from the end nodes of B. For an arbitrary chain corresponding to the element $b \in B$ just considered, apply the Proposition 2 to find all admissible chains starting from elements of Π_0 and ending in a final branch of the anticipatory tree. Apply the ordering and immediate admissible predecessors coding as in Algorithm 1.*

Step. 6k. *For each k-th final branch β_k corresponding to the bifurcation unit $b \in B$, apply Steps 4m and 5m,n of Algorithm 1 to find the anticipatory chains starting at Π_0 and ending at the end node of β_k.*

Remove from the tree T the final branch of this chain of optimizers for which the anticipatory chains have been found.

If *T* consist of O_0 only, **stop**

else go to Step 5k.   ∎

An application of Algorithm 2 to find all anticipatory chains in a simple tree of optimizers is given in Skulimowski (2014a). The Algorithm 2 can be extended to any decision units by replacing the set of nondominated decisions with another decision selection rule.

Example. Let us consider the anticipatory tree *T* shown in Fig. 4 below. Observe that the Step 1 of Algorithm 2 need not be illustrated in this example because we analyze the optimal decisions only, without taking into account how these were derived from, constraints, the criteria functions and preference structures. To eliminate irrelevant feedback relations, all anticipatory feedbacks are checked whether they link weakly causally dependent decision units in an appropriate order. For instance, if an anticipatory feedback links O_3 and O_1, this can be accomplished by an iterative search in the list of causal predecessors of O_3 until either O_1 or O_0 is reached. In the latter case, the feedback would be irrelevant. In Fig. 4, the feedback between O_9 and O_{11} is identified as irrelevant and eliminated from further consideration. There are five end nodes in the tree, namely, O_4, O_6, O_9, O_{10}, and O_{11}. According to Definition 6, O_1 is the bifurcation unit for the end nodes O_4 and O_6, while O_8 is the bifurcation unit for O_9 and O_{10} and O_7 is the bifurcation unit for O_9, O_{10}, and O_{11}. After surveying all end nodes we find out that $B = \{O_1, O_7, O_8\}$. Pursuing the procedure outlined in Step 3 of Algorithm 2, we remove the final branches of *T* which correspond to the bifurcation units identified so far, or – equivalently – all decision units causally dependent only on either O_1, O_7, or O_8.

The only bifurcation decision unit in the tree so reduced which is now added to *B* is O_0. Thus *B* consists of four bifurcation optimizers: O_1, O_7, O_8, and O_0. In Step 4 of Algorithm 2, they are ordered according to the causal order inherited from *T*. The further calculations in Steps 5k and 6k follow this order.   ∎

Generally, in a network of active decision units, there may exist nodes that are directly causally influenced by two or more predecessors (cf. Figs. 1 and 7). Such problems emerge often when, for example, an input to an investment decision comes from two or more independent economic, social, or technological processes, which are optimized with respect to the same criteria. In order to deal with such a situation, observe first that the causal dependences in form of constraints on the set of admissible decisions in a subsequent problem O_k, which come from two or more causally independent decision units yield, in fact, just an intersection of constraints. For example, if the units are optimizers $O_i=(U_i, F_i, P_i)$ and $O_j=(U_j, F_j, P_j)$ influencing another unit with the constraint multifunctions Y_i and Y_j, respectively, their joint influence can be represented as a new multifunction Y defined on the Cartesian product of $F_i(U_i)$ and $F_j(U_j)$, namely,

$$Y(u_{ip}, u_{jr}) := Y_i(u_{ip}) \bigotimes Y_j(u_{jr}), \tag{16}$$

where "$\bigotimes$" denotes an arbitrary set theoretical combination of the arguments of Y, characteristic to their joint influence (e.g. the union of sets corresponds to a "permissive" influence, while the intersection occurs in a restrictive Y). Based on this observation, in case of arbitrary networks, one has to survey all decision units which are causally influenced by two or more predecessors. The above process can be repeated iteratively in a similar way as Algorithms 1 and 2. The Problem 1 can be regularized for a case where no solution exists, by solving the relaxed Problem 2 as proposed in section "Anticipatory Chains."

From the above remarks, we conclude that a solution scheme based on Algorithms 1 and 2 as subroutines can be used to solve general anticipatory networks.

Generalizations and Extensions of Anticipatory Networks

The aim of this section is to present further ideas concerning anticipatory network theory and basic hints on how to analyze them. There exists a variety of network architectures, potential anticipatory feedback rules, and resulting solution rules. Below we discuss some of these extensions and directions for further research.

Interactive Optimizers and Sustainable Decisions

The principal application of the decision model presented in this chapter is to assist the decision-maker in choosing a compromise decision at an initial decision unit O_0. This decision will be selected taking into account all the anticipatory information encoded in the network's structure.

The above theory can also be applied to model interactive solution process in multicriteria decision problems. The latter can be represented as a self-feedback loop in a causal graph provided that a multicriteria decision unit O_χ is endowed with an interactive solution selection mechanism

$$\chi : \Pi(U, F, P) \times I \rightarrow \Pi(U, F, P), \tag{17}$$

where $\Pi(U, F, P)$ is the set of nondominated solutions for the problem (1) and I is the set states of knowledge of an external agent. These evolve according to the equation $s_{i+1} := \zeta(s_i, \pi_i)$, where ζ is a transition function that assigns a new state of knowledge s_{i+1} based on the former state s_i and on the assessment of the current nondominated output π_i generated by the multicriteria optimizer O_χ. The actions of O_χ and ζ are repeated iteratively for different states of knowledge. For an appropriately defined transition function ζ the sequence of nondominated solutions thus generated converges to a compromise solution in $\Pi(U, F, P)$. There may be multiple external agents ('advisors') involved in the decision making process as well as the latter may depend on the random states of nature $\mathbf{N}$. The unit O_χ will be termed a *repetitive optimizer.* Its scheme is shown in Fig. 5.

Another class of decision units related to interactive optimizers is referred to as *sustainability units.* Instead of modeling an interaction on a separate time scale, assuming the identity preservation of the decision-makers, sustainability units are stretched in time, and the parameters of the subsequent-stage units evolve following predefined modification rules. Unlike as in the classical anticipatory network model, it is assumed that the decision-makers responsible for future decisions in a sustainability unit may be the same as at the previous stages. The decision-makers may also vary but remain closely related to their predecessors. Only the outputs from the last-stage units are taken into account in the optimization process and as sources of anticipatory feedback information for other units in the network.

Hybrid Networks

Hybrid anticipatory networks have been introduced in Skulimowski (2012). They may contain nodes modeling different types of future decision problems, apart from optimization problems. Hybrid network nodes can model the choice of a mixed strategy in games with conflicts that may eventually lead to Nash equilibria, subset selection problems, rankings, or predetermined, random, or irrational decisions. Although hybrid anticipatory networks may contain nodes of all above types, their structure is similar to networks of optimizers as the nodes are connected by edges modeling causal and anticipatory feedback relations. All nodes in an anticipatory network are termed *decision units*, while optimizers and game units are additionally termed *active.* Decision units of all kinds produce output decisions based on the inputs fed by units preceding them in the causal order. In Fig. 6, we present the schemes of the most frequently occurring decision problems that can be modeled as nodes in hybrid anticipatory networks.

Fig. 5 A repetitive optimizer – an interactive anticipatory decision-making agent in an AN

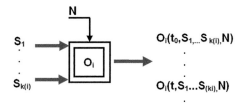

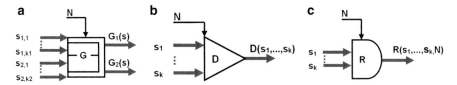

Fig. 6 Decision units occurring in hybrid anticipatory networks: **a** two-player game unit with $s = (s_{1,1}, \ldots, s_{1,k1}, s_{2,1}, \ldots, s_{2,k2})$, **b** a predetermined algorithmic decision unit with no freewill, and **c** random decisions with a known distribution function. Output from all units may depend on the states of nature N (source: Skulimowski 2012)

Similarly as in networks of optimizers, the inputs to all units presented in Fig. 6 depend on the outputs from other units except the initial node, which has no inputs unless it is influenced by the external environment (the nature) N. This dependence may have the form of a multifunction φ that defines an influence relation r, or another relation that, e.g., modifies the preference structure of a decision unit. Every decision unit has two functions:

(i) It transforms the input signals into the mapping that modifies the parameters of the decision problem to be solved; this transformation is a characteristic feature of a particular decision unit.

(ii) It solves its decision problem with modified parameters and produces the output, which can be identified with the solution of the decision unit's characteristic problem; the output is unique except the game units, where the number of outputs equals the number of players.

For example, the aggregation of input signals represented by multifunctions $\varphi_1, \ldots, \varphi_k$ that restrict the choice of an admissible decision at a decision unit O_i by imposing additional constraints may be defined as an intersection $\varphi = \varphi_1 \cap \ldots \cap \varphi_k$. If U_i is the decision set at O_i and the outputs at the decision units causally preceding O_i are $x_1, \ldots, x_k$ then $\varphi(x_1, \ldots, x_k) = \varphi_1(x_1) \cap \ldots \cap \varphi_k(x_k) \subset U_i$. In general, aggregations can be defined by arbitrary Boolean and algebraic operations, depending on modeling purposes.

Recall that a decision unit O_i is termed *active* if a decision-maker associated to O_i is able to perform a free choice (Skulimowski 2011). Otherwise it is termed *passive*. The operations of decision units, including those described in section "Interactive Optimizers and Sustainable Decisions," are summarized in Table 1.

An example of a hybrid anticipatory network where the influence relations form the causal graph Γ is shown in Fig. 7 below.

Timed Anticipatory Networks

Timed anticipatory networks have been introduced and analyzed in Skulimowski (2016b, 2017a). Their definition requires two time scales: one is for the anticipatory

Table 1 Decision units occurring in hybrid anticipatory networks

Decision unit	Type	Internal parameters	Output function(s)
Multicriteria optimizer	Active	The feasible decision set U, the (vector) criterion F, preference structure P	A single optimal solution or a subset of the Pareto set
n-player game unit	Active	Strategy sets for all players, information sets, payoff functions	The values of payoff functions G_i for all players
Algorithmic decision unit	Passive	The deterministic output function D. The value of D on the decision set U is calculated with a known algorithm	A unique value of D on $V \subset U$, or a subset of $D(U)$ determined by the inputs
Random decision unit	Passive	Probability distributions describing the random decision generation	A random number or a random output subset
Repetitive decision unit	Active	An interaction algorithm to assess anticipated own decisions (cf. section "Interactive Optimizers and Sustainable Decisions")	Compromise decision made within an interaction
Sustainability unit	Active	A unit is stretched in time, the parameters of the subsequent-stage units follow a modification rule	Outputs from the last-stage units only
Other units	Active or passive	Uncertainty characteristics (fuzzy, possibilistic, fuzzy-random variables, etc.) and decision sets	Different types of outputs, depending on the specificity of the decision unit

Source: classification based on Skulimowski (2012), *extended*

network evolution; the other one is required for modeling the anticipatory solution process at each time step of the first scale. Consequently, we will define first the discrete solution time interval T and assume that there exists an optimization problem to be solved for all $t \in T$ modeled as an initial node of the network. Moreover, in a *timed anticipatory networks (TAN)*, the anticipatory multigraph may vary in time. The formal definition of a TAN is given below (Skulimowski 2016b).

Definition 8 *A timed anticipatory network $A(t)$ is a directed-multigraph-valued time series defined for $t \in T = \{t_0, t_1, \ldots, t_n\}$, $t_{i-1} < t_i$ for $i = 1,\ldots,n$, such that*

(a) *For each $t \in T$, $A(t)$ is an anticipatory network where each decision is to be made within a prescribed time interval termed decision time horizon.*

(b) *For each i, $i = 0,\ldots,n-1$, t_{i+1} corresponds to certain decision time horizon in $A(t)$.*

(c) *The decisions made and solutions implemented in the network $A(t_i)$ by all agents until the time t_{i+1} comply with the structure of the network $A(t_{i+1})$.*

(d) *The initial node and at least one other node in $A(t_{i+1})$ inherit the multigraph structure from $A(t_i)$.* ∎

There are many more specific structures of TANs modeling different decision situations. In a TAN considered in the following sections, any unit's decision is a sequence of simple decisions made by the same evolving agent at subsequent moments of time. The decisions made by future agents at a moment t_i become

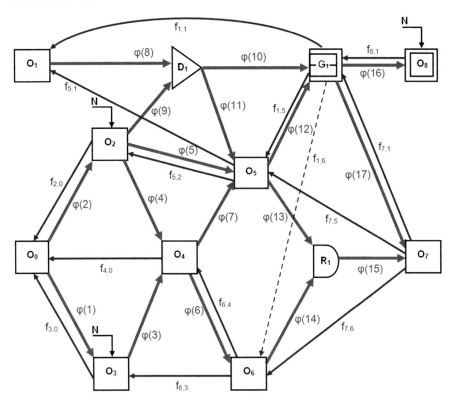

Fig. 7 An example of a hybrid anticipatory network with 12 units. The *dotted line* shows an induced anticipatory feedback (cf. Skulimowski 2016a). Observe that the unit O_8 is a repetitive optimizer (based on Skulimowski 2012)

known to their predecessors at time t_{i+1} and may be used for supervisory learning of decision rules, supplementing the anticipatory feedback information.

The following principles, derived from real-life interpretations of timed ANs as anticipatory robot formations, will serve to model the evolution and compute the optimal solutions of structured TANs:

- A finite discrete time interval $T = [t_0, t_f]$ plays the role of evolution period.
- For every $t \in T$, the causal subgraph of $A(t)$ is embedded in a given structure graph $S(A)$ that is characteristic for this TAN, $S(A)$ is a finite digraph with no cycles, and non-isolated nodes with no predecessors are termed *initial nodes*.
- The functions of TAN's units are characterized by their positions in the structure graph, i.e., different physical units and decision-makers may be substituted for the same specific node in the structure graph during the network evolution.
- All TAN units, $V_i(t_k)$, $i = 1, \ldots, N$, $k := k(i)$, are initially homogeneous and anonymous; this may change for $t_k > t_0$.

- At least one decision, namely, at an initial node, is made, and at least one causal impact is executed at each time step t (*nontrivial progress principle*).
- If a unit $V_i(t_k)$ remains in the network at time t_{k+1}, then its native decision scope U_i and performance criteria F_i remain unchanged (*network stationarity principle*).
- Some units may be deleted, and some new ones may be admitted to the network as time changes from t_k to t_{k+1}.
- The decision-maker responsible for the unit $V_i(t_k)$ can remain in the network at time t_{k+1} as the decision-maker at a new unit $V_j(t_{k+1})$.

As an example, we describe the situation where each of the anticipatory decision problems modeled by the networks $A(t)$, $t = t_0$, ... , t_f is solved either independently from problems occurring at the following moments or it takes into account the resources needed by the next-step problem only. The latter situation may happen exclusively if the decision-maker corresponding to the initial node at t_k knows which unit will play the role of the robot network coordinator at the next moment t_{k+1}. This case is investigated in more detail in Skulimowski (2016b).

Observe that the above-presented rules are less restrictive than the incremental evolutionary building of ANs, where the *causality preservation* principle must be satisfied, i.e., units along a causal chain cannot change their order from the t_k-*th* to the t_{k+1}-*th* modeling step.

The solution concept of a TAN is in a natural way a combination of solutions of $A(t)$ for $t \in T$. One can consider additive, multiplicative (in case of relative growth criteria), and Bayesian probability combination rules.

Now, we will provide the following three anticipatory optimization problem formulations for a TAN with corresponding solution principles:

(**P1**) A temporal combination of momentary criteria values is calculated for the initial node acting as an optimizer for all $t \in T$, irrespectively whether which different V_i's play the role of $V_0(t)$. All or only some selected criteria G of $V_0(t)$ are taken into account.

(**P2**) A temporal combination of momentary criteria values is calculated for the same physical unit that preserves its identity for different moments of time in a TAN. This procedure may be performed for all or only for some selected units.

(**P3**) The performance criteria are split into two groups: for each $t \in T$, the first group $G=(G_1,...,G_{nl})$ is optimized on the set of admissible decisions of $A(t)$, and a temporal combination of their momentary nondominated values is calculated; the second group of criteria, $F_i=(F_{i1},...,F_{i,m})$, describes the performance of V_i irrespective of its current role in $A(t)$; the F_i and their optimal (nondominated) values for $A(t)$ are assigned to the fixed physical units and combined for all $t \in T$.

An example of solving an anticipatory robot swarm optimization problem with the mixed principle P3 has been presented in Skulimowski (2016b). There exist a variety of multigraph-transforming rules $A(t + 1) = a(A(t))$ that satisfy the principles P1, P2, or P3 and such that for each $t \in T \cdot A(t) \subset S(A)$. The rules of TAN evolution based on the above-cited example are illustrated in Fig. 8.

Observe that a temporal combination of nondominated momentary criteria values needs not be nondominated. Therefore a post-optimal selection of Pareto-optimal decisions should be executed to find an optimal solution for the entire evolution period.

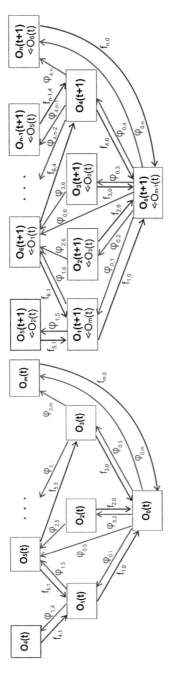

Fig. 8 An example of evolution of a timed anticipatory network from t (*left*) to $t + 1$ (*right*)

Vehicle routing, traffic coordination, supervision, and search for efficient equilibrium algorithms (cf., e.g., Huang et al. 2016) can benefit from the anticipatory decision-making principles in TANs; see Skulimowski (2016b) for further references.

Nested Anticipation and Superanticipatory Systems

Nested properties of anticipation are directly implied by the definition of the modern anticipatory systems (Rosen 1985). They were noted and discussed since the dawn of the anticipatory system theory. Rosen's definition assumes the existence of a *model* of itself and of the environment. If another anticipatory system is contained in the environment, its model should contain the first system, including its model. Here, we will show that a quantitative analysis of nested and recursive properties of anticipatory systems leads to the idea of superanticipation (Skulimowski 2014b, 2016a) that is closely related to anticipatory networks and can be described in formal and quantitative terms. In anticipatory networks, when making a decision, decision-maker(s) at a starting decision node can take into account the network of its successors and their models. Thus, the model of future environment available to a decision-maker contains models of agents acting in the future, including their own future models. The formal definition of a superanticipatory system can be formulated in the following way (Skulimowski, 2014b, 2016a).

Definition 9 *A **superanticipatory system** is an anticipatory system that contains at least one model of another future anticipatory system.* ∎

By the above definition, the notion of superanticipation is idempotent, i.e., the inclusion of other superanticipatory systems in the model of the future of a super-anticipatory system does not extend this class of systems since every super-anticipatory system is also anticipatory. However, superanticipatory systems can be distinguished by a grade of nested superanticipation.

Definition 10 *A superanticipatory system S is **of grade n** if it contains a model of an external superanticipatory system of grade n-1 and does not contain any model of a superanticipatory system of grade n except itself. An anticipatory system which does not contain any model of another anticipatory system may be termed super-anticipatory of grade 0.* ∎

The estimation of the grade n of a superanticipatory system S depends on its knowledge of the grade of other anticipatory systems modeled by S. When constructing its model of the environment, S is likely to underestimate the actual power of other system models. Thus, according to Definition 6, the grade of superanticipation of S derived from its anticipatory model is a grade of this model and an estimation from below of the actual grade of S as a biological, social, or an artificial autonomous system. In conflicting real-life environments without a perfect information exchange, modeled systems may have models of a higher grade than S could estimate. The exact value of the grade can be attributed to artificial collaborative systems only.

It turns out that anticipatory networks constitute a relevant subclass of super-anticipatory systems. Specifically, Thm.1 in (Skulimowski 2014b, 2016a) states that a finite anticipatory network is a superanticipatory system of grade n if it contains an anticipatory chain with at least n decision units and exactly n nested anticipatory feedbacks, and n is maximal with this property. For example, an anticipatory chain on n optimizers, each one linked with all its causal predecessors with an anticipatory feedback, is a superanticipatory system of grade n. The converse theorem is not true, for instance, two coupled superanticipatory systems of grade 1, S_1, and S_2, where S_1 contains a model of S_2 and vice versa, do not form an anticipatory network because if an anticipatory chain from S_1 to S_2 exists, then by acyclicity of anticipatory networks, there is no such a chain from S_2 to S_1.

Further development of superanticipatory systems, and nested anticipation in general, can greatly benefit from the relations to the notion of self-referentiality and other fundamental ideas of autonomous system theory (cf. Varela 1979).

Applications of Anticipatory Networks

The principal motivation to admit assumptions used in the definitions of networked discrete optimizers presented in the previous sections of this chapter came from the need to formalize scenario building and roadmapping processes in technological foresight (cf. Skulimowski 2014c) based on the identification of future decision-making processes. Anticipatory networks can model both hierarchical decision structures and horizontal links between decision problems, taking into account a large number of economic, environmental, social, and technological criteria. The other motivating application areas were:

- Multicriteria decision-making theory, where the use of scalar utility values is often insufficient
- Decision algorithms for artificial autonomous systems (AADS, cf. Skulimowski 2014d, 2016b)
- Financial decisions related to long-term resource allocation and their impact models

Following Skulimowski (2014a, b, c, d), two of them are presented in this chapter (sections "Timed Anticipatory Networks" and "Scenario Building and Other Foresight Applications"). Discussion of further anticipatory networks' applications is given in section "Discussion and Further Applications" below.

Scenario Building and Other Foresight Applications

The notion of scenario referred to in this section should be meant as alternative visions of the future similarly as foresight or strategic planning scenarios (Godet 2001; Skulimowski 2014c). The actual appearance of a specific scenario depends on the choice of economic, technological, or political decisions made by external agents in one or more present and/or future problems or on random or external trends and events, where the decision agents cannot be identified uniquely. This is why scenarios can be regarded as conditional forecasts.

When decision units with forecasted parameters are included in an anticipatory network, they allow us to generate decision rules taking into account alternative network structures depending on different variants of external influence. The influence of the decision made at O_i on future constraints and preferences can itself generate scenarios identified with the sequences of plausible outcomes from future decision problems following O_i. Assuming that each decision unit is rational and there are no conflicts with other units, one can apply multicriteria optimization methods to find all potential variants of anticipated rational future problem outcomes as either a nondominated point or Pareto equilibria in cooperative games. The admissible chains can be regarded as elementary scenarios (Skulimowski 2008) of the future values of optimization criteria and other indicators that characterize decision units in an anticipatory network. The anticipatory feedbacks can be used to filtering out non-plausible elementary scenarios, contributing thus to an efficient and rational building of foresight scenarios.

Game-theoretic models can also be applied to select and filter elementary scenarios defined in the same way as for the optimizers based on multicriteria optimization principles.

The Computational Methods for Anticipatory Decision-Making

As estimated from computational evidence – the Algorithms 1 and 2 based on forward-looking surveys of anticipatory feedbacks allow us to efficiently manage problems with up to 10^3 alternatives in up to 10^2 optimizers. The analysis of larger or more specialized problems can be accomplished with tailored decision support systems capable of using anticipatory information.

A discussion of the "anytime" property of Algorithms 1 and 2 is given in Skulimowski (2014a). This property can also be regarded as an ability to include more and more predicative aspects of a real-life system into a computational model. When referring to engineering and many economic applications, one can assume that this computational property is fulfilled.

A related problem of searching in a dynamic graph considered by Likhachev et al. (2008) is of particular importance to the problem of planning autonomous mobile robot activity, where the external circumstances change in real time. The autonomous agent that models anticipatory systems in the network should be capable of acquiring the information about the environment and other systems and to update their models in real time. The design of such an algorithm for real-time implementations of anticipatory planning of robot operations requires an estimation of the expected information flow from the environment and other robots in the swarm and to confront it with the computational and communication capacities of the mobile robots. The qualitative analysis of network topology, including discovery of new units, emergence of new anticipatory feedbacks, and causal influences, has to be accomplished in real time as well. A more profound analysis of cooperating robot systems is presented in the paper (Skulimowski 2016b), devoted to anticipatory autonomous vehicle swarms.

Discussion and Further Applications

Apart from the abovementioned inspirations coming from the potential uses in technological foresight, sustainable knowledge platform planning (Skulimowski 2017a), medicine, finance, and environmental modeling, as well as applications of timed networks to adaptive robot control systems with feedback, discussed briefly in section "The Computational Methods for Anticipatory Decision-Making," there are further potential areas of basic and applied research, where the ANs may provide competitive solutions. These include:

- Modeling the behavioral decision-making mechanisms in systems biology with nested anticipatory systems (cf. Baliga 2008; Terenzi 2008; Skulimowski 2014b)
- Extending the theory of n-level multicriteria programming (Nishizaki and Sakawa 2009) and merging it with the variable and flexible contraints optimization
- Investigating relations of anticipatory network models to predictive and anticipatory control (Kaczorek 2002)
- Analysis of anticipation phenomena in queuing networks as well as their applications in telecommunications

The latter field attracts an ample attention of researchers recently. For example, Mayora and Osmani (2014) defined the concept of Human-Aware Networking (HAN). The main idea behind HAN is to utilize the sensed context and the recognized human behaviors mostly based on the use of mobile devices in order to feed the network with the interaction patterns of users to better set up and optimize network parameters. With HAN, the goal is to maximize the relationship between provided quality of service. The AN-based models provide a new approach to modelling decision making, forecasting and foresight processes (Skulimowski 2014c). Skulimowski (2014c, 2017b) presented an application of anticipatory networks to build the development strategy for a regional creativity support center. Another real-life application is the sustainable exploitation strategy planning for an innovative knowledge platform elaborated within a Horizon 2020 research project (cf. www.moving-project.eu), where anticipatory networks are used to define the framework of the roadmapping process of the platform.

Further potential real-life applications of the model extensions presented in this chapter include:

- Modeling the impact of social innovations, including open innovation and knowledge platforms (Skulimowski 2017a)
- Planning long-term financial investment decisions, cf. Sec. 6.4 in (Skulimowski 2014a) for a more detailed discussion of this class of applications

- Environmental sustainability modeling, where the anticipatory feedback corresponds to the classical "ensuring a sustainable future for next generations" principle

ANs may also be useful to invent novel analysis approaches and new architectures of multilayer artificial neural networks, where active decision units and other anticipatory systems modeled in an AN coexist with neurons and fed them anticipatory information to adaptively optimize their structure and parameters. Hybrid networks could also be useful to model the anticipatory functions of the brain (cf. Antle and Silver 2009; Ghajar and Ivry 2009; Pezzulo and Rigoli 2011; Hassabis et al. 2014), where AN components are black box models of anticipatory functions evidenced in brain but with unknown or imprecise location in the cortex (Fiebach and Schubotz 2006).

We expect that further application in the medicine and health care will emerge in the next years, along with further progress in the AN theory. Anticipatory planning clinical therapy paths belong to the relevant motivating applications of the overall anticipatory network theory. ANs can be particularly useful to model therapy results and to select the best clinical path when patients will undergo different medical interventions and diagnostic examinations at hospital departments, as well as ambulant and home treatments. In such a case, the results of a recommended therapy depend to a large extent to the trust of anticipated rational behavior of the patient, in a networked environment of influences from other medical personnel as well as from home and working conditions impact.

Summary

The theory of anticipatory networks combines the features of causal and influence modeling (cf., e.g., Sloman and Hagmayer 2006) with the anticipatory system theory and new concepts of anticipatory feedback relation and superanticipation. The well-known ideas of modeling linked decision problems has been endowed with additional modeling power by adding the qualitative and quantitative characteristics of anticipation. This has made possible first to define new methods of anticipatory preference modeling to solving multicriteria optimization problems linked by causal relations. Then, it emerged a number of further fruitful applications of this theory, specifically in the areas of autonomous systems, foresight, and strategic planning.

Applying the anticipatory models presented in this chapter needs heterogeneous analytic techniques, combining forecasting to define the parameters of future problems, with foresight-based techniques, optimization, uncertainty analysis, and knowledge engineering. This will push the researchers to build complex models that are likely to require new insights into the decision theory, computational methods, and cognitive science.

Unlike as in the supervisory models of multicriteria decision-making, with just one source of recommendations, the decision-maker embedded in an anticipatory network may update the decision choice depending on the anticipated decisions and anticipatory behavior of other decision units. This is why a key role in an anticipatory network is played by trust between decision agents. This is particularly relevant in networks modeling cooperating autonomous robots together with some human operators. An in-depth analysis of different anticipation and trust levels, partial anticipation, and further information flows in the network should shed new light on the trust, confidence, and cooperation theory of autonomous agents. A better cooperation of robots, either individual, such as mobile rehabilitation robots cooperating with a handicapped human, robot formations, and swarms, using supervisory control to form ad hoc anticipatory networks as presented in Skulimowski (2016b) can bring new benefits from anticipatory network modeling.

For the sake of parsimony, this chapter did not refer to those anticipation aspects and anticipation-related concepts which do not have an interpretation in the AN theory yet. As an exception, we will mention a speculative yet potentially high-impact application area of anticipatory networks in its contribution to modeling of quantum consciousness (Hameroff and Penrose 2014; Skulimowski 2013). The hypothesis concerning quantum entanglement across time (cf., e.g., Olson and Ralph 2011) can interplay with the synchronization phenomena in macroscopic physical systems (Dubois 2001; Sun and Bollt 2014). Further extensions of the anticipatory network models, including continuous and stochastic decision problems, as well as a possibility of constructing a time-space model consisting of linked elementary decision problems, by an analogy to entangled qubit models in quantum information theory may provide new challenges to further researchers, see Tuszynski (2006, ed.) for a review of related ideas.

Finally, we have to stress that the concept of anticipation encompasses many different aspects and application fields, and not all of them can be or are intended to be converted into a computational science area. This is why the approach to quantify the anticipation presented in this chapter cannot be regarded neither as universal nor unique. As emphasized in sections "Introduction" and "Anticipatory Decision-Making in Multicriteria Problems," building a computable anticipatory network presumes an availability of forecasts and the knowledge of parameters that can be taken for granted in some areas of application only, related predominantly to ICT, engineering, economy, and finance. In humanities, literature, or some branches of social sciences, anticipation may play a relevant role despite a lack of quantitative models. In addition, every model referring to human decisions is by its nature approximate, as it merely simulates some aspects of human thinking that are fundamental for the decision-making process. Nevertheless, the above disclaimer may gradually lose its validity along with the future development of artificial intelligence tools and artificial creativity that are sometimes supposed to invade the areas traditionally restricted to human creative activity during the next century, cf. Skulimowski (2014d). As the theory of anticipatory networks will be further developed, one can expect that more fruitful relations to other areas of the science of anticipation will be discovered, more constructive tools will be created, and more real-life applications found.

References

Antle, M., & Silver, R. (2009). Neural basis of timing and anticipatory behaviors European. *Journal of Neuroscience, 30*, 1643–1649.

Baliga, N. (2008). The scale of prediction. *Systems Biology, 320*(5881), 1297–1298.

Christofides, N. (1975). *Graph theory: An algorithmic approach* (p. 415). New York: Academic.

Debreu, G. (1959). *Theory of value*. New Haven: Yale University Press.

Dubois, D. M. (2001). Theory of incursive synchronization and application to the anticipation of a delayed Pearl-Verhulst chaotic system. *Systems Science, 27*(1), 71–86.

Ehrgott, M. (2005). *Multicriteria optimization* (2nd ed.p. 323). Berlin: Springer-Verlag.

Fiebach, C., & Schubotz, R. (2006). Dynamic anticipatory processing of hierarchical sequential events: A common role for Broca's area and ventral premotor cortex across domains? *Cortex, 42*(4), 499–502.

Ghajar, J., & Ivry, R. (2009). The predictive brain state: Asynchrony in disorders of attention? *The Neuroscientist, 15*(3), 232–242.

Godet, M. (2001). *Creating futures – scenario planning as a strategic management tool*. London: Economics.

Hameroff, S., & Penrose, R. (2014). Consciousness in the universe: A review of the 'Orch OR' theory. *Physics of Life Reviews, 11*, 39–78.

Hassabis, D., Spreng, R. N., Rusu, A. A., Robbins, C. A., Mar, R. A., & Schacter, D. L. (2014). Imagine all the people: How the brain creates and uses personality models to predict behavior. *Cerebral Cortex, 24*(8), 1979–1987. https://doi.org/10.1093/cercor/bht042.

Huang, W., Viti, F., & Tampère, C. M. J. (2016). Repeated anticipatory network traffic control using iterative optimization accounting for model bias correction. *Transportation Research Part C, 67*, 243–265.

Kaczorek, T. (2002). Elimination of anticipation of singular linear systems. In D. M. Dubois (Ed.), *5th International Conference on Computing Anticipatory Systems, Liège, Belgium, August 13–18, 2001. AIP Conference Proceedings 627* (pp. 107–118).

Kaliszewski, I. (2006). *Soft computing for complex multicriteria decision making*. New York: Springer.

Likhachev, M., Ferguson, D., Gordon, G., Stentz, A., & Thrun, S. (2008). Anytime search in dynamic graphs. *Artificial Intelligence, 172*, 1613–1643.

Mayora, O., Osmani, V. (2014). From ubiquitous computing to human aware networking: Exploiting the know-how of Ubicomp Research for improving networked-user experience. In *Proceedings of the 3rd International Conference on Context-Aware Systems and Applications (ICCASA'14), Dubai, October 7–9, 2014* (pp. 110–113). Brussels: ICST. http://dl.acm.org/citation.cfm?id=2762744

Nishizaki, I., & Sakawa, M. (2009). *Cooperative and noncooperative multi-level programming, Operations research/computer science interfaces series* (Vol. 48). Dordrecht: Springer.

Olson, S. J., & Ralph, T. C. (2011). Extraction of timelike entanglement from the quantum vacuum. *Physical Review Letters, 106*, 110404.

Pezzulo, G., & Rigoli, F. (2011). The value of foresight: How prospection affects decision making. *Frontiers in Neuroscience, 5*, 79. Art. #79, p. 15, https://doi.org/10.3389/fnins.2011.00079.

Poli, R. (2017). Introducing anticipation. In R. Poli (Ed.), *Handbook of anticipation. Theoretical and applied aspects of the use of future in decision making* (pp. 1–14). Heidelberg: Springer. https://doi.org/10.1007/978-3-319-31737-3_1-1.

Rosen, R. (1985). *Anticipatory systems – philosophical, mathematical and methodological foundations* (2nd ed.). London: Pergamon Press, Springer. 2012.

Skulimowski, A. M. J. (1985). Solving vector optimization problems via multilevel analysis of foreseen consequences. *Foundations of Control Engineering, 10*(1), 25–38.

Skulimowski, A.M.J. (1986). Foreseen utility in multi-stage multicriteria optimization. In J. Kacprzyk (Ed.), *Seminar on nonconventional problems of optimization, Warsaw, May 9–11, 1984. Proceedings, Part III. Prace IBS PAN 136* (pp. 365–386).

Skulimowski, A. M. J. (1987). An interactive modification of the decision set to attain a target point in vector optimization problems. In Y. Sawaragi, K. Inoue, & H. Nakayama (Eds.), *Toward interactive and intelligent decision support systems, 1, Proceedings, VII-th International Conference on Multicriteria Decision Making, Kyoto, Japan, 18–08.1986, Lecture Notes in Economics and Mathematical Systems* (Vol. 285, pp. 142–153). Berlin: Springer. https://doi.org/10.1007/978-3-642-46607-6_16

Skulimowski, A. M. J. (1997). Methods of multicriteria decision support based on reference sets. In R. Caballero, F. Ruiz, & R. E. Steuer (Eds.), *Advances in multiple objective and goal programming, Lecture notes in economics and mathematical systems* (Vol. 455, pp. 282–290). Berlin: Springer. https://doi.org/10.1007/978-3-642-46854-4_31

Skulimowski, A. M. J. (2008). Application of dynamic rankings to portfolio selection. In J. O. Soares, J. P. Pina, & M. Catalão-Lopes (Eds.), *New developments in financial modelling. Proceedings of the 41st Meeting of the Euro Working Group on Financial Modelling. Lisbon, Portugal, November 8–9, 2007* (pp. 196–212). Newcastle: CSP Cambridge Scholars Publishing.

Skulimowski, A. M. J. (2011). Freedom of choice and creativity in multicriteria decision making. In T. Theeramunkong, S. Kunifuji, V. Sornlertlamvanich, & C. Nattee (Eds.), *Knowledge, information, and creativity support systems: KICSS'2010 revised selected papers, Lecture notes in artificial intelligence* (Vol. 6746, pp. 190–203). Berlin: Springer. https://doi.org/10.1007/978-3-642-24788-0_18.

Skulimowski, A. M. J. (2012). Hybrid anticipatory networks. In L. Rutkowski et al. (Eds.), *Proc. ICAISC 2012, lecture notes in artificial intelligence 7268* (pp. 706–715). Berlin: Springer. https://doi.org/10.1007/978-3-642-29350-4_83.

Skulimowski, A. M. J. (2013). Exploring the future with anticipatory networks. In P. L. Garrido et al. (Eds.), *Physics, computation, and the mind – advances and challenges at interfaces, Proceedings of the 12th Granada Seminar on Computational and Statistical Physics: La Herradura, Spain, 17–21 September 2012. AIP Conference Proceedings* (Vol. 1510, pp. 224–233). https://doi.org/10.1063/1.4776525

Skulimowski, A. M. J. et al (2013). *Scenarios and development trends of selected Information Society Technologies until 2025 (SCETIST), Final report* (Contract No. UDA-POIG.01.01.01-00-021/09-00, p. 656). Kraków: Progress & Business Publishers. www.ict.foresight.pl.

Skulimowski, A. M. J. (2014a). Anticipatory network models of multicriteria decision-making processes. *International Journal of Systems Science, 45*(1), 39–59. https://doi.org/10.1080/00207721.2012.670308.

Skulimowski, A. M. J. (2014b). Anticipatory networks and superanticipatory systems. *International Journal of Computing Anticipatory Systems, 30*, 117–130. CASYS'11: 10th International Conference on Computing Anticipatory Systems: Liège, Belgium, August 8–13, 2011, Dubois, D.M. (ed.), Liège, CHAOS Centre for Hyperincursion and Anticipation in Ordered Systems. Institute of Mathematics. University of Liège.

Skulimowski, A. M. J. (2014c). Applying anticipatory networks to scenario planning and backcasting in technological foresight. In *Fifth International Conference on Future-Oriented Technology Analysis (FTA) – Engage today to shape tomorrow, Brussels, 27–28 Nov 2014* (p. 10). https://ec.europa.eu/jrc/en/event/site/fta2014/programme/panel-session/cutting-edge-fta-approaches#28-Nov

Skulimowski, A. M. J. (2014d). Future prospects of human interaction with artificial autonomous systems. In A. Bouchachia (Ed.), *Adaptive and intelligent systems, Third International Conference, ICAIS 2014, Bournemouth, UK, September 8–10, 2014. Proceedings, Lecture notes in artificial intelligence* (Vol. 8779, pp. 131–141). Heidelberg: Springer. https://doi.org/10.1007/978-3-319-11298-5_14.

Skulimowski, A. M. J. (2016a). The art of anticipatory decision making. In S. Kunifuji, G. A. Papadopoulos, A. M. J. Skulimowski, & J. Kacprzyk (Eds.), *Knowledge, information and creativity support systems, Advances in intelligent systems and computing* (Vol. 416, pp. 19–37). Heidelberg: Springer. https://doi.org/10.1007/978-3-319-27478-2_2.

Skulimowski, A. M. J. (2016b). Anticipatory control of vehicle swarms with virtual supervision. In C.-H. Hsu et al. (Eds.), *IOV 2016, Lecture notes in computer science* (Vol. 10036, pp. 65–81). Heidelberg: Springer. https://doi.org/10.1007/978-3-319-51969-2_6.

Skulimowski, A. M. J. (2017a, July). *Multicriteria decision planning with anticipatory networks.* Paper presented at the 24th International Conference on MCDM, Ottawa.

Skulimowski, A. M. J. (2017b). *Selected methods, applications, and challenges of multicriteria optimization, Series: Monographs* (Vol. 19, p. 380). Kraków: Committee for Automation and Robotics of the Polish Academy of Sciences, AGH Publishers.

Sloman, S. A., & Hagmayer, Y. (2006). The causal psycho-logic of choice. *Trends in Cognitive Sciences, 10*(9), 407–412.

Steuer, R. (1987). *Multiple criteria optimization: Theory, computation and application, Wiley series in probability & mathematical statistics.* New York: Wiley.

Sun, J., & Bollt, E. M. (2014). Causation entropy identifies indirect influences, dominance of neighbors and anticipatory couplings. *Physica D: Nonlinear Phenomena, 267,* 49–57.

Terenzi, G. (2008). Anticipation in biological and cognitive systems: The need for a physical theory of biological organization. In I. Licata & A. Sakaji (Eds.), *Physics of emergence and organization* (pp. 371–388). Singapore: World Scientific Publishing.

Tuszynski, J. A. (Ed.). (2006). *The emerging physics of consciousness* (p. 487). Berlin: Springer.

Varela, F. J. (1979). *Principles of biological autonomy.* New York: Elsevier.

Future Scenario Generation, Minimum Regret Decisions, and Linear Programming

48

Stefano Benati

Contents

Abstract

After determining the set of future scenarios that an organization may encounter, practitioners must also provide the organization with the decision rule it should adopt for exploiting, or hedging against, anticipated scenarios. This paper argues that the most advantageous rule available is the minimum regret decision rule. Regret is defined as the difference between the decision taken and the optimal one given the contingency. The larger the difference, the greater the sense of regret that decision-makers will feel for having failed to make the (unpredictable) right choice. The minimum regret decision is the one that minimizes the maximum of this difference. It is a decision rule that was first proposed in the very early days of operations research (in the 1950s) in the works of Wald and Savage, to temper the extremely pessimistic view of the min-max decision rule. Later, in the early 1980s, some authors proved that the rule satisfies a set of axioms, providing an alternative to the expected utility model for modeling real and behavioral decision-making. As a consequence, one can develop operational decision models that are based on regret computations. The application of minimum regret as a normative tool for operational problems obliges practitioners to design all scenarios and feasible decisions carefully, as regret does not satisfy the transitivity

S. Benati (✉)
Department of Sociology and Social Research, University of Trento, Trento, Italy
e-mail: stefano.benati@unitn.it

© Springer Nature Switzerland AG 2019
R. Poli (ed.), *Handbook of Anticipation*,
https://doi.org/10.1007/978-3-319-91554-8_86

principle of the expected utility. As such, mathematical programming tools are needed to solve minimum regret models. We discuss these mathematical tools by analyzing a flood management problem, based on a real-life application to the Iowa River.

Keywords

Scenario generation · Minimum regret decision · Linear programming · Flood management

Introduction: Scenarios and Decision-Making

The first step in any exercise regarding the future is to define a set of scenarios $S = \{s_j, j = 1, \ldots, n\}$, representing in broad terms the medium-, or long-, term evolution of a system (see Poli 2010). The scenarios are predictions regarding the future of a social, economic, or physical system. But it must be recognized immediately that these predictions lack the analytical precision of short-term forecasting. The latter is ruled by the clear mathematical representation of the system, using deterministic or stochastic dynamic models to elicit the most probable future states. The former is a technique in which the mathematical representation is combined with expert views to reach a consensus on the possible future state of the world. It follows that the dimensions, which are described as continuous random variables with some specific probability distributions in short-term predictions, are modeled as discrete scenarios in future studies. For example, when deciding optimal investment levels on a weekly or monthly basis, the investor can rely on predictions based on probability distributions. But when the decisions involve long-term planning, the investor can rely only on general scenarios representing growth, stagnation, and other economic conditions.

After building the set of scenarios S for a practical application, the question that typically lingers in the air between advisers and stakeholders is: "... and now, what should we do?" Stakeholders soon realize they can exploit occurrences from S by preparing long-term plans to fit the economic environments specified. They realize they can take decisions so that the future economic outcome will depend on both the implemented decision and the occurred future scenario. We assume that decisions are represented though the set $D = \{d_i, i = 1, \ldots, m\}$ and that there is a profit function $u_{ij} = u(d_i, s_j)$ that maps pairs (d_i, s_j) on the utility scale, $U: S \times D \rightarrow R$. Comparing values u_{ij}, the organization is able to make an informed decision. But is decision-making an activity that should be left to stakeholders creativity? Or should advisers extend their analyses to include the decision support system? We are convinced that the answer to the latter question should be yes and that the natural decision rule we advocate is the minimum regret formula. To support this view, in section "The Mathematics of Decision-Making," we will revise last century's mathematics of decision-making to show in which sense minimum regret is an optimization framework that is alternative to expected utility, and in section "Min Regret and Optimization," we will show how minimum regret decisions can be calculated though large-scale linear programming problems.

The Mathematics of Decision-Making

The broad taxonomy of mathematical decision-making, presented in classic textbooks such as (Luce and Raiffa 1957), distinguishes between decisions in conditions of:

- Full knowledge
- Risky environments
- Uncertainty

When we speak about full knowledge, we mean that everything is predictable and deterministic. All the parameters affecting decisions are known and treated as if they could be measured precisely and not subject to random variations or even uncertainty. More subtly, what is not taken into consideration is the fact that implementing the best decision may be difficult and involve adapting and readjusting organizational elements, a task that may also be subject to randomness and uncertainty. More formally, these models assume that:

- Profit and cost parameters are deterministic.
- No random variables are involved.
- There is no systemic reaction to the decisions from other independent decision-makers.
- The decision-maker has full control over decision implementation.
- There are no future scenarios.

The decision methodology used in such applications is mathematical programming and optimization. The decision-maker formulates a profit function $f : \mathbb{B} \to \mathbb{R}$ that depends on variables x belonging to a decision space $\mathbb{B} \subseteq \mathbb{R}^n$. The space $\mathbb{B}$ is defined using mathematical constraints, such as equations, inequalities, and so on, to model the links between the x variables. The optimal decision is the solution to the mathematical programming problem $\max \{f(x) : x \in \mathbb{B}\}$.

This kind of model constitutes the bulk of operations research, one of its most successful applications. Routine activities like vehicle routing, crew scheduling, timetables, and so on are formulated through linear equations that can be solved in a few seconds even when problems are formulated with thousands of variables (see Eksioglu et al. 2009; Van den Bergh et al. 2013). The interest here is the computational power of these models. They can handle problems with thousands of variables; therefore, the decision-maker can try to formulate the application as a mathematical programming problem in which variables are scenario-dependent and then use existing software to calculate the optimal decisions.

When we speak about risky environments, the literature usually calls them "lotteries." Here, the scenario set $S = \{s_j, j = 1, \ldots, n\}$ is the set of elementary events, pair-wise incompatible, that are the outcome of an experiment. The experiment is the lottery, and the outcome are characterized by probabilities $p_j = \Pr[s = s_j]$. Then, there are the decisions $D = \{d_i, i = 1, \ldots, m\}$ that, jointly with random occurrences, determine the economic outcomes u_{ij}. If decision-makers agree with the axioms of Von Neumann and Morgenstern (1944), or the axioms of Savage (1954), then they should maximize their expected utility. For non-practitioners, it is important to remark that the correct interpretation of expected utility is the following: if decision-makers agree with the content of the axioms (that are the logical rules by which lotteries should be compared), then they should behave *as if* they are maximizing their expected utility. To clarify the point, one of the axioms is transitivity. It states that if for three decisions d_i, d_j, d_k the decision-maker reveals that he prefers d_i over d_j, that is $d_i \succ d_j$ (The binary relation $\succ$ stands for the actual choice of the decision-maker; it is not the consequence of some mathematical manipulation.), and he reveals that he prefers $d_j \succ d_k$ too, then he must agree that d_i is better than d_k, so $d_i \succ d_k$.

In a practical application, we must replace the economic outcome u_{ij}, formerly referred to as a generic profit, with the utility function $U(x(d_i, s_j))$, in which $x(d_i, s_j)$ is the tangible economic outcome. So, the mathematical features of the utility function reflect the decision-maker's characteristics, such as his risk aversion, non-satiety, and so on. For example, the second derivative $U''(\cdot)$ is negative for any investor that is risk adverse. Using the probabilities p, one can calculate the optimal decision that solves the stochastic programming problem, $\max\{E_p[U(x(d_i, s_j))]: d \in D\}$. The most famous application of this approach is probably Markowitz's portfolio model (Markowitz 1952). This model involves the decision-maker having to choose which are the best assets to invest his/her wealth on. Asset returns are modeled as random variables, so the number of future scenarios is uncountable. With regard to risk aversion, the decision-maker is represented as a utility maximizer, and then, after certain technical assumptions have been made, the standard deviation of the investment, e.g., the risk, is minimized on the condition that the expected return is higher than a fixed threshold. The standard deviation and the expectation are calculated by maximum likelihood estimators, and the mathematical formulation of the problem is one of the first examples of quadratic programming. As noted before, it is essential that a decision rule is implementable, as indicated by Markowitz's quadratic problem, which can be solved quickly even if thousands of variables are included. It is this level of practicality that has made the model so popular.

When we speak about uncertainty, we mean that we cannot really assign probabilities to scenarios, not even subjective ones. (Uncertainty can sometimes be resolved by using subjective probabilities, as illustrated by Savage (1954).) In some applications, the source of uncertainty explicitly prevents the possibility of probabilities. For example, the system dynamic of social and physical systems is the outcome of many interdependent variables, in which nonlinear equations, feedbacks, and bifurcations are common features (Strogatz 2014). In this case, even if all the necessary information about the structural equations governing the system is available, making accurate predictions using probabilities may still prove impossible. Moreover, scenarios always refer to medium- or long-term planning, so any probability assessment is completely arbitrary. For example, a little later, we will look at decisions concerning flood prevention in a hydrological basin. These decisions involve major investments in dams and embankments, which are dependent on predictions regarding rain precipitation. As with all phenomena related to climate change, the time scale available is never long enough to permit reliable probability assessments, as discussed in Hall (2007).

In the event of uncertainty, the main decision-making elements are, once again, the decision space D, the scenario space S, and the gains and losses u_{ij} associated with the decision/scenario pairs. Our purpose is to determine which decision rule should be used to select the best decision $d \in D$, and in order to give a straight answer right from the beginning, we will adopt the minimum regret rule. The regret rule works as follows: if the decision-maker has known that scenario s_i will occur for sure, then he will choose the optimal $d_k = d(s_i) = \arg\max\{u_{ij}|s = s_i\}$. But, as the future cannot be predicted, it is likely that sub-optimal decision d_j, different to d_k, has been chosen instead. As a consequence, after implementing d_j and observing s_i, the following difference will emerge:

$$L\big(d_i, s_j\big) = u_{kj} - u_{ij} \tag{1}$$

As documented by many psychological observations, for example, in Zeelenberg and Pieters (2007) and the citations therein, the loss $L(d_i, s_j)$ provokes an unconscious uneasiness in decision-makers, who tend to blame themselves for having made the wrong decision. The higher the loss, the greater the sense of regret. This is why this difference (1) is called *regret*. Since advisers cannot predict the future, the least they can do for stakeholders is to alleviate their sense of regret. Which is why we advocate that optimal decision should be calculated minimizing the maximum regret:

$$\min_{d_i \in D} \quad \max_{s_j \in S} \quad L\big(d_i, s_j\big) \tag{2}$$

Depending on applications, problem (2) can be easily described in matrix form or should be formulated as a mathematical programming problem. Next, we will provide some examples.

Example: Peak Flow and Flood Management. The following example shows how minimum regret can be calculated in a practical setting. This is a real case example that came to our attention in an H2020 research project we are currently involved and is inspired by a mathematical flood management model developed for Iowa City, documented in Spence and Brown (2016). Here, the model has been significantly simplified for computation purposes. The Iowa River that runs through Iowa City has water flow peaks that are both volatile and potentially dangerous. These peaks are managed using local water reservoirs, such as the Coralville Lake, located upstream from the city, and by the controlled flooding of agricultural land downstream. Recent peak flow events, however, have raised concerns regarding the efficacy of existing defenses given the increasing risk of flooding. One possible solution is a public works project that would update the existing reservoir operations, raise the river embankments, and buy more inundation options from farmers. The costs of the alternatives are different and scenario-dependent, but there is no consensus regarding the future of water flow in the area, as it is not clear whether climate change will cause water levels to increase, decrease, or remain the same.

The elements of the decision are the predicted scenarios s:

- Increasing peak flows (R+)
- Stationary conditions (R=)
- Decreasing peak flows (R-)

and the available decisions d:

- Do nothing (N)
- Reservoir reoperation (D)
- Raise embankment (E)

For every pair (d, s), we can calculate the payoff (the gain for the decision-maker). The following table is justified by the fact that every decision is optimal for a particular scenario (optimal scenario-dependent decisions are written in bold) (Table 1).

A close look at the table reveals that raising embankments is anti-economic if peak flow decreases, as is doing nothing in the event of an increase in peak flows (on account of flood damage), whereas reservoir reoperation is an intermediate decision that is less expensive, but less effective too.

Using formula (1), values $L(\cdot,\cdot)$ are reported on the table (Table 2).

The last column indicates the maximum regret score of each decision. For example, the maximum regret of N is 5. This is calculated by comparing the loss of doing nothing in the increased flow scenario and the optimal decision (the loss of -1 compared to the gain of 4). It is therefore easy to calculate that the minimum regret decision is E, raising embankments.

For the sake of completeness, it is worth comparing this method with the expected utility model. We have assumed that the decision-maker is characterized by the linear utility function $U(x) = x$, representing risk neutrality. Moreover, the city administration agrees with the conservative probability distribution $p = [1/6, 4/6, 1/6]$. The expected utility calculation is therefore:

Table 1 Flood management matrix

	R−	R=	R+
N	1	0	−1
D	0	2	1
E	−1	1	4

Table 2 Regret table

	R−	R=	R+	Regret
N	0	2	5	5
D	1	0	3	3
E	2	1	0	2

$$U\,[\text{raising embankments}] = (1/6) \times (-1) + (4/6) \times 1 + (1/6) \times 4 = 7/6;$$
$$U\,[\text{doing nothing}] = (1/6) \times 1 + (4/6) \times 0 + (1/6) \times (-1) = 0; \quad (3)$$
$$U\,[\text{reservoir reoperation}] = (1/6) \times 0 + (4/6) \times 2 + (1/6) \times 1 = 9/6.$$

Administrators therefore infer that U [reservoir reoperation] $>$ U [raising embankments] $>$ U [doing nothing].

The decision supported by the maximum utility principle has a slightly immaterial quality. Firstly, probabilities are such an uncertain attribution to scenarios that a decision relying so heavily upon them leaves the administrators open to severe criticism in the event of an unfavorable outcome. Secondly, the utility principle claims that decision-makers behave as if. But real-life fiscal budget discussions do not follow the utility principle as specific interests always play a role in committees and votes. Here, the rationale of a decision must be readily understood by an audience, and public opinions are unlikely to be easily convinced by the mathematical rationality of expected utility. Conversely, the minimum regret decision cannot be questioned for its probability assumptions, as it does not use any.

The minimum regret approach is similar to the max-min criterion, and both were formulated in the same time period (Savage 1951; Von Neumann and Morgenstern 1944). In fact, minimum regret was motivated by the empiric adjustment of the max-min criterion, as the latter was considered too conservative. The max-min criterion proceeds as follows: firstly, a security threshold is calculated for every decision: $l(d_i) = \min\{u_{ij}|s_j \in S, d = d_i\}$, $l(d_i)$ is the worst-case scenario outcome of decision d_i. So the max-min criterion becomes arg $\max\{l(d_i)|d \in D\}$, i.e., the decision that maximizes the worst-case outcome. When applied to the Iowa City example, the result is the following (Table 3).

The max-min decision rule provides results that are overly conservative. As a matter of fact, max-min decisions are rational in zero-sum games, where they are used to calculate the Nash equilibrium of the game. For this kind of game, what is gained by one player is lost by the other, so maximizing security levels is justified by the fact that players will always oppose their opponents' gains. In our applications, however, models have nothing to do with zero-sum games, and there is no reason to believe that one is playing against a diabolical Mother Nature, who is trying to take advantage of our weakness. By focusing on this situation, authors, such as Savage (1951) and Wald (1950), created the first elaboration of the minimum regret criterion, which was known at the time as min-max risk (see Luce and Raiffa 1957).

Table 3 Worst-case table

	R−	R=	R+	Worst-case
N	1	0	−1	**−1**
D	0	2	1	**0**
E	−1	1	4	**−1**

where in bold number are reported the values $l(N)$, $l(D)$, $l(E)$. Then, the optimal decision is D, as $l(D) = 0 = \max\{-1, 0, -1\}$.

A formal treatment of regret theory was put forward in three independent papers, all published in 1982 (Bell 1982; Fishburn 1982; Loomes and Sugden 1982). The origin of these contributions was the contradiction between what is dictated by the expected utility principle and the experimental results on real decision-making. People choices do not always conform to expected utilities, Allais's paradox being one of the most famous counterexamples (Kahneman and Tversky 1979), showing the epistemic difference between risk and uncertainty. However, there was still much debate about which principle should be used to replace utility maximization. An explanation of human decisions can be both descriptive and normative. It is descriptive, when the outcomes of laboratory experiments are matched by the mathematical model, be it in the form of numeric formulas or heuristic algorithms. One example of a descriptive theory is the prospect theory, put forward by Kanheman and Tversky (1979). In order to fit experiment results, this theory contemplates probability overweighting and underweighting, discrete numerical approximations, choice functions with inflection points, and even more mathematical machinery. Such a huge amount of sophistication, however, is of little help when building decision models or, more simply, when we want a normative model to replace the expected utility principle in a decision support system. In a case like this, regret theory is both descriptive and normative. It is also powerful enough to encompass many decision paradoxes that are not explained by an expected utility while keeping the mathematics simple enough to be used in algorithmic applications.

At first, the predictive and explicative power of regret theory was tested in risk situations, i.e., in cases where probabilities are linked to events. Regret is therefore expressed in mathematical terms as a decision function penalty. According to the original terminology (Loomes and Sugden 1982), the empiric decision function is characterized by the choiceless and cardinal utility function $C(\cdot)$, eventually weighted by probabilities, if they are present in the problem. This function is choiceless because it represents the utility the individual would get from a consequence without having chosen it, for example, the plain utility of finding a sum of money on the sidewalk or, more generally, the psychological pleasure associated with the satisfaction of a desire. When comparing two choiceless outcomes, one experiences a feeling of regret. The result is a handy mathematical function that can replace the expected utility with a minimum amount of complication.

Some psychologists and behavioral economists have analyzed the neurological origin of regret using functional magnetic resonance imaging to determine the orbito-frontal cortex's role in its appearance (Camille et al. 2004, 2005). The results show that people tend to anticipate their potential regret before making a decision. Psychologists have also observed that cerebral activity is triggered by the prediction of a possible feeling of sorrow, in the case of things not going right. Behavioral economists have also found that regret is the learning process individuals most rely on when making decisions in complex situations, for example, in scenarios where the outcome is affected by other people's decisions. The experiments in Marchiori and Warglien (2008) also reveal a tendency to learn from experienced regrets, as people shift from old regretful decisions to safer new ones. All these findings have far-reaching philosophical consequences about the evolutive appearance of regret, how emotions shape our rationality and intelligence, and, more deeply, what we are like as human beings. For the moment, though, we will continue to focus on more trivial (operational) advice.

To summarize the discussion so far, the reasons to support the regret decision rule are:

- **Political reasons:** Minimum regret is easy to explain, as mathematical sophistication is minimal, and any audience can easily understand the methodology behind the decision.
- **Methodological reasons:** Minimum regret uses a minimum amount of information to justify a decision. It uses losses and gains only and does not involve any other parameters, such as probabilities, utilities, and so on, that may be questioned or rejected by stakeholders.
- **Psychological reasons:** Regret is a feeling that exists and affects human behavior, as has been demonstrated in many experiments. In complex situations it often dictates human behavior and is therefore a natural and understandable algorithm to follow.

Min Regret and Optimization

For as much it can be contested by experiments, nevertheless the expected utility axioms are hard to reject. So what is the axiom that we must refuse if we want to replace max expected utility with min-max regret? In the following example, we will show that we must reject the transitivity axiom. To begin with, we just rewrite Table 1 with different numbers (Table 4).

Here, we can see that regret is attributed a value of 3 for all the decisions, so they are all, in theory, the same. However, if we make pair-wise comparisons, the results are quite surprising. Take decision N and D, for example, and decide which one is better using regret. The matrix is the following (Table 5).

Looking at the regret column, we can readily determine $D \succ N$. If we repeat the regret analysis between E and D only, we find $E \succ D$ too. Therefore, it is normal to expect that, after comparing N and E, we should find $E \succ N$. In fact, this is the logical condition expressed by the transitivity axiom. But if we do the calculation, it is not the case: we find $N \succ E$. When these pair-wise comparisons are summarized, the results are:

- $D \succ N$ (regret when R= occurs)
- $E \succ D$ (regret when R+ occurs)
- $N \succ E$ (regret when R− occurs)

A cycle of pair-wise preferences is obtained, which shows that regret decisions do not satisfy the transitivity axiom. In fact, the axioms on which the regret theory is based are different to the expected utility ones (see Bell 1982). This is unavoidable, if we want to create a descriptive theory of experimental choices. But, can it still be used as a normative tool? Can regret be used to model potential individual choices? And can it be embedded in a decision support algorithm to replace the expected

Table 4 Flood management matrix

	R−	R=	R+	Regret
N	3	0	1	**3**
D	1	3	0	**3**
E	0	1	3	**3**

Table 5 Regret pair-wise comparison

	R−	R=	R+	Regret
N	3	0	1	**3**
D	1	3	0	**2**

utility for an operational application? The mathematics of regret is still simple enough to be formalized as an optimization problem. But the lack of transitivity is, nevertheless, a warning about how we should implement the decision model. We must keep in mind that we cannot simplify the analysis by making pair-wise comparisons and discarding apparently useless decisions. Rather, we must always consider all scenarios and all decisions as well! This is a mathematical challenge, because in many applications (e.g., the ones in which decisions are real numbers), describing all the alternatives means having to formulate and solve a mathematical programming problem. (Regret theory may be seen as being particularly sensitive to model building, especially with regard to the scenarios and decisions description, as expected utility is sensitive to probability assessments.)

If the application considers a finite number of scenarios and a finite set of decisions, as in the previous example, the user must define the optimal decisions for each scenario and use them as the benchmarks against all others decisions, including a list of nonoptimal decisions. There are also cases in which decisions are analytically highly complex, because decisions may consist of interacting variables, and any discrete approximation may hide erroneous calculations and unpredicted consequences. In this case, linear programming problem may help, as in applications like scheduling, routing, location, and so on, mentioned at the beginning of the paper. Some of those problems have been already formulated as minimum regret optimization (Aissi et al. 2009), and in some of them, minimum regret has been motivated by parameter uncertainty, as in Conde (2007), or by multi-objective optimization, as in Ehrgott et al. (2014). An example of a plain application, the p-median problem of an optimization problem that considers a discrete set of scenario, is discussed in Serra and Marianov (1998).

To demonstrate the mathematical sophistication needed to build a minimum regret optimization model, we will continue to use the example of flood management outlined in the previous paragraph. But, here, we will focus our attention on the problem of locating and dimensioning detention dams along a particular river catchment area in order to prevent flood emergencies, as described in Bellu et al. (2016) and Yazdi and Neyshabouri (2014). The aforementioned models show that there are so many variables involved in this decision that we cannot rely only on the finite matrix shown in Table 1. Operational decisions include long-term variables, such as the location and dimensioning of dams, and short-term scenario-dependent variables, such as filling dams or allowing the partial flooding of flatlands. The scenarios also include rainfall predictions and territorial changes, such as deforestation, urbanization, and economic spillovers. In our example, we have included some simplified assumptions regarding the models presented in Bellu et al. (2016) and Yazdi and Neyshabouri (2014), to obtain a manageable optimization model. We also assume that the city administrators have a budget to invest in new detention basins, or dams, along the river and its tributaries. With regard to this budget, the city can decide to invest the whole sum on a single gigantic project or spread the sum over a series of smaller dams, located along the river and its tributaries. The sole purpose of the administrators is to mitigate the damage caused by peak water flows, which often cause flooding. The administrators have some scenarios in hand, such as peak flow predictions in the form of rainfall forecasts divided by time and area.

To create a minimum regret optimization model, the first step is to build a linear programming model that calculates optimal dam location and dimensioning for one fixed scenario only. This is a deterministic model that we can then extend to multiple scenarios using the regret as objective function. When dams are built, peak flows are diverted to overflow reservoirs, so a model of river behavior during an emergency is required. The river and its tributaries are described as a directed tree $T = (V, E)$ (see Fig. 1), in which V is the node set and E is the arc set, and the direction of an arc is consistent with the direction of the water flow. One of the nodes, such as t, has a peculiar meaning as it refers to the river estuary. Other nodes, such as the nodes $S \subset V$, are the sources of the river and its tributaries. The intermediate river nodes are then classified as $A = V - (S \cup \{t\})$. The potential location of the basins is represented by the set B (not shown in the figure). We assume that any potential location $k \in B$ can be linked to any node $i \in A$ with the potential arc (i, k) (not shown in Fig. 1). If necessary, the flow in i can be diverted to basin k until the capacity of the basin is filled.

The flow entering and leaving a node i, $i \in A$ must obey the flow conservation constraint, that is, the quantity of water entering the node must be equal to the quantity leaving. Here we introduce a discrete time step to model the temporal

Fig. 1 River watershed described as a directed tree

STEFANO BENATI

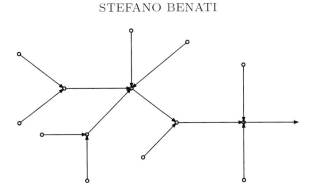

evolution of the peak flow. Let $f_{ij,t}$ be the flow along arc (i, j) in time i, let E_j be the arcs entering node j, then the flow conservation principle in node j is formulated as the equality:

$$\sum_{(i, j) \in E_j} f_{ij,t} = f_{jq,t+1}, \tag{4}$$

that is, what is flowing in time t along arcs (i, j) will flow along arc (j, k) in time $t + 1$.

Now we have to modify formula (4) to take into account that any arc receives additional water from its watershed, in the form of rain and small tributary streams. Let $r_{ij,t}$ be the additional water received by the river along arc (i, j) in time t, and consider that part of the flow can be diverted to the (planned) artificial basin k: let $x_{jk,t}$ be the quantity of water diverted from node j to the basin k in time t. Next, overflow is modeled as follows: if the capacity C_{ij} of the arc (i, j) is exceeded, part of the water overflows, damaging the surrounding area. Let $z_{ij,t}$ be the quantity of the overflown water along arc (i, j) in time t. Then, the flow conservation law (4) in node j can be rewritten as follows:

$$\sum_{(i,j) \in E_j} \left(f_{ij,t} + r_{ij,t} - z_{ij,t} \right) = f_{jq,t+1} + x_{jk,t+1}. \tag{5}$$

The administrators can mitigate flood damage by building detention basins B. The relevant decisions are the capacities y_k, $k \in B$ that are the detention capacity of basin k. In case of peak flow, the quantity of water x that can be diverted cannot exceed the basin capacity so that for all t:

$$\sum_{l=1}^{t} x_{ik,l} \leq y_k. \tag{6}$$

Flood along one arc occurs when the flow exceeds the arc capacity C_{ij}:

$$z_{ij,t} = \max\left\{ f_{ij,t} + r_{ij,t} - C_{ij}, 0 \right\} \tag{7}$$

The max operator of Eq. (7) guarantees that $z_{ij,t}$ will not take negative values. As we will see later, since the problem is in minimization form, the nonlinear Eq. (7) can be described by the two linear inequalities:

$$\begin{aligned} z_{ij,t} &\geq f_{ij,t} + r_{ij,t} - C_{ij} \\ z_{ij,t} &\geq 0 \end{aligned} \tag{8}$$

We have assumed that the unitary capacity cost of basin k is m_k and that the administrators have a budget M. The unitary flood cost along arc (i, j) is d_{ij}. So, putting together the Eqs. (5), (6), and (8) for all the nodes, we have the set of constraints describing river flow. The problem decision variables are the vectors z, f, x, y, the problem parameters are the vectors C, r and budget M. The first model built represents the simplest case in which r is considered fixed and deterministic for the times $t = 1, \ldots, T$. The optimal location and dimensioning of the dams are calculated minimizing the cost with the following linear programming problem:

$$P1 : \min_{y,x,f,z} \sum_{t=1}^{T} \sum_{(i,j) \in E} d_{ij} z_{ij,t} \tag{9}$$

$$\text{s.t.} \sum_{k \in B} m_k y_k \leq M; \tag{10}$$

$$\sum_{(i,j) \in E_j} \left(f_{ij,t} + r_{ij,t} - z_{ij,t} \right) = f_{jq,t+1} + x_{jk,t+1} \tag{11}$$
$$\text{for all } j \in A, t = 1, \ldots, T;$$

$$\sum_{l=1}^{t} x_{ik,l} \leq y_k \quad \text{for all } i \in A, k \in B, t = 1, \ldots, T; \tag{12}$$

$$z_{ij,t} \geq f_{ij,t} + r_{ij,t} - C_{ij}$$
$$\text{for all } (i,j) \in E, \ t = 1, \ldots, T; \tag{13}$$

$$z_{ij,t} \geq 0 \text{ for all } (i,j) \in E, \ t = 1, \ldots, T; \tag{14}$$

$$f_{ij,t} \geq 0 \text{ for all } (i,j) \in E, \ t = 1, \ldots, T; \tag{15}$$

$$x_{ik,t} \geq 0 \text{ for all } i \in A, \ k \in B, \ t = 1, \ldots, T; \tag{16}$$

$$y_k \geq 0 \text{ for all } k \in B. \tag{17}$$

The objective function (9) is the minimization of flood damages. Constraint (10) is the budget allocation. Constraints (11) are the flow conservation constraints along all the intermediate nodes, previously discussed as Eq. (5). Constraints (12) are the capacity constraints previously described in Eq. (6). Constraint pairs (13) and (14) describe the flood variable discussed in inequalities (8). It can be seen that, since the problem is in minimization form, in the optimal solution, at least one of constraints (13) and (14) is tight. Finally, constraints (15), (16), and (17) impose non-negativity to all variables.

Problem P1 is an instance of linear programming. This formulation has been reached using various simplified assumptions, but the advantage is that existing software, like Gurobi and others, can calculate an optimal solution to a problem with thousands of variables in only a few seconds Meindl and Templ (2013). This is an important strategic tool when calculating minimum regret decisions, as it can be applied to cases with thousands of scenarios and variables. Hence, we describe how problem P1 can be modified to include different scenarios on r and the minimum regret decision.

Experts provided the city administrators with some scenarios, denoted as ω, describing possible rain patterns during the peak flows. Scenarios are a finite set Ω, and each scenario $\omega \in \Omega$ describes the rain precipitation $r_{ij,t}^{\omega}$ for all $(i, j) \in A$

during the time interval, $t = 1, \ldots, T$. Many variables of problem P1 are now scenario-dependent. They are the flows $f_{ij,t}^{\omega}$ and $x_{ij,t}^{\omega}$ and the overflows $z_{ij,t}^{\omega}$. Conversely, the capacity variables y_k remain the same for all scenarios. To calculate the minimum regret decision, the decision-maker must first calculate the value w^{ω} of the optimal decisions for each scenario ω, solving an instance of P1 with input r^{ω}. Then the minimum regret decision defined in (1) is calculated as:

$$P2: \quad \min_{y,x,f,z} \quad \eta \tag{18}$$

$$\text{s.t. } \eta \geq \sum_{(i,j) \in E} \left(\sum_{t=1}^{T} d_{ij} z_{ij,t}^{\omega} \right) - w^{\omega} \text{ for all } \omega \in \Omega; \tag{19}$$

$$\sum_{k \in B} m_k y_k \leq M; \tag{20}$$

$$\sum_{(i,j) \in E_j} \left(f_{ij,t}^{\omega} + r_{ij,t}^{\omega} - z_{ij,t}^{\omega} \right) = f_{jq,t+1}^{\omega} + x_{jk,t+1}^{\omega}$$
$$\text{for all } j \in A, \ t = 1, \ \ldots, \ T, \ \omega \in \Omega; \tag{21}$$

$$\sum_{l=1}^{t} x_{ik,l}^{\omega} \leq y_k \text{ for all } i \in A, \ k \in B, \ t = 1, \ \ldots, \ T, \ \omega \in \Omega; \tag{22}$$

$$z_{ij,t}^{\omega} \geq f_{ij,t}^{\omega} + r_{ij,t}^{\omega} - C_{ij}$$
$$\text{for all } (i,j) \in E, \ t = 1, \ \ldots, \ T, \ \omega \in \Omega; \tag{23}$$

$$z_{ij,t}^{\omega} \geq 0 \text{ for all } (i,j) \in E, \ t = 1, \ \ldots, \ T, \ \omega \in \Omega; \tag{24}$$

$$f_{ij,t}^{\omega} \geq 0 \text{ for all } (i,j) \in E, \ t = 1, \ \ldots, \ T, \ \omega \in \Omega; \tag{25}$$

$$x_{ij,t}^{\omega} \geq 0 \text{ for all } i \in A, \ k \in B, \ t = 1, \ \ldots, \ T, \ \omega \in \Omega; \tag{26}$$

$$y_k \geq 0 \text{ for all } k \in B. \tag{27}$$

The objective function (18) contains just a single term, η, that is the maximum regret to minimize. The value η appears in the left side of constraints (19), constrained to be greater than the right side, that describes the regret for every scenario as the difference between the occurred output, that is the scenario-dependent summation, and the optimal solution w^{ω}. Constraint (20) is the same as constraint (10), as y_k are not scenario-dependent variables, while constraints (21), (22), (23), (24), (25), and (26) are homologous to the respective constraints of problem P1. As P1, P2 is a huge linear programming problem, but again, its solution is not a hard task for modern solvers.

In problem P2 we took advantage that scenarios are a finite number, but things get more complicated when one wants to consider an infinite number of scenarios. For example experts can provide the administrator a continuous range of values

$r \in R \subset \mathbb{R}^{|E| \times T}$. For example, the rain fall can be any value between a minimum value l and an upper value u: $l \leq r \leq u$. In this case, one cannot calculate all values w^{ω}, as they are an infinite number, and we must devise some problem-dependent specific technique, like Benders' cut and column generation (see Ben-Tal and Nemirovski 2002). In the following, we just sketch the general problem framework. In mathematical programming terminology, let D be the set of the decisions and Ω be the set of the scenarios. Suppose, as in problem P2, that the decision-maker wants to minimize the costs but that they are scenario-dependent. Let $f(x, \omega)$, with $x \in D$ and $\omega \in \Omega$, be the cost function. One can calculate the regret of decision x with respect to the optimal scenario contingent optimal decision as:

$$\text{regret of } x \text{ in } \omega := d(x, \omega) = f(x, \omega) - \left[\min_{y \in D} f(y, \omega) \right]. \tag{28}$$

Then calculate the maximum regret:

$$\text{max regret} := r(x) = \max_{\omega \in \Omega} d(x, \omega). \tag{29}$$

The optimal decision is calculated as:

$$\min_{x \in D} r(x) = \min_{x \in D} \left[\max_{\omega \in \Omega} \left[\left[f(x, \omega) - \left[\min_{y \in D} f(y, \omega) \right] \right] \right] \right] \tag{30}$$

As can be seen, the problem (30) is the most general representation of regret decision-making. The formulation clarifies that there are three maximum or minimum problems nested one in the other, and up to now, we can solve problem (30) only within some specific instances (Aissi et al. 2009). Surely, further investigation on real cases and applications is needed.

Summary

In order to consolidate our view that minimum regret is the correct rule to adopt when making decisions in situations where probabilities cannot be fully assessed, we have carefully analyzed the rules' roots and foundations. We have also indicated how mathematical programming models can be modified to include scenarios and the regret objective function. In doing this, we hope to stimulate further discussion and achieve new applications for this fascinating and useful topic.

References

Aissi, H., Bazgan, C., & Vanderpooten, D. (2009). Min–max and min–max regret versions of combinatorial optimization problems: A survey. *European Journal of Operational Research, 197*(2), 427–438.

Bell, D. E. (1982). Regret in decision making under uncertainty. *Operations Research, 30*(5), 961–981.

Bellu, A., Fernandes, L. F. S., Cortes, R. M. V., & Pacheco, F. A. L. (2016). A framework model for the dimensioning and allocation of a detention basin system: The case of a flood-prone mountainous watershed. *Journal of Hydrology, 533*, 567–580.

Ben-Tal, A., & Nemirovski, A. (2002). Robust optimization–methodology and applications. *Mathematical Programming, 92*(3), 453–480.

Camille, N., Coricelli, G., Sallet, J., Pradat-Diehl, P., Duhamel, J.-R., & Sirigu, A. (2004). The involvement of the orbitofrontal cortex in the experience of regret. *Science, 304*(5674), 1167–1170.

Conde, E. (2007). Minmax regret location–allocation problem on a network under uncertainty. *European Journal of Operational Research, 179*(3), 1025–1039.

Coricelli, G., Critchley, H. D., Joffily, M., O'Doherty, J. P., Sirigu, A., & Dolan, R. J. (2005). Regret and its avoidance: A neuroimaging study of choice behavior. *Nature Neuroscience, 8*(9), 1255–1262.

Ehrgott, M., Ide, J., & Schöbel, A. (2014). Minmax robustness for multi-objective optimization problems. *European Journal of Operational Research, 239*(1), 17–31.

Eksioglu, B., Vural, A. V., & Reisman, A. (2009). The vehicle routing problem: A taxonomic review. *Computers & Industrial Engineering, 57*(4), 1472–1483.

Fishburn, P. C. (1982). Nontransitive measurable utility. *Journal of Mathematical Psychology, 26*(1), 31–67.

Hall, J. (2007). Probabilistic climate scenarios may misrepresent uncertainty and lead to bad adaptation decisions. *Hydrological Processes, 21*(8), 1127–1129.

Kahneman, D., & Tversky, A. (1979). Prospect theory: An analysis of decision under risk. *Econometrica: Journal of the Econometric Society, 47*, 263–291.

Loomes, G., & Sugden, R. (1982). Regret theory: An alternative theory of rational choice under uncertainty. *Economic Journal, 92*(368), 805–824.

Luce, R. D., & Raiffa, H. (1957). *Games and decisions: Introduction and critical survey.* New York: Wiley.

Marchiori, D., & Warglien, M. (2008). Predicting human interactive learning by regret-driven neural networks. *Science, 319*(5866), 1111–1113.

Markowitz, H. (1952). Portfolio selection. *The Journal of Finance, 7*(1), 77–91.

Meindl, B., & Templ, M. (2013). Analysis of commercial and free and open source solvers for the cell suppression problem. *Transactions Data Privacy, 6*(2), 147–159.

Poli, R. (2010). The many aspects of anticipation. *Foresight, 12*(3), 7–17.

Savage, L. J. (1951). The theory of statistical decision. *Journal of the American Statistical Association, 46*(253), 55–67.

Savage, L. J. (1954). *The foundations of statistics.* New York: Wiley.

Serra, D., & Marianov, V. (1998). The p-median problem in a changing network: The case of Barcelona. *Location Science, 6*(1), 383–394.

Spence, C. M., & Brown, C. M. (2016). Nonstationary decision model for flood risk decision scaling. *Water Resources Research, 52*(11), 8650–8667.

Strogatz, S. H. (2014). *Nonlinear dynamics and chaos: With applications to physics, biology, chemistry, and engineering.* Boulder: Westview Press.

Van den Bergh, J., Beliën, J., De Bruecker, P., Demeulemeester, E., & De Boeck, L. (2013). Personnel scheduling: A literature review. *European Journal of Operational Research, 226*(3), 367–385.

Von Neumann, J., & Morgenstern, O. (1944). *Theory of games and economic behavior.* Princeton: Princeton University Press.

Wald, A. (1950). *Statistical decision functions.* Oxford: Wiley.

Yazdi, J., & Neyshabouri, S. (2014). Adaptive surrogate modeling for optimization of flood control detention dams. *Environmental Modelling & Software, 61*, 106–120.

Zeelenberg, M., & Pieters, R. (2007). A theory of regret regulation 1.0. *Journal of Consumer Psychology, 17*(1), 3–18.

Printed by Printforce, the Netherlands